Y0-EHZ-615

Contemporary Authors®

NEW REVISION SERIES

ISSN 0275-7176

Contemporary Authors®

A Bio-Bibliographical Guide to Current Writers in Fiction, General Nonfiction, Poetry, Journalism, Drama, Motion Pictures, Television, and Other Fields

NEW REVISION SERIES volume 91

Detroit
San Francisco
London
Boston
Woodbridge, CT

Staff

Library of Congress Catalog Card Number 62-52046
ISBN 0-7876-3214-7
ISSN 0275-7176
Printed in the United States of America

10 9 8 7 6 5 4 3 2 1

Contents

Indexing note: All *Contemporary Authors* entries are indexed in the *Contemporary Authors* cumulative index, which is published separately and distributed twice a year.

As always, the most recent *Contemporary Authors* cumulative index continues to be the user's guide to the location of an individual author's listing.

Preface

The *Contemporary Authors New Revision Series* (*CANR*) provides updated information on authors listed in earlier volumes of *Contemporary Authors* (*CA*). Although entries for individual authors from any volume of *CA* may be included in a volume of the *New Revision Series*, *CANR* updates only those sketches requiring significant change. However, in a response to requests from librarians and library patrons for the most current information possible on high-profile writers of greater public and critical interest, *CANR* revises entries for these authors whenever new and noteworthy information becomes available.

Authors are included on the basis of specific criteria that indicate the need for a revision. These criteria include a combination of bibliographical additions, changes in addresses or career, major awards, and personal information such as name changes or death dates. All listings in this volume have been revised or augmented in various ways and contain up-to-the-minute publication information in the Writings section, most often verified by the author and/or by consulting a variety of online resources. Many sketches have been extensively rewritten, often including informative new Sidelights. As always, a *CANR* listing entails no charge or obligation.

How to Get the Most out of *CA*: Use the Index

The key to locating an author's most recent entry is the *CA* cumulative index, which is published separately and distributed twice a year. It provides access to *all* entries in *CA* and *Contemporary Authors New Revision Series* (*CANR*). Always consult the latest index to find an authors most recent entry.

For the convenience of users, the *CA* cumulative index also includes references to all entries in these Gale literary series: *Authors and Artists for Young Adults, Authors in the News, Bestsellers, Black Literature Criticism, Black Writers, Children's Literature Review, Concise Dictionary of American Literary Biography, Concise Dictionary of British Literary Biography, Contemporary Authors Autobiography Series, Contemporary Authors Bibliographical Series, Contemporary Literary Criticism, Dictionary of Literary Biography, Dictionary of Literary Biography Documentary Series, Dictionary of Literary Biography Yearbook, DISCovering Authors, DISCovering Authors: British, DISCovering Authors: Canadian, DISCovering Authors: Modules* (including modules for Dramatists, Most-Studied Authors, Multicultural Authors, Novelists, Poets, and Popular/Genre Authors), *Drama Criticism, Hispanic Literature Criticism, Hispanic Writers, Junior DISCovering Authors, Major Authors and Illustrators for Children and Young Adults, Major 20th-Century Writers, Native North American Literature, Poetry Criticism, Short Story Criticism, Something about the Author, Something about the Author Autobiography Series, Twentieth-Century Literary Criticism, World Literature Criticism,* and *Yesterday's Authors of Books for Children.*

A Sample Index Entry:

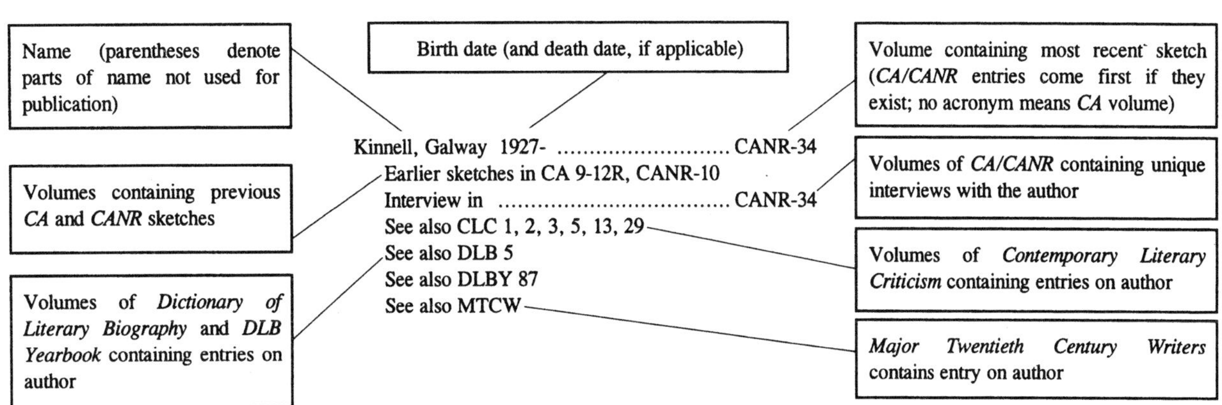

How Are Entries Compiled?

The editors make every effort to secure new information directly from the authors; listees' responses to our questionnaires and query letters provide most of the information featured in *CA.* For deceased writers, or those who fail to reply to requests for data, we consult other reliable biographical sources, such as those indexed in Gale's *Biography and Genealogy Master Index,* and bibliographical sources, including *National Union Catalog, LC MARC,* and *British National Bibliography.* Further details come from published interviews, feature stories, and book reviews, as well as information supplied by the authors' publishers and agents.

An asterisk (*) at the end of a sketch indicates that the listing has been compiled from secondary sources believed to be reliable but has not been personally verified for this edition by the author sketched.

What Kinds of Information Does An Entry Provide?

Sketches in *CA* contain the following biographical and bibliographical information:

- **Entry heading:** the most complete form of author's name, plus any pseudonyms or name variations used for writing

- **Personal information:** author's date and place of birth, family data, ethnicity, educational background, political and religious affiliations, and hobbies and leisure interests

- **Addresses:** author's home, office, or agent's addresses, plus e-mail and fax numbers, as available

- **Career summary:** name of employer, position, and dates held for each career post; resume of other vocational achievements; military service

- **Membership information:** professional, civic, and other association memberships and any official posts held

- **Awards and honors:** military and civic citations, major prizes and nominations, fellowships, grants, and honorary degrees

- **Writings:** a comprehensive, chronological list of titles, publishers, dates of original publication and revised editions, and production information for plays, television scripts, and screenplays

- **Adaptations:** a list of films, plays, and other media which have been adapted from the author's work

- **Work in progress:** current or planned projects, with dates of completion and/or publication, and expected publisher, when known

- **Sidelights:** a biographical portrait of the author's development; information about the critical reception of the author's works; revealing comments, often by the author, on personal interests, aspirations, motivations, and thoughts on writing

- **Interview:** a one-on-one discussion with authors conducted especially for *CA*, offering insight into authors' thoughts about their craft

- **Autobiographical Essay:** an original essay written by noted authors for *CA*, a forum in which writers may present themselves, on their own terms, to their audience

- **Photographs:** portraits and personal photographs of notable authors

- **Biographical and critical sources:** a list of books and periodicals in which additional information on an author's life and/or writings appears

- **Obituary Notices** in *CA* provide date and place of birth as well as death information about authors whose full-length sketches appeared in the series before their deaths. The entries also summarize the authors' careers and writings and list other sources of biographical and death information.

Related Titles in the *CA* Series

Contemporary Authors Autobiography Series complements *CA* original and revised volumes with specially commissioned autobiographical essays by important current authors, illustrated with personal photographs they provide. Common topics include their motivations for writing, the people and experiences that shaped their careers, the rewards they derive from their work, and their impressions of the current literary scene.

Contemporary Authors Bibliographical Series surveys writings by and about important American authors since World War II. Each volume concentrates on a specific genre and features approximately ten writers; entries list works written by and about the author and contain a bibliographical essay discussing the merits and deficiencies of major critical and scholarly studies in detail.

Available in Electronic Formats

CD-ROM. Full-text bio-bibliographic entries from the entire *CA* series, covering approximately 100,000 writers, are available on CD-ROM through lease and purchase plans. The disc combines entries from the *CA, CANR,* and *Contemporary Authors Permanent Series* (*CAP*) print series to provide the most recent author listing. The *CA CD-ROM* is searchable by name, title, subject/genre, nationality/ethnicity, personal data, and as well as by using Boolean logic. The disc is updated every six months. For more information, call 1-248-699-4253.

Contemporary Authors is also available on CD-ROM from SilverPlatter Information, Inc.

Online. The *Contemporary Authors* database is made available online to libraries and their patrons through online public access catalog (OPAC) vendors. Currently, *CA* is offered through Ameritech Library Services' Vista Online (formerly Dynix).

GaleNet. *CA* is available on a subscription basis through GaleNet, an online information resource that features an easy-to-use end-user interface, the powerful search capabilities of the BRS/Search retrieval software, and ease of access through the World-Wide Web. For more information, call 1-248-699-4253.

Magnetic Tape. *CA* is available for licensing on magnetic tape in a fielded format. The database is available for internal data processing and nonpublishing purposes only. For more information, call 1-248-699-4253.

Suggestions Are Welcome

The editors welcome comments and suggestions from users on any aspect of the *CA* series. If readers would like to recommend authors for inclusion in future volumes of the series, they are cordially invited to write the Editors at *Contemporary Authors*, Gale Group, 27500 Drake Rd., Farmington Hills, MI 48331-3535; or call at 1-248-699-4253; or fax at 1-248-699-8054.

CA Numbering System and Volume Update Chart

Occasionally questions arise about the *CA* numbering system and which volumes, if any, can be discarded. Despite numbers like "29-32R," "97-100" and "184," the entire *CA* print series consists of only 203 physical volumes with the publication of *CA* Volume 185. The following charts note changes in the numbering system and cover design, and indicate which volumes are essential for the most complete, up-to-date coverage.

***CA* First Revision**

- 1-4R through 41-44R (11 books)
  Cover: Brown with black and gold trim.
  There will be no further First Revision volumes because revised entries are now being handled exclusively through the more efficient *New Revision Series* mentioned below.

***CA* Original Volumes**

- 45-48 through 97-100 (14 books)
  Cover: Brown with black and gold trim.
- 101 through 185 (85 books)
  Cover: Blue and black with orange bands.
  The same as previous *CA* original volumes but with a new, simplified numbering system and new cover design.

***CA* Permanent Series**

- *CAP*-1 and *CAP*-2 (2 books)
  Cover: Brown with red and gold trim.
  There will be no further Permanent Series volumes because revised entries are now being handled exclusively through the more efficient *New Revision Series* mentioned below.

***CA* New Revision Series**

- CANR-1 through CANR-91 (91 books)
  Cover: Blue and black with green bands.
  Includes only sketches requiring significant changes; **sketches are taken from any previously published *CA*, *CAP*, or *CANR* volume.**

If You Have:	You May Discard:
CA First Revision Volumes 1-4R through 41-44R and *CA Permanent Series* Volumes 1 and 2.	*CA* Original Volumes 1, 2 ,3, 4 Volumes 5-6 through 41-44
CA Original Volumes 45-48 through 97-100 and 101 through 185	**NONE:** These volumes will not be superseded by corresponding revised volumes. Individual entries from these and all other volumes appearing in the left column of this chart may be revised and included in the various volumes of the *New Revision Series.*
CA New Revision Series Volumes *CANR*-1 through *CANR*-91	**NONE:** The *New Revision Series* does not replace any single volume of *CA*. Instead, volumes of *CANR* include entries from many previous *CA* series volumes. All *New Revision Series* volumes must be retained for full coverage.

A Sampling of Authors and Media People Featured in This Volume

Mitch Albom
An award-winning sports columnist for the *Detroit Fress Press*, Albom scored both critical and popular success with the book *Tuesdays with Morrie: An Old Man, a Young Man, and Life's Greatest Lesson*. A national bestseller, *Tuesdays with Morrie* is based on the weekly visits Albom made to his dying, yet inspirational, college mentor Morrie Schwartz. Albom is also the author of *The Bo Schembechler Story* and *Fab Five: Basketball, Trash Talk, the American Dream.*

Ric Burns
Filmmaker Burns, known for such documentaries as *The Donner Party* and *Coney Island*, was a key collaborator with his brother Ken Burns on the eleven-hour, Emmy Award-winning documentary *The Civil War*. Burns also co-wrote, produced, and directed *New York*, a film history of New York City from its Dutch immigrant origins through its evolution as a modern metropolis of the twentieth century. Burns also co-authored the illustrated books *The Civil War* and *New York*, which were both based on the documentary films.

Stephen Dixon
A novelist and prolific author of short fiction, Dixon often writes on the personal dynamics between men and women and examines the minutiae of existence in a large cosmopolitan city like New York. Dixon, winner of three O. Henry awards and a Best American Short Stories award among numerous other honors, has authored the novels *Frog, 30: Pieces of a Novel,* and *Tisch,* and the short story collections *The Stories of Stephen Dixon* and *Sleep*.

Nikki Giovanni
Among the prominent African American poets to have matured during the late 1960s and early 1970s, Giovanni authors verse for children as well as adults. Her work, which is known for its strong expressions of racial pride and respect for family, is collected in such volumes as *My House, Cotton Candy on a Rainy Day,* and *Blues: For All the Changes: New Poems*. Giovanni's poetry collections for youth include *Ego-Tripping and Other Poems for Young People* and *Vacation Time*.

Seamus Heaney
Nobel laureate Heaney, considered one of the world's finest twentieth-century poets, has achieved both high stature among critics and popularity with "the common reader." Much of what defines Heaney's poems spring from his Northern Ireland surroundings and his witness to the civil strife dividing Catholics and Protestants. His poetry has been collected in *Selected Poems, 1966-1987* and *Opened Ground: Selected Poems, 1966-1996*, as well as in the volumes *Seeing Things* and *The Spirit Level*. In 2000, Heaney was awarded the Whitbread Award for his translation of the epic poem *Beowulf*.

Ruth Prawer Jhabvala
novelist who is also known for her screenplays—particularly two adaptations from the works of E. M. Forster, *A Room with a View* and *Howard's End*—Jhabvala has received numerous honors for her writing, including a Booker Prize for the novel *Heat and Dust*. Long known in Europe and India for the quality of her fiction, it was not until she received an Academy Award for the screenplay to *A Room with a View* that she became prominent in the U.S. as well. Among Jhabvala's other works of fiction are *Three Continents, Shards of Memory,* and *East into Upper East: Plain Tales from New York and New Delhi.*

V. S. Naipaul
Born in Trinidad to the descendants of Hindu immigrants from India and educated at England's Oxford University, Naipaul is considered one of the world's most gifted novelists. Winner of a Booker Prize for *In a Free State*, which writer Paul Theroux described as "a masterpiece in the fiction of rootlessness," Naipaul is known for setting his stories in emerging Third World countries, caught in the throes of creating new national identities from the remnants of native and colonial cultures. In 2000, he released the volumes *Between Father and Son: Selected Correspondence of V. S. Naipaul and His Family, 1949-1953* and *Reading and Writing: A Personal Account*.

Simon Schama

Schama, the Mellon Professor of History at Harvard University, authors unique volumes of narrative history that often focus on a distinct historical period or place, such as seventeenth-century Dutch society or the French Revolution. Schama also interweaves historical scholarship with analyses of the fine arts, as in his biography *Rembrandt's Eyes.* Among his other works is *Landscape and Memory*, an often controversial discourse on the relationship between humanity and nature.

Acknowledgments

Grateful acknowledgment is made to those publishers, photographers, and artists whose work appear with these authors' essays. Following is a list of the copyright holders who have granted us permission to reproduce material in this volume of *CANR*. Every effort has been made to trace copyright, but if omissions have been made, please let us know.

Photographs/Art

Helen Gurley Brown: Brown, photograph by Marty Lederhandler. AP/Wide World Photos. Reproduced by permission.

Deepak Chopra: Chopra, photograph. AP/Wide World Photos. Reproduced by permission.

Clive Cussler: Cussler, photograph by Ron Semrod. AP/Wide World Photos. Reproduced by permission.

Stephen Dixon: Dixon, photograph. AP/Wide World Photos. Reproduced by permission.

Charles Alexander Eastman: Eastman, photograph. The Library of Congress.

Nikki Giovanni: Giovanni, photograph. AP/Wide World Photos. Reproduced by permission.

Eric Idle: Idle, photograph by Chris Pizzello. Reproduced by permission.

John Nance: Nance, photograph by Patricia Davenport. © Patricia Davenport. Reproduced by permission.

Felice Picano: Picano, photograph. AP/Wide World Photos. Reproduced by permission.

William Safire: Safire, photograph. UPI/Corbis-Bettmann. Reproduced by permission.

A

Indicates that a listing has been compiled from secondary sources believed to be reliable, but has not been personally verified for this edition by the author sketched.

ABRAHAMS, Peter 1947-

PERSONAL: Born in 1947, son of a dentist; married Diana Gray (a teacher), 1978; children: Seth, Ben, Lily. *Education:* Williams College, B.A., 1968.

ADDRESSES: *Agent*—c/o Ballantine Publishing Group, 201 East 50th St., New York, NY 10022. *E-mail*—pa@cape.com.

CAREER: Writer. Worked as a spear fisherman in the Bahamas, 1968-70; Canadian Broadcasting Co., Toronto, Canada, producer.

AWARDS, HONORS: Edgar Award nomination for best novel of 1994, for *Lights Out.*

WRITINGS:

THRILLERS

The Fury of Rachel Monette, Macmillan (New York City), 1980.
Tongues of Fire, M. Evans (New York City), 1982.
Hard Rain, Dutton (New York City), 1988.
Pressure Drop, Dutton, 1989.
(With Sidney D. Kirkpatrick) *Turning the Tide: One Man against the Medellin Cartel* (nonfiction), Dutton, 1991.
Revolution #9: A Thriller, Mysterious Press (New York City), 1992.
Lights Out, Mysterious Press, 1994.
The Fan, Warner (New York City), 1995.
A Perfect Crime, Ballantine (New York City), 1998.
Crying Wolf, Ballantine, 2000.

Also author of *Red Message,* 1986.

ADAPTATIONS: *The Fan* was adapted for film by Frank Darabont and Phoef Sutton and released by Tri-Star, 1996.

SIDELIGHTS: Peter Abrahams is the author of many suspenseful novels that have become favorites with readers and critics alike. "Abrahams' thrillers, generally first-rate, . . . usually hinge on the sins of the past (Nazi intrigue, etc.) staining the present," according to a critic for *Kirkus Reviews.* In an interview with Kay Longcope of the *Boston Globe,* Abrahams explained: "They're all sorts of thrillers, but defining them isn't easy. . . . I think of them as novels but the suspense element plays a strong role. I like to lead my main character to something the reader will dread, then say, 'Given characteristics of that particular character, that had to happen.' I like a bit of humor, too. Generally, thrillers provide a humorless terrain."

Abrahams' books often feature ordinary heroes and heroines, complicated plot twists, and political intrigue. His first, *The Fury of Rachel Monette,* follows the title character to Morocco, France, and Israel as she attempts to solve her husband's murder, discover the secret of a 1942 German letter he left behind, and recover her young son, who has been kidnapped by a man posing as a rabbi. *The Fury of Rachel Monette* garnered praise from critics: A *Publishers Weekly* reviewer commented that its "[s]teadily sustained suspense and smooth writing keep the reader hooked"; and *Spectator* contributor Harriet Waugh called the book "well written, fast moving, constantly surprising and jolly exciting."

An Israel connection also figures prominently in *Tongues of Fire,* Abrahams' second novel. In it, Isaac Rehv, a former Israeli soldier, flees to the United States after his country is destroyed by Arab invaders. There, Rehv conspires to assassinate an Arab leader and attracts the attention of a zealous CIA agent who tails Rehv around the world, from Canada to Sudan and Mecca. Although some reviewers considered *Tongues of Fire* to be a bit implausible, many praised Abrahams' skill nonetheless. A *Publishers Weekly* reviewer termed the book "fast-paced and exciting," while *Los Angeles Times Book Review* contributor Raymond Mungo called it "a wickedly clever and intricate mystery." According to a *West Coast Review of Books* critic, Abrahams' "gripping prose can best be described as throat-grabbing."

Abrahams' third thriller to catch the attention of critics was *Hard Rain,* which conjures up the atmosphere of the late 1960s and takes its title from a Bob Dylan tune. In it, Jessie Shapiro is caught up in political intrigue as she searches for her ex-husband and young daughter, who have failed to return from a weekend trip. Defining events of the past, such as Woodstock and the Vietnam War, haunt the present as Jessie treks from Los Angeles to Vermont in search of clues. Writing in the *Los Angeles Book Review,* Charles Champlin praised *Hard Rain* as a "top-rank adventure." *Publishers Weekly* critic Sybil Steinberg called the book "an intricate, convincing thriller." *New York Times Book Review* contributor William J. Harding was also enthusiastic, commenting that *Hard Rain* has the elements of "a good thriller": "style, atmosphere and a surprising plot."

Pressure Drop, Abrahams' follow-up to *Hard Rain,* also generated approval from critics. According to *Quill & Quire* contributor Paul Stuewe, "*The Fury of Rachel Monette* and *Hard Rain* were competent thrillers, but Peter Abrahams' latest novel breaks to the front ranks of this extremely crowded field." In *Pressure Drop,* Abrahams sets up two seemingly unrelated plot lines that eventually collide. In one, suspicious and dangerous circumstances develop around Nina Kitchener, whose baby boy, conceived through artificial insemination, is kidnapped from the hospital shortly after birth. In the other, N. H. "Matt" Matthias investigates nagging questions surrounding a scuba-diving accident that took place at his resort in the Bahamas, uncovering a connection between the accident and Nina's tragedy. Reviewing *Pressure Drop* in the *Armchair Detective,* William J. Schafer praised Abrahams' writing as "highly literate, brisk, and graphic," and his characterizations as "fresh and uncliched."

Flashbacks to 1960s Vietnam War protests provide a backdrop for Abrahams' next thriller, *Revolution #9.* The main character is Charlie Ochs, a Cape Cod lobsterman who has been lying low since a campus protest bombing he was involved in accidentally killed a young boy. Ochs, who has spent nearly twenty years living underground, is finally tracked down by federal agents the night before his wedding. He is given an ultimatum: help the government find the bombing's mastermind, Rebecca Klein, or serve time for his own role in the attack. According to Chicago *Tribune Books* contributor Richard Martins: "Charlie's hunt through the past is an often painful but always gripping story. Abrahams weaves in and out of time and temperament with considerable skill." Although finding *Revolution #9* a bit "uneven," a *Publishers Weekly* reviewer nonetheless noted that "expert pacing and an intriguing plot hold the reader's interest."

Abrahams followed *Revolution #9* with *Lights Out,* which received an Edgar Award nomination for best novel of 1994. The book's main character is Eddie Nye, who, despite his innocence, has spent fifteen years in prison on drug charges. He is not free long before he is again plunged into dangerous intrigue while investigating his frame-up. According to *Publishers Weekly* critic Sybil Steinberg, Abrahams "creates a fascinating and memorable character in Eddie Nye." Steinberg further noted: "Consistently interesting and suspenseful, his thriller's shocking outcome is revealed only on the very last page."

In his eighth book, *The Fan,* Abrahams focuses on Gil Renard, a down-and-out traveling salesman, and Bobby Rayburn, an arrogant and successful baseball player who is riding out a batting slump. Renard, a baseball fanatic, has lost his job and wife and has slid into committing petty crimes. He becomes obsessed with Rayburn, managing to become the caretaker on the ballplayer's estate while he plans to murder the star on the field. *The Fan* was a hit with critics; *Booklist* contributor Wes Lukowsky called it a "first-rate thriller," and *Library Journal* reviewer Marylaine Block termed it an "excellent novel." A *Rapport* critic proclaimed that if "you're not a fan of Peter Abrahams by now, *The Fan* will make you one." *The Fan* was filmed in 1996 by action pro Tony Scott, and starred Robert DeNiro and Wesley Snipes.

In 1998, Abrahams' *A Perfect Crime* was released. This thriller tells of Roger Cullingwood's murderous plot against his wife. Though in a marriage that lacks depth and on unemployment for months, Roger's idyllic perception of his life is not shattered until he learns that his wife, Francie, is romantically involved with a well-known local psychologist. Roger, an extremely intelligent person desperate to restore his enormous ego, engineers a "perfect" plan to kill his wife. He loses control of his plot after he enlists the help of a previously convicted murderer. Although a *Publishers Weekly* critic complained that Roger and his cohort were unrealistic characters who "lack dimension," the critic felt the other major characters were "well-drawn." In contrast, *Booklist* contributor Thomas Gaughan uniformly praised Abrahams' characterizations as well as complimenting the author's "complex and compelling [plotting]" and "sharp and almost flawless [dialogue]." Gaughan notes, however, that the "satisfying" novel has "a subtle sense of the mathematical certainty to the denouement." Despite its perceived flaws, the "initially absorbing but somewhat contrived thriller" was recommended by the *Publishers Weekly* critic, who asserted: "As he explores Francie's emotional terrain in the wake of tragedy, Abrahams will keep readers very much engaged." "*A Perfect Crime* is fast-paced, tense, even witty as it careens to its bloody conclusion," declared Karen Anderson's *Library Journal* review.

The ethics of four young adults from various social classes are exposed and tested in actions and reactions associated with acquiring money and material goods. What will a middle-class kid from a small Colorado town do to pay for a prestigious university education in New England? Abrahams presents one scenario in *Crying Wolf,* "a suspense novel built around kidnapping, extortion and youthful stupidity," related a *Publishers Weekly* reviewer. Nat, a high school valedictorian, uses his $2,000 essay contest winnings to help his mother cover the tuition for his freshman year at Inverness. When his mother loses her job, Nat must find another way to subsidize his education. He sets up a kidnapping plot with the help of Grace and Izzie, the wealthy twins Nat becomes involved with at Inverness. As Vanessa Bush indicated in *Booklist,* the trio's plan is devised to be "a 'victimless' crime with one of [the twins] as the kidnapping subject, to get the money from an indifferent father." The father prevents the kidnapping, however, and Freedy, a thief and suspected rapist from the "wrong side" of the college town, takes the trio's kidnapping idea and adapts it, making a more dangerous kidnapping plan. When Nat tries to expose Freedy's plans people think that he is just "crying wolf." "Freedy makes for an interesting villain, but his rages can't sustain the book," assessed the writer for *Publishers Weekly,* who faulted *Crying Wolf* for having a slow pace and poor characterizations. However, Bush more positively concluded in a review of *Crying Wolf:* "Abrahams ably builds suspense in this novel about secret lives, madness, and mistrust."

Commenting on his books to Kay Longcope in the *Boston Globe,* Abrahams stated: "I'm interested in putting ordinary people into extraordinary situations, as Alfred Hitchcock did, rather than making James Bond-type superheroes and putting them in life and death situations. You can generate a lot more dread. I want to directly attack the imagination, to ensnare it. That's the way a good book works for me."

BIOGRAPHICAL/CRITICAL SOURCES:

PERIODICALS

Armchair Detective, spring, 1990, p. 238.

Booklist, August, 1992, Peter Robertson, review of *Revolution #9,* p. 1998; February 1, 1994, Wes Lukowsky, review of *Lights Out,* p. 996; January 15, 1995, Wes Lukowsky, review of *The Fan,* p. 868; July, 1998, Thomas Gaughan, review of *A Perfect Crime,* p. 1827; August, 1999, Karen Harris, review of *A Perfect Crime,* p. 2075; January 1, 2000, Vanessa Bush, review of *Crying Wolf,* p. 833.

Boston Globe, February 22, 1988.

Entertainment Weekly, April 21, 1995, Gene Lyons, review of *The Fan,* p. 49.

Kirkus Reviews, June 15, 1980, pp. 789-90; September 1, 1989, p. 1264; June 1, 1992, pp. 682-83; January 1, 1994, p. 2.

Library Journal, August, 1980, Samuel Simons, review of *The Fury of Rachel Monette,* p. 1655; April 15, 1982, review of *Tongues of Fire,* p. 823; December, 1987, A. M. B. Amantia, review of *Hard Rain,* p. 126; May 1, 1991, review of *Turning the Tide,* p. 89; July, 1992, Michele Leber, review of *Revolution #9,* p. 119; February 1, 1994, Dan Bogey, review of *Lights Out,* p. 109; February 1, 1995, Marylaine Block, review of *The Fan,* p. 97; August, 1998, Karen Anderson, review of *A Perfect Crime,* p. 128; December, 1998, Danna Bell-Russel, review of *A Perfect Crime,* p. 173.

Los Angeles Times, July 20, 1992, p. E3.

Los Angeles Times Book Review, June 27, 1982, p. 10; January 17, 1988, p. 10.

New Republic, September 9, 1996, Stanley Kauffmann, review of *The Fan,* p. 37.

New York, July 5, 1982, Rhoda Koenig, review of *The Fury of Rachel Monette,* p. 103.

New York Times Book Review, February 21, 1988, William J. Harding, review of *Hard Rain,* p. 20; October 11, 1998, Marilyn Stasio, review of *A Perfect Crime,* p. 28.

Penthouse, February, 1981, Marilyn Stasio, review of *The Fury of Rachel Monette,* p. 48.

Playboy, June, 1991, Digby Diehl, review of *Turning the Tide,* p. 38.

Publishers Weekly, June 27, 1980, review of *The Fury of Rachel Monette,* p. 79; April 9, 1982, Barbara A. Bannon, review of *Tongues of Fire,* p. 43; November 6, 1987, Sybil Steinberg, review of *Hard Rain,* p. 58; September 29, 1989, review of *Pressure Drop,* p. 60; April 19, 1991, review of *Turning the Tide,* p. 54; June 1, 1992, p. 50; January 10, 1994, review of *Lights Out,* pp. 43-44; January 23, 1995, review of *The Fan,* pp. 58-59; July 3, 1995, p. 26; July 20, 1998, review of *A Perfect Crime,* p. 206; January 10, 2000, review of *Crying Wolf,* p. 42.

Quill & Quire, February, 1990, p. 27.

Rapport, volume 19, number 6, p. 29.

Spectator, January 30, 1982, pp. 22-23.

Tribune Books (Chicago), August 2, 1992, p. 5; March 20, 1994, p. 7; March 19, 1995, p. 6.

Washington Post Book World, August 16, 1992, p. 6.

West Coast Review of Books, July, 1982, p. 33.*

* * *

ADLER, H. G. 1910-

PERSONAL: Born July 2, 1910, in Prague, Czechoslovakia; son of Emil and Alice (Fraenkel) Adler; married Gertrude Klepetar (died October 14, 1944); married Bettina Gross; children: (second marriage) Jeremy David. *Education:* German University of Prague, Dr.Phil. *Religion:* Jewish.

ADDRESSES: Home—47 Wetherby Mansions, London SW5 9BH, England.

CAREER: Freelance writer and scholar.

MEMBER: PEN.

AWARDS, HONORS: Leo Baeck Prize, 1958; Prix Charles Veillon, 1969, for *Panorama;* Buber-Rosenzweig Medal, 1974; honorary Dr.Phil., University of Berlin, 1980.

WRITINGS:

(Editor) Franz Baermann Steiner, *Unruhe ohne Uhr: Gedichte aus dem Nachlass,* Lambert Schneider, 1954.

Theresienstadt, 1941-1945: Das Antlitz einer Zwangsgemeinschaft, J. C. B. Mohr, 1955.

Die verheimlichte Wahrheit: Theresienstaedter Dokumente, J. C. B. Mohr, 1958.

Der Kampf gegen die "Endloesung der Judenfrage," Bundeszentrale, 1958.

Die Juden in Deutschland, Koesel, 1960, translation published as *The Jews in Germany,* University of Notre Dame Press, 1969.

Unser Georg und andere Erzaehlungen, Bergland Verlag, 1961.

Eine Reise: Erzaehlung, Bibliotheca Christiana, 1962, reprinted with postscript by son, Jeremy Adler, Zsolnay (Vienna), 1999.

(Editor with Hermann Langbein and Else Lingens-Reiner)*Auschwitz: Zeugnisse und Berichte,* Europaeische Verlagsanstalt, 1962.

Der Fuerst des Segens (short prose), Bibliotheca Christiana, 1964.

(Editor) Franz Baermann Steiner, *Eroberungen: Ein lyrischer Zyklus,* Lambert Schneider, 1964.

Die Erfahrung der Ohnmacht; Beitraege zur Soziologie unserer Zeit, Europaeische Verlagsanstalt, 1964.

Sodoms Untergang (short prose), Bibliotheca Christiana, 1965.

Panorama (novel), Walter-Verlag, 1968.

Ereignisse, Erzachlungen, Walter-Verlag, 1969.

Kontraste und Variationen (essay and photographs), Echter, 1969.

Der verwaltete Mensch: Studien sur Deportation der Juden aus Deutschland, J. C. B. Mohr, 1974.

Fenster (poems), Alphabox Press, 1974.

Viele Jahreszeiten (poems), Wienand, 1975.

Die Freiheit des Menschen (essays), J. C. B. Mohr, 1976.

Shuren und Pfeiler (poems), Alphabox Press, 1978.

Blicke (poems), Verlag Europaeische Ideen, 1979.

Stimme und Zonuf (poems), Knaus, 1980.

Vorschule fuer eine Experimentaltheologie: Betrachtungen uber Wirklichkeit und Sein, Steiner Verlag (Stuttgart), 1987.

(With Hermann Langbein and Ella Lingens-Reiner) *Auschwitz: Zeugnisse und Berichte,* Athenaum (Frankfort), 1988.

Hausordnung: Wortlaut und Auslegung, Edition Atelier (Vienna), 1988.

Die unsichtbare Wand, Zsolnay (Vienna), 1989.

SIDELIGHTS: H. G. Adler is a Czech poet and novelist who survived the Nazi concentration camps of World War II. Adler has written about his experiences during that time in nonfiction books, autobiographies, and the novel *Eine Reise.* Written at a time when the existence of the concentration camps was little known, Adler's novel took some twelve years to find a publisher. Even then, it was little regarded. Although a Jew, Adler came from a secular rather than religious family and his book reflects that background. Because of this, the Jewish community paid little attention to his story. "In his isolation," remarks Peter Demetz in the *Times Literary Supplement,* "[Adler] wrote a pioneering book, under tremendous pressure."

Eine Reise tells the story of a Jewish family of five who are shipped from their native Czechoslovakia to a Nazi concentration camp during World War II. The father soon dies, and the mother, daughter, and aunt die in the camp, leaving only the son as a survivor. The son's account of his time as a prisoner and in the immediate post-war period include his meetings with good Germans who help him and with American soldiers who liberate the camp. Demetz especially praises Adler's use of the daughter's point of view to show the shifting levels of fantasy, fear, and desperation felt by those trapped within the death camp; Demetz explains that "the close web of delusions, healing daydreams and false consolations constitutes a masterpiece of modern fiction."

BIOGRAPHICAL/CRITICAL SOURCES:

BOOKS

Hubmann, Heinrich, and Alfred O. Lanz, *Zu Hause im Exil: zu Werk und Person H. G. Adler,* Steiner Verlag (Stuttgart), 1987.

PERIODICALS

Times Literary Supplement, December 17, 1999, p. 25.*

* * *

ADRIAN, Frances
See POLLAND, Madeleine A(ngela Cahill)

* * *

ALAYA, Flavia (M.) 1935-

PERSONAL: Surname is pronounced Ah-*lah*-ya; born May 16, 1935, in New Rochelle, NY; daughter of Mario Salvatore (a teacher) and Maria (a teacher; maiden name, Spagnola [or Spagnuolo]) Alaya; married Sandy Feddema, 1993; children: (with Henry J. Browne) Harry Mario, Christopher Robert, Nina Maria Browne. *Education:* Barnard College, B.A., 1956; University of Padua, graduate study, 1957-58; Columbia University, M.A., 1960, Ph.D., 1965; Certificate in Integrated Territorial and Urban Conservation, ICCROM (Rome), 1997.

ADDRESSES: Office—School of Social Science, Ramapo College of New Jersey, Mahwah, NJ 07430.

CAREER: University of North Carolina at Greensboro, instructor in English, 1959-60; Barnard College, New York City, lecturer and assistant in English, 1960-62; Hunter College of the City University of New York, New York City, lecturer in English, 1962-66; New York University, New York City, instructor, 1966-67, assistant professor of English, 1967-71; Ramapo College of New Jersey, School of Intercultural Studies, Mahwah, NJ, associate professor of English and comparative literature and founding director, 1971-74, professor, 1974-80; Ramapo College, School of Social Science, professor of literature and cultural history, 1981-99, emeritus, 1999—. City of Paterson Historic Preservation Commission, NJ, commissioner, 1989-98, chair, 1990-98; National Trust for Historic Preservation, advisor, 1991-2000; New Jersey Historic Sites Council, member, 1998—.

MEMBER: National Writers Union, Modern Language Association of America, Northeast Victorian Studies Association (president, 1977-81), Passaic County Historical Society (trustee, 1973-84; president, 1978-82), National Trust for Historic Preservation (advisor, 1991-2000), Association for Union Democracy, Amnesty International.

AWARDS, HONORS: Fulbright and Italian Government scholar in Italy, 1957-58; Guggenheim Foundation fellow, 1974-75; National Endowment for the Humanities Summer Stipend, 1985; Kress Foundation ICCROM Fellow, 1997; Geraldine R. Dodge Foundation, New Jersey Writers scholarship award, 1997.

WRITINGS:

William Sharp—"Fiona Macleod," 1855-1905, Harvard University Press (Cambridge, MA), 1970.

(General editor, with Charles Savage as the art and technical editor, and with Henry J. Browne and Lynda Price) *Gaetano Federici: The Artist as Historian,* Passaic County Historical Society (Paterson, NJ), 1980.

(With Dolores Van Rensalier) *Bridge Street to Freedom: Landmarking a Station on the Underground Railroad,* Ramapo College of New Jersey (Mahwah, NJ), 1998.

Under the Rose: A Confession (memoir), Feminist Press at the City University of New York (New York City), 1999.

Also author of *The Imagination Is a Square Wheel,* 1977; *Silk and Sandstone,* 1984; and *Signifying Paterson,* 1989. Contributor to periodicals, including *Victorian Poetry, Journal of the History of Ideas, Victorian Studies,* and *CHOICE;* frequently anthologized.

WORK IN PROGRESS: Research toward major article on Feminism and Catholicism; studies in Victorian publicity and celebrity; fiction.

SIDELIGHTS: In her 1999 memoir, *Under the Rose: A Confession,* Alaya describes her early life as a sheltered Italian-American daughter, and tells of meeting Henry J. (Harry) Browne, a thirty-eight-year-old Irish-American Roman Catholic priest, on a Fulbright year abroad in 1957. Out of this meeting the rest of her life evolved, from a secret love affair into an enduring partnership that eventually produced three children and lasted until Browne died from leukemia in 1980. The bond begun in Italy between the clandestine lovers, both of them scholars and political activists, grew after they returned to New York City. To protect the secrecy of their liaison, Alaya had her first baby in Italy and later moved to New Jersey. But in 1970, ten years before his death, Browne resigned from his parish and chose to live with her and their children. Alaya justly faults "a regressive church" for Browne's "divided loyalties," according to a *Publishers Weekly* critic, calling her "less convincing, however, in her protestations that their domestic situation allowed her the freedom to be herself." Margaret Flannagan in a *Booklist* review called *Under the Rose* "a hauntingly beautiful memoir. . . . an honest examination . . . [and analysis] of [Alaya's] lifestyle choice."

BIOGRAPHICAL/CRITICAL SOURCES:

PERIODICALS

Booklist, October 15, 1999, p. 396.
Publishers Weekly, September 20, 1999, p. 65.

* * *

ALBOM, Mitch (David) 1958-

PERSONAL: Born May 23, 1958, in Passaic, NJ; son of Ira (a corporate executive) and Rhoda (an interior designer) Albom; married Janine Sabino (a singer), 1995. *Education:* Brandeis University, B.A. (sociology), 1979; Columbia University, M.J., 1981, M.B.A., 1982.

ADDRESSES: *Home*—Farmington Hills, MI. *Office*—*Detroit Free Press,* 321 West Lafayette, Detroit, MI 48226-2721. *E-mail*—mitch@albom.com.

CAREER: *Queens Tribune,* Flushing, NY, editor, 1981-82; contributing writer for *Sport, Philadelphia Inquirer,* and *Geo,* 1982-83; *Fort Lauderdale News and Sun Sentinel,* Fort Lauderdale, FL, sports columnist, 1983-85; *Detroit Free Press,* Detroit, MI, sports columnist, 1985—; WLLZ-radio, Farmington Hills, MI, sports director, beginning 1985, co-host of sports talk show, *Sunday Sports Albom,* 1988-99; WDIV-TV, Detroit, broadcaster and commentator, beginning 1987; *Monday Sports Albom* (originally *Sunday Sports Albom*; nationally-syndicated weekly sports talk show), host, 1999—; *The Mitch Albom Show* (nationally syndicated sports talk show), host; *Sports Reporters,* ESPN, panelist. Piano player; composer of a song for the television movie *Christmas in Connecticut,* 1992.

MEMBER: Baseball Writers of America, Football Writers of America, Tennis Writers of America.

AWARDS, HONORS: Award for best sports news story in the United States, 1985; named number one sports columnist in Michigan, Associated Press (AP) and United Press International (UPI), 1985, 1986, 1987, and 1988; named number-one sports columnist in the United States, AP Sports Editors, 1987, 1988, 1989, 1990, 1991, 1992, 1993, 1994, 1995, 1996, 1997, and 1998; named number-one sports columnist in Michigan, National Association of Sportswriters and Broadcasters, 1988 and 1989; number two outstanding writer, National Headliners Award, 1989; award for best feature writing, AP Sports Editors, 1993, for article on University of Michigan basketball player Juwan Howard.

WRITINGS:

The Live Albom: The Best of Detroit Free Press Sports Columnist Mitch Albom, Detroit Free Press (Detroit), 1988.

(With Bo Schembechler) *Bo: The Bo Schembechler Story,* Warner Books (New York City), 1989.

Live Albom II, foreword by Ernie Harwell, Detroit Free Press, 1990.

Live Albom III: Gone to the Dogs, Detroit Free Press, 1992.

Fab Five: Basketball, Trash Talk, the American Dream, Warner Books, 1993.

Live Albom IV, foreword by Dave Barry, Detroit Free Press, 1995.

Tuesdays with Morrie: An Old Man, a Young Man, and Life's Greatest Lesson, Doubleday (New York City), 1997.

Contributor to periodicals, including *Gentlemen's Quarterly, Sports Illustrated, New York Times,* and *Sport.*

ADAPTATIONS: Tuesdays with Morrie: An Old Man, a Young Man, and Life's Greatest Lesson was adapted by Oprah Winfrey as a television movie, aired by ABC, 1999; *Bo: The Bo Schembechler Story* and *Tuesdays with Morrie* have been adapted as audio books.

SIDELIGHTS: Mitch Albom, a journalist for the *Detroit Free Press,* has earned national attention and awards for his sports columns distinguished by insight, humor, and empathy. These writings have been collected in *The Live Albom: The Best of Mitch Albom, Live Albom II, Live Albom III: Gone to the Dogs,* and *Live Albom IV.* Disdaining the questionable ethical conduct, drug problems, and over-inflated egos often found in the sports world, Albom highlights instances of athletic courage and determination while providing honest commentary on a team's performance. After stints in New York and Florida, Albom arrived in Detroit, Michigan, in 1985 as a staff member of the *Detroit Free Press.* Introducing himself to his new audience in his first column, he explained that readers could expect "some opinion, some heart, some frankness. Some laughs. Some out of the ordinary." Albom also made a good first impression with area sports fans by rejecting the negative stereotype—a crime-ridden and dying city—that Detroit held for the nation. He added, "Some people apparently look at a new job in Detroit as something to be endured or tolerated. . . . I, for one, am thrilled to be here. For sports, they don't make towns any better than this one."

One of Albom's most distinguished traits as a columnist is his sympathy with disappointed fans when local professional teams struggle unsuccessfully for championships. He commiserated with area readers in 1988 when Detroit's basketball team, the Pistons, battled to the National Basketball Association (NBA) finals and pushed Los Angeles to a full seven-game series, only to lose the last game by three points. He reasoned, "They went further than any Pistons team before them. They came onto the stage as brutes and left with an entire nation's respect—for their courage, for their determination, for their talent. . . . They took on all comers. . . . They could beat any team in the league. They just couldn't beat them all." A year earlier, when the underdog Red Wings reached the National Hockey League (NHL) semifinals but lost, Albom reported how, on the long flight home, the players dealt with this defeat. Upon learning that a devoted fan—who was riding the team's charter plane home—had flown to Edmonton to watch the game, Detroit players chipped in to reimburse him for his ticket. They also joined in on a chorus of that fan's favorite cheer. Witnessing this, Albom wrote, "Amazing. Here were these bruising, scarred, often toothless men, on the night of a season-ending loss, singing a high school cheer. Simply because it made an old guy happy. Many people will remember goals and saves and slap shots from this season. I hope I never forget that cheer."

With columns such as these, Albom earned a loyal following and a reputation as a blue-collar sports fan. His success in print carried over to other media, including radio and television. He joined the staff of rock station WLLZ in 1985, initially serving as sports director. In 1988 he and co-host Mike Stone began a weekly program, *The Sunday Sports Albom.* Guests included both local and national sports figures and the program's format allowed calls by listeners. His stellar guest list was evidence of the comfortable rapport Albom shared with many area athletes and coaches. This accord extended beyond interviews; in 1987 he was even a good luck charm for Detroit's Red Wings. As he explained in a column reprinted in *The Live Albom,* "I am not sure when my car and the fortunes of the Red Wings actually became intertwined. I do know [coach] Jacques Demers and I have now driven to five playoff games together and Detroit has won all five, and now even Demers, who is not superstitious, is asking me what time we're leaving."

Albom's relationship with another state sports figure, former University of Michigan football coach Bo Schembechler, led to a collaboration on Schembechler's autobiography, *Bo: The Bo Schembechler Story.* Respected as a top college coach for his Big Ten championships and frequent bowl appearances, Schembechler reputedly had a quick temper and churlish personality. In *Bo,* Albom presents Schembechler as a sincere family man whose demeanor was a deliberate act and who inspired love and respect from his football players. Albom credits Schembechler with turning the Michigan football program around. When he began as coach, Michigan was a perennial runner-up to Ohio State. Bo promised championships, and he delivered without ever suffering through a losing season. Albom notes a greater accomplishment, however, is that Schembechler ran a program free from rules violations and saw his athletes graduate. A reviewer for the *New York Times Book Review* concluded that while *Bo* did not offer much new information about Schembechler, the work strengthened Schembechler's position as a role model for college athletes.

While Albom has reigned as the darling of the Detroit sports scene, he has also been involved with his share of controversy. He raised the ire of a Detroit Tigers pitcher with a column and, eleven months later, had a bucket of ice water dumped over his head in the Tigers' clubhouse (the pitcher blamed his disintegrating effectiveness on Albom's commentary). Albom also broke the 1988 story of the after-curfew bar visits of several Red Wings players. He reported that, when confronted with the news, the coach "looked as if he was going to cry." Albom added that this black mark on the team's accomplishments was "not the story I wanted to write. Not the one you wanted to read." In these instances, a prediction Albom made in his first column came true: "I try to be honest. . . . This is not always a pretty job. Sometimes you have to write that the good guys lost, or that somebody's favorite baseball hero in the whole world just checked into the rehab clinic. Still, sports are the only show in town where no matter how many times you go back, you never know the ending. That's special."

Albom expanded his writing beyond the realm of sports with his 1997 publication *Tuesdays with Morrie: An Old Man, a Young Man, and Life's Greatest Lesson.* The book, which was the top-selling nonfiction title of 1998, sprang from Albom's weekly visits with his former professor, Morrie Schwartz. While a student at Brandeis University, Albom was strongly influenced by the unconventional Schwartz, who urged his students to disdain high paying careers and follow their hearts instead. Upon graduating, Albom promised to keep in touch with his teacher, but he never called or visited Schwartz for the next sixteen years. Watching television one night, he saw Schwartz on the ABC program *Nightline.* The professor had been diagnosed with amyotrophic lateral sclerosis (ALS), commonly known as Lou Gehrig's disease. A hasty trip to Massachusetts to see his old mentor led to a weekly meeting for the rest of Schwarz's life. Albom was struck by the realization that although he was young, healthy, and wildly successful, his old, dying teacher was a much happier, more peaceful person. He began to write a book based on their conversations, in part to help defray Schwartz's medical expenses.

Tuesdays with Morrie is "a slender but emotionally weighty account of Albom's final seminar with Schwartz," in the words of *People* contributor William Plummer. Albom relates the way in which, without even realizing it, he had slowly abandoned his youthful ideals to become cynical, spiritually shallow, and materialistic. Working around the clock to maintain his career left him little time for reflection. Schwartz helped his former student to refocus his life and in chapters that focus on fear, aging, greed, family, forgiveness, and other topics, "the reader hears Morrie advise Mitch to slow down and savor the moment . . . to give up striving for bigger toys and, above all, to invest himself in love," explains Plummer. "Familiar pronouncements, of course, but what makes them fresh is Morrie's eloquence, his lack of self-pity . . . and his transcendent humor, even in the face of death."

"One gets whiffs of Jesus, the Buddha, Epicurus, Montaigne and Erik Erikson" from Schwartz's discourses, relates Alain de Botton in the *New York Times Book Review.* Yet that reviewer objects that the "true and sometimes touching pieces of advice" dispensed by Schwartz "don't add up to a very wise book. Though Albom insists that Schwartz's words have transformed him, it's hard to see why. . . . Because Albom fails to achieve any real insight into his own previously less-than-exemplary life, it's difficult for the reader to trust in his spiritual transformation." That opinion was not shared by a *Publishers Weekly* reviewer, who assures: "Far from being awash in sentiment, the dying man retains a firm grasp on reality." The writer concludes that *Tuesdays with Morrie* is "an emotionally rich book and a deeply affecting memorial to a wise mentor."

BIOGRAPHICAL/CRITICAL SOURCES:

BOOKS

Albom, Mitch, *The Live Albom,* Detroit Free Press, 1988, pp. 12, 208, 218.

Albom, *Live Albom II,* Detroit Free Press, 1990, pp. 33, 35, 44.

PERIODICALS

Books, Christmas, 1998, p. 22.

Bookwatch, February, 1998, p. 11.

Christian Science Monitor, April 30, 1998, Robin Whitten, review of audio version of *Tuesday with Morrie,* p. B4.

Crain's Cleveland Business, September 27, 1999, Brian Tucker, "Two Speakers Capture Local Audiences," p. 10.

Detroit Free Press, March 30, 1993, p. 1C.

Kirkus Reviews, July 1, 1997, p. 993.

Kliatt, May, 1998, p. 56.

Lancet, October 17, 1998, Faith McLellan, "A Teacher to the Last," p. 1318.

New York Times, September 6, 1995, James Bennet, "In 7th Week, Detroit Strike Turns Violent; Newspaper Workers Clash with Police," September 6, 1995, p. A13.

New York Times Book Review, November 19, 1989, Charles Salzberg, review of *Bo: The Bo Schembechler Story,* p. 44; November 23, 1997, Alain de Botton, review of *Tuesdays with Morrie,* p. 20.

People, January 12, 1998, William Plummer, "Memento Morrie: Morrie Schwartz, while Dying, Teaches Writer Mitch Albom the Secrets of Living," p. 141.

Publishers Weekly, October 5, 1990, review of audio version of *Bo: The Bo Schembechler Story,* p. 73; June 30, 1997, review of *Tuesdays with Morrie,* p. 60; March 2, 1998, review of audio version of *Tuesdays with Morrie,* p. 30.

Sports Illustrated, May 15, 1995, "Record Albom," p. 22; December 20, 1999, "Morrie Glory: His Bestseller Now a Hit TV Movie, Sportswriter Mitch Albom Continues His Crossover Act," p. 28.

Tribune Books (Chicago), December 12, 1993, p. 3.

TV Guide, December 4, 1999, "These Days with Morrie," p. 39.

Wall Street Journal, March 14, 1988, Bradley A. Stertz, "It's Probably Not Too Smart for Us to Publicize This Kind of Revenge," p. 29.

OTHER

Albom Online, http://www.albom.com (June 14, 2000).*

* * *

ALEXANDER, Adele Logan 1938-

PERSONAL: Born January 26, 1938, in New York, NY; daughter of Arthur C. (a physician) and Wenonah (a social worker; maiden name, Bond) Logan; married Clifford L. Alexander, Jr. (a consultant), July 11, 1959; children: Elizabeth, Mark Clifford. *Education:* Radcliffe College, B.A., 1959; Howard University, M.A., 1987. *Politics:* Democrat.

ADDRESSES: *Office*—Department of History, George Washington University, 2121 Eye St. NW, Washington, DC, 20052.

CAREER: Instructor in history and Afro-American studies at University of Maryland at College Park, and Howard University, Washington, DC; George Washington University, Washington, DC, professor of history.

WRITINGS:

Ambiguous Lives: Free Women of Color in Rural Georgia, 1789-1879, University of Arkansas Press (Fayetteville, AR), 1991.

Homelands and Waterways: The American Journey of the Bond Family, 1846-1926, Pantheon (New York City), 1999.

SIDELIGHTS: "Women are the keepers of the stories," Adele Logan Alexander said in a recent *Detroit Free Press* article, "which ironically also makes them protectors of family secrets." As columnist Desiree Cooper relates, "It wasn't until her own mother's death that Adele felt she finally had permission to unlock her family's past." What resulted for Alexander, a professor of history at George Washington University, was two books: *Ambiguous Lives: Free Women of Color in Rural Georgia,* and *Homelands and Waterways: The American Journey of the Bond Family, 1946-1926.*

The latter work came as a revelation to its author: While researching *Ambiguous Lives,* Alexander learned her paternal grandmother had been an outspoken suffragist. As Cooper quotes Alexander, "When she realized she knew as little about the women's suffrage movement as she did about her grandmother's politics, [the author] 'sidled from genealogy into American history.' "

Homelands and Waterways recounts three generations of Alexander's African-American ancestry, beginning with the arrival of her paternal great-grandfather, John Robert Bond, the mulatto son of a black dockhand and a white Irish woman. Bond left his native Liverpool for a new life in the United States in 1862, distinguishing himself in the U.S. Navy during the Civil War. Bond married a freed slave, Emma Thomas, and the family settled in Hyde Park, Massachusetts. From that generation and future ones came Bonds who were involved in suffrage and anti-lynching campaigns, the Spanish-American War and Booker T. Washington's Tuskegee Institute.

What the author finds unique about her family's story, she says, is the melting-pot aspect of her forebears. "When most people think of African-Americans, we think only of the stories of slavery, and in fact, that was Emma's story, and the whole idea of somebody who became African-American," Alexander told David Gergen in an *Online NewsHour* interview. "And John had to become a naturalized citizen, just as so many other Irish-English immigrants during that period did. But [once] he moved into this country, he could not really be part of the white immigrant community, but he was adopted by the African-American community, and he became part of that."

In her research, Alexander learned that her great-grandfather, though he had been poorly treated following the Civil War, became an honored American patriot. "He is included among 20 of [his] small New England town's . . . wounded veterans of the Civil War. And today, in Hyde Park, there is this wonderful monument [including] the gravestones of the 20 of their townsmen who were wounded in service to the country. And John Bond, U.S. Navy, is one of them."

Library Journal lauds *Homelands and Waterways* as "a saga of struggle and achievement against stereotype" and calls Alexander's work "an exemplary mix of history, genealogy and biography." The same view is taken by *Booklist*'s Margaret Flanagan, who called the book "an epic portrait of a strong family's determined passage from poverty to middle-class respectability."

BIOGRAPHICAL/CRITICAL SOURCES:

PERIODICALS

Booklist, August, 1999, Margaret Flanagan, review of *Homelands and Waterways,* p. 2016.

Detroit Free Press, September 3, 1999, Desiree Cooper, "Two Women Dig into the Past, Refreshingly."

Library Journal, July, 1999, Thomas J. Davis, review of *Homelands and Waterways,* p. 110.

Publishers Weekly, June 14, 1999, review of *Homelands and Waterways,* p. 60.

OTHER

Online NewsHour, interview with Adele Logan Alexander, http://web-cr05.pbs.org/newshour (December 30, 1999).*

* * *

ALEXANDER, Charles C(omer) 1935-

PERSONAL: Born October 24, 1935, in Cass County, TX; son of Charles Comer (an educator) and Pauline (Pynes) Alexander; married JoAnn Erwin, June 2, 1960; children: Rachel Camille. *Education:* Lamar State College of Technology (now Lamar University), B.A., 1958; University of Texas, M.A., 1959, Ph.D., 1962. *Politics:* Republican.

ADDRESSES: Home—8 Ann, Athens, OH, 45701. *E-mail*—alexande@oak.cats.ohiou.edu.

CAREER: University of Houston, Houston, TX, instructor, 1962-64, assistant professor of history, 1964-66; University of Georgia, Athens, associate professor of history, 1966-70; Ohio University, Athens, professor, 1970-89, distinguished professor of history, 1989—. University of Texas, visiting associate professor, 1968-69.

MEMBER: Organization of American Historians, American Historical Association, Southern Historical Association, Phi Alpha Theta, Phi Kappa Phi, Pi Sigma Alpha.

WRITINGS:

Crusade for Conformity: The Ku Klux Klan in Texas, 1920-30, Texas Gulf Coast Historical Association, 1962.

The Ku Klux Klan in the Southwest, University Press of Kentucky (Lexington, KY), 1965.

(With Loyd S. Swenson) *This New Ocean: A History of Project Mercury,* U.S. Government Printing Office (Washington, DC), 1966.

Nationalism in American Thought, 1930-1945, Rand McNally (Chicago, IL), 1969.

Holding the Line: The Eisenhower Era, 1952-1961, Indiana University Press (Bloomington, IN), 1975.

Here the Country Lies: Nationalism and the Arts in Twentieth-Century America, Indiana University Press, 1980.

Ty Cobb, Oxford University Press (New York City), 1984.

John McGraw, Viking (New York City), 1988.

Our Game: An American Baseball History, Holt (New York City), 1991.

Roger Hornsby: A Biography, Holt, 1995.

Contributor to periodicals.

* * *

ALLINSON, Gary D(ean) 1942-

PERSONAL: Born August 12, 1942, in Webster City, IA; son of Everette J. (in business) and Grace Lucille

(Winnie) Allinson; married Patricia Susan Bush (a genetic counselor), December 27, 1965; children: Robin John. *Ethnicity:* "Caucasian." *Education:* Attended University of Iowa, 1960-62; Stanford University, B.A. (with honors), 1964, M.A., 1966, Ph.D., 1971. *Avocational interests:* Jogging, travel, swimming, music.

ADDRESSES: Home—102 Cannon Pl., Charlottesville, VA 22901. *Office*—Corcoran Department of History, Randall Hall, University of Virginia, Charlottesville, VA 22903; fax 804-924-7891.

CAREER: University of Pittsburgh, Pittsburgh, PA, assistant professor, 1971-75, associate professor, beginning in 1975, then professor of history, until 1983; University of Virginia, Charlottesville, Ellen Bayard Weedon Professor of East Asian Studies, 1983—.

MEMBER: Association for Asian Studies, International House of Japan, Phi Beta Kappa, Phi Eta Sigma, Omicron Delta Kappa.

AWARDS, HONORS: Fulbright scholarship, 1975-76; fellow of Social Science Research Council, 1977, Japan Foundation, 1978-79, and Woodrow Wilson International Center for Scholars, 1983; grant from Japan-U.S. Friendship Commission, 1990; award from Suntory Cultural Foundation, 1993.

WRITINGS:

Japanese Urbanism: Industry and Politics in Kariya, 1872-1972, University of California Press (Berkeley, CA), 1975.
Suburban Tokyo: A Comparative Study in Politics and Social Change, University of California Press, 1979.
Political Dynamics in Contemporary Japan, Cornell University Press (Ithaca, NY), 1993.
Japan's Postwar History, Cornell University Press, 1997.
The Columbia Guide to Modern Japanese History, Columbia University Press (New York City), 1999.

Contributor to history, social science, and Asian studies journals.

* * *

ARDOIN, John (Louis) 1935-

PERSONAL: Born January 8, 1935, in Alexandria, LA; son of Louis and Ruth (Herren) Ardoin. *Education:* University of Texas, B.M., 1955; University of Oklahoma, M.M., 1956; University of North Texas, Ph.D., 1987.

ADDRESSES: Home—4305 Travis St., Dallas, TX 75205.

CAREER: Musical America (magazine), New York City, assistant editor, 1959-62, associate editor, 1962-64, editor, 1964; *Saturday Review* (magazine), New York City, member of music staff, 1965-66; *Dallas Morning News,* Dallas, TX, music editor and amusements critic, 1966-98. Guest lecturer at University of Southern California, 1967, 1968, Indiana University, 1971, 1972, Eastman School of Music, 1973, 1983, and American Institute of Music Studies, 1973, 1986. Music consultant for Great Performances, 1981—, PBS Online, 1997—.

WRITINGS:

(With Gerald Fitzgerald) *Callas,* Holt, 1974.
(With others) *The Tenors,* Macmillan, 1974.
The Callas Legacy, Scribner (New York City), 1977, revised edition published as *The Callas Legacy: A Biography of a Career,* 1982, released on compact disc, Scribner, 1991.
The Stages of Menotti, photographs edited by Gerald Fitzgerald, Doubleday (Garden City, NY), 1985.
The Callas Legacy: The Complete Guide to Her Recordings, foreword by Terrance McNally, Scribner, Maxwell Macmillan International (New York City), 1991, 4th edition reprinted as *The Callas Legacy: The Complete Guide to Her Recordings on Compact Disk,* Amadeus Press (Portland, OR), 1995.
The Furtwangler Record, discography by John Hunt, Amadeus Press, 1994.
Valery Gergiev and the Kirov, Amadeus Press, 2001.

EDITOR

Callas at Juilliard: The Master Classes, Knopf (New York City), 1987, revised edition, Amadeus Press, 1988.
The Philadelphia Orchestra: A Century of Music, Temple University Press (Philadelphia, PA), 1999.

OTHER

Contributor to music journals. New York music critic for London *Times,* 1964-66, and *Opera,* 1965-66; managing editor of *Philharmonic Hall Program,* 1965-66. Contributor to PBS Online's *Great Performances* Web site: writer for site devoted to performances of the San Francisco Opera.

SIDELIGHTS: John Ardoin edited *Callas at Juilliard: The Master Classes,* a book that details famed opera singer Maria Callas' role presiding over a series of classes in "The Lyric Tradition," working with a select group of twenty-five young professional singers, performing seventy-five arias. She was invited to host these master classes by New York City's Juilliard Music School President Peter Mennin from October, 1971, to March, 1972. Her class performed for sold-out audiences of fans, students, the press, and such honored colleagues as Franco Zeffirelli, Tito Gobbi, Bidu Sayao, and Elisabeth Schwartzkopf. *National Review* critic Chilton Williamson deems *Callas at Juilliard: The Master Classes* "a truly superb book." And Charles H. Parsons, writing in *American Record Guide,* notes "The text is a cornucopia of information, insight and tradition—an inspiration even to the non-musician," and continues, "This book is a must for musicians and opera lovers."

In *The Furtwangler Record,* Ardoin explores the work of controversial German conductor Wilhelm Furtwangler (1886-1954), who, during his lifetime, was widely regarded as the caretaker of the German musical tradition, and is still considered by many as one of the greatest conductors of the twentieth century. While Furtwangler's spiritually intense, introspective interpretations cast their spell through sound recordings even today, in his broadcasts during World War II, patriotism—a complex mix with his revulsion toward Hitler—lent to his work a peculiar edge. His decision not to leave Nazi Germany, but to remain as director of the Berlin Philharmonic, has cast a stigma upon his reputation.

While Ardoin provides a helpful overview of Furtwangler's career, the book is primarily a study of Furtwangler's recorded legacy. The works are grouped according to musical period (classical, baroque, etc.). Ardoin supplies exhaustive information regarding variant recordings of each score and utilizes excerpts from Furtwangler's correspondence and diaries to shed light upon the musician's interpretive approach to individual scores and composers. *Booklist* contributor John Shreffler writes, "Ardoin's exhaustive study will be valuable in any library with patrons deeply interested in classical music." And David McKee comments in *Opera News,* "As with his earlier studies of Maria Callas, John Ardoin has produced a book that will prove a valuable resource to anyone wishing to come to grips with a legendary artist. Discussions of specific performances have a charming mix of practical detail and Toveyesque philosophizing. Ardoin also takes great pains to elucidate the why of Furtwangler's music-making, drawing heavily on the conductor's own words."

Ardoin's radio documentary *Callas* allows opera's most controversial and beloved diva tell much of her story through the extensive use of excerpts from her own interviews, interviews with associates such as Renata Tebaldi, Franco Zeffirelli, and Rudolf Bing, her rehearsals, live performances, and recordings. Peter Josyph notes in *Library Journal,* that these excerpts "are connected chronologically by a narrative that is sensitive and succinct," and lauds the program as "highly recommended."

BIOGRAPHICAL/CRITICAL SOURCES:

PERIODICALS

American Record Guide, March-April, 1999, Charles H. Parsons, review of *Callas at Juilliard,* p. 329.

Booklist, August, 1994, John Shreffler, review of *The Furtwangler Record,* p. 2011.

Library Journal, February 1, 1988, Peter Josyph, review of *Callas,* p. 128.

National Review, August 19, 1988, Chilton Williamson Jr., review of *Callas at Juilliard,* p. 47; July, 1995, p. 58.

Opera News, July, 1995, David McKee, review of *The Furtwangler Record,* p. 58; February 11, 1998, p. 128.

Washington Post Book World, December 5-11, 1999, review of *The Philadelphia Orchestra,* p. 12.

OTHER

Great Performances: A Streetcar Named Desire, http://www.wnet.org.gperf (February 14, 2000).

* * *

ARGUELLES, Ivan (Wallace) 1939-

PERSONAL: Born January 24, 1939, in Rochester, MN; son of Enrique and Ethel Pearl (Meyer) Arguelles; married Claire Birnbaum, August, 1958 (divorced, 1960); married Marilla Calhoun Elder (a fabric art designer and teacher, and founder of Consensus, a brain trauma rehabilitation center), October 27, 1962; children: Alexander, Max. *Education:* University of Chicago, B.A., 1961; Vanderbilt University, M.L.S., 1968;

attended University of Minnesota and New York University. *Avocational interests:* Languages, classics, travel.

ADDRESSES: Home—740 Walnut St., No. 4, Berkeley, CA 94709.

CAREER: Poet, publisher, and librarian. Midwest Interlibrary Loan Center, Chicago, clerk, 1961; Columbia University Library, New York City, bindery clerk, 1961; Kroch & Brentano's Bookstore, Chicago, IL, clerk, 1963, promoted to head of Personal Shopping Services; Brentano's Bookstore, New York City, night manager, 1967; Elder's bookstore, Nashville, TN, clerk, 1967-68; New York Public Library, cataloguer, 1968-78; University of California at Berkeley Library, head of serial cataloging division, 1978—. Also worked as dishwasher, St. Mary's Hospital, Rochester, MN, 1957; English instructor in an aeronautical school, Macerata, Italy, 1967; private tutor in Spanish, Italian, and French, New York, c. 1970s; teacher of beginning Spanish, Brooklyn College adult education division, c. 1970s; guest lecturer, Ramapo College, New Jersey, 1978. Has given numerous poetry readings; founded poetry reading series at University Library, Berkeley, c. mid-1980s. Co-founder (with Craig Stockfleth), Rock Steady Press, San Francisco, 1988; co-founder, Pantograph Press, Berkeley, 1992.

AWARDS, HONORS: National high school poetry contest, award, 1955; first *Silverfish Review* Chapbook Award, 1985, for *Manicomio; Yellow Silk* Award for erotic poetry, 1985; William Carlos Williams Award for best book of poetry published by a noncommercial press, Poetry Society of America, 1989, for *Looking for Mary Lou: Illegal Syntax.*

WRITINGS:

POEMS

Instamatic Reconditioning, Damascus Road (Wescoville, PA), 1978.
The Invention of Spain, Downtown Poets Co-op (Brooklyn, NY), 1978.
Captive of the Vision of Paradise, graphics by Linda Strickland, Hartmus Press (Mill Valley, CA), 1983.
The Tattooed Heart of the Drunken Sailor, Ghost Pony (Madison, WI), 1983.
Manicomio, Silverfish Review (Eugene, OR), 1984.
Nailed to the Coffin of Life, Ruddy Duck (Fremont, CA), 1985.
What Are They Doing to My Animal?, Ghost Dance (East Lansing, MI), 1986.
The Structure of Hell, Grendahl (Lompoc, CA), 1986.
Pieces of the Bone-Text Still There, NRG Press (Portland, OR), 1987.
Baudelaire's Brain, Sub Rosa (Teaneck, NJ), 1988.
Looking for Mary Lou: Illegal Syntax, photographs by Craig Stockfleth, Rock Steady (San Francisco, CA), 1989.
"THAT" Goddess, Pantograph (Berkeley, CA), 1992.
Hapax Legomenon, Pantograph, 1993.
Enigma & Variations: Paradise Is Persian for Park, Pantograph, 1996.

OTHER

Contributor of play *The Tragedy of Momus* in *Terminal Velocities,* Pantograph, 1993. Contributor to anthologies, including *Voices of Brooklyn,* American Library Association (Chicago, IL), 1973; *Doctor Generosity Poets,* Damascus Road, 1975; *A Decade of Spanish Literature,* Arte Publico Press, c. 1980; *American Poetry since 1970,* Four Walls Eight Windows, 1987; *American Poetry Confronts the '90s,* Black Tie Press, 1990; *Yellow Silk: Erotic Arts and Letters,* Harmony Books (New York City), 1990; and *New Chicano/Chicana Writing,* University of Arizona Press (Tucson), 1992. Also contributor to *American Poets Say Goodbye to the Twentieth Century,* 1996. Contributor of more than five hundred individual poems to magazines, including *Poetry USA, Velocities, Kayak, Abraxas, Ally, Berkeley Poetry Review, Osiris, Revista Chicano/Riquena, Kansas Quarterly,* and *Minnesota Review.*

SIDELIGHTS: Surrealist poet Ivan Arguelles is a professional librarian at the University of California, Berkeley, who has managed to write successfully during breaks in his job as a serials cataloguer. Although never allied with any academic creative writing program, Arguelles has earned several prestigious awards—including the William Carlos Williams Award from the Poetry Society of America—while supporting himself and his family in an entirely different profession. In *American Libraries* magazine, Arguelles explained how he manages to balance the duties of librarian and father with the urge to create poetry. "I work very intensely," he said. "The minute I walk out of the library, I'm working on a poem. I basically have lunch hour and my afternoon break to create. When it's time, I write like mad."

Arguelles's life has been a self-described American odyssey, and he provided a full account, up to the year 1996, in his confessional sketch for the *Contemporary Authors Autobiography Series* (*CAAS*). Born in Rochester, Minnesota, he spent his earliest years in Mexico City, where his father—in Arguelles's words a "failed artist,"—associated with such personages as Leon Trotsky, Diego Rivera, and Frida Kahlo. Arguelles and his twin brother Joe (who later changed his name to Jose and became a Buddhist affiliated with the Naropa Institute in Colorado) received the benefit of early exposure to the arts and music.

A return to Minnesota, where Arguelles's Minnesota-born mother could receive treatment for tuberculosis, was in some ways traumatic, but as a teenager, he became a star Latin student and won a scholarship to the University of Minnesota. He had already discovered within himself a linguistic gift that enabled him to master several Romance languages with apparent ease, and to take pleasure in the most obscure tongues, such as Romanian, Catalan, and Provencal. Given a copy of Irish author James Joyce's *Ulysses* by his girlfriend at age fifteen, he had his eyes opened to modernist literature.

At the University of Chicago, where he had transferred as a sophomore, Arguelles spent much of his time discovering blues music and soaking up the Bohemian atmosphere of the era. The descriptions of his student life in the late 1950s and early 1960s resemble something out of Richard Farina's *Been Down So Long It Looks like Up to Me:* experience-hungry collegians "digging scenes," sampling mind expansion, and crisscrossing the nation in an effort to emulate the characters in Beat writer Jack Kerouac's *On the Road.*

Arguelles, while an undergraduate, was married to a Holocaust survivor of Romanian origin; the marriage lasted two years. He became briefly acquainted with life inside psychiatric hospitals, and at one point he attempted suicide. On Halloween, 1960, he met the woman who would share his future, Marilla Calhoun Elder, a Nashville resident whose father ran an esteemed bookstore in that city. Arguelles's preference to be a "difficult young man" (as eminent lawyer Telford Taylor called him) continued, but he was also continuing to explore modern literature and was taking the first steps toward a career as a university librarian. Travel was a major part of his development as well, and the list of his stopping points includes Italy, England, Switzerland, Portugal, Spain, Morocco, Srinigar, and Ladakh. The list of languages he was fluent in grew, concomitantly, to include such exotics as Indoeuropean, Sanskrit, Hittite, Persian, Hindi, Arabic, and Greek.

A son, Alexander, was born in Chicago in 1964, and a second son, Max, in New York in 1968, at the beginning of what Arguelles calls "the most felicitous" ten years "of my life." He was working at the New York Public Library, living in an artsy neighborhood in Brooklyn, and writing and publishing poems at a feverish pace. It was in 1978 that tragedy struck: young Max succumbed to viral encephalitis. The boy survived, but with severe, permanent brain damage, and the family's life was irrevocably altered, its focus now caring for the disabled Max.

Soon afterward, the family moved to Berkeley, California, where Arguelles had landed a job running the Serial Cataloging division of the university library. Although he had, at first, fewer contacts on the West Coast than on the East, Arguelles made his way into the Bay Area poetry scene, giving readings, having his books and chapbooks published by small presses, and ultimately founding, with a friend, his own small Pantograph Press. "The long line, oneiric distance, and an erotic mysticism were becoming characteristics of my poetry," he writes in his autobiographical sketch. He was at times associated, at least in the minds of critics and editors, with Mexican-American poets because of his background, but Arguelles regards himself as primarily a surrealist. Romanian-American poet and critic Andrei Codrescu said in a review of the 1984 *Tattooed Heart,* "Unlike the more superficial image makers who lay claim to the surrealist label out of sheer laziness or because 'it looks easy,' Arguelles is genuine."

A 1985 collection of Arguelles's best poems to that point, *Manicomio,* won a prize from the *Silverfish Review.* New books emerged regularly and won praise from critics. As Christina Zawadiwsky noted in *Small Press Review,* with reference to the 1989 *Pieces of the Bone-Text Still There,* "Arguelles may only have two eyes but in those eyes are a million mirrors with which he dazzles us as he introduces the inside world to the outside world and both of these to worlds that haven't even been born yet."

Reviewing *Looking for Mary Lou: Illegal Syntax* in 1990, Zawadiwsky described it as "a book about the wounded," and applauded: "What remains pervasive and absolutely remarkable about Arguelles's writing is his beauty of language. . . . Few poets today write on any topic with such immense skill and imagination. Arguelles is a surgeon opening up our pain-racked psyches and whispering and singing to us that everything will be all right as he forcefully wields his scalpel of words."

In February, 1990, Arguelles experienced a major inspiration: he came upon the idea for his continuing, "obsessive" epic, *Pantograph,* and wrote the first volume, *"THAT" Goddess,* "in a white heat of two months." Unable to find a publisher for it, Arguelles would turn this setback into an opportunity by establishing Pantograph Press, with *"THAT" Goddess* as one of its first three titles. *Small Press Review* contributor Dennis Formento responded to the book, proclaiming it an "incredibly dense work" and "an alchemical treatise on the properties of the fem[ale] as engendered by language." *Sulfur* reviewer Keith Tuma acknowledged the poem's obsession with female figures, but interpreted it as essentially an expression of male attitudes. He found in it "more pure raw undiluted gushing spastic energy than I have encountered in some time," and, assessing the influence of Allen Ginsberg upon Arguelles, said, "Arguelles is much more the mandarin and classicist than Ginsberg ever was, and in some ways is more interesting for it." Although commenting that *"THAT" Goddess* was too long and contained too much digressive material, Tuma averred, "there's no denying the power of the poem."

Fundamentally a long poem influenced by those of Ezra Pound and Charles Olson, *Pantograph* could vary widely in form: the fourth volume, *The Tragedy of Momus,* was an Elizabethan play that followed strictly the classical unities. The author's progress on the epic was such that a ninth volume, *Hapax Legomenon,* was published in 1993.

Summing up his life and work in *CAAS,* Arguelles described himself as perennially "dipping my finger in the broth of knowledge." Pantograph Press, he hoped, would "better establish us on the map" by virtue of "generating a 'California School,' post-Olson, post-Language, and definitely nonacademic, a mix of experiment with language and passion." On a personal level, he added, "I recall my strong sense of inferiority growing up in Minnesota, of being an outsider, of being unsure of myself and of my talents [and] suddenly here I am with some kind of reputation, and with some kind of conviction of my own art."

BIOGRAPHICAL/CRITICAL SOURCES:

BOOKS

Contemporary Authors Autobiography Series, Volume 24, Gale (Detroit, MI), 1996, pp. 1-30.

PERIODICALS

American Libraries, November, 1991, Ron Chepsiuk, "In Pursuit of the Muse: Librarians Who Write," p. 988.

Small Press Review, September, 1987, p. 1; June, 1990, p. 38; May, 1994, p. 11.

Sulfur, spring, 1993, pp. 339-343.*

* * *

ARMITAGE, Simon 1963-

PERSONAL: Born May 26, 1963, in Huddersfield, West Yorkshire, England; son of Peter (a probation officer) and Audrey (a teaching assistant; maiden name, Ashton) Armitage. *Education:* Portsmouth Polytechnic, B.A. (with honors), 1984; Victoria University of Manchester, Certificate of Qualification in social work and M.A., both 1988. *Politics:* "Occasional socialist." *Religion:* Church of England.

ADDRESSES: Home—110 Mount Rd., Marsden, Huddersfield, West Yorkshire HD7 6HN, England.

CAREER: Probation officer in Manchester, England, 1988—; poetry editor at Chatto and Windus in London. Gives poetry readings and workshops.

AWARDS, HONORS: Eric Gregory Award, Society of Authors, 1988, and shortlisted for Whitbread Award, 1989, both for *Zoom!;* Sunday Times Young Writer of the Year, 1993; commission from New Millennium Experience Company to write *Killing Time,* 1999.

WRITINGS:

Human Geography, Smith/Doorstop, 1986.
The Distance between the Stars, Wide Skirt Press, 1987.
The Walking Horses, Slow Dancer (Nottingham, England), 1988.
Zoom! (Poetry Book Society choice), Bloodaxe Books, 1989.
Around Robinson, Slow Dancer, 1991.
Kid, Faber (Boston), 1992.
Xanadu, Bloodaxe Books, 1992.
Book of Matches, Faber, 1993.
The Dead Sea Poems, Faber, 1995.
Moon Country, Faber, 1996.
(Editor with Robert Crawford) *The Penguin Book of Poetry from Britain and Ireland since 1945,* Viking, 1998.
Killing Time, Faber, 1999.

Also author of poetry pamphlets. Contributor of poems and reviews to periodicals, including *Orbis.*

SIDELIGHTS: Simon Armitage is known for his distinctly northern British vernacular and deadpan delivery. In his first full-length volume of poetry, *Zoom!,* Armitage concerns himself with such divergent subjects as the world fish market and the dumping of an elderly woman in the hospital to die. Brian Macaskill points out in *Contemporary Poets:* "Bringing to mind Philip Larkin's late-career use of vernacular, slang locutions, and telling obscenities, Armitage often turns the commonplace or, especially, the vulgar phrase to epigrammatic effect." In his *Times Literary Supplement* review of *Zoom!,* Lawrence Norfolk characterizes Armitage's poems as "postmodern, post-industrial and steeped in the culture of the past decade," but he notes that the poems "swap the usual celebration of mall-and-arcade glitz for a searching, sympathetic gaze down the debit column of the economic miracle." He adds that "the poems are revelatory rather than reflexive, their author has plenty to say and says it with wit and sympathy."

According to *New Statesman* reviewer David Herd, Armitage revisits in *Xanadu* the first place he was posted as a probation officer. Herd notes: "As the poem journeys round the estate, it shifts rapidly through a series of registers, or rather conceits. The effect of this combination of high style and low idiom is first to soften, then harden, the impact of urban decay."

In *New Statesman,* John Hartley Williams describes Armitage's fourth book, *The Dead Sea Poems,* as "energetic" and possessing "a demonic man-in-the-street astuteness." He observes: "[Armitage's] voice is that of the all-too-knowing chap in the pub leaning over to tell you some urban myth. . . . He has just the vocabulary an armchair expert needs to persuade you his storytelling is true." The poems display Armitage's "wide formal range, [and] willingness to tackle any subject," according to Lachlan MacKinnon of the *Times Literary Supplement.*

Armitage was commissioned to write *Killing Time* in celebration of the new millennium. A 1,000-line poem that presents a wide-ranging look at present-day British society, *Killing Time* contains accounts of recent news events, meditations on religion and politics, and satiric asides. It is, writes Robert Potts in the *Times Literary Supplement,* "a big poem for a big occasion, an epic in miniature."

BIOGRAPHICAL/CRITICAL SOURCES:

BOOKS

Contemporary Poets, sixth edition, St. James Press (Detroit), 1996.

PERIODICALS

Economist, December 12, 1998, "Verse: Mixed Marriages," p. 6.

New Statesman, November 24, 1989, p. 37; August 28, 1992, p. 36; October 27, 1995, John Hartley Williams, review of *The Dead Sea Poems,* p. 46; November 15, 1996, p. 45.

Times Literary Supplement, January 5, 1990, p. 19; July 3, 1992, p. 27; October 13, 1995, Lachlan MacKinnen, review of *The Dead Sea Poems,* p. 28; December 24, 1999, Robert Potts, "The Baggage of One Man's Mind," p. 21.*

B

BABITZ, Eve 1943-

PERSONAL: Born May 13, 1943, in Hollywood, CA; daughter of Sol (a musician) and Mae (an artist; maiden name, LaViolette) Babitz. *Education:* Graduated from Hollywood High School, CA.

ADDRESSES: Agent—Erica Spellman, International Creative Management, 40 West 57th St., New York, NY 10019.

CAREER: East Village Other, office manager, 1966; *Ramparts,* office manager, 1967; free-lance illustrator and designer of covers for record albums, 1967-72; writer, beginning 1967.

WRITINGS:

Eve's Hollywood, Seymour Lawrence, 1974.
(Editor) *Los Angeles Manifesto* (stories), privately printed, 1976.
Slow Days, Fast Company: The World, the Flesh, and L.A. Tales (stories), Knopf, 1977.
Sex and Rage (novel), Knopf, 1979.
Fiorucci, the Book, Harlin Quist, 1980.
L.A. Woman (novel), Linden Press, 1982.
Black Swans (stories), Knopf, 1992.
Two by Two: Tango, Two-Step, and the L.A. Night (nonfiction), Simon & Schuster, 1999.

Contributor of stories to magazines, including *Cosmopolitan, Rolling Stone, Elle, Saturday Evening Post, L.A. Weekly,* and *Vogue.*

SIDELIGHTS: Eve Babitz, says a *Kirkus Reviews* article, is an "acquired taste"; the Los Angeles author's "slewing style, bad-girl postures, and sad-funny takes on hedonism can be deliciously shocking but don't always blend-up right." In several collections of stories and nonfiction, Babitz offers a distinctly personal slant to life in America's most glamorously shallow city.

Regarding Eve Babitz's 1977 collection of stories about Southern California, *Slow Days, Fast Company: The World, the Flesh, and L.A. Tales,* Julia Whedon wrote in the *New York Times Book Review:* "The author's sensibility presides and prevails throughout, threading together restaurants and landscape, friendship and fornication, diets and death, as if they were all set out en buffet. . . . Her enthusiastic prose style. . . . has the bright, nutty, incisive quality of good gossip." A reviewer for *Time* added that while Babitz's "style is often derivative of Tom Wolfe and Joan Didion . . . [she] has the one indispensable quality for her kind of work: true glitz."

Babitz's Los Angeles—"full of grand malls and petit ones," as she puts it in *Black Swans*—is as much a character as the show-biz-wannabe types who prowl its streets with little more than their hedonistic interests in mind. Alice Joyce in *Booklist* asks readers to imagine a couple engaging in a romantic night at the faded luxury hotel Chateau Marmont, "unaware that the Rodney King verdict has released half the population . . . into the streets."

In the novel *L.A. Woman,* Babitz takes on a portrait of a self-centered, undereducated denizen who speaks in a disjointed first-person narrative. Sophie Lubin has seen and done it all: from trips to Paris to an affair with Jim Morrison. But for all her adventures, says P. J. O'Rourke in *New York Times Book Review,* Sophie is "too blase to give details. And since she has very few internal conflicts, no important conflicts with others, and no ambition worthy of the name, I can't see why anyone would bother to tell her story." Still, adds O'Rourke, if anyone is suited to tell Sophie's tale, it's Babitz: She's given her protagonist "a style of declamation that is perfect *fin de siecle* Southern California." The reviewer notes the strong sense of irony in Babitz's prose, as if she's "giving us a study of a tinsel-skulled modern type." James Kaufmann, in the *Los Angeles Times Book Review,* described the novel as "more a collection of vignettes stitched together like a crazy quilt and possessed of . . . enigmatic logic." Kaufmann praised Babitz's prose as being "calculated, breathy, glib and precocious," adding that "her eclectic approach to plotting gives the novel hyperkinesis."

Modern types also figure into *Black Swans,* a collection of first-person stories built around the L.A. social scene. Besides the hard-partying "Eve" (a name that suggests *roman-a-clef*), other characters include Warren, a bit actor who abandons his true love to take up with a wealthy widow who promises a more privileged lifestyle; Albert, a surfer-turned-artist; and Kate, the idealistic New Yorker who plunges into the schlock-filmmaking world courtesy of her husband. " 'Fun' [in the form of sex, drugs, booze and rock music] is an operative word in these people's lives," writes Michiko Kakutani in a *New York Times* critique. But "it's tiresome, reading a whole book of stories about ninnies as self-absorbed and self-deluded as this, and some of the shorter tales in [*Black Swans*] are little more than depressing sketches of narcissists in extremis." What redeems the book, Kakutani continues, is Babitz's full-tilt irony and "her gift for the odd, unexpected observation."

Another *New York Times* reviewer, Donna Rifkind, examined *Black Swans* and has this to say of Babitz: "Like all of her writing, the new volume offers a lush, sensual, David Hockneyish view of fashionable life in Los Angeles." Rifkind calls one story, "Expensive Regrets," the most revealing in the collection. This is the story revolving around the aftermath of the Rodney King ruling, which sparked civil unrest in the city. The story's narrator, unaware of the turmoil outside her hotel window, "is most outraged," as Rifkind describes it, "when she ventures into the streets to survey the damage, about the looting of Frederick's of Hollywood. 'Except for the National Guard and the fear,' she assures us, 'it wasn't really so bad.' "

Entering the dance scene of Los Angeles, Babitz spent two years taking dance lessons and researching her 1999 book, *Two By Two: Tango, Two-Step, and the L.A. Night.* "Along the way she meets obsessed dancers and listens night after night as they pour out the secrets of their style—who the best teachers are, where to find the perfect dancing shoes, and how to fall in love with your partner," relates a writer for the Simon and Schuster Internet site. Tom Nolan of the *Wall Street Journal* described the work as a "chronicle of the writer's progress through her city's vibrant proliferation of partner-dance milieus."

Babitz once wrote: "I became a writer when I felt I was too old to design rock 'n' roll album covers any more. As I could no longer drink Southern Comfort till three o'clock A.M. with nineteen-year-old bass players from Mississippi, I felt that my days in rock 'n' roll were numbered. I knew I'd be a writer eventually, and I decided to write stories about Los Angeles that weren't depressing. And I did."

BIOGRAPHICAL/CRITICAL SOURCES:

PERIODICALS

Atlantic, April, 1974.
Booklist, September 1, 1993.
Kirkus Reviews, July 15, 1993.
Los Angeles Times, May 1, 1977; February 8, 1980.
Los Angeles Times Book Review, May 30, 1982.
Ms., May, 1975; February, 1980; June, 1982.
New Yorker, November 12, 1979; May 10, 1982.
New York Times, July 15, 1977; October 1, 1993; October 17, 1993.
New York Times Book Review, June 19, 1977; December 2, 1979; May 2, 1982, P. J. O'Rourke, "Not a Bad Girl, But Dull One," p. 12; October 17, 1993, Donna Rifkind, "L.A. Lore."
Publishers Weekly, July 26, 1993, review of *Black Swans,* p. 57.
Saturday Review, May, 1982.
Time, July 4, 1977.
Village Voice, June 27, 1977; October 15, 1979.

OTHER

SimonSays.com, http://www.simonsays.com (July 6, 2000).*

* * *

BAIN, David Haward 1949-

PERSONAL: Born February 23, 1949, in Camden, NJ; son of David (in business) and Rosemary (Haward)

Bain; married Mary Smyth Duffy (a painter), June 6, 1981. *Education:* Boston University, B.S., 1971.

ADDRESSES: Agent—Ellen Levine Literary Agency Inc., 15 East 26th St. Suite 1801, New York City, NY 10010.

CAREER: Alfred A. Knopf, Inc., New York City, editorial assistant, 1973-76; Stonehill Publishers, New York City, editor, 1976-77; Crown Publishers, New York City, editor, 1977-78; writer, 1978—. Bread Loaf Writers' Conference at Middlebury College, member of faculty, 1981-88, admissions board, 1987—; visiting lecturer at various institutions, including Middlebury College, 1987—.

MEMBER: Authors Guild, PEN, National Writers Union.

AWARDS, HONORS: Grants from Rinehart Foundation, 1979, for *Aftershocks,* and Lebensburger Foundation, 1982, and New York State Council for the Arts/ PEN Center, 1983, for *Sitting in Darkness;* prose fellowship from Bread Loaf Writers' Conference, 1980.

WRITINGS:

Aftershocks, Methuen (New York City), 1980.
Sitting in Darkness: Americans in the Philippines, Houghton (Burlington, MA), 1984.
Empire Express: Building the First Transcontinental Railroad, Viking (New York City), 1999.

EDITOR

(With Sydney Landon Plum) *At an Elevation: On the Poetry of Robert Pack,* Middlebury College Press (Middlebury, VT), 1994.
(With wife, Mary Smyth Duffy) *Whose Woods These Are: A History of the Bread Loaf Writers' Conference,* Bread Loaf Writers' Conference of Middlebury College, 1994.

OTHER

Contributor to periodicals, including *Baltimore Sun, Esquire, Los Angeles Times, Newsday, New York Times,* and *Philadelphia Inquirer.*

SIDELIGHTS: David Haward Bain told *CA:* "At this stage, if there is a thread that runs through my books on Vietnam, on the Philippines, and on the building of the first transcontinental railroad, and certain short writings (such as an article about the U.S. misadventure in Nicaragua in the late Twenties), it is to probe with questions about the nature of the American civilization. Why the inability to meaningfully remember our own past? Which events get left out of the history books? Why have we been condemned to repeat our own mistakes? What is the source of our cultural disinterest in points of view not of mainstream America? How can we learn from all of this?

"*Sitting in Darkness* takes its title from a passionate essay of American humorist Mark Twain in which he lambasted the William McKinley-Theodore Roosevelt presidential administration for its misadventures in the Philippines, and the other 'superpowers' of the era for their own colonial misdeeds. Twain was one of my most formidable literary influences: that cantankerous generosity I first came across, at eight years of age, in *Huckleberry Finn* and his other fictions, later graduating to the iron-backboned essays, most of them too angry or profane to be published in his own lifetime. I happened upon either *Europe and Elsewhere* or the collection edited by American writer Bernard DeVoto, *Letters from the Earth,* some time in my mid-teens, and Twain's thoughts on social justice, disorganized and splenetic as they were, made a tremendous impression.

"Around the same time as I located Twain and some twentieth-century Christian philosophers (not so much an impossible confluence as one might immediately think), I heard another literary voice that, in my mid-teens, helped shape my direction. In that era of atomic drills in the public schools, an English class assignment was American author and journalist John Hersey's *Hiroshima,* still a classic of penetrating, sensitive reportage. It must have been my first sampling of the best sort of *New Yorker* journalism, though the magazine was always present on family coffee tables and must have previously made some sort of impression. The book whetted my appetite for nonfiction artfully written, and instilled in me a curiosity about how other cultures perceived events in which the United States had a hand.

"I chose these examples because of their immeasurable importance in locating my world-view and literary direction as a humanist and citizen of the world. But one cannot stress enough the equal importance of my family atmosphere: literate, book-devouring parents who imparted love of the written and spoken word to their four children. From them I developed an all-encompassing insatiability for books, which knew no limitation of subject matter; I remember a complex stew, including English poet and playwright A. A. Milne, English novelist Charles Dickens, All-Abouts and Landmarks, Twenties-era debunkers, American poet Robert Frost (of course!), American author Philip Wylie's overlooked *Finley Wren,* science fiction visionaries from French writer Jules Verne and English author Herbert George Wells to English author and scientist Arthur Charles Clarke and American author Ray Bradbury, Civil War centennials, *The Conquest of Mexico,* C. W. Ceram's archaeological *Gods, Graves and Scholars,* English satirist Jonathan Swift, swashbucklers from *The Prisoner of Zenda* to American writer Edgar Rice Burroughs. Good heavens, once tapped, this list could go on!

"Jump ahead, again, to my five or six years in publishing—most particularly, the three years put in at Alfred A. Knopf, where I sat literally in Mr. Knopf 's shadow (having sold his firm to Random House some years before, and having relinquished editorial control to a gifted trio of enfants terrible from Simon & Schuster, Alfred made ceremonial appearances twice a week, and between dictated letters would venture past the desks of young fools such as myself, showing great patience with my attempts at conversation; on his days off, I would nap lunchtimes in his Barcalounger). The old traditions of careful publishing were still observed at Knopf. I was expected to have a junior-level hand in a good number of Knopf 's more serious projects—its histories, mostly (many of which, despite my flailings-about with galley proofs and transmittal forms, survived my meddlings and gained recognition in the outside world). Through my small association with these books, I think I learned more *care* with regard to both scholarship and the literary process. Three years at Knopf was equal to any number of graduate degrees. (The subsequent three years in book publishing, divided between two full-time jobs and a forgotten number of free-lance positions, made an impression only in that I was persuaded that business was not for me.)

"Since I've been proceeding in this Henry Adams-manner, I should mention a process which began back in college, when I was introduced to the historical writings of DeVoto, and has continued over the nearly eight years of my full-time writing. I keenly appreciate DeVoto's notion of synecdochic writing whereby the whole is inferred from a treatment of its part, and find great inspiration in how he moves from theme to theme, producing an enviable panorama of history. Other influences are American historian, educator, and author Arthur M. Schlesinger, Jr., and Barbara Tuchman in history; and a number of journalists often identified with *New Yorker* from Edmund Wilson and Joseph Mitchell to John McPhee, Michael Arlen, and Peter Matthiessen. The last, with his political progressivism and his concerns for the natural world, is probably the most inspirational of this group of journalists.

"A significant part of my meager income while writing my first book was derived from playing piano in a wine and cheese cafe; at one time I was a professional musician (last years of college and for a year or thereabouts after graduation)—played piano in a blues band in Massachusetts, did some unimportant session work, and picked up occasional free-lance band jobs when people like John Lee Hooker and T-Bone Walker came to town.

"The most significant travel to date was for my second book, *Sitting in Darkness*—one-third of the interwoven narrative involved the physical retracing of the turn-of-the-century routes of Brigadier General Frederick Funston and Philippine leader Emilio Aguinaldo. Therefore, in 1982 I put together an expedition for six Americans (myself, my brother, who is a professional photographer, and four of our hometown friends who were skilled in mountaineering and backpacking), assuming the costs myself. Using guides from the aboriginal Agta (or Negrito) tribe, who knew almost no English, wore loincloths, and employed spears or bows and arrows, we hiked a good deal over one-hundred miles through the mountains, jungles, and coastal trails from Baler, Aurora Quezon Province, to Palanan, Isabela Province, having nearly as many adventures as our historical predecessors."

Sitting in Darkness: Americans in the Philippines received an overall very favorable review from Jonathan Kwitney in *Nation.* Bain's book is a study of U.S. Brigadier General Frederick Funston, from his childhood on the Kansas prairie to adventures and misadventures as a government biologist embarked on long, dangerous trips collecting specimens, from Death Valley to Alaska's snowbound wilderness, to other exotic locales abroad. As Kwitney says, "Gripped by a sense of national destiny, he conquered all he challenged. For the best and worst reasons, he was a quintessential American hero." Kwitney lauds the "treasure-trove of first-hand accounts by Funston and his contemporaries that bring all those adventures to life." However, these same accounts condemn actions taken under Funston's command of what, today, would certainly be considered war-crime atrocities, during his long and bloody campaign against the Filipinos during the Spanish-American war. In 1982, Bain, accompanied by his brother (a professional photographer) and four hometown friends skilled in mountaineering, set out to follow the long and tortuous march taken by Funston and his troops as they sought the remote mountain stronghold of Emilio Aguinaldo. Former president of the short-lived Philippine Republic, Aguinaldo had become the guerrilla-leader of the Filipinos resisting American aggression and conquest. The book interweaves passages from Funston's era with Bain's current point of view. Kwitney finds: "The contemporary stuff sometimes works, but sometimes not, and therein lie the book's flaws, forgivable as they are." But Kwitney concludes that *Sitting in Darkness: Americans in the Philippines* is "a tale of great people, wonderfully told."

Whose Woods These Are: A History of the Bread Loaf Writers' Conference was edited in collaboration with Bain's wife, Mary Smyth Duffy, a painter and curator. The annual Bread Loaf Writers' Conference is a two-week event sponsored by Middlebury College in Vermont. Over the years, it has attracted many of the most prestigious writers in America, both as faculty and as students. Such now-famous authors as Anne Sexton, Joan Didion, Howard Fast, among numerous others, were nurtured there at the beginnings of their careers. Visiting writers have included such notables as Robert Frost, Archibald Macleish, Truman Capote, Linda Pastan, Harry Crews, Donald Justice, and Julia Child. Its directors have included Joe Battell, Ted Morrison, John Ciardi, and Robert Pack. A *Publishers Weekly* reviewer says, "Bain . . . provides an interesting historical overview of the conference, anecdotal rather than evaluative." Greg Buckman of *Booklist* describes the Bread Loaf Writers' Conference itself as "hilarious, outrageous, gossip-ridden, exhausting, and egotistical," and he notes that the book portrays the conference "at its best: Young writers can actually learn how to make a living writing fiction and poetry, as well as how to improve their craft." Buckman commented, "At its worst: hierarchical, arrogant, bickering, conniving."

Bain's next book *Empire Express: Building the First Transcontinental Railroad* also received critical praise. Robert M. Utley writes in *New York Times Book Review,* "The building of the Pacific Railroad is an epic story, often recounted, but never so thoroughly, authoritatively and engagingly as in 'Empire Express.' " Bain's story follows two trajectories—one in the power centers of the nation, including corporate boardrooms, state and federal political arenas, and the U.S. Congress and judicial system; the other is, in the words of Utley, "in the towering Sierra Nevada, the deserts of Utah and Nevada, the rugged canyons of Utah's Wasatch and the Nebraska plains." Bain digs deeply into the political corruption that so tainted this epic endeavor. Utley says, "Even by the loose standards of the 1860s, every ranking official could be labeled a crook, as most ultimately were. Bain probes the financial, legal and political skullduggery in all its complexity. He nimbly spins the kaleidoscope of stocks, bonds, securities, first and second mortgages, slush funds and piles of cash. He exposes the artifice of the Credit Mobilier and the Contract and Finance Company, by which the railroad directors let padded construction contracts to themselves. Bain's attempt to untangle the tangle is sometimes bewildering but always fascinating." Bain also addresses the pawns in this great contest, such as Chinese laborers imported by the thousands from Canton and Irish immigrants and former Civil War soldiers, still led by ex-Union Generals Dodge and Casement.

A *Publishers Weekly* reviewer enthuses: "Displaying energetic research and enthusiasm for the subject matter, Bain brings the linking of the Atlantic and Pacific coasts, and the era that produced it, back to life." And *Library Journal* critic Randall M. Miller praises: "He captures all that energy and enthusiasm in a book almost as big as the dreams of the empire builders. With Bain, one can stand astride the continent like a colossus." And Utley concludes: "*Empire Express* is well researched, well written, refreshingly revisionist where the sources indicate. . . . The book promises to endure as the standard history of the Pacific railroad."

BIOGRAPHICAL/CRITICAL SOURCES:

PERIODICALS

Booklist, October 15, 1993, Greg Burkman, review of *Whose Woods These Are,* p. 411.

Library Journal, October 1, 1999, Randall M. Miller, review of *Empire Express,* p. 107.

Nation, December 1, 1984, Jonathan Kwithy, review of *Sitting in Darkness,* p. 592.

New York Times Book Review, December 12, 1999, Robert M. Utley, "The Spike Wasn't Golden," p. 10.

Publishers Weekly, August 9, 1993, review of *Whose Woods These Are,* p. 440; October 4, 1999, review of *Empire Express,* p. 51.*

* * *

BANE, Diana

See DAY, Dianne

BARKAN, Joanne
(J. B. Wright)

PERSONAL: Born in Chicago, IL; married Jon R. Friedman (a painter and sculptor). *Education:* Goucher College, B.A.; University of Wisconsin, M.A.; also attended Ecole des Hautes Etudes de Sciences Politiques, Paris, and Johns Hopkins University. *Politics:* "Leftist/ democratic socialist." *Avocational interests:* Art, dance, movies, politics, European travel.

ADDRESSES: Home and Office—711 West End Ave., No. 5-AN, New York, NY 10025. *E-mail*—barkanj@ aol.com.

CAREER: Prentice-Hall, Inc., Englewood Cliffs, NJ, editor of curriculum materials for teachers, 1976-78; Jim Henson Productions, book editor and staff writer for "The Muppets," 1985-87; Brooke-House Publishing, editor and project coordinator, 1988-92; freelance writer and editor. USA-Europe/Locarno Seminar on Politics and Society, member, 1994, 1995, and 1996; I Seminari di Dissent & Reset ad Abano Terme, member, 1998—.

MEMBER: Democratic Socialists of America, National Writers Union, Phi Beta Kappa.

AWARDS, HONORS: Grant for Sweden, Swedish-American Bicentennial Fund, 1988; Children's Choices selection, 1990, for *Anna Marie's Blanket;* Parents Choice Reference Book Honor and joint award for outstanding science trade book, National Association of Science Teachers and Children's Book Council, 1991, both for *Creatures That Glow;* grant for Sweden, Swedish Institute, 1991; Bogliasco fellow at Liguria Study Center for the Arts and Humanities, Bogliasco, Italy, 2000.

WRITINGS:

(Editor) *Kick Up Your Heels* (stories for beginning readers), Scott, Foresman (Glenview, IL), 1980.

(Contributor) *The Politics of Eurocommunism,* South End Press (Boston, MA), 1980.

Visions of Emancipation: The Italian Workers' Movement since 1945 (adult nonfiction), Praeger (Westport, CT), 1984.

Baby Piggy and the Thunderstorm, Muppet Press, 1987.

The Christmas Toy, Scholastic, Inc. (New York City), 1987.

Kermit's Mixed-up Message, illustrated by Lauren Attinello, Scholastic, Inc., 1987.

Baby Gonzo's Unfinished Dream, illustrated by Tom Cooke, Muppet Press, 1988.

Baby Kermit's Old Blanket, illustrated by Tom Brannon, Muppet Press, 1988.

Boober's Colorful Soup, illustrated by John Nez, Longmeadow Press, 1988.

Doozers Big and Little, illustrated by Nez, Longmeadow Press, 1988.

My Cooking Pot, illustrated by Jody Wheeler, Warner Books (New York City), 1989.

My Cooking Spoon, illustrated by Wheeler, Warner Books, 1989.

My Frying Pan, illustrated by Wheeler, Warner Books, 1989.

My Measuring Cup, illustrated by Wheeler, Warner Books, 1989.

My Rolling Pin, illustrated by Wheeler, Warner Books, 1989.

My Spatula, illustrated by Wheeler, Warner Books, 1989.

What's So Funny, illustrated by Normand Chartier, Houghton (Boston), 1989.

Nancy Drew Mystery: The Girl Who Couldn't Remember, Simon & Schuster (New York City), 1989.

The New Bobbsey Twins: The Secret of the Sunken Treasure, Simon & Schuster, 1989.

Abraham Lincoln: A Biography, illustrated by Lyle Miller, Silver Burdett (Morristown, NJ), 1990.

Air, Air, All Around, illustrated by Heidi Petach, Silver Burdett, 1990.

Fire, Fire, Burning Bright, illustrated by Petach, Silver Burdett, 1990.

Rocks, Rocks, Big and Small, illustrated by Petach, Silver Burdett, 1990.

Water, Water, Everywhere, illustrated by Petach, Silver Burdett, 1990.

My Pruning Shears, illustrated by Wheeler, Warner Books, 1990.

My Rake, illustrated by Wheeler, Warner Books, 1990.

My Trowel, illustrated by Wheeler, Warner Books, 1990.

My Watering Can, illustrated by Wheeler, Little, Brown (Boston), 1990.

Whiskerville Bake Shop, illustrated by Karen L. Schmidt, Grosset, 1990.

Whiskerville Firehouse, illustrated by Schmidt, Grosset, 1990.

Whiskerville Post Office, illustrated by Schmidt, Grosset, 1990.

Whiskerville School, illustrated by Schmidt, Grosset, 1990.

Anna Marie's Blanket, illustrated by Deborah Mase, Barron's (Woodbury, NY), 1990.

Glow in the Dark Spooky House, illustrated by Rose Mary Berlin, Western Publishing (New York City), 1990.

Creatures That Glow, Doubleday (New York City), 1991.

My Birthday Adventure with TeddyO (computer-personalized picture book), illustrated by Wheeler, Franco American Products, 1991.

A Very Scary Haunted House, illustrated by Wheeler, Scholastic, Inc., 1991.

A Very Scary Jack O'Lantern, illustrated by Wheeler, Scholastic, Inc., 1991.

Easter Egg Fun, illustrated by Betsy Franco-Feeney, Warner Books, 1991.

Easter Surprise, illustrated by Franco-Feeney, Warner Books, 1991.

Where Do I Put My Toys?, illustrated by Laura Rader, Scholastic, Inc., 1991.

Where Do I Put My Clothes?, illustrated by Rader, Scholastic, Inc., 1991.

Where Do I Put My Books?, illustrated by Rader, Scholastic, Inc., 1991.

Where Do I Put My Food?, illustrated by Rader, Scholastic, Inc., 1991.

Whiskerville Train Station, illustrated by Schmidt, Grosset, 1991.

Whiskerville Theater, illustrated by Schmidt, Grosset, 1991.

Whiskerville Grocery, illustrated by Schmidt, Grosset, 1991.

Whiskerville Toy Shop, illustrated by Schmidt, Grosset, 1991.

(Under pseudonym J. B. Wright) *Dinosaurs,* illustrated by Gene Biggs, Western Publishing, 1991.

Box Car, illustrated by Richard Walz, Macmillan (New York City), 1992.

Caboose, illustrated by Walz, Macmillan, 1992.

Locomotive, illustrated by Walz, Macmillan, 1992.

Passenger Car, illustrated by Walz, Macmillan, 1992.

A Very Merry Santa Claus Story, illustrated by Cristina Ong, Scholastic, Inc., 1992.

A Very Merry Snowman Story, illustrated by Ong, Scholastic, Inc., 1992.

A Very Scary Ghost Story, illustrated by Wheeler, Scholastic, Inc., 1992.

A Very Scary Witch Story, illustrated by Wheeler, Scholastic, Inc., 1992.

That Fat Hat, illustrated by Maggie Swanson, Scholastic, Inc., 1992.

Animal Car, illustrated by Ong, Macmillan, 1993.

Circus Locomotive, illustrated by Ong, Macmillan, 1993.

Clown Caboose, illustrated by Ong, Macmillan, 1993.

Performers' Car, illustrated by Ong, Macmillan, 1993.

The Magic Carpet's Secret, illustrated by Brooks Campbell and Kenny Thompkins, Walt Disney Co., 1993.

Elves for a Day, Walt Disney Co., 1993.

Numbers Add Up at Home, illustrated by Peggy Tagel, Book Club of America, 1993.

(Reteller) *The Velveteen Rabbit,* Allan Publishers, 1993.

The Ballet Mystery, Simon & Schuster, 1994.

The Krystal Princess and the Grand Contest, Scholastic, Inc., 1994.

(Contributor) *Legacy of Dissent,* Simon & Schuster, 1994.

(Contributor) *Why Market Socialism?,* M. E. Sharpe (Armonk, NY), 1994.

Nala's Dare, Grolier Books, 1994.

Shopping Surprises, Joshua Morris, 1994.

Ride All Around, Joshua Morris, 1994.

Look What I Found, Joshua Morris, 1994.

Big Wheels, Little Wheels, Joshua Morris, 1994.

Home, Creepy Home, Steck-Vaughn, 1995.

Nancy Drew Notebooks: Bad Day for Ballet, Simon & Schuster, 1995.

Nancy Drew Notebooks: The Ice Cream Snoop, Simon & Schuster, 1995.

Nancy Drew Notebooks: The Best Detective, Simon & Schuster, 1995.

A Boy across the Sea, Grolier Books, 1995.

Merry Christmas, Santa!, Troll (Mahwah, NJ), 1995.

Lost Little Bunny, Scholastic, Inc., 1995.

Tooth Fairy Magic, Scholastic, Inc., 1995.

The Adventures of Wishbone: A Tale of Two Sitters, Lyrick Publishing, 1995.

The Switching Hour, Simon & Schuster, 1996.

Fire Truck, Simon & Schuster, 1996.

Tanker, Simon & Schuster, 1996.

Tractor-Trailer, Simon & Schuster, 1996.

Recycler, Simon & Schuster, 1996.

Big Wheels, Troll (Mahwah, NJ), 1996.

Big Fire Trucks, Troll, 1996.

Help! It's Halloween!, Simon & Schuster, 1996.

The Strangest Halloween, Simon & Schuster, 1996.

Binya Binya Hide-and-Seek: Lift the Flap, Simon & Schuster, 1996.

The Witch's Hat, Simon & Schuster, 1997.

Zeena's Cat, Simon & Schuster, 1997.

Donkey Kong Country: My Very First Nintendo Game Boy, Simon & Schuster, 1997.

Super Mario's Adventures: My Very First Nintendo Game Boy, Simon & Schuster, 1997.

The Adventures of Wishbone: A Pup in King Arthur's Court, Lyrick Publishing, 1998.

Cat's Birthday, Children's Television Workshop, 1998.

Textures, Random House (New York City), 1998.

Patterns, Random House, 1998.
Colors, Random House, 1998.
Splish! Splash!: Magic Bath Book, Random House, 1998.
Scrub-a-Dub-Dub: Magic Bath Book, Random House, 1998.
Barnum's Animals: ABC, Simon & Schuster, 1998.
Barnum's Animals: Counting 1 to 10, Simon & Schuster, 1998.
Barnum's Animals: Shapes, Simon & Schuster, 1998.
Barnum's Animals: Opposites, Simon & Schuster, 1998.
Barnum's Animals ABC Puzzle Pack, Simon & Schuster, 1999.
The Santa Claus Nutcracker, Simon & Schuster, 1999.
The Toy Soldier, Simon & Schuster, 1999.
Voyage to Rados, Grolier Books, 1999.
Wishbone SuperMysteries: Riddle of the Lost Lake, Lyrick Publishing, 2000.
Andy and the Lion, Lyrick Publishing, 2000.

Contributor to anthologies, including *Kick Up Your Heels,* Scott, Foresman, 1981; *On Stage,* Riverside Publishing, 1986; *Blue Ribbon,* Riverside Publishing, 1986; and *Tails of Terror,* Lyrick Publishing, 1999. Contributor (sometimes under undisclosed pseudonyms) of original stories to reading textbooks for Scott, Foresman, and Riverside Publishing; author of social studies textbooks for Holt and for Ginn and Co. (Lexington, MA). Contributor to periodicals, including *Storyworks, Kids,* and *Roboforce;* contributor of articles on politics and economics to *Attenzione, Progressive, Commonweal, Monthly Review, Dissent, In These Times,* and other publications in the United States, and to *Renewal* (England), *Tiden* (Sweden), and *Il Manifesto,* a daily newspaper in Italy. National news editor, *Seven Days,* 1978; member of executive committee and editorial board, *Dissent,* 1986—.

SIDELIGHTS: Joanne Barkan is a prolific author of both fiction and nonfiction children's books. Her award-winning *Creatures That Glow* is a science book for young readers that explains bioluminescence. The book features color photographs that glow in the dark and a text that was praised for its clear, straightforward presentation of a complicated but fascinating topic.

Barkan is also the author of *Abraham Lincoln,* a biography for first readers that reviewers noted reads like fiction. Other nonfiction titles for this age group include *Air, Air, All Around* and *Water, Water, Everywhere,* books which feature riddles and simple experiments as a way to introduce youngsters to science topics.

Barkan's fiction titles include board books such as *Locomotive, Box Car, Passenger Car,* and *Caboose.* This series contains information about trains that is geared for the youngest of children. The books, which are shaped like the train car they depict, may be joined together end-to-end like a train. Another board book series includes such titles as *Whiskerville Bake Shop, Whiskerville Firehouse, Whiskerville Post Office,* and *Whiskerville School,* and introduces young children to the workings of various public institutions. A reviewer for *Publishers Weekly* commented: "This hospitable town is worth a stop on any young traveler's itinerary."

The list of Barkan's picture books includes two Halloween tales, *A Very Scary Witch Story* and *A Very Scary Ghost Story,* both of which feature glow-in-the-dark illustrations and friendly supernatural beings in search of fun. *Anna Marie's Blanket* is a more realistic story concerning a young girl whose excitement about starting school is tempered by the realization that she will have to leave her beloved blanket at home.

BIOGRAPHICAL/CRITICAL SOURCES:

PERIODICALS

Booklist, November 1, 1991, p. 511.
Publishers Weekly, March 30, 1990, p. 60; April 27, 1990, p. 59; April 13, 1992, pp. 85-86; September 7, 1992, p. 59.
School Library Journal, July, 1990, p. 67; March, 1991, p. 181; January, 1992, pp. 118, 123.

* * *

BECK, Aaron T(emkin) 1921-

PERSONAL: Born July 18, 1921, in Providence, RI; son of Harry S. and Elizabeth (Temkin) Beck; married Phyllis Harriet Whitman (a lawyer), June 4, 1950; children: Roy, Judith, Daniel, Alice. *Education:* Brown University, A.B. (magna cum laude), 1942; Yale University, Ph.D. (in psychiatry), 1946; Philadelphia Psychoanalytic Institute, graduate, 1956.

ADDRESSES: *Home*—406 Wynmere Rd., Wynnewood, PA 19096. *Office*—133 South 36th St., Room 602, Philadelphia, PA 19104.

CAREER: Rhode Island Hospital, Providence, intern, 1946, resident in pathology, 1947; Cushing Veterans Administration Hospital, Framingham, MA, resident in neurology, 1948, resident in psychiatry, 1949-50; Austen Riggs Center, Stockbridge, MA, fellow, 1950-52; University of Pennsylvania, Philadelphia, 1954—, assistant professor, 1956-67, associate professor, 1967-70, professor of psychiatry, 1970—; Philadelphia General Hospital, Philadelphia, chief of section in department of psychiatry, 1958—. Member of visiting staff, Institute of the Pennsylvania Hospital, 1956—; consultant, Veterans Administration Hospital, Philadelphia, 1967—. President, Beck Institute for Cognitive Therapy and Research. *Military service:* U.S. Army, 1943-46, 1952-54; became captain.

MEMBER: American Psychiatric Association, American Academy of Psychoanalysis, Philadelphia County Medical Society, Philadelphia Psychiatric Society, Phi Beta Kappa.

AWARDS, HONORS: Cummings PSYCHE Award, the Nicholas and Dorothy Cummings Foundation in collaboration with Institute for Behavioral Healthcare, for "significant contributions which have reshaped the fields of psychiatry, social work and behavioral health."

WRITINGS:

Depression: Clinical, Experimental, and Theoretical Aspects, Harper (New York City), 1967.

Diagnosis and Management of Depression, University of Pennsylvania (Philadelphia, PA), 1973.

Prediction of Suicide, Charles Press (Bowie, MD), 1974.

Cognitive Therapy and the Emotional Disorders, International Universities Press (New York City), 1976.

Cognitive Therapy of Depression, Guilford Press (New York City), 1979.

Anxiety and Phobias: Cognitive Approaches, Basic Books (New York City), 1983.

(With Gary Emory and Ruth L. Greenberg) *Anxiety Disorders and Phobias: A Cognitive Perspective,* Basic Books, 1985.

(With Robert A. Steer) *BDI-II, Beck Depressive Inventory* (manual), Psychological Corp. (San Antonio, TX) and Harcourt (New York City), 1987, (with Steer and Gregory K. Brown), 2nd edition, 1996.

(With Steer) *BHS, Beck Hopelessness Scale* (manual), Psychological Corp. and Harcourt, 1988.

Love is Never Enough: How Couples can Overcome Understandings, Resolve Conflicts, and Solve Relationship Problems through Cognitive Therapy, Harper (New York City), 1988.

(Author of foreword and editor with Jan Scott and J. Mark G. Williams) *Cognitive Therapy in Clinical Practice: An Illustrative Casebook,* Routledge (New York City), 1989.

(With Steer) *BAI, Beck Anxiety Inventory,* (manual), Psychological Corp. and Harcourt,1990.

(With Arthur Freeman and associates) *Cognitive Therapy of Personality Disorders,* Guilford Press, 1990.

(With Steer) *BSI, Beck Scale for Suicide Ideation* (manual), Psychological Corp. and Harcourt, 1991.

Cognitive Therapy of Substance Abuse, Guilford Press, 1993.

(With Brad A. Alford) *The Integrative Power of Cognitive Therapy,* Guilford Press, 1997.

Prisoners of Hate: The Cognitive Basis of Anger, Hostility, and Violence, Harper (New York City), 1999.

(With David A. Clark and Brad A. Alford) *Scientific Foundations of Cognitive Theory and Therapy of Depression,* John Wiley (New York City), 1999.

Also author of sound recording, *Rational Thinking—An Antidote to Depression,* American Psychological Association (Washington, DC), 1984. Contributor of more than three hundred seventy-five articles to professional journals.

SIDELIGHTS: Aaron T. Beck was honored as "one of the major figures of 20th Century psychotherapy" when he won the Cummings PSYCHE Award. During the Korean War Beck served as Assistant Chief of Neuropsychology at Valley Forge Hospital. Following his graduation in 1956 from the Philadelphia Psychoanalytic Institute, Beck devoted himself to a research program to validate psychoanalytic theories. However, when his research failed to validate his hypotheses, he rejected the psychoanalytic approach and began developing a cognitive therapy for depression—a program that seeks to reverse depressive moods through reason and problem-solving.

In a 1986 *People Weekly* interview with Beck, correspondent Giovanna Breu asked him, "Are there personality traits that identify people as a suicide risk?" Beck reportedly replied, "There is no single profile. In general they don't like to feel bad and they look for quick fixes to avoid feeling bad. They have less control over their angry feelings and violent impulses. They also have low serotonin, a neural biochemical substance in the brain that has a dampening effect on impulses, like shock absorbers on a car. Other factors include a low capacity for solving problems—and alcoholism."

Breu also asked Beck, "What is the system of treatment that you call 'cognitive therapy'?" Beck reportedly explained: "Depressed and suicidal people start off by not seeing any solution to their problems. At our Center for

Cognitive Therapy, we try to define the problems for them and generate a variety of probable solutions or approaches. Most psychological problems center on incorrectly appraising life's stresses, reasoning on the basis of false assumptions and jumping to self-defeating conclusions. You help patients apply reason and logic to their problems so they can confront them consciously, here and now." Beck further detailed, "You don't have to extinguish totally the wish to die. You just have to lobby to swing the vote the other way. If you intervene properly, you can save lives."

Beck's *Prisoners of Hate* strives to apply the same problem-solving approaches taken by cognitive therapy in one-on-one encounters with individual patients to the international level, in dealing, country to country, people to people. The book is divided into three sections. Part One examines the beliefs and cognitive distortions underlying the psychology of anger in individual, everyday life. Part Two examines violence, both on an individual level and in groups, from persons who commit assault, rape, child abuse, and other violent crimes, to the group level, including collective illusions legitimizing prejudice and war. Part Three examines the possibility of harnessing the universal needs for altruism, cooperation and attachment, through cognitive intervention, to reduce hate and anger and violence, between individuals, groups, or nations.

Albert Mobilio, a *Fortune* magazine critic, in his essay "Death by Psychobabble," a most uncomplimentary, even hostile, review of Beck's *Prisoners of Hate* and Richard Rhodes Knopf 's *Why They Kill: The Discoveries of a Maverick Criminologist,* takes both books severely to task. "Why did the killer cross the road? To get to the other side, stab you in the face, and carve a pentagram on your forehead. The answer may be obvious to you and me, but we're not sociologists or psychologists. For members of these unworldly tribes, the ready answer rarely comes readily. Study must be done. Only then can they reach the same conclusion we would." Mobilio assesses that Beck and Rhodes "both labor mightily in these flawed books to explain why people do violent things, yet their similar verdicts—those who smack were smacked themselves—are no shockers."

In a *Times Literary Supplement* review, Carol Tavris states, "However, the methods that might work for an angry couple are unlikely to work on the grand scale that Beck envisions in *Prisoners of Hate.* Beck succumbs to the fallacy of the misleading similarity; if two phenomena share certain features, the phenomena must have the same causes and be modifiable by the same interventions." Having observed in both individual and group behavior similar elements of primal thinking, she cites Beck's conclusion: "This is not surprising, since group behaviour represents the cumulative effect of the individuals members' thinking." To which Tavris responds: "This is plain wrong; group behaviour is far more than the sum of its members' thoughts or even their individual wishes or personalities. Cognitive distortions and stereotypes about the enemy do indeed 'activate the motivation to fight and kill', but, at a group level, so do many other forces, including conformity, group pressure, cultural values, loyalty to fellow soldiers, self-defense, fear and direct orders." Tavris notes: "Beck believes that the interventions that work for warring couples are appropriate for warring groups and nations: deactivate hostility with a cooling-off period; encourage empathy; teach both sides that they may actually be abysmally wrong in their characterizations of one another's motives and intentions; and emphasize the satisfaction of cooperation and altruism." To which Tavris then rhetorically replies: "How sane, how nice, how . . . unlikely! Cognitive therapy as a method, and Aaron Beck as a clinician, have a sweet optimism and rationality to them that are appealing, yet will strike many as naive." Tavris concludes: "Individuals and couples in conflict will benefit enormously from reading this book; but it will take more than reason to make governments reasonable."

BIOGRAPHICAL/CRITICAL SOURCES:

PERIODICALS

Fortune, October 11, 1999, Albert Mobilio, "Death by Psychobabble," p. 84.

Library Journal, August, 1999, E. James Lieberman, review of *Prisoners of Hate,* p. 120.

People Weekly, April 7, 1986, "When Hopelessness sets in, Warns Psychiatrist Aaron Beck, Suicide Can Be Close Behind," p. 93.

Times Literary Supplement, December 17, 1999, Carol Tavris, "Hanging on to Our Hatred," p. 26.

OTHER

Aaron T. Beck, Honorary President, http:///www.personal.kent.edu/, (February 14, 2000).

Biography: Aaron T. Beck, http://www.duskin.com/connectext/, (February 14, 2000).*

BECKETT, Ian F(rederick) W(illiam) 1950-

PERSONAL: Born June 7, 1950, in Whitchurch, Buckinghamshire, England; son of R. Alexander (an engineer) and Anne Patricia (Beer) Beckett; married Trina Margaret Willis, October 4, 1975; children: Andrea Charlotte, Mark Frederick William. *Ethnicity:* "English." *Education:* University of Lancaster, B.A. (with honors), 1971; King's College, London, Ph.D., 1975.

ADDRESSES: Office—Department of Literature and History, University of Luton, 75 Castle St., Luton, Bedfordshire LU1 3AJ, England. *E-mail*—ian-beckett@luton.ac.uk.

CAREER: University of Salford, Salford, England, administrator and historian, 1974-79; Open University, Milton Keynes, England, administrator, 1979; Royal Military Academy, Sandhurst, Camberley, England, senior lecturer in war studies, 1979-94; University of Luton, professor of modern history, 1995—, head of School of Literature and History, 1994-96, head of history, 1996—. U.S. Naval War College, visiting professor, 1992-93.

MEMBER: North American Conference on British Studies, Royal Historical Society (fellow), Institute of Historical Research, Society for Army Historical Research, Army Records Society, Western Front Association, Society of Friends of the National Army Museum, Buckinghamshire Record Society, Buckinghamshire Archaeological Society, Custer Battlefield Historical and Museum Association (United States).

WRITINGS:

Marlborough's Campaigns, Shire, 1973.
History in Camera: Victoria's Wars, Shire, 1974.
(Editor with John Gooch) *Politicians and Defence: Studies in the Formulation of British Defence Policy,* Manchester University Press, 1981.
Riflemen Form, Ogilby Trusts, 1982.
(Editor with Keith Simpson) *A Nation in Arms,* Manchester University Press, 1985.
(Editor with John Pimlott) *Armed Forces and Modern Counter-Insurgency,* St. Martin's (New York City), 1985.
The Buckinghamshire Posse Comitatus, 1798, Buckinghamshire Record Society, 1985.
Call to Arms, Barracuda, 1985.
(Editor) *The March of Communism,* Military Press, 1985.
The Army and the Curragh Incident, 1914, Bodley Head, 1986.
Buckinghamshire, Shire, 1987.
Johnnie Gough, V.C., Tom Donovan, 1989.
Amateur Military Tradition in Britain: 1640-1940 (monograph), Manchester University Press, 1991.
The Judgement of History: Smith-Dorrien, Lord French and 1914, Tom Donovan, 1993.
The War Correspondents: The American Civil War, Alan Sutton, 1993.
(Editor with David Chandler) *The Oxford Illustrated History of the British Army,* Oxford University Press (New York City), 1994.
Discovering British Regimental Traditions, Shire, 1999.
Encyclopedia of Guerrilla Warfare, American Bibliographical Center-Clio Press (Santa Barbara, CA), 1999.

Other books include *Whitchurch in Camera,* 1989. General editor of the series "History of the British Army" and "War, Armed Forces, and Society," both Manchester University Press, 1987-97.

WORK IN PROGRESS: The Politics of Command in the Victorian Army, 1872-99.

SIDELIGHTS: Ian F. W. Beckett once told *CA:* "My interest in military history stems from my boyhood and my interest in local history in Buckinghamshire. I attended some lectures in my village on local history, at about the age of thirteen or fourteen, in which the auxiliary forces—militia, yeomanry, and volunteers—were mentioned casually, and I began to go to the County Record Office to look at the documents myself.

"Local military units provided me with an entree into the wider field of military studies, and they remain my abiding interest. Few British historians have researched the auxiliary forces and their relationship with the local county communities. I believe, however, with the regular army being small and mostly overseas, it has been the auxiliaries who provided the essential link between army and society in England. They were far more visible to society than the regulars and were an integral part of life from the seventeenth century to at least the beginning part of the Second World War. In all this, there is a considerable element of continuity from period to period, hence the concept of an amateur military tradition—for, of course, auxiliaries were part-time soldiers only temporarily in uniform. There is actually a close parallel with the United States and, originally, I derived much information on how to approach the English auxiliary forces from work on the United States militia (the militia was taken to the colonies by the English settlers) and volunteers.

"I have a particular fascination for 'last stands' in military history, and my hobby has been to read about, rather than to do deep research on, such incidents as the Alamo and Custer's Last Stand. It probably stems from watching too many films of John Wayne and Errol Flynn!"

BIOGRAPHICAL/CRITICAL SOURCES:

PERIODICALS

Times Literary Supplement, September 4, 1981.

* * *

BEISTLE, Shirley
See CLIMO, Shirley

* * *

BLACK, David 1945-

PERSONAL: Born April 21, 1945, in Boston, MA; son of Henry Arnold (a teacher) and Zelda Edith (a social worker; maiden name, Hodosh) Black; married Deborah Hughes Keehn (a teacher), June 22, 1968; children: Susannah Haden, Tobiah Samuel McKee. *Education:* Amherst College, B.A. (with honors), 1967; Columbia University, M.F.A., 1971. *Religion:* Jewish.

ADDRESSES: Home and Office—150 West 95th St., 5B, New York, NY 10025. *Agent*—David Wirtschafter, International Creative Management, 8899 Beverly Blvd., Los Angeles, CA 90048.

CAREER: Writer. Mount Holyoke College, South Hadley, MA, writer in residence, 1982-86; story editor for television series *Hill Street Blues,* National Broadcasting Company, Inc. (NBC-TV), 1986-87, and *Miami Vice,* American Broadcasting Companies, Inc. (ABC-TV), 1987-88; producer of television series *Lou Gossett Show,* 1988; co-creator and supervising producer of *The Nasty Boys,* NBC-TV, 1990; supervising producer of *H.E.L.P.,* ABC-TV, 1990, and *Law and Order,* NBC-TV, 1990.

MEMBER: PEN, Writers Guild, Mystery Writers of America.

AWARDS, HONORS: First Award from *Atlantic Monthly,* 1973; honorable mention in *Best Short Stories of the Year,* 1974, for "Laud"; *Like Father* was named a notable book of the year by the *New York Times* and listed as one of the seven best novels of the year by the *Washington Post,* both 1978; National Endowment for the Arts grant, 1980; award for best article, *Playboy,* 1980; *The King of Fifth Avenue: The Fortunes of August Belmont* was named a notable book of the year by the *New York Times, New York Magazine,* and Associated Press, all 1981; Edgar Allan Poe Award nomination, Mystery Writers of America, best fact crime book, 1984, for *Murder at the Met;* Science-in-Society Award, National Association of Science Writers, 1985, and Pulitzer Prize nomination, both for *The Plague Years: A Chronicle of AIDS, the Epidemic of Our Times;* reporting award from *National Magazine,* 1986; honorable mention in *Best Essays of the Year,* 1986, for "Walking the Cape."

WRITINGS:

Ekstacy, Bobbs-Merrill (New York City), 1975.

Like Father (novel), Dembner (New York City), 1978.

The King of Fifth Avenue: The Fortunes of August Belmont (nonfiction), Dial (New York City), 1981.

Minds (novel), Harper (New York City), 1982.

Medicine Man: A Young Doctor on the Brink of the Twenty-First Century (nonfiction), F. Watts (New York City), 1985.

The Plague Years: A Chronicle of AIDS, the Epidemic of Our Times(nonfiction), Simon & Schuster (New York City), 1986.

Peep Show (novel), Doubleday (New York City), 1986.

The Actor's Audition, foreword by Eli Wallach, Vintage Books (New York City), 1990.

The Magic of Theater: Behind the Scenes with Today's Leading Actors, Collier Books (New York City), 1993.

(Editor and narrator) *In His Own Words: John Curtin's Speeches and Writings,* Paradigm Books Curtin University (Bentley, WA), 1995.

An Impossible Life: A Bobeh Myseh (novel), Moyer Bell (Wakefield, RI), 1998.

Also author of *Murder at the Met* (novel), 1983; *An Impossible Life* (play), 1990; author of scripts for television series, including *Hill Street Blues,* 1986; and author of unproduced screenplays. Contributor to periodicals, including *Atlantic Monthly, Cosmopolitan, Granta, Harper's, New York Times Magazine, New York, Playboy, Rolling Stone, Transatlantic Review,* and *Village Voice.* Contributing editor of *Rolling Stone,* 1986—.

SIDELIGHTS: David Black is a versatile, multi-media writer who has distinguished himself in both fiction and nonfiction. As a novelist, he is probably best known for *Like Father,* which the *New York Times* ranked among the best novels of 1978. *Like Father* tells of Dennis Moses, a middle-aged man attempting to find his father who has run away after reading a biography of Russian novelist and philosopher Leo Tolstoy. In conducting his search the son reconsiders his own life, particularly his childhood and his marriage. Elizabeth F. Halley, reviewing *Like Father* in the *Washington Post Book World,* deemed it "a narrative rich with incident and alive with full-blooded characters."

In *Murder at the Met,* a fictional work based on an actual crime, Black focused on the apprehension of Craig S. Crimmins, killer of Helen Hagnes Mintiks, a thirty-year-old violinist whose naked, bound corpse was found in an air shaft at New York City's Metropolitan Opera House in 1980. The work also describes the developing bond between two detectives, Mike Struk and Jerry Giorgio, assigned to the case. The two have contrasting personalities and each is used to a different work environment, but the men realize that cooperation will bring success and further their respective careers. The book concludes with a lengthy account of Crimmins's court trial, where his lawyers futilely try to discredit the police investigation. *New York Times Book Review* contributor M. S. Kaplan maintained that the "courtroom episodes lack the macabre fascination of the book's behind-the-scenes glimpse at the Police Department's workaday world." Kaplan conceded, however, that in describing the victim's autopsy and the chase for the killer, "Black uses his skill and sensibility as a novelist to its most chilling effect."

Black has also received recognition for his nonfiction. Among his works in this genre is *The King of Fifth Avenue: The Fortunes of August Belmont,* which is about the Jewish immigrant who became a prominent New York City socialite in the nineteenth century. John Brooks, in his *New York Times Book Review* appraisal, described the work as a "rich biography," and he noted that it "has the absorbing quality of a first-rate historical novel."

Medicine Man: A Young Doctor on the Brink of the Twenty-First Century is Black's often disturbing account of an actual medical student's third year of study. In this book Black notes that much of the information learned by the student will soon be out of date. Black also indicates that the technological developments in the field of medicine may be outpacing the handling capacities of many physicians. Carole Horn wrote in the *Washington Post* that *Medicine Man* is a "graphic, rather bleak account of medical education."

Black is also author of *The Plague Years: A Chronicle of AIDS, the Epidemic of Our Times,* expanded from articles originally appearing in *Rolling Stone* magazine. Transmitted by bodily fluids, acquired immune deficiency syndrome (AIDS) is a fatal disease which attacks the body's immune system, eventually halting the victim's ability to fight infection. Initially the AIDS epidemic in the United States seemed restricted to homosexual men, but the disorder has since extended to other areas of the population, including intravenous drug users, children of infected mothers, and heterosexual men and women. Because of the disease's deadly nature and its lingering association with the homosexual community, AIDS victims have often been treated as social outcasts and shunned as highly contagious. Black, who reported on the AIDS crisis for nearly a year, is appalled by such reactions and in *The Plague Years* denounces those who use AIDS to justify their homophobia. Noting this sentiment, *Los Angeles Times* contributor Lee Dembart stated that the work "sears with emotion." And Richard Davenport-Hines, in his review for the *Times Literary Supplement,* affirmed that "Black's book displays sensitivity, and its research clearly caused him anguish."

BIOGRAPHICAL/CRITICAL SOURCES:

PERIODICALS

Best Sellers, September, 1986, p. 233.
Booklist, February 1, 1986, p. 785; June 15, 1986, p. 1478.
Journal of American Culture, spring, 1993, p. 73.
Kirkus Reviews, October 1, 1985, p. 1056; April 1, 1986, p. 486; April 15, 1986, p. 596.
Library Journal, November 1, 1985, p. 104; July, 1986, p. 97.
Los Angeles Times, August 12, 1986.
National Review, December 28, 1984, p. 53.
New York Times Book Review, October 25, 1981, pp. 12, 54; October 21, 1984, p. 18; January 5, 1986, p. 28; June 8, 1986, p. 36; July 27, 1986, p. 12.
Publishers Weekly, October 4, 1985, p. 65; November 29, 1985, p. 45; April 4, 1986, p. 48; May 2, 1986; April 25, 1994, p. 70; February 3, 1997, p. 95.
Quill & Quire, September, 1986, p. 90.
Times Educational Supplement, May 9, 1986, p. 26.
Times Literary Supplement, July 18, 1986, p. 780.
Voice Literary Supplement, September, 1986, p. 16.
Washington Post, December 18, 1985.

Washington Post Book World, December 3, 1978; December 17, 1978, pp. 1, 14.*

* * *

BLECKER, Robert A. 1956-

PERSONAL: Born November 17, 1956, in Philadelphia, PA; son of Sol (a government worker) and Luba Krasnov-Rein (an art teacher; maiden name, Allen) Blecker; married Elizabeth J. Greenberg (a social science analyst), December 26, 1982; children: Matthew, Emily. *Education:* Yale University, B.A. (summa cum laude), 1978; graduate study at El Colegio de Mexico, 1978-79; Stanford University, M.A., 1983, Ph.D., 1987.

ADDRESSES: Home—12607 Taylor Ct., Silver Spring, MD 20904. *Office*—Department of Economics, American University, 4400 Massachusetts Ave. N.W., Washington, DC 20016-8029. *E-mail*—blecker@american.edu.

CAREER: American University, Washington, DC, instructor, 1985-86, assistant professor, 1986-92, associate professor, 1992-98, professor of economics, 1998—, and member of Global Development Network. Economic Policy Institute, research associate, 1991—; public service work includes testimony before the U.S. Congress on the U.S. trade deficit.

MEMBER: American Economic Association, Phi Beta Kappa.

AWARDS, HONORS: Fulbright fellow in Mexico, 1978-79; grants from Economic Policy Institute, 1990-91 and 1998-99, International Labor Affairs Bureau, U.S. Department of Labor, 1993-94, Center for Economic Policy Analysis, New School University, 1998-99, and Council on Foreign Relations, 1999.

WRITINGS:

(Contributor) Bob Cherry and other editors, *The Imperiled Economy: Left Perspectives on Macroeconomics,* Union for Radical Political Economists, 1987.

Are Americans on a Consumption Binge? The Evidence Reconsidered, Economic Policy Institute (Washington, DC), 1990.

(Contributor) Robert S. McIntyre and Bruce L. Fischer, editors, *Growth and Equity: Tax Policy Challenges for the 1990s,* Citizens for Tax Justice, 1990.

(Contributor) Paul Davidson and Jan A. Kregel, editors, *Economic Problems of the 1990s: Europe, the Developing Countries, and the United States,* Edward Elgar (Brookfield, VT), 1991.

Beyond the Twin Deficits: A Trade Strategy for the 1990s, M. E. Sharpe (Armonk, NY), 1992.

(With Stephen D. Cohen and Joel R. Paul) *Understanding U.S. Foreign Economic Policy,* Westview (Boulder, CO), 1996.

(Editor) *Trade Policy and Global Growth,* M. E. Sharpe, 1996.

(Contributor) Philip Arestis, editor, *Essays in Honour of Paul Davidson,* Volume I: *Keynes, Money, and the Open Economy,* Edward Elgar, 1996.

(Contributor) Robert Pollin, editor, *The Macroeconomics of Finance, Saving, and Investment,* University of Michigan Press (Ann Arbor, MI), 1997.

Taming Global Finance: A Better Architecture for Growth and Equity, Economic Policy Institute, 1999.

(Contributor) Candace Howes and Ajit Singh, editors, *Competitiveness Matters: U.S. Industry, Industrial Policy, and Economic Performance,* University of Michigan Press, 1999.

(Contributor) John T. Harvey and Johan Deprez, editors, *Foundations of International Economics: Post Keynesian Perspectives,* Routledge (New York City), 1999.

Contributor of articles and reviews to economic journals, including *Journal of Post Keynesian Economics, International Review of Applied Economics, Structural Change and Economic Dynamics,* and *Economica.*

* * *

BOLGER, Dermot 1959-

PERSONAL: Born February 6, 1959, in Finglas, Ireland; son of Roger and Bridie (Flanagan) Bolger; married, wife's name, Bernadette, 1988; children: Donnacha, Diarmuid. *Education:* Attended Beneavin College Secondary School.

ADDRESSES: Agent—A. P. Watt, 20 John St., London WC1N 2DR, England.

CAREER: Editor, poet, and novelist. Raven Arts Press, Finglas, Dublin, Ireland, founder and editor, 1979-92; New Island Books, executive editor, 1992—. Member, Arts Council of Ireland, 1989-93, and Aosdana, 1991.

AWARDS, HONORS: A. E. Memorial Prize, 1986, for *Night Shift;* Macaulay fellowship, 1987, for *The*

Woman's Daughter; Samuel Beckett Award, Stewart Parker BBC Award, and Edinburgh Fringe First Award, all for *The Lament for Arthur Cleary;* A. Z. Whitehead Prize, for *Blinded by the Light;* Edinburgh Fringe First Award, for *The Holy Ground.*

WRITINGS:

NOVELS

Night Shift, Brandon (Dingle, Ireland), 1985.
The Woman's Daughter, Raven Arts Press (Dublin, Ireland), 1987, expanded edition, Viking (New York City), 1991.
The Journey Home, Viking, 1990.
Emily's Shoes, Viking, 1992.
A Second Life, Viking, 1994.
Father's Music, Flamingo, 1997.
Finbar's Hotel (collaborative novel), Picador, 1997.
Temptation, Flamingo, 2000.

POETRY

The Habit of Flesh, Raven Arts Press, 1979.
Finglas Lilies, Raven Arts Press, 1980.
No Waiting America, illustrated by Syd Bluett, Raven Arts Press, 1981.
Internal Exiles (includes "The Lament for Arthur Cleary"), Dolmen Press (Mountrath, Portlaoise, Ireland), 1986.
Leinster Street Ghosts, Raven Arts Press, 1989.
Taking My Letters Back: New and Selected Poems, New Island Books (Dublin), 1998.

EDITOR

(And author of introduction) Madeleine Stuart, *Manna in the Morning: A Memoir 1940-1958,* Raven Arts Press, 1986.
The Dolmen Book of Irish Christmas Stories, Dolmen Press, 1986.
The Bright Wave: Poetry in Irish Now, Raven Arts Press, 1986.
16 on 16: Irish Writers on the Easter Rising, Raven Arts Press, 1988.
Invisible Cities: The New Dubliners; A Journey through Unofficial Dublin, Raven Arts Press, 1988.
Invisible Dublin: A Journey through Dublin's Suburbs, Raven Arts Press, 1991.
Francis Ledwidge: Selected Poems, introduction by Seamus Heaney, New Island Books, 1992.
Wexford through Its Writers, New Island Books, 1992.
The Picador Book of Contemporary Irish Fiction, Picador, 1993.
(With Aidan Murphy) *12 Bar Blues,* Raven Arts Press, c. 1993.
The New Picador Book of Contemporary Irish Fiction, Picador, 2000.

Editor of the book *Ladies Night at Finbar's Hotel,* 1999.

PLAYS

The Lament for Arthur Cleary (adapted by Bolger from the author's poem of the same title), produced in Dublin, Ireland, at Dublin Theatre Festival, 1989.
Blinded by the Light, produced in Dublin, at Abbey Theatre, 1990.
In High Germany, produced at Dublin Theatre Festival, 1990.
The Holy Ground, produced at Gate Theatre with *In High Germany* under the title *The Tramway End,* 1990, produced under original title, Abbey Theatre, 1998.
One Last White Horse, produced at Dublin Theatre Festival, 1991.
A Dublin Quartet (contains the plays *The Lament for Arthur Cleary, In High Germany, The Holy Ground,* and *One Last White Horse*), introduction by Fintan O'Toole, Penguin (London), 1992.
The Dublin Bloom (adapted from the novel *Ulysses* by James Joyce), produced in Philadelphia, PA, at Annenberg Theater, 1994.
April Blight, produced at Abbey Theatre, 1995.
The Passion of Jerome, produced at Abbey Theatre, 1999.
Consenting Adults, produced in Dublin, at Fishamble Theatre, 2000.
Plays 1, Methuen, 2000.

OTHER

(With Michael O'Loughlin) *A New Primer for Irish Schools,* Raven Arts Press, 1985.

Work represented in anthologies, including *The Inherited Boundaries: Younger Poets of the Republic of Ireland,* edited by Sebastian Barry, Dolmen Press, 1988.

SIDELIGHTS: Dermot Bolger is a prolific writer of novels, plays, and poems, and the editor of several collections of writings by Irish authors. He is considered by critics to be one of the foremost modern writers in Ireland, and much of his work is devoted to the portrayal of the contemporary Irish lifestyle.

Internal Exiles, Bolger's 1986 volume of poetry, depicts life and love in the working class suburbs of Dublin. Included in the collection are "The Lament for Arthur Cleary," in which a young woman remembers her dead biker lover, as well as other poems written from a woman's perspective. Clair Wills, in a review of Irish poetry for *Times Literary Supplement,* asserted that with *Internal Exiles* Bolger "builds on his skill at writing strangely erotic poems about love in the deprived atmosphere of Dublin tenements and hotel rooms. . . . [He] has the rare ability to describe ordinary pain with both wit and affection." Among Bolger's numerous plays is his stage adaptation of "The Lament for Arthur Cleary." Critic Martin Hoyle noted in the London *Times* that the drama is a "wryly affectionate and ruefully despairing glance at Irishness."

Bolger's next publication, the 1987 novel *The Woman's Daughter,* is also set in the somber suburbs of Dublin, and deals with such issues as incest and child abuse. The first portion of the narrative is composed of a woman's monologue, in which the character details her painful childhood memories and rationalizes the abuse of her own daughter. Interspersed are the thoughts of the daughter, whom the mother has confined to a bedroom since birth. In her seventeen years, the girl has had no contact with anyone and no sense of identity. She therefore fills the lonely hours by fantasizing about the people she hears her mother describe in her babbling monologues. Eventually the nameless girl's spirit travels back in time to haunt a child from a previous century, demanding facts and names from which the girl might develop a self-history.

In a *Times Literary Supplement* review of *The Woman's Daughter,* Anne-Marie Conway noted that despite the book's elements of horror, madness, and murder, "to read Dermot Bolger's novel as no more than a chilling tale, well told, would be an injustice to a subtle and extraordinary novel." Conway went on to say: "*The Woman's Daughter* does not reveal its secrets easily. The intricate cat's cradle of relationships later revealed, the half-rhymed lives, the recurring names and nightmares, the many narrative voices spliced together across the centuries, all demand great concentration from the reader, and each reading reveals new threads to follow."

Also set in a seedy Dublin suburb is *The Journey Home,* Bolger's 1990 novel about nineteen-year-old Francis Hanrahan's encounters with an assortment of characters: a streetwise runaway, the spirit of a murdered man, and the local, crooked family of politicians responsible for the man's death. *The Journey Home,* opined *Times Literary Supplement* reviewer David Montrose, "is a grim and angry novel written in appropriately terse, muscular prose. . . . Powerful scenes abound." Frances Hill, in a critique of the book for the London *Times,* deemed *The Journey Home* "a profound and subtle lament for a heritage well lost. It is also a fast-paced adventure story."

The strong influence of the Catholic church on Irish life is often evident in Irish literature, and *Emily's Shoes,* another of Bolger's novels, follows in this tradition. *Emily's Shoes* is the story of Michael McMahon, an orphan in the care of an aunt who leaves him alone at night while she works. To pass the time, Michael plays with his aunt's shoes, teetering about the apartment in her spiked heels. His play becomes a fetish, and Michael becomes a lonely, troubled adult with an unusual love of women's footwear. When a charlady envisions the Virgin Mary's face in the grain of Michael's bedroom door, Michael begins, finally, to find meaning in life apart from his love affair with shoes. An *Observer* critic deemed *Emily's Shoes* an "original, fiercely well written book."

As an editor and publisher, Bolger displays a keen interest in promoting the work of modern Irish writers. *The Picador Book of Contemporary Irish Fiction* contains Bolger's selection of works by numerous contemporary authors, many of whom have broken away from the stereotypes of the Irish set forth by England and the United States and are part of the newly emerging Irish literary scene. Bolger includes in this collection literature from the late 1960s and onward, since "he calculates that Ireland began to emerge from stagnation and the difficult adjustment to independence at the end of the 1960s," according to Penelope Fitzgerald in *Times Literary Supplement.* In an *Observer* review of *The Picador Book of Contemporary Irish Fiction,* a critic noted: "Like all the best anthologies this is not just a selection but a cumulative argument on behalf of a cause." The critic also deemed Bolger "an ideal editor" to deal with imposed stereotypes. Nick Hornby, writing in the London *Times,* elaborated on a story by Eilis Ni Dhuibhne included in the anthology: "This is a shiny modern European literature, as relevant as anything currently being written in the English language, and Bolger's collection is a welcome and necessary confirmation of its vibrancy."

Bolger told *CA:* "Dublin is not only a city with an extraordinary literary heritage, but, far more importantly, one with the youngest population of any European capital. In my poetry, novels, and plays I have tried to capture the shifting social and political realities of that city, and of country, and of my generation (both at home and forced to scatter abroad). I am however as much a poet as a political writer; all my work has a strong spiritual aspect which interests me as much, if not more, than the more obvious political aspects which create far more controversy and comment.

"In 1977, at the age of eighteen, I started a publishing house, The Raven Arts Press, supporting it by working at first in a welding rod factory. I felt at the time the Irish writing that was being published did not fully reflect the reality of people's lives in Ireland. The press ran for fifteen years, publishing over 130 books. It is not my place to say whether it was a success or a failure (although many of its authors have gone on to become quite famous), beyond saying that it was never a business but more a loose movement for change, and that, for me, its major success was that the face of Irish writing has changed so much by 1992 that there seemed no reason for it to continue."

BIOGRAPHICAL/CRITICAL SOURCES:

PERIODICALS

New Statesman, January 16, 1987, p. 30; April 2, 1993, p. 26.

Observer, April 18, 1993, p. 61; July 11, 1993, p. 63.

Times (London), October 4, 1990; July 4, 1991, p. 16; July 30, 1992; March 21, 1993, pp. 8-9.

Times Literary Supplement, March 4-10, 1988, p. 254; July 6, 1990, p. 731; June 28, 1991, p. 19; June 12, 1992, p. 20; March 12, 1993.

* * *

BONINGTON, (Sir) Chris(tian John Storey) 1934-

PERSONAL: Born August 6, 1934, in London, England; son of Charles (a journalist) and Helen Anne (Storey) Bonington; married Muriel Wendy Marchant (an illustrator), May 26, 1962; children: Daniel, Rupert. *Education:* Attended Royal Military Academy, Sandhurst, 1954-56. *Religion:* Agnostic. *Avocational interests:* Mountaineering, squash, orienteering.

ADDRESSES: Home and Office—Badger Hill, Nether Row, Hesket Newmarket, Wigton, Cumbria CA7 8LA, England; fax: + 44 (0) 169-74-78238. *Agent*—Curtis Brown, 4th Floor, Haymarket House, 28/29 Haymarket, London SW1Y 4SP, England. *E-mail*—Chris@Bonington.com.

CAREER: British Army, troop commander of Royal Tank Regiment, 1956-58, instructor in Army Outward Bound School, 1958-61; Unilever, London, England, management trainee, 1961-62; free-lance writer, photographer, and mountaineer, 1962—. Member of team making first descent of Blue Nile, 1968; leader or co-leader of Annapurna South Face Expedition, 1970, British Everest Expedition, 1972, Everest South West Face Expedition, 1975, first ascent of Ogre, 1977, first ascent of Kongur, South West China, 1981, first ascent of Shivling West, 1983, and Vinson, Antarctica, 1983; reached Everest summit, 1985. Fellow, University of Manchester Institute of Science and Technology, 1976.

MEMBER: 1983 Royal Geographic Society (fellow), British Mountaineering Council (vice-president, 1976-79, 1985-88; president, 1988-91), Army Mountaineering Association (vice-president, 1980—), British Orienteering Federation (president, 1985—), Alpine Climbing Group (president, 1964-66), LEPRA (president, 1985—), Alpine Club (president, 1995-98), Army and Navy Club, Border Liners Club, Climbers Club, Fell and Rock Climbing Club.

AWARDS, HONORS: Honorary M.A., Salford University, 1973; Royal Geographic Society Founders Medal, 1974; Commander, Order of the British Empire, 1976; Honorary D.Sc., Sheffield University, 1976, Lancaster University, 1983; Lawrence of Arabia Medal, Royal Society for Asian Affairs, 1986; Livingstone Medal, Royal Scottish Geographical Society; honorary D.L.L., University of Northumbria.

WRITINGS:

I Chose to Climb, Doubleday, 1966.

Annapurna South Face, McGraw, 1970.

The Next Horizon, Gollancz (London), 1972.

The Ultimate Challenge: The Hardest Way up the Highest Mountain in the World, Stein & Day (New York City), 1973, published in England as *Everest South West Face,* Hodder & Stoughton (London), 1973.

Everest the Hard Way, Vikas Publications (New Delhi), 1976, Random House (New York City), 1977.

Quest for Adventure, Hodder & Stoughton, 1981, C. N. Potter (New York City), 1982.

Kongur, China's Elusive Summit, Hodder & Stoughton, 1982.

(With Charles Clarke) *Everest, the Unclimbed Ridge,* Hodder & Stoughton, 1983, Norton, 1984.

The Everest Years: A Climber's Life, Hodder & Stoughton, 1986, Viking (New York City), 1987.

Mountaineer: Thirty Years of Climbing on the World's Great Peaks, Diadem, 1989.

(With Robin Knox-Johnston) *Sea, Ice, and Rock: Sailing and Climbing Above the Arctic Circle,* Sheridan House (Dobbs Ferry, NY), 1993.

The Climbers: A History of Mountaineering (see below), BBC/Parkwest (Jersey City, NJ), 1994.

(General editor) *Heroic Climbs: A Celebration of World Mountaineering,* edited by Audrey Salkeld, Mountaineers (Seattle, WA, 1994, originally published in Britain as *Great Climbs: A Celebration of World Mountaineering,* M. Beazley (London), 1994.

(With Charles Clarke) *Tibet's Secret Mountain: The Triumph of Sepu Kangri,* Weidenfeld & Nicolson (London), 1999.

Also author of six-part television series and accompanying book (see above), *The Climbers: A History of Mountaineering,* British Broadcasting Company, c. 1994.

SIDELIGHTS: A veteran of numerous mountain-climbing expeditions, Chris Bonington has detailed his experiences in numerous books; his accounts, however, are more than mere recitations of events. In a review of *The Next Horizon,* Robin James of *Books and Bookmen* notes that "the author is as energetic in his writing as he is in his life. . . . Gripped by the danger of some climb or expedition, I found that we were either at the top of the mountain or at the end of the journey while my mind was still catching mental breath." *The Ultimate Challenge,* an account of Bonington's expedition to Mount Everest's southwest face, similarly involves the reader in events; a *Times Literary Supplement* critic comments that as the party approaches their climb "the expedition begins to come to life; some of the minor personality problems are brought out into the open frankly and naturally, which gives the reader the feeling of getting to know the climbers individually."

Bonington's successful 1975 climb of the southwest face is recounted in *Everest the Hard Way. New York Times Book Review* contributor Raymond A. Sokolov notes that "even amateur writers do well with the Everest story, and Chris Bonington . . . is a writer of real competence—and an even better editor." The author "quotes liberally not only from his own journal but from those of other climbers," J. D. Moorhead explains in the *Christian Science Monitor.* "This gives the reader glimpses into the thoughts of its participants while they are actually contending with the mountain." John Naughton of the *Times Literary Supplement* contends that "this book will confirm the worst suspicions of those who believe that all mountaineers are crazy," remarking on the difficulty and riskiness in ascending the southwest face. But, Naughton observes, "Bonington is acutely aware of this [danger], and the cautious, self-effacing, almost apologetic, tone of [*Everest the Hard Way*] is the result. . . . [It] is an admirable book."

Although the bulk of his work consists of reports of his own adventures, Bonington has also authored *Quest for Adventure,* "a nonfictional account of men and women who have endured incredible physical and mental hardships—even death itself—to conquer challenges of nature," as Robert Rector describes it in the *Los Angeles Times Book Review.* The author writes inspiringly about attempts to circumnavigate the globe by boat, cross deserts and climb mountains alone or with minimal equipment; D. J. R. Bruckner states in the *New York Times Book Review* that while Bonington is known as a climber, he "is also a good reporter. He conducted many interviews and did a lot of research for this book." The critic concludes that Bonington's "writing is masterly, assured and urbane and his tales have great emotional power."

What happens when two British adventurers, a world-famous sailor and a renowned mountain-climber, meet on a television program? In the case of Robin Knox-Johnston and Sir Chris Bonington, the result is a collaborative adventure in which the sailor learns to climb and the mountaineer learns to sail, detailed in their book, *Sea, Ice, and Rock: Sailing and Climbing Above the Arctic Circle.* The initial suggestion they share their skills was Knox-Johnston's. Aboard Knox-Johnston's 40-foot ketch, Suhaili, they followed the same course set by famed sailing mountaineer H. W. Tilman—from England to Greenland's east coast. They then endured a brutal forty-mile inland trek to The Cathedral, a previously unscaled 7,800-foot peak. The pair spent nearly twenty-five hours of climbing, attempting to reach their goal but were finally forced to give up. Bonington, accompanied by another climber, made a second attempt on their goal, but, again, were forced to turn back before reaching the summit—the events of which were a major cliffhanger of an adventure in its own right. Back aboard the Suhaili, the party was delayed off the coast of Iceland for more than a week when they encountered quite unfavorable winds. A *Publishers Weekly* reviewer deemed the book an "engaging account of camaraderie and of a grand escapade."

In *The Climbers: A History of Mountaineering,* Bonington details the development of the high-risk sport of mountain climbing, from the early exploits of Edward Whymper and A. F. Mummery to the daredevil adventures of today. Bonington begins by recounting the major expeditions of the 1920s and 1930s, then documents the successful assaults on the great peaks that began with Sir Edmund Hillary's ascent of Mt. Everest in 1953. The 1980s established a new, near-saturation level of fevered interest in scaling the major peaks of the Himalayas, and in attempting ever more dangerous conquests in their desire to make and break new records—new routes, solo climbs and winter ascents. In 1986, no less than nine expeditions attempted two new routes up K-2—although twenty-seven people successfully scaled the summit, another thirteen climbers died in their attempts. Among the record-holders, in 1986, Jerry Messher scaled all fourteen 8,000-meter peaks, while Jerzy Kukuczka followed suit in 1987. A *Publishers Weekly* reviewer lauded, "These are gripping stories of men and women who pushed themselves to the outer limits of endurance."

Tibet's Secret Mountain: The Triumph of Sepu Kangri is told in alternating chapters between co-authors Bonington and fellow veteran Himalayan climber Charles Clark, a British neurologist specializing in high-altitude medicine. The story began in 1982, when, during a mutual plane ride over the Tibetan plateau, the two spotted a "secret" mountain, not shown on any of their maps—known to Tibetans as "The Great White Snow God"—incredibly, a mountain, at some 22,800 feet, just slightly shorter than Mt. Everest! In 1996, they made their reconnaissance expedition; then, during 1997 and 1998, the pair made two attempts to achieve the never-before-scaled summit of Sepu Kangri. They were aided by USAF photos and a high-tech team and accompanying film crew equipped with such state-of-the-art equipment as a satellite communication hookup for instant transmission of their unprecedented adventure as it occurred direct to their website. Although they narrowly missed the actual summit, the book details their amazing adventure—all three expeditions—and includes such fascinating accounts as their witnessing a "Devil Dance," a ritual enactment by masked dancers of good's frenzied victory over evil, as well as participation in the annual quest for caterpillar fungus, the rare ingredient of a medicinal elixir. Jospeph L. Carson, writing in *Library Journal* deemed the book "a mesmerizing journey via prose." And a *Publishers Weekly* reviewer praised, "Mountaineering emerges here as a delicate balancing act between risk and ecstasy, a test of friendship and self."

BIOGRAPHICAL/CRITICAL SOURCES:

PERIODICALS

Books and Bookmen, August, 1973.

Christian Science Monitor, February 20, 1974; April 11, 1977.

Library Journal, January, 2000, Joseph L. Carlson, review of *Tibet's Secret Mountain,* p. 141.

Los Angeles Times Book Review, November 28, 1982.

New York Times Book Review, April 17, 1977; December 12, 1982; December 6, 1987.

Publishers Weekly, May 3, 1993, review of *Sea, Ice, and Rock,* p. 289; January 23, 1995, review of *The Climbers,* p. 57; December 6, 1999, review of *Tibet's Secret Mountain,* p. 64.

Spectator, September 29, 1973.

Times Literary Supplement, November 2, 1973; October 21, 1977.

* * *

BRADBURY, Malcolm (Stanley) 1932-

PERSONAL: Born September 7, 1932, in Sheffield, England; son of Arthur and Doris Ethel (Marshall) Bradbury; married Elizabeth Salt, October, 1959; children: Matthew, Dominic. *Education:* University College, University of Leicester, B.A. (first class honors), 1953; Queen Mary College, University of London, M.A., 1955; attended Indiana University, 1955-56, University of Manchester, 1956-58, Yale University, 1958-59; Ph.D., University of Manchester, 1962.

ADDRESSES: Agent—Curtis Brown Literary Agents, Haymarket House, Haymarket London, W1, England.

CAREER: University of Hull, Hull, England, staff tutor in literature and drama in department of adult education, 1959-61; University of Birmingham, Birmingham, England, lecturer in English language and literature, 1961-65; University of East Anglia, Norwich, England, lecturer, 1965-67, senior lecturer, 1967-69, reader in English, 1969-70, professor of American studies, 1970-95, professor emeritus, 1995—. Teaching fellow, Indiana University, 1955-56; junior fellow, Yale University, 1958-59; fellow, Harvard University, 1965-66; visiting professor, University of California, Davis, 1966; visiting fellow, All Souls College, Oxford University, 1969; visiting professor, University of Zurich, 1972; Fanny Hurst Professor of Writing, Washington University, 1982; Davis Professor, University of Queensland, and visiting professor, Griffith University, 1983; Senior Visiting Research Fellow, St. John's College, Oxford, 1994; Wells Professor, Indiana University, 1997. Chair of British Council English Studies Seminar, 1976-84; Booker-McConnell Prize for Fiction, chair of judges, 1981, member of management committee, 1984-91; member of management committee, Book Trust, 1987-89; judge of Royal Television Society Drama Awards, 1993; judge for British Academy of Film and Television Arts, 1995, 1998; chair of judges, Whitbread Prize, 1997. Founding director of Radio Broadland (independent radio station), 1984-96; director, East Anglian Radio, 1990-96.

MEMBER: British Association of American Studies, Society of Authors, PEN (executive committee, 1973-75), Royal Society of Literature (fellow).

AWARDS, HONORS: British Association of American Studies junior fellow in United States, 1958-59; American Council of Learned Societies fellow, 1965-66; Heinemann Prize, Royal Society of Literature, 1975, for *The History Man*; named among twenty best British writers by Book Marketing Council, 1982; shortlisted for Booker-McConnell Prize for Fiction, 1983, for *Rates of Exchange;* International Emmy Award, 1987, for *Porterhouse Blue;* Decorated Commander of the Order of the British Empire, 1991; Silver Nymph award for best screenplay for a series, Monte Carlo Television Festival, 1991, for *The Gravy Train;* Writers' Guild Macallan Award nomination, best drama serial for television, 1993, for *The Gravy Train Goes East;* best film made for television award, Banff Film Festival, 1995, for *Cold Comfort Farm;* Edgar Award nomination for best television feature, Mystery Writers of America, 1997, for *An Autumn Shroud.* D. Litt., University of Leicester, 1987, Birmingham University, 1989, University of Hull, 1994, Nottingham University, 1996.

WRITINGS:

Eating People Is Wrong (novel), Secker & Warburg, 1959, Knopf, 1960.
Phogey!; or, How to Have Class in a Classless Society (also see below), Parrish, 1960.
All Dressed Up and Nowhere to Go: The Poor Man's Guide to the Affluent Society (also see below), Parrish, 1962.
Evelyn Waugh (critical study), Oliver & Boyd, 1962.
Stepping Westward (novel), Secker & Warburg, 1965, Houghton, 1966.
(With Allan Rodway) *Two Poets* (verse), Byron Press, 1966.
What Is a Novel?, Edward Arnold, 1969.
The Social Context of Modern English Literature (criticism), Schocken, 1971.
Possibilities: Essays on the State of the Novel, Oxford University Press, 1972.
The History Man (novel), Secker & Warburg, 1975, Houghton, 1976.
Who Do You Think You Are?: Stories and Parodies, Secker & Warburg, 1976.
The Outland Dart: American Writers and European Modernism, Oxford University Press, 1978.
Saul Bellow (critical study), Methuen, 1982.
All Dressed Up and Nowhere to Go (contains revised versions of *Phogey!* and *All Dressed Up and Nowhere to Go*), Pavilion, 1982.
Rates of Exchange (novel), Knopf, 1983.
The Modern American Novel (criticism), Oxford University Press, 1983, revised edition, Viking, 1993.
Why Come to Slaka?, Secker & Warburg, 1986.
Cuts: A Very Short Novel (novella), Harper, 1987.
My Strange Quest for Mensonge, Penguin, 1988, also issued as *Mensonge: Structuralism's Hidden Hero.*
No, Not Bloomsbury (collected essays), Columbia University Press, 1988.
Unsent Letters: Irreverent Notes from a Literary Life, Penguin, 1988.
The Modern World: Ten Great Writers (criticism), Penguin, 1989.
(With Richard Ruland) *From Puritanism to Postmodernism: A History of American Literature* (criticism), Viking Penguin, 1991.
Doctor Criminale (novel), Viking Penguin, 1992.
The Modern British Novel (criticism), Penguin Books (New York City), 1994.
Dangerous Pilgrimages: Trans-Atlantic Mythologies and the Novel (criticism), Secker & Warburg (London), 1995.

Contributor of more than 1,500 articles and reviews to periodicals, including *Punch, New Yorker, New York Times, Times* (London), *Times Literary Supplement, New York Review of Books, Spectator,* and *New Republic.*

DRAMA

(With David Lodge and James Duckett) *Between These Four Walls* (stage revue), first produced in Birmingham, England, 1963.
(With Lodge, Duckett, and David Turner) *Slap in the Middle* (stage revue), first produced in Birmingham, England, 1965.
(With Chris Bigsby) *The After Dinner Game* (television play), British Broadcasting Corporation (BBC), 1975.
(With Bigsby) *Stones* (television play), BBC, 1976.
Love on a Gunboat (television play), BBC, 1977.
The Enigma (television play based on a story by John Fowles), BBC, 1980.

Standing In for Henry (television play), BBC, 1980.

Congress (radio play), BBC, 1981.

The After Dinner Game: Three Plays for Television, Arrow Books, 1982, revised edition, 1989.

Rates of Exchange (television series based on Bradbury's novel of the same title), BBC, 1985.

Blott on the Landscape (television series; adapted from novel by Tom Sharpe), BBC, 1985.

Porterhouse Blue (television series; adapted from the novel by Tom Sharpe), Channel 4, 1987.

Imaginary Friends (television series; adapted from the novel by Alison Lurie), Thames, 1987.

The Green Man (television series; adapted from the novel by Kingsley Amis), BBC, 1990.

Cold Comfort Farm (television series; adapted from the novel by Stella Gibbons), BBC, 1996.

Cold Comfort Farm (screenplay; based on the novel by Stella Gibbons), BBC, 1996.

Inside Trading: A Comedy in Three Acts (drama; produced at the Norwich Playhouse, November-December, 1996), Methuen Drama, 1996.

In the Red (television series; adapted from the novel by Mark Tavener), BBC2, 1998.

Author of plays *Scenes from Provincial Life,* based on the novel by William Cooper, and *Pemberton Billing and the Little Black Book.* Author, with wife, Elizabeth Bradbury, of radio play *This Sporting Life,* 1974-75. Author of six episodes of series *Anything More Would Be Greedy,* Anglia, 1989; four episodes of *The Gravy Train,* Channel 4, 1991; and four episodes of *The Gravy Train Goes West,* Channel 4, 1992. Adaptor of works by Reginald Hill, including *An Autumn Shroud,* BBC1, 1996, for the series *Dalziel and Pascoe.* Also author or adaptor of episodes of television series *A Touch of Frost, Kavanagh QC, Dalziel and Pascoe,* and *Inspector Morse.* Literary advisor for South Bank Show television series *The Modern World: Ten Great Writers,* LWT, 1988.

EDITOR

E. M. Forster: A Collection of Critical Essays, Prentice-Hall, 1965.

Mark Twain, *"Pudd'nhead Wilson" and "Those Extraordinary Twins,"* Penguin, 1969.

E. M. Forster, A Passage to India: A Casebook, Macmillan, 1970.

(With David Palmer) *Contemporary Criticism,* Edward Arnold, 1970, St. Martin's, 1971.

(With Eric Mottram and Jean Franco) *The Penguin Companion to American Literature,* McGraw, 1971 (published in England as *The Penguin Companion to Literature, Volume III: U.S.A.,* Allen Lane, 1971), published as *The Avenal Companion to English and American Literature,* Avenal Books, 1981.

(With Palmer) *Metaphysical Poetry,* Indiana University Press, 1971.

(With Palmer) *The American Novel and the Nineteen Twenties,* Edward Arnold, 1971.

(With Palmer) *Shakespearean Comedy,* Edward Arnold, 1972.

(With James McFarlane) *Modernism: A Guide to European Literature, 1890-1930,* Penguin, 1976, revised edition, 1990.

The Novel Today: Contemporary Writers on Modern Fiction, Rowman & Littlefield, 1977, revised edition, 1991.

(With Palmer) *Decadence and the 1890s,* Edward Arnold, 1979.

(With Palmer) *The Contemporary English Novel,* Edward Arnold, 1979.

(With Palmer) *Contemporary Theatre,* Holmes & Meier, 1979.

(With Howard Temperley) *An Introduction to American Studies,* Longman, 1980, revised edition, 1997.

Stephen Crane, *The Red Badge of Courage* (critical edition), Dent, 1983.

(With Palmer) *Shakespearean Tragedy,* Holmes & Meier, 1984.

(With Sigmund Ro) *Contemporary American Fiction,* E. Arnold, 1987.

The Penguin Book of Modern British Short Stories, Penguin, 1988.

(With Judy Cooke) *New Writing,* Heinemann, 1992.

(With Andrew Motion) *New Writing 2,* Heinemann, 1993.

Washington Irving, *The Sketch Book of Geoffrey Crayon, Gent.,* J. M. Dent, 1993.

Present Laughter: An Anthology of Modern Comic Fiction, Weidenfeld & Nicolson, 1994.

Class Work: An Anthology of University of East Anglia Stories (anthology), Sceptre, 1995.

The Atlas of Literature, D'Agostini (New York City), 1996.

Henry James, *The American,* Everyman, 1997.

(Introduction and notes) E. M. Forster, *A Room with a View,* Penguin Books, 2000.

General editor, "Stratford-upon-Avon Studies" series, Edward Arnold, 1970-81, and "Contemporary Writers" series, Methuen. Associate editor, Leicester University literary magazine, *Luciad,* 1952-53, Indiana University literary magazine, *Folio,* 1955-56; joint editor of *Yale Penny Poems,* Yale University, 1958-59; advisory and guest editor to several literary magazines.

WORK IN PROGRESS: A novel about philosopher Denis Diderot; adaptations of Virginia Woolf 's *Flush,* and Noel Coward's *The Vortex.*

ADAPTATIONS: The History Man was adapted as a four-part television series by Christopher Hampton, BBC, 1979.

SIDELIGHTS: Herbert Burke calls Malcolm Bradbury's first novel, *Eating People Is Wrong,* "a novel . . . about how weary academic life is in the English Midlands of the '50s—but this is not a weary novel. Often truly comic, its satire has many barbs and they often draw blood. . . . If seriousness of intent—a sociology of the British establishment of the times as seen through the microcosm of the academy—gets in the way of hearty satire, bawdiness is not lacking." According to Martin Tucker, the author "has written a first novel that is sloppy, structurally flabby, occasionally inane, frequently magnificent and ultimately successful. It is as if [Charles] Dickens and Evelyn Waugh sat down together and said 'Let's write a comic novel in the manner of Kingsley Amis about a man in search of his lost innocence who finds it.' The result is one of the most substantial and dazzling literary feasts this year." Not all reviewers have been so generous in their appraisal of the book, however. Patrick Dennis writes: "While Malcolm Bradbury's first novel is brilliant, witty, sensitive, adult, funny and a lot of other pleasant and desirable things, it is not a good novel. And I know why: Mr. Bradbury has been so busy entertaining himself with his brilliance, wit, etc., that he has quite forgotten about those less gifted people who are expected to buy, read and enjoy his book. . . . While his knaves and fools are elegantly written, his 'sympathetic' characters are so feckless or so grotesque that one has almost no feeling for them." And a *New Yorker* critic finds that "there are no funny situations, and the few comic episodes that occur are much too light, and perhaps also too tired, to stand up against the predominant, tragic predicament that is [the main character's] life . . . and even if this spectacle were more richly decorated than it is with jokes and puns and so on, it would not be good enough. Mr. Bradbury has created a serious and very human character, and has obscured him with jugglers."

Stepping Westward, Bradbury's second novel, also about university life, has been hailed by a *Times Literary Supplement* reviewer as "a *vade mecum* for every youthful or aspiring first visitor to the United States. Every situational joke, every classic encounter is exactly and wittily exploited. The dialogue is often marvellously acute, the tricks of American speech expertly 'bugged.' " On the other hand, however, Rita Estok says that "the school, faculty and students do not ring true; in fact, it is almost a travesty on university life. James Walker, the principal character, never becomes believable and remains unsympathetic throughout the story. *Stepping Westward,* be it a travesty or satire on university life, fails to hit the mark as either." And Bernard McCabe writes: "Within this very funny book Mr. Bradbury proposes a serious novel about freedom and community and friendship's inevitable failures. The result is interesting, but too schematic and analytical to be really successful. The comedy works, though, thanks to Bradbury's artful writing. I leave to some future scholar the precise significance of the recurrent buttocks-motif and ear-motif. . . . [The author's] exaggerated versions of [university life] work by lending a British ear and eye to the oddities of the American scene."

Robert Nye says that Bradbury, in his third novel, *The History Man,* "achieves some charming comic efforts—and not a few cruel ones. Bradbury has a baleful eye for human weakness. He describes with skill and obvious relish. The result is a clever, queer, witty, uncomfortable sort of book—a book whose prose possesses considerable surface brilliance but with a cutting edge concealed beneath." Margaret Drabble calls the book "a small narrative masterpiece," and she feels that "one of the reasons why this novel is so immensely readable is its evocation of physical reality; it may be a book about ideas, but the ideas are embodied in closely observed details. . . . A thoroughly civilized writer, [Bradbury] has written a novel that raises some very serious questions about the nature of civilization without for a moment appearing pretentious or didactic—a fine achievement."

Bradbury's fourth novel, *Rates of Exchange,* was published in 1983 to praise from critics such as *New York Times Book Review* contributor Rachel Billington, who labels it "an astonishing tour de force." The tale of a linguist traveling to a fictive Eastern bloc country, *Rates of Exchange* takes on the subject of language itself and "manages to be funny, gloomy, shrewd and silly all at once," according to Joel Conarroe in the *Washington Post Book World.* Bradbury's inventive use of language—both the locals' fractured English and their native Slakan, a hybrid of several European languages—is a highlight for many reviewers. Notes Anatole Broyard in the *New York Times,* "Bradbury is in such virtuoso form that he can even make you enjoy an entire book in which the majority of the characters speak various degrees of broken English." Although some critics take issue with the book's pacing, characterization, and sometimes uneasy mixture of humor and seriousness, many value its wit and pungent observations on travel. Writes *Los Angeles Times* reviewer Elaine Kendall, "Hilarious and accurate, deepened by the author's concern for subtle political and social factors, *Rates of Exchange* turns tour de force into an unequivocal compliment, elevating the genre to a major literary category."

In the 1992 novel *Doctor Criminale,* Bradbury returns to the intellectual circuit for a satirical look at the charming and worldly Dr. Criminale, a fictional "superpower of contemporary thought." The doctor's shadowy past contributes to his mysterious appeal; students, scholars, and virtually all available members of the female gender are dazzled by his social, political, economic, philosophical, and literary wisdom. When a young journalist lands the job of researching the doctor's life for a TV documentary, the hunt for the *real* Criminale begins. This is, according to Michiko Kakutani of the *New York Times,* "an ambitious novel about large, unwieldly ideas. Mr. Bradbury raises questions about Criminale's past to examine the meaning of political commitment, the relationship between moral responsibility and esthetic principles, and the consequences of ethical pragmatism in an individual's public and private lives. . . . The . . . novel," she concludes, "is provocative and smart but also somehow bloodless." And other reviewers felt that the character of Dr. Criminale needed fleshing out. "The eponymous subject is meant to be absolutely intriguing, but he is so 'elusive' that we have to attend instead to a thwarted narrator, in whom we're allowed no interest at all," asserts Mick Imlah in the *Times Literary Supplement.*

In 1994 Bradbury's sweeping literary survey *The Modern British Novel* was published to mixed reviews. *Times Literary Supplement* critic Peter Kemp lists several instances in which the names of characters and the titles of books under discussion are cited incorrectly; furthermore, he calls the author's accounts of various literary movements "little more than reaccumulations of the hackneyed. . . . As original critical analysis, [this book] is virtually non-existent." But, Kemp concedes, "where it does briefly spark into life is as polemic. . . . Bradbury stirs into energetic and eloquent defence of the twentieth-century British novel's variety, versatility, and vitality. With comic regularity, he demonstrates, jeremiahs throughout the century have been announcing the death of the novel, only to be elbowed aside by the emergence of vigorous new practitioners of the genre."

Dangerous Pilgrimages: Trans-Atlantic Mythologies and the Novel, Bradbury's 1996 look at the reciprocal influence of British and American literary content and style, is generally regarded as an impressive and much-needed addition to the study of literary history. The book focuses largely on about a dozen American novelists and a half dozen Europeans (a couple of French writers along with British heavyweights of the last three centuries) and concludes that myths, rather than mimicry, have fueled the rich flow of ideas that make up "trans-Atlantic fiction." John Sutherland proclaims in the *Times Literary Supplement:* "Academic criticism of American literature is currently densely theorized, introverted and, for anyone not professionally obliged to work with it, repugnant. This book is clearly a tool for the scholar but is generously accessible to any generally literate reader."

Bradbury has also written numerous stage revues and television mini-series and teleplays, including the original television series *Anything More Would Be Greedy, The Gravy Train,* and *The Gravy Train Goes East.* In addition to writing original episodes for well-known television series, including *A Touch of Frost, Kavanagh QC, Dalziel and Pascoe,* and *Inspector Morse,* Bradbury has adapted numerous works as teleplays. Bradbury's adaptation of Tom Sharpe's *Porterhouse Blue* garnered an International Emmy award; his adaptation of Stella Gibbons' *Cold Comfort Farm,* later released as a full-length motion picture directed by John Schlesinger, based on the screenplay by Bradbury, received the best film made for television award at the Banff Film Festival.

Bradbury commented: "As a novelist, I achieved four novels (and a volume of short stories) in twenty-five years. It may seem a slow record, but then I have been a critic, reviewer, and professor of American studies too, as well as a regular writer for television. I believe the writer has a responsibility for literary study, and this belief has gone into my teaching of creative writing and my editorship of series like Methuen's *Contemporary Writers,* where I and my fellow editor Chris Bigsby have sought to show that we live in a major period of literary creation very different from that of the earlier part of the century. I believe in fact we live in a remarkable international age of fiction, and this has affected my own writing. Though I started with provincial themes and in a relatively realistic mode I have grown vastly more international in preoccupation and far more experimental in method. Looking back over my books, they now seem to me to follow the curve of the development of British fiction from the 1950s: from the comic social realism of the postwar period through to a much harsher, more ironic vision which involves the use of fictiveness and fantasy—though always, in my case, with an edge of tragic commentary on the world we live in as this dark century moves to its end. I think I have grown far more exact as a writer, more concerned to deal with major themes, to escape provincial limitations, and to follow the fate of liberal hopes through the many intellectual, moral, and historical challenges it has now to face. As I said earlier: 'Serious writing is not an innocent act; it is an act of connection with the major acts of writing achieved by others. It is also . . . a new set of grammars, forms, and styles for the age we live in.'

"My books have been widely translated and are set-texts in schools and universities, and two—*The History Man* and *Rates of Exchange*—have been made into British Broadcasting Corporation television series. This has done a good deal to free me of the unfortunate label of being a 'university novelist,' since my aims are wider. I have myself been considerably influenced by writing for television, and I think the imagery and grammar of film and television has brought home new concepts of presentation and perception to the novel. I have also been influenced by (and perhaps also have influenced) younger writers like Ian McEwan and Clive Sinclair who have been in my creative writing classes at the University of East Anglia. I have fought for a view of the novel in Britain as a serious and experimental form, and I believe it has increasingly become so. I believe in our great need for fiction; in *Rates of Exchange,* set in Eastern Europe, I have tried to relate our awareness of an oppressive modern reality forged by the fictions of politicians and the structures of ideology to our need for true fictions that can challenge them. My basic themes, though, remain the same: the conflict between liberal humanism and the harsh systems and behaviorisms of the modern world, and the tragic implications, which, however, I believe must be expressed in comic form. In an age when the big ideologies grow tired, I think we need the abrasive vision of the writer, and in some of our great contemporaries of the novel, from Saul Bellow to Milan Kundera, I think we find that. So the novel is what gives me hope, and lasting pleasure."

BIOGRAPHICAL/CRITICAL SOURCES:

BOOKS

Bigsby, Christopher, and Heide Ziegler, editors, *The Radical Imagination and the Liberal Tradition: Interviews with English and American Novelists,* Junction Books, 1982.

Contemporary Literary Criticism, Volume 32, Gale, 1985.

Dictionary of Literary Biography, Volume 14: *British Novelists since 1960,* Gale, 1983.

Morace, Robert A., *The Dialogic Novels of Malcolm Bradbury and David Lodge,* Southern Illinois University Press, 1989.

PERIODICALS

Atlantic, November, 1992, p. 162.

Booklist, April 15, 1960; July, 1996, p. 1796; December 15, 1996, p. 745.

Books and Bookmen, April, 1983.

California, October, 1988.

Christian Science Monitor, February 18, 1976.

Commentary, September, 1989.

Commonweal, April 22, 1960.

Globe and Mail (Toronto), September 12, 1987; August 20, 1988.

Library Journal, March 1, 1960; June 1, 1966; May 15, 1988; June 15, 1988; January, 1989; November 15, 1991.

Literary Review, October, 1983.

London Review of Books, September 24, 1992, p. 18; November 18, 1993, p. 23.

Los Angeles Times, October 21, 1983; December 9, 1988.

Los Angeles Times Book Review, October 18, 1987; September 25, 1988.

Mother Jones, October, 1987.

National Review, May 2, 1960; June 17, 1996, p. 57.

New Leader, January 11, 1988, pp. 20-21.

New Republic December 14, 1987; May 27, 1996, pp. 28-29.

New Statesman, October 31, 1959; April 17, 1987; August 28, 1987.

New Statesman and Society, October 12, 1990.

Newsweek, October 24, 1983.

New Yorker, July 16, 1960; May 3, 1976.

New York Times, April 10, 1960; October 1, 1983; November 7, 1987; January 30, 1989.

New York Times Book Review, February 8, 1976; November 20, 1983; October 18, 1987; September 25, 1988; October 6, 1992, p. C-15; October 25, 1992.

People Weekly, May 27, 1996, p. 19.

Publishers Weekly, September 11, 1987; May 27, 1988; November 18, 1988; July 20, 1992, p. 220; June 10, 1996, p. 80.

San Francisco Chronicle, April 26, 1960.

Saturday Review, April 9, 1960; May 21, 1966.

Spectator, September 12, 1992, p. 37; October 30, 1993, p. 29; April 15, 1995, p. 35.

Time, June 3, 1966; November 14, 1983; July 18, 1988, p. 70.

Times (London), April 7, 1983; January 14, 1988; May 12, 1988; June 4, 1988.

Times Literary Supplement, November 13, 1959; August 5, 1965; November 7, 1975; September 3, 1982; April 8, 1983, February 22, 1985; October 24, 1986; June 12, 1987; November 12, 1987; May 13, 1988; September 11, 1992, p. 23; November 12, 1993, p. 24; April 28, 1995, p. 21.

Tribune Books (Chicago), August 28, 1988.

Washington Post, October 14, 1987.

Washington Post Book World, November 20, 1983; July 3, 1988; October 25, 1992, p. 5.*

* * *

BRANCH, Edgar Marquess 1913-

PERSONAL: Born March 21, 1913, in Chicago, IL; son of Raymond Sydney (a publisher) and Marian (Marquess) Branch; married Mary Josephine Emerson, April 29, 1939; children: Sydney Elizabeth (Mrs. James A. Diez), Robert Marquess, Marian Emerson. *Education:* University College, London, student, 1932-33; Beloit College, A.B., 1934; Brown University, graduate study, 1934-35; University of Chicago, M.A., 1938; University of Iowa, Ph.D., 1941. *Politics:* Democrat. *Religion:* Episcopalian. *Avocational interests:* Tennis, golf, gardening, and camping with his family.

ADDRESSES: *Home*—4810 Bonham Rd., Oxford, Ohio 45056. *Office*—352 King Library, Miami University, Oxford, Ohio 45056. *E-mail*—ebranch@lib.mu ohio.edu.

CAREER: Miami University, Oxford, Ohio, instructor, 1941-43, assistant professor, 1943-49, associate professor, 1949-57, professor, 1957-64, chairman of English Department, 1959-64, research professor of English, 1964-78, research professor of English emeritus and research associate in American literature, 1978—. Visiting associate professor, University of Missouri, 1949; literary executor, James T. Farrell estate, 1975—; Mark Twain Project, Berkeley, CA, member of board of directors, 1980-90; Mark Twain Home Foundation Advisory Panel, consultant, 1992—.

MEMBER: Modern Language Association of America, National Council of Teachers of English, American Studies Association (member of executive board for Ohio-Indiana, 1961-62), College English Association of Ohio, English Association of Ohio (member of executive board, 1959-60), Beta Theta Pi, Phi Beta Kappa.

AWARDS, HONORS: Beloit College, junior foreign fellow, 1932-33; summer fellow, American Council of Learned Societies, 1969; senior fellow, National Endowment for the Humanities, 1971-72, for edition of Mark Twain's *Early Tales and Sketches;* Outstanding Educators of America Award, 1975; senior fellow, National Endowment for the Humanities, 1976-77, for biography of James T. Farrell; dedication of the Branch Seminar Room, Miami University, 1978; Benjamin Harrison Award, Miami University, 1978; Distinguished Service Citation, Beloit College, 1979; Guggenheim Fellow, 1979; Nancy Dasher Book Award, College English Association of Ohio, 1981, for *Mark Twain's Early Tales and Sketches, Volume 1;* Second Lifetime Achievement Award, Mark Twain Circle of America, 1991; Mid-America Award, Society for the Study of Midwestern Literature, 1994; First Prize for a Distinguished Scholarly Edition, Modern Language Association of America, 1995, for Mark Twain's *Roughing It;* Pegasus Award, Ohio Library Association, 1996.

WRITINGS:

The Literary Apprenticeship of Mark Twain, University of Illinois Press (Urbana, IL), 1950.

A Bibliography of James T. Farrell's Writings, 1921-1957, University of Pennsylvania Press (Philadelphia, PA), 1959.

James T. Farrell, University of Minnesota Press (Minneapolis, MN), 1963.

(Author of introduction) Mark Twain, *Adventures of Huckleberry Finn,* edited by James K. Bowen and Richard VanDerBeets, Scott, Foresman (Glenview, IL), 1970.

James T. Farrell, Twayne (Boston, MA), 1971.

(With Frederick Anderson) *The Great Landslide Case,* Friends of the Bancroft Library, 1972.

(Author with Robert H. Hirst of an account of Mark Twain's literary use of the bloody encounters at Compromise, KY) *The Grangerford-Shepherdson Feud: Life and Death at Compromise,* Mark Twain (facsimile of that episode's first publication prior to *The Adventures of Huckleberry Finn*), Friends of the Bancroft Library, University of California Press (Berkeley, CA), 1985.

Men Call Me Lucky: Mark Twain and the Pennsylvania, Friends of the Library Society, Miami University (Oxford, OH), 1985.

Mark Twain and the Starchy Boys, Elmira Center for Mark Twain Studies (Elmira, NY), 1992.

Studs Lonigan's Neighborhood and the Making of James T. Farrell, Arts End Books (Newton, MA), 1996.

A Paris Year: Dorothy and James T. Farrell, 1931-1932, Ohio University Press (Athens, OH), 1998.

EDITOR

Mark Twain's Letters in the Muscatine Journal (monograph), Mark Twain Association of America, 1942, 2nd edition, (and author of introduction), R. West (Philadelphia, PA) 1977.

(And author of introduction and preface) *Clemens of the "Call,"* University of California Press, 1969.

(With Robert H. Hirst, with the assistance of Harriet Elinor Smith) Mark Twain, *Early Tales and Sketches,* five volumes, published for the Iowa Center for Textual Studies by University of California Press (Berkeley, CA), Volume I: *1851-64,* 1979, Volume II: *1864-65,* 1981.

(With Michael B. Frank and Kenneth M. Sanderson; associate editors Harriet Elinor Smith, Lin Salamo and Richard Bucci) *Mark Twain's Letters,* University of California Press, Volume 1: *1853-1866,* Volume 2: *1867-1868,* Volume 5: *1872-1873,* 1988-1997.

(With H. E. Smith; associate editors, L. Salamo and Robert Pack Browning) Mark Twain, *Roughing It,* illustrated by True Williams, Edward F. Mullen and others, University of California Press, 1993, 2nd edition, 1995.

OTHER

Contributor to books, including *Essays on Determinism in American Literature,* Kent State University Press, 1964; *Seven Novelists in the American Naturalist Tradition: An Introduction,* edited by Charles C. Walcutt, University of Minnesota Press, 1974; and *A Question of Quality,* edited by Louis Filler, 1976. Contributor to literary journals, including *American Book Collector, American Literature, American Quarterly, College English, PMLA, American Literary Realism, Nineteenth Century Literature, Twentieth Century Literature, American Book Collector, Mark Twain Journal,* and *University of Kansas City Review.*

WORK IN PROGRESS: (With Robert H. Hirst) *Mark Twain's Early Tales and Sketches,* volumes 3, 4, and 5, for the Mark Twain Project, University of California Press (Berkeley, CA), 2001-06.

SIDELIGHTS: Edgar Marquess Branch has had a distinguished career as a professor of English, as a scholar studying both Samuel Clemens/Mark Twain and James T. Farrell, and as a prolific author and editor specializing in the works of these two great American writers.

In 1971, Branch's *James T. Farrell,* a critical biography, was published as part of Twayne's United States Authors Series—this was, reportedly, the first such book written about Farrell. James T. Farrell, best known for his "Studs Lonigan" series *(Young Lonigan,* 1932; *The Young Manhood of Studs Lonigan,* 1934; *Judgment Day,* 1935), a trilogy concerned with the lower middle class Irish of Chicago's declining south side, an exhaustive analysis of a portion of urban American life noted for the scrupulous consistency with which it documented social and speech idioms. A lesser figure from the "Studs Lonigan" series, Danny O'Neill, became the subject of a later, five-volume series (1936-53), and Farrell wrote another trilogy, centered around yet another Irish-American protagonist, Bernard Clare. Despite the popular and critical fame of the "Studs Lonigan" series, some critics feel Farrell's "proletarian novel," *Gas-House McGinty,* a surprisingly experimental work, employing stream-of-consciousness passages and montage effects, to be his finest creation. Farrell also wrote other novels and numerous collections of short stories and critical essays.

Mark Twain's Letters, Volume 1: 1853-1866, for which Branch was one of the editors, received some very positive reviews. Critic Charles Nicol paid due tribute to this massive editorial undertaking, stating in *National Review:* "The Letters are part of the University of California's monumental edition of the Mark Twain papers. The editorial apparatus is a bit overwhelming, but very useful: counting introductions, exhaustive footnotes, appendices, textual commentaries, etc., more than half of these pages have been written by the editors, but everything seems justified." Gerald Weales, writing in *Smithsonian,* said, "This is an admirable book for Twain addicts, scholars or not."

Branch's status as dean of Farrell studies at Miami University, along with his friendship with both Farrells—which provided him with access to Farrell's papers, a prodigious trove of diaries, letters and unpublished manuscripts—lends him a uniquely qualified vantage point in writing *A Paris Year: Dorothy and James T. Farrell, 1931-1932.* When Farrell and his wife of four days, the former Dorothy Butler—already pregnant—set sail for Paris in 1931, the first wave of American expatriate writers, including Fitzgerald and Hemingway, had already returned to the United States. But he was eager to escape his hometown of Chicago and the Great Depression. This year in Paris, living as an outsider, saw immense productivity on the part of Farrell: revision of *Young Lonigan,* after its acceptance by James Herle—due in large part to the help of Ezra Pound and Sam Putnam; mapping out the balance of the trilogy; the writing of *Gas-House McGinty,* originally entitled *The Madhouse,* its first draft of 329 pages completed in a mere month and a half; and many short stories, including contributions of experimental fiction to the avant-garde, published in Bob Brown's *Readies.* But it was also a time of deep poverty, of personal tragedy with the death of their three-day-old son, Sean, all made the more painful and depressing because the couple had to keep their marriage and her pregnancy secret from her disapproving parents. Barry Wallenstein, writing in *American Book Review,* notes, "In addition, the book *[Young Lonigan]* had to be protected from the censors. The story of literary censorship, both in the US and in Great Britain, makes for a fascinating, albeit lamentable, subplot in the book." Sanford E. Marovitz, writing in the *NOBS Newsletter* notes that *A Paris Year* confirms that "Edgar M. Branch is a scholar's scholar and a master of facts." A *Publishers Weekly* reviewer deemed the book "an in-depth study that brings the artist-in-the-garret cliche to life and shows the tenacity and talent that would help make Farrell an important American writer." Wallenstein terms *A Paris Year: Dorothy and James T. Farrell, 1931-1932* a "treasure of a book," and cites "the elegantly presented evidence in Branch's detailed account of the Farrells' year in the city of dreams" that is "remarkable for its exhaustive scholarship, its commitment to and connection with its subject."

BIOGRAPHICAL/CRITICAL SOURCES:

PERIODICALS

American Book Review, January-February, 2000, Barry Wallenstein, "American in Paris," p. 23.

NOBS Newsletter, spring, 1999, Sanford E. Marovitz, review of *A Paris Year,* pp. 15-17.

National Review, July 22, 1988, Charles Nicol, review of *Mark Twain's Letters, Volume 1,* p. 47.

Publishers Weekly, September 14, 1998, review of *A Paris Year,* p. 62.

Smithsonian, April, 1989, Gerald Wade, review of *Mark Twain's Letters, Volume 1,* p. 170.

Time, June 6, 1988, Stefan Kanfer, review of *Mark Twain's Letters, Volume 1,* p. 87.

BRANTLINGER, Patrick (Morgan) 1941-

PERSONAL: Born March 20, 1941, in Indianapolis, IN; son of Morgan Wilson (a journalist) and Lavon Ruth (a musician; maiden name, Patrick) Brantlinger; married Ellen Carleen Anderson (a professor), June 21, 1963; children: Andrew Morgan, Susan Rachel, Jeremy Zoar. *Education:* Antioch College, B.A., 1963; Harvard University, M.A., 1965, Ph.D., 1968.

ADDRESSES: *Office*—Department of English, Indiana University, Bloomington, IN 47405; fax 812-855-9535. *E-mail*—brantli@indiana.edu.

CAREER: Indiana University—Bloomington, assistant professor, 1968-72, associate professor, 1972-78, professor of English, 1978—, chairperson of department, 1990-94, director of Victorian Studies Program, 1978-90.

MEMBER: Modern Language Association of America, American Association of University Professors, American Federation of Teachers, Midwest Victorian Studies Association.

AWARDS, HONORS: Guggenheim fellowship, 1978; summer fellowship, National Endowment for the Humanities, 1983.

WRITINGS:

The Spirit of Reform: British Literature and Politics, 1832-1867, Harvard University Press (Cambridge, MA), 1977.

Bread and Circuses: Theories of Mass Culture as Social Decay, Cornell University Press (Ithaca, NY), 1984.

Rule of Darkness: British Literature and Imperialism, 1830-1914, Cornell University Press, 1988.

(Editor) *Energy and Entropy: Science and Culture in Victorian Britain; Essays from Victorian Studies,* Indiana University Press (Bloomington), 1989.

Crusoe's Footprints: Cultural Studies in Britain and America, Routledge (New York City), 1990.

(Editor with James Naremore) *Modernity and Mass Culture* (essays), Indiana University Press, 1991.

Fictions of State: Culture and Credit in Britain, 1694-1994, Cornell University Press, 1996.

The Reading Lesson: The Threat of Mass Literacy in Nineteenth-Century British Fiction, Indiana University Press, 1998.

Editor of *Victorian Studies,* 1980-90.

SIDELIGHTS: As a professor of English and scholar of Victorian studies, Patrick Brantlinger has published several volumes linking Victorian issues and literature with theories of modern culture. In his *Bread and Circuses: Theories of Mass Culture as Social Decay,* the author discusses what he terms "negative classicism," or the theory that society is weakened and eventually destroyed by its dependence on mass culture, such as religion, television, literature, and numerous other influences. Underlying the thoughts of all the individuals Brantlinger studies is the common belief that progress breeds decay, and "that there had once been a better age, somewhere in the past," according to *Voice Literary Supplement* critic Laurie Stone.

Brantlinger traces negative classicism from the French Revolution to the late twentieth century, starting with Victorian reactions to the modernization of their culture, and moves chronologically, drawing from the works of many writers, including Friedrich Nietzsche, Soeren Kierkegaard, Karl Marx, Sigmund Freud, Albert Camus, T. S. Eliot, and Marshall McLuhan. In his discussion of each writer, Brantlinger points out that subject's concern about his society's future based on then-current trends, and examines how each saw a better model somewhere in the past.

In her *Voice Literary Supplement* review, Laurie Stone writes that *Bread and Circuses* "is a joy to read. Brantlinger is learned, witty, and, best of all, inviting of conversation. Pleasure in the play of his mind smiles from nearly every sentence, and he is wonderfully generous, noting intelligence and plausibility, where they exist, in the anti-democratic theories of Nietzsche and Kierkegaard, and esteeming the Frankfurt philosophers, despite their gloom, for sniffing out oppression in places liberals seldom think to look." The critic also declares that Brantlinger's "work in the 19th century has steered him wisely and well to his current subject, which could be described as a history of reactions to modernization."

Another of Brantlinger's works, *Rule of Darkness: British Literature and Imperialism, 1830-1914,* is what the author describes as "cultural history," depicting how Victorian literature affected the building of the British Empire and supported the Empire's prevalent racism. Again, Brantlinger interrelates historical facts with the observations of numerous writers, among them William Makepeace Thackeray. "The results are illuminating," writes John Sutherland in *Times Literary Supplement,* "not because of any new critical wrinkle but because Brantlinger is a sound critic and a well-read historian who writes clearly on topics with complex interrelations." Sutherland adds: "Brantlinger's is an important book whose effect will be felt on a number of fronts."

Brantlinger's *Crusoe's Footprints: Cultural Studies in Britain and America* describes the way in which universities and the media are adapting to an ever-changing society, one in which women, people of color, and other minorities are given a voice and represented in literature and art, and are thus empowered in society. Brantlinger sees the need for cultural studies to embody the mosaic whole of society, for "unless the ideals expressed in great works of literature and art . . . can and do become politically empowered," he asserts, "there seems to be no point in teaching them." *Times Literary Supplement* critic Wendy Steiner declares *Crusoe's Footprints* "excellent both as an introduction and as a sourcebook to the cultural studies movement."

BIOGRAPHICAL/CRITICAL SOURCES:

PERIODICALS

Los Angeles Times Book Review, August 11, 1985, p. 8.

Times Literary Supplement, September 9, 1988, p. 996; January 25, 1991, p. 7.

Voice Literary Supplement, February, 1984, pp. 10-12.

* * *

BRINGHURST, Robert 1946-

PERSONAL: Born October 16, 1946, in Los Angeles, CA; son of George H. and Marion (Large) Bringhurst; married Miki Cannon Sheffield, June 3, 1974 (divorced, 1981); children: Piper Laramie. *Education:* Attended Massachusetts Institute of Technology, 1963-64, 1970-71, and University of Utah, 1964-65; studied Arabic language and Islamic history at Defense Language Institute, Monterey, CA, 1966-67; Indiana University, B.A. (comparative literature), 1973; University of British Columbia, M.F.A. (poetry), 1975.

ADDRESSES: Office—Box 357, 1917 West 4th Ave., Vancouver, British Columbia V6J 1M7, Canada. *Agent*—c/o Douglas & McIntyre Ltd., 2323 Quebec St., Suite 201, Vancouver, British Columbia, Canada.

CAREER: Worked as journalist in Beirut, Lebanon, 1965-66, and in Boston, MA, 1970-71; dragoman in Israel and Palestine, 1967-68; law clerk in Panama Canal

Zone, 1968-69; University of British Columbia, Vancouver, British Columbia, visiting lecturer, 1975-77, lecturer in English department, 1979-80; School of Fine Arts, Banff, Alberta, poet-in-residence, 1983; Simon Fraser University, Vancouver, adjunct lecturer, 1983-84; Ojibway & Cree Cultural Centre Writers' Workshops, Atikokan & Espanola, Ontario, poet-in-residence, 1985; University of Winnipeg, Winnipeg, Manitoba, writer-in-residence, 1986; University of Edinburgh Scotland, Canada/Scotland Exchange Fellow and writer-in-residence, 1989-90; Trent University, Peterborough, Ontario, Ashley Fellow, 1994; University of Western Ontario, London, Ontario, writer-in-residence, 1998-99; Frost Centre for Native Studies and Canadian Studies, Trent University, conjunct professor, 1998—. *Military service:* U.S. Army Intelligence, seconded to Israeli Defense Force, 1966-68; Judge Advocate General's Corps., 1968-69.

MEMBER: Writers Union of Canada (national council member, 1985-87), Charles Taylor Foundation (founding trustee).

AWARDS, HONORS: Macmillan Prize for Poetry, 1975; Canada Council Arts Grant, 1975-76; Canada Council Travel Grant, 1977; Canada Council Arts Grant, 1980-81; Ontario Arts Council Literary Grant, 1982; Canada Council Travel Grant, 1983; Alcuin Society Design Award, 1984; Canada Council Senior Arts Grant, 1984-85; Alcuin Society Design Award, 1985; Canadian Broadcasting Corporation Poetry Prize, 1985; Canada Council Nonfiction Grant, 1986-87; Guggenheim Fellow in poetry, 1987-88; Canada Council & Scottish Arts Council Canada/Scotland Exchange Fellow, 1989-90; Alcuin Society Design Award, 1993; TIA International design award, 1993; Canada Council Senior Arts Grant, 1993-94; Canada Council Travel Grant, 1995; Rocky Mountain Publishers Association Design Award, 1997; Symons Trust Fund for Canadian Studies, major research grant, 1999; Charles Watts Award, 1999, for "outstanding endeavor in the polity of poetry."

WRITINGS:

The Shipwright's Log, Kanchenjunga Press, 1972.
Cadastre, Kanchenjunga Press, 1973.
Deuteronomy, Sono Nis Press, 1974.
Eight Objects, Kanchenjunga Press, 1975.
Bergschrund, Sono Nis Press, 1975.
Jacob Singing, Kanchenjunga Press, 1977.
The Stonecutter's Horses, Standard Editions, 1979.
Tzuhalem's Mountain, Oolichan Books, 1982.
The Beauty of the Weapons: Selected Poems 1972-82, McClelland & Stewart, 1982, Copper Canyon Press, 1985.
(Editor with others) *Visions: Contemporary Art in Canada,* Douglas & McIntyre (Vancouver), 1983.
Ocean/Paper/Stone, William Hoffer, 1984.
(With Bill Reid) *The Raven Steals the Light,* Douglas & McIntyre/University of Washington Press, 1984.
Tending the Fire, Alcuin Society, 1985.
The Blue Roofs of Japan, Barbarian Press, 1986.
Pieces of Map, Pieces of Music, McClelland & Stewart, 1986, Copper Canyon Press, 1987.
Shovels, Shoes and the Slow Rotation of Letters, Alcuin Society, 1986.
Conversations with a Toad, Lucie Lambert, 1987.
The Black Canoe: Bill Reid and the Spirit of Haida Gwaii, photographs by Ulli Steltzer, Douglas & McIntyre/University of Washington Press, 1991.
The Calling: Selected Poems, 1970-1995, McClelland & Stewart (Toronto), 1995.
Elements (poetry), with drawings by Ulf Nilsen, Kuboaa Press (New York City), 1995.
The Elements of Typographic Style, Hartley & Marks (Point Roberts, WA), 1996.
Boats Is Saintlier than Captains: Thirteen Ways of Looking at Morality, Language, and Design, Edition Rhino (New York City), 1997.
A Story as Sharp as a Knife: The Classical Haida Mythtellers and Their World, Douglas & McIntyre, 1999.
(With Warren Chappell) *A Short History of the Printed Word,* Hartley & Marks, 1999.

CONTRIBUTOR TO ANTHOLOGIES

The New Oxford Book of Canadian Verse, Oxford University Press (Toronto), 1982.
Oxford Anthology of Canadian Literature in English, Oxford University Press, 1983.
The Penguin Book of Canadian Verse, Penguin Books, 1984.
The New Canadian Poets, edited by Dennis Lee, McClelland & Stewart (Toronto), 1985.
Canadian Short Fiction, edited by W. H. New, Prentice-Hall (Scarborough, Ontario), 1986.
Fifteen Canadian Poets Times Two, edited by Gary Geddes, Oxford University Press, 1988.
The Second Macmillan Anthology, edited by John Metcalf and Leon Rooke, Macmillan (Toronto), 1989.
Native Writers and Canadian Writing, edited by W. H. New, University of British Columbia Press, 1990.
The Norton Introduction to Poetry, edited by J. Paul Hunter, Norton (New York City), 1991, sixth edition, 1995.

Inside the Poem, edited by W. H. New, Oxford University Press, 1992.

World Poetry: An Anthology of Verse from Antiquity to Our Time, edited by Katharine Washburn, John S. Major, and Clifton Fadiman, Norton, 1998.

OTHER

The Spirit of Haida Gwaii (television documentary), CBC, 1992.

(Editor, and author of introduction and notes) Bill Reid, *Solitary Raven: Selected Writings,* Douglas & McIntyre, 2000.

(Translator and editor) Ghandl of the Qayahl Llaanas, *Nine Visits to the Mythworld,* University of Nebraska Press (Lincoln, NE), 2000.

Guest editor of Arabic literature and Greek issues of *Contemporary Literature in Translation,* 1974, 1976; contributing editor, *Fine Print,* beginning 1985.

SIDELIGHTS: In an online article for *The Reader,* Canadian poet Crispin Elsted recalls being sold a "modest pamphlet of a poem" by a bookseller "whose sales pitch consisted of handing me the pamphlet and saying, 'Guy named Bringhurst. Three bucks. You'll like it. It's intelligent.' " Elsted goes on to relate how right the bookseller was: Elsted's colleague Robert Bringhurst, he says, "is one of the very few poets of my generation who write poetry as if it were important, addressing the mind and the heart rather than the glands. More than this, he couples his intelligence with a deeply effective sense of rhetoric—the voice of his poems is characterful and engaging—and a recognition that the notation of poetry, its visual inflection on the page, is a powerful element in a poem's success."

Elsted stresses that the high level of Bringhurst's poetry does not imply a lack of heart. Indeed, "It would be wrong to give the impression . . . that it is professorial, didactic, and austere. Although it makes profession of thought, and teaches, and does so often with a pared, winnowed simplicity of language . . . it is the clarity, the simplicity of the writing that holds the attention. Teaching in college, I found that Bringhurst, more than any other contemporary poet, would hold a classroom of tin-eared adolescents quiet. He is, finally, a vastly entertaining poet."

Linking to the Bringhurst affinity for words on a page is his interest in the type style of those words. In 1992 he published *The Elements of Typographic Style,* a book "packed with design wisdom," according to Roy Johnson's online review. "It is obvious from almost every word that [the author] has thought profoundly about the fundamental issues of printed words on the page, and he often has insights to offer on topics most of us take for granted. He can conjure poetry out of the smallest detail, and he offers a scholarly yet succinct etymology of almost every mark that can be made—from the humble hyphen to the nuances of serifs on Trajan Roman or a Carolingian Majuscule."

Bringhurst is also a literary historian, specializing in works about native tribes of Canada. In *A Story as Sharp as a Knife,* he examines the native Haida of British Columbia's Queen Charlotte Islands. A civilization nearly wiped out by smallpox in the early 20th century, the Haida were a people rich in cultural and oral tradition. Many of the tales they told "were entertaining and historically important," according to *Maclean's* writer John Bemrose. "But the best were poetry of a high order—evocations of the myths that had once sustained the Haida's deep links to the sea and forests."

In assessing the ancient poetry, Bemrose continues, Bringhurst shows "that the Haida poets had their own individual styles. And while they often used similar plots, characters and formulaic phrases, they were no different, he maintains, than those Renaissance artists who all painted crucifixions or annunciations." As Bringhurst writes, "Haida poetry is not folk tales any more than the sculpture of Donatello is folk art or the sonatas of Beethoven are folk music. This is art made by individuals who knew what they were doing, and did it in their own way."

BIOGRAPHICAL/CRITICAL SOURCES:

BOOKS

Contemporary Poets, 6th edition, St. James (Detroit, MI), 1996.

Inside the Poem, edited by W. H. New, Oxford University Press (Toronto, Ontario), 1992, pp. 93-100.

Oxford Companion to Canadian Literature, 2nd edition, Oxford University Press, 1997.

Oxford Companion to Twentieth-Century Poetry, Oxford University Press, 1997.

PERIODICALS

Antognish Review, volume 85-86, 1991, Peter Sanger, "Poor Man's Art: On the Poetry of Robert Bringhurst," pp. 151-169.

Books in Canada, 1995, Scott Ellis, review of *The Calling,* pp. 30-31.

Canadian Dimension, July-August, 1996, Terren Ilana Wein, review of *The Black Canoe,* p. 42.

Globe and Mail (Toronto), December 24, 1983; June 24, 1995, Chris Dafoe, "Robert Bringhurst: In Ink and Paper," pp. C1-C2.

Journal of Canadian Poetry, volume 12, 1998, Iain Higgins, review of *The Calling,* pp. 27-46.

Library Journal, volume 101, 1976, Norman Stock, review of *Bergschrund,* p. 819.

Maclean's, July 12, 1996, John Bemrose, "The Timely Wisdom of Traditional Tales," p. 56; July, 1999, John Bemrose, review of *A Story as Sharp as a Knife,* pp. 56-57.

New York Times Book Review, September 28, 1986, Jorie Graham, "Making Connections," pp. 32-33; February 9, 1992, Karal Ann Marling, "A Noah's Ark of the North," p. 13.

Poetry, volume 144, 1984, Robin Skelton, "Recent Canadian Poetry," pp. 297-307.

Quill & Quire, volume 61.5, 1995, Michael Redhill, review of *The Calling,* p. 36.

Star (Toronto), April, 1995, Philip Marchand, "Simplicity Motivates Poet's Work of a Lifetime," p. H6.

Whig-Standard Magazine (Kingston, Ontario), March 26, 1988, Larry Scanlan, "Notebook: Interview with Robert Bringhurst," p. 25.

OTHER

The Reader Winter 1995—Robert Bringhurst, http://collection.nlc-bnc.ca, (March 6, 2000).

Review of *The Elements of Typographic Style,* http://www.mantex.co.uk/reviews. (March 6, 2000).

* * *

BROCKINGTON, J(ohn) L(eonard) 1940-

PERSONAL: Born December 5, 1940, in Oxford, England; son of L. H. (a university teacher and minister) and F. E. (Woodward) Brockington; married Mary Fairweather (a researcher), August 2, 1966; children: Anne, Michael. *Ethnicity:* "British." *Education:* Corpus Christi College, Oxford, B.A. (with honors), 1963, M.A., 1966, Ph.D., 1968.

ADDRESSES: *Office*—School of Asian Studies, University of Edinburgh, 7 Buccleuch Pl., Edinburgh EH8 9LW, Scotland; fax +131-651-1258. *E-mail*—j.l.brockington@ed.ac.uk.

CAREER: University of Edinburgh, Edinburgh, Scotland, assistant lecturer, 1965-67, lecturer, 1967-82, senior lecturer, 1982-89, reader, 1989-98, professor of Sanskrit, 1998—, director of studies, 1969-75, department head, 1975-99. Guest lecturer, Cambridge University, 1979, Utkal University, 1981 and 1994, Sri Jagannatha Sanskrit University, 1981 and 1994, University of Calcutta, 1981, University of Zagreb, 1987, London School of Oriental and African Studies, London, 1993, and Jadavpur University, 1993.

MEMBER: International Association of Sanskrit Studies (secretary general, 2000—), Traditional Cosmology Society.

WRITINGS:

The Sacred Thread: Hinduism in Its Continuity and Diversity, Edinburgh University Press (Edinburgh, Scotland), 1981.

Righteous Rama: The Evolution of an Epic, Oxford University Press (Delhi, India), 1985.

(Contributor) Geoffrey Carnall and Colin Nicholson, editors, *The Impeachment of Warren Hastings: Papers from a Bicentenary Commemoration,* Edinburgh University Press, 1989.

Hinduism and Christianity, Macmillan (London, England), 1992, and St. Martin's (New York City).

(Compiler with P. Flamm, Heinrich von Stietencron, and others) *Epic and Puranic Bibliography: Up to 1985,* Purana Research Publications (Tuebingen, Germany), 1992.

(Contributor) Roy Willis, editor, *World Mythology,* Simon & Schuster (New York City), 1993.

The Sanskrit Epics, E. J. Brill (Leiden, Netherlands), 1998.

A Catalogue of the Chandra Shum Shere Collection, Part II: *Epics and Puranas,* Oxford University Press (Oxford, England), 1999.

Epic Threads: John Brockington on the Sanskrit Epics, edited by Greg Bailey and wife, Mary Brockington, Oxford University Press (Delhi), 2000.

Contributor to reference books, including; *The Penguin Encyclopedia of Classical Civilizations,* edited by Arthur Cotterell, Penguin, 1993. Contributor of more than forty articles to learned journals. Member of editorial board, *Indologica Taurinensia, Jagannath Jyotih,* and *Cosmos.*

WORK IN PROGRESS: Translating the core of the Ramayana, with M. Brockington, for Penguin (New York City).

SIDELIGHTS: J. L. Brockington told *CA:* "My research so far has been concerned mainly with the Ramayana, the Puranas, and the development of Vaisnavism. I collaborated for several years with the Tuebingen Purana Project of the Seminar fuer Indologie und vergleichende Religionswissenschaft at the University of Tuebingen. In 1984 I was invited by the Sahitya Akademi in New Delhi to participate in the critical inventory of Ramayana studies throughout the world by compiling information on holdings of manuscripts and other materials relating to any version of the Ramayana located in Britain.

"I am continuing my studies on textual problems of the Ramayana, and I am also widening my epic research, with studies on the Ramayana tradition in India and the rest of Asia, and with an edition of Varadaraja's commentary."

* * *

BROWN, Helen Gurley 1922-

PERSONAL: Born February 18, 1922, in Green Forest, AR; daughter of Ira M. (a teacher and member of Arkansas State Legislature) and Cleo F. (a teacher; maiden name, Sisco) Gurley; married David Brown (a motion picture producer and executive), September 25, 1959. *Education:* Attended Texas State College for Women (now Texas Woman's University), 1939-41; Woodbury College, graduate, 1942; also took extension courses in writing at University of California, Los Angeles. *Politics:* Independent. *Religion:* Protestant.

ADDRESSES: Home—One West 81st St., New York, NY 10024. *Office—Cosmopolitan,* The Hearst Corp., 959 8th Ave., New York, NY 10019.

CAREER: Music Corp. of America, executive secretary, 1942-45; William Morris Agency, executive secretary, 1945-47; Foote, Cone & Belding (advertising agency), Los Angeles, CA, copywriter, 1948-58; Kenyon & Eckhardt (advertising agency), Hollywood, CA, advertising writer and account executive, 1958-62; *Cosmopolitan* magazine, New York City, editor-in-chief, 1965-97, editorial director of international editions, 1972—. Supervising editor, *EYE* magazine, 1967-68. Host of syndicated daily television show *Outrageous Opinions,* WOR-TV, New York City, 1967-68; has appeared as a guest on numerous television and radio programs. Lecturer.

MEMBER: Authors Guild, Authors League of America, American Society of Magazine Editors, American Federation of Television and Radio Artists, Eta Upsilon Gamma.

Helen Gurley Brown

AWARDS, HONORS: Frances Holmes Achievement Awards for outstanding work in advertising copywriting, 1956-59; Distinguished Achievement Award, University of Southern California School of Journalism, 1971; special award for editorial leadership, American Newspaper Woman's Club, 1972; named one of the twenty-five most influential women in the United States by *World Almanac,* 1976-81; Distinguished Achievement Award in journalism and honorary alumnus, Stanford University, 1977.

WRITINGS:

Sex and the Single Girl, Geis (New York City), 1962, revised edition published as *Sex and the New Single Girl,* Geis, 1970.
Sex and the Office, Geis, 1964.
Outrageous Opinions, Geis, 1966.
Single Girl's Cookbook, drawings by Frank Daniel, Geis, 1969.

(Author of foreword) *Cosmopolitan's Love Book: A Guide to Ecstasy in Bed,* Wilshire, 1978.

Having It All: Love, Success, Sex, Money, Even If You're Starting with Nothing, Linden (New York City), 1982, abridged recording of book read by Brown, Newman Books-on-Cassette (Albuquerque, NM), 1985.

The Late Show: A Semiwild but Practical Survival Plan for Women over Fifty, Morrow (New York City), 1993.

The Writer's Rules: The Power of Positive Prose—How to Create It and Get It Published, Morrow, 1998.

I'm Wild Again: Snippets from My Life and a Few Brazen Thoughts, St. Martin's (New York City), 2000.

Also author of foreword to *Cosmopolitan's New Etiquette Guide,* Borden Publishing Co. Author of column "Woman Alone," distributed by Los Angeles Times Syndicate to over fifty newspapers throughout the world, 1963-65.

ADAPTATIONS: *Sex and the Single Girl* was adapted by Joseph Heller and David R. Schwartz for film, produced by William T. Orr, directed by Richard Quine, and released by Warner Bros. in 1964.

SIDELIGHTS: Judy Klemesrud of the *New York Times* has called Helen Gurley Brown "the woman who, by her outspoken advice, has probably removed more girls from their virginity than anyone else in the world." An exaggeration, perhaps, but it is true that when *Sex and the Single Girl* was published in 1962, Brown became famous for her promotion of a concept that many considered shocking at the time: that sex can be fun, even for single women.

However, as Brown told Claudia Dreifus in a 1975 *Miami Herald* interview, the single women to whom the book was directed were not the ones who were shocked, "because girls have been sleeping with boys without being married to them *forever.* The ones who were not participating—older women, fathers—were horrified." Besides, as she says, she was not advocating promiscuity. She told Roy Newquist (in an interview for his book, *Conversations):* "I don't believe in 'sleeping around.' I don't think it's fun to have too many lovers; it gets very confusing. Therefore, I would never lead a girl toward that kind of activity, nor even encourage her to have one affair (although it certainly can work out well)." On the other hand, she does believe that "a girl who is terrified that a man is going to deflower her before her wedding night has a problem, socially. She sets up icy waves around her, and perhaps she can't help it. Something has made her believe that men are dangerous until you marry them, and then they are okay. . . . This is a rather incendiary subject, and it sounds as though I'm pushing sex, saying, 'Go out there and get your share.' I'm not, really. I dare say that there are girls so anesthetized that they are happier not doing anything about sex; they would be desperately unhappy if they tried to change, so they should stay as they are."

Brown also explained to Newquist that she sees "a different moral code for young girls, even girls in their twenties, and women in their thirties and forties. A girl of thirty-six is not a girl of sixteen, yet in this country some persons believe girls of all ages live by the same rules. I'm all for girls staying chaste as long as they can, really, up to a reasonable age. There's no hurry. I think that being innocent when you're young is desirable and lovely. You can make love to a man until you're seventy, so what's the rush? However, to carry innocence past a certain age may defeat its purpose."

The idea for *Sex and the Single Girl* was provided by Helen's husband, motion picture producer *(Jaws, Deep Impact)* David Brown. He had come across some copies of old letters his wife had written to a former boyfriend and, impressed by her bright, witty style, encouraged her to attempt a book on a subject she was well acquainted with: the life of a single woman. Having been single until the age of thirty-seven, she felt comfortable advising others in such matters as careers, money, apartments, wardrobe, make-up, diet, and—particularly—men. These were all areas that she felt had been neglected by other publications, most of which were aimed at married women, or at least at women who wanted to be married. "At the time I wrote about single girls," she told Newquist, "nobody was championing them. Volumes had been written about this creature, but they all treated the single girl like a scarlet-fever victim, a misfit, and . . . you can't really categorize one-third of the female population [of the United States] as misfits. . . . I picked up a torch, I guess you'd say, and became the standard-bearer for this particular group."

The combination of helpful, constructive advice and, as Brown puts it "the inherent sexiness of the subject and fairly easy-to-take writing," worked so well that the book sold in the millions of copies and led to a second book, *Sex in the Office,* as well as a syndicated newspaper column, "Woman Alone," and eventually to her position as editor-in-chief of *Cosmopolitan* magazine. The idea for a magazine devoted to the needs of single women was inspired, to a great extent, by the enormous amount of mail generated by *Sex and the Single Girl.* The number of letters soliciting advice on personal problems left little doubt that a large segment of the population was not being reached by the women's magazines of the day. David and Helen worked out a format for a publication, tentatively entitled *Femme,* which would serve to answer some of the questions being asked by the readers of her first book; but initially they were unable to find a publisher willing to back the rather expensive project.

Luckily, Bernard Geis, who had published Helen's first two books, knew the president of the Hearst Corp. and was able to arrange a meeting. The Hearst people were not particularly interested in starting a new magazine, but they were willing to turn over editorial control of their ailing *Cosmopolitan,* a periodical whose sales had dwindled by twenty percent in the past year. Helen changed the format of the magazine, moving its appeal away from the housewives of its previous incarnation toward the new "*Cosmo* girl," someone who, she told Dreifus, "looks as good as she can, works as hard as she can, and the smarter she is, the better off she is." When Brown took over in 1965, *Cosmopolitan* sales did not exactly skyrocket overnight, but the magazine did begin a steady rise from a circulation of around 800,000 to over three million copies (with a readership of approximately twelve million), making it one of the most successful periodicals in the world.

Although *Cosmo* has articles on make-up and grooming, apartments and decorating, diet, health, pets, finance, fashion, and celebrities, the magazine's premier topic is male-female relationships. Brown explained to Newquist that "we do a lot of stuff about men and women because about ninety percent of the mail I get is about a man's relationship with a woman or the other way around. . . . I'd say that seventy percent of this mail is from women who are mixed up with the wrong man but they won't admit it; they can't stand to hear it. So we have a great deal to say about divorce, about the man who won't marry, the homosexual man, the lukewarm boy." She says that "we deal with all subjects of emotion, because I think emotions come first. They really motivate everything we do. I think most decisions are visceral, really. Therefore, every month *Cosmopolitan* has an article on jealousy, shyness, the uncontrollable temper, or insecurity—things that stem from emotional states."

One topic that is assiduously avoided in *Cosmopolitan* is the domestic scene; articles about natural childbirth, babies, and child-rearing are definitely *not* part of the *Cosmo* image. Brown recognizes that a lot of her readers are mothers but chooses to disregard that area of their lives because, as she mentioned in the Newquist interview, "my format says we do not do children and domesticity." And, she notes, the format has worked, so why tamper with it? The closest *Cosmo* might come to an article about children would be one advising single women on how to deal with a divorced lover's offspring, or perhaps one on how to get along with a friend's kids for a weekend. This philosophy has led to some comparisons between *Cosmopolitan* and *Playboy,* which similarly ignores the family life of men. Although *Cosmo* is "less racy by far" than *Playboy,* Brown acknowledges the comparison and says that she is not in the least offended by it. "Nothing gets into *Playboy* that is not presumably for the *Playboy* man," she told Newquist, and "every single thing that goes into *Cosmopolitan* is for the consumption and enjoyment and self-improvement" of the *Cosmo* girl.

Brown, who through the decades as has proudly maintained her status as the ultimate *Cosmo* girl, wrote a book directed at women over fifty years old. In *The Late Show: A Semiwild but Practical Survival Plan for Women over Fifty,* Brown offers the type of advice she and her magazine have historically dished out. She presents her thoughts on physical appearance, sex, and values "in her trademark exhortative, chirpy, ad-copy style," described Joanne Kaufman in *People Weekly,* noting that the Cosmo queen "unabashedly parades her neuroses, parsimony . . . split ends and plastic surgery." Regardless of age, being skinny and wealthy and maintaining a sex life (even if you have to resort to relations with a married man) are among Brown's high priorities. According to Jay Scott's *Chatelaine* review, the book is "so out of touch with reality" and Brown's words, which lean into "sexism and dubious ethics," should "be pitied, not perused." A *Publishers Weekly* assessment more positively appraised *The Late Show,* concluding: "However frothy, this little advisory offers comfort and cheer—possibly even for those who have neither sex nor money."

After more than three decades leading *Cosmopolitan,* in 1997 Brown unwantingly left her position as the magazine's editor-in-chief. The following year she published *The Writer's Rules: The Power of Positive Prose—How to Create It and Get It Published.* The 1998 release received some unenthusiastic reviews. A *Publishers Weekly* critic called it a "mish-mash. . . . pockmarked by . . . [the] trademarks of her style and of the gossipy, rhetorical, narcissistic voice of ads for that certain magazine, *Cosmo.*" The *Publishers Weekly* critic felt her advice was neither novel nor, at times, sensible. Though weaker than other how-to-write publications, Brown's "fluffy little book on writing" offers her "positive attitude" and "knowledge of what magazine editors want," assessed *Library Journal* contributor Lisa J. Cihlar.

In 2000, with *I'm Wild Again: Snippets from My Life and a Few Brazen Thoughts,* Brown once again gave readers a look at her perspective of life, this time adding more of her life history. "A savvy seductress, Brown, 78, wastes not time titillating her readers in this frisky, off-the-cuff memoir," remarked Paula Chin, judging *I'm Wild Again* for *People Weekly.* After reading the book, Chin described Brown as "refreshingly self-deprecating." In a "relentlessly candid" manner, observed a *Publishers Weekly* reviewer, "Brown muses over her life, career and philosophy." "Brown's voice is uniquely hers, although the book feels padded and repetitions," asserted the reviewer for *Publishers Weekly.* According to *Booklist* contributor Ilene Cooper, the "collection of Brown's all-too-random thoughts . . . is part rehash . . . part dish . . . and part (way too big a part) intimate details about the author's body."

INTERVIEW:

Jean W. Ross conducted a telephone interview with Brown on April 3, 1981. An abridged version of the interview, which was published in an earlier volume of CA, follows.

CA: Back in 1962, when the polite pretense was that nice single girls didn't know anything about sex, you startled a lot of people with your first book, Sex and the Single Girl. *Did it take a certain amount of courage to write that book?*

BROWN: No, it absolutely didn't. Emotionally speaking, it always takes courage to sit down and do anything assiduously week after week, month after month, for some writers year after year; but in terms of saying the things I said it seemed perfectly natural to me. I had been in group therapy, where people discuss personal matters very frankly and almost casually, plus the fact that the idea of the whole book was that people are all doing things and everybody's pretending they aren't, so I never for a moment really felt I was doing anything brave. The brave part was getting the work done.

CA: The mail from readers in this country led to the syndicated newspaper column "Woman Alone." What sorts of response did you get from the other countries in which the book was published?

BROWN: I still get response from them and it's gratifying. I think it was twenty-eight countries, eighteen languages, and of course *Cosmopolitan* has an edition in many of these countries where the book was published. In England and France, particularly, I still hear from people who read the book. It was also popular in Germany. The response is the same as it is to *Cosmo* . . . people found it said something reassuring because they were sexual creatures and had been having a sexual life for a long time, but nobody could ever admit that publicly. The book readers found it gratifying that there were lots of other young women all over the world doing just what they were; it made them feel good.

CA: In 1965 you became editor of Cosmopolitan *and, with your new format, made that dying magazine a financial success. Were you confident when you took the job that you could accomplish that near-miracle?*

BROWN: Absolutely not. I had no idea what I was doing, and it seemed highly unlikely I'd succeed. I'd written two books at that point—*Sex and the Single Girl* and *Sex in the Office*—and hadn't really intended to become a magazine editor. This is how it happened: I got all this mail from people who'd read the books and were reading my column, "Woman Alone," and they all needed advice. David, my husband, said, "You really ought to have your own magazine," and we were going to start one of our own. We did up a format and took it around to a few people, but nobody wanted to start a magazine. We did get to the Hearst Corporation, however, where they said they wouldn't start a new magazine, but *Cosmo* (one of their old-line magazines) was not doing very well, and I could have a fling at that. I think they were about to close it down anyway, so they weren't taking too much of a chance with me.

The night before I was to report to work, I remember walking down Park Avenue with David and Irving Wallace—Irving is a close friend. Tears were streaming down my face, and I said, "Why can't I *write?*" I was sort of envious of Irving because he had had so many best-selling books, and he never had to do anything but be a writer as long as he lived, and here I was being stuffed into an office. I felt this proved I was not really a *Writer* whereas Irving *was.* I thought, well, I'll just think of it like I'm going to jail and I'll serve out a year, and if it doesn't work I'll get out. As for knowing what I was doing or having any idea how to do what was required, I didn't. I learned fairly quickly, however. I had David to help. He'd worked on a magazine before, and bailed me out that first year.

CA: "I was a mouseburger," you've said more than once. Do you think Cosmopolitan *has helped a lot of women become more than mouseburgers?*

BROWN: I hope so. It would be pretentious of me to say, "We have helped millions of women." Millions of women see *Cosmo* every month—we have a readership of twelve million, a circulation of three, and I would assume that if not all have been *helped,* at least they've been encouraged, possibly inspired. I want a woman to feel better about herself when she finishes reading. I believe we do achieve that. I think it's important when you put the magazine down to say, "Yes, I can; I believe I can work on that situation and make it come out better. I'm going to try anyway."

CA: You've angered certain key figures in the women's liberation movement. How do you feel about women's liberation, about the movement itself and the progress it's making?

BROWN: I consider myself a feminist, and I don't think the women's movement and I have any great differences at this stage of the game. Gloria Steinem is a good friend. We'd be closer if she had more time, perhaps, but I honor and respect her totally. The movement is here to stay, it's not going to go away. The Equal Rights Amendment may be defeated; we don't know yet. But there is no way that womankind is going to return to its previous parameters. I don't think a house in America hasn't been affected by women's lib. Women are still traditional homemakers in many instances, but they are aware now that other possibilities are open for them. They may not want to take advantage of them, but they are there.

I was talking to an executive of a five-billion-dollar firm yesterday—I sell advertising once a week—and he was asking me if I knew anybody who had been doing a study or could do a study about how companies could help women maintain their various roles. I thought that was so enlightened of him. This is a very conservative company; their top executives probably think women should go back home and get pregnant and stop fooling around with executive jobs, and yet they know that's not going to happen. He acknowledged that women are a tremendous resource, and he was trying to figure out what he could do to help his women work more successfully for his company. Most women want to have children, and men are not taking over the nurturing of children as we thought they might, so women are still stuck with that—or maybe they want to be stuck with it. But if they're also going to work at a job, things have to be a little bit different than they were. There has to be a way for them not to worry so much about whether their children are okay. This man thought there might be a bus or some means of picking up children in an emergency to take them to the doctor or do whatever a mother might do in the circumstances, sort of a mother's helper.

CA: How do you most want to use your influence as an award-winning journalist and author?

BROWN: How I would most like to use my influence? Simply something we talked about earlier—to convince any so-called average woman that she can get further than she now is, have a lot more in her life than she now has, not by doing anything spectacular, but just by getting *on* with it, by doing whatever she is *able* to do . . . using *her* special skills, however modest, sticking to her project and not getting too bored or restless, or having such grandiose ideas that she can't live up to them. I want to convince women that so much is *possible,* not on a grand scale, but just by doing a little every day. And pretty soon you get further, you make more money, people are listening to you more, and you have more friends, it just all falls into place. I want to inspire and encourage.

BIOGRAPHICAL/CRITICAL SOURCES:

BOOKS

Diamonstein, Barbaralee, *Open Secrets,* Viking, 1972.

Leterman, Ehner G., and T. W. Carila, *They Dare to Be Different,* Meredith, 1968.

Newquist, Roy, *Conversations,* Rand McNally, 1967.

PERIODICALS

50 Plus, November, 1982, p. 68.

Advertising Age, October 19, 1981, p. S2; September 9, 1996, p. 3.

ADWEEK Eastern Edition, March 4, 1996, p. MR40.

Book Week, October 18, 1964.

Booklist, December 15, 1999, p. 738.

Cosmopolitan, November, 1982, p. 66; October, 1983, p. 56; February, 2000, p. 132.

Esquire, February, 1970.

Financial World, April 15, 1997, 128.

Folio: The Magazine for Magazine Management, August, 1985, p. 73.

Fortune, November 26, 1984, p. 11; October 28, 1996, p. 181.

Harper's Bazaar, August, 1983, p. 34.

Harper's Magazine, May, 1984, p. 37.

Interavia, May, 1983, p. 42.

Library Journal, December 1, 1982, p. 2261; September 15, 1998, p. 88.
Life, March 1, 1963, November 19, 1965, March 12, 1971.
Los Angeles Magazine, December, 1982, p. 322.
Maclean's, January 29, 1996, p. 40; February 17, 1997, p. 60.
McCall's, July, 1997 ,p. 18.
MEDIAWEEK, January 29, 1996, p. 17.
Miami Herald, August 24, 1975.
Modern Maturity, May-June, 1997, p. 54.
Newsweek, January 29, 1996, p. 46.
New York, July 6, 1981, p. 56; September 27, 1982, p. 36.
New York Herald Tribune Book Review, June 17, 1962.
New York Herald Tribune Magazine, November 22, 1964.
New York Post, June 15, 1962, November 3, 1963, December 30, 1967.
New York Times Book Review, October 10, 1982, p. 34; October 31, 1982, p. 39.
New York Times, December 31, 1967.
New York Times Magazine, August 11, 1974.
Omni, October, 1980, p. 124.
People Weekly, November 1, 1982, p. 54; March 6, 2000, p. 55.
Playboy, November, 1981, p. 215; March, 1997, Stephen Randall, "Was Helen Gurley Brown the Silliest Editor in America—or the Smartest?," p. 24.
Psychology Today, March/April, 1994, "Bad Girl Helen Gurley Brown, the Original Cosmo Girl, Defies Every Label," p. 22.
Publishers Weekly, September 10, 1982, p. 70; September 23, 1983, p. 71; August 3, 1998, p. 68; December 20, 1999, p. 65.
San Francisco Chronicle, May 24, 1962.
Saturday Evening Post, January 30, 1965.
Time, March 26, 1965; November 1, 1982, p. 72; January 29, 1996, p. 19.
Variety, October 12, 1998 ,p. NY5.
Washington Monthly, October, 1982, p. 57.
Washington Post, May 17, 1969.
Working Woman, June, 1980, p. 38.
WWD, August 27, 1999, Lisa Lockwood, "Just Call Her Helen 'Girly' Brown," p. 14.*

* * *

BROWN, Robert Fath 1941-

PERSONAL: Born June 6, 1941, in St. Louis, MO; son of John P. (in business) and Georgia (a secretary; maiden name, Fath) Brown; married Ann Lee Werthmuller (a teacher), 1963 (marriage ended); married Mary Ann Harkins (a secretary), 1997; children: (first marriage) Nathan, Kristy, Grace. *Ethnicity:* "Caucasian." *Education:* Attended Union Theological Seminary, New York City, 1963-70; DePauw University, B.A., 1963; Columbia University, M.A., 1967, Ph.D., 1971.

ADDRESSES: Office—Department of Philosophy, University of Delaware, Newark, DE 19716; fax 302-831-6321. *E-mail*—rfbrown@udel.edu.

CAREER: University of Delaware, Newark, instructor, 1970-71, assistant professor, 1971-75, associate professor, 1975-86, professor of philosophy, 1986—, acting chairperson of department, 1983-84, director of university honors program, 1989-98. University of Hull, visiting lecturer, 1980-81. Delaware Humanities Council, member, 1976-79, 1983-87, chairperson, 1977-79.

MEMBER: American Academy of Religion, American Philosophical Association, Society of Christian Philosophers, Hegel Society of America, Society for Philosophy of Religion.

WRITINGS:

The Later Philosophy of Schelling: The Influence of Boehme on the Works of 1809-1815, Bucknell University Press (Lewisburg, PA), 1977.
Schelling's Treatise on "The Deities of Samothrace": A Translation and an Interpretation, Scholars Press (Missoula, MT), 1977.
(Translator with Peter Hodgson and J. M. Stewart) Peter Hodgson, editor, *Hegel: Lectures on the Philosophy of Religion,* University of California Press (Berkeley, CA), Volume I, 1984, Volume III, 1985, Volume II, 1987, abridged edition in one volume, 1988.
(Translator with Stewart, and editor) *Hegel: Lectures on the History of Philosophy,* Volume III: *Medieval and Modern Philosophy,* University of California Press, 1990.

Contributor to philosophy and theology journals.

WORK IN PROGRESS: Editing and translating (with Stewart) *Hegel: Lectures on the History of Philosophy,* Volume I: *Introduction and Oriental Philosophy* and Volume II: *Greek Philosophy,* for University of California Press.

SIDELIGHTS: Robert Fath Brown told *CA:* "I pursue the problems of philosophy of religion in a historical way; that is, mainly by grappling with the views of great thinkers of the past rather than trying to start from scratch. The period of German idealism is the high point of creativity in Western religious thought, not so much because of the way its great philosophers and theologians solved problems, but because of the enduring interest and value of the way they posed them. I came to be fascinated with Schelling through studying the writings of the theologian Paul Tillich. Shelling remains a central concern, though recently I have worked more on Hegel. I particularly enjoy translating because it has taught me much about the nature and use of language, particularly about how to write and speak with greater precision and less ambiguity."

"I am convinced that we humans have free will, and that it is our most important feature, the very center of what we are (though we are ingenious at trying to evade facing that fact). The centrality of human free will in the Christian theological tradition is a particular interest of mine, especially in relation to doctrines that have the (sometimes unwitting) effect of undercutting it, such as original sin, predestination, and divine omnipotence. I explore such issues with a strong commitment to their importance, though not necessarily to the correctness of traditional Christian solutions. A collateral interest is in conceptions of divine will that treat it as genuinely free (indeed, capable of evil), rather than, as in so much classical theism, a meaningless appendage to a divine nature that is of necessity good. To me, these are the great issues that make philosophy and theology of perennial interest and importance."

* * *

BUCHOLZ, Arden 1936-

PERSONAL: Born May 14, 1936, in Chicago, IL; son of Arden (a journalist) and Betty (a radio personality; maiden name, Lutz) Bucholz; married Sue Tally, July 7, 1962; children: Merritt, Mark. *Education:* Dartmouth College, B.A., 1958; University of Vienna, diploma, 1960; University of Chicago, M.A., 1965, Ph.D., 1972.

ADDRESSES: *Home*—356 Roosevelt Highway, Waterport, NY 14571. *Office*—Department of History, State University of New York College at Brockport, Brockport, NY 14420; fax 716-682-7536.

CAREER: Amerikan Orta Okulu, Talas-Kayseri, Turkey, teacher of English, 1958-60; Latin School of Chicago, Chicago, IL, teacher of history, 1965-70; State University of New York College at Brockport, professor of history, 1970—, codirector of program at Brunel University, Uxbridge, England, 1987-88. *Military service:* U.S. Army, Counterintelligence, 1961-64; served in Germany; became lieutenant.

AWARDS, HONORS: *Moltke, Schlieffen, and Prussian War Planning* was named "one of outstanding books in military history" by International Commission on Military History, 1991.

WRITINGS:

Hans Delbruck and the German Military Establishment, University of Iowa Press (Iowa City, IA), 1985.

Moltke, Schlieffen, and Prussian War Planning, Berg Publishers (Oxford, England), 1991.

Delbruck's Modern Military History, University of Nebraska Press (Lincoln, NE), 1997.

Moltke and the German Wars, Macmillan (London, England), in press.

Contributor to history journals.

* * *

BURLING, William J. 1949-

PERSONAL: Born January 27, 1949, in Ladysmith, WI; son of Wesley G. (in insurance business) and Patricia (a secretary; maiden name, Buckles) Burling; married Brenda Gunnes (divorced, 1976); married Debby Drake (an accountant), July 11, 1980; children: Andrew, Amanda. *Education:* University of Wisconsin—Eau Claire, B.S., 1972, M.A., 1974; Pennsylvania State University, Ph.D., 1985. *Religion:* Unitarian-Universalist. *Avocational interests:* Astronomy, gardening.

ADDRESSES: *Home*—1030 East Portland St., Springfield, MO 65807. *Office*—Department of English, Southwest Missouri State University, 901 South National, Springfield, MO 65804; fax 417-836-4226. *E-mail*—wjb692f@mail.smsu.edu.

CAREER: Auburn University, Auburn, AL, assistant professor of English, 1985-89; Southwest Missouri State University, Springfield, associate professor, 1989-94, professor of English, 1994—. Producer, codirector, audio engineer, and musical director of the documentary videotape *The Spirit of Pioneer Women,*

1993; codirector and musical director of the documentary videotape *Give the Ballot to the Mothers: Songs of the Suffragists,* 1996.

MEMBER: American Society for Eighteenth Century Studies.

AWARDS, HONORS: Silver Telly Award, 1994, for the videotape *The Spirit of Pioneer Women.*

WRITINGS:

A Checklist of New Plays and Entertainments on the London Stage, 1700-1737, Fairleigh Dickinson University Press (East Brunswick, NJ), 1992.

Summer Theatre in London, 1661-1820, and the Rise of the Haymarket Theatre, Fairleigh Dickinson University Press, 2000.

(With Odai Johnson) *The Colonial American Stage, 1665-1774: A Documentary Calendar,* Fairleigh Dickinson University Press, in press.

Contributor to scholarly journals.

WORK IN PROGRESS: Editing *The Plays of Colley Cibber,* with Timothy J. Viator.

SIDELIGHTS: William J. Burling told *CA:* "After attempting, during the seventies, to write poetry and fiction in Wisconsin, I discovered at Penn State the pleasures of scholarly research and writing. I had originally planned to specialize in twentieth-century American literature when Professor Robert D. Hume introduced me to the possibilities of the London stage of the seventeenth and eighteenth centuries. After intensive work with manuscripts and printed sources from 1660 to 1800, I began to develop possibilities for projects, which resulted in the *Checklist of New Plays and Entertainments.*

"I am now at work on an edition of the plays of Colley Cibber, 1671-1757, a leading actor, playwright, and manager in London, and Poet Laureate from 1730 until his death."

* * *

BURNS, James MacGregor 1918-

PERSONAL: Born August 3, 1918, in Melrose, MA; son of Robert Arthur (a businessman) and Mildred (Bunce) Burns; married Janet Thompson Dismorr (a college administrator), May 23, 1942 (divorced, 1968); married Joan Simpson (a writer), September 7, 1969 (divorced, 1991); children: David MacGregor, Timothy Stewart, Deborah Edwards, Margaret Rebecca Antonia. *Education:* Williams College, B.A., 1939; attended National Institute of Public Affairs, 1939-40; Harvard University, M.A., 1947, Ph.D., 1947; postdoctoral study, London School of Economics, 1949. *Politics:* Democrat. *Religion:* Congregational.

ADDRESSES: Office—Department of Political Science, Williams College, Williamstown, MA 01267.

CAREER: Williams College, Williamstown, MA, assistant professor of political science, 1947-50, associate professor, 1950-53, professor of political science, 1953-86, Woodrow Wilson Professor of Government, 1962-86, professor emeritus, 1986—. Faculty member, Salzburg Seminar in American Studies, 1954, 1961; lecturer, Institute of History of the Soviet Academy of Sciences, Moscow and Leningrad, 1963; senior scholar, Jepson School of Leadership Studies, University of Richmond, 1990-93. Member of staff, Hoover Commission, 1948; Massachusetts delegate to Democratic National Convention, 1952, 1956, 1960, 1964; democratic candidate for Congress, 1958. Member of advisory board, Berkshire Community College, 1963-64. *Military service:* U.S. Army, 1943-45; served as combat historian in the Pacific; received four battle stars and Bronze Star.

MEMBER: International Society of Political Psychology (president, 1982-83), American Political Science Association (president, 1975-76), American Historical Association, American Philosophical Association, New England Political Science Association (president, 1960-61), American Civil Liberties Union, American Legion, Phi Beta Kappa, Delta Sigma Rho.

AWARDS, HONORS: Tamiment Institute award for best biography and Woodrow Wilson prize, both 1956, for *Roosevelt: The Lion and the Fox;* Francis Parkman Prize, Society of American Historians, Pulitzer Prize in history, and National Book Award for history and biography, all 1971, for *Roosevelt: The Soldier of Freedom;* Sarah Josepha Hale Award for general literary achievement, 1979; nominated for *Los Angeles Times* Book Prize, 1982, for *The American Experiment,* Volume I: *The Vineyard of Liberty;* Christopher Award, 1983.

WRITINGS:

POLITICAL HISTORY

Congress on Trial: The Legislative Process and the Administrative State, Harper (New York City), 1949.

Roosevelt: The Lion and the Fox, Harcourt (Boston), 1956.

John Kennedy: A Political Profile, Harcourt, 1960.

The Deadlock of Democracy: Four-Party Politics in America, Prentice-Hall, 1963.

Presidential Government: The Crucible of Leadership, Houghton, 1966.

Roosevelt: The Soldier of Freedom (sequel to *Roosevelt: The Lion and the Fox*), Harcourt, 1970.

Uncommon Sense, Harper, 1972.

Edward Kennedy and the Camelot Legacy, Norton, 1976.

State and Local Politics: Government by the People, Prentice-Hall, 1976, revised with David B. Magleby, Thomas E. Cronin, and J. W. Peltason, Prentice Hall, 1998.

Leadership, Harper, 1978.

The American Experiment, Knopf, Volume I: *The Vineyard of Liberty,* 1982, Volume II: *The Workshop of Democracy,* 1985, Volume III: *The Crosswinds of Freedom,* 1989.

The Power to Lead: The Crisis of the American Presidency, Simon & Schuster, 1984.

(With L. Marvin Overby) *Cobblestone Leadership: Majority Rule, Minority Power,* University of Oklahoma Press, 1990.

(With Stewart Burns), *A People's Charter: The Pursuit of Rights in America,* Knopf (New York City), 1991.

(With Georgia Jones Sorenson, Robin Gerber, and Scott W. Webster) *Dead Center: Clinton-Gore Leadership and the Perils of Moderation,* Scribner (New York City), 1999.

Also author of *Guam: Operations of the 77th Infantry Division,* 1944; co-author of *Okinawa: The Last Battle,* 1947.

WITH JACK WALTER PELTASON

Government by the People: The Dynamics of American National Government, Prentice-Hall, 1952, 12th edition, 1985.

Government by the People: The Dynamics of American State and Local Government, Prentice-Hall, 1952, 12th edition, 1985.

EDITOR

(With Peltason) *Functions and Policies of American Government,* Prentice-Hall, 1958, 3rd edition, 1967.

Lyndon Baines Johnson, *To Heal and to Build: The Programs of Lyndon B. Johnson,* McGraw, 1968.

(With Patricia Bonomi and Austin Ranney) *The American Constitutional System under Strong and Weak Parties,* Praeger, 1981.

(With others) *The Democrats Must Lead,* Westview Press, 1992.

CONTRIBUTOR

Dialogues in Americanism, Regnery, 1964.

Our American Government Today, 2nd edition, Prentice-Hall, 1966.

RECORDINGS

James MacGregor Burns Discusses Government Planning and Change, Center for Cassette Studies, c. 1975.

(With Peltason) *Resurrection of the Party System through Control of Campaign Financing,* Center for the Study of Democratic Institutions (Santa Barbara), 1976.

SIDELIGHTS: "To some historians [James MacGregor] Burns is a fine political scientist. To some political scientists he is a fine historian. In fact," wrote Walter Johnson in the *Washington Post Book World,* "he is the best of both disciplines." For more than forty years, Burns has written effective blends of history and political analysis. As Austin Ranney noted in the *Reporter,* Burns is also "the co-author of the most popular postwar college textbook in American government," *Government by the People: The Dynamics of American National Government,* and is a champion of the leadership that holds the best interests of the governed high above political gain. Gordon S. Wood commented in the *New York Review of Books* that "although [Burns] . . . is writing history, [he] is still the political scientist and has the political problems of our recent past, our present and our future very much on his mind."

Whether the subject is history, politics, or a combination of the two, Burns's books focus on the nature of political leadership. In a *New York Times* interview with Herbert Mitgang, Burns discussed his theory of leadership and its importance in *The American Experiment,* a three-volume survey of U.S. history from the New Deal to the present that includes *The Vineyard of*

Liberty, The Workshop of Democracy, and *The Crosswinds of Freedom.* "What I . . . emphasize is the role of leadership," Burns said, "but I don't believe in the great-man theory of history. . . . What impresses me as I do my research is the importance of the second and third level of leaders—the staff people. It isn't just a story of Presidents and generals."

Many reviewers have commented on Burns's theory of leadership, especially as outlined in *The American Experiment.* As Pauline Maier noted in the *New York Times Book Review:* "Burns . . . has written a very different kind of history . . . in that his is much less a history of great white men. . . . He has conceived of leaders as falling into three tiers: national power-wielders, notable persons on the state and local level and what he calls 'grass roots activists'. . . . As a result of this expanded focus, women, laboring people, blacks and Indians become part of the story." And in the *New Yorker,* Naomi Bliven further observed that Burns "astutely pays particular attention to what he calls the 'third cadre' of political leadership. . . . Burns thinks of the third cadre as 'country politicians, circuit-riding lawyers, money-minded men of commerce, cracker-barrel philosophers' whose decisions about accepting or rejecting the Constitution influenced their neighbors' votes."

With the publication of *The Crosswinds of Freedom* in 1989, Burns completed *The American Experiment.* Commenting on this achievement in the *New York Times Book Review,* John A. Garraty wrote, "Mr. Burns possesses a keen eye and ear for anecdote and quotation. He is a master at summarizing clearly the most complex events, and he is capable of brilliant capsule descriptions of broad historical trends." The unifying theme of *The American Experiment* is Burns's concept of leadership. Wrote Garraty: "Again and again [in *The Crosswinds of Freedom*] . . . Mr. Burns returns to his thesis about the American experiment and to his belief in the central importance of leadership if the nation's problems are to be solved." Michael Kazin, who in the *Washington Post Book World* described Burns as "one of our most skilled interpreters of the lives of 20th-century liberal heroes," observed that social movements and cultural changes serve as briefing papers for these heroes. "For Burns," wrote Kazin, "the evolution of modern America is largely a matter of how leaders like FDR, Truman, Kennedy, Johnson, Carter and an occasional non-president like Martin Luther King, Jr., attempted to realize the lofty, yet often contradictory, vision of 'individual liberty and equality of opportunity for all.' "

According to William B. Logan in the *Saturday Review,* Burns's theory of leadership "allows him to write almost as though history were a set of linked biographies." Burns's historical narrative is complemented by short vignettes that focus on particular personalities—including relatively unknown people—involved in the shaping of U.S. history. A portrait of Mercy Warren, an influential writer of the late 1700s, appears alongside one of George Washington because Burns believes that all citizens had a hand in the shaping of America. "Burns enlivens his text," wrote Robert V. Remini in *Tribune Books,* "with insightful character sketches of the leading figures of his narrative. But he also includes the not-so-famous . . . whose contribution to the American experiment was nonetheless significant."

According to many reviewers these biographies make Burns's historical writing better than most. "Some may object," claimed Bernard A. Weisberger in the *Detroit News,* "to Burns' work precisely on the ground that this focus on leaders . . . and 'scenes' is outdated. . . . But such critics forget that professional historians and political scientists who have forsaken philosophy and myth in favor of 'behavioral models' . . . have produced a body of work so remote from what moves ordinary people that they have deservedly lost their audience." "Here is history as it should be written," Remini concurred. "Not the awful stuff of many academics these days who submerge the Jeffersons and Jacksons . . . beneath a sea of statistical tables, distribution curves and computer analyses. Here is history with sweep and grandeur." Mitgang added: "Burns . . . brings an extra dimension to historical writing. [He is unlike those] who revise history by emphasizing statistical data instead of human expression."

In his two-part biography of Franklin Roosevelt, Burns's ability both as an historian and a teller of tales merge to produce award-winning nonfiction. Part 1, *Roosevelt: The Lion and the Fox,* was considered "thorough, scholarly, [and] incisive in its analysis," by W. V. Shonnon in his *Commonweal* review; in the *New Republic* Richard Marshall called it "the best Roosevelt study by far." Critics were even more enthusiastic about the second part, *Roosevelt: The Soldier of Freedom,* which won the Pulitzer Prize and the National Book Award when it was published in 1971. G. W. Johnson wrote in *Washington Post Book World:* "About James MacGregor Burns as a literary craftsman there can be no two opinions. . . . To style he adds the rare gift of ability to sort out from a tangled skein the significant threads that enable him to present in a consistent, coherent narrative the period he has chosen to study. There is not, and may never be a better one-volume presentation of the diplomatic and political aspects of the great war that raged in those years."

In his preface to *Roosevelt: The Soldier of Freedom,* Burns explains both the theme of the book and his personal theory of leadership: "The proposition of this work is that Franklin D. Roosevelt as a war leader was . . . divided between the man of principle of ideals, of faith . . . and . . . the man of *Realpolitik,* of prudence, of narrow, manageable short-run goals." This concept of leadership was expanded into a 530-page study Burns published in 1978. In *Leadership* Burns explains that he believes there are two kinds of leaders: transactional and transformational. In democracies, most political leaders are transactional. As Richard J. Walton explained in *Chicago Tribune,* "They lead by making political bargains (transactions), by serving as political brokers, giving this to gain that." What America needs are transformational leaders. "Such leadership occurs," Burns writes, "when one or more persons engage with others in such a way that leaders and followers raise one another to higher levels of motivation and morality." He cites Mao Tse-tung and Mahatma Gandhi as examples, noting of the latter that he was a leader who "aroused and elevated the hopes and demands of millions of Indians and whose life and personality were enhanced in the process."

In *Uncommon Sense* Burns lists the national goals that a transformational leader would pursue and how these goals should be accomplished. The three underlying values that all Americans and their leaders should be committed to, according to Burns, are defense of civil liberties, the abolition of poverty, and the protection of the environment. Wrote Milton R. Konvitz in the *Saturday Review,* "Burns warns . . . [that] because [these] problems are complex, many factors must be dealt with simultaneously and with equal energy. It is not, therefore, merely a question of spending more money but of reordering priorities in such a way that adequate means will be employed to achieve the desired ends." The means suggested by Burns include the strengthening of certain Presidential powers and the creation of "presidential agencies" to coordinate Executive policy decisions down through state and local levels of government.

Together with his son Stewart, Burns tackles the issue of leadership from a slightly different perspective in *A People's Charter,* published in 1991. The book explores the evolution of the rights of those who are led, following their historical development in the United States from the eighteenth century to the present. Alan Wolfe, writing in the *Washington Post Book World,* found the volume well-timed—*A People's Charter* was published on the two hundredth anniversary of the incorporation of the Bill of Rights into the U.S. Constitution—and well intentioned. However, Wolfe faulted the Burnses for relying too heavily on their own liberal political agenda and thereby giving short shrift to the more complex and nuanced issues that a debate on rights and responsibilities should engender. "They tell the story of rights in America," he wrote, "as a simple morality play in which their own sense of morality stars." However, in the *New Republic,* Sean Wilentz described the book as "an ambitious synthesis of virtually everything connected to the pursuit of rights in America." He continued, "Taking a left-populist approach not normally associated with the senior Burns, the books shows how rights talk . . . has galvanized virtually every democratic movement in the nation's history."

A year after *The People's Charter* came an essay collection—a manifesto of sorts—edited by Burns and others. In *The Democrats Must Lead: The Case for a Progressive Democratic Party,* various authors and pundits argue the need for the Democratic leaders of the 1990s return to what *Nation* critic Ronnie Dugger called "their liberal roots." Burns et. al., Dugger continues, "argue convincingly 'that the Democrats can win by appealing to a liberal constituency with liberal issues. . . . A Democratic Party that addresses the country's real problems can win.' "

Burns "believes the party's history shows that when progressive Democrats ran for the residency they usually won and, in winning, obtained above all 'the moral right to act,' " noted Dugger. "He concedes that since World War II the progressive George McGovern lost and Jimmy Carter, running as a liberal on many issues, won, but then presided 'on dead center.' Published just prior to the 1992 presidential election, when Democrat Bill Clinton took the win, ending twelve years of Republican rule, *The Democrats Must Lead* points out that by 1991 polls were showing that the public agreed by a three-to-one margin that the Republicans were perceived as overly focused on "[protecting] the interest of the rich and big business." "Burns asks, logically, 'Why is the [Democratic] party being told to go "centrist"?' " as Duggar wrote.

Burns took the centrist idea into his next two books. The second, published in 1999 near the end of Bill Clinton's second term in office, is *Dead Center: Clinton-Gore Leadership and the Perils of Moderation.* This book bears the stamp of the author's disapproval over what a *Publishers Weekly* reviewer terms the administration's "vanilla political behavior." Burns and co-author Georgia J. Sorenson compare Clinton to the progressive Democrats of the past—Theodore and Franklin Roosevelt, Harry Truman—"and, not surprisingly, [they find] the man from Hope wanting."

"From the outset, Clinton was a centrist, moving slightly to the left or right as expedience necessitated but always returning to an ill-defined middle ground," wrote a *Kirkus Reviews* contributor. In *Dead Center,* the authors go as far as calling Clinton a chameleon, "more concerned about winning elections and maintaining his popularity than transforming the nation," notes a reviewer for *Business Week.* The problem, says Burns, is the philosophy of centrism, aimed at moderation that the author finds both "intellectually bankrupt and politically inert," in the words of *Business Week.* The review goes on to say that the great presidents of the past governed in bold strokes that dared to go against public opinion to achieve the greater good. By contrast, a newer political style based on trying to please and appease everybody has compromised executive leadership. Burns and Sorenson, liberals both, "view Ronald Reagan as the only president in the second half of the twentieth century to come close to greatness as a leader. Their reasoning: He stuck to his philosophical guns and transformed both American politics and the world."

The *Business Week* reviewer concluded by calling *Dead Center* "often dead right when it comes to assessing Bill Clinton's leadership on domestic issues. But the political center is not nearly as dead as Burns and Sorenson believe." "This is neither a 'fair' nor an impartial book," penned a *Kirkus Reviews* critic. "It is a call for boldness and courage in public life, written with a passion the authors find so missing in Clinton."

Burns told *CA:* "My central intellectual concern throughout my adult life has been leadership, especially political and intellectual leadership, whether I was doing political science, history, psychology, or biography. We face, together as Americans or world citizens, the most intractable circumstances about which we can do far too little, but one thing Americans *can* do is to exercise their right to vote and choose leaders who can face up to the daunting problems, not only in rhetoric but in action."

BIOGRAPHICAL/CRITICAL SOURCES:

BOOKS

Beschloss, Michael R., and Thomas E. Cronin, editors, *Essays in Honor of James MacGregor Burns,* Prentice-Hall, 1989.

PERIODICALS

American Prospect, February 28, 2000, Thomas B. Edsall, review of *Dead Center: Clinton-Gore Leadership and the Perils of Moderation,* p. 48.

Annals of the American Academy of Political and Social Science, November, 1949.

Atlantic Monthly, March, 1979.

Best Sellers, September 15, 1970.

Book Week, January 30, 1966.

Business Week, December 27, 1999, review of *Dead Center,* p. 33.

Chicago Tribune, September 10, 1978.

Christian Science Monitor, January 31, 1963; October 22, 1970.

Commentary, April, 1971.

Commonweal, December 7, 1956; November 24, 1978.

Critic, November 15, 1978.

Detroit News, April 4, 1982.

Harper's, January, 1971; May, 1976.

Kirkus Reviews, September 1, 1999, p. 1364.

Library Journal, September 15, 1999, p. 98.

Los Angeles Times, April 11, 1984.

Los Angeles Times Book Review, November 14, 1982; April 16, 1989, p. 9.

Nation, July 20, 1992, Ronnie Dugger, review of *The Democrats Must Lead,* p. 110

National Review, November 3, 1970.

New Republic, January 11, 1960; February 2, 1963; February 5, 1966; May 13, 1972; July 24, 1976; December 23, 1978; December 23, 1991.

Newsweek, October 26, 1970.

New Yorker, August 18, 1956; January 9, 1971; May 17, 1982; June 25, 1984.

New York Review of Books, March 31, 1966; May 20, 1971; April 29, 1976; February 18, 1982; January 20, 2000, Lars-Erik Nelson, "Clinton & His Enemies," p. 18.

New York Times, July 17, 1949; August 12, 1956; September 12, 1970; March 11, 1979; April 10, 1984; April 18, 1984; September 24, 1985; January 9, 1982; April 19, 1989; January 8, 1992.

New York Times Book Review, January 24, 1960; January 23, 1966; September 1, 1968; September 13, 1970; April 18, 1976; December 24, 1978; February 21, 1982; April 29, 1984; September 29, 1985; May 14, 1989; May 6, 1990; June 30, 1991; March 15, 1992, p. 19.

Publishers Weekly, July 26, 1985; November 1, 1999, review of *Dead Center,* p. 66.

Reporter, March 14, 1963.

Saturday Review, August 11, 1956; January 19, 1963; February 5, 1966; September 21, 1968; September

12, 1970; February 12, 1972; May 1, 1976; February, 1982.
Time, September 28, 1970.
Times Literary Supplement, March 5, 1971.
Tribune Books (Chicago), February 21, 1982, April 29, 1990, p. 8.
Virginia Quarterly Review, autumn, 1990; summer, 1992.
Washington Post, September 9, 1970.
Washington Post Book World, June 13, 1976; September 17, 1978; February 14, 1982; May 6, 1984; April 23, 1989, p. 1; January 12, 1992.

* * *

BURNS, Ric 1955-

PERSONAL: Born in 1955; son of Robert Kyle (an anthropology professor) and Lyla (a homemaker; maiden name, Tupper) Burns; married Bonnie Lafave; children: two sons. *Education:* Columbia College, B.A. (English literature, summa cum laude), 1978; Cambridge University, first-class honors degree (English literature), 1980; Columbia University, M.Phil. (English literature), 1982.

ADDRESSES: Office—c/o Steeplechase Films, 2095 Broadway, Rm. 503, New York, NY 10023.

CAREER: Filmmaker and author.

AWARDS, HONORS: Television Producer of the Year, Producers Guild of America, 1991, Humanitas Prize, documentaries—special awards category, 1991, Christopher Award, Alfred I. DuPont-Columbia Award, and two Emmy Awards, all for *The Civil War;* John Jay Award, Columbia College, 2000, for "distinguished professional achievement"; Peabody Award, for *The Donner Party.*

WRITINGS:

(With brother Ken Burns and Geoffrey C. Ward) *The Civil War: An Illustrated History,* Knopf, 1990.
(With James Sanders and Lisa Ades) *New York: An Illustrated History,* Knopf, 1999.

DOCUMENTARIES

(Contributor) *The Statue of Liberty,* 1985.
(With Geoffrey C. Ward; and producer with Ken Burns) *The Civil War,* PBS, 1990.
(Also producer and director) *The Donner Party,* PBS, 1992.
(Also director) *Coney Island,* PBS, 1994.
(With Lisa Ades) *The Way West,* PBS, 1995.
(With James Sanders; also executive producer/director) *New York: A Documentary Film,* PBS, 1999.

SIDELIGHTS: Ric Burns helped his older brother Ken Burns and author Geoffrey C. Ward create one of the most heralded events in television history—the acclaimed 1990 public television documentary series *The Civil War.* Spanning eleven hours and shown over five consecutive nights, the program drew rave reviews from critics, including Tom Shales of the *Washington Post,* who called it "a grippingly powerful film about who we were, who we are, and who we yet may be." Burns also helped pen the companion book to the series, which was published by Knopf in 1990.

The Civil War series used authentic diaries, letters, and photographs of the period to create an in-depth feeling of what life was like for the people who lived through the conflict that occurred between 1861 and 1865. Not only were famous historical figures such as U.S. President Abraham Lincoln and Confederate General Robert E. Lee discussed and quoted from, but the documents of ordinary soldiers and their wives from both sides of the conflict were used as building blocks for *The Civil War.* Ric Burns explained to Elizabeth Kastor in the *Washington Post:* "I think that's what makes the war come alive, when you realize each name is really just the lid of an extraordinary package. And once you start looking at the smaller figures, you can see that the larger figures so encrusted with cliche—Robert E. Lee, Ulysses Grant—were real people."

Burns also confided to Kastor that working with his brother Ken for five years on *The Civil War* was such a transformative experience that he decided to leave his Ph.D unfinished and pursue his own career in film. He described what it was like collaborating with his brother, who has created several previous film documentaries, including projects about artist Thomas Hart Benton and Louisiana politician Huey Long, as well as a film about the Statue of Liberty that Ric contributed to as a writer. "I think Ken would agree that there was constant creative friction, not just between him and me, but also with Geoffrey Ward, the principle writer," Burns revealed to Kastor. "As brothers it was tough at times, but I think it's fruitfully tough. . . . It is a close relationship. Now, however, I think having worked together for five years, we'll give it a rest." After completing *The Civil War,* Ric Burns went on to pursue his own projects concerning the history of Coney Island and the ill-fated Donner Party that became stranded in the Sierra Nevada mountains en route to California in the 1800s. With his own production company, Steeplechase Films, Burns created the documentaries *Coney Island, The Donner Party,* and *The Way West.* This last title was lauded by Rick Marin in *Newsweek* as "long, but deeply involving. It has a cumulative payoff—the more you watch, the more you want to watch."

One of Burns' later projects, *New York: A Documentary Film,* a seven-part, fourteen-hour television documentary which he produced, co-wrote with James Sanders, and directed, aired on the Public Broadcasting System (PBS) in November, 1999—but only the first ten hours. Burns is working on the final episodes. "More than any other place in America, New York is the city Americans love to love, and love to hate," Burns said in a PBS online interview. The occasion was the premiere of *New York.*

With *New York,* Burns traced the history of America's most recognized city from the arrival of Dutch colonists in 1609, through the burgh's rise as a cultural center and its turmoil during the Civil War. Further episodes turn the spotlight on the city as a metropolis of wealth and greed toward the end of the nineteenth century, the rise of immigration at the turn of the next century, and the African American experience during the "Harlem Renaissance" period of the 1920s. The film is punctuated with voiceover narration by actors who read the words of the men and women of New York's fabled past. Present-day "witnesses" to the city's glory and strife include E. L. Doctorow, Martin Scorsese, Pete Hamill, Mayor Rudolph Giuliani, Donald Trump, and Senator Daniel Patrick Moynihan.

Regarding *New York, Time*'s James Poniewozik noted "slow pacing, reverent interviewees, soothing strings and custardy voice-overs. It may seem harsh to call this sentimental and dull, but something in this pledge-drive-friendly aesthetic belittles the [film's] intense, contentious [subject]." However, some reviewers saw *New York* as a worthy successor to *The Civil War.* The city itself is one "defined by muchness, and so it should come as no surprise that Ric Burns' documentary . . . embraces the same principle," David Mermelstein wrote in *Variety.* "There is a surfeit of information here. But Burns' mammoth effort, which might have played as too much of a good thing, proves nothing short of gripping." Who knew, added Mermelstein, "that Wall Street was so named because the avenue replaced a long wall? Or that Jews first came to the city in 1654? Or that 'skyscraper' is a sailor's term? Burns and company turn up an endless supply of such factoids."

Burns produced a companion book to his documentary. *New York: An Illustrated History* is a "fat, rich history," according to Gay Daly in *Entertainment Weekly,* that "offers two kinds of pleasure: hundreds of carefully chosen photographs and a thoughtful, well-written text." Likewise, a *Publishers Weekly* reviewer lauded the print effort as "an engaging and intelligent work in its own right, presenting a coherent overview without ever glossing over thorny historical or political questions."

BIOGRAPHICAL/CRITICAL SOURCES:

PERIODICALS

American Heritage, February-March, 1994, p. 104; July-August, 1994, p. 106; November, 1999, Frederick Allen, "The Supreme Laboratory of the American Experiment," p. 68.

Booklist, November 1, 1999, Gilbert Taylor, review of *New York: An Illustrated History,* p. 482.

Commonweal, November 5, 1999, Celia Wren, review of *New York: A Documentary Film,* p. 20.

Entertainment Weekly, December 17, 1999, Gay Daly, review of *New York: An Illustrated History,* p. 78.

Hollywood Reporter, November 12, 1999, Barry Garron, review of *New York: A Documentary Film,* p. 10.

Library Journal, December, 1999, Harry Frumerman, review of *New York: An Illustrated History,* p. 157.

Los Angeles Times Book Review, April 23, 1990, pp. 1, 12.

National Review, December 17, 1990, Paul Hubbard, review of *The Civil War: An Illustrated History,* p. 51.

New Republic, February 18, 1991, Alfred Kazin, review of *The Civil War: An Illustrated History,* p. 61.

Newsweek, May 8, 1995, Rick Marin, review of *The Way West,* p. 62.

New York Times, September 5, 1990.

New York Times Book Review, September 9, 1990, p. 26.

People, November 12, 1990, pp. 28-29.

Publishers Weekly, August 3, 1990, Genevieve Stuttaford, review of *The Civil War: An Illustrated History,* p. 66; November 1, 1999, review of *New York: An Illustrated History,* p. 61.

Time, November 8, 1999, James Poniewozik, "Thoroughly Burned Out: The Suffragists and New York City as Docu-dozes," p. 135.

Variety, November 15, 1999, David Mermelstein, review of *New York: A Documentary Film,* p. 37.

Washington Post, September 23, 1990, pp. G1, G5, G10-G11.

Washington Post Book World, October 14, 1990, p. 9.

OTHER

The Indie Scene: New York: A Documentary Film, http://www.pbs.org/independents, (December 30, 1999).*

C

CAIRNS, Scott 1954-

PERSONAL: Born November 19, 1954, in Tacoma, WA; son of Bud Clifford Eugene (a teacher) and Irene Elizabeth Cairns Laursen (an accountant; maiden name, Stubbs) Cairns; married Barbara Lunke (divorced, June 1982); married Marcia Vanderlip (a journalist), March 12, 1983; children: Elizabeth Vanderlip, Benjamin Vanderlip. *Education:* Western Washington University, B.A., 1977; Hollins College, M.A., 1979; Bowling Green State University, M.F.A., 1981; University of Utah, Ph.D., 1990. *Politics:* Progressive Democrat. *Religion:* Eastern Orthodox. *Avocational interests:* Metaphorical theology, "theosis, apocatastasis."

ADDRESSES: *Home*—Columbia, MO. *Office*—Department of English, University of Missouri—Columbia, Columbia, MO 65201; fax: 573-882-5785. *E-mail*—cairnss@missouri.edu.

CAREER: Kansas State University, Manhattan, instructor, 1981-84; Westminster College, Salt Lake City, assistant professor, 1987-90; University of North Texas, Denton, assistant professor of English and director of creative writing, 1990-94; Old Dominion University, Norfolk, VA, associate professor of English and director of creative writing, 1994-99; University of Missouri—Columbia, associate professor of English, 1999—.

MEMBER: International PEN, Modern Language Association of America, Associated Writing Programs.

WRITINGS:

The Theology of Doubt, Poetry Center, Cleveland State University (Cleveland, OH), 1985.
The Translation of Babel, University of Georgia Press (Athens), 1990.
Figures for the Ghost, University of Georgia Press, 1994.
Recovered Body, Braziller (New York City), 1998.

WORK IN PROGRESS: *Which Tribe? Which River?,* a collection of poems; research on the Kabbalah, gnostic and other non-canonical gospels, Midrashim, and other revisionary sacred texts.

SIDELIGHTS: Scott Cairns told *CA:* "As the poet W. H. Auden put it in *Archaeology:* 'Knowledge may have its purposes, but guessing is always more fun than knowing.' I spend most of my 'writing time' reading English translations of ancient texts, more often than not *sacred* texts. While I suppose that much of the time I am reading in order to know something, what I savor most about these texts are those moments when their rhetorics fail, when their coherences are compromised, when incommensurate and appalling *wrongness* disrupts the narrative. That's when I start guessing, and this guesswork becomes my next poem.

"Even so, it would be misleading to imply that *making poems* is all I want out of the practice. What I actually want, what I have always wanted, is—forgive the audacity—to see God. In those moments when the god-talk fails to convince, one is able to suspect something of the enormity which will not be confined to likely stories."

* * *

CALDER, John (Mackenzie) 1927-

PERSONAL: Born January 25, 1927; son of James and Lucianne (Wilson) Calder; married Mary Ann Simmonds, 1949 (marriage ended); married Bettina Jonic, 1960 (divorced, 1975); children: (first marriage) one daughter; (second marriage) one daughter. *Ethnicity:* "White." *Education:* Attended McGill University, Sir George Williams College, Concordia University, and University of Zurich. *Avocational interests:* Music, theater, opera, reading, chess, lecturing and conversation, travel, good food, wine.

ADDRESSES: Office—John Calder Publications Ltd., 126 Cornwall Rd., London SE1 8TQ, England.

CAREER: Former director of Calder Ltd. (timber company); John Calder Publishers Ltd. (now John Calder Publications), London, England, founder, 1950, managing director, 1950—. Managing director, Calder & Boyars Ltd., 1950—. Organizer of literary conferences; founder, Ledlanet Nights (music and opera festival), 1963; chair, Federation of Scottish Theatres, 1972-74; director of Operabout Ltd., Riverrun Press, Inc. (United States), and Canadian International Library Ltd. Candidate for Parliament for Kinross and West Perthshire, 1970, and Hamilton, 1974; candidate for European Parliament for Mid Scotland and Fife, 1979.

MEMBER: Royal Society of Arts (fellow), Defence of Literature and the Arts Society (co-founder), Caledonian Club, Scottish Arts Club, Scottish Liberal Club, Shadow Arts Council.

AWARDS, HONORS: Chevalier des Arts et des Lettres, 1975.

WRITINGS:

(Editor) *A Henry Miller Reader,* Picador, 1983.
(Editor) *A Samuel Beckett Reader,* Picador, 1984.
(Editor with Martin Esslin, Billie Whitelaw, and David Warrilow) *As No Other Dare Fail: Festschrift for Samuel Beckett's Eightieth Birthday,* Riverrun Press (New York City), 1986.
(Editor with John Fletcher) *The Nouveau Roman Reader,* Riverrun Press, 1986.
The Philosophy of Samuel Beckett, Calder Publications (London), 1996.

Also author of plays. Editor of *Beckett at Sixty.* Contributor of articles, stories, translations, and reviews to periodicals. Editor of *Gambit International Drama Review.*

BIOGRAPHICAL/CRITICAL SOURCES:

PERIODICALS

Management Today, March, 1987, Anna Foster, "The Battle of Britain's Books," p. 38.
Publishers Weekly, May 12, 1989, Joseph Barbato, "John Calder: A Sturdy Survivor," p. 254.

* * *

CARPENTER, (J.) Delores Bird 1942-

PERSONAL: Born December 6, 1942, in Chattanooga, TN; daughter of Basil Ivan and Hazel (Hawkins) Bird; married Joe Keith Carpenter (a Methodist minister and elementary schoolteacher), December 27, 1959 (divorced July 21, 1987); married Keith William Bull; children: Frederic Keith. *Ethnicity:* "Small part Cherokee." *Education:* Attended University of Mississippi; Boston University, B.A. (summa cum laude), 1967; University of Hartford, M.A., 1974; University of Massachusetts at Amherst, Ph.D., 1978. *Politics:* Democrat. *Religion:* "Spiritual."

ADDRESSES: Office—Department of English, Cape Cod Community College, 2240 Iyanough Rd., West Barnstable, MA 02668; fax 508-477-7561. *E-mail*—DBird@capecod.mass.edu.

CAREER: Junior high school English teacher in Shrewsbury, MA, 1967-70; University of Hartford, Hartford, CT, member of adjunct faculty, 1971-73; Tunxis Community College, Farmington, CT, member of adjunct faculty, 1973-74; Springfield College, Springfield, MA, member of adjunct faculty, 1974; high school teacher in Suffield, CT, 1974-75; Springfield Technical Community College, Springfield, member of adjunct faculty, 1975; University of Massachusetts at Amherst, member of adjunct faculty, 1976-77; Cape Cod Community College, West Barnstable, MA, instructor, 1977-80, assistant professor, 1980-84, associate professor, 1984-88, professor of English, 1988—. Southeastern Association for Cooperation in Higher Education, lecturer in southeastern Massachusetts, 1985-86; guest on television programs.

MEMBER: Emily Dickinson Society, Ralph Waldo Emerson Society, Thoreau Society, Hawthorne Society, Phi Beta Kappa, Appalachian Mountain Club's 4000 Footer Club.

WRITINGS:

(Editor) Ellen Tucker Emerson, *The Life of Lidian Jackson Emerson,* G. K. Hall (Boston, MA), 1980, revised edition, Michigan State University Press (East Lansing, MI), 1992.

(Contributor) *Studies in the American Renaissance,* Twayne (Boston), 1980.

(Editor and author of introduction) *The Selected Letters of Lidian Jackson Emerson,* University of Missouri Press (Columbia), 1987.

The Early Days of Cape Cod Community College, Cape Cod Community College (West Barnstable, MA), 1989.

Early Encounters: Native Americans and Europeans in New England from the Papers of W. Sears Nickerson, Michigan State University Press, 1994.

(Editor and author of introduction) *Inside Out: The Poetry of George Hoar,* Sullwold Printer, 1994.

(Editor) W. Sears Nickerson, *Land Ho!-1620, a Seaman's Story of the Mayflower, Her Construction, Her Navigation, and Her First Landfall,* Michigan State University Press, 1997.

Contributor to *Bulletin of the Massachusetts Archaeological Society.*

SIDELIGHTS: Delores Bird Carpenter told *CA:* "Lidian Jackson Emerson was the wife of Ralph Waldo Emerson for forty-six years, the mother of their four children, and the hostess to the Transcendentalist circle. She gave herself to at least four causes, including active membership in the Massachusetts Society for the Prevention of Cruelty to Animals, serving as its vice president for Concord in 1872. She could conjure up in her mind's eye real or imagined sufferings of animals, making their agonies more intense than her own. Something as inconsequential as the sun in Bossy's eye might distress her. The sufferings of humans also touched both her heart and mind. She worked for the Anti-Slavery Society, and got out of her sickbed to go to meetings in Boston. She worked on behalf of the Cherokee and Modoc Indians, and was an ardent advocate of woman's suffrage. Locally, for forty years she received school children at New Year's with gifts and admonitions concerning her favorite causes.

"A well-rounded woman of the nineteenth century emerges from Lidian Emerson's letters. They trace the growth of her independent and incisive mind, reveal her active influence on her husband's thought, and present a domestic view of the lives of the Emersons, their children, and their friends, including such notable contemporaries as Henry David Thoreau, Margaret Fuller, Thomas Carlyle, Amos Bronson Alcott, Jones Very, and many others."

BIOGRAPHICAL/CRITICAL SOURCES:

PERIODICALS

New England Quarterly, Vol. LXVIII, no. 3, September, 1995.

New York Times Book Review, November 29, 1987.

* * *

CHESNOFF, Richard Z(eltner) 1937-

PERSONAL: Born June 4, 1937, in New York, NY; son of Lewis (a musician) and Martha (Zeltner) Chesnoff; married Yora Yedlin (a ceramicist), June 14, 1959 (divorced, March, 1968); married Susan M. Warburg, September 10, 1972; children: (first marriage) Adam Louis, (stepchildren from second marriage) Ian Edward Warburg, Paul Jason Warburg. *Education:* Studied at New York University, 1955-57, and Hebrew University of Jerusalem, 1957-60. *Religion:* Jewish.

ADDRESSES: *Home*—3 Comp. Pkwy., Westport, CT 06880; and Casa Willi, Klosters, Switzerland.

CAREER: Correspondent in Israel for *New York Herald Tribune,* 1964-66, and for *Newsweek* and National Broadcasting Co. News, 1965-66; *Newsweek,* New York, NY, associate editor for foreign news, 1966-68, correspondent, specializing in Middle East affairs, and deputy bureau chief, Paris, France, 1968-72, Newsweek International, general editor, 1973-74, assistant managing editor, 1974-75, executive editor, 1975-78; Richesu, Inc., president, beginning 1979. Senior correspondent, *U.S. News and World Report.*

WRITINGS:

(With Edward Klein and Robert Littell) *If Israel Lost the War,* Coward, 1969.

AWOL (screenplay), produced by BFB Productions, 1972.

Philippines, Abrams, 1978, concise edition, 1980.

Pack of Thieves: How Hitler and Europe Plundered the Jews and Committed the Greatest Theft in History, Doubleday, 1999.

Also contributor of articles to *GEO, Esquire, WorldPaper,* and other periodicals.

WORK IN PROGRESS: Imelda Marcos, a political biography, for Prentice-Hall; *Arabella,* a novel.

SIDELIGHTS: "Terrible things are happening outside. At any time of night and day, poor helpless people are being dragged out of their homes. They're allowed to take only a knapsack and a little cash, and even then, they're robbed of these possessions on the way." Those words, excerpted from Anne Frank's famous wartime diary, are a touchpoint in journalist Richard Chesnoff 's acclaimed book, *Pack of Thieves.*

In this 1999 publication, Chesnoff, a senior correspondent for *U.S. News and World Report,* contends that it was not only the Nazis who stole money and possessions from their Jewish prisoners during and after World War II. In fact, the powers-that-be in many nations—including Swiss bankers, French museums, Italian insurance companies, and Sweden's influential Wallenberg family—took advantage of political turmoil to "plunder," as the author puts it, Europe's Jews in what Chesnoff calls history's largest robbery.

Pack of Thieves begins with an examination of Germany, providing "a summary of how Berlin developed models for spoliation, most of which is already known," as Milton Goldin states in the online *H-Net Reviews.* Chesnoff, Goldin continues, "is more original in discussions of seven countries allied with or occupied by Germany, five neutral countries and the Vatican." The author "argues that whether among communist atheists in Poland or the faithful in Rome during the postwar ear, ideology might be dead, but greed was very much alive . . . and receivers of stolen property or property left for safekeeping held tight to what they had."

Using interviews, documentation, and evidence, Chesnoff examines the lingering effects of "homes taken . . . of life insurance unpaid, of recompense for slave labor ignored," and property stolen across Europe, according to Anne Roiphe's *New York Observer* review. While the author asserts that *Pack of Thieves* is not an inventory of what was stolen, he is careful to keep track of the extent of the theft through documentation.

Not every critic found *Pack of Thieves* engrossing. *Kirkus Reviews* saw the work as "unfocused and underdocumented," maintaining that Chesnoff 's anecdotal approach adds little new information on the goings-on in Austria, the Netherlands, Norway, France, Poland, and Hungary. But many critics took a different view. Roiph contends that the book "makes the blood boil" in its unrelenting picture of the lingering social crimes that accompanied the slaughter of six million. Bloomfield declared the volume an "excellent" effort "well worth reading [and] as current as the headlines."

In his argument for restitution, a reviewer for *Publishers Weekly* explains, Chesnoff "criticizes as perverse those who argue that [these demands reinforce] the stereotype of the money-grubbing Jew." As quoted by *New York Jewish Week,* Chesnoff asks, "What do these people prefer, that the money remain with those who stole it?"

BIOGRAPHICAL/CRITICAL SOURCES:

PERIODICALS

New York Jewish Weekly, December 10, 1999, Sandee Brawarsky, review of *Pack of Thieves.*

New York Observer, January 10, 2000, Anne Roiphe, review of *Pack of Thieves.*

Publishers Weekly, October 25, 1999, review of *Pack of Thieves,* p. 59.

U.S. News and World Report, November 15, 1999, review of *Pack of Thieves.*

OTHER

Bloomfield, Douglas, syndicated column, http://www.amazon.com, (March 14, 2000).

Chesnoff, Richard, http://www.amazon.com, (October 10, 1999).

H-Net Reviews: Pack of Thieves, http://www.ess.uwe.ac.uk/genocide, (March 14, 2000).

Kirkus Reviews, http://www.amazon.com, (March 14, 2000).*

* * *

CHILTON, John (James) 1932-

PERSONAL: Born July 16, 1932, in London, England; son of Thomas W. (a singer) and Eileen (Burke) Chilton; married Teresa Macdonald (a bookseller); children: Jennifer, Martin, Barnaby. *Education:* Attended schools in England.

ADDRESSES: Home—London, England. *Office*—3 Great Ormond St., London WC1, England.

CAREER: Employed in advertising, and with the *Daily Telegraph,* 1953-57; professional musician, bandleader, 1957-59, member of Bruce Turner's Jump

Band, 1959-63; worked in public relations and free-lance writing, 1963-67; Bloomsbury Book Shop, London, England, co-manager, 1967-73; full-time musician, band-leader, 1973—. Jazz historian and composer. *Military service:* Royal Air Force, 1950-52; became senior aircraftsman.

MEMBER: National Union of Journalists, Musicians Union, Performing Rights Society.

WRITINGS:

(With Max Jones) *Salute to Satchmo,* International Publishing, 1970.
(With Jones) *Louis: The Louis Armstrong Story,* Little, Brown (Boston), 1971.
Who's Who of Jazz, Bloomsbury Book Shop (London), 1970.
Billie's Blues, Stein & Day, 1975.
McKinney's Music, Bloomsbury Book Shop, 1978.
Teach Yourself Music, McKay, 1979.
A Jazz Nursery, Bloomsbury Book Shop, 1980.
(Contributor) *Giants of Jazz,* Time-Life, 1981-82.
(Contributor) *A Biographical Dictionary of Modern Thought,* Fontana Books (Center Point, NY), 1982.
Who's Who of Jazz: Storyville to Swing Street, Da Capo Press, 1985.
The Song of the Hawk: The Life and Recordings of Coleman Hawkins, University of Michigan Press (Ann Arbor, MI), 1990.
Let the Good Times Roll: The Story of Louis Jordan and His Music, University of Michigan Press, 1992.
Sidney Bechet: The Wizard of Jazz, Oxford University Press (New York City), 1987.
Who's Who of British Jazz, Cassell (New York City), 1997.
Ride, Red, Ride: The Life of Henry "Red" Allen, Cassell, 1998.

SIDELIGHTS: John Chilton is not just a jazz composer but an historian as well. The British-born Chilton is in fact a major chronicler of the most American of musical forms. A former advertising professional, he got early experience playing with Bruce Turner's Jump Band and, after a stint managing the Bloomsbury Book Shop in London, became a full-time leader of his own jazz combo, the Feetwarmers.

Chilton's books center on the greats of the art form: Louis Armstrong, Billie Holliday, Coleman Hawkins, and many more. In 1995 he produced a definitive biography of a top name in jazz: sax man Louis Jordan. *Let the Good Times Roll* is the story of the musician who is thought to have bridged the gap between the big-band stylings of the 1940s and the emerging sound of rock-and-roll a decade later. After a brief career as a sideman with Charlie Gaines and Chick Webb (accompanying a then-unknown Ella Fitzgerald), Jordan toured the United States. with his own band, the Tympany Five, which boasted such names as Wild Bill Davis, Bill Doggett, Dallas Bartley, and Chris Columbus.

In the 1940s and 1950s, Jordan saw dozens of his songs turn into hits for his band and others. The songs that distinguish his sound—like "Buzz Me," "Choo Choo Ch' Boogie" and "Caldonia"—are characterized by a jumpy beat, clever lyrics and infectious melody. But beneath the jive is something at least one critic has identified as subtle.

In *Let the Good Times Roll* Chilton uses extensive research and numerous interviews to examine the life and work of this complicated musician, revealing what a *Publishers Weekly* reviewer calls "the moody and difficult taskmaster" within the flamboyant showman. The reviewer lauds the author's "painstaking attention to every detail of Jordan's story," a view shared by *Booklist* critic Aaron Cohen. While Cohen notices a lack of deeper understanding of the subject's psychology, Chilton, he says, still delivers "fascinating stories of the swinging 'battles' between big bands and the struggles of touring in the [still-segregated] South."

Thanks to the success of "Five Guys Named Moe," an extensively toured musical review based around Jordan's music, the jazzman has found a new audience. *Down Beat*'s Frank-John Hadley notes the resurgence of Jordan in reviewing Chilton's book. Readers, he says, can rely on the author's "even-tempered, carefully ordered words" and numerous photos that help reveal "the amazing magneticism of the rock & roll pioneer whose name . . . is no longer obscure."

BIOGRAPHICAL/CRITICAL SOURCES:

PERIODICALS

Booklist, June 1, 1994, Aaron Cohen, review of *Let the Good Times Roll,* p. 1752.
Down Beat, February, 1995, Frank-John Hadley, review of *Let the Good Times Roll,* p. 53.
Publishers Weekly, May 20, 1994, review of *Let the Good Times Roll,* p. 44.*

CHOPRA, Deepak (K.) 1946-

PERSONAL: Born in 1946, in New Delhi, India; immigrated to United States, 1970; naturalized U.S. citizen; son of Krishan Chopra (a physician); married; wife's name, Rita; children: Mallika (daughter), Gautam (son). *Education:* All India Institute of Medical Science, M.D.

ADDRESSES: Office—The Chopra Center for Well Being, 7630 Fay Ave., La Jolla, CA 92307. *Agent*—Muriel Nellis, Literary and Creative Artists, 3543 Albemarle St. NW, Washington, DC 20008; c/o The Ford Group, 872 La Jolla Rancho Rd., La Jolla, CA 92037.

CAREER: Physician, lecturer, and writer. Muhlenbert Hospital, Plainfield, NJ, intern, c. 1970-71; established private endocrinology practice in Boston, MA, 1971; affiliated with Tufts University, Medford, MA, Harvard University, Cambridge, MA, and Boston University, Boston, MA, 1971-c. 1985; New England Memorial Hospital (now Boston Regional Medical Center), Stoneham, MA, chief of staff, 1981-85; Maharishi Ayur-Veda Products International, Inc. (produces herbal remedies), co-founder, 1985, sole stockholder, 1985-87, president, treasurer, and clerk, 1985-88; Maharishi Ayur-Veda Health Center for Behavioral Medicine and Stress Management, Lancaster, MA, director, 1985-93; Sharp Institute for Human Potential and Mind/Body Medicine, La Jolla, CA, executive director, 1993—; Center for Mind/Body Medicine at L'Auberge, Del Mar, CA, director, 1993-95; The Chopra Center for Well Being (learning center and day spa), La Jolla, founder and chief executive officer, 1995—. Lecturer and speaker, including appearances on public television programs, the *Oprah Winfrey Show,* and numerous radio shows. Member of alternative medicine board of National Institute of Health, 1992. Co-producer of video *Growing Younger,* 1994.

MEMBER: American Association of Ayurvedic Medicine (founder).

AWARDS, HONORS: Christened Dhanvantari of Heaven on Earth by Maharishi Mahesh Yogi, 1989; named one of the "Top 100 Icons and Heroes of the [Twentieth] Century," *Time* magazine, 1999.

WRITINGS:

Creating Health: The Psychophysiological Connection, Houghton (Boston), 1985, published as *Creating Health: Beyond Prevention, toward Perfection,* 1987, new edition with new introduction published with a new introduction by Chopra as *Creating Health: How to Wake up the Body's Intelligence,* 1991.

Deepak Chopra

Total Health: The Rediscovery of Ayurveda (sound recording), Maharishi Vedic Publications International (Fairfield, IA), 1986.

Return of the Rishi: A Doctor's Search for the Ultimate Healer (autobiography), Houghton, 1988, new edition with new introduction published as *Return of the Rishi: A Doctor's Story of Spiritual Transformation and Ayurvedic Healing,* 1991.

Quantum Healing: Exploring the Frontiers of Mind/Body Medicine, Bantam (New York City), 1989.

(With Richard Averbach and Stuart Rothenberg) *Perfect Health: Maharishi Ayurveda, the Mind/Body Program for Total Well-Being,* Crown/Harmony (New York City), 1990.

Perfect Health: The Complete Mind/Body Guide, illustrations by Stephen Van Damme, Harmony, 1991.

Unconditional Life: Mastering the Forces That Shape Personal Reality, Bantam, 1991, published as *Unconditional Life: Discovering the Power to Fulfill Your Dreams,* Bantam, 1992.

Creating Affluence: Wealth Consciousness in the Field of All Possibilities, New World Library (San Rafael, CA), 1993, associated with *The A-to-Z Steps to a Richer Life* and *The Seven Spiritual Laws of Success: A Practical Guide to the Fulfillment of Your Dreams* (see below).

Ageless Body, Timeless Mind: The Quantum Alternative to Growing Old, Crown/Harmony, 1993.

Restful Sleep: The Complete Mind/Body Program for Overcoming Insomnia, Harmony, 1994.

The A-to-Z Steps to a Richer Life (special edition based on Chopra's *Creating Affluence*), Barnes & Noble (New York City), 1994.

The Seven Spiritual Laws of Success: A Practical Guide to the Fulfillment of Your Dreams (based on Chopra's book *Creating Affluence*), Amber-Allen (San Rafael, CA), 1994.

Perfect Weight: The Complete Mind/Body Program for Achieving and Maintaining Your Ideal Weight, Harmony, 1994.

Body, Mind, and Soul: The Mystery and the Magic (video; 2 volumes), PBS Home Video (Alexandria, VA), 1995.

Journey into Healing: Awakening the Wisdom within You, Harmony (New York City), 1994, published as *Journey into Healing: A Step-by-Step Personal Guide Compiled from the Timeless Wisdom of Deepak Chopra, M.D.,* Crown/Harmony, 1994.

Perfect Digestion: The Key to Balanced Living, Harmony, 1995.

The Return of Merlin (novel), Harmony, 1995.

Living without Limits, American Medical Association Library, 1995.

Boundless Energy: The Complete Mind/Body Program for Overcoming Chronic Fatigue, Crown/Harmony, 1995.

The Way of the Wizard: Twenty Spiritual Lessons for Creating the Life You Want, Harmony, 1995.

The Path to Love: Renewing the Power of Spirit in Your Life, Harmony, 1997, published as *The Path to Love: Spiritual Strategies for Healing,* Three Rivers, (New York City), 1998.

The Seven Spiritual Laws for Parents: Guiding Your Children to Success and Fulfillment, Harmony, 1997.

Overcoming Addictions: The Spiritual Solution, Harmony, 1997.

(Editor, and translator with Fereydoun Kia) Maulana Jalal al-Din Rumi, *The Love Poems of Rumi,* Harmony, 1998.

Healing the Heart: A Spiritual Approach to Reversing Coronary Artery Disease, Harmony, 1998.

Deepak Chopra: World of Infinite Possibilities, Random House (Australia), 1998, published as *A Deepak Chopra Companion: Illuminations on Health and Human Consciousness,* edited by Leon Nacson, Three Rivers (New York City), 1999.

Everyday Immortality: A Concise Course in Spiritual Transformation, Harmony, 1999.

(With Martin Greenberg) *The Lords of Light* (adventure novel), St. Martin's (New York City), 1999.

(Selector) Rabindranath Tagore, *On the Shores of Eternity: Poems from Tagore on Death and Immortality,* Harmony, 1999.

(With Rosa Parks) *Secrets of Inner Power: A Profile in Courage* (sound recording; profile of and interview with Rosa Parks), Hay House Audio, 1999.

How to Know God: The Soul's Journey into the Mystery of Mysteries Crown (New York City), 2000.

(With David Simon) *The Chopra Center Herbal Handbook: Natural Prescriptions for Perfect Health,* Three Rivers, 2000.

Contributor to periodicals, including *Journal of the American Medical Association.* Member of scientific advisory board of *Longevity.* Interviewed in film *Rumi: Poet of the Heart,* Magnolia Films (San Anselmo, CA), 1999. Associated with the album/sound recording *A Gift of Love,* c. 1998. Author of more than one hundred audio and video series.

ADAPTATIONS: The Lords of Life is being adapted for a film by London Films. Several of Chopra's books have been adapted as audio books, including *Quantum Healing,* Bantam Audio, 1989; *Unconditional Life,* Banatam Audio, 1991; and *The Lords of Light,* Audio Renaissance, 1999.

SIDELIGHTS: Deepak Chopra is a prolific author and speaker who promotes alternative approaches to mental and physical well-being. His works include numerous books (primarily nonfiction, but some novels), sound recordings, videotapes, and appearances in various media, including public television and the *Oprah Winfrey Show.* Chopra, who "has been called everything from a modern-day prophet to the swami of the rich hip and famous" noted *Los Angeles Magazine*'s J. W., began his career as a physician. After studying in India, he came to the United States in 1970 and completed his education, served a residency, and then opened a private practice. In addition, he taught at various institutions, including Tufts University and Boston University, and served as the chief of staff for the New England Memorial Hospital.

By 1980 Chopra became increasingly concerned with Western medicine's—and thus his own practice's—reliance on pharmaceuticals as a major means of restoring, or merely maintaining, healthy individuals. Chopra's search for alternatives to standard Western approaches eventually led him to the Maharishi Mahesh Yogi, an Indian spiritualist who teaches transcendental meditation. Through the Maharishi, who had gained celebrity status in the 1960s with his counseling of several notable celebrities, including the music group the Beatles, Chopra became profoundly involved in transcendental meditation. In addition, he learned about Ayurvedic medicine, an holistic approach in which a patient's surroundings and general attitude are considered in addition to more conventional mental and physical conditions.

In 1985 Chopra established the Maharishi Ayur-Veda Health Center for Behavioral Medicine and Stress Management. Here Chopra began applying his understanding of both Ayurvedic and Western practices. Two years later, he published *Creating Health: The Psychophysiological Connection,* the first of many works in which Chopra detailed his holistic perspective on various health-related subjects. This initial work, which had multiple reprintings, first as *Creating Health: Beyond Prevention, toward Perfection,* and then as *Creating Health: How to Wake up the Body's Intelligence,* launched Chopra as a leading figure in alternative medicine, and his ensuing writings have established him as one of the most successful, and charismatic, figures in the counter-culture health movement.

Creating Health proved immensely successful with book-buyers eager to discover an alternative to Western medicine and its reliance on drug medications. An ensuing volume, the autobiographical *Return of the Rishi: A Doctor's Search for the Ultimate Healer* (reprinted as *Return of the Rishi: A Doctor's Story of Spiritual Transformation and Ayurvedic Healing*) realized similar success and furthered Chopra's reputation as an accessible, credible physician with insights somewhat unique in Western medicine. The book chronicles Chopra's path to enlightenment, from his early days as an intern at a New Jersey hospital, to his discovery of Ayurveda methods, to his current success. Judith Hooper wrote in the *New York Times Book Review:* "Chopra's talent as a storyteller and his eye for the exemplary detail make this a rich and compelling book."

In ensuing volumes Chopra has continued to elaborate on various aspects of holistic health. In 1991's *Perfect Health: The Complete Mind/Body Guide,* he emphasizes the health benefits gained by considering all aspects—as opposed to merely the ailing aspects—of given patients. And in *Unconditional Life: Mastering the Forces That Shape Personal Reality* (reprinted as *Unconditional Life: Discovering the Power to Fulfill Your Dreams*), he relates the manner in which individuals can realize greater health and stability by adjusting personal perspectives.

Among Chopra's most popular, and most controversial, publications is *Ageless Body, Timeless Mind: The Quantum Alternative to Growing Old,* a 1993 volume in which he contends that the aging process can be significantly affected and modified through such means as meditation, nutrition, and even personal expression. Aging, Chopra argues, is not necessarily a process of degeneration; it is, rather, a culmination of experiences and perceptions. As such, the elderly, for Chopra, constitute the storehouse for humankind's most profound knowledge and understanding. A contributor to *Kirkus Reviews* called the book "thoughtful" and "sometimes inspiring," while a reviewer for *Publishers Weekly* stated that despite Chopra's "inspirational conviction" in his material, the book was periodically "thin on substance."

Chopra's relatively radical insights into aging and the elderly appealed to a substantial segment of the American public, and the book eventually topped numerous bestseller lists. Chopra has enjoyed further success with such volumes as *The Seven Spiritual Laws of Success: A Practical Guide to the Fulfillment of Your Dreams* and *Journey into Healing: Awakening the Wisdom within You.* In addition, he has addressed specific health issues in such works as *Perfect Digestion: The Key to Balanced Living, Perfect Weight: The Complete Mind/Body Program for Achieving and Maintaining Your Ideal Weight,* and *Restful Sleep: The Complete Mind/Body Program for Overcoming Insomnia.* In 1998 Chopra gave readers his insights on caring for their heart. *Healing the Heart: A Spiritual Approach to Reversing Coronary Artery Disease* outlines "the Ayurvedic view of health" and how "the three doshas, or Ayurvedic metabolic types" can be understood in the context of dealing with heart disease, reported *Booklist* contributor Ray Olson, who referred to Chopra as "a master of metaphor and instruction" and judged his presentation in *Healing the Heart* to be "logical" given the Ayurvedic foundation.

Among Chopra's less characteristic publications is *The Return of Merlin,* a novel in which an apprentice to the Arthurian wizard Merlin travels through time to the twentieth century, where he helps a police officer solve a crime. "This is a bold, occasionally brilliant retelling of Arthurian lore," wrote a critic in *Publishers Weekly.* Pam Lambert, writing in *People Weekly,* declared: "Chopra weaves an intriguing story that also offers plenty to ponder." Chopra explained to a *Publishers*

Weekly interviewer that he felt fiction was truthful in that "it reveals your innermost feelings and fantasies about situations, circumstances, people and events." He added, "If you write fiction and you do it with intensity and passion, you reveal yourself—and you write the truth."

Although he followed *The Return of Merlin* with the more characteristic *The Way of the Wizard: Twenty Spiritual Lessons for Creating the Life You Want,* Chopra disclosed that he has become increasingly inclined toward writing fiction. In 1999, he co-authored with Mark Greenberg the adventure novel *The Lords of Light.* Originally conceived by Chopra as a film, the book release is the first of "an ongoing brand author franchise series, much like Tom Clancy's Op-Center and Politka series," indicated Judy Quinn in *Publishers Weekly,* noting that "[p]ackager Martin Greenberg, who is also involved in those Clancy books, will work on the Chopra/SMP [St. Martin's Press] tides." According to a *Publishers Weekly* critic's review of the audio version of *The Lords of Light,* the story is "action-adventure served up as a life lesson for the ages."

Chopra benefits from widespread celebrity as a prolific writer whose new works regularly rank among national bestsellers. He is also a prominent figure on television, whether appearing as a guest on interview programs such as *The Oprah Winfrey Show* or as principal lecturer on public television broadcasts. In 1995, the Chopra Center for Well Being opened. With this institution, noted a writer for the *Los Angeles Magazine,* Chopra, the founder and CEO, gives the public a learning center and day spa "for battling chronic illness as well as exploring one's 'full human potential' says Chopra." In alliance with his writings and speaking appearances, Chopra's center advocates Ayurvedic teachings and attracts celebrities. Chopra's center, his novel series, his company's production of herbal remedies, his lectures and appearances, and future books all contribute to his continual public visibility.

Prior to the wide release of *How to Know God: The Soul's Journey into the Mystery of Mysteries* (2000), *Booklist*'s Ilene Cooper acknowledged: "Chopra's status as a spiritual guru will prompt heavy media coverage, which in turn will spur demand for the book." Cooper was not impressed with *How to Know God.* However, a *Publishers Weekly* reviewer believed it had value for readers interested in spiritual writing. In the work Chopra asserts that there are seven different perspectives people can take when approaching God, each giving rise to different concepts of, experiences with, and gifts from God. "Like most theories that claim to be all-encompassing, Chopra's scheme is often reductive, but this will nonetheless be a worthwhile addition to the spiritual seeker's library," judged the *Publishers Weekly* critic. "If God is to be found, Chopra believes, He will emerge through the sciences," remarked Morgan Murphy in *Forbes* article. In *How to Know God,* as in past works, Chopra highlights findings from the scientific community that blend with spiritual thought. Specifically, Chopra discusses how quantum physics identifies a realm that merges with the spiritual world.

BIOGRAPHICAL/CRITICAL SOURCES:

PERIODICALS

Advocate, June 30, 1998, p. 43.
American Health, January-February, 1990, p. 106; January-February, 1992, p. 43.
Billboard, December 6, 1997, p. 1.
Booklist, January 15, 1987, p. 783; March 15, 1992, p. 1398; September 1, 1992, p. 74; May 15, 1993, p. 1650; June 1, 1995, p. 1683; October 1, 1995, p. 240; December 1, 1995, p. 586; January 1, 1996, p. 856; February 15, 1996, p. 1036; November 15, 1996, p. 546; July, 1997, p. 1770; April 15, 1998, p. 1354; December 1, 1999, p. 659.
Chicago Tribune, September 13, 1995.
Entertainment Weekly, May 24, 1996, p. 12; November 20, 1998, p. 130.
Esquire, October, 1995, p. 118.
Forbes, April 11, 1994, p. 132; March 22, 1999, p. 238.
Fortune, December 9, 1996, p. 54.
Hippocrates, January-February, 1989, p. 83.
In Health, May-June, 1990, p. 78.
Insight on the News, July 16, 1990, p. 50.
In Style, November 1, 1999, p. 326.
Kirkus Reviews, April 15, 1990, p. 571; July 1, 1991, p. 833; May 15, 1993, p.636.
Library Journal, December, 1985, p. 135; June 1, 1988, p. 128; June 1, 1990, pp. 160, 162; October 1, 1991, p. 125; January, 1992, p. 200; June 15, 1993, p. 90; September 1, 1994, p. 233; May 1, 1995, p. 152; July, 1995, p. 118; January, 1996, p. 106; July, 1996, p. 94; January, 1997, pp. 78, 125; September 1, 1997, p. 210; May 1, 1999, p. S16; February 1, 2000, pp. 131, 134.
Los Angeles Magazine, December, 1999, p. 244.
McCall's, July, 1997, p. 18.
Men's Fitness, November, 1996, p. 136.
Money, December, 1993, p. 20.
National Catholic Reporter, August 9, 1996, p. 15.
New England Journal of Medicine, December 14, 1989, p. 168.
New York, August 14, 1995, p. 28.

New Yorker, July 28, 1997, p. 80.
New York Times Book Review, March 27, 1988, p. 39.
New York Times Magazine, September 20, 1998, p. 92.
Newsweek, October 20, 1997, p. 52.
People Weekly, November 15, 1993, p. 169; August 14, 1995, p. 27; October 28, 1996, p. 126; August 11, 1997, p. 41.
Psychology Today, November-December, 1993, p. 36.
Publishers Weekly, December 18, 1987, p. 48; April 20, 1990, p. 73; December 6, 1991, p. 45; June 28, 1993, 74; April 11, 1994, p. 132; September 26, 1994, p. 67; May 8, 1995, p. 283; July 24, 1995, pp. 43-44; September 1, 1996, p. 17; November 5, 1996, p. 64; December 2, 1996, p. 31; February 17, 1997, p. 206; July 28, 1997, p. 63; March 2, 1998, p. 18; May 3, 1999, p. 35; May 17, 1999, p. 71; January 10, 2000, p. 61; March 6, 2000, p. 24.
San Diego Business Journal, October 20, 1997, p. 8.
School Library Journal, September, 1999, p. 242.
Science, October 11, 1991, p. 188.
Time, June 24, 1996, p. 64; September 29, 1997, p. 64.
Town & Country, January, 2000, p. 143.
USA Today, January 4, 1990.
Vegetarian Times, July, 1994, p. 112; July, 1997, p. 70.

OTHER

Deepak Chopra Home Page, http://www.chopra.com (June 22, 2000).*

* * *

CHRIST, Karl 1923-

PERSONAL: Born April 6, 1923, in Ulm, Germany; son of Karl (in business) and Rosa (a homemaker; maiden name, Sterk) Christ; married Gisela Hartmann (a homemaker), December 28, 1954; children: Thomas, Susanne, Elisabeth. *Ethnicity:* "German." *Education:* Attended University of Zurich, 1950; University of Tuebingen, Ph.D., 1953. *Religion:* Roman Catholic.

ADDRESSES: Home—26-1/2 Rotenberg, Marburg L D-35037, Germany.

CAREER: University of Marburg, Marburg, Germany, assistant professor, 1959, associate professor, 1959-65, professor of ancient history, 1965-1988. *Military service:* German Army, 1940-45; became first lieutenant; received Iron Cross, first and second class.

MEMBER: German Archaeological Institute, Historical Commission of Hessen, Accademia di Scienze Morali e Politiche (Naples), Istituto Lombardo (Milan).

AWARDS, HONORS: Dr. Phil., Free University of Berlin.

WRITINGS:

TRANSLATED INTO ENGLISH

Die Roemer: Eine Einfuehrung in ihre Geschichte und Zivilisation, Beck (Munich, Germany), 1979, translation by Christopher Holme published as *The Romans: An Introduction to Their History and Civilization,* University of California, 1984.
(With others) *The Italian World: History, Art, and the Genius of a People,* edited by John Julius Norwich, Thames & Hudson, 1983.

IN GERMAN

Antike Numismatik: Einfuehrung und Bibliographie (title means "Ancient Numismatics: Introduction and Bibliography"), Wissenschaftliche Buchgesellschaft, 1967, 3rd edition, 1991.
Von Gibbon zu Rostovtzeff: Leben und Werk fuehrender Althistoriker der Neuzeit (title means "From Gibbon to Rostovtzeff: Life and Work of Important Scholars in Ancient History") Wissenschaftliche Buchgesellschaft, 1972, 3rd edition, 1989.
Das Roemische Weltreich: Aufstieg und Zerfall einer antiken Grossmacht (title means "The Roman Empire: Dawn and Decline of an Ancient World Power"), Herder, 1973, 2nd edition, 1981.
Roemische Geschichte: Einfuehrung, Quellenkunde, Bibliographie (title means "Roman History: Introduction, Sources, Bibliography"), Wissenschaftliche Buchgesellschaft, 1973, 5th edition, 1994.
(With Reinhard Anders, Marianne Gaul, and Bettina Kreck) *Roemische Geschichte: Eine Bibliographie* (title means "Roman History: A Bibliography"), Wissenschaftliche Buchgesellschaft, 1976.
Krise und Untergang der Roemische Republik (title means "Crisis and Decline of the Roman Republic"), Wissenschaftliche Buchgesellschaft, 1979, 4th edition, 2000.
Roemische Geschichte und deutsche Geschichtewissenschaft (title means "Roman History and German Historiography"), Beck, 1982.
Roemische Geschichte und Wissenschaftsgeschichte (title means "Roman History and History of Sciences"), three volumes, Wissenschaftliche Buchgesallschaft, 1982-84.
Geschichte der roemischen Kaiserzeit: von Augustus bis zu Konstantin (title means "A History of the Roman Empire: From Augustus to Constantine"), Beck, 1988, 3rd edition, 1995.

Neue Profile der Alten Geschichte (title means "New Profiles of Ancient History"), Wissenschaftliche Buchgesellschaft (Darmstadt, Germany), 1990.
Geschichte und Existenz (title means "History and Existence"), Wagenbach (Berlin, Germany), 1991.
Caesar: Annaeherungen an einen Diktator (title means "Caesar: Approaches to a Dictator"), Beck, 1994.
Von Caesar zu Konstantin: Beitraege zur roemischen Geschichte und ihrer Rezeption (title means "From Caesar to Constantine: Studies in Roman History and Its Reception"), Beck, 1996.
Griechische Geschichte und Wissenschaftsgeschichte (title means "Greek History and History of Sciences"), Steiner (Stuttgart, Germany), 1996.
Hellas: Griechische Geschichte und deutsche Geschichtswissenschaft (title means "Greek History and German Historiography"), Beck, 1999.

EDITOR

Der Untergang des Roemischen Reiches (title means "The Fall of the Roman Empire"), Wissenschaftliche Buchgesellschaft, 1970, 2nd edition, 1986.
Hannibal, Wissenschaftliche Buchgesellschaft, 1974.
Jacob Burckhardt, *Die Zeit Constantins des Grossen,* C. H. Beck, 1982.
(With Theodore Mommsen) *Roemische Geschichte* (title means "Roman History"), Deutscher Taschenbuch Verlag, 1976, 5th edition, 1993.
Sparta, Wissenschaftliche Buchgesellschaft, 1986.
(With Arnaldo Momigliano) *Die Antike im 19. Jahrhundert in Italien und Deutschland* (title means "Antiquities in the Nineteenth Century in Italy and Germany"), Il Mulino (Bologna, Italy), 1988.
(With Emilio Gabba) *Roemische Geschichte und Zeitgeschichte in der deutschen und italienischen Altertumswissenschaft waehrend des 19. und 20. Jahrhunderts* (title means "Roman History and Current History in the German and Italian Humanities during the Nineteenth and Twentieth Centuries"), two volumes, Edizioni New Press (Como), 1989, 1991.

SIDELIGHTS: Karl Christ once told *CA:* "As my friend Arnaldo said, 'I am a student of the ancient world, and my primary aim is to understand and evaluate the Greek and Roman historians and the modern historians of the ancient world.' "

CHRISTOPHER, Nicholas 1951-

PERSONAL: Born February 28, 1951, in New York, NY; married Constance (a writer), November 21, 1980. *Education:* Harvard College, A.B. (English literature, cum laude), 1973. *Avocational interests:* Travel, film, ancient history.

ADDRESSES: Agent—c/o Anne Sibbald, Janklow & Nesbit Associates, 645 Park Ave., New York, NY 10022.

CAREER: Poet and novelist. New York University, New York City, former adjunct professor of English; Columbia University, New York City, lecturer, then associate professor in writing division of school of the arts.

MEMBER: PEN, Poetry Society of America.

AWARDS, HONORS: Amy Lowell Poetry traveling scholarship, 1985; fellowship, New York Foundation for the Arts, 1986; fellowship, National Endowment for the Arts, 1987; Peter I. B. Lavan Award, Academy of American Poets, 1991; Guggenheim fellowship in poetry, 1993.

WRITINGS:

On Tour with Rita (poems), Knopf (New York City), 1982.
A Short History of the Island of Butterflies (poems), Viking (New York City), 1986.
The Soloist (novel), Viking, 1986.
Desperate Characters (poems), Viking, 1988.
In the Year of the Comet (poems), Viking, 1992.
Five Degrees and Other Poems, Penguin (New York City), 1995.
Veronica (novel), Dial Press (New York City), 1996.
Somewhere in the Night: Film Noir and the American City, Free Press (New York City), 1997.
The Creation of the Night Sky: Poems, Harcourt (New York City), 1998.
Atomic Field: Two Poems, Harcourt (New York City), 2000.
A Trip to the Stars (novel), Dial Press, 2000.

Work represented in anthologies, including *New York: Poems,* Avon, 1980, *The Morrow Anthology of Younger American Poets,* Morrow, 1985, and *The Grand Street Reader,* Summit, 1986. Contributor to magazines, including *Grand Street, Esquire, Nation, New Republic, New Yorker, New York Review,* and *New York Times Book Review.*

EDITOR

Under Thirty-Five: The New Generation of American Poets, Doubleday (New York City), 1989.

Walk on the Wild Side: Urban American Poetry since 1975, Scribner (New York City), 1994.

WORK IN PROGRESS: Franklin Flyer, a novel, to be published by Dial Press, 2002.

SIDELIGHTS: In his first published collection of poems, *On Tour with Rita,* Nicholas Christopher presents a transcontinental nomad's fleeting glimpses of landscapes ranging from Mexico, Rome, and New Orleans to the Greek Islands. Reading like a series of postcards, according to J. D. McClatchy in *Poetry,* the poems are lucid dreams "in which Rita, the poet's muse and mirror, reflects the life around her." In his attempt to "capture the elusiveness of objects of desire," says Bruce Bennett in *Nation,* Christopher's shimmering, phantasmagorical images provide "little of substance to grasp." Richard Tillinghast in *New York Times Book Review,* however, states that though "one may experience a dizziness and exasperation" with some of the poems, "the wit and panache of passages . . . make reading Mr. Christopher a delight."

A Short History of the Island of Butterflies draws on similar themes and styles as *On Tour with Rita.* Opting again for exotic settings—Italy and the Greek Islands—Christopher "approaches the world with a hedonist's exuberance," says David Wojahn in *New York Times Book Review.* Though Christopher's Byronic tone is "apt to become excessive and grandiloquent," claims Wojahn, "his poems are lushly textured, astutely detailed and above all sensuous," devoid of the "naive sensuality" that marked *On Tour with Rita.* J. P. White, reviewing the book in *Poetry,* notes Christopher's "sensualist's eye for detail" and his "profusion of lush pictorial elements," but prefers the "grittier emotional range" of several of the poems ("Winter Night," "The Partisan," "Losing Altitude," and "Notes at Summer's End") that provide "a welcome relief from the tropical narcosis" of the other works.

In *Desperate Characters,* Christopher alters his previous poetic style and combines it with a novelistic narrative to create what *Virginia Quarterly Review* dubs "an absurdist's detective fiction." The story is summarized by Jane Mendelsohn in *Village Voice:* "The noir victim hangs out. He waits. Before he can say *Maltese Falcon,* people lie to him, the police suspect him, and women, for no apparent reason, fling themselves at him." Robert B. Shaw in *Poetry* comments that the stylized situations knowingly parody the film noir genre to create "a sense of purgatory with no exit and no redemptive purpose." Declaring the urban setting in *Desperate Characters* "vapid" but possessing an "irresistible neon intensity," *New York Times Book Review* critic Andy Brumer says the "punk-rococo imagery" is "a phantasmagorical collage reminiscent of the film *Blade Runner."* Mendelsohn lauds Christopher's "cool melancholy voice" that conveys "a remarkable mix of accessible outrageous humor with subtle psychological insight."

Harriet Zinnes, reviewing the collection of poems *In the Year of the Comet,* in *Washington Post Book World,* notes that Christopher's "language is always accessible, and though his internal structures can be calculating . . . he writes with a contemporary conscience." *Poetry* critic J. D. McClatchy places Christopher in good company when he summarizes that the poet "has a style in which are folded strands of Apollinaire, Frank O'Hara, James Tate, and Nanzia Nunzio." David Baker in *Poetry* further describes Christopher's style as approaching "contemporary neoclassicism" in his use of "erudition to express experience." Renowned poet Anthony Hecht, in *New York Times Book Review,* says, "Mr. Christopher's poetry is not merely extraordinarily good, but seems to me altogether in a class by itself."

In Christopher's 1995 collection, *Five Degrees and Other Poems,* the titular work is actually an interlinked series of thirty-five poems with allegorical elements, all centered in a single night in an imaginary permutation of New York City where the current temperature is five degrees. It explores themes of magic, history, and spiritual transcendence, and features a quirky cast of characters and situations—among them, Harry Houdini as an aviation pioneer who performs magic only as a hobby, Arctic adventurer John Davis, the historian Herodotus, the friendship of painters Van Gogh and Gauguin, the occupation of an Aegean island by the Nazis, the goddess Inanna's descent into the underworld down a flight of slippery, razor-sharp steps, and an angel who, with blue light, writes a man's signature on a black wall. Twenty-five additional, primarily lyrical poems, set in milieus from Bosnia to Vietnam, round out the book. *Booklist* contributor Elizabeth Gunderson says of the title poem: "For the most part, the ambitious sequence succeeds, and Christopher's language is as bewitching as the inhabitants of his fantasized metropolis," and states of all the poems, "Christopher beautifully combines empathy and distance, mystery and exploration." And a *Publishers Weekly* critic deems the title poem "a dense and stunning, often elliptical sequence . . . each [segment] shimmering with immediacy."

Individual interpretations of the structure of Christopher's sixth collection, *The Creation of the Night Sky: Poems,* vary widely from reviewer to reviewer, no doubt due to the poet's nonlinear approach which presents individual pieces which can be recontextualized, puzzle-like, as a cohesive whole, creating and illuminating the experiences of a single night, or be perceived as separate, unrelated units. Some perceive the book as beginning with a number of individual poems and concluding with another lengthy, interlinked poem sequence, "Night Journal: January 1-September 24," which either weaves together the parallel lives of three characters whose physical and psychic paths cross in the passage of a single night, linked by, in the words of a *Publishers Weekly* contributor, "clinical snapshots of an anonymous physician's death." Others see "Night Journal" as a centerpiece to which the other poems, which flow from New York City to Naxos, the Kyi Valley of Tibet, Las Vegas, and, finally, back to New York City, in a rush of fantasy, dream, memory, and simultaneous realities, all relate. The *Publishers Weekly* contributor finds the poems "full of apocalyptic foreboding" and feels that, although "Christopher's noirish manner. . . won't convince everyone[,]. . . fans of his five previous collections . . . will find the mix of deadpan detail and mystical wonder familiar and welcome." Melanie Rehak writes in the *New York Times,* "his poems document a recurring awareness of another world toward which the human spirit is ultimately directed," and finds "Night Journal" to be a "haunting, multifaceted work filled with astonishing, surreal images."

Christopher trades in the lush tropical settings of his poetry for the backdrop of the classical music scene in his first novel, *The Soloist.* Max Randal is a former child prodigy who, at age thirty-three, attempts to revive his stalled career as a concert pianist. Surrounded by all the trappings of his early success—beautiful women, eccentric friends, and excessive luxury—Max seeks solace for his tortured soul by maintaining an arduous rehearsal schedule, hoping to recover his inspiration in time for his Carnegie Hall comeback. Although Christopher Zenowich in *Chicago Tribune* characterizes Max's angst as "self-conscious soul-searching and Byronic posturing," he praises "Christopher's instinct for the power of a good tale [that] overcomes the occasional awkwardness of narration." Laura Kuhn in *Los Angeles Times* calls *The Soloist* "melodramatic . . . in a commonplace way," but asserts that the only serious flaw of this first novel "is . . . perpetuating the notion that the Romantic hero needs to be obsessed." However, "it is not character . . . that provides motive and momentum for 'The Soloist'," says Isa Kapp in the *New York Times Book Review,* "but music."

Veronica, Christopher's second novel, although nominally set in Manhattan, as *New York Times*' contributor David Guy states, it "really unrolls in its author's wild mind." What at first appears to be merely another story about a young man (Leo—named by his mother for her zodiacal sign) who meets a mysterious and enticing woman (the titular Veronica), albeit at the "dragon-point" intersection where Waverly Place crosses Waverly Place, soon develops into a far stranger tale when we learn she is the daughter of a famous magician whose act incorporated time travel. It is a kaleidoscope of odd visions, including a perhaps fatal fall from the top of the Empire State Building, triangular mirrors that peer into other worlds, Tibetan restaurants, Elizabethan England, a Manhattan apartment with an aquarium in which the surrounding room is duplicated down to the single blind fish paralleling the room's sole, blind occupant, and chalk with which one can sketch a ship and then use it to sail off into another dimension. The story is a quest, wherein Leo and Veronica search for her lost father, who disappeared into a rift in time when his act was sabotaged by a villainous rival. Guy finds that "Mr. Christopher has . . . done his homework: on magic, British history, Tibetan mysticism, feng shui. 'Veronica' is a hip, sexy, trendy fantasy novel." Janet St. John, writing in *Booklist,* notes that while there may be perceived similarities to novelist Daphne Du Maurier's "disorienting blurring of time" in *House on the Strand,* the "chess-game strategizing and breathtaking pace" of Catherine Neville's *The Eight,* and the "strongly visual, rhythmic transitions, both jarring and elliptical," found in such films as *Strange Days, Jacob's Ladder* and *Blink,* that "Christopher reconfigures, stretches, and re-envisions such techniques with grace and ingenuity, making this no copycat novel but a fresh and innovative novel for our times." She further praises, "This is an alchemist's fiction . . . creating a novel of great force, a nonstop, exciting page-turner, and more."

A Trip to the Stars begins in 1965, when ten-year-old orphan Loren is kidnaped while celebrating his birthday by visiting a planetarium with Alma Verell, his twenty-year-old adoptive aunt—a classics major in college, and herself an orphan. Loren is taken to meet Junius Samax, his benevolent and wealthy uncle. His uncle transports him to Las Vegas, where he resides in the luxurious Hotel Canopus. Loren learns his true name is Enzo. He lives a privileged life, there, receiving a unique and varied education from his contacts with distinguished scholars visiting Uncle Samax, not only a patron of the arts but a tireless seeker of arcane knowledge. Meanwhile, frantic about Loren's disappearance, Aunt Alma alerts the police; however, their investigation hits a dead end. Alma then flees to New Orleans, assumes the name Mala Revell, and lets herself be bitten by a rare Stellarum spider, whose venom imbues her with psychic ability. These are only some of the initial, convoluted twists and turns of plot. A *Publishers Weekly* reviewer praised, "As background to this intricate narrative, Christopher interweaves erudite details of such subjects as arachnology, vampire lore, quincuxes, architecture, celestial navigation and space exploration, Zuni legends, Greek philosophy—to touch on only a few." In the words of this same *Publishers Weekly* reviewer, "Breathtaking coincidences, magical occurrences, dramatic confrontations, mystical beliefs, the influence of astrological phenomenon and the intriguing confluence of fate and chance are plot elements that bubble like champagne in Christopher's . . . brilliantly labyrinthine new novel."

In *Somewhere in the Night: Film Noir and the American City,* Christopher sets out to prove that film noir, rather than simply being a style, is a Weltanschauung, a "dark mirror reflecting the dark underside of American urban life," an "utterly homegrown modern American form," that "inevitably appears in, and emblematizes, times of deep stress." Christopher's research included viewing over 350 films. In the typical noir formula, Christopher writes, "It is night, always. The hero enters a labyrinth on a quest. He is alone and off balance." The object of this solitary hero's quest "is elusive, often an illusion," and during this quest, he is inevitably joined by a seductive, Circean figure of a woman, "at a critical juncture, when he is most vulnerable," as he descends "downward, into an underworld, on a spiral." Unlike the heroes of earlier mythologies, they rarely return from the quests into this underworld intact—if not destroyed, the hero "is left a burnt-out case." Christopher also explores the symbolic, contextual meaning of the places and objects the hero meets along his way—the cars, telephones, casinos, night clubs, and office buildings.

Michiko Kakutani notes in the *New York Times* that, "Mr. Christopher also argues that film noir mythologized the American city as a kind of modern-day Babylon, a Darwinian jungle where crime pays, and killers, con-men and extortionists prey upon the vulnerable and weak." And Kakutani states, "Such movies turn the labyrinthine streets and office corridors of the city into a metaphor for the psychological mazes their heroes travel in search of self-knowledge, and in doing so, create a potent image of the modern American metropolis as a forbidding (and alluring) den of iniquity and sin. The noir city is a place devoid of the small-town consolation of neighborliness and compassion, a place where misfits and malcontents lead lives of sullen desperation, eager to use whatever means necessary to get their crack at the American dream." Kakatani cautions that "This tendency on Mr. Christopher's part to try to fit a vast array of films into a single schematic formula can warp his reading of individual films." A *Booklist* reviewer finds that "Throughout, Christopher moves fluidly from the films to the real world and back again, ruminating suggestively on the appeal of film noir to psychically wounded postwar Americans and on why the genre is currently enjoying a renaissance." And a *Publishers Weekly* critic lauds, "Christopher writes with the mind of a scholar and the heart of a poet—incisive, metaphorical, illuminating and artful, yet without conceit or grandiosity. This fascinating book will be a treat for film buffs, film professionals and everyone in between."

Christopher told *CA:* "I write daily, whether at home or traveling."

BIOGRAPHICAL/CRITICAL SOURCES:

PERIODICALS

Booklist, April 1, 1994, Donna Seaman, review of *Walk on the Wild Side,* p. 1418; December 15, 1994, Elizabeth Gunderson, review of *Five Degrees and Other Poems,* p. 731; December 15, 1995, Janet St. John, review of *Veronica,* p. 686; March 15, 1997, Bill Ott, review of *Somewhere in the Night,* p. 1218; March 1, 1998, Janet St. John, review of *The Creation of the Night Sky,* p. 1086.

Chicago Tribune, February 9, 1986.

Library Journal, March 15, 1997, Neal Baker, review of *Somewhere in the Night,* p. 65; February 15, 1998, Tim Gavin, review of *The Creation of the Night Sky,* p. 145.

Los Angeles Times, April 3, 1986.

Nation, March 26, 1983; June 13, 1994, Matthew Flamm, review of *Walk on the Wild Side,* p. 839.

New York Times, February 11, 1996, David Guy, review of *Veronica;* March 28, 1997, Michiko Kakutani, "A Nation's Nightmares Hurled onto the Screen"; May 3, 1998, Melanie Rehak, review of *The Creation of the Night Sky;* May 25, 1997, Patricia Ryan, review of *Somewhere in the Night.*

New York Times Book Review, May, 1 1983; April 20, 1986; June 8, 1986; February 11, 1990.

Poetry, December, 1983; December, 1986; August, 1989; November, 1992; December, 1995, Bruce Murphy, review of *Five Degrees and Other Poems,* p. 160.

Publishers Weekly, January 31, 1994, review of *Walk on the Wild Side,* p. 77; February 27, 1995, review of *Five Degrees and Other Poems,* p. 98; November 6, 1995, review of *Veronica,* p. 82; February 17, 1997, review of *Somewhere in the Night,* p. 204; March 30, 1998, review of *The Creation of the Night Sky,* p. 78; December 6, 1999, review of *A Trip to the Stars,* p. 51.

Village Voice, September 27, 1988.

Virginia Quarterly Review, winter, 1989.

Washington Post Book World, February 16, 1992.

* * *

CIORAN, E(mil) M. 1911-1995

PERSONAL: Born April 8, 1911, in Rasinari, Rumania; died of complications from Alzheimer's Disease, June 20, 1995, in Paris, France; son of Emilian (a priest of the Greek Orthodox Church) and Elvira (Comaniciu) Cioran. *Education:* Studied philosophy at the University of Bucharest, 1929-31. *Religion:* Greek Orthodox. *Avocational interests:* Walking, "my only real passion."

CAREER: Author, living in Paris beginning in 1937.

WRITINGS:

Precis de decomposition, Gallimard (Paris), 1949, translation by Richard Howard published as *A Short History of Decay,* Viking (New York City), 1975.

Syllogismes de l'amertume, Gallimard, 1952.

La Tentation d'exister, Gallimard, 1956, translation by Howard published as *Temptation to Exist,* introduction by Susan Sontag, Quadrangle Books (Chicago), 1968.

Joseph de Maistre, Editions du Rocher (Monaco), 1957.

Histoire et utopie, Gallimard, 1960, translation by Howard published as *History and Utopia,* reprinted, University of Chicago Press, 1987.

La Chute dans le temps, Gallimard, 1964, translation by Howard published as *The Fall into Time,* Quadrangle, 1970.

Le Mauvais demiurge, Gallimard, 1969, translation by Howard published as *The New Gods,* Quadrangle, 1974.

De l'inconvenient d'etre ne, Gallimard, 1973, translation by Howard published as *The Trouble with Being Born,* Viking, 1976.

Drawn and Quartered, translated by Howard, Seaver Books, 1983.

Cahiers, 1957-1972 (diaries), Gallimard, 1997.

All Gall Is Divided: Gnomes and Apothegms, translation by Howard, Arcade (New York City), 1999.

SIDELIGHTS: "What is there to know about Emile Cioran?" asked Stephen Mitchelmore in an essay in *Spike* magazine. "He was born in Romania in 1911." Mitchelmore went on to explain how the son of a Greek Orthodox priest eventually "lost his religion," became an insomniac, wandered Paris during World War II, created a series of classic philosophical works, gave up writing later in life, to avoid "slander[ing] the universe" any more, and died in 1995, "a few years after an encounter with an over-excited dog." Finally, said Mitchelmore, "I hope none of this helps."

Cioran, whose works, according to a *Guardian* obituary, were characterized by American novelist William Gass as variations on themes of "alienation, absurdity, boredom, futility, decay, the tyranny of history," belonged to a rarified group of literary artists, an existentialist talent rivaling Freiderich Nietzsche, but far less publicly celebrated. The French-language writer was best known as a writer of aphorisms—short, concise statements—a producer of "dark words" and as "our century's great connoisseur of atrophy, unreason and despair," as a *Kirkus Reviews* critic put it. A survivor of war and exile, Cioran was never one to sugarcoat his feelings. He made his stance on life known through his titles alone: *The Trouble with Being Born; Drawn and Quartered; On the Heights of Despair; A Short History of Decay.* "Inside every citizen nowadays," he wrote, according to a *Publishers Weekly* contributor, "lies a future alien." To hope, Cioran noted, "is to contradict the future."

The philosopher's cynical stance made him a cult figure. Indeed, "in some impossibly erudite television sitcom of the imagination," wrote Albert Mobilio in the *New York Times,* Cioran could be cast as the wacky neighbor, "who bursts through the door and says something like . . . 'Any and all water is the color of drowning.' " To Mitchelmore, Cioran's aphorisms "are unlike the smug, bourgeois exponents of the nineteenth century. They open wounds."

Daniel Stern in *Washington Post Book World* called Cioran "a sort of final philosopher of Western civilization, the creator of a curving pessimism so profound and ironic as to almost meet a serious optimism at the other end of its arc." Richard Gilman wrote in a *New Republic* review of Cioran's "autobiography," the collection of essays titled *Temptation to Exist:* "He has a claim, although he would be the last to do anything to press it and might even think it and might even think it horrifying, to be regarded as among the handful of forceful and original minds writing." His original mind was, according to Stern, "a mind in revolt against mind itself, which best expresses itself in such statements as: 'The only free mind is the one that, pure of all intimacy with beings of objects, plies its own vacuity.' "

More than merely continue "that melancholy parade of European intellectuals in revolt against the intellect," Susan Sontag noted in her introduction to *Temptation to Exist* that Cioran reached toward a total abnegation, at the very roots of aware thought, to deny consciousness itself which he defined as "that nonparticipation in what one is that faculty of not coinciding with anything." Furthermore, he insisted that "to be conscious is to be divided from oneself, is to hate oneself. This hatred seethes at our roots at the same time as it furnishes sap to the Tree of Knowledge." His primary concern in *Temptation to Exist,* as Gilman understood it was with "consciousness as the supreme achievement and value of Western civilization, with the crisis that such celebration has brought about." In addition, Gilman observed these essays, "by the very fact of their having been written, participate in the crisis and bear all the marks of its bitter and ludicrous agony."

"Negation is the mind's first freedom," asserted Cioran. How did he come to affirm such a conclusive emptiness? He began with the classic conflict of the mind-body polarities, but as Gilman pointed out, "he manages to stand on a Platonic base and yet not build the structures one would expect to arise." He was also "a child of Nietzsche," as Stern observed. Although William Gass in the *New York Review of Books* may say "Nietzsche, who made so many of the same observations . . . was altogether wiser," Cioran was, according to Bernard Murchland in *Commonweal,* "proposing a transvaluation of all values that is just as radical as Nietzsche's." Cioran was "not only in revolt against the Enlightenment, with its sterile rationalism," noted Stern, "but against the metaphysical revolution that followed it."

Initially, Cioran called reason "the rust of vitality," while he recognized, too that it was part of man's nature to reason. However, he challenged such a normal function, saying, "We cannot be normal and alive." If he does not accept normal thought as valuable, neither does he welcome abnormal, irrational thought without reservation. In fact he chastised Dostoevsky, Baudelaire, and similar rebel thinkers for their dependence upon abnormal impulses. He despised the way the "malcontents, triflers, and fanatics" have self-consciously shaped their identities in terms of their deviations, thus helping to establish the familiar modern self image that relies on aberrations for its substance. In fact, it was this "manner in which Cioran manages to distinguish necessary abnormality from that which we cultivate as neurotic self-definition," that Gilman felt was "one of the primary sources of his originality."

"Each time I catch myself assigning some importance to things, I incriminate my mind I challenge it and suspect it of some weakness, of some depravity. I try to wrest myself from everything, to raise myself by uprooting myself; in order to become futile, we must sever our roots, must become metaphysically alien," said Cioran, revealing his disgust not only for conscious thought but also for the whole process of "history." He refused to accept the way "history" established habitual ways for us to be conscious of ourselves, as "results" or "products." He said, "History is a monster we have called up against ourselves," and he strove to disassociate himself and his philosophy from this "monster."

Such statements as these might cause *Temptation to Exist* to "become a new cultic text for the alienated," observed Murchland, who added: "The young in particular, at least important numbers of them are reluctant to accept the acquired as valid guides to self-definition." Cioran appeared to be prophetic, particularly for some of the more anarchic demonstrators when he stated: "Everything is virtue that leads us to live against the stream of our civilization, that invites us to compromise and sabotage its progress." However it was a mistake to interpret his philosophy in a political way, because, as Gilman explained, it never comes "to grips directly with political actualities."

Gass described *Temptation to Exist* as "a philosophical romance on modern themes: alienation, absurdity, boredom, futility, decay, the tyranny of history, the vulgarities of change, awareness as agony, reason as disease." Indeed, Stern said, "you will need all the tired old arguments from alienation to crisis theology," but, he added, "they have been transformed by the most subtle of ironic minds into statements that have the compression of poetry and the audacity of cosmic clowning." Cioran went beyond past philosophers who, according to Stern, "were concerned with the absence of usable values: he questions the very use of thought and language with which to couch either the loss of old values or the creation of new ones. Despair? Kid stuff. They treated hopelessness: he breathes it as if it were air." Cioran was "committed with all the force of his intellect to struggle against the irreconcilabilities that the mind by its very nature opens up between men and the world," said Gilman, recognizing that "he embodies the dilemma in its most acute form."

As a Rumanian exile in Paris in 1937, Cioran made the conscious decision to write in French. According to George Woodcock, reviewing *The Fall into Time* for the *New Leader,* "he has become as astonishingly well grafted to the French tradition. . . . France has a long history of philosophers who proceed by self-analysis, psychological explorers who inevitably find, as Cioran remarks, that they 'cannot believe we are free when we are always with ourselves, facing ourselves, the same.' It is the condition of those who have, as the book's title suggests, 'fallen out of time.' For the earlier representatives of this tradition, there was an escape route . . . toward eternity." Woodcock called Cioran "the reverse of an optimist. At times he seems to suggest that hope vanished for humanity with the triumph of literacy. Man's 'capacity to degenerate,' he says, 'is limitless.' Yet one cannot call him a pessimist, for he tells also of the ways man can defy and evade the despoilment that the loss of eternity and the extremity of wisdom have brought upon him. Cioran attacks and probes and criticizes constantly, baring our—or his—shamefulness in its most intimate forms; he cries out against civilization. . . . It is even hard to maintain the label of skeptic that often seems appropriate to Cioran. For there is a difference between the true skeptic and the man who can say, 'I become aware of myself, indeed I am, only when I deny.' "

In the *New York Times Book Review* Peter Caws called Cioran "a brilliant and original exponent of a rare genre, the philosophical essay. . . . We may not think it either desirable or necessary to follow or agree with Cioran," Caws continued. "He tends to overdo his detachment, his style may come to seem too rich. . . . But once read, Cioran cannot fail to provoke reflection; in fact, he insistently demands it. And that . . . is no small service."

Four years after Cioran's death, the aphoristic volume *All Gall Is Divided* was published in English (the work had originally appeared in a French edition in 1952). A *Publishers Weekly* reviewer writing about *All Gall* found that Cioran's lines have "staying power," particularly those covering "his thirst for doubt and his despairing delight in the world's contradictions."

To Mitchelmore, "the violence in Cioran's work, its verbosity and arrogance, results from a struggle with inevitable positivism. The use of aphorism is also born of this. It demands our opposition. The blank following the sentences rises up before us. Our exasperation leaves the same silent space hovering there. This is the placeless heaven or hell Cioran is always returning us to. It is pointless to oppose or argue—or explain."

BIOGRAPHICAL/CRITICAL SOURCES:

BOOKS

Cioran, E. M., *The Temptation to Exist,* introduction by Susan Sontag, translated by Richard Howard, Quadrangle Books (Chicago), 1968, pp. 7-29.

PERIODICALS

Books Abroad, summer, 1970, spring, 1971.
Booklist, October 15, 1995, p. 365.
Commonweal, December 27, 1968, Bernard Murchland, review of *The Temptation to Exist,* pp. 446-447.
Georgia Review, fall, 1969.
Kirkus Reviews, June 1, 1999, p. 848.
National Review, December 25, 1995, Matthew Carolan, review of *Tears and Saints,* p. 58.
New Leader, March 22, 1971, George Woodcock, "Combating Wisdom," pp. 22-23.
New Republic, May 18, 1968, Richard Gilman, "The Revolt against Becoming," pp. 25-27.
New York Review of Books, August 22, 1968, William H. Gass, "The Evil Demiurge," pp. 18-20.
New York Times Book Review, March 14, 1971, Peter Caws, "When Adam Ate the Apple, God Lost His Head," p. 28; October 3, 1999, Albert Mobilio, review of *All Gall Is Divided.*
Publishers Weekly, March 15, 1991, p. 49; May 11, 1992, p. 63; June 21, 1999, review of *All Gall Is Divided,* p. 47.
Tri-Quarterly, winter, 1968.
Washington Post Book World, September 22, 1968, Daniel Stern, "Ironies of a Cosmic Clown," p. 6.

OTHER

E. M. Cioran: To Infinity and Beyond, http://www.spikemagazine.com (March 16, 2000).

OBITUARIES:

PERIODICALS

Guardian, June 23, 1995.

Los Angeles Times, June 22, 1995, p. A24.*

* * *

CLAWSON, James G. 1947-

PERSONAL: Born August 7, 1947, in Pocatello, ID; stepson of Leo R. (in sales construction) and R. Ruth (a medical receptionist) Clawson; son of Gordon Schlafke; married, wife's name Susan K. (a homemaker), April 16, 1977; children: Rudger, Carrie, Caitlin, Suba. *Education:* Stanford University, A.B. (with great distinction), 1971; Brigham Young University, M.B.A., 1973; Harvard University, D.B.A., 1981. *Avocational interests:* Golf, basketball.

ADDRESSES: *Home*—125 Ivy Ridge Rd., Charlottesville, VA 22901. *Office*—Darden School, University of Virginia, Northgrounds, Box 6550, Charlottesville, VA 22906. *E-mail*—jimclawson@virginia.edu.

CAREER: Mormon missionary in Hong Kong and Japan, 1967-69; Wells Fargo Bank, San Francisco, CA, international credit officer, 1973-75; Harvard University, Business School, Boston, MA, assistant professor, 1979-81; University of Virginia, Charlottesville, began as associate professor, became professor, 1981—. International University of Japan, visiting faculty member, 1991.

MEMBER: Academy of Management, Organizational Behavior Teaching Society.

WRITINGS:

Self-Assessment and Career Development, Prentice-Hall (Englewood Cliffs, NJ), 1986, now in 3rd edition.
An MBA's Guide to Self-Assessment and Career Development, Prentice-Hall, 1987.
Level Three Leadership, Prentice-Hall, 1999.

WORK IN PROGRESS: Research on leadership, teaching management, and leadership profiles east and west.

* * *

CLIMO, Shirley 1928-
(Shirley Beistle)

PERSONAL: Born November 25, 1928, in Cleveland, OH; daughter of Morton J. (a paving contractor) and Aldarilla (a writer; maiden name, Shipley) Beistle; married George F. Climo (a corporate historian), June 17, 1950; children: Robert, Susan, Lisa. *Ethnicity:* "Caucasian." *Education:* Attended DePauw University, 1946-49. *Politics:* "Variable." *Religion:* Protestant.

ADDRESSES: *Home*—24821 Prospect Ave., Los Altos, CA 94022.

CAREER: WGAR-Radio, Cleveland, OH, scriptwriter for weekly juvenile series *Fairytale Theatre*, 1949-53; freelance writer, 1976—. Morning Forum of Los Altos, president, 1971-73.

MEMBER: Society of Children's Book Writers and Illustrators, Author's Guild.

AWARDS, HONORS: Parents Choice Award and Pick of the Lists citation, American Booksellers, 1982, for *The Cobweb Christmas;* Storytelling World Award, 1997, for *A Treasury of Mermaids;* books cited as "notable books in the field of social studies" by American Library Association include *King of the Birds, Egyptian Cinderella,* and *Korean Cinderella;* citation for "notable book in the field of science," American Library Association, and Teachers Choice selection, National Association of English Teachers, both for *Someone Saw a Spider;* nominations for state awards in Minnesota, Indiana, Oklahoma, and North Carolina, for *A Month of Seven Days;* nomination for state awards in Georgia and Nevada, for *The Korean Cinderella.*

WRITINGS:

FOR CHILDREN

Piskies, Spriggans, and Other Magical Beings: Tales from the Droll-Teller, Reteller, illustrated by Joyce Audy dos Santos, Crowell (New York City), 1981.
The Cobweb Christmas (picture book), illustrated by Joe Lasker, Crowell, 1982.
Gopher, Tanker, and the Admiral, illustrated by Eileen McKeating, Crowell, 1984.
Someone Saw a Spider, illustrated by Dirk Zimmer, Crowell, 1985.
A Month of Seven Days (historical novel), Crowell, 1987.
King of the Birds (picture book), illustrated by Ruth Heller, Harper (New York City), 1988.
T. J.'s Ghost, Crowell, 1988.
The Egyptian Cinderella (picture book), illustrated by Heller, Crowell, 1989.
City! San Francisco, photographs by George Ancona, Macmillan (New York City), 1990.

City! New York, photographs by Ancona, Macmillan, 1990.

City! Washington, D.C., photographs by Ancona, Macmillan, 1991.

The Match between the Winds, illustrated by Roni Shepherd, Macmillan, 1991.

The Korean Cinderella (picture book), illustrated by Heller, HarperCollins (New York City), 1993.

Stolen Thunder: A Norse Myth, illustrated by Alexander Koshkin, Clarion (New York City), 1994.

Atalanta's Race: A Greek Myth, illustrated by Koshkin, Clarion, 1995.

The Little Red Ant and the Great Big Crumb, illustrated by Francisco X. Mora, Clarion, 1995.

The Irish Cinderlad, HarperCollins, 1996.

(Collector and reteller) *A Treasury of Princesses: Princess Tales from around the World,* illustrated by Ruth Sanderson, HarperCollins, 1996.

(Collector and reteller) *A Treasury of Mermaids: Mermaid Tales from around the World,* illustrated by Jean and Mou-sien Tseng, HarperCollins, 1997.

The Persian Cinderella, HarperCollins, 1999.

Magic and Mischief, Clarion, 1999.

OTHER

(Contributor) Sylvia K. Burack, *Writing and Selling Fillers, Light Verse, and Short Humor,* Writer, Inc. (Boston, MA), 1982.

Contributor to anthologies, including *Explorations,* Houghton (Burlington, MA), 1986; *Family Read-aloud Christmas Treasury,* Little, Brown (Boston, MA), 1989; and *Teacher's Read-aloud Anthology,* McGraw (New York City), 1993. Contributor to magazines, including *Cricket, Family Weekly, Ranger Rick, Seventeen, Short Story International,* and *Writer,* and to newspapers. Some writings appear under the name Shirley Beistle.

WORK IN PROGRESS: Monkey Business, for Holt (New York City); *Tuko the Gecko,* Holt, completion expected in 2001; revising *The Cobweb Christmas,* HarperCollins, 2001; *Pandora and the Giant's Box,* HarperCollins, 2002.

SIDELIGHTS: Shirley Climo told *CA:* "To write children's books always seemed the most wonderful goal in the world to me—and the most natural. My earliest memory is rocking in a creaky wicker porch swing while my mother, a children's author, recited her stories. Long before I could read, I'd begun telling my own tales to anyone willing to listen.

"When I was sixteen, my first magazine story for children was published. Since then, when I wasn't scribbling grocery lists or PTA bulletins, I've completed more than twenty-two books for children and have three more in the works. Although I've written picture books for the 'just-in-school' set, story collections for middle grades, nonfiction, and novels for preteens, I never stray far away from the favorite folk tales of my childhood. Researching folklore fascinates me, and retelling it to entertain today's young people without losing yesterday's flavor is both a pleasure and a challenge.

"Folklorist Andrew Lang once said, 'Nobody can write a new fairytale; you can only mix up and dress the old stories and put characters into new dresses.' For me, playing dress-up is fun at any age."

Climo added: "Recently, comparative folklore has caught my eye—and my ear. By that I mean focusing on a specific subject or theme and seeing how people in different areas dealt with it in their stories. *Someone Saw a Spider,* a collection of arachnid tales from around the globe, launched me in this direction. My four Cinderella retellings—Egyptian, Korean, Irish, and Persian—carried on this interest. *A Treasury of Princesses* looks at diverse royalty from the South Pacific to South America, while *A Treasury of Mermaids* enumerates the world's water people—such as the sirens that Odysseus encountered and the Swiss nixie that convinced a cowherd to join her at the bottom of Lake Zug.

"*Monkey Business,* a work in progress, samples monkey lore in Asia, Africa, and Latin America, and I plan to follow that book with *Birds of a Feather,* a compilation of bird stories. I am also researching a volume of horse stories.

"My recent publication *Magic and Mischief* concentrates on Cornwall and the giants, ghosts, piskies, spriggans, knackers, mer-people, witches (good and bad), fairies, and the nasty little buccas once thought to inhabit that corner of England."

BIOGRAPHICAL/CRITICAL SOURCES:

PERIODICALS

Booklist, November, 1980; May 1, 1993; May 1, 1994; July 1, 1999; August, 1999.

Bulletin of the Center for Children's Books, March, 1986; October, 1987; February, 1988, p. 114; October, 1989, p. 30; June, 1993, p. 311; October, 1999.

Kirkus Reviews, March 15, 1989, pp. 460-461; April 15, 1999; August, 1999.

Los Angeles Times Book Review, March 27, 1988, p. 12.
New York Times Book Review, July 5, 1981; November 12, 1989, p. 50; October 31, 1993, p. 26.
Publishers Weekly, June 7, 1999.
School Library Journal, February, 1981; December, 1985, p. 87; December, 1987, p. 84; August, 1988, p. 79; November, 1989, p. 105; March, 1991; December, 1991; July, 1994; July, 1999.
Tribune Books (Chicago), December 12, 1982.
Writer, June, 1978; December, 1979.

* * *

COLE, Robert 1939-

PERSONAL: Born August 24, 1939, in Harper, KS; son of Charles Edgar (a farmer) and Olive Gertrude (a teacher; maiden name, Columber) Cole; married first wife, Glenda, August 9, 1963 (divorced); married Ilona Jappinen (a professor), September 14, 1990; children: Teresa Cole-Das. *Ethnicity:* "Anglo-American." *Education:* University of Ottawa, B.A., 1961; Kansas State University, M.A., 1967; Claremont Graduate School (now University), Ph.D., 1970. *Politics:* Liberal Democrat. *Religion:* Episcopalian. *Avocational interests:* Skiing, singing, cooking.

ADDRESSES: Home—999 Sumac Dr., Logan UT 84321. *Office*—Department of History, Utah State University, Logan, UT 84322-0710; fax: 435-797-3899. *E-mail*—rcole@hass.usu.edu.

CAREER: Utah State University, Logan, professor of history, 1970—.

MEMBER: North American Conference on British Studies, Western Conference on British Studies (past president).

WRITINGS:

(Editor) *The Dissenting Tradition,* Ohio University Press (Athens), 1975.
A Traveller's History of France, Windrush Press, 1988, 3rd edition, 1994.
Britain and the War of Words in Neutral Europe, 1939-45, Macmillan (New York City), 1990.
A. J. P. Taylor: The Traitor within the Gates, Macmillan, 1993.
A Traveller's History of Paris, Windrush Press, 1994.
Twentieth-Century Political and War Propaganda: An Annotated Bibliography, Scarecrow (Metuchen, NJ), 1995.
(Editor) *The Encyclopedia of Propaganda,* three volumes, M. E. Sharpe (Armonk, NY), 1998.

WORK IN PROGRESS: Research on Anglo-American propaganda in neutral Ireland, 1939-45.

SIDELIGHTS: Robert Cole told *CA:* "Writing has many venues. Mine is historical, for the most part, including a short story 'Water Music,' a tongue-in-cheek version of the first performance of the G. F. Handel composition on a barge in the Thames. Otherwise, I have written serious history and popular history such as the travelers' histories. The serious works are the sort of archive-based monographs that professional historians write as part of their jobs. *France* and *Paris,* on the other hand, were a labor of love—general histories of one of my two favorite countries and cities, which required the integration of enormous amounts of detail into readable and interpretive summaries. *Paris* has been particularly well received, I am happy to say.

"Students are usually perplexed over how to write history. It seems so obvious when they read what a historian has written; how it is done is another matter. The answer is that students must find their own way. What they put on paper has to come from their own perceptions of what they have found and what it means—and, of course, they have to find their own styles. There is, as A. J. P. Taylor once put it, 'no reason why history can't be written so that someone wants to read it.' That is what I have tried to do in my work. If any single historical writer has been my mentor, at least in terms of style, it has been Taylor.

"I started out to be an artist; at least, I majored in art at university. Looking back at what survives of my early efforts, I do not expect the Guggenheim to come knocking at my door. In any case, I was much better at art history than at painting or drawing. Some of this came from my father, who seemed always to see things in the perspective of the passage of time, and who was also an avid reader. A Kansas farmer, he would sometimes arrive late in the fields because he could not tear himself away from a magazine article he had started over breakfast. I inherited his instincts in this regard, and that, together with a preference for historical novels over anything else and the enjoyment of expressing myself on paper, turned me into a professional historian. I have never regretted it for a moment."

CONNELLY, Michael 1956-

PERSONAL: Born in 1956; married. *Education:* Attended University of Florida, Gainesville.

ADDRESSES: *Agent*—Philip G. Spitzer Literary Agency, 50 Talmage Farm Lane, East Hampton, NY 11937.

CAREER: Worked as a newspaper reporter in Florida and for *Los Angeles Times;* became a full-time novelist.

AWARDS, HONORS: Pulitzer Prize finalist for feature writing, (with two other reporters), 1986, for an article in the *Sun-Sentinel* about a major airline crash and its survivors; Edgar Award for best first novel, Mystery Writers of America, 1993, for *The Black Echo.*

WRITINGS:

NOVELS

The Black Echo, Little, Brown (Boston, MA), 1992.
The Black Ice, Little, Brown, 1993.
The Concrete Blonde, Little, Brown, 1994.
The Last Coyote, Little, Brown, 1995.
The Poet, Little, Brown, 1996.
Trunk Music, Little, Brown, 1997.
Blood Work, Little, Brown, 1998.
Angels Flight, Little, Brown, 1999.
Void Moon, large-print edition, Random House (New York City), 1999, Little, Brown, 2000.

A sound recording of *Blood Work,* was issued by Brilliance Corp., 1998, read by Dick Hill.

SIDELIGHTS: "Sheeesh! This guy can write a thriller!" remarked novelist Lucian Truscott IV, reviewing Michael Connelly's sixth novel, *The Poet,* for the *Los Angeles Times Book Review.* Critics have been expressing essentially the same approval ever since Connelly's first novel, *The Black Echo,* came out in 1992. That book, which won the Edgar Award as the best first mystery novel of its year, marked the initial appearance of Connelly's signature detective-hero, Hieronymous "Harry" Bosch of the L.A.P.D.

Bosch, a gloomy man raised as an orphan after having been born to a prostitute, is haunted by his memories of Vietnam, and is possessed of a romantically self-dramatizing but not burnt-out nature. Faced with the apparently drug-related death of an old Marine buddy, he investigates with the help of F.B.I. agent Eleanor Wish, and finds himself involved in an increasingly complicated plot that several reviewers praised for its convolutions and its sociological and psychological details. *People* magazine reviewer Lorenzo Carcaterra called Bosch "the best new protagonist in crime fiction since . . . the late '70s," and hailed the book as "a most impressive first novel." Christine Watson of *Rapport* called it "a mystery to savor." Marilyn Stasio of the *New York Times Book Review* commended *The Black Echo* as "one of those books you read with your knuckles—just hanging on until it's over." A *Publishers Weekly* reviewer adjudged that Connelly had "transcend[ed] the standard L.A. police procedural with this original and eminently authentic first novel."

Many novelists would have been hard-pressed to follow up that kind of success, but Connelly met the challenge with *The Black Ice* the following year. The ice in question is a new drug, a mixture of heroin, crack, and PCP, and one of Bosch's fellow officers has apparently been involved with it to the point of suicide. "Strong and sure," commented a *Publishers Weekly* contributor after reading *The Black Ice;* "This novel establishes him as a writer with a superior talent for storytelling." In *Booklist,* Wes Lukowsky called *The Black Ice* "[a] powerful novel in a series that seems destined for wide popularity," and advised readers, "Plan ahead before you read this buzz saw of a novel. Don't start unless you have the next day off." In the *Los Angeles Times Book Review,* Charles Champlin praised "Connelly's command of police workings and his knowledge of the turf from L.A. south and across the border"; *The Black Ice,* he affirmed, was "a terrific yarn, extending the boundaries of the police procedural in the ingenuity of the plot and the creation of a character."

When Connelly's *The Concrete Blonde* was issued in 1994, Champlin responded, "Connelly joins the top rank of a new generation of crime writers." This novel placed Bosch on trial for having killed a suspected serial killer when the suspect was reaching for a toupee rather than for the presumed pistol. Bosch feels that the man he killed was really the serial killer, but the female district attorney goes after him, seeing police brutality in the case; and while Bosch is on trial, new murder victims crop up, bearing the *modus operandi* of the psychopath Bosch supposedly put out of action. "The new one is a police procedural of crackling authenticity," wrote Champlin. "But it is also a courtroom drama worthy of any of those from the current crop of lawyer-novelists. And finally it is a cunningly conceived mystery in which, in the Agatha Christie tradition, a series of quite convincing suspects are set up and cast aside before the ultimate perpetrator is revealed." The *Chicago Tribune*'s Gary Dretzka called *The Concrete*

Blonde "extremely satisfying." And Stasio, praising Connelly for keeping "a tight grip" on his material, cracked, "Bosch deserves the Kafka medal for holding on to his sanity while stumbling from one nightmare to the other."

In Connelly's 1995 novel, *The Last Coyote,* Bosch investigates, retrospectively, the 1961 death of his mother. Bosch himself is the creature in the title—he sees himself as a wild animal, and has, in his cliffside, earthquake-damaged house, recently had a traumatic confrontation with a real coyote. His search for his mother's killer, a quest Bosch has time for while suspended from the department for pushing a superior through a window, leads him into the upper reaches of local politics. Stasio comments, in regard to Bosch's author, that he "has the tough, taut writing style to see him through his perilous and lonely search for justice." *Booklist*'s Lukowsky said of the novel's plot and setting that it was "heady territory for a cop novel, but Edgar winner Connelly handles it with style and grace."

In *The Poet,* Connelly parted company from Bosch—temporarily—and joined that of crime reporter Jack McEvoy, whose twin brother, a homicide detective, has apparently committed suicide. The brother, however, is in fact the victim of a fiendishly clever serial killer who has dispatched a half-dozen other homicide detectives in various states, and who leaves clues, in the form of quotations from Edgar Allan Poe, at each death site. McEvoy pursues the case for personal and professional reasons, and worms his way into the F.B.I.'s investigation. "The F.B.I. bureaucracy is rendered with an expert eye," commented *Los Angeles Times Book Review* contributor Truscott. Among the suspects is a serial killer named Gladden, who, according to Truscott, "makes Hannibal Lecter look like a child-care worker," but who is not the killer of the cops. Praise for the novel was high. Dick Adler in the *Chicago Tribune* welcomed the change of pace from Bosch, and said, "Each quote from Poe left by the killer cuts to the bone, revealing the true psychosis of the poet and the killer." Stasio, despite finding peripheral aspects of the plot implausible (the romantic subplot, and the ease with which McEvoy joins the investigation), said, "The villain's flamboyant character may be unbelievable, but his methods of killing and eluding detection are infernally ingenious, adding an intellectual charge to the visceral kick of the hunt." Truscott delivered perhaps the ultimate praise, not only saying, "Talent like this is rare and delicious," but adding, "This guy writes commercial fiction so well, he's going to end up on the 'literature' shelves along with Poe if he plays his cards right."

Connelly's 1997 *Trunk Music,* was "his best yet," in the opinion of a *Publishers Weekly* contributor. This one marked a return to Harry Bosch and his Los Angeles turf, after the redoubtable detective's "involuntary stress leave." The plot begins when the body of a would-be Hollywood player is found in the trunk of his Rolls Royce with two bullets in his head then winds through Las Vegas mob connections, F.B.I. and L.A.P.D. machinations, and Hollywood dealmaking before coming to rest on a Hawaiian beach. The obvious overtones of mob executions and money-laundering provided the spark for something more complicated and original; the novelist, said Thomas Gaughan in *Booklist,* "has taken traditional motifs from crime, cop, private-eye, mystery, and noir novels and created a terrific read." Gaughan called *Trunk Music* "one of the year's best entertainments." Stasio also used the word "terrific" to describe the book. *Library Journal* reviewer Rex E. Klett applauded the presence of "clear, crisp prose, intricate plotting, and ever-increasing suspense in yet another masterful procedural."

Blood Work again temporarily parts ways with series protagonist Harry Bosch; this time the story centers on retired FBI agent Terrell "Terry" McCaleb, who had specialized in tracking down Los Angeles-area serial killers while with the Bureau. Suffering from cardiac problems, after an agonizing two-year wait, Terry is finally the lucky recipient of a heart transplant. Terry is under doctor's orders to avoid any stress, particularly such as his anxiety-laden investigations that precipitated his heart problems. He is puttering around on his houseboat in San Pedro's harbor, preparing the boat and himself for a planned trip back to his boyhood home on Catalina Island, when his relaxed life is suddenly thrown into turmoil. The very attractive Graciella Rivers steps aboard his boat and asks him to investigate the murder of her sister, Gloria, which the L.A.P.D. has placed in back-burner status as a convenience-store robbery gone tragically wrong. Terry gives her a flat "no" response, until she drops her bombshell—sister Gloria was the heart donor who, through her selfless gift, saved McCaleb's life. Against doctor's orders, sans license, and with little help from the police, Terry studies the evidence and determines there is a second murder linked to Gloria's. Moreover, he learns there were "souvenirs" taken from both victims, a surprise tip-off he's actually on the trail of a serial killer. In the plot twists that ensue, Terry himself is nearly indicted as the murderer, and an intimate connection between hunter and hunted is revealed.

Booklist contributor Thomas Gaughan found *Blood Work* "solid entertainment but not up to Connelly's last two novels: *The Poet* (1996) and the superb *Trunk Music* (1997)," and stated, "Frankly, many readers will see the shattering truth coming a long time before the sleuth does." A *Publishers Weekly* critic praised *Blood Work* as "a tautly paced, seductively involving thriller. . . . [W]orking with seemingly shopworn material, Connelly produces fresh twists and turns, and, as usual, packs his plot with believable, logical surprises." Rebecca House Stankowski, in *Library Journal,* cites, "High suspense, masterful plotting, and smart prose make this a superior thriller." And Pam Lambert, in *People Weekly,* lauded Connelly for "the sharp eye of the Los Angeles reporter he used to be and the power of the ever-more stylish writer he is becoming with each outing."

With *Angels Flight,* Connelly returns the action to hard-boiled homicide detective Harry Bosch and his L.A.P.D. partners, Jerry Edgar and Kizmin "Kiz" Rider, a female African-American officer. This time they are embroiled in highly sensitive murder investigation that could set the city, still healing from the Rodney King bloodbath, ablaze in its wake—the slaying of a controversial, high-profile black lawyer named Howard Elias, who has built his reputation and fortune suing L.A.P.D. officers for racially motivated police brutality. Elias is shot while in downtown L.A., on the eve of his biggest case yet, while taking a short train ride up a steep hill known as Angels Flight. The logical suspect, of course, could be any one of thousands of L.A. police officers, with particular motivation for one of Elias's numerous L.A.P.D. defendants. His case early on saddled with unwanted "help" from Internal Affairs, the F.B.I., and L.A.P.D.'s independently appointed inspector general, impeded by an obstructive and secretive departmental leadership, personal stress builds for Harry as his year-old marriage begins to dissolve as his wife returns to her former gambling habit, while he tries to quit smoking. The case takes twist upon twist as Harry finds himself deep in racial tension, politics and police corruption—he uncovers signs of evidence tampering by the first police officers to arrive at the crime scene, his ex-partner's apparent links to the crime, the civilian attorney who serves as inspector general is discovered to have been Elias's lover, and, then, the investigation's focus veers to a celebrated child-murder case, tied to wealthy and powerful Internet pedophiles. The denouement sees Harry stepping far beyond the rules and following the moral code of a reckless crusader when he finally uncovers the ugly truth that motivated the killing.

Thomas Gaughan of *Booklist* faulted *Angels Flight* as "Connelly at less than his best," and feared "Bosch fans may feel that the author works too hard to create the tightest rat hole yet." A *Publishers Weekly* contributor found: "the finale, set against riots, delivers a brutal, anti-establishment sort of justice. This isn't Connelly's best ;. . . Bosch seems to be evolving from the true character of early books into a sort of icon, a Dirty Harry for our times." However, Rebecca House Stankowski, writing in *Library Journal,* lauded the book as "another gripping police procedural," and found that *Angels Flight* "explores the underbelly of the human soul with the usual tight prose and swirling plot twists that Connelly's legions of fans have come to expect."

In *Void Moon,* the protagonist is crack burglar and ex-con Cassie Black, who has sustained herself though her six-year prison stretch with dreams of one last big score. Cassie's certainly had a hard-luck life. Her father abandoned her family for the Las Vegas casinos. Max, Cassie's lover, lost his life when plunged from a casino penthouse through a glass ceiling while they were attempting to rob a rich high roller. And, due to a twist of Nevada law, she found herself charged with manslaughter in Max's deadly accident. Now free and trying to go straight while dealing with her tormented past, she eventually succumbs to the temptation of trying to get payback for Max's death while she robs yet another high roller—at the same casino where Max fell to his death. But her intended victim turns out to be a bagman for the Chicago mob who was carrying the 2.5-million-dollar downpayment for the Cleopatra Casino, and Cassie finds herself hunted by Jack Karsh, a highly skilled and techno-savvy private eye in the employment of the casino. Cassie has a secret she will do anything to protect, while the brutal, psychopathic Karsh leaves no witnesses alive. A stolen child is instrumental in their showdown, which results in an unexpected and unabashed tear-jerker of an ending.

A *New York Times Book Review* critic found "Connelly makes shrewd work of the manhunt, cranking up the suspense to keep Cassie a whisker ahead of her pursuer." *Library Journal* contributor Jeff Ayer praised, "Connelly has written his best book to date . . . [a] fastpaced thriller. . . . In astrology, a void moon is considered bad luck, but Connelly's *Void Moon* is better than a four-leaf clover." And Thomas Gaughan and Gilbert Taylor, writing in *Booklist,* found Cassie "a wonderfully engaging character," Jack Karsh a "chilling sicko," "Casino boss Victor Grimaldi is spectacularly reptilian," and "Lesser characters are finely drawn, too." Regarding the details of casinos' security systems and "Cassie's criminal tradecraft," they noted, "Connelly really does his homework." The critics' final assessment wass highly laudatory: "the pacing of this thriller is as good as you'll find in the genre. *Void Moon* offers readers a full house of entertainment."

BIOGRAPHICAL/CRITICAL SOURCES:

PERIODICALS

Booklist, April 1, 1993, p. 1413; June 1 & 15, 1995, p. 1733; October 1, 1996, p. 290; January 1, 1998, Thomas Gaughan, review of *Blood Work,* p. 742, Bill Ott, review of *The Poet,* p. 783; October 15, 1998, Thomas Gaughan, review of *Angels Flight,* p. 371; October 1, 1999, Thomas Gaughan and Gilbert Taylor, review of *Void Moon,* p. 308.

Entertainment Weekly, February 4, 2000, Charles Winecoff, review of *Void Moon,* p. 66.

Library Journal, October 1, 1996, p. 130; March 15, 1998, Rebecca House Stankowski, review of *Blood Work,* p. 91; July, 1998, Joanna M. Burkhardt, review of *Blood Work,* p. 152; November 15, 1998, Rebecca House Stankowski, review of *Angels Flight,* p. 95; March 15, 1999, Michael Adams, review of *Angels Flight,* p. 128; October 15, 1999 Jeff Ayers, review of *Void Moon,* p. 104.

Los Angeles Times Book Review, September 12, 1993, p. 8; July 10, 1994, p. 8; February 18, 1996, p. 4.

Newsweek, April 13, 1998, Malcoln Jones Jr., review of *Blood Work,* p. 77; February 1, 1999, Katrine Ames, review of *Angels Flight,* p. 66.

New York Times Book Review, January 19, 1992, p. 20; June 12, 1994, p. 42; June 18, 1995, p. 31; January 5, 1996, p. 20 January 21, 1996, p. 31; January 09, 2000, review of *Void Moon,* p. 24.

People, February 10, 1992, p. 23.

People Weekly, March 9, 1998, Pam Lambert, review of *Blood Work,* p. 39; February 1, 1999, Pam Lambert, review of *Angels Flight,* p. 41.

Publishers Weekly, May 24, 1993, p. 83; March 22, 1993, p. 68; October 21, 1996, p. 73; February 2, 1998, review of *Blood Work,* p. 80; November 2, 1998, review of *Angels Flight,* p. 73.

Rapport, August-September, 1992, p. 19.

Tribune Books (Chicago), August 7, 1994, p. 7; January 7, 1996, p. 6.

* * *

COOLEY, John Kent 1927-

PERSONAL: Born November 25, 1927, in New York, NY; son of John Landon and Ruth (Robinson) Cooley; married April 2, 1950 (divorced); married second wife, 1970; children: (first marriage) Katherine Anne; (second marriage) Alexander. *Education:* Attended University of Zurich, 1948-49, University of Vienna, 1951-53; Dartmouth College, A.B. (cum laude), 1952; graduate study at New School for Social Research, 1954, and Columbia University, 1964-65.

ADDRESSES: Office—c/o *Christian Science Monitor,* Hotel St. George, Beirut, Lebanon.

CAREER: Began as reporter, 1948; freelance foreign correspondent, 1949-57; civilian clerk, editor, and interpreter with U.S. military groups and Department of State in Austria, 1949-51, 1952-53; personnel clerk for civilian contractor, and editor of weekly newspaper for construction workers on U.S. air base, Ben Guerir, Morocco, 1953; *New York Herald Tribune,* editorial writer, 1954; U.S. Army Engineers (Mediterranean), Nouasseur, Morocco, 1955-57, civilian translator, then intelligence analyst and public information officer; *Christian Science Monitor,* Boston, MA special North Africa correspondent with assignments in other Mediterranean countries, 1958-64, staff correspondent based in Beirut, Lebanon, 1965—. Also freelance correspondent for *New York Herald Tribune* in central Europe, 1949-51, 1952-53, Morocco, 1953, for *Christian Science Monitor,* 1954-58, Radio Press International, 1957-60, *Observer* and Observer Foreign News Service, 1960-64, Canadian Broadcasting Corp., 1961-64, *Newsweek,* 1962-64, and *New York Times,* 1964. *Military service:* U.S. Army, Signal Corps, cryptographer in Vienna, Austria, 1946-47.

MEMBER: Phi Beta Kappa.

AWARDS, HONORS: Foreign correspondent fellowship, Council on Foreign Relations, 1964-65; citations from Overseas Press Club of America, 1967 and 1969, for best interpretive reporting of foreign affairs.

WRITINGS:

Baal, Christ, and Mohammed: Religion and Revolution in North Africa, Holt (New York City), 1965.

East Wind over Africa: Red China's African Offensive, Walker (New York City), 1965.

Green March, Black September: The Story of the Palestinian Arabs, International Scholarly Book Services (Beaverton, OR), 1973.

Libyan Sandstorm, Holt (New York City), 1982.

Payback: America's Long War in the Middle East, foreword by Pierre Salinger, Brassey's (Washington, DC) and Macmillan (Riverside, NJ), 1991.

Unholy Wars: Afghanistan, America, and International Terrorism, Pluto Press (Sterling, VA), 1999.

Contributor to textbooks and encyclopedias; also contributor of articles on current affairs and literature and the arts to *American Abroad* (Paris), *Books Abroad, Commonweal, Musical Courier, Reporter,* and *This Week, Wort und Wahrheit* (Vienna).

WORK IN PROGRESS: A book on the Kurds and Kurdistan.

SIDELIGHTS: Well-travelled journalist John Kent Cooley speaks French, German, Spanish, and Russian, and has reading competence in Arabic, Portuguese, and Italian. His report on Chinese communism in Africa, *East Wind over Africa,* was termed by reviewers to be both objective and valuable. James Kritzeck wrote of *Baal, Christ, and Mohammed:* "For the first time in English, the history of civilization in North Africa is written here, by the distinguished correspondent of *The Christian Science Monitor,* with all the hard coin and delicate vision often missing in historians' work. . . . Mr. Cooley's focus is sharply upon the cultural force of religion . . . such a focus provides us with a uniquely illuminating method of ordering and understanding the masses of unwieldy facts which make up the long, checkered history of that region."

Cooley's theme in *Payback: America's Long War in the Middle East* is that during the critical era from the inception of the Iranian revolution until the present, the United States has been "paid back" for its poor judgment and often disastrous policy errors regarding the Middle East. He places within a logical framework the abductions of Associated Press bureau chief Terry Anderson and the CIA's William Buckley, the hijacking of TWA Flight 847, the attacks on the U.S. Embassy and the Marine barracks in Lebanon, and various other retaliatory acts committed during what Cooley terms "the Khomeini Decade." The book contends that from 1988, at the end of the Iran-Iraq War, until 1990, with Saddam Hussein's invasion of Kuwait, U.S. President George Bush's administration was engaged in "a strange love affair" with Iraq's dictator. This "affair" was finally brought to a violent close with Desert Storm. According to Cooley, the final payback was the dreadful burden of responsibility placed on the Bush administration by the plight of those millions of Kurds forced to flee annihilation by Saddam Hussein's military forces. A *Publishers Weekly* reviewer praises, "The book is essential reading for its authoritative overview of the Middle East and the recent role of the U.S. in the region."

Donald Johnson, writing in *Library Journal,* notes that Cooley refers to his book, *Unholy Wars: Afghanistan, America, and International Terrorism,* as a "narration," and agrees that "indeed it reads more like a conversation than a traditional book." The book provides a detailed investigation of intricately related Middle Eastern events: the 1979 Russian invasion of Afghanistan, the intensive American and Muslim support for the war against the Soviet Union by the mujahedeen's guerrilla forces, and the international consequences, including the unleashing of radical Islamic militarism throughout the entire Muslim world, the flood tide of narcotics from the now-uncontrolled Afghan-Pakistani territory, the criminalization of political structures and regional anarchy prevalent throughout many of the former Soviet Union's new republics, and the creation and proliferation of an international cadre of fanatic Islamic terrorists whose activities continue to impact the United States, now, and into the immediate future. Cooley unfolds an intricately complex tapestry of relationships linked, directly or indirectly, to the Afghan events, and involving a cast of statesmen, businessmen, bankers, sheiks, religious fanatics from various countries, intelligence officers, weapons merchants, international adventurers, terrorists, and drug runners. The book also points out the little-known involvement of China in the Afghan War, and the dangerous impact this had upon its own Muslim populace.

New York Times Book Review critic Graham E. Fuller feels "The book ultimately disappoints. . . . First, Cooley is unable to conceal a powerful bias against anything the C.I.A. touches, and his distaste for the agency infuses nearly every page." And, while admitting "there is much that the C.I.A. can be faulted for," he points out that "one searches for any balance, a few things that maybe went right in American policy . . . but we get none." Fuller further states, "More seriously, Cooley superficially attributes to Washington's 'holy war' in Afghanistan the emergence of most subsequent regional viciousness, ignoring the deep roots of most of these crises. . . . Cooley tends to turn a broad range of diverse regional events into simplistic cause-and-effect relationships." Fuller admonishes, "Cooley furthermore indiscriminately lumps conservative and radical, violent and nonviolent, authoritarian and moderate Islamic movements all into the same the-Muslims-are-coming basket."

While Johnson feels that "this provocative book certainly will provide insight into many events in the Middle East for the general reader," Fuller concludes, "the topic awaits a more thoughtful and balanced treatment than the present effort, which often goes barely beyond journalistic muckraking."

BIOGRAPHICAL/CRITICAL SOURCES:

PERIODICALS

Library Journal, May 1, 1999, Donald Johnson, review of *Unholy Wars,* p. 96.
New York Times Book Review, January 9, 2000, Graham E. Fuller, "Our Own Islamic Radicals," p. 33.
Publishers Weekly, November 15, 1991, review of *Payback,* p. 55.*

* * *

CUSHMAN, Stephen B. 1956-

PERSONAL: Born December 17, 1956, in Norwalk, CT; son of Bigelow P. (a college teacher) and Anne (a librarian; maiden name, Toffey) Cushman; married Sandra Bain (a teacher), June 19, 1982; children: Samuel Bain, Simon Bain. *Education:* Cornell University, B.A., 1978; Yale University, M.A., 1980, M.Phil., 1981, Ph.D., 1982.

ADDRESSES: Home—3650 Lonesome Mountain Rd., Charlottesville, VA 22911. *Office*—Department of English Language and Literature, University of Virginia, Box 400121, Charlottesville, VA 22904-4121.

CAREER: University of Virginia, Charlottesville, assistant professor, 1982-88, associate professor, 1988-94, professor of English, 1994—, Mayo Distinguished Teaching Professor, 1994-97.

MEMBER: William Carlos Williams Society.

AWARDS, HONORS: Fellow of American Council of Learned Societies, 1986-87; Fulbright lecturer in Greece, 1993.

WRITINGS:

William Carlos Williams and the Meanings of Measure, Yale University Press (New Haven, CT), 1985.
Fictions of Form in American Poetry, Princeton University Press (Princeton, NJ), 1993.
Blue Pajamas (poems), Louisiana State University Press (Baton Rouge), 1998.
Bloody Promenade: Reflections on a Civil War Battle, University Press of Virginia (Charlottesville), 1999.

WORK IN PROGRESS: Cussing Lessons, poems.

SIDELIGHTS: Stephen B. Cushman told *CA:* "Since the publication of *Fictions of Form in American Poetry,* I have been concentrating on my own poems. Although there are many poet-critics writing in the United States today, they constitute a relatively small percentage of either poets or critics. For me the writing of poetry complements other kinds of writing, and I would feel incomplete if I had to stick to only verse or prose. Meanwhile, after two books about the formal aspects of poetry, my research has shifted to the study of narrative representations of the American Civil War, both in verse and prose, fiction and nonfiction. In particular, I am especially interested in the various kinds of memoirs that leaders on both sides felt compelled to write after the war. In the near future, I will be exploring this genre, as well as its relation to later narratives of the war."

BIOGRAPHICAL/CRITICAL SOURCES:

PERIODICALS

American Literature, May, 1986.
Choice, March, 1994.
Chronicle of Higher Education, November 12, 1999.
Journal of Modern Literature, November, 1986.
Times Literary Supplement, June, 1994.
Virginia Quarterly Review, spring, 1986.

* * *

CUSSLER, Clive (Eric) 1931-

PERSONAL: Born July 15, 1931, in Aurora, IL; son of Eric E. and Amy (Hunnewell) Cussler; married Barbara Knight, August 28, 1955; children: Teri, Dirk, Dana. *Education:* Attended Pasadena City College, 1949-50, and Orange Coast College, California. *Politics:* Nonpartisan. *Religion:* None. *Avocational interests:* Collecting automobiles, searching for historic shipwrecks.

ADDRESSES: Home—Telluride, CO, and Paradise Valley, AZ. *Agent*—Peter Lampack, The Lampack Agency, 551 Fifth Ave., New York, NY 10017.

CAREER: Bestgen & Cussler Advertising, Newport Beach, CA, owner, 1961-65; Darcy Advertising, Hollywood, CA, creative director, 1965-68; Mefford, Wolff and Weir Advertising, Denver, CO, vice president and creative director of broadcast, 1970-75; Aquatic Marine Dive Equipment, Newport Beach, CA, member of sales staff; National Underwater & Marine Agency, founder

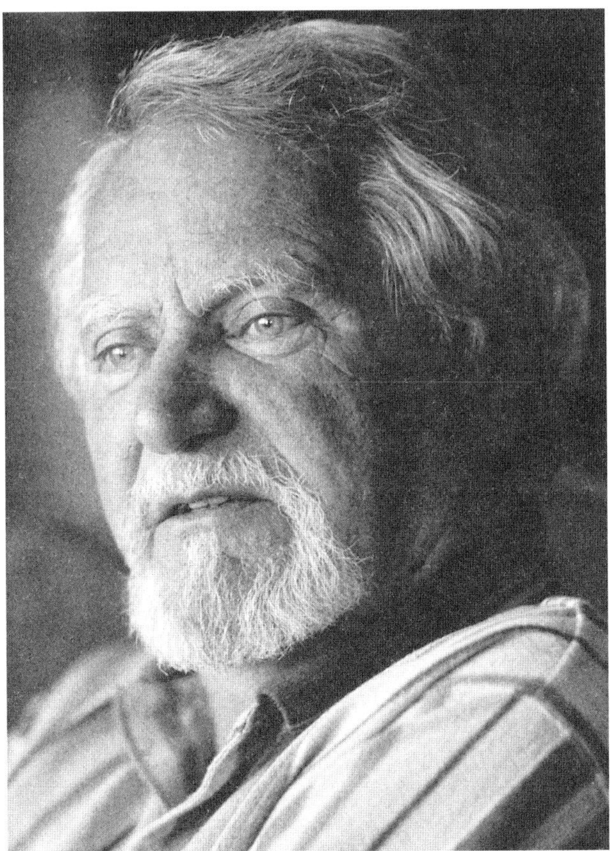

Clive Cussler

and chair. Discoverer of more than sixty shipwrecks. Has worked for a supermarket and a gas station. *Military service:* U.S. Air Force, 1950-54; served as aircraft mechanic, became sergeant.

MEMBER: National Society of Oceanographers (fellow), Classic Car Club of America, Royal Geographic Society (London; fellow), Explorers Club of New York (fellow).

AWARDS, HONORS: Ford Foundation Consumer Award, 1965-66, for best promotional campaign; first prize, Chicago Film Festival, 1966, for best thirty-second live action commercial; International Broadcasting Awards, 1964, 1965, 1966, 1972, 1973, for year's best radio and TV commercials; first place award, Venice Film Festival, 1972, for sixty-second live commercial; Clio Awards, 1972, 1973, 1974, for TV and radio commercials; Lowell Thomas Award, Explorers Club of New York, for underwater exploration; numerous honors for work in shipwreck discoveries and marine archaeology.

WRITINGS:

"DIRK PITT" ADVENTURE NOVELS

The Mediterranean Caper, Pyramid Publications (New York City), 1973, published as *May Day.*
Iceberg, Dodd, Mead (New York City), 1975.
Raise the Titanic, Viking (New York City), 1976.
Vixen 03, Viking, 1978.
Night Probe, illustrations by Errol Beauchamp, Bantam (New York City), 1981.
Pacific Vortex!, Bantam, 1983.
Deep Six, Simon & Schuster (New York City), 1984.
Cyclops, Simon & Schuster, 1986.
Treasure, Simon & Schuster, 1988.
Dragon, Simon & Schuster, 1990.
Sahara, Simon & Schuster, 1992.
Inca Gold, Simon & Schuster, 1994.
Shock Wave, Simon & Schuster, 1996.
(With Craig Dirgo) *The Sea Hunters,* Simon & Schuster, 1996.
Flood Tide, Simon and Schuster (New York City), 1997.
Atlantis Found, Putnam (New York City), 1999.

OTHER NOVELS

(With Paul Kemprecos) *Serpent: A Novel from the NUMA Files,* Wheeler (Rockland, MA), 1999.
(With Paul Kemprecos) *Blue Gold: A Novel from the NUMA Files,* Pocket Books (New York City), 2000.

OTHER

Clive Cussler and Dirk Pitt Revealed, Pocket Books, 1998.

ADAPTATIONS: Raise the Titanic, based on Cussler's novel and starring Jason Robards and Richard Jordan as Dirk Pitt, was released by Associated Film Distribution in 1980; Cussler's books are available on audiotape.

SIDELIGHTS: Clive Cussler earned his living writing award-winning advertising copy until the success of his underwater adventure novels featuring his hero, Dirk Pitt, enabled him to leave the business world and pursue his writing interests full-time. Since then, his adventure tales have sold over seventy million copies in more than forty languages and a hundred countries. Some sources cite the best-selling author as having more than ninety million fans, a number of which eagerly attend his book-signings and ask for his "famous" "personalized inscription[s]," informed Daisy Maryless in a 1999 *Publishers Weekly* article recognizing the remarkable initial demand for Cussler's fifteenth Dirk Pitt novel, *Atlantis Found.* In a *People Weekly* review of that book, J. D. Reed described Cussler's writing, deciding that it has two-dimensional characters, predictable story-lines, and "dialogue as sticky as Mississippi mud." "Still," qualified Reed, "we can't put down a Cussler Opus." Noting that Cussler "typically [exerts a] make-no-apologies enthusiasm," a *Publishers Weekly* critic declared: "For muscle-flexing, flag-waving, belief-suspending fare, [Cussler] has no equal." The *Publishers Weekly* critic's review specifically referred to *Atlantis Found* as "another wickedly engrossing yet predictably scripted tale of bravery against all odds."

"'There are many things I'd rather be doing than writing a book,' " Cussler once said, according to Rebecca Ascher-Walsh in a 1997 *Entertainment Weekly* article. Acquiring cars and discovering ship wrecks are among his passions. Cussler has built a premier collection of over eighty-five classic and vintage automobiles. From European classic body styles to American town cars to 1950s convertibles, they are all carefully restored by Cussler and his crew of experts to concours d'elegance condition.

Cussler almost lives the same sort of adventurous life as his best-selling protagonist, Dirk Pitt: tramping the Southwest deserts and mountains in search of lost gold mines and ghost towns, as well as funding and leading more than thirty expeditions in search of lost ships and aircraft. Cussler and his team of NUMA scientists and engineers (his fictional National Underwater and Marine Agency became a reality) have discovered and surveyed nearly seventy historically significant shipwrecks around the world, including the long-lost Confederate submarine *Hunley,* the German submarine *U-20* which sank the *Lusitania,* the famous Confederate raider *Florida,* the Navy dirigible *Akron* which crashed at sea during a storm in 1933, and the troop transport *Leopoldville* which was torpedoed on Christmas Eve of 1944 off the coast of Cherbourg, France, killing over eight hundred American soldiers. Cussler has donated all of his recovered artifacts from the archaeological sites to museums and universities.

Cussler's chosen genre, his avocations, and even his entry into publishing reveal his willingness to take risks. Almost thirty years ago, after his first manuscript received numerous rejections, the author created a clever ploy to promote his second work: he printed up stationery with the name of a fabricated West Coast literary agent and used it to send recommendations for his books to major New York agencies. Within a month he had a contract, and has remained with the same agent, Peter Lampack, ever since. After *Flood Tide,* his fourteenth Dirk Pitt adventure, however, he split with his long-time publisher Simon & Schuster. The Phoenix, Arizona *Business Journal* reported that he left his former publisher in hopes of getting more respect through his new contract with G. P. Putnam & Sons: "Cussler would joke that Simon & Schuster executives lavished their attention on Mary Higgins Clark. . . . Cussler said. 'I get less respect than Rodney Dangerfield.' "

Cussler's widely read "Dirk Pitt" novels relate the adventures of a handsome, witty, courageous, devil-may-care character who, like his creator, collects classic cars and searches for lost ships. *Armchair Detective* reviewer Ronald C. Miller offered this description: "Dirk Pitt has the archeological background of Indiana Jones and the boldness of James Bond. He is as skilled and comfortable underwater as Jacques Cousteau, and, like Chuck Yeager, he can fly anything with wings." Yet Pitt is far from superhuman, Chicago's *Tribune Books* contributor David E. Jones observed: "Cussler has created a caring, cared-about, flesh and blood human being" who takes wrong turns and suffers from lapses in judgment, but who "also thinks faster on his feet than most and has an uncanny ability to turn negative situations into positive ones." This combination has proved to be tremendously appealing to readers, even though reviewers have often faulted Cussler's writing style and his improbable storylines. *New York Times Book Review* critic Newgate Callendar cited Cussler as "the cliche expert nonpareil" in a review of *Raise the Titanic* and asserted that "Cussler has revived the cliche and batters his reader with choice specimens: 'the cold touch of fear'; 'a set look of determination in the deep green eyes'; 'before death swept over him'; 'narrow brush with death.' " *Best Sellers* contributor Ralph A. Sperry dismissed the author's prose in *Cyclops* as "the prosaic in the service of the implausible."

Cussler also shrugs off negative responses to his work. "Because I was locked in for eighteen years writing the short, snappy ad copy, I could never sit down and write a Fitzgerald-Hemingway-Bellow-type Great American Novel," he once told *CA*. "But [that experience] did prepare me to write easy, understandable prose, and also to look at writing and publishing from a marketing angle."

Cussler once recalled to *CA* that at the beginning of his writing career, "blood and guts adventure" was not universally accepted in the publishing field. Initially he was told that his adventures would never sell and that critical opinion was against him, but these views have softened with the growth of the author's popular appeal. When Cussler complained to his agent, Peter Lampack, about negative reviews, Lampack, Cussler said, "came back with a classic statement: 'Listen, when we start getting good literary reviews, we're in big trouble.' "

While early reviews of Cussler may have been dismissive, reviews of his later works have recognized his stories as full of action, fun to read, and extremely popular, while nonetheless pointing out the incredibility of his plots. Discussing *Dragon,* the author's 1990 release, *Publishers Weekly* critic Sybil Steinberg admitted that although the storyline was "improbable," Cussler had still come up with "a page-turning romp that achieves a level of fast-paced action and derring-do that . . . practitioners of modern pulp fiction might well envy." Peter L. Robertson, in his *Tribune Books* review of *Treasure,* placed Cussler's stories "in the tradition of Ian Fleming's James Bond," and added, "Cussler has developed and patented a vibrant, rollicking narrative style that seldom shows signs of relenting." *Inca Gold,* which finds Pitt in the Amazonian jungles on a quest to thwart a group of smugglers, is "pure escapist adventure,with a wry touch of humor and a certain self-referential glee (Cussler himself makes a cameo appearance)," a *Publishers Weekly* reviewer noted, "but the entertainment value meets the gold standard." *Booklist* reviewer Joe Collins noted that the author's fans "are already familiar with his gift for hyperbole," and recommended that new readers take Cussler's "breathless approach with a grain of salt and just relax and enjoy the adventures of Pitt and company" in *Inca Gold.*

In 1997's *Flood Tide* Pitt's vacation plans go by the way side as he uncovers a Chinese immigrant smuggling ring in waters near Seattle—an operation that is linked, through it's leader, Qin Shang, to an attempt to cause "ecological and economic destruction from New Orleans to eastern Texas," related a *Publishers Weekly* reviewer that also noted Cussler leveraged "right-winged fears of a flood tide of nonwhite immigrants." The *Publishers Weekly* reviewer, as well as many other critics, determined that *Flood Tide* will please Cussler's fans. As Gilbert Taylor concluded in *Booklist,* "This bombastically scripted tale will satisfy Cussler faithfuls." The story is "[p]acked with meticulous research and wonderfully quirky characters," remarked *People Weekly* contributor Cynthia Sanz, judging *Flood Tide* to be "as fun as it is formulaic." "*Cussler's* story is entertaining, but suspending disbelief may be a problem," asserted Ray Vignovich in a *Library Journal* assessment of a sound recording of the novel.

In an interview with Connie Lauerman in the *Chicago Tribune,* Cussler reflected on his work. "I look upon myself more as an entertainer than merely a writer. It's my job to entertain the reader in such a manner that he or she feels that they received their money's worth when they reach *the end* of the book." Cussler also considers the impact of his books on children. "I have quite a large following of young people," he once told *CA.* "That's why I don't believe in using four-letter words, and any sex is simply alluded to, never detailed. I've had letters from kids as young as eight who enjoy Pitt and his adventures. And because I try to write my stories in a simple, forward manner, I'm especially pleased by letters from mothers and school teachers, who tell me their children and students had refused to read before they were given one of my books. Now they read everything in sight and are hooked on reading."

Cussler found that his readers enjoy the pictures of Pitt's cars included on the backs of his book jackets. *Clive Cussler and Dirk Pitt Revealed* provides a guide to the world of Pitt, including summaries of each novel of the Dirk Pitt series as well as details on weapons, vehicles, and locations from the writings. Cussler also once told *CA* that he takes great fun in his cameo appearances. He and Pitt always meet up, with Cussler often supplying his hero with vital information before sending him on his way to subdue the villains. While his stories may seem tailor-made for Hollywood, Cussler emphasized that he refuses to sell them for adaptation until he can be assured of a quality production.

Asked how he comes up with his intricate plots, the author once told *CA:* "First comes the overall concept. This is, of course, the old cut-and-dried, time-tested *What-if.* What if, for example, they raise the *Titanic*? In *Night Probe,* what if Canada and the United States became one country? I also use a prologue that describes something in the past that sets up the plots in the present. Then I end with an epilogue that sews all the corners together. My plots are pretty convoluted; I usually juggle one main plot and as many as four subplots. Then the trick is to thread the needle in the end and give the readers a satisfying conclusion." Cussler has continually succeeded in giving readers a plot to escape in—even with his fifteenth "Dirk Pitt" adventure, published in 1999, twenty-three years after the series debut. Of *Atlantis Found,* Ronnie H. Terpening proclaimed in *Library Journal:* "Brilliantly conceived and boldly plotted. . . . his most imaginative yet. . . . [A] fascinating story . . . backed by meticulous research."

In the same year that *Atlantis Found* was released, Cussler introduced new protagonists in the first of a projected series. A collaboration with Paul Kemprecos, *Serpent: A Novel from the NUMA Files* tells of the adventures of Kurt Austin and his NUMA colleague Joe Zavala. A *Publishers Weekly* reviewer described the duo as "two young bucks without the seasoning and panache of Pitt but worthy successors, nonetheless." The co-authors used "the 1956 sinking of the Andrea Doria as the springboard for [this] thriller," stated Roland Green in *Booklist.* In *Serpent,* Austin and Zavala "are trying to find out why top archeologists are being killed, some of them butchered, at dig sites," recounted the writer for *Publishers Weekly* who judged the novel to be "great fun, if not a little top-heavy at times from flabby subplots and excessive detail." The story contains Cussler's "trademarks," reassured Green, predicting that the novel will "prove eminently satisfactory to Cussler fans."

BIOGRAPHICAL/CRITICAL SOURCES:

PERIODICALS

Americana, September-October, 1987, p. 10.

Armchair Detective, fall, 1994, p. 496.

Best Sellers, August, 1981; May, 1986.

Booklist, April 1, 1992, p. 1411; April 1, 1994, p. 1404; December 15, 1995, p. 667; August, 1997, p. 1846; June 1, 1999, p. 1741; November 15, 1999, p. 579.

Books and Bookmen, May, 1984.

Business Journal (Phoenix), December, 1999, p. 8.

Chicago Tribune, February 10, 1980; August 13, 1984.

Critic, summer, 1977.

Denver Business Journal, May 27, 1994, p.14A.

Entertainment Weekly, October 17, 1997, p. 66.

Far Eastern Economic Review, December 18, 1997, p. 47.

Globe and Mail (Toronto), August 10, 1985.

Inside Books, November, 1988, pp. 31-34.

Library Journal, July, 1981, p. 1442; June 1, 1984, p. 1144; October 15, 1990, p. 116; November 1, 1990, p. 139; April 15, 1994, p. 111; April 1, 1995, p. 142; February 1, 1996, p. 97; September 1, 1996, p. 229; November 1, 1997, p. 130; November 15, 1999, p. 97.

Los Angeles Magazine, September, 1990, p. 183; September, 1981, p. 259.

Los Angeles Times, June 21, 1979; September 25, 1981; March 21, 1986.

Los Angeles Times Book Review, August 5, 1984; March 20, 1988.

New Choices for the Best Years, March, 1991, p. 58.

New Yorker, June 27, 1994, p. 87.

New York Times Book Review, December 19, 1976; September 25, 1977; October 18, 1981, p. 46; February 16, 1986, p. 16; May 29, 1988, p. 14; June 17, 1990, p. 19; May 22, 1994, p. 39; January 21, 1996, p. 21.

People Weekly, July 2, 1984, p. 61; July 27, 1992, p. 25; September 21, 1992, p. 93; December 16, 1996, p. 36; November 10, 1997, p. 41; March 20, 2000, p. 47.

Playboy, April, 1986, p. 32.

Publishers Weekly, August 23, 1976; June 12, 1981, p. 46; February 26, 1982, p. 146; November 12, 1982, p. 64; April 13, 1984, p. 50; August 31, 1984, p. 312; January 3, 1986, p. 41; January 15, 1988, p. 69; March 18, 1988, p. 71; September 2, 1988, p. 71; May 4, 1990, p. 51; July 6, 1990, p. 46; April 13, 1992, p. 40; August 3, 1992, p. 26; March 28, 1994, p. 80; July 11, 1994, p. 58; September 19, 1994, p. 11; October 9, 1995, p. 18; December 18, 1995, p. 42; May 20, 1996, p. 37; August 26, 1996, p. 87; August 25, 1997, p. 46; March 16, 1998, p. 10; September 28, 1998, p. 20; March 1, 1999, p. 14; May 31, 1999, p. 65; November 22, 1999, p. 44; December 20, 1999, p. 17.

School Library Journal, October 1981, p. 160; October, 1990, p. 150; March, 1997, p. 217; December, 1997, p. 150; April, 1999, p. 130.

Skin Diver, November, 1984, p. 20; May, 1987, p. 151.

Tribune Books (Chicago), March 20, 1988; June 21, 1992, p. 6; May 22, 1994, p. 6.

U.S. News & World Report, August 27, 1984, p. 45.

Washington Post, October 24, 1978; August 10, 1981; June 22, 1984; April 11, 1988.

Washington Post Book World, March 2, 1986; June 7, 1992, p. 8.

Writer, September, 1996, p. 15.

Writer's Digest, April, 1988, p. 31.*

D-E

DANIELS, James R(aymond) 1956-
(Jim Daniels)

PERSONAL: Born June 6, 1956, in Detroit, MI; son of Raymond J. and Mary T. (Rivard) Daniels; married Kristin Kovacic, September 28, 1985; children: Ramsey, Rosalie. *Education:* Alma College, B.A. (with honors), 1978; Bowling Green State University, M.F.A., 1980.

ADDRESSES: Home—3419 Parkview Ave., Pittsburgh, PA 15213. *Office*—Department of English, Carnegie-Mellon University, Pittsburgh, PA 15213; fax: 412-268-7989. *E-mail*—jd6s@andrew.cmu.edu.

CAREER: Bowling Green State University, Bowling Green, OH, lecturer in English, 1980-81; Carnegie-Mellon University, Pittsburgh, PA, visiting writer-in-residence, 1981-84, assistant professor, 1984-86, associate professor, 1986-94, professor of English, 1995—. Judge of poetry competitions; gives readings at schools, libraries, and on National Public Radio.

AWARDS, HONORS: Winner of Signpost Press chapbook contest, 1980, for *On the Line;* first prize from *Passages North* poetry contest, 1983, for "My Father Worked Late"; fellow of National Endowment for the Arts, 1985; Wisconsin/Brittingham Prize for Poetry from University of Wisconsin Press, 1985, for *Places/ Everyone;* literature fellowships from Pennsylvania Council on the Arts, 1987 and 1990.

WRITINGS:

UNDER NAME JIM DANIELS

Factory Poems (chapbook), Jack-in-the-Box Press, 1979.

On the Line (chapbook), Signpost Press (Menomonee Falls, WI), 1981.

Places/Everyone (poems), University of Wisconsin Press (Madison), 1985.

The Long Ball (chapbook), Pig-in-a-Poke Press, 1988.

Digger's Territory (chapbook), Adastra Press (Easthampton, MA), 1989.

Punching Out (poems), Wayne State University Press (Detroit, MI), 1990.

Hacking It (chapbook), Ridgeway Press (St. Clair Shores, MI), 1992.

M-80 (poems), University of Pittsburgh Press (Pittsburgh, PA), 1993.

(Co-editor) *The Carnegie-Mellon Anthology of Poetry,* Carnegie-Mellon University Press (Pittsburgh), 1993.

Niagara Falls (chapbook), Adastra Press, 1994.

No Pets (screenplay), Braddock Films, 1994.

(Editor) *Letters to America: Contemporary Poetry on Race,* Wayne State University Press, 1995.

Blessing the House (poems), University of Pittsburgh Press, 1997.

No Pets (stories), Bottom Dog Press, 1999.

Blue Jesus (poems), Carnegie-Mellon University Press, 2000.

(Co-editor) *American Poetry: The Next Generation,* Carnegie-Mellon University Press, 2000.

Contributor of poems and stories to magazines, including *Paris Review, Cimarron Review, Iowa Review, Gettysburg Review, Kenyon Review,* and *Prairie Schooner.*

WORK IN PROGRESS: New poems, stories, and essays.

SIDELIGHTS: James R. Daniels once told *CA:* "Much of my poetry has focused on blue-collar life in my native Detroit. I feel that there is little poetry being written about the world I come from and the people I care about. I try to give a voice to those who are often shut out of poetry, to explore their lives both in and out of the workplace. If nothing else, I'm trying to say that these people are important, that their lives have value and meaning."

* * *

DANIELS, Jim
See DANIELS, James R(aymond)

* * *

DAY, Dianne 1938-
(Diana Bane, Madelyn Saunders: pseudonyms)

PERSONAL: Born July 5, 1938, in Greenville, MS; daughter of Herman and Anita (a social worker; maiden name, Sanders) Day; married Christopher Brookhouse (a professor and writer; divorced); children: Stephen Christopher, Nathaniel. *Education:* Stanford University, A.B. (English, with honors), 1959; graduate study at University of North Carolina at Chapel Hill, 1968-75, 1980; Lone Mountain College, M.A., 1975; Duke University, certificate in health administration, 1980; studied psychology at Tufts University.

ADDRESSES: *Agent*—Harvey Klinger, 301 West 53rd St., New York, NY 10019. *E-mail*—dianneday@aol.com.

CAREER: Alamauer Mental Health Center, Burlington, NC, psychologist, 1975-76; North Carolina Memorial Hospital, Chapel Hill, administrator, 1976-82; Carol Woods Health Center, Chapel Hill, administrator, 1982-84; writer and secretary, 1984—.

AWARDS, HONORS: Macavity Award, best first mystery, 1995, for *The Strange Files of Fremont Jones.*

WRITINGS:

NOVELS

Obsidian, Pocket Books (New York City), 1987.
The Stone House, Pocket Books, 1989.

FREMONT JONES MYSTERIES; PUBLISHED BY DOUBLEDAY (NEW YORK CITY)

The Strange Files of Fremont Jones, 1995.
Fire and Fog, 1996.
The Bohemian Murders, 1997.
Emperor Norton's Ghost, 1998.
Death Train to Boston, 1999.
Beacon Street Mourning, 2000.

UNDER PSEUDONYM MADELYN SAUNDERS; ROMANTIC SUSPENSE NOVELS

Author of *Under Venice, Sarabande, Darkness at Cottonwood Hall,* and *Laird's Mount,* all for Harlequin Intrigue.

UNDER PSEUDONYM DIANA BANE

Author of *Eyes of Night,* Berkley, *Jove,* and *Lovers of the Golden Drum.*

WORK IN PROGRESS: An historical thriller.

SIDELIGHTS: Novelist Dianne Day's "Fremont Jones" mysteries are set in northern California in the first decade of the twentieth century. "Independent, unconventional, curious, and intelligent—that's amateur sleuth Fremont Jones. . . . [She] is the epitome of the strong-minded, ahead-of-her-time woman," states Emily Melton in *Booklist.*

In the first novel of the series, *The Strange Files of Fremont Jones,* Carolyn Fremont Jones is introduced as a Wellesley-educated young woman from a conservative Boston background. Jones soon drops her first name and moves to San Francisco to start her own business, a typing service. When one of her clients, the venerable Li Wong, turns up dead, and another, horror writer Edgar Allan Partridge, disappears, Jones becomes suspicious of one of the other tenants in her rooming house, Michael Archer, whom she also thinks is a spy. Archer is innocent, and eventually emerges as Jones' romantic interest and cohort in sleuthing, both here and in subsequent books in the series. A *Publishers Weekly* reviewer notes: "While the plot plays out credibly, Day shines brightest at horror writing: the excerpts from Partridge's stories are truly frightening."

Fire and Fog, the second Fremont Jones entry, is set against the drama of the 1906 San Francisco earthquake. In the immediate aftermath of the quake, Jones volunteers as a Red Cross nurse. Meanwhile, she has discovered a secret cache of samurai swords in the

walls of her office. Michael Archer is once again on hand, to loan Jones his automobile, and, when a double murder takes place, to help her solve the crime. Melton describes *The Bohemian Murders* as "a complex mystery . . . [h]umorous, cleverly plotted, and thoroughly engaging." A reviewer from *Publishers Weekly* remarks: "The strong-willed, intelligent Jones shines, whether she's helping her friend, fending off suitors or fleeing the clutches of ninja smugglers."

In *The Bohemian Murders* the action moves south along the California coast to the artist colony of Carmel where Jones has taken a job as a lighthouse keeper. Much to her consternation, Archer has also moved to Carmel, where he is living under an alias with a new lover. After the body of an unidentified woman in a red dress washes up on shore, Jones' investigation leads her through the world of bohemian artists to a mysterious land speculator. She not only discovers the woman's identity and solves her murder, but also uncovers the secret to Archer's transformation. "Mysteries of the heart," a *Publishers Weekly* reviewer comments, "feature large in the latest adventures of an outspoken heroine whose assured demeanor sometimes masks a pleasantly vulnerable interior."

Returning to San Francisco in *Emperor Norton's Ghost,* Jones and Archer start their own detective agency. The plot revolves around the deaths of two well-known mediums. The book provides a portrait of San Francisco in the course of rebuilding after the earthquake. It also sports a host of subsidiary characters, including the supposed ghost of the famous San Francisco eccentric Emperor Norton. Cyndy Burt of *The Book Report* finds "a great deal of humor as well as mystery" in *Emperor Norton's Ghost.* "There are nuggets of San Francisco history buried in the stories of Fremont's wanderings," comments Burt, "and her tour of San Francisco's exclusive clubs—disguised as a young man—is especially entertaining." A *Publishers Weekly* reviewer feels that the success of the Fremont Jones mysteries can be attributed to "[t]he interplay between the two principals and Day's superior handling of period detail and supporting characters."

The sleuthing couple's detective agency is hired by the Southern Pacific Railroad to discover the identities of vandals in *Death Train to Boston* (1999). The vandals eventually destroy a bridge in use by a train on which Jones and Archer are passengers, causing many deaths. Jones is taken in by a local Mormon and Archer tries to locate her. Rex. E. Klett for *Library Journal* calls the work "great story-telling." A reviewer for *Publishers Weekly* describes the story as "swift and upbeat," noting that the immediate mystery is less important because "the ongoing adventures of the sharply defined and appealing cast of characters carry the lively story."

Day once told *CA:* "I write intentionally to entertain; my goal is to take the reader with me into another world for awhile. I believe my books are well-written, even if they are 'only' entertainment, and I hope they teach a little bit while they entertain."

BIOGRAPHICAL/CRITICAL SOURCES:

PERIODICALS

Book Report, August 30, 1998.

Booklist, April 1, 1995, p. 1380; July, 1996, p. 1807; July 1997, p. 180; May 1, 2000, Grace Anne A. DeCandido, review of *Death Train to Boston,* p. 1599.

Library Journal, July, 1997, p. 131; October 1, 1999, Rex E. Klett, review of *Death Train to Boston,* p. 138.

New York Times Book Review, September 19, 1999, Marilyn Stasio, review of *Death Train to Boston,* p. 28.

Publishers Weekly, March 6, 1995, p. 62; July 1, 1996, p. 46; May 19, 1997, p. 69; June 29, 1998, p. 38; August 23, 1999, review of *Death Train to Boston,* p. 52.

OTHER

Dianne Day Home Page, http://members.aol.com/dianneday (June 13, 2000).*

* * *

DAYTON, Charles (W.) 1943-

PERSONAL: Born September 17, 1943, in New York; son of A. W. and Flora B. Dayton; married Laurie Harrison (an education consultant), August 12, 1978; children: Elizabeth, William. *Ethnicity:* "White." *Education:* State University of New York at Binghamton, B.A., 1966; Syracuse University, M.A., 1968; San Jose State University, M.A., 1979.

ADDRESSES: *Office*—Graduate School of Education, University of California, Berkeley, CA 94720; and Foothill Associates, 230 Main St., Nevada City, CA 95959.

CAREER: Cayuga Community College, Auburn, NY, English teacher, 1968-71; American Institutes for Research, Palo Alto, CA, research scientist, 1972-84; Foothill Associates, Nevada City, CA, education consultant, 1984-98; University of California, Berkeley, coordinator of public programs and director of Career Academy Support Network, Graduate School of Education, 1998—. Stanford Urban Coalition, director of Peninsula Academies, 1982-84; California New Youth Apprenticeship Project, past staff member.

WRITINGS:

(With J. A. Hamilton, J. M. Wolff, and S. M. Jung) *Safeguarding Your Education: A Student's Consumer Guide to College and Occupational Education,* Houghton (Hanover, NH), 1977.
(Contributor) C. Hatcher and B. S. Brooks, editors, *New Horizons in Counseling Psychology,* Albion Publishers (San Francisco, CA), 1977.
The Job Search and Youth Employment, American Institutes for Research (Palo Alto, CA), 1980.
(Contributor) P. M. Insel, editor, *Environmental Variables and the Prevention of Mental Illness,* Lexington Books (Lexington, MA), 1980.
(With R. J. Rossi and K. J. Gilmartin) *Agencies Working Together: A Guide to Coordination and Planning,* Sage Publications (Beverly Hills, CA), 1982.
(With D. Stern and M. Raby) *Career Academies: Partnerships for Reconstructing American High Schools,* Jossey-Bass (San Francisco, CA), 1992.
Net Impact Evaluation of School-to-Work: Exploring Alternatives, U.S. Department of Labor (Washington, DC), 1996.
(With Raby) *Career Academies and High School Reform,* University of California, Berkeley, 1998.
(With Raby) *Youth Development in Career Academies,* University of California, Berkeley, 1999.

Contributor to periodicals, including *School Safety, Vocational Education Journal, Phi Delta Kappan, Journal of Counseling Psychology, Journal of Employment Counseling,* and *Counselor Education and Supervision.*

SIDELIGHTS: Charles Dayton told *CA:* "The focus of my work has been youth employment, primarily assisting and evaluating programs designed to improve the school-to-work transition of at-risk youth. I coordinate a statewide effort among fourteen California Partnership Academies to develop an integrated curriculum between academic subjects and the career themes around which they are structured. I have developed a variety of manuals and handbooks, staffed the school-to-work committee of the California High School Task Force, and helped to write a California guide for the Vocational Education Act."

DE ARMAS, Frederick A(lfred) 1945-

PERSONAL: Born February 9, 1945, in Havana, Cuba; naturalized U.S. citizen; son of Alfredo and Ana (Galdos) De Armas. *Ethnicity:* "Hispanic." *Education:* Stetson University, B.A. (magna cum laude), 1965; University of North Carolina at Chapel Hill, Ph.D., 1969.

ADDRESSES: *Office*—Department of Romance Languages, University of Chicago, 1050 East 59th St., Chicago, IL 60637; fax 773-834-1095.

CAREER: Louisiana State University, Baton Rouge, assistant professor, 1968-73, associate professor, 1973-78, professor of Spanish, 1978-88; Pennsylvania State University, University Park, professor, 1988-91, distinguished professor, 1991-98, Edwin Erle Sparks Professor of Spanish and Comparative Literature, 1998-2000, fellow of Institute for the Arts and Humanistic Studies, 1989-2000; University of Chicago, Chicago, IL, professor of Spanish, 2000—.

MEMBER: Modern Language Association of America, American Association of Teachers of Spanish and Portuguese, American Comparative Literature Association, Renaissance Society of America, Asociacion Internacional de Hispanistas.

WRITINGS:

The Four Interpolated Stories in the "Roman comique," University of North Carolina Press (Chapel Hill), 1971.
Paul Scarron, Twayne (Boston, MA), 1972.
(Editor) Luis de Belmonte Bermudez, *El sastre del campillo,* Estudios de Hispanofila, 1975.
The Invisible Mistress: Aspects of Feminism and Fantasy in the Golden Age, Biblioteca Siglo de Oro, 1976.
(Coeditor) *Critical Perspectives on Calderon de la Barca,* Society for Spanish and Spanish-American Studies, 1981.
The Return of Astraea: An Astral-Imperial Myth in Calderon, University Press of Kentucky (Lexington), 1986.
(Editor) *The Prince in the Tower: Perceptions of "La vida es sueno,"* Bucknell University Press (Lewisburg, PA), 1993.
(Editor) *Heavenly Bodies: The Realms of "La estrella de Sevilla,"* Bucknell University Press, 1996.
(Editor) *A Star-Crossed Golden Age: Myth and the Spanish Comedia,* Bucknell University Press, 1998.
Cervantes, Raphael, and the Classics, Cambridge University Press (New York City), 1998.

Contributor to literary journals.

WORK IN PROGRESS: Co-editor of *Western Literary Careers: Classical, Medieval, Renaissance; Quixotic Frescoes: Cervantes and Italian Renaissance Art; Murder in Madrid (1622): The Death of Villamediana in the Literature of the Spanish Golden Age.*

* * *

DELGADO, Ramon (Louis) 1937-

PERSONAL: Born December 16, 1937, in Tampa, FL; son of Eloy Vincent (a grocer) and Hildegard (Chapman) Delgado. *Ethnicity:* "Hispanic." *Education:* Stetson University, B.A. (cum laude), 1959; Baylor University, M.A., 1960; Yale University, M.F.A., 1967; Southern Illinois University at Carbondale, Ph.D., 1976.

ADDRESSES: *Home*—16 Forest St., Apt. 107, Montclair, NJ 07042. *Office*—Department of Theater and Dance, Montclair State University, Upper Montclair, NJ 07043. *E-mail*—delgador@mail.montclair.edu.

CAREER: Chipola Junior College, Marianna, FL, instructor in speech and theater, 1962-64; Kentucky Wesleyan College, Owensboro, assistant professor, 1967-69, associate professor of speech and theater, 1969-72; Hardin-Simmons University, Abilene, TX, associate professor of speech and theater, 1972-74; St. Cloud State College (now University), St. Cloud, MN, assistant professor of theater, 1976-78; Montclair State University, Upper Montclair, NJ, began as associate professor, became professor of speech and theater, 1978—. Play director for Act Two, 1971-72, Stearns County Theatrical Company, 1978, and American College Theatre Festival, 1982.

MEMBER: Nashville Songwriters Association International, Association for Theatre in Higher Education, National Theatre Conference, Dramatists Guild (associate member), Phi Kappa Phi.

AWARDS, HONORS: First place awards from Theta Alpha Phi, 1959, for *Waiting for the Bus,* Baylor University, 1966, for *Nest among the Stars,* and University of Missouri, 1971, for *The Knight-Mare's Nest;* award from *Earplay,* 1973, for *The Longest Day of the Year;* first place award from Southern Illinois University at Carbondale, 1975, for *The Fabulous Jeromes,* and 1976, for *A Little Holy Water;* fellow of Dale Wasserman's Midwest Professional Playwrights Workshop, 1978; INTAR playwright-in-residence, International Arts Relations, 1980; regional winner, American College Theatre Festival, 1982, for directing Sam Shepard's *Curse of the Starving Class;* Grand Prize, lyric category, Music City Song Festival, 1988.

WRITINGS:

PUBLISHED PLAYS

Waiting for the Bus (one-act play; first produced in DeLand, FL, at Stetson University, November, 1958; produced in New York City at No Smoking Playhouse, June 8, 1977), Walter H. Baker (Boston, MA), 1972.

The Little Toy Dog (one-act play; first produced in Longwood, FL, at Lyman High School, March, 1960), Walter H. Baker, 1972.

Sparrows of the Field (one-act play; first produced in Carbondale, IL, at Lutheran Center, May 7, 1975), Walter H. Baker, 1973.

Omega's Ninth (one-act play; first produced in New Haven, CT, at Playwright's Lab Theatre, Yale School of Drama, March, 1967), I. E. Clark (Schulenburg, TX), 1975.

(Editor) *The Best Short Plays,* Chilton (Radnor, PA), 1981-85.

A Little Holy Water (three-act play; first produced in St. Cloud, MN, at St. Cloud State University, October 20, 1976), I. E. Clark, 1983.

Acting with Both Sides of Your Brain, Holt (New York City), 1985.

Author of *Once below a Lighthouse* (first produced in New York City at Glines, February 2, 1977), anthologized in *Best Short Plays,* Chilton, 1972; work represented in other anthologies, including *Ten Great One-Act Plays,* Bantam (New York City), 1968; *Themes in the One-Act Play,* McGraw (New York City), 1971; *Best Short Plays, 1972,* Chilton, 1972; *A Pocket Full of Wry,* I. E. Clark, 1974; *New Beats: Seven One-Act Hispanic American Plays,* SLUSA Press, 1990; and *The Good Parts,* Department of Theater, Southern Illinois University, 1997. Author of *The Youngest Child of Pablo Peco* (one-act play), published in *Stetson Review;* contributor of articles, plays, and poems to theater and speech journals.

PRODUCED PLAYS

Time out for Love (three-act musical), first produced at Lyman High School, April, 1961.

Nest among the Stars (three-act), first produced in Marianna, FL, at Chipola Junior College, June 11, 1964.
Hedge of Serpents (three-act), first produced in Owensboro, KY, at Kentucky Wesleyan College, November 19, 1969.
Brambles on the Sheepskin (three-act), first produced at Kentucky Wesleyan College, November 18, 1970.
Brother of Dragons (three-act), first produced in Abilene, TX, at Hardin-Simmons University, October 23, 1973.
Snowbird (one-act), first produced in Washington, DC, at American Theatre Association, August 11, 1975.
Bug on a Sweet Potato Vine (one-act), first broadcast in Carbondale, IL, on WSIU-TV, August, 1975.
Song of the Goose (one-act), first broadcast on WSIU-TV, August, 1975.
Lady Crickets Don't Sing (one-act), first broadcast on WSIU-TV, April, 1976.
The Fabulous Jeromes (two-act), first produced at St. Cloud State University, November 12, 1978.
The Jerusalem Thorn, first produced in New York City at Shandal Theatre, July 26, 1979.
Stones, first produced in Upper Montclair, NJ, at Montclair State College (now University), December 2, 1983.
Remembering Booth (two-act), first produced at Montclair State University, September 17, 1998.

UNPRODUCED PLAYS

Fear of Angels (three-act), 1966.
Farewell to the Curlew (three-act), 1975.
The Great American (Southern-Fried) Ice Cream Party (two-act musical), 1978.
The Fabulous Jennie, (two-act musical), 1984.

Also author of *The Knight-Mare's Nest* and *The Longest Day of the Year.*

WORK IN PROGRESS: A full-length play, *The Iron Corset.*

SIDELIGHTS: Ramon Delgado told *CA:* "Subject matter for my plays has run the gamut from historical drama to contemporary social and psychological material; style ranges from the ironic tragedy in *Brother of Dragons* to the black farce of *The Knight-Mare's Nest.* As a theater director and occasional actor I have developed an appreciation for the concept of the playscript as the score for a theatrical event. The playwright, then, must use words economically, revealing only the tip of the dramatic iceberg while the unspoken inner actions of the characters are brought to the surface through performance."

DIXON, Stephen 1936-

PERSONAL: Born Stephen Ditchik, June 6, 1936, in New York, NY; son of Abraham Mayer (a dentist) and Florence (an interior decorator; maiden name, Leder) Ditchik; married Anne Frydman (a translator and lecturer), January 17, 1983; children: Sophia, Antonia. *Education:* City College of New York (now City College of the City University of New York), B.A., 1958. *Avocational interests:* Reading, writing, listening to serious music, "reading the *New York Times* over several cups of black coffee."

ADDRESSES: Office—The Writing Seminars, Johns Hopkins University, Baltimore, MD 21218.

CAREER: Writer. Worked variously as fiction consultant, junior high school teacher, tour leader, school bus driver, department store sales clerk, artist's model, waiter, bartender, reporter for a radio news service, magazine editor, and assistant producer of a television show, *In Person,* for the Columbia Broadcasting System (CBS); New York University, School of Continuing Education, New York City, instructor, 1979; Johns Hopkins University, Baltimore, MD, assistant professor, 1980-83, associate professor, 1984-89, professor of fiction, 1989—.

AWARDS, HONORS: Stegner fellow, Stanford University, 1964-65; National Endowment for the Arts grants for fiction, 1974-75 and 1991-92; O. Henry Awards, 1977, for "Mac in Love," 1982, for "Layaways," and 1993, for "The Rare Muscovite"; Pushcart Prizes, 1977, for "Milk Is Very Good for You," and 1999, for "The Burial"; American Academy Institute of Arts and Letters prize for literature, 1983; Guggenheim fellowship for fiction, 1984-85; John Train Humor Prize, *Paris Review,* 1986; National Book Awards finalist in fiction, 1991, and PEN/Faulkner finalist in fiction, 1992, both for *Frog;* Best American Short Stories award, 1993, for "Man, Woman, and Boy"; National Book Awards finalist in fiction, 1995, for *Interstate*; Best American Short Stories award, 1996, for "Sleep"; New Stories of the South award, 1998, for "The Poet."

WRITINGS:

SHORT STORY COLLECTIONS

No Relief, Street Fiction Press (Newport, RI), 1976.
Quite Contrary: The Mary and Newt Story, Harper (New York City), 1979.
Fourteen Stories, Johns Hopkins University Press (Baltimore, MD), 1980.
Movies, North Point Press (Berkeley, CA), 1983.

Stephen Dixon

Time to Go, Johns Hopkins University Press, 1984.

The Play and Other Stories, Coffee House Press(Minneapolis, MN), 1989.

Love and Will, British American Publishing (Willits, CA), 1989.

All Gone, Johns Hopkins University Press, 1990.

Friends: More Will and Magna Stories, Asylum Arts, 1990.

Long Made Short, Johns Hopkins University Press, 1994.

The Stories of Stephen Dixon, Holt (New York City), 1994.

Man on Stage: Playstories, Hi Jinx (Davis, CA), 1996.

Sleep, Coffee House Press, 1999.

NOVELS

Work, Street Fiction Press (Newport, RI), 1977.

Too Late, Harper (New York City), 1978.

Fall and Rise, North Point Press, 1985.

Garbage, Cane Hill Press (New York City), 1988.

Frog, British American Publishing, 1991.

Interstate, Holt, 1995.

Gould: A Novel in Two Novels, Holt (New York City), 1997.

Thirty: Pieces of a Novel, Holt, 1999.

Tisch, Red Hen Press (Palmdale, CA), 2000.

OTHER

Contributor to anthologies, including *Making a Break,* Latitudes Press (New York City), 1975. Contributor of more than 450 short stories to periodicals, including *American Review, Atlantic, Boulevard, Chicago Review, Esquire, Glimmer Train, Harpers, Paris Review, Pequod, Playboy, South Carolina Review, Triquarterly, Viva, Western Humanities Review,* and *Yale Review.*

SIDELIGHTS: Stephen Dixon has published more than 450 pieces of short fiction and nine novels. His work has appeared in a wide variety of magazines, from the venerable *Paris Review* to such popular glossies as *Playboy* and *Esquire,* to little magazines with a few hundred subscribers. Some critics have seen the success of his published short story collections as an indication of a "boomlet" of interest in that genre. Dixon, who worked odd jobs for years while trying to sell his fiction, admitted in a *Baltimore Sun* article that he didn't really start publishing books until he was forty. "By being published late, I learned I could endure and survive and still write," he said. "If I lost my job [as professor of creative writing at Johns Hopkins University], . . . I would get a job as a waiter or a bartender and go on writing."

Pervasive themes in Dixon's work include "relationships of couples, complexities of even the simplest jobs, and ways in which information so easily becomes misinformation or even disinformation," to quote Jerome Klinkowitz in the *Dictionary of Literary Biography.* A native New Yorker, Dixon often sets his fiction's action in that city. Paul Skenazy notes in the *San Francisco Chronicle* that Dixon "writes about people who live in rundown apartments. . . . he gives a reader the irritating, wearing feel of city life. He captures that rubbing of noise and excitement against the grain of one's inertia, that constant intrusion of human traffic. But at its best the tone is less tough than worn-at-the-cuffs, frayed and slightly frantic from observing people who let their pride escape while they were watching TV or doing the laundry." "Dixon's imagination sticks close to home," writes John Domini in the *New York Times Book Review.* "His principal subject is the clash of the mundane and aberrant, those unsettling run-ins with wackos or former lovers all too familiar to anyone who's ever lived in a city." Skenazy feels that Dixon's urban stories "frequently have a powerful impact that, while distasteful, is bracing; and there is something of the feel of that part of life too often ignored by fiction."

Much of Dixon's work also chronicles the pitfalls and problems of male-female relationships, painting "a harrowing portrait of therapeutic man and therapeutic woman trying to experience love," according to Anatole Broyard in the *New York Times.* A *Kirkus Reviews* critic writes that the author's theme becomes clear: "love affairs are like fiction—stories that are added to, rubbed out, obsessively changed, matters of chosen order and nuance and correction." His male protagonists "are generally so yearning and irritably hungry for sex and/or intimacy that they either don't look before they leap, or if they do look, leap anyway no matter what they see ahead," claims David Aitken in the *Baltimore Sun.* "As a result, their lives are almost always in uncontrollable comic disarray."

This theme is apparent in Dixon's novel *Fall & Rise,* in which the leading character tries, through a long New York night, to woo a woman he met at a party earlier in the evening. It is also the controlling idea behind Dixon's O. Henry Award-winning short story "Mac in Love," in which a repulsed suitor yells wistful nonsense at his date's balcony until the beleaguered woman calls the police. The final effect in many of Dixon's male-female imbroglios is, in Aitken's opinion, "vaguely Woody Allenish. Dixon's comedy is stronger than Allen's though, in being less stylized and drawn with a fresher eye for the particulars of life."

Some critics have found fault with aspects of Dixon's work. In his review of *Time to Go,* Aitken comments: "One wishes Dixon didn't republish so many of his weaker stories. It dilutes the impression his best work makes." Domini similarly finds that in *Time to Go,* "all Mr. Dixon's encounters lack any but the most general physicality. . . . The repression of rhetoric and an emphasis on the trivial are hallmarks of many contemporary short stories. But Mr. Dixon is so unrelenting in both regards that he ends up compounding a lack of imagination with a near absence of passion." James Lasdun writes in the *Times Literary Supplement:* "One has the feeling that Dixon begins most of his stories with little more in mind than a vague idea, a couple of characters, or a briefly observed scene, relying on his ready wit to transform it into a convincing piece of fiction. This is fine when it works, but occasionally the initial impulse is too flimsy and the story fails to take off."

In general, however, Dixon's literary output has elicited considerable critical approval. Lasdun notes: "The best of these stories have a certain manic quality about them, caused largely by Dixon's delight in speeding life up and compressing it, to the point where it begins to verge on the surreal." In Chicago's *Tribune Books,* George Cohen concludes: "Dixon's best is superb, tragic, funny, cynical. He's telling us all the bizarre things we already know about ourselves, and he's right on the mark." "Every overworked adjective of praise in the literary criticism business applies to Dixon's writing, beginning with versatile," comments a reviewer in the *Baltimore Sun.* Richard Burgin, in an article for the *St. Petersburg Times,* calls Dixon "a prolific and versatile writer whose strong vision balances anxiety and darkness with humor and compassion. . . . It is high time that the larger American literary community recognized that he is one of our finest writers of short fiction."

The Stories of Stephen Dixon, a collection of many of the author's favorite and most representative work, was published in 1994 and shows the writer playing "intelligent variations on a few great themes," observes William Ferguson in the *New York Times Book Review.* Ferguson also notes Dixon's penchant for characters who "reinvent themselves, time and again, in a retractile language that always seems to be more substantial than they are."

Praising Dixon's stories generally for their depth of feeling and their technical merit, Klinkowitz notes: "Although their humor is often based on the inanity of human needs caught up in and mangled by the infernal machinery of systematics, his narratives can also use this same facility to convey great sensitivity and emotion." Concludes Klinkowitz: "Like a jazz soloist improvising exuberantly, yet within the contours of melody and progressions of chords, Dixon uses the structures of language and circumstance to produce effective prose."

Dixon's *Sleep* collects twenty-two stories written by him during the last twenty-five years of the twentieth century—until then uncollected. Jerome Klinkowitz writes in *American Book Review:* "There's plenty of well-made stuff in *Sleep,* and lots of deep thinking, too. One can imagine Dixon putting together this volume with an eye toward showing all he can do." The title story, the closing piece of the collection, concerns a man troubled because, at the moment of his wife's death, a thought flashes through his mind, "Now I can get some sleep." His heartbreak is rendered all the more poignant by his self-perceived betrayal. A *Publishers Weekly* critic terms this story "powerful," and Klinkowitz says, "pulls all [the varied] themes and techniques together like a good repertory company's signature performance, as a protagonist examines his feelings about his wife's death. Are they love or just simple relief? To decide, he tries remembering the sequence of events, and in that memory comes the full panoply of Dixonian fictive techniques." The two most traditional, straight-forward narratives, "Heat" and "The Hairpiece," are nestled at the book's center, surrounded by the edgier, more inventive fictions. Several of the stories are metafictional—"The Elevator," "Tails," and "The Stranded Man." Frank Caso, writing in *Booklist,* says, "His style might not be to everyone's taste, but the slow, deliberate pacing and self-reflection of these stories absolutely focus the reader's attention on worries, neuroses, an even sentiments that other writers take for granted." Klinkowitz assesses: "Dixon works with language the way a painter handles paint and textures on a canvas—this way, that way, sometimes declaratively, as we'd hope to live our own lives, other times optatively or subjunctively, in the shoulda-coulda-woulda moods where too much existence resides. The truths of his subjects are not *in* their representations, but in *how* they are presented."

The same distinctive style Dixon employs in his short stories can also be found in his novels. A reviewer for the *Virginia Quarterly Review* explains that Dixon "writes rapid-fire fiction; the action is fast and unceasing." Once again mostly employing urban settings, the author often moves the action along via run-on sentences that imitate real-life speech and thought patterns, complete with pauses, self-contradictions, and digressions. "One doesn't exactly read a story by Stephen Dixon, one submits to it," claims Alan H. Friedman in the *New York Times Book Review.* "An unstoppable prose expands the arteries while an edgy, casual nervousness overpowers the will."

In one of Dixon's longer works, the novel titled *Garbage,* this quick-paced delivery intensifies the action of the plot, helping to create a dark and hopeless mood. An average bar owner, Shaney Fleet, has two choices when a garbage collection service tries to extort money—pay or fight. Fleet decides to fight, and in the process his apartment is burned down and he goes to jail where he is so badly beaten that he ends up in the hospital, at which point his neighbors help themselves to whatever he has left. The police are remote and unable to help. In the end, Fleet loses his bar, but retains his fighting spirit. "In *Garbage,* the good guys don't triumph over the bad guys. What triumphs is simply the human spirit," declares Margo Hammond in the *Baltimore Sun. Library Journal* contributor Albert E. Wilhelm calls *Garbage* "a well-wrought parable of modern urban life," and Cleveland *Plain Dealer* correspondent Michael Heaton concludes: "More than an entertainment, Dixon's novel is an achievement. He is a writer's writer whose mastery of the mundane elevates the common life experience to high art. Put simply, *Garbage* is glorious."

In *Frog,* a National Book Award finalist, Dixon brings together a collection of short stories, novellas, letters, essays, poems, and two novels surrounding the life of one protagonist—Howard Tetch, a teacher and family man. The stories, or chapters, are arranged without regard to chronology, so Tetch's marriage, childhood, anecdotes of his children's lives, and aging and death intermix, creating a conglomeration of his fantasies and memories. Episodes overlap, variations on the same story are presented, and the reader is often left to decipher the "truth." Within the space of two chapters, for example, Tetch's daughter Olivia is lost forever at the beach, only to show up as a member of the family at his funeral, without the separation indicated. "Events rotate in a kaleidoscope, the bright fragments fall, and the author's eye focuses on his protagonist's self-absorption, through chains of immense paragraphs, each a story in itself," describes Friedman. Sybil Steinberg in *Publishers Weekly* advises: "Readers attuned to the author's run-on style may warm to a cunning, sexy, audacious performance; others will find this an arty bore." Jim Dwyer in the *Library Journal* praises *Frog* for its "labyrinthine structure, rapid-fire wordplay, vivid descriptions, and raw emotional power." *Washington Post Book World* contributor Steven Moore concludes: "For readers who can see through such bad writing and relish the immediacy it offers, its vitality, its feel of catching life on the wing as Dixon's characters endlessly try to explain themselves to others or to themselves, *Frog* will be a memorable experience."

The same permutations of repetitious event and imagery form the basis of Dixon's 1995 novel *Interstate.* Through eight divergent versions of the story, a father named Nathan Frey grapples with the horror of losing a daughter in a freak murder on the highway. Over and over again the events of the shooting are re-visited, each time from an entirely different perspective. "Italo Calvino and Alain Robbe-Grillet have also written novels that begin again and again, revising themselves, but the subjects of these novels are only themselves," observes George Stade in the *New York Times Book Review.* "Neither of them has brought off anything like the broken eloquence of Nathan's voice, which is as distinct and original and American as Mark Twain's, if otherwise very different." In the *Los Angeles Times Book Review,* Allen Barra commends Dixon for his experimental style, noting: "In this, his 17th book, Stephen Dixon has honed his radical techniques to their finest sheen." Barra concludes: "There is the intriguing possibility that the narrator, in recounting the story, can't recall all the details himself and keeps changing its landscape slightly. There is also the even more intriguing possibility that each narrative is simply a blueprint of the father's subconscious fears for his children and his own helplessness to protect them in the outside world."

Gould: A Novel in Two Novels presents the stories of Gould Bookbinder, a New York City college instructor and book reviewer, in a form typically Dixon's: nontraditional and nonlinear, subverting the conformist expectation of the novel into fragments that, when studied and considered together, create a multi-faceted whole. This time, the novel is comprised of two novels: "Abortions" and "Evangeline." The first tells of five affairs over a span of forty years, from his first, fumbling, manipulative, and self-centered sexual experience at age seventeen, to a self-centered and manipulate affair in his late-fifties—each of which produced an abortion or miscarriage. The second is a long flashback exploring his troubled relationship with Evangeline, a divorcee with a young son. Their relationship is held together primarily by good sex and his genuine affection for and devotion to her son, Brons, who is the reason why Gould fails to break off his affair with the unpredictable-tempered Evangeline, who, among other endearing qualities, effusively hates New York and is casually anti-Semitic. All the while Gould maintains a marriage and two daughters, but is insatiable in his urge to engender yet a third offspring, over the overt protestations of his seriously ill wife, Sally, suffering from multiple sclerosis. Gould is obsessed with the desire, not only to have sex, but to procreate—generally achieved through coercion and trickery, increasingly aggressive in his to block any objections to his desires, regardless of the consequences to the women embroiled in his life.

A *Publishers Weekly* reviewer notes that, "Characteristically, Dixon . . . writes looping run-on sentences filled with dialogue, a style that captures the manic momentum of Gould's consciousness. Dixon's subject is human malleability. He excels at depicting men who try many versions of themselves." Jim Dwyer states in *Library Journal,* "Dixon has created a deeply flawed and fascinating character. Highly recommended." And Anthony Quinn writes in *New York Times Book Review,* "Stephen Dixon's novel seems at times to be paddling around in that stream of consciousness—sentences that snake on interminably, multiple elisions of speech and thought, a cavalier way with names and pronouns—but there is enough rigor and discipline in the writing to maintain a general coherence without sacrificing fluency. And while the book may not have an altogether reader-friendly style, its chronicle of one man's life and loves is never less than absorbing." Quinn further notes, "Mr. Dixon, plainly is not entering his protagonist in a popularity contest; but he is creating an intimate, vivid, emotionally truthful and often funny portrait of an educated and sexually voracious American male in the second half of the 20th century." Quinn concludes, "Given that his (anti)hero starts the narrative as a repellant, sex-driven creep, Stephen Dixon has effected a strange turnaround by the close of this remarkable book: we may not like Gould Bookbinder, but after being privy to the minutest contortions of his interior life, we may at least feel stirrings of forgiveness, if not outright sympathy."

Thirty: Pieces of a Novel revisits the life of Gould Bookbinder, in thirty more chapters of Gouldiana, this time exploring the neuroses, regrets, hopes, and anxieties from his earliest childhood (in "The Dinner Table") to his older years, his mother's death, and his divorce, and beyond. Actually, nothing ever being quite as it might seem at first when dealing with the ever-tricksterish Dixon, there are indeed twenty-nine stories, plus a thirtieth segment, which consists of fifteen additional stories, all with separate titles, gathered together under the subcategory, "Ends." The still sex-obsessed Gould may be obsessed with bedding nubile strangers, but he now displays he can be loving and loyal (albeit in his own peculiar fashion) and tenderly caring for his slowly dying mother, his wife, who, like his mother, is now wheelchair-bound, and in his relationship with his pair of sharp-witted daughters. The vignettes are connected by the common thread of sex: Gould is wolfishly ogling some female bypasser and engaging in elaborate, pre-masturbatory sexual fantasies—a waitress at a Maine vacation resort or a girl playing frisbee in the park—or trying to seduce the twenty-three-year-old daughter of an academic colleague, or chasing a belly dancer aboard a cruise ship, or remembering an episode from his youth where, on the way to his girlfriend's house, he became uncontrollably aroused spying in the window of a parked car at a teenaged couple engaging in intercourse. The stories in "Ends" present alternate, incompatible endings to the novel, including variants on Gould's own death.

A *Publishers Weekly* reviewer says that "Dixon's fiction never stops. Not only does he write lots of it . . . but his insights into motive, emotion, interaction, speech and thought are as prodigious as his output." This reviewer also notes, "Dixon's prose can be brilliantly accurate, or draining, or excruciating, or all three. . . . Sometimes the novel feels vertiginously dense, like a three-hour movie consisting of all close-ups. At other times it's simply more demanding, and more rewarding, than ordinary, ordinarily plotted novels." In *New York Times Book Review,* Vince Passaro criticizes: "Dixon's problem is that over a long career he has relied on [his] strengths too heavily and repeated them too often; he has turned them into mere effect. The run-on sentences, the rapid-fire but mundane stream of consciousness, the apparently frank but merely amphetamined dialogue that goes back and forth and back and forth within page after page of unbroken paragraphs that stretch as far as the eye can SEE: these devices are no longer energized by an author who has anything fresh to say." He adds that "Gould's lascivious nature is supposed to propel these stories and give them what little power to shock they have. But the sexuality is bland and unsurprising; the cleaning up, one senses, takes longer than the act."

"My writing comes first in my work," Dixon once told *CA*. "But to get to my writing, I first must finish all my school work. And I have lots of school work to do, but I never feel free to write, and I have to feel free and unburdened of looming work of other kinds, so I do all my school work before I do my writing. That sometimes means I'll stay up to 3:00 a.m. finishing student papers; I'll go to bed tired but I wake up liberated, and ready to write. I must teach in order to pay the bills. I like teaching, but I'd prefer just to read and write. I've a lot to write and I write every single day. New ideas always come when I'm writing, so the process of writing is very important for me. . . . I write only for myself, my writing has to excite me or it's worthless, boring, and I then have to try something else; and I must always do something new. If I ever find myself going over familiar ground in a familiar way, meaning my familiar or other writers, I'd give up writing—that wouldn't be so hard; I've written plenty, more than anyone would ever want to read—and try something else, or just read, walk, think, and keep my manual typewriter polished and clean for possible future writing days."

BIOGRAPHICAL/CRITICAL SOURCES:

BOOKS

Contemporary Literary Criticism, Gale (Detroit, MI), Volume 52, 1989.

Dictionary of Literary Biography, Volume 130: *American Short-Story Writers since World War II,* Gale, 1993.

Short Story Criticism, Volume 16, Gale, 1994.

PERIODICALS

American Book Review, January-February, 2000, Jerome Klinkowitz, "Little Things Mean a Lot," p. 6.

Baltimore Sun, January 22, 1984; July 22, 1984, pp. F1, F8-9; October 19, 1988; April 31, 1989, pp. F8, F11, F13-15.

Booklist, March 1, 1999, Donna Seaman, review of *Gould,* p. 1154; March 15, 1999, Frank Caso, review of *Sleep,* p. 1289.

Chicago Sun-Times, June 4, 1978.

Kansas City Star, August 12, 1984.

Kirkus Reviews, May 1, 1979.

Library Journal, August, 1988, p. 173; December, 1989, p. 166; January, 1992, p. 172; January, 1997, Jim Dwyer, review of *Gould,* p. 145; May 15, 1999, Edward B. St. John, review of *30,* p. 124.

Los Angeles Times Book Review, December 3, 1989, p, 2; May 28, 1995, pp. 1, 11.

New York Times, June 9, 1979.

New York Times Book Review, July 31, 1977; May 7, 1978; October 14, 1984; July 7, 1985, p. 16; June 4, 1989, Jennifer Levin, review of *The Play and Other Stories,* p. 19; December 17, 1989, Joyce Reiser Kornblatt, review of *Love and Will,* p. 23; July 1, 1990, Steve Erickson, review of *All Gone,* p. 18; November 17, 1991, Alan H. Friedman, review of *Frog,* p. 14; February 20, 1994, Linda Barrett Osborne, review of *Long Made Short,* p. 22; September 4, 1994, William Ferguson, review of *The Stories of Stephen Dixon,* p. 12; May 21, 1995, George Stade, review of *Interstate,* p. 46; April 20, 1997, Anthony Quinn, "The Jerk," p. 12; May 16, 1999, Vince Passaro, "S.A.S.E.," p. 12.

North American Review, March, 1981, pp. 54-56.

Plain Dealer (Cleveland), January 22, 1988.

Publishers Weekly, September, 29, 1989, p. 58; November 8, 1991, p. 48; June 19, 1995, pp. 40-41; January 6, 1997, review of *Gould,* p. 64; February 1, 1999, review of *Sleep,* p. 74; February 15, 1999, review of *30,* p. 85.

Review of Contemporary Fiction, fall, 1992, Marilyn Moss, review of *Frog,* p. 184; fall, 1997, Thomas Howe, review of *Gould,* p. 235; fall, 1999, Irving Malin, review of *Thirty: Pieces of a Novel,* p. 161.

St. Petersburg Times, August 26, 1984.

San Francisco Chronicle, January 29, 1984.

Small Press, May/June 1985.

Soho Weekly News, December 2, 1976.

South Carolina Review, November, 1978.

Studies in Short Fiction, summer, 1990, Peter La Salle, review of *All Gone,* p. 421; winter, 1990, Christopher Metress, review of *Love and Will,* p. 115.

Time, August 13, 1984.

Times Literary Supplement, May 29, 1981.

Tribune Books, (Chicago) July 15, 1979, January 4, 1981, June 11, 1995, p. 6.

Virginia Quarterly Review, autumn, 1988.

Washington Post Book World, February 22, 1981, p. 10; August 5, 1984, pp. 8-9; July 20, 1985; January 19, 1992, pp. 6-7.

OTHER

JHU's Stephen Dixon Reflects on His Life's Work, http://www.jhu.edu (October 16, 1997).

Johns Hopkins University Book Center—Stephen Dixon, http://www.bkstore.com/johns-hopkins (February 14, 2000).

* * *

DOWNS, Robert C. S. 1937-

PERSONAL: Born November 23, 1937, in Chicago, IL; son of Norbert Henry (an executive) and Laura C. (Smith) Downs; married Barbara Lewry, September 6, 1968; children: Christina Elizabeth, Susan Laura. *Education:* Harvard University, A.B., 1960; University of Iowa, M.F.A., 1965.

ADDRESSES: Office—Department of English, 764 West Hamilton Ave., State College, PA 16801. *Agent*—Don Congdon, Harold Matson Co., Inc., 22 East 40th St., New York, NY 10016.

CAREER: Phillips Exeter Academy, Exeter, NH, instructor in English, 1962-63; Hunter College of the City University of New York, New York City, lecturer in English, 1965-66; *Life,* New York City, sales promotion writer, 1966-68; Colby Junior College, New London, NH, assistant professor of English, 1968-73; University of Arizona, Tucson, associate professor of English and director of creative writing program, 1973-80; Pennsylvania State University, University Park, professor of English and director of writing program, 1980—.

AWARDS, HONORS: Guggenheim fellowship, 1979-80.

WRITINGS:

NOVELS

Going Gently, Bobbs-Merrill (Indianapolis), 1973.

Peoples, Bobbs-Merrill, 1974.

Country Dying, Bobbs-Merrill, 1976.

White Mama (also see below), Ballantine (New York City), 1980.

Living Together, St. Martin's Press (New York City), 1983.

The Fifth Season, Counterpoint (Washington, DC), 2000.

Contributor of short fiction to periodicals. Author of screenplay, *White Mama* (based on novel of same title), CBS-TV, 1980.

ADAPTATIONS: Peoples was adapted by Stephen Gethers as *Billy: Portrait of a Street Kid,* a 1977 NBC-TV World Premier Movie. *Going Gently* was adapted by Thomas Ellice for production by BBC-TV.

SIDELIGHTS: Robert C. S. Downs's novel *The Fifth Season* tells the story of Ted Neel, a sixty-year-old professor of literature, and the ways he copes with the sudden decline of his aging parents. Ted's father, Abel, is mentally alert, but he is recovering from the removal of a cancerous kidney. The two men's relationship has been strained for many years. It is only upon coming to visit Abel in the hospital that Ted realizes his mother, Lillian, is in the advanced stages of Alzheimer's disease. For years, Abel has been caring for and protecting her, while remaining in denial about her worsening condition. Ted's parents, aging and dealing with health problems, "consume and disrupt his staid life with their sudden degeneration," reported a *Publishers Weekly* reviewer. In *The Fifth Season,* Downs examines many issues related to dying, and shows the change that Ted sees has taken place in his parents. The *Publishers Weekly* reviewer noted: "Never maudlin or trite, Downs rises admirably to the difficult challenge of writing an honest and gently forthright novel about dying." Danise Hoover in *Booklist* concluded: "Well written and not maudlin, this is a story worth reading."

BIOGRAPHICAL/CRITICAL SOURCES:

PERIODICALS

Booklist, February 15, 2000, Danise Hoover, review of *The Fifth Season,* p. 1079.

New York Times Book Review, March 12, 2000, Jeff Waggoner, review of *The Fifth Season,* p. 23.

Publishers Weekly, June 10, 1983, review of *Living Together,* p. 55; January 24, 2000, review of *The Fifth Season,* p. 293.*

* * *

DOYLE, Robert C(harles) 1946-

PERSONAL: Born January 20, 1946, in Philadelphia, PA; son of Edward J. and Arvella W. Doyle; married Beate T. Engel (an assistant professor), August 23, 1986. *Education:* Pennsylvania State University, B.A.,

1967, M.A., 1976; Bowling Green State University, Ph.D., 1987.

ADDRESSES: Home—1317 Ridge Ave., Steubenville, OH 43952. *E-mail*—bdoyle@uov.net.

CAREER: Substitute teacher at public schools in Philadelphia, PA, 1972; Checkered Flag Motor Car Co., Norfolk, VA, automobile salesperson, 1972; Pennsylvania State University, University Park, lecturer in American studies, 1974-77; Bob Doyle Talent Agency, State College, PA, owner, 1978-86; Pennsylvania State University, lecturer in American studies, 1987-94; Westfaelische Wilhelms-Universitaet, Munster, Germany, Fulbright lecturer in American studies, 1994-95; Universite Marc Bloch, Strasbourg, France, professor of American civilization, 1995-98; Joint Personnel Recovery Agency, Fort Belvoir, VA, historical consultant. Professional musician and band leader, 1972-86; appeared in television documentary programs, including *In Search of Fiddlers and Their Tunes,* broadcast by WPSX-TV, 1981; and *Secrets of War: American Prisoners of War* and *Escape from a Living Hell,* both for the History Channel, 2000. Universite Robert Schuman, Strasbourg, instructor, 1996-97; visiting lecturer at Monash University, University of Melbourne, University of New South Wales, Warrnambool Institute, and Macquarie University, 1989; guest on radio and television programs. Central Pennsylvania Festival of the Arts, director of Fiddlers Competition, 1975-86; Vietnam Veterans Memorial Moving Wall, member of regional committee. *Military service:* U.S. Naval Reserve, 1967-80, active duty in Vietnam, 1968, 1970-71.

MEMBER: American Studies Association, American Culture Association, Society for Military History, German Association for the Study of the Western, American Federation of Musicians (member of executive board, Local 660, 1987-93), American Legion, Veterans of Foreign Wars, Pennsylvania State Alumni Association (life member), Mobile Riverine Association, Fulbright Association.

AWARDS, HONORS: Grants from Pennsylvania Council on the Arts, 1974, and Central Pennsylvania Center for Cultural Heritage Conservation, 1991; Fulbright grants for Germany, 1994-95.

WRITINGS:

(Author of introduction) Matthew G. Guntharp, *Learning the Fiddler's Ways,* Pennsylvania State University Press (University Park, PA), 1980.

Voices from Captivity: Interpreting the American POW Narrative, University Press of Kansas (Lawrence), 1994.

(Contributor) Susan R. Rusinko, editor, *Shaw and Other Matters,* Susquehanna University Press (Selinsgrove, PA), 1998.

A Prisoner's Duty: Great Escapes in U.S. Military History, Naval Institute Press (Annapolis, MD), 1999.

(Contributor) Thomas Schneider, editor, *War and Literature,* Volume II, Rasch Universitaetsverlag (Osnabruck, Germany), 1999.

Contributor of articles and reviews to periodicals, including *Journal of American Culture, Folklore Historian, Perspectives on Film, Popular Music and Society, Bluegrass Unlimited,* and *Pickin'.*

WORK IN PROGRESS: Prisoners in American Hands, an analysis of narratives and documents of prisoners of war taken and held by American forces, from colonial wars through Vietnam; *War through a Looking Glass,* a study of images of prisoners of war found in folklore, popular narrative fiction, theater, and film.

* * *

DROWN, Merle 1943-

PERSONAL: Born January 14, 1943, in York, ME; son of Merle F. and Hazel (Gallagher) Drown; married; wife's name, Patricia; children: James, Matthew, Devin. *Education:* Macalester College, B.A., 1965; attended University of Washington, Seattle, 1965-66; Goddard College, M.F.A., 1978.

ADDRESSES: Home—60 West Parish Rd., Concord, NH 03301. *Agent*—Jack Scovil, Scovil, Chichak, Galen, 381 Park Ave., Suite 1020, New York, NY 10016.

CAREER: Writer.

WRITINGS:

NOVELS

Plowing up a Snake, Dial (New York City), 1982.

The Suburbs of Heaven, Soho Press (New York City), 2000.

(Editor, with John Cawelti) Leon Forrest, *Meteor in the Madhouse* (novellas), Northwestern University Press (Evanston, IL), 2000.

SIDELIGHTS: Merle Drown's fiction illustrates the grisly side of life in backwoods New England. The author, who was born in rural Maine and lives in New Hampshire, told *CA* that his first novel, *Plowing up a Snake,* "is about an actual murder in a small town, a murder that remained unsolved, although many apparently knew the murderers' identities. What stimulated me to write about this event was that for twenty years I had been hearing people talking about it, making stories about it. They were groping to find the truth, not of the murder, but of the human spirit." In a *San Francisco Chronicle* review of *Plowing up a Snake,* Bruce Colman wrote: "First-time novelist Merle Drown is so good with characters, weather and landscape that we can practically walk the streets of Enoch, New Hampshire, where this story takes place. . . . [It] is compelling reading, the kind of fiction you can stay up with half the night."

Drown's second novel, *The Suburbs of Heaven,* is an "antic, tender and bittersweet" story, in the words of a *Publishers Weekly* reviewer. It portrays the Hutchins family, a New Hampshire clan struggling to recover from many recent tragedies. Jim Hutchins' sister died in a fall down the cellar steps, and his daughter drowned in a neighbor's cow pond. His older son is mentally disturbed, believing that a snake is eating through his brain; the younger son is a brutal, aggressive man who lands in jail for beating his girlfriend. Jim's daughter Lisa, who turns tricks to get liquor, is also involved with an abusive man, one who believes God directs his aggression. Jim's beloved wife Pauline has a strange relationship with her wealthy, widowed brother-in-law Emory, who is widely suspected of killing Helen for insurance money. Pauline lets Emory pay her to dance naked while he films her. A misplaced videocassette sparks the book's climax. Jim—who always dreamed of getting his family out of trouble, getting ahead financially, and escaping his sordid world—explodes into violence. The *Publishers Weekly* reviewer praised Drowns's work: "Narrated in the convincing voices of the five Hutchinses, the story veers from ribald to tragic, with consistently amazing plot twists: guns are lost and found; intimate moments are spied upon; revenge is swift, creative and nasty. Throughout, Drown's language shines, and even [his] most misguided characters are fully alive, resonant, and original, speaking with quiet, piercing wisdom."

Drown concluded: "It is when characters come alive that fiction can reveal the truth of ideals and ideas. For me that means finding an occurrence, whether it is a personal experience or an anecdote or a news item, that can provide the situation for my characters to become themselves and to live out their lives, separate from me. It is what I believe is creativity."

BIOGRAPHICAL/CRITICAL SOURCES:

PERIODICALS

Library Journal, July, 1982, review of *Plowing up a Snake,* p. 1343.

New York Times Book Review, March 5, 2000, Jean Thompson, "New Hampshire Primary: This Novel Features a Disaster-prone yet Enduring Backwoods Family," p. 16.

People, September 20, 1982, review of *Plowing up a Snake,* p. 12.

Publishers Weekly, November 22, 1999, review of *Suburbs of Heaven,* p. 41.

San Francisco Chronicle, September 8, 1982.

* * *

DRURY, S(hadia) B(asilious) 1950-

PERSONAL: Born May 27, 1950, in Cairo, Egypt; immigrated to Canada, 1962; daughter of Anwar Basilious and Nazli Shenouda; married Dennis Drury, 1973; children: Kelly Anne. *Education:* York University, B.A. (with honors), 1971, Ph.D., 1977; Queen's University, Kingston, Ontario, M.A., 1972.

ADDRESSES: *Office*—Department of Political Science, University of Calgary, 2500 University Dr. N.W., Calgary, Alberta, Canada T2N 1N4. *E-mail*—drury@ucalgary.ca.

CAREER: University of Calgary, Calgary, Alberta, assistant professor, 1977-80, associate professor of legal and political theory, 1980-89, professor, 1989—.

MEMBER: Canadian Political Science Association (chairman of political theory, 1982), American Political Science Association, Conference for the Study of Political Thought.

WRITINGS:

The Political Ideas of Leo Strauss, St. Martin's (New York City), 1988.

Alexandre Kojeve: The Roots of Postmodern Politics, St. Martin's, 1994.

Leo Strauss and the American Right, St. Martin's, 1997.

Contributor of articles and reviews to journals in politics and philosophy.

WORK IN PROGRESS: "Terror and Civilization."

SIDELIGHTS: Professor of political philosophy Shadia B. Drury has made an extensive study of the life work of Leo Strauss, the "godfather of the conservative revolution." Strauss's teachings were absorbed by such conservative and neo-conservative political scientists as Allan Bloom, William Bennett, and Irving Kristol. In her 1988 book *The Political Ideas of Leo Strauss,* and her more recent work, *Leo Strauss and the American Right,* Drury offers a scholarly but nonetheless passionate critique of Strauss, his disciples, and the modern conservative movement.

In a review of *Leo Strauss and the American Right* for *Reason* magazine, Loren E. Lomasky observed that it is from a liberal perspective that Drury mounts her attack on Strauss. Lomasky wrote: "Although she lands some accurate shots, the ratio of hits to misses is conspicuously smaller than should be expected from an obviously intelligent and sophisticated critic intimately familiar with her quarry." The critic added that Drury "is undone by the intense animus she holds toward Strauss and all that is associated with him. She is outraged by what he says, what he intimates, and what he disclaims but is really nonetheless thinking." Conversely, a *Publishers Weekly* reviewer noted that although Drury's prose "is occasionally dry and academic, her evidence is persuasive and her research is impeccable. . . . Her interest seems to lie in exploration rather than conversion."

BIOGRAPHICAL/CRITICAL SOURCES:

PERIODICALS

American Political Science Review, September, 1998, James F. Ward, review of *Leo Strauss and the American Right.*

Choice, November, 1999, D. J. Maletz, review of *Leo Strauss and the American Right,* p. 618.

Library Journal, December, 1997, Patricia Hatch, review of *Leo Strauss and the American Right,* p. 125.

Political Theory, December, 1998, John P. McCormick, "Political Theory and Political Theology."

Publishers Weekly, December 1, 1997, review of *Leo Strauss and the American Right,* p. 39.

Reason, November, 1998, Loren E. Lomasky, "Straussed Out," p. 71.

Washington Monthly, November, 1997, Michael Lind, review of *Leo Strauss and the American Right,* p. 52.

Washington Times, February 11, 1998, Ken Masugi, "A Leo Straussian Conspiracy."

* * *

DUCKER, Bruce 1938-

PERSONAL: Born August 10, 1938, in New York, NY; son of Allen (a lawyer) and Lillian (Goldner) Ducker; married Jaren Jones; children: Foster, Penelope, John. *Education:* Dartmouth College, A.B., 1960; Columbia University, M.A., 1963, LL.B., 1964.

ADDRESSES: Office—Ducker, Montgomery & Lewis, P.C., Denver, CO 80202.

CAREER: Lawyer in private practice, 1964—.

AWARDS, HONORS: Colorado Book Award for fiction, for *Lead Us Not into Penn Station.*

WRITINGS:

Rule by Proxy, Crown (New York City), 1976.

Failure at the Mission Trust, Freundlich Books (New York City), 1986.

Bankroll, Dutton (New York City), 1989.

Marital Assets, Permanent Press (Sag Harbor, NY), 1993.

Lead Us Not into Penn Station, Permanent Press, 1994.

Bloodlines, Permanent Press, 2000.

Contributor to legal journals and law reviews. Poetry and short fiction in periodicals, including *The Yale Review, Commonweal, Appalachia,* and *The Literary Quarterly.*

SIDELIGHTS: Bruce Ducker's novels explore many types of human relationships. In *Marital Assets,* his characters are well-to-do people whose emotionally repressed lives do not prevent their story from being "poignant," in the estimation of a *Publishers Weekly* reviewer. In *Marital Assets,* a sixty-one-year-old New York City banker named Charles Meredith writes journal entries concerned with events that started fifteen years earlier, when he and his wife Evelyn were vacationing in the Caribbean. There they befriended another New York couple, Claudia and William "Weemo" Abbott. Over the years that followed, adulterous feelings developed. Claudia and Charles keep their romance chaste, while Weemo and Evelyn have a brief physical affair. Charles's memoirs are "full of both regret and acceptance," and Ducker "surveys the subtle, treacherous landscape of love and betrayal" effectively, according to the *Publishers Weekly* writer.

The love between a father and son is central to Ducker's next novel, *Lead Us Not into Penn Station.* A contributor to *Publishers Weekly* calls this book an "evocative bildungsroman" focusing on Danny Meadoff, a teenager in Brooklyn, New York, during the 1950s. Devoted to literature, baseball, and his friends Angie and Rick, Danny is increasingly aware of his parents' human frailties and the difficulties they struggle with. Danny gives up a summer literature course to work as a Fuller Brush salesman in order to help his family. "*Lead Us Not into Penn Station* captures a long, eventful summer that has significant lessons to teach a young man on the brink of adulthood," asserted Mary Carroll in *Booklist.* The *Publishers Weekly* writer noticed that Ducker "maintains a difficult balance in his narrative, penetrating characters' complex thoughts and emotions while never losing the feeling of a summer break in a simpler time. . . . Danny's many moments of discovery . . . are genuine and often moving."

With *Bloodlines,* Ducker created a "suspenseful, well-crafted, and riveting novel," in the words of *Library Journal* reviewer Lisa Rohrbaugh. The protagonist is Peter Steinmuller, a young American jazz pianist who ends up looking for work in Europe. Instead he discovers a mystery about his own heritage, involving the true identity of his grandfather; the story behind an unseaworthy boat that sank during the war, drowning the Jewish refugees on board; and the illegal, but possibly noble, actions of an aristocrat in control of Peter's inheritance. "By the time Peter unravels the mystery, readers have learned about the nefarious dealings of people who profited from the Holocaust," advised a *Publishers Weekly* reviewer. "And although Ducker's prose sometimes lacks vibrancy, he deftly interpolates background material about jazz and neatly evokes such settings as Geneva and Budapest." Rohrbaugh concluded that *Bloodlines* is an "intriguing novel in which friendships are easily betrayed," and noted, "The underlying musical motifs lend special meaning to the protagonist."

BIOGRAPHICAL/CRITICAL SOURCES:

PERIODICALS

Booklist, May 1, 1994, Mary Carroll, review of *Lead Us Not into Penn Station,* p. 1582; January 1, 2000, James Klise, review of *Bloodlines,* p. 876.

Library Journal, December, 1986, James B. Hemesath, review of *Failure at the Mission Trust,* p. 135; March 15, 1993, Michele Leber, review of *Marital Assets,* p. 104; April 15, 1994, Edwin B. Burgess, review of *Lead Us Not into Penn Station,* p. 111; February 1, 2000, Lisa Rohrbaugh, review of *Bloodlines,* p. 116.

Publishers Weekly, December 5, 1986, Sybil Steinberg, review of *Failure at the Mission Trust,* p. 62; June 30, 1989, Sybil Steinberg, review of *Bankroll,* p. 87; January 25, 1993, review of *Marital Assets,* p. 77; April 18, 1994, review of *Lead Us Not into Penn Station,* p. 47; December 20, 1999, review of *Bloodlines,* p. 54.

* * *

DUNANT, Sarah 1950-

PERSONAL: Born August 8, 1950, in London, England; daughter of David (an airline manager) and Estelle (a teacher; maiden name, Joseph) Dunant; children: Zoe Willox Dunant. *Education:* Cambridge University, degree in history, 1972.

ADDRESSES: Home and Office—17 Tytherton Rd., London N19 4QB, England. *Agent*—Gillon Aitken, 29 Fernshaw Rd., London SW10 0TG, England.

CAREER: BBC-Radio, London, England, producer, 1974-76; freelance writer and broadcaster, 1977—.

AWARDS, HONORS: Golden Dragon Award nomination, Crime Writers Association, 1987, for *Intensive Care;* Dagger Award, British Crime Writers' Association, 1993, for *Fatlands.*

WRITINGS:

NOVELS

(With Peter Dunant) *Exterminating Angels,* Deutsch (England), 1983.

(With Peter Dunant) *Intensive Care,* Deutsch, 1986.

Snow Storms in a Hot Climate, Random House (New York City), 1988.

Transgressions, Virago (London), 1997, ReganBooks (New York City), 1998.
Mapping the Edge, Virago, 1999.

HANNAH WOLFE MYSTERY SERIES

Birth Marks, Doubleday (New York City), 1992.
Fatlands, O. Penzler Books (New York City), 1994.
Under My Skin, Scribner (New York City), 1995, Thorndike Press (Thorndike, ME), 1996.

OTHER

Thin Air (television serial), broadcast by BBC-TV, 1988.
(Editor) *The War of the Words: The Political Correctness Debate,* Virago, 1994.
(Editor with Roy Porter) *The Age of Anxiety,* Virago, 1996.

WORK IN PROGRESS: A book and a film script.

SIDELIGHTS: British author Sarah Dunant's first solo novel, *Snow Storms in a Hot Climate,* is a psychological thriller set in the United States. Michael Freitag, writing in the *New York Times Book Review,* notes: "While American readers may not find the settings—cramped, gritty New York City and the vast, sparkling California coast, among others—particularly exotic, they will find the writing refreshingly economical and astute." Oxford professor Marla, protagonist and narrator of the novel, travels to New York to come to the aid of an old friend who has become emotionally involved with a mysterious cocaine dealer who may also be a murderer. According to Freitag, Marla "finds that she too has become caught in a complex web of emotions: friendship, romance, curiosity, jealousy and revenge." Freitag finds *Snow Storms in a Hot Climate* to be an "intelligent and rarely predictable" novel with some "truly breathtaking" scenes. On the downside, he feels that Dunant "relies too heavily on secondhand storytelling to advance her plot."

In *Birth Marks* Dunant launched a mystery series featuring the female private detective Hannah Wolfe. Reviewing the novel for the *New York Times Book Review,* Marilyn Stasio calls Dunant an "author with a streak of independence," and describes Hannah as "entirely refreshing among her treacly peers . . . [a] coolly pragmatic London operative, [who] uses brains over charm, relies on psychology rather than intuition and does not confuse compassion with sentimentality." Hannah's first case involves a runaway ballerina who turns up floating in the Thames: dead, pregnant, and probably a suicide. The subsequent investigation reveals the woman's sad double life. The book's surprise ending, according to Stasio, leads to "a real education" for Hannah.

Hannah Wolfe returns in *Fatlands,* the tale of a scientist who uses animals in his experiments. The scientist's fourteen-year-old daughter is killed by a car bomb, probably meant for him, most likely planted by radical animal-rights activists. Hannah's investigation reveals corporate and scientific skulduggery fueled by runaway greed. Emily Melton of *Booklist* comments: "Dunant's writing is smooth, polished, funny, and sophisticated, with an inventive plot and some sharp-edged commentary about the ethics of the modern-day business/science community." A reviewer for *Publishers Weekly* finds Hannah's observations to be "frequently funny, occasionally poignant and always insightful." The third Hannah Wolfe entry, *Under My Skin,* is set against the backdrop of an exclusive health and beauty spa. Someone is out to sabotage the spa and Hannah is hired to uncover the culprit. Melton finds the book somewhat disappointing: "Not to say . . .[it] is a bad book. It just never quite reaches the pinnacle of excellence that *Fatlands* achieved." However, Melton concludes that the novel's "keep-'em-guessing plot, dry wit, and a revealing look at society's expectations about beauty and youth make this one an entertaining and educational read."

In *Transgressions,* a non-series mystery, Dunant explores the themes of sexual obsession, power, and violence. Elizabeth Skvorecky, deserted by her lover of eight years, isolates herself in her London mansion and spends her time translating a Czech police thriller that is rife with images of sadistic pornography. At first she finds the book disgusting, but then begins to realize it has "burrowed its way under her skin." When objects begin disappearing from the mansion, Elizabeth suspects either her former lover or a poltergeist, yet she is soon confronted by the real intruder, a serial rapist, whom she proceeds to seduce. Elizabeth subsequently "stalks" the rapist-stalker by baiting him with pornographic passages purportedly excerpted from the Czech police thriller, but which she has actually written herself. Much of this material appears in the text of the novel. Dunant's stated purpose with *Transgressions* was "to breathe life into the victims [of rape]." However, a *Publisher Weekly* reviewer feels that "it's hard to distinguish between what Lizzie writes and the ill-conceived, poorly disguised appeal to prurience Dunant has penned." Vicky Hutchings of the *New Statesman* comments: "I don't believe a word of it."

Dunant is also the editor of and a contributor to *The War of the Words: The Political Correctness Debate,* a collection of essays that argues the relevance of gender and ethnic issues to any contemporary political debate, and attempts to put forth a methodology as to how these issues can best be raised.

Sarah Dunant once told *CA:* "I have a dual career. In one incarnation I am a television journalist, presenting an arts and culture live show on BBC-TV 2. In the other I am a novelist and screenplay writer. My preoccupations are history, travel, and trying to combine work, home, and bringing up a small child."

BIOGRAPHICAL/CRITICAL SOURCES:

PERIODICALS

Booklist, November 1, 1994, p. 480; September 15, 1995, p. 142.
Guardian, October 3, 1994, p. 2.10.
New Statesman, July 11, 1997, p. 49.
New Statesman & Society, October 21, 1994, p. 40.
New York Times Book Review, January 1, 1989, p. 14; October 25, 1992.
Publishers Weekly, October 17, 1994, p. 67; August 21, 1995, p. 49; February 16, 1998, p. 203.*

* * *

DYER, Joyce 1947-

PERSONAL: Born July 20, 1947, in Akron, OH; daughter of Thomas William (a supervisor at a rubber factory) and Edna Annabelle (a board of education clerk; maiden name, Haberkost) Coyne; married Daniel Osborn Dyer (a freelance writer), December 20, 1969; children: Stephen Osborn. *Education:* Wittenberg University, St. Louis, MO, B.A., 1969; Kent State University, Ph.D., 1977. *Politics:* Democrat.

ADDRESSES: *Home*—30 Church St., Hudson, OH 44236. *Office*—Hinsdale Hall, Hiram College, Hiram, OH 44234; fax: 330-342-9952. *E-mail*—dyerja@hiram.edu.

CAREER: Teacher at a private school in Hudson, OH, 1979-90; Hiram College, Hiram, OH, associate professor of English and director of writing, 1990—. Wittenberg University, visiting writer, 1998; Radford University, writer in residence, summer, 2000.

MEMBER: Modern Language Association of America, Associated Writing Programs, Appalachian Studies Association, National Alzheimer's Association, Hudson Library and Historical Society, Friends of the Hiram College Library.

AWARDS, HONORS: National Endowment for the Humanities, fellow, 1987 and 1988, grant, 1990-91; Paul E. Martin Award for excellence in teaching, 1993; *The Awakening* was named one of the best academic books of the year by *Choice,* 1993; first place award in nonfiction category, Midwest Writers' Conference, 1995; Appalachian Studies Award, 1997, for *Bloodroot;* grant from Ohio Arts Council, 1997; resident, Appalachian Writers Workshop, 1999.

WRITINGS:

The Awakening: A Novel of Beginnings (nonfiction), Twayne (New York City), 1993.
In a Tangled Wood (nonfiction), introduction by Ian Frazier, Southern Methodist University Press (Dallas, TX), 1996.
(Editor) *Bloodroot: Reflections on Place by Appalachian Women Writers,* University Press of Kentucky (Lexington, KY), 1998.

Contributor of more than a hundred articles to magazines and newspapers, including *Appalachian Journal, Teachers and Writers, Cleveland Plain Dealer, Southern Literary Journal,* and *Seventeen.*

WORK IN PROGRESS: Home Fires Burning (tentative title), literary nonfiction about a house fire in Chautauqua, NY; *Firestone Park* (tentative title), a memoir of growing up in a company town designed for rubber workers at Firestone Tire and Rubber Company; *Letters from the Region* (tentative title), a collection of letters by writers of Appalachia.

SIDELIGHTS: Joyce Dyer told *CA:* "My roots are in coal (the Coyne side of my family migrated from the anthracite mines of the northern Appalachians in Pennsylvania) and rubber (my grandfather and father gave a total of sixty-seven years service to the Firestone Tire and Rubber Company in Akron, Ohio). For a long while, I fought hard not to admit that I had grown up in South Akron, in an industrial subdivision—a company town—created in 1915 by Harvey S. Firestone for his rubber workers. It took me quite a few years to realize that familiar ground is the richest ground available to a writer. For over thirty years I hadn't even known that the sixteen-acre city park at the center of Firestone Park was designed by Firestone's landscape architect in the shape of the Firestone company shield. If you look at an aerial map, you see this instantly. The park is as perfect as a patch on a blazer. That shield may as well have been my family crest (*everything* was Firestone), but I never knew it was there until I left—and then returned to survey the land again, using memory and research as the lenses in my transit.

"Writing my way to the center of familiar experience has taken many circuitous routes, but they have all been important. They have all permitted me to bore closer to the center of mystery I know is there—the mystery of family history, or American vision gone wrong, of class arrogance, of illness and disease, of brave and frugal parents, of six generations of Haberkosts who a million times have walked Grant Street—the street that connects Goosetown and Firestone Park.

"In 1996 my writing excursions took me inside my mother's Alzheimer's unit, one of the strangest and most miraculous places I have ever known. Through literary nonfiction, my favorite genre, I recorded what I saw there, and what I learned. The book, *In a Tangled Wood,* began with an invitation to write from two mute swans that suddenly appeared in the pond that bordered my mother's unit. It ended, months later, in a manuscript that I'd like to say I wrote for my mother, but I know was really a gift from her to me. I was merely her scrivener.

"I am currently completing a memoir about my growing-up years in Firestone Park and have found, as I often do when I write, that I have been forced to go to odd and difficult places—the corner of Cross and Grant where my cousin Eddie was killed at age five, the house on Grant Street where August Haberkost tormented his wife and seven children, the Firestone Memorial where I slept in the arms of a huge bronze statue of Harvey Firestone, the site of a two-hundred-year-old American elm tree (the only one in Akron that survived Dutch elm disease), the rubber plant where my father rose for a while in management but finally ended his career on clock as a janitor.

"I also enjoy editing collections. My Appalachian roots—both through my grandfather Coyne's experience in northern mines and the experiences of many uncles from West Virginia who came to Akron to work in the rubber plants (then married my aunts)—are important to me. It was probably this personal connection that led me to the literature of Appalachia over twenty years ago. I have come to realize that Appalachian letters have suffered serious neglect—like the region itself. I have also come to realize that Appalachian literature is at the heart of America's most recent literary renaissance—a powerful and diverse literature of enormous importance. I have tried to do the little I can to celebrate the achievement of Appalachian letters and draw attention to Appalachian art. *Bloodroot,* for example, is a collection of original essays by contemporary Appalachian women writers about the influence of place on their work. I am currently trying to mount a new project called *Letters from the Region* that collects correspondence from Appalachian writers. Both of these projects are intended, in part, to provide a better understanding and definition of the region than the country has had in the past. The writers I ask to contribute are insiders who live and work in the mountains, not outsiders just traveling through.

"I continue to believe that writers must be susceptible to metaphor, unafraid to see those invisible strands that hold the whole world together. It's that task, primarily, that calls us to this profession, rather than some other."

* * *

EAKIN, Paul John 1938-

PERSONAL: Born March 8, 1938, in Cleveland, OH; son of Paul James (an investment banker) and Jean (a social worker and naturalist; maiden name, Gibson) Eakin; married Sybil Shepard (a freelance writer and editor), 1964; children: Marion C., Emily J., Hallie C., Hugh G. *Education:* Harvard University, A.B., 1959, A.M., 1961, Ph.D., 1966.

ADDRESSES: Office—Department of English, Indiana University—Bloomington, Bloomington, IN 47405; fax: 812-855-9535. *E-mail*—eakin@indiana.edu.

CAREER: Indiana University—Bloomington, assistant professor, 1966-72, associate professor, 1972-79, professor, 1979-99, Ruth N. Halls Professor of English, 1999—. University of Paris XII, senior Fulbright lecturer, 1972-73, 1991; University of Athens, senior Fulbright lecturer, 1978-79.

MEMBER: Modern Language Association of America, American Association of University Professors.

WRITINGS:

The New England Girl: Cultural Ideals in Hawthorne, Stowe, Howells, and James, University of Georgia Press (Athens, GA), 1977.

Fictions in Autobiography: Studies in the Art of Self-Invention, Princeton University Press (Princeton, NJ), 1985.

(Editor and author of introduction) Philippe Lejeune, *On Autobiography,* University of Minnesota Press (Minneapolis, MN), 1987.

(Editor and author of introduction) *American Autobiography: Retrospect and Prospect,* University of Wisconsin Press (Madison, WI), 1991.

Touching the World: Reference in Autobiography, Princeton University Press, 1992.

How Our Lives Become Stories: Making Selves, Cornell University Press (Ithaca, NY), 1999.

Contributor to literature journals.

SIDELIGHTS: Paul John Eakin once told *CA:* "I expect to continue my research and writing on autobiography for a good many years to come, for I find in it an opportunity to confront questions—the nature of the self, the meaning and the shape of a life—that are of the deepest import to me in my personal, as well as professional, life. I suspect that I am, in this sense, a kind of crypto-autobiographer, working indirectly through my study of the lives of others to understand my own."

BIOGRAPHICAL/CRITICAL SOURCES:

PERIODICALS

Times Literary Supplement, January 10, 1986.

* * *

EASTMAN, Charles A(lexander) 1858-1939 (Ohiyesa)

PERSONAL: Sioux name, Ohiyesa (name means "Winner"); born February 19, 1858, on the Santee reservation near Redwood Falls, MN; died January 8, 1939; buried in Detroit, MI; son of Jacob (a homesteader; Sioux name, Ite Wakanhdi Ota [name means "Many Lightnings"]) and Mary Nancy (Sioux name, Wakantankanwin [name means "Goddess"]) Eastman; married Elaine Goodale (a teacher and poet), June, 1891 (separated, 1921); children: Dora Winona, Irene Taluta, Virginia, Ohiyesa II, Eleanor, Florence. *Education:* Attended Beloit College and Knox College; Dartmouth College, B.S., 1887; Boston University, M.D., 1890.

CAREER: Writer, physician, and lecturer. Indian Health Service, Pine Ridge Reservation, SD, agency physician, 1890-93; private medical practice in St. Paul, MN, beginning 1893. Active in Young Men's Christian Association (YMCA), 1894-97; lobbyist for

Charles A. Eastman

Santee Sioux in Washington, D.C., 1897-99; outing agent for Carlisle Indian School, PA, 1899; Crow Creek Agency, SD, agency physician, 1900-03; worked for U.S. government, 1903; associated with the Boy Scouts of America beginning 1910; U.S. Indian inspector, 1923-25; lecturer.

MEMBER: Society for American Indians (co-founder, 1911; president, 1918).

AWARDS, HONORS: Indian Achievement Award, 1933.

WRITINGS:

Indian Boyhood (autobiography), McClure, Philips (New York), 1902.

Red Hunters and the Animal People (legends), Harper (New York), 1904.

Old Indian Days (legends), McClure (New York), 1907.

(With wife, Elaine Goodale Eastman) *Wigwam Evenings: Sioux Folk Tales Retold* (legends), Little,

Brown (Boston), 1909, republished as *Smoky Day's Wigwam Evenings: Indian Stories Retold,* Little, Brown, 1910.

The Soul of the Indian: An Interpretation, Houghton Mifflin (Boston), 1911.

Indian Child Life (nonfiction), Little, Brown (Boston), 1913.

Indian Scout Talks: A Guide for Boy Scouts and Campfire Girls (nonfiction), Little, Brown (Boston), 1914, republished as *Indian Scout Craft and Lore,* Dover (New York), 1974.

The Indian Today: The Past and Future of the First American, Doubleday, Page (Garden City, NY), 1915.

From the Deep Woods to Civilization: Chapters in the Autobiography of an Indian, Little, Brown (Boston), 1916.

Indian Heroes and Great Chieftains, Little, Brown (Boston), 1918.

The Soul of an Indian and Other Writings from Ohiyesa (Charles Alexander Eastman), edited and arranged by Kent Nerburn, New World Library (San Rafael, CA), 1993.

Contributor to periodicals, including *Chautauquan, Craftsman, Boys' Life, Lippincott's Magazine, Popular Science Monthly, Quarterly Journal of the Society of American Indians,* and *American Indian Magazine.*

SIDELIGHTS: Charles A. Eastman, a physician, writer, and spokesman for Indian affairs, was the first well-known Native American author. In eleven books and many articles, Eastman told the story of his own life and gathered Sioux myths, legends, and history in such a way that made them accessible to a mainstream white audience. The unique perspective apparent in Eastman's work—that of an American Indian who was acculturated into white society without forsaking his heritage—made Eastman's a voice that was respected by his readers, much in keeping with the respect he held for his subject.

When Eastman was four years old, just after the Sioux Indian Uprising of 1862, he fled to Canada with his family. Since his father, Many Lightnings, was presumed dead in the fracas and his mother had died at his birth, Eastman's uncle adopted the boy and raised him, with the boy's grandmother's help, in the traditional Indian ways. Young Ohiyesa (his Sioux name, meaning "The Winner") was fully trained as a hunter and warrior. His father reappeared with a new name, Jacob Eastman, and a new religion: Christianity. He had not died during the uprising; instead, he had been imprisoned, sentenced to death, and then pardoned. When he saw Ohiyesa, he invited his son to return with him to the homestead he had built in Dakota Territory.

Thus began Eastman's formal education, which took him through Dartmouth and medical school at Boston University. In 1890, he returned to the Pine Ridge Reservation in South Dakota, where he treated victims at Wounded Knee. That year he met Elaine Goodale, an educator, social worker, and writer who would become his wife and collaborator in his writings.

With his wife's editing and encouragement, Eastman began writing about his childhood in 1893 and began to publish the resulting pieces in *St. Nicholas: An Illustrated Magazine for Young Folks.* These articles were the basis of Eastman's first book, *Indian Boyhood* (1902), an autobiography written for children. In recalling his childhood, Eastman gave special emphasis to his grandmother and his uncle, documenting with loving detail the care and instruction these two bestowed upon him until his father's return. Eastman presented idyllic elements of life among his people alongside objective accounts of the struggles of Indian life—conflicts with whites and other Indians, sickness, hunger. Raymond Wilson, in *Dictionary of Literary Biography,* submitted that the balance of the work was skewed more toward "idealizing and romanticizing his past and investing it with an atmosphere of childlike simplicity . . . [conveying] a longing to return to a world in which nearly every activity helped develop courage, endurance, generosity, or patience."

Over the next few years, Eastman released three collections of Sioux stories that clarified Indian, and particularly Sioux, ways. In 1904, Eastman's first collection appeared. In twelve stories about various animals, *Red Hunters and the Animal People* revealed the special relationship between the Sioux and animals. "Indian hunters," Wilson summed, "learn from animals in the hope of acquiring their resourcefulness, while whites indiscriminately kill the animals." Eastman's second collection, *Old Indian Days* (1907), offered more exciting fare, with stories about warriors and women, making Eastman, Wilson stated, "one of the first authors to provide a comprehensive and accurate view of the major roles women played in Sioux society." Both *Red Hunters* and *Old Indian Days* offered glossaries of Sioux words. *Wigwam Evenings: Sioux Folk Tales Retold* (1909), which Eastman co-authored with his wife, had an Indian storyteller telling tales to Sioux children in a structure reminiscent of the Uncle Remus tales. As in Aesop, each tale had a moral attached. As a whole, the book offered clear statements of Indian values as well as conveying further understanding of Sioux spiritual beliefs.

Eastman wrote a more direct explanation of Indian beliefs in *The Soul of the Indian* (1911). Religious instruction was primarily in the hands of the women, who passed on to Indian children natural lore, Indian virtues, and prayer, as Eastman's grandmother Uncheedah did for him. (Interestingly, Eastman's wife was a staunch assimilationist and once gave a speech decrying Indian grandmothers' role in propagating the old ways, thwarting assimilation.) Eastman gave significant attention to the contradictions implicit between the whites' Christianity and their actions, and he described Indian bewilderment when whites met Indian openness to miraculous Christian tales by unilaterally dismissing Indian creation stories.

In 1915 Eastman wrote *The Indian Today: The Past and Future of the First American,* a chronicle of Indian history up to the then present. The book documented "how white contact destroyed Indian societies," Wilson related, particularly the destruction wrought by alcohol and guns, and the terrible reservation conditions. This powerful invective on the behalf of the American Indian served as a platform from which Eastman strongly supported enactment of the Dawes Act of 1887, as it might have made it possible for Indians to gain citizenship and its attendant rights. He also called for the elimination and replacement of the Bureau of Indian Affairs with a more racially balanced group to ensure fair representation.

From the Deep Woods to Civilization: Chapters in the Autobiography of an Indian (1916), picking up where *Indian Boyhood* left off, clarified Eastman's personal development from young warrior into a tireless proponent of Indian rights. It is an account of the growth of an idealistic young warrior into a cynical adult. According to a contributor for the *Encyclopedia of World Biography,* Eastman's "pervasive tone of innocence in *Indian Boyhood* was now replaced by one of frustration." Eastman's final book, *Indian Heroes and Great Chieftains* (1918), is a collection of short biographies of Indian leaders whose actions displayed a loyalty to their cultures and their people. In this volume, Eastman set straight the whites' lack of acknowledgment of Indian military skill and condemned them for their unfairness in matters of land and war.

In 1921, Eastman and his wife separated and he did not publish anymore writings. While the nature of the split was unclear, according to Wilson one thing was clear: "They had been, despite their problems, an excellent writing team: he had furnished the experiences and ideas, and she had supplied the literary skill."

Eastman's was a career in which he promoted his culture and his people as well as himself. Writing was one facet of his career. Throughout his life, he spent years doctoring on reservations, lobbying for the Santee Sioux in Washington, DC, and working with the Bureau of Indian Affairs to rename thousands of Sioux in order to protect their property rights. He began a long association with the Boy Scouts in 1910, contributing to their magazine *Boys' Life,* and he and his wife opened and ran a camp for girls for several years. He helped found the Society of American Indians in 1911. There was once even talk of his installation as Woodrow Wilson's commissioner of Indian affairs. Once he stopped writing books, Eastman maintained an active, international lecturing schedule for the rest of his life. He died January 8, 1939. Wilson finished his essay: "[Eastman] was the first major Indian author to write Indian history from the Indian perspective; the main objective of his publications was to tear down the wall of prejudice that separated Indians and whites."

BIOGRAPHICAL/CRITICAL SOURCES:

BOOKS

Copeland, Marion W., *Charles Alexander Eastman (Ohiyesa),* Caxton Printers, 1978.

Dictionary of Literary Biography, Volume 175: *Native American Writers of the United States,* Gale, 1997, pp. 75-83.

Encyclopedia of World Biography, second edition, Volume 5, Gale, 1998, pp. 183-185.

Wilson, Raymond, *Ohiyesa: Charles Eastman, Santee Sioux,* University of Illinois Press, 1983.

PERIODICALS

American Indian Quarterly, autumn, 1977, pp. 199-208.

Great Plains Quarterly, spring, 1988, pp. 89-101.

South Dakota Historical Review, July, 1937, pp. 171-184.

South Dakota History, winter, 1975, pp. 55-73.*

* * *

EBERSTADT, Nicholas (Nash) 1955-

PERSONAL: Born December 20, 1955, in New York, NY; son of Frederick (a photographer) and Isabel (a writer; maiden name, Nash) Eberstadt; married Mary Tedeschi (a writer), October 24, 1987; children: Frederick William, Catherine Nash, Isabel. *Education:* Harvard University, B.A., M.P.A., Ph.D.; London School of Economics and Political Science, M.Sc. *Politics:* "Classical liberal."

ADDRESSES: Home—3511 Lowell St. N.W., Washington, DC 20016. *Office*—American Enterprise Institute for Public Policy Research (AEI), 1150 17th St. N.W., Washington, DC 20036. *E-mail*—eberstadt@aei.org.

CAREER: American Enterprise Institute for Public Policy Research, Washington, DC, visiting scholar, then Wendt Chair in Political Economy, 1985—. Harvard University, visiting fellow, 1980—; consultant to government and private organizations, including U.S. Bureau of the Census, World Bank, and State Department.

WRITINGS:

Foreign Aid and American Purpose, AEI Press (Washington, DC), 1988.
The Poverty of Communism, Transaction Books (New Brunswick, NJ), 1988.
(With J. Banister) *The Population of North Korea,* University of California Press (Berkeley, CA), 1992.
Korea Approaches Reunification, M. E. Sharpe (Armonk, NY), 1995.
The Tyranny of Numbers: Mismeasurement and Misrule, AEI Press, 1995.
The End of North Korea, AEI Press, 1999.

Also contributor of articles to periodicals, including *Wall Street Journal, New Republic, New York Times, Times Literary Supplement, New York Review of Books, National Review, Atlantic Monthly, Foreign Affairs,* and *Commentary.*

SIDELIGHTS: Nicholas Eberstadt, who holds the Wendt Chair in Political Economy at the American Enterprise Institute, is versed in a number of important fields. He has written and spoken on demographic and foreign aid issues, on ways to improve poverty and reduce famine, on politics in East Asia with emphasis on North Korea, and on issues affecting Russia and other former Soviet republics. His speaking duties have taken him before congressional committees, international summit meetings, and onto radio and television as a commentator. Eberstadt has been particularly attentive to events in North Korea, a communist nation born during the Cold War that today suffers from isolationism, famine, and a reputation as a terrorist state.

In *The End of North Korea,* Eberstadt describes the beleaguered country's plight at the end of the twentieth century, maintaining that it is "less a nation-state than a shakedown state," to quote *New York Times Book Review* correspondent Aaron L. Friedberg. Eberstadt demonstrates how North Korea has used the threat of nuclear terrorism to extort outside assistance from South Korea, Japan, and the United States, assistance that has done little to stave off mass starvation and economic decline within its borders. Friedberg wrote: "Eberstadt argues persuasively that prolonging North Korea's life may actually increase the costs and the dangers of its inevitable demise." The author "brilliantly challenges the conventional wisdom that North Korea is ruled by madmen," to quote Lucian W. Pye in *Foreign Affairs.* Pye added: "Eberstadt convincingly argues that the inherent flaws in communism will inevitably doom North Korea—and it is time to start preparing for the eventual reunification with the South."

Eberstadt once told *CA:* "I come from a family with a literary tradition. When I was quite young, I tried writing fiction. This proved too difficult; I have stuck with nonfiction ever since. Most of my writing is in the realm of what is somewhat pretentiously called 'social science.' Using numbers as a cane, rather than a cudgel, I try to help my readers traverse contemporary social and economic problems. I enjoy writing. It forces me to clarify."

BIOGRAPHICAL/CRITICAL SOURCES:

PERIODICALS

Foreign Affairs, November-December, 1999, Lucian W. Pye, "Recent Books on International Relations: Asia and the Pacific," p. 139.
New York Times Book Review, December 12, 1999, Aaron L. Friedberg, "Loose Cannon," p. 23.

* * *

ELFSTROM, Gerard 1945-

PERSONAL: Born February 26, 1945, in Rockford, IL; son of LeRoy and June Elfstrom. *Ethnicity:* "Caucasian." *Education:* Cornell College, Mount Vernon, IA, B.A., 1967; Emory University, M.A., 1969, Ph.D., 1975.

ADDRESSES: Home—306 East Magnolia Ave., Apt. 113, Auburn, AL 36830. *Office*—Department of Philosophy, 6080 Haley Center, Auburn University, Auburn, AL 36489-5210. *E-mail*—elfstga@mail.auburn.edu.

CAREER: Morris Brown College, Atlanta, GA, assistant professor of philosophy and head of department, 1976-80; Emory University, Atlanta, visiting assistant professor of philosophy, 1981-84; Agnes Scott College, Decatur, GA, assistant professor of philosophy, 1985-88; Auburn University, Auburn, AL, assistant professor, 1988-92, associate professor, 1992-97, professor of philosophy, 1997—.

MEMBER: American Philosophical Association, Society for the Advancement of American Philosophy, Law and Philosophy Study Group, Southern Society for Philosophy and Psychology, Alabama Philosophical Society, Georgia Philosophical Society (vice president, 1981-82; president, 1982-83).

WRITINGS:

(With Nicholas Fotion) *Military Ethics,* Routledge (New York City), 1986.
Ethics for a Shrinking World, St. Martin's (New York City), 1989.
Moral Issues and Multinational Corporations, St. Martin's, 1991.
(With Fotion) *Toleration,* University of Alabama Press (University), 1992.
New Challenges for Political Philosophy, St. Martin's, 1997.
International Ethics: A Reference Handbook, American Bibliographical Center-Clio Press (Santa Barbara, CA), 1998.

Contributor of articles and reviews to periodicals.

* * *

EMERSON, Caryl (Geppert) 1944-

PERSONAL: Born August 30, 1944, in Highland Park, IL; son of David Geppert and Bonnie Pfanstiehl; married Ivan Zaknic. *Education:* Cornell University, B.A., 1966; Harvard University, M.A. and M.A.T., both 1968; University of Texas at Austin, Ph.D., 1980.

ADDRESSES: Home—67 Dempsey Ave., Princeton, NJ 08540. *Office*—Department of Slavic Languages and Literatures, Princeton University, Princeton, NJ 05844.

CAREER: Windham College, Putney, VT, instructor, 1970-75, assistant professor of Russian language, literature, and history, 1975-76; University of Texas at Austin, assistant instructor in Russian language, 1976-80; Cornell University, Ithaca, NY, assistant professor, 1980-86, associate professor of Russian literature, 1986-87; Princeton University, Princeton, NJ, professor of Slavic languages and literatures, beginning 1987, currently A. Watson Armour, III University Professor of Slavic Languages and Literatures.

MEMBER: American Association for the Advancement of Slavic Studies, Modern Language Association of America, American Association of Teachers of Slavic and East European Languages.

WRITINGS:

(Translator with Michael Holquist) *The Dialogic Imagination: Four Essays by M. M. Bakhtin,* University of Texas Press (Austin, TX), 1981.
Boris Godunov: Transpositions of a Russian Theme, Indiana University Press (Bloomington, IN), 1986.
(Editor with Holquist) M. M. Bakhtin, *Speech Genres and Other Late Essays,* University of Texas Press, 1987.
(Editor with Gary Saul Morson) *Rethinking Bakhtin: Extensions and Challenges,* Northwestern University Press (Evanston, IL), 1989.
(With Gary Saul Morson) *Mikhail Bakhtin: Creation of a Prosaics,* Stanford University Press (Stanford, CA), 1990.
(With William Oldani) *Modest Musorgsky and Boris Godunov: Myths, Realities, Reconsiderations,* Cambridge University Press (Cambridge, England), 1994.
The First Hundred Years of Mikhail Bakhtin, Princeton University Press (Princeton, NJ), 1997.
(Editor) *Critical Essays on Mikhail Bakhtin,* G. K. Hall (New York City), 1999.
The Life of Musorgsky, Cambridge University Press (New York City), 1999.

Also author of *Boris Godunov Opera Handbook,* for Cambridge University Press. Contributor to literature and Slavic studies journals.

SIDELIGHTS: Caryl Emerson has published widely on Russian literature, literary critics, opera, and composers. She is best known for her extensive work on Mikhail Bakhtin (1895-1975), a literary theorist and philosopher whose works have been intensely studied in Russia and Eastern Europe. "Caryl Emerson is arguably the most knowledgeable and gifted Bakhtin scholar in the United States," declared Tomas Venclova in the *New Republic.* "Emerson deals with Russian history and culture with admirable ease; she is at home in areas that many native [Russian] scholars would consider unfamiliar and esoteric."

Emerson's *The First Hundred Years of Mikhail Bakhtin* offers a centennial overview of Russian criticism on Bakhtin. According to Venclova, the book "provides us with fascinating glimpses of [Bakhtin's] life and his character, and with a history of his intellectual career in Russia and in the West, and with a serious discussion of the problematic areas of his thought." The critic added: "After giving the reader a clear picture of recent Russian criticism on Bakhtin, Emerson proceeds to her own opinions, which, as a rule, are very well-reasoned and tend toward the golden mean." In *Nation,* Scott McLemee cited *The First Hundred Years of Mikhail Bakhtin* as "one of the three or four most important works on the theorist now available in English. Emerson, a leading translator and interpreter of Bakhtin's writings, has prepared a detailed report on the state of Bakhtinology in the former Soviet Union. . . . But the core of Emerson's book lies not in the addition of new details about Bakhtin himself but rather in her precis of the debates and discordant readings his work has inspired over the years." McLemee concluded that the book "makes the rereading of Bakhtin not one bit easier or less troubling, which is the highest praise I can think to give."

BIOGRAPHICAL/CRITICAL SOURCES:

PERIODICALS

Nation, December 29, 1997, Scott McLemee, review of *The First Hundred Years of Mikhail Bakhtin,* p. 16.

New Republic, May 18, 1998, Tomas Venclova, review of *The First Hundred Years of Mikhail Bakhtin,* p. 25.

New York Times Book Review, March 22, 1987.

Times Literary Supplement, July 17, 1987; August 21, 1987; December 31, 1999, Marina Frolova-Walker, review of *The Life of Musorgsky,* p. 28.*

F

FISHER, Angela 1947-

PERSONAL: Born September 17, 1947, in Adelaide, Australia; daughter of Henry (a chartered accountant) and Kate (a dress designer; maiden name, Gibson) Fisher. *Education:* Adelaide University, social studies degree, 1967.

ADDRESSES: *Home*—42 Belsize Ave., Belsize Park, London NW3 4AH, England.

CAREER: Social worker, Darwin, Australia, 1968-70; researcher of traditional jewelry and jewelry designer, various African and Middle Eastern countries, 1970-77; photographer and writer, 1977—; freelance jewelry designer in Australia, England, the United States, and Kenya, 1984—.

WRITINGS:

Africa Adorned, Abrams (New York City), 1984.
(With Carol Beckwith and Graham Hancock) *African Ark: People and Ancient Cultures of Ethiopia and the Horn of Africa,* Abrams, 1990.
(With Beckwith) *African Ceremonies,* 2 volumes, Abrams, 1999.

SIDELIGHTS: Angela Fisher's career has taken her to some of the remotest corners of Africa, and the photographer and jewelry designer's vivid experiences have inspired her three illustrated books. Fisher left her native Australia in 1970 after two years as a social worker and arrived in Africa as a tourist. She soon found herself captivated by the rich pageantry of body and jewelry ornamentation that is a vital part of most of that continent's cultures. Fisher then began documenting, with her camera and a notebook, the wide variety of personal adornment practiced by each of the peoples she encountered. She remained in Africa for seven years and traveled through nearly every country in her quest to chronicle the hairstyles, clothing, jewelry, body-piercing, and tattooing of such groups as the Fali of Cameroon, the Masai of Kenya, and the Berbers of the northern countries. Often making her way on foot, horseback, or canoe, Fisher overcame language and culture barriers in documenting this vanishing art.

The result was her first book, *Africa Adorned,* a 1984 work illustrated with some 457 of her own photographs. Fisher's accompanying text examines the history and cultural significance relative to each of the styles depicted. She relates the essential sociological role that hair, jewelry, and make-up play among the individual cultures, and discusses how they are used in both everyday life and in the more formal traditional rituals. A multitude of bracelets, elaborately plaited hair, lip plugs, or a painted face may denote much about the wearer's social or sexual status, family wealth, or age.

Fisher's text explores African attitudes about ornamentation that may seem difficult for an outsider to comprehend—painful processes such as ritual scarring or the stretching of lips and earlobes are an important part of certain cultures. The author also discusses the means by which modern African governments have discouraged these centuries-old tribal practices, denouncing them as "primitive." *Voice Literary Supplement* contributor Guy Trebay remarked: "Fisher's eye for spirited invention leavens this book, whose serious task it is to record vanishing ways and a depleted store of art and artifact." Beverly Beyette, writing in the *Los Angeles Times Book Review,* noted that *Africa Adorned* is "not just another beautiful book" and found many of Fisher's photographs "riveting."

The expertise Fisher gained from studying the jewelry of Africa led to a career as a jewelry designer. She divides her time between London and Kenya, where her brother was also living in the mid-1980s. His chance encounter with Carol Beckwith, an American photographer whose book on the Masai was completed around the same time as *Africa Adorned,* led to a meeting and a merging of interests. The two women soon began a five-year trek together in order to gather photographs for *African Ark: People and Ancient Cultures of Ethiopia and the Horn of Africa.* The 1990 book concentrates primarily on the inhabitants and cultures of Ethiopia, Kenya, and Somalia. Fisher and Beckwith traveled with native guides and discovered ingenious methods to win over the trust and camaraderie of their subjects. The two photographers shared photo credits for the illustrations, and the text was written by Graham Hancock.

The success of *African Ark* led to an even more daunting enterprise. Over a period of ten years, Fisher and Beckwith journeyed the length and breadth of Africa, making a photographic record of forty-three public ceremonies from twenty-six different countries. The two-volume *African Ceremonies* was published in 1999, with more than 800 color photographs that capture important moments from birth to death, and beyond to a communication with the spirit world. "These are sumptuous photographs—a visual feast—and they reflect both the photographers' gift for gaining the trust of their subjects and the reciprocal generosity of all sorts of African men and women," declared K. Anthony Appiah in the *New York Times Book Review.* "If these ceremonies are familiar, they have seldom been as elegantly photographed. But even more impressive are the pictures from behind the scenes, in the more intimate events when ceremony comes to focus on a single moment in a human life."

Selected by the Book-of-the-Month Club, *African Ceremonies* drew particular praise for its attention to vanishing rituals. A *Washington Post Book World* reviewer deemed the work "a stunning collection of 847 full-color photographs that, in some cases, document ways of life and worship that are no longer practiced." A *Publishers Weekly* correspondent likewise wrote: "Ten years in the making, the volumes also represent an important anthropological achievement—some of the rituals have never been seen by outsiders and many others are disappearing under the cumulative pressure of drought, famine, political upheaval and Western influence." While himself expressing doubt about the extinction of regional African ceremonies, Appiah nevertheless observed that the Africa presented by Fisher and Beckwith "is not just a fantasy of our authors: it is also something that many Africans have come to believe in. When Beckwith and Fisher say that they are seeking to capture ceremonies that may soon disappear, this rhetoric of rescue is not just theirs, it is the rhetoric of many of the people whom they are photographing." For his part, Appiah concluded: "What [the photographers] show is not how African ceremonies are dying, but how alive so many of them are."

Fisher told *CA:* "The Horn of Africa is like a microcosm of the entire continent, with peoples of all different life styles and spiritual beliefs, including Islam, Christianity, Animism, and Judaism.

"My work, *African Ceremonies,* is a five-year study of rites of passage—from birth, initiation, courtship, and marriage to religious festivals across the African continent."

BIOGRAPHICAL/CRITICAL SOURCES:

PERIODICALS

Economist, October 9, 1999, "Africa's Vanishing Ceremonies," p. 106.
Library Journal, December, 1999, Eugene C. Burt, review of *African Ceremonies,* p. 148.
Los Angeles Times Book Review, December 2, 1984.
National Geographic, November, 1984; February, 1991; September, 1994.
Newsweek, December 10, 1984, p. 90.
New York Times Book Review, December 5, 1999, K. Anthony Appiah, "The Rite Stuff," p. 13.
People, November 12, 1990, pp. 159-60.
Publishers Weekly, October 25, 1999, review of *African Ceremonies,* p. 57; December 13, 1999, review of *African Ceremonies,* p. 44.
Washington Post Book World, December 2, 1984, pp. 7-8; December 5-11, 1999, review of *African Ceremonies,* p. 5.
Voice Literary Supplement, November, 1984, p. 3.*

* * *

FLAHERTY, Michael G. 1952-

PERSONAL: Born March 15, 1952; U.S. citizen. *Ethnicity:* "Irish/Italian." *Education:* University of South Florida, B.A. (with honors), 1975, M.A., 1977; University of Illinois at Urbana-Champaign, Ph.D., 1982.

ADDRESSES: Office—Department of Sociology, Eckerd College, 4200 54th Ave. S., St. Petersburg, FL 33711.

CAREER: Eckerd College, St. Petersburg, FL, assistant professor, 1980-87, associate professor, 1987-92, professor of sociology, 1992—.

WRITINGS:

(Editor with Carolyn Ellis) *Investigating Subjectivity: Research on Lived Experience,* Sage Publications (Beverly Hills, CA), 1992.
(Editor with Ellis) *Social Perspectives on Emotions,* Volume III, JAI Press (Greenwich, CT), 1995.
A Watched Pot: How We Experience Time, New York University Press (New York City), 1999.

Contributor to sociology journals.

* * *

FORMAN, Robert K. C. 1947-

PERSONAL: Born August 3, 1947, in Baltimore, MD; son of Leonard (a business owner) and Rosalind (a psychotherapist and homemaker; maiden name, Michaelson) Forman; married, wife's name Yvonne K. C. (an artist and au pair coordinator), November 20, 1975; children: Rosha, Avram. *Education:* University of Chicago, B.A., 1969; Columbia University, M.A., M.Phil., Ph.D., 1988. *Religion:* "Idiosyncratic and polyglot." *Avocational interests:* Meditation, singing, chopping wood, fixing up his old house (built in 1735).

ADDRESSES: Home—Hastings on Hudson, NY. *Office*—Program in Religion, 1241 HW, Hunter College of the City University of New York, 695 Park Ave., New York, NY 10021.

CAREER: Vassar College, Poughkeepsie, NY, faculty member, 1987-89; Hunter College of the City University of New York, New York City, began as assistant professor, became associate professor of religious studies, 1989—. Forge Institute for Spirituality and Social Change, computer consultant, 1984-89, executive director, 1991—.

MEMBER: American Academy of Religion (chairperson of Mysticism Group, 1985-93), Association for Transpersonal Psychology, Institute of Noetic Science, Association for Asian Studies.

AWARDS, HONORS: Grants from New World Foundation, 1992, 1993, Fetzer Institute, 1998, Infinity Institute, 2000, and American Council of Learned Societies; merit awards from Columbia University.

WRITINGS:

(Editor) *The Problem of Pure Consciousness,* Oxford University Press (New York City), 1990.
Master Eckhart: Mystic as Theologian, Element, 1992.
(Editor) *Religions of the World,* 3rd edition, St. Martin's (New York City), 1993.
(Editor) *Religions of Asia,* St. Martin's, 1993.
The Innate Capacity, Oxford University Press, 1999.
Mysticism, Mind, and Consciousness, State University of New York Press (Albany, NY), 1999.

WORK IN PROGRESS: Letting Go, a study of spiritual transformation; research on myth and mysticism.

SIDELIGHTS: Robert K. C. Forman told *CA:* "I've been practicing a form of Hindu meditation for twenty-five years now. It has been profoundly important to me, helping me move from a nearly useless social fallout to a productive and, indeed, rather satisfied person. Though I've had many experiences I would call mystical over the years, the important part of a path like this is the way it changes one's life, one's image of oneself, and one's heart; for me, it has done all this. Thus it breaks my heart to see mysticism and spiritual development so poorly understood, so misrepresented in the literature, both academic and trade. It is a truly deep loss, for mysticism could help many. I have been attempting to help create a new academic view of mysticism, which allows its inherently surprising nature to shine through.

"I continue that effort today, but recently I've begun working on a more accessible account of the spiritual process, as seen in the full panoply of cultures, religions, and ages. I believe that a new approach to spirituality is deeply needed in our age, and I want to contribute to that new view in some way. What has happily surprised me is how deeply satisfying it has been to try to formulate my own account of spirituality. Indeed, I find that writing and articulating thoughts about spiritual growth has become my path toward a more complete life."

* * *

FORRESTER, Michael A. 1953-

PERSONAL: Born March 21, 1953, in Glasgow, Scotland; son of John (a teacher) and Moira (a teacher; maiden name, Martin) Forrester. *Ethnicity:* "White." *Education:* Attended St. Aloysius College, 1960-69;

University of Strathclyde, B.A. (with honors), 1983, Ph.D., 1986.

ADDRESSES: Home—Canterbury, Kent, England. *Office*—Department of Psychology, University of Kent at Canterbury, Canterbury CT2 7NP, England. *E-mail*—m.a.forrester@ukc.ac.uk.

CAREER: Loughborough University of Technology, Leicestershire, England, research associate, 1986-87; University of Kent at Canterbury, Canterbury, England, lecturer, 1987-94, senior lecturer in psychology, 1995—.

MEMBER: British Society for Research into Learning Mathematics, British Psychological Society.

WRITINGS:

The Development of Young Children's Social-Cognitive Skills, Lawrence Erlbaum (Hillsdale, NJ), 1992.

Psychology of Language: A Critical Introduction, Sage (London, England), 1996.

Psychology of the Image, Routledge (New York City), 2000.

SIDELIGHTS: In the first section of his 1992 book, *The Development of Young Children's Social-Cognitive Skills,* Michael A. Forrester presents the history of research and theory on the development of social cognition —(the ability to participate in conversation)— in children, citing and analyzing the research and ideas of such noted psychologists as George Herbert Mead and Jean Piaget. After presenting this overview, Forrester goes on to present his own theory, which is comprised of five "essential components involved in the study of children's early developing social-cognitive skills," drawn from and based upon a variety of theories and schools of thought. The final section of *The Development of Young Children's Social-Cognitive Skills* contains several case studies in which Forrester illustrates his theories in action and then extrapolates meaning from them.

BIOGRAPHICAL/CRITICAL SOURCES:

PERIODICALS

Journal of Child Language, 1993, pp. 725-27.

Times Educational Supplement, 1992.

G

GARAFOLA, Lynn 1946-

PERSONAL: Born December 12, 1946, in New York, NY; daughter of Louis (a printer) and Rose Joan (a homemaker; maiden name, Marchione) Garafola; married Eric Foner (a historian), May 1, 1980; children: Daria Rose. *Education:* Barnard College, A.B., 1968; Graduate School and University Center, City University of New York, M.Phil., 1979, Ph.D., 1985.

ADDRESSES: *Home*—606 West 116th St., New York, NY 10027.

CAREER: Berlitz Translation Service, New York City, translator and assistant director, 1970-72; Brooklyn College, City University of New York, Brooklyn, part-time lecturer, 1975-77; Columbia University, New York City, lecturer, 1985 and 1986, adjunct assistant professor, 1988-89; *Dance Magazine,* New York City, critic, feature writer, and editor, 1985—; New York State Council on the Arts, New York City, dance department auditor, 1985—; writer. Reader for Duke University Press, Princeton University Press, Oxford University Press, and *Dance Research Journal;* coordinator of various dance seminars; guest on and consultant for *Eye on Dance,* WNYC-TV.

MEMBER: Society of Dance History Scholars, Dance Critics Association (treasurer, 1985-87; co-president, 1987-88).

AWARDS, HONORS: Fulbright fellow, 1968-69; Social Science Research Council fellow, 1978-79; Getty fellowship in the history of art and the humanities, 1986-87; De la Torre Bueno Prize, 1990, for *Diaghilev's Ballets Russes;* scholar-in-residence, Getty Center for the History of Art and the Humanities, 1991-92.

WRITINGS:

Diaghilev's Ballets Russes, Oxford University Press (New York City), 1989.

(Editor with Joan Acocella) *Andre Levinson on Dance: Writings from Paris in the Twenties,* Wesleyan University Press (Middletown, CT), 1991.

(Editor) *Rethinking the Sylph: New Perspectives on the Romantic Ballet,* University Press of New England (Hanover, NH), 1997.

(Editor) Jose Limon, *Jose Limon: An Unfinished Memoir,* University Press of New England, 1998.

(Editor with Nancy Van Norman Baer) *The Ballets Russes and Its World,* Yale University Press (New Haven, CT), 1999.

(With husband, Eric Foner) *Dance for a City: Fifty Years of the New York City Ballet,* Columbia University Press (New York City), 1999.

Contributer to *Martin Scorsese: The First Decade,* Redgrave (South Salem, NY), 1980; *Lydia Lopokova,* Weidenfeld & Nicolson (London), 1983; and *New York, 1940-1965,* Rizzoli International (New York City), 1988.

Also editor, with Vicente Garcia-Marquez, of the exhibition catalogue *Espana y los Ballets Russes,* 1989. Contributor to *International Dance Encyclopedia* and *Reader's Encyclopedia of American History;* contributor of numerous articles and reviews to periodicals, including *Commonweal, Nation, Ballet Review, Dance Research Journal, Women's Review of Books,* and *Dance Magazine.* Co-editor, *Studies in Dance History;* dance editor, *Encyclopedia of New York City;* assistant editor, *American National Biography.*

WORK IN PROGRESS: A biography of Russian dancer/patron/producer Ida Rubinstein.

SIDELIGHTS: Lynn Garafola's *Diaghilev's Ballets Russes* explores the economic, social, and artistic history of the avant-garde Russo-French ballet company Ballets Russes and the life of its producer, Serge Diaghilev. Founded in 1909, the Ballets Russes dominated the dance world for twenty years; under Diaghilev's direction its productions were renowned for innovative music, choreography, costumes, and set designs—elements that Diaghilev believed should share equal importance in a dance production. *Washington Post Book World* contributor Robert Craft remarked that throughout Garafola's book, "Diaghilev's intuitive genius and genius in artistic matchmaking, his depth of culture and manifold musical and theatrical talents are in evidence." The work of Diaghilev and Ballets Russes is remembered favorably, and *Diaghilev's Ballets Russes* received generally positive reviews. Garafola's research was lauded by *New York Times Book Review* contributor Alastair Macauley as "awesomely thorough," and he described the book as "dense with new findings, connections, scrutiny." Writing in the *New Republic,* Richard Taruskin pronounced the book "surely the most detached (and therefore the most valuable) account of [Diaghilev's] extraordinary career. . . . This is the first study of the impresario and his accomplishments to be informed by sophisticated historical methods, the first to meet professional historiographical standards." Some reviewers took exception to the frequent repetition and the lack of clear chronology in the text. *Times Literary Supplement* contributor Robert Orledge granted, however, that *Diaghilev's Ballets Russes* is, "a major contribution to dance scholarship which no one interested in the subject can afford to ignore." Craft praised the book as "skillfully written, critically perceptive and compendious," deeming it "the most comprehensive and intelligent book so far published about Diaghilev's Ballets Russes."

Garafola has also edited, with Nancy Van Norman Baer, *The Ballets Russes and Its World,* a compendium of essays on the artistic impact of the company and its lasting implications for twentieth century art. According to Carolyn M. Mulac in *Library Journal,* Garafola and Van Norman Baer "have assembled a distinguished group of dance and music shoclars and critics to assess the importance of the Ballets Russes." London's *Sunday Times* reviewer Colin McDowell wrote of the work: "This [is] not just another lightly written, highly illustrated superficial skim—the bane of art books at the end of the century—but something very much more substantial. This is a scholarly and broad-based assessment not only of Diaghilev's spectacular ballet company but also of the artistic and creative background that formed both him and it; a modern reappraisal of the figures who worked with him to make it so artistically triumphant and unassailable; and a measured examination of its continuing influence."

In 1999, Garafola and her husband, historian Eric Foner, published *Dance for a City: Fifty Years of the New York City Ballet.* The book was a companion volume to an exhibit mounted at the New York Historical Society to celebrate the fiftieth anniversary of the highly regarded dance company. The work's text includes six essays on the New York City Ballet and transcripts of interviews with its founder and principal choreographer, George Balanchine. Illustrations and rare photographs of staged works round out the volume. In *Booklist,* Michael Spinella suggested that *Dance for a City* "captures the beauty and reverie of the world of dance that ballet itself evokes. Garafola and Foner have compiled a lovely and interesting look at this amazing company and its lush history." *New York Times Book Review* correspondent Terry Teachout declared: "The pictures are so good that you may want to buy two copies of 'Dance for a City,' one for reading and the other for clipping and framing."

BIOGRAPHICAL/CRITICAL SOURCES:

PERIODICALS

Booklist, August, 1999, Michael Spinella, review of *Dance for a City,* p. 2007.

Library Journal, September 15, 1999, Carolyn M. Mulac, review of *The Ballets Russes and Its World,* p. 84.

New Republic, October 9, 1989, pp. 26-32.

New York Times Book Review, December 24, 1989, p. 12; April 18, 1999, Francis Mason, "Struck by Lightning," p. 23; August 15, 1999, Terry Teachout, "What Balanchine Wrought."

Publishers Weekly, January 11, 1999, review of *Jose Limon,* p. 62.

Sunday Times (London), August 25, 1990; January 2, 2000, Colin McDowell, "Setting the Pace for the Music of Time," pp. 40-41.

Times Literary Supplement, September 28, 1990, p. 1035.

Washington Post Book World, November 12, 1989, pp. 6-7.

OTHER

Dance for a City, http://www.cc.columbia.edu/ (February 13, 2000).

GERMOND, Jack W. 1928-

PERSONAL: Born January 30, 1928, in Newton, MA; son of John W. (an engineer) and Lottie (Clift) Germond; married Barbara Wippler (an investor), December 30, 1951; children: Jessica. *Education:* University of Missouri, B.S., 1951, B.A., 1951.

ADDRESSES: *Home*—Charles Town, WV. *Office*—Baltimore Sun, 501 North Calvert St., P.O. Box 1277, Baltimore, MD 21278.

CAREER: *Evening News,* Monroe, MI, reporter, 1951-53; reporter with Gannett Newspapers, 1953-73, chief of Washington Bureau, 1969-73; *Washington Star,* Washington, DC, political editor, 1974-81, assistant managing editor and columnist, 1977; *Baltimore Evening Sun,* Baltimore, MD, columnist, 1981—. Co-author of political column for *Chicago Tribune*—New York News Syndicate, beginning in 1977. Guest panelist and political analyst on television shows, including *NBC-Today* and *The McLaughlin Group. Military service:* U.S. Army, 1946-47.

WRITINGS:

(With Jules Witcover) *Blue Smoke and Mirrors: How Reagan Won and Why Carter Lost the Election of 1980,* Viking (New York City), 1981.

(With Witcover) *Wake Us When It's Over: Presidential Politics of 1984,* Macmillan (New York City), 1985.

(With Witcover) *Whose Broad Stripes and Bright Stars?: The Trivial Pursuit of the Presidency, 1988,* Warner Books (New York City), 1989.

(With Witcover) *Mad as Hell: Revolt at the Ballot Box, 1992,* Warner Books, 1993.

Fat Man in a Middle Seat: Forty Years of Covering Politics, Random House (New York City), 1999.

Also author, with Witcover, of bimonthly newsletter, *Germond-Witcover Political Report,* beginning 1981. Contributor to periodicals, including *New York Times Magazine, New Republic,* and *National Journal.* Political editor of *Washingtonian Magazine,* 1981.

SIDELIGHTS: Jack W. Germond is a syndicated columnist who has covered presidential politics for more than four decades. Germond and co-author Jules Witcover have published a series of books about specific presidential campaigns and have been dubbed the "dynamic duo of many an Op-Ed page" by a critic in the *Washington Post Book World.* More recently Germond has struck out on his own, covering politics for the *Baltimore Sun* and serving as a regular commentator on *The McLaughlin Group.* A *Publishers Weekly* reviewer wrote of the journalist: "Rumpled, cantankerous and blessed with a sense of humor as dry as the best martini, Germond tells great political stories and tells them expertly."

Germond and Witcover began working together on a political column in the late 1970s, when Germond was at the *Washington Star* and Witcover at the rival *Washington Post.* Theirs was a fruitful collaboration in which they took turns producing five columns a week for syndication, as well as a newsletter and their various books. "You have only two goals in the newspaper business," Germond once told *CA.* "One is, obviously, to make a decent living. There are only two ways to do that in this business: to get syndicated or to become an editor. If you want to stay free, syndication is the answer. The second goal—and this is more important—is to have control of your own schedule, so that no one else assigns you. That's a luxury I've had for quite a long time now."

Germond and Witcover published their first tandem book in 1981, a study of campaign tactics titled *Blue Smoke and Mirrors: How Reagan Won and Why Carter Lost the Election of 1980.* The book focuses on critical events during the election, including key primaries and debates, consequences of the Iranian hostage crisis and the Soviet invasion of Afghanistan, Reagan's knack for handling Carter's negative campaign tactics, and what Lee Walczak in a *Business Week* review called Carter's "fatal predilection to obscure rather than correct his political errors." In presenting these incidents, Germond and Witcover argue that the presidential election of 1980 was won not by the "new political technology" but by "unforseen events [which] were so dominant, compelling, and uncontrollable that they overwhelmed the professionals' efforts to shape and confine the presidential campaign and assure victory for the man of their choice." Walczak considered *Blue Smoke and Mirrors* "one of the better campaign books to come along in some time," while critic Jeff Greenfield recommended the book in the *Saturday Review* as "an absorbing glimpse back into our recent political past."

Subsequent Germond-Witcover collaborations have followed a similar pattern. The two print journalists immerse themselves in a political campaign and, when it has ended, draw from their notes, interviews, and columns to produce a book. A contributor to *The Economist,* reviewing *Whose Broad Stripes and Bright Stars?: The Trivial Pursuit of the Presidency,* described the two authors as "seasoned campaign journalists, informed, industrious, and intuitive. . . . Comprehensive and gossipy, the Germond-Witcover chronicle is rich in insider detail. If you want to know the what, the when and the how of the Republican and Democratic campaigns, it is all here."

In 1999 Germond—alone this time—published *Fat Man in a Middle Seat: Forty Years of Covering Politics.* The memoir offers vignettes on presidents from John F. Kennedy to Bill Clinton, documents Germond's foray onto television in *The McLaughlin Group,* and casts a jaundiced eye on the changes in campaign tactics and reportage in the last decades of the twentieth century. Noting in a *Booklist* review that Germond "doesn't pull any punches," Ilene Cooper and Gilbert Taylor commented: "Still, Germond raking a deserving politician over the coals makes for good fun. . . . His prose is witty, his anecdotes are amusing in that bitter kind of way, his points are well taken, and overall, he's as hard on himself as he is on anyone else." In the *National Review,* Robert D. Novak characterized Germond as "a knee-jerk, even bleeding-heart liberal," but the conservative journalist went on to note that Germond "can be relied on to pick out the phonies." Novak concluded that he hoped younger journalists would read the book "to discover how a great reporter operated—and had fun doing it." *New York Times Book Review* correspondent Michael Tomasky wrote of *Fat Man in a Middle Seat:* "Germond knew everyone, went everywhere, saw everything; his droll style keeps the plot hustling along and can sometimes be quite moving. . . . [The book] is . . . a good one to have on the shelf for handy reference, to settle bets or to marvel at how many Irish coffees those guys could knock back of an evening."

BIOGRAPHICAL/CRITICAL SOURCES:

BOOKS

Germond, Jack, *Fat Man in a Middle Seat: Forty Years of Covering Politics,* Random House (New York City), 1999.

PERIODICALS

American Spectator, December, 1981.

Booklist, October 1, 1999, Ilene Cooper and Gilbert Taylor, review of *Fat Man in a Middle Seat,* p. 306.

Business Week, August 24, 1981.

Christian Science Monitor, September 14, 1981.

Economist, November 18, 1989, review of *Whose Broad Stripes and Bright Stars?,* p. 104.

Library Journal, October 15, 1999, Thomas H. Ferrell, review of *Fat Man in a Middle Seat,* p. 86.

Nation, December 26, 1981.

National Review, November 8, 1999, Robert D. Novak, "Reliable Source," p. 58.

New Republic, December 30, 1981.

Newsweek, January 24, 1977.

New York Times Book Review, December 26, 1993, Ronnie Dugger, "The Year Bill Clinton Won the Pennant"; November 28, 1999, Michael Tomasky, "Boy on the Bus," p. 19.

Progressive, December, 1981.

Publishers Weekly, October 18, 1999, review of *Fat Man in a Middle Seat,* p. 38.

Saturday Review, September, 1981; October, 1981.

Washington Monthly, September, 1981; September, 1993, Walter Shapiro, review of *Mad as Hell,* p. 54.

Washington Post Book World, August 30, 1981.*

* * *

GIOVANNI, Nikki 1943-

PERSONAL: Born Yolande Cornelia Giovanni Jr., June 7, 1943, in Knoxville, TN; daughter of Gus Jones (a probation officer) and Yolande Cornelia (a social worker; maiden name, Watson) Giovanni; children: Thomas Watson. *Education:* Fisk University, B.A. (with honors), 1967; postgraduate studies at University of Pennsylvania School of Social Work and Columbia University School of Fine Arts, 1968.

ADDRESSES: Office—English Department, Virginia Tech, Blacksburg, VA 24061.

CAREER: Poet, writer, and lecturer. Queens College of the City University of New York, Flushing, assistant professor of black studies, 1968; Rutgers University, Livingston College, New Brunswick, NJ, associate professor of English, 1968-72; Ohio State University, Columbus, visiting professor of English, 1984; College of Mount St. Joseph on the Ohio, Mount St. Joseph, Ohio, professor of creative writing, 1985-87; Virginia Tech, Blacksburg, VA, professor, 1987—; Texas Christian University, visiting professor in humanities, 1991. Founder of publishing firm, NikTom Ltd., 1970; participated in "Soul at the Center," Lincoln Center for the Performing Arts, 1972; Duncanson Artist-in-Residence, Taft Museum, Cincinnati, 1986; Co-chair, Literary Arts Festival for State of Tennessee Homecoming, 1986; director, Warm Hearth Writer's Workshop, 1988—; appointed to Ohio Humanities Council, 1987; member of board of directors, Virginia Founda-

Nikki Giovanni

tion for Humanities and Public Policy, 1990-93; participant in Appalachian Community Fund, 1991-93, and Volunteer Action Center, 1991-94; featured poet, International Poetry Festival, Utrecht, Holland, 1991. Has given numerous poetry readings and lectures worldwide and appeared on numerous television talk shows.

MEMBER: National Council of Negro Women, Society of Magazine Writers, National Black Heroines for PUSH, Winnie Mandela Children's Fund Committee, Delta Sigma Theta (honorary member).

AWARDS, HONORS: Grants from Ford Foundation, 1967, National Endowment for the Arts, 1968, and Harlem Cultural Council, 1969; named one of ten "Most Admired Black Women," *Amsterdam News,* 1969; outstanding achievement award, *Mademoiselle,* 1971; Omega Psi Phi Fraternity Award, 1971, for outstanding contribution to arts and letters; Meritorious Plaque for Service, Cook County Jail, 1971; Prince Matchabelli Sun Shower Award, 1971; life membership and scroll, National Council of Negro Women, 1972; National Association of Radio and Television Announcers Award, 1972, for recording *Truth Is on Its Way;* Woman of the Year Youth Leadership Award, *Ladies' Home Journal,* 1972; National Book Award nomination, 1973, for *Gemini: An Extended Autobiographical Statement on My First Twenty-five Years of Being a Black Poet;* "Best Books for Young Adults" citation, American Library Association, 1973, for *My House;* "Woman of the Year" citation, Cincinnati Chapter of YWCA, 1983; elected to Ohio Women's Hall of Fame, 1985; "Outstanding Woman of Tennessee" citation, 1985; Post-Corbett Award, 1986; Woman of the Year, National Association for the Advancement of Colored People (Lynchburg chapter), 1989.

Honorary Doctorate of Humanities, Wilberforce University, 1972, and Fisk University, 1988; Honorary Doctorate of Literature, University of Maryland (Princess Anne Campus), 1974, Ripon University, 1974, and Smith College, 1975; Honorary Doctorate of Humane Letters, The College of Mount St. Joseph on the Ohio, 1985, Indiana University, 1991, Otterbein College, 1992, Widener University, 1993, Albright College, 1995, Cabrini College, 1995, and Allegheny College, 1997. Keys to numerous cities, including Dallas, TX, New York, NY, Cincinnati, OH, Miami, FL, New Orleans, LA, and Los Angeles, CA; Ohioana Book Award, 1988; Jeanine Rae Award for the Advancement of Women's Culture, 1995; Langston Hughes Award, 1996.

WRITINGS:

POETRY

Black Feeling, Black Talk, Broadside Press (Detroit), 1968, 3rd edition, 1970.

Black Judgement, Broadside Press, 1968.

Black Feeling, Black Talk/Black Judgement (contains *Black Feeling, Black Talk* and *Black Judgement*), Morrow, 1970, selection published as *Knoxville, Tennessee,* illustrated by Larry Johnson, Scholastic, 1994.

Re: Creation, Broadside Press, 1970.

Poem of Angela Yvonne Davis, Afro Arts (New York City), 1970.

Spin a Soft Black Song: Poems for Children, illustrated by Charles Bible, Hill & Wang (New York City), 1971, illustrated by George Martins, Lawrence Hill (Westport, CT), 1985, revised edition, Farrar, Straus, 1987.

My House, foreword by Ida Lewis, Morrow, 1972.

Ego-Tripping and Other Poems for Young People, illustrated by George Ford, Lawrence Hill (Chicago), 1973.

The Women and the Men, Morrow, 1975.

Cotton Candy on a Rainy Day, introduction by Paula Giddings, Morrow, 1978.

Vacation Time: Poems for Children, illustrated by Marisabina Russo, Morrow, 1980.

Those Who Ride the Night Winds, Morrow, 1983.

The Genie in the Jar, illustrated by Chris Raschka, Holt, 1996.
The Selected Poems of Nikki Giovanni (1968-1995), Morrow, 1996.
The Sun Is So Quiet, illustrated by Ashley Bryant, Holt, 1996.
Love Poems, Morrow, 1997.
Blues: For All the Changes: New Poems, Morrow, 1999.

Sound recordings by the author of her works include *Truth Is on Its Way,* 1971; *Like a Ripple on a Pond,* 1973; *The Way I Feel,* 1974; and *Legacies: The Poetry of Nikki Giovanni* and *The Reason I Like Chocolate,* both 1976.

OTHER

(Editor) *Night Comes Softly: An Anthology of Black Female Voices,* Medic Press (Newark, NJ), 1970.
Gemini: An Extended Autobiographical Statement on My First Twenty-five Years of Being a Black Poet, Bobbs-Merrill (Indianapolis, IN), 1971.
(With James Baldwin) *A Dialogue: James Baldwin and Nikki Giovanni,* Lippincott (Philadelphia), 1973.
(With Margaret Walker) *A Poetic Equation: Conversations between Nikki Giovanni and Margaret Walker,* Howard University Press (Washington, DC), 1974.
(Author of introduction) *Adele Sebastian, Intro to Fine* (poems), Woman in the Moon, 1985.
Sacred Cows . . . and Other Edibles (essays), Morrow, 1988.
(Editor, with C. Dennison) *Appalachian Elders: A Warm Hearth Sampler,* Pocahontas Press (Blacksburg, VA), 1991.
(Author of foreword) *The Abandoned Baobob: The Autobiography of a Woman,* Chicago Review Press, 1991.
Racism 101 (essays), Morrow, 1994.
(Editor) *Grand Mothers: Poems, Reminiscences, and Short Stories about the Keepers of Our Traditions,* Holt, 1994.
(Editor) *Shimmy Shimmy Shimmy like My Sister Kate: Looking at the Harlem Renaissance through Poems,* Holt, 1995.
(Editor) *Grand Fathers: Reminiscences, Poems, Recipes, and Photos of the Keepers of Our Traditions,* Holt, 1999.

Contributor to numerous anthologies. Contributor of columns to newspapers. Contributor to magazines, including *Black Creation, Black World, Ebony, Essence, Freedom Ways, Journal of Black Poetry, Negro Digest,* and *Umbra.* Editorial consultant, Encore American and Worldwide News.

A selection of Giovanni's public papers is housed at Mugar Memorial Library, Boston University.

ADAPTATIONS: Spirit to Spirit: The Poetry of Nikki Giovanni (television film), 1986, produced by Corporation for Public Broadcasting, and Ohio Council on the Arts.

SIDELIGHTS: One of the best-known African American poets to reach prominence during the late 1960s and early 1970s, Nikki Giovanni has continued to create poems that encompass a life fully experienced. Her unique and insightful verses testify to her own evolving awareness and experiences as a woman of color: from child to young woman, from naive college freshman to seasoned civil rights activist, and from daughter to mother. Frequently anthologized, Giovanni's poetry expresses strong racial pride and respect for family. Her informal style makes her work accessible to both adults and children. In addition to collections such as *Re: Creation, Spin a Soft Black Song,* and *Those Who Ride the Night Winds,* Giovanni has published several works of nonfiction, including *Racism 101* and the anthology *Grand Mothers: Poems, Reminiscences, and Short Stories about the Keepers of Our Traditions.* A frequent lecturer and reader, Giovanni has also taught at Rutgers University, Ohio State University, and Virginia Tech.

Giovanni was born in Knoxville, Tennessee, in 1943, the youngest of two daughters in a close-knit family. Having gained an intense appreciation for her African American heritage from her outspoken grandmother, Louvenia Terrell Watson, Giovanni had a reputation for being strong-willed even as a child. "I come from a long line of storytellers," she once explained in an interview, describing how her family influenced her poetry through oral traditions. "My grandfather was a Latin scholar and he loved the myths, and my mother is a big romanticist, so we heard a lot of stories growing up." This early exposure to the power of spoken language would influence Giovanni's career as a poet, particularly her tendency to sprinkle her verses with colloquialisms such as curse words. "I appreciated the quality and the rhythm of the telling of the stories," she once commented, "and I know when I started to write that I wanted to retain that—I didn't want to become the kind of writer that was stilted or that used language in ways that could not be spoken. I use a very natural rhythm; I want my writing to sound like I talk."

When Giovanni was a young child, she moved with her parents from Knoxville to a predominantly black suburb of Cincinnati, Ohio. She remained close to her outspoken grandmother, however, spending both her sophomore and junior years of high school at the family home in Knoxville. Encouraged by several schoolteachers, Giovanni enrolled at Fisk University, a prestigious, all-black college in Nashville, Tennessee. Unaccustomed to Fisk's traditions, the outspoken young woman inevitably came into conflict with the school's dean of women and was asked to leave. She returned to Fisk in 1964, however, determined to be an ideal student. She accomplished her goal, becoming a leader in political and literary activities on campus during what would prove to be an important era in black history.

Giovanni had experienced racism firsthand during her childhood in the South. Random violence that erupted in and near Knoxville "was frightening," she later recalled in an autobiographical essay for *CA*. "You always felt someone was trying to kill you." Yet when Giovanni re-entered the freshman class at Fisk she was decidedly conservative in her political outlook. During high school she had been a supporter of Republican presidential candidate Barry Goldwater, as well as an avid reader of books by Ayn Rand, who was famous for her philosophy of objectivism (based on self-assertion and competition). The poet credits a Fisk roommate named Bertha with successfully persuading her to embrace revolutionary ideals. In the wake of the civil rights movement and demonstrations against U.S. involvement in the Vietnam conflict, demands for social and political change were sweeping college campuses around the country. "Bertha kept asking, 'how could Black people be conservative?,' " Giovanni wrote in *Gemini: An Extended Autobiographical Statement on My First Twenty-five Years.* " 'What have they got to conserve?' And after a while (realizing that I had absolutely nothing, period) I came around."

While Giovanni was at Fisk, a black renaissance was emerging as writers and other artists of color were finding new ways of expressing their distinct culture to an increasingly interested public. In addition to serving as editor of the campus literary magazine, *Elan,* and participating in the Fisk Writers Workshop, Giovanni worked to restore the Fisk chapter of the Student Non-Violent Coordinating Committee (SNCC). At that time, the organization was pressing the concept of "black power" to bring about social and economic reform. Giovanni's political activism ultimately led to her planning and directing the first Black Arts Festival in Cincinnati, which was held in 1967.

Later that year, Giovanni graduated magna cum laude with a degree in history. She decided to continue her studies at the University of Pennsylvania School of Social Work under a grant from the Ford Foundation, and then take classes at Columbia University's School of Fine Arts. This period was punctuated by tragedy, however, when Giovanni's beloved grandmother died. The loss "stirred in her a sense of guilt and shame both for the way in which society had dealt with this strong, sensitive woman, to whom she had been so close and who had deeply influenced her life, as well as for the way she herself had left her alone to die," according to Mozella G. Mitchell in *Dictionary of Literary Biography.*

Giovanni's first published volume of poetry grew out of her response to the assassinations of such figures as Martin Luther King Jr., Malcolm X, Medgar Evers, and Robert Kennedy. *Black Feeling, Black Talk* and *Black Judgement* display a strong, almost militant African American perspective as Giovanni recounts her growing political and spiritual awareness. These early books, which were followed by *Re: Creation,* quickly established Giovanni as a prominent new African American voice. *Black Feeling, Black Talk* sold more than ten thousand copies in its first year alone, making the author an increasingly visible and popular figure on the reading and speaking circuit. Because of Giovanni's overt activism, her fame as a personality almost preceded her critical acclaim as a poet. She gave the first public reading of her work at Birdland, a trendy New York City jazz club, to a standing-room-only audience. Mitchell described the poems Giovanni produced between 1968 and 1970 as "a kind of ritualistic exorcism of former nonblack ways of thinking and an immersion in blackness. Not only are they directed at other black people whom [Giovanni] wanted to awaken to the beauty of blackness, but also at herself as a means of saturating her own consciousness."

Critical reaction to Giovanni's early work focused on her more revolutionary poetry. Some reviewers found her political and social positions to be unsophisticated, while others were threatened by her rebelliousness. "Nikki writes about the familiar: what she knows, sees, experiences," Don L. Lee observed in *Dynamite Voices I: Black Poets of the 1960s.* "It is clear why she conveys such urgency in expressing the need for Black awareness, unity, solidarity. . . . What is perhaps more important is that when the Black poet chooses to serve as political seer, he must display a keen sophistication. Sometimes Nikki oversimplifies and therefore sounds rather naive politically." *Dictionary of Literary Biography* contributor Alex Batman heard in Giovanni's verse the echoes of blues music. "Indeed the rhythms of her verse correspond so directly to the syncopations of black music that her poems begin to show a potential for becoming songs without accompaniment," Batman noted.

Giovanni's first three volumes of poetry were enormously successful, taking into account the relatively low public demand for modern poetry. *Black Judgement* alone sold six thousand copies in three months, almost six times the sales level expected of a book of its type. As she traveled to speaking engagements at colleges around the country, Giovanni was often hailed as one of the leading black poets of the new black renaissance. The prose poem "Nikki-Rosa," Giovanni's reminiscence of her childhood in a close-knit African American home, was first published in *Black Judgement.* As it became her most beloved and most anthologized work, "Nikki-Rosa" expanded her appeal to an audience well beyond fans of her more activist poetry.

In 1969, Giovanni took a teaching position at Rutgers University. That year she also gave birth to her son, Thomas. Her decision to bear a child out of wedlock was understandable to anyone who knew her. Even as a young girl she had determined that the institution of marriage was not hospitable to women and would never play a role in her life. "I had a baby at twenty-five because I *wanted* to have a baby and I could *afford* to have a baby," she told an *Ebony* interviewer. "I did not get married because I didn't *want* to get married and I could *afford* not to get married."

Despite her success as a poet of the black revolution, Giovanni's work exhibited a shift in focus after the birth of her son. Her priorities had expanded and now encompassed providing her child with the security of a stable home life. As she remarked to an interviewer for *Harper's Bazaar,* "To protect Tommy there is no question I would give my life. I just cannot imagine living without him. But I can live without the revolution." During this period Giovanni produced a collection of autobiographical essays, two books of poetry for children, and two poetry collections for adults. She also made several recordings of her poetry set against a gospel music backdrop. Reviewing these works, Mitchell commented that "we see evidence of a more developed individualism and greater introspection, and a sharpening of her creative and moral powers, as well as of her social and political focus and understanding."

In addition to writing her own poetry, Giovanni sought exposure for other African American women writers through NikTom, Ltd., a publishing cooperative she founded in 1970. Gwendolyn Brooks, Margaret Walker, Carolyn Rodgers, and Mari Evans were among those who benefited from Giovanni's efforts. Travels to other parts of the world, including the Caribbean, also filled much of the poet's time and contributed to the evolution of her work. As she broadened her perspective, Giovanni began to review her own life. Her introspection led to *Gemini: An Extended Autobiographical Statement on My First Twenty-five Years of Being a Black Poet,* which earned a nomination for the National Book Award.

Gemini is a combination of prose, poetry, and other "bits and pieces." In the words of a critic writing in *Kirkus Reviews,* it is a work in which "the contradictions are brought together by sheer force of personality." From sun-soaked childhood memories of a supportive family to an adult acceptance of revolutionary ideology and solo motherhood, the work reflected Giovanni's internal conflict and self-questioning. "I think all autobiography is fiction," Giovanni once observed in an interview, expressing amazement that readers feel they learn something personal about an author by reading a creative work. "[T]he least factual of anything is autobiography, because half the stuff is forgotten," she added. "Even if you [write] about something terribly painful, you have removed yourself from it. . . . What you have not come to terms with you do not write." While she subtitled *Gemini* an autobiography, Giovanni denied that it offered a key to her inner self. The essays contained in the volume—particularly one about her grandmother—were personal in subject matter and "as true as I could make it," she commented. But, as Giovanni noted in an interview several decades later, "I also recognize that there are [parts of] the book in which I'm simply trying to deal with ideas. I didn't want it to be considered *the definitive.* It's far from that. It's very selective and how I looked at myself when I was twenty-five."

In addition to writing for adults in *Gemini* and other works during the early 1970s, Giovanni began to compose verse for children. Among her published volumes for young readers are *Spin a Soft Black Song, Ego-Tripping and Other Poems for Young People,* and *Vacation Time.* Written for children of all ages, Giovanni's poems are unrhymed incantations of childhood images and feelings. *Spin a Soft Black Song,* which she dedicated to her son Tommy, covers a wealth of childhood interests, such as basketball games, close friends, moms, and the coming of spring. "Poem for Rodney" finds a young man contemplating what he wants to be when he grows up. "If " reflects a young man's daydreams about what it might have been like to participate in a historic event. In a *New York Times Book Review* article on *Spin a Soft Black Song,* Nancy Klein noted, "Nikki Giovanni's poems for children, like her adult works, exhibit a combination of casual energy and sudden wit. No cheek-pinching auntie, she explores the contours of childhood with honest affection, sidestepping both nostalgia and condescension."

Ego-Tripping and Other Poems for Young People contains several poems previously published in *Black Feeling, Black Talk.* Focusing on African American history, the collection explores issues and concerns specific to black youngsters. In "Poem for Black Boys," for example, Giovanni wonders why young boys of color do not play runaway slave or Mau-Mau, thereby identifying with the brave heroes of their own race rather than the white cowboys of the Wild West. "Revolutionary Dreams" and "Revolutionary Music" speak to the racial strife of the 1960s and 1970s and look toward an end to racial tension. Commenting on *Ego-Tripping,* a *Kirkus Reviews* contributor claimed: "When [Giovanni] grabs hold . . . it's a rare kid, certainly a rare black kid, who could resist being picked right up."

Vacation Time contrasts with Giovanni's two earlier poetry collections for children by being "a much more relaxed and joyous collection which portrays the world of children as full of wonder and delight," according to Kay E. Vandergrift in *Twentieth-Century Children's Writers.* In *Vacation Time* Giovanni uses more traditional rhyme patterns than in *Spin a Soft Black Song.* Reviewing the work for the *Bulletin of the Center for Children's Books,* Zena Sutherland noted that the rhythms often seem forced and that Giovanni uses "an occasional contrivance to achieve scansion." Yet other critics praised the poet's themes. "In her singing lines, Giovanni shows she hadn't forgotten childhood adventures in . . . exploring the world with a small person's sense of discovery," wrote a *Publishers Weekly* reviewer. Mitchell, too, claimed: "One may be dazzled by the smooth way [Giovanni] drops all political and personal concerns [in *Vacation Time*] and completely enters the world of the child and brings to it all the fanciful beauty, wonder, and lollipopping."

Giovanni's later works for children include *Knoxville, Tennessee* and *The Sun Is So Quiet.* The first work, a free-verse poem originally published in *Black Feeling, Black Talk, Black Judgement,* celebrates the pleasures of summer. Many of the warm images presented in the picture book again came directly from the author's childhood memories. Ellen Fader, writing in *Horn Book,* called *The Sun Is So Quiet* "a celebration of African-American family life for all families." Published in 1996, *The Sun Is So Quiet* offers a collection of thirteen poems, ranging in topics from snowflakes to bedtime to missing teeth. "The poems," wrote a *Publishers Weekly* reviewer, "hover like butterflies, darting in to make their point and then fluttering off."

Giovanni has found writing for children to be particularly fulfilling because she is a mother who reads to her son. "Mostly I'm aware, as the mother of a reader, that I read to him," she once observed in an interview. "I think all of us know that your first line to the child is going to be his parent, so you want to write something that the parent likes and can share." According to Mitchell, the children's poems have "essentially the same impulse" as Giovanni's adult poetry—namely, "the creation of racial pride and the communication of individual love. These are the goals of all of Giovanni's poetry, here directed toward a younger and more impressionable audience."

Throughout the 1970s and 1980s Giovanni's popularity as a speaker and lecturer increased along with her success as a poet and children's author. She received numerous awards for her work, including honors from the National Council of Negro Women and the National Association of Radio and Television Announcers. She was featured in articles for such magazines as *Ebony, Jet,* and *Harper's Bazaar.* She also continued to travel, making trips to Europe and Africa.

In *My House* Giovanni began to exhibit increased sophistication and maturity. Her viewpoint had broadened beyond a rigid black revolutionary consciousness to balance a wide range of social concerns. Her rhymes had also become more pronounced, more lyrical, more gentle. The themes of family love, loneliness, and frustration, which Giovanni had defiantly explored in her earlier works, find much deeper expression in *My House.* In a review for *Contemporary Women Poets,* Jay S. Paul called the book "a poetic tour through . . . a place rich with family remembrance, distinctive personalities, and prevailing love." And in the foreword to *My House,* Ida Lewis observed that Giovanni "has reached a simple philosophy more or less to the effect that a good family spirit is what produces healthy communities, which is what produces a strong (Black) nation." Noting the focus on self-discovery throughout *My House,* critic John W. Conner suggested in *English Journal* that Giovanni "sees her world as an extension of herself . . . sees problems in the world as an extension of her problems, and . . . sees herself existing amidst tensions, heartache, and marvelous expressions of love." "*My House* is not just poems," added Kalumu Ya Salaam in *Black World.* "*My House* is how it is, what it is to be a young, single, intelligent Black woman with a son and no man. It is what it is to be a woman who has failed and is now sentimental about some things, bitter about some things, and generally always frustrated, always feeling frustrated on one of various levels or another." *My House* contained the revelations of a woman coming to terms with her life. *The Women and the Men* continued this trend.

When Giovanni published *Cotton Candy on a Rainy Day,* critics viewed it as one of her most somber works. They noted the focus on emotional ups and downs, fear and insecurity, and the weight of everyday responsibilities. Batman also sensed the poet's frustration at aims unmet. "What distinguishes *Cotton Candy on a Rainy Day* is its poignancy," the critic maintained. "One feels throughout that here is a child of the 1960s mourning the passing of a decade of conflict, of violence, but most of all, of hope."

During the year *Cotton Candy* was published, Giovanni's father suffered a stroke. She and her son immediately left their apartment in New York City and returned to the family home in Cincinnati to help her mother cope with her father's failing health. After her father passed on, Giovanni and her son continued to stay in Cincinnati with her aging mother. She thus built the same secure, supportive, multigenerational environment for Tommy that she had enjoyed as a child.

The poems in *Vacation Time* reflect, perhaps, the poet's growing lightness of spirit and inner stability as she enjoys her family. Similarly, *Those Who Ride the Night Winds* reveals "a new and innovative form," according to Mitchell, who added that "the poetry reflects her heightened self-knowledge and imagination." *Those Who Ride the Night Winds* tends to echo the political activism of Giovanni's early verse as she dedicates various pieces to Phillis Wheatley, Martin Luther King Jr., and Rosa Parks. In *Sacred Cows . . . and Other Edibles* she presents essays on a wide range of topics: African American political leaders, national holidays, and termites all come under her insightful and humorous scrutiny. Such essays as "Reflections on My Profession," "Four Introductions," and "An Answer to Some Questions on How I Write" are described by *Washington Post Book World* critic Marita Golden as "quintessential Nikki Giovanni—sometimes funny, nervy and unnerving with flashes of wisdom."

As Giovanni moved through her middle years, her works continued to reflect her changing concerns and perspectives. *The Selected Poems of Nikki Giovanni,* which spans the first three decades of her career, was heralded by *Booklist* critic Donna Seaman as a "rich synthesis [that] reveals the evolution of Giovanni's voice and charts the course of the social issues that are her muses, issues of gender and race." Twenty of the fifty-three works collected in *Love Poems* find the writer musing on subjects as diverse as friendship, sexual desire, motherhood, and loneliness, while the remainder of the volume includes relevant earlier works. "Funny yet thoughtful, Giovanni celebrates creative energy and the family spirit of African American communities," Frank Allen wrote of *Love Poems* in a *Library Journal* review.

Giovanni continues to supplement her poetry with occasional volumes of nonfiction. In *Racism 101* she looks back over the past thirty years as one who has influenced the civil rights movement and its aftermath. Characterized by a *Publishers Weekly* reviewer as "fluid, often perceptive musings that beg for more substance," this collection of essays touches on diverse topics. Giovanni gives advice to young African American scholars who are just starting an academic career, and she reflects on her own experiences as a teacher. She also provides a few glimpses into her personal life—for instance, she admits to being a confirmed "Trekkie." The book is a rich source of impressions of other black intellectuals, including writer and activist W. E. B. DuBois, writers Henry Louis Gates Jr. and Toni Morrison, Supreme Court Justice Clarence Thomas, and filmmaker Spike Lee. "Giovanni is a shrewd observer and an exhilarating essayist," maintained Seaman in *Booklist,* "modulating her tone from chummy to lethal, hilarious to sagacious as smoothly as a race-car driver shifts gears." In addition to publishing original writings, Giovanni has edited poetry collections like the highly praised *Shimmy Shimmy Shimmy like My Sister Kate.* A compilation of works composed by African American writers during the Harlem Renaissance of the early twentieth century, *Shimmy* helps students of black writing to gain an understanding of the past.

"Most writers spend too much time alone; it is a lonely profession," Giovanni once explained. "I'm not the only poet to point that out. Unless we make ourselves get out and see people, we miss a lot." Teaching, lecturing, sustaining close family ties, and remaining active in her community have allowed the poet to balance the loneliness of writing with a myriad of life experiences. "[Teaching] enriches my life, I mean it keeps reminding all of us that there are other concerns out there," Giovanni said. "It widens your world. . . . I have certain skills that I am able to impart and that I want to, and it keeps me involved in my community and in a community of writers who are not professional but who are interested. I think that's good."

"Writing is . . . what I do to justify the air I breathe," Giovanni wrote, explaining her choice of a vocation in *CA*. "I have been considered a writer who writes from rage and it confuses me. What else do writers write from? A poem has to say something. It has to make some sort of sense; be lyrical; to the point; and still able to be read by whatever reader is kind enough to pick up the book." Giovanni believes one of her most important qualities is to have experienced life and to have been able to translate those experiences into her work—"apply the lessons learned," as she termed it in *CA*. "Isn't that the purpose of people living and sharing? So that others will at least not make the same mistake, since we seldom are able to recreate the positive things in life." She continues to look back on her contributions to American poetry with pride. "I think that I have grown; I feel that my work has grown a lot," she once told an interviewer. "What I've always wanted to do is something different, and I think each book has made a change. I hope that the next book continues like that. Like all writers, I guess, I keep looking for the heart. . . ." She concluded, "human beings fascinate me. You just keep trying to dissect them poetically to see what's there."

BIOGRAPHICAL/CRITICAL SOURCES:

BOOKS

Contemporary Literary Criticism, Volume 64, Gale, 1991.

Contemporary Poets, St. James Press, 1996, pp. 390-91.

Dictionary of Literary Biography, Gale, Volume 5: *American Poets since World War II,* 1980, Volume 41: *Afro-American Poets since 1955,* Gale, 1985, pp. 135-51.

Evans, Mari, editor, *Black Women Writers, 1950-1980: A Critical Evaluation,* Doubleday, 1984.

Fowler, Virginia, *Nikki Giovanni,* Twayne, 1992.

Fowler, Virginia, editor, *Conversations with Nikki Giovanni,* University Press of Mississippi (Jackson), 1992.

Giovanni, Nikki, *Gemini: An Extended Autobiographical Statement on My First Twenty-five Years of Being a Black Poet,* Bobbs-Merrill, 1971.

Lee, Don L., *Dynamite Voices I: Black Poets of the 1960's,* Broadside Press, 1971, pp. 68-73.

Lewis, Ida, introduction to *My House,* Morrow, 1972.

Tate, Claudia, editor, *Black Women Writers at Work,* Crossroads Publishing, 1983.

Twentieth-Century Children's Writers, 4th edition, St. James Press, 1995, p. 388.

Twentieth-Century Young Adult Writers, St. James Press, 1994, pp. 245-46.

PERIODICALS

Black World, July, 1974.

Booklist, December 1, 1993, p. 658; September 15, 1994, p. 122; December 15, 1995, p. 682.

Bulletin of the Center for Children's Books, October, 1980, p. 31; June, 1996, p. 334.

Ebony, February, 1972, pp. 48-50.

English Journal, April, 1973, p. 650.

Harper's Bazaar, July, 1972, p. 50.

Horn Book, September/October, 1994, p. 575.

Jet, April 4, 1994, p. 29.

Kirkus Reviews, September 15, 1971, p. 1051; January 1, 1974, p. 11; March 15, 1996, p. 447.

Library Journal, January, 1996, p. 103; February 1, 1997, p. 84.

New York Times Book Review, November 28, 1971, p. 8.

Publishers Weekly, May 23, 1980, p. 77; December 13, 1993, p. 54; December 18, 1995, pp. 51-52; October 21, 1996, p. 83.

School Library Journal, April, 1994, p. 119; October, 1994, p. 152; May, 1996, p. 103.

Voice of Youth Advocates, December, 1994, p. 298; October, 1996, pp. 229-30.

Washington Post Book Review, February 14, 1988, p. 3.

* * *

GODWIN, Joscelyn 1945-

PERSONAL: Born January 16, 1945, in Kelmscott, Oxford, England; immigrated to the United States, 1966, naturalized 1980; son of Edward (an artist and writer) and Stephanie (an artist and writer; maiden name, Allfree; later surname Godwin) Scott-Snell; married Sharyn Louise Cook (a musician), July 31, 1971 (divorced, 1979); married Janet Matthews, November 21, 1979; children: (second marriage) Ariel. *Education:* Magdalene College, Cambridge, B.A., 1965, Mus.B., 1966, M.A., 1970; Cornell University, Ph.D., 1969.

ADDRESSES: *Office*—Department of Music, Colgate University, Hamilton, NY 13346.

CAREER: Cleveland State University, Cleveland, OH, instructor in music, 1969-71; Colgate University, Hamilton, NY, assistant professor, 1971-76, associate professor, 1976-82, professor of music, 1982—. Church organist, 1969-75.

AWARDS, HONORS: Harding Prize from Royal College of Organists, 1965; Abingdon Prize from Cambridge University, 1966, for "String Trio"; grant from American Council of Learned Societies, 1985.

WRITINGS:

NONFICTION

Robert Fludd: Hermetic Philosopher and Surveyor of Two Worlds, Shambhala (Boulder, CO), 1979.
Athanasius Kircher: A Renaissance Man and the Quest for Lost Knowledge, Thames & Hudson (New York City), 1979.
Mystery Religions in the Ancient World, Harper (San Francisco, CA), 1981.
Harmonies of Heaven and Earth: The Spiritual Dimensions of Music from Antiquity to the Avant-Garde, Inner Traditions International (Rochester, VT), 1987, 2nd edition, 1995.
L'Esoterisme musical en France, 1750-1950, Albin Michel (Paris, France), 1991, revised English edition published as *Music and the Occult: French Musical Philosophies, 1750-1950,* University of Rochester Press (Rochester, NY), 1995.
The Mystery of the Seven Vowels in Theory and Practice, Phanes Press (Grand Rapids, MI), 1991.
Arktos: The Polar Myth in Science, Symbolism, and Nazi Survival, Phanes Press, 1993.
The Theosophical Enlightenment, State University of New York Press (Albany, NY), 1994.
(With Michael Embach) *Johann Friedrich Hugo von Dalberg (1760-1812): Schriftsteller, Musiker, Domherr,* Gesellschaft fuer mittelrheinische Kirchengeschichte (Mainz, Germany), 1998.

TRANSLATOR

Werner Walcker-Meyer, *The Roman Organ of Aquincum,* Musikwissenschaftliches Verlagsgesellschaft (Ludwigsburg, Germany), 1973.
Salomon Trismosin, *Splendor Solis,* Magnum Opus Hermetic Sourceworks (Edinburgh, Scotland), 1981, Phanes Press, 1991.
Rene Guenon, *The Multiple States of Being,* Larson (Burdett, NY), 1984.
Fabre d'Olivet, *Music Explained as Science and Art,* Inner Traditions International, 1988.
The Chemical Wedding of Christian Rosenkreuz, Phanes Press, 1991.
Antoine Faivre, *The Eternal Hermes,* Phanes Press, 1995.
Francesco Colonna, *Hypnerotomachia Poliphili: The Strife of Love in a Dream,* Thames & Hudson, 1999.

AUTHOR OF FOREWORD

The Pythagorean Sourcebook, Phanes Press, 1987.
D. P. Walker, *La Magie spirituelle et angelique de Ficin a Campanella,* Albin Michel, 1987.
Iamlichus, *The Exhortation to Philosophy,* Phanes Press, 1988.
Basarab Nicolescu, *Science, Meaning, and Evolution,* Parabola Books (New York City), 1991.
Antoine Faivre, *The Golden Fleece and Alchemy,* State University of New York Press, 1993.
Paul Johnson *The Masks of the Masters,* State University of New York Press, 1994.

EDITOR

Alessandro Scarlatti, *Marco Attilio Regolo* (opera), Harvard University Press (Cambridge, MA), 1975.
Schirmer Scores: A Repertory of Western Music, Schirmer Books (New York City), 1975.
(And translator) *Music, Mysticism, and Magic: A Sourcebook,* Routledge & Kegan Paul (New York City), 1986.
(And recording producer) Michael Maier, *Atalanta Fugiens,* Magnum Opus Hermetic Sourceworks (Tysoe, United Kingdom), 1987, Phanes Press, 1989.
(And co-translator) Marius Schneider, Rudolph Haase, and Hans Erhard Lauer, *Cosmic Music: Three Musical Keys to the Interpretation of Reality,* Inner Traditions International, 1988.
(With Paul Cash and Timothy Smith) Paul Brunton, *Essential Readings,* Crucible Books (Wellingborough, England), 1990.
(And translator) *Harmony of the Spheres: A Sourcebook of the Pythagorean Tradition in Music,* Inner Traditions International, 1993.
(With Christian Chanel and John Patrick Deveney) *The Hermetic Brotherhood of Luxor: Historical and Initiatic Documents of an Order of Practical Occultism,* Samuel Weiser (York Beach, ME), 1995.

OTHER

Composer of "String Trio," "Epistle 1 to Harmodius," and "A Few Thoughts for Treble Recorder." Contributor to *Dictionary of Twentieth-Century Music* and *Dictionary of the Middle Ages.* Contributor to music, religion, and esoteric journals, including *American Recorder, American Theosophist, The Consort, Early*

Music, Golden Blade, Gnosis, Hermetic Journal, Journal of Rosicrucian Studies, Lapis, Lute Society Journal, Music and Letters, Musical Quarterly, Studies in Comparative Religion, and *Temenos.*

WORK IN PROGRESS: The Pagan Dream of the Renaissance, for Phanes Press.

SIDELIGHTS: Joscelyn Godwin told *CA:* [My work] "describes the circuitous route I am having to take in order to reach a better understanding of music in the light of my philosophical interests." Those interests encompass a broad range of time and thought, and include such subjects as hermeticism (the study of the astrological and occult writings attributed to Hermes Trismegistus), the role of music in the universe, and the "Perennial Philosophy," a concept central to Godwin's work that attempts to unify and find a common purpose in man's religious experience.

One of Godwin's most widely reviewed works, *Mystery Religions in the Ancient World,* is described by Mary Beard in the *Times Literary Supplement* as "a book not of history, but of theosophy. Ancient religion has been rescued from the hands of 'unbelieving academics' and 'Christian chauvinists,' and the Mysteries are seen to play their part in the 'Perennial Philosophy,' as 'attempts, each valid for its time and place, to point the way to the true goal of human existence!' "

Godwin defined for *CA* the relationship between *Mystery Religions in the Ancient World* and two of his previous works, *Robert Fludd: Hermetic Philosopher and Surveyor of Two Worlds* and *Athanasius Kircher: A Renaissance Man and the Quest for Lost Knowledge:* "Fludd and Kircher were two universal men of the Renaissance for whom music was a fundamental element of their attempt to grasp the cosmos as a whole. Both were deeply concerned with hermeticism, and Kircher especially with the mystery religions of antiquity. Hence [*Mystery Religions in the Ancient World*], which approaches these religions with the question, 'how are we to empathize with these believers?' "

Although Beard faults Godwin's approach, she nevertheless points out the value of his purpose, declaring of *Mystery Religions in the Ancient World:* "There is something of interest here. [As a work of mysticism] this book is, I suspect, quite par for the course. Moreover, the recurring and shifting notion of the 'Perennial Philosophy,' from its inception in sixteenth-century Italy, through Leitniz, Huxley, and beyond, is certainly worth attention as is also . . . the intellectual make-up of Godwin himself."

Having explored the religious implications of his earlier work through the writing of *Mystery Religions in the Ancient World,* Godwin has returned to music. He explains the present and future course of his work: "I have assembled in my sourcebook a continuous stream of 'musical hermeticism' as it appears in the West, Judaism, and Islam. *Harmonies of Heaven and Earth: The Spiritual Dimensions of Music from Antiquity to the Avant-Garde* presents my own ideas about this material. Although I have written exclusively about Western esotericism, I hope to move in spirit to the East, where I feel more at home philosophically. My current research focuses on the meeting of the Western and Eastern esoteric streams around 1900."

Godwin provided an update on his activities for *CA:* "My earliest writings were in my professional field of musicology. After I received tenure I felt free to branch out, producing three illustrated books. Two of these *(Robert Fludd, Athanasius Kircher)* treated the problem of universal knowledge; the third *(Mystery Religions in the Ancient World)* was an exercise in empathy with strange and alien religious forms. All were influenced by my encounter with the books and person of Paul Brunton, a British orientalist and philosopher, to whom I later paid tribute by compiling a volume of his *Essential Readings.*

"The 1980s were devoted to writing, translating, and editing materials on the mystical, magical, cosmological, and occult aspects of music. My object was to provide a body of work from which others could develop their own ideas and opinions.

"My recent work is also encyclopedic, but nonmusical. Some of it pursues out-of-the-way topics, such as the polar myth, vowel-lore, and Nineteenth-century occultism. Some is concerned with neglected figures of the past, especially ones who aspired to universal knowledge, such as the alchemist Michael Maier and the musician-philosophers Dalberg and Fabre d'Olivet. I feel something very like friendship for these people.

"I love to travel, and to work in European libraries. Most of my research is done there, then made into books at home in upstate New York. A perpetual curiosity drives me to discover ever new vistas, which I describe and interpret for those with less facility in languages and less time on their hands. My profession is the teaching of undergraduates, and all my work is didactic; I simply make the kind of books that I would have enjoyed learning from when I was younger."

Godwin's books have been translated into Czech, French, German, Greek, Japanese, and Spanish.

BIOGRAPHICAL/CRITICAL SOURCES:

PERIODICALS

A.R.I.E.S., number 7, 1988.
Gnosis, summer, 1988; spring, 1996.
International Herald Tribune, February 12, 2000.
Literary Review, August, 1988.
Nature, April, 1993, pp. 665-66.
New York Times, April 23, 1987.
Temenos (London), number 10, 1988.
Theosophical Enlightenment, summer, 1995, pp. 44-45.
Times Literary Supplement, January 15, 1982; July 31, 1987; April 12, 1993, p. 31; March 3, 2000.

* * *

GOETZ, Ignacio L. 1933-

PERSONAL: Born August 10, 1933, in Caracas, Venezuela; son of Federico L. (a banker) and Ilse (Roemer) Goetz; married Katherine Griggs, August 21, 1965; children: Christine, Mariella, Sonya. *Education:* Pontifical Athenaeum, Poona, India, B.A. (with honors), 1956; St. Mary's College, Kurseong, India, B.D. (with honors), 1963; Columbia University, M.A., 1965; New York University, Ph.D., 1968.

ADDRESSES: Home—386 California Ave., Uniondale, NY 11553. *Office*—107 Barnard Hall, Hofstra University, Hempstead, NY 11550; fax: 516-463-4832. *E-mail*—ignaciolleo@cs.com.

CAREER: Ordained Roman Catholic priest, 1962; teacher of English at a junior high school in Baroda, India, 1957-59; St. Stanislaus' College, Hazaribagh, India, lecturer in exegesis, 1963-64; Hofstra University, Hempstead, NY, special assistant professor, 1966-68, assistant professor of philosophy of education, 1968—, professor of philosophy and director of special studies program, 1972—.

MEMBER: Philosophy of Education Society, American Association of University Professors, American Teilhard de Chardin Association, Middle Atlantic States Philosophy of Education Society, Kappa Delta Pi, Sigma Delta Pi.

AWARDS, HONORS: Hofstra University, Teacher of the Year Award, 1971, and Faculty Distinguished Service Award, New College, 1977.

WRITINGS:

(Translator) *Pavitra Gulabmala,* Anand Press (Anand, India), 1961.
(Editor) *No Schools,* MSS Educational Publishing, 1971.
The Psychedelic Teacher, Westminster (Philadelphia, PA), 1972.
Creativity: Theoretical and Socio-cosmic Reflections, University Press of America (Lanham, MD), 1978.
Zen and the Art of Teaching, J. L. Wilkerson, 1988.
Conceptions of Happiness, University Press of America, 1995.
The Culture of Sexism, Praeger (Westport, CT), 1999.
Manners and Violence, Praeger, 2000.

Contributor to education, philosophy, and theology journals, including *Journal of Aesthetics and Art Criticism, Educational Theory, Teilhard Review,* and *Journal of Negro Education.*

SIDELIGHTS: Ignacio L. Goetz told *CA:* "I love to write. Always have, since I published my first opinion piece on peace at the end of World War II in 1945. Over the years I have written lots but published less, for in these matters one is dependent on the taste of editors and the fickle advice of advertising departments. I have written two novels and many short stories, but I have no agent, therefore cannot get them published. My academic writing has been luckier. About seventy articles have appeared, along with nine books.

"In my nonfiction work I aim at clarity, conciseness, and style. I think I subconsciously seek to duplicate in English the directness and sparseness of Latin. I look for the catchy phrase that may remain after all else is forgotten. I try to balance my paragraphs as Cicero did in his orations, mindful of the fact that Plato was a prose stylist of great accomplishment (lost in translation). From Blanshard and Camus I learned that nothing prevents delighting while we tell the truth.

"I write to put across a point of view, usually that of the underdog. I espouse lost causes, and this undoubtedly has cost me readership over the years, but I believe that the truth is not always palatable, like a spoonful of honey, and that nothing is really true that forces one to exclude (Camus).

"I am also aware of the fact that I write because I do not want to die. Like Horace, I hope to leave behind a monument more lasting than bronze, for as long as I am read I will not altogether die; but just in case, I also had children."

Goetz speaks French, Gujarati, Latin, and Hindi, and reads Italian, Greek, Portuguese, Sanskrit, and German.

* * *

GOODMAN, Susan 1951-

PERSONAL: Born March 20, 1951, in Boston, MA; daughter of Ralph (in business) and Rhoda (an artist; maiden name, Cohen) Rudnick; married Gregory Goodman (divorced, 1991). *Ethnicity:* "Anglo." *Education:* University of New Hampshire, B.A., 1972, M.Ed., 1974, M.A., 1987, Ph.D., 1989.

ADDRESSES: Home—105 Bent Lane, Newark, DE 19711. *Office*—Department of English, University of Delaware, Newark, DE 19711; fax: 302-831-1586. *E-mail*—sgoodman@udel.edu.

CAREER: Public school teacher, 1972-83, including English teacher, high school reading specialist, and coordinator of English as a second language; California State University, Fresno, professor of English, 1990-94; University of Delaware, Newark, professor of English, 1994—. Dorothy M. Healy Visiting Professor, 2000.

MEMBER: Modern Language Association of America, American Library Association, Edith Wharton Society, Ellen Glasgow Society.

AWARDS, HONORS: Fellow of Virginia Humanities Foundation, 1994, and Houghton Library, 2000-01.

WRITINGS:

Edith Wharton's Women: Friends and Rivals, University Press of New England (Hanover, NH), 1990.
Edith Wharton's Inner Circle, University of Texas Press (Austin, TX), 1994.
(Editor with Daniel Royot) *Femmes de Conscience: Aspects du Feminisme Americain, 1848-1875,* Sorbonne Press (Paris, France), 1994.
Ellen Glasgow: A Biography, Johns Hopkins University Press (Baltimore, MD), 1998.
(Editor with Clare Colquitt and Candace Waid) *Edith Wharton: A Forward Glance,* University of Delaware Press (Newark, DE), 1999.
(Author of introduction) Ellen Glasgow, *The Battle-Ground* (novel), University of Alabama Press (University), 2000.

SIDELIGHTS: Susan Goodman told *CA:* "My work has focused on the lives and works of women writers, primarily Edith Wharton and Ellen Glasgow. In trying to relate another's past, I have looked at those intersections between fact and imagination, knowing that what I offer is itself a kind of embroidery, a piecing together of separate appliques. Commenting on history, I cannot wholly escape making it. Living as we all do, in both real and fictive worlds, both inside and outside history, I echo Alain Besancon in arguing that historical research, indeed all writing, is a form of introspection, *la recherche de soi-meme.* The relationship between writer and subject is an exchange that evolves in its various stages. How much so is illustrated by a dream I had at the beginning of my research on Edith Wharton. She had invited me for a motor-flight, after which I elatedly skipped down a hill, secure in the knowledge that she liked me. Since then, I have read a letter she wrote to her sister-in-law, stating that women scholars would be better off staying home and having babies. Although the dream illustrates the danger of filtering another's story through one's own, it also gave me permission to explore Wharton's life.

"Writing the life of someone who must, in large part, remain unknown raises questions about the construction of identity and the nature of biography itself. In *The Woman Within,* Ellen Glasgow asks a question that haunts all writers: 'How can one tell where memory ends and imagination begins?' This question has particular significance for a biographer. The 'truth' of biography, like that of autobiography, is necessarily evolving. It grows from a process of amendment and revision. If we accept that any writer tells, as Glasgow believed of herself, his or her own disguised story, then the biographer is also an autobiographer, whose personal narrative develops within, alongside, or in opposition to that of the subject.

"Leon Edel describes the biographer's dilemma as twofold: 'he must apprise the life of another by becoming that other person; and he must be scrupulously careful that in the process the other person is not refashioned in his image.' The relationship—subtle, intimate, and ambivalent—is complicated by any number of factors. A biographer may choose a subject who seems a soul mate in need of rescue, or who represents the values of a secretly envied class or a bygone era. In other cases, a biographer may be motivated by a kind of self-righteous, usually termed 'moral' wrath. Perhaps the nearest approach to another's life is through the divination of an inexplicable presence, whether a verbal mood or an emotional aura."

GOTZ, Ignacio L.
See GOETZ, Ignacio L.

* * *

GREEN, Scott E. 1951-

PERSONAL: Born June 2, 1951, in Boston, MA; son of Meyer (an attorney) and Peggy (a typist; maiden name, Berle) Green. *Ethnicity:* "Jewish." *Education:* Bates College, B.A., 1973; Rhode Island College, M.A., 1985. *Politics:* Democrat. *Religion:* Jewish. *Avocational interests:* Collecting books and art, history, public affairs.

ADDRESSES: Home—47 Byledge Rd., Manchester, NH 03104. *E-mail*—sgreen@grolen.com.

CAREER: Merrimack Valley Business, Randolph, MA, freelance writer primarily in field of antiques and collectibles with nationally syndicated column on collectors. Worked variously as book dealer, substitute teacher, manuscript processor, interviewer, and archival consultant. Former member of New Hampshire House of Representatives. Past chairman, Security Deposit Loan Fund of Greater Manchester; past chairman, Mayor's Committee on Restoring Rail Passenger Service; delegate to First Governor's Conference on the Arts. Member of Manchester Safety Review Board, Manchester United Way Low Income Housing Network Committee, Manchester Caregivers (past vice president), and the New Hampshire Snowmobile Museum Association. Past librarian of Manchester Boys and Girls Club, secretary of the Friends of the Manchester City Library, Manchester Ward 1 Clerk (an elected office).

MEMBER: Science Fiction Writers of America, Science Fiction Poetry Association, Small Press Writers and Artists Organization (past vice president), National Association of Railroad Passengers, National Writers Union/U.A.W. #1981 (Grievance Officer, Steering Committee of the Boston Local).

WRITINGS:

Private Worlds (poems), Bedouin Press, 1983.
Baby Sale at the 7-11 (poems), Bloom Books, 1985.
Science Fiction, Fantasy, and Horror Poetry: A Resource Guide and Biographical Directory, Greenwood Press (Westport, CT), 1989.
Directory of Repositories of Family History in New Hampshire, Clearfield, 1993.
Isaac Asimov, Greenwood Press, 1995.

Author of nationally syndicated column on collectors. Contributor to science fiction anthologies, including *The Williamson Effect,* TOR, 1995, and *Project Solarsail,* Penguin Roc, 1990. Contributor to magazines, including *Amazing, Space and Time, Star*Line, Isaac Asimov's Science Fiction Magazine, Midnight Graffiti,* and *American Fantasy.* Editor and publisher of *Rising Star.*

SIDELIGHTS: Scott E. Green once told *CA:* "While I work as a journalist, my avocation as a writer is science fiction, fantasy, and horror. I do it as a poet, not as a prose writer. I never had the urge to write the great American science fiction novel, but to create the great American science fiction poem."

* * *

GREENE, Naomi 1942-

PERSONAL: Born Naomi Greenstein, June 18, 1942, in New York City; name legally changed in 1970; daughter of Milton (a lawyer) and Beatrice (Zutty) Greenstein. *Education:* Brown University, B.A., 1963; New York University, Ph.D., 1967.

ADDRESSES: Home—633 Por la Mar Circle, Santa Barbara, CA 93103. *Office*—Department of French and Italian, University of California, Santa Barbara, CA 93106.

CAREER: University of California at Santa Barbara, first assistant professor of French, later emeritus, beginning in 1968.

MEMBER: Phi Beta Kappa.

AWARDS, HONORS: Fulbright scholar, 1965-66.

WRITINGS:

Antonin Artaud: Poet without Words (originally published in 1970), introduction by Janet Flanner, Simon & Schuster (New York City), 1971.
Rene Clair: A Guide to References and Resources, Hall (Boston), 1985.
Pier Paolo Pasolini: Cinema as Heresy, Princeton University Press (Princeton, NJ), 1990.
Landscapes of Loss: The National Past in Postwar French Cinema, Princeton University Press, 1999.

SIDELIGHTS: Naomi Greene has written works on Antonin Artaud, Rene Clair, and Pier Paolo Pasolini. More recently Greene published a book focused on the French cinema. Released in 1999, *Landscapes of Loss: The National Past in Postwar French Cinema* is "a work of informed theory and sensitive analysis," praised M. Yacowar in *Choice.* Yacowar asserted: "[*Landscapes of Loss*] should prove influential and engrossing to both film and history scholars."

BIOGRAPHICAL/CRITICAL SOURCES:

PERIODICALS

Choice, November, 1999, M. Yacowar, review of *Landscapes of Loss: The National Past in Postwar French Cinema,* p. 546.

Film Quarterly, summer, 1992, p. 56.

Wilson Library Bulletin, January, 1991, p. 128.*

* * *

GURALNICK, Peter 1943(?)-

PERSONAL: Born c. 1943; son of an oral surgeon; married; wife's name, Alexandra; children: Jake, Nina. *Education:* Attended Columbia University; Boston University, B.A., 1967.

ADDRESSES: Home—Massachusetts. *Agent*—Richard McDonough, P.O. Box 1950, Boston, MA 02130.

CAREER: Music journalist, nonfiction writer, and novelist. Boston University, Boston, MA, classics instructor, c. 1960s-73

AWARDS, HONORS: American Book Award, Before Columbus Foundation, 1983, for *Lost Highway: Journeys and Arrivals of American Musicians;* Grammy Award for best album notes, National Academy of Recording Arts and Sciences, 1985, for *Sam Cooke Live at the Harlem Square Club, 1963;* first place, Ralph J. Gleason Music Book Awards, 1995, for *Last Train to Memphis: The Rise of Elvis Presley,* and 1999, for *Careless Love: The Unmaking of Elvis Presley.*

WRITINGS:

Feel like Going Home: Portraits in Blues and Rock 'n Roll, Outerbridge & Dienstfrey (New York City), 1971.

Lost Highway: Journeys and Arrivals of American Musicians, Vintage(New York City), 1979.

Nighthawk Blues: A Novel, Thunder's Mouth Press (New York City), 1980.

The Listener's Guide to the Blues, Facts on File (New York City), 1982.

Sweet Soul Music: Rhythm and Blues and the Southern Dream of Freedom, Harper (New York City), 1986.

Searching for Robert Johnson (originally published in *Living Blues*), Dutton (New York City), 1989.

Last Train to Memphis: The Rise of Elvis Presley, Little, Brown (Boston), 1994.

Careless Love: The Unmaking of Elvis Presley, Little, Brown, 1999.

(With Ernst Jorgensen) *Elvis Day by Day,* Ballantine (New York City), 1999.

(Editor, with Douglas Wolk) *Da Capo Best Music Writing 2000,* Da Capo Press (Cambridge, MA), 2000.

Work represented in the anthology *New Writing,* edited by Faith Sale, 1967. Contributor to periodicals, including *Rolling Stone.* Author of the television script "Sam Phillips: The Man Who Invented Rock 'n' Roll," *A&E Biography,* A&E, 2000.

WORK IN PROGRESS: A novel titled *Democracy;* a work on musician Sam Cooke, for Little, Brown.

SIDELIGHTS: Peter Guralnick has developed a reputation as one of the foremost experts on the history of American popular music. Though he knew he wanted to write fiction from the age of five, Guralnick has made a name for himself as a nonfiction writer and chronicler of influential figures in the worlds of blues, country, rock, and soul music. He is noted for his extensive reliance on personal interviews and his measured representation of all sides of an issue. Guralnick discussed his journalistic approach with Wendy Smith in *Publishers Weekly:* "You have to recognize the legitimacy of people's experience, that whatever formulations you have made about a subject and however much the person you're talking to may be contradicting those formulations, they have a very personal, vivid memory that is valid for them. Then the problem is trying to bring all these different versions together."

In 1971 Guralnick issued his first book, *Feel like Going Home: Portraits in Blues and Rock 'n Roll.* As he would in his later nonfiction works on musical topics, the author focuses both on the broad outlines of a musical period—in this case, the blues as it fed into and became early rock and roll—and on the major figures within the movement. A *Publishers Weekly* reviewer described Guralnick's history as "rich in insights" and his portraits of individuals as "vividly evocative" of the period itself, dubbing the combination "an appealing panoply in muted tones."

Feel like Going Home had become something of a classic, according to *Rolling Stone* critic Greil Marcus, by the time Guralnick published his next nonfiction effort, *Lost Highway: Journeys and Arrivals of American Musicians,* a 1979 collection of interviews and portraits of musicians on the country, rockabilly, and rhythm and blues scenes. Critical reaction to *Lost Highway* was mixed, however, with a *Kirkus Reviews* contributor complaining of a lack of focus and the author's occasional "corny-mawkish" veneration of his subjects. British critic Russell Davies of the *Times Literary Supplement,* however, found the book instructive on country music and its connection between its sometimes bathetic lyrics and the lives of country music performers. Marcus, highlighting the author's "seamless" interweaving of interviews, biography, reporting, and musicology, concluded: "Guralnick has produced more than a tribute to the lost highway that carries the music he loves best: he has come through with a map of it."

The publication of *Sweet Soul Music: Rhythm and Blues and the Southern Dream of Freedom,* Guralnick's 1986 nonfiction work, marked the completion of a trilogy on American music. Again placing material from numerous interviews in a broader historical context, Guralnick focuses on the rise of soul music in the mid-1950s and its fall from the music charts by the early 1970s, tracing the music's themes, aspirations, and ultimate decline to the concurrent civil rights movement. Several critics highlighted Guralnick's revelations regarding the harmonious collaborative efforts of Southern white and black musicians in making the best known of the era's soul music. "Like the best pop music," observed Daniel Brogan in the *Chicago Tribune,* "Guralnick makes his point without preaching. The message is woven into the stories, and only occasionally overtly surfaces. Thus, *Sweet Soul Music* is at once a scholarly work and a whole lotta fun." Michiko Kakutani of the *New York Times* was less impressed. "Guralnick's attempts to underscore the social and cultural implications of his subject occasionally feel strained and overly intellectualized," she stated. *Newsweek*'s Jim Miller, on the other hand, was enthusiastic, calling *Sweet Soul Music* "one of the best books ever written on American popular music."

Guralnick's next musical subject was blues singer/songwriter Robert Johnson, who is often described as "legendary" not merely for his influence on other blues singers but also for his short and mysterious life. Published in 1989, *Searching for Robert Johnson* briefly examines the rumors and stories that surround the shy young man who recorded less than thirty songs during his lifetime, yet came to be known as the "king of the Mississippi Delta blues singers." Although faulting Guralnick for frequently referring to Johnson's "shadowy" world, John Litweiler concluded in the *Chicago Tribune* that *Searching for Robert Johnson* "is a rewarding appetizer" for the reader waiting for a more definitive biography of the blues musician.

In 1994 Guralnick published *Last Train to Memphis: The Rise of Elvis Presley,* the first volume of a two-volume biography. In this highly acclaimed work, Guralnick restricts himself to the early career of the man commonly known as "the king of rock and roll," when Presley's musical roots in Southern gospel and blues music were unadulterated by the influences of pop and Hollywood musicals. The book covers Presley's first twenty-three years, from his birth in Mississippi in 1935, through his adolescence as a shy but energetic mama's boy, to his rapid ascent to stardom after the 1954 release of his first single, "That's All Right Mama," and concluding with Elvis's departure for Germany in 1958 to fulfill his military obligation. Guralnick originally intended to complete the biography in one volume, but his compilation of interviews and notes on the singer's life became so voluminous that he was forced to split the project into two books. The result is that *Last Train to Memphis* is a detailed, 560-page narrative praised by reviewers for its objective presentation of the American popular culture hero.

Characterizing Guralnick's prose in *Last Train to Memphis* as "calm and meticulous," Frank Rose of the *Los Angeles Times Book Review* compared *Last Train to Memphis* favorably with the numerous other biographies of Presley. "[Guralnick's] Elvis is neither dumb yokel nor rock 'n' roll messiah," Rose commented, "just a pimply, poor white mama's boy from the Mid-South, untutored and inarticulate, whose vague yearning to be a star lands him in worlds he never dreamed of." And although Rose noted that Guralnick sheds little light on Presley's passivity in directing his career or his "mother-fixation," the critic concluded: "The virtue of Guralnick's approach is that it forces us to forget what might have been and see what was. Only then can we trace the intricate contradictions beneath the surface simplicity that turned Elvis into the mirror we still can't put down today." *New York Times Book Review* contributor Stephen Wright offered similar praise for *Last Train to Memphis:* "Try to pass twenty-four hours in the United States without hearing Elvis Presley's name or seeing his image. It's virtually impossible. This profound and moving book, a triumph of biographical art, will show you why." In a *New York Times* piece, Kakutani declared the book "a model of biographical scholarship: erudite and ardent and almost novelistic in its conjuring of Elvis's spectacular rise."

The concluding volume of Guralnick's Presley biography, *Careless Love: The Unmaking of Elvis Presley,* offers the grim account of the musician's creative and personal decline, culminating in a drug-induced death in 1977. In her *New York Times* review of the work, Kakutani wrote: "By the very nature of its subject matter this volume tells a far more depressing tale than its predecessor, chronicling Elvis's long, slow slide, despite his 1968-69 comeback, into maudlin commercialism and self-loathing." Many salacious Presley biographies have covered the same time period, but Guralnick's book was particularly praised for its reasoned approach and avoidance of sensationalism. As Kakutani put it, "Unlike . . . earlier Elvis biographers, . . . Mr. Guralnick manages to recount . . . events without indulging in the faintest bit of voyeurism."

Careless Love earned reviews similar to its companion volume. *Insight on the News* correspondent Eric Peters commented: "The new work is meticulously researched and beautifully written, captures the achievement, the wasted potential and pervasive sadness of Elvis' life after his return to Memphis in the spring of 1960." In *Maclean's,* Nicholas Jennings concluded: "Masterfully and movingly told, *Careless Love* stands as the definitive chronicle of the King's downfall. Although clearly a fan of Presley's best work and appreciative of his extraordinary talent, Guralnick does not avert his eyes from his subject's failings." *Esquire* critic Greil Marcus noted of Guralnick: "In both books, he has realized that remarkable ambition. But what if the air his characters breathe is itself oppressive, their everyday culture itself a form of bondage? That is the air the reader, the characters, must breathe all through *Careless Love,* so perfectly named for an old folk song about how idly hearts are broken." Marcus continued: "The story has been told before, but never so convincingly or with such an absence of glee or condescension." An *Entertainment Weekly* reviewer found *Careless Love* to be "the story of a man who gave up his creative life for the security of wealth and unquestioning friends. . . . Where *Last Train to Memphis* spoke of a miracle—how an impoverished young man became a revolutionary artist and a king of popular culture—*Careless Love* documents the life of a sheltered boy who turned his miracle into a tragedy as well as a joke. Guralnick tells that joke with eloquent sorrow and muted poignance."

Perhaps no reviewer of Guralnick's work on Presley was more enthusiastic than Gerald Marzorati in the *New York Times Book Review.* "Peter Guralnick's two-volume life of Elvis Aron Presley . . . is not simply the finest rock-and-roll biography ever written," Marzorati stated. "It must be ranked among the most ambitious and crucial biographical undertakings yet devoted to a major American figure of the second half of the 20th century."

Though Guralnick has written a number of novels, to date only one has been published—*Nighthawk Blues,* appearing in 1980. Dubbed "a realistic and at times wrenching novel which illuminates the bright and dark sides of seminal blues musicians," by Harry Sumrall in the *Washington Post, Nighthawk Blues* centers on the rise and fall of Screamin' Nighthawk, a down-and-out blues musician whose career is briefly revived in the late 1960s with the help of a young white jazz historian. Sumrall praised the authenticity that marks Guralnick's depiction of the musician's way of speaking and living.

BIOGRAPHICAL/CRITICAL SOURCES:

PERIODICALS

American History, December, 1999, Joe Gustaitis, review of *Careless Love,* p. 66.

Booklist, November 1, 1998, Benjamin Segedin, review of *Careless Love,* p. 450; August, 1999, Ted Hipple, review of *Careless Love,* p. 2075; September 1, 1999, Benjamin Segedin, review of *Elvis Day by Day,* p. 4.

Business Wire, July 19, 1999, "Presley Biography Wins First Place at 10th Annual Ralph J. Gleason Music Book Awards," p. 1650.

Chicago Tribune, August 6, 1986; January 5, 1990.

Economist (US), November 5, 1994, review of *Last Train to Memphis: The Rise of Elvis Presley,* p. 90.

Entertainment Weekly, January 8, 1999, "Heartbreak Hotel," p. 60; October 15, 1999, Ken Tucker, review of *Elvis Day by Day,* p. 74; June 23, 2000, "Between the Lines: The Inside Scoop on the Book World."

Esquire, February, 1999, Greil Marcus, "The Building Has Left Elvis," p. 72.

Globe and Mail (Toronto), November 29, 1986.

Hollywood Reporter, January 19, 2000, Michele Greppi, "Rock Pioneer on 'Biography,' " p. 37.

Insight on the News, March 1, 1999, Eric Peters, "Long Live the King," p. 36.

Kirkus Reviews, October 15, 1979, p. 1239.

Library Journal, January, 1999, Carol J. Binkowski, review of *Careless Love,* p. 100; April 1, 1999,

Nancy R. Ives, review of *Careless Love,* p. 147; September 1, 1999, Michael Rogers, reviews of *Feel like Going Home* and *Lost Highway,* p. 238.

Los Angeles Times Book Review, October 15, 1989, p. 6; October 2, 1994, pp. 1, 12-13.

Maclean's, March 1, 1999, Nicholas Jennings, "Sex, Drugs, and the Rock King," p. 59.

Mother Jones, January, 1999, review of *Careless Love: The Unmaking of Elvis Presley,* p. 73.

Nation, December 5, 1994, pp. 695-98.

National Review, February 6, 1995, Terry Teachout, review of *Last Train to Memphis,* p. 70; March 8, 1999, D. Keith Mano, "A King's Demise," p. 52.

Newsweek, August 4, 1986, p. 60.

New York Review of Books, August 11, 1994, p. 49.

New York Times, June 7, 1986; October 26, 1994; January 8, 1999, Michiko Kakutani, "The Final Years: When Elvis Left the Building."

New York Times Book Review, November 5, 1989, p. 25; October 30, 1994, pp. 1, 18-21; January 3, 1999, Gerald Marzorati, "Heartbreak Hotel," p. 4.

People, October 18, 1993, p. 23; January 30, 1995, Steve Dougherty, "When the King Was King," p. 82.

Publishers Weekly, September 20, 1971, p. 47; October 17, 1980, p. 54; October 3, 1994, pp. 47-48; June 22, 1998, review of *Elvis Presley,* p. 79; November 9, 1998, review of *Careless Love,* p. 62; September 13, 1999, "Shake, Rattle & Roll," p. 74; November 1, 1999, review of *Careless Love,* p. 50.

Rolling Stone, April 17, 1980, p. 29; January 21, 1999, p. 32.

Time, January 11, 1999, Jay Cocks, "The Fall of the King," p. 100.

Times Literary Supplement, June 6, 1980, p. 633; July 27, 1990, p. 793.

Washington Post, December 11, 1980, p. C9.

Washington Post Book World, July 12, 1986; December 5-11, 1999, review of *Elvis Day by Day,* p. 12.*

H-I

HARDESTY, Von 1939-

PERSONAL: Born March 16, 1939, in Byesville, OH; son of Wilford W. and Florentine (Decker) Hardesty; married, wife's name Judith, December 22, 1962 (divorced, 1976); married, wife's name Patricia, 1987; children: (first marriage) Stephen Walter. *Education:* Bluffton College, B.A., 1961; Case Western Reserve University, M.A., 1964; Ohio State University, Ph.D., 1974. *Religion:* Eastern Orthodox.

ADDRESSES: *Home*—2374 North Oakland St., Arlington, VA 22207. *Office*—National Air and Space Museum 3308, Smithsonian Institution, Washington, DC 20560; fax: 202-786-2447. *E-mail*—von.Hardesty@nasm.si.edu.

CAREER: Ohio Wesleyan University, Delaware, instructor in history, 1969-70; Bluffton College, Bluffton, OH, associate professor of history, 1970-78; Smithsonian Institution, Washington, DC, curator of National Air and Space Museum, 1979—. Oxford University, visiting fellow of Worcester College, 1988-89, senior associate of St. Antony's College, 1995.

AWARDS, HONORS: Guggenheim fellowship, 1978-79; Regents fellow, Smithsonian Institution, 1994.

WRITINGS:

Red Phoenix: The Rise of Soviet Air Power, 1941-1945, Smithsonian Institution Press (Washington, DC), 1982.

(With Dominick A. Pisano) *Black/Wings: The American Black in Aviation,* National Air and Space Museum (Washington, DC), 1983.

Conflict and Stability in the Development of Modern Europe, 1870-1970, Open University Press, 1983.

(Contributor) Paul Murphy, editor, *The Soviet Air Forces,* McFarland and Co. (Jefferson, NC), 1984.

(Editor) Alexander Riaboff, *Gatchina Days: Reminiscences of a Russian Pilot,* Smithsonian Institution Press, 1986.

(Translator and adapter, and editor with K. N. Finne and Carl J. Bobrow) *Igor Sikorsky: The Russian Years,* Smithsonian Institution Press, 1987.

(With Dorothy Cochrane and Russell Lee) *The Aviation Careers of Igor Sikorsky,* University of Washington Press (Seattle, WA), 1989.

(Editor and author of introduction) Georgiy Baidukov, *Russian Lindbergh: The Life of Valery Chkalov,* translated by Peter Belov, Smithsonian Institution Press, 1991.

(Editor) James J. Fahey, *Pacific War Diary, Illustrated,* University of Washington Press, 1993.

(Editor) *An Early Black Aviator's Own Story: William J. Powell's Black Wings,* Smithsonian Institution Press, 1994.

(Editor and contributor) Fahey, *Pacific War Diary,* University of Washington Press, 1995.

(Coeditor) *Russian Air Power and Aviation,* Frank Cass (London, England), 1998.

Contributor to periodicals, including *Smithsonian.*

WORK IN PROGRESS: *Headwinds: The Story of African Americans in Aerospace,* publication by Little, Brown (Boston, MA) expected in 2002; *Epic Flights,* Hugh Levin Associates (New York City), 2003.

SIDELIGHTS: Writing in the *Washington Post Book World,* critic Martin Caidin praised *Red Phoenix: The Rise of Soviet Air Power, 1941-1945,* deeming historian

Von Hardesty's chronicle of Soviet military air power during World War II "a brilliant study" and commending its "wealth of detail on structure, policy, organization and statistical data." In the book, which contains many never-before-seen photographs, Hardesty "recounts the slow, painful transformation," according to George Alexander of the *Los Angeles Times Book Review,* "of the Voyenno vosdushnyye sily, or Soviet air force, from a 1941 pushover to a 1945 strongman."

BIOGRAPHICAL/CRITICAL SOURCES:

PERIODICALS

Los Angeles Times Book Review, December 5, 1982.
Washington Post Book World, January 23, 1983.

* * *

HARE, David 1947-

PERSONAL: Born June 5, 1947, in St. Leonards, Sussex, England; son of Clifford Theodore (a sailor) and Agnes (Gilmour) Hare; married Margaret Matheson (a theatrical agent), 1970 (divorced, 1980); married Nicole Farhi (a designer), 1992; children: (first marriage) Joe, Lewis and Darcy (twins). *Education:* Attended Lancing College, Sussex, England; Jesus College, Cambridge, M.A. (with honors), 1968.

ADDRESSES: Agent—c/o Casarotto Ramsay Ltd., National House, 60-66 Wardour St., London W1V 3HP, England.

CAREER: Playwright, director, and filmmaker. Portable Theatre (traveling company), founder with Tony Bicat, and director, 1968-71; Royal Court Theatre, London, literary manager, 1969-70, resident dramatist, 1970-71; Nottingham Playhouse, Nottingham, England, resident dramatist, 1973; Joint Stock Theatre (traveling company), founder with David Aukin and Max Stafford-Clark and director, 1975-80; Greenpoint Films, founder, 1982; National Theatre, London, associate director, 1984-88, 1989—.

MEMBER: Royal Society of Literature (fellow), Dramatists Club.

AWARDS, HONORS: Evening Standard Drama awards, 1970, for *Slag,* and 1985, for *Pravda: A Fleet Street Comedy;* John Llewellyn Rhys Memorial Award, 1975, for *Knuckle;* British Academy of Film and Television Arts (BAFTA) award for best play of the year, 1978, for *Licking Hitler;* New York Drama Critics Circle award for best foreign play and Antoinette Perry ("Tony") award nomination for best play, both 1983, both for *Plenty; Plays and Players* Best Play of the Year and City Limits award, both 1985, both for *Pravda: A Fleet Street Comedy;* Golden Bear award from Berlin Film Festival, 1985, for *Wetherby; Plays and Players* Award for best new play, 1988 and 1990; *Drama* magazine award for best play, 1988; London Critics Poll best play award, 1990; Time out Theatre Award, 1990; Laurence Olivier Award for best play, 1990.

WRITINGS:

PUBLISHED PLAYS

How Brophy Made Good (one-act; first produced in Brighton, England, at Brighton Combination Theatre, 1969), published in *Gambit,* 1970.
Slag (two-act; first produced in London at Hampstead Theatre Club, April 6, 1970; produced on Broadway at Public Theatre, March, 1971), Faber, 1971.
(With Howard Brenton, Brian Clark, Trevor Griffiths, Stephen Poliakoff, Hugh Stoddart and Snoo Wilson) *Lay By* (one-act; first produced in Edinburgh, Scotland, at Traverse Theatre, 1971; produced in London at Open Space Theatre, 1971), Calder & Boyars, 1972.
The Great Exhibition (two-act; first produced at Hampstead Theatre Club, February 28, 1972), Faber, 1972.
(With Brenton) *Brassneck* (three-act; first produced in Nottingham, England, at Nottingham Playhouse, 1973), Methuen (London), 1974.
Knuckle (two-act; first produced in the West End at Comedy Theatre, 1974; produced Off-Broadway at Phoenix Theatre, 1975; also see below), Faber, 1974, revised edition, 1978.
Fanshen (two-act; adapted from the book *Fanshen: A Documentary of Revolution in a Chinese Village* by William Hinton; first produced in London at ICA Theatre, 1975; also see below), Faber, 1976.
Teeth 'n' Smiles (two-act; first produced in London at Royal Court Theatre, 1975), Faber, 1976.
Plenty (two-act; first produced in London at National Theatre, 1978; produced in Washington, DC, at Arena Stage, 1980; also see below), S. French, (New York City), 1978.
(With others) *Deeds* (produced in Nottingham, 1978), published in *Plays and Players,* 1978.
Licking Hitler (also see below), Faber, 1978.

A Map of the World (produced at Adelaide Festival, 1982; also see below), Faber, 1982, revised edition, 1983.

(With Brenton) *Pravda: A Fleet Street Comedy* (produced at National Theatre, 1985), Methuen, 1985.

The Bay at Nice [and] *Wrecked Eggs* (double bill; produced at National Theatre, 1986), Faber, 1986.

The Asian Plays: Fanshen, Saigon, A Map of the World, Faber, 1986.

The History Plays: Plenty, Knuckle, Licking Hitler, Faber, 1986.

The Secret Rapture (produced in London, 1988; produced Off-Broadway, 1989; produced on Broadway, 1989), Grove (New York City), 1989.

The Rules of the Game (three-act; translated and adapted from a play by Luigi Pirandello; first produced at National Theatre, June 15, 1971), Absolute Classics (London), 1993.

Skylight, Faber, 1995, S. French, 1997.

Mother Courage and Her Children (adaptation of Bertolt Brecht's *Mutter Courage und Ihre Kinder*), Arcade (New York City), 1996.

Plays Two (includes *Fanshen, Saigon, A Map of the World, The Bay at Nice,* and *The Secret Rapture),* introduction by Hare, Faber (Boston), 1997, published as *The Secret Rapture and Other Plays,* Grove, 1997.

The Blue Room: Freely Adapted from Arthur Schnitzler's La Ronde, Grove, 1998.

Amy's View (first produced in London at the Royal National Theater, 1997), Faber, 1998.

The Judas Kiss (produced in London at The Playhouse, 1998), Grove, 1998, S. French, 1999.

UNPUBLISHED PLAYS

(With Tony Bicat; and director) *Inside Out* (one-act; adapted from diaries of Franz Kafka), first produced in London at Arts Laboratory, 1968.

What Happened to Blake? (one-act), first produced at Royal Court Theatre, September 29, 1970.

Deathsheads (one-act), first produced in Edinburgh at Traverse Theatre, 1971.

(With others) *England's Ireland* (two-act), first produced in Amsterdam, Netherlands, at Mickery Theatre, 1972, produced in London at Roundhouse Theatre, 1972.

The Madman Theory of Deterrence (sketch), produced in London, 1983.

(Author of libretto and director) *The Knife* (opera), produced Off-Broadway at Public Theatre, 1987.

Racing Demon, first produced in London at the National Theatre (Olivier Theatre), 1990.

Murmuring Judges, first produced at the National Theatre, 1991.

Absence of War, first produced at the National Theatre, 1993.

The Life of Galileo (adaptation of Bertolt Brecht), produced in London at Almeida Theatre, 1994.

(And performer) *Via Dolorosa* (monologue), produced in New York City at Boom Theater, 1999.

Also author of *Ivanov* (adaptation of play by Anton Chekhov), 1997.

SCREENPLAYS

Man above Men, first broadcast on British Broadcasting Corp. (BBC), 1973.

(And director) *Licking Hitler* (based on his play of the same title; first broadcast on BBC, January 10, 1978), Faber, 1978.

(And director) *Dreams of Leaving* (first broadcast on BBC, January 17, 1980), Faber, 1980.

Saigon: Year of the Cat (first broadcast on Thames Television, 1983), Faber, 1983.

(And director) *Wetherby* (released by Metro-Goldwyn-Mayer/United Artists Classics, 1985), Faber, 1985.

Plenty (based on his play of the same title), Twentieth Century-Fox, 1985.

Paris by Night, Twickenham Film Studios, 1988.

(And director) *Strapless,* Granada, 1989.

Also author of the television film, *Heading Home,* 1991, and the screenplay *Damage,* 1992.

OTHER

Writing Left-Handed (essays), Faber (London), 1991.

Asking Around: Background to the David Hare Trilogy (notes on plays), Faber, 1993.

Acting Up: A Diary, Farrar, Straus (New York City), 1999.

WORK IN PROGRESS: A Gift of Honey, a three-act stage play.

SIDELIGHTS: Following in the footsteps of the group of English writers who became known in the 1950s as the "angry young men," several authors have emerged since the 1970s to challenge the traditional values of British society. Among them, playwright David Hare has become the most prominent and successful as a result of such plays as *Knuckle, Plenty,* and *Pravda: A Fleet Street Comedy.* His plays are noted for their strong female characterizations, cinematic technique, witty dialogue, and, above all, their concern for social and political problems. An author with a strong faith in socialism, Hare has been most interested in writing about life in England as it has evolved since World War II. He often addresses such issues "as the collapse of the English empire, the debilitating effects of the class system, the myths of patriotism, [and] the loss of personal freedom," according to a *New York Times Magazine* article by Mel Gussow. But despite "Hare's position as a dramatist with a confirmed left-wing political consciousness," writes one *New York Times* critic, "in his plays it is not immediately evident which side he supports. He places his characters in conflict and encourages us to decide who is our spokesman while subtly nudging us in what he considers to be the morally responsible direction."

Hare is an important figure in the theater not only for his plays, but also for his work as a director and founder of the Portable Theatre Company and for his continued support of serious theater. *Dictionary of Literary Biography* contributor Roger N. Cornish relates that "Hare wrote his first three plays for the Portable Theatre and established it as one of the forces in England's fringe theater movement, a loose collection of small semiprofessional groups that might be likened to New York's Off-Off-Broadway." Directing and sometimes commissioning the plays of other budding playwrights such as Snoo Wilson, Tony Bicat, and Howard Brenton, Hare managed to help their controversial works gain acceptance, paving the way for productions at London theaters like the Royal Court and National.

As for Hare, it was his first full-length play, *Slag,* that brought him to the attention of critics and audiences. *Slag* is a farce about three teachers who run a school for girls. As a metaphor for the decline of England as a world power, the play traces the women's increasingly bizarre behavior as they try to maintain control of the school while slowly losing the entire enrollment. A number of reviewers have praised *Slag* for the author's ability to entertain, but have also felt, as *New Republic* contributor Stanley Kauffmann notes, that the play is "unfocussed and sometimes boring." Kauffmann later elaborates that this is because "Hare never clarifies his viewpoint, he just has fun," or, as Clive Barnes puts it in the *New York Times,* Hare "is clever. He is also a genuine playwright with more ideas than his thought can handle."

The "stinging wit followed by undercutting honesty" that *Drama* critic Jonathan Myerson considers to be the playwright's forte is an integral part of Hare's plays. *Slag* was followed by similarly satirical plays like *The Great Exhibitionist,* a wry look at one socialist politician's disillusionment with his work at Parliament, and *Brassneck,* which concerns three generations of crooked businessmen. But it was the 1974 play *Knuckle* that Gussow says "confirmed [Hare's] hope to be a playwright, and it also branded him as controversial." Originally, the playwright intended *Knuckle* to simply be a mystery like the ones he enjoyed reading. "However," writes Richard Christiansen in the *Chicago Tribune,* "by the time the play had its premiere in London in 1974, he had arrived at a different goal: 'to subvert the form of the thriller to a serious end.' " The result is a play that is only superficially about Curly Delafield's search for his missing sister. "The real point of the play," Gussow explains in a *New York Times* review, "is not the mystery but the subtext, the casual corruption of Guildford, a decaying city whose burghers are presented as swindlers and blackmailers." Hare attempts to show that the real criminals in society are the ones hiding behind the wealthy sheen of respectability that Curly unveils during the course of his investigation. In the end, overwhelmed by cynicism and suspicions that his own father is guilty of the crime, Curly misses out on his one chance to discover the truth about his sister.

The character of Curly illustrates a pervasive theme in Hare's plays: the inability of most people to change themselves or society for the better. Hare applies this theme toward the entire 1960s generation in his first West End hit, *Teeth 'n' Smiles,* which concerns "the challenge of pop music in the '60s to the way privilege has re-grouped itself in Britain since 1945," according to *Plays and Players* contributor Ronald Bryden. The conclusion of the play, says Bryden, "is as disillusioned and scathing an epitaph for the Beatle decade's army of mercenaries as any ['angry young men' playwright John] Osborne could devise. But [Hare] understands what the battle was about and mourns for its lost cause with a harsh tenderness which sometimes touches poetry."

Moving away from England in the play *Fanshen,* Hare shows how change is indeed possible when given another culture and political system. The play is set in a small Chinese village right after the Communist revolution. Over the course of the story, as Cornish relates, the "village peasants learn to stand up for their new rights, acquire political consciousness and the habits of group criticism and discussion, develop indigenous cadres, redistribute wealth, abuse their powers, and correct themselves." But although Hare clearly disapproves of the English system of government, "he makes no strong judgment, pro or con, about the ultimate wisdom of Maoism," according to Frank Rich in the *New York*

Times. "[*Fanshen*] is a microscopic view of one embryonic moment in history, so free of ideological pleading and so intimate that it could be a paradigm of almost any newborn society's struggle to govern itself equitably, anywhere and any time."

One of Hare's most successful plays and the one with which he is most often associated, *Plenty,* returns to the now familiar setting of post-World War II England, where the playwright explores the effects of a suffocating English culture on a woman named Susan Traherne. Susan, who experienced her glory days when she worked for the French Resistance, finds only a banal existence when she marries a diplomat after the war. In a society where everyone around her sacrifices their beliefs for those of the majority, she is the only person with a genuine—though unfocussed—desire to change the world. She eventually "has to resort to violence, in word and deed, in order to make herself heard above the din of double-talk that Hare sees as the official tongue of England," relates Gene Siskel, who reviewed Hare's screenplay adaptation of *Plenty* for the *Chicago Tribune.* Susan's frustration causes her to attempt suicide several times. "In the end," comments Cornish, "her idealism, expressed as it is through extreme behavior, ruins her husband, and the audience is left to ponder a woman of the best potential achieving only the worst."

Some critics have complained that *Plenty* never effectively links Susan's personal problems with those of society, believing that it also fails to clarify whether or not her fate was inevitable. Robert Brustein, for example, writes in the *New Republic* that "the most uncertain aspect of the play . . . [is that] it assigns purely social causes to problems that may at least be partially existential." Hare, however, does not actually place all the blame on society. Susan, who is in this respect reminiscent of Curly in *Knuckle,* is also to blame. Rich remarks in another *New York Times* article: "If the author believes that idealists have a right to 'a kind of impatience' with a world that betrays their noble, hard-won victories, [Hare] also seems to feel that Susan should have struggled anew for those ideals rather than 'lose control' by giving in to bitterness and cynicism."

Plenty did not receive resounding acclaim in Britain at first, but it slowly won audiences over several years, and, upon its release in the United States, was an immediate hit. Film critics were also very receptive to Hare's screenplay version of *Plenty,* which starred Meryl Streep. Charles Champlin of the *Los Angeles Times,* for example, writes, "I can't remember a film in recent months that has seemed so continuously startling, affecting and ultimately satisfying," and the *Washington Post*'s Paul Attanasio remarks: "You resent it for the work it makes you do, and recognize it by the rules it breaks—you recognize it as greatness." Many reviewers also specifically praised Hare for his characterization of the protagonist. For example, Steve Grant, a contributor to Sandy Craig's *Dreams and Deconstructions: Alternative Theatre in Britain,* asserts that "in this creation of Susan, Hare has written his most colossal role to date."

Yet the problem of Hare's ability to illustrate universal concerns through his plays remains, in some critics' opinion. According to John Hope Mason in the *Times Literary Supplement,* early plays like *Plenty* risk the "danger that the general view, the overall verdict, would collapse into a purely local and personal reaction." But Mason later comments that with *A Map of the World* Hare "has confronted this difficulty—the relationship between individual experience and general judgement—in the context not of England but of the world. The difficulty is not completely resolved . . . [but] in the end the play lives up to its high ambition." Set at an UNESCO conference to address world poverty, *A Map of the World* pits the arguments of a respected right-wing comic novelist reminiscent of V. S. Naipaul with those of a brilliant left-wing journalist and a leader of a new African country. "Though they are disparate in their points of view," reports one *New York Times* critic, "all three are essentially allied in opposition to an UNESCO official, a centrist who sacrifices principle in order to sustain the political status quo. The play is not so much in favor of any of the alternatives as it is opposed to the pragmatist at the center." Hare, therefore, never allows any of his debaters a decisive victory. "In *Map of the World,*" the playwright tells Gussow in the *New York Times Magazine,* "I'm trying to say that no intellectual will ever be able to organize the world in the way he wants to organize it. Life will always seep back up and spoil his sand castle."

Even though Hare does not guide his audience toward any specific alternative, his plays generally demonstrate that supporting the establishment usually leads to the abandonment of truth, the acceptance of lies for the sake of convenience or profit. But to defend one's ideals often results in defeat at the hands of corrupt people, as the playwright illustrates in works like *Pravda: A Fleet Street Comedy* and *The Secret Rapture.* With *Pravda,* a work that became "the most talked about play in London," according to Gussow in the *New York Times Magazine,* Hare and coauthor Howard Brenton lambaste what they see as one of the chief perpetrators of the status quo: the newspaper industry. Despite the title, which is taken from the Russian newspaper of that name and ironically means "truth," the subtitle reveals that the play actually concerns an English newspaper. Lambert Le Roux is a former tabloid editor who now runs an important London paper, upon which he imposes his philosophy: "Why go to the trouble of producing good papers when bad ones are so much easier, and they sell better too?" When a young editor decides to challenge the newspaper baron's policies, Le Roux effectively crushes the opposition. The satirical approach that Hare and Brenton use to tell this story makes it "superb high-energy entertainment," according to *Time* contributor William A. Henry III, but in a *New York Times* review, Rich complains that the second act loses it satirical punch and lends itself to "authorial preaching about political tactics." Henry, however, maintains that "*Pravda* . . . given its bitter convictions, could not have a happy ending."

According to Benedict Nightingale, Hare's next play, *The Secret Rapture* is his "most personal and private work, the one in which he exposes his emotions most completely." The play is about a gentle, moral woman named Isobel whose family takes advantage of her by stripping her of her assets and business after her father dies. Isobel, who never judges her family harshly for their actions, is nevertheless subjected to "outrageously unjust accusations that she is criticizing or patronizing them," relates Irving Wardle in the London *Times.* This touches on Hare's belief that, as he tells Nightingale, "goodness tends to make people shifty, and make those with bad consciences feel judged even when they're not being judged at all." Toward the end of the play, the family's demands upon Isobel finally turn her into "an exhausted emotional refugee," to use Wardle's words. The play concludes with a crime of passion that results in Isobel's death. Several critics have deemed this conclusion unconvincing, however. Wardle calls this the play's "one big miscalculation" and *Chicago Tribune* critic Matt Wolf remarks that it "seems melodramatic and wrong." Nevertheless, Wolf declares *The Secret Rapture* "is on its way to becoming a great play."

"The play [*Skylight*] is a love story constructed on the kinds of ideological polarities that often underpin Mr. Hare's dramas," comments Warren Hoge in the *New York Times.* The story revolves around Kyra and Tom, once lovers for six years although he was twenty years older, married, and her boss. The two ended their relationship when Tom's wife found out about the affair, but after his wife's death, Tom visits Kyra to win her back. According to David Jays in *New Statesman,* "Hare's writing twinges with sadness, with a sorrow so poignant it must be love." Yet Jays faults the way Hare attempts to address cultural issues. He writes: "Hare argues his case for the citizen's entitlement to respect, opportunity, from too lordly a distance. Politically, *Skylight* is obvious and inconsistent, it works best as a sad romance." Richard Zoglin of *Time* observes that the "play's sparseness leaves the audience with entirely too much time to admire the acting," while *New Leader* reviewer Stefan Kanfer, critical of Hare's political posturing in *Skylight,* concludes: "A happy ending for everyone except those in search of significance."

In *Asking Around: Background to the David Hare Trilogy,* Hare shares the research he conducted for his *State of the Nation* trilogy, written for the National Theatre. Michael Coveney describes the book in the *Observer* as "a compelling volume that is part work-book, part voyage of discovery: an anatomical, wryly amused look at our institutions of church, law, and state." Hare interviewed and observed officials at the General Synod and inner-city vicarages for *Racing Demon* about the Church of England; police officers, lawyers, and prison governors for *Murmuring Judges* about the law; and reporters and politicians and their advisers for *Absence of War* about the Labour Party. "His notes on all this are quite interesting," writes Frances Wheen in *The Spectator,* "but not quite interesting enough, since they cover ground that has already been well-trodden by many a journalist and sociologist." Coveney concludes: "The book is not a template for drama, but you can trace bits of scenes and characters, and a few jokes, right through to the National's stage."

Hare's prolific output continued in the late 1990s with three new plays, a dramatic monologue, and a book, all in the space of two years. The 1997 *Amy's View* covers the ups and downs of a stage actress, Esme Allen, through sixteen years of her life. Also central to the drama are Esme's daughter Amy, and Amy's film-critic boyfriend, Dominic. While Esme's career gradually declines, the facile Dominic carves out a successful notch for himself as a media savant. According to Matt Wolf of *Variety,* the themes of the play include "such Hare constants as the changing fortunes of Britain, the unreliability of journalists, and the volatility of love." Wolf faults the body of the play as lacking on several counts, including Hare's tendency to have his characters "personify points of view" that are announced rather than dramatized. Yet Wolf finds the conclusion of *Amy's Voice,* in which "Hare surpasses even himself," to be its saving grace, noting: "Hare is altogether more successful away from domestic and social harangue and into the passionate defense of the theater that brings the play to its tumultuous close." Charles Isherwood, also of *Variety,* observes that "even when the play's characters are behaving like linguistic pugilists, Hare's elegant witty language and the allure of his ideas entertain," while *Back Stage* critic David Rosenberg characterizes *Amy's View* as "engrossing, if somewhat engorged . . . a head-spinning work full of anger and passion, humor and vitriol."

The Blue Room, Hare's "freely adapted" version of Austrian dramatist Arthur Schnitzler's *Riegen,* fared less well with critics. *Riegen,* which translates as "Merry-Go-Round," was considered scandalous when it first appeared shortly after 1900 and in several subsequent productions, provoking riots in its German premier of 1921. It later surfaced as a 1950 film, *La Ronde,* by Max Ophul. Mark Steyn of *New Criterion* describes the play as "a roundelay of transitory sex, in which the Whore lures the Soldier, the Soldier picks up the Chambermaid, the Chambermaid seduces the Young Gentleman, and so on, until the whole thing comes full circle and the Count catches the eye of the Whore." The New York production of *The Blue Room* attracted considerable attention, selling out its twelve-month run and proving a windfall for ticket scalpers even before its first appearance. Seats first priced at $35 were soon going for as high as $300. Such attention had more to do with the fact that film star Nicole Kidman would appear nude in the play than it did with Hare's reputation as an author. Reviewers, while often admiring Kidman's form both as an actress (she assumes five different roles) and woman, remained unimpressed with Hare's updated adaptation. In his discussion of the play for *National Review,* Rod Dreher pans it as "pure theatrical saltpeter." Richard Scholem of *LI Business News* calls it "a lightweight piece by a heavyweight playwright," and for Zoglin it represents "the kind of hype which great letdowns are made of." In what could be considered backhanded praise, Steyn concludes that "in reducing Schnitzler to the sad, perfunctory, non-erotic sex bouts on display here, Hare has provided an uncanny mirror of the pitiful state of sexual adventure in our own times."

Hare's *The Judas Kiss,* a drama about homosexual author Oscar Wilde and his affair with the young Lord Alfred (Bosie) Douglas, appeared in New York in 1998, simultaneously with two other plays about Wilde. Kanfer finds it to be "the weakest" of the three presentations, noting that "the play never comes to life." Though Kanfer and other critics blame much of the play's failure on the miscasting of Liam Neeson as Wilde—"a footballer attempting to play a voluptuary"—Hare also comes under fire. Isherwood believes that "Neeson's performance combines with Hare's exactingly unsentimental portrait of Wilde to drain the play of all emotional weight." While Wolf praises the second act of *The Judas Kiss,* which portrays Wilde in decline after two years at hard labor for sexual crimes, he finds the relationship between Wilde and Bosie to be completely unconvincing. "In *The Judas Kiss,*" he concludes, "we're left with a merely odd couple even as the lethal potential of love lies . . . outside the production's embrace."

In 1997, at the behest of the Royal Court Theater, Hare embarked on a series of trips to the Middle East. The aim of his travels was to gather material for a play on the conflicts that continued to plague the region. Hare ended up writing not a play but a dramatic monologue, for which he turned "actor." In the course of the ninety-minute production he relates the views of more than thirty different people, both Arabs and Israelis, he met during his travels. The title of the piece, *Via Dolorosa,* refers to a cobblestone route in Jerusalem that is sacred to Christians. Critical response to *Via Dolorosa* ranges across a broad spectrum. Steyn observes: "About two minutes in, you suddenly realize you've paid Broadway prices to hear an English public schoolboy talk about what he did in his holidays. . . . He [Hare] has no great insights into Arabs and Israelis." In contrast, Brustein feels that "Hare deals eloquently, compassionately, and feelingly with most of the issues currently roiling this stormy area. . . . Given the enormity of his subject, Hare does a sound if synoptic job with his material." While Brustein faults Hare's talents as a performer—"hunching his shoulders, clenching and rubbing his hands, jerking his body spasmodically like a car idling on one cylinder." Jack Kroll of *Newsweek* notes that "Hare uses eloquent shifts of voice, body language and eyes that reflect anger, sorrow and (not much) hope to portray the struggle," and Isherwood remarks that "Hare's dramatic gifts combine happily with the passionate personalities he enthusiastically impersonates to turn the complexities of the narrative into engaging theater." Hare's Middle-East travels and the production of *Via Dolorosa* also led to his 1999 book, *Acting Up: A Diary.* The book is not about the Arab-Israel conflict but, as a *Publishers Weekly* reviewer puts it, concerns "discovering what it's like to be an actor who must incarnate a writer's words in the flesh for a live audience." Barry X. Miller of *Library Journal,* extolls *Acting Up* for its "delightfully stimulating insights, connections, arguments, and ideas," and deems it: "A stunning work; essential for theater collections in all libraries." The *Publishers Weekly* critic concludes that "Hare's love for theater flows from every page, most notably in a thrillingly exact description of the magic of live performance: 'The great wind of an audience blows through, and nothing is what you thought it was going to be.' "

Although most of his plays do not offer an optimistic view of human potential, Hare consistently encourages his audiences to question the establishment that governs it. As he says to *New York Times* writer Christine Pittel: "My interest as a writer has always been to try and break down conventional responses to things. People walk around thinking they know what they think about things, but first of all, people rarely examine their beliefs. . . . And secondly, when they are confronted with a real work of art, then they discover that they don't believe what they thought they believed all along. In a way, the great art, the great subversive art, is art that makes you realize that you don't think what you thought you did." But Hare maintains that he "is not a social doctor prescribing remedies for our national ills," writes Ludlow. Instead, his primary concern lies in creating engrossing theater, and Cornish writes that Hare feels "that the theater is at its best when portraying lies, and he believes that the moment when the audience sees the ironic contrast between what is professed and what is done is one of the most exciting in theater."

BIOGRAPHICAL/CRITICAL SOURCES:

BOOKS

Ansorge, Peter, *Disrupting the Spectacle: Five Years of Experimental and Fringe Theatre in Britain,* Pitman, 1975.

Contemporary Literary Criticism, Volume 29, Gale (Detroit, MI), 1984.

Craig, Sandy, editor, *Dreams and Deconstructions: Alternative Theatre in Britain,* Amber Lane Press, 1980.

Dean, Joan Fitzpatrick, *David Hare,* Twayne (Boston), 1990.

Dictionary of Literary Biography, Volume 13: *British Dramatists since World War II,* Gale, 1982.

Donesky, Finlay, *David Hare: Moral and Historical Perspectives,* Greenwood Press (Westport, CT), 1996.

Hare, David, and Harold Brenton, *Pravda: A Fleet Street Comedy,* Methuen, 1985.

Hare, David, *Writing Left-Handed* (essays), Faber, 1991.

Hayman, Ronald, *British Theatre since 1955: A Reassessment,* Oxford University Press (New York City), 1979.

Homden, Carol, *The Plays of David Hare,* Cambridge University Press (New York City), 1995.

Kerensky, Oleg, *The New British Drama,* Taplinger (New York City), 1977.

Zeifman, Hersh, editor, *David Hare: A Casebook,* Garland (New York City), 1994.

PERIODICALS

America, May 22, 1999, James S. Torrens, "Triple Play," p. 27.

Back Stage, April 30, 1999, David Rosenberg, review of *Amy's View,* p. 56; April 2, 1999, David A. Rosenberg, review of *Via Dolorosa,* p. 48.

Books Magazine, January, 1994, p. 14.

Chicago Tribune, September 25, 1985; September 27, 1985; August 13, 1988; November 13, 1988; January 15, 1989; April 7, 1989.

Cue, March 6, 1971.

Drama, winter, 1975; summer, 1978; autumn, 1983.

Entertainment Weekly, January 29, 1993, p. 38.

Film Comment, October, 1985.

Hudson Review, summer, 1971.

Library Journal, November 1, 1999, review of *Acting Up,* p. 84.

LI Business News, January 15, 1999, Richard Scholem, review of *The Blue Room,* p. 26A.

London Magazine, July, 1978.

Los Angeles Times, September 6, 1985; September 18, 1985; September 28, 1985; December 19, 1989; May 18, 1990.

Ms., October, 1985.

Nation, March 8, 1971; December 18, 1989, p. 766; November 2, 1992, p. 518.

National Review, January 25, 1999, Rod Dreher, "Theater: The Bottom Line," p. 51.

New Criterion, February, 1999, Mark Steyn, "Sad, Perfunctory, Mechanical," p. 44; June, 1999, Mark Steyn, "Saying Nothing at Great Length," p. 39.

New Leader, April 6, 1981; October 7, 1996, Stefan Kanfer, review of *Skylight,* p. 22; May 4, 1998, Stefan Kanfer, review of *The Judas Kiss,* p. 22.

New Republic, March 13, 1971; November 29, 1982; November 20, 1989, p. 29; February 17, 1992, p. 28; June 7, 1999, Robert Brustein, "Robert Brustein on Theater-Spring Roundup," p. 34.

New Statesman, June 4, 1971; June 21, 1991, p. 45; May 12, 1995, p. 32.

Newsweek, March 23, 1981; August 5, 1985; September 23, 1985; March 15, 1999, Jack Kroll, "In a Land without Pity," p. 70.

New York, March 22, 1971; November 1, 1982; December 14, 1992, p. 89.

New Yorker, March 6, 1971; January 25, 1993, p. 96; December 4, 1995, p. 48.

New York Times, May 7, 1971; November 4, 1977; March 18, 1979; August 14, 1979; March 10, 1981; October 17, 1982; October 22, 1982; October 31, 1982; January 13, 1983; January 31, 1983; February 3, 1983; March 13, 1983; May 20, 1983; June 20, 1985; July 19, 1985; September 19, 1985; October 2, 1985; October 4, 1985; October 11, 1985; October 13, 1985; May 29, 1986; March 8, 1987; March 11, 1987; March 15, 1987; July 31, 1988; June 30, 1989; September 23, 1989; October 22, 1989; October 27, 1989; August 29, 1990; November 19, 1996.

New York Times Magazine, September 29, 1985.

Observer, October 17, 1993, p. 18.

Plays and Players, May, 1970; July, 1971; November, 1975; April, 1978; March, 1983.

Publishers Weekly, October 25, 1999, review of *Acting Up,* p. 64.

Spectator, November 6, 1993, p. 53.

Stage, June 24, 1971; March 2, 1972.

Theatre Quarterly, September-November, 1975.

Time, June 10, 1985; October 28, 1985; January 11, 1993, p. 50; October 7, 1996, Richard Zoglin, review of *Skylight,* p. 95; December 28, 1998, Richard Zoglin, "Room for Improvement: Nicole Kidman Is Here! Now Stop the Hype!" p. 184.

Times (London), April 23, 1975; January 31, 1983; March 2, 1985; March 8, 1985; May 4, 1985; November 22, 1985; September 11, 1986; October 6, 1988; May 25, 1991.

Times Educational Supplement, February 4, 1983.

Times Literary Supplement, January 25, 1980; February 11, 1983.

Variety, June 30, 1997, Matt Wolf, review of *Amy's View,* p. 72; March 22, 1999, Charles Isherwood, review of *Via Dolorosa,* p. 46; March 23, 1998, Matt Wolf, review of *The Judas Kiss,* p. 100; April 19, 1999, Charles Isherwood, review of *Amy's View,* p. 54.; May 4, 1999, Charles Isherwood, review of *The Judas Kiss,* p. 93.

Washington Post, April 5, 1983; May 21, 1983; August 26, 1985; September 20, 1985; November 27, 1988.*

* * *

HARJO, Joy 1951-

PERSONAL: Born May 9, 1951, in Tulsa, OK; daughter of Allen W. and Wynema (Baker) Foster; children: Phil, Rainy Dawn. *Education:* University of New Mexico, B.A., 1976; University of Iowa, M.F.A., 1978; attended Anthropology Film Center, Santa Fe, 1982. *Ethnicity:* "American Indian; Muskoke." *Avocational interests:* Performing on the saxophone with band Joy Harjo and Poetic Justice.

ADDRESSES: Home—1140-D, Alewa Dr., Honolulu, HI 96817. *E-mail*—katcvpoet@aol.com.

CAREER: Institute of American Indian Arts, Santa Fe, NM, instructor, 1978-79, 1983-84; Arizona State University, Tempe, lecturer in creative writing and poetry, 1980-81; University of Colorado, Boulder, assistant professor, 1985-88; University of Arizona, Tucson, associate professor, 1988-90; University of New Mexico, Albuquerque, professor, 1991-97. Visiting professor of creative writing at the University of Montana, 1985. Writer and consultant for Native American Public Broadcasting Consortium, National Indian Youth Council, and National Endowment for the Arts, all 1980-83. Member of steering committee of En'owkin Centre International School of Writing. Writer-in-residence at schools, including Navajo Community College, 1978; University of Alaska Prison Project, 1981; and Institute of Alaska Native Arts, 1984. Recordings with band, Joy Harjo and Poetic Justice, include *Furious Light,* 1986, *The Woman Who Fell from the Sky,* 1994, and *Letter from the End of the Twentieth Century,* 1997.

MEMBER: PEN (member of advisory board), PEN New Mexico (member of advisory board).

AWARDS, HONORS: Academy of American Poetry Award and University of New Mexico first place poetry award, both 1976; National Endowment for the Arts fellow, 1978; named one of the Outstanding Young Women in America, 1978, 1984; first place in poetry, Santa Fe Festival for the Arts, 1980; Arizona Commission on the Arts Creative Writing fellow, 1989; American Indian Distinguished Achievement Award, 1990; Josephine Miles Award for excellence in literature, PEN Oakland, William Carlos Williams award, Poetry Society of America, and American Book Award, Before Columbus Foundation, all 1991, for *In Mad Love and War;* Wittner Bynner Poetry fellowship, 1994; Lifetime Achievement award, Native Writers' Circle of America, 1995; Oklahoma Book Arts award, 1995, for *The Woman Who Fell from the Sky;* Delmore Schwartz Memorial award, and Mountains and Plains Booksellers' award, both 1995, both for *In Mad Love and War;* Bravo Award, Albuquerque Arts Alliance, 1996; New Mexico Governor's Award for excellence in the arts, 1997; Lila Wallace/*Reader's Digest* Fund Writers' Award, 1998; National Council on the Arts, presidential appointment, 1998; Honorary doctorate, St. Mary-in-the-Woods College, 1998.

WRITINGS:

POETRY

The Last Song (also see below), Puerto Del Sol Press (Las Cruces, NM), 1975.

What Moon Drove Me to This? (contains *The Last Song*), I. Reed Books (New York City), 1980.

She Had Some Horses, Thunder's Mouth Press (New York City), 1983.

Secrets from the Center of the World, illustrated by Steven Strom, University of Arizona Press (Tucson), 1989.

In Mad Love and War, Wesleyan University Press (Middletown, CT), 1990.

The Woman Who Fell from the Sky, Norton (New York City), 1994.

A Map to the Next World: Poetry and Tales, Norton, 2000.

OTHER

(Editor with Gloria Bird) *Reinventing the Enemy's Language: North American Native Women's Writing,* Norton, 1997.

The Good Luck Cat (children's fiction), illustrated by Paul Lee, Harcourt (San Diego, CA), 2000.

Also author of the film script *Origin of Apache Crown Dance,* Silver Cloud Video, 1985; co-author of the film script *The Beginning,* Native American Broadcasting Consortium; author of television plays, including *We Are One, Uhonho,* 1984, *Maiden of Deception Pass,* 1985, *I Am Different from My Brother,* 1986, and *The Runaway,* 1986. Contributor to numerous anthologies and to several literary journals, including *Conditions, Beloit Poetry Journal, River Styx, Tyuoyi,* and *Y'Bird.*

WORK IN PROGRESS: A collection of personal essays.

SIDELIGHTS: Strongly influenced by her Muskogee Creek heritage, feminist and social concerns, and her background in the arts, Joy Harjo frequently incorporates Native American myths, symbols, and values into her writing. Her poetry additionally emphasizes the Southwest landscape and the need for remembrance and transcendence. She asserts: "I feel strongly that I have a responsibility to all the sources that I am: to all past and future ancestors, to my home country, to all places that I touch down on and that are myself, to all voices, all women, all of my tribe, all people, all earth, and beyond that to all beginnings and endings. In a strange kind of sense [writing] frees me to believe in myself, to be able to speak, to have voice, because I have to; it is my survival."

Harjo's work is largely autobiographical, informed by her love of the natural world and her preoccupation with survival and the limitations of language. Her first volume of poetry was published in 1975 as a nine-poem chapbook titled *The Last Song.* These early compositions, mainly set in Oklahoma and New Mexico, reveal Harjo's remarkable power and insight, especially as evident in the title poem, "The Last Song," and "3 AM." Harjo writes in "3 AM" about an exasperating airport experience: "the attendant doesn't know / that third mesa / is a part of the center / of the world / and who are we just two indians / at three in the morning trying to find our way back home." Commenting on "3 AM" in *World Literature Today,* John Scarry writes that the poem "is a work filled with ghosts from the Native American past, figures seen operating in an alien culture that is itself a victim of fragmentation. . . . Here the Albuquerque airport is both modern America's technology and moral nature—and both clearly have failed. Together they cannot get these Indians to their destination, a failure that stretches from our earliest history to the sleek desks of our most up-to-date airline offices."

What Moon Drove Me to This?, Harjo's first full-length volume of poetry, appeared four years later and contains the entire contents of *The Last Song.* "With this collection," C. Renee Field writes in *Dictionary of Literary Biography,* "Harjo continued to refine her ability to find and voice the deep spiritual truths underneath everyday experiences, especially for the Native American." In an interview with Laura Coltelli in *Winged Words: American Indian Writers Speak,* Harjo shares the creative process behind her poetry: "I begin with the seed of an emotion, a place, and then move from there. . . . I no longer see the poem as an ending point, perhaps more the end of a journey, an often long journey that can begin years earlier, say with the blur of the memory of the sun on someone's cheek, a certain smell, an ache, and will culminate years later in a poem, sifted through a point, a lake in my heart through which language must come."

The search for freedom and self-actualization considered central to Harjo's work, is particularly noted in her third book of poetry, *She Had Some Horses,* in which she frequently incorporates prayer-chants and animal imagery. For example, in "The Black Room," a poem about childhood rape, Harjo repeats the mantric line "She thought she woke up." In the title poem, "She Had Some Horses," one of Harjo's most highly regarded and anthologized poems, she describes the "horses" within a woman who struggles to reconcile contradictory personal feelings and experiences to achieve a sense of oneness. The poem concludes: "She had some horses she loved. / She had some horses she hated. / These were the same horse." As Field observes, "The horses are spirits, neither male nor female, and, through them, clear truths can be articulated." As Scarry observes, "Harjo is clearly a highly political and feminist Native American, but she is even more the poet of myth and the subconscious; her images and landscapes owe as much to the vast stretches of our hidden mind as they do to her native Southwest."

Nature is central to Harjo's works, as evident in her 1989 prose poetry collection *Secrets from the Center of the World.* Each poem in this volume is accompanied by a color photograph of the Southwest landscape, which, as Margaret Randall notes in *Women's Review of Books,* works to "create an evocative little gem, intensely personal, hauntingly universal." Offering praise for the volume in the *Village Voice,* Dan Bellm writes, "*Secrets* is a rather unlikely experiment that turned into a satisfying and beautiful book. . . . As Harjo notes, the pictures 'emphasize the "not-separate" that is within and that moves harmoniously upon the landscape.' " According to Randall, "There is no alteration in these photographs, nor do the poems lack a word or possess one too many. Language and visual image are perfectly tuned and balanced, producing an experience in which neither illustrates the other but each needs its counterpart." Bellm similarly adds, "The book's best poems enhance this play of scale and perspective, suggesting in very few words the relationship between a human life and millennial history."

Her best-known volume, the multi-award-winning *In Mad Love and War,* is more overtly concerned with politics, tradition, remembrance, and the transformational aspects of poetry. In the first section, which relates various acts of violence, including others' attempts to deny Harjo her heritage as well as the murder of an Indian leader, Harjo explores the difficulties many Native Americans face in modern American society: "*we have too many stories to carry on our backs like houses, we have struggled too long to let the monsters steal our sleep, sleep, go to sleep.* But I never woke up. Dogs have been nipping at my heels since I learned to walk. I was taught to not dance for a rotten supper on the plates of my enemies. My mother taught me well." The second half of the book frequently emphasizes personal relationships and change.

"Harjo's range of emotion and imagery in this volume is truly remarkable," writes Scarry. "She achieves intimacy and power in ways that send a reader to every part of the poetic spectrum for comparisons and for some frame of reference." In the poem "Autobiography," a mother describes to her daughter how God created humans to inhabit the earth. In another, "Javelina," Harjo invokes the strong voice of "one born of a blood who wrestled the whites for freedom, and I have since lived dangerously in a diminished system." Leslie Ullman notes in *Kenyon Review,* "Like a magician, Harjo draws power from overwhelming circumstance and emotion by submitting to them, celebrating them, letting her voice and vision move in harmony with the ultimate laws of paradox and continual change." Commenting on "Javelina," Ullman adds that Harjo's "stance is not so much that of a representative of a culture as it is the more generative one of a storyteller whose stories resurrect memory, myth, and private struggles that have been overlooked, and who thus restores vitality to the culture at large." Praising the volume in *Prairie Schooner,* Kathleene West writes, "*In Mad Love and War* has the power of beauty and prophecy and all the hope of love poised at its passionate beginning. It allows us to enter the place 'we haven't imagined' and allows us to imagine what we will do when we are there."

In 1994, Harjo followed *In Mad Love and War* with *The Woman Who Fell from the Sky,* another book of prose poetry. The title is based on an Iroquois myth about the descent of a female creator. As Frank Allen notes in *Library Journal,* Harjo is concerned with the vying forces of creation and destruction in contemporary society, embodied in such symbolism as wolves and northern lights contrasted with alcoholism and the Vietnam War. *Booklist* reviewer Pat Monaghan praises the poems as "stunning, mature, wholehearted, musical," and the collection together as a "brilliant, unforgettable book."

In addition to her fictional works, Harjo has worked to popularize the work of other Native American women writers. An interview with Laura Coltelli published as *Spiral of Memory: Interviews: Joy Harjo,* appeared in 1997 and offers additional insight into the writer's background, art, and views on poetry. And in *Reinventing the Enemy's Language: North American Native Women's Writing* she presents a collection of stories that act to spur readers to social and political activism. The works, from such authors as Louise Erdrich and diarist Mary Brave Bird, present a new genre, according to *Progressive* contributor Mark Anthony Rolo, but rather than faddish, it is "a new sphere of storytelling, part of a larger hidden culture."

Consistently praised for the depth and thematic concerns in her writings, Harjo emerged as a major figure in contemporary American poetry. Though, for taking a position on numerous political, social, economic, and humanitarian issues, she has received criticism for being overly "politically correct." As Field notes, "She does not tell her reader how to feel but simply tells the truth she sees. Harjo's poetry is not so much about 'correctness' as it is about continuance and survival." While Harjo's work is often set in the Southwest, emphasizes the plight of the individual, and reflects Creek values, myths, and beliefs, her oeuvre has universal relevance. Bellm asserts: "Harjo's work draws from the river of Native tradition, but it also swims freely in the currents of Anglo-American verse—feminist poetry of personal/political resistance, deep-image poetry of the unconscious, 'new-narrative' explorations of story and rhythm in prose-poem form." According to Field, "To read the poetry of Joy Harjo is to hear the voice of the earth, to see the landscape of time and timelessness, and, most important, to get a glimpse of people who struggle to understand, to know themselves, and to survive."

Commenting on her writing as a means of survival, Harjo told Coltelli, "I don't believe I would be alive today if it hadn't been for writing. There were times when I was conscious of holding onto a pen and letting the words flow, painful and from the gut, to keep from letting go of it all. Now, this was when I was much younger, and full of self-hatred. Writing helped me give voice to turn around a terrible silence that was killing me. And on a larger level, if we, as Indian people, Indian women, keep silent, then we will disappear, at least in this level of reality." Field notes, "As Harjo has continued to refine her craft, her poems have become visions, answers to age-old questions, keys to understanding the complex nature of twentieth-century American life, and guides to the past and the future."

Harjo told *CA:* "I agree with Gide that most of what is created is beyond us, is from that source of utter creation, the Creator, or God. We are technicians here on Earth, but also co-creators. I'm still amazed. And I still say, after writing poetry for all this time, and now music, that ultimately humans have a small hand in it. We serve it. We have to put ourselves in the way of it, and get out of the way of ourselves. And we have to hone our craft so that the form in which we hold our poems, our songs in attracts the best.

"My particular road is not about taking established forms and developing them. I admire a finely constructed sonnet but I do not wish to work in that Euro-classical form. I honor that direction, but I am working to find my own place and one who is multi-cultural, multi-racial. I am influenced by Muscogean forms, European and African forms, as well as others that have deeply moved me, say for instance, Navajo. When I began writing poetry as a painting major at the University of New Mexico, I was learning Navajo language. It influenced me deeply because intimate to the language were the shapes of the landscape, the history. I became aware of layers of meaning marked by sandhills, by the gestures of the earth.

"African-American influences in poetry and music have been critical to my development as a writer and musician. This is not something new. There is history and a relationship between Africans and Muscogean peoples begun in the southeastern U.S. We've influenced each other, yet this influence is rarely talked about. I can hear the African influence in our stomp dance music, and can hear Muscogean influence in jazz, the blues, and rock. It's all there.

"I have also taken up saxophone and perform professionally with my band. I am asked often about how music has informed my poetry, changed it. It's difficult to say exactly, except to acknowledge that of course it has all along. The first poetry I heard and recognized as pure poetry was the improvised line of a trumpet player on a jazz tune on the radio when I was four-years-old. That was it. I've been trying to get it right ever since. Sometimes I hear the origin of that line when I'm at the stomp grounds. One of these days I'll be able to sing it, write it."

BIOGRAPHICAL/CRITICAL SOURCES:

BOOKS

Allen, Paula Gunn, *The Sacred Hoop: Recovering the Feminine in American Indian Traditions,* Beacon Press (Boston), 1986.

Bruchac, Joseph, editor, *Survival This Way: Interviews with American Indian Poet,* University of Arizona Press (Tucson), 1987.

Coltelli, Laura, editor, *Winged Words: American Indian Writers Speak,* University of Nebraska Press, 1990.

Coltelli, Laura, editor, *The Spiral of Memory: Interviews: Joy Harjo,* University of Michigan Press (Ann Arbor), 1996.

Contemporary Literary Criticism, Volume 83, Gale (Detroit), 1994.

Contemporary Women Poets, St. James Press (Detroit), 1997.

Crawford, John, and Patricia Clark Smith, *This Is about Vision: Interviews with Southwestern Writers,* edited by William Balassi, John F. Crawford, and Annie O. Eysturoy, University of New Mexico Press, 1990.

Dictionary of Literary Biography, Gale, Volume 120: *American Poets since World War II,* 1992, Volume

175: *Native American Writers of the United States,* 1997.
Harjo, Joy, *She Had Some Horses,* Thunder's Mouth, 1983.
Harjo, Joy, *In Mad Love and War,* Wesleyan University Press, 1990.
Hobson, Geary, editor, *The Remembered Earth: An Anthology of Contemporary Native American Literature,* Red Earth, 1979.
Pettit, Rhonda, *Joy Harjo,* Boise State University (Boise, ID), 1998.
Swann, Brian, and Arnold Krupat, editors, *I Tell You Now: Autobiographical Essays by Native American Writers,* University of Nebraska Press, 1987.

PERIODICALS

American Book Review, April-May, 1991, pp. 10-11.
American Indian Quarterly, spring, 1983, pp. 27-40.
Belles Lettres, summer, 1991, pp. 7-8.
Bloomsbury Review, March-April, 1996.
Booklist, November 15, 1994, p. 573.
Kenyon Review, spring, 1991, pp. 179-83; summer, 1993, pp. 57-66.
Library Journal, October 15, 1994, p. 72; November 15, 1994, p. 70; June 1, 1997, p. 100.
Los Angeles Times, February 10, 1989, section 5, pp. 1, 14-16.
MELUS, spring, 1989-90.
Ms., July-August, 1991; September-October, 1991, p. 73.
North Dakota Quarterly, spring, 1985, pp. 220-34.
Poetry, August, 1996, pp. 281-302.
Prairie Schooner, summer, 1992, pp. 128-32.
Progressive, December, 1997, p. 42.
Publishers Weekly, November 28, 1994, p. 54; April 21, 1997, p. 57.
Small Press Review, March, 1983, p. 8.
Village Voice, April 2, 1991, p. 78.
Whole Earth Review, summer, 1995, p. 43; summer, 1998, p. 99.
Women's Review of Books, July, 1990, pp. 17-18.
World Literature Today, winter, 1991, p. 167-68; spring, 1992, pp. 286-91.*

* * *

HARLEMAN, Ann 1945-

PERSONAL: Born October 28, 1945, in Youngstown, OH; daughter of Samuel Thomas and Mary (Hagan) Harleman; married Bruce Rosenberg (a folklorist), June 20, 1981; children: four. *Ethnicity:* "German/Russian/Irish/French Canadian." *Education:* Rutgers University, B.A., 1967; Princeton University, Ph.D., 1972; Brown University, M.F.A. (creative writing), 1988. *Politics:* Independent. *Religion:* "Lapsed Catholic." *Avocational interests:* Painting, languages.

ADDRESSES: Home—55 Summit Ave., Providence, RI 02906. *Office*—Department of American Civilization, Brown University, Providence, RI 02912. *Agent*—Richard P. McDonough, 34 Pinewood, Irvine, CA 92604. *E-mail*—Ann—Harleman@brown.edu.

CAREER: Rutgers University, New Brunswick, NJ, assistant professor of English, 1973-74; University of Washington, Seattle, assistant professor, 1974-79, associate professor of English, 1979-84; Massachusetts Institute of Technology, Cambridge, visiting associate professor of English, 1984-86; Brown University, Providence, RI, research associate in American civilization, 1986—. Wheaton College, Wheaton, IL, Cole Distinguished Professor, 1992-93; visiting professor at Dartmouth College, 1981-82, Northeastern University, Wesleyan University, Middletown, CT, and Rhode Island School of Design.

MEMBER: PEN American Center, Poets and Writers.

AWARDS, HONORS: Guggenheim fellow, 1976-77; American Council of Learned Studies, fellow, 1976-77, senior fellow, 1992-93; fellow, Huntington Library, 1979-80; Fulbright fellow, 1980-81; Raymond Carver Short Story Prize, 1986, for "It Was Humdrum"; McDowell Colony fellow, 1988 and 1999; National Endowment for the Humanities grant, Institute for Literary Translation, 1988; Chris O'Malley fiction prize from *Madison Review,* 1989, for "Life Class"; fellow of Rockefeller Foundation, 1989, and Rhode Island State Arts Council, 1989-90 and 1998; Pushcart Prize nomination, 1990, for "Salvage"; Judith Siegal Pearson award for fiction, 1991, for "How It Is"; PEN syndicated fiction award, 1991, for "Nothing"; Wurlitzer Foundation fellowship, 1992; John Simmons Short Fiction Award, University of Iowa, 1993, for *Happiness;* fellowships from Princeton University, 1968-72, National Science Foundation, 1969-70, University of Wisconsin Humanities Institute, 1972, University of Washington Research Council, 1975, Bread Loaf Writers' Conference, 1991, Djerassi Foundation, 1997, and Bogliasco Foundation, 1998.

WRITINGS:

FICTION

Happiness (short stories; contains "Eve and Adam," "In Damascus," "Happiness,""Urban Fishing," "Dancing Fish,""Salvage," "Someone Else," "It Was Humdrum," "The White Hope of Cleveland," "Imagined Colors," "Nothing" and "The Cost of Anything"), University of Iowa Press (Iowa City), 1994.

Bitter Lake (novel), Southern Methodist University Press (Dallas, TX), 1996.

Work represented in anthologies, including *Best American Short Stories,* 1993. Contributor of stories to periodicals, including *Ploughshares, New England Review, Greensboro Review, Virginia Quarterly Review, American Fiction, Story, Shenandoah,* and *Southwest Review.*

OTHER

Graphic Representation of Models in Linguistic Theory, Indiana University Press (Bloomington), 1976.

(Contributor) Martin Tucker, editor, *The Critical Temper IV,* Ungar (New York City), 1979.

(With Bruce A. Rosenberg) *Ian Fleming: A Critical Biography,* Twayne (Boston, MA), 1989.

(Contributor) Sylvia K. Burack, editor, *The Writer's Handbook,* Writer, Inc. (Boston), 1989, revised edition, 1993.

(Translator from Russian) Ruth Zernova, *Mute Phone Calls,* selected by Helen Reeve, Rutgers University Press (New Brunswick, NJ), 1991.

(Contributor) Marina Ledkovsky, editor, *Russia according to Women,* Hermitage (Ann Arbor, MI), 1991.

Contributor of poems, articles, and reviews to periodicals, including *Southern Review, Kansas Quarterly, Greensboro Review, High Plains Literary Review, Ascent, Bellingham Review, Apalachee Quarterly,* and *Yankee.*

WORK IN PROGRESS: A novel, *Acts of Light;* a story collection, *Lovers Made Men;* a novella about Harleman's great-grandfather, "who murdered for love."

SIDELIGHTS: Ann Harleman, the first woman at Princeton to receive a doctorate in linguistics, published largely academic work until the late 1980s when, after turning down tenure at three universities, she returned to Brown University to earn her master of fine arts degree in creative writing. She told *CA:* "For a decade and a half I struggled to be a respectable academic, publishing no fiction but rather books with titles like *Graphic Representation of Models in Linguistic Theory.* This made me restless. I lived in Russia for six months (went there as the single parent of a three-year-old daughter), in Poland for a year. I am probably the only academic in America who has relinquished tenure at three different universities. The third time, I had the good sense to go back to school myself, earning an M.F.A. in creative writing from Brown University."

Harleman cites personal tragedy as the reason she turned to storytelling. In a span of only five years, she experienced her father's death and sister's suicide, and later learned both her husband and daughter had contracted chronic illnesses.

Despite her relatively late entry into the world of fiction (she was forty before publishing a story), Harleman has made her mark, earning several important literary awards for her short stories. Twelve of these are contained in the collection *Happiness,* winner of the 1993 John Simmons Short Fiction Award. Many of the stories in *Happiness* depict the emotions, passions, and frustrations of everyday people as they experience life: a terminally ill woman, for instance, seeks her daughters' forgiveness for an adulterous affair; a boy introduces his black girlfriend to his disapproving white parents; a childless couple drift apart, the husband turning to someone else for love; a woman recovers from an attack by a gang; a detective seeks the mother he never knew, while his wife is cheating behind his back. All of these situations, as well as many others, are told in a "rich, melancholy voice that shows remarkable control and summons meticulous detail in stories that are poignant and assured," according to *Publishers Weekly*'s Sybil S. Steinberg.

BIOGRAPHICAL/CRITICAL SOURCES:

PERIODICALS

Boston Globe, May 17, 1994.

New York Times Book Review, February 13, 1994.

Publishers Weekly, October 18, 1991, p. 58; November 8, 1993, p. 58.

Tribune Books (Chicago), October 4, 1987, p. 7.

Washington Post Book World, February 6, 1994.

HARUF, Kent 1943-

PERSONAL: Surname rhymes with "sheriff"; born February 24, 1943, in Pueblo, CO; son of Louis A. (a Methodist preacher) and Eleanor V. (a teacher and homemaker; maiden name, Shaver) Haruf; married Virginia K. Koon (divorced); married Cathy Dempsey; children: Sorel, Whitney, Chaney (daughters). *Education:* Nebraska Wesleyan University, B.A., 1965; University of Iowa, M.F.A., 1973.

ADDRESSES: *Home*—P. O. Box 1580, Salida, CO 81201. *Agent*—Peter Matson, Sterling Lord Literistic, 65 Bleecker St., New York, NY 10012.

CAREER: Worked odd jobs, including farm laborer, construction worker, rural paper route carrier, hospital orderly, railroad worker, librarian, and orphanage house parent; served in the Peace Corps in Turkey, 1965-67; taught high school English in Wisconsin and Colorado, 1976-86; Nebraska Wesleyan University, Lincoln, assistant professor, 1986-91; Southern Illinois University, Carbondale, associate professor, 1991-2000.

AWARDS, HONORS: PEN/Hemingway Foundation Special Citation, 1985; American Library Notable Books Award, 1985; Whiting Writer's Award, Mrs. Giles Whiting Foundation, 1986, for *The Tie That Binds;* Maria Thomas Award, 1991; National Book Award finalist in fiction, 1999, Mt. Plains Booksellers Award, 2000, *Salon.com* Award, 2000, Alex Award, 2000, *New Yorker* Fiction Award finalist, 2000, *Los Angeles Times* Fiction Award finalist, 2000, and *Book Sense* Award finalist, 2000, all for *Plainsong.*

WRITINGS:

NOVELS

The Tie That Binds, Holt (New York City), 1984.
Where You Once Belonged, Summit Books (New York City), 1991.
Plainsong, Knopf (New York City), 1999.

Also contributor of short stories to periodicals, including *Puerto del Sol, Grand Street, Prairie Schooner,* and *Gettysburg Review.* Stories have appeared in *Best American Short Stories,* Houghton, 1987; and *Where Past Meets Present,* University of Colorado Press, 1994.

ADAPTATIONS: Haruf 's short story "Private Debts/ Public Holdings" was adapted into a short film by Nancy Cooperstein for Chanticleer Films, 1987.

SIDELIGHTS: The son of a Methodist minister, Kent Haruf was born and raised in the flatlands of northeastern Colorado, an environment that provides the background for his fiction. Haruf 's career path to his longtime ambition of writing was a slow and convoluted one, involving attendance at several universities, a stint in the Peace Corps in Turkey, and numerous odd jobs. After graduating from the prestigious University of Iowa Writers Workshop at the age of thirty, Haruf did not make his first appearance in print, a short story in a literary magazine, until eleven years later at the age of forty-one. That same year, 1984, his first novel was published. Speaking with John Blades of *Publishers Weekly,* Haruf described Holt, the fictional town that provides the setting for his novels, as his own "little postage stamp of native soil." Holt is a small Colorado farming community, close to the Kansas and Nebraska borders and more akin to the rural environments of those states than it is to cosmopolitan Denver to the west. Blades noted: "Along with its surrounding farms and homesteads, Holt has proved as fertile—and will perhaps be as inexhaustible—for Haruf 's fiction as the apocryphal Yoknapatawpha County was for Faulkner's"

Haruf 's first novel, *The Tie That Binds,* chronicles the long, hard life of Edith Goodnough, born near the turn of the twentieth century. Edith's story is told by Sanders Roscoe, the son of the man Edith loved but refused to marry, giving up her chance at happiness to care for a tyrannical but crippled father. *The Tie That Binds* garnered Haruf several honors, including the 1986 Whiting Writer's Award. The novel was praised by critics as well; Ruth Doan MacDougall in the *Christian Science Monitor* observed that Haruf 's "characters live, and the voice of his narrator reverberates after the last page: humorous, ironic, loving." Chris Wall in the *Los Angeles Times Book Review* hailed *The Tie That Binds* as "an impressive, expertly crafted work of sensitivity and detail, absent the hokum that usually accompanies sad tales of simple women and their domineering fathers." Haruf also won accolades from Perry Glasser in the *New York Times Book Review.* The critic declared that the author's "work is rooted in a sense of place; his eye and ear are faithful to his subject."

Haruf followed *The Tie That Binds* with his 1991 effort, *Where You Once Belonged.* This book centers on Jack Burdette, a villainous former high school football hero who manages to ruin many lives in his home town of Holt, Colorado. Narrating Jack's story is a man with a stake in the events told, newspaper editor Pat Arbuckle. Richard Eder in the *Los Angeles Times Book Review* offered a laudatory assessment of *Where You Once Be-*

longed, calling it "taut and deadly," and applauding the "disciplined economy" of "Haruf 's writing." The critic concluded that the author's second novel is a "stirring and remarkable book." A *Publishers Weekly* reviewer called the book a "deeply affecting novel," and noted that "not a word is wasted in [Haruf 's] brooding drama." A commentator for *Kirkus Reviews* observed that Haruf "does a beautiful job of capturing small-town life."

Haruf wrote his first two novels by conventional means. With his third he tried a radically different approach. Removing his glasses and placing a stocking cap over his eyes, he typed his first draft blind. Haruf 's aim, as related by Blades, was "to achieve freshness and spontaneity without being distracted by the sight of words on the page." The result was *Plainsong,* a novel subsequently lauded by critics even more highly than Haruf 's earlier books. Even before its publication, *Plainsong* began drawing special attention. According to Daisy Maryles of *Publishers Weekly:* "Knopf 's enthusiasm for [the novel] began last spring with the manuscript being passed around in-house; for a while, it was the most photocopied manuscript on Knopf 's fall list." On the basis of editorial response to the book, a larger first printing was planned, along with increased publicity that included a twelve-city tour for Haruf.

In the epigraph to *Plainsong,* Haruf states that the title of the book refers to the "simple and unadorned" vocal melodies, sometimes sung by alternating voices, that have been used in Christian churches for centuries. The novel tells the story of six major characters and several subsidiaries ones, and like a plainsong, the action is related from alternating perspectives of different characters in different chapters. Once again the setting is Holt, Colorado, and its environs. The plot begins with three separate tales that ultimately intertwine. A pregnant teenager, Victoria Roubideaux, is kicked out of her home by her mother. A local high school history teacher, Tom Guthrie, is abandoned by his wife and left to raise his two young sons alone. Two elderly bachelor brothers, Harold and Raymond McPherson, have consigned themselves to an isolated existence on their cattle ranch miles from town. "Although the intersection of these three sets of lonely lives might normally have all the melodramatic makings of a provincial soap opera," noted Michiko Kakutani in the *New York Times Book Review,* "Mr. Haruf orchestrates their convergence with such authority and grace that their stories materialize before the reader's eyes without a shred of contrivance."

Writing in a lean prose style that several reviewers compared to that of Hemingway's, Haruf portrays the lives of his characters from the fall of one year through the spring of the next, often using images from the natural world and the changing seasons to complement the changes they experience. "A fugue upon weather and light plays throughout the novel," observed Verlyn Klinkenborg in a glowing review of the novel for the *New York Times,* while Donna Seaman of *Booklist* commented: "Haruf 's narrative voice is spare and procedural, and his salt-of-the-earth characters are reticent almost to the point of mannerism until it becomes clear that their terseness is the result of profound shyness and an immensity of feeling. Haruf 's unforgettable tale is both emotionally complex and elemental, following, as it so gracefully does, the cycle of life, death, and rebirth." Although less overcome with the power of *Plainsong* than most reviewers, Robin Nesbitt of *Library Journal* nevertheless found it to be both "[l]yrical and well crafted" and a "tight narrative about how families can be made between folks who are not necessarily blood relatives [that] makes for enjoyable reading."

Knopf 's confidence in *Plainsong* was justified when the novel became a National Book Award finalist and appeared on the *Publishers Weekly* bestseller lists, prompting further paperback reprints of Haruf 's earlier novels. Discussing his "sudden" success, at the age of fifty-six, with Blades, Haruf noted: "This country's crazy in terms of fame and what people think it means. They expect a writer to be something between a Hollywood starlet and the village idiot. . . . Fame is very seductive and can be very dangerous if you're trying to get your work done."

BIOGRAPHICAL/CRITICAL SOURCES:

BOOKS

Contemporary Literary Criticism, Volume 34, Gale, 1985.

PERIODICALS

Booklist, August, 1999, Donna Seaman, review of *Plainsong,* p. 1986.
Christian Science Monitor, December 7, 1984, p. B12.
Entertainment Weekly, November 5, 1999, Megan Harlan, "The Week," p. 76.
Kirkus Reviews, November 15, 1989, pp. 1618-1619.
Los Angeles Times Book Review, January 27, 1985, p. 4; February 11, 1990, pp. 3, 7.
Library Journal, October 1, 1984, review of *The Tie That Binds,* p. 1861; January, 1990, Joseph Levan-

doski, review of *Where You Once Belonged,* p. 148; September 1, 1999, Robin Nesbitt, review of *Plainsong,* p. 232.

Newsweek, October 4, 1999, Jeff Giles, "The Heart of the Country," p. 67.

New York Review of Books, October 21, 1999, Joyce Carol Oates, "Wearing out the West," p. 30.

New York Times, October 3, 1999, Verlyn Klinkenborg, "The Sheltering Sky: Kent Haruf 's Novel Describes a Season of Changes Great and Small in a Colorado Plains Town," p. 7.

New York Times Book Review, January 6, 1985, Perry Glasser, review of *The Tie That Binds,* p. 16; October 8, 1999, Michiko Kakutani, "Everyone's a Neighbor in a Small Prairie Town."

Publishers Weekly, August 24, 1984, review of *The Tie That Binds,* p. 74; December 1, 1989, Sybil Steinberg, review of *Where You Once Belonged,* p. 47; August 2, 1999, review of *Plainsong,* p. 70; October 25, 1999, Daisy Maryles, "This Novel Just Sings," p. 19; November 1, 1999, review of *Plainsong,* p. 46, John Blades, "Kent Haruf: Home on the Plains," p. 59.

Time, October 25, 1999, Elizabeth Gleick, review of *Plainsong,* p. 130.

* * *

HARVEY, Hazel (Mary) 1936-

PERSONAL: Born July 27, 1936, in Princes Risborough, Buckinghamshire, England; daughter of Edward Douglas (a scientist) and Doris Marie (a teacher; maiden name, Carpenter) van Rest; married David Harvey (a university lecturer), September 5, 1964; children: Francis Edward Victor, Miffy Hazel Louisa. *Education:* Bedford College, London, B.A. (with honors), 1957, M.A., 1961. *Politics:* "Green." *Religion:* Church of England.

ADDRESSES: Home—53 Thornton Hill, Exeter, Devon EX4 4NR, England.

CAREER: Harrap (publisher), lexicographer, 1957-58; University of Exeter, Exeter, England, lecturer, 1961-64; University of London, National Extension College, tutor, 1975—. Member of Devon Transport 2000, International Tree Foundation, and Campaign for Nuclear Disarmament.

MEMBER: Friends of the Earth, Exeter Civic Society (chairperson, 1992—).

AWARDS, HONORS: Shared Schlegel-Tieck Prize with David Harvey, 1980, for translation of Karl Reinhardt's *Sophocles.*

WRITINGS:

(Translator with husband David Harvey) Karl Reinhardt, *Sophocles,* Basil Blackwell, 1979.

(Translator with D. Harvey and Fred Robertson) Richard Heinze, *Virgil's Epic Technique,* Bristol Classical Press, 1993.

Exeter Past, Phillimore, 1996.

A Better Provision: The Royal Devon & Exeter Hospital, 1948-1998, Royal Devon & Exeter Healthcare, 1998.

Author of booklets for the Exeter Civic Society, including *Discovering Exeter, Pennsylvania,* 1984, *Discovering Exeter: Sidwell Street,* 1986, *Discovering Exeter: West of the River,* 1989, and *Discovering Exeter: Community Mosaics,* 1998.

WORK IN PROGRESS: Research on the history of Exeter.

SIDELIGHTS: Hazel Harvey told *CA:* "Trained in German translation and married to a classicist, I was entrusted with the translation of major German works on the classics. I did not train as a historian, but Exeter has been a city since Roman times, and its history is visible at every turn. I was so fascinated by Joyce Greenaway's *Discovering Exeter Number 1: St. David's* that I was persuaded to write a booklet about one suburb of Pennsylvania, and then I could not stop until I had covered two other outlying suburbs of the city. I have now been commissioned to produce a volume showing Exeter's history in old pictures. I work at home at the kitchen table, between family demands. For research I cycle to the nearby city libraries."

* * *

HAYDEN, Brian (Douglas) 1946-

PERSONAL: Born February 14, 1946, in Flushing, NY; son of F. Douglas and Constance Hayden; married Huguette Sansonnet, August 26, 1970; children: three. *Education:* University of Bordeaux, Certificate de Prehistoire, 1967; University of Colorado, B.A., 1969; University of Toronto, M.A., 1970, Ph.D., 1976.

ADDRESSES: Home—8338 196th St., Langley, British Columbia, Canada V3A 6Y3. *Office*—Department of

Archaeology, Simon Fraser University, Burnaby, British Columbia, Canada V5A 1S6. *E-mail*—bhayden@sfu.ca.

CAREER: American Stock Exchange, New York City, research worker, 1964; Virginia Commonwealth University, Richmond, instructor in sociology and anthropology, 1973-74; Simon Fraser University, Burnaby, British Columbia, instructor, 1974-76, assistant professor, 1976-78, associate professor, 1978-84, professor of archaeology, 1984—. Dinosaur National Monument, field assistant, 1965-66; field assistant for archaeological excavations in Tunisia, 1967, Guatemala, 1970, Lebanon, 1970, and in the United States and Canada; principal investigator and field director of Coxoh ethno-archaeological project in Mexico and Guatemala, 1977-85; Villatoro Mastodon Site, Guatemala, principal investigator, 1978; conducted archaeological field research in France and British Columbia.

MEMBER: Canadian Archaeological Association, Society for American Archaeology, Current Anthropology (associate), Sociedad de Antropologia de Mexico, Simon Fraser University Faculty Association, Phi Beta Kappa.

AWARDS, HONORS: Fulbright fellow in Australia, 1971-72; grants from Wenner-Gren Foundation for Anthropological Research, UNESCO, Leakey Foundation, Canada Council, and Canadian Department of External Affairs.

WRITINGS:

(Editor and contributor) *Lithic Use-Wear Analysis,* Academic Press (San Diego, CA), 1979.

Paleolithic Reflections: Lithic Technology of the Western Desert Aborigines, Australian Institute of Aboriginal Studies, 1979.

(With Aubrey Cannon) *The Structure of Material Systems: Ethnoarchaeology in the Maya Highlands,* Society for American Archaeology, 1984.

(Editor and contributor) *Lithic Studies among the Contemporary Highland Maya,* University of Arizona Press (Tucson), 1987.

(Contributor) O. Soffer, editor, *The Pleistocene Old World,* Plenum (New York City), 1987.

(Contributor) Ellen Kroll and Douglas Price, editors, *The Interpretation of Archaeological Spatial Patterning,* Plenum, 1991.

(Editor and contributor) *A Complex Culture of the British Columbia Plateau: Traditional Stl'atl'imx Resource Use,* University of British Columbia Press (Vancouver, British Columbia), 1992.

(Contributor) Cheryl Claassen, editor, *Exploring Gender through Archaeology,* Prehistory Press, 1992.

Archaeology: The Science of Once and Future Things, W. H. Freeman (New York City), 1993.

(Contributor) T. D. Price and G. Feinman, editors, *Foundations of Social Inequality,* Plenum, 1995.

The Pithouses of Keatley Creek, Harcourt (Austin, TX), 1997.

The Ancient Past of Keatley Creek, Archaeology Press (Burnaby, British Columbia), 2000.

(Coeditor and contributor) *Feasts,* Smithsonian Institution (Washington, DC), in press.

Contributor to the book *Last Foragers, First Farmers,* edited by Price and A. Gebauer, School of American Research Press (Santa Fe, NM). Contributor of articles and reviews to archaeology and anthropology journals.

WORK IN PROGRESS: Research on the archaeological occurrence of corporate groups in British Columbia, on feasting as a key component of non-egalitarian societies, and on material conditions favoring competition and cooperation.

SIDELIGHTS: Brian Hayden told *CA:* "I consider myself a cultural ecologist studying past and traditional contemporary societies; that is, pre-industrial societies. I am most concerned with what people actually did and how their behavior (past or present) is affected by the environment and resources that they depend upon. This is the major theme of my books *A Complex Culture of the British Columbia Plateau* and *Archaeology.* The concern with behavior is also present in the volume I edited on lithic use-wear analysis and the ethnoarchaeological study I conducted of the use of stone tools by modern Australian aborigines. The theme of what material culture can reveal about behavior is also the central focus of my writings on the highland Maya. At present, my main topic of interest within cultural ecology is the transition from egalitarian societies to hierarchical ones, and particularly the role that feasting plays in this transition."

* * *

HEADRICK, Daniel R. 1941-

PERSONAL: Born August 2, 1941, in Bay Shore, NY; son of William Cecil (a civil servant) and Edith (a homemaker; maiden name, Finkelstein) Headrick; married first wife, Rita, June 20, 1965 (died February 14, 1988); married Kate Ezra (a curator), August 23, 1992;

children: Isabelle, Juliet, Matthew. *Education:* Attended University of Madrid, 1960-61; Swarthmore College, B.A., 1962; attended Johns Hopkins University, Bologna Center, 1962-63; Johns Hopkins School of Advanced International Studies, M.A., 1964; Princeton University, Ph.D., 1971.

ADDRESSES: Home—5483 Hyde Park Blvd., Chicago, IL 60615. *Office*—University College, Roosevelt University, 430 South Michigan Ave., Chicago, IL 60605. *E-mail*—dan.headrick@worldnet.att.net.

CAREER: Tuskegee Institute, Tuskegee, AL, instructor, 1968-71, assistant professor, 1971-73, associate professor of history, 1973-75; Roosevelt University, Chicago, IL, associate professor, 1975-82, professor of social sciences and history, 1982—.

MEMBER: Society for the History of Technology, American Historical Association, American Association of University Professors.

AWARDS, HONORS: National Endowment for the Humanities, fellow, 1983-84, 1988-89, grants, 1986, 1987, 1990; Burlington Northern Awards, 1988, 1992; grant from National Research Council, 1989; Guggenheim fellow, 1994-95.

WRITINGS:

Ejercito y politica en Espana, 1866-1898 (title means "The Army and Politics in Spain, 1866-1898"), Editorial Tecnos (Madrid, Spain), 1981.

The Tools of Empire: Technology and European Imperialism in the Nineteenth Century, Oxford University Press (New York City), 1981.

(Contributor) Steven Ozment and Frank M. Turner, editors, *The Many Sides of History: Readings in the Western Heritage,* Macmillan (New York City), 1987.

The Tentacles of Progress: Technology Transfer in the Age of Imperialism, 1851-1945, Oxford University Press, 1988.

(Contributor) B. L. Turner II and other editors, *The Earth as Transformed by Human Action: Global and Regional Changes in the Biosphere over the Past Three Hundred Years,* Cambridge University Press (New York City), 1990.

The Invisible Weapon: Telecommunications and International Politics, 1851-1945, Oxford University Press, 1991.

(Coauthor) *The Earth and Its Peoples,* Houghton (Boston, MA), 1997.

When Information Came of Age: Technologies of Knowledge in the Age of Reason and Revolution, Oxford University Press, 2000.

Contributor of articles and reviews to scholarly journals, including *Journal of Modern History, African Studies Review, European Studies Review,* and *History and Technology.*

SIDELIGHTS: Daniel R. Headrick told *CA:* "My original career goal was to become a professor of history, writing only what I needed to get and keep a teaching position. I soon discovered, however, that writing is an interesting activity in itself.

"While professional historians typically mark out areas of specialization in which they can express their expertise in monographs, I have always been driven to broaden my interests and roam into fields where I am no expert, in the hope of finding new connections. Teaching world history at Tuskegee Institute broadened my interests from European history to the relations between Europeans, on the one hand, and Asians and Africans, on the other. In this I was inspired by the works of William McNeill, Leften Stavrianos, and other global historians. Meanwhile, a latent interest in the history of technology was awakened when I read Lynn White, Jr.'s *Medieval Technology and Social Change.* I resolved to bring these two interests together by studying the relationship between technological change and European imperialism. The result was two books: *The Tools of Empire* and *The Tentacles of Progress.*

"Of all the technological systems involved in the formation of the modern world, and in the terrible disparities between the rich and the poor countries, the one that I found most intriguing was telecommunications. After reading a great deal on the subject, I wrote *The Invisible Weapon.*

"Meanwhile, the study of telecommunications led me to a larger issue, namely the role of information in social change. While information is a fashionable concept to describe the current situation and future direction of the world, it is seldom applied to the past. The problem is that the 'information age' is widely understood to be the result of certain technical innovations (in the narrow sense of hardware): the telegraph, the printing press, the computer. I am questioning these assumptions and investigating the role of cultural changes in bringing about both the technical innovations and the broader 'information revolution' in which we live."

HEANEY, Seamus (Justin) 1939-

PERSONAL: Born April 13, 1939, in County Derry, Northern Ireland; son of Patrick (a farmer) and Margaret Heaney; married Marie Devlin, 1965; children: Michael, Christopher, Catherine. *Education:* Attended St. Columb's College, Derry; Queen's University of Belfast, B.A. (first class honors), 1961, St. Joseph's College of Education, teacher's certificate, 1962.

ADDRESSES: Office—Department of English and American Literature and Language, Harvard University, Warren House, 11 Prescott St., Cambridge, MA 02138.

CAREER: Poet, 1960—. Worked as secondary school teacher in Belfast, 1962-63; St. Joseph's College of Education, Belfast, Northern Ireland, lecturer, 1963-66; Queen's University of Belfast, lecturer in English, 1966-72; freelance writer, 1972-75; Carysfort College, Dublin, Ireland, lecturer, 1976-82; Harvard University, Cambridge, MA, visiting lecturer, 1979, visiting professor, 1982-86, Boylston Professor of Rhetoric and Oratory, 1986—; Oxford University, Oxford, England, professor of poetry, 1990-94. Visiting lecturer, University of California, Berkeley, 1970-71. Has given numerous lectures and poetry readings at universities in England, Ireland, and the United States.

MEMBER: Irish Academy of Letters, Royal Dublin Society, American Academy of Arts and Letters (honorary foreign member), American Academy of Arts and Sciences.

AWARDS, HONORS: Eric Gregory Award, 1966, Cholomondeley Award, 1967, Somerset Maugham Award, 1968, and Geoffrey Faber Memorial Prize, 1968, all for *Death of a Naturalist;* Poetry Book Society Choice citation, 1969, for *Door into the Dark;* Irish Academy of Letters award, 1971; writer in residence award from American Irish Foundation and Denis Devlin Award, both 1973, both for *Wintering Out;* E. M. Forster Award, American Academy and Institute of Arts and Letters, 1975; W. H. Smith Award, Duff Cooper Memorial Prize, and Poetry Book Society Choice citation, all 1976, all for *North;* Bennett Award, *Hudson Review,* 1982; D.H.L., Fordham University and Queen's University of Belfast, both 1982; *Los Angeles Times* Book Prize nomination, 1984, and PEN Translation Prize for Poetry, 1985, both for *Sweeney Astray: A Version from the Irish;* Whitbread Award, 1987, for *The Haw Lantern;* Lannam Foundation award, 1990; Premio Mondello (International Poetry Prize), Mondello Foundation, Palermo, Sicily, 1993; Nobel Prize for Literature, 1995; Whitbread Award, 1997, for *The Spirit Level;* Whitbread Award for poetry and book of the year, 1999, for *Beowulf.*

WRITINGS:

POETRY COLLECTIONS

Death of a Naturalist, Oxford University Press (New York City), 1966.
Door into the Dark, Oxford University Press, 1969.
Wintering Out, Faber (London), 1972, Oxford University Press, 1973.
North, Faber, 1975, Oxford University Press, 1976.
Field Work, Farrar, Straus (New York City), 1979.
Poems: 1965-1975, Farrar, Straus, 1980.
(Adapter) *Sweeney Astray: A Version from the Irish,* Farrar, Straus, 1984, revised edition, with photographs by Rachel Giese, published as *Sweeney's Flight,* 1992.
Station Island, Farrar, Straus, 1984.
The Haw Lantern, Farrar, Straus, 1987.
New and Selected Poems, 1969-1987, Farrar, Straus, 1990, revised edition published as *Selected Poems, 1966-1987,* 1991.
Seeing Things: Poems, Farrar, Straus, 1991.
The Midnight Verdict, Gallery Books (Old Castle, County Meath, Ireland), 1993.
The Spirit Level, Farrar, Straus (New York City), 1996.
Opened Ground: Selected Poems, 1966-1996, Farrar, Straus, 1998.

POETRY CHAPBOOKS

Eleven Poems, Festival Publications (Belfast), 1965.
(With David Hammond and Michael Longley) *Room to Rhyme,* Arts Council of Northern Ireland, 1968.
A Lough Neagh Sequence, edited by Harry Chambers and Eric J. Morten, Phoenix Pamphlets Poets Press (Manchester), 1969.
Boy Driving His Father to Confession, Sceptre Press (Surrey), 1970.
Night Drive: Poems, Richard Gilbertson (Devon), 1970.
Land, Poem-of-the-Month Club, 1971.
Servant Boy, Red Hanrahan Press (Detroit), 1971.
Stations, Ulsterman Publications (Belfast), 1975.
Bog Poems, Rainbow Press (London), 1975.
(With Derek Mahon) *In Their Element,* Arts Council of Northern Ireland, 1977.
After Summer, Deerfield Press, 1978.
Hedge School: Sonnets from Glanmore, C. Seluzichi (Oregon), 1979.
Sweeney Praises the Trees, [New York], 1981.

PROSE

The Fire i' the Flint: Reflections on the Poetry of Gerard Manley Hopkins, Oxford University Press, 1975.

Robert Lowell: A Memorial Address and Elegy, Faber, 1978.

Preoccupations: Selected Prose, 1968-1978, Farrar, Straus, 1980.

The Government of the Tongue: Selected Prose, 1978-1987, Farrar, Straus, 1988.

The Place of Writing, Scholars Press, 1989.

The Redress of Poetry, Farrar, Straus (New York City), 1995.

EDITOR

(With Alan Brownjohn) *New Poems: 1970-71,* Hutchinson (London), 1971.

Soundings: An Annual Anthology of New Irish Poetry, Blackstaff Press (Belfast), 1972.

Soundings II, Blackstaff Press, 1974.

(With Ted Hughes) *The Rattle Bag: An Anthology of Poetry* (juvenile), Faber, 1982.

The Essential Wordsworth, Ecco Press (New York City), 1988.

Also editor of *The May Anthology of Oxford and Cambridge Poetry,* 1993.

OTHER

(With John Montague) *The Northern Muse* (sound recording), Claddagh Records, 1969.

(Contributor) *The Writers: A Sense of Ireland,* O'Brien Press (Dublin), 1979.

Advent Parish Programme, State Mutual Book & Periodical Service, 1989.

Lenten Parish Programme: Renewal of Personal and Community Life through Prayer and Scripture, State Mutual Book & Periodical Service, 1989.

The Cure at Troy: A Version of Sophocles Philotetes (drama), Farrar, Straus, 1991.

(Translator with Stanislaw Baranczak) *Laments,* Farrar, Straus, 1995.

(With Joseph Brodsky and Derek Walcott) *Homage to Frost,* Farrar, Straus, 1996.

Crediting Poetry: The Nobel Lecture, Farrar, Straus (New York City), 1996.

(Contributor) *Canopy: A Work for Voice and Light in Harvard Yard,* Harvard University Art Museums, 1997.

(Translator) *Beowulf: A New Verse Translation,* Farrar, Straus, 2000.

(Translator) Leos Janacek, *Diary of One Who Vanished: A Song Cycle,* Farrar, Straus, 2000.

Contributor of poetry and essays to periodicals, including *New Statesman, Listener, Guardian, Times Literary Supplement,* and *London Review of Books.*

SIDELIGHTS: Nobel laureate Seamus Heaney has been widely recognized as one of the world's finest twentieth-century poets. A native of Northern Ireland who divides his time between a home in Dublin and a teaching position at Harvard University, Heaney has attracted a readership on two continents and has won prestigious literary awards in England, Ireland, and the United States. As Blake Morrison notes in his work *Seamus Heaney,* the author is "that rare thing, a poet rated highly by critics and academics yet popular with 'the common reader.' " Part of Heaney's popularity stems from his subject matter—modern Northern Ireland, its farms and cities beset with civil strife, its natural culture and language overrun by English rule. *Washington Post Book World* contributor Marjorie Perloff suggests that Heaney is so successful "because of his political position: the Catholic farm boy from County Derry transformed into the sensitive witness to and historian of the Irish troubles, as those troubles have shaped and altered individual lives." Likewise, *New York Review of Books* essayist Richard Murphy describes Heaney as "the poet who has shown the finest art in presenting a coherent vision of Ireland, past and present." Heaney's "is, after all," writes Robert Buttel in the *Concise Dictionary of British Literary Biography* (*CDBLB*), "a poetry manifestly regional and largely rural in subject matter and traditional in structure—a poetry that appears to be a deliberate step back into a premodernist world of William Wordsworth and John Clare and to represent a rejection of most contemporary poetic fashions."

Inevitably, Heaney has been compared with the great Irish poet William Butler Yeats; in fact, several critics have called Heaney "the greatest Irish poet since Yeats." Such praise-by-comparison makes the poet uncomfortable, and it serves to obscure the uniqueness of his work. *New York Review of Books* contributor Richard Ellmann once wrote: "After the heavily accented melodies of Yeats, and that poet's elegiac celebrations of imaginative glories, Seamus Heaney addresses his readers in a quite different key. He does not overwhelm his subjects; rather he allows them a certain freedom from him, and his sharp conjunctions with them leave their authority and his undiminished." Elizabeth Jennings makes a similar observation in the *Spectator.* To Jennings, Heaney is "an extremely Irish poet most especially in language, but he is not a poet in the Yeatsian mould; not for him high-mannered seriousness or intentional rhetoric. He is serious, of course, but it is the gravity which grows in his roots, not one which is obtrusive in the finished artefact." In the *Listener,* Conor Cruise O'Brien analyzes the source from which the comparison might have stemmed. "Heaney's writing is modest, often conversational, apparently easy, low-pitched, companionably ironic, ominous, alert, accurate and surprising," notes O'Brien. "An Irish reader is not automatically reminded of Yeats by this cluster of characteristics, yet an English reader may perhaps see resemblances that are there but overlooked by the Irish—resemblances coming, perhaps, from certain common rhythms and hesitations of Irish speech and non-speech."

Heaney is well aware of the dual perspective afforded him by his upbringing and subsequent experiences. He once described himself in the *New York Times Book Review* as one of a group of Catholics in Northern Ireland who "emerged from a hidden, a buried life and entered the realm of education." This process began for Heaney at age eleven; that year he left the family farm to study on scholarship at a boarding school in Belfast. Access to the world of English, Irish, and American letters—first at St. Columb's College and then at Queen's University of Belfast—was "a crucial experience," according to the poet. He was especially moved by artists who created poetry out of their local and native backgrounds—authors such as Ted Hughes, Patrick Kavanagh, and Robert Frost. Heaney said: "From them I learned that my local County Derry [childhood] experience, which I had considered archaic and irrelevant to 'the modern world' was to be trusted. They taught me that trust and helped me to articulate it." Searching his cultural roots, but also letting his English literary education enrich his expression, Heaney began to craft "a poetry concerned with nature, the shocks and discoveries of childhood experience on a farm, the mythos of the locale—in short, a regional poetry," to quote Robert Buttel in his book *Seamus Heaney.* This sort of poetry, Buttel continues, was, in the early 1960s, "essentially a counter-poetry, decidedly not fashionable at the time. To write such poetry called for a measure of confidence if not outright defiance."

According to Morrison, a "general spirit of reverence towards the past helped Heaney resolve some of his awkwardness about being a writer: he could serve his own community by preserving in literature its customs and crafts, yet simultaneously gain access to a larger community of letters." Indeed, Heaney's earliest poetry collections—*Death of a Naturalist* and *Door into the Dark*—evoke "a hard, mainly rural life with rare exactness," in the words of *Parnassus: Poetry in Review* contributor Michael Wood. Using descriptions of rural laborers and their tasks and contemplations of natural phenomena—filtered sometimes through childhood and sometimes through adulthood—Heaney seeks the self by way of the perceived experience, celebrating the life force through earthly things. Buttel writes in *Seamus Heaney:* "Augmenting the physical authenticity and the clean, decisive art of the best of the early poems, mainly the ones concerned with the impact of the recollected initiatory experiences of childhood and youth, is the human voice that speaks in them. At its most distinctive it is unpretentious, open, modest, and yet poised, aware." *Newsweek* correspondent Jack Kroll notes that in these first poems, Heaney "makes you see, hear, smell, taste this life, which in his words is not provincial, but parochial; provincialism hints at the minor or the mediocre, but all parishes, rural or urban, are equal as communities of the human spirit. So Heaney's poems dig away, filled with a grunting vowel music that evokes the blunt ecstasy of physical work."

In *Northern Voices: Poets from Ulster,* Terence Brown expresses the view that it is a mistake "to think of Heaney as merely a descriptive poet, endowed with unusual powers of observation. From the first his involvement with landscape and locale, with the physical world, has been both more personal and more remarkable in its implications than any mere act of observation and record could be." Heaney's early poems are not burdened with romantic notions about nature; rather they present nature "as a random power that sometimes rewards but more often frustrates human [efforts]," to quote Arthur E. McGuinness in *Eire-Ireland. New York Times Book Review* correspondent Nicholas Christopher likewise finds "no folksy, down-home or miniaturist tendencies in [Heaney's] presentation of natural subjects. His voice is complex and his eye keen, but as with any inspired poet, he is after transformations, not reproductions. Nature is neither antagonist nor sounding board but a component of the human imagination." This latter description outlines the direction Heaney's poetry has taken since he "began to open, both to the Irish, and to his own abyss," in the words of *Times Literary Supplement* reviewer Harold Bloom.

"Seamus Heaney comes from the north of Ireland, and his career has almost exactly coincided with the present span of the 'Troubles,' " claims Seamus Deane in the *Sewanee Review.* The "Troubles" to which Deane refers are, of course, the violent political struggles between some Northern Irish Protestants and their British allies and the militant Irish Republican Army. Heaney was living in Belfast when the fighting erupted in 1969; as a Catholic partisan, notes Morrison, "he felt the need to write poetry that would be not necessarily propagandist but certainly urgent in tone." In *Critical Quarterly,* Damian Grant suggests that Heaney "is no protest poet, but nor can he remain indifferent to the bombs, snipers, and internment camps that maim the body of his land." The poet has sought, therefore, to weave the current Irish troubles into a broader historical frame embracing the general human situation. Deane writes that in *Wintering Out* and *North,* "the ancient past and the contemporary present, myth and politics, are in fact analogues for one another. . . . Mr. Heaney is very much in the Irish tradition in that he has learned, more successfully than most, to conceive of his personal experience in terms of his country's history. . . . Accent, etymologies, old ritual murders and invasions, contemporary assassinations and security systems—these and other related elements swarm now more and more thickly, the lethal infusoria in this pellucid verse." *New York Review of Books* correspondent Richard Murphy suggests that the poetry "is seriously attempting to purge our land of a terrible blood-guilt, and inwardly acknowledging our enslavement to a sacrificial myth. I think it may go a long way toward freeing us from the myth by portraying it in its true archaic shape and color, not disguising its brutality."

Heaney has found a powerful metaphor for current violence in the archaeological discoveries made in peat bogs in Ireland and northern Europe. The chemical nature of the water in the bogs preserves organic material buried in them—including human beings. In 1969 Heaney read *The Bog People,* by P. V. Glob, an archaeologist who had unearthed the preserved remains of several ritually slaughtered Iron Age Europeans. Terrence Des Pres, in a *Harper's* essay, quotes Heaney on the impact this work had on his poetry: "The unforgettable photographs of these victims blended in my mind with photographs of atrocities, past and present, in the long rites of Irish political and religious struggles." Although the first of the well-known "bog poems" appeared in *Wintering Out,* published in 1972, Heaney continued the sequence in *North,* published in 1975. Eight of the poems in that sequence were brought together in a limited edition entitled *Bog Poems* that same year.

Heaney's bog poems, according to Murphy, trace "modern terrorism back to its roots in the early Iron Age, and mysterious awe back to the 'bonehouse' of language itself. . . . He looks closely . . . at our funeral rites and our worship of the past. . . . The central image of this work, a symbol which unifies time, person, and place, is bogland: it contains, preserves, and yields up terror as well as awe." "What makes Heaney different is the archetypal dimension of his poetic involvement with Irish culture," writes Gregory A. Schirmer in *Eire-Ireland.* "Nowhere is this more evident—and nowhere is Heaney's art more transcendent—than in the poems that Heaney has written about the peat bogs of Ireland and Jutland and the treasures and horrors that they have preserved. Heaney has developed the image of the bog into a powerful symbol of the continuity of human experience that at once enables him to write about the particularities of his own parish, past and present, and to transcend, at the same time, those particularities." In 'Punishment,' for instance, Heaney interprets one of the victims (a young girl) as an adulteress. Buttel explains in *CDBLB:* "The speaker's sympathy for the [young girl] pulls him erotically: 'I almost love you'; 'I am the artful voyeur / of your brain's exposed / and darkened combs, / your muscles' webbing.' But as he compares her with 'your betraying sisters' in the present who have presumably been punished, 'cauled in tar,' for consorting with British soldiers, he feels himself caught between the 'civilized outrage' at which he 'would connive' and his understanding of 'the exact / and tribal, intimate revenge' to which the Iron Age adulteress had been subjected."

Morrison suggests that the role of political spokesman has never particularly suited Heaney. The author "has written poems directly about the Troubles as well as elegies for friends and acquaintances who have died in them; he has tried to discover a historical framework in which to interpret the current unrest; and he has taken on the mantle of public spokesman, someone looked to for comment and guidance," notes Morrison. "Yet he has also shown signs of deeply resenting this role, defending the right of poets to be private and apolitical, and questioning the extent to which poetry, however 'committed,' can influence the course of history." In the *New Boston Review,* Shaun O'Connell contends that even Heaney's most overtly political poems contain depths that subtly alter their meanings. "Those who see Seamus Heaney as a symbol of hope in a troubled land are not, of course, wrong to do so," O'Connell states, "though they may be missing much of the undercutting complexities of his poetry, the backwash of ironies which make him as bleak as he is bright."

In 1972 Heaney left Belfast for the opportunity to live in a cottage outside Dublin, where he could write full time. The move had political overtones even though Heaney made it for financial reasons; Morrison observes that the subsequent poetry in *Field Work* "is deeply conscious of that move into the countryside."

Morrison adds: "It was not surprising that the move should have been seen by some as a betrayal of the Northern Catholic community and should have aroused in Heaney feelings of unease and even guilt. One important consequence was the new seriousness he brought to his thinking about the writer and his responsibilities." At his retreat in Glanmore, Heaney reasserted his determination to produce fresh aesthetic objects, to pursue his personal feelings as member of—and not spokesman for—church, state, and tribe.

A further liberating experience occurred at Glanmore when Heaney began to undertake the translation and adaptation of the Irish lyric poem *Buile Suibhne.* The work concerns an ancient king who, cursed by the church, is transformed into a mad bird-man and forced to wander in the harsh and inhospitable countryside. Heaney's translation of the epic was published as *Sweeney Astray: A Version from the Irish.* In the *Dictionary of Literary Biography* Buttel contends that the poem "reveals a heartfelt affinity with the dispossessed king who responds with such acute sensitivity, poetic accuracy, and imaginative force to his landscape." *New York Times Book Review* contributor Brendan Kennelly also deems the poem "a balanced statement about a tragically unbalanced mind. One feels that this balance, urbanely sustained, is the product of a long, imaginative bond between Mr. Heaney and Sweeney." Indeed, this bond is extended into Heaney's 1984 volume *Station Island,* where a series of poems titled "Sweeney Redivivus" take up Sweeney's voice once more. Buttel sees these poems as part of a larger theme in *Station Island;* namely, "a personal drama of guilt, lost innocence, and lost moral and religious certainty played against the redemptions of love, faith in the integrity of craft and of dedicated individuals, and ties with the universal forces operating in nature and history."

Station Island also introduces a spiritual theme that Heaney had not developed strongly before. "The tone," declares Buttel in *CDBLB,* "is devout and properly purgatorial." Buttel quotes *Times Literary Supplement* contributor Blake Morrison as calling the volume "a religious book and no getting around it—intense, superstitious, pantheistic, even mystical, and at times very difficult to decipher. . . . it gives us a rather different poet from the one we thought we knew."

This fascination with words and the spirit is evident in *The Haw Lantern,* published in 1987. *Times Literary Supplement* reviewer Neil Corcoran feels that the poems in that work "have a very contemporary sense of how writing is elegy to experience." W. S. DiPiero explains Heaney's intent in the *American Scholar:* "Whatever the occasion—childhood, farm life, politics and culture in Northern Ireland, other poets past and present—Heaney strikes time and again at the taproot of language, examining its genetic structures, trying to discover how it has served, in all its changes, as a culture bearer, a world to contain imaginations, at once a rhetorical weapon and nutriment of spirit. He writes of these matters with rare discrimination and resourcefulness, and a winning impatience with received wisdom." Heaney, declares Buttel in *CDBLB,* remains "in a long tradition of Irish writers who have flourished in the British literary scene, showing the Britons new possibilities for poetry in their mother tongue."

With the publication of *Selected Poems, 1966-1987,* Heaney marked the beginning of a new direction in his career. Michael Dirda, writing in the *Washington Post Book World,* notes that a collection of "selected poems" is almost redundant for a poet of Heaney's stature and popularity. The reviewer points out that "where a 'Collected Poems' is a monument, a 'Selected' is an invitation, a sometimes needed ice-breaker for shy new readers." "In truth," Dirda concludes, Heaney "is probably one of the few poets who doesn't really need a Selected Poems. Anyone who cares for poetry already knows that he should be reading him. And anyone who likes his work will want to own it all." *Poetry* contributor William Logan questions how successful the poet has been in this new direction, saying, "The younger Heaney wrote like a man possessed by demons, even when those demons were very literary demons; the older Heaney seems to wonder, bemusedly, what sort of demon he has become himself."

In another poetry collection, *Seeing Things,* Heaney demonstrates even more clearly the direction in which he is taking his career. Jefferson Hunter, reviewing the book for the *Virginia Quarterly Review,* shows that in some of the poems in *Seeing Things* Heaney has taken a more spiritual, less concrete approach than had been his habit previously. "Words like 'spirit' and 'pure,' as opposed to words like 'reek' and 'hock,' have never figured largely in Heaney's poetry," the critic explains. In the portion of the book titled "Squarings," "they create a new distanced perspective and indeed a new mood . . . [in which] 'things beyond measure' or 'things in the offing' or 'the longed-for' can sometimes be sensed, if never directly seen." Heaney also creates a direct link between himself and some of his ancient predecessors, Hunter continues. " 'The Golden Bough' translates the famous passage of *Aeneid* VI wherein the Sybil tells the hero what talisman he must carry on his trip to the underworld, while 'The Crossing' translates

Dante's and Virgil's confrontation with the angry Charon in *Inferno* III."

The Spirit Level is Heaney's first collection of poetry since he was awarded the 1995 Nobel Prize for Literature. The book explores the themes of politics, humanism, and nature. "Heaney's latest collection is a moving and human book, one that includes in its composition a plea for hope, for innocence, for balance, and to seek eventually that 'bubble for the spirit level,' " writes *World Literature Today* reviewer Sudeep Sen. Donna Seaman remarks in *Booklist:* "Heaney navigates skillfully from the personal to the universal, from life to death, seeking that precious equilibrium that only poetry can possess."

In 1998, Heaney offered another hand-picked selection of his verse: *Opened Ground: Selected Poems, 1966-1996. New York Times Book Review* commentator Edward Mendelson comments of that book: "With the prospect of decades of work ahead of him, Heaney has assembled a collection with a satisfying heft and more than enough variety of subject and style to delineate the shape of a long and constantly evolving career. It eloquently confirms his status as the most skillful and profound poet writing in English today." *New York Times* critic Michiko Kakutani concurs that the collection demonstrates "the consummate virtuosity of his work."

In an interview published in *Viewpoints: Poets in Conversation with John Haffenden,* Heaney offered some insight into his craftsmanship. "One thing I try to avoid ever saying at readings is '*my* poem,' " he said, "—because that sounds like a presumption. The poem *came, it came.* I didn't go and fetch it. To some extent you wait for it, you coax it in the door when it gets there. I prefer to think of myself as the host to the thing rather than a big-game hunter." Elsewhere in the same interview he commented: "You write books of poems because that is a fulfillment, a making; it's a making sense of your life and it gives achievement, but it also gives you a sense of growth."

In his review of *The Redress of Poetry* in the *Nation,* James Longenbach explains that "Heaney wants to think of poetry not only as something that intervenes in the world, redressing or correcting imbalances, but also as something that must be redressed—re-established, celebrated as itself." The book contains a selection of lectures Heaney delivered as Oxford Professor of Poetry on subjects ranging from Christopher Marlowe to Philip Larkin. *New York Times Book Review* contributor J. D. McClatchy calls the lectures "a meditation on the uses of art and power, a fresh and astute defense of poetry against any attempt to reduce it to a relevant or useful commodity." However, in the *Times Literary Supplement,* John Bayley criticizes Heaney for not providing fresh ideas about poetry, saying the book "gives the impression of being adjusted with courtly discretion to an audience who expect the familiar rather than the new." He continues: "The poet as diplomat is an honourable and unusual role . . . but the critic exercising the same kind of function runs the risk of giving pleasure without surprise or illumination."

In addition to writing his own poetry, Heaney has made his mark as a translator of other poets' work. His version of Sophocles' *Philoctetes* earned praise from numerous critics when it was performed at the Yale Repertory Theater in 1998. His translation of the epic Anglo-Saxon poem *Beowulf* was considered groundbreaking because of the freedom he took in using modern language. Several reviewers noted that *Beowulf* has become something of a tired chestnut in the literary world, but credited Heaney with breathing new life into the ancient classic. Malcolm Jones in *Newsweek* states: "As rendered by Heaney, the bardic saga of a Danish prince's epic battles with the monster Grendel, Grendel's mother, and a 50-foot dragon is as vivid as a tabloid headline and as visceral as a nightmare. Heaney's own poetic vernacular—muscular language so rich with the tones and smell of earth that you almost expect to find a few crumbs of dirt clinging to his lines—is the perfect match for the Beowulf poet's Anglo-Saxon. . . . As retooled by Heaney, 'Beowulf ' should easily be good for another millennium." Readers responded to recommendations such as these, making Heaney's *Beowulf* a surprising entry on the bestseller lists.

The popular translation stirred up some controversy when in 2000 it was awarded the Whitbread Award, one of Great Britain's top literary honors. Stiff competition for Heaney's book came in the form of a book in J. K. Rowling's "Harry Potter" series, *The Prince of Azkaban.* Rowling's wildly popular stories of a teenage apprentice wizard have earned their author over $22 million and sold more than twenty-seven 27 million copies worldwide. Rowling's supporters on the Whitbread judges panel felt that as a translation, *Beowulf* was not eligible for consideration; others argued that the award should be given to a more fresh, modern work than *Beowulf.* Gary McKeone, the head of the literature department at the Arts Council of England, was quoted in *Christian Science Monitor* as saying that Heaney's translation has "true literary merit. This is translation at its potent best. . . . Heaney's subtle, luminous vernacular ignites the poem for a new generation of readers."

BIOGRAPHICAL/CRITICAL SOURCES:

BOOKS

Allen, Michael, editor. *Seamus Heaney,* St. Martin's Press, 1997.

Brown, Terence, *Northern Voices: Poets from Ulster,* Rowman & Littlefield (Totowa, NJ), 1975.

Buttel, Robert, *Seamus Heaney,* Bucknell University Press (Cranbury, NJ), 1975.

Concise Dictionary of British Literary Biography: Contemporary Writers, 1960 to the Present, Gale, 1992.

Contemporary Literary Criticism, Gale (Detroit), Volume 5, 1976, Volume 7, 1977, Volume 14, 1980, Volume 25, 1983, Volume 37, 1986, Volume 74, 1993, Volume 91: *Yearbook 95,* 1996.

Curtis, Tony, editor, *The Art of Seamus Heaney,* Wolfhound Press (Dublin), 1994.

Dictionary of Literary Biography, Volume 40: *Poets of Great Britain and Ireland since 1960,* Gale, 1985.

Durkan, Michael J., *Seamus Heaney: A Reference Guide,* G. K. Hall (New York City), 1996.

Garratt, Robert F., *Critical Essays on Seamus Heaney,* G. K. Hall, 1995.

Harmon, Maurice, editor, *Image and Illusion: Anglo-Irish Literature and Its Contexts,* Wolfhound Press, 1979.

Malloy, Catharine and Phyllis Carey, editors, *Seamus Heaney—The Shaping Spirit,* University of Delaware Press (Newark), 1996.

McGuinness, Arthur E., *Seamus Heaney: Poet and Critic,* P. Lang (New York City), 1994.

Molino, Michael R., *Questioning Tradition, Language, and Myth: The Poetry of Seamus Heaney,* Catholic University of America Press (New York City), 1994.

Morrison, Blake, *Seamus Heaney,* Methuen (London), 1982.

Newsmakers 96, Gale, 1997.

Viewpoints: Poets in Conversation with John Haffenden, Faber, 1981.

Weathers, William, editor, *The Nature of Identity: Essays Presented to Donald E. Haydon by the Graduate Faculty of Modern Letters,* University of Tulsa Press (Tulsa, TX), 1981.

PERIODICALS

America, October 11, 1997, p. 8; December 20, 1997, p. 24; July 31, 1999, John F. Desmond, "Measures of a Poet," p. 24.

American Scholar, autumn, 1981.

Antioch Review, spring, 1993.

Back Stage, December 19, 1997, review of *The Cure at Troy: A Version of Sophocles Philotetes,* p. 34.

Booklist, May 1, 1996, p. 1485; October 15, 1998, review of "Opened Ground," p. 388; February 15, 2000, Ray Olson, "A New Verse Translation," p. 1073.

Books for Keeps, September, 1997, p. 30.

Christian Science Monitor, April 22, 1999, Elizabeth Lund, "The Enticing Sounds of This Irishman's Verse," p. 20; February 3, 2000, "'Harry Potter' Falls to a Medieval Slayer," p. 1.

Critical Inquiry, spring, 1982.

Critical Quarterly, spring, 1974; spring, 1976.

Economist, September 12, 1998, review of *Opened Ground,* p. 14; November 20, 1999, "Translations of the Spirit," p. 101.

Eire-Ireland, summer, 1978; winter, 1980.

Encounter, November, 1975.

Globe and Mail (Toronto), September 3, 1988.

Harper's, March, 1981.

Irish Literary Supplement, fall, 1997, p. 14.

Kliatt, March, 1998, p. 57.

Library Journal, May 15, 1997, review of *The Spirit Level,* p. 120; September 1, 1997, review of *The Spirit Level,* p. 235; April 1, 1999, Barbara Hoffert, review of *Opened Ground,* p. 96; December, 1999, Thomas L. Cooksey, review of *Beowulf,* p. 132.

Listener, December 7, 1972; November 8, 1973; September 25, 1975; December 20-27, 1984.

London Review of Books, November 1-14, 1984; May 27, 1999, review of *Opened Ground,* p. 20.

Los Angeles Times, May 16, 1984; January 5, 1989.

Los Angeles Times Book Review, March 2, 1980; October 21, 1984; June 2, 1985; October 27, 1987; August 26, 1990; December 27, 1992.

Nation, November 10, 1979; December 4, 1995, p. 716; January 4, 1999, Jay Parini, review of *Opened Ground,* p. 25.

New Boston Review, August-September, 1980.

New Republic, March 27, 1976; December 22, 1979; April 30, 1984; February 18, 1985; January 13, 1997, review of *Homage to Robert Frost,* p. 14; February 28, 2000, Nicholas Howe, "Scullionspeak," p. 32.

New Statesman, April 25, 1997; September 18, 1998, review of *Opened Ground,* p. 54.

Newsweek, February 2, 1981; April 15, 1985; February 28, 2000, Malcolm Jones, "'Beowulf' Brawling: A Classic Gets a Makeover," p. 68.

New Yorker, September 28, 1981; September 23, 1985.

New York Review of Books, September 20, 1973; September 30, 1976; March 6, 1980; October 8, 1981;

March 14, 1985; June 25, 1992; March 4, 1999, Fintan O'Toole, review of *Opened Ground,* p. 43.

New York Times, April 22, 1979; January 11, 1985; November 24, 1998, Michiko Kakutani, review of *Opened Ground: Selected Poems, 1966-1996;* January 30, 1999, Joyce Jensen, "As Anthologies Duel, Women Gain Ground," p. B11; January 20, 2000, Sarah Lyall, "Wizard vs. Dragon: A Close Contest, but the Fire-Breather Wins," p. A17; January 27, 2000, William Safire, "Besotted with Potter," p. A27; February 22, 2000, Richard Eder, "Beowulf and Fate Meet in a Modern Poet's Lens," p. B8; March 20, 2000, Mel Gussow, "An Anglo-Saxon Chiller (with an Irish Touch)," p. B1.

New York Times Book Review, March 26, 1967; April 18, 1976; December 2, 1979; December 21, 1980; May 27, 1984; March 10, 1985; March 5, 1989; December 14, 1995, p. 15; June 1, 1997, p. 52; December 20, 1998, review of *Opened Ground,* p. 10; June 6, 1999, review of *Opened Ground,* p. 37; February 22, 2000, "Beowulf and Fate Meet in a Modern Poet's Lens"; February 27, 2000, James Shapiro, "A Better 'Beowulf' " p. 6.

New York Times Magazine, March 13, 1983.

Observer (London), September 6, 1998, review of *Opened Ground,* p. 17.

Parnassus, spring-summer, 1974; fall-winter, 1977; fall-winter, 1979.

Partisan Review, Number 3, 1986.

Poetry, June, 1992.

Publishers Weekly, April 29, 1996, p. 63; January 27, 1997, p. 14; November 2, 1998, review of *Opened Ground,* p. 74; February 7, 2000, Jana Riess, "Heaney Takes U.K.'s Whitbread Prize," p. 18; February 14, 2000, Judy Quinn, "Will Readers Cry 'Wulf '?," p. 86; February 21, 2000, review of *Beowulf,* p. 84; March 13, 2000, Daisy Maryles, "A Real Backlist Mover," p. 22.

Saturday Review, July-August, 1985.

Sewanee Review, winter, 1976.

Southern Review, January, 1980.

Spectator, September 6, 1975; December 1, 1979; November 24, 1984; June 27, 1987; September 16, 1995, p. 39; September 5, 1998, review of *Opened Ground,* p. 36.

Time, March 19, 1984; February 25, 1985; October 16, 1995; March 20, 2000, Paul Gray, "There Be Dragons: Seamus Heaney's Stirring Translation of Beowulf Makes Waves on Both Shores of the Atlantic," p. 84.

Times (London), October 11, 1984; January 24, 1985; October 22, 1987; June 3, 1989.

Times Educational Supplement, November 7, 1997, p. 2; September 11, 1998, review of *Opened Ground,* p. 11.

Times Literary Supplement, June 9, 1966; July 17, 1969; December 15, 1972; August 1, 1975; February 8, 1980; October 31, 1980; November 26, 1982; October 19, 1984; June 26, 1987; July 1-7, 1988; December 6, 1991; October 20, 1995, p. 9.

Tribune Books (Chicago), April 19, 1981; September 9, 1984; November 8, 1987; November 25, 1990.

Twentieth-Century Studies, November, 1970.

U.S. News & World Report, March 20, 2000, Brendan I. Koerner, "Required Reading," p. 68.

Variety, May 4, 1998, Markland Taylor, review of "The Cure at Troy," p. 96.

Virginia Quarterly Review, autumn, 1992.

Wall Street Journal, April 2, 1999, review of *Opened Ground,* p. W6; March 10, 2000, "Slaying Dragons," p. W17; February 24, 2000, Elizabeth Bukowski, "Seamus Heaney Tackles 'Beowulf,' " p. A16.

Washington Post Book World, January 6, 1980; January 25, 1981; May 20, 1984; January 27, 1985; August 19, 1990.

World Literature Today, summer, 1977; autumn, 1981; summer, 1983; autumn, 1996, p. 963.*

* * *

HERBERGER, Charles F. 1920-

PERSONAL: Born February 29, 1920, in Ilion, IL; son of Charles F., Sr. (an industrial manager) and Florence (Hunt) Herberger; married Melvina Crosby, August 10, 1946; children: Melvina Herberger Brock. *Education:* Dartmouth College, A.B., 1942; University of Cincinnati, M.A., 1948; Boston University, Ph.D., 1960. *Politics:* Republican. *Religion:* Protestant. *Avocational interests:* Travel, watercolor painting.

ADDRESSES: *Home*—445 Main St., Centerville, MA 02632-2913.

CAREER: University of Cincinnati, Cincinnati, OH, instructor, 1946-50; Framingham State Teachers College (now State College), Framingham, MA, instructor, 1952; Colby Junior College (now Colby-Sawyer College), New Hampshire, instructor, 1953-54; Wayne State University, Detroit, MI, instructor, 1954-58; Nasson College, Springvale, ME, began as assistant professor, became professor, 1958-82, George Nasson Lecturer, 1971 and 1982, professor emeritus, 1982—, coordinator of Humanities Division, 1964-80, director of Humanities Study Abroad Program in Vienna, Austria, 1971, 1974, 1976, and 1979. University of New Hampshire, visiting professor, summer, 1967; Deree College, Athens, Greece, visiting professor, 1977. *Military service:* U.S. Navy, administrative officer, 1942-46; became commander.

MEMBER: Shakespeare Oxford Society, Centerville Library Association (second vice president), New England Antiquities Research Association, Midwestern Epigraphic Society.

AWARDS, HONORS: Victor Moseley Award, Midwestern Epigraphic Society, 1999.

WRITINGS:

The Back of Your Neck (play), produced in Springvale, ME, by Little Theater Group, 1965.
Shadrach, Meshach, and Abednego (play), produced in Springvale, by Nasson College Dramatic Club, 1966.
The Thread of Ariadne: The Labyrinth of the Calendar of Minos, Philosophical Library (New York City), 1972.
Paradise Glossed (play), produced in Springvale, by Nasson College Dramatic Club, 1973.
The Riddle of the Sphinx: Calendric Symbolism in Myth and Icon, Vantage (New York City), 1979, 2nd edition, Efstathiades Group (Athens, Greece), 1988.
Three Centuries of Centerville Scenes: Vignettes of a Cape Cod Village, Centerville Historical Society (Barnstable, MA), 1989.
(Editor) *A Yankee at Arms: The Diary of Lieutenant Augustus D. Ayling, 29th Massachusetts Volunteers,* University of Tennessee Press (Knoxville, TN), 1999.

Contributor to periodicals, including *Humanitas, New England Antiquities Research Association Journal, Ancient American, Archaeoastronomy, Griffith Observer, Chrysalis, Epigraphic Society Papers,* and *Revue Kadath.*

WORK IN PROGRESS: Morning, Noon and Night: The Hinges of the Day, poetry; *Remembrances and Reflections: An American Scholar's Odyssey,* a memoir.

HERNDON, Ursule Molinaro
See MOLINARO, Ursule

* * *

HOLZMAN, Red
See HOLZMAN, William

* * *

HOLZMAN, William 1920-1998
(Red Holzman)

PERSONAL: Born August 10, 1920, in New York, NY; died of leukemia, November 13, 1998, in Long Island, NY; son of Abraham (a tailor) and Sophie Holzman; married in 1942, wife's name Selma; children: Gail. *Education:* Attended City College (now of the City University of New York).

CAREER: Professional basketball player, 1945-54; St. Louis Hawks, St. Louis, MO, coach, 1954-57; New York Knicker-bockers, New York City, scout, 1958-67, coach, 1967-77, general manager, 1970-75, consultant, 1977-79, coach, 1979-82, consultant, 1982-98. Vice president of Winner World championship, 1970 and 1973; coach of National Basketball Association (NBA) East All-Star Team, 1970-71. *Military service:* U.S. Navy, 1942-44.

AWARDS, HONORS: Named coach of the year by National Basketball Association, 1970; voted into Basketball Hall of Fame, 1991.

WRITINGS:

UNDER NAME RED HOLZMAN

(With Leonard Lewin) *The Knicks,* Dodd, Mead (New York City), 1971.
(With Lewin) *Holzman's Basketball: Winning Strategy and Tactics,* Macmillan (New York City), 1973.
(With Lewin) *A View from the Bench,* Norton (New York City), 1980.
(With Harvey Frommer) *Red on Red,* Bantam (New York City), 1987.
(With Frommer) *Holzman on Hoops: The Man Who Led the Knicks through Two World Championships Tells It like It Was,* Taylor Publishing (Dallas, TX), 1991.
(With Lewin) *My Unforgettable Season—1970,* TOR (New York City), 1993.

SIDELIGHTS: The late William "Red" Holzman guided the New York Knicks to two National Basketball Association championships, in 1970 and 1973, and retired from the NBA with 696 victories in regular season play. A member of the Basketball Hall of Fame, Holzman served as the Knicks' head coach from 1967 until 1977, and again from 1979 until 1982. Even when not at the team's helm he played an important role in the franchise, variously serving as a scout, general manager, and consultant up until his death from leukemia in 1998. According to Ira Berkow in the *New York Times,* Holzman "was the molder, conductor and architect of one of the most unusual, most thrilling and, for the involved basketball fan, most gratifying teams ever assembled."

Born in Manhattan and raised in Brooklyn by Jewish immigrant parents, Holzman excelled in sports from a young age. He earned his nickname based on the thick, bright red hair that covered his head. In the early 1940s he was twice named an All-America guard at the City College of New York, and after his wartime service in the U.S. Navy he played nine seasons of professional basketball with the Rochester Royals and Milwaukee Hawks in the fledgling NBA. In 1954 he became head coach of the St. Louis Hawks, a job he held until 1957. Two years later he signed with the Knicks as a scout, and, according to Berkow, he "beat the bushes, traveling across the country in search of talent. His recommendations included players like [Willis] Reed and [Walt] Frazier."

In December of 1967 Holzman took over head coaching duties with the Knicks, where he became widely admired for melding a talented squad of individual stars—including future senator Bill Bradley—into a selfless team marked by an aggressive defense. The Knicks won the 1970 NBA championship in a grueling seven-game matchup against a Los Angeles Lakers team featuring Wilt Chamberlain, Jerry West, and Elgin Baylor. At the end of the series, Holzman was named NBA coach of the year. Again in 1973 the Knicks met the Lakers for the championship, and this time the Knicks sealed the title in five games.

Thereafter Holzman was always associated with the Knicks, either as head coach or as a respected consultant. His fame brought opportunities for speaking and writing, and—with two co-authors, Leonard Lewin and Harvey Frommer—he published a series of books on coaching, the Knicks, and his personal reminiscences. *Red on Red,* his 1988 title, offers anecdotes from his career and his personal life, which included a long and happy marriage to his high school sweetheart. In a *New York Times Book Review* of *Red on Red,* Joyce Howe commended the work as "the entertaining account of a man's life in the sport that made him a legend." Howe added: "A keen observer of today's game, the coach recalls his winning players with respect and affection. Oh, what a time. What a team!"

On the occasion of Holzman's death in 1998, NBA Commissioner David Stern told the *Washington Post:* "Red represented the best of our game. He was a fan-friendly player and coach but most of all, a gentleman who treated his players with dignity and respect and received their loyalty and love in return."

BIOGRAPHICAL/CRITICAL SOURCES:

BOOKS

Hickok, Ralph, *Who's Who of Sports Champions,* Houghton Mifflin (Boston, MA), 1995.

Holzman, Red, and Harvey Frommer, *Red on Red,* Bantam (New York City), 1987.

LaBlanc, Michael, editor, *Professional Sports Team Histories: Basketball,* Gale (Detroit, MI), 1994, pp. 73-92.

PERIODICALS

Library Journal, February 1, 1981, p. 366; November 15, 1987, p. 88; September 15, 1991, p. 86.

New York Times Book Review, January 31, 1988, Joyce Howe, review of *Red on Red,* p. 25.

Publishers Weekly, September 5, 1980, 60; November 6, 1987, p. 54.

OBITUARIES:

PERIODICALS

Los Angeles Times, November 15, 1998, "Former Knick Coach Holzman Dead at 78," p. D5.

New York Times, November 15, 1998, Ira Berkow, "Red Holzman, Hall of Fame Coach, Dies at 78," p. A46, George Vecsey, "Red Holzman, the Modest Assistant, Always Had a Plan," and "Former Players and Peers Fondly Recall Holzman, a Friend and a Professional," p. SP1; November 27, 1998, p. D1.

Washington Post, November 15, 1998, "Hall of Fame Coach Holzman Dies," pp. B6, D6.*

HOUGHTON, Katharine 1945-

PERSONAL: Surname is pronounced "*Hoe*-ton"; born March 10, 1945, in Hartford, CT; daughter of Ellsworth Strong (a documentary filmmaker) and Marion (an historian; maiden name, Hepburn) Grant. *Education:* Sarah Lawrence College, B.A., 1965.

ADDRESSES: *Home*—134 Steele Rd., West Hartford, CT 06119.

CAREER: Professional actress on stage, screen, and television, 1965—. Stage appearances in New York productions include *A Very Rich Woman, The Front Page, A Scent of Flowers,* and *To Heaven in a Swing;* film appearances include *Guess Who's Coming to Dinner, The Gardener, Eyes of the Amaryllis, Ethan Frome,* and *Mr. North;* television appearances include *The Hawk, The Adams' Chronicles, Judd for the Defense, The Confession, The Color of Friendship, All My Children,* and *One Life to Live.* Co-founder of Pilgrim Repertory Company, 1971-80.

MEMBER: Dramatists Guild.

AWARDS, HONORS: *Theatre World* Award, 1969-70, for the role of Zoe in *A Scent of Flowers.*

WRITINGS:

(With brother, J. B. Grant) *Two Beastly Tales,* illustrated by Joan Patchen, Lamplighters Roadway Press, 1975.

To Heaven in a Swing (two-act play), first produced in New York City at American Place Theatre, March 21, 1984.

Merlin (children's play), first produced in Kansas City, MO, at Coterie Theatre, February 20, 1985.

Buddha (one-act play), first produced in New York City at West Bank Cafe, January 27, 1987.

On the Shady Side (one-act play), first produced in New York City at West Bank Cafe, March 31, 1987.

The Right Number (one-act play), first produced in New York City at West Bank Cafe, May 19, 1987.

The Hooded Eye (play), first produced in New York City at West Bank Cafe, September 25, 1987.

Phone Play (one-act play), first produced in New York City at 44th Street Playhouse, May 10, 1988.

Mortal Friends (one-act play), first produced in New York City at West Bank Cafe, November 3, 1988.

MHG: A Biography, Fenwick Productions, 1989.

Best Kept Secret: A Dangerous Liason in the Cold War (two-act play; autobiographical), first produced at the Ivoryton Playhouse, Ivoryton, CT, 1998.

Also author of the children's play *The Wizard's Daughter;* the book for the musical *The Marry Month of May,* 1988; the play *Good Grief,* 1988; and the screenplay *The Heart of the Matter,* 1995. Co-author of the screenplays *Acting in Concert,* with A. Littles, 1994, and *Spot,* with E. Rose, 1996. Work represented in anthologies, including *Best Short Plays of 1988.*

BIOGRAPHICAL/CRITICAL SOURCES:

BOOKS

Almanac of Famous People, sixth edition, Gale (Detroit, MI), 1999.

PERIODICALS

New York Times, August 30, 1984; January 23, 1987.

Variety, April 3, 2000, p. 173.*

* * *

HUSKEY, Eugene 1952-

PERSONAL: Born December 2, 1952, in Leesburg, FL; son of Everette (a realtor) and Suzanne Rasmussen (a homemaker; maiden name, Stratton) Huskey; married Janet Martinez (an attorney), January 10, 1979; children: Sarah Emilia, Charlotte Louisa. *Education:* Vanderbilt University, B.A., 1974; University of Essex, M.A., 1976; attended Moscow State University, 1979-80; London School of Economics and Political Science, London, Ph.D., 1983.

ADDRESSES: *Home*—415 East Pennsylvania Ave., DeLand, FL 32724. *Office*—Stetson University, Box 8313, DeLand, FL 32720; fax: 904-822-7569. *E-mail*—ehuskey@stetson.edu.

CAREER: Colgate University, Hamilton, NY, visiting instructor, 1981-83; Bowdoin College, Brunswick, ME, assistant professor, 1983-89; Stetson University, DeLand, FL, associate professor, 1989-96, professor, 1996—, William R. Kenan, Jr. Professor of Political Science and Russian Studies, 1999—.

WRITINGS:

Russian Lawyers and the Soviet State, Princeton University Press (Princeton, NJ), 1976.

(Editor) *Executive Power and Soviet Politics: The Rise and Decline of the Soviet State,* M. E. Sharpe (Armonk, NY), 1992.

Presidential Power in Russia, M. E. Sharpe, 1999.

Contributor to academic journals.

WORK IN PROGRESS: Research on the politics of Kyrgyzstan and on Russian bureaucracy.

SIDELIGHTS: Eugene Huskey told *CA:* "My interest in things Russian emerged, strangely enough, in Florida in the 1960s. In October, 1962, as a boy in a small central Florida town, I experienced nuclear attack drills and the drone of tanks and planes massing for what we all assumed would be an attack on Cuba. A few years later, I found myself in one of the first high school programs in Russian language in the state. I was hooked.

"My intellectual baptism in Russian studies came during the 1979-80 academic year, which I spent in the law faculty of Moscow State University. I had gone to Russia to research a dissertation on the Russian Bar and its destruction by the Bolsheviks. The subject revealed two important elements of Russian history in the period from the Great Reforms of the 1860s through the Stalin era: the strength of liberal thought and institutions in late imperial Russia, and the methods used by the Bolsheviks to destroy an incipient Russian liberalism.

"I have continued to work on the formation and development—and now the dismantling—of Communist legal institutions, with articles on historical subjects, and on contemporary questions of law and justice. The study of law spawned related work on the rise of a new Russian state. A book on the Yeltsin presidency attempts to explain why Russia has been unable to construct a liberal state, which is a prerequisite for market and democratic reforms. I have also written recently on politics in the new states of central Asia, castoffs from the old Soviet Union."

* * *

IDLE, Eric 1943-
(Monty Python, a joint pseudonym)

Eric Idle

PERSONAL: Born March 29, 1943, in South Shields, Durham, England; son of Ernest (a Royal Air Force sergeant) and Norah (a health visitor; maiden name, Sanderson) Idle; married Lyn Ashley (an actress), July 7, 1969 (divorced, 1978); married Tania Kosevich (a model), 1981; children: (first marriage) Carey (son), (second marriage) Lily. *Education:* Pembroke College, Cambridge, degree (English literature, with honors), 1965.

ADDRESSES: *Agent*—William Morris Agency, 151 El Camino Dr., Beverly Hills, CA 90212.

CAREER: Actor, writer, composer, and director. British Broadcasting Corp. (BBC) television programs, writer, 1960s; writer and performer with Graham Chapman, John Cleese, Terry Gilliam, Terry Jones, and Michael Palin as Monty Python comedy troupe, 1969—; co-founder and president of Prominent Features, a production company. Cambridge Footlights, president, 1964-65.

Actor in television series, including various roles, *Do Not Adjust Your Set,* BBC, 1968-69; various roles, *Monty Python's Flying Circus,* BBC, 1969-74, PBS, 1974-82; various roles, *Rutland Weekend Television,* BBC, 1975-76; Grant Pritchard, *Nearly Departed,* NBC, 1989; voice of Parenthesis, *Hercules* (also known as *Disney's Hercules*), 1998; and Ian Maxtone-Graham, *Suddenly Susan,* NBC, 1999-2000. Actor in television miniseries, including as Passepartout, *Around the World in Eighty Days,* NBC, 1989. Actor in television movies, including *Ken Russell's Isadora The Biggest Dancer in the World,* BBC, 1966; *Jona-*

than Miller's Alice in Wonderland, BBC, 1966; *No, That's Me over Here,* London Weekend Television, 1967; *We Have Ways of Making You Laugh,* London Weekend Television, 1968; *Pythons in Deutschland,* Bavaria Atelier, 1971; various roles, *Monty Python's Fliegende Zircus,* Bavaria TV, 1971, 1972; (and director) Dirk McQuickley, narrator, and S. J. Krammerhead, *The Rutles* (also known as *All You Need Is Cash*), NBC, 1978; Ko-Ko, *The Mikado,* Thames TV, 1987; various roles, *Parrot Sketch Not Included,* 1989; and himself, *Thirty Years of Python: A Revelation,* 1999.

Actor in films, including *Albert Carter Q.O.S.O.,* Dormer, 1968; various roles, *And Now for Something Completely Different,* Columbia, 1971; Sir Robin and other roles, *Monty Python and the Holy Grail,* Cinema V, 1975; himself, *Side by Side,* 1976; Stan, Harry the Haggler, Mr. Cheeky, Jailer's assistant, and Mr. Frisbee III, *Life of Brian* (also known as *Monty Python's The Life of Brian*), Warner Bros., 1979; various roles, *Monty Python Live at the Hollywood Bowl,* Paramount, 1982; himself, *Group Madness,* 1983; various roles, *Monty Python's The Meaning of Life,* Universal, 1983; Commander Clement, *Yellowbeard,* Orion, 1983; himself, *The Secret Policeman's Private Parts,* 1984; Bike Rider, *European Vacation* (also known as *National Lampoon's European Vacation*), Warner Bros., 1985; voice of Wreck-Gar, *The Transformers: The Movie,* DEG, 1986; Desmond/Berthold, *The Adventures of Baron Munchausen,* Columbia/TriStar, 1988; Brian Hope, *Nuns on the Run,* Twentieth Century-Fox, 1990; Wendal, *Missing Pieces,* HBO Home Video, 1991; Sonny, *Too Much Sun,* RCA/Columbia Home Video, 1991; King Raff, *Mom and Dad Save the World,* Warner Bros., 1992; Tommy Patel, *Splitting Heirs,* Universal, 1993; Dr. Niles Channing, *Honey, I Shrunk the Audience,* 1995; Dibs, *Casper,* Universal, 1995; Rat, *The Wind in the Willows* (also known as *Mr. Toad's Wild Ride*), Columbia, 1996; Alan Smithee, *An Alan Smithee Film: Burn, Hollywood, Burn,* Buena Vista, 1997; voice of Devon, *Quest for Camelot,* Warner Bros., 1998; voice of Slyly the Fox, *Rudolph the Red-nosed Reindeer: The Movie,* Legacy Releasing, 1998; voice of "New and Improved" Martin, *The Secret of NIMH 2: Timmy to the Rescue,* MGM/UA Home Video, 1998; Dr. Niles Channing, *Journey into Your Imagination,* 1999; voice of Dr. Vosknocker, *South Park: Bigger, Longer, and Uncut,* Paramount, 1999; and Prospector Kim Jay Darling, *Dudley Do-Right,* Universal, 1999.

Actor in theatre, including *Footlights '63,* Edinburgh Festival, 1963; *My Girl Herbert,* Lyric Hammersmith Theatre, London, 1963; *I'm Just Wild about Harry,* Henry Miller Theatre, Edinburgh Festival, 1963; *The Tempest,* Edinburgh Festival, 1964; *Footlights '64,* Edinburgh Festival, 1964; *One for the Pot,* Leicester Phoenix Theatre, 1965; *Oh What a Lovely War,* Leicester Phoenix Theatre, 1965; Coventry Festival, 1972; *Monty Python's First Farewell Tour,* Canada, then United Kingdom, 1973; *Monty Python Live at Drury Lane,* 1974; *Monty Python Live at City Centre,* 1976; and *Monty Python Live at the Hollywood Bowl,* 1980. Also performed in opera, including as Ko-Ko, *The Mikado,* English National Opera, 1987, then Houston Grand Opera, 1989.

Performed voice-over work for video games and computer games, including as various roles, *Monty Python's Complete Waste of Time,* 1994; *Discworld,* 1995; *Discworld II: Mortality Bytes,* 1996; Sir Robin and other roles, *Monty Python and the Quest for the Holy Grail,* 1996; and various roles, *Monty Python's The Meaning of Life,* 1997.

AWARDS, HONORS: Silver Rose, Montreux Television Festival, 1971, for *Monty Python's Flying Circus;* ACE Cable Award for Best Cable Show of the Year, 1982, for "The Frog Prince"; Grand Prix Special du Jury award, Cannes Film Festival, 1983, for *Monty Python's The Meaning of Life;* Michael Balcon Award for Outstanding British Contribution to Cinema (with Monty Python), British Academy of Film and Television Arts, 1987.

WRITINGS:

Hello Sailor (novel), Weidenfeld & Nicolson (London), 1974.

The Rutland Dirty Weekend Book, Methuen, 1976.

Pass the Butler (play; produced at Globe Theatre, London, 1982), Methuen, 1982.

The Quite Remarkable Adventures of the Owl and the Pussycat (children's fiction; based on the works of Edward Lear), illustrated by Edward Lear and Wesla Weller, Dove Kids (Los Angeles, CA), 1996.

The Road to Mars: A Post Modem Novel, Pantheon Books (New York City), 1999.

Author, with Neil Innes, of recording *Rutland Dirty Weekend Songbook,* 1975.

SCREENPLAYS

Albert Carter Q.O.S.O., Dormer, 1968.

Splitting Heirs, Universal, 1992.

Welcome to the Family, Savoy, 1994.

The Remains of the Piano, Miramax, 1995.

TELEPLAYS

(With Chapman and Cryer) *No, That's Me over Here,* London Weekend Television, 1967.
The Frost Report, BBC, 1967.
Twice a Fortnight, BBC, 1967.
Frost on Sunday, Wednesday, Thursday, Friday, etc., London Weekend Television, 1967-68.
Marty Feldman, BBC, 1968-69.
Rutland Weekend Television (series), BBC-TV, 1975-76.
All You Need Is Cash (movie), NBC, 1978, televised in Britain as *The Rutles,* BBC-TV, 1978.
(And director) "The Frog Prince," *Faerie Tale Theatre,* Showtime, 1982.
Nearly Departed, NBC, 1989.

RADIO PLAYS

I'm Sorry I'll Read That Again, BBC, 1966, 1968.
(With John Du Prez) *Behind the Crease,* BBC, 1990.

Also author of *Radio Five* (two series), c. 1970s.

CO-AUTHOR WITH MONTY PYTHON; SCREENPLAYS

And Now for Something Completely Different (adapted from *Monty Python's Flying Circus*), Columbia, 1972.
Monty Python and the Holy Grail (also see below), Cinema V, 1975.
Monty Python's Life of Brian (also see below), Warner Bros., 1979.
Monty Python Live at the Hollywood Bowl, Columbia, 1982.
Monty Python's The Meaning of Life (also see below), Universal, 1983.

CO-AUTHOR WITH MONTY PYTHON; BOOKS

(And editor) *Monty Python's Big Red Book,* Methuen, 1972, Warner Books, 1975.
(And editor) *The Brand New Monty Python Bok,* illustrations by Gilliam (under pseudonym Jerry Gillian) and Peter Brookes, Methuen, 1973, published as *The Brand New Monty Python Papperbok,* 1974.
Monty Python and the Holy Grail (also published as *Monty Python's Second Film: A First Draft*), both by Methuen, 1977.
(And editor) *Monty Python's Life of Brian* [and] *Montypythonscrapbook,* Grosset, 1979.
The Complete Works of Shakespeare and Monty Python: Volume One—Monty Python (contains *Monty Python's Big Red Book* and *The Brand New Monty Python Papperbok*), Methuen, 1981.
Monty Python's The Meaning of Life, Grove Press, 1983.
The Complete Monty Python's Flying Circus: All the Words, two volumes, Pantheon, 1989.
Monty Python Speaks!: John Cleese, Terry Gilliam, Eric Idle, Terry Jones, and Michael Palin Recount an Amazing, and Silly, Thirty-Year Spree in Television and Film—in Their Own Words, Squire!, interviewed by David Morgan, Spike (New York City), 1999.

CO-AUTHOR WITH MONTY PYTHON; TELEPLAYS

Do Not Adjust Your Set, BBC, 1968-69.
Monty Python's Flying Circus (series), BBC-TV, 1969-74, PBS, 1974-82.
Pythons in Deutschland (movie), Bavaria Atelier, 1971.

C0-AUTHOR WITH MONTY PYTHON; RECORDINGS; AND PERFORMER

Monty Python's Flying Circus, BBC, 1970.
Another Monty Python Record, Charisma, 1970.
Monty Python's Previous Record, Charisma, 1972.
Monty Python Matching Tie and Handkerchief, Charisma, 1973.
Monty Python Live at the Theatre Royal, Drury Lane, Charisma, 1974.
The Album of the Soundtrack of the Trailer of the Film of Monty Python and the Holy Grail (film soundtrack; includes additional material), Charisma, 1975.
Monty Python Live at City Center, 1976.
The Worst of Monty Python, 1976.
The Monty Python Instant Record Collection, Charisma, 1977.
(And co-producer) *Monty Python's Life of Brian* (film soundtrack), WEA, 1979.
(And producer) *Monty Python's Contractual Obligation Album,* Charisma, 1980.
Monty Python's The Meaning of Life (film soundtrack), CBS, 1983.
Monty Python's the Final Ripoff (compilation), Virgin, 1987.
(And producer) *Monty Python Sings,* Virgin, 1989.
Always Look on the Bright Side of Life (single), Virgin, 1991.

WORK IN PROGRESS: Screenplays.

SIDELIGHTS: Eric Idle is one of six members of Monty Python, a group of British comedians whose absurd humor has earned them a large following in Europe and North America. The group first appeared together in 1969 in the television series *Monty Python's Flying Circus,* which regularly featured such offbeat skits as "Hell's Grannies," in which Idle and cohorts play obscene and rowdy old women, and "The Upper Class Twit of the Year," in which aristocratic morons compete on an obstacle course. Among Idle's most memorable roles on the show are leering rogues, obsequious television hosts, and fussy old women. Idle has also undertaken a number of successful solo projects in writing and acting.

Many of the Python troupe's most renowned skits from the *Flying Circus*'s first two seasons, including "Hell's Grannies" and the twit contest, have been collected in the film *And Now for Something Completely Different.* This work contains such celebrated Python material as "Dead Parrot," in which a pet store proprietor and a customer debate the state of a recently purchased parrot, and "The Lumberjack Song," which begins with a lumberjack boastfully singing the virtues of manly work but ends with him confessing to transvestism. Blaine Allen, reviewing the film in *Take One,* calls it "one of the most hilarious and original movies to come along in a while."

As *Monty Python's Flying Circus* became increasingly popular, the Pythons began recording and publishing some of their material. Idle has edited many of the Python books, including *Monty Python's Big Red Book* (which has a blue cover) and *The Brand New Monty Python Bok,* incorporating new and old material with graphics and stills from the series and films. The results have provided Python fans with hard copy of their favorite sketches while giving the Pythons themselves enough additional revenue to work independently.

Their first independent venture was the 1975 movie *Monty Python and the Holy Grail,* which follows the legendary King Arthur and his knights on their quest to find the sacred cup of Christ. Idle is particularly memorable as Sir Robin the Not-So-Brave, who wets his armor at the first sign of danger and is accompanied by a troupe of minstrels who sing odes to his cowardice. "The whole film, which is often recklessly funny and sometimes a matter of comic genius, is a triumph of errancy and muddle," *New Yorker* critic Penelope Gilliatt remarks. "Its mind strays like an eye, and it thrives on following false trails. The Monty Python people have won a peculiar right to be funny even when they make a mess of things, because their style accepts floundering as a condition of life." While "there are the usual sillies—phrases repeated endlessly, nonsense syllables, and sight gags plentiful enough to warm the cockles of a hitter's heart," Richard Goldstein similarly comments in the *Village Voice,* there is also "a great deal of gratuitous cruelty, much of it occasioned by the presence of poverty and plague. The film's anger at these occurrences adds dimension to its anarchy, and makes it matter more than the tv show."

After the last season of *Flying Circus* in 1974, Idle persuaded the BBC to air his program *Rutland Weekend Television,* a parody of a small independent television station. The show only ran for two seasons, but provided the idea for the "Rutles," a takeoff of the Beatles. With the assistance of Neil Innes, a regular contributor of music to Python projects, Idle constructed a thorough "re-creation" of a pop music group's trials and triumphs. After the group appeared with Idle on an episode of *Saturday Night Live* in 1977, NBC offered Idle the chance to make a Rutles television movie. *All You Need Is Cash* featured cameos by such recording stars as Mick Jagger, Paul Simon, and even former Beatle George Harrison. "The growth of the ersatz quartet's career and ultimate breakup is followed in a take-off of that you-are-actually-making-history-this-very-moment approach to documentary reporting," *Village Voice* writers Howard Smith and Leslie Harlib state. The reviewers also find that the program has a "sneaky power" to its satire and praise in particular its "fifteen slyly brilliant parody songs of well-known Beatles tunes."

Idle rejoined the Pythons to film *Monty Python's Life of Brian,* a satire along biblical lines. The title character is a poor fellow who is mistaken for the messiah and spends his life frantically trying to evade his "followers." Notable among the Monty Python members—each of whom portrays numerous characters in the film—is Idle as a nonchalant crucifixion victim who jokes with his executioners and leads his fellow convicts in a sing-along from the cross, "Always Look on the Bright Side of Life." The film, with its irreverent portrayal of religion and its followers, drew protesters in many places. But "Jesus isn't singled out for ridicule," Gene Siskel of the *Chicago Tribune* observes, explaining that *Life of Brian* "is simply the Python response to such pompous pictures as 'King of Kings.' " The critic adds that "the protests of religious groups against the film, however well-intentioned, are simply missing the point of the picture." Many people agreed, for the film proved a success at the box office. And Barry Took, in a review for *Punch,* described *Life of Brian* as "a film to be cherished."

After appearing in Chapman's film *Yellowbeard,* in 1983 Idle and the rest of the Pythons completed another celebrated film, *Monty Python's The Meaning of Life.* There were problems getting the script together, for the group had grown unaccustomed to writing in collaboration. Nevertheless, the difficulties helped to produce a stronger film. As Idle pointed out to George Perry in *The Life of Python,* the group's self-criticism was essential: "I think it's the important thing—we do all keep a strong critical eye on what everyone else is doing. It's healthy, and if you're reading scripts out to everyone and something doesn't work, it's better to get that sort of criticism while you're still making the film than when it is out—at least you have a chance to make it better."

Monty Python's The Meaning of Life, which was honored at the Cannes Film Festival, is comprised of sketches on topics such as birth, sex, and death. As in the previous films, members of the troupe played several characters, with Idle most striking as he emerges, clad in pink long-tailed tuxedo, from a refrigerator to disrupt a "live" organ transplant by serenading the unwilling donor with facts about the universe. Siskel describes the film as "fresh and original and delightfully offensive," while *Newsweek* reviewer Katrine Ames calls it "the best movie to date from England's satirical sextet." The critic further praises the group's humor as "never . . . more incisive—they've become savagely hilarious observers of the human condition." And *Time* writer Richard Schickel believes that *The Meaning of Life* overcomes any minor flaws: "In their assaults on conventional morality, [the Pythons] generate a ferocious and near Swiftian moral gravity of their own," the critic concludes. "It is this quality that distinguishes their humor from the competition, rescues it from its own excesses and makes braving it an exhilarating experience."

Idle undertook solo writing projects as well. *Hello Sailor* (1974) was his first novel. Frank Pike for the *Times Literary Supplement* described the novel "as 'rude' and 'silly' as the [Monty Python] detractors would expect." The novel involves a large amount of sexual humor. In 1976, Idle wrote *The Rutland Dirty Weekend Book.* D. A. N. Jones for the *Listener* felt that the book was not as funny as it intended to be. Jones related that: "*The Rutland Dirty Weekend Book* is based on the television show and has many panto-dame jokes about sex—that is, 'sexy' sexlessness." In 1996, Idle offered a children's work with *The Quite Remarkable Adventures of the Owl and the Pussycat.* A critic for *Kirkus Reviews* reviewing Idle's adaptation of *The Quite Remarkable Adventures of the Owl and the Pussycat* (1996) wrote: "When a Monty Python alum offers a novelization of an Edward Lear poem, it's practically guaranteed to be a Silly Walk." The book is a mixture of the familiar and the novel. Idle's Monty Python antics infiltrate the classic story in a much more subdued form appropriate for children. The reviewer continued: "Illustrated with a mix of Lear's sketches and new pen-and-ink drawings in the same spirit, this delivers the kind of funny business for which Idle is known, and will probably appease adult Python fans who wish to pass on a gentler form of the lunacy to their children."

In another medium, an *Amusement Business* article regarding Idle's "3-D Pirates Stranded at Sea World" reveals what Sea World and Renaissance Entertainment and Creative Services Production stated about the fifteen-minute film written by and featuring Idle and Leslie Nielsen. Eric Miles, corporate manager of production for Busch Entertainment Company and executive producer of the film said, "This film is instant magic. The energy between Eric Idle and Leslie Nielsen is amazing." The article reports that Jim Timon of Renaissance Entertainment and Creative Services Production and the executive heading the production of this film concurs with Miles: "Unlike many 3-D films, this one has a progressive plot and is not used strictly to 'wow' viewers with effects."

The Monty Python comedy troupe created and released the *Monty Python and the Quest for the Holy Grail* CD-ROM game (1996). Stanley Young for *Publishers Weekly* records Idle's involvement in the project "as the person 'responsible to make sure it's Pythonic,' Idle says he especially enjoyed reworking *Grail,* one of his favorite movies, into a CD-ROM replete with goofy games like Spank the Virgin. It's very cheeky, very fresh, silly and juvenile—in an endearing way."

Pursuing his solo work again, Idle wrote the novel *The Road to Mars* (1999). Gary Kamiya for the *New York Times* expresses that Idle's adept physical comedy makes an inadequate comic novel, but recognizes the more favorable aspects in the book, "Idle handles plot competently, even displaying some genuine narrative quirkiness." For Kamiya, the basic problem of *The Road to Mars* is the fact that an actor wrote the book, rather than a writer: "His terse prose lacks the robust, cunning, luxurious stupidity that comedy needs." A reviewer for *Publishers Weekly* felt the writing lacked as well: "The narrative meanders for long stretches with scene after scene whose only point is to set up a weak joke—the sort of thing that works so well as TV farce but when passed off as a novel, is tedious." Devon

Thomas for *Library Journal,* however, disagrees with both Kamiya and the critic for *Publishers Weekly:* "Idle . . . has written an engaging and amusing work of speculative fiction with fully developed characters, a taut plot, and a thoughtful and entertaining analysis of humor's part in human development. A joy to read; highly recommended."

Idle also busied himself with acting and developing scripts. He won an ACE Cable Award for writing and directing "The Frog Prince" for Showtime's *Faerie Tale Theatre;* he later created the short-lived NBC series *Nearly Departed* and appeared as Passepartout in the television mini-series *Around the World in Eighty Days.* In film, he has co-starred in the comedy *Nuns on the Run* and had a supporting role as Berthold, the fastest man alive, in Gilliam's *The Adventures of Baron Munchausen.* He also played a role on the American sitcom *Suddenly Susan* and performed voiceover work for animated films, including *Quest for Camelot* and *South Park: Bigger, Longer, and Uncut.*

Despite his solo success, Idle looks back fondly as his days as a Python. Expressing amazement at the enduring popularity of the group, he noted for *People:* "It's astounding. Here we are twenty years on, and people are still watching the same silly stuff. They're fascinated by the program."

BIOGRAPHICAL/CRITICAL SOURCES:

BOOKS

Authors and Artists for Young Adults, Volume 7, Gale, 1991.

Contemporary Literary Criticism, Volume 21, Gale, 1982.

Hewison, Robert, *Monty Python: The Case Against,* Methuen, 1981.

Hewison, Robert, *Footlights!,* Methuen, 1983.

Johnson, Kim Howard, *The First 200 Years of Monty Python,* St. Martin's, 1989.

Perry, George, *The Life of Python,* Pavilion, 1983.

Thompson, John O., editor, *Monty Python: Complete and Utter Theory of the Grotesque,* University of Illinois Press, 1982.

Wilmut, Roger, *From Fringe to Flying Circus,* Methuen, 1980.

PERIODICALS

Amusement Business, March 17, 1997, Tim O'Brien, "Eric Idle's 3-D Pirates Stranded at Sea World," p. 26.

Chicago Tribune, September 21, 1979; April 1, 1983.

Entertainment Weekly, September 6, 1996, Erin Richter, review of *Missing Pieces,* p. 84.

Library Journal, August, 1999, Devon Thomas, review of *The Road to Mars,* p. 139.

Listener, December 23, 1976.

Nation, March 27, 1989, Stuart Klawans, review of *The Adventures of Baron Munchausen,* p. 427.

New Republic, May 24, 1975; April 16, 1990, Stanley Kauffmann, review of *Nuns on the Run,* p. 27; June 7, 1993, Stanley Kauffmann, review of *Splitting Heirs,* p. 27.

Newsweek, April 4, 1983.

New Yorker, May 5, 1975; May 12, 1975; March 31, 1983.

New York Times, April 16, 1976; April 18, 1976.

People, August 2, 1982; July 11, 1983, review of *Yellowbeard,* p. 10; April 17, 1989, John Stark, review of *Around the World in Eighty Days,* p. 13; April 24, 1989, Susan Schindehette, "Puzzling out His Post-Python Life Leaves Eric Idle with Hands Full," p. 59; February 11, 1991, Ralph Novak, review of *Too Much Sun,* p.12; August 10, 1992, Ralph Novak, review of *Mom and Dad Save the World,* p. 20; July 1, 1996, Stanley Young, "Older and Wiseacre," p. 35.

Publishers Weekly, July 19, 1999, review of *The Road to Mars,* p. 188.

Punch, October 12, 1977; November 29, 1978.

Stereo Review, October, 1975; October, 1976; January, 1981.

Take One, May-June, 1971.

Time, September 17, 1979; March 28, 1983; June 12, 1995, Richard Corliss, review of *Casper,* p. 68.

Times Literary Supplement, March 21, 1975.

Variety, October 6, 1997, Deborah Young, review of *An Alan Smithee Film—Burn, Hollywood, Burn,* p. 54; November 3, 1997, Todd McCarthy, review of *The Wind in the Willows,* p. 99; May 11, 1998, Joe Leydon, review of *Quest for Camelot,* p. 58.

Village Voice, May 5, 1975; March 20, 1978.

Washington Post, April 4, 1983.

OTHER

Welcome to PythOnline!, http://www.pythonline.com/ (June 6, 2000).*

J

JAKLE, John A(llais) 1939-

PERSONAL: Born May 16, 1939, in Terre Haute, IN; son of John D. and Irene (Allais) Jakle; married Cynthia Powell (a librarian), 1958; children: Stephanie Jakle Movahedi-Lankarani, Barbara. *Education:* Western Michigan University, B.B.A., 1961; Southern Illinois University, M.A., 1963; Indiana University, Ph.D., 1967.

ADDRESSES: Home—405 West Michigan, Urbana, IL 61801. *Office*—Department of Geography, 220 Davenport Hall, University of Illinois, Urbana, IL 61801.

CAREER: University of Maine, Orono, assistant professor of geography, 1965-66; Western Michigan University, Kalamazoo, instructor in geography, 1966-67; University of Illinois, Urbana, assistant professor, 1967-70, associate professor, 1970-82, professor of geography, 1982—.

MEMBER: Association of American Geographers, American Historical Association, Pioneer America Society, National Trust for Historic Preservation.

WRITINGS:

(With Stanley Brunn and Curtis Roseman) *Human Spatial Behavior: A Social Geography,* Wadsworth, 1976, reprinted, Waveland (Prospect Heights, IL), 1985.

Images of the Ohio Valley: An Historical Geography of Travel, 1740-1860, Oxford University Press (New York City), 1977.

The American Small Town: Twentieth-Century Place Images, Archon Books (Hamden, CT), 1981.

The Tourist: Travel in Twentieth-Century America, University of Nebraska Press, 1985.

The Visual Elements of Landscape, University of Massachusetts Press (Amherst), 1987.

(With Robert Bastian and Douglas Meyer) *Common Houses in America's Small Towns: The Atlantic Seaboard to the Mississippi Valley,* University of Georgia Press (Athens), 1989.

(With David Wilson) *Derelict Landscapes: The Wasting of America's Built Environment,* Rowman & Littlefield (Savage, MD), 1992.

(With Keith A. Sculle) *The Gas Station in America,* Johns Hopkins University Press (Baltimore, MD), 1994.

(With Sculle and Jefferson Rogers) *The Motel in America,* Johns Hopkins University Press, 1996.

(With Sculle) *Fast Food: Roadside Restaurants in the Automobile Age,* Johns Hopkins University Press, 1999.

CONTRIBUTOR

Ralph E. Ehrenberg, editor, *Pattern and Process: Research in Historical Geography,* Howard University Press (Washington, DC), 1975.

Lachlan F. Blair and John A. Quinn, editors, *Historic Preservation: Setting, Legislation, and Techniques,* University of Illinois (Urbana), 1977.

Ruth E. Knack, editor, *Preservation Illinois: A Guide to State and Local Resources,* Illinois Department of Conservation (Springfield, IL), 1977.

Carl Patton and Barry Checkoway, editors, *The Metropolitan Midwest,* University of Illinois Press (Urbana), 1985.

Martin S. Kenzer, editor, *On Becoming a Professional Geographer,* C. E. Merrill (Columbus, OH), 1989.

Michael Conzen, editor, *The Making of the American Landscape,* Unwin Hyman (Boston, MA), 1990.

Leo Zonn, editor, *Place Images in the Media,* Rowman & Littlefield, 1991.

Robert L. Reid, editor, *Always a River,* Indiana University Press (Bloomington), 1991.

David Wilson and James O. Huff, editors, *Marginalized Places and Populations: A Structuralist Agenda,* Praeger (Westport, CT), 1994.

Karl Raitz, editor, *A Guide to the National Road,* Johns Hopkins University Press, 1996.

Contributor to history and geography journals, including *Journal of Geography, Journal of Cultural Geography, Environmental Review, Pioneer America Society Proceedings, Annals of Tourism Research, Agricultural History,* and *American Historical Review.* Editor, Volume 7 of *Proceedings of the Association of American Geographers* (Washington, DC), 1975.

SIDELIGHTS: John A. Jakle is a landscape historian whose focus rests on America's evolving built environments. Whether studying the fast food industry, the gas station, or the advent of motels, he is concerned with the functional and aesthetic aspects of traveler-based commodities. An interest in travel and tourism has sparked much of Jakle's scholarly work, as he examines America's changing landscapes in the twentieth century. According to Tom Hanchett in the *Business History Review,* Jakle's books meld "business history with architectural history, cultural geography, and social history."

Jakle and co-author Keith A. Sculle have completed three books about travel-based architecture: *The Gas Station in America, The Motel in America,* and *Fast Food: Roadside Restaurants in the Automobile Age.* As the titles suggest, these works all contribute to scholarship on changes to the American landscape (and the American mindset) that have originated or blossomed since the advent of pervasive automobile travel. In a *New York Times Book Review* piece on *The Gas Station in America,* Thomas Hine observed: "Mr. Jakle and Mr. Sculle argue . . . that the gas station and the roadside are entitled to serious study, and that theirs is an attempt to go beyond the mere description that has characterized the field thus far. *The Gas Station in America* does advance that study. It provides important information and insights for those who will explain more fully the American landscape of consumption." In the *Journal of Travel Research,* Jonathan N. Goodrich called *The Motel in America* "a well-written and informative book about the origins, evolution, geographical distribution, changing social meanings, architecture designs, and marketing of motels." The critic added that the book "is fun to read. It also indirectly offers lessons in geography, history, business acumen, and sociology."

Jakle's *Fast Food* is a chronicle of the evolution of roadside restaurants that ties together "a nation's passion for eating with its love of the automobile," to quote Bruce Heydt in *American History. New York Times Book Review* correspondent Karal Ann Marling deemed *Fast Food* a "meticulously detailed study of the origins and growth of fast-food chains in the 20th century." The critic further noted that *Fast Food* "has enough incident, comedy and tragedy for any two novels. . . . To be perfectly honest, we have all had bad pie out there on the blue highways of nostalgia, along with regional specialties that challenge the recuperative powers of the average digestive tract. But enough nostalgia. Jakle and Sculle offer a refreshing draft of realism."

Jakle once told *CA:* "I bring the orientations of the geographer and the historian to bear on the concept of place. My interest in small towns as a distinctive part of the American experience, and my interest in tourism and the common landscapes created to serve tourists will lead, I hope, to the fuller comprehension of how and why people create and use places as setting for particular kinds of behavior.

"In recent decades, academic geographers have turned away from the concept of place as an integrating concept. They have neglected whole categories of place (including small towns) and have ignored the impulse to travel as a significant research subject. My work seeks to remedy this neglect. As I see it, the discipline of geography was originally rooted in a healthy concern for exploring places. Today's geographical exploration should treat common behaviors in common places. Place exploration should be the geographer's objective."

BIOGRAPHICAL/CRITICAL SOURCES:

PERIODICALS

American Historical Review, June, 1996, p. 937.

American History, February, 2000, Bruce Heydt, review of *Fast Food,* p. 67.

American Scholar, summer, 1986, p. 429.

Business History Review, autumn, 1997, Tom Hanchett, review of *The Motel in America,* p. 488.

Entertainment Weekly, January 14, 2000, Nikki Amdur, review of *Fast Food,* p. 70.

Journal of American History, December, 1985, p. 717.

Journal of Travel Research, May, 1999, Jonathan N. Goodrich, review of *The Motel in America,* p. 411.

Journal of Urban History, November, 1998, Joseph C. Bigott, review of *The Gas Station in America,* p. 103.
New York Times Book Review, October 30, 1994, Thomas Hine, "University Presses; Gasoline Dreams," p. 36; January 9, 2000, Karal Ann Marling, "Sameness Is Glorious," p. 34.
Pacific Historical Review, February, 1998, Marguerite S. Shaffer, review of *The Motel in America,* p. 141.

* * *

JAMIE, Kathleen 1962-

PERSONAL: Born May 13, 1962, in Renfrewshire, Scotland. *Education:* Attended University of Edinburgh.

ADDRESSES: *Home*—Newburgh-on-Tay, Fife, Scotland.

CAREER: Poet. Writer-in-residence at Midlothian District Libraries.

AWARDS, HONORS: Gregory Award, 1981; Scottish Arts Council, Book Award, 1982, for *Black Spiders,* grant, 1985, Book Award, 1988, for *The Way We Live.*

WRITINGS:

Black Spiders (poems), Salamander (Edinburgh), 1982.
(With Andrew Greig) *A Flame in Your Heart* (poems), Bloodaxe (Newcastle Upon Tyne), 1986.
The Way We Live (poems), Bloodaxe, 1987.
The Golden Peak: Travels in Northern Pakistan, Virago (London), 1992.
The Queen of Sheba (poems), Bloodaxe, 1994.
Jizzen (poems), Picador (London), 1999.

Also author of radio dramas. Contributor of articles and reviews to periodicals, including *Scotsman, New Edinburgh Review,* and *Lines Review.*

SIDELIGHTS: Kathleen Jamie has published many poetry collections, among them 1994's *The Queen of Sheba* and 1999's *Jizzen.* According to Bill Greenwell's *New Statesman* review of the 1994 volume, Jamie has created remarkably "startling, special poems." "The title poem [of *The Queen of Sheba*]—the first printed, regrettably, because it would have made a brilliant climax—confronts the erotic biblical hussy with a suspicious Presbyterian audience," commented Greenwell, who added: "This wonderful piece of glee is matched by 'School Reunion,' a poem full of disbelieving energy as present and past collide." Although Greenwell remarked that Jamie at times appears to lose her "inspirations" in her poetry, resulting in occasional poems that he called "patchy," the critic maintained: "I'd eat the Pope and his hat for the poems I have mentioned, and dose myself happily on her contagious energy."

In a *Times Literary Supplement* assessment of Jamie's "exhilarating new collection"—*Jizzen,* Patrick Crotty analyzed: "Jamie's bringing the materials of one room of life to bear on the goings on of another is fuelled by a deep, strikingly unpostmodern faith in the possibility of arriving at a unitary apprehension of experience through engineering unfamiliar relationships between its disparate parts." Crotty continued: "[Jamie's] poems are unabashedly democratic in their directness of address and in their urge to give witness to the lives of ordinary people." Crotty's concluding remarks positively attached the descriptors "energy," "earnestness and good humour," and "panache" to Jamie's work in *Jizzen.* Jamie also penned the poetry collections *Black Spiders* (1982), *A Flame in Your Heart* (1986; with Andrew Greig), and *The Way We Live* (1987).

BIOGRAPHICAL/CRITICAL SOURCES:

BOOKS

Contemporary Poets, sixth edition, St. James Press, 1996.
Contemporary Women Poets, St. James Press, 1999.

PERIODICALS

New Statesman, January 29, 1988, Robert Sheppard, review of *The Way We Live,* p. 32; May 13, 1994, Bill Greenwell, review of *The Queen of Sheba,* p. 38.
Times Literary Supplement, November 19, 1999, Patrick Crotty, review of *Jizzen.*
Yomiuri Shimbun/Daily Yomiuri, March 20, 2000.*

* * *

JHABVALA, Ruth Prawer 1927-

PERSONAL: Born May 7, 1927, in Cologne, Germany; immigrated to England, 1939; naturalized British citizen, 1948; naturalized U.S. citizen, 1986; daughter of

Marcus (owner of a clothing business) and Eleonora (Cohn) Prawer; married Cyrus S. H. Jhabvala (an architect), 1951; children: Renana, Ava, Firoza. *Education:* Queen Mary College, London, M.A., 1951.

ADDRESSES: Home and Office—400 East 52nd St., New York, NY 10022. *Agent*—Harriet Wasserman, 137 East 36th St., New York, NY 10016.

CAREER: Fulltime writer, 1951—. Producer of documentary film *Courtesans of Bombay,* New Yorker, 1982.

MEMBER: Royal Society of Literature (fellow), Authors Guild.

AWARDS, HONORS: Booker McConnell Prize for Fiction, England's Book Trust, 1975, for *Heat and Dust;* Guggenheim fellow, 1976; Neil Gunn International fellow, 1979; British Academy Award, best screenplay, British Academy of Film and Television Arts, 1983, for *Heat and Dust;* Literary Lion award, New York Public Library, 1983; MacArthur Foundation fellow, 1984-89; Writers Guild of America Award, best adapted screenplay, 1986, and British Academy Award nomination, best adapted screenplay, and Academy Award, best screenplay adaption, both 1987, all for *A Room with a View;* New York Film Critics Award, best screenplay, 1990, for *Mr. and Mrs. Bridge;* Academy Award, best screenplay adaption, British Academy Award nomination, best adapted screenplay, Writers Guild of America Award nomination for best screenplay based on material previously produced or published, and Golden Globe Award nomination, best screenplay—motion picture, all 1993, all for *Howards End;* Academy Award nomination, best writing—screenplay based on material from another medium, British Academy Award nomination, best adapted screenplay, Writers Guild of America Award nomination, best screenplay based on material previously produced or published, and Golden Globe Award nomination, best screenplay—motion picture, all 1994, all for *The Remains of the Day;* Laurel Award for Screen Writing Achievement, Writers Guild of America, 1994; D.Litt. and L.H.D., London University.

WRITINGS:

FICTION

To Whom She Will, Allen & Unwin (London), 1955, published as *Amrita,* Norton (New York City), 1956.
The Nature of Passion, Allen & Unwin, 1956.
Esmond in India, Allen & Unwin, 1957.
The Householder (also see below), Norton, 1960.
Get Ready for Battle, J. Murray (London), 1962.
Like Birds, Like Fishes and Other Stories, J. Murray, 1963.
A Backward Place, Norton, 1965.
A Stronger Climate: Nine Stories, J. Murray, 1968.
An Experience of India (stories), J. Murray, 1971.
A New Dominion, J. Murray, 1972, published as *Travelers,* Harper (New York City), 1973.
Heat and Dust (also see below), J. Murray, 1975.
How I Became a Holy Mother and Other Stories, J. Murray, 1975.
In Search of Love and Beauty, Morrow, 1983.
Out of India: Selected Stories, Morrow, 1986.
Three Continents, Morrow, 1987.
Poet and Dancer, Doubleday (New York City), 1993.
Shards of Memory, Doubleday, 1995.
East into Upper East: Plain Tales from New York and New Delhi, Counterpoint Press, 1998.

Contributor of short stories to periodicals, including *New Yorker, Encounter, Kenyon Review, Yale Review,* and *New Statesman.* Work represented in anthologies, including *Penguin Modern Stories 2,* Penguin, 1972.

SCREENPLAYS

The Householder (based on her novel), Royal, 1963.
(With James Ivory) *Shakespeare Wallah* (produced by Merchant-Ivory Productions, 1966), Grove, 1973.
(With Ivory) *The Guru,* Twentieth Century-Fox, 1968.
(With Ivory) *Bombay Talkie,* Merchant-Ivory Productions, 1970.
Autobiography of a Princess, Cinema V, 1975, published in *Autobiography of a Princess: Also Being the Adventures of an American Film Director in the Land of the Maharajas,* Harper, 1975.
Roseland, Merchant-Ivory Productions, 1977.
Hullabaloo over Georgie and Bonnie's Pictures, Contemporary, 1978.
(With Ivory) *The Europeans* (based on the novel by Henry James), Levitt-Pickman, 1979.
Jane Austen in Manhattan, Contemporary, 1980.
(With Ivory) *Quartet* (based on the novel by Jean Rhys), Lyric International/New World, 1981.
Heat and Dust (based on her novel), Merchant-Ivory Productions, 1983.
The Bostonians (based on the novel by James), Merchant-Ivory Productions, 1984.
The Courtesans of Bombay, Channel 4, England/New Yorker Films, 1985.
A Room with a View (based on the novel by E. M. Forster), Merchant-Ivory Productions, 1986.

(With John Schlesinger) *Madame Sousatzka* (based on the novel by Bernice Rubens), Universal, 1988.

Mr. and Mrs. Bridge (based on the novels *Mrs. Bridge* and *Mr. Bridge* by Evan S. O'Connell), Miramax, 1990.

Howards End (based on the novel by Forster), Merchant-Ivory Productions, 1992.

The Remains of the Day (based on the novel by Kazuo Ishiguro), Merchant-Ivory Productions, 1993.

Jefferson in Paris (an original screenplay), Merchant-Ivory Productions, 1995.

Surviving Picasso, Merchant-Ivory Productions, 1997.

(With James Ivory) *A Soldier's Daughter Never Cries* (based on the novel by Kaylie Jones), October Films, 1998.

The Golden Bowl (based on the novel by Henry James), Miramax, 2000.

OTHER

A Call from the East (play), produced in New York at the Manhattan Theatre Club, 1981.

SIDELIGHTS: Although Ruth Prawer Jhabvala has long been celebrated in Europe and India for her quality fiction and screenplays, it was not until she captured an Academy Award for her screenplay adaptation of E. M. Forster's *A Room with a View* that she began winning widespread attention in the United States for her work. As a German-born British citizen who lived in India for over twenty years, and in New York for over a decade, Jhabvala brings a unique perspective to her novels and stories of East-West conflict. "With a cool, ironic eye and a feeling for social nuance," asserts Bernard Weinraub in a *New York Times Magazine* article, Jhabvala "[has] developed a series of themes—families battered by change in present-day India, the timeless European fascination with the subcontinent—that were probably both incomprehensible and inconsequential to readers who were not intrigued with India in the first place. And yet," continues the critic, "as Mrs. Jhabvala's work darkened and turned more melancholy, as her detachment grew chilling in her later work, critics began to notice that the writer's India had become as universal as Faulkner's Yoknapatawpha and Chekhov's czarist Russia." "Like Jane Austen," notes *Saturday Review* contributor Katha Pollitt, Jhabvala "treats satirically and intimately a world in which conventions are precisely defined and widely accepted, even by those who are most harmed by them."

Jhabvala herself has led a rather unconventional life. She and her family narrowly escaped the Nazi persecution of the Jews, fleeing to relative safety in England in 1939. All her father's relatives died in the Holocaust. Ten years after the family's flight into exile she met the man who became her husband, the architect Cyrus S. H. Jhabvala. After their marriage, the couple left Europe to live in newly independent India. "I was twenty-four," Jhabvala stated in an interview with David Streitfeld in the *Washington Post Book World,* "and just at the age when one really starts to write seriously. There was so much subject matter for me. I hardly finished a book before I started a new one. I was so full of energy, I immediately wrote as if I were an Indian, from inside." Yet, she added, she wasn't truly an Indian writer. "I wasn't even really anything when I was in India, because I was a foreigner there. People are always asking where my roots are, and I say I don't have any."

Indeed, since the appearance of her first work in 1955, *Amrita* (published in England as *To Whom She Will*), Jhabvala has frequently been compared to English writers like Jane Austen, due to her cutting portrayals of the foibles of the Indian middle-class. In *Amrita,* comments Nancy Wilson Ross in the *New York Herald Tribune Book Review,* Jhabvala "has written a fresh and witty novel about modern India. It is not necessary to know anything about the customs and habits of . . . New Delhi—the setting of Mrs. Jhabvala's lively comedy of manners—to enjoy her ironic social commentary." And in a *Times Literary Supplement* review of *A Backward Place,* one critic maintains that while Jhabvala "has not the sustained brilliance that Jane Austen often rises to . . . all the same her many excellent qualities are nearly all Austenish ones, and they make her a most interesting and satisfactory writer." "At least three British reviewers have compared her to Jane Austen," observes J. F. Muehl in his *Saturday Review* account of Jhabvala's debut novel, "and the comparison is not only just; it is inevitable."

Although Jhabvala had been securing a name for herself as one of the foremost modern writers about India after the publication of *Heat and Dust,* she was finding it difficult both to remain in and write about her adopted country. Critics began observing an increasing amount of ambivalence toward India in Jhabvala's writing, a change evident in her retrospective collection of stories, *Out of India. The New York Times*'s Michiko Kakutani, for example, comments that "bit by bit, . . . the stories in *Out of India* darken, grow denser and more ambiguous. In choosing narrative strategies that are increasingly ambitious," explains the reviewer, "Mrs. Jhabvala gradually moves beyond the tidy formulations of the comedy of manners, and a strain of melancholy also begins to creep into her writing."

Village Voice contributor Vivian Gornick similarly sees a sense of "oppressiveness" in Jhabvala's writing, and speculates that "Jhabvala is driven to separate herself from India." The critic believes that this need undermines the author's work: "That drive deprives her of empathy and, inevitably, it deprives her characters of full humanness." In contrast, Paul Gray claims in his *Time* review that the stories in *Out of India* "do not demystify India; they pay the place tributes of empathy and grace." "Reading [these stories] is like watching a scene through an exceptionally clear telescope," states Rumer Godden in the *New York Times Book Review.* This distance, however, "does not take away from the stories sureness of touch," Godden continues. "They have a beginning, middle and end, but fused so subtly we drift into them—and are immediately at home—and drift out again."

Some of Jhabvala's more recent works, while eschewing the familiar Indian setting, still explore some of her usual themes, such as the search for spiritual fulfillment. *Three Continents,* for example, relates the story of nineteen-year-old twins Michael and Harriet Wishwell, heirs to a large fortune who are drawn to the promises of a trio of supposed spiritual philosophers. The twins become obsessed with the Rawul, his consort the Rani, and their "adopted son" Crishi, and turn over control of their lives and fortune to the swindlers. "In its geographical scope, its large and far-flung cast and its relentless scrutiny of both sexual and intellectual thralldom," maintains Laura Shapiro in *Newsweek, Three Continents* "is Jhabvala's most ambitious and impressive work." *Los Angeles Times* reviewer Elaine Kendall similarly calls the novel "perhaps [Jhabvala's] most ambitious work," remarking that it "not only confronts these issues [from her previous work] directly but in a more contemporary context."

Poet and Dancer, like *Three Continents,* is a non-Indian novel; it is, in fact, set in New York. Jhabvala told Streitfeld that the novel was inspired by the story of a double suicide, two sisters who killed themselves without any perceptible reason. "I was wondering how this could have happened—it was a very dark deed, a dark relationship," she stated. The relationship as Jhabvala depicts it is between two cousins, Angel and Lara. Angel (the poet) has lived her entire life in New York City, while Lara (the dancer) has travelled all over the world. "As the reader might expect," states Claire Messud in the *Times Literary Supplement,* "Angel, to whom Lara appears an exotic and precious butterfly, devotes herself adoringly to her cousin; but Lara proves dangerous and ultimately mad, and the result of their closeness is their mutual destruction." Some critics express puzzlement over Angel's fascination with Lara, who, they feel, is depicted very unsympathetically. A critic writing for *Rapport,* calls their association a "chilling relationship between hunter and prey where the boundary between love and obsession is crossed so many times it is blurred beyond recognition." "There's something lacking in this small, well-made novel," declares *New Statesman and Society* reviewer Wendy Brandmark, "some moral centre, some emotional touchstone. . . . We do not know why we should care about these characters and their destructive search for the perfect life, the perfect art, the perfect love."

"In her twelfth novel . . . Jhabvala once again addresses the themes of family and history through the premise of a set of old papers," writes Molly E. Rauch in the *Nation.* The novel, *Shards of Memory,* follows successive generations of a family who follow the charismatic spiritual guru known only as "the Master." Weaving multiple memories in the narrative, according to *Booklist* critic Ilene Cooper, is what makes the novel "intensely personal." But, Cooper argues, the "beguiling" structure of the novel is not the only positive aspect of the novel: "At the forefront are the characters, and here Jhabvala has outdone herself." Critics laud Jhabvala's narrative skill in handling the various ways in which each character's life was affected or touched by the Master. "Jhabvala handles this highly sophisticated, complicated story with sinuous skill," writes a *Publishers Weekly* critic.

Jhabvala followed *Shards of Memory* with a collection of short fiction titled *East into Upper East: Plain Tales from New York and New Delhi.* The stories, some of which were originally published in the *New Yorker,* were written over the span of twenty years. In these stories, writes a *Publishers Weekly* reviewer, Jhabvala "depicts characters struggling to reconcile dependency and accommodation in their relationships." A *Library Journal* critic lauds Jhabvala's "expert observation and unique insight." Deborah Mason, in the *New York Times Book Review,* claims that the collection "reaffirms [Jhabvala] as a spell-binding urban fabulist."

While Jhabvala has been a consistent force on the literary scene, she is also a member of the longest producer-director-writer partnership in film history. Along with Ismail Merchant and James Ivory, Jhabvala has helped create numerous movies that, while not hits at the box office, have been praised by critics for their consistent literary quality. Their association dates back to 1963, when Ivory and Merchant telephoned the author, then living in India, and asked her to write a screenplay from her fourth novel *The Householder.* "That gave me the opportunity I otherwise would never have had," Jhabvala tells Streitfeld. "I was so lucky. Merchant and Ivory are like a shield for me. I don't have to bother with the things that are so gruesome for other screenwriters, like story conferences."

Although the author was initially reluctant to attempt screenplays, critic Yasmine Gooneratne thinks that the dramatic qualities necessary for films have always been present in Jhabvala's work. Writing in *World Literature Written in English,* Gooneratne states that the author's early novels have "the tight structure of stage plays, and even [contain] casts of characters. The process by which the comparative simplicities of satiric drama yield to the complexity of ironic fiction is hastened, it would appear, through her experience of working repeatedly within the narrow limits of a screenplay." The critic cites the film-like structure of *Heat and Dust* as an example, and adds that "despite the fact that Mrs. Jhabvala's increasing technical skill as a writer of screenplays has helped her to devise ways and means to make the cinema screen yield workable equivalents for her established fictional techniques, it is probable that her artistry as a fiction-writer still outstrips her achievement as a writer for film. So rapid has her development been, however," Gooneratne continues, "that this is unlikely to be the case for very long." This prediction has proved accurate, for several recent Merchant-Ivory-Jhabvala productions have been popular as well as critical successes.

About *The Bostonians,* the 1984 adaptation of Henry James's novel, Vincent Canby of the *New York Times* remarks that "it's now apparent [that the trio has] enriched and refined their individual talents to the point where they have now made what must be one of their best films as well as one of the best adaptations of a major literary work ever to come onto the screen." The best—until Jhabvala and her collaborators produced the film that would earn the author her first Oscar nomination, 1986's *A Room with a View.* Director Ivory and screenwriter Jhabvala "have taken E. M. Forster's 1908 novel and preserved its wit, irony and brilliant observation of character," states Lawrence O'Toole in *Maclean's.* "And they never allow its theme—the importance of choosing passion over propriety—to escape their grasp." Calling the trio's film "an exceptionally faithful, ebullient screen equivalent to a literary work that lesser talents would embalm," Canby notes that "maybe more important than anything else [in the film] is the narrative tone." He explains that Ivory and Jhabvala "have somehow found a voice for the film not unlike that of Forster, who tells the story of *A Room with a View* with as much genuine concern as astonished amusement. That's quite an achievement." Audiences found the film entertaining as well, for *A Room with a View* became one of the most popular Merchant-Ivory-Jhabvala collaborations ever, setting house records at many theaters.

For their next film, *Mr. and Mrs. Bridge,* Jhabvala, Merchant, and Ivory chose a different author, but a similar theme—the foibles of the American, rather than the English, upper-middle class. But Jhabvala's version of Evan S. Connell's two novels "is not social satire as much as a melancholy, delicate and gently funny look at the ordinariness of American life," declares Richard A. Blake in *America.* "In her adaptation, Jhabvala has tried to balance highlights of the Bridges' lives with dailiness," Stanley Kauffmann states in the *New Republic,* "though inevitably there's less of the non-dramatic in the film than in the novels." The end result, Blake concludes, "is a charming, elegant and literate film, beautifully embellished by finely balanced, sensitive ensemble acting."

Yet "for all the respect [the trio's] films garnered," explains *Newsweek* contributor David Ansen, "there were always detractors who dismissed their works as enervated 'Masterpiece Theatre' gentility." The dichotomy is especially evident in the diversity of critical commentary that greeted the three's version of Forster's *Howards End*—the film that brought Jhabvala her second Oscar nomination. John Simon, writing in *National Review,* terms the movie "inept." Anne Billson states in her *New Statesman and Society* review of the film, "If *Howards End* is supposed to be an indictment of snobbery and greed, it fails, because it revels in the snobbish and greedy way of life." "The qualities of such illustrated English Lit are not cinematic, but are those of the Edwardian theme park," she continues. "This film should be bought up by the National Trust, though it doesn't need to be preserved. It has already been pickled in the formaldehyde of nostalgia." *New Yorker* contributor Terrence Rafferty calls the film well-done, but adds, "those of us who love Forster might miss the sense of strain, the awkward human beauty of his artistic failure."

In the opinion of *Commonweal* contributor Richard Alleva, Jhabvala, Merchant, and Ivory actually improved on author Kazuo Ishiguro's novel *The Remains of the Day* by making it into a film. Alleva points out that Ishiguro, by seeing his story about a butler whose sense of self-worth rests wholly on his usefulness to his employer only through the butler's eyes, makes the novel "predictable." "It's a stunt," Alleva says, "and you soon learn the mechanics of the stunt." But Jhabvala's "film adaptation is not a stunt, just a good movie," the reviewer continues, because it takes the story away from the butler-only point of view and presents the plot in a linear fashion. "The stoic poignancy of the title, *The Remains of the Day,*" he concludes, "is more fully earned by the movie than by the book." Simon enjoys the film as well, stating that "*The Remains of the Day* will long remain in your memory as a portrait of heroic futility, heartbreaking fatuity, and purblind doggedness, as they become the downfall of a society, an empire, and, worst of all, a single human soul."

Jhabvala's screenplay for Merchant-Ivory's *Surviving Picasso* was loosely based on Arianna Huffington's 1989 biography of the Spanish painter. The film follows the ten-year relationship between Picasso and Francoise Gilot, a young ingenue he met in Nazi-occupied Paris in 1943. Jhabvala's script is less concerned with the artistic muse behind Picasso's works than on the artist's love life and how it influenced his imagination. The film received mixed reviews. Bruce Williamson of *Playboy* found it "an elegant, uncompromising" look at a man who was "a cruel, self-serving womanizer." John Simon of the *National Review,* on the other hand, thought the film sacrificed Picasso's passion on the altar of middlebrow civility. Labeling Jhabvala and Ivory "two old routiners," Simon observed that they "have by now achieved a certain slickness and fluency, but without the spark of inspiration that makes the whole world kin."

In some ways, Jhabvala says, the two forms of writing—fiction and screenplays—enhance each other. "I certainly don't think I could write screenplays very well if I didn't, most of the time, work at creating characters and dialogue and situations of my own in my fiction," she tells Ross. "Then whatever I've accumulated of experience in that, I bring to the screenplays. And in writing novels you also get a certain feel for structure which you have to have in constructing a screenplay. But I also think the screenwriting has definitely influenced my fiction. For instance, I think you can see it in *Heat and Dust,* and in *In Search of Love and Beauty* in the way I've juggled scenes and time sequences around. That's something I learned in films."

While she has been compared to several classic writers, Jhabvala has achieved a prominent literary standing with her consistently excellent work, and critics no longer need comparisons to describe its quality. "How does one know when one is in the grip of art, of a literary power?" asks Rabinowitz in the *New York Times Book Review.* "One feels, amongst other things, the force of personality behind the cadence of each line, the sensibility behind the twist of the syllable. One feels the texture of the unspoken, the very accents of a writer's reticence." Jhabvala, maintains the critic, "seems to come naturally by a good deal of that reticence." Godden similarly praises the author for her original voice: "Time has proved [her unique]; she has written [numerous works] . . . and I could wager there is not in any of them one shoddy line or unnecessary word, a standard few writers achieve. Each book," Godden continues, "has her hallmark of balance, subtlety, wry humor and beauty." And Weinraub, in assessing Jhabvala's reputation in the literary community, quotes the late novelist C. P. Snow: "Someone once said that the definition of the highest art is that one should feel that life is this and not otherwise. I do not know of a writer living who gives that feeling with more unqualified certainty than Mrs. Jhabvala."

BIOGRAPHICAL/CRITICAL SOURCES:

BOOKS

Contemporary Literary Criticism, Gale (Detroit), Volume 4, 1975, Volume 8, 1978, Volume 29, 1984, Volume 94, 1997.

Dictionary of Literary Biography, Volume 194: *British Novelists since 1960, Second Series,* Gale, 1998.

Gooneratne, Yasmine, *Silence, Exile, and Cunning: The Fiction of Ruth Prawer Jhabvala,* Orient Longman (New Delhi), 1983.

Pritchett, V. S., *The Tale Bearers: Literary Essays,* Random House (New York City), 1980.

Shepherd, Ronald, *Ruth Prawer Jhabvala in India: The Jewish Connection,* Chanakya, 1994.

Sucher, Laurie, *The Fiction of Ruth Prawer Jhabvala,* St. Martin's (New York City), 1988.

PERIODICALS

America, March 2, 1991, p. 242.

Booklist, September 1, 1995, p. 40.

Commonweal, December 17, 1993, pp. 14-16.

Entertainment Weekly, April 7, 1995, p. 61; September 27, 1996.

Globe and Mail (Toronto), July 26, 1986; October 17, 1987.

Library Journal, October 1, 1998, p. 138.

Los Angeles Times, November 9, 1983; September 4, 1987.

Los Angeles Times Book Review, April 12, 1992, p. 14; March 14, 1993, p. 3.

Maclean's, March 31, 1986.

Modern Fiction Studies, winter, 1984.

Nation, September 11, 1995, p. 244.

National Review, December 13, 1993, pp. 61-63; November 11, 1996, p. 59.

New Republic, December 24, 1990, p. 26.

New Statesman, October 31, 1975; April 15, 1983.

New Statesman and Society, May 29, 1992, pp. 32-33; April 9, 1993, p. 56.

Newsweek, April 19, 1976; March 10, 1986; August 24, 1987; March 16, 1992, p. 66.

New Yorker, May 4, 1992, pp. 74-76; March 22, 1993, p. 106.

New York Herald Tribune Book Review, January 15, 1956.

New York Review of Books, July 15, 1976.

New York Times, August 30, 1973; July 19, 1983; September 15, 1983; August 2, 1984; August 5, 1984; March 7, 1986; May 17, 1986; July 5, 1986; August 6, 1987.

New York Times Book Review, January 15, 1956; February 2, 1969; July 8, 1973; April 4, 1976; June 12, 1983; May 25, 1986; August 23, 1987; March 28, 1993, p. 106; September 17, 1995, p. 12; November 29, 1998, p. 20.

New York Times Magazine, September 11, 1983.

People Weekly, March 17, 1986; September 28, 1987; April 10, 1995, p. 15; October 7, 1996.

Playboy, November, 1996.

Publishers Weekly, June 6, 1986; July 17, 1995, p. 217; August 31, 1998, p. 48.

Saturday Review, January 14, 1956; March 1, 1969; April 3, 1976; October 30, 1976.

Spectator, April 23, 1983; October 24, 1987; April 24, 1993, p. 28.

Time, May 12, 1986; October 6, 1986; April 10, 1995, p. 82.

Times (London), February 4, 1983; April 14, 1983; October 15, 1987.

Times Literary Supplement, May 20, 1965; November 7, 1975; April 15, 1983; April 24, 1987; November 13, 1987; April 16, 1993, p. 20.

Tribune Books (Chicago), February 28, 1993, p. 6.

Village Voice, August 2, 1983; May 8, 1986; September 30, 1986.

Washington Post, October 7, 1983; September 22, 1984; April 5, 1986.

Washington Post Book World, September 12, 1976; September 18, 1983; May 25, 1986; February 21, 1993, p. 9; March 28, 1993, p. 15.

World Literature Written in English, April, 1978; November, 1979.*

JIN, Xuefei 1956-
(Ha Jin)

PERSONAL: Born February 21, 1956, in Liaoning, China; son of Danlin (an officer) and Yuanfen (a worker; maiden name, Zhao) Jin; married Lisah Bian, July 6, 1982; children: Wen. *Ethnicity:* "Han." *Education:* Heilongjiang University, B.A., 1981; Shangdong University, M.A., 1984; Brandeis University, Ph.D., 1992. *Politics:* "None." *Religion:* "None."

ADDRESSES: Office—Department of English, Callaway Memorial Center, 302 North Callaway, Emory University, Atlanta, GA 30322; fax: 404-727-2605. *Agent*—Christina Ward, P.O. Box 515, North Scituate, MA 02060.

CAREER: Emory University, Atlanta, GA, assistant professor of creative writing, 1993—. *Military service:* Chinese People's Army, 1987-95.

AWARDS, HONORS: Three Pushcart Prizes for fiction; prize from *Kenyon Review;* Agni Best Fiction Prize; PEN Hemingway Award for first fiction, 1998, for *Ocean of Words;* Flannery O'Conner Award, 1998, for *Under the Red Flag;* National Book Award, 1999, and PEN/Faulkner Award for Fiction, 2000, both for *Waiting.*

WRITINGS:

UNDER NAME HA JIN

Between Silences (poems), University of Chicago Press (Chicago, IL), 1990.

Facing Shadows (poems), Hanging Loose Press (Brooklyn, NY), 1996.

Ocean of Words: Army Stories, Zoland Books (Cambridge, MA), 1996, Vintage (New York City), 1998.

Under the Red Flag (stories), University of Georgia Press (Athens), 1997, Zoland Books, 1999.

In the Pond (novel), Zoland Books, 1998.

Waiting (novel), Pantheon (New York City), 1999.

Quiet Desperation (stories), Pantheon, 2000.

WORK IN PROGRESS: Man to Be: Country Stories, short fiction; *Crazed,* a novel about madness.

SIDELIGHTS: In 1986 thirty-year-old Xuefei Jin, who writes under the name Ha Jin, emigrated from his native China to begin working on a Ph.D. in English at Brandeis University in Waltham, Massachusetts. Before taking his degree in 1992, Jin had already published his first book of poems in English, *Between Silences.* The next year he began teaching at Emory University in Atlanta, Georgia, and another book of poetry, *Facing Shadows,* appeared a few years later in 1996. In the next three years Jin published two story collections and two novels, all written in English, all set in the People's Republic of China. Jin's work has received nearly universal acclaim from American critics and garnered numerous awards.

Jin's second collection of stories, *Under the Red Flag,* won the Flannery O'Connor Award for Short Fiction. The book is set in a rural town, Dismount Fort, during the Cultural Revolution that swept across China in 1966. This was a time when fanatical beliefs gained sway and those who did not embrace them were often persecuted. In what Paul Gray of *Time* singled out as the best story in the book, "Winds and Clouds over a Funeral," a communist official is torn between conflicting loyalties. His mother's last request upon her death bed was that she not be cremated. However, it is the official policy of the Communist Party that all dead bodies should be cremated in order to conserve arable land. In another story, the Communist Party has arrested a woman accused of being a whore and are planning a public humiliation and punishment for her. A young boy, the narrator of the story, looks forward to the event. In another, a man castrates himself to gain admission to the Communist Party. Gray noted: "Ha Jin is not a preachy author. He offers his characters choices that are incompatible and potentially destructive and then dispassionately records what they do next." Frank Caso of *Booklist* found *Under the Red Flag* to be a "powerful" collection, but also remarked "there is . . . an undisguised cynicism, in . . . many of the . . . tales, that the truth must first be shaped to a political purpose." A *Publishers Weekly* reviewer, though stating of Jin that "sometimes his allegories are too simple," maintained that the stories are used by Jin "to explore larger themes about human relationships and the effect of government on individual lives."

Jin's first novel, *In the Pond,* is the tale of a talented artist, Shao Bin, who must spend his time working at a fertilizer plant to support his family. After being assigned inferior housing, Bin protests by drawing a series of cartoons that criticize his supervisors at work, the villains of the story. After a series of conflicts with the supervisors, spurred on by more cartoons, Bin eventually receives a promotion to the propaganda office. A writer reviewing *In the Pond* for *Publishers Weekly* found that Jin "offers a wise and funny first novel that gathers meticulously observed images into a seething yet restrained tale of social injustice in modern China." The reviewer also applauded the complexity of the book's characters, such as the supervisors, and concluded by stating that the novel goes beyond its setting of Communist China to "engagingly illustrat[e] a universal conundrum."

A National Book Award winner, *Waiting* generated considerable critical attention. "[A] deliciously comic novel . . . [told] . . . in an impeccably deadpan manner," exclaimed Gray, again writing in *Time.* One *Publishers Weekly* reviewer deemed *Waiting* "quiet but absorbing . . . powerful," while another remarked that besides its "affecting love story," *Waiting* "presents a trenchant picture of Chinese life under communism." According to Shirley N. Quan of *Library Journal:* "This touching story about love, honor, duty, and family speaks feelingly to readers on matters of the heart." The plot of *Waiting* centers on three individuals: Lin, a medical student who later becomes a doctor; Shuyu, the woman his ailing parents force him to marry so they will have someone to care for them; and Manna Wu, a nurse with whom Lin falls in love. According to communist law, a couple must be separated for eighteen years before they can legally divorce. The novel covers twenty years, including the eighteen during which Lin and Manna maintain their relationship but decide to wait until they can marry before they will consummate it. Assessing the strengths and weaknesses of the book for *Entertainment Weekly,* Megan Harlan stated: "Jin overexplains the story's background. But the lengthy finale . . . resounds with elegant irony." Francine Prose of the *New York Times Book Review* noted: "Character is fate, or at least some part of fate, and Ha Jin's achievement is to reveal the ways in which character and society conspire."

Irene Wanner of the *Seattle Times* credited the success of Jin's work to its "skill, compassion and enlightening aspects." Gray felt Jin's success is in part due to the "accident of his birth." Having been born in another country, Gray explained, Jin was "protected from the homogenizing and potentially trivializing influences that afflict so many U.S.-born aspiring authors." However, Gray concluded that although "exotic subject matter" has helped Jin's career, his "narrative talent proves victorious."

Jin once told *CA:* "Because I failed to do something else, writing in English became my means of survival, of spending or wasting my life, of retrieving losses, mine and those of others. Because my life has been a constant struggle, I feel close in my heart to the great Russian masters, including Chekhov, Gogol, and

Babel. As for poetry, some ancient Chinese influences are Tu Fu, Li Po, and Po Chu-I.

"Since I teach full time, my writing process has been adapted to my teaching. When I have a large piece of time, I write drafts of stories, or a draft of a novel, which I revise and edit when I teach. Each draft is revised thirty times before it is finished.

"If I am inspired, it is from within. Very often I feel that the stories have been inside me for a long time, and that I am no more than an instrument for their manifestation. As for the subject matter, I guess we are compelled to write about what has hurt us most."

BIOGRAPHICAL/CRITICAL SOURCES:

PERIODICALS

Booklist, November 1, 1997, Frank Caso, review of *Under the Red Flag,* p. 454.

Entertainment Weekly, October 29, 1999, Megan Harlan, review of *Waiting,* p. 106; December 3, 1999, Lori Tharps and Clarissa Cruz, "Between the Lines," p. 93.

Library Journal, October 15, 1999, Shirley N. Quan, review of *Waiting,* p. 105.

New York Times Book Review, October 24, 1999.

Progressive, March, 2000, John McNally, review of *Waiting,* p. 44.

Publishers Weekly, February 26, 1996, review of *Ocean of Words: Army Stories,* p. 98; October 3, 1997, review of *Under the Red Flag,* p. 58; October 12, 1998, review of *In the Pond,* p. 58; August 23, 1999, review of *Waiting,* p. 42; November 1, 1999, review of *Waiting,* p. 46.

Seattle Times, October 31, 1999, Irene Wanner, review of *Waiting.*

Time, December 1, 1997, Paul Gray, review of *Under the Red Flag,* p. 94; November 8, 1999, Paul Gray, "Divorce, Chinese-Style," p. 144.

World Literature Today, autumn, 1997, Timothy C. Wong, review of *Ocean of Words: Army Stories,* p. 862; autumn, 1997, K. C. Leung, review of *Facing Shadows,* p. 861; spring, 1998, Fatima Wu, review of *Under the Red Flag,* p. 454; spring, 1999, Jeffrey C. Kinkley, review of *In the Pond,* p. 389.

OTHER

Emory Magazine: Spring 1998: Ha Jin, http://www.emory.edu/ (June 6, 2000).

Ha Jin Page, http://worldwriters.english.sbc.edu/ (June 6, 2000).

PEN/Faulkner Award for Fiction, http://www.folger.edu/ (June 6, 2000).*

* * *

JOHNSON, Richard
See RICHARDSON, John

* * *

JONES, Amelia 1961-

PERSONAL: Born July 14, 1961, in Durham, NC; daughter of Edward E. (a professor) and Virginia S. Jones; married Anthony Sherin (a film editor), March 7, 1987; children: Evan E., Vita B. *Ethnicity:* "Caucasian." *Education:* Harvard University, B.A. (magna cum laude), 1983; University of Pennsylvania, M.A., 1987; University of California, Los Angeles, Ph.D., 1991. *Politics:* "Left/democrat."

ADDRESSES: Home—339 South Orange Dr., Los Angeles, CA 90036. *Office*—Department of the History of Art, University of California, Riverside, CA 92521; fax 323-939-1830. *E-mail*—jonessher@aol.com.

CAREER: Art Center College of Design, Pasadena, CA, instructor and adviser, 1990-91; University of California, Riverside, began as assistant professor, became professor of contemporary art and theory and the history of photography, 1991—. Curator of exhibitions at California Museum of Photography and Armand Hammer Museum of Art; public speaker, including lectures at Otis College of Art and Design, Cornell University, and University of London. Los Angeles Center for Photographic Studies, member of board of directors; member of California Museum of Photography, Riverside, Highways Performance Space, Los Angeles, and Los Angeles Contemporary Exhibitions.

MEMBER: International Association of Art Critics, College Art Association, Society for Photographic Education, Los Angeles Film Forum, National Organization for Women, Teachers for a Democratic Culture.

AWARDS, HONORS: Fellow of American Council of Learned Societies, 1994-95, and National Endowment for the Humanities, 2000-01; Guggenheim fellow, 2000.

WRITINGS:

(Contributor) Kathleen Adler and Marcia Pointon, editors, *The Body Imaged,* Cambridge University Press (New York City), 1993.
(Contributor) Kim Levin, editor, *Beyond Walls and Wars: Art, Politics, and Multiculturalism,* Midmarch Arts Press, 1993.
(Contributor) Cassandra Langer, Joanna Frueh, and Arlene Raven, editors, *New Feminist Criticisms: Art/Identity/Action,* HarperCollins (San Francisco, CA), 1994.
Postmodernism and the En-Gendering of Marcel Duchamp, Cambridge University Press, 1994.
(Editor and contributor) *Sexual Politics: Judy Chicago's "Dinner Party" in Feminist Art History,* University of California Press (Berkeley, CA), 1996.
(Contributor) Paul Duro, editor, *The Rhetoric of the Frame: Essays on the Boundaries of the Artwork,* Cambridge University Press, 1996.
Body Art/Performing the Subject, University of Minnesota Press (Minneapolis, MN), 1998.
(Contributor) Donald Preziosi, editor, *Art History Past and Future,* Oxford University Press (New York City), 1998.
(Editor with Andrew Stephenson, and contributor) *Performing the Body/Performing the Text,* Routledge (New York City), 1999.
(Contributor) Naomi Sawelson-Gorse, editor, *Women in Dada,* MIT Press (Cambridge, MA), 1999.
(Contributor) Steve Edwards, editor, *Art and Its Histories: A Reader,* Yale University Press (New Haven, CT), 1999.
(Contributor) Erika Suderburg, editor, *Space, Site, and Intervention: Issues in Installation and Site-Specific Art,* University of Minnesota Press, 2000.
(Contributor) Philip Brett, Sue-Ellen Case, and Susan Leigh Foster, editors, *Decomposition: Post-Disciplinary Performance,* Indiana University Press (Bloomington, IN), 2000.
(Contributor) Clare Manchester, editor, *The Artist's Body,* Phaidon (London, England), 2000.
(Contributor) Jim Drobnick and Jennifer Fisher, editors, *Living Display,* University of Chicago Press (Chicago, IL), 2000.
(Contributor) Emory Elliott, editor, *Aesthetics and Difference,* Oxford University Press, 2000.
(Contributor) Julia Watson and Sidonie Smith, editors, *InterFaces: Visualizing and Performing Women's Lives,* University of Michigan Press (Ann Arbor, MI), 2000.

Contributor to exhibition catalogs. Contributor of articles and reviews to art and history journals, including *Atzlan: Journal of Chicano Studies, Art Journal, New Observations, Afterimage,* and *Camera Obscura: Journal of Feminism and Film History.* Executive editor, *Framework,* 1995-98; contributing editor in charge of West Coast coverage, *Artscribe,* 1991-92.

WORK IN PROGRESS: Editing and contributing to the Internet web site project *WomEnhouse,* http://www.cmp.ucr.edu/womenhouse/

SIDELIGHTS: Amelia Jones told *CA:* "Initially inspired to write the great American novel, I realized in my early twenties that academic prose offered a more direct (and less frightening) path toward becoming a writer, and was better suited to my polemical writing style. After studying art history in college and graduate school, I became increasingly comfortable writing about contemporary art and culture.

"It seemed to me that I can do a great deal in this area, especially by diversifying my writing into a wide range of venues, in order to reach academics, the non-academic art world, and (ideally) the general public. In diverse publications I have enjoyed attacking subjects ranging from postfeminism, representations of women in Hollywood films, and feminist art from the 1970s to the construction of the French-turned-American avant-garde artist Marcel Duchamp as a father figure for U.S. postmodern art and the contemporary use of the artist's body in or *as* the work of art.

"My goal with all of these publications has been to open areas of accepted thought in contemporary culture to critical analysis and to disrupt traditional narratives of art history by insisting on the inclusion of women and artists of color. In my writing, as in my teaching, I encourage readers and students to take a critical distance from the information that bombards them in the contemporary world. I have been motivated by the importance of communicating the powerful relevance of art history (understood in this broad sense as the study of culture through historical and theoretical models) to everyone who lives in the imagery-saturated contemporary world. I try to convince readers and students that, by grasping the inevitably ideological ways in which visual culture is made to mean, they can become empowered in relation to these representations and can potentially find ways to intervene in, critique, or encourage various representations in progressive ways.

"I believe in writing as polemic, but also as a kind of seduction. While some may try to veil it, all writers have a point of view, and the best favor we can do our readers is to make that point of view as clear as possible. To this end, my favorite writers are philosophers whose main project has been the poeticizing of academic writing (bell hooks, Jacques Derrida, Luce Irigaray) and fiction writers—especially black women who have negotiated with passion and eloquence the commingling of oppressiveness and potentially liberatory magic in the English language—Alice Walker and Toni Morrison especially. Norman Rush is, for me, one of the great contemporary authors, in that he, too, writes in that ephemeral but fabulous space in which the gorgeousness of language, the complexity of intellectual and political ideas regarding race and gender, and profound emotional and sensual meanings intersect.

"My long-standing love of fiction has held me in good stead with my academic prose. Recently, I have enjoyed opening up this usually rather formulaic kind of writing to fictionalized and playful modes of expression. In doing so, I not only answer my own desire to merge my emotional, personal self with my academic, rational self, but also expose the illusion of objectivity thrown up by the mannered poses of academic prose. Looking at art and experiencing culture are always emotionally invested processes. For this, I have been called—sometimes derisively, sometimes in praise—a 'new art historian' and a 'poststructuralist feminist.'

"Writing is the process that has allowed me to exist. Without writing I would have nothing to say."

* * *

JONES, J. Gwynfor 1936-

PERSONAL: Born November 22, 1936, in Conwy Valley, North Wales; children: two sons, one daughter. *Ethnicity:* "Welsh (white)." *Education:* Attended University of Wales, University College, Cardiff, 1955-60, and University College of North Wales, Bangor, 1960-62. *Religion:* Presbyterian.

ADDRESSES: Home—1 Westminster Dr., Cyncoed, Cardiff CF2 6RD, Wales. *Office*—School of History and Archaeology, University College, University of Wales, Cardiff, Wales; fax 02-92-087-4929. *E-mail*—shajgj@forest.cf.ac.uk.

CAREER: University of Wales, University College, Cardiff, began as senior lecturer, 1975, professor of Welsh history, 1997—.

WRITINGS:

Wales and the Tudor State, 1534-1605, University of Wales Press (Cardiff, Wales), 1989.

(Editor) *The Memoirs of Sir John Wynn,* Gomer Press, 1990.

Concepts of Order and Gentility in Wales, 1540-1640, Gomer Press, 1992.

Early Modern Wales, 1526-1640, Macmillan (New York City), 1994.

The Wynn Family of Gwydir c. 1490-1674, [Aberystwyth, Wales], 1995.

Law, Order, and Government in Caernarfonshire, 1558-1640, University of Wales Press, 1996.

The Welsh Gentry, 1536-1640, University of Wales Press, 1998.

Conflict, Continuity, and Change in Wales, c. 1500-1603, Faculty of Education, University College of Wales, Aberystwyth, 1999.

WORK IN PROGRESS: A new edition of George Owens's *Dialogue of the Government of Wales* (1594), with notes, introduction, and text; a volume of essays on aspects of social history in Wales, c. 1450-1750; a volume of essays on religious history in Wales, c. 1559-1750.

* * *

JONES, Mervyn 1922-

PERSONAL: Born February 27, 1922, in London, England; son of Ernest (a psychoanalyst) and Katharine (Jokl) Jones; married Jeanne Urquhart, April 2, 1948; children: Jacqueline, Marian, Conrad. *Education:* Attended New York University, 1939-41. *Politics:* Socialist. *Religion:* None.

ADDRESSES: Home—10 Waterside Place, Princess Rd., London NW1, England. *Agent*—Christine Bernard, 7 Well Rd., London NW3, England.

CAREER: Freelance journalist and novelist, 1947—; *Tribune,* London, England, assistant editor, 1955-60, drama critic, 1958-66; *New Statesman,* assistant editor, 1966-68. *Military service:* British Army, 1942-47; became captain.

AWARDS, HONORS: Traveling scholarship, Society of Authors, 1982.

WRITINGS:

NOVELS, EXCEPT AS NOTED

No Time to Be Young, J. Cape (London), 1952.
The New Town, J. Cape, 1953.
The Last Barricade, J. Cape, 1953.
Helen Blake, J. Cape, 1955.
On the Last Day, J. Cape, 1958.
A Set of Wives, J. Cape, 1965.
John and Mary, J. Cape, 1966, Atheneum (New York City), 1967.
A Survivor, Atheneum, 1968.
Joseph, Atheneum, 1970.
Mr. Armitage Isn't Back Yet, J. Cape, 1971.
Twilight of Our Day, Simon & Schuster (New York City), 1973, published as *Holding On,* Quartet, 1973.
The Revolving Door, Quartet, 1973.
Strangers, Quartet, 1974.
Lord Richard's Passion, Knopf (New York City), 1974.
The Pursuit of Happiness, Quartet, 1975, Mason/Charter, 1976.
Scenes from Bourgeois Life (short story collection), Quartet, 1976.
Nobody's Fault, Mason/Charter, 1977.
Today the Struggle, Quartet, 1978.
The Beautiful Words, Deutsch, 1979.
A Short Time to Live, Deutsch, 1980, St. Martin's Press (New York City), 1981.
Two Women and Their Man, Deutsch, 1981, St. Martin's Press, 1982.
Joanna's Luck, Piatkus (London), 1984.
Coming Home, Piatkus, 1986.

NONFICTION

(With Michael Foot) *Guilty Men, 1957,* Rinehart, 1957.
Potbank (documentary), Secker & Warburg, 1961.
The Antagonists, C. N. Potter, 1962, published as *Big Two: Life in America and Russia,* J. Cape, 1962.
Two Ears of Corn: Oxfam in Action, Hodder & Stoughton, 1965, published as *In Famine's Shadow: A Private War on Hunger,* Beacon Press (Boston), 1967.
(Editor) *Kingsley Martin: Portrait and Self-Portrait,* Humanities, 1969.
Life on the Dole, Davis-Poynter, 1972.
(Translator) K. S. Karol, *The Second Chinese Revolution,* Hill & Wang (New York City), 1974.
(Editor) *Privacy,* David & Charles (North Pomfret, VT), 1974.
The Oil Rush, photographs by Fay Godwin, Quartet, 1976.
The Sami of Lapland, Minority Rights Group (London), 1982.
Chances: An Autobiography, Verso (New York City), 1987.
(Author of introduction) Ernest Jones, *Free Associations: Memories of a Psycho-Analyst,* Transaction Publishers (New Brunswick, NJ), 1990.
(With Patrick D. Wall) *Defeating Pain: The War Against a Silent Epidemic,* Plenum Press (New York City), 1991.
A Radical Life: The Biography of Megan Lloyd George, Hutchinson (London), 1991.
Michael Foot (biography), Gollancz (London), 1994.

OTHER

The Shelter (play), first produced in London, 1982.

Also author of radio plays, including *Anna,* 1982, *Taking Over,* 1984, *Lisa,* and *Generations,* 1986. Work represented in *English Story* anthologies numbers 8 and 10, edited by Woodrow Wyatt, Collins, 1948 and 1950. Contributor to periodicals, including *Bananas, Encounter, Sunday Times, Woman,* and London *Observer.*

ADAPTATIONS: John and Mary was filmed by Twentieth Century-Fox Film Corp. in 1969.

SIDELIGHTS: British writer Mervyn Jones is the author of numerous novels and nonfiction works, many of which address Jones's fervent political liberalism. One of the most noticeable features of Jones's novels, according to critics, is a meticulous writing style combined with a decidedly leftist political or sociological approach to his subject matter. A typical Jones character, rather than being endowed by the author with a distinctly individual personality, usually serves as a representation or embodiment of a general human quality common to the setting in question. As a result of such preoccupations, some commentators criticize Jones for writing novels which seem "lifeless and contrived," as a *Times Literary Supplement* reviewer described *Lord Richard's Passion. Today the Struggle,* a chronicle tracing the lives of several related English families from the 1930s to the 1970s, also garnered criticism for its focus on causes and types rather than on "real" people, but not all critics panned it. Valentine Cunningham, writing in *New Statesman,* called the book "so engrossing that it's hard to put down." Admitting that "it's bound, of course, occasionally to seem a bit too schemed-for, too shrewdly schematising," Cunningham nonetheless deemed such criticism "midget grouses.

Many of the people are wonderfully believable in themselves. . . . they are, what's more, placed most convincingly in their time."

Commenting on the author's work in general, a London *Observer* critic stated, "One thing that Mervyn Jones can certainly do is tell a story: his straightforward narrative technique looks simple, reads easily, and keeps you reading. At the same time, he has a good old-fashioned novelist's way with characters. There is no authorial presence, no overt trickery or tricksiness. And such things aren't unimportant to the ordinary reader."

In 1982's *Two Women and Their Man,* Jones uses his "straightforward narrative technique" to tell the story of a love triangle between a Welsh man, his wife, and his mistress—an American. Set in Wales in 1939, the novel displays Jones's commitment to leftist political causes with its World War II backdrop of political tension. Noting that the novel is Jones's twenty-first work of fiction, *Listener* contributor John Mellors remarked that the author's "inventiveness and narrative powers show no signs of flagging." His 1986 novel, *Coming Home,* also received positive reviews for its quiet, understated prose and its moving story line. The novel concerns a long-delayed love affair between Owen and Vera, once young lovers who ended their affair when Owen was sent to Malaya as part of his military service. After thirty years living in the Far East, having never married but having enjoyed a successful professional life and the company of numerous women, Owen returns to the British Isles. He tracks down Vera at the group home that she maintains for handicapped people, and the two fall in love again and marry. Unfortunately, Vera dies, leaving Owen to assume her duties and run the group home. "Mervyn Jones tells his story in a plain, straightforward way that convinces by its evenness of tone and avoidance of histrionics," commented John Grigg in *Listener.*

In his 1991 nonfiction volume, *Defeating Pain: The War Against a Silent Epidemic,* written in collaboration with physiologist Patrick D. Wall, Jones explores the subject of physical pain: what causes it, how people react to it, and the different means of treating it. The text points out that the degree of pain a person experiences is not always related to the severity of an injury or condition; minor stimuli can sometimes generate severe pain. A *Publishers Weekly* reviewer found the book "especially enlightening in discussing the varied ways people react to pain . . . and in evaluating pain-relieving options."

Jones has produced many other volumes of nonfiction, including several biographies. His 1991 *A Radical Life: The Biography of Megan Lloyd George* traces the life of the Labour Party politician and daughter of legendary British Prime Minister David Lloyd George. The 1994 *Michael Foot* tells the story of the former British Labour Party leader, a left-wing moderate who was thoroughly trounced by the Conservative Party in an election in the early 1980s. Jones and Foot were both long-time friends and former colleagues on the Socialist-oriented *Tribune.* Jones was unapologetic in expressing his affection for his friend's life and political views in *Michael Foot,* but a number of reviewers found that Jones was too close and too sympathetic to his subject to present a comprehensive and insightful book. Steven Fielding of *History Today* characterized *Michael Foot* as "a competent, if very conventional, narrative of the period," going on to note that Jones offers "little insight" into Foot's ideas and accepts their validity "virtually without question." Reviewing *Michael Foot* for *New Statesman,* Bernard Crick commented: "Not wholly uncritical, not wholly adulatory, it is nonetheless written in the Roman and Victorian tradition of exemplary lives. But the biographer would have done well . . . to prevent his book appearing as so much a tale of a personal struggle whose outcome leaves us puzzled whether to see the two lives of Michael Foot, the literary and the political, as triumphant fusion, tragic contradiction, or even farce." A critic for the *Economist* granted that the connection between the two men gave the book "warmth and immediacy" yet at the same time felt that it resulted in "a certain loss of perspective." The critic concluded: "Except for these disastrous three years as Labour leader, Mr. Foot was a fairly minor figure with little influence on events. Portraying him as a man of significance has the odd effect of diminishing him still further." In contrast, Crick remarked: "This friendly biography may not be good history, but it is a noble tribute."

In his 1987 autobiography, *Chances,* Jones recounts his interesting, varied life, including his early life in an intellectual, middle-class household (his father, Ernest Jones, was Sigmund Freud's biographer); his commitment to communism at age sixteen; his expulsion from school and travel to the United States to attend college, an experience that was cut short when he was drafted to serve in World War II; his later wide travels on behalf of leftist causes to places such as the Soviet Union and France; and the blossoming of his literary career.

Jones once told *CA:* "In a forbidding, almost windowless medieval tower by the coast of southern France, Catholic rulers in the eighteenth century imprisoned

Protestant women who refused to renounce their faith. The special torment was that each of them could go free, any day, by accepting conversion. One, Marie Durand, stayed in the tower from the age of fifteen to the age of fifty-three, when the persecution ended. Visitors can still read, carved in stone, the word *resister.* I have taken this as the conclusive symbol in my novel *Today the Struggle.* In all my writing, my theme is the defense and possible survival of the integral human personality, assailed by multiform varieties of cruelty and temptation. How difficult it is to live—that is the subject of all serious novels, I suppose, and certainly of mine. I am concerned with both the dignity and the irony of idealism. Even the good are sometimes absurd and sometimes dishonest; but to know this of oneself is part of the difficulty.

"Critics generally define me as a political writer. Perhaps this reflects the general avoidance, especially by British writers, of what's seen as the contamination of politics. Wearing other hats, as a citizen and a journalist, I've made clear my socialist convictions and my concern with the threat of nuclear war. Politics, in the direct sense, does bulk large in my best-known novels. *Joseph* is based on the life of Joseph Stalin and is an attempt to explain the degeneration of revolutionary ideals. *Twilight of the Day* is a record of working-class life in the East End of London. *Today the Struggle* chronicles the experiences of the politically obsessed and the politically involved—Communists, liberals, pro-Nazis—from the time of the Spanish civil war to the recent past. Yet I don't think that the boundaries of the political can be neatly drawn, if the setting of the novel is the *polis*—city or community. *The Beautiful Words* is a simple story of a mentally handicapped boy trying to survive in the bewildering urban jungle. None of the characters could be imagined demonstrating or even voting, and there's no mention of what we normally call politics, but this novel seems to me as political as any of my others.

"I also believe that the problems with which I'm concerned—problems of integrity, loyalty, and self-realization—can be explored within the framework of intimate personal relationships. In this zone, men and women have to resolve the conflict between externally imposed conventions and authentic desires. In the only novel which I have set in an earlier century, *Lord Richard's Passion,* I sought to exploit a Victorian literary cliche, the dilemma of love and ambition, in order to illuminate this dichotomy. (Reviewers, and perhaps other readers, took it too straight—'a tender evocative story, full of compassion and understanding,' one of them said.) In *Nobody's Fault,* which I personally consider to be my best novel, the central situation is that of a woman fatally and inextricably attached to two contrasted men. In *Two Women and Their Man* it is the affection between women who, on conventional assumptions, should be rivals and enemies. I ask myself, are these, too, political novels? It was a surprise to me, on reading an essay collection called *The Socialist Novel in Britain,* to find that a Marxist critic, Kiernan Ryan, singled out *John and Mary* as the Jones novel he found most significant. In this novel, of which the only subject is the mutual interrogation of two young people who have spent the night together, I deliberately omitted all reference to their social or economic background or indeed their work—an omission remedied with predictable clumsiness in the film made from the book. For Ryan, the achievement of this novel was to dramatize 'the power of men and women to surmount the acquired illusions, fears and prejudices barring their way to mutual self-realization.' I should say that—not only in *John and Mary* but in all my writing—this has been my aim."

BIOGRAPHICAL/CRITICAL SOURCES:

BOOKS

Contemporary Authors Autobiography Series, Volume 5, Gale, 1987.

Contemporary Literary Criticism, Gale, Volume 10, 1979, Volume 52, 1989.

Contemporary Novelists, sixth edition, St. James Press, 1996.

Jones, Mervyn, *Chances: An Autobiography,* Verso, 1987.

Klaus, H. Gustav, editor, *The Socialist Novel in Britain,* St. Martin's Press, 1982.

PERIODICALS

Books and Bookmen, August, 1979.

British Book News, July, 1986, p. 423.

Contemporary Review, July, 1994, Paul B. Rose, review of *Michael Foot,* p. 52.

Economist (US), April 9, 1994, review of *Michael Foot,* p. 97.

Guardian (London), July 9, 1979.

History Today, January, 1992, p. 56; January, 1996, Steven Fielding, review of *Michael Foot,* p. 56.

Library Journal, April 15, 1974.

Listener, December 11, 1975; July 12, 1979; March 11, 1982, p. 23; May 29, 1986, p. 25.

London Review of Books, September 18, 1986, p. 14; September 15, 1988, p. 15; March 24, 1994, p. 13.

New Statesman, February 17, 1978; July 13, 1979; February 12, 1982, p. 23; February 15, 1985, p. 30;

May 24, 1991, p. 43; March 25, 1994, Bernard Crick, review of *Michael Foot,* p. 45.
New York Times Book Review, October 16, 1977.
Observer (London), July 22, 1979; February 3, 1985; June 22, 1986; November 1, 1987, p. 27; June 23, 1991; March 20, 1994, p. 18.
Publishers Weekly, September 13, 1991, review of *Defeating Pain,* p. 69.
Spectator, August 7, 1976; February 18, 1978; February 9, 1985, p. 25; March 26, 1994, p. 37.
Times (London), February 7, 1985.
Times Literary Supplement, October 25, 1974; November 7, 1975; August 19, 1977; October 3, 1980; December 19, 1986; November 20, 1987, p. 1277; September 6, 1991, p. 10; April 15, 1994, p. 15.*

* * *

JOPPKE, Christian 1959-

PERSONAL: Born September 6, 1959, in Langenhagen, Germany; son of Lothar (in business) and Irene (an executive secretary; maiden name, Dechow) Joppke; married Catherine Kratz, January 1, 1999; children: Benjamin. *Education:* Attended Free University of Berlin, 1978-80; University of Frankfurt, diploma, 1984; University of California, Berkeley, Ph.D., 1989.

ADDRESSES: Office—Department of Political and Social Sciences, European University Institute, Via del Roccettini 9, I-50016 San Domenico di Fiesole, Florence, Italy. *E-mail*—Jopple@datacomm.iue.it.

CAREER: University of Southern California, Los Angeles, assistant professor of sociology, 1990-94, Zumberge fellow, 1992; European University Institute, Florence, Italy, associate professor of sociology and political science, 1995—. University of California, Berkeley, John L. Simpson fellow at Institute of International Studies, 1989; Georgetown University, research associate at Center for German and European Studies, 1993-94.

AWARDS, HONORS: German Academic Exchange fellow, 1985-86.

WRITINGS:

Mobilizing against Nuclear Energy: A Comparison of Germany and the United States, University of California Press (Berkeley, CA), 1993.
East German Dissidents and the Revolution of 1989: Social Movement in a Leninist Regime, Macmillan (New York City), 1995.
(Editor) *Challenge to the Nation-State: Immigration in Western Europe and the United States,* Oxford University Press (New York City), 1998.
(Editor with Steven Lukes) *Multicultural Questions,* Oxford University Press, 1999.
Immigration and the Nation-State: A Comparison of the United States, Germany, and Great Britain, Oxford University Press, 1999.

Contributor of articles and reviews to sociology and political science journals.

K

KAPLAN, Fred 1937-

PERSONAL: Born November 4, 1937, in Bronx, NY; son of Isaac (an attorney) and Bessie (Zwirn) Kaplan; married Gloria Taplin (a teacher), May 28, 1959 (divorced, 1989); children: Benjamin, Noah, Julia. *Education:* Brooklyn College (now Brooklyn College of the City University of New York), B.A., 1959; Columbia University, M.A., 1961, Ph.D., 1966.

ADDRESSES: *Home*—151 Bergen Street, Brooklyn, NY 11217. *Office*—Department of English, Queens College of the City University of New York, Flushing, NY 11367; Graduate School and University Center of the City University of New York, 33 West 42nd St., New York, NY 10036.

CAREER: Lawrence University, Appleton, WI, instructor in English, 1962-64; California State College (now University), Los Angeles, assistant professor of English, 1964-67; City University of New York, Queens College, Flushing, NY, associate professor, 1967-71, professor of English, 1971-90; Queens College and Graduate Center, New York City, distinguished professor of English, 1990—. Graduate School and University Center, New York City, professor of English, 1979—. University of Copenhagen, Fulbright professor, 1973-74; University of Paris, visiting professor, 1986-87; Bar-Ilan University, Israel, visiting professor, 1987.

MEMBER: International Association of University Professors of English, Modern Language Association of America, PEN, Dickens Society (president, 1990-91).

AWARDS, HONORS: City University of New York research grant, 1968-69, 1976-78, 1980-85; Guggenheim fellow, 1976-77; National Endowment for the Humanities, fellowship at Huntington Library, 1981-82, grant, 1983; *Thomas Carlyle: A Biography* was a nominee for National Book Critics Circle award, 1983, and a jury-nominated finalist for Pulitzer Prize, 1984; fellow at National Humanities Center, NC, 1985-86; fellow, Rockefeller Study Center, Bellagio, Italy, 1990.

WRITINGS:

NONFICTION

Miracles of Rare Device: The Poet's Sense of Self in Nineteenth-Century Poetry, Wayne State University Press (Detroit, MI), 1972.

Dickens and Mesmerism: The Hidden Springs of Fiction, Princeton University Press (Princeton, NJ), 1975.

Thomas Carlyle: A Biography, Cornell University Press (Ithaca, NY), 1983.

(With Michael Goldberg and K. J. Fielding) *Lectures on Carlyle and His Era,* edited and compiled by Jerry D. James and Rita B. Bottoms, University of California Press (Santa Cruz), 1985.

Sacred Tears: Sentimentality in Victorian Literature, Princeton University Press, 1985.

Dickens: A Biography, Morrow (New York City), 1988.

Henry James: The Imagination of Genius, Morrow, 1992.

Gore Vidal: A Biography, Doubleday (New York City), 1999.

EDITOR

Dickens' Book of Memoranda: A Photographic and Typographic Facsimile of the Notebook Begun in

January, 1855, New York Public Library (New York City), 1981.

John Elliotson on Mesmerism, Da Capo Press (New York City), 1982.

(General editor) *The Readers' Advisor: A Layman's Guide to Literature,* 13th edition, Bowker (New York City), 1985.

Carlyle's "The French Revolution," annotated edition, University of California Press, 1990.

Charles Dickens, *Oliver Twist: Authoritative Text, Backgrounds and Sources, Early Reviews, Criticism,* Norton Critical Education (New York City), 1993.

Traveling in Italy with Henry James (essays), Morrow, 1994.

(And author of introduction) Gore Vidal, *The Essential Gore Vidal: A Gore Vidal Reader,* Random House (New York City), 1999.

Editor, *Dickens Studies Annual,* 1980—.

OTHER

Contributor to *Carlyle Newsletter, Dickens Studies Annual, Journal of the History of Ideas, Journal of Narrative Techniques, New York Times Book Review, Nineteenth-Century Fiction, Studies in English Literature,* and *Victorian Newsletter.*

SIDELIGHTS: Fred Kaplan is the author of several books of nonfiction, including biographies, and he has edited several works as well. Kaplan's *Thomas Carlyle: A Biography* "tells the story of Carlyle's life with descriptive skill, conviction, and a sure sense of history," commented Donald Thomas in a *New York Times Book Review* article. As John Clive noted in the *Times Literary Supplement,* Kaplan focuses on Carlyle's childhood in Scotland, his strained marriage, and his chronic gastric disorders, but offers little detail of his works. Carlyle's complicated personality has inspired extreme opinions on his life and works, but Clive wrote of Kaplan, "He is sympathetic to his subject, but at the same time does not let his judgements depend on any particular bias." Maureen Corrigan observed in a *Village Voice* article that Kaplan's *Thomas Carlyle* "doubtless will be the definitive [Carlyle] biography for decades, displacing the one written by James Anthony Froude in 1884." Kaplan's 1988 *Dickens: A Biography,* reissued in an updated edition in 1999, was also well received by reviewers, as a critic for *Library Journal* noted the "kudos" it was given by several reviewers.

In 1999 Kaplan published a biography of Gore Vidal and served as the editor for a comprehensive retrospective collection of the celebrated author's work. Consisting of nearly 1,300 pages, *The Essential Gore Vidal: A Gore Vidal Reader* contains the complete texts of Vidal's once-scandalous transgender novel, *Myra Breckenridge,* and his John F. Kennedy-inspired drama, *The Best Man;* excerpts from his six novels of American history (*Burr, Lincoln, 1876,* etc.), arranged to form a narrative sequence; excerpts from six other novels, including *Duluth, Julian,* and *The City and the Pillar;* and twenty-five assorted reviews and essays that include political commentary, satire, tributes to Eleanor Roosevelt and Montaigne, and four previously unpublished entries. In addition to writing an introduction to the volume as a whole, Kaplan introduces each section and provides both a bibliography of Vidal's work and a biographical chronology of his life. Paul Mattick of the *New York Times Book Review* commented: "Fred Kaplan . . . must . . . be congratulated for the job he has done in distilling Vidal's writing for *The Essential Gore Vidal."* However, a *Publishers Weekly* reviewer felt that "Kaplan actually deadens the pleasure of Vidal's prose by constant interruptions that didactically guide readers through a disparate body of work." A writer from *Kirkus Reviews,* though, stated about Kaplan's book: "Essential work, indeed, and a good deal more fun to read than the work of many other highly esteemed writers who take themselves much more seriously."

Kaplan's *Gore Vidal: A Biography,* based on access to Vidal's personal papers and interviews with Vidal and his friends, recounts a life that has been largely defined by privilege and controversy, hard work and extravagant socializing. Vidal's maternal grandfather was an Oklahoma senator, his father a West Point graduate who is considered a pioneer in aviation. He is related by blood or marriage to prestigious and powerful American families, including the Kennedys and the Gores. Growing up in a mansion on the Potomac, Vidal expressed an interest in writing at an early age. In the course of his long and prolific career, he has tried nearly every form of literary expression, including a profitable stint in Hollywood as a scriptwriter. Vidal's open homosexuality and outspoken political views once caused commentator William F. Buckley to denounce him during a television interview. His ongoing feud and competition with Norman Mailer has taken on legendary proportions in literary circles. Vidal has run for public office twice, both times unsuccessfully. Since 1971 he has lived as an expatriate at his villa in Ravello, Italy. His many friends and acquaintances have included Princess Margaret, Anais Nin, Claire Bloom, Christopher Isherwood, and Tennessee Williams. "The way Fred Kaplan tells it in his enormous new biography," stated a writer for the *Economist,* "it sounds like an enviable life."

Critical reaction to *Gore Vidal: A Biography* varied greatly. A *Publishers Weekly* reviewer felt that Kaplan "showcases erudition at the expense of selection, and the book drowns in encyclopedic detail." The *Economist* writer found Kaplan's account to be indiscriminate in its praise of both Vidal's work and his friends, "plodding and not wholly reliable." Yet Brad Hooper of *Booklist* described Gore Vidal as an "edifying portrait," and praised Kaplan for "his ability to weave considerable information into a smooth, interpretive account," while David W. Henderson of *Library Journal* deemed the book to be "wide-ranging and thorough . . . a fascinating account."

BIOGRAPHICAL/CRITICAL SOURCES:

PERIODICALS

Advocate, March 30, 1999, Robert Plunket, "Vital Vidal," p. 76.

Booklist, September 15, 1999, Brad Hooper, review of *Gore Vidal: A Biography,* p. 196.

Economist (US), December 11, 1999, "American Literature: Comeback Kid," p. 78.

Kirkus Reviews, December 15, 1998.

Library Journal, February 15, 1999, Michael Rogers, review of *Dickens: A Biography,* p. 189; October 15, 1999, David W. Henderson, review of *Gore Vidal: A Biography,* p. 71.

Los Angeles Times Book Review, January 29, 1984; October 23, 1988, p. 3.

Maclean's, April 17, 1989, John Bemrose, review of *Dickens: A Biography,* p. 60.

Modern Language Review, April, 1978.

National Review, May 3, 1999, "Hard-Core Gore-Christopher Caldwell," p. 51.

New Statesman, November 1, 1999, Andrew Biswell, review of *Gore Vidal: A Biography,* p. 58.

New Yorker, January 16, 1984.

New York Times Book Review, January 8, 1984; November 13, 1988, p. 3; April 29, 1990, p. 37; February 14, 1999, p. 13.

Publishers Weekly, September 21, 1992, review of *Henry James: The Imagination of Genius,* p. 84; November 30, 1998, review of *The Essential Gore Vidal: A Gore Vidal Reader,* p. 58; October 25, 1999, review of *Gore Vidal: A Biography,* p. 65.

Sewanee Review, October, 1977.

Smithsonian, November, 1989, Bruce Allen, review of *Dickens: A Biography,* p. 243.

Times (London), November 17, 1988.

Times Literary Supplement, April 2, 1976; June 3, 1983; April 20, 1984.

Village Voice, February 21, 1984.

Washington Post Book World, August 15, 1982.*

* * *

KERMAN, Joseph (Wilfred) 1924-

PERSONAL: Born April 3, 1924, in London, England; U.S. citizen; married Vivian Shaviro, September 12, 1945; children: Jonathan, Peter, Lucy. *Education:* New York University, A.B., 1943; Princeton University, Ph.D., 1950.

ADDRESSES: *Home*—107 Southampton Ave., Berkeley, CA 94707. *Office*—Department of Music, University of California, Berkeley, CA 94720.

CAREER: Westminster Choir College, Princeton, NJ, director of graduate studies, 1949-51; University of California, Berkeley, assistant professor, 1951-56, associate professor, 1956-60, professor of music, 1960—, chairman of department, 1961-64. Visiting fellow, All Souls College, Oxford, 1966-67, Cornell University, 1971, and Clare Hall, Cambridge, 1971; Heather Professor of Music, Oxford University, 1971-74. *Military service:* U.S. Naval Reserve, 1946.

MEMBER: American Musicological Society, Royal Academy of Music (honorary fellow), American Academy of Arts and Sciences (fellow), British Academy (corresponding fellow).

AWARDS, HONORS: National Institute and American Academy award in literature, 1956; Hodder junior fellowship, 1957-58; Guggenheim fellowship, 1960; Fulbright fellowship, 1966-67; L.H.D., Fairfield University, 1970.

WRITINGS:

Opera as Drama, Knopf (New York City), 1956, revised edition, University of California Press (Berkeley), 1988.

The Elizabethan Madrigal: A Comparative Study (no. 4 in "American Musicological Society's Studies and Documents" series), American Musicological Society, 1962.

The Beethoven Quartets, Knopf, 1967.

(With Horst W. Janson and Dora Jane Janson) *A History of Art and Music,* Prentice Hall (Englewood Cliffs, NJ), 1968.

(Editor) Ludwig von Beethoven, *Autograph Miscellany from Circa 1786 to 1799: British Museum Additional Manuscript 29801, ff. 39-162 (The Kafka Sketchbook),* two volumes, British Museum (London), 1970.

(With wife, Vivian Kerman) *Listen* (includes sound recording), Worth (New York City), 1972, third edition, 1980, third brief edition, 1996.

(Editor with Alan Tyson) *Beethoven Studies,* Norton, 1973.

The Masses and Motets of William Byrd (Volume 1 of "The Music of William Byrd" series), University of California Press, 1981.

(With Tyson) *The New Grove Beethoven* (first published in *New Grove Dictionary of Music and Musicians . . . 1980*), Norton, 1983.

Contemplating Music: Challenges to Musicology, Harvard University Press (Cambridge, MA), 1985.

Musicology, Fontana (London), 1985.

(Editor) *Music at the Turn of the Century: A Nineteenth-Century Music Reader,* University of California Press, 1990.

Write All These Down: Essays on Music, University of California Press, 1994.

Concerto Conversations (includes an accompanying sound recording; part of "The Charles Eliot Norton Lectures" series, 1997-98), Harvard University Press, 1999.

Also, sound recording *In Memory of Gertrude Clarke Whittall: A Lecture,* recorded April 6, 1987, in the Coolidge Auditorium at the Library of Congress in Washington, D.C., sponsored by the Gertrude Clarke Whittall Poetry and Literature Fund. Contributor of articles and reviews to journals in his field, including *Hudson Review* and *New York Review,* and to newspapers, including *San Francisco Chronicle.* Co-editor, *Nineteenth-Century Music,* 1977—.

SIDELIGHTS: Musicologist Joseph Kerman has authored and edited numerous publications, among them 1985's *Contemplating Music: Challenges to Musicology* and *Write All These Down: Essays on Music,* published in 1994. *Contemplating Music* is "a very good book. . . . a passionate polemic. . . . [that] goes beyond polemic to provide a lucid overview of important developments on the postwar musical scene," praised Terry Teachout in a *National Review* assessment, declaring Kerman "a first-rate musicologist" who "has been writing exquisitely about [music] for several decades." In addition to recognizing that Kerman's writing is jargon-free, Teachout described the musicologist's text as "a witty, contentious prose." David McKee also remarked on Kerman's wit, judging in an *Opera News* review of *Write All These Down:* "Kerman, whose 1956 *Opera as Drama* remains a touchstone, has collected twenty far-flung essays into one weighty tome. . . . decidedly for the serious musicologist rather than the average listener. . . . A schoolmasterly frown pervades much of Kerman's prose. . . . Yet whenever he threatens to turn tendentious, shafts of wit help to sell his point of view."

Kerman is "appreciate[d]" for his "erudition and accessibility" as well as his ability to give "imaginative . . . connections," according to Bonnie Jo Dopp's *Library Journal* review of *Concerto Conversations,* a 1999 publication originating from Harvard University's 1997-98 Charles Eliot Norton lecture series. In *Concerto Conversations,* which includes an accompanying sound recording, Kerman presents "conversations in words about conversations in music," stated Ray Olson in a *Booklist* review, concluding, "this is a marvelous book for music lovers, especially because Kerman is such a good conversationalist." "What a pity this engaging, intelligent book is not a multimedia CD or video series," declared Dopp, complaining about the logistics related to the publication's layout and integration of music and text. Without a mention of *Concerto Conversations*' interplay between text and sound recording, *Times Literary Supplement* contributor Judith Weir heralded the work, instructing: "Present-day composers should pay particular heed to Kerman's illuminating ideas." *Concerto Conversations,* asserted Weir, is a "persuasive little book [that] argues very successfully for an end to . . . self-denial [of the concerto], and suggests that the concerto could have an ebullient creative future." Weir also remarked, "Kerman's view of concerto form consists basically of two opposing principles: polarity and reciprocity."

One of Kerman's first books focuses on quartets, specifically Beethoven's quartets. In an issue of *Times Literary Supplement,* a critic wrote about *The Beethoven Quartets:* "The main attraction of the new book is its scale and scope. Mr. Kerman's actual knowledge is formidable, and he preserves a just balance between technical analysis and artistic result. As a handbook for the intelligent listener desirous of deepening his understanding, or of refreshing his mind about 'what happens,' the volume is important, and the copious music examples are excellently reproduced." Composer Igor Stravinsky remarked of Kerman in the *New York Review of Books:* "I recommend him to high-minded readers, as well as to credit-minded students in need of a crib. The book is rich in insights. . . . Mr. Kerman has an acute grasp of the powers of Beethoven's tonality instrument." Stravinsky added: "Nor is Mr. Kerman's study of the other aspects of the quartets, and of Beethoven in general, less perspicacious, valuable observations on such matters as the proprieties of the genres, and the rarity of relationships based on the augmented triad, being found on every page."

Kerman's 1981 study of the music of early English composer William Byrd (*The Masses and Motets of William Byrd*) delves into the issue of how Byrd was able to achieve success writing church music with Latin texts in a period when the language had been banned from liturgical services. Robert Donington stated in the *Times Literary Supplement:* "Byrd survived and prospered, acknowledged Catholic though he was; and Joseph Kerman has taught us far more than we knew before about that aspect of this very great Englishman's career. He earns our gratitude . . . for publishing, with appropriate excellence, this major enterprise of musical scholarship."

BIOGRAPHICAL/CRITICAL SOURCES:

PERIODICALS

Booklist, October 15, 1999, p. 407.
High Fidelity, July, 1982, p. MA19; November, 1985, p. MA17.
Library Journal, November 1, 1988, p. 91; October 1, 1999, p. 97.
Music & Letters, August, 1995, review of *Write All These Down: Essays on Music,* p. 413.
Musical Quarterly, winter, 1983, p. 144; winter, 1984, p. 134; spring, 1985, p. 38; summer, 1986, p. 416.
National Review, May 23, 1986, p. 51.
New Republic, February 14, 2000, Alex Ross, review of *Concerto Conversations,* p. 47.
New York Review of Books, September 26, 1968; July 18, 1985, p. 23.
New York Times Book Review, May 26, 1985, p. 19; April 13, 1986, p. 38.
Notes, December, 1995, Renee Cox Lorraine, review of *Write All These Down: Essays on Music,* p. 505.
Opera News, April 15, 1989, p. 44; March 18, 1995, p. 47.
Times Literary Supplement, August 17, 1967; October 23, 1981; November 19, 1999, Judith Weir, review of *Concerto Conversations.*
Yale Review, spring, 1986, p. 437.*

KESSLER, Ronald (Borek) 1943-

PERSONAL: Born December 31, 1943, in New York, NY; son of Ernest Borek (a biochemist) and Minuetta (a pianist; maiden name, Shumiatcher) Kessler; married second wife, Pamela Johnson (an author), 1979; children: Greg, Rachel. *Education:* Attended Clark University, 1962-64.

ADDRESSES: Home and Office—2516 Stratton Dr., Potomac, MD 20854.

CAREER: Worcester Telegram, Worcester, MA, reporter, 1964; *Boston Herald,* Boston, editorial writer and reporter, 1964-67; *Wall Street Journal,* New York City, reporter, 1967-70; *Washington Post,* Washington, DC, investigative reporter, 1970-87. Notable stories include Richard Nixon's finances, F.B.I. wiretapping, General Services Administration scandal, and problem loans at New York banks.

AWARDS, HONORS: First prize award in news writing, United Press International, 1965; Sevellon Brown Award, Associated Press, 1965; Freedoms Foundation Award, 1966; public affairs award, American Political Science Association, 1967; science award, American Dental Society, 1968; Washingtonian of the Year award, *Washingtonian* Magazine, 1972; Baltimore-Washington Newspaper Guild Front Page Award, 1972; George Polk Memorial awards, 1972, for community service, and 1979, for national reporting; public affairs award, American Association of University Women, 1973; top prize for business and financial reporting, Washington Chapter of Sigma Delta Chi; first place award in investigative reporting, Association of Area Business Publications.

WRITINGS:

The Life Insurance Game, Holt (New York City), 1985.
The Richest Man in the World: The Story of Adnan Khashoggi, Warner (New York City), 1986.
Spy vs. Spy: Stalking Soviet Spies in America, Scribner (New York City), 1987.
Moscow Station: How the KGB Penetrated the American Embassy, Scribner, 1989.
The Spy in the Russian Club: How Glenn Souther Stole America's War Plans and Escaped to Moscow, Scribner, 1990.
Escape from the CIA: How the CIA Won and Lost the Most Important KGB Spy Ever to Defect to the U.S., Pocket Books (New York City), 1991.
Inside the CIA: Revealing the Secrets of the World's Most Powerful Spy Agency, Pocket Books, 1992, Blackstone Audio Books, 1998.

The FBI: Inside the World's Most Powerful Law Enforcement Agency, Pocket Books, 1993, revised and updated edition, 1994.

Inside the White House: The Hidden Lives of the Modern Presidents and the Secrets of the World's Most Powerful Institution, Pocket Books, 1995, revised and updated edition, 1996.

The Sins of the Father: Joseph P. Kennedy and the Dynasty He Founded, Warner, 1996.

Inside Congress: The Shocking Scandals, Corruption, and Abuse of Power behind the Scenes on Capitol Hill, Pocket Books, 1997.

The Season: Inside Palm Beach and America's Richest Society, HarperCollins (New York City), 1999.

SIDELIGHTS: Former *Washington Post* and *Wall Street Journal* reporter Ronald Kessler has used his skills as an investigative journalist to pen a number of best-selling exposes, including books on the White House, the KGB, the CIA, and the FBI. Kessler's 1998 volume, *Inside Congress: The Shocking Scandals, Corruption, and Abuse of Power behind the Scenes on Capitol Hill,* depicts, according to Don Wismer of *Library Journal,* "an institution out of control, which exempted itself from the laws under which we live and spent rampantly, on behalf of those special interests that funded the members' elections." Raymond L. Fischer of *USA Today Magazine* notes: "Kessler terms the one-man, one-vote system a cruel joke. Instead of people at large, Congressmen represent the special interests that can raise the most money. . . . [He] documents not only the trips, junkets, and pork-barrel projects, but the lack of accountability and the lavish individual spending." In the course of writing the book, Kessler interviewed 350 Capitol Hill insiders. He includes eyewitness accounts from police officers, doormen, clerks, pages, and many others to substantiate his charges of not only financial chicanery but sexual misconduct and general lawlessness. Declaring that "Kessler has catalogued decades' worth of corruption and scandal involving our nations's elected officials," Alex Tresniowski of *Publishers Weekly* also notes that he "isn't shy about naming names. . . . Republicans and Democrats alike." In contrast, Wismer finds *Inside Congress* to be "an uneven effort that [bogs] down in salacious detail and anti-Gingrich partisanship." Wismer feels that the true value of the book lies not in its expose of Congressional misconduct, but in Kessler's argument, based in part on the Clean Elections Act adopted by Maine voters in 1996, "that public financing of elections would remove much of the tendency toward Congressional corruption."

In the course of researching a book on Joseph P. Kennedy, Kessler spent some time in the wealthy resort community of Palm Beach, Florida. He found life in Palm Beach to be so bizarre that he felt it warranted its own book. The result is *The Season: Inside Palm Beach and America's Richest Society.* An island off the east coast of Florida, Palm Beach first became a winter retreat for America's very rich in the late nineteenth century when it hosted multimillionaires such as John D. Rockefeller, Andrew Carnegie, and J. P. Morgan. In 1999 the names have changed to those such as Donald Trump, Roxanne Pulitzer, and Rod Stewart, but the wealth and conspicuous consumption remain the same. Kessler's stays revealed that Jews are excluded from some of the island's private clubs, mistresses are commonplace, until recently those servants belonging to certain ethnic groups were legally required to be fingerprinted, and "that the super-rich can be as painfully insecure . . . as the rest of us," relates a reviewer for *Publishers Weekly.* "While all of that may be nothing new," the *Publishers Weekly* writer concludes, "this is a fun and frothy glimpse into a world that, despite its surface glitter, is, as Kessler astutely observes, characterized by almost as much cliquishness, pettiness and gossip as high school."

BIOGRAPHICAL/CRITICAL SOURCES:

PERIODICALS

Library Journal, April 15, 1998, Don Wismer, review of *Inside Congress,* p. 135; August, 1998, Don Wismer, review of sound recording *Inside the C.I.A.,* p. 154.

People Weekly, August 18, 1997, Alex Tresniowski, review of *Inside Congress,* p. 34.

Publishers Weekly, November 1, 1999, review of *The Season,* p. 70.

Times Literary Supplement, May 17, 1996, p. 36.

USA Today, January, 1998, Raymond L. Fischer, review of *Inside Congress,* p. 80.

* * *

KITT, Sandra (E.) 1947-

PERSONAL: Born June 11, 1947, in New York, NY; daughter of Archie B. and Ann (Wright) Kitt. *Ethnicity:* "African American." *Education:* Bronx Community College of the City University of New York, A.A.; City College of the City University of New York, B.A., 1969, M.F.A., 1975; also attended School of Visual

Arts, New School for Social Research, and University of Guadalajara. *Religion:* Methodist.

ADDRESSES: Home—New York City. *Agent*—Ling Lucas, Nine Muses and Apollo Agency, 2 Charlton St., New York, NY 10014.

CAREER: Philip Gips Studios, Inc., art assistant, 1970-72; New York City Board of Education, New York City, teacher in Cloisters Workshop Program, 1972-73; *Information Specialist,* New York City, librarian, 1974-92; American Museum of Natural History, New York City, manager of library services at Richard S. Perkin Library, Hayden Planetarium, 1992—. Museum of Contemporary Arts, assistant to the registrar and assistant coordinator at Children's Art Center, 1972-73; New York City Office of Cultural Affairs, teacher at Printmaking Workshop, 1974-80. Freelance graphic artist and illustrator, with work exhibited throughout the United States and represented in corporate collections, including American Institute of Graphic Arts and African-American Art Museum of Los Angeles; greeting card designer for UNICEF; printmaker. Guest on television programs, including *NBC Today,* and on the Black Entertainment Television cable network.

MEMBER: Special Libraries Association, Published Authors Network, Romance Writers of America, Novelists INK, American Library Association (Black Caucus).

AWARDS, HONORS: NIA Woman of Excellence Award from the mayor of New York City, 1993.

WRITINGS:

ROMANCE NOVELS

Rites of Spring, Harlequin American (Tarrytown, NY), 1984.
Adam and Eva, Harlequin American, 1984.
All Good Things, Doubleday (New York City), 1984.
Perfect Combination, Harlequin American, 1985.
Only with the Heart, Harlequin American, 1985.
With Open Arms, Harlequin American, 1987.
An Innocent Man, Harlequin American, 1989.
The Way Home, Harlequin American, 1990.
Someone's Baby, Harlequin American, 1991.
Love Everlasting, Odyssey Books, 1993.
Love Is Thanks Enough (also known as *Friends, Families, and Lovers*), Harlequin, 1993.
Serenade, Pinnacle Books (New York City), 1994.
Sincerely, Pinnacle Books, 1995.
The Color of Love, Dutton (New York City), 1995.
Significant Others, Onyx Books (New York City), 1996.
Between Friends, Signet Books (New York City), 1998.
Family Affairs, Signet Books, 1999.
Close Encounters, Signet Books, 2000.

OTHER

(Illustrator) Isaac Asimov, *Asimov's Guide to Halley's Comet,* Walker and Co. (New York City), 1985.
(Illustrator) Asimov, *Beginnings: The Story of Origin. . .,* Walker and Co., 1986.

Author of the unreleased screenplays *Forgiving,* 1988, and *Snatched!* 1992. Contributor of articles and reviews to museum and library journals.

* * *

KLEMENT, Frank L(udwig) 1908-1994

PERSONAL: Born August 19, 1908, in Leopolis, WI; died in 1994; son of Jacob and Barbara (Kutil) Klement; married Laurel Marie Fosnot, 1938; children: Paul Francis, Richard Eugene, Kenneth Raymond. *Education:* Central State College (now Wisconsin State College at Stevens Point), B.E., 1935; University of Wisconsin, Ph.M., 1938, Ph.D., 1946. *Avocational interests:* Camping, fishing.

CAREER: High school teacher in Beloit, WI, 1938-41; Lake Forest College, Lake Forest, IL, instructor, 1943-45; Wisconsin State College, Eau Claire, assistant professor of history, 1945-48; Marquette University, Milwaukee, WI, professor of history, then emeritus, 1948-94. National Civil War Centennial Commission, member of advisory council; Wisconsin Civil War Centennial Commission, chairman of education committee.

MEMBER: American Historical Society, Mississippi Valley Historical Association, American Catholic Historical Association (executive council, 1957-60), Wisconsin Historical Society, Civil War Round Table of Milwaukee, Phi Alpha Theta (national councilor, 1963—).

AWARDS, HONORS: Ford Foundation fellowship, 1952-53.

WRITINGS:

Lincoln's Critics in Wisconsin: Address at Annual Meeting, Lincoln Fellowship of Wisconsin, Madi-

son, February 14, 1955 (lecture), Lincoln Fellowship of Wisconsin, 1956.

The Copperheads in the Middle West, University of Chicago Press (Chicago), 1960.

Wisconsin and the Civil War, State Historical Society of Wisconsin (Madison), 1963.

The Limits of Dissent: Clement L. Vallandigham and the Civil War, University Press of Kentucky (Lexington), 1970, with a preface by Steven K. Rogstad, Fordham University Press (New York City), 1998.

Dark Lanterns: Secret Political Societies, Conspiracies, and Treason Trials in the Civil War, Louisiana State University Press (Baton Rouge), 1984.

The Gettysburg Soldiers' Cemetery and Lincoln's Address: Aspects and Angles, introduction by Rogstad, White Mane (Shippensburg, PA), 1993.

Wisconsin in the Civil War: The Home Front and the Battle Front, 1861-1865, State Historical Society of Wisconsin (Madison), 1997.

Lincoln's Critics: The Copperheads of the North, edited and introduced by Rogstad, White Mane, 1999.

Contributor to a score of professional journals, mainly on historical subjects. Editorial board member, *Proceedings* of Wisconsin Academy of Science, Arts, and Letters.

SIDELIGHTS: Frank L. Klement, who died in 1994 as professor emeritus at Marquette University, became "the premier historian of Lincoln's opponents in the North," reported Ray Olson in a *Booklist* review of *Lincoln's Critics: The Copperheads of the North,* published in 1999. Drawn from the Civil War historian's previously published papers as well as unpublished material, *Lincoln's Critics* is a culmination of Klement's lifetime of scholarly work. *Lincoln's Critics* "provides the fullest statement of Klement's thesis. . . . [and] insights into Klement's development as a scholar," maintained P. F. Field in *Choice.* The posthumously published volume presents a case for Klement's belief that "copperheads" have been historically misrepresented. In Klement's opinion, they were not traitors. They were not like the image furthered by "Republican propaganda" and "nationalist mythologizing about Lincoln"; rather they were a generally democratic group weary of change and concerned about "Lincoln administration's abuse of Constitutional rights," recounted Olson. Among Klement's other publications are *The Copperheads in the Middle West* (1960), *Wisconsin and the Civil War* (1963), *The Limits of Dissent: Clement L. Vallandigham and the Civil War* (1970), *Dark Lanterns: Secret Political Societies, Conspiracies, and Treason Trials in the Civil War* (1984), and *Wisconsin in the Civil War: The Home Front and the Battle Front, 1861-1865* (1997).

BIOGRAPHICAL/CRITICAL SOURCES:

PERIODICALS

American Historical Review, October, 1985, p. 1017.

Booklist, September 1, 1999, Ray Olson, review of *Lincoln's Critics: The Copperheads of the North,* p. 65.

Choice, November, 1999, P. F. Field, review of *Lincoln's Critics: The Copperheads of the North,* p. 603.

Civil War History, December, 1999, Richard R. Duncan, review of *The Limits of Dissent: Clement L. Vallandigham and the Civil War,* p. 350; March, 2000, Steven Deyle, review of *Lincoln's Critics: The Copperheads of the North,* p. 77.

Journal of American History, December, 1985, p. 692.

Library Journal, February 1, 1994, p. 96.*

* * *

KLIMA, Ivan 1931-

PERSONAL: Born September 14, 1931, in Prague, Czechoslovakia; son of Ing Vilem and Marta (Synkova) Klima; married Helena Mala (a psychotherapist), September 24, 1958; children: Michal, Hana. *Education:* Charles University, M.A., 1956. *Avocational interests:* Lawn tennis, picking mushrooms.

ADDRESSES: Agent—(books) Brombergs Bokforlag Industrigatan, 4a Box 12886 S-11298, Stockholm, Sweden; (plays) Projekt, Theater & Medien Verlag, Karolimgerring 31, 5000 Cologne 1, Germany.

CAREER: Writer. Ceskoslovensky Spisovatel (publishers), Prague, Czechoslovakia, editor, 1959-63; *Literarni noviny* (weekly publication of Union of Writers), Prague, deputy and editor-in-chief, 1963-69. University of Michigan, Ann Arbor, visiting professor, 1969-70; University of California at Berkeley, visiting professor, 1997; *Lidove Noviny* (daily newspaper), former member of editorial board; *Literarni noviny,* member of board; State Fund of Culture of Czech republic, member of board.

MEMBER: Union of Czechoslovak Writers (member of central committee 1963-70,during by Czech government; council member, 1989—), Club of Rome (Czech branch), Czech PEN Centre (president, 1990-93), Greenpeace (member of voting membership of Czech section), Ambassador Club.

AWARDS, HONORS: Awards from Ministry of Culture, 1960, 1965, and from Ceskoslovensky Spisovatel, 1963; Hostovsky Award, New York, 1986, for *My First Loves;* George Theiner Prize, 1993, for *My Golden Trades;* Best Books of 1995 citation, *Publishers Weekly,* for *Waiting for the Dark, Waiting for the Light.*

WRITINGS:

NONFICTION

Mezi tremi hranicemi (book on Slovakia), Ceskoslovensky Spisovatel (Prague), 1960.

Karel Chapek (essay), Ceskoslovensky Spisovatel, 1962.

The Spirit of Prague (essays), Granta (London), 1994.

Kruh nepratel ceskeho jazyka: fejetony, Hynek (Prague), 1998.

(With Bedrich Fritta) *O chlapci ktery se nestal cislem,* Zidovske muzeum (Prague), 1998.

Between Security and Insecurity, translated by Gerald Turner, Thames & Hudson (New York City), 1999.

SHORT STORIES

Bezvadny den (title means "The Wonderful Day"), Ceskoslovensky Spisovatel, 1962.

Milenci na jednu noc, Ceskoslovensky Spisovatel, 1964, translation by Turner published in expanded edition with more recent stories as *Lovers for a Day,* Grove Press (New York City), 1999.

Ma vesela jitra, Ceskoslovensky Spisovatel, 1978, translation by George Theiner published as *My Merry Mornings: Stories from Prague,* Readers International, 1985.

My First Loves, translation by Ewald Osers, Chatto and Windus, 1987, Harper (New York City), 1988, originally published in Czech as *Moje prvni lasky.*

Ostrov mrtvych kralu (title means "The Island of Death Kings"), Rozmluvy (Prague), 1991.

My Golden Trades, translation by Paul Wilson, Granta, 1992, originally published in Czech as *Moje zlata remesla.*

NOVELS

Hodina ticha (title means "The Hour of Silence"), Ceskoslovensky Spisovatel, 1963.

Lod jmenem nadeje, Ceskoslovensky Spisovatel, 1969, translation by Edith Pargeter published as *A Ship Named Hope,* Gollancz (London), 1970.

Milostne leto, Sixty-Eight Publishers, 1973, translation by Osers, published as *A Summer Affair,* Chatto & Windus, 1987.

Love and Garbage, Chatto & Windus, 1990, Knopf (New York City), 1991, originally published in Czech as *Laska a smeti.*

Judge on Trial, translation by A. G. Brain, Chatto & Windus, 1991, Knopf, 1993, originally published in Czech as *Soudce z milosti.*

Waiting for the Dark, Waiting for the Light, translation by Wilson, Granta, 1994, St. Martin's Press, 1996, originally published in Czech as *Cekani na tmu, cekani na svetlo.*

Posledni stupen duvernosti, Hynek, 1996, translation by A. G. Brain published as *The Ultimate Intimacy,* Grove Press, 1997.

PLAYS

Zamek, first produced in Prague, Czechoslovakia, at Theatre Na Vinohradech, 1964, produced as *The Castle* in Ann Arbor, MI, at Lydia Mendelssohn Theatre, University of Michigan, December 3, 1968, produced for television in Austria, Finland, and the Netherlands.

Porota (title means "The Jury"), first produced in Prague, April 17, 1969, adaptation for radio produced by NDR Radio, West Germany, English radio version produced by the British Broadcasting Corporation (BBC), London, England, 1970.

Zenich pro Marcelu (title means "A Bridegroom for Marcela"), translation by Ruth Willard first produced Off-Broadway, spring, 1969, produced for television in Austria and West Germany.

Klara, translation by Willard first produced Off-Broadway, spring, 1969, produced for television in Austria and West Germany.

Ministr a andel (title means "President and the Angel"), broadcast by BBC, London, 1973.

Hry (title means "The Games"), first produced in Vancouver, Canada, 1975.

Also author of *Mistr* (title means "The Master"), 1967; *Cafe Myrian* (title means "The Sweetshoppe Myriam"), 1968; *Franz a Felice,* translation by Jan Drabek as *Kafka and Felice,* 1985; *Uz Se Blizi Mece: Eseje, Fejetony, Rozhovory,* Novinar (Prague), 1990; (with others) *Uzel Pohadek: Pohadky, Soucasnych Ceskychautoru,* Lidove Noviny, 1991.

Contributor to periodicals, including *New York Review of Books, National, Granta,* and *Index on Censorship.* Contributor to *This Side of Reality: Modern Czech Writing,* edited by Alexandra Buchler, Serpent's Trail, 1996. Klima's works have been translated into twenty-eight languages, including German, Swedish, Italian, Spanish, Hebrew, French, Korean, Norwegian, Russian, Danish, Dutch, Polish, Portuguese, Chinese, Japanese, Hungarian, and Serbocroatian.

SIDELIGHTS: Ivan Klima is a Czech writer who was banned in his own country by the communist government after the 1968 Prague Spring reforms. One of about two hundred banned Czech writers, Klima chose not to emigrate, unlike his fellow dissidents Milan Kundera and Josef Skvorecky, preferring to stay at home and write as best he could under the existing constraints. "Ivan Klima," according to Eva Hoffman in the *New York Times Book Review,* "is among those urbane, plain-spoken literary spirits whose work travels successfully across political systems, as well as across continents."

During the communist government's ban on writers' work, an underground movement was formed in Czechoslovakia to circulate typewritten manuscripts among interested readers. The Russian term for writing circulated in this fashion is *samizdat,* generally translated as "writing for the desk-drawer." Circulating and reading *samizdat* writings were considered criminal offenses, so the reader as well as the writer took a risk in participating in the movement. After the collapse of the Czech communist government, restrictions loosened and efforts were made to reintegrate banned writers into Czech society and liberalize controls on the arts. Klima was an active member and spokesperson for the revived Czech branch of PEN; in 1990 he became its president.

Both Michiko Kakutani of the *New York Times* and *Los Angeles Times* reviewer Richard Eder have noted the effects that government bans can have on writing style. Eder observed that "writing accomplished through censorship and the prospect of punishment can take on a primal urgency. There is a nerviness to it. It comes partly from the act of defiance, and partly from the hunger of readers to hear voices and messages denied them by the official monopoly." As an example, Eder pointed to Klima's short-story collection *My Merry Mornings: Stories from Prague,* which he called "a work of jittery truth . . . gritty, passionate and starved." Kakutani noted that "in the work of . . . Milan Kundera and Ivan Klima, people *do* make an attempt to create a personal life that will be free from state control. They do so mainly by engaging in frenetic and promiscuous sex, but they discover that even sex has been colored by the duplicities and manipulations of the political life around them. For them, too, the line between the public and the personal has been erased."

The plot of Klima's *A Summer Affair* supports Kakutani's point, at least in part. It is the story of a research scientist who, in the words of *Times Literary Supplement*'s Lesley Chamberlain, "shamelessly and unreasonably . . . abandons his family and his work for a humiliating and temperamental sexual arrangement." Summing up the author's treatment of his protagonist's behavior, Chamberlain stated: "Though Ivan Klima does not quite condone, these are facts, not matters inviting judgment. Love is a condition, not a controllable sin, and Klima writes about it with disconcerting Flaubertian wisdom."

My First Loves, a collection of four stories, was published in the United States in 1988. "At first glance," Eder remarked, "the tone is delicately nostalgic, even pastoral. . . . The longings, delusions, and losses of young love become a code language for an alien and crimped reality. The code works sporadically; the result is writing that is haunting at times, but that can be cloudy and bland." Jack Sullivan, writing in the *New York Times Book Review,* commented that "Klima is most compelling when he is willing to trust the power and odd lucidity of his hero's adolescent musing. He is least so when he occasionally . . . explains the work's symbolism and significance. No explanations are necessary, for these stories carry the burning authority and desperate eloquence of a survivor."

Several reviewers unhesitatingly labeled the stories autobiographical. Andrew Sinclair noted in the London *Times* that Klima spent several of his childhood years in the Czech barracks camp of Terezin. In one story of the collection, a boy is emotionally attracted to and then disappointed by the young woman who doles out the daily milk rations and initially gives the child an extra portion every day. In the *New York Review of Books,* D. J. Enright offered the example of another story in which the boy's father—like Klima's, an engineer—"voices the idealistic Communist vision of a future in which poverty and exploitation will be no more, heavy labor will be done by marvelous machines, the people will govern, and, since there is no reason for war, an age of universal peace and trust will dawn."

Klima's novel *Love and Garbage* focuses on a middle-aged dissident writer in Prague who had lived in the Terezin camp as a child. Unable to make a living at his profession because his work is banned, he becomes a street-sweeper. The tales of his fellow laborers become part of the material for his fiction, along with memories of people who were close to him and an account of his present struggle to choose between his wife and his mistress. The book turns on many allegories, most of which are centered around the question of what is trash. In the London *Times,* Barbara Day explained that "Klima was writing before the 'gentle revolution' which swept away the tainted ideals of his country's old government, and brought in a new one. Now he is amongst those who are working—a little less gently—to clear up the rubbish of the past." In the opinion of Alberto Manguel in the *Washington Post Book World, "Love and Garbage* announces [the] world's essential dichotomy: We create in order to destroy, and then build from the destruction. Our emblem is the phoenix."

In the *New Republic,* Stanislaw Baranczak criticized the author's style, noting that "Klima does his thing with utmost seriousness, with heavy-handed directness; even his symbols seem to have a sign that reads ATTENTION: SYMBOL attached to them, lest we overlook their exfoliating, larger-than-life implications. . . . It is . . . the arbitrariness, the sententiousness and the priggishness of Klima's observations, which leave no room for the reader's own interpretation of the matters under discussion." Hoffman found that the author's "sincerity sometimes slides toward banality. The novel's fragmentary method makes for a certain stasis." She concluded, however, that these defects "do not substantially affect the import or the impact of Mr. Klima's work," which "affords the experience, rare in today's fiction, of being in the presence of a seasoned, measured perspective, and a mind that strives honestly to arrive at a wisdom sufficient to our common condition."

Judge on Trial centers around a judge who earlier in his career wrote against the death penalty and withdrew from the Community Party, acts that have brought his loyalty to the government increasingly into question. As he presides over the trial of a petty criminal accused of gassing his landlady and her granddaughter, the judge realizes that he is equally on trial. "The novel's subject is suffocation. Like all of Ivan Klima's fiction," wrote Peter Kemp in the *Times Literary Supplement,* "it takes you into an atmosphere of choking oppressiveness." In a *Times Literary Supplement* review, Roger Scruton called *Judge on Trial* "one of the saddest novels to have been written in contemporary Czechoslovakia." Kemp concluded that Klima demonstrates in this novel how, "even in a climate thickly polluted by cynicism, integrity can't be entirely asphyxiated."

Set in the post-communist Czech Republic, the novel *The Ultimate Intimacy* considers the lives of the citizens of Prague under their new democracy. At the story's center is Daniel Vedra, a Protestant minister, who is left disoriented by the dissolution of the communist government, which, as the people's common enemy, provided a clear distinction between good and evil. "Bereft of his old certainties and lacking a single metaphysical hook on which to hang his surplice," explained Scott Bradfield in the *Los Angeles Times Book Review,* "Daniel eventually begins to question everything: his family, his faith, and his political beliefs." Unable to forget his first wife, Daniel cheats on his second by having an affair with a married woman. His search for intimacy involves his examining the relationships he has not only with the women in his life but also with his children and God.

Critical reception to *The Ultimate Intimacy* was rather mixed. Commenting in the *Washington Post Book World,* Steven Moore, citing the "standard themes of adultery and religious doubt," felt that a "predictability dogs Klima's novel." He averred that "the most interesting aspect of *The Ultimate Intimacy* is its elegant, formal structure." Peter Sherwood in the *Times Literary Supplement* asserted: "Disillusionment with some aspects of life after 1989 is not uncommon in Central and Eastern Europe, but Klima's simplistic nostalgia is disappointing, and it makes for bad art." Bradfield, while finding that the author's "narratives tend to get mired in introspection" and that "his characters tend to be swallowed up by their own rampant subjectivity," argued that the novel "establishes its own special intimacy with readers." He concluded that the work "is an absorbing account of people seeking faith in an age of faithlessness."

In 1999 Klima's 1964 story collection, *Lovers for a Day,* (expanded to include more recent stories from the 1980s and 90s) appeared in English-language translation. Reviewing the work for *Booklist,* Brad Hooper lauded Klima as "a master of significant detail—telling only that which is essential." As the title indicates, the twelve stories in the collection are linked by the theme of love. In "The White Horse" a student falls in love with a blind girl, and insists he is going to abandon her. In "Rich Men Tend to Be Strange" a dying man plans to leave his life's savings to a nurse who has been kind to him. "Execution of a Horse" tells of a woman who learns a lesson about love by seeing a horse put down. According to Lisa Rohrbaugh of *Library Journal,* Klima demonstrates "precise prose and an uncanny ability to write conversations between husband and wife or lovers." In marked contrast a *Publishers Weekly* reviewer, unsure whether to blame Klima or the Turner translation, described the prose in the book as "clunky," and faulted Klima for his tendency "to stop and spell out the point he's making, in a manner alien to most modern English-language fiction." However, the reviewer granted that " 'The White Horse' is brilliant by any reckoning."

Between Security and Insecurity presents a series of interrelated essays by Klima that deal with what he considers the major malady of our age: existential emptiness. "With broad strokes," a *Publishers Weekly* reviewer remarked, "Klima offers philosophically informed diagnoses of current ills," including the "breakdown" of families and marriages. Klima blames many of these problems on the materialism of Western culture, which he feels stresses consumption and productivity at the expense of values such as love and a sense of community. On the positive side, he praises the environmental movement and the increased participation of women in society, both of which he sees as hopeful signs. Though the *Publishers Weekly* reviewer felt that *Between Security and Insecurity* "comes off as hastily written and oddly bland," the critic also maintained that the work "is at times morally incisive and fluent."

In 1999 Mark Schapiro interviewed Klima at his home in Prague for an article that appeared in the *Nation.* "With thin hair hanging over his head in a bowl cut," Schapiro stated, "and eyes bulging behind spectacles, he wears a loose sweater—the uniform of Czech intellectuals—and comes across as a mischievous, grandfatherly figure." Central to Schapiro's line of questioning were his observations about the declining interest in serious literature in the contemporary Czech Republic. After the overthrow of the communist government in 1989, dissident writers had enjoyed an unprecedented popularity as their works were openly published and freely circulated on their own soil for the first time in more than thirty years. A number of Klima's books, such as *My Merry Mornings* and *Love and Garbage,* had sales in excess of 100,000 copies, "enormous in a country of 15 million people," as Schapiro noted. Yet with the ascendancy of capitalism and the increased influence of Western culture, this popularity soon began to wane. The Czech bestseller list began to resemble that in most other countries; it was topped by authors such as Ed McBain, Jackie Collins, and Stephen King. "Today," Schapiro observed, "ironically, those writers who sustained the country's cultural lifeblood in the underground face an audience not dramatically different or expanded from the days when their works could be obtained only on the sly." While granting the validity of Schapiro's statements, Klima did not seem "particularly perturbed by this development." "Most of this society collaborated with the regime from the first moment [in 1948]," Klima commented during the interview. "Later, *samizdat* did not represent them. *Samizdat* was for a small number of people, a few thousand at most, who opposed the regime and lived according to their own beliefs. And it's no different now in terms of who reads the [quality] literature." Klima added: "I argue with those who complain about how writers are less important today. . . . For some people, it has been difficult to accept. They are less famous, less heroic than they were before. On the other hand, you might have been famous for your bravery, but not for your mastery."

BIOGRAPHICAL/CRITICAL SOURCES:

BOOKS

Almanac of Famous People, sixth edition, Gale (Detroit, MI), 1999.

Goetz-Stankiewicz, Marketa, *The Silenced Theatre,* University of Toronto Press, 1979.

Kienzle: Modernes Welttheatre, Kroner Verlag, 1966.

PERIODICALS

Booklist, January 1, 1998, Jim O'Laughlin, review of *The Ultimate Intimacy,* p. 777; August, 1999, Brad Hooper, review of *Lovers for a Day,* p. 2026.

Economist(US), November 9, 1991, p. 107.

Library Journal, November 1, 1997, Marc A. Kloszewski, review of *The Ultimate Intimacy,* p. 116; August, 1999, Lisa Rohrbaugh, review of *Lovers for a Day,* p. 144.

London Review of Books, December 19, 1991.

Los Angeles Times, June 19, 1985; January 13, 1988.

Los Angeles Times Book Review, May 19, 1991; January 25, 1998, p. 8.

Nation, December 30, 1991; May 17, 1999, Mark Schapiro, "Fading Czech Velvet," p. 38.

New Republic, July 29, 1991.

New York Review of Books, May 18, 1989; April 12, 1990; July 15, 1993.

New York Times, August 4, 1989; February 8, 1990.

New York Times Book Review, February 21, 1988; May 12, 1991; April 18, 1993.

Publishers Weekly, March 22, 1991, Sybil Steinberg, review of *Love and Garbage,* p. 69; March 8, 1993, review of *Judge on Trial,* p. 67; August 15, 1994, review of *My Golden Trades,* p. 85; February 6, 1995, review of *Waiting for the Dark, Waiting for the Light,* p. 74; July 10, 1995, review of *The Spirit of Prague,* p. 54; June 10, 1996, review of *This Side of Reality: Modern Czech Writing,* p. 95; November 10, 1997, review of *The Ultimate Intimacy,* p. 55; July 12, 1999, review of *Lovers for a Day,* p. 71; December 6, 1999, review of *Between Security and Insecurity,* p. 62.

Times Literary Supplement, July 5, 1985; January 23, 1987; August 28, 1987; March 30, 1990; October 25, 1991; October 16, 1992; October 31, 1997, p. 26.

Times (London), November 30, 1986; April 5, 1990.

Washington Post Book World, June 23, 1991; April 18, 1993; January 11, 1998, p. 8.

World Literature Today, autumn, 1994, Karen von Kunes, review of *Judge on Trial,* p. 848; summer, 1995, Peter Z. Schubert, review of *My Golden Trades,* p. 609; autumn, 1997, B. R. Bradbrook, review of *Posledni stupen duvernosti,* p. 827.

* * *

KNIGHT, Theodore O. 1946-

PERSONAL: Born October 14, 1946, in Providence, RI; son of Monroe O. (an electrician) and Lilla (a librarian; maiden name, Taudvin) Knight; married Norma Aldrich (a special education teacher), August 10, 1968, children: Matthew Monroe, Anne Aldrich. *Ethnicity:* "White." *Education:* Brown University, B.A. (with honors), 1968; State University of New York at Buffalo, Ph.D., 1975; further study at Rhode Island College and Roger Williams College. *Politics:* Independent. *Religion:* "Varies." *Avocational interests:* Hiking, canoeing, family, travel, music, reading.

ADDRESSES: Home and Office—89 Johnson Rd., Foster, RI 02825. *E-mail*—tknight@loa.com.

CAREER: College Hill Book Store, Providence, RI, manager, 1975-81; Jamestown Publishers, Providence, RI, senior editor, 1982-88; freelance writer/editor, 1989-95; Brookline Books, Cambridge, MA, editorial director, 1995-96; Atlantic Group (book development and editorial service), co-owner and president, 1996—. Dushkin/McGraw-Hill, acquisition editor and list manager, 1998—. Instructor in literature and writing at colleges and universities, including Quinebaug Valley Community College, Nichols College, University of Massachusetts at Boston, Tufts University, and State University of New York at Buffalo, 1971-89.

WRITINGS:

(Editor) Jerry Silbert, Douglas Carnine, and Marcy Stein, *Direct Instruction Mathematics* (textbook), C. E. Merrill (Columbus, OH)/Custom Publishing, 1989.

(Editor) Deborah Greh, *Computers in the Artroom,* Davis Publications (Worcester, MA), 1989.

Silver Burdett and Ginn Social Studies—World Cultures, teacher's edition, Silver Burdett (Morristown, NJ)/Ginn-Mazer, 1990.

Heath Composition and Grammar, Grade 12, teacher's edition, Heath (Lexington, MA)/Boultinghouse & Boultinghouse, 1990.

(Editor) David Henley, *Therapeutic Art Education,* Davis Publications, 1990.

The Olympic Games, Lucent Books-Greenhaven Press (St. Paul, MN), 1991.

(Editor) *Glencoe English, Grade 12,* teacher's edition, Glencoe (New York City)/Ligature, 1991.

(Editor) *Macmillan Reading, Grade 8,* teacher's edition, Macmillan (New York City), 1991.

(Editor) Andrea Vierra, *Reading Educational Research,* Gorsuch Scarisbrick, 1991.

Study Strategies for Career Programs (textbook), Irwin (Homewood, IL), 1993.

Study Strategies for College Programs (textbook), Irwin, 1993.

(Editor) *Houghton Mifflin Social Studies,* Grade 6: *World Culture,* teacher's edition, Houghton (Boston, MA), 1993.

Pioneer Women (juvenile), Rourke Publishing, 1993.

The Language Arts Handbook, Heath, 1993.

Mastering College Reading, Irwin, 1994.

Expressions 2, with teacher's manual, Contemporary Books, 1994.

Viewpoints 2, with teacher's manual, Contemporary Books, 1994.

(Editor) *Beacham's Encyclopedia of Popular Fiction,* Beacham, 1995.

(Contributor) *Reading and Writing Strategies,* Grades 5, 7, and 8, Options, Inc., 1996.

(With Christine Lund Orciuch) *Fifty Strategies to Build Better Study Skills,* Options, Inc., 1997.

(With Orciuch) *Understanding Literature,* Books 6, 7, and 8, Options, Inc., 1997.

Voyager: Reading and Writing for Today's Adult, Book 8, New Readers Press/Learning Unlimited, 1997.

(With Orciuch) *Best Nonfiction, Introductory Level,* Contemporary Books/Jamestown Publishers (Providence, RI), 1998.

(With Orciuch) *Best Nonfiction: Middle Level,* Contemporary Books/Jamestown Publishers, 1998.

(With Orciuch) *Best Nonfiction: Advanced Level,* Contemporary Books/Jamestown Publishers, 1998.

Editor of "ACTION Anthology" series of remedial reading anthologies, Scholastic, Inc. (New York City). Contributor to reference books, including *Encyclopedia of World Biography,* Gale (Detroit, MI), 1997. Book review columnist, *Buffalo Spree,* 1972-99; reviewer for *Magill's Book Reviews* (online service), 1991—.

SIDELIGHTS: Theodore O. Knight commented: "As a freelance writer who works in several areas, I'm constantly trying to combine my knowledge and background with my interests and the need to earn a living. I enjoy doing young adult non-fiction, because it gives me an opportunity to learn more about all sorts of subjects that excite my interest. Writing about things so that they are clear to young adult readers is a great exercise in really learning a subject."

* * *

KOHN, Alan J(acobs) 1931-

PERSONAL: Born July 15, 1931, in New Haven, CT; son of Curtis I. and Harriet J. Kohn; married Marian S. Adachi, August 28, 1959; children: Lizabeth Sawyer, Nancy, Diane Neil, Stephen. *Ethnicity:* "White." *Education:* Princeton University, A.B., 1953; Yale University, Ph.D., 1957.

ADDRESSES: *Home*—18300 Ridgefield Rd. N.W., Shoreline, WA 98177. *Office*—Department of Zoology, University of Washington, Seattle, WA 98195; fax 206-543-3041. *E-mail*—kohn@u.washington.edu.

CAREER: Hopkins Marine Station, laboratory assistant, 1951; Narragansett Marine Laboratory, junior assistant in marine biology, 1952; Marine Biological Laboratory, Woods Hole, MA, technician, 1953; Hawaii Marine Laboratory, associate in research, 1954, visiting collaborator, 1955-56; Yale University, New Haven, CT, W. W. Anderson Fellow at Bingham Oceanographic Laboratory, 1958; Florida State University, Tallahassee, assistant professor of zoology, 1958-61; University of Washington, Seattle, assistant professor, 1961-63, associate professor, 1963-67, professor of zoology, 1967-98, professor emeritus, 1998—, adjunct professor at Quaternary Research Center, 1986—. Thomas Burke Memorial Washington State Museum, affiliate curator of malacology, 1965-70, adjunct curator, 1971—. Smithsonian Institution, National Research Council senior postdoctoral research associate, 1967, research associate at National Museum of Natural History, 1985—, senior fellow of the museum, 1990; University of Hawaii at Manoa, visiting professor, 1968. Visiting investigator at Mid-Pacific Marine Laboratory, Enewetak, 1957 and 1971-73, Bernice P. Bishop Museum, 1961, and University of the Ryukyus, 1982-83; participant in Yale Seychelles Expedition to the Indian Ocean, 1957-58, and U.S. Biology Program of the International Indian Ocean Expedition, 1963. Council for the International Exchange of Scholars, member, 1986-90, chairperson of Australasia Area Committee, 1986-90, member of executive committee, 1988-89.

MEMBER: International Society for Reef Studies, American Association for the Advancement of Science (fellow), Society for Integrative and Comparative Biology (president, 1997-98), American Malacological Union (president, 1982-83), Marine Biological Association of the United Kingdom, Marine Biological Association of India (fellow), Malacological Society of Japan, Pacific Science Association, Linnean Society of London (fellow), Malacological Society of London, Sigma Xi (president of University of Washington chapter, 1971-72).

AWARDS, HONORS: Guggenheim fellow, 1975-76.

WRITINGS:

A Chronological Taxonomy of Conus, 1758-1840, Smithsonian Institution Press (Washington, DC), 1992.

(Editor with F. W. Harrison) *Microscopic Anatomy of Invertebrates,* Wiley (New York City) Volume 5: *Mollusca I,* 1994, Volume 6: *Mollusca II,* 1997.

(With F. E. Perron) *Life History and Biogeography: Patterns in Conus,* Oxford University Press (New York City), 1994.

(With D. Roeckel and W. Korn) *Manual of the Living Conidae,* Christa Hemmen Verlag, 1995.

Contributor of more than a hundred articles to scientific journals. Member of editorial board, *American Zoologist,* 1973-77 and 1999—, *Malacologia,* 1974—, *American Naturalist,* 1976-78, *Journal of Experimental Marine Biology and Ecology,* 1981-84, *Coral Reefs,* 1981-87, *American Malacological Bulletin,* 1983—, and *Marine Research,* 1993—.

KOTLER, Neil G. 1941-

PERSONAL: Born April 17, 1941, in Chicago, IL; son of Maurice (in business) and Betty (a homemaker; maiden name, Bubar) Kotler; married Wendy I. Abrams (a teacher), December 19, 1971; children: Jena J. *Education:* Brandeis University, A.B., 1962; University of Wisconsin—Madison, M.S., 1963; University of Chicago, Ph.D., 1974. *Politics:* Independent. *Religion:* Jewish. *Avocational interests:* Drawing, art, piano.

ADDRESSES: Home—1135 North Kirkwood Rd., Arlington, VA 22210. *Office*—Office of the Undersecretary for Science, Smithsonian Institution, Washington, DC 20560; 202-786-2642.

CAREER: U.S. Peace Corps, Washington, DC, volunteer teacher of Ethiopian history in Asmara, Ethiopia, 1964-66; De Paul University, Chicago, IL, instructor in American government and political science, 1967-71; Dartmouth College, Hanover, NH, instructor in American government and political science, 1971-73; University of Texas at Austin, instructor, 1974-75; U.S. House of Representatives, Washington, DC, began as legislative assistant, became legislative director, 1975-84; Smithsonian Institution, Washington, DC, special assistant and program officer, 1986—, coproducer of the documentary videotapes *Democracy and Rights: One Citizen's Challenge,* 1989, and *Citizen Stories: Democracy and Responsibility in American Life,* 1991. Georgetown University, instructor, 1979.

MEMBER: Phi Beta Kappa.

WRITINGS:

(Editor) Philip Kotler and Eduardo L. Roberto, *Social Marketing: Strategies for Changing Public Behavior,* Free Press (New York City), 1989.

(Editor) *Completing the Food Chain: Strategies for Combating Hunger and Malnutrition,* Smithsonian Institution Press (Washington, DC), 1989.

Democracy and Rights: One Citizen's Challenge (documentary videotape), Smithsonian Institution and Close Up Foundation, 1989.

(Editor) *Sharing Innovation: Global Perspectives on Food, Agriculture, and Rural Development,* Smithsonian Institution Press, 1990.

Citizen Stories: Democracy and Responsibility in American Life (documentary videotape), Smithsonian Institution and Close Up Foundation, 1991.

(Editor) *Frontiers of Nutrition and Food Security in Asia, Africa, and Latin America,* Smithsonian Institution Press, 1992.

(Coeditor) *The Statue of Liberty Revisited: Making a Universal Symbol,* Smithsonian Institution Press, 1994.

(With P. Kotler) *Museum Strategy and Marketing: Designing Missions, Building Audiences, Generating Revenue and Resources,* Jossey-Bass (San Francisco, CA), 1998.

WORK IN PROGRESS: A book on politicians and politics.

SIDELIGHTS: Neil G. Kotler told *CA:* "My books and other writings reflect my lifelong concern for teaching and public service. As a Peace Corps volunteer in Ethiopia, I wrote articles and monographs on Ethiopian and Eritrean history that I hope were of value to my students; this I did, through articles, as a university instructor in political science and American politics. Opportunities at the Smithsonian allowed me to edit a series of books on world food and agriculture and on innovations adopted in non-industrialized nations of the world to feed their peoples. I want to devote the next several years as a writer to advancing museums as centers for enlightenment, education, and historical and cultural understanding. As a political science instructor, I want to help rehabilitate the standing of politics and politicians in the United States and other democratic societies."

* * *

KRIEG, Robert Anthony 1946-

PERSONAL: Born February 8, 1946, in Hackensack, NJ; son of Anthony Benedict (a business systems analyst) and Helen Adele (an editor; maiden name, Battista) Krieg. *Ethnicity:* "German-Italian." *Education:* Stonehill College, B.A., 1969; University of Notre Dame, Ph.D., 1976.

ADDRESSES: Home—Moreau Seminary, University of Notre Dame, Notre Dame, IN 46556. *Office*—Department of Theology, University of Notre Dame, 327 O'Shaughnessy, Notre Dame, IN 46556-5639; fax: 219-631-9238. *E-mail*—krieg.1@nd.edu/.

CAREER: Entered Congregation of the Holy Cross, 1966, ordained Roman Catholic priest, 1973; King's College, Wilkes-Barre, PA, assistant professor of theology, 1975-77; University of Notre Dame, Notre Dame, IN, assistant professor, 1977-85, associate professor, 1985-97, professor of theology, 1997—, director of field education for the ministry, 1978-84, director of Master of Divinity Program, 1985-91, director of doctoral studies, 1995-97.

MEMBER: Catholic Theological Society of America, College Theology Society, Karl Rahner Society.

WRITINGS:

Story-shaped Christology, Paulist Press (Mahwah, NJ), 1988.

Karl Adam: Catholicism in German Culture, University of Notre Dame Press (Notre Dame, IN), 1992.

(Associate editor) *Encyclopedia of Catholicism,* HarperCollins (San Francisco, CA), 1995.

(Editor) *Romano Guardini: Proclaiming the Sacred in a Modern World,* Liturgy Training Publications, 1995.

Romano Guardini: A Precursor of Vatican II, University of Notre Dame Press, 1997.

Contributor to theology journals.

WORK IN PROGRESS: A book on the political views of Catholic theologians in the Third Reich.

SIDELIGHTS: Robert Anthony Krieg told *CA:* "I became a member of a Catholic religious order in 1966 and was ordained a Catholic priest in 1973. This involvement in the life of the church has shaped my scholarly interests and writings. At the same time, my desire to understand the unfolding of modern German theology has brought me into fruitful dialogue with scholars in Munich, Tuebingen, Mainz, Paderborn, and Bochum."

He added: "Although most Catholic theologians in Germany gave no support to Adolf Hitler and his Nazi movement, very few of them made public statements against the *Fuehrer* or overtly defended the dignity and rights of Jews. I am currently doing research toward a book on the link between Catholic theology and politics in Germany from 1933 to 1945."

* * *

KUSHNER, Howard I(rvin) 1943-

PERSONAL: Born July 21, 1943, in Camden, NJ; son of Samuel and Gertrude (Slotnikoff) Kushner; married Carol Rubin (a teacher), August, 1965; children: Peter Evan. *Education:* Rutgers University, A.B. (cum laude), 1965; Cornell University, M.A., 1968, Ph.D., 1970.

ADDRESSES: *Home*—4415 Hingston Ave., Montreal, Quebec, Canada H4A 2J8. *Office*—Department of History, Concordia University, 7141 Sherbrooke St. West, Montreal, Quebec, Canada H4B 1R6.

CAREER: State University of New York College at Fredonia, assistant professor, 1970-74, associate professor of history, 1975-76; Cornell University, Ithaca, NY, visiting associate professor of history, 1976-77; Concordia University, Montreal, Quebec, Canada, associate professor of history, 1977—. Visiting assistant professor at San Francisco State University, 1973-74.

MEMBER: Canadian Association of American Studies, American Studies Association, American Historical Association, Organization of American Historians, Inter-University Centre for European Studies.

WRITINGS:

Conflict on the Northwest Coast: American-Russian Rivalry in the Pacific Northwest, 1790-1867, Greenwood (Westport, CT), 1975.

(With Anne Hummel Sherrill) *John Milton Hay: The Union of Poetry and Politics,* Twayne (Boston), 1977.

Self-Destruction in the Promised Land: A Psychocultural Biology of American Suicide, Rutgers University Press (New Brunswick, NJ), 1989.

A Cursing Brain?: The Histories of Tourette Syndrome, Harvard University Press (Cambridge, MA), 1999.

Contributor to history and American studies journals.

SIDELIGHTS: Howard I. Kushner is the author of 1999's *A Cursing Brain?: The Histories of Tourette Syndrome,* "a compassionate and absorbing work of medical history," praised *Library Journal* contributor Kathleen Arsenault. Tourette Syndrome is a disorder characterized by "involuntary gestures and vocalizations, sometimes shocking or obscene," related Arsenault. In Kushner's "fascinating narrative," described William Beatty in a complimentary *Booklist* review, he "combines the virtues of a detective story with those of a well-documented medical history." "Kushner follows the winding trail of recurrent ticcing through hysteria and hypnosis, masturbation and moral treatment, through to the still controversial suggestion that Tourette syndrome might be an auto-immune disease that follows streptococcal infection," stated John C. Marshall, assessing the work for the *Times Literary Supple-*

ment. While presenting the etiology, treatment, and medical and social perspectives of Tourette syndrome throughout time, Kushner asserts that the direct voice of people with Tourette syndrome has remained relatively silent. Although Marshall referred to Kushner's historical presentation of the disorder as "expertly summarized," the *Times Literary Supplement* critic questioned why *A Cursing Brain?* contained "no mention of a *literary* history of Tourette syndrome. . . . [nor] the nineteenth-century English neurologist John Hughlings Jackson." Furthermore, Marshall wondered why "Kushner stresses very firmly that Tourette syndrome is an *organic* disorder." This emphasis is inane, according to Marshall, because "the old distinction between functional and organic conditions can no longer be drawn." Both Arsenault and Beatty highly recommended *A Cursing Brain?.* Other books by Kushner include *Conflict on the Northwest Coast: American-Russian Rivalry in the Pacific Northwest, 1790-1867* (1975), *John Milton Hay: The Union of Poetry and Politics* (1977; co-authored with Anne Hummel Sherrill), and *Self-Destruction in the Promised Land: A Psychocultural Biology of American Suicide* (1989).

BIOGRAPHICAL/CRITICAL SOURCES:

PERIODICALS

American Historical Review, December, 1990, p. 1611.

Annals of the American Academy of Political and Social Science, Volume 514, 1991, p. 203.

Booklist, April 15, 1999, William Beatty, review of *A Cursing Brain?: The Histories of Tourette Syndrome,* p. 1496.

Journal of the American Medical Association, November 24, 1990, p. 2933.

Journal of American History, December, 1990, p. 981.

Journal of Social History, spring, 2000, Gerald N. Grob, review of *A Cursing Brain?: The Histories of Tourette Syndrome,* p. 741.

Library Journal, June 1, 1989, p. 130; April 15, 1999, Kathleen Arsenault, review of *A Cursing Brain?: The Histories of Tourette Syndrome,* p. 137.

New England Journal of Medicine, July 29, 1999, p. 379.

Science, October 1, 1999, p. 56.

Times Literary Supplement, October 29, 1999, John C. Marshall, review of *A Cursing Brain?: The Histories of Tourette Syndrome.**

L

LAURSEN, John Christian 1952-

PERSONAL: Born in 1952, in Asheville, NC. *Education:* Harvard University, B.A., 1973, J.D., 1977; Johns Hopkins University, M.A., 1981, Ph.D., 1985.

ADDRESSES: *Office*—Department of Political Science, University of California, Riverside, CA 92521. *E-mail*—laursen@wizard.ucr.edu.

CAREER: University of California, Riverside, professor of political science, 1991—.

WRITINGS:

The Politics of Skepticism in the Ancients, Montaigne, Hume, and Kant, E. J. Brill (Long Island City, NY), 1992.

(Editor) *New Essays on the Political Thought of the Huguenots of the Refuge,* E. J. Brill, 1995.

(Editor with Cary J. Nederman) *Difference and Dissent: Theories of Toleration in Medieval and Early Modern Europe,* Rowman & Littlefield (Totowa, NJ), 1996.

(Editor with Nederman) *Beyond the Persecuting Society: Religious Toleration before the Enlightenment,* University of Pennsylvania Press (Philadelphia, PA), 1998.

(Editor) *Religious Toleration: "The Variety of Rites" from Cyrus to Defoe,* St. Martin's (New York City), 1999.

(Editor and translator, with Johan van der Zande) Carl Friedrich Bahrdt, *The Edict of Religion: A Comedy, and History and Diary of My Imprisonment,* Lexington Books (Lexington, MA), 2000.

(Editor with Richard Popkin) *Continental Millenarians: Protestants, Catholics, Heretics,* Kluwer Academic (Hingham, MA), 2000.

LEASKA, Mitchell A(lexander) 1934-

PERSONAL: Surname is pronounced Lee-*as*-ka; born September 8, 1934, in Putnam, CT; son of Nicholas Naum (a real estate agent) and Flora (Ginalis) Leaska. *Education:* Brown University, B.A., 1956; New York University, Ph.D., 1968.

ADDRESSES: *Home*—2 Washington Square Village, Apt. 8H, New York, NY 10012-1706. *Office*—New York University, 735 East Building, New York, NY 10003.

CAREER: Teacher at private school in New York City, 1958-64; Brooklyn College of the City University of New York, Brooklyn, NY, lecturer in English, 1964-66; New York University, New York City, instructor, 1966-68, assistant professor, 1968-70, associate professor, 1970-72, professor of English education, 1972—, director of humanities program in Paris, summer, 1974, director of Study Abroad Center in Athens.

MEMBER: Modern Language Association of America, National Council of Teachers of English.

WRITINGS:

The Voice of Tragedy, Robert Speller (New York City), 1964.

Virginia Woolf's Lighthouse: A Study in Critical Method, Columbia University Press (New York City), 1970.

(Editor) *The Pargiters by Virginia Woolf: Novel-Essay Portions of the Years,* New York Public Library (New York City), 1977.

The Novels of Virginia Woolf: From Beginning to End, John Jay Press (New York City), 1977.

(Editor) *Pointz Hall: The Earlier and Later Typescripts of Between the Acts by Virginia Woolf,* John Jay Press, 1981.

(Editor) *The Virginia Woolf Reader,* Harcourt (San Diego), 1984.

(Co-editor) *The Letters of Vita Sackville-West to Virginia Woolf,* Morrow (New York City), 1985.

(Co-editor) *Violet to Vita: The Letters of Violet Trefusis to Vita Sackville-West,* Methuen (London), 1989, Penguin (New York City), 1991.

(Co-editor with Louise DeSalvo) Virginia Woolf, *A Passionate Apprentice: The Early Journals, 1897-1909,* Harcourt, 1990.

Granite and Rainbow: The Hidden Life of Virginia Woolf, Farrar, Straus (New York City), 1998.

Contributor to library journals and *Virginia Woolf Quarterly.* Consultant for *Psychoanalytic Review,* 1984—.

SIDELIGHTS: Among countless studies of writer Virginia Woolf published every year, Mitchell A. Leaska's contributions are significant. In addition to publishing several critical studies of Woolf 's writings, Leaska has also added to Woolf scholarship by editing *A Passionate Apprentice: The Early Journals, 1897-1909,* the author's previously unpublished diaries and letters. Lauded as a skillful editor, Leaska has won critics' praise for his graceful and sensitive introductions, as well as for his deft handling of journals and correspondence.

Woolf, who is perhaps best known as a prominent member of the intellectually elite "Bloomsbury Group" at the turn of the twentieth century, kept numerous volumes of diaries in addition to publishing boldly original novels, short stories, and essays. Although most of Woolf 's letters and journals had already been published, in 1990 Leaska edited a series of diaries from the author's early, formative years. Compiled into a single volume, the seven notebooks, which span from 1897 to 1909, "have been scrupulously edited and most sensitively introduced and linked" by Leaska, wrote Isabel Colegate in the *New York Times Book Review.* Valuable in their portrait of a young woman who was deeply devastated by the early deaths of both her parents, a half-sister, and her beloved older brother, these diaries "show Virginia Woolf forming the habits of hard work that lasted all her life," Colegate noted. The diaries also show that Woolf—who suffered periodic nervous breakdowns and bouts of depression, the worst of which led to her suicide in 1941—was "exceptionally sane" for most of her life, added Colegate.

Leaska has also contributed to Woolf scholarship by editing the correspondence of Vita Sackville-West—the close friend who inspired Woolf 's mythical novel, *Orlando*—to produce *The Letters of Vita Sackville-West to Virginia Woolf.* The letters, which chronicle the brief affair and decades-long friendship between these two writers, expand not only understanding of Woolf but of Sackville-West, as well. *Washington Post Book World* reviewer Anthony Hecht noted that the volume of letters rounds out "the documentation of the brief but sufficiently literary-historical lesbian flirtation between the novelist of the subjective world [Woolf] and the less brilliant and more earth-bound novelist of upper-crust Britain [Sackville-West]." Although Hecht remarked that the inclusion of both women's complete correspondence in one volume would be ideal, he complimented Leaska for grafting excerpts of Woolf 's letters with Sackville-West's "in a useful way." *New York Times Book Review* critic Thomas Mallon said that Leaska and co-editor Louise DeSalvo "have included enough of Woolf 's side of the correspondence to give its emotional flavor and eliminate scores of footnotes." Other critics found the liaison between Woolf and Sackville-West less interesting. The volume of letters, wrote Fiona MacCarthy in the London *Times,* "is, if not quite dull as ditchwater, a little unenthralling." MacCarthy added that the book "is an example of the madness which takes over when a love affair becomes the material for research."

The letters' focus on the affair between the writers, however, is the very reason other critics commended Leaska for collecting, editing, and publishing them. "Among the greatest pleasures provided by these two decades of well-edited letters," stated Mallon, "is the chance to recall every love affair's keenest intoxication." The volume, he added, "reads like a book, not just a gathering of marvelous scraps." Penned by a well-known and prolific writer of witty correspondence, Woolf 's letters to Sackville-West are considered among her very best. For those interested in the Woolf-Sackville-West relationship in particular, this volume of letters will prove "informative, useful, readable, and entertaining," Hecht concluded.

In *Granite and Rainbow: The Hidden Life of Virginia Woolf,* Leaska seeks to relate Woolf 's life to her work, including the extent to which her manic-depressive illness, love affairs, and sexual abuse by her half-brother informed her writing. Leaska concludes that Woolf 's "manic periods may have accelerated her productivity" and that she derived more satisfaction from her fiction writing than from her life. *Times Literary Supplement* contributor P. N. Furbank referred to Leaska's approach as "the . . . fatal theory that knowledge of [a writer's life] will help one respond to the works." To Furbank, "Such explanations can only ever be pure guesswork. They might be better left to the reader." Michael Anderson, writing in the *New York Times Book Review,* expressed a similar reservation, saying, "Leaska conflates Woolf 's fiction with her life reductively and clumsily." Anderson saw no need for another biography of Woolf and asserted that Leaska "uses the form as a catchall for stray critical observations," which are "oddly ham-handed." Furbank also had a problem with Leaska's literary criticism; in Furbank's opinion, Leaska's admiration of Woolf 's work is justified, but he has exaggerated her role as an innovator. Furbank noted that some authors had preceded Woolf in using unconventional narrative techniques. Furbank added, however, that Leaska "has a fluent, vivid, and at times compelling narrative style. . . . If one had never read a Life of Woolf before, one would, certainly, find *Granite and Rainbow* engrossing and entertaining as well as moving." In *Library Journal,* Ronald Ray Ratliff also noted that several biographies on Woolf have already been published, but he commented that Leaska's work is "solidly written and well done" and concluded that *Granite and Rainbow* is "for comprehensive collections."

BIOGRAPHICAL/CRITICAL SOURCES:

BOOKS

Leaska, Mitchell A., *Granite and Rainbow: The Hidden Life of Virginia Woolf,* Farrar, Straus (New York City), 1998.

PERIODICALS

Ariel: A Review of International English Literature, January, 1971.

Chicago Tribune, March 17, 1985.

Economist (US), January 19, 1991, review of *A Passionate Apprentice: The Early Journals, 1897-1909,* p. 80.

Globe and Mail (Toronto), January 5, 1985; March 9, 1991.

Library Journal, February 1, 1998, Ronald Ray Ratliff, review of *Granite and Rainbow: The Hidden Life of Virginia Woolf,* p. 86.

Los Angeles Times Book Review, December 23, 1984, p. 6.

New York Times Book Review, December 16, 1984, p. 34; February 17, 1991; September 27, 1998.

Publishers Weekly, December 14, 1990, Genevieve Stuttaford, review of *A Passionate Apprentice: The Early Journals, 1897-1909,* p. 57.

Time, January 19, 1998.

Times (London), December 20, 1984; December 29, 1990, pp. 18-19.

Times Literary Supplement, December 21, 1984, p. 1480; December 14, 1990; December 11, 1998, p. 9.

Washington Post Book World, December 9, 1984, p. 1; February 2, 1986, p. 12; January 13, 1991.

OTHER

Faculty Biographies, http://www.nyu.edu/ (July 7, 1999).*

* * *

LEKSON, Stephen H(enry) 1950-

PERSONAL: Born May 18, 1950, in West Point, NY; son of John Stephan (in the U.S. Army) and Gladys Mae (a homemaker) Lekson; married Catherine M. Cameron (an archaeologist), January 12, 1979. *Education:* Case Western Reserve University, B.A., 1972; Eastern New Mexico University, M.A., 1978; University of New Mexico, Ph.D., 1988.

ADDRESSES: Home—7279 West Kentucky #B, Lakewood, CO 80226. *Office*—Crow Canyon Archaeological Center, 23390 County Rd. K, Cortez, CO 81321.

CAREER: Case Western Reserve University, project director of Upper Gila Project, 1971-73, principal investigator for Redrock Valley Survey, 1974; University of Tennessee, crew chief for Columbia Reservoir Survey Project, 1973, project director of Hartsville Reactor Mitigation Project, 1973; Eastern New Mexico University, Portales, NM, assistant director of ceramics laboratory of San Juan Valley Archaeological Project, 1974, and Puerco River Valley Project, 1975; National Park Service, Chaco Canyon National Monument, archeologist, 1976-86; Arizona State Museum, research associate, 1986-90; Museum of New Mexico, curator of archaeology, 1991-92; Crow Canyon Archaeological Center, president, 1992—. Chairperson or organizer of various archaeological conferences and symposia.

MEMBER: World Archaeological Congress, American Anthropological Association, American Association of Museums, Archaeological Institute of America (Denver Chapter), Council for Museum Anthropology, Society for American Anthropology, Archaeological Society of New Mexico, Arizona Archaeological and Historical

Society, Arizona Archaeological Council, Colorado Archaeological Society, Colorado Council of Professional Archaeologists, New Mexico Archaeological Council.

WRITINGS:

The Architecture and Dendrochronology of Chetro Ketl, U.S. Government Printing Office (Washington, DC), 1983.

(With Robert P. Powers and William B. Gillespie) *The Outliers Survey: A Regional View of Settlement in the San Juan Basin,* Division of Cultural Research, National Park Service, U.S. Department of the Interior (Albuquerque), 1983.

(With contributions by Gillespie and Thomas C. Windes) *Great Pueblo Architecture of Chaco Canyon, New Mexico,* National Park Service, U.S. Department of the Interior (Albuquerque), 1984.

Nana's Raid: Apache Warfare in Southern New Mexico, 1881, Texas Western Press (El Paso), 1987.

Mimbres Archaeology of the Upper Gila, New Mexico, University of Arizona Press (Tucson), 1990.

Ethnohistory of the Warm Spring Apache Reservation and Its Region (prepared for the National Park Service Southwestern Region), Human Systems Research (Las Cruces, NM), 1992.

(With Rina Swentzell and Catherine M. Cameron) *Ancient Land, Ancestral Places,* Museum of New Mexico Press (Santa Fe), 1993.

Archaeological Overview of Southwestern New Mexico: Final Draft (prepared for New Mexico State Historic Preservation Division), New Mexico Historic Preservation Division (Santa Fe), 1992.

(Author, with John R. Stein and Simon J. Ortiz, of essays) Mary Peck, *Chaco Canyon: A Center and Its World,* Museum of New Mexico Press (Santa Fe), 1994.

(With Richard P. Lozinsky and Richard W. Harrison) *Elephant Butte, Eastern Black Range Region: Journeys from Desert Lakes to Mountain Ghost Towns,* New Mexico Bureau of Mines & Mineral Resources (Socorro), 1995.

The Chaco Meridian: Centers of Political Power in the Ancient Southwest, AltaMira (Walnut Creek, CA), 1999.

Also author of research papers and reports. Contributor to books, including volume two of *Ceramics, Lithics, and Ornaments of Chaco Canyon: Analysis of Artifacts from the Chaco Project, 1971-1978,* three volumes, edited by Frances Joan Mathien, 1997. Contributor to scholarly journals and popular periodicals, including *American Antiquity, Archaeology, Artifact, Expedition, Kiva, New Mexico Magazine, New Mexico Archaeological Council Newsletter, New Mexico Journal of Science, El Palacio, Pottery Southwest, Scientific American,* and *Southwestern Lore.*

SIDELIGHTS: In Chaco Canyon, New Mexico, there are structures remaining from the eleventh through the thirteenth centuries. Specifically, there are remnants of an 800-room, three-story building made of sandstone. In *The Chaco Meridian: Centers of Political Power in the Ancient Southwest,* archaeologist Stephen H. Lekson speculates about the society that created this structure. He explores why it vanished, why the city existed where it did, and what its relation was to other societies of its time. Lekson "presents his hypothetical answers convincingly," maintained N. C. Greenberg in *Choice,* who described *The Chaco Meridian* as "remarkable." "Lekson overwhelms readers with his answers," complimented Greenberg.

Among Lekson's earlier titles are *The Architecture and Dendrochronology of Chetro Ketl* (1983), *Nana's Raid: Apache Warfare in Southern New Mexico, 1881* (1987), *Mimbres Archaeology of the Upper Gila, New Mexico* (1990), and *Archaeological Overview of Southwestern New Mexico: Final Draft* (1992). Lekson collaborated with others to create works such as *The Outliers Survey: A Regional View of Settlement in the San Juan Basin* (1983), *Ancient Land, Ancestral Places* (1993), and *Elephant Butte, Eastern Black Range Region: Journeys from Desert Lakes to Mountain Ghost Towns* (1995). In addition to publishing many books focused on the New Mexico region, Lekson has contributed numerous works to scholarly journals and popular periodicals.

Lekson once told *CA:* "I am primarily a research archaeologist, working with the Pueblo Indian ruins of the North American Southwest. My principal writings, about places like Chaco Canyon and Mesa Verde, have been monographs and articles in scholarly journals. For the last five years, however, I've devoted about one-third of my time to non-technical works: essays in photo books, magazine articles, copy for museum exhibits. Archaeology has a great deal to say to our times, and I plan to write more for larger audiences."

BIOGRAPHICAL/CRITICAL SOURCES:

PERIODICALS

American Antiquity, April, 1999, Arthur W. Vokes, review of *Ceramics, Lithics, and Ornaments of*

Chaco Canyon: Analysis of Artifacts from the Chaco Project, 1971-1978, p. 389.

Archaeology, May-June, 1987, p. 22; November-December, 1990, p. 44; September-October, 1995, p. 54; January-February, 1997, p. 52; May-June, 1999, p. 67.

Choice, November, 1999, p. 583.

Scientific American, July, 1988, p. 100.*

* * *

LIU, Eric 1968-

PERSONAL: Born November 1, 1968, in Poughkeepsie, NY; son of Chao-Hua (a manager at IBM) and Julia Liu; married. *Education:* Yale University, B.A. (summa cum laude), 1990; Harvard University, J.D. (cum laude), 1999.

ADDRESSES: Agent—Raphael Sagalyn, The Sagalyn Literary Agency, 4825 Bethesda Ave., Suite 302, Bethesda, MD.

CAREER: Next Progressive, Cambridge, MA, founder, 1991, editor, 1991-96; MS-NBC-TV, commentator, 1996-97; White House, Washington, DC, deputy domestic policy adviser, 1999-2000. Speechwriter for President Bill Clinton and the National Security Council, 1993-94.

WRITINGS:

(Editor) *Next: Young American Writers on the New Generation,* Norton (New York City), 1994.

The Accidental Asian: Notes of a Native Speaker (memoir), Random House (New York City), 1998.

SIDELIGHTS: Author Eric Liu, a deputy domestic policy adviser to President Bill Clinton, has been a speechwriter for Clinton and the National Security Council, editor of *Next Progressive,* which he founded, and a television commentator. Liu is also the editor of *Next: Young American Writers on the New Generation,* and the author of 1998's *The Accidental Asian: Notes of a Native Speaker.*

The anthology *Next,* published in 1994, features selections that examine the topic of Generation X from writers such as David Greenberg, Lalo Lopez, Ted Kleine, Elizabeth Wurtzel, and Liu himself. *Next* received some criticism from reviewers, such as one in *Publishers Weekly,* who noted, "Most of the writers collected here fall deep into muddy generalizations," and added, "Surely we can expect more from 'Young Writers.' " However, the same reviewer admitted, "Not all the selections are dim." Jeffrey Bloom, writing in *Commentary,* stated that with *Next,* "Eric Liu . . . hopes to move beyond the 'superficial stereotypes' that characterize his generation." However, Bloom noted, "Liu's essayists tend toward uniformity," further commenting that the essayists "are largely captive to the conventional wisdom of their time and place." Bloom concluded: "In an odd sense, the *Next* anthology does go beyond the media stereotypes about Generation X: when one hears the X-ers in their own 'unfiltered' voices, they sound, if anything, even worse off than advertised. Still, to judge by these essays, for at least some of them there may now, at long last, be nowhere to go but up."

The Accidental Asian: Notes of a Native Speaker, Liu's second work, was described by a *Publishers Weekly* reviewer as "candid" and "well-crafted," a memoir in which the author "explores his identity as a second-generation Chinese American." In the book Liu relates his childhood feelings and experiences concerning what it was like growing up as a Chinese American, explores the 'Asian American' concept, and discusses assimilation challenges. In *Library Journal,* Kitty Chen Dean referred to *The Accidental Asian* as "poignant" and "well-written," maintaining that Liu "researched his topic well." Dean concluded that the "book is especially recommended for non-Asian readers." Romesh Ratesar in a *Time* review offered: "*The Accidental Asian* provides a perspective on race often ignored in America's black-white conversation. It is in part a collection of essays on racial identity and the place in American life occupied by the 10 million Americans who claim Asian descent. But it is also a family narrative." Though feeling that Liu rushed his coverage of the affirmative action subject, Ratesar maintained that Liu offers "careful, balanced views on race" in "a unique . . . memoir, suffused with smarts, elegance, and warmth."

BIOGRAPHICAL/CRITICAL SOURCES:

PERIODICALS

Commentary, June, 1994, Jeffrey Bloom, review of *Next: Young American Writers on the New Generation,* p. 59.

Library Journal, May 1, 1998, Kitty Chen Dean, review of *The Accidental Asian: Notes of a Native Speaker,* p. 124.

National Review, August 3, 1998, John Derbyshire, "Asian Minor," p. 50.

Newsweek, June 22, 1998, Yahlin Chang, "Asian Identity Crisis," p. 68.

Publishers Weekly, March 28, 1994, review of *Next: Young American Writers on the New Generation,* p. 92; April 6, 1998, review of *The Accidental Asian: Notes of a Native Speaker,* p. 67.

Time, June 22, 1998, Romesh Ratesar, review of *The Accidental Asian: Notes of a Native Speaker,* p. 76.*

* * *

LOCKER, Thomas 1937-

PERSONAL: Born June 26, 1937, in New York, NY; son of Bernard (a lobbyist) and Nan (a book dealer; maiden name, Alpern) Locker; married Marea Panares Teske, 1964 (divorced, 1971); married Maria Adelman; children: (first marriage) Anthony; (second marriage) Aaron, Josh, Jonathan, Gregory. *Education:* University of Chicago, B.A., 1960; American University, M.A., 1963. *Politics:* Democrat. *Religion:* Jewish.

ADDRESSES: *Home*—Stuyvesant, NY. *Office*—119 Warren St., Hudson, NY 12534.

CAREER: Author and illustrator. Franklin College, Franklin, IN, professor of art, 1963-68; Shimer College, Mount Carroll, IL, professor or humanities, 1968-73; full-time landscape painter, 1973-84. Associated with Chicago Arts Council, 1964—. Work has been shown in major galleries in Chicago, London, Los Angeles, Atlanta, and New York City. *Military service:* U.S. Army, 1955-56.

MEMBER: Authors League of America.

AWARDS, HONORS: Ten Best Illustrated Books of the Year selection, *New York Times,* Notable Book Award, *New York Times,* and Parents' Choice Award from Parents' Choice Foundation, all 1984; Outstanding Science Trade Book for Children designation, National Science Teacher's Foundation, Children's Reviewer's Choice, *Booklist,* Pick of the List Award from American Booksellers Association, and Children's Books of the Year Award from Child Study Association, all 1985, all for *Where the River Begins;* Children's Books of the Year Award, 1985, and Colorado Children's Book Award runner-up, University of Colorado, 1986, both for The Mare on the Hill; American Institute of Graphic Arts Book Award, Ten Outstanding Picture Books Award selection, *New York Times,* and Editor's Choice Award from *Booklist,* all 1987, all for *Sailing with the Wind;* New Jersey Institute of Technology Award, 1988, for *The Boy Who Held Back the Sea;* Christopher Award, 1989, for *Family Farm.*

WRITINGS:

SELF-ILLUSTRATED; FOR CHILDREN

Where the River Begins, Dial (New York City), 1984.

The Mare on the Hill, Dial, 1985.

Sailing with the Wind, Dial, 1986.

Family Farm, Dial, 1988.

The Young Artist, Dial, 1989.

The Land of Gray Wolf, Dial, 1991.

Anna and the Bagpiper, Philomel Book, 1994.

Miranda's Smile, Dial, 1994.

(With Candace Christiansen) *Sky Tree: Seeing Science through Art,* HarperCollins (Scranton, PA), 1995.

(With Candace Christiansen) *Water Dance,* Harcourt, 1997.

(Editor with Candace Christiansen) *Home: A Journey through America,* Harcourt, 1998.

Cloud Dance, Harcourt, 2000.

In Blue Mountains: An Artist's Return to America's First Wilderness, Bell Pond Books, 2000.

ILLUSTRATOR; FOR CHILDREN

Hans Christian Andersen, *The Ugly Duckling,* Macmillan, 1987.

Lenny Hort, reteller, *The Boy Who Held Back the Sea,* Dial, 1987.

Washington Irving, *Rip van Winkle,* Dial, 1988.

Josette Frank, editor, *Snow toward Evening: A Year in a River Valley,* Dial, 1990.

Herman Melville, *Catskill Eagle,* Philomel Books, 1991.

Joseph Bruchac, *Thirteen Moons on Turtle's Back: A Native American Year of Moons,* Philomel Books, 1992.

Hans Christian Christiansen, *Calico and Tin Horns,* Dial, 1992.

Hans Christian Christiansen, *The Ice Horse,* Dial, 1993.

Jean Craighead George, *The First Thanksgiving,* Philomel Books, 1993.

Jean Craighead George, *To Climb a Waterfall,* Philomel Books, 1995.

Joseph Bruchac, *The Earth Under Sky Bear's Feet: Native American Poems of the Land,* Philomel Books, 1995.

Joseph Bruchac, *Between Earth and Sky: Legends of Native American Sacred Places,* Harcourt, 1996.

Keith Strand, *Grandfather's Christmas Tree,* Harcourt, 1999.

SIDELIGHTS: Thomas Locker is an American author and illustrator of children's books whose works are noted for their studio-quality art. A landscape painter for two decades before turning his hand to children's books, Locker brings to the medium painterly skills that set his books apart from the mainstream.

Leigh Dean, assessing Locker's work in *Children's Book Review Service,* remarked, "Besides painting exquisite Constable-esque country scenes, Mr. Locker carefully chooses a particular rhythm to Nature to illustrate the passage of time and to provide his palette with the full spectrum of color, light and shadow." Dean further noted, "What makes his books so spectacularly successful is the harmonious marriage of textual theme and nature's theme."

With his initial self-illustrated title, *Where the River Begins,* Locker established himself "nearly instantly as an important figure in the world of children's books," according to Joyce Maynard, writing in the *New York Times Book Review.* His lush landscapes, reminiscent of the Hudson River School and nineteenth-century romanticism, serve as the backdrop for this simple story of two boys and their grandfather who set out to find the source of the river that flows past their house.

In subsequent books Locker has confirmed this early promise, winning awards and delighting readers young and old. He tells simple and gentle stories of children and their adult relatives, of receiving an animal's trust, of the passage and rhythm of seasons, of Native American themes, and of the simple joys of art, and illustrates these tales with panoramic landscape paintings that often depict the eastern United States where he makes his home. Locker was born in New York City in 1937, and earned his masters at American University. Thereafter, he taught both art and humanities at colleges in Indiana and Illinois before returning to his native New York state and becoming a full-time painter. But while reading children's books to his five sons, he discovered the world of children's book illustration and began to see how his brand of landscape painting might fit into such a medium.

With his first book, *Where the River Begins,* Locker announced one of his primary themes: how children learn from and grow with nature. Naming the two boys in his story Josh and Aaron after two of his own boys, Locker provides a simple, straightforward text. The two live in a big yellow house by a river, and as they watch its gentle course, they begin to wonder where it comes from. Their grandfather agrees to take them on a camping trip to find out. "The boys and their grandfather do find the pond where the river begins, a satisfying quest in itself," noted a reviewer for *Kirkus Reviews.* "But the only real drama is that of entering into this particular 19th-century romantic imagining." *Booklist* contributor Denise M. Wilms remarked, "Spectacular paintings reminiscent of nineteenth-century landscape art are a unique and riveting anchor for this simple story."

John Seelye, reviewing this first title in the *New York Times Book Review,* declared simply, "Here is a truly beautiful book." Seelye further commented on the "Thoureauvian vein" in Locker's idyll, noting the many "anachronistic" details—no phone lines, no air conditioners protruding from the windows of the house, no cars or even bicycles visible—that give the book such a pleasant nineteenth-century feel. "The real story here," decided Ross Drake in a *People* magazine review, "is the play of light and the changing moods of the countryside." Amanda J. Williams, reviewing the title in *School Library Journal,* thought it was a "sensitive and peaceful story which parallels a strong and constant river to the relationship between two brothers and their grandfather." Williams further commented, "The glorious full-page landscapes, in alkyd and oil, depict the action of the simple text." And Jean F. Mercier, writing in *Publishers Weekly,* is typical of the critical reception: "Locker's first book is a treasure. . . . This is a book for the entire family."

The same two boys and their grandfather are featured in Locker's second self-illustrated title, *The Mare on the Hill.* This time the adventure is closer to home when the grandfather brings a mare home to breed with their own stallion. This mare has been mistreated by its owner, and the boys plead with their grandfather to let it run free in the pasture. The grandfather tells them that they will never be able to catch her if he does so, but finally consents to their wishes, and over the course of a year the boys slowly gain the animal's trust. "Again it is the paintings that linger in the mind," noted Maynard. "The pictures are oil paintings rather than illustrations—deep, richly textured landscapes that might almost have emerged from the Hudson River School." Maynard's one negative criticism of Locker's work had to do with his painting of people. "If a weakness exists," Maynard wrote, "it is probably Locker's portrayal of figures; they never possess the same lifelike quality as his landscapes. . . . One can imagine they were painted in last."

School Library Journal contributor Patricia Dooley, in a review of *The Mare on the Hill,* called particular attention to the "splendid oil paintings that face each page of text in this book." As other critics have also observed, Dooley pointed out that because of the conscious lack of modern details in the paintings—no power lines or cars—"we might be at any point in the past 200 years." A reviewer for *Publishers Weekly* likewise applauded the "artist's rich colors" which "emphasize changes wrought by the four seasons in the country, largely undisturbed by 'progress,' where people live in harmony with nature." *Horn Book*'s Mary M. Burns declared *The Mare on the Hill,* like classics such as *My Friend Flicka,* "has sure-fire appeal." Burns concluded that "the book is as memorable as it is splendid."

Locker featured the bond between a young girl and her sailor uncle in *Sailing with the Wind,* his third title. The young girl has always longed to see the ocean, and one day she sails with her uncle along the river by her home through a variety of New England riverscapes to find the end of the river, only to be threatened by stormy seas once they arrive. Something of a reverse of the journey in *Where the River Begins,* this third book was again welcomed by critics and readers alike. "Locker's high level of technical proficiency, excellence of design and careful detail are rare in books for children," noted a *Kirkus Reviews* critic, who concluded that the book was "a rewarding visual experience." "This book is Locker's most visually stunning to date," declared a reviewer for *Publishers Weekly.* "Locker has created an enduring work of art." Betsy Hearne, writing in *Bulletin of the Center for Children's Books,* felt that "[e]ach scene is arrestingly rich with dramatic colors in sky and deep shadings in foliage," while Wilms remarked, "Locker's striking, luminous landscape paintings are again the stunning backdrop for what is perhaps his strongest story." Reviewing the title in the *New York Times Book Review,* Christopher Lehmann-Haupt commented that Locker "tells an evocative story of a young person's first venture into adulthood, full of unstated threats and promises."

For his fourth book, *Family Farm,* Locker moved afield from his eastern seaboard landscapes, setting his story in the American heartland, where he lived for fifteen years. Young Mike and Sarah and their whole family are worried about the low prices for corn and milk and fear they may lose their farm. To cover the lean times, the two children try selling pumpkins and flowers, but the family still needs more money to survive. Covering a year in the life of a small farm, *Family Farm* won a 1989 Christopher Award for Locker.

In *The Young Artist,* Locker once again blends his strong oil paintings with a direct story line to create a memorable experience. Twelve-year-old Adrian is apprenticed to a master artist who teaches him to paint his subjects with real depth and honesty. But a problem results when a royal family demands he paint them as they wish the world to see them, and not as they really are. Another Locker picture book with art at its center is 1994's *Miranda's Smile.* The title character's father is an artist who cannot quite capture his daughter's smile. Finally, he understands that the smile is really in her eyes. "This is a quiet story," commented Wendy Lukehart in *School Library Journal.* Lukehart went on to note, "As with all of Locker's titles, whatever their plots, the subject is art. Here, his style evokes 17th-century Dutch portraiture and domestic genre scenes."

Locker has also created self-illustrated titles with a Native American theme in *The Land of the Gray Wolf,* and with a romantic and mystical air in *Anna and the Bagpiper.* In the former title, Running Deer listens to a wolf howl. As he grows up with his family, hunting in the forests, the whites increasingly encroach on the Native American hunting lands until Running Deer, on the reservation, can no longer hear the wolf howl at night. A reviewer for *Publishers Weekly,* while admiring Locker's landscapes, felt that "[t]ext and art unfortunately do not reach Locker's usual standards." In *Anna and the Bagpiper,* a young girl is summoned by the sound of a bagpipe. Finally, Anna finds the old man playing the bagpipe and listens to him until the sun sets.

But later she wonders if this has not all been a dream. "The shifting light, from dusk to sunset to moonlight, permeates the full-page paintings and is as much a presence as Anna or the piper," noted Karen James in a *School Library Journal* review of the book. James concluded, "This brief account of a magical encounter glows with visual appreciation of the natural world."

Locker has also illustrated the work of several other writers, including Candace Christiansen, Joseph Bruchac, and Jean Craighead George. Working with Christiansen, he illustrated two of her titles dealing with Hudson Valley history, *Calico and Tin Horns* and *The Ice Horse.* Reviewing *Calico and Tin Horns,* Carolyn Phelan commented in *Booklist* that "Locker's oil paintings, with their richly colored, well-composed depictions of landscape and characters, are often striking as individual works of art as well as in the context of the book." Locker and Christiansen blend science and art in *Sky Tree* and *Water Dance,* both titles which take a look at the natural cycle. And in *Home: A Journey through America,* the two co-edit a pilgrimage to various sights in America that are linked with certain writers.

Locker's collaborations with Joseph Bruchac have also allowed him to represent nature in the illustration of Native American tales. Reviewing *Thirteen Moons on Turtle's Back,* Karen Hutt noted in *Booklist,* "Locker, well known for his landscapes, has created a dramatic oil painting for each short tale." A *Publishers Weekly* reviewer commented of that same title that Locker's "oil paintings are eye-catching in their depth of color reflecting dramatic seasonal changes."

Teaming up with George, Locker provided the illustrations to *The First Thanksgiving* and *To Climb a Waterfall.* Reviewing the former title in *Booklist,* Phelan remarked, "Locker's dramatic landscapes and seascapes set the tone for this handsome version of the Pilgrim's story." Another holiday is featured in Keith Strand's 1999 work *Grandfather's Christmas Tree,* with illustrations from Locker. *Booklist* contributor Shelley Townsend-Hudson felt that "Locker's resplendent illustrations express the characters' devotion and capture the beauty of the landscape."

Whether illustrating his own stories or those of others, Locker is noted for his painterly approach and his depiction of nature in all its moods. "I rejoice in the expressive potential of joining words with images and painting in narrative order," Locker once told *CA.*

BIOGRAPHICAL/CRITICAL SOURCES:

BOOKS

Authors of Books for Young People, third edition, Scarecrow Press, 1990.

Children's Literature Review, Volume 14, Gale, 1988.

Locker, Thomas, *The Man Who Paints Nature,* Richard C. Owens, 1999.

PERIODICALS

Booklist, December 15, 1984, Denise M. Wilms, review of *Where the River Begins,* p. 591; September 1, 1986, Denise M. Wilms, review of *Sailing with the Wind,* p. 64; March 1, 1992, Karen Hutt, review of *Thirteen Moons on Turtle's Back,* p. 1281; July, 1993, Carolyn Phelan, review of *The First Thanksgiving,* p. 1970; February 1, 1996, p. 927; April 1, 1996, p. 1358; March 1, 1997, p. 1164; November 1, 1998, p. 488; September 1, 1999, Shelley Townsend-Hudson, review of *Grandfather's Christmas Tree,* p. 151.

Bulletin of the Center for Children's Books, Betsy Hearne, September, 1986, review of *Sailing with the Wind,* p. 13.

Children's Book Review Service, September, 1986, Leigh Dean, review of *Sailing with the Wind,* p. 7.

Horn Book, March-April, 1986, Mary M. Burns, review of *The Mare on the Hill,* pp. 193-94; May-June, 1996, pp. 341-42.

Kirkus Reviews, September 1, 1984, review of *Where the River Begins,* p. J63; July 15, 1986, review of *Sailing with the Wind,* pp. 1119-20.

New York Times Book Review, November 11, 1984, John Seelye, review of *Where the River Begins,* p. 49; December 17, Ross Drake, review of *Where the River Begins,* 1984, p. 45; October 27, 1985, Joyce Maynard, review of *The Mare on the Hill,* p. 36; October 19, 1986, Christopher Lehmman-Haupt, review of *Sailing with the Wind,* p. 44.

Publishers Weekly, December 14, 1984, Jean F. Mercier, review of *Where the River Begins,* p. 54; December 20, 1985, review of *The Mare on the Hill,* p. 66; July 25, 1986, review of *Sailing with the Wind,* p. 182; August 10, 1990, p. 442; May 24, 1991, review of *The Land of the Gray Wolf,* p. 58; February 10, 1992, review of *Thirteen Moons on Turtle's Back,* p. 80; July 26, 1993, p. 72; July 11, 1994, p. 77; January 23, 1995, p. 70; September 18, 1995, p. 133; May 17, 1997, p. 83; September 7, 1998, p. 95; September 27, 1999, p. 61.

School Library Journal, December, 1984, Amanda J. Williams, review of *Where the River Begins,* p. 73; November, 1985, Patricia Dooley, review of *The Mare on the Hill,* p. 74; May, 1988, p. 69; September, 1992, p. 200; July, 1993, p. 76; June, 1994, Karen James, review of *Anna and the Bagpiper,* p. 109; September, 1994, Wendy Lukeheart, review of *Miranda's Smile,* p. 189; August, 1995, p. 122; October, 1995, p. 128; November, 1995, p. 87; April, 1997, p. 128.*

* * *

LORCA de TAGLE, Lillian 1914-

PERSONAL: Born December 11, 1914, in San Francisco, CA; daughter of Arturo (a diplomat) and Rosa (a homemaker; maiden name, Bunster) Lorca; widowed and divorced; children: Monica Tagle Allen, Rosa Tagle Glenn-Reilly. *Ethnicity:* "White." *Education:* Catholic University, Santiago, Chile, B.A., 1936; also attended schools in Belgium, Switzerland, and Germany. *Politics:* Independent. *Religion:* Roman Catholic.

ADDRESSES: Home and Office—5006 Summer Forest Dr., Houston, TX 77091-5024. *E-mail*—lolarco@aol.com.

CAREER: Ercilla, Santiago, Chile, translator and reporter, 1939-40; independent translator, 1936-49; Bacteriological Institute of Chile, scientific translator in epidemiology department, 1950-52; Organization of American States, assistant editor, 1952-54; League of Women Voters, Chattanooga, TN, public relations officer, 1956-62; U.S. Department of State, Washington, DC, escort interpreter, 1962-64; Voice of America, Washington, DC, chief of field services branch in American Republics Division, 1964-89, coordinator of evening air show, 1970-73, cultural affairs officer in Honduras, 1973-76; independent translator, 1989—.

MEMBER: American Literary Translators Association, U.S. Information Agency Alumni Association, Rotary Club.

AWARDS, HONORS: Translation award, International PEN, for Spanish translation of Somerset Maugham's *Of Human Bondage;* Order of Morazan, government of Honduras, for cultural relations improvement and raising funds for victims of Hurricane FiFi.

WRITINGS:

(Translator) Rima de Vallbona, *Flowering Inferno: Tales of Sinking Hearts,* Latin American Literary Review Press, 1994.

Honorable Exiles (memoir), University of Texas Press (Austin, TX), 1999.

Translator into Spanish of *Mariano Moreno,* (title means "The Undying Flame") by Ellen Garwood, 1992; translator of *Moonstruck* by Enrique Araya, 1991, *Of Human Bondage* by Somerset Maugham, and *People on the Prowl* (stories) by Jaime Collyer, Latin American Literary Review Press; translator of nearly forty other books from English, French, and German into Spanish for publishers in Chile and Argentina. Assistant editor, *Americas,* 1952-54.

WORK IN PROGRESS: Translating into English *Dawn,* an historical novel by Julio Escoto.

SIDELIGHTS: Lillian Lorca de Tagle told *CA:* "Writing is to me as natural and compulsive as breathing. I have been privileged by circumstances and career experiences that provided me with an insight on this century's most significant events. As a member of the Voice of America staff I had to reflect political events and issues in my writing. Now that I am retired, my writing responds to events and people that surround me. Reading is part of my life. Styles and insights of different authors teach me modes of expression. I return sometimes to translations because, being of Latin American origin, I want to make our authors known by the best of their work. From now on, I expect to slow down on translations and write more of my own stories."

* * *

LOUDEN, Robert B. 1953-

PERSONAL: Born April 8, 1953, in Lafayette, IN; son of Robert K. (a computer consultant) and Anne (Zimmerman) Louden; married Tama Silverstein, May 19, 1985; children: Elizabeth Mary, Sarah Rebecca. *Education:* University of California, Santa Cruz, B.A. (with honors), 1975; University of Chicago, M.A., 1976, Ph.D., 1981.

ADDRESSES: Home—167 Coyle St., Portland, ME 04103. *Office*—Department of Philosophy, University of Southern Maine, 96 Falmouth St., Portland, ME 04103; fax: 207-780-4226. *E-mail*—louden@maine.edu.

CAREER: Indiana University Northwest, Gary, adjunct lecturer, 1977-80; Iowa State University, Ames, visiting assistant professor of philosophy, 1980-82; University of Southern Maine, Portland, assistant professor, 1982-88, associate professor, 1988-96, professor of philosophy, 1996—, chairperson of department, 1988-89, 1992-96, and 1998-2000. Barat College, adjunct lecturer, 1979-80; University of Goettingen, visiting associate professor, 1992; Emory University, visiting associate professor, 1995; speaker at colleges and universities in the United States and abroad, including Keene State College, University of Santa Clara, Radcliffe College, University of South Carolina—Columbia, University of Maine at Orono, University of San Diego, and Bernard M. Baruch College of the City University of New York; guest on radio and television programs. Council for Philosophical Studies, fellow at Summer Institute, 1983 and 1988.

MEMBER: North American Kant Society, American Philosophical Association, American Society for Eighteenth Century Studies, Alexander von Humboldt Association of America, Society for Ancient Greek Philosophy, Society for Philosophy and Public Affairs, Northern New England Philosophical Association (president, 1986-87), Maine Philosophical Institute (president, 1985-86).

AWARDS, HONORS: Grants from American Philosophical Association, 1983, and National Endowment for the Humanities, 1983, 1985, 1988, 1989, 1993, 1996, and 2000; fellow of American Council of Learned Societies, 1989-90; Alexander von Humboldt Foundation fellow at University of Marburg and University of Goettingen, 1991-92, and at University of Muenster, 1996-97.

WRITINGS:

(Contributor) Robert B. Kruschwitz and Robert C. Roberts, editors, *The Virtues: Contemporary Essays on Moral Character,* Wadsworth Publishing (Belmont, CA), 1987.

(Contributor) Louis P. Pojman, editor, *Ethical Theory: Classical and Contemporary Readings,* Wadsworth Publishing, 1989.

(Contributor) John Anton and Anthony Preus, editors, *Essays on Ancient Greek Philosophy,* Volume 4: *Aristotle's Ethics and Politics,* State University of New York Press (Albany, NY), 1991.

Morality and Moral Theory: A Reappraisal and Reaffirmation, Oxford University Press (New York City), 1992.

(Contributor) Ruth F. Chadwick, editor, *Kant: Critical Assessments,* Routledge (New York City), 1992.

(Editor with Paul Schollmeier, and contributor) *The Greeks and Us: Essays in Honor of Arthur Adkins,* University of Chicago Press (Chicago, IL), 1996.

(Contributor) Heiner F. Klemme and Manfred Kuehn, editors, *Immanuel Kant,* Ashgate (Hampshire, England), 1999.

Kant's Impure Ethics: From Rational Beings to Human Beings, Oxford University Press, 2000.

(Editor and translator, with Allen Wood) Immanuel Kant, *Lectures on Anthropology,* Cambridge University Press (New York City), in press.

(Editor and translator, with Guenter Zoeller) Kant, *Anthropology, History, Education,* Cambridge University Press, in press.

(Contributor) Bryan William Van Norden, editor, *Essays on the Analects of Confucius,* Oxford University Press, in press.

(Contributor) Brian Jacobs, editor, *Essays on Kant's Anthropology,* Cambridge University Press, in press.

(Contributor) Alan Thomas, editor, *Bernard Williams,* Cambridge University Press, in press.

General editor of the series "Ethical Theory," State University of New York Press, 1988-94. Contributor of articles and reviews to scholarly journals and newspapers, including *Journal of Education, Ancient Philosophy, Journal of the History of Philosophy, Journal of Philosophical Research, Journal of Value Inquiry,* and *American Philosophical Quarterly.* Editorial assistant and book review editor, *Ethics,* 1976-79.

WORK IN PROGRESS: The World We Want: A Defense of the Moral Ideals of the Enlightenment.

M

MacDONOGH, Steve 1949-

PERSONAL: Born September 3, 1949, in Dublin, Ireland; son of Jack Albert Middleton (a minister and teacher) and Barbara Kathleen (Sullivan) MacDonogh. *Ethnicity:* "Irish." *Education:* University of York, B.A., 1971.

ADDRESSES: *Office*—Brandon/Mount Eagle Publications, Dingle, County Kerry, Ireland.

CAREER: Irish Writers Cooperative, Dublin, chairperson, 1977-81; Brandon Book Publishers Ltd., Dingle, Ireland, publisher, 1982-97; Brandon/Mount Eagle Publications, Dingle, publisher, 1997—.

WRITINGS:

York Poems, Cosmos, 1972.
My Tribe, Beaver Row Press, 1982.
Green and Gold: The Wrenboys of Dingle, Brandon (Dingle, Ireland), 1983.
A Visitor's Guide to the Dingle Peninsula, Brandon, 1985.
By Dingle Bay and Blasket Sound, Brandon, 1991.
The Dingle Peninsula, Brandon, 1993, color edition, 2000.
(Editor) *The Rushdie Letters: Freedom to Speak, Freedom to Write,* University of Nebraska Press (Lincoln, NE), 1993.
(Editor) *The Brandon Book of Irish Short Stories,* Brandon, 1998.
Open Book: One Publisher's War, Brandon, 1999.

SIDELIGHTS: Steve MacDonogh told *CA:* "A major theme in both my writing and my publishing has been freedom of expression. In neither Ireland nor Britain is there anything even approaching the U.S. First Amendment tradition. I do not mean to suggest that either the First Amendment or U.S. society are perfect, but what is so important is the starting point. The British start from a monarchist model, with the citizen viewed as a 'subject.' The state takes upon itself enormous powers to suppress information, especially in the area of its intelligence services. This culture of suppression spreads widely through society, leading to a highly undeveloped acceptance of the citizens' right to know what is being done in their name.

"In Ireland, although the independent state which makes up twenty-six of its thirty-two counties describes itself as a republic, we have inherited many elements from the British; in particular, most of our governmental, parliamentary, and legal apparatus, structures, and traditions. Added to this, the formerly crucial influence of a very authoritarian Roman Catholicism has left us with a tradition of starting from the assumption that 'if in doubt it is not permitted.' Still in operation are wartime (1939) emergency measures suspending the right to trial by jury, and still on the statute books are draconian measures of political censorship of the broadcast media. In addition, our defamation laws have a strongly chilling effect on investigative journalism and prevent the proper scrutiny of the conduct of public figures. In the northern six counties, still under British rule, the particular Protestant traditions of the area have been at least as inclined to suppression as the Roman Catholic tradition.

"I have sought in my publishing and writing to challenge the pervasive censorship, and this has led to conflicts with the British government, the Irish government, and the Irish broadcasting authorities. Among my authors since 1982 has been Gerry Adams, president of the Sinn Fein party; for most of the time I have been publishing him, the public have been prevented by Irish and British government banning orders from hearing him speak on radio or television. However, by challenging the broadcasting censorship, we succeeded eventually in breaching the political censorship provisions. I have documented this struggle for freedom of expression in *Open Book: One Publisher's War.*"

* * *

MACHADO de ASSIS, Joaquim Maria 1839-1908

PERSONAL: Born June 21, 1839, in Rio de Janeiro, Brazil; died of arterio-sclerosis, September 29, 1908, in Rio de Janeiro, Brazil; son of a house painter; married, 1869; wife's name, Carolina.

CAREER: Worked as a printer, typesetter, and proofreader before joining Brazilian civil service in 1860, where he eventually attained the directorship of the Ministry of Agriculture.

MEMBER: Brazilian Academy of Letters (named president for life, 1897).

WRITINGS:

NOVELS

Resurreicao, 1872, W. M. Jackson, 1937.

A mao e a luva, 1874, Garnier, 1922, translation by Albert I. Bagby, Jr., published as *The Hand and the Glove* with an introduction by Helen Caldwell, University Press of Kentucky (Lexington), 1970.

Helena, 1876, Garnier, 1929, translation by Helen Caldwell published under same title, University of California Press, 1984.

Iaia Garcia, 1878, Garnier, 1899, translation by R. L. Scott-Buccleuch published as *Yaya Garcia,* P. Owen (London), 1976.

Memorias posthumas de Braz Cubas, 1881, Garnier, 1914, translation by William L. Grossman published as *Epitaph of a Small Winner,* Noonday Press, 1952, translation by E. Percy Ellis published as *Posthumous Reminiscences of Braz Cubas,* Instituto Nacional do Livro, 1955, translation by Gregory Rabassa published as *The Posthumous Reminiscences of Bras Cubas,* Oxford University Press (New York City), 1998.

Quincas Borba, 1891, 3rd edition, Garnier, 1899, translation by Clotilde Wilson published as *Philosopher or Dog?,* Noonday Press, 1954, and as *The Heritage of Quincas Borba,* W. H. Allen (London), 1954, translation by Gregory Rabassa, with an introduction by David T. Haberly and an afterword by Celso Favaretto, published as *Quincas Borba,* Oxford University Press, 1998.

Dom Casmurro, 1899, Garnier, 1924, translation by Helen Caldwell published under same title with an introduction by Waldo Frank, University of California Press (Berkeley), 1953, translation by R. L. Scott-Buccleuch published as *Dom Casmurro: Lord Taciturn,* P. Owen, 1992, edited translation by John Gledson, with an afterword by Joao Adolfo Hansen, published as *Dom Casmurro,* Oxford University Press, 1997.

Esau e Jaco, 1904, Garnier, 1924, translation by Helen Caldwell published as *Esau and Jacob,* University of California Press, 1965.

Memorial de Ayres (also published as *Memorial de Aires*), 1908, Garnier, 1923, translation by Helen Caldwell published as *Counselor Ayres' Memorial,* University of California Press, 1972, translation by R. L. Scott-Buccleuch published as *The Wager: Aires' Journal,* P. Owen, 1990.

SHORT STORIES

Contos fluminenses, 1870, Garnier, 1924.

Historias de meia-noite, 1873, Garnier, 1923.

Historias sem data, 1884, revised edition, Garnier, 1924.

Papeis avulos, 1884, W. M. Jackson, 1937.

Varias historias, 1895, Garnier, 1924.

Paginas recolhidas, 1899, W. M. Jackson, 1937.

Reliquas de casa velha, 1906, Garnier, 1921.

The Psychiatrist, and Other Stories, translation by William L. Grossman and Helen Caldwell, University of California Press, 1963.

What Went on at the Baroness': A Tale with a Point, translation by Helen Caldwell, Magpie Press (Santa Monica, CA), 1963.

The Devil's Church, and Other Stories, translation by Jack Schmitt and Lorie Ishimatsu, University of Texas Press (Austin), 1977.

PLAYS

Desencantos, produced in Rio de Janeiro, 1861.

Quase ministro, produced in Rio de Janeiro, 1864.

Os deuses de casaca, produced in Rio de Janeiro, 1866.

Tu, so tu, puro amor, Impresso por Lombaerts, 1881, translation published as *You, Love, and Love Alone,* 1972.

POETRY

Americanas, Garnier, 1875.
Poesias completas, Garnier, 1901.

Also the author of *Crisalidas,* [Rio de Janeiro], 1864, and *Phalenas,* [Rio de Janeiro], 1869.

OTHER

Teatro (essays), 1863, W. M. Jackson, 1937.
Novas reliquias, Editora Guanabara, Waissman, Koogan, 1932.
Conceitos e pensamentos, compilacao de Julio Cesar da Silva, Companhia editors nacional, 1934.
Chronicas (1859-1888), W. M. Jackson, 1937.
Correspondencia; colligida e annotada por Fernando Nery, W. M. Jackson, 1937.
Historias romanticas, W. M. Jackson, 1937.
O alienista e outras historias, Saraiva, 1957.

Also the author of *Occidentais,* 1901.

SIDELIGHTS: Joaquim Maria Machado de Assis is widely considered Brazil's greatest writer. Although he wrote in many genres, he achieved his greatest literary successes in both the novel and short-story forms. A complex blend of psychological realism and symbolism, Machado's fiction is marked by pessimism, sardonic wit, an innovative use of irony, and an ambiguous narrative technique. These qualities have contributed to the perception of Machado as a peculiarly modern, or even postmodern, writer of the nineteenth century, for critics have found echoes of his radical skepticism, his playfulness with narrative form, and his iconoclasm in the works of Beckett, Thomas Mann, and James Joyce. Machado often used satire to illuminate trivial human vanities and selfishness, particularly among the white Brazilian upper middle classes; he rarely addresses his own mulatto culture. Although his works, particularly the novels *Memorias postumas de Bras Cubas* and *Dom Casmurro* are among the most highly prized in Western literature, Machado is remarkably little known. This situation is only gradually changing as the centenary of Machado's death nears. In 1989 Earl E. Fitz remarked in his biography of the author that "whether we consider him primarily as a short story writer or as a novelist, Machado de Assis deserves—and is beginning to receive—recognition as one of the true modern masters of Western narrative."

Machado was born in Rio de Janeiro to a Portuguese mother who died when he was ten and a mulatto father who worked as a house painter. After the death of his mother, he was raised by his mulatto stepmother, Maria Ines, who is credited with introducing the youth to literature. Machado had epilepsy and a speech impediment, which are thought to have made him very self-conscious. During his teens he met many prominent literary figures while working as a printer's apprentice. These acquaintances helped Machado get his first works published. He was an early success, and his work was highly acclaimed by the time he was twenty-five. In 1860, he entered the civil service, to which he dedicated himself, and he eventually attained the directorship of the Ministry of Agriculture. Over the next decade, while working for the Ministry, Machado wrote mostly poetry and several comedies—the theater being his first literary passion—before he gave more serious attention to narrative fiction. During the 1880s and 1890s Machado wrote what many critics consider his greatest fiction: the novels *Epitaph of a Small Winner, Quincas Borba,* and *Dom Casmurro;* and the stories in *Papeis avulsos, Historias sem data, Varias historias,* and *Paginas recolhidas.* In 1897 Machado was named the first president in perpetuity of the Brazilian Academy of Letters, of which he was a founding member. He held this title until his death in 1908.

Machado began his literary career by writing dramas and poetry. Most of these works went unpublished or unproduced, but his poetry collection *Occidentais,* which appeared in 1901 in *Poesias completas,* was well received. Critics have noted that while these poems are often stylistically mundane, they nevertheless faithfully reflect the belief that life is essentially meaningless, a theme prominent in Machado's mature novels. They also convey the author's characteristic attitude of ironic resignation. These beliefs and attitudes are first displayed extensively and with some artistic success in Machado's early novels. His first four—*Ressurreicao, A mao e a luva, Helena,* and *Iaia Garcia*—are products of the Romantic movement in Brazilian literature and are considered inferior to his later fiction. Like other works of this movement, Machado's novels, which center on thwarted love or ambition, are often criticized for their unrealistic situations and lack of character motivation. In these works Machado presented detailed portraits of female characters, meticulously examining the moral and social implications of the marriage of convenience. In his later works he abandoned both female protagonists and his concern with the delineation of class and social distinctions.

As far as Machado is known to twentieth-century English-speaking audiences, his reputation rests in great measure on *Epitaph of a Small Winner.* In an essay in the *New Yorker,* Susan Sontag wrote: "*Epitaph of a*

Small Winner is probably one of those thrillingly original, radically skeptical books which will always impress readers with the force of a private discovery." *Epitaph of a Small Winner* is the autobiography of a dead writer—"I am a deceased writer not in the sense of one who has written and is now deceased," writes the narrator, Bras Cubas, "but in the sense of one who has died and is now writing." This often humorous novel features a garrulous, unreliable narrator, and has been likened to Laurence Stern's *Life and Opinions of Tristram Shandy.* In *Epitaph of a Small Winner,* Machado explores the effects of egotism, focusing on the extremes of self-love, and on the absurdity of life and inevitability of death. Machado viewed human nature as fundamentally irrational and found self-love to be the only consistent motivating force in human behavior. While characterizing this worldview as pessimistic, critics have also noted that Machado's fiction conveys amusement rather than bitterness toward the folly of selfish, passion-driven humanity. Throughout his novels, and particularly in *Epitaph of a Small Winner,* Machado mockingly challenges the accepted beliefs of society. In his introduction to his translation of this work, William L. Grossman argued that *Epitaph of a Small Winner* affirms important human values by destroying many false gods and illusions.

Like *Epitaph of a Small Winner,* the story of *Dom Casmurro* is conveyed by an unreliable narrator. This novel, which is considered Machado's masterpiece, is full of deception and ambiguity. Helen Caldwell, one of Machado's most important English-language critics and translators, wrote in *Machado de Assis: The Brazilian Master and His Novels:* "Assis's seventh novel, *Dom Casmurro,* is the culmination of the six that preceded it. Not only does it surpass the others as an artistic work, but elements of the first six novels appear here in more perfect form: composition of characters, narrative structures, theme developments—the whole novelist's art." Dom Casmurro's self-destructive conviction—that his wife and best friend cuckolded him, and that his son is in fact theirs—was long accepted as a central fact of the novel. But critics have recently questioned whether the narrator's conclusion was perhaps based merely on suspicion, circumstantial evidence, and unfounded jealousy—all prevalent themes in Machado's novels. More recent commentators surmise that the narrator seems to be pleading his case before a jury of readers in an attempt to let them decide for themselves, and for him, if his cruelty toward those closest to him may be justified.

In *Quincas Borba,* the central character from *The Posthumous Memoirs of Bras Cubas,* whose name is Quincas Borba, bequeaths all his earthly possessions, as well as his dog (whom he named after himself), to his faithful servant Rubiao de Alvarenga. The character of Rubiao is said to embody the author's skepticism about Brazil's pretensions to constitutional democracy without abolishing slavery, and to resemble no one so much as the country's last emperor, Pedro II. The newly enriched heir travels to Rio de Janeiro in order to associate with other wealthy people and snub those who had earlier snubbed him, but descends into madness when, in his inescapable naivete, he is constantly taken advantage of by the urban sophisticates. Jonathan Keates commented in the *New York Times Book Review* that "such plot elements may seem simple enough, but the author is constantly trying to detach us from the mere exercise of threading together a sequential narrative." This detachment is achieved primarily through frequent authorial interruptions that highlight the artificiality of the fictional world and just as often mock the reader. Referring to contributions to the 1998 Oxford University Press edition by Celso Favaretto and David T. Haberly, Keates stated: "Both commentators maintain that it is not hard to grasp the book's fascination, whether as a political allegory, a drama of solitude amid multitudes, a critique of Brazil's failure to reconcile the imperatives of past and present or a celebration of skepticism. Features like these brought Machado his earliest constituency of English-speaking readers when *Bras Cubas* was translated in 1952. For some its sequel, *Quincas Borba,* consolidates the triumph of a Latin American proto-modernist."

Machado's last two novels, *Esau e Jaco* and *Memorial de Aires,* are considered extended allegorical interpretations of turn-of-the-century Brazilian social conflicts. The warring twins of *Esau and Jacob,* for example, have been interpreted as symbols of the emancipation period in Rio de Janeiro; they represent conflicts between liberal and conservative factions, between tradition and modern values, and between colonial life and the birth of an independent Brazil. In *Counselor Ayres' Memorial,* Machado again metaphorically evoked Brazil, but this time he expresses hope for his country, provided Brazilians learn to be guided by selfless love—the force that rejuvenates the jaded ambassador Ayres in the novel. Machado's affirmations of life and love in *Counselor Ayres' Memorial* are regarded as foils for the total pessimism expressed in his earlier works.

Machado is also considered a master of the short story. Having a much broader range than his novels, Machado's short fiction is concerned with the destructiveness of time, the nature of madness, the isolation of the individual, conflicts between self-love and love for others, and human inadequacy. Often humorous, Machado's stories portray the thoughts and feelings, rather than the actions, of characters who often exemplify Brazilian social types. Machado's stories deal satirically with cultural institutions and contemporary social conditions. His short fiction eschews descriptions or narration in favor of self-revealing dialogue and monologue. Unlike his novels, very few of Machado's more than two hundred short stories have been translated into English, but those that have represent his most accomplished works in the genre. These include "The Psychiatrist," which struggles with the twin questions of who is insane and how one can tell; "Alexandrian Tale," a satirical attack on the tendency to use science to cure human problems; "The Companion," one of Machado's most anthologized tales, in which a man hired to care for a cantankerous old invalid is driven to murder him instead; and "Midnight Mass," regarded as his best work of short fiction, which relates the events surrounding an ambiguous love affair between the young narrator and a married woman.

Critics have found Machado's racial heritage problematic in analyzing his works. In his book *The Negro in Brazilian Literature* Raymond S. Sayers commented: "One of the strange paradoxes of literature is that the greatest Brazilian novelist, Joaquim Maria Machado de Assis . . ., was a mulatto who wrote very little about his fellow Negros and their lives but instead drew most of his material for his novels from the lives of the upper classes of Carioca society, which were predominantly white." Because blacks and mulattoes rarely have more than minor roles in Machado's works, some critics have accused the author of denying that he was a *mestizo*—a person of mixed race—and condemned him for not decrying slavery in Brazil, which was not abolished until the author was fifty years old. Yet Machado was at least partially black and certainly encountered discrimination in his life. David T. Haberly remarked in his *Three Sad Races: Racial Identity and National Consciousness in Brazilian Literature* that among "the catalogue of social and physical handicaps that late nineteenth-century Brazilian would have defined as *taras,* or hereditary defects," Machado had not only weak health and epilepsy but, most importantly, he "was not white." Haberly argued that Machado consequently tried to construct a social identity that would be perceived as white, and while noting the dangers of identifying the author's life with his work, continued: "[Machado's] works can be seen as a highly evasive and ambiguous journal of his passage from non-whiteness to whiteness, a journal that focuses upon three central problems: the nature of identity, the nature of time, and the character and meaning of the transformations in identity that occur as an individual moves through time and through society." Sayers, however, emphasized that Machado was interested in satirizing Brazilian society, not in rejecting his race, and blacks and mulattoes could not reasonably be targets for his satire. Sayers explained: "The Negro could not serve as subject for the irony of Machado, for the Negro could never determine his own conduct or fix his own position in society; he was not a free agent, and therefore he could not be made a subject for satire."

Most commentators agree that Machado is one of the greatest, if critically neglected, writers of Latin America. "I am astonished," exclaimed Sontag, "that a writer of such greatness does not yet occupy the place he deserves." This lack of recognition is reflected in the paucity of short stories that have been translated, relative to Machado's body of work in this genre. Machado's small presence on the scene of world literature may be attributed in part to the fact that Portuguese is not widely accepted as a literary language and thus Brazilian literature comprises only a small part of the traditional Western canon. According to Fitz, "had [Machado] written in French, German, or English, for example, [he] would be as well-known today as Flaubert, Goethe, or Shakespeare." The appearance of Machado's major novels in new translations from Oxford University Press in the late 1990s was viewed as welcome, though the new editions have little to improve upon in the older translations, according to *New York Times Book Review* contributor K. David Jackson. "A larger question is why there is no indication of an intention to translate some of Machado's great short stories, most of which have never been translated into English at all. . . . These are the truly 'lost' works of the master."

BIOGRAPHICAL/CRITICAL SOURCES:

BOOKS

Bacarisse, Salvador, and others, editors, *What's Past Is Prologue: A Collection of Essays in Honour of L. J. Woodward,* Scottish Academic Press, 1984, pp. 57-69.

Black Literature Criticism, Volume 2, Gale, 1992, pp. 1290-1305.

Caldwell, Helen, *Machado de Assis: The Brazilian Master and His Novels,* University of California Press, 1970.

The Brazilian Othello of Machado de Assis: A Study of "Dom Casmurro," University of California Press, 1960.

Fitz, Earl E., *Machado de Assis,* Twayne Publishers, 1989.

Grossman, William L., Introduction to Joaquim Maria Machado de Assis, *Epitaph of a Small Winner,* Noonday Press, 1952, pp. 11-14.
Haberly, David T., *Three Sad Races: Racial Identity and National Consciousness in Brazilian Literature,* Cambridge University Press, 1983, pp. 70-98.
Loos, Dorothy Scott, *The Naturalistic Novel of Brazil,* Hispanic Institute of the United States, 1963.
Machado, Jose Bettencourt, *Machado of Brazil: The Life and Times of Machado de Assis, Brazil's Greatest Novelist,* second edition, Charles Frank Publications, 1962.
Machado de Assis, Joaquim Maria, *Epitaph of a Small Winner,* translated by William L. Grossman, Noonday Press, 1952.
Magill, Frank N., editor, *Critical Survey of Short Fiction,* Salem Press, 1993, pp. 1548-53.
Pritchett, V. S., *A Man of Letters: Selected Essays,* Chatto & Windus, 1985, pp. 259-63.
Putnam, Samuel, *Marvelous Journey: A Survey of Four Centuries of Brazilian Writing,* Knopf, 1948, pp. 176-92.
Sayers, Raymond S., *The Negro in Brazilian Literature,* Hispanic Institute in the United States, 1956, pp. 201-22.
Schmitt, Jack, and Lorie Ishimatsu, Introduction to Joaquim Maria Machado de Assis, *The Devil's Church, and Other Stories,* University of Texas Press, 1977, pp. ix-xiii.
Short Story Criticism, Volume 24, Gale, 1997, pp. 126-56.
Sole, Carlos A., editor, *Latin American Writers,* Scribner's, 1989, pp. 253-68.
Twentieth-Century Literary Criticism, Volume 10, Gale, 1983, pp. 277-307.
Verissimo, Erico, *Brazilian Literature: An Outline,* Macmillan, 1945, pp. 55-73.

PERIODICALS

Arizona Quarterly, spring, 1968, pp. 5-22.
Booklist, December 1, 1997, p. 609.
CLA Journal, September, 1983, pp. 187-96.
Comparative Literature Studies, winter, 1982, pp. 442-49.
Hispania, March, 1965, pp. 76-81; March, 1966, pp. 81-87; May, 1966, pp. 211-17; December, 1966, pp. 778-86; September, 1967, pp. 430-41; May, 1970, pp. 198-206.
Journal of Inter-American Studies, January, 1968, pp. 154-58.
Library Journal, November 1, 1997, p. 116; November 15, 1997, p. 77.
Luso-Brazilian Review, December, 1972, pp. 47-57; summer, 1982, pp. 31-38.
Modern Language Journal, April, 1975, pp. 186-89.
New Republic, May 25, 1998, p. 36.
New Statesman, February 25, 1996, pp. 261-62; August 15, 1997, p. 47.
New Yorker, May 7, 1990, pp. 102-8.
New York Times Book Review, February 22, 1998, p. 14; December 20, 1998.
Romance Quarterly, May, 1989, pp. 213-21.*

* * *

MacLEAN, Sorley 1911-1996

PERSONAL: Name also given in Gaelic as Somhairle MacGhill-Eain; born in 1911, in Osgaig, Raasay Island, Scotland; died November, 1996; married Renee Cameron, 1946; children: three daughters. *Education:* University of Edinburgh, B.A. (honors; English); Moray House College of Education, Edinburgh, teaching diploma.

CAREER: Portree High School, English teacher, 1934-37; Tobermory Secondary School, English teacher, 1938; English teacher in Boroughmuir, Edinburgh, 1947-56; Plockton Secondary School, Wester Ross, headmaster, 1956-72; University of Edinburgh, writer-in-residence, 1973-74; Sabhal Mor Ostaig Gaelic college, Isle of Skye, writer-in-residence, 1975-76. *Military service:* Signal Corps, 1940-43.

AWARDS, HONORS: Scottish Arts Council award, 1990. D.Litt.: University of Dundee, 1972; National University of Ireland, 1979; University of Edinburgh, 1980.

WRITINGS:

POETRY

(With Robert Garioch) *17 Poems for Sixpence,* Chalmers Press (Edinburgh), 1940.
Dain do Eimhir agus Dain Eile, Maclellan (Glasgow), 1943, English translation by Iain Crichton Smith published as *Poems to Eimhir and Other Poems,* Gollancz-Northern House (London), 1971.
(With George Campbell Hay, William Neill, and Stuart MacGregor) *Four Points of a Saltire,* Reprographia (Edinburgh), 1970.
Spring Tide and Neap Tide: Selected Poems, 1932-1972, Canongate (Edinburgh), 1977.

Ris a'bhruthaich: The Criticism and Prose Writings of Sorley MacLean, edited by William Gillies, Acair (Stornoway, Isle of Lewis), 1985.

O Choille Gu Bearradh/From Wood to Ridge: Collected Poems in Gaelic and English, translated by the author, Carcanet (Manchester), 1989.

Aisling Agus Toir, An Sagart (Maigh Nuad), 1992.

RECORDINGS

Barran agus Asbhuain: Poems by Sorley MacLean Read by Himself, Claddagh, 1973.

OTHER

Also contributor to anthologies, including *Nuabhardachd Ghaidhlig/ Modern Scottish Gaelic Poems,* edited by Donald MacAulay.

SIDELIGHTS: In works such as *Dain do Eimhir agus Dain Eile* (1943), *Ris a'bhruthaich: The Criticism and Prose Writings of Sorley MacLean* (1985), *O Choille Gu Bearradh* (1990), and *Aisling Agus Toir* (1992), the late Scottish poet Sorley MacLean "established him-[self] as the preeminent Gaelic poet of the century," wrote *World Literature Today* contributor G. Ross Roy. "It was not until 1977 that many of his best poems were available in English," Roy explained, adding that most of the author's prose writing suffered a similar neglect because of their publication in periodicals not easily accessible outside the Gaelic world.

Yet critics have compared MacLean's work with that of the best modern poets in its impact on both a genre and on an entire language. "The finest poetry written by British citizens during the years 1939-45," explained *London Review of Books* contributor Robert Crawford, "was produced by T. S. Eliot and by Sorley MacLean. Each was a British citizen in a very different way. . . . MacLean, a Gael born on the Hebridean island of Raasay in 1911, almost gave his life in the service of the British Crown when he was blown up by a land-mine at El Alamein in 1942." Both Eliot (born an American) and MacLean, Crawford continued, were "impelled by a duty to his language, by the necessity of modernizing its capacities and fighting its insularities; each was to become a cultural figurehead, the quintessential representative of poetry in his language." With *Dain do Eimhir agus Dain Eile* (1943), stated Colin Nicholson in *Contemporary Poets,* MacLean "effected a transformation in Gaelic poetry, which had been largely a retrospective art. MacLean modernized its focus, introducing international conflict and contemporary political and social perspectives of radical kinds as appropriate contexts for intensely personal expression." "Through his master of the aural techniques of Gaelic poetry, including complex schemas of internal, end-, and cross-rhyming, as well as cumulative, alternating, and constrasting structures of rhythm," Nicholson concluded, "he achieves an individual resonance as he extends his tradition."

BIOGRAPHICAL/CRITICAL SOURCES:

BOOKS

Contemporary Poets, 6th edition, St. James Press (Detroit, MI), 1996.

Matheson, Ann, *Sorley MacLean,* National Library of Scotland (Edinburgh), 1981.

Sorley MacLean: Critical Essays, Scottish Academy Press (Edinburgh), 1986.

PERIODICALS

Books and Bookmen, October, 1971, p. 68.

London Review of Books, May 24, 1990, pp. 17-18.

New Statesman, November 20, 1981, p. 20.

Times Literary Supplement, September 9, 1977, p. 1087; June 5, 1987, p. 611; September 28, 1990, p. 1041.

World Literature Today, autumn, 1986, pp. 676-77; summer, 1998, p. 666.

OBITUARIES:

PERIODICALS

New York Times, November 27, 1996, p. A13.*

* * *

MAGINN, Simon 1961-

PERSONAL: Born November 6, 1961, in Wallasey, Merseyside, England; son of Jerome (a lecturer) and Winifred Isabella (a teacher; maiden name, McGee) Maginn. *Education:* Attended St. Mary's R. C. College; University of Sussex, B.A., 1984. *Politics:* "Labour voter." *Religion:* "Rationalist." *Avocational interests:* Improvising at the piano.

ADDRESSES: Home—Hove, East Sussex. *Office*—c/o Transworld Publishers, 61-63 Uxbridge Rd., London W5 5SA, England. *Agent*—Corgi Books, Carole Blake,

Blake Friedmann, 37-41 Gower St., London WC1E 6HH, England.

CAREER: Singer and songwriter for popular bands, 1981-90; worked variously in clerical, factory, and cleaning jobs, 1984-90; music teacher in Hove, England, 1990—.

WRITINGS:

NOVELS

Sheep, Corgi (London), 1994, White Wolf (Atlanta), 1996.
Virgins and Martyrs, Corgi, 1995, White Wolf, 1996.
A Sickness of the Soul, Corgi, 1995.
Methods of Confinement, Black Swan (London), 1996.

Contributor to magazines, including *Interzone. Sheep* has been translated into Dutch and German; *Virgins and Martyrs* has appeared in Dutch.

ADAPTATIONS: Sheep is being adapted for film by the Welsh production company Tiger Bay.

SIDELIGHTS: Simon Maginn told *CA:* "I started writing purely as a way of filling time. I sleep during the day and have to entertain myself at night. Writing is cheap, clean, free from health risk, and has no identifiable side- or after-effects, unlike most of the other things you can do at night.

"I am fascinated by irrationality. I have living relatives who have *personally* seen statues of virgins fly across rooms, speak, and so on. I particularly like well-organized belief systems, such as religions, schizophrenic thought processes, and extreme political beliefs. I write, mostly, about mad people.

"The writers I most admire are all British: Evelyn Waugh, Graham Greene, Beryl Bainbridge, Peter Ackroyd, and Doris Lessing."*

* * *

MAIDEN, Jennifer 1949-

PERSONAL: Born April 7, 1949, in Penrith, New South Wales, Australia; married David Toohey, 1984; children: one daughter. *Education:* Macquarie University, B.A., 1974.

ADDRESSES: Home—P.O. Box 4, Penrith, New South Wales 2750, Australia.

CAREER: Tutor in creative writing, Outreach, Evening College Movement, and Blacktown City Council, all New South Wales, Fellowship of Australian Writers, and University of Western Sydney, 1976-91. Writer-in-residence, Australian National University, Canberra, New South Wales, State Torture and Trauma Rehabilitation Unit, and University of Western Sydney, all 1989.

AWARDS, HONORS: Australia Council grant or fellowship, 1974, 1975, 1977, 1978, 1983, 1984, 1986; Harri Jones memorial prize; Butterly-Hooper award.

WRITINGS:

POETRY

Tactics, University of Queensland Press (St. Lucia), 1974.
The Occupying Forces, Makar Press (St. Lucia), 1975.
The Problem of Evil, Poetry Society of Australia (Sydney), 1975.
Birthstones, Angus & Robertson (Sydney), 1978.
The Border Loss, Angus & Robertson, 1979.
For the Left Hand, South Head Press (Sydney), 1981.
The Trust, Black Lightning Press (Wentworth Falls, New South Wales), 1988.
The Winter Baby, Angus & Robertson, 1990.
Bastille Day, National Library of Australia (Canberra), 1990.
Selected Poems of Jennifer Maiden, Penguin (New York City), 1990.
Acoustic Shadow, Penguin, 1993.

Also contributor of poetry to periodicals, including *Southerly.*

NOVELS

The Terms, Hale & Iremonger (Sydney), 1982.
Play with Knives, Allen & Unwin (Sydney), 1990.

SHORT STORIES

Mortal Details, Rigmarole (Melbourne), 1977.

OTHER

Also contributor of essays to periodicals, including *Australian Literary Studies.*

SIDELIGHTS: Australian poet and novelist Jennifer Maiden often writes about violence and uncertainty within a suburban setting—sometimes Australian, but also in the United States. " 'Ambivalent, ambidextrous, androgynous, amorous, ironic'—so Jennifer Maiden characterizes her poetry," explains *Contemporary Poets* contributor Nan Bowman Albinski. " 'Teasing, intellectual irony, too has always seemed to me a humane new channel toward pensive seduction for what otherwise, in more direct poetry, can be a jealous urge for power over the reader.' Such poetic intent suggests demanding work, resistant to easy interpretation," Albinski concludes.

"Often, my fiction is not inspired by actual experience," Maiden reveals in an essay on her work published in the *Australian Literary Review.* "I was amazed, for example, that when my novel *Play with Knives*—about a suburban girl who has killed her younger siblings at the age of eleven, and also about her relationship with her male probation officer—was published in 1991, one intelligent female reviewer explained to her readership that I was a poet who had been so changed by my work as writer-in-residence at the N.S.W. Torture and Trauma Rehabilitation Unit that I had written this novel! In fact, I took on the residency because of my pre-existing interest in the topic of political and other forms of violence. . . . The novel was written almost a decade before the residency." The concept of suburbia is one that Maiden finds especially enriching, in contrast to many other writers. "Cities are planned and tend to lack what Nye Began called 'the gift of the unexpected,' " Maiden states in the *Australian Literary Review.* "This is not true of the suburbs. Nowhere else can the essential, eternal and eternally reversing dialectic between icon and iconoclasm be observed and experienced so well."

BIOGRAPHICAL/CRITICAL SOURCES:

BOOKS

Contemporary Poets, 6th edition, St. James Press (Detroit, MI), 1996.

PERIODICALS

Australian Literary Studies, October, 1998, p. 115.*

* * *

MALIN, David (Frederick) 1941-

PERSONAL: Surname is pronounced *May*-lin; born March 28, 1941, in Bury, England; son of Fred (a decorator) and Mary (a homemaker; maiden name, Milburn) Malin; married Phillipa Jones (a teacher), August 26, 1967; children: James, Jenny and Sara (twins). *Education:* Bury Technical College, Higher National Certificate, 1965.

ADDRESSES: Home—2 Wongala Ave., Elanora Heights, New South Wales 2101, Australia. *Office*—Anglo-Australian Observatory, Box 296, Epping, New South Wales 2121, Australia.

CAREER: Ciba-Geigy Ltd., Manchester, England, chemist, 1957-75, microscopist and photographer, 1964-75; Anglo-Australian Observatory, Epping, Australia, photographer and astronomer, 1975—.

MEMBER: International Astronomical Union (chairman of Photographic Working Group, 1985—), Astronomical Society of Australia, Royal Photographic Society (fellow).

AWARDS, HONORS: Professor Henri Chreitien Award from the American Astronomical Society, 1985.

WRITINGS:

(With Paul Murdin and David Allen) *Catalogue of the Universe,* with photographs by David Malin, Crown (New York City), 1979.

(With Murdin) *Colours of the Stars,* with photographs by Malin, Cambridge University Press (New York City), 1984.

A View of the Universe, Cambridge University Press, 1993.

(With David J. Frew) *Hartung's Asronomical Objects for Southern Telescopes: A Handbook for Amateur Observers,* revised 2nd edition, Cambridge University Press, 1995.

The Invisible Universe, Little, Brown (Boston), 1999.

Contributor of numerous articles and photographs to magazines and scientific journals.

WORK IN PROGRESS: Articles and scientific papers for periodicals, books, and journals.

SIDELIGHTS: David Malin is one of the world's best known professional astrophotographers. Based in Australia, Malin uses photographic techniques he refined as a chemist to bring vivid color to celestial bodies both near and far. "One could call David Malin the Ansel Adams of modern astrophotography," wrote Robert Bunge in *Astronomy.* "As Adams did with nature photography, Malin combines the hard science behind photography with the artist's eye to produce many of the most stunning photographs of the universe." Bunge added that Malin's work "has led to a better understanding of our universe."

Malin's photographs have appeared in most of the major science magazines, and they are collected in books such as *Colours of the Stars, The Invisible Universe,* and *A View of the Universe. Astronomy* contributor Peter Bond maintained that Malin's "spectacular color photographs of celestial objects have revealed unprecedented detail in many star clusters and gas clouds in our Galaxy as well as others. The photos are the result of experiments which photographic techniques that continue to influence astrophotography." In a *Sky & Telescope* review of *A View of the Universe,* H. J. P. Arnold commended Malin for his "very down-to-earth and occasionally humorous approach to his profession," adding that the book "is a joy to have and an inspiration for all amateur astrophotographers."

In *Astronomy,* Malin reflected upon his profession and the growing body of information on the visible and invisible universe. "This new understanding has changed our outlook on society as well as stars and galaxies," he commented. "Astronomers have provided the raw information that's forced the change. I think the human race has benefited from astronomy and I'm proud to be associated with that."

Malin told *CA:* "I fell into astronomy late in life, after a career in chemistry. I was helped enormously by colleagues like my co-authors to find my way in a new science. Since then I have made valuable photographic and astronomical discoveries, and I have established a reputation as an astronomical photographer. I have a strong desire to communicate the beauty and excitement of astronomy to anyone who will listen. This is the purpose of my books and a steady stream of lectures."

BIOGRAPHICAL/CRITICAL SOURCES:

PERIODICALS

Astronomy, August, 1994, Robert Bunge, "A View of the Universe," p. 98; July, 1995, Peter Bond, "David Malin's Universe," p. 30.

Earth Science, winter, 1987, "Splendors of the Universe," p. 36.

Library Journal, review of *Colours of the Stars,* p. 1764.

Popular Photography, October, 1999, Sunshine Flint, "Space Photos Take Off," p. 10.

Science, August 27, 1999, "The Art of Science," p. 1418.

Scientific American, May, 1985, Philip Morrison, review of *Colours of the Stars,* p. 40; August, 1991, Philip Morrison, "A Celebration of Colour in Astronomy," p. 110; April, 1994, Philip Morrison, review of *A View of the Universe,* p. 126.

Sky & Telescope, July, 1985, Andrew T. Young, review of *Colours of the Stars,* p. 33; August, 1989, Dennis di Cicco, "Astrophotography's Rise and Fall," p. 124; June, 1994, H. J. P. Arnold, "The Master of Astrophotography," p. 56; May, 1996, William Liller, review of *Hartung's Asronomical Objects for Southern Telescopes,* p. 54.

Washington Post Book World, Kathy Sawyer, "Cosmic Delights," p. 14.

Wilson Library Bulletin, Charles Bunge, review of *Catalogue of the Universe,* p. 463.

OTHER

David Malin's Home Page, http://www.aao.gov.au/ (February 16, 2000).*

* * *

MAN, John 1941-

PERSONAL: Born May 15, 1941, in Tenterden, England; son of John Henry Garnet (a farmer) and Peggy (a tennis coach; maiden name, Durnford) Man; married Angela Strange (an actress), January 27, 1967 (divorced, 1991); married Timberlake Wertenbaker (a playwright), June 30, 1991; children: (first marriage) Jonathan, Thomas, Emily, William, (second marriage) Dushka. *Education:* Keble College, Oxford, B.A. (languages); diploma in history and philosophy of science; one year post-graduate course in Mongolian at School of Oriental and African Studies, London.

ADDRESSES: Home—90 Oakfield Rd., London N4, England.

CAREER: Reuters, London, England, correspondent in London and in Bonn, West Germany, 1965-68; British Publishing Corp., London, editor, 1968-69; Time-Life Books, New York City, editor in London, 1969-72, European editor in London, 1972-74, senior editor, 1974-75; director of John Man Books Ltd., London, 1975-81; writer, including television, film, and radio writings. Interviewer for *Survive,* a six-part television series, 1984.

WRITINGS:

Berlin Blockade, Ballantine (New York City), 1973.
(With Henry Kyemba) *State of Blood,* Ace Books (New York City), 1977.
The Day of the Dinosaur, Dutton (New York City), 1978.
Assault at Mogadishu, Corgi, 1978.
Walk! It Could Change Your Life, Paddington, 1979.
The Lion's Share, St. Martin's (New York City), 1982.
Gold-Dive, Corgi, 1982.
Jungle Nomads of Ecuador, Time-Life (Alexandria, VA), 1982.
The Survival of Jan Little, I. B. Tauris (London), 1985, Viking (New York City), 1987.
(Editor) Christian Schmidt-Haeuer, *Gorbachev: The Path to Power,* I. B. Tauris, 1986.
(With Pin Yathay) *Stay Alive, My Son,* Free Press (New York City), 1987.
Exploration and Discovery (juvenile), Gareth Stevens (Milwaukee, WI), 1990.
Zwinger Palace, Dresden, with photographs by Nicolas Sapieha, Tauris Parke Books (London), 1990.
The Facts on File D-Day Atlas: The Definitive Account of the Allied Invasion of Normandy, Facts on File (New York City), 1994.
The Penguin Atlas of D-Day and the Normandy Campaign, Penguin (New York City), 1994.
(With Jayne Torvill) *Torvill & Dean: The Autobiography of Ice Dancing's Gold Medal Winners,* Carol Publishing Group (New York City), 1996.
Battlefields Then and Now, Macmillan (New York City), 1997.
The Birth of Our Planet, Reader's Digest (London), 1997, Reader's Digest (Pleasantville, NY), 1999.
Gobi: Tracking the Desert, Orion (London), 1997, Yale University Press (New Haven, CT), 1999.
The Traveler's Atlas: A Global Guide to the Places You Must See in a Lifetime, Barron's (Hauppauge, NY), 1998.
(With Jayne Torvill) *Torvill & Dean: The Autobiography of Ice Dancing's Gold Medal Winners,* Carol Publishing (Secaucus, NJ), 1998.
The War to End Wars, 1914-18, Reader's Digest (London), 1998.
The Space Race, Reader's Digest (London), 1999.
Atlas of the Year 1000, Harvard University Press (Cambridge, MA), 1999.
Alpha Beta, Headline (London), 2000.

SIDELIGHTS: John Man is an author who has published a plethora of nonfiction titles: as-told-to adventure tales, travel books, historical volumes, biographies, and science works for non-technical readers. He has a specialist interest in Mongolia. Among his most popular works are *Stay Alive, My Son, The D-Day Atlas,* and *Gobi: Tracking the Desert.*

In *Stay Alive, My Son* Man and co-author Pin Yathay chronicle Yathay's experiences in his native Cambodia following the takeover of the country by communist guerrillas. The genocidal tactics of the new regime led to the deaths of several million Cambodians in a campaign of deliberate starvation. Yathay describes how one communist official explained the slaughter: "In the new [society], one million is all we need to continue the revolution. We don't need the rest. We prefer to kill ten friends rather than keep one enemy alive." Joseph Sobran, reviewing the book for the *National Review,* calls it "moving and harrowing."

Man's *The D-Day Atlas* "is a concise history illustrated with color maps and black-and-white photographs," according to Sandy Whiteley in *Booklist.* Man's account of the pivotal battle of World War II, in which Allied forces crossed the English Channel and successfully won a beachhead in the French province of Normandy, provides an overview of the complex and treacherous operations of the invasion. John Bemrose in *Maclean's* finds that the book, "with its colorful maps, fine photographs and clear, energetic text, creates a stimulating overview of the Normandy battlefields."

Man details a journey he made across the desolate Gobi Desert of Mongolia in his travel book *Gobi: Tracking the Desert.* Combining an account of his own adventures with historical background of early explorers in the region and recountings of local myths and legends, Man creates a "fascinating and informative book that is hard to put down," as Stephanie Papa notes in *Library Journal.* The critic for *Publishers Weekly* concludes that *Gobi* is "an exhilarating blend of travel, history and adventure" by "a graceful and companionable travel writer."

Man's *Atlas of the Year 1000* is a portrait of the world at a moment which, as he writes, "marked the first time in human history when it was possible to pass a message, or an object, right around the world. . . . it does not seem too fanciful to look for the roots of today's 'one world' in the world of 1,000 years ago." Robert Bartlett of the *Times Literary Supplement* said "it introduces the astonishing range of human activity of the time," while Felipe Fernandez-Armesto, in the London *Times,* called it "an amusing, quirky conspectus spattered with surprises."

BIOGRAPHICAL/CRITICAL SOURCES:

PERIODICALS

Booklist, June 1, 1994, Sandy Whiteley, review of *The D-Day Atlas,* p. 1874.

Country Living, April, 1998, Tom Claire, review of *Battlefields Then and Now,* p. 50.

Far Eastern Economic Review, November 20, 1997, Alan Sanders, review of *Gobi: Tracking the Desert,* p. 57.

Library Journal, February 1, 1987, Joan W. Gartland, review of *The Survival of Jan Little,* p. 74; October 15, 1999, Stephanie Papa, review of *Gobi: Tracking the Desert,* p. 92.

Maclean's, June 6, 1994, John Bemrose, review of *The D-Day Atlas,* p. 57.

National Review, October 23, 1987, Joseph Sobran, review of *Stay Alive, My Son,* p. 54.

Publishers Weekly, May 21, 1982, Barbara A. Bannon, review of *The Lion's Share,* p. 65; January 23, 1987, Genevieve Stuttaford, review of *The Survival of Jan Little,* p. 57; July 17, 1987, Genevieve Stuttaford, review of *Stay Alive, My Son,* p. 45; August 16, 1999, review of *Gobi: Tracking the Desert,* p. 67.

School Library Journal, December, 1994, Susan H. Woodcock, review of *The D-Day Atlas,* p. 146.

Times (London), December 9, 1999, Felipe Fernandez-Armesto, "How Not to Set the World on Fire."

Times Literary Supplement, December 31, 1999, Robert Bartlett, "The Way It Was," p. 31.

* * *

MARAINI, Dacia 1936-

PERSONAL: Born November 13, 1936, in Florence, Italy; daughter of Fosco (an Orientalist) and Topazia (a painter; maiden name, Alliata) Maraini; married Lucio Pozzi (divorced). *Education:* Studied at Collegio S. S. Annunziata, Florence.

ADDRESSES: Home—Via Beccaria 18, 00196, Rome, Italy.

CAREER: Writer. La Maddalena, co-founder. Film director of *Conjugal Love,* 1970.

AWARDS, HONORS: Prix Formentor, 1962, for *L'Eta del malessera;* Premio Saint Vincent, 1972; Premio Riccione, 1978; Aghof award, 1982; Premio Arta Terme, 1983; Telemone premio, 1984; Fregene premio, 1985; Efebo d'Oro, 1985; Citta' Di Rapallo premio, 1986; Premio Mediterraneo and Premio Citta di Penna, 1991, for *Viaggiando con Passo di Volpe.*

WRITINGS:

NOVELS, EXCEPT AS INDICATED

La vacanza, Lerici (Milan), 1962, translation by Stuart Hood published as *The Holiday,* Weidenfeld & Nicolson (London), 1966.

L'eta del malessera, Einaudi (Turin), 1963, translation by Frances Frenaye published as *The Age of Malaise,* Grove (New York City), 1963, published in England as *The Age of Discontent,* Weidenfeld & Nicolson, 1963.

A memoria (title means "From Memory"), Bompiana (Milan), 1967.

Mio marito (short stories; title means "My Husband"), Bompiana, 1968, enlarged edition, 1974.

Memorie di una ladra, Bompiana, 1972, translation by Nina Rootes published as *Memories of a Female Thief,* Abelard-Schuman (London), 1973, Transatlantic Arts (Levittown, NY), 1974.

Donna in guerra, Einaudi, 1975, translation by Mara Benetti and Elspeth Spottiswood published as *Woman at War,* Lighthouse Books (London), 1984, Italica Press (New York City), 1988.

Lettere a Marina, Bompiana, 1981, translation by Dick Kitto and Spottiswood published as *Letters to Marina,* Crossing Press (Freedom, CA), 1987.

Il treno per Helsinka, Einaudi, 1984, translation by Kitto and Spottiswood published as *The Train,* Camden (London), 1989.

La lunga vita di Marianna Ucria, Rizzoli (Milan), 1990, translation by Kitto and Spottiswood published as *The Silent Duchess,* Flamingo (London), 1993, Feminist Press (New York City), 1998.

Bagheria, Rizzoli, 1993, translation by Kitto and Spottiswood published as *Bagheria,* Peter Owens, 1994.

Voci (title means "Voices"), Rizzoli, 1994.

Un clandestine a bordo (title means "A Stowaway on Board"), Rizzoli, 1996.

Dolce per se (title means "Sweet by Itself"), Rizzoli, 1997.

POETRY

Crudelte all' aria aperta (title means "Cruelty in the Open Air"), Feltrinelli, 1966.

Donne mie (title means "Oh, My Women"), Einaudi, 1974.

Mangiami pure, Einaudi, 1978, translation by Genni Donati Gunn published as *Devour Me Too,* Guernica (Montreal), 1987.

Dimenticato di dimenticare, Einaudi, 1982.

Viggiando con passo di volpe: poesies, 1983-1991, Rizzoli, 1991, translation by Gunn published as *Traveling in the Gait of a Fox,* Quarry Press (Kingston, Ontario), 1992.

PLAYS

Recitare, first produced at Teatro Centouno, 1969.

Il ricatto a teatro e alter commedie (title means "Blackmail on the Stage and Other Plays"), Einaudi, 1970.

Viva l'Italia (title means "Long Live Italy"), Einaudi, 1973.

Dialogo di una prostituta col cliente (first produced at Teatro Alberico in Rome), Images, 1975.

La Donna perfetta, Seguito da il Cuore di una Vergine, Einaudi, 1975.

Don Juan, Einaudi, 1976.

I sogni di Clitennestra (first produced at Teatro Tendra, Prato; title means "Clytemnestra's Dream"), Bompiana, 1981.

Maria Stuarda (produced in Holland by Publieketheatre and in Spain by Teatro Espanol de Madrid; title means "Mary Stuart"), Bompiana, 1981.

Lezioni d'amore e alter commedia, Bompiana, 1982.

Veronica, meretrice e scrittora (title means "Veronica, Prostitute and Writer"), Bompiana, 1992.

Only Prostitutes Marry in May. Four Plays, edited and with an introduction by Rhoda Helfman Kaufman, Guernica (New York City), 1994.

Also author of *La famiglia normale* (one-act play), 1967, and *Il manifesto.*

SCREENPLAYS

(With Piera Degli Esposti and Marco Ferreri) *The Story of Piera,* Faso Film S.R.L., T. Films, Sara Films, and Ascot, 1983.

OTHER

(With Salvatore Samperi) *Cuore di mamma,* Forum (Milan), 1969.

Nikto sa nepamata, B. Bystrica (Bratislava), 1969.

Et tu chi eri? Interviste sull'infanzia (interviews; title means "And Who Were You? Interviews on Childhood"), Bompiana, 1973.

Fare teatro. materiali, testi, interviste (interviews), Bompiana, 1974.

Donna, cultura e tradizione, G. Mazotta (Milan), 1976.

Donne in poesia, Savelli (Rome), 1976.

(With Piera deli Espositi) *Storia di Piera* (biography), Bompiana, 1980, Rizzoli, 1997.

Il bambino Alberto (title means "The Child Alberto"), Bompiana, 1986.

Stravaganza, Sercangeli (Rome), 1987.

La bionda, la bruna e l'asino, Rizzoli, 1987.

Mariani Stein, Il ventaglio (Rome), 1987.

Delitto, Marco (Lungro di Cosenza), 1990.

L'uomo tatuato, Guida (Naples), 1990.

Erzbeth Bathory; Il geco; Norma 44, Editori & Associati (Rome), 1991.

Cercando Emma (literary criticism), Rizzoli, 1993, translation published as *Searching for Emma: Gustave Flaubert and Madame Bovary,* University of Chicago Press (Chicago), 1998.

Il sommacco: piccolo inventario dei teatri parlermitani trovati e persi, Flaccovio (Palermo), 1993.

Mulino, Orlove e Il gatto che si crede pantera, Stampa alternativa (Rome), 1994.

Isolina: la donna tagliata a pezzi (investigative journalism), Mondadori (Milan), 1985, translation by Sian Williams published as *Isolina,* Peter Owen (Chester Springs, PA), 1993.

La casa tra due palme, Sottotraccia (Salerno), 1995.

Conversazione con Dacia Maraini, Omicron (Rome), 195.

Silvia, Edizioni del girasol (Ravenna), 1995.

Storie di cani per una bambina, Bompiana, 1996.

Nuovi racconti campani, Guida, 1997.

Dizionarietto quotidian. Da "amare" a "zonzo": 229 voci raccolte da Gioconda Marinelli, Bompiana, 1997.

Se amando troppo, Rizzoli (Milan), 1998.

Buio (short stories; title means "Darkness"), Rizzoli, 1999.

Contributor to Italian newspapers and magazines, including *Corriere della Sera, L'Unita,* and *Noi Donne.*

SIDELIGHTS: Dacia Maraini is considered one of the foremost literary and cultural figures of contemporary Italy. In a career spanning forty years, Maraini has published in nearly every conceivable form, including novels, stories, books of poetry, plays, literary criticism, biographies, collections of interviews, investigative journalism, and other nonfiction. Her work is noted in part for its strong feminist and progressive political views. In addition to her books, Maraini has written for Italian newspapers, taught creative writing, hosted a television show, been active in the Italian feminist movement, founded both a theater group and a women's cultural center, and currently heads a foundation dedicated to the memory of the famous Italian writer Albert Moravia, with whom she was romantically involved for eighteen years.

The daughter of noted Orientalist and ethnologist Fosco Maraini and Sicilian noblewoman Topazia Alliata, Maraini spent the first nine years of her life in Japan. Two of these (1943-45) were spent in a Japanese concentration camp because of her family's opposition to fascism. After World War II the family returned to Italy virtually impoverished. Later describing this period of her life to an interviewer from *Panorama,* Maraini stated: "At home I was exposed to culture and hunger." After her parents separated in 1954, Maraini followed her father to Rome where she was exposed to the literary circles of the time, inclusive of such writers as Moravia and Pier Paolo Pasolini. In a publishing climate where women writers were seldom taken seriously, Maraini published her first novel, *The Vacation,* in 1962 at the age of twenty-six. However, the publisher only agreed to take the book after Maraini obtained an introduction from Moravia.

Writing in the *Encyclopedia of World Literature,* essayist Stefania Lucamente divides Maraini's literary career into three distinct periods. In the first, the years 1962-70, Maraini produced psychological novels in which the central characters were young women facing complex moral issues such as abortion. Her work already demonstrated a marked feminist slant and portrayed Italian society as one in which women were oppressed by patriarchal values rooted in a traditional family structure. In the second period, 1970-89, Lucamente notes a "stronger political engagement . . . active participation in social activities regarding women's rights" reflected in Maraini's work. Most of Maraini's plays were written during this period and are perhaps the most overtly political of any of her work.

One of her most acclaimed novels at this time was *Memoirs of a Female Thief* (1974). Based on the life of an actual thief Maraini met during her investigations of Italian prisons, the novel demonstrates how childhood deprivation, unrelieved by inadequate social services, can create an adult criminal who is unlikely to be rehabilitated. Maraini's second book of poems, *Oh, My Women,* also appeared in 1974. Writing in the *Dictionary of Literary Biography,* Augustus Pallotta characterizes *Oh, My Women* as "a feminist manifesto in verse, containing a passionate appeal to women to break free from the centuries-old stereotypes fashioned by men and assert themselves as independent beings."

The third period that Lucamente delineates in Maraini's career, from 1990 onward, is marked by a shift in her fiction toward both more experimental forms and semi-autobiographical work. The 1990 novel, *La lunga vita di Marianna Ucria* (translated as *The Silent Duchess*), described by Lucamente as an "historiographic metafiction," is set in eighteenth century Italy and explores the repressed condition of women at that time as exemplified by one of Maraini's own ancestors. The 1995 *Bagheria*—titled after the town where Maraini lived with her parents after returning from Japan—not only presents a novelistic portrait of her own childhood, but interweaves this with both Sicilian history and a depiction of how the town is despoiled by corrupt developers and the Mafia.

Without defining distinct periods, Pallotta also sees a progression in Maraini's work closely linked to changes in her feminist perspectives. Pallotta notes that in the earliest novels, *The Vacation* and *The Age of Malaise,* "the distinctive trait of Maraini's female characters is a lack of self-consciousness." The 1967 *From Memory* marks a transitional stage, portraying a heroine who is outwardly "assertive and independent" yet still "incapable of giving her life structure and a purposeful direction." According to Pallotta it is the 1975 *Women at War,* set during the widespread and often violent feminist protests that rocked Italy in the late 1960s, that stands as Maraini's "first fully coherent feminist novel." Vannina, the protagonist of the book, becomes involved in those protests and eventually leaves her husband to begin a new life "with a healthy consciousness." Unlike Maraini's previous female characters, Vannina "make[s] responsible individual choices rather than acting to appease social expectations." Despite this progression tied to feminist concerns, Pallotta maintains: "it would be a mistake to view her [Maraini's] work only through a feminist lens. She is a contemporary writer committed to feminism who offers a socially provoking view of the human condition, often focusing on but not limited to women. . . . There is little doubt she has earned an important place in contemporary Italian literature and that some of her works, such as *Donna in guerra* [*Women at War*] and *La lunga vita di Marianna Ucria* [*The Silent Duchess*], will stand the test of time." Lucamente concludes that in addition to its feminist insights, Maraini's "work also provides an implacable analysis of Italian society during the latter half of the twentieth century."

In the works of Maraini that have been translated, English-language reviewers have found much to appreciate. Reviewing *The Silent Duchess* for *Library Journal,* Lisa Rohrbaugh comments: "Mariani's writing is elegant, and her graphic descriptions of the luxurious life of the aristocracy in sharp contrast to the squalor of the majority living in poverty are quite realistic." Kathryn Harrison of the *New York Times Book Review* finds the book to be "a story of grace and endurance" that "acquires a slyly suspenseful quality." Maraini's 1985 *Isolina,* a journalistic investigation of a murder that occurred in 1900, is described by Michele Roberts of *New Statesman* as "powerful and sensitively created." Deanna Larson of *Booklist* remarks concerning *Bagheria:* "Bittersweet memoirs make the most interesting reading. This one . . . is full of contradiction and as pungent as black olives grown in Mediterranean soil."

BIOGRAPHICAL/CRITICAL SOURCES:

BOOKS

Dictionary of Literary Biography, Volume 196, *Italian Novelists since World War II, 1965-1995,* Gale (Detroit), 1999, pp. 189-200.

Encyclopedia of World Literature, Volume 3, St. James Press (Detroit), 1999, pp. 200-201.

PERIODICALS

Booklist, March 15, 1995, p. 1301; February 1, 1998, p. 893; March 15, 2000, Sylvia S. Goldberg and Hung-yun Chang, "Italian Books," p. 1336.

Choice, June, 1998, L. A. Russell, review of *Searching for Emma: Gustave Flaubert and Madame Bovary,* p. 1714.

Economist, May 17, 1997, p. S13; July 17, 1999, review of *Buio,* p. 14.

Library Journal, May 15, 1988, Lisa Mullenneaux, review of *Letters to Marina,* p. 92; September 15, 1998, p. 113.

Modern Language Review, July, 1998, Sharon Wood, "Dacia Maraini and the Written Dream of Women in Italian Literature," p. 855.

New Statesman, July 6, 1984, Marion Glastonbury, review of *Woman at War,* p. 27; October 8, 1993, p. 36.

New York Times, February 24, 1987, D. J. R. Bruckner, review of *Mary Stuart,* p. 22.

New York Times Book Review, April 9, 1995, James Marcus, "Broken Promises," p. 13; December 13, 1998, Kathryn Harrison, "The Silence," p. 8.

Parade, June 28, 1998, Herbert Kupferberg, review of *Searching for Emma: Gustave Flaubert and Madame Bovary,* p. 18.

Publishers Weekly, February 26, 1988, Penny Kaganoff, review of *Letters to Marina,* p. 190; October 31, 1994, p. 43; March 20, 1995, p. 53; October 5, 1998, p. 81.

Theatre Journal, October, 1990, Tony Mitchell, " 'Scrittura femminile': Writing the Female in the Plays of Dacia Maraini," p. 332.

Variety, March 26, 1969; June 24, 1970; July 8, 1970.

Women's Review of Books, March, 1999, Marion Lignana Roseberg, review of *The Silent Duchess,* p. 7.

World Literature Today, spring, 1991, Patricia M. Gathercole, review of *La lunga vita di Marianna Ucria,* p. 286.

OTHER

IRT: Dacia Maraini, http://www.mbnet.mb.ca/ (May 13, 1999).*

* * *

MARIUS, Richard (Curry) 1933-1999

PERSONAL: Born July 29, 1933, in Martel, TN; died of pancreatic cancer, November 5, 1999, in Belmont, MA; son of Henri (a foundryman) and Eunice (a journalist; maiden name, Henck) Marius; married Gail Smith, June 28, 1955 (divorced); married Lanier Smythe, March 21, 1970; children: (first marriage) Richard, Fred; (second marriage) John. *Ethnicity:* "Greek-American." *Education:* University of Tennessee, B.S. (summa cum laude), 1954; Southern Baptist Theological Seminary, B.D., 1958; Yale University, M.A., 1959, Ph.D., 1962. *Politics:* Liberal Democrat. *Religion:* Unitarian.

CAREER: Newspaper reporter while attending college, and worked at odd jobs to pay for further education; Gettysburg College, Gettysburg, PA, assistant professor of history, 1962-64; University of Tennessee, Knoxville, assistant professor, 1964-68, associate professor, 1968-73, professor of history, 1973-78; Harvard University, Cambridge, MA, director of expository writing, beginning in 1978.

MEMBER: American Association of University Professors, Authors League of America, Authors Guild.

AWARDS, HONORS: The Coming of Rain was designated the best novel of 1969 by Friends of American Writers; *Thomas More: A Biography* was nominated for the 1984 American Book Award in nonfiction.

WRITINGS:

The Coming of Rain (novel), Knopf (New York City), 1969.

Bound for the Promised Land (novel), Knopf, 1976.
After the War (novel), Knopf, 1992.

NONFICTION

(Co-editor) Thomas More, *Confutations,* three volumes, Yale University Press (New Haven, CT), 1973.
Luther (biography), Lippincott (Philadelphia, PA), 1974.
(Editor with Thomas M. C. Lawler and Germain Marc'hadour, and contributor) *The Complete Works of St. Thomas More,* Volume 6, Yale University Press, 1982.
(Editor with others, and contributor) *The Yale Edition of the Complete Works of St. Thomas More,* Volume 8, Yale University Press, 1983.
Thomas More: A Biography, Knopf, 1984.
A Writer's Companion, Knopf, 1985, 4th edition, McGraw (New York City), 1999.
(With Harvey S. Wiener) *The McGraw-Hill College Handbook* (with annotated teacher's supplement), McGraw, 1985, 4th edition, 1994.
(With J. Bean) *The McGraw-Hill Self-Study Workbook,* McGraw, 1985.
A Short Guide to Writing about History, Little, Brown (Boston, MA), 1987, 3rd edition, HarperCollins (New York City), 1995, 4th edition, Longman (New York City), 1999.
(Editor) *The Columbia Book of Civil War Poetry,* Columbia University Press (New York City), 1994.
Martin Luther: The Christian between God and Death, Harvard University Press (Cambridge, MA), 1999.

Featured on the sound recording *The Writer and Human Values,* Tennessee Library Association, 1973. Contributor to scholarly journals and other periodicals, including *Daedalus, Moreana, Traditio, Sewanee Review, Boston Sunday Globe, Christian Century, Esquire,* and *National Forum.* Contributor to *Quincentennial Essays on St. Thomas More,* edited by Michael J. Moore, Albion, 1962; and *Pioneer Spirit 76: Commemorative BicenTENNial Portrait,* edited by Dolly Berthelot, 1975.

SIDELIGHTS: Richard Marius, an historian, educator, and author of novels and nonfiction who died in 1999, once told *CA:* "I write because I have had a compulsion to write since I was in the fifth grade and began a newspaper in my little country school by typing every copy on my mother's typewriter. My work is most influenced by my observation of people, but my authors who draw me again and again are Shakespeare, Twain, Faulkner, Conrad, Dickens, Proust, Balzac, Joyce, and Tolstoy. My work probably needs a little more levity. I love to write first with a pen or pencil and then to type the draft into the computer. I revise far too much, too compulsively, often by printing out my drafts and filling in revisions by hand and afterwards plugging them back into the computer. I also revise directly off the screen. All my work has an autobiographical cast, but it is autobiography filtered through a screen of the surreal and the dream world of imagination. I have kept a journal since I was fifteen, recording what I see of people, and the almost daily process of writing my observations feeds my fictional imagination. My mother was a religious fanatic, and I spent three years in two Southern Baptist seminaries, one in New Orleans and one in Louisville, Kentucky. They were stupid, hateful places. But I still write about religious themes."

Marius wrote extensively about the Renaissance and its personages; but he was also a novelist who "classifie[d] both fiction and nonfiction as 'creative writing' and applie[d] the same criteria of writing to both: ideas must 'make sense' and be real and 'memorable,' " reported Nancy G. Anderson in the *Dictionary of Literary Biography Yearbook, 1985.* As Marius once explained in *National Forum:* "Writers observe in a world of restless change. In setting their observations on paper, all writers create something—a design that makes the observations make sense, something that relates them to the rest of our thought and feeling, something that may make them memorable." As director of expository writing at Harvard University, Marius also authored student textbooks on the subject which, according to Anderson, are "praised for their commonsensical approach to writing, their readable and even humorous style." Although Marius's stylistic approach was informal and personal, his work is often cited for its clarity and precision. "The levels of language and tone vary with the subject and audience," observed Anderson, "but readable style, use of memorable details, the sense of drama, and, when appropriate, humor persist."

Luther, Marius's biography of Martin Luther, evolved out of his "opposition to the Vietnam War and his efforts at that time to teach the Reformation," noted Anderson. And while *Christian Science Monitor* contributor J. G. Harrison objected to "gratuitous references to the 'dirty war' in Vietnam," he simultaneously believed that the biography "is a serious, well-written and—most important of all—understandable history of a complex subject and time." Commending its "historical authenticity" and its author's efforts to discover a "relevance for our own times," *Library Journal* contributor J. S. Nelson considered *Luther* "interesting, lively, and informative." However, Anderson mentioned that Marius's informal, personal style and the conclusions he draws (that help comes from within the individual rather than from arcane theology, and that life itself is but a process in which one makes peace with death) provoked critical objections. Finding "little admiration expressed by the author for anyone," Roland H. Bainton claimed in a *Christian Century* review that *Luther* is "an indictment not so much of a man as of a century." Moreover, said Bainton, "I hear in Marius's book the reverberations of an agonized cry of frustration because the contemporary church has let the author down." Conversely, though, Harrison believed that the biography accomplishes its informative task clearly, simply, and directly: "Luther's struggles, his anguish, his world-upsetting insights, his medieval prejudices, his human shortcomings are set forth without either adulation or prejudice. From here emerges a man, not a symbol."

Marius's scholarly writings about Thomas More, which emanated from his graduate studies and dissertation, analyze "More's beliefs and his place in the political and religious developments of his day," according to Anderson. Whatever his audience, she continued, Marius's "argument, often complex or abstract, is carefully reasoned and developed with documented evidence from primary sources." *Thomas More: A Biography,* which was nominated for the American Book Award, resulted from his work on the Yale University Press edition of *The Complete Works of St. Thomas More,* and represents "the culmination of Richard Marius's research on More, the Reformation, and the sixteenth century," stated Anderson. *Library Journal* contributor Bennett D. Hill asserted that "this sympathetic but judicious, sensitively written work" appeals to the lay person and scholar alike, but "as popular biography, it's absolutely first-rate." Finding that it "sparkles with epigrams," Carl Banks added in *Christian Century:* "Wry comments and pointed parallels enliven the biography." And as Jack Miles expressed it in the *Los Angeles Times Book Review,* "When smart people talk about other people, this is how they do it. . . . It is as subtle and satisfying a portrait as I have encountered in years."

In contrasting the public figure with the private one, Marius pursues a dual purpose in *Thomas More,* observed Nicolas Barker in the *Times Literary Supplement.* "To peel away the hagiography . . . and to present him in terms that today's reader, unfamiliar with the historic background, will grasp as real and lively. This is not easy," Barker declared. Acknowledging the difficulty Marius faced in crafting such a biography, *New Republic* reviewer Robert M. Adams pointed out: "Thomas More is one of those historical figures who are easy to take a piece at a time, but hard to assemble." Critics frequently compared *Thomas More* with a 1935 biography by R. W. Chambers, which Adams deemed "an elegantly written but patently unctuous piece of sentimental hagiography." Adams suggested that Marius's study of More is "just as hagiographic . . . since he represents More as a lifelong advocate of, and finally a martyr to, a particularly noble ideal of the church." However, unlike that of Chambers, Marius's portrait of More lacks charm, decried Adams, who then summarized his estimation of Marius's antithetical perspective: "Marius gives us a thoroughly disagreeable More, a domestic tyrant, neurotically afraid of sex, a quarrelsome and self- important writer, a vicious and dishonest controversialist, an obsequious sycophant, a man quite without sympathy for the poor or concern over the slaughter of innocent men in brutally expensive and futile wars." In *Thomas More,* the subject "receives tremendous sympathy, but without suppression of the dark ambiguities of his life and character," observed Banks. Similarly, *Newsweek*'s Peter S. Prescott suggested that Marius considers a wealth of new evidence and, "careful not to reject the prevailing image," he develops another, darker one. "Marius's More is in public an actor, creating his own role on a stage of his own devising," wrote Prescott, adding that "the More he gives us is the last medieval man, a failed monk who by necessity chose marriage and a secular career in London, a merciless scourge of heretics who was forever preoccupied with death and fearing for his soul." *Time*'s Melvin Maddocks thought that "it is Marius's persuasive thesis that, far from being the serene humanist, . . . More was a soul tormented by the little death knells of ticktocking time, and haunted even more by the silences of eternity." But as O. B. Hardison, Jr., explained in *Book World,* although Marius shows us the infallible More, "In the end, and almost in spite of Marius's effort to identify his defects, More the saint eclipses More the man."

Marius's "unrivaled knowledge of More's works . . . serves him very well," declared Paul Johnson in the *New York Times Book Review,* adding that Marius "is the first writer to stress the central importance of More's unfinished biography of Richard III," which, as Johnson posited, "expresses not so much Tudor propaganda as More's political philosophy." Citing Marius's frequent use of "the image of More as an actor on stage," Anderson wrote that Marius "records his life against the rich setting of the Renaissance and the nascent Reformation, with the full drama of a fall from power and relative luxury. . . . And, even for an audience that knows the ending, Marius builds to the climax of the final scene of the scaffold, where, having apparently conquered his fear of death, More gave his best performance." Maddocks suggested that, "without presuming to answer, the author raises a question: Did More die for what he believed or for what he wanted to believe?" Calling *Thomas More* "an iconoclastic book which yet recognizes the ultimate greatness of Thomas More," G. R. Elton proclaimed in the *New York Review of Books:* "The debate about More will now continue because Marius has helped to reopen it after More threatened to get embalmed, and that debate will be different through this book."

Agreeing that *Thomas More* is "clearly a work of authority and scholarship," Prescott averred that it "nonetheless contains a multitude of unsupported assertions and misleading generalizations." Elton recognized that Marius's achievement "is not perfect; with a writer so deeply involved in everything he says it could hardly be." However, acknowledging that "avowed conjecture abounds . . . and not all of that conjecture carries conviction," Elton maintained that "genuine mistakes are very few." And Barker, who believed that Marius "succeeds in forcing his mind into the sixteenth-century mentality, without losing sight of his twentieth-century reader," proposed: "What faults there are come from Marius's determination . . . to see for himself with his own eyes." Moreover, said Elton, "Marius has written a very remarkable book, full of knowledge and understanding. He has written a very personal book, full of wrestling with intractable material and the overwhelming problem of comprehending a man, 450 years dead, who lived in a world and by rules that the present day finds it hard even to contemplate." And, concluded Elton, Marius should be particularly pleased that "he replaces Chambers not only because he knows much more and thinks far more deeply, but also because he writes infinitely better." Prescott also admitted that "if Marius too often writes about more than he knows, what he knows is impressive."

"Richard Marius's Renaissance-like interests [developed] naturally from his background and education," remarked Anderson, who perceived that just as "history is a focus of Marius's scholarly publications, . . . attitudes toward history are also concerns in his fiction." Marius's novels are set in the fictional city of Bourbonville, based upon the nearby town of his childhood, Lenoir City, Tennessee. *The Coming of Rain,* described by D. C. Taylor in *Library Journal* as an "ambitious and successful first novel about love and violence and family pride and murder and coming of age in post-Civil War eastern Tennessee," explores what Marius once described in "The Middle of the Journey," an autobiographical essay in *Sewanee Review,* as the "Confederate myth of the Lost Cause." The novel recounts the events of only two days in 1885 but, as R. V. Cassill declared in *Book World,* "Threads of action and subplots intertwine so luxuriously that one almost needs a concordance to keep them from entangling hopelessly in his mind." Commenting that the novel "contains multitudes," and is "superbly plotted," a *Times Literary Supplement* contributor especially lauded Marius's ability to "convey vividly the feeling of a rough, sweat-soiled, primitive society overawed by tub-thumping preachers and haunted by the still rankling evils of slavery and civil war." And although Joyce Carol Oates suggested in the *New York Times Book Review* that the novel is "betrayed by [its] melodramatic complications," she discerned within it a "slender, tragic, perhaps beautiful story of the ruins of dreams."

"I always ponder history in my fiction," Marius stated in *Sewanee Review.* "In *The Coming of Rain* the real conflict is one between good history and bad history." Marius also explained that in his second novel, *Bound for the Promised Land,* "the conflict between illusion and reality is such that one must wonder if writing history is even possible. Nothing in that book is what it first seems to be." In this novel about a family's journey from Tennessee to California forty years earlier during the 1850s, "Marius uses a journey comparable to Chaucer's pilgrimage to bring together disparate, and desperate, characters," explained Anderson, adding that the novel explores "the discrepancy between the appearance of people and things and their reality, and about the meaning—or meaninglessness—of life." While Marius may have crafted his fiction in multiple layers of meaning, critics have also appreciated his ability to tell a story: "It's a good solid story, colorful, lively and authentic," maintained a *Publishers Weekly* contributor about *Bound for the Promised Land.* "A sound if somewhat exhausting read," concurred a *Booklist* reviewer.

"Ultimately, [*The Coming of Rain* and *Bound for the Promised Land*] are quite similar philosophically or thematically," stated Anderson, explaining that "characters in both novels search for meaning and purpose in life." Anderson also noted that Marius's unhappy "seminary experiences and the fundamentalist religious environment of his childhood are reflected in both of his novels as religious fanatics cause death and destruction." And although both novels speak about Southern lives and the romantic traditions of the South, Marius, whose maternal ancestry can be traced to the American Revolution, and whose grandfather fought for the Union in the Civil War, indicated in *Sewanee Review:* "I bristle when anyone calls me a 'southern' writer. I am a novelist of the border, and in both my novels the romantic traditions of the old South take a good beating. I shall beat those traditions still more in my third." "As best I can tell," continued Marius, "three things seem to have contributed most to my fiction: a love for the English language, the experiences of a vividly remembered childhood, and my profession as a historian." Anderson suggested that "after a study of his essays, his novels, and his biographies, one must complete the list with the influence of religion." In his autobiographical essay, Marius recalled his family's move to a farm as well as his own happy, if somewhat isolated, childhood. They moved, he said, partly to be nearer to his father's work, but also to avoid the "curious and reproachful attention of near neighbors in town" upon his older, mentally impaired brother, whom his mother believed to have been a divine punishment for her failure to become a missionary. Marius described his mother as having been "cursed by religion"; and although he entered the seminary essentially because of her religiosity, he related that the isolation of his childhood was relieved by the pleasure of listening to his mother read aloud—especially the Bible—and he credited this with having given him a love for the English language. "To this day I read aloud everything that I write, and if the rhythms are not right, I write again," he said. "I rewrote every page of both my novels at least ten times, and there are some scenes . . . in *The Coming of Rain* that I rewrote as many as thirty times. It is a burden to rewrite so much because it takes me years to finish a book."

In his controversial work *Martin Luther: The Christian between God and Death,* Marius offers a close examination of Luther's life from his birth into the mid-1520s, suggesting that Luther's search for a "believable faith" was motivated by a consuming fear of death. To make his case, Marius undertakes a close reading of Luther's early writings and reminiscences, also speculating on the formative influence of Luther's parents. "Richard Marius's fine new biography of Luther resumes the traditional focus of interest in a life first prepared for in 'years of silence' to 1517 (when Luther was thirty-four), and then lived at centre stage in the period down to the 1520s," wrote Michael Mullett in the *Times Literary Supplement.* "The early years, which are relatively well documented . . . are illuminatingly covered, Professor Marius having some particularly imaginative speculations to make about parental, if not psychological, influences, on Luther." In the *New Republic,* Heiko A. Oberman felt that *Martin Luther: The Christian between God and Death* bears a strong thematic resemblance to Marius's biography of Thomas More. Oberman noted: "Placing Thomas More and Martin Luther side by side reveals what may easily escape even critical readers reading either volume in isolation: Marius bridges the gap between 'then' and 'now,' past and present. . . . In his hands, the English saint . . . and the German reformer become 'one of us,' driven by the same indomitable sexual drives and perplexed by our own fear of Death as the End, all threatened by a deeply unsettling climate of skepticism, and by the creeping realization that the Bible is merely a waxen nose and the Heavens are no longer the domain of the Almighty." Oberman continued: "All of these pronouncements circle around Marius's great psychological discovery: that More and Luther . . . are victims of the same daunting dawn of doubt that propelled Marius himself from the pulpit to the classroom."

Oberman was not convinced by the arguments Marius marshalls in *Martin Luther: The Christian between God and Death.* "A truly hard-hitting criticism of Luther must rest on more than speculation about his unconscious life," the critic stated. "Marius's book is what the Romans called a *pia fraus,* a 'pious fraud.' After all, its motivation is openly admitted: the intense fervor of the lapsed believer who is intent on rejecting his past." Mullett came to a different conclusion in his review of the book. "To a considerable extent," noted the reviewer, "[the book] is an investigation of Luther's intellectual evolution during [a] critical decade." Mullett maintained: "Understandably, Luther is one of the most heavily studied figures in history, and, arguably, the leading Western figure of the second millennium. . . . Richard Marius writes vividly and clarifies complex matters for students." Likewise, a *Christian Science Monitor* contributor declared: "There can be no doubt that this book is destined to become a classic."

"In all of his works, as eclectic as the interests of the Renaissance which he [studied] and about which he [wrote], Marius strives to achieve 'memorability,' " Anderson once declared. "He claims that he writes because 'I am going to die, and I don't want to perish completely from this earth.' " And in his autobiographical essay, Marius had contemplated his responsibility as an historian, educator, and writer: "Anyone who has taught and written about the past, as I do regularly, must ponder some awesome questions. Any historian is perhaps nothing more than a weaver of glittering illusion as fragile as light and as dangerous as poison." Offering, however, a slight modification to Marius's statement, Anderson concluded: "And a memorable novelist is perhaps nothing more than a good historian with a love of language."

BIOGRAPHICAL/CRITICAL SOURCES:

BOOKS

Dictionary of Literary Biography Yearbook 1985, Gale (Detroit, MI), 1986, pp. 402-12.

PERIODICALS

Best Sellers, November 1, 1969, pp. 281-82; January 1, 1975.
Booklist, June 1, 1976; February 1, 1999, Steven Schroeder, review of *Martin Luther,* p. 946.
Book World, September 14, 1969.
Boston Book Review, May, 1999, review of *Martin Luther.*
Boston Globe, March 14, 1999, review of *Martin Luther.*
Boston Globe Magazine, December 11, 1983, pp. 12, 38, 42, 44, 48, 52, 54.
Boston Sunday Globe, November 11, 1984, pp. A18, A20.
Christian Century, February 19, 1975, pp. 173-75; October 6, 1976, pp. 842-43; July 3-10, 1985.
Christianity Today, July 12, 1999, Mark Galli, "New and Noteworthy: Biography," p. 63.
Christian Science Monitor, December 24, 1974; April 8, 1999, review of *Martin Luther.*
Commonweal, May 3, 1985, pp. 286-87.
Library Journal, September 1, 1969; December 1, 1974; September 1, 1984; January, 1999, David Bourquin, review of *Martin Luther,* p. 106; February 15, 1999, review of *Martin Luther.*
Life, September 6, 1969, p. 16.
Los Angeles Times Book Review, October 28, 1984.
National Forum, fall, 1985.
New Republic, January 21, 1985, pp. 38-40; August 16, 1999, Heiko A. Oberman, "Varieties of Protest," p. 40.
Newsweek, October 29, 1984.
New York Review of Books, January 31, 1985, pp. 7-9.
New York Times, November 20, 1979, p. B7; June 16, 1985, p. 48.
New York Times Book Review, September 21, 1969, p. 5; January 6, 1985, p. 11.
Sewanee Review, summer, 1977.
Spectator, February 2, 1985.
Time, December 24, 1984.
Times Literary Supplement, August 21, 1970; April 12, 1985; June 18, 1999, Michael Mullett, "Luther and the Fear of Death," p. 11.
USA Today, December 14, 1984, p. 3D.

OBITUARIES:

PERIODICALS

New York Times, November 8, 1999; November 14, 1999.*

* * *

MARKSON, David M(errill) 1927-

PERSONAL: Born December 20, 1927, in Albany, NY; son of Samuel A. (a newspaper editor) and Florence (a school teacher; maiden name, Stone) Markson; married Elaine Kretchmar (a literary agent), September 30, 1956; children: Johanna Lowry, Jed Matthew. *Education:* Union College, Schenectady, NY, B.A., 1950; Columbia University, M.A., 1952. *Politics:* Liberal Democrat. *Religion:* Jewish.

ADDRESSES: Home and Office—215 West 10th St., New York, NY 10014. *Agent*—Elaine Markson, 44 Greenwich Ave., New York, NY 10011.

CAREER: Albany Times-Union, Albany, NY, staff writer, 1944-46, 1948-50; Weyerhauser Timber Co., Molalla, OR, rigger, 1952; Dell Publishing Co., New York City, editor, 1953-54; Lion Books, New York City, editor, 1955-56; freelance writer, 1956-64; Long Island University, Brooklyn Center, Brooklyn, NY, assistant professor of English, 1964-66; freelance writer, 1966—. Part-time lecturer, Columbia University, 1979-87. *Military service:* U.S. Army, 1946-48; became staff sergeant.

MEMBER: Louis Norman Newsom Memorial Society (executive secretary, 1973-80).

AWARDS, HONORS: Fellow of Centro Mexicano de Escritores, 1960-61.

WRITINGS:

NOVELS

Epitaph for a Tramp, Dell (New York City), 1959, published as *Fannin,* Belmont (New York City), 1971.
Epitaph for a Dead Beat, Dell, 1961.
Miss Doll, Go Home, Dell, 1965.
The Ballad of Dingus Magee, Bobbs-Merrill (Indianapolis, IN), 1966.
Going Down, Holt (New York City), 1970.
Springer's Progress, Holt, 1977.

Wittgenstein's Mistress, Dalkey Archive Press (Normal, IL), 1988.
Springer's Progress, Dalkey Archive Press, 1990.
Reader's Block, Dalkey Archive Press, 1996.

POETRY

Collected Poems, Dalkey Archive Press, 1993.

OTHER

(Editor) *Great Tales of Old Russia* (anthology), Pyramid Publications, 1956.
Face to the Wind (screenplay), Brut Productions, 1974.
Malcolm Lowry's Volcano: Myth, Symbol, Meaning (literary criticism), New York Times Co., 1978.

Contributor to magazines and newspapers, including *Saturday Evening Post, Nation, Atlantic,* and *Village Voice.*

ADAPTATIONS: The Ballad of Dingus Magee was filmed as *Dirty Dingus Magee* by Metro-Goldwyn-Mayer in 1970, starring Frank Sinatra and George Kennedy.

SIDELIGHTS: David Markson is best known as a writer of experimental fiction. *San Francisco Review of Books* contributor Joseph Tebbi notes that Markson is "among the few working novelists decisively to have carried the modernist tradition into the present, post-modern literature; a writer who, without claiming any particular knowledge of, or even affinities with, the more programmatic expounders of post-modernism, in recent work exemplifies many of the period's most vital developments." Since the publication in 1959 of *Epitaph for a Tramp* (later released under the title *Fannin*), he has published seven novels, has seen a play and screenplay produced, and has written a book of literary criticism centering on the works of his friend, the writer Malcolm Lowry. Markson, writes *Contemporary Novelists* contributor Barry Lewis, "found it easy to form friendships with well-known writers such as Lowry, Dylan Thomas, and Jack Kerouac in his youth, but only found widespread success for his own work with *Wittgenstein's Mistress,* a book rejected 54 times before its publication in 1988."

Markson achieved a modicum of notoriety with the publication in 1966 of *The Ballad of Dingus Magee,* a parody of the Western novel complete with a ruthless young gunfighter, a corruptible sheriff, and a prosperous town bordello. According to a *Time* critic, the book "is stacked with enough sagebrush cliches to make it high Campfire. . . . Parts of the book are rollickingly funny parody, while other parts are slapstick." In a somewhat tongue-in-cheek review, Piers Brendon of *Books and Bookmen* writes: "Everyone has a cache of conviction inside him, however small, where to admit humour is to commit sacrilege. Personally, I can take jokes about the Virgin Mary, about disease, even about incest. But I do draw the line at laughing at the Wild West. . . . If God is dead one must have faith in something. I believe in John Wayne. However, Dingus Magee has shaken my simple faith. I feel rather like one of the Disciples who suddenly discovers that Christ has been secretly bottling the water which he has changed into wine and selling it at an exorbitant price." Dispelling his outrage, Brendon concludes that "there is plenty of action, plenty of bawdy and plenty of highly irreverent amusement in this novel."

In a review of *Going Down, Newsweek's* S. K. Oberbeck writes: "A volcanic pretension bubbles at the bottom of the drama of a *menage a trois* of damaged U.S. expatriates nearing their doom in Mexico. It stumbles and stutters along in a dreamy barrage of elegant, unfinished sentences and unanswered rhetorical questions nipped at mid-phrase." Markson's unique style appears to be a favorite target for some critics who feel that it tends to detract from the underlying quality of his work. A *Virginia Quarterly Review* writer, for instance, calls him "an intelligent writer, often a humorous one, whose mannerisms tend to conceal his very solid attributes." But Christopher Lehmann-Haupt, writing in the *New York Times,* offers a possible explanation: "It may be that Mr. Markson is up to something here. On the other hand, it is equally possible that he is not. My reasoning runs as follows: If the prose style of fiction doesn't serve to illuminate the action it's describing, then it's either incompetent or it's meant to call attention to itself. . . . The prose of *Going Down* is by no means incompetent. It draws one's attention inexorably to the narrator, who turns out to be no one but the author himself." However, after arriving at this conclusion, Lehmann-Haupt decides that the illusion created by this method "is of a novelist, with nothing to say, trying to tell a story he doesn't believe for a minute."

Wittgenstein's Mistress is the story that takes the form of an interior monologue given by Kate, a former painter who believes that she is the last person left alive on earth. Markson leaves ambiguous the notion of whether Kate is actually insane or the only survivor of a global catastrophe. "*Wittgenstein's Mistress,*" writes Evelin E. Sullivan in the *Review of Contemporary Fiction,* "addresses the question of how memory works. . . . Throughout the book, Kate moves by mental associations from topic to topic: who was who's student, who knew whom, who lived in the same city as who, died of the same disease as who, had eccentricities similar to whose?" "As Kate finally realizes," Sullivan concludes, "what anything and everything brings to her mind are things too painful to think about."

BIOGRAPHICAL/CRITICAL SOURCES:

BOOKS

Breit, Harvey, and Margerie Bonner Lowry, editors, *Selected Letters of Malcolm Lowry,* Lippincott (Philadelphia), 1965.
Contemporary Novelists, 6th edition, St. James Press (Detroit, MI), 1996.
Contemporary Literary Criticism, Volume 67, Gale Research (Detroit, MI), 1992.
Day, Douglas, *Malcolm Lowry,* Oxford University Press, 1974.
Fiedler, Leslie A., *The Return of the Vanishing American,* Stein & Day (New York City), 1968.

PERIODICALS

Books and Bookmen, May, 1967.
Newsweek, April 6, 1970.
New York Times, April 24, 1970.
Publishers Weekly, August 9, 1993, p. 472; August 12, 1996, p. 79.
Punch, April 5, 1966.
Review of Contemporary Fiction, summer, 1990, pp. 240-46.
San Francisco Review of Books, summer, 1988, p. 32.
Time, April 22, 1966.
Union College Symposium, winter, 1970-71.
Virginia Quarterly Review, summer, 1970.*

* * *

MASSIE, Allan (Johnstone) 1938-

PERSONAL: Born October 19, 1938, in Singapore; son of Alexander Johnstone and Evelyn Jane Wilson (Forbes) Massie; married Alison Agnes Graham Langlands, 1973; children: two sons, one daughter. *Education:* Attended Trinity College, Glenalmond; Trinity College, Cambridge, B.A. *Avocational interests:* Rugby, reading, lunching, watching cricket, horse-racing, and equestrian events.

ADDRESSES: Home—Thirladean House, Selkirk TD7 5LU, England. *Agent*—Sheil Land Associates, 43 Doughty St., London WC1N 2LF, England.

CAREER: Drumtochty Castle School, England, schoolteacher, 1960-71; teacher of English as a second language, Rome, Italy, 1972-75; *The Scotsman,* fiction reviewer, 1976—; *Glasgow Herald,* Glasgow, Scotland, creative columnist, 1985-88; *Sunday Times Scotland,* 1987—; *Daily Telegraph,* 1991—. Edinburgh University, creative writing fellow, 1982-84; Glasgow and Strathclyde Universities, creative writing fellow, 1985-86.

MEMBER: Scottish Arts Council.

AWARDS, HONORS: Niven Award, 1981; Scottish Arts Council Award, 1982; fellow, Royal Society of Literature.

WRITINGS:

NOVELS

Change and Decay in All around I See, Bodley Head (London), 1978.
The Last Peacock, Bodley Head, 1980.
The Death of Men, Bodley Head, 1981, Houghton (Boston), 1982.
One Night in Winter, Bodley Head, 1984.
Augustus: The Memoirs of the Emperor, Bodley Head, 1986, published as *Let the Emperor Speak: A Novel of Caesar Augustus,* Doubleday, 1987, published as *Augustus: A Novel,* Sceptre (London), 1987.
A Question of Loyalties, Hutchinson (London), 1989.
The Hanging Tree, Heinemann, 1990.
Tiberius: The Memoirs of the Emperor, Hodder & Stoughton, 1991, Carroll & Graf (New York City), 1993.
The Sins of the Father, Hutchinson, 1991.
These Enchanted Woods, Hutchinson, 1993.
Caesar, Hodder & Stoughton, 1993.
The Ragged Lion, Hutchinson, 1994.
King David, Sceptre, 1995.
Nero's Heirs, Sceptre, 1999.

OTHER

Muriel Spark, Ramsay Head Press (Edinburgh), 1979.
Ill Met by Gaslight: Five Edinburgh Murders, Harris (Edinburgh), 1980.
The Caesars, Secker & Warburg (London), 1983, F. Watts (New York City), 1984.
(Editor and author of introduction) *Edinburgh and the Borders: In Verse,* Secker & Warburg, 1983.
A Portrait of Scottish Rugby, Polygon (Edinburgh), 1984.

(Author of text) *Eisenstaedt: Aberdeen, Portrait of a City* (photographs by Alfred Eisenstaedt), Louisiana State University Press, 1984.

Colette: The Woman, the Writer, and the Myth (part of the "Lives of Modern Women" series), Penguin (New York City), 1986.

101 Great Scots, Chambers (Edinburgh), 1987.

(Editor) *PEN New Fiction: Thirty-two Short Stories,* Quartet (London), 1987.

How Should Health Services Be Financed? A Patient's View, Aberdeen University Press (Aberdeen), 1988.

The Novelist's View of the Market Economy, David Hume Institute, 1988.

Byron's Travels, Sidgwick & Jackson (London), 1988.

Glasgow: Portraits of a City, Barrie & Jenkins (London), 1989.

The Novel Today: A Critical Guide to the British Novel, 1970-1989, Longman/British Council (London), 1990.

Author of plays *Quintet in October* and *The Minstrel and the Shirra;* the short story "In the Bare Lands" appeared in *Modern Scottish Short Stories,* edited by Fred Urquhart and Giles Gordon, Hamish Hamilton, 1978; contributor to *Spectator* and *Sunday Telegraph.*

SIDELIGHTS: A prolific author with a wide-ranging list of titles to his credit, Allan Massie taught school for a number of years before turning to full-time writing in the mid-1970s. In addition to writing books, Massie is also a regular contributor such newspapers as the *Glasgow Herald* and the *Daily Telegraph,* and he has taught creative writing at the university level.

Massie's body of work encompasses several themes, and prominent among these is his interest in Scotland. A number of his novels have been set in the windswept northern reaches of this land, and many of his nonfiction titles include such subjects as famous Edinburgh crimes, notable Scottish personalities, and the city of Glasgow. Another profound influence on Massie's writings was a 1970s sojourn in Italy: one of his novels is set in modern-day Rome, while others hearken back to the city's ancient days. Additionally, Massie has written one general historical work on the leaders of imperial Rome and four fictionalized biographies of well-known emperors. Historical events, whether of centuries past or more recent, permeate much of Massie's writing, and his characters, whether wholly created or elaborated upon, struggle to fathom areas of personal morality through introspection. According to Brian Morton in *These Enchanted Woods,* Massie "has emerged as a historical novelist in the truest vein." Morton noted that the author "has been attacked in Scotland as a latter-day representative of [Sir Walter] Scott: hostile to democracy and urbanism, a defensive Unionist committed to High Tory pastorals. However true that might be of his newspaper columns, which reveal an able controversialist, it is far less true of his fiction. If his novels recall anyone from [the twentieth] century, it has to be Andre Malraux, whose awareness of how characters behave within tightly knit ideological groups is unparalleled."

Change and Decay in All around I See, Massie's first novel, was published in 1978. Set in 1950s London, the work introduces a cast of disparate and dissolute characters. At the center of this group is Atwater, recently released from prison, and his revolutionary friend Horridge. Atwater haunts London's seedy back streets, intermingling with the novel's cast, and everyone's atrocious behavior is observed with irony. Through humorous dialogue, *Change and Decay in All around I See* particularly inveighs against all types of literary pretensions. "Becking and nodding frantically in an odd assortment of literary directions," wrote Valentine Cunningham of the *Times Literary Supplement,* ". . . Massie's whippy little first novel manages at the same time a self-possessed talent to amuse."

Massie's second novel, *The Last Peacock,* appeared in 1980. Although the setting of this book is very different from *Change and Decay,* the characters, once again, appear as a metaphor for society in general. A clan has gathered at a Scottish country estate to be present at their matriarch's deathbed. The descendants who occupy the largest role in the novel are two of the dowager's grandchildren: Belinda, a confused divorcee who lives in London, far removed from her family and the tradition-bound rural Scottish landscape, and her dissolute brother Colin, with whom she holds many alcohol-fueled discussions. Both Colin and Belinda are perplexed by the modern age, and their dissonance with it has been brought to the fore by the act of returning to their ancestral home and the ritual of the deathwatch itself. Their quandary—feeling out of place in the contemporary world, wistfully longing for an earlier time—marks them as members of the same dying breed represented by their grandmother. Yet the action of *The Last Peacock* also involves other characters, such the brother-in-law with whom Belinda illicitly engages in an affair, and other ideas, such as talk of forming a right-wing political faction that would reinstate traditional morals and behavior. Admitting strong reservations about Massie's first book, Mary Hope of the *Spectator* declared that she was elated by *The Last Peacock.* Praising it as "serious, sensitive, witty, moving and accomplished," Hope asserted that Massie's book is "a subtle comedy of manners and an impressive attempt to say many uncomfortable things. It is also a delight to read."

In *Ill Met by Gaslight: Five Edinburgh Murders,* Massie turns to the subject of true crime. In this work of nonfiction, he recounts—with adjunct social and historical commentary—the tales of five heinous Scottish criminals. Most of the crimes took place in the nineteenth century, and Massie quotes from the murderers' own accounts as well as from previously published interpretations by criminologists. Although the first malefactor presented in the book was only a thief and burglar, two others were found guilty of murdering their wives and another was charged with slaying and then hiding several infants.

Massie returned to the novel format for his next work, 1981's *The Death of Men.* Loosely based upon the actual kidnapping and murder of Italian politician Aldo Moro, all the action of the book takes place in Rome, and Massie integrates his knowledge of the city into many passages of the novel. The central character of *The Death of Men* is Corrado Dusa, a respected political leader who becomes embroiled in an ideological struggle between Italy's established bourgeois order and the shadowy netherworld of terrorists. Dusa is kidnapped by a small leftist group whose members include his own son; their aim is to expose the corruption of Italian politics. The novel is related through the separate but ultimately interlocking viewpoints of three other characters. The first of these is Dusa's diplomat brother, who tacitly aids the kidnappers by not fully cooperating with the police investigation. The second character is a jaded journalist with former ties to the left, primarily interested in advancing his own career. The final member of the trio is Tomaso, a representative of the left itself and one of Dusa's captors. Tomaso's dialogues in particular provide insight into the motives of terrorist faction, and through this Massie presents the eternal conflict between the status quo and those who seek to dismantle it. The Italian government, whose fictional members are portrayed as immoral and avaricious, refuses to negotiate Dusa's release, knowing he will be more valuable to them as a martyr than a bridge toward political reconciliation. The plot culminates in a desperate last-minute attempt at rescue and Dusa's lengthy conversation with his captor Tomaso about the nature of political struggle. The novel's title is part of a quote from former United States Supreme Court justice Oliver Wendell Holmes, who died in 1935 a respected jurist but sometimes condemned for his mildly fascist views on human nature. The quote, reprinted in the epigraph, reads in part: "Man at present is a predatory animal . . . the sacredness of human life is a purely municipal ideal of no validity outside the jurisdiction . . . every society rests on the death of men."

The Death of Men received mixed reviews. *Times Literary Supplement* critic Anne Duchene complained that at times, "Massie's pen seems clogged in all the richly crumbling Roman *impasto,* and the central, passionate enquiry comes to seem incidental in a way he cannot have intended." A *New Yorker* reviewer praised Massie's handling of the complexities of the tale, noting that "although his aims are dead serious, his moves are tensely entertaining, dryly comedic, ruthlessly moving." In an essay in *Contemporary Novelists,* Trevor Royle asserted that with *The Death of Men* the author "discovered his true voice," noting that Massie "keeps open his moral options. Terrorism is roundly condemned, but he never loses sight of the question which is central to its occurrence: what are the political conditions which bring it into existence?"

Massie's fourth novel, 1984's *One Night in Winter,* is set in modern Scotland and allows the author to explore a variety of topics—from slick London bourgeoisie to dangerous nationalist tendencies in the British Isles. The protagonist, Dallas Graham, is a dissipated London antiques dealer married to an icy television producer. Graham is jolted out of the stupor of his life when his wife brings home a subject she plans to interview, a woman recently released from prison. Graham knew the woman twenty years before, when she was part of a circle of hedonists with whom he became involved after leaving college. As *One Night in Winter* relates through flashbacks, the young Graham returned to the family estate in northern Scotland and in a local pub met the enigmatic Fraser Donnelly, a blustery self-made sort who vociferously espoused a peculiar doctrine blending promiscuous sex with Scottish nationalism. Graham's involvement with Donnelly and his cohorts has haunted him for the last twenty years, since the sect's activities culminated in a deed of grisly violence and a well-publicized scandal. His introspection occupies a large part of the novel, and through this Massie dramatizes the conflict between a somnolent past haunting an often-superficial present in modern Great Britain. Graham attempts to run away from his present life with the ex-convict, but resignedly returns. Toby Fitton of the *Times Literary Supplement* praised Massie's characters, assessing Donnelly as "entirely convincing as a kenspeckle provincial 'character'," and describing the novel as the author's "best book to date. He is fully at home in the Scotland of his story, at several social levels, and has a good command of strong vernacular dialogue, not least its obscenities." *Spectator* critic Mary Hope also praised Massie's portrayals, declaring that "the second-league, sleazy provincial power-seekers and their cronies are cutting cameos which leave just the right nasty taste in the mouth." Hope summarized *One Night in Winter* as "technically flawed but always probing and intelligent."

In *Augustus: The Memoirs of the Emperor,* Massie overturned the standard biographical format completely for his fictionalized account of a Roman emperor. The book first appeared in 1986, but was subsequently reissued under the titles *Let the Emperor Speak: A Novel of Caesar Augustus* and *Augustus: A Novel.* Blending actual historical events into a dramatized narrative account, *Augustus* is fashioned into several segments: an introduction by Massie as the supposed translator of the long-lost journals, the memoirs themselves, and another section told from the point of view of a fictional scholar of the Roman Empire, Professor Aeneas Fraser-Graham. By utilizing this multiple-vantage device, Massie explores the inner motivations behind the successful Caesar and first emperor. Augustus lived from 63 BCE to 14 CE and was known chiefly as the architect of the Roman Empire. The memoirs, supposedly translated by Massie into colloquial English, touch upon the successes and failures of the Augustan Age. This includes a cast of real-life characters such as Augustus's daughter Julia, who brought scandal upon the family name for her sexual proclivities, and Mark Antony, the military general led astray by the Egyptian queen Cleopatra. Through the structural ruse Massie also provides a critical commentary on the pretensions of modern-day historical scholarship. Savkar Altinel of the *Times Literary Supplement* disparaged *Augustus* for its contrivances, remarking that the fictional professor "is the first of the novel's many problems." The critic also found fault with the wooden characters, various anachronisms and Massie's overall portrayal of the emperor, stating that "Augustus' pronouncements on various subjects . . . have a banality which should perhaps be expected from a man of action, but which does not exactly make for good literature." Conversely, *Times* reviewer Andrew Sinclair lauded *Augustus* for its unusual admixture of fact and fiction. Sinclair asserted that Massie "makes Augustus credible as a man: wily, ruthless, shrewd, generous, admirable," and that the tome "proves that Massie is the best novelist north of the Scots border where the Roman Empire reached its limits."

Byron's Travels marks Massie's return to the straightforward biographical format he first visited in 1979's *Muriel Spark* and 1986's *Colette: The Woman, the Writer, and the Myth. Byron's Travels* is a study of Lord Byron, the aristocratic English poet who died in 1824, and it coincided with commemorative celebrations marking the bicentennial of the writer's birth. The illustrated work is divided into three parts, titled "The Adventurer," "The Exile," and "The Hero." Massie primarily concentrates on the nobleman's later wanderings through Europe, chronicling his sojourn in Italy, where he was feted by the Venetians, and his final stop in Greece during the midst of a war for independence from Turkey. It was here that Byron worked tirelessly for the Greek revolutionaries before his unexpected death. Peter Manning of the *Times Literary Supplement* described *Byron's Travels* as "a concise biography . . . enlighteningly sketching the landscapes and societies through which Byron moved." Manning praised the author as "a crisp writer," commenting that he "nicely plays . . . [Byron's] life against the poetry, and by not confusing them enriches both."

Massie's sixth novel is *A Question of Loyalties,* in which the author tackles the complex moral issue of patriotism, collaboration and a nation's spiritual self-image. Set in present-day Switzerland, the tale unfolds when an aged man named Etienne is pestered by an investigative journalist for details about the retired banker's father, whom Etienne barely knew. Grudgingly, he begins to unearth information on his father Lucien, a French diplomat. During World War II Lucien worked as a speechwriter for Marshal Petain, the vilified leader of the provisional Vichy government during the Nazi occupation of France. Much of the action of this period is told through extant letters exchanged by Etienne's parents during the war. This journey of discovery is a painful one for Etienne, corresponding to Lucien's ultimate decision to exchange humanist ideals for patriotic sentiments in order to join the Vichy regime. *A Question of Loyalties* was published just as France was marking the fiftieth anniversary of the German invasion. The book addresses the dilemma faced by those who helped the Vichy government and the Nazis to send French Jews to concentration camps, in contrast to those who furtively joined the Resistance. Gerald Mangan of the *Times Literary Supplement* declared "the interweaving of fact and fiction is deft and largely plausible, and the complex moral spectrum is as finely etched as the landscapes and cultural backgrounds that shape many of the characters' motives." *A Question of Loyalties* also won praise from Nicci Gerrard of the *Observer,* who lauded its "heavy charm" and described the narrative as "sombre and dense, like an oil whose colours have darkened with time."

Tiberius: The Memoirs of the Emperor is Massie's follow-up to his tale of the Roman leader Augustus. This 1991 volume is the fictionalized autobiography of Augustus's stepson, who commanded the Roman Empire from 14 to 37 CE. Actual historical accounts portrayed Tiberius as a depraved soul, but Massie sets out to depict him in a more favorable light. As his emperor looks back on his life, Massie sketches a lonely man overwhelmed by both the power struggles in Rome and within his own clan. Noted figures who appear in the book include Livia, his scheming mother, his estranged wife Julia, and his degenerate grandnephew Caligula who would succeed him. Throughout the action, Tiberius questions the moral judgements of those around him as well as his own motivations, while simultaneously taking care of the more mundane bureaucratic details of running an empire. In the end he flees the palace intrigue for the Mediterranean isle of Capri. Mary Beard of the *Times Literary Supplement* suggested that *Tiberius* "fails to convince." She criticized its "flat narrative style" and remarked that some of Massie's passages are similar to a previously-published account of Tiberius' life. However, in the *Observer* Cunningham stated: "Massie's narrative moves with zest and confidence. . . . [*Tiberius* is] most engagingly readable, as captivating an historical novel as anyone in Britain is currently capable of producing."

In 1991's *The Sins of the Father,* as with *A Question of Loyalties,* Massie places his younger characters against turmoil brought on by their parents' involvement in World War II. In this story, Becky, the daughter of a blind survivor from Auschwitz, falls in love with the handsomely Teutonic Franz. Their affair takes place during the 1960s in Argentina, where their parents emigrated from Germany after the war. At a party, Becky's father Eli recognizes the voice of Kestner, Franz's estranged father, as a former Nazi officer and killer. Eli denounces him to the government as a war criminal, and a gang of former Nazis kidnaps Becky in an attempt at retaliation. She is released when Franz's stepfather, an Argentinean general, intervenes. The rest of the novel takes place in Israel at Kestner's trial, which all the participants travel to witness. A *Publishers Weekly* reviewer lauded the book as a "tale of one generation's painful legacy to the next."

Massie returned to the subject of ancient Rome for two more novels in the 1990s. His eleventh fiction, *Caesar,* appeared in 1993, and his fourteenth, *Nero's Heirs,* closed out the decade in 1999. *Caesar* chronicles the last years of Julius Caesar (the predecessor of both Tiberius and Augustus) who was infamously assassinated by his own men in 44 BCE. Events during a five-year span of Julius Caesar's life are related through the memoirs of his killer, Decimus Brutus. During this period, Decimus accompanied him on a military expedition that resulted in civil war and the proclamation of Caesar's dictatorship. Meanwhile the two men became close confidants, sharing both numerous military victories as well as wives and other lovers. In the book, Decimus explains his reasons for turning on Caesar amid the backdrop of political intrigue, and into this drama Massie incorporates other actual events and characters such as Cleopatra and Mark Antony. Christopher Kelly of the *Times Literary Supplement* faulted Massie's characterization of Caesar as "a cardboard king at whose brutal slaughter it is difficult to feel either revulsion or sympathy," but praised the attempt to put a new spin on a well-told tale by narrating it through the voice of his murderer Decimus. Kelly asserted that "it is this arresting and disturbing perspective on an old story which makes *Caesar* worth reading." In a review of the work for the *Sunday Times,* Lucy Hughes-Hallett lauded the author's style, noting: "The narrative is swift and the tone racy."

Nero's Heirs explores the "year of four emperors," 68-69 CE, and the turmoil that gripped Rome after the death of the despotic emperor Nero. The events are described by a cynical exile named Scaurus who had been intimate with two aspiring emperors, Titus and Domitian of the Flavian dynasty. Corresponding with the Roman historian Tacitus, Scaurus recalls in detail the scandals and political maneuvers that marked the period after Nero's death. "*Nero's Heirs* is full of names and details, as generals, senators and emperors crisscross the stage, mostly wielding knives for each other's backs," observed Adam Lively in the *Sunday Times.* The critic concluded: "*Nero's Heirs* is an entertaining, gripping read, but in the end it is the potboiler that wins the day, leaving behind those shadows and shadings that had suggested a deeper, richer novel."

Commenting on Massie's fiction of ancient Rome, Hughes-Hallett asserted that "his Roman novels . . . are full of vital, complex characters dug up out of the ancient historians and given new life." Lively likewise credited Massie with an "encyclopedic knowledge of Roman history."

Both *These Enchanted Woods* and *The Ragged Lion* present readers with pictures of Scotland, but the two novels are distinct from one another through theme and tone. Set in the present, *These Enchanted Woods,* characterized by Morton as a "condition-of-Scotland" novel, offers a grim tale of a cadre of hard-drinking Scottish aristocrats. "It is clear that the [characters'] primary dependency is an economic one: a profound social and cultural shortfall that can only be bridged by excess," Morton conceded. The reviewer found *These Enchanted Woods* to be "a painful, often funny, but also searingly accurate diagnosis of Scotland's needs." *The Ragged Lion* purports to be an unpublished memoir by Sir Walter Scott, in which Scott takes stock of his life and ruminates upon the decline of his fame. "Allan Massie is here on home ground," declared Christian Hasketh in *History Today*. "What *The Ragged Lion* succeeds best in conveying are the two contradictory sides of Sir Walter's character. . . . In *The Ragged Lion* we see both sides of a very rare coin." *New Statesman* correspondent David McVey found *The Ragged Lion* to be "a sombre picture of a melancholy man, mourning his wife and many of his friends, fully aware that his creative powers are waning." McVey concluded: "Massie's principal triumph is to make his narrator full, rounded and convincing. Authenticity will be a matter of argument, but it really does not matter. Massie's Scott holds water."

BIOGRAPHICAL/CRITICAL SOURCES:

BOOKS

Contemporary Novelists, Gale (Detroit, MI), 1986.

Massie, Alan, *The Death of Men,* Bodley Head (London), 1981.

PERIODICALS

Contemporary Review, February, 1981, pp. 109-110.

History Today, June, 1995, Christian Hesketh, review of *The Ragged Lion,* p. 48.

Los Angeles Times Book Review, July 18, 1982, p. 6; October 18, 1987, p. 4.

New Statesman, December 20, 1991, p. 45; August 6, 1993, Brian Morton, review of *These Enchanted Woods,* p. 37; June 24, 1994, David McVey, review of *The Ragged Lion,* p. 39.

New Yorker, April 19, 1982, p. 176.

Observer (London), May 8, 1988, p. 43; August 27, 1989, p. 43; January 6, 1991, p. 47.

Publishers Weekly, August 1, 1986, p. 74; July 24, 1987, p. 172; May 25, 1992, p. 39; August 2, 1993, p. 63.

Spectator, May 27, 1978, p. 25; May 3, 1980, p. 24; November 21, 1981, p. 23; July 21, 1984, pp. 27-28; December 6, 1986, p. 34.

Sunday Times, May 16, 1993; January 2, 2000, Adam Lively, "Smells like a Cauldron Boiler," p. 44.

Times (London), January 19, 1982; November 3, 1983; September 25, 1986; November 29, 1986; July 4, 1987; November 22, 1990.

Times Literary Supplement, August 8, 1978, p. 925; May 9, 1980, p. 537; March 13, 1981, p. 284; October 16, 1981, p. 1193; June 8, 1984, p. 632; October 3, 1986, p. 1115; August 12, 1988, p. 886; September 8, 1989, p. 969; January 18, 1991, p. 11; October 4, 1991, p. 27; May 28, 1993, p. 22.*

* * *

MEYER, Karl E(rnest) 1928-

PERSONAL: Born May 22, 1928, in Madison, WI; son of Ernest L. (a journalist) and Dorothy (Narefsky) Meyer; married Sarah Neilson Peck, 1959; married Shareen Blair Brysac; children (first marriage): Ernest Leonard, Heather, Jonathan. *Education:* University of Wisconsin, B.S., 1951; Princeton University, Ph.D., 1956. *Avocational interests:* Archaeology, music, and reading.

ADDRESSES: *Office—New York Times,* 229 West 43rd St., New York, NY 10036.

CAREER: *New York Times,* New York City, general assignment reporter, 1952; *Washington Post,* Washington, DC, member of editorial staff, 1956-64, London correspondent, beginning 1965, *Saturday Review,* New York City, senior editor, 1976-79; *New York Times,* member of editorial board, beginning 1979; writer. Washington correspondent for *New Statesman,* 1962-65.

MEMBER: American Newspaper Guild, Federal City Club.

AWARDS, HONORS: Citation for excellence on Latin-American reporting, Overseas Press Club; Sigma Delta Chi award, 1964.

WRITINGS:

The New America, Basic Books (New York City), 1961.

(With Tad Szulc) *The Cuban Invasion: The Chronicle of a Disaster,* Praeger (New York City), 1962.

Fulbright of Arkansas, Robert B. Luce (Bridgeport, CT), 1963.

The Pleasures of Archaeology: A Visa to Yesterday, Atheneum (New York City), 1970.

The Plundered Past, Atheneum, 1973.

Teotihuacan, Newsweek (New York City), 1973.

The Art Museum: Power, Money, and Ethics, Morrow (New York City), 1979.

(Editor and author of introduction and notes) *Pundits, Poets, and Wits: An Omnibus of American Newspaper Columns,* Oxford University Press (New York City), 1990.

(With wife, Shareen Blair Brysac) *Tournament of Shadows: The Race for Empire in Central Asia,* Counterpoint (Washington, DC), 1999.

Contributor to many magazines.

SIDELIGHTS: Karl E. Meyer, a former editorial writer for the *New York Times,* has frequently been commended for bringing much-needed information on subjects of current interest to the attention of the general public. Meyer's roots as a journalist reach back two generations. His grandfather ran a German-language daily newspaper in Milwaukee, and his father was a newspaper columnist. Meyer's own career includes long associations with such important periodicals as the *New York Times,* the *Washington Post,* and the *Saturday Review,* for which he wrote everything from foreign correspondence to book reviews. His book-length works range across disciplines from politics to history, to archaeology and a concern for ancient and modern art works. Diana Loescher heralded one of Meyer's titles, *The Plundered Past,* as a "finely documented, highly readable book, . . . the first major work on the illegal international traffic in works of art." In his review of the same title, Ian Graham wrote that the author "has obviously put an immense amount of energy into unraveling the antecedents of several important objects recently purchased by museums and private collections . . . all this he accomplished in urbane style and with sufficient detachment, even though an underlying sense of outrage is apparent."

Even Meyer's detractors have been willing to make some concessions about his style. R.R. Brunn called him a "clever phrasemaker" and admitted that "often his judgments are accurate," although he warned that Meyer "is busy taking things apart and seldom stops to put things together again." In the same way, Charles Rolo's review of *The New America* deemed the work "cleverly packaged, eminently 'consumable' " and noted that it "has the appearance of seriousness." Rolo added, however, that the book "really is quite lacking in ideas of any depth or originality." Hilton Kramer similarly noted that, in *The Art Museum,* Meyer fails to "break new ground or, indeed, add anything to what has been conspicuously reported."

Other reviewers have found much to admire in Meyer's books. As a *Newsweek* correspondent pointed out, in *The Pleasures of Archaeology* Meyer "is writing as a passionate hobbyist, genially, with love, and with much lively information." Also in Meyer's defense, John Canaday declared in a review of *The Art Museum:* "I never felt for a moment that Mr. Meyer's book was old news warmed over. Rather, I found that half-faded events were freshened with details I had quite forgotten plus some that I had never managed to ferret out for myself."

Meyer's *Pundits, Poets, and Wits: An Omnibus of American Newspaper Columns* explores column-writing from the days of Benjamin Franklin to the present, seeking to prove the literary qualities of the genre through some of its best practitioners. "As Karl Meyer makes clear in this indispensable collection of newspaper columns, the art form has had a glorious past," observed Edwin Diamond in *Washington Monthly.* "There were, in fact, several golden ages, each skillfully mined by Meyer. . . . His contemporary examples bestow as much pleasure as the earlier ones." The book grew out of a class Meyer taught on the history of the newspaper column at Yale University in 1983, and not all of the practitioners he cites are widely read or nationally known. While noting that many of the selections "suffer from being removed from their original context," David R. Boldt concluded in the *New York Times Book Review:* "Still, it is a tribute to both Mr. Meyer and the American columnist that so many of the columns included here retain the power to stir the heart and stretch the mind."

Tournament of Shadows: The Great Game and the Race for Empire in Central Asia covers more than a century in its explanation of a military movement called the Great Game. Beginning in the eighteenth century and stretching into the early twentieth, the imperial powers of Great Britain and Russia both sought to consolidate control of a vast region of Asia, including Tibet and Afghanistan. Working with his wife, Shareen Blair Brysac, Meyer tells the story of intrigue and quest by force "from the perspective of the explorers, soldiers and archeologists . . . who planted their nations' flags in the steppes and mountain passes of Afghanistan, Turkestan and Tibet," to quote a *Publishers Weekly* correspondent. In the *New York Times Book Review,* Jason Goodwin stated: "As the authors of this brilliant history point out, the Great Game was a dry run for the cold war, avoiding outright conflict but marked by the same search for influence and the same displays of bravery and cussedness, though whether the story of the cold war will ever seem as exciting as this, I doubt." The critic added that *Tournament of Shadows* "is much more than a magisterial work of scholarship: it is an absorbing inquiry into men and motives that is one part

[John] le Carre, one part Indiana Jones. . . . It is written with elegant assurance."

BIOGRAPHICAL/CRITICAL SOURCES:

PERIODICALS

Atlantic, June, 1961.
Christian Science Monitor, June 14, 1961; November 28, 1973.
Natural History, December, 1973.
New Republic, May 21, 1967; March 3, 1979.
New York Times Book Review, June 10, 1962; December 9, 1973; March 4, 1979; September 23, 1990, David R. Boldt, "Keeping up the Conversation," p. 7; January 9, 2000, Jason Goodwin, "The Playing Fields of Asia," p. 8.
Publishers Weekly, December 11, 1978; October 18, 1999, review of *Tournament of Shadows: The Race for Empire in Central Asia and the Great Game,* p. 59.
Washington Monthly, June, 1990, Edwin Diamond, review of *Pundits, Poets, and Wits: An Omnibus of American Newspaper Columns,* p. 60.
Washington Post Book World, February 18, 1979.*

* * *

MILLER, Anita 1926-

PERSONAL: Born August 31, 1926, in Chicago, IL; daughter of Louis and Clara (Ruttenberg) Wolfberg; married Jordan Miller (a publisher), December 19, 1948; children: Mark Crispin, Bruce Joshua, Eric Lincoln. *Education:* Roosevelt University, B.A., 1948; Northwestern University, M.A., Ph.D., 1972.

ADDRESSES: Office—Academy Chicago Publishers, 363 West Erie St., Chicago, IL 60610.

CAREER: University of Wisconsin—Parkside, Kenosha, lecturer in English, 1969-70; Northwestern University, Evanston, IL, lecturer in English, 1970-77; Academy Chicago Publishers, Chicago, IL, editorial director, 1976—.

WRITINGS:

NONFICTION

Arnold Bennett: An Annotated Bibliography, 1887-1932, Garland Publishing (New York City), 1972.
(With Jean M. Weiman) *The Fair Women,* Academy Chicago (Chicago), 1981.
Georges Perec: Zwischen Anamnese und Struktur, Romanistischer Verlag (Bonn, Germany), 1996.
Uncollecting Cheever: The Family of John Cheever vs. Academy Chicago Publishers, Rowman & Littlefield (Lanham, MD), 1998.

EDITOR

Beyond the Front Page, Academy Chicago, 1983.
Feminismo!, Academy Chicago, 1988.
The Trial of Levi Weeks, Academy Chicago, 1989.
Four Classic Ghostly Tales, Academy Chicago, 1993.
Complete Transcripts of the Clarence Thomas-Anita Hill Hearings, Academy Chicago, 1994.
(With J. Papp) Augustus Hare, *Peculiar People: The Story of My Life,* Academy Chicago, 1995.

TRANSLATOR

Hella S. Haasse, *In a Dark Wood Wandering: A Novel of the Middle Ages,* Academy Chicago, 1989.
Haasse, *The Scarlet City: A Novel of 16th-Century Italy,* Academy Chicago, 1990.
(With Nina Blinstrub) Haasse, *Threshold of Fire: A Novel of Fifth-Century Rome,* Academy Chicago, 1994.

Editor, *Arnold Bennett Newsletter;* contributing editor, *English Literature in Translation.*

SIDELIGHTS: Anita Miller and her husband, Jordan, were veterans of the publishing business when, in 1987, their company approached John Cheever's widow about publishing a book of Cheever's uncollected short stories. The Millers, who had owned and operated Academy Chicago Publishers since the 1970s, envisioned the collection as a companion volume to *The Stories of John Cheever,* published in 1978 by Knopf. The widow, Mary Cheever, signed a contract approving the publication; however, the contract's vagueness soon caused her and other Cheever family members to feel they had been duped, that the book was going to be a much larger project than they had expected—a project that would be more lucrative for the Cheevers if it were published by a larger company. The family's efforts to get out of the contract resulted in a court battle that Anita Miller chronicles in *Uncollecting Cheever: The Family of John Cheever vs. Academy Chicago Publishers.*

Miller is not an objective narrator, and this is both the book's "biggest weakness" and its "main attraction," according to Richard Dooling, writing in the *New York Times Book Review.* "'Uncollecting Cheever,' " he reports, "vividly shows us what acrimonious civil litigation looks like from the perspective of the acrimonious litigant." The courts eventually ruled in the Cheever family's favor and allowed Academy Chicago to bring out a book of only thirteen Cheever stories, as opposed to the nearly seventy the the firm had hoped to publish. Dooling notes that Miller intended *Uncollecting Cheever* "in part as the story of a small publishing house struggling against the corporate, big-money, big-book mentality of East Coast publishers," but he thinks it does not quite come off that way. "Despite what Studs Terkel says in a blurb on the jacket, this book does not read like 'a case of a small press bullied into defeat,' " Dooling contends. "It sounds more like the tale of a small publisher that carelessly drafted an important contract (without consulting a lawyer) and the family of a renowned author who foolishly signed it (without consulting a lawyer)." A *Publishers Weekly* reviewer, though, believes that Miller's "account has the ring of truth, and there seems no doubt that Academy started out with a valid contract," adding that the story features "exhaustive yet endlessly fascinating detail." *Entertainment Weekly* contributor Vanessa Friedman, while finding Miller occasionally guilty of "taking petty potshots at her opponents," believes she has made a "valid point" about the threat posed to small publishers by the decisions in the Cheever case.

Miller has numerous other books to her credit, and she once told *CA:* "I have been writing since I was in grade school. I became a translator of Dutch literature by accident, when I was sent a poorly translated historical novel by Hella Haasse, and went to a dictionary to attempt to improve the translation; eventually I completely rewrote the English version. This was followed by two other Haasse novels, the English versions of which have been well received by critics and the public. . . . I am also interested in reviving interest in worthwhile but now neglected writers, by writing critical introductions to their work and seeing that they are reprinted."

BIOGRAPHICAL/CRITICAL SOURCES:

PERIODICALS

Entertainment Weekly, January 8, 1999, p. 62.
New York Times Book Review, December 27, 1998.
Publishers Weekly, October 5, 1998, p. 63.*

MILLER, Heather Ross 1939-

PERSONAL: Born September 15, 1939, in Albemarle, NC; daughter of Fred E. (a novelist and newspaper editor) and Geneva (Smith) Ross; married Clyde H. Miller (a park superintendent), February 14, 1960 (deceased); children: Melissa Martha, Kirk Alexander. *Education:* University of North Carolina at Greensboro, B.A., 1961, M.F.A., 1969.

ADDRESSES: Office—c/o Department of Speech and Writing, Pfeiffer College, Misenheimer, NC 28109.

CAREER: Pfeiffer College, Misenheimer, NC, instructor in creative writing, 1965-67, assistant professor of English and head of department of speech and writing, beginning in 1977; Southeastern Community College, Whiteville, NC, instructor in English, 1969-72; teacher and consultant to North Carolina's "Poetry in the Schools" program, 1972-74; Stanly Technical Institute, Albemarle, NC, writer-in-residence, 1974-77.

MEMBER: Phi Beta Kappa, Phi Delta Sigma.

AWARDS, HONORS: Best Book Award, National Association of Independent Schools, 1964, for *The Edge of the Woods;* fellowships from National Endowment for the Arts, 1968-69, 1973-74; Distinguished Alumni Award, University of North Carolina at Greensboro, 1976; United States-United Kingdom exchange fellow, 1979-80; Danforth associate, 1980-86.

WRITINGS:

The Edge of the Woods (novel), Atheneum (New York City), 1964.
Tenants of the House (novel), Harcourt (New York City), 1966.
The Wind Southerly (poems), Harcourt, 1967.
Gone a Hundred Miles (novel), Harcourt, 1968.
Horse Horse, Tyger Tyger (poems), Red Clay Books, 1973.
A Spiritual Divorce and Other Stories, Blair, 1974.
Confessions of a Champeen Fire-Baton Twirler (novel), North Carolina Review Press, 1976.
Adam's First Wife (poems), Briarpatch Press (Davidson, NC), 1983.
Hard Evidence (poems), University of Missouri Press (Columbia, MO), 1990.
Friends and Assassins (poems), University of Missouri Press, 1993.
In the Funny Papers (stories), University of Missouri Press, 1995.
Champeen (novel), Southern Methodist University Press (Dallas, TX), 1999.

Crusoe's Island: A Story of a Writer and a Place, Coastal Carolina Press (Wilmington, NC), 2000.

Contributor to periodicals, including *Impetus, Southern Poetry Review, Reflections, New York Times, Carolina Quarterly, American Scholar, Raleigh News and Observer, Red Clay Reader,* and *Vogue.* Some of Miller's work has been translated into French.

BIOGRAPHICAL/CRITICAL SOURCES:

PERIODICALS

Library Journal, January, 2000, Kimberly G. Allen, review of *Champeen,* p. 161.
New York Times Book Review, May 30, 1993, p. 14.
Publishers Weekly, May 30, 1993, p. 14; October 25, 1999, p. 49.*

* * *

MILLER, Linda Lael 1949-

PERSONAL: Maiden name rhymes with "sale"; born June 10, 1949, in Spokane, WA; daughter of Grady Eugene (a U.S. Park Service foreman) and Hazel (Bleecker) Lael; married Rick M. Miller (a shipyard painter), October 12, 1968 (divorced July, 1987); children: Wendy, Diane. *Education:* Attended high school in Northport, WA. *Politics:* Independent. *Religion:* Methodist.

ADDRESSES: Home and Office—2295 Woods Rd. S.E., Port Orchard, WA 98366. *Agent*—Irene Goodman, Irene Goodman Literary Agency, 521 Fifth Ave., 17th Floor, New York, NY 10017.

CAREER: Rockwood Clinic, Spokane, WA, clerk, 1968-71; Aetna Insurance Co., Spokane, clerk, 1978-79; Pan American World Airways, Bangor, WA, clerk, 1980-81; writer, 1981—.

AWARDS, HONORS: Most Sensual Historical Romance Award, *Romantic Times* Reviewer's Choice, 1987, for *Wanton Angel.*

WRITINGS:

Fletcher's Woman, Pocket Books (New York City), 1983.
Desire and Destiny, Pocket Books, 1983.
Snowflakes on the Sea, Silhouette (New York City), 1984.
Banner O'Brien, Silhouette, 1984.
Willow, Silhouette, 1984.
Part of the Bargain, Silhouette, 1985.
Corbin's Fancy, Silhouette, 1985.
State Secrets, Silhouette, 1985.
Memory's Embrace, Silhouette, 1986.
Ragged Rainbows, Silhouette, 1986.
Lauralee, Pocket Books, 1986.
Wanton Angel, Pocket Books, 1987.
Moonfire, Pocket Books, 1988.
Used-to-Be Lovers, Silhouette, 1988.
Angelfire, Silhouette, 1989.
Just Kate, Harlequin (Toronto, Ontario), 1989, Silhouette, 1990.
My Darling Melissa, Silhouette, 1990.
Daring Moves, Silhouette, 1990.
Mixed Messages, Silhouette, 1990.
Lily and the Major (first volume in "Orphan Train" trilogy), Silhouette, 1990.
Escape from Cabiz, Harlequin, 1990, Silhouette, 1991.
Glory, Glory, Harlequin, 1991, Silhouette, 1992.
Emma and the Outlaw (second volume in "Orphan Train" trilogy), Silhouette, 1991.
Wild about Harry, Harlequin, 1991, Silhouette, 1992.
There and Now, Silhouette, 1992.
Caroline and the Raider (third volume in "Orphan Train" trilogy), Silhouette, 1992.
Here and Then, Silhouette, 1992.
Daniel's Bride, Thorndike Press (Thorndike, ME), 1993.
Taming Charlotte, Pocket Books, 1993.
For All Eternity, Berkley (New York City), 1994.
Princess Annie, Pocket Books, 1994.
Forever and the Night, Thorndike Press, 1994.
The Legacy, Thorndike Press, 1995.
Pirates, Pocket Books, 1995.
Knights, Pocket Books, 1996.
My Outlaw, Pocket Books, 1997.
Springwater Seasons: Rachel, Pocket Books, 1998.
Heatwave, Harlequin, 1998.
Two Brothers: The Lawman & the Gunslinger, Simon & Schuster (New York City), 1998.
The Vow, Pocket Books, 1998.
In Our Dreams, Kensington Publishing, 1998.
Springwater Seasons: Miranda, Pocket Books, 1999.
A Springwater Christmas, Pocket Books, 1999.

Contributor of about thirty stories to confession magazines and *Woman's World.* Also contributor to anthologies and collections, including Jayne Ann Krentz, *Forever and the Night,* Berkley, 1993; Jayne Ann Krentz, *Everlasting Love,* Pocket Books, 1997; Linda Howard, *Summer Sensations,* Harlequin, 1998; and Linda Howard, *Always & Forever,* Harlequin, 1998.

SIDELIGHTS: "As an author of both historical and contemporary romances," writes Barbara E. Kemp in *Twentieth-Century Romance and Historical Writers,* "Linda Lael Miller is acknowledged to write some of the genre's most explicitly sensual love scenes." Miller's historicals are often set in her native Pacific Northwest, while her novels set in contemporary times feature elements such as time travel and supernatural visitations, including ghosts and vampires. Her works have proved their attraction to both readers and critics. The author, states a *Publishers Weekly* reviewer about *Springwater Seasons: Rachel,* "provides all the necessary components, including well-defined subplots and characters, to create a warm and cozy love story." "Miller," declares another *Publishers Weekly* contributor, writing about *My Outlaw,* "tugs at the heart-strings as few authors can."

Whatever the circumstances surrounding her heroines, Miller's works almost invariably build to climaxes realized in torrid physical encounters. In her historicals, including *Corbin's Fancy, My Darling Melissa, Lily and the Major,* and *Daniel's Bride,* Miller "follow[s] a familiar storyline of romance novels," explains Kemp. "A feisty heroine and a proud, hard-headed man meet, and are paired into an unlikely couple. Sparks begin to fly when she insists on declaring or maintaining her independence, no matter how superficially. They disagree on just about everything and seem incompatible except in bed. They are so involved in mutual pleasure that they forget their differences." Similar encounters mark Miller's contemporary and fantasy romances, such as *Wild about Harry,* in which a woman is visited by the ghost of her dead husband, or *Knights,* in which a young girl finds herself transported to thirteenth-century England, or even *Time without End,* in which a 600-year-old vampire reencounters a woman he knew in one of her past incarnations. "Once consummated, the relationship flares into passion at almost every opportunity," Kemp states. "Occasionally, the heroine gets to take charge and torment her man to the point of exhaustion, but usually he controls the situation. With such a style it is no wonder that Miller was named 'the Most Outstanding Writer of Sensual Romance.' "

Miller once told *CA:* "I consider Norman Vincent Peale's books invaluable to anyone, writer or non-writer. I've read them all. I read a lot of history, of course, and books on the writing craft. I would love to travel and intend to."

BIOGRAPHICAL/CRITICAL SOURCES:

BOOKS

Twentieth-Century Romance and Historical Writers, 3rd edition, St. James Press (Detroit, MI), 1994.

PERIODICALS

Booklist, November 1, 1994, p. 478; June 1, 1995, p. 1730.

Publishers Weekly, January 19, 1990, p. 104; October 26, 1990, p. 63; May 3, 1991, p. 69; July 20, 1992, p. 244; September 27, 1994, p. 59; October 3, 1994, p. 66; May 29, 1995, p. 67; September 25, 1995, p. 53; March 25, 1996, p. 61; March 17, 1997, p. 80; February 8, 1999, p. 210.*

* * *

MILLER, Sue 1943-

PERSONAL: Born November 29, 1943; daughter of James Hastings (a minister and educator) and Judith Beach Nichols; married second husband Doug Bauer (a writer), c. mid-1980s; children: (first marriage) Ben. *Education:* Radcliffe College, B.A., 1964; received master's degrees from Harvard University, Boston University, and Wesleyan University.

ADDRESSES: *Home*—Boston, MA. *Agent*—Maxine Groffsky, Maxine Groffsky Literary Agency, 2 Fifth Ave., New York, NY 10011.

CAREER: Writer. Teacher of creative writing courses at universities. Worked variously as a day-care worker, high school teacher, waitress, model, and researcher.

MEMBER: PEN New England (chairman, 2000).

AWARDS, HONORS: Boston University creative writing fellowship, 1979; Pushcart Press honorable mention, 1984; National Book Critics Circle Award nomination, 1991, for *Family Pictures;* Bunting Institute fellowship, Radcliffe College; grant from Massachusetts Artists Foundation; MacDowell fellowship; Guggenheim fellowship.

WRITINGS:

The Good Mother, Harper (New York City), 1986.

Inventing the Abbotts, and Other Stories (contains "Leaving Home" and "Appropriate Affect"), Harper, 1987.

Family Pictures, Harper, 1990.
For Love, Harper, 1993.
The Distinguished Guest, Harper, 1995.
While I Was Gone, Knopf (New York City), 1999.

Contributor of short stories to periodicals, including *Atlantic, Mademoiselle,* and *Ploughshares.*

WORK IN PROGRESS: The World Below, a novel, publication by Knopf expected in 2002.

ADAPTATIONS: The Good Mother was adapted as a motion picture, written by Michael Bortman, directed by Leonard Nimoy, starring Diane Keaton and Liam Neeson, Buena Vista, 1988; *Family Pictures* was adapted as a television movie, written by Jennifer Miller, directed by Philip Saville, starring Anjelica Huston and Sam Neill, 1993; *Inventing the Abbotts* was adapted as a motion picture, written by Ken Hixon, directed by Pat O'Connor, Twentieth-Century-Fox, 1997.

SIDELIGHTS: Fiction writer Sue Miller earned immediate acclaim with her first novel, *The Good Mother.* In her appraisal of the book for the *New York Times Book Review,* Linda Wolfe asserted, "Every once in a while, a first novelist rockets into the literary atmosphere with a novel so accomplished that it shatters the common assumption that for a writer to have mastery, he or she must serve a long, auspicious apprenticeship." Such profuse praise surprised Miller, who did not begin writing seriously until she was thirty-five when she took a writing course and her first story was published. Since deciding to pursue a writing career, Miller has distinguished herself by producing works fraught with bittersweet emotion that provide insight into family life, particularly nontraditional families with divorced mothers. *Publishers Weekly* contributor Rosemary Herbert lauded the author's rendition of such scenes, calling Miller "an extraordinarily accomplished writer who is particularly skilled in the use of visual images and homey detail." Likewise, *Booklist* reviewer Brad Hooper observed: "The domestic scene is Miller's terrain, a place where steadiness is hoped for by all parties involved but where earthquakes are bound to come along and disassemble the landscape."

The daughter of a minister, Miller grew up in a boisterous family of five in Chicago. She was a precocious student who entered Radcliffe College at age sixteen and emerged with a bachelor's degree in 1964. Not long after that she married a medical student who later became a psychiatrist. Her only child, Ben, was born of this union. As a divorced single parent in the 1970s, Miller taught preschool children at the Harvard Day Care Centers, a position that she later found invaluable for her fiction-writing. She was in her mid-thirties before she began publishing short stories and writing novels, and in 1979 she earned a fellowship to Boston University. "They paid me almost as much as I had been making working in daycare," Miller recalled in *The Writer.* "That one-year program really turned things around for me because after that I got another one-year fellowship. . . . I learned from writing [unpublished novels] . . . what I needed to do as a corrective in my own writing. And, in a way, *The Good Mother* was me teaching myself to write a novel that had a plot."

Miller explained to Herbert that her inspiration for *The Good Mother* was her dissatisfaction with "a number of postfeminist novels which suggested that all you need to do is shed your husband and then you enter this glorious new life of accomplishment and ease." *The Good Mother* is the saga of a divorced woman embroiled in a custody battle. This fight is based on her lover's alleged improper sexual contact with her daughter. At the story's beginning, narrator Anna Dunlap realizes her dissatisfaction with her role as a dutiful wife and extricates herself from an apathetic marriage. She then attempts to create a new life for herself and her four-year-old daughter, Molly. With this move, Anna hopes to focus on self-fulfillment and continue to build an open, loving relationship with her daughter. Soon she meets Leo, a sculptor, and embarks upon a fervent love affair that offers the passion and spontaneity her marriage lacked. The relationship progresses and Leo becomes a fixture in the household, even helping to care for Molly. Anna's domestic bliss is shattered, however, when her ex-husband serves court papers citing an improper relationship—with sexual overtones—between Molly and Leo and charging Anna with negligence.

The remainder of *The Good Mother* addresses the trial and its outcome. Crediting Miller's rendering of suspense, *USA Today* correspondent Robert Wilson noted that she "makes the court case both dramatic and convincing, and effectively interweaves the impersonal legal machinations with the almost devastatingly intense emotions Anna feels for Molly and Leo." In the book Anna explains her alleged remissness to the court-appointed social worker: "I was very caught up in my feelings about Leo, and I just didn't give enough thought to Molly, to what might be confusing or difficult for her in all of it." Ultimately Anna loses custody of Molly, but earns her title as a "good mother" by accepting the painful ruling for the sake of her child's well-being. In a *Publishers Weekly* interview, Miller commented that her narrator was "a person who thought she could make her life like someone else's, who thought she could be in control of her life. And that seems to me to be a false thing to believe in this world."

The Good Mother rested atop the bestseller lists for six months, and Miller earned widespread acclaim for the book. *New York Times* contributor Michiko Kakutani deemed the work "a remarkably assured first novel" and added: "Thanks to Sue Miller's gift for precise psychological detail, her sure sense of narrative and her simple compassion for ordinary lives, this powerful novel proves as subtle as it is dramatic, as durable—in its emotional afterlife—as it is instantly readable." Catherine Petroski, writing in *Chicago Tribune,* remarked that the story "mesmerizes the reader till the last page is turned."

A few critics, however, charged that in *The Good Mother* Miller needlessly makes her protagonist a victim. She betrays Leo by agreeing with the court that he acted irresponsibly. Confronting these criticisms, Josephine Humphreys, writing in *Nation,* countered, "Because . . . Anna is, in the end, human rather than heroic, the novel is all the more disturbing and powerful." The author, however, did view Anna as a heroic character. She told Beth Austin of the *Chicago Tribune* that with *The Good Mother* "I was trying . . . to establish what I regard as a very female notion of heroism and, I think, a very feminist notion of heroism." Miller noted that her character's choices may be more valiant than what she believes is the typical male response of fighting despite the consequences. Anna realized how her battle might adversely effect her daughter and instead chose to protect her child from that emotional trauma.

Miller followed *The Good Mother* with a collection of short fiction titled *Inventing the Abbotts, and Other Stories.* Ellen Lesser, in her *Village Voice* appraisal, stated: "The new volume demonstrates that Miller doesn't need the breadth of a novel to chart the complex and confusing topography of families after divorce." In "Leaving Home," Leah, a divorced mother, realizes that the behavior she prompted from her son while he was growing up corresponds to his present problem of standing up to his wife. Observing his marital problems, she regrets that he no longer turns to her for advice. Another story, "Appropriate Affect," documents a quiet grandmother with a sad, sweet smile who turns surly after suffering a stroke. This unexpected—though truthful—behavior drives her family away. In the title piece of the volume, Doug narrates his older brother Jacey's romantic liaisons with three sisters from a higher socio-economic class in a dull, Midwestern town. In this story, noted *Times Literary Supplement* reviewer Roz Kaveney, "Miller writes with genuine power."

Miller's second novel, *Family Pictures,* was also a bestseller. Using third-person narration, the author chronicles the history of an upper-middle-class family living in Chicago from the end of World War II to the mid-1980s. The author told Laura Shapiro of *Newsweek* that she wanted the book "to be about a whole family almost as a character, and to trace the way everybody contributes to this mutual reality." *Family Pictures* concerns David and Lainey Eberhardt and their six children. The couple's early marital happiness is tested after learning that their third child, son Randall, is autistic. David is a psychiatrist who sides with other experts in the medical field to blame Lainey for her son's autism, citing some form of subconscious rejection. Lainey feels betrayed by her husband's charges but subdues her anger. Instead, in an attempt to prove that Randall's autism is not her fault, she bears three more healthy children against David's wishes.

Based on this undercurrent of anger and blame, *Family Pictures* describes how Randall defines the family and how the directions of the other family members have been altered because of his plight. Fourth child Nina, a photographer, serves as a frequent narrator. She likens her family's situation to that of a photograph in which the main subject is shown in sharp detail while the background remains a blur. As he grows older, Randall's behavior becomes less predictable, and when he demonstrates abusive tendencies, the family is forced to institutionalize him. Previously held together by the tragedy of his condition and the strain of caring for him, the family begins to crumble and David and Lainey separate.

Shapiro called *Family Pictures* "a big, wonderful, deeply absorbing novel that retains the vivid domestic focus of *The Good Mother* while spiraling far beyond it." Michael Dorris, writing in the *Detroit News,* judged that "the entire novel, in fact, is packed with . . . moments of wisdom and insight, and suffused with terrific writing." Dorris added: "*Family Pictures* is rich with complexity and paradox. It makes no easy judgments of right and wrong about its embattled protagonists." In his *New York Times* review, Christopher Lehmann-Haupt declared: "Miller is particularly good at dramatizing scenes of domestic chaos and the complex interplay of adults and children. . . . Each child, each of the family members, is wounded by the presence of Randall in a different way. Yet the reader is irresistably drawn through their pain by the author's exquisite eye for psychological detail and sexual nuance, and also by her method of keeping the narrative slowed down in that way that suggests something explosive is about to happen."

Praising the author's adept handling of several narrative shifts in *Family Pictures, Chicago Tribune* contributor Anne Tyler noted, "in tone it is absolutely flawless. It captures perfectly the sass and grit of family life." In a *New York Times Book Review* article, Jane Smiley concluded that *Family Pictures* is "profoundly honest, shapely, ambitious, engrossing, original and true, an important example of a new American tradition that explores what it means . . . to make a home, live at home and learn what home is."

Miller's third novel, titled simply *For Love,* explores the complexity of emotion faced by a woman approaching her middle years. In youth, protagonist Lottie Gardner had specialized in reinventing herself—changing her name from Char to Charlotte to Lottie, marrying and divorcing and marrying again. In her forties, Lottie realizes that, through "the many lenses of her life: daughter, sister, mother, lover and wife" she must continually try "to understand the rules of love, even as they appear to be changing," according to Ron Carlson in the *New York Times Book Review.* Carlson maintained that Miller writes with the kind of realism "that takes us by the shoulders and says, '*Look at this!*' " Similarly, *Chicago Tribune* critic Madison Smartt Bell praised Miller for a body of work that is "remarkably free of politically motivated distortion. She is in no sense an ideologue but a strong believer in reality." Bell, however, added that the realism in *For Love* is marred by the lack of a central plot point. Calling the novel "cloudy and hard to grasp," Gail Pool, a *Women's Review of Books* writer, similarly saw insufficient power in Lottie's character to carry a whole novel. Still, Pool admitted, *For Love,* "despite its problems, is a very readable book, largely because Miller is a good storyteller."

Bringing out private conflicts in a public forum sets the stage for Miller's fourth novel, *The Distinguished Guest.* The title character is Lily Maynard—in her eighties, frail and ill, but with her detailed (and perhaps embellishing) memory intact. Ten years before the start of the narrative, Lily has authored a feminist bestseller based on her marriage to a civil rights activist in the 1960s. Now, divorced, debilitated, and estranged from her two eldest children, she takes refuge in the home of her resentful youngest, Alan, and his family. Alan and his wife, Gaby, have only begun to work out their own marital difficulties; the presence of Lily only exacerbates the tension. The small circle is joined by a journalist, Linnett, who has arrived to write Lily's life story for a magazine. In relating her life to Linnett, Lily dredges all manner of family conflict. It is in the character of Linnett that Miller—so often lauded for her realistic portrayals—hits a false note, in the view of Kakutani. Writing in the *New York Times,* Kakutani opined that the author's creation of Linnett "must surely rank as one of the more unbelievable depictions of a journalist to appear in a novel in a long time." Kakutani also faulted the novel for "[diluting the] portrait of a mother and her middle-aged son with lots of extraneous talk about race relations and middle-class guilt." "Where Miller fumbles a bit is in her effort to plop the issue of racism into her characters' hands," agreed *Detroit Free Press* correspondent Susan Hall-Balduf. The author, she continued, "doesn't speak plainly of the issue until she brings in the book's only black character." But the parallels drawn between the conflict between the races, and the conflicts within a single family, are just what critic Roxana Robinson found compelling. In her *Los Angeles Times Book Review* article, she noted that both issues "are complex and highly charged, both provoke public debate and private anguish. Both raise the question of personal debt: what one owes, and is owed." To Robinson, *The Distinguished Guest* presents "no simple resolutions to these conflicts between idealism and realism, parent and child, black and white. But Miller's compassionate narrative explores the problems and reveals the possibilities for change."

One powerful moment in the novel was noted by several reviewers. In this scene, a dinner-table discussion reveals Lily's offhanded cruelty when, in the presence of Alan and Alan's grown son, the matriarch says, "There's no surer or shorter route to heartbreak than having high expectations for your children." This remark, *Chicago Tribune* critic Penelope Mesic averred, "amounts to indicting Alan both as an overfond parent and a failure himself." "The various responses . . . form a sort of paradigm for the novel's larger construction," wrote Richard Bausch in his *New York Times Book Review* assessment. "We move through the moment, and its aftermath, with all sorts of insights that lend weight and richness to what glides by on the surface."

Overall, Miller's fourth novel was well received for its gripping—if uncomfortable—take on the strained dynamics between adult children and their aging parents. Praising the author's ability to avoid "flattering" her audience, Mesic summarized that reading *The Distinguished Guest* is "a rueful pleasure—akin to poking a sore tooth with an exploratory tongue, or trying on clothes, fearing they're unflattering from behind, and backing up to a three-fold mirror. In such cases the best we can feel is that we know the worst." *The Distinguished Guest,* concluded Bausch, "is a very moving book about—and for—grown-ups who are willing to consider, with honesty and intelligence, some unavoidable grown-up predicaments."

While I Was Gone, Miller's fifth novel, again "talks about the dangerous intersection of motherhood and desire," to quote Kathleen Jacobs in *Redbook.* Narrator Jo Becker is a veterinarian, married to a minister, and the mother of three grown daughters. All appearances indicate that Jo is happy and successful, but she has begun to chafe at the complacency and predictability of her existence. The predictability is shattered when an old friend, Eli Mayhew, arrives at Jo's office with a pet in need of care. Her re-acquaintance with Eli reminds Jo of an idyllic year she spent in a communal house in Cambridge, a brief interlude that ended with the brutal murder of the commune's other female resident. As she is drawn to Eli, Jo revisits the past, and Eli's revelations about the murder bring moral dilemma and emotional turmoil to Jo and her family. *New York Times Book Review* contributor Jay Parini wrote of Miller: "Through a collection of stories and a string of novels, she has used her fiction to explore the artificially tamed emotional wilderness inhabited by husbands and wives. Her latest novel, 'While I Was Gone,' continues this preoccupation. A painstaking meditation on marital fidelity, it swoops gracefully between the past and the present, between a woman's complex feelings about her husband and her equally complex fantasies—and fears—about another man."

A *Publishers Weekly* reviewer wrote of *While I Was Gone:* "Miller's narrative is a beautifully textured picture of the psychological tug of war between finding integrity as an individual and satisfying the demands of spouse, children and community." The reviewer further stated that Miller "renders the details of quotidian domesticity with bedrock veracity and a sensitivity to minute calibrations of family dynamics." In *Newsday,* Dan Cryer remarked: "Scene after Miller scene is an artfully staged mini-drama of those painful or delightful moments that reveal humanity in all its awkward, muddled splendor." Cryer deemed the book "gripping, close-to-the-bone fiction." Lehmann Haupt, in his *New York Times* piece on *While I Was Gone,* suggested that Miller "has once again taken a morally extreme position and made it seem both plausible and questionable, as she has done often in her previous fiction." Lehmann-Haupt added: "Ms. Miller does many things well in this novel. She shows a deep respect for all her characters. . . . The narrative pacing is masterly, building tension even in its most psychologically subtle passages. The story is at once so well made and vividly imagined that one might call it an exercise in spontaneous craftsmanship."

In her fictional works, Miller presents poignant and authentic portraits of family life. Reviewers credit the author with matching the promise she showed in her first book. In addition, some critics singled out Miller's rendering of female characters for special praise. The author, though, objects to being tagged a "women's writer" because of the inherent limitations and suggestion that her work would not appeal to men. Miller explained to Shapiro: "Women are beginning to use the experience of being female, of being a mother, and they're using it metaphorically. I don't want to let men off the hook. They need to learn how to read women's metaphors just the way women have learned to read men's metaphors." Asked to comment on the rigors of the writing life in the *Arizona Republic,* Miller said: "I knew a woman who compared writing a novel to knitting an argyle sock the size of a football field. I think that is very apt. It's just such a struggle to shape it all up. And then it's published, and I worry about it making its way in the world. And then I worry about getting another idea. It's always something."

BIOGRAPHICAL/CRITICAL SOURCES:

BOOKS

Bestsellers 90, Issue 3, Gale (Detroit), 1990.

Biggs, Melissa E., editor, *In the Vernacular: Interviews at Yale with Sculptors of Culture,* McFarland (Jefferson, NC), 1991, pp. 169-77.

Contemporary Literary Criticism, Gale, Volume 44, 1987.

Dictionary of Literary Biography, Volume 143: *American Novelists since World War II, Third Series,* Gale, 1994, pp. 151-58.

Newsmakers 1999, Gale, 2000.

Pearlman, Mickey, editor, *Mother Puzzles: Daughters and Mothers in Contemporary American Life,* Greenwood Press (Westport, CT), 1989, pp. 11-22.

Pearlman, Mickey, *Listen to Their Voices: Twenty Interviews with Women Who Write,* Norton (New York City), 1993, pp. 162-71.

PERIODICALS

America, November 17, 1990.

Antioch, fall, 1988, pp. 450-461.

Arizona Republic, March 7, 1999, p. E15.

Atlanta Journal and Constitution, March 7, 1999, p. L11.
Booklist, January 1, 1993; November 1, 1998, Brad Hooper, review of *While I Was Gone,* p. 452.
Boston Globe, March 28, 1993, p. B38.
Boston Magazine, August, 1990.
Chatelaine, September, 1990; June 1993.
Chicago Tribune, April 27, 1986; July 19, 1989.
Christian Century, June 13, 1990; April 28, 1993.
Christian Science Monitor, April 30, 1986; May 9, 1995, p. 13.
Commonweal, October 12, 1990; December 7, 1990; September 24, 1999, Suzanne Keen, review of *While I Was Gone,* p. 25.
Cosmopolitan, March, 1987; April, 1993.
Detroit Free Press, April 23, 1995, p. 7F.
Detroit News, August 8, 1986; April 25, 1990.
Economist, April 17, 1993.
Entertainment Weekly, May 11, 1990, p. 50; april 9, 1993, p. 46.
Globe and Mail (Toronto), November 22, 1986.
Kirkus Reviews, November 15, 1998, review of *While I Was Gone.*
Library Journal, May 1, 1987; April 15, 1990; October 15, 1990; February 15, 1993; January, 1999, Karen Anderson, review of *While I Was Gone,* p. 156.
Los Angeles Times, April 14, 1986; May 4, 1990.
Los Angeles Times Book Review, May 7, 1995, p. 2.
Maclean's November 14, 1988; August 6, 1990; June 7, 1993.
Modern Fiction Studies, autumn, 1988, pp. 405-12.
Nation, May 10, 1986.
National Catholic Reporter, November 9, 1990.
New Statesman, November 23, 1990.
Newsday, February 1, 1999, p. B2.
Newsweek, April 30, 1990; April 19, 1993; April 24, 1995, p. 62.
New York, May 14, 1990; March 22, 1993.
New York Review of Books, August 16, 1990.
New York Times, April 23, 1986, p. C20; September 15, 1986; April 30, 1990, p. C15; April 5, 1993; April 21, 1995; January 28, 1999, Christopher Lehmann-Haupt, "When Your Past Comes Calling, There's No Escape"; March 8, 1999, p. B1.
New York Times Book Review, April 27, 1986, pp. 1, 40; April 19, 1987; May 24, 1987; April 22, 1990, p. 1; April 11, 1993, p. 7; May 7, 1995; February 21, 1999, Jay Parini, review of *The Good Wife.*
Publishers Weekly, May 2, 1986, pp. 60-61; March 27, 1987; February 23, 1990; September 7, 1990; May 3, 1993; November 2, 1998, review of *While I Was Gone,* p. 68.
Redbook, March, 1999, Kathleen Jacobs, "A Mother's Secret Life," p. G1.
Time, July 21, 1986, p. 72; June 25, 1990; January 11, 1993; May 3, 1993; February 22, 1999, Jill Smolowe, review of *While I Was Gone,* p. 91.
Times Literary Supplement, July 17, 1987; December 21, 1990; March 22, 1996, p. 23.
Tribune Books (Chicago), April 22, 1990; April 11, 1993, p. 3; April 16, 1995, p. 5.
USA Today, April 4, 1986; January 21, 1999, p. 4D.
Village Voice, June 23, 1987.
Washington Post, June 19, 1986; May 15, 1990.
Washington Post Book World, May 4, 1986; May 17, 1987.
Wilson Library Bulletin, November, 1990.
Women's Review of Books, July, 1993, p. 33.
Writer, June, 1999, p. 11.

OTHER

A Conversation with Sue Miller, http://www.randomhouse.com/ (March 24, 2000).*

* * *

MILOSZ, Czeslaw 1911-
(J. Syruc)

PERSONAL: Surname pronounced *Mee*-wosh; born June 30, 1911, in Szetejnie, Lithuania; defected to the West, 1951; came to the United States, 1960; naturalized citizen, 1970; son of Aleksander (a civil engineer) and Weronika (Kunat) Milosz. *Education:* University of Stephan Batory, M. Juris, 1934.

ADDRESSES: Office—Department of Slavic Languages and Literatures, University of California, 5416 Dwinelle Hall, Berkeley, CA 94720.

CAREER: Poet, critic, essayist, novelist, and translator. Programmer with Polish National Radio, 1935-39; worked for the Polish Resistance during World War II; cultural attache with the Polish Embassy in Paris, France, 1946-50; freelance writer in Paris, 1951-60; University of California, Berkeley, visiting lecturer, 1960-61, professor of Slavic languages and literature, 1961-78, professor emeritus, 1978—.

MEMBER: American Association for the Advancement of Slavic Studies, American Academy and Institute of Arts and Letters, PEN.

AWARDS, HONORS: Prix Litteraire Europeen, 1953, for novel *La Prise du pouvoir;* Marian Kister Literary

Award, 1967; Jurzykowski Foundation award for creative work, 1968; Institute for Creative Arts fellow, 1968; Polish PEN award for poetry translation, 1974; Wandycz Award, 1974; Guggenheim fellow, 1976; Litt. D., University of Michigan, 1977; Neustadt International Literary Prize for Literature, 1978; University Citation, University of California, 1978; Zygmunt Hertz literary award, 1979; Nobel Prize for literature, 1980; honorary doctorate, Catholic University, Lublin, 1981; honorary doctorate, Brandeis University, 1983; Bay Area Book Reviewers Association Poetry Prize, 1986, for *The Separate Notebooks;* Robert Kirsch Award for poetry, 1990; National Medal of Arts, 1990.

WRITINGS:

Zniewolony umysl (essays), Instytut Literacki (Paris), 1953, translation by Jane Zielonko published as *The Captive Mind,* Knopf (New York City), 1953, reprinted, Octagon (New York City), 1981.

Rodzinna Europa (essays), Instytut Literacki, 1959, translation by Catherine S. Leach published as *Native Realm: A Search for Self-Definition,* Doubleday (New York City), 1968.

Czlowiek wsrod skorpionow: Studium o Stanislawie Brzozowskim (title means "A Man among Scorpions: A Study of St. Brzozowski"), Instytut Literacki, 1962.

The History of Polish Literature, Macmillan (New York City), 1969, revised edition, University of California Press (Berkeley), 1983.

Widzenia and Zatoka San Francisco, Instytut Literacki, 1969, translation by Richard Lourie published as *Visions from San Francisco Bay,* Farrar, Straus (New York City), 1982.

Prywatne obowiazki (essays; title means "Private Obligations"), Instytut Literacki, 1972.

Moj wiek: Pamietnik nowiony (interview with Alexander Wat; title means "My Century: An Oral Diary"), edited by Lidia Ciolkoszowa, two volumes, Polonia Book Fund (London), 1977.

Emperor of the Earth: Modes of Eccentric Vision, University of California Press, 1977.

Ziemia Ulro, Instytut Literacki, 1977, translation by Louis Iribarne published as *The Land of Ulro,* Farrar, Straus, 1984.

Ogrod nauk (title means "The Garden of Knowledge"), Instytut Literacki, 1980.

Dziela zbiorowe (title means "Collected Works"), Instytut Literacki, 1980—.

Nobel Lecture, Farrar, Straus, 1981.

The Witness of Poetry (lectures), Harvard University Press (Cambridge, MA), 1983.

The Rising of the Sun, Arion Press (San Francisco, CA), 1985.

Unattainable Earth, translation from the Polish manuscript by Milosz and Robert Hass, Ecco Press (New York City), 1986.

Beginning with My Streets: Essays and Recollections (essays), translation from the Polish manuscript by Madeline G. Levine, Farrar, Straus, 1992.

Year of the Hunter, translation from the Polish manuscript by Levine, Farrar, Straus, 1994.

Legendy nowoczesno'sci: eseje okupacyjne, Literackie, 1996.

Szukanie ojczyzny, Znak, 1996.

Traktat moralny: traktat poetycki (interviews), Literackie, 1996.

Striving towards Being: The Letters of Thomas Merton and Czeslaw Milosz, edited by Robert Faggen, Farrar, Straus, 1997.

Piesek przydroczny, Znak, 1997, translation published as *Roadside Dog,* Farrar, Straus (New York City), 1998.

Czycie na wyspach (essays), Znak, 1997.

(Contributor) *Winter Dialogue,* Hydra Books, 1997.

Dar = Gabe, Literackie, 1998.

Inne abecadlo, Literackie, 1998.

Zaraz po wojnie: korespondenczja z pisarzami 1945-1950 (correspondence), Znak, 1998.

POEMS

Poemat o czasie zastyglym (title means "Poem of the Frozen Time"), [Vilnius, Lithuania], 1933.

Trzy zimy (title means "Three Winters"), Union of Polish Writers, 1936.

(Under pseudonym J. Syruc) *Wiersze* (title means "Poems"), published by the Resistance in Warsaw, Poland, 1940.

Ocalenie (title means "Salvage"), Czytelnik (Poland), 1945.

Swiatlo dzienne (title means "Daylight"), Instytut Literacki, 1953.

Trak tat poetycki (title means "Treatise on Poetry"), Instytut Literacki, 1957.

Kontynenty (title means "Continents"), Instytut Literacki, 1958.

Krol Popiel i inne wiersze (title means "King Popiel and Other Poems"), Instytut Literacki, 1962.

Gucio zaczarowany (title means "Bobo's Metamorphosis"), Instytut Literacki, 1965.

Lied vom Weltende (title means "A Song for the End of the World"), Kiepenheuer & Witsch, 1967.

Wiersze (title means "Poems"), Oficyna Poetow i Malarzy (London), 1969.

Miasto bez imienia (title means "City without a Name"), Instytut Literacki, 1969.

Selected Poems, Seabury (New York City), 1973, revised edition published as *Selected Poems: Revised,* Ecco Press, 1981.

Gdzie wschodzi slonce i kedy zapada (title means "From Where the Sun Rises to Where It Sets"), Instytut Literacki, 1974.

Utwory poetyckie (title means "Selected Poems"), Michigan Slavic Publications (Ann Arbor), 1976.

The Bells in Winter, translation by Milosz and Lillian Vallee, Ecco Press, 1978.

Hymn O Perle (title means "Hymn to the Pearl"), Michigan Slavic Publications, 1982.

The Separate Notebooks, translation by Robert Hass and Robert Pinsky, Ecco Press, 1984.

The Collected Poems, 1931-1987, Ecco Press, 1988.

The World, translation by the author, Arion Press, 1989.

Provinces: Poems, 1987-1991, translation by Milosz and Hass, Ecco Press, 1991.

Facing the River: New Poems, translation by Milosz and Hass, Ecco Press, 1995.

Swiat: poema naiwne (based on a 1943 manuscript), Literackie, 1999.

NOVELS

La Prise du pouvoir, translation from the Polish manuscript by Jeanne Hersch, Gallimard (Paris), 1953, original Polish edition published as *Zdobycie wladzy,* Instytut Literacki, 1955, translation by Celina Wieniewska published as *The Seizure of Power,* Criterion, 1955, published in England as *The Usurpers,* Faber (London), 1955.

Dolina Issy, Instytut Literacki, 1955, translation by Louis Iribarne published as *The Issa Valley,* Farrar, Straus, 1981.

EDITOR

(With Zbigniew Folejewski) *Antologia poezji spolecznej* (title means "Anthology of Social Poetry"), [Vilnius], 1933.

Piesn niepodlegla (Resistance poetry; title means "Invincible Song"), Oficyna, 1942, Michigan Slavic Publications, 1981.

(And translator) Jacques Maritain, *Drogami Kleski,* [Warsaw], 1942.

(And translator) Daniel Bell, *Praca i jej gorycze* (title means "Work and Its Discontents"), Instytut Literacki, 1957.

(And translator) Simone Weil, *Wybor pism* (title means "Selected Works"), Instytut Literacki, 1958.

(And translator) *Kultura masowa* (title means "Mass Culture"), Instytut Literacki, 1959.

(And translator) *Wegry* (title means "Hungary"), Instytut Literacki, 1960.

(And translator) *Postwar Polish Poetry: An Anthology,* Doubleday, 1965, revised edition, University of California Press, 1983.

Lettres inedites de O. V. de L. Milosz a Christian Gauss (correspondence of Milosz's uncle, the French poet Oscar Milosz), Silvaire, 1976.

(With Drenka Willen) *A Book of Luminous Things: An International Anthology of Poetry,* Harcourt, 1996.

Founder and editor, *Zagary* (literary periodical), 1931.

TRANSLATOR

(With Peter Dale Scott) Zbigniew Herbert, *Selected Poems,* Penguin (New York City), 1968.

Alexander Wat, *Mediterranean Poems,* Ardi, 1977.

Ewangelia wedlug sw. Marka (title means "The Gospel According to St. Mark"), Znak, 1978.

Ksiega Hioba (title means "The Book of Job"), Dialogue (Paris), 1980.

Also translator of Anna Swir's *Happy as a Dog's Tail,* Harcourt and, with Leonard Nathan, *With the Skin: Poems of Aleksander Wat.*

RECORDINGS

Czeslaw Milosz Reading from His Poems in the Montpelier Room, Library of Congress, 1997.

SIDELIGHTS: One of the most respected figures in twentieth-century Polish literature, Czeslaw Milosz was awarded the Nobel Prize for literature in 1980. Born in Lithuania and raised in Poland, Milosz has lived in the United States since 1960. His poems, novels, essays, and other works are written in his native Polish and translated by the author and others into English. Having lived under the two great totalitarian systems of modern history, national socialism and communism, Milosz writes of the past in a tragic, ironic style that nonetheless affirms the value of human life. Terrence Des Pres, writing in the *Nation,* states that "political catastrophe has defined the nature of our century, and the result—the collision of personal and public realms—has produced a new kind of writer. Czeslaw Milosz is the perfect example. In exile from a world which no longer exists, a witness to the Nazi devastation of Poland and the Soviet takeover of Eastern Europe, Milosz deals in his poetry with the central issues of our time: the impact of history upon moral being, the search for ways to survive spiritual ruin in a ruined world."

Although Milosz writes in several genres, it is his poetry that has attracted the most critical acclaim. Several observers, writes Harold B. Segel in the *Washington Post Book World,* consider Milosz to be "the foremost Polish poet of this century." Similarly, Paul Zweig of the *New York Times Book Review* claims that Milosz "is considered by many to be the greatest living Polish poet." But Joseph Brodsky goes further in his praise for Milosz. Writing in *World Literature Today,* Brodsky asserts: "I have no hesitation whatsoever in stating that Czeslaw Milosz is one of the greatest poets of our time, perhaps the greatest."

Born in Lithuania in 1911, Milosz spent much of his childhood in Czarist Russia, where his father worked as a civil engineer. After World War I the family returned to their hometown, which had become a part of the new Polish state, and Milosz attended local Catholic schools. He published his first collection of poems, *Poemat o czasie zastyglym* ("Poem of the Frozen Time"), at the age of twenty-one. Milosz was associated with the catastrophist school of poets during the 1930s. Catastrophism concerns "the inevitable annihilation of the highest values, especially the values essential to a given cultural system. . . . But it proclaims . . . only the annihilation of certain values, not values in general, and the destruction of a certain historical formation, but not of all mankind," Aleksander Fiut explains in *World Literature Today.* The writings of this group of poets ominously foreshadowed the Second World War.

When the war began in 1939, and Poland was invaded by Nazi Germany and Soviet Russia, Milosz worked with the underground Resistance movement in Warsaw, writing and editing several books published clandestinely during the occupation. One of these books, a collection titled *Wiersze* ("Poems"), was published under the pseudonym of J. Syruc. Following the war, Milosz became a member of the new communist government's diplomatic service and was stationed in Paris, France, as a cultural attache. In 1951, he left this post and defected to the West.

The Captive Mind explains Milosz's reasons for defecting and examines the life of the artist under a communist regime. It is, maintains Steve Wasserman in the *Los Angeles Times Book Review,* a "brilliant and original study of the totalitarian mentality." Karl Jaspers, in an article for the *Saturday Review,* describes *The Captive Mind* as "a significant historical document and analysis of the highest order. . . . In astonishing gradations Milosz shows what happens to men subjected simultaneously to constant threat of annihilation and to the promptings of faith in a historical necessity which exerts apparently irresistible force and achieves enormous success. We are presented with a vivid picture of the forms of concealment, of inner transformation, of the sudden bolt to conversion, of the cleavage of man into two."

Milosz's defection came about when he was recalled to Poland from his position at the Polish embassy. He refused to leave. Joseph McLellan of the *Washington Post* quotes Milosz explaining: "I knew perfectly well that my country was becoming the province of an empire." In a speech before the Congress for Cultural Freedom, quoted by James Atlas of the *New York Times,* Milosz declares: "I have rejected the new faith because the practice of the lie is one of its principal commandments and socialist realism is nothing more than a different name for a lie." After his defection Milosz lived in Paris, where he worked as a translator and freelance writer. In 1960 he was offered a teaching position at the University of California at Berkeley, which he accepted. He became an American citizen in 1970.

In *The Seizure of Power,* first published as *La Prise du pouvoir* in 1953, Milosz renders as fiction much of the same material found in *The Captive Mind.* The book is an autobiographical novel that begins with the Russian occupation of Warsaw at the close of the Second World War. That occupation is still a matter of controversy in Poland. As the Russian army approached the Nazi-held city, the Polish Resistance movement rose against the German occupation troops. They had been assured that the Russian army would join the fight the day after their uprising began. But instead, the Russians stood by a few miles outside of the city, allowing the Nazis to crush the revolt unhindered. When the uprising was over, the Russian army occupied Warsaw and installed a communist regime. The novel ends with the disillusioned protagonist, a political education officer for the communists, emigrating to the West.

The Seizure of Power "is a novel on how to live when power changes hands," Andrew Sinclair explains in the London *Times.* Granville Hicks, in an article for the *New York Times Book Review,* sees a similarity between *The Captive Mind* and *The Seizure of Power.* In both books, "Milosz appeals to the West to try to understand the people of Eastern Europe," maintains Hicks. Told in a series of disjointed scenes meant to suggest the chaos and violence of postwar Poland, *The Seizure of Power* is "a novel of ineffable sadness, and a muffled sob for Poland's fate," writes Wasserman. Michael Harrington, in a review for *Commonweal,* calls *The Seizure of Power* "a sensitive, probing work, far better than most political novels, of somewhat imperfect realization but of significant intention and worth."

After living in the United States for a time, Milosz began to write of his new home. In *Native Realm: A Search for Self-Definition* and *Visions from San Francisco Bay,* Milosz compares and contrasts the West with his native Poland. *Native Realm,* Richard Holmes writes in the London *Times,* is "a political and social autobiography, shorn of polemic intent, deeply self-questioning, and dominated by the sense that neither historically nor metaphysically are most Westerners in a position to grasp the true nature of the East European experience since the First War." A series of personal essays examining events in Milosz's life, *Native Realm* provides "a set of commentaries upon his improbable career," as Michael Irwin maintains in the *Times Literary Supplement.* Milosz "has written a self-effacing remembrance composed of shards from a shattered life," believes Wasserman. "He tells his story with the humility of a man who has experienced tragedy and who believes in fate and in destiny. It is a work that reflects the stubborn optimism of his heart, even as it dwells on the pessimism of his intellect." Irving Howe, writing in the *New York Times Book Review,* finds *Native Realm* "beautifully written." Milosz, Howe continues, "tries to find in the chaos of his life some glimmers of meaning."

In *Visions from San Francisco Bay,* Milosz examines his life in contemporary California, a place far removed in distance and temperament from the scenes of his earlier life. His observations are often sardonic, and yet he is also content with his new home. Milosz "sounds like a man who has climbed up, hand over hand, right out of history, and who is both amazed and grateful to find that he can breathe the ahistorical atmosphere of California," Anatole Broyard states in the *New York Times.* The opening words of the book are "I am here," and from that starting point Milosz describes the society around him. "The intention," notes Julian Symons in the *Times Literary Supplement,* "is to understand himself, to understand the United States, to communicate something singular to Czcslaw Milosz." Broyard takes this idea even further, arguing that Milosz "expresses surprise at 'being here,' taking this phrase in its ordinary sense of being in America and in its other, Heideggerian sense of being-in-the-world."

Although Milosz's comments about life in California are "curiously oblique, deeply shadowed by European experience, allusive, sometimes arch and frequently disillusioned," as Holmes points out, he ultimately embraces his adopted home. "Underlying all his meditations," comments Leon Edel in the *New York Times Book Review,* "is his constant 'amazement' that America should exist in this world—and his gratitude that it does exist." "He is fascinated," explains Symons, "by the contradictions of a society with enormous economic power, derived in part from literally non-human technical achievement, which also contains a large group that continually and passionately indicts the society by which it is maintained." Milosz, P. J. Kavanagh remarks in the *Spectator,* looks at his adopted country with "a kind of detached glee—at awfulness; an ungloomy recognition that we cannot go on as we are—in any direction. He holds up a mirror and shows us ourselves, without blame and with no suggestions either, and in the mirror he himself is also reflected." Edel believes that Milosz's visions "have authority: the authority of an individual who reminds us that only someone like himself who has known tyranny . . . can truly prize democracy."

The story of Milosz's odyssey from East to West is also recounted in his poetry. Milosz's "entire effort," Jonathan Galassi explains in the *New York Times Book Review,* "is directed toward a confrontation with experience—and not with personal experience alone, but with history in all its paradoxical horror and wonder." Speaking of his poetry in the essay collection *The Witness of Poetry,* Milosz stresses the importance of his nation's cultural heritage and history in shaping his work. "My corner of Europe," he states, "owing to the extraordinary and lethal events that have been occurring there, comparable only to violent earthquakes, affords a peculiar perspective. As a result, all of us who come from those parts appraise poetry slightly differently than do the majority of my audience, for we tend to view it as a witness and participant in one of mankind's major transformations." "For Milosz," Helen Vendler explains in the *New Yorker,* "the person is irrevocably a person in history, and the interchange between external event and the individual life is the matrix of poetry." Writing in *TriQuarterly,* Reginald Gibbons states that Milosz "seems to wonder how good work can be written, no matter how private its subject matter, without the poet having been aware of the pain and threat of the human predicament."

Milosz sees a fundamental difference in the role of poetry in the capitalist West and the communist East. Western poetry, as Alfred Kazin of the *New York Times*

Book Review writes, is " 'alienated' poetry, full of introspective anxiety." But because of the dictatorial nature of communist government, poets in the East cannot afford to be preoccupied with themselves. They are drawn to write of the larger problems of their society. "A peculiar fusion of the individual and the historical took place," Milosz writes in *The Witness of Poetry,* "which means that events burdening a whole community are perceived by a poet as touching him in a most personal manner. Then poetry is no longer alienated."

For many years Milosz's poetry was little noticed in the United States, though he was highly regarded in Poland. Recognition in Poland came in defiance of official government resistance to Milosz's work. The communist regime refused to publish the books of a defector; for many years only underground editions of his poems were secretly printed and circulated in Poland. But in 1980, when Milosz was awarded the Nobel Prize for Literature, the communist government was forced to relent. A government-authorized edition of Milosz's poems was issued. It sold a phenomenal 200,000 copies. One sign of Milosz's widespread popularity in Poland occurred when Polish workers in Gdansk unveiled a monument to their comrades who were shot down by the communist police. Two quotations were inscribed on the monument: one was taken from the Bible; the other was taken from a poem by Milosz.

The Nobel Prize also brought Milosz to the attention of a wider audience in the United States. Since 1980 a number of his earlier works have been translated into English and released in this country, while his new books have received widespread critical attention. The poet's image has graced a postage stamp in Poland. Some of this public attention has focused less on Milosz's work as poetry than "as the work of a thinker and political figure; the poems tend to be considered en masse, in relation either to the condition of Poland, or to the suppression of dissident literature under Communist rule, or to the larger topic of European intellectual history," as Vendler maintains. But most reviewers comment on Milosz's ability to speak in a personal voice that carries with it the echoes of his people's history. Zweig explains that Milosz "offers a modest voice, speaking an old language. But this language contains the resources of centuries. Speaking it, one speaks with a voice more than personal. . . . Milosz's power lies in his ability to speak with this larger voice without diminishing the urgency that drives his words."

Because he has lived through many of the great upheavals of recent history, and because his poetry fuses his own experiences with the larger events in his society, many of Milosz's poems concern loss, destruction, and despair. "There is a very dark vision of the world in my work," he told Lynn Darling of the *Washington Post.* And yet Milosz went on to say that he is "a great partisan of human hope." This essential optimism comes from his religious convictions.

Milosz believes that one of the major problems of contemporary society—in both the East and the West—is its lack of a moral foundation. Writing in *The Land of Ulro,* Milosz finds that twentieth-century man has only "the starry sky above, and no moral law within." Speaking to Judy Stone of the *New York Times Book Review,* Milosz stated: "I am searching for an answer as to what will result from an internal erosion of religious beliefs." Michiko Kakutani, reviewing *The Land of Ulro* for the *New York Times,* finds that "Milosz is eloquent in his call for a literature grounded in moral, as well as esthetic, values. Indeed, when compared with his own poetry, the work of many Westerners—from the neurotic rantings of the Romantics to the cerebral mind games of the avant-gardists—seems unserious and self-indulgent."

Because of his moral vision Milosz's writings make strong statements, some of which are inherently political in their implications. "The act of writing a poem is an act of faith," Milosz claimed in *The History of Polish Literature,* "yet if the screams of the tortured are audible in the poet's room, is not his activity an offense to human suffering?" His awareness of suffering, writes Joseph C. Thackery of *Hollins Critic,* makes Milosz a "spokesman of the millions of dead of the Holocaust, the Gulags, the Polish and Czech uprisings, and the added millions of those who will go on dying in an imperfect world."

But Milosz also warns of the dangers of political writing. In a PEN Congress talk reprinted in the *Partisan Review,* he stated: "In this century a basic stance of writers . . . seems to be an acute awareness of suffering inflicted upon human beings by unjust structures of society. . . . This awareness of suffering makes a writer open to the idea of radical change, whichever of many recipes he chooses. . . . Innumerable millions of human beings were killed in this century in the name of utopia—either progressive or reactionary, and always there were writers who provided convincing justifications for massacre."

In *The Witness of Poetry* Milosz argues that true poetry is "the passionate pursuit of the Real." He condemns those writers who favor art for art's sake or who think of themselves as alienated. Milosz suggests, as Adam

Gussow writes in the *Saturday Review,* that poets may have "grown afraid of reality, afraid to see it clearly and speak about it in words we can all comprehend." What is needed in "today's unsettled world," Gussow explains, are poets who, "like Homer, Dante, and Shakespeare, will speak for rather than against the enduring values of their communities."

This concern for a poetry that confronts reality is noted by Thackery, who sees Milosz searching "for a poetry that will be at once harsh and mollifying, that will enable men to understand, if not to rationalize, the debasement of the human spirit by warfare and psychic dismemberment, while simultaneously establishing a personal *modus vivendi* and a psychology of aesthetic necessity." Des Pres also sees this unifying quality in Milosz's poetry, a trait he believes Milosz shares with T. S. Eliot. "The aim of both Milosz and Eliot," Des Pres states, "is identical: to go back and work through the detritus of one's own time on earth, to gather up the worst along with the best, integrate past and present into a culminating moment which transcends both, which embraces pain and joy together, the whole of a life and a world redeemed through memory and art, a final restoration in spirit of that which in historical fact has been forever lost." Vendler believes that "the work of Milosz reminds us of the great power that poetry gains from bearing within itself an unforced, natural, and long-ranging memory of past customs; a sense of the strata of ancient and modern history; wide visual experience; and a knowledge of many languages and literatures. . . . The living and tormented revoicing of the past makes Milosz a historical poet of bleak illumination."

Upon receiving the Nobel Prize in 1980, Milosz hoped to "continue with my very private and strange occupation," as McLellan quotes him. He has continued to publish books—some new titles and some older books appearing in English for the first time—and has spoken out at meetings of PEN, the international writers' organization, on such topics as censorship and totalitarianism. Darling explains that Milosz lives in Berkeley and writes, "under the benevolent light of the California sun, in a country of easy consummation and temporary passion, poems about the past, about horror, about life in the abyss of the 20th century."

Because Milosz writes of recent Polish history, and decries the nation's political tragedies of the past thirty-five years, his work embodies a spirit of freedom that speaks powerfully to his countrymen as well as to others. "Polish independence exists in this poet's voice," Brodsky maintains in the *New York Times.* "This, at least, is one way to account for the intensity that has made him perhaps the greatest poet of our time." Norman Davies notes in the *New York Times Book Review* that Milosz is one of three Poles who have come to international prominence during the 1980s. Milosz, Pope John Paul II, and Lech Walesa, the leader of the Solidarity trade union challenging the Polish communist government, have "each served in different ways to illuminate the depth and richness of their native Polish culture," Davies writes. In 1981, during his first visit to Poland in thirty years, Milosz met with Lech Walesa and the two men acknowledged their mutual indebtedness. "I told him that I considered him my leader," Milosz recounted to Darling. "He said that he had gone to jail because of my poetry."

With the publication in 1986 of *Unattainable Earth,* Milosz continued to show himself as a poet of memory and a poet of witness, for, in the prose footnote to "Poet at Seventy," he writes of his continued "un-named need for order, for rhythm, for form, which three words are opposed to chaos and nothingness." The book uses what Stanislaw Baranczak in *Threepenny Review* calls, a "peculiar structure of a modern*silva rerum*" which "consists in including a number of prose fragments, notes, letters, verses of other poets." *Unattainable Earth* was the first of several lauded collaborative translations between the author and American poet Robert Hass.

A year later, *The Collected Poems, 1931-1987* was published, bringing together *Selected Poems, Bells in Winter, The Separate Notebooks,* and *Unattainable Earth* in one volume. The book contains one hundred and eighty poems ranging in size from two lines to sixty pages. Forty-five poems appear for the first time in English in this edition, of which twenty-six are recently translated older poems and twenty are new poems. Warren W. Werner in *Southern Humanities Review* calls the work "a big, varied, and important book . . . a feast of poetry." P. J. M. Robertson in *Queen's Quarterly* lauds the collection as "a gift to cherish, for it contains the song of a man . . . passionately affirming the daily miracle of life and its continuity even now on our battered earth," and affirms that *The Collected Poems* "reveal Milosz's answer to the question of the role of poetry and of art in the twentieth century . . . . a responsibility to see and express beauty: that is, the truth about life in its miraculous complexity." *New York Times Book Review* contributor Edward Hirsch finds the volume "one of the monumental splendors of poetry in our age." Baranczak believes that it is a book that can "finally give the English-speaking reader a fairly accurate idea of what [Milosz's] poetry really is, both in the sense of the largeness of its thematic and stylistic range and the uniqueness of his more than half-century-long creative evolution." Don Bogan of *Nation* finds that "with its clarity, historical awareness and moral vision, *The Collected Poems* is among the best guides we have" to help remind us that "poetry can define and address the concerns of an age."

Milosz followed in 1991 with *Provinces: Poems, 1987-1991.* For Milosz, the life in each individual seems made up of provinces, and one new province which he must now visit is the province of old age. He explores getting older in the thirteen-part sequence titled, "A New Province," reporting that "not much is known about that country / Till we land there ourselves, with no right to return." Hirsch finds that these poems about old age have "a penetrating honesty" derived from "a powerful dialectical tension, a metaphysical dispute at work . . . about the conflicting claims of immanence and transcendence, the temporal and the eternal." Ben Howard, in *Poetry,* comments on the inclusion of Milosz's "abiding subjects—the loss of his native Lithuania, the suffering of Eastern Europe, the wrenching upheavals of a long and difficult life," and suggests that the poet through his verse is "asserting his affinity with the common people and his closeness to the soil." *New York Review of Books* contributor Helen Vendler calls *Provinces* a collection of "many of Milosz's central themes—including the strangeness of human life (where in the blink of an eye absurdity can turn to bravery, or tranquillity to war), exile, sensuality, memory, Platonic idealism, and iron disbelief." Bill Marx of *Parnassus* describes *Provinces* as "an inner landscape of clashing contraries and times. Valleys of sensuous admiration for the earth's delights are broken up by notched peaks of traumatic memory; deserts formed by perceptions of nature's indifference are dotted with oases rooted in intimations of the transcendent."

Beginning with My Streets: Essays and Recollections, published in 1992, is a collection of essays, philosophical meditations, literary criticism, portraits of friends and writers, and a genre which Sally Laird in London's *Observer* identifies as " 'chatty narratives' in the Polish tradition." Donald Davie in *New Republic* deems the book "more a medley than a collection, with a deceptive air of being 'thrown together'," made up, as Vendler points out, of essays in which Milosz "moves with entire naturalness from Swedenborg to Robinson Jeffers, from Lithuanian scenery to Meister Eckhart, from the Seven Deadly Sins to Polish Marxism." Laird praises in particular the essay "Saligia," in which Milosz takes on two multiple perspectives, that of poet and of engaged historian. The book contains accounts of the poet's childhood in Vilnius and closes with his 1980 Nobel lecture. *Washington Post Book World* contributor Alberto Manguel concludes, "Milosz excels in recounting, in finding the happy phrase for a scene or a concept. The invention of the past, the elusiveness of reality, the fluidity of time, the apparent banality or apparent importance of philosophical inquiries are traditional (some would say intrinsic) poetic fodder, and Milosz arranges the questions on the page with economy and elegance."

A Year of the Hunter, published in 1994, is a journal Milosz penned between August of 1987 and August of 1988. John Simon in *Washington Post Book World* points out that these entries were "written on airplanes zooming to lecture engagements, poetry readings, literary congresses and the like." Ian Buruma praises the work in the *Los Angeles Times Book Review* as "a wonderful addition to [Milosz's] other autobiographical writing. The diary form, free-floating, wide-ranging . . . is suited to a poet, especially an intellectual poet, like Milosz," allowing for his entries to range from gardening to translating, from communism to Christianity, from past to present. Indeed, as Michael Ignatieff states in the *New York Review of Books, A Year of the Hunter* is successful "because Milosz has not cleaned it up too much. Its randomness is a pleasure."

In 1995, Milosz produced the poetry collection *Facing the River: New Poems.* This volume includes verse that deals largely with Milosz's return to Vilnius, the city of his childhood, now the capital of the free republic of Lithuania. In returning, Ignatieff points out, Milosz found himself in an ironic circumstance: "Having been a poet of exile, he had now become the poet of the impossible return of the past." The poet recognized many streets, buildings, and steeples in his homeland, but the people from his past were gone. This left Milosz to "bring the absent dead back to life, one by one, in all their aching singularity," as Ignatieff states. *Facing the River* is not just about Milosz's return to Lithuania and the people that he misses; it also addresses the poet's accomplishments and his views on life. In "At a Certain Age," Milosz declares that old men, who see themselves as handsome and noble, will find: "later in our place an ugly toad/ Half-opens its thick eyelid/ And one sees clearly: 'That's me.' "*Facing the River,* which ends with Milosz wondering "If only my work were of use to people," leaves Ignatieff speaking for many readers of Milosz when he writes: "Those like myself who see the world differently because of him hope he will continue to stand facing the river, and tell us what he sees."

In 1999, at age eighty-eight, Milosz offered a collection, *Roadside Dog,* "that at first encounter seems an invitation to revisit the remembered landscapes of his life," as Jaroslaw Anders notes in a *New Republic* article. In "maxims, anecdotes, meditations, crumbs of worldly wisdom, introspections . . . [and] poems," Milosz takes readers on a trip through the sounds and images that have shaped his life as a poet. "Some of these morsels are perfectly finished," Anders finds, "others appear sketchy, tentative, even commonplace: assertions in search of proof, thoughts that should become essays, plot lines that need to be tested in a novel. Is this the writer's scrap-book offered generously—but also a little self-indulgently—to his readers, the literary equivalent of a rummage sale?"

David S. Gross saw *Roadside Dog* differently. In his essay, part of a 1999 salute to Milosz published in *World Literature Today,* Gross admits that it's "hard to say what these little pieces are. Prose poems, I suppose, after Baudelaire and others." Still, the work as a whole "constantly reexamines questions of politics, religion, the nature of poetry, issues of consciousness and meaning, and more, always toward the end of understanding, even reinventing, the self, in order to understand and reinvent the world." Again and again in *Roadside Dog,* says Gross, the poet "tries to get at that which links him with the suffering and the excluded, even though he has not for years had to suffer the same consequences."

Into his ninth decade, Milosz remained in touch with his readers. In *World Literature Today,* Jerzy Maciuszko recalls how in 1970 the poet divided his time between writing and teaching at various universities. "He established a very good rapport with students and interacted with them beautifully," Maciuszko notes. "The students not only learned a great deal but came to love and greatly respect the future Nobel Prize laureate, as though they sensed that, fascinating and inspiring as we was at that time, greater things were still to come." In 1999, adds Maciuszko, Milosz agreed to meet students again, this time at the University of Oklahoma. "It came as no surprise to read in a letter of 1 March 1999 from Dr. Riggen the following statement: 'Even at age 87 Milosz is still remarkably active and vigourous, and he seems to have enjoyed his visit every bit as much as we did, even confessing to me at week's end that he had not realized how much he missed teaching and interacting with eager, interested students and faculty.' "

"Milosz's work is something so extraordinary in our epoch, that it seems to be a phenomenon that he has appeared on the surface of contemporary art from the mysterious depths of reality," declares Krzysztof Dybciak in *World Literature Today.* "At a time when voices of doubt, deadness, and despair are the loudest; when writers are outstripping each other in negation of man, his culture, and nature; when the predominant action is destruction . . ., the world built by the author of 'Daylight' crates a space in which one can breathe freely, where one can find rescue. It renders the world of surfaces transparent and condenses being. It does not promise any final solutions to the unleashed elements of nature and history here on earth, but it enlarges the space in which one can await the Coming with hope. Milosz does not believe in the omnipotence of man, and he has been deprived of the optimistic faith in the self-sufficiency of a world known only through empirical experience. He leads the reader to a place where one can see—to paraphrase the poet's own formula regarding time—Being raised above being through Being."

BIOGRAPHICAL/CRITICAL SOURCES:

BOOKS

Czerni, Irena, *Czeslaw Milosz laureat literackiej nagrody Nobla 1980: katalog wystawy,* Nakl. Uniwersytety Jagiellonskiego (Krakow), 1993.

Contemporary Literary Criticism, Gale (Detroit), Volume 5, 1976, Volume 11, 1979, Volume 22, 1982, Volume 31, 1985, Volume 56, 1989, Volume 82, 1994.

Czarnecha, Ewe, *Prdrozny swiata: Rosmowy z Czeslawem Miloszem, Komentane,* Bicentennial, 1983.

Czarnecha, Ewa, and Alexander Fiut, translation by Richard Lourie, *Conversations with Czeslaw Milosz,* Harcourt (San Diego, CA), 1988.

Dompkowski, Judith Ann, *"Down a Spiral Staircase, Never-ending: Motion as Design in the Writing of Czeslaw Milosz,* P. Lang (New York City), 1990.

Dudek, Jolanta, *Gdzie wschodzi slonce i kedy zapada—europejskie korzenie poezji Czeslawa Milosza,* Nakl. Univwersytetu Jagiellonskiego, 1991.

Fiut, Aleksander, *Rozmowy z Czeslawem Miloszem,* Wydawnictwo Literackie (Kracow), 1981.

Fiut, Aleksander, *The Eternal Moment: The Poetry of Czeslaw Milosz,* University of California Press, 1990.

Gillon, A., and L. Krzyzanowski, editors, *Introduction to Modern Polish Literature,* Twayne (Boston), 1964.

Gocmoeri, G., *Polish and Hungarian Poetry, 1945 to 1956,* Oxford University Press (New York City), 1966.

Hass, Robert, *Twentieth Century Pleasures: Prose on Poetry,* Ecco Press, 1984.

Malinowska, Barbara, *Dynamics of Being, Space, and Time in the Poetry of Czeslaw Milosz and John Ashbery,* P. Lang, 1997.

Milosz, Czeslaw, *The Captive Mind,* Knopf, 1953.

Milosz, *The History of Polish Literature,* Macmillan, 1969, revised edition, University of California Press, 1983.

Milosz, *The Witness of Poetry,* Harvard University Press, 1983.

Milosz, *The Land of Ulro,* Farrar, Straus, 1984.

Mozejko, Edward, *Between Anxiety and Hope: The Poetry and Writing of Czeslaw Milosz,* University of Alberta Press (Edmonton), 1988.

Nathan, Leonard and Arthur Quinn, *The Poet's Work: An Introduction to Czeslaw Milosz,* Harvard University Press, 1992.

Nilsson, Nils Ake, editor, *Czeslaw Milosz: A Stockholm Conference, September 9-11, 1991,* Kungl. Vitterhets (Stockholm, Sweden), 1992.

Volynska-Bogert, Rimma, and Wojciech Zaleswski, *Czeslaw Milosz: An International Bibliography 1930-80,* University of Michigan Press (Ann Arbor), 1983.

PERIODICALS

America, December 18, 1982; December 15, 1984, p. 409; May 12, 1990, pp. 472-75; February 1, 1997, Robert Coles, "Secular Days, Sacred Moments," p. 6.

American Book Review, March, 1985, p. 22.

American Poetry Review, January, 1977.

Atlanta Journal/Constitution, April 2, 1989, p. N11; April 12, 1992, p. N11; April 23, 1995, p. M13; April 25, 1995, p. B7; April 26, 1995, p. D1.

Booklist, April 15, 1988, p. 1387; November 1, 1991, p. 497; January 1, 1992, p. 806; March 1, 1992, p. 1191; November 1, 1998, Ray Olson, review of *Roadside Dog,* p. 465.

Book Report, November 1988, p. 39.

Books Abroad, winter, 1969; spring, 1970; winter, 1973; winter, 1975.

Book Week, May 9, 1965.

Book World, September 29, 1968; August 31, 1986, p. 8; March 8, 1992, p. 9; October 9, 1994, p. 10.

Boston Globe, October 16, 1987, p. 91; August 28, 1994, p. 62.

Canadian Literature, spring 1989, pp. 183-84.

Chicago Tribune, October 10, 1980; September 6, 1987, p. 6; December 4, 1989, p. 2; March 15, 1992, p. 6; December 18, 1994, p. 5.

Christian Science Monitor, July 2, 1986, p. 21; October 5, 1990, p. 10; January 17, 1992, p. 14.

Commonweal, July 8, 1955; March 22, 1985, p. 190; November 6, 1992, p. 33-34.

Denver Quarterly, summer, 1976.

Eastern European Poetry, April, 1967.

English Journal, January, 1992, p. 16.

Globe and Mail (Toronto), March 16, 1985.

Guardian Weekly, October 2, 1988, p. 28.

Hollins Critic, April, 1982.

Hudson Review, autumn, 1992, p. 509.

Ironwood, Number 18, 1981.

Journal of Religion, January, 1987, pp. 141-42.

Library Journal, November 15, 1984, p. 2114; April 15, 1986, p. 84; April 15, 1988, p. 83; January, 1989, p. 45; October 15, 1991, p. 80.

Los Angeles Times, January 14, 1987; September 13, 1987, p. 14.

Los Angeles Times Book Review, May 10, 1981; August 22, 1982; June 5, 1983; August 24, 1984; June 24, 1990, p. 12; November 4, 1990, p. 10; August 15, 1993, pp. 19-20; August 14, 1994, p. 3.

Modern Age, spring, 1986, p. 162.

Nation, December 30, 1978; June 13, 1981; December 22, 1984, p. 686; December 19, 1988, pp. 688-91.

New Leader, October 15, 1984, p. 14; September 19, 1988, p. 19; March 24, 1997, Pheobe Pettingell, review of *Striving towards Being,* p. 13.

New Perspectives Quarterly, fall, 1988, p. 55; spring, 1990, p. 44.

New Republic, May 16, 1955; August 1, 1983; October 3, 1988, pp. 26-28; March 16, 1992, pp. 34-37; April 12, 1999, Jaroslaw Anders, "Beauty and Certainty," p. 48.

New Statesman, October 24, 1980; December 17-24, 1982; August 30, 1985, p. 27; August 5, 1988, p. 38.

Newsweek, June 15, 1981; October 4, 1982.

New Yorker, November 7, 1953; March 19, 1984; October 24, 1988, p. 122; July 16, 1990, p. 80.

New York Review of Books, April 4, 1974; June 25, 1981; February 27, 1986, p. 31; June 2, 1988, p. 21; August 13, 1992, pp. 44-46; August 11, 1994, p. 41; August 28, 1994, p. 9; May 11, 1995, p. 15; March 23, 1995, pp. 39-42.

New York Times, June 25, 1968; October 10, 1980; September 4, 1982; August 24, 1984; July 26, 1987; June 2, 1988, p. 21.

New York Times Book Review, April 17, 1955; July 7, 1974; March 11, 1979; February 1, 1981; June 28, 1981; October 17, 1982; May 1, 1983; September 2, 1984; October 20, 1985, p. 60; May 25, 1986, p. 2; July 6, 1986; June 2, 1988, p. 21; June 19, 1988, p. 6; December 8, 1988, p. 26; April 26, 1992, p. 20; May 17, 1992, p. 7; May 31, 1992, p. 22; August 28, 1994, p. 9.

New York Times Magazine, January 14, 1990, p. 22.
Observer (London), December 2, 1984, p. 19; August 11, 1985, p. 20; July 24, 1988, p. 42; November 22, 1992, p. 64.
Parnassus, fall, 1983, p. 127; 1989, p. 67; 1992, pp. 100-20.
Partisan Review, November, 1953; spring, 1977; fall, 1985, p. 448; 1986, pp. 177-19; 1990, p. 145.
Poetry, April, 1980; December, 1986, p. 168; January 1993, pp. 223-26; February, 1997, John Taylor, review of *Facing the River,* p. 293; August, 1999, Christian Wiman, review of *Roadside Dog,* p. 286.
Progressive, March, 1985, p. 40.
Publishers Weekly, October 24, 1980; January 31, 1986, p. 362; February 26, 1988, p. 187; January 13, 1992, p. 37; June 6, 1994, p. 49; August 28, 1994, p. 48; September 28, 1999, review of *Roadside Dog,* p. 95; September 28, 1998, p. 95.
Queen's Quarterly, winter, 1989, pp. 954-56.
Reflections, winter, 1985, p. 14.
San Francisco Review of Books, spring, 1985, p. 22.
Saturday Review, June 6, 1953; May-June, 1983.
Southern Humanities Review, fall, 1989, pp. 382-86.
Spectator, December 4, 1982.
Stand, summer, 1990, p. 12.
Theology Today, January, 1984.
Threepenny Review, summer, 1989, p. 23.
Times (London), July 16, 1981; January 6, 1983; May 19, 1983; February 9, 1985; May 27, 1987.
Times Literary Supplement, December 2, 1977; August 25, 1978; July 24, 1981; December 24, 1982; September 9, 1983; October 3, 1986, p. 1092; February 8, 1988, pp. 955-56; September 2, 1988, p. 955.
Tribune Books (Chicago), May 31, 1981; March 15, 1992, p. 6; December 6, 1992, p. 13; December 18, 1994, p. 5.
TriQuarterly, fall, 1983.
Village Voice, May 2, 1974.
Virginia Quarterly Review, spring, 1975; autumn, 1991, p. 125; summer, 1992, p. 99.
Wall Street Journal, July 24, 1992, p. A10.
Washington Post, October 10, 1980; April 29, 1982; September 20, 1989, p. D1; April 26, 1995, p. C1.
Washington Post Book World, June 14, 1981; December 22, 1991, p. 15; March 8, 1992, p. 9; October 9, 1994, p 10.
World Literature Today, winter, 1978; spring, 1978, pp. 372-76; winter, 1985, p. 126; winter, 1987, p. 127; summer, 1987, p. 467; autumn, 1991, p. 735; winter, 1993, p. 210; autumn, 1999 (a celebration of Milosz), pp. 617-692.
Yale Review, spring, 1990, p. 467.*

MINARIK, Else Holmelund 1920-

PERSONAL: Born September 13, 1920, in Aarhus, Denmark; daughter of Kaj Marius and Helga Holmelund; immigrated to the United States, 1925; married Walter Minarik, July 14, 1940 (died, 1963); married Homer Bigart (a journalist), October 3, 1970 (deceased); children: (first marriage) Brooke Ellen. *Education:* Attended Paltz College of the State University of New York; Queens College (now Queens College of the City University of New York), B.A., 1942. *Avocational interests:* Gardening.

ADDRESSES: Home—Rural Delivery, Barrington, NH 03825. *Office*—c/o Greenwillow Books, 1350 Avenue of the Americas, New York, NY 10019.

CAREER: Children's author. Reporter for *Daily Sentinel,* Rome, NY, 1940s; first-grade and art teacher in Commack Public Schools, Commack, Long Island, NY, 1950-54.

MEMBER: PEN.

AWARDS, HONORS: Best Illustrated Children's Books of the Year, *New York Times,* 1959, for *Father Bear Comes Home,* and 1968, for *A Kiss for Little Bear; Little Bear's Visit* was named a Caldecott honor book, 1962.

WRITINGS:

FOR CHILDREN

Little Bear, illustrated by Maurice Sendak, Harper (New York City), 1957, with audiocassette, HarperCollins (New York City), 1986.
No Fighting, No Biting!, illustrated by Sendak, Harper, 1958.
Father Bear Comes Home, illustrated by Sendak, Harper, 1959, HarperCollins, 1978.
Cat and Dog, illustrated by Fritz Siebel, Harper, 1960.
Little Bear's Friend, illustrated by Sendak, Harper, 1960, with audiocassette, HarperCollins, 1985.
Little Bear's Visit, illustrated by Sendak, Harper, 1961, with audiocassette, HarperCollins, 1985.
The Little Giant Girl and the Elf Boy, illustrated by Garth Williams, Harper, 1963.
The Winds That Come from Far Away, and Other Poems, illustrated by Joan P. Berg, Harper, 1964.
A Kiss for Little Bear, illustrated by Sendak, Harper, 1968.
(Translator) Jan Loeoef, *My Grandpa Is a Pirate,* Harper, 1968.

What If?, illustrated by Margaret Bloy Graham, Greenwillow (New York City), 1987, with audiocassette, Random House, 1988.

It's Spring!, illustrated by Graham, Greenwillow, 1989.

Percy and the Five Houses, illustrated by James Stevenson, Greenwillow, 1989.

The Little Girl and the Dragon, illustrated by Martine Gourbault, Greenwillow, 1991.

Am I Beautiful?, illustrated by Yossi Abolafia, Greenwillow, 1992.

Some of Minarik's books have appeared in Spanish and Braille editions.

ADAPTATIONS: Minarik's *Little Bear* has been animated and broadcast on Nickelodeon since 1995; it is also available on videocassette.

SIDELIGHTS: Else Holmelund Minarik has written many acclaimed books for children, but she is probably best known for her beloved "Little Bear" series, which began with *Little Bear,* published in 1957. Her work has attracted some of the most outstanding children's illustrators, including Maurice Sendak and Garth Williams. In addition to the "Little Bear" books, Minarik has charmed children and critics with titles including *No Fighting, No Biting!, Cat and Dog,* and *Percy and the Five Houses.*

Minarik's daughter, Brooke, first inspired her to write for children. When Brooke expressed an early interest in reading, Minarik discovered a shortage of easy-to-read children's books for her. She began writing books for Brooke and continued the practice with the first-graders she was then teaching. She considered it especially important that young readers have books to read during the summers, so as not to lose the skills they had gained during the school year.

Eventually, Minarik submitted some of the stories she had written to Ursula Nordstrom of Harper and Row. Nordstrom was impressed and used Minarik's *Little Bear* to begin the publisher's "I Can Read" series. *Little Bear,* illustrated by Maurice Sendak, noted illustrator of *Where the Wild Things Are,* features a bear cub who acts much like a child of preschool age. The book quickly stole the hearts of readers and critics alike. Though Minarik's next effort, *No Fighting, No Biting!,* centered on tales of an alligator family rather than Little Bear, she continued his story with her third book, *Father Bear Comes Home.* Other titles about Little Bear include *Little Bear's Friend,* in which he becomes friends with a little girl named Emily; *Little Bear's Visit,* in which he goes to see his grandparents; and *A Kiss for Little Bear,* which chronicles his grandmother's attempts to send him a kiss via some animal friends. *Little Bear's Visit* was named a runner-up for the prestigious Caldecott Medal in 1962.

It is still the "Little Bear" stories for which Minarik remains best known. Little Bear's popularity has exploded in the years since an animated version of his adventures has begun broadcasting on Nickelodeon in 1995. Little Bear has also become a fixture on videotape. "The quality animation, pleasant, reassuring vocal talent and relaxed pace of the simple story lines," says a *Publishers Weekly* reviewer, writing about the video release of *Meet Little Bear,* "have proven to be an endearing and enduring formula on television and are sure to win many new fans in this format." Christine McDonnell in *Twentieth-Century Children's Writers* explains Little Bear's popularity, comparing him to "a preschool child. Minarik's genius lies in her ability to create three-dimensional characters and humorous plots within the limits of a very simple text, accessible to beginning readers." "In the Little Bear books," McDonnell continues, "she focuses on the crucial concerns of young children: the tug and pull between the need for independence and taking risks and the need for reassurance and security . . . the need for acceptance and for friendship." Little Bear is accompanied by patient and understanding parents, Mother Bear and Father Bear; by unconditionally-loving grandparents; and by a variety of playmates, including a human girl named Emily. "The Little Bear books are notable for the graceful simplicity of the language, which avoids the choppy repetition characteristic of most books for beginning readers," McDonnell states. "And they are remarkable for their wealth of warmth, humor, and understanding."

Minarik's *Percy and the Five Houses* uses the enticement of the "House of the Month Club" to teach Percy the beaver, and in turn, youthful readers, that "there's no place like home." In the *New York Times Book Review,* Daniel Meier compares it to the "Little Bear" series: "I grew up on Else Holmelund Minarik's classic 'Little Bear' books for beginning readers. As a teacher, I have shared all her books with my young students. Her direct yet gentle language can inject interest into even the most ordinary of Little Bear's adventures. . . . I was pleased to find some of these qualities in *Percy and the Five Houses.*" Likewise, the hippo protagonist of *Am I Beautiful?* echoes one of Little Bear's major themes, writes a *Publishers Weekly* contributor: "unconditional parental love."

BIOGRAPHICAL/CRITICAL SOURCES:

BOOKS

Twentieth-Century Children's Writers, 4th edition, St. James Press (Detroit, MI), 1995.

PERIODICALS

Commonweal, November 22, 1968.
New Yorker, November 23, 1957.
New York Times, September 8, 1957; October 5, 1958.
New York Times Book Review, March 25, 1990.
Publishers Weekly, July 20, 1992, p. 247; May 12, 1997, p. 38.
Storytime, spring, 1987.*

* * *

MITCHELL, Jay
See ROBERSON, Jennifer

* * *

MOLINARO, Ursule

PERSONAL: Full name, Ursule Molinaro Herndon. *Avocational interests:* Painting (neo-Haitian primitive; oil on wood) and philosophy (any system of self-knowledge).

ADDRESSES: Home—New York City. *Agent*—c/o McPherson & Co., P.O. Box 1126, Kingston, NY 12402.

CAREER: United Nations, New York City, multilingual proofreader, 1946-51; writer, 1950—. Ecole Libre des Hautes Etudes, New York, teacher of creative and literary translation, 1971-72; University of Idaho, member of creative writing workshop, 1979.

MEMBER: Coordinating Council of Literary Magazines.

AWARDS, HONORS: Creative Artists Public Service grants, 1972-73 and 1980-81; MacDowell fellowship, 1977; National Endowment for the Arts grant, 1981-82; awards from New York Foundation for the Arts and PEN American Center.

WRITINGS:

POETRY

Rimes et raisons, Regain (Monte Carlo, Monaco), 1954.
Mirrors for Small Beasts, Noonday, 1960.

NOVELS

L'un pour l'autre, translation from the English manuscript by Edith Fournier, Julliard (Paris, France), 1964, published as *The Borrower: An Alchemical Novel,* Harper (New York City), 1970.
Green Lights Are Blue: A Pornosophic Novel, New American Library (New York City), 1967.
Sounds of a Drunken Summer, Harper, 1969.
The Autobiography of Cassandra, Princess and Prophetess of Troy, Archer Editions Press (Danbury, CT), 1979.
Positions with White Roses, McPherson (New Paltz, NY), 1983.
The New Moon with the Old Moon in Her Arms: A True Story Assembled from Scholarly Hearsay, Women's Press Ltd. (London, England), 1990, McPherson (Kingston, NY), 1993.
Power Dreamers: The Jocasta Complex, McPherson, 1994.

Also author of unpublished novel "That Which Is Bright Rises Twice," excerpts from which have appeared in *The Little Magazine,* Volume 10, numbers 3-4, 1976, and in *Gallimaufry,* 1978.

COLLECTIONS

Encores for a Dilettante, Braziller (New York City), 1978.
Bastards: Footnotes to History (two short stories; illustrated), Treacle Press, 1979.
Nightschool for Saints, Second Floor, Ring Bell: 11 Short Stories, Archer Editions Press, 1981.
Thirteen: Stories, McPherson, 1989.
A Full Moon of Women: 29 Word Portraits of Notable Women from Different Times and Places, Dutton (New York City), 1990.
Demons and Divas: Three Novels (contains *Angel on Fire, Saint Boy,* and *April in Paris*), McPherson, 1999.

NONFICTION

The Zodiac Lovers, Avon (New York City), 1969.

Life by the Numbers: A Basic Guide to Learning Your Life through Numerology, Morrow (New York City), 1971.

PLAYS

The Abstract Wife, Hill & Wang (New York City), 1961.

Breakfast Past Noon (one-act), published in *New Women's Theatre,* Random House (New York City), 1977.

Also author of one-act plays *The Engagement, After the Wash,* and *The Sundial,* all published or produced; author of unpublished and unproduced plays *The Mine* (one-act), *Antiques* (one-act), *The Great Emancipation,* and *The Happy Hexagon.*

OTHER

Translator from German, Italian, Spanish, and Portuguese into French and English of work by Dino Buzzati, Ugo Carrega, Hermann Hesse, Michael Horbach, Uwe Johnson, Reinhard Lettau, Claude Ollier, Nathalie Sarraute, Jean Vauthier, Christa Wolf, and many others. Also translator of film subtitles from and into French and from Italian into English. Work represented in anthologies, including *Statements 1,* Braziller, 1975, *Statements 2,* Braziller, 1977, both compiled by Jonathan Baumbach, and *Superfiction,* edited by Joe David Bellamy, Vintage, 1975. Contributor of short stories and articles to journals, including *Benzene, Contemporary Quarterly, Epoch, Evergreen, Fiera letteraria, Iowa Review, Lettres nouvelles, New Boston Review, New Directions, Panache, Top Stories, TriQuarterly,* and *Village Voice.*

SIDELIGHTS: Ursule Molinaro once told *CA* that her basic interest is "the position of the individual, regardless of ethnic background, sex, or age."

BIOGRAPHICAL/CRITICAL SOURCES:

PERIODICALS

Book World, September 7, 1969.

New Yorker, June 24, 1967.

New York Review of Books, August 24, 1967.

New York Times, August 25, 1971.

New York Times Book Review, May 21, 1967; September 2, 1990, p. 24.

Village Voice, December 19, 1968.

MOLINARO HERNDON, Ursule
See MOLINARO, Ursule

* * *

MULDOON, Paul 1951-

PERSONAL: Born June 20, 1951, in Armagh, Northern Ireland; son of Patrick (a laborer and gardener) and Brigid (a schoolteacher; maiden name, Regan) Muldoon; married Jean Hannff Kovelitz, 1987; children: Dorothy Aoife, Asher Malachi. *Education:* Received B.A. from Queen's University, Belfast, Northern Ireland.

ADDRESSES: Office—c/o Faber & Faber, 3 Queen Sq., London WC1N 3AU, England; Princeton University, Creative Writing Program, Princeton, NJ 08544.

CAREER: Poet. British Broadcasting Corporation (BBC Radio), Belfast, Northern Ireland, radio producer, 1973-78; senior producer, 1978-85; television producer, 1985-86; Columbia University, School of Arts, part-time teacher, 1987-88; Princeton University, Princeton, NJ, lecturer in writing, 1987—, part-time teacher, 1987-88, director of creative writing program, 1993—, professor, 1995—; University of California, Berkeley, Roberta Holloway Lecturer, 1989; University of Massachusetts, visiting professor, 1989-90; University of Oxford, Professor of Poetry, 1999—.

MEMBER: Royal Society of Literature (fellow), Aosdana; American Academy of Arts and Sciences.

AWARDS, HONORS: Eric Gregory Award, Society of Authors, 1972; Geoffrey Faber Memorial Prize, 1982, for *Why Brownlee Left;* fellowship, John Simon Guggenheim Memorial, 1990; T. S. Eliot Prize, 1994; Academy Awards in Literature, American Academy of Arts and Letters, 1996.

WRITINGS:

POETRY, EXCEPT AS INDICATED

Knowing My Place, Ulsterman, 1971.

New Weather, Faber (London), 1973.

Spirit of Dawn, Ulsterman, 1975.

Mules (also see below), Faber, 1977.

Names and Addresses, Ulsterman, 1978.

Why Brownlee Left (includes "Immram"), Faber, 1980, Wake Forest University Press (Winston-Salem, NC), 1981.

Immram, illustrations by Robert Ballagh, Gallery Press (Dublin), 1980.
Out of Siberia, illustrations by Timothy Engelland, Deerfield Press (Deerfield, MA), 1982.
Quoof, University of North Carolina Press (Chapel Hill), 1983.
The Wishbone, Gallery, 1984.
Mules, and Early Poems, Wake Forest University Press, 1985.
Selected Poems: 1968-86, Faber, 1986, Ecco Press (New York City), 1987.
Meeting the British, Faber, 1987.
Madoc: A Mystery, Farrar, Straus (New York City), 1991.
The Annals of Chile, Farrar, Straus, 1995.
Kerry Slides, photographs by Bill Doyle, Gallery Press,(Loughcrew, Ireland), 1996.
(With Daron Hagen) *The Waking Father: A Song Cycle in Twelve Movements* (printed music), lyrics by Muldoon, music by Hagen, Roger Dean Publishing (Dayton, OH), 1996.
New Selected Poems: 1968-94, Faber (London), 1996.
Hay, Farrar, Straus, 1998.
Bandanna (libretto), Faber, 1999.

EDITOR

The Scrake of Dawn: Poems by Young People from Northern Ireland, Blackstaff (Belfast), 1979.
The Faber Book of Contemporary Irish Poetry, Faber, 1986.
The Essential Byron, Ecco Press, 1988.
Czeslaw Milosz and Paul Muldoon Reading Their Poems (sound recording), Archive of Recorded Poetry and Literature, 1991.
(Translator) Nuala Ni Dhomhnaill, *The Astrakhan Cloak,* Gallery Press, 1992, Wake Forest University Press, 1993.
The Faber Book of Beasts, Faber, 1997.
(Translator with Richard Martin) Aristophanes, *The Birds,* Gallery Press, 1999.

SIDELIGHTS: Paul Muldoon is one of Ireland's leading contemporary poets. His short lyrics, modified sonnets and ballads, and dramatic monologues touch on themes of love, maturation, and self-discovery, as well as Irish culture and history. Terse and highly original, Muldoon's poetry is noted for its multiplicity of meaning. In a *Stand* review, Rodney Pybus asserted that the poet's works reveal a "quirky, off-beat talent for sudden revelatory flights from mundane consequences. . . . He found very early a distinctively wry and deceptively simple-sophisticated lyric voice.

Muldoon is the youngest member of a group of Northern Irish poets—including Seamus Heaney, Michael Longley, and Derek Mahon—which gained prominence in the 1960s and 1970s. As a student at Queen's University, Muldoon studied under Heaney, and refined his own analytical and critical skills in weekly discussions with other poets. In 1971, at the age of nineteen, Muldoon had completed his first short collection, *Knowing My Place.* Two years later, he published *New Weather,* his first widely reviewed volume of poetry. The book secured Muldoon's place among Ireland's finest writers and helped establish his reputation as an innovative new voice in English-language poetry.

The poems in *New Weather* generally illuminate the complexities of seemingly ordinary things or events. Several critics have noted that the collection's multilayered, heavily imagistic, and metaphoric verse explores psychological development with apparent simplicity and eloquence while offering keen insights into the subjective nature of perception. Calling the collection "the result of continuous age and aging," Roger Conover suggested in a review for *Eire-Ireland,* "Muldoon's is a poetry which sees *into* things, and speaks of the world in terms of its own internal designs and patterns." A *Times Literary Supplement* reviewer, however, felt that the poems in Muldoon's "highly promising collection are flawed by a vagueness of focus that dissipates the strength of original ideas."

Muldoon followed *New Weather* with the 1977 collection *Mules,* which opens with a poem reflecting Northern Ireland's civil strife. Recurring themes of political and social relevance inform the other pastorals and ballads in *Mules.* "The Narrow Road to the North," for instance, depicts the debilitating effects of war on a Japanese soldier who emerges from hiding, unaware that World War II has ended. The poem subtly parallels the soldier's deadened emotional state with the toll that the struggle in Ireland has taken on its citizens. As Peter Scupham noted in his *Times Literary Supplement* review, "Muldoon's taste for anecdote, invention, and parable shows strongly [in *Mules*]," and claimed that the collection is "a handsome promise of good poems to come." In *Preoccupations: Selected Prose, 1968-1978,* Heaney deemed *Mules* "a strange, rich second collection" and judged the poet "one of the very best."

By the time Muldoon's next volume of poetry, *Why Brownlee Left,* was published in 1980, the poet had attracted considerable attention for his technical acumen, dry verbal wit, and provocative use of language. Some critics considered *Why Brownlee Left* a more mature effort than Muldoon's earlier collections. According to

Alan Hollinghurst in *Encounter,* "the key to the book" lies in a seemingly straightforward and elemental poem titled "October 1950." Chronicling the poet's own conception, the poem reflects Muldoon's preoccupation with the search for self and acknowledges, noted Hollinghurst, that life "refute[s] any philosophical attempts to organize or direct it." Feeling that Muldoon's poetry in *Why Brownlee Left* was composed mainly of "blueprints, sketches, [and] fragments," and that Muldoon is not "a truly satisfying poet," *Anglo-Welsh Review*'s David Annwn nonetheless praised Muldoon for his "unnerving knack of capturing most elusive atmospheres, manipulating the inflexions of Anglo-Irish . . . and conveying a whole spectrum of humour."

Muldoon's 1983 collection, *Quoof,* takes its title from his family's name for a hot-water bottle. The imaginative poems in the volume offer varying perceptions of the world. "Gathering Mushrooms" opens the book with the narrator's drug-induced reminiscences of his childhood, his father, and the turmoil in Ireland. "The More a Man Has the More a Man Wants," the final poem and the volume's longest, is a narrative that follows the exploits of the mercenary-like figure Gallogly as he voyages through Northern Ireland. Writing in the *London Review of Books,* John Kerrigan asserted that the poetry in *Quoof* is "a bewildering display of narrative invention . . . written with that combination of visual clarity and verbal panache which has become the hallmark of Paul Muldoon." Muldoon, in an interview with Michael Donaghy in *Chicago Review,* commented on the violence in *Quoof:* "I don't think it's a very likeable or attractive book in its themes."

Meeting the British, Muldoon's 1987 collection, contains several poems of recollection as well as more unusual selections such as "7, Middagh Street," which, according to Terry Eagleton in the *Observer,* blends fantasy and history with "dramatic energy and calculated irony . . . to produce a major poem." A series of imaginary monologues by such prominent artistic and literary figures as W. H. Auden, Salvador Dali, Gypsy Rose Lee, Carson McCullers, and Louis MacNeice, "7, Middagh Street" contains provocative commentary on the importance of politics in Irish art. Comparing *Meeting the British* with *Quoof,* Mark Ford in the *London Review of Books* found that whereas "*Quoof* tended to push its metaphors, trance-like, to the point of no return, its mushroom hallucinations not deviation from but a visionary heightening of reality: the poems in *Meeting the British* seem more self-aware. . . . *Meeting the British* adds some wonderful new tricks to Muldoon's repertoire." Deeming *Meeting the British* Muldoon's "most ambitious collection," Mick Imlah, writing in the *Times Literary Supplement,* noted that the volume proves an innovative addition "to a difficult and delightful body of poetry." Responding to several critics' attempts to compare the poet's style to that of his contemporaries, Conover proclaimed that Muldoon's "poems are too individual to characterize very effectively in terms of anyone else's work. . . . [His] conception of the poem is unique."

Muldoon's next collection was the ambitious *Madoc: A Mystery,* summarized by Geoffrey Stokes in the *Village Voice* as "quite funny, very difficult, highly ambitious, more than a little unsettling, and . . . subtitled 'A Mystery.' Which it surely is." Named after the title of a Robert Southey poem concerning a Welsh prince who discovers America in the twelfth century, the narrative flow of *Madoc* revolves around "what might have happened if the Romantic poets Robert Southey and Samuel Taylor Coleridge had indeed come (as they planned in 1794) to America and created a 'pantisocracy' ('equal rule for all') on the banks of the Susquehanna River in Pennsylvania," commented Lucy McDiarmid in her *New York Times Book Review* piece on *Madoc.* Coleridge becomes entranced by peyote and Native American culture while Southey becomes vengeful and tyrannical after a loss of idealism. The question, in the words of Thomas M. Disch in *Poetry,* is whether or not *Madoc*'s "helter-skelter narrative pattern, with its excursions into such parallel lives as those of Thomas Moore, Lord Byron, Lewis and Clark, Aaron Burr, Thomas Jefferson, and George Catlin, add up either to a memorable drama or to a coherent vision of history?" Despite finding *Madoc* "readable for its entire length," Disch's answer remained: "I don't think so." Michael Hoffman in the *London Review of Books* concluded, however, that each "reading—and still more, every new bit of information—makes *Madoc* a cleverer and more imposing piece of work." Stokes countered Disch, and commented: "The question is whether it's worth stepping into *Madoc* even once; the answer is an unqualified yes."

"*The Annals of Chile* is easier of access and more emotionally direct than *Madoc,* while more allusive and arcane than [Muldoon's] earlier work," argued Richard Tillinghast in the *New York Times Book Review.* "Incantata," one of two central poems in *The Annals of Chile,* remembers Muldoon's lover Mary Farl Powers in a "beautiful and heartfelt elegy" in the words of *Times Literary Supplement* reviewer Lawrence Norfolk. "It is Muldoon's most transparent poem for some time, and also his most musical." "Yarrow," the second, "jazzily juxtaposes swashbuckling daydreams . . .

with real life's painful memories of a druggy girlfriend's breakdown and the death of [Muldoon's] mother," commented Michael Dirda in a *Washington Post Book World* review. Mark Ford, in a review of *Annals* in the *London Review of Books,* found the themes of "less scope for the kinds of all-synthesizing wit characteristic of Muldoon." William Pratt concluded in *World Literature Today* that for those readers "who enjoy having a leg pulled, Muldoon is your man; to those who expect something more substantial from poetry, Muldoon rhymes with buffoon." *Los Angeles Times Book Review*'s Katherine McNamara, however, found that in *Annals,* "every word, every reference, every allusion, carries meaning. Muldoon never flinches in his brilliant verbal workings." In his review of *The Annals of Chile* for *Poetry,* F. D. Reeve characterized Muldoon as "a juggler, a handspringing carny, a gandy dancer, a stand-up comic, and intellectual muckraker," and went on to state: "He bends language as easily as Geller, the psychic, bent spoons."

The 1996 *Kerry Slides,* in which Muldoon's poems are accompanied by the photographs of Bill Doyle, received significant praise from Patricia Monaghan of *Booklist* who dubbed it "an inspired collaboration." The title of the book refers both to the Irish dance of that name and to Doyle's photos of Kerry County in southwestern Ireland. "Muldoon's short poems," Monaghan remarked, "are only obliquely connected to Doyle's black-and-white photos," yet at the same time she felt that their "wild rhymes and witty wordplay encapsulate history, myth, language, and landscape." Monaghan found Doyle's photos to be "dreamlike despite their sharpness," and went on to note "his eye sees beyond the picturesque to the archetypal."

Muldoon's 1998 *Hay* is a diverse collection, covering subjects from the personal to the political and the universal, offering a range of forms and styles that includes sonnets, sestinas, haiku, and much more. William Logan of *New Criterion* observed: "Poems shift and ratchet, one time slipping into another, one place substituting for another, scenes turning themselves inside out, lines jolting and stuttering, mysteriously repeating according to some Masonic code, subject to sudden outcries of 'hey' or 'wheehee' or 'tra la.' " The dust jacket for the book describes Muldoon as a "prodigy" who has now become a "virtuoso." It is Muldoon's technical virtuosity that some reviewers of *Hay* fastened upon as a drawback in the work. Reviewing the book for *The New Republic* Adam Kirsch noted: "if virtuosity is all that a poet can display, if his poems demand attention simply because of their elaborateness and difficulty, then he has in some sense failed. . . . It is true that Muldoon sometimes writes directly, with plain emotion, even sentimentality. But those are not his most characteristic poems, nor his best. When he is at his most original, Muldoon is rather a kind of acrobat, piling up strange rhymes, references, and conceits in a way that is disorienting and exhilarating." According to Logan: "Muldoon is . . . in love (not wisely but too well) with language itself. . . . Too often the result is tedious foolery, the language run amok with Jabberwocky possibility (words, words, monotonously inbreeding), as if possibility were reason enough for the doing." Yet almost as if in spite of themselves, both Logan and Kirsch also offered praise for *Hay.* Logan concluded: "Everyone interested in contemporary poetry should read this book. . . . In our time of tired mirrors and more-than-tiresome confession, Muldoon is the rare poet who writes through the looking glass." In a similar vein, Kirsch remarked: "at a time when poetry has all but forgotten the possibilities of adventurous form, when the majority of poets are trivially self-expressive and the minority with higher ambitions pursue a formless complexity, Muldoon's ability to construct his poems is rare, and admirable."

Muldoon once told *CA:* "I started [writing poetry] when I was fifteen or sixteen. I'd written a few poems before then, as I suppose most people do. It seems to me that children of eight or nine—though I don't remember writing anything myself when I was that age—are in a way some of the best poets I've come across. Poems by children of that age are quite fresh, untrammeled by any ideas of what a poem might be or what a poem should look like. While I think it's perhaps a little romantic to suggest it, I believe it's something of that quality that people a little older are trying to get back to, something of that rinsed quality of the eye.

"I wrote lots of poems as a teenager, many of them heavily under the influence of T. S. Eliot, who seemed to me to be quite a marvelous person. I devoured Eliot and learned everything I could about him. He's a bad person, though, for anyone trying to write to learn from, since his voice is so much his own; I ended up doing parodies of Eliot. I read a lot of poetry, modern poetry as well as poetry by writers all the way through in English and indeed in Irish. And gradually I began to learn, particularly from writers who were round about, like Seamus Heaney, Michael Longley, Derek Mahon, and other Irish writers who were writing about things I knew about. I think it's quite important to have people round about who remind one that writing poetry is not an entirely weird occupation, that one isn't the only one trying to do it.

"As to choosing poetry rather than some other form of writing, in a way I chose poetry over the weekly essay. We had a teacher who used to assign an essay every week, and rather than an essay, I wrote a poem one week because it seemed to me a much easier, certainly a shorter, thing to do. In a way it was out of laziness that I felt I might try to write poems, and I continued to do it. I'd love to be able to write prose, and I've written the occasional little autobiographical piece for radio or whatever, but I find it takes me so long to write a sentence, or to write anything. I don't have a natural fluency in writing. The poems I do try to write are aimed to sound very off-the-cuff, very simple and natural, as if they were spoken, or as if they were composed in about the same time as it takes to speak them. But I spend a lot of time getting that effect; it doesn't come naturally.

"There is a school of thought that holds that the writer is dead, and really anyone can read whatever they like into this text, as they insist on calling it nowadays. I think one of the jobs of a writer is to contain and restrict the range of possible meanings and readings and connotations that a series of words on a page can have. There's an element of the manipulative about the process of writing. The writer is very truly a medium if things are ideal. The writer should be open to the language and allowing the language to do the work. I don't want to sound like somebody who's heavily into Zen, but I really do believe in all of that; I believe in inspiration in some way.

"On the other hand, there is this other part involved in the writing, the part that is marshaling and is looking on as an acute, intense reader. When I am writing, I'm in control of this uncontrollable thing. It's a combination of out of control and in control. What I'm interested in doing, usually, is writing poems with very clear, translucent surfaces, but if you look at them again, there are other things happening under the surface. And I am interested in poems that go against their own grain, that are involved in irony, that seem to be saying one thing but in fact couldn't possibly be saying that. I am interested in what's happening in those areas, and I do try to control that and hope that I have controlled it. But sometimes when I reread a poem much later (which I don't usually do), I wonder, What on earth was I thinking of there?"

BIOGRAPHICAL/CRITICAL SOURCES:

BOOKS

Kendall, Tim, *Paul Muldoon,* Dufour, 1996.

PERIODICALS

Anglo-Welsh Review, 1981, p. 74.
Booklist, January 1, 1997, Patricia Monaghan, review of *Kerry Slides,* p. 809.
Chicago Review, autumn, 1985, p. 76.
Concerning Poetry, Volume 14, number 2, 1981, p. 125.
Eire-Ireland, summer, 1975, p. 127; Volume 13, number 2, 1978; spring, 1984, p. 123; spring, 1989, p. 79.
Encounter, February-March, 1981; March, 1984.
Kenyon Review, summer, 1988, p. 127.
Listener, October 13, 1977.
London Magazine, October, 1977.
London Review of Books, February 16, 1984; December 10, 1987, p. 20; December 20, 1990, p. 18; August 19, 1993, p. 22; January 12, 1995, p. 19.
Los Angeles Times Book Review, November 11, 1994, p. 13.
New Criterion, December, 1998, William Logan, "Sins & Sensibility," p. 69.
New England Review and Bread Loaf Quarterly, winter, 1989, p. 179.
New Republic, November 30, 1998, Adam Kirsch, review of *Hay,* p. 56.
New Statesman, September 26, 1980.
New York Review of Books, May 30, 1991, p. 37.
New York Times Book Review, July 28, 1991, p. 14; December 11, 1994, p. 25.
Observer (London), May 3, 1987, p. 25.
Poetry, May, 1992, p. 94; November, 1994, p. 101; April, 1997, F. D. Reeve, review of *The Annals of Chile,* p. 37.
Shenandoah, summer, 1974.
Stand, Volume 22, number 3, 1981.
Times Literary Supplement, April 20, 1973, p. 442; July 1, 1977, p. 801; March 28, 1980; November 14, 1980, p. 1287; May 30, 1986; September 4, 1987; October 12, 1990, p. 1105; October 7, 1994, p. 32.
Village Voice, July 30, 1991, p. 68.
Voice Literary Supplement, March, 1984.
Washington Post Book World, January 31, 1988; January 1, 1995, p. 8.
World Literature Today, spring, 1995, p. 365.*

N-O

NAIPAUL, V(idiadhar) S(urajprasad) 1932-

PERSONAL: Born August 17, 1932, in Chaguanas, Trinidad; son of Seepersad (a journalist and writer) and Dropatie Capildeo Naipaul; married Patricia Ann Hale, 1955. *Education:* Attended Queen's Royal College in Trinidad, 1943-48; University College, Oxford, B.A., 1953.

ADDRESSES: *Agent*—c/o Aitken & Stone Ltd., 29 Fernshaw Rd., London SW10, England.

CAREER: Writer. Also worked as a freelance broadcaster for the British Broadcasting Corp. (BBC), 1954-56.

MEMBER: Society of Authors, Royal Society of Literature (fellow).

AWARDS, HONORS: John Llewellyn Rhys Memorial Prize, 1958, for *The Mystic Masseur;* grant from government of Trinidad for travel in Caribbean, 1960-61; Somerset Maugham Award, 1961, for *Miguel Street;* Phoenix Trust Award, 1963; Hawthornden Prize, 1964, for *Mr. Stone and the Knights Companion;* W. H. Smith Award, 1968, for *The Mimic Men;* Booker Prize, 1971, for *In a Free State;* D. Litt, St. Andrew's College, 1979, Columbia University, 1981, Cambridge University, 1983, London University, 1988, and Oxford University, 1992; Bennett Award from *Hudson Review,* 1980; T. S. Eliot Award for Creative Writing, Ingersoll Foundation, 1986; knighted, 1990.

WRITINGS:

The Mystic Masseur, Deutsch (London), 1957, Vanguard (New York City), 1959.
The Suffrage of Elvira, Deutsch (London), 1958.
Miguel Street, Deutsch, 1959, Vanguard, 1960.
A House for Mr. Biswas, Deutsch, 1961, McGraw (New York City), 1962.
The Middle Passage: Impressions of Five Societies—British, French and Dutch in the West Indies and South America (nonfiction), Deutsch, 1962, Macmillan (New York City), 1963.
Mr. Stone and the Knights Companion, Deutsch, 1963, Macmillan, 1964.
An Area of Darkness (nonfiction), Deutsch, 1964, Macmillan, 1965.
The Mimic Men, Macmillan, 1967.
A Flag on the Island (short story collection), Macmillan, 1967.
The Loss of El Dorado: A History (nonfiction), Deutsch, 1969, Knopf (New York City), 1970.
In a Free State, Knopf, 1971.
The Overcrowded Barracoon and Other Articles, Deutsch, 1972, Knopf, 1973.
Guerrillas, Knopf, 1975.
India: A Wounded Civilization (nonfiction), Knopf, 1977.
The Perfect Tenants and The Mourners, Cambridge University Press (Cambridge, England), 1977.
A Bend in the River, Knopf, 1979, introduction by Elizabeth Hardwick, Modern Library, 1997, large print edition, G. K. Hall (Thorndike, ME), 1999.
The Return of Eva Peron (nonfiction), Knopf, 1980.
A Congo Diary, Sylvester & Orphanos (Los Angeles, CA), 1980.
Among the Believers: An Islamic Journey, Knopf, 1981.
Finding the Center, Knopf, 1986.
The Enigma of Arrival, Knopf, 1987.
A Turn in the South, Knopf, 1989.
India: A Million Mutinies Now, Heinemann (London), 1990, Viking (New York City), 1991.

A Way in the World, Knopf, 1994.

Beyond Belief: Islamic Excursions among the Converted Peoples, Random House (New York City), 1998.

(Edited by Gillon Aitken) *Between Father and Son: Selected Correspondence of V. S. Naipaul and His Family, 1949-1953,* Knopf, 2000.

Reading and Writing: A Personal Account, New York Review of Books (New York City), 2000.

Contributor to *New York Review of Books, New Statesman,* and other periodicals. Contributor to *Island Voices: Stories from the West Indies,* edited by Andrew Salkey, Liveright, 1970. Fiction reviewer, *New Statesman,* 1958-61.

SIDELIGHTS: Born in Trinidad to the descendants of Hindu immigrants from northern India and educated at England's Oxford University, V. S. Naipaul is considered one of the world's most gifted novelists. As a *New York Times Book Review* critic writes: "For sheer abundance of talent there can hardly be a writer alive who surpasses V. S. Naipaul. Whatever we may want in a novelist is to be found in his books: an almost Conradian gift for tensing a story, a serious involvement with human issues, a supple English prose, a hard-edged wit, a personal vision of things. Best of all, he is a novelist unafraid of using his brains. . . . His novels are packed with thought, not as lumps of abstraction but as one fictional element among others, fluid in the stream of narrative. . . . [He is] the world's writer, a master of language and perception, our sardonic blessing."

The idea of Naipaul as "the world's writer" comes largely, as he has pointed out himself, from his rootlessness. Unhappy with the cultural and spiritual poverty of Trinidad, distanced from India, and unable to relate to and share in the heritage of each country's former imperial ruler (England), Naipaul describes himself as "content to be a colonial, without a past, without ancestors." As a result of this nonattachment to region and tradition, most of his work deals with people who, like himself, feel estranged from the societies they are ostensibly part of and who desperately seek ways to belong or "to be someone." The locales Naipaul chooses for his stories represent an extension of this same theme, for most take place in emerging Third World countries in the throes of creating new national identities from the remnants of native and colonial cultures.

Naipaul's early works explore the comic aspects of these themes. Essentially West Indian variations on the comedy of manners, these works present almost farcical accounts of an illiterate and divided society's shift from colonial to independent status, emphasizing the multiracial misunderstandings and rivalries and various ironies resulting from the sudden introduction of such democratic processes as free elections. In *The Mystic Masseur, The Suffrage of Elvira,* and *Miguel Street,* Naipaul exposes the follies and absurdities of Trinidadian society; his tone is detached yet sympathetic, as if he is looking back at a distant past of which he is no longer a part. The tragic aspects of the situation are not examined, nor is there any attempt to involve the reader in the plight of the characters. Michael Thorpe describes the prevailing tone of these early books as "that of the ironist who points up the comedy, futility and absurdity that fill the gap between aspiration and achievement, between the public image desired and the individual's inadequacies, to recognize which may be called the education of the narrator: 'I had grown up and looked critically at the people around me.' "

A House for Mr. Biswas marks an important turning point in Naipaul's work; his attention to psychological and social realism foreshadows the intensive character studies of his later works. In addition, *A House for Mr. Biswas* has a universality of theme that the earlier books lacked because of their emphasis on the particularities of Trinidadian society. As a consequence of these "improvements," many critics regard *A House for Mr. Biswas* as Naipaul's masterpiece. Robert D. Hamner wrote in 1973 that with "the appearance in 1961 of *A House for Mr. Biswas,* Naipaul may have published his best fiction. It is even possible that this book is the best novel yet to emerge from the Caribbean. It is a vital embodiment of authentic West Indian life, but more than that, it transcends national boundaries and evokes universal human experiences. Mr. Biswas' desire to own his own house is essentially a struggle to assert personal identity and to attain security—thoroughly human needs."

The *New York Herald Tribune Books* reviewer notes that "Naipaul has a wry wit and an engaging sense of humor, as well as a delicate understanding of sadness and futility and a profound but unobtrusive sense of the tragi-comedy of ordinary living. . . . His style is precise and assured. In short, he gives every indication of being an important addition to the international literary scene. [*A House for Mr. Biswas*] is funny, it is compassionate. It has more than 500 pages and not one of them is superfluous." Paul Theroux writing in the *New York Times Book Review* admits that "it is hard for the reviewer of a wonderful author to keep the obituarist's assured hyperbole in check, but let me say that if the silting-up of the Thames coincided with a freak monsoon, causing massive flooding in all parts of South London, the first book I would rescue from my library would be *A House for Mr. Biswas.*"

Michael Thorpe agrees that the novel is "a work of rare distinction . . . [it is] a 'novelist's novel,' a model work. . . . The book's popularity must be largely due to its universality of subject and theme, the struggle of one ordinary man to climb—or cling on to—the ladder of life; the ordinariness lies in his ambitions for home, security, status, his desire to live through his son, yet he remains an individual. . . . At first sight Mr. Biswas seems an abrupt departure from Naipaul's previous fiction: in its concentration upon the life history of a single protagonist it goes far deeper than *The Mystic Masseur* and the mood is predominantly 'serious,' the still pervasive comedy being subordinated to that mood. Yet on further consideration we can see *Mr. Biswas* as the natural and consummate development of themes that ran through the first three books: the perplexing relation of the individual to society, his struggle to impress himself upon it through achievement—or defy its pressures with a transforming fantasy that puts a gloss upon life and extracts order from the rude chaos of everyday existence. . . . We should not doubt that the narrative is to be heroic, the quest for the house—however flawed in its realization—a victory over the chaos and anonymity into which the hero was born. The novel is such a man's celebration, his witness, the answer to the dismal refrain, 'There was nothing to speak of him.' " In short, Thorpe concludes, "for West Indian literature *A House for Mr. Biswas* forged [the] connection [between literature and life] with unbreakable strength and set up a model for emulation which no other 'Third World' literature in English has yet equaled."

After the success of *A House for Mr. Biswas,* Naipaul increasingly sought broader geographic and social contexts in which to explore his themes. At the same time, his earlier light-hearted tone gradually faded as he examined the more tragic consequences of alienation and rootlessness through the eyes of various "universal wanderers." As Thomas Lask reports in the *New York Times:* "V. S. Naipaul's writings about his native Trinidad have often enough been touched with tolerant amusement. His is an attitude that is affectionate without being overly kind. . . . On his own, Mr. Naipaul [has] made no secret of his alienation from his native island. . . . [*In a Free State*] takes the story one step further. How does the expatriate fare after he leaves the island?. . . [The author] lifts the argument above and beyond material success and social position. These new stories focus on the failure of heart, on the animal-like cruelty man exhibits to other men and on the avarice that . . . is the root of all evil. . . . What the author is saying is that neither customs nor color nor culture seems able to quiet that impulse to destruction, that murderous wantonness that is so much part of our make-up. . . . Mr. Naipaul's style in these stories seems leaner than in the past and much more somber. There is virtually none of the earlier playfulness. He appears to have settled for precision over abundance. Each detail and each incident is made to carry its weight in the narrative. The effect is not small-scaled, for in the title story he has created an entire country. He has not tidied up every loose strand. . . . But there is nothing unfinished in these polished novellas."

Paul Theroux calls *In a Free State* "Naipaul's most ambitious work, a story-sequence brilliant in conception, masterly in execution, and terrifying in effect—the chronicles of a half-a-dozen self-exiled people who have become lost souls. Having abandoned their own countries (countries they were scarcely aware of belonging to), they have found themselves in strange places, without friends, with few loyalties, and with the feeling that they are trespassing. Worse, their lives have been totally altered; for them there is no going back; they have fled, each to his separate limbo, and their existence is like that of souls in a classical underworld. . . . The subject of displacement is one few writers have touched upon. Camus has written of it. But Naipaul is much superior to Camus, and his achievement—a steady advance through eleven volumes—is as disturbing as it is original. *In a Free State* is a masterpiece in the fiction of rootlessness."

Alfred Kazin writing in the *New York Review of Books* claims that "Naipaul writes about the many psychic realities of exile in our contemporary world with far more bite and dramatic havoc than Joyce. . . . No one else around today, not even Nabokov, seems able to employ prose fiction so deeply as the very choice of exile. . . . What makes Naipaul hurt so much more than other novelists of contemporary exodus is his major image—the tenuousness of man's hold on the earth. The doubly unsettling effect he creates—for the prose is British—chatty, proper yet bitter—also comes from the many characters in a book like [*In a Free State*] who don't 'belong' in the countries they are touring or working in, who wouldn't 'belong' any longer in the countries they come from, and from the endless moving about of contemporary life have acquired a feeling of their own unreality in the 'free state' of endlessly moving about. . . . Naipaul has never encompassed so much, and with such brilliant economy, with such a patient though lighthanded ominousness of manner, as in [*In a Free State*]. The volume of detail is extraordinary. . . . I suppose one criticism of Naipaul might well be that he covers too much ground, has too many representative types, and that he has an obvious desolation about homelessness, migration, the final placelessness of those who have seen too much, which he tends to turn into a mysterious accusation. Though he is a marvelous technician, there is something finally modest, personal, openly committed about his fiction, a frankness of personal reference, that removes him from the godlike impersonality of the novelist. . . . Naipaul belongs to a different generation, to a more openly tragic outlook for humanity itself. He does not want to play God, even in a novel."

A *New Statesman* critic, on the other hand, suggests that Naipaul's outlook may not be completely bleak. The critic writes: "Each piece [in *In a Free State*] is a tour de force. . . . I don't know any writer since Conrad who's exposed the otherness of Africa so starkly, and Naipaul leaves his readers freer by his massacre of obstinate illusions. But his vision excludes elements of growth and hope which are, palpably, there. . . . Naipaulia remains a kingdom of cryptic anti-climax. I wonder, though, if the 'cryptic' final section is nudging away from pessimism."

With the publication of *Guerrillas,* however, the novel that established Naipaul's reputation in the United States, most reviewers noted that his outlook is indeed grim. Notes Theroux: "*Guerrillas* is a violent book in which little violence is explicit. . . . It is a novel, not of revolt, but of the play-acting that is frequently called revolt, that queer situation of scabrous glamour which Naipaul sees as a throw-back to the days of slavery. . . . *Guerrillas* is one of Naipaul's most complex books; it is certainly his most suspenseful, a series of shocks, like a shroud slowly unwound from a bloody corpse, showing the damaged—and familiar—face last. . . . This is a novel without a villain, and there is not a character for whom the reader does not at some point feel deep sympathy and keen understanding, no matter how villainous or futile he may seem. *Guerrillas* is a brilliant novel in every way, and it shimmers with artistic certainty. It is scarifying in the opposite way from a nightmare. One can shrug at fantasy, but *Guerrillas*—in a phrase Naipaul himself once used—is, like the finest novels, 'indistinguishable from truth.' "

Paul Gray of *Time* believes that *Guerrillas* "proves [Naipaul] the laureate of the West Indies. . . . [He] is a native expatriate with a fine distaste for patriotic rhetoric. . . . [The novel] is thus conspicuously short of heroes. . . . The native politicians are corrupt, the foreign businessmen avaricious, and the people either lethargic or criminal. When an uprising does flare, it is nasty and inept. Perhaps no one but Naipaul has the inside and outside knowledge to have turned such a dispirited tale into so gripping a book. His island is built entirely of vivid descriptions and offhand dialogue. At the end, it has assumed a political and economic history, a geography and a population of doomed, selfish souls. . . . *Guerrillas* is not a polemic (polemicists will be annoyed) but a Conradian vision of fallibility and frailty. With economy and compassion, Naipaul draws the heart of darkness from a sun-struck land."

Noting that Naipaul takes a "hackneyed" theme ("incipient Black Power") and manages to produce "a more significant treatment of it than most of his contemporaries with similar concerns," Charles R. Larson of the *Nation* writes that *Guerrillas* "builds so slowly and so skillfully that until the final scene bursts upon us, we are hardly aware of the necessary outcome of the events; it is only in retrospect that we see that the desultory action has in fact been charged with fate. . . . No one writes better about politics in the West Indies than V. S. Naipaul. Nor is there anyone who writes more profoundly about exiles, would-be revolutionaries and their assorted camp followers. Written in a deliberately flat style, *Guerrillas* is a deeply pessimistic novel, telling us that we have seen about as much political change in the West Indian island republics as we are likely to see."

In *A Bend in the River,* Naipaul returns to Africa as a locale (the scene of *In a Free State*) and confirms his basic pessimism. John Leonard comments in the *New York Times:* "This is not an exotic Africa [in *A Bend in the River*]. . . . [The author] despises nostalgia for the colonial past, while at the same time heartlessly parodying . . . the African future. . . . *A Bend in the River* is a brilliant and depressing novel. It is no secret by now, certainly not since *Guerrillas* . . . that V. S. Naipaul is one of the handful of living writers of whom the English language can be proud, if, still, profoundly uneasy. There is no consolation from him, any more than there is sentiment. His wit has grown hard and fierce; he isn't seeking to amuse, but to scourge."

John Updike, writing in the *New Yorker,* asserts that *A Bend in the River* "proves once more that Naipaul is incomparably well situated and equipped to bring us news of one of the contemporary world's great subjects—the mingling of its peoples. *A Bend in the River* struck me as an advance—broader, warmer, less jaded and kinky—over the much-praised *Guerrillas,* though not quite as vivid and revelatory as the fiction of *In a Free State. A Bend in the River* is carved from the same territory [as *In a Free State*]—an Africa of withering colonial vestiges, terrifyingly murky politics, defeated pretensions, omnivorous rot, and the implacable undermining of all that would sustain reason and safety. . . . Rage . . . is perhaps the deepest and darkest fact Naipaul has to report about the Third World, and in this novel his understanding of it goes beyond that shown in *Guerrillas*. . . . In *A Bend in the River,* the alien observer—white bureaucrat or Asian trader—is drawn closer into the rationale of the riots and wars that seethe in the slums or the bush beyond his enclave. The novel might be faulted for savoring a bit of the visiting journalist's worked-up notes: its episodes do not hang together with full organic snugness; there are a few too many clever geopolitical conversations and scenically detailed car rides. . . . [But] the author's embrace of his tangled and tragic African scene seems relatively hearty as well as immensely knowledgeable. Always a master of fictional landscape, Naipaul here shows, in his variety of human examples and in his search for underlying social causes, a Tolstoyan spirit, generous if not genial."

Walter Clemons of *Newsweek* calls *A Bend in the River* "a hurtful, claustrophobic novel, very hard on the nerves, played out under a vast African sky in an open space that is made to feel stifling. . . . Naipaul's is a political novel of a subtle and unusual kind. . . . [It] is about tremors of expectation, shifts in personal loyalty, manners in dire emergency. . . . As an evocation of place, [the novel] succeeds brilliantly. . . . *A Bend in the River* is by no means a perfected work. . . . But this imperfect, enormously disturbing book confirms Naipaul's position as one of the best writers now at work." And Irving Howe writes in the *New York Times Book Review:* "On the surface, *A Bend in the River* emerges mostly as a web of caustic observation, less exciting than its predecessor, *Guerrillas;* but it is a much better and deeper novel, for Naipaul has mastered the gift of creating an aura of psychic and moral tension even as, seemingly, very little happens. . . . [But in the end,] Naipaul offers no intimations of hope or signals of perspective. It may be that the reality he grapples with allows him nothing but grimness of voice. . . . A novelist has to be faithful to what he sees, and few see as well as Naipaul; yet one may wonder whether, in some final reckoning, a serious writer can simply allow the wretchedness of his depicted scene to become the limit of his vision. . . . Naipaul seems right now to be a writer beleaguered by his own truths, unable to get past them. That is surely an honorable difficulty, far better than indulging in sentimental or ideological uplift; but it exacts a price. . . . Perhaps we ought simply to be content that, in his austere and brilliant way, he holds fast to the bitterness before his eyes."

Naipaul chose a different setting for his novel *The Enigma of Arrival.* John Thieme explains in the *Dictionary of Literary Biography* that in the years between the publication of *A Bend in the River* and *The Enigma of Arrival,* the author "suffered from a serious illness and was deeply moved by the deaths of his younger sister and his brother, Shiva." *The Enigma of Arrival,* Thieme continues, reflects his somber personal experience and "is pervaded by a sense of personal loss and fragility." The novel examines the impact of imperialism on a native English estate, slowly decaying along with its reclusive landlord, who is suffering from a degenerative disease. "Characteristically for Naipaul," Thieme declares, "the narrator identifies with his landlord's sense of inertia, which is symbolized by his allowing ivy to proliferate and gradually strangle the trees on his grounds. The colonial man has found a haven in a landscape that seems 'benign' to him, but the manor is a semiruin, without the traditional appendages of farms and lands, and the remains of the older management that it represents crumble during the course of the narrative." The decay of the manor and its owner causes the novel's autobiographical narrator to ponder the inevitability of his own death. "The novel is full of intimations of mortality," Thieme concludes, "and ultimately it is as much a generalized lament for human transience and an expression of the writer's all-pervasive sense of vulnerability as an elegy for any particular person or community."

With *A Turn in the South* and *India: A Million Mutinies Now,* Naipaul turned to nonfiction. *A Turn in the South* tells of a journey through the southern United States, ostensibly looking for similarities between Naipaul's own Trinidadian culture and that of the American South. "Consequently 'the race issue' is high on his agenda at the outset," Thieme explains, "but it is increasingly less so as the work proceeds." Instead, Naipaul finds himself drawn deeper and deeper into a description of the culture of the modern American south, including country western music, strict, conservative Christianity, and the enduring fascination with Elvis Presley. *India: A Million Mutinies Now* represents Naipaul's third consideration of his ancestral homeland. Unlike the first two times, in which Naipaul expressed pessimism about India's ability to overcome centuries of religious and ethnic strife, in *India: A Million Mutinies Now* the author "takes heart in what he sees," declares Thomas D'Evelyn in the *Christian Science Monitor.* "As the details accumulate, the reader becomes more deeply involved in a growing appreciation for a life lived under extreme circumstances. Reading Naipaul," D'Evelyn concludes, "one becomes as optimistic about mankind as the author is about India." "His cautious optimism represents the primary value of the book," states Douglas J. Macdonald in *America.* "Pessimism can too easily lead to inertia and despair. . . . Naipaul's message is that despite the problems, despite the obstacles, the Indians, and by extension the rest of us, must continue to try." "Whether or not they know it," asserts *New York Review of Books* contributor Ian Buruma, "the millions of mutineers, wrestling with their fates, are all on the road forever. That is the truth of Naipaul's excellent book."

A Way in the World mixes elements of Naipaul's fiction and nonfiction, merging his Indian and West Indian heritage with the English history and culture he assumed when he immigrated to England at the age of eighteen. "His project is simultaneously to construct his own literary inheritance and the legacy he will leave to the world," explains Philip Gourevitch in *Commentary.* "The book . . . combines memoir, historical scholarship, and imaginative writing in a series of nine independent but thematically interlocking narratives. These narratives accumulate to form a dramatic portrait gallery of people—historical and fictionalized—whose lives have been formed and transformed by their encounters with Trinidad. And through the echo chamber of their stories there emerges a portrait of the artist, Naipaul himself, at the apex of his literary consciousness." "Now, near the end of his days," declares Caryl Phillips in the *New Republic,* "Naipaul is clearly . . . deliberating over the question of whether he ever left home in the first place, for whatever else it is *A Way in the World* is a beautiful lament to the Trinidad he has so often denigrated."

Naipaul labels each of these early narratives "An Unwritten Story." He includes under that title tales about the sixteenth century sea dog and explorer Sir Walter Raleigh traveling down a branch of the Orinoco River in Guyana in search of gold (and not finding it), and a nineteenth century South American revolutionary named Francisco Miranda plotting a Venezuelan revolution that never materializes. However, he also traces the careers of other notable characters—the Trinidadian Marxist revolutionary Naipaul calls Lebrun, for instance, who served as advisor to several independence movements, but was discarded as irrelevant after the regimes were established. "Once in power," declares *Los Angeles Times Book Review* contributor Richard Eder, "[the nationalists] had no use for him; his ideology was good for building up their strength but they had no intention of actually setting up a Marxist regime." Instead, Lebrun found himself exiled to the fringes of society, spending his life in exile, speaking to leftist groups in Great Britain and the United States.

"If there is one thing that unifies the chapters in [*A Way in the World*]," declares Amit Chaudhuri in the *Spectator,* "it is its attempt to explore and define the nature of the colonial's memory." Chaudhuri contrasts Naipaul's fiction in this volume with the work of the British novelist Joseph Conrad, whose work often looked darkly at the spreading colonialism of Great Britain at the end of the nineteenth and the beginning of the twentieth centuries. The reviewer suggests that Naipaul retraces the colonialism that Conrad depicted in his work and shows in *A Way in the World* how British imperialism created not just colonies but colonials—men and women with unique sensibilities and memories. "The river, in these 'stories,' no longer remains simply a Conradian image of Western exploration and territorial ambition," Chaudhuri concludes, "but becomes an emblem of the colonial memory attempting to return to its source."

With his 1998 *Beyond Belief: Islamic Excursions among the Converted Peoples,* Naipaul returned to nonfiction with a sequel to his 1981 *Among the Believers.* Discussing the earlier book, Naipaul told Jeffrey Myers of *American Scholar* that it "is about people caught at a cultural hinge moment: a whole civilization is on the turn. . . . It seeks to make that change clear, and to make a story of it." The later book, like the earlier one, deals with Islamic countries that are non-Arabic: Indonesisa, Iran, Pakistan, and Malaysia. Both books relate stories from individuals Naipaul encountered while traveling extensively through these countries. Comparing the two books, a *Booklist* reviewer observes that in *Beyond Belief* "Naipaul is more dispassionate, letting the people he meets take center stage as they express their struggles with family, religion, and nation." Meyers also observes this dispassionate quality and goes on to state: "The author of *Guerillas* and *A Bend in the River* has done what I thought impossible: written a book as boring as its bland gray jacket." Meyers also finds Naipaul's central thesis in the book that "everyone not an Arab who is a Muslim is a convert" to be "radically flawed." Edward Said of the *Progressive* agrees strongly on that count, observing: "This ridiculous argument would suggest by extension that only a native of Rome can be a good Roman Catholic. . . . In effect, the 400-page *Beyond Belief* is based on nothing more than this rather idiotic and insulting theory. . . . The greater pity is that Naipaul's latest book will be considered a major interpretation of a great religion, and more Muslims will suffer and be insulted."

In support of his thesis, Naipaul points out how Islam came late to these nations and remains in conflict with older native traditions. He also shows how the revival of Islamic fundamentalism in recent years has had a negative impact on these "converted" countries. Yet most critical response to the book remains unconvinced. In a reaction slightly more tempered than Meyers or Said, Jane I. Smith of *Christian Century* remarks: "Naipaul's picture of Islam among the converted peoples is not necessarily inaccurate; it is simply incomplete. And his presupposition that Muslims in the countries he visits have sacrificed their native traditions for a religion in which they can never fully share is a partial truth at best. The whole picture is both broader and considerably more hopeful than this artful but melancholy presentation might have us believe." While also questioning Naipaul's thesis and his generally negative views of Islam, L. Carl Brown of *Foreign Affairs* takes a different slant on *Beyond Belief:* "In-depth interviews with a handful of the near-great and the obscure from each country produce brilliant writing and somber stories. . . . *Beyond Belief* is rewarding. His [Naipaul's] subjects are memorable."

Between Father and Son: Selected Correspondence of V. S. Naipaul and His Family, 1949-1953, presents letters from a young Naipaul to his father, Seepersad, and other members of his family during the time when Naipaul was studying in England on a scholarship. During the course of the correspondence, Naipaul's father suffers a heart attack, loses his job at a local newspaper, and dies at the age of forty-seven. Reviewing the compilation for *Publishers Weekly,* a critic notes: "More memorable than the ambitious son, who is often consumed by anxiety, is the pragmatic father, who assure Vido that he will be 'a great writer' and advises him to 'be aware of undue dissipation.' but not to be 'a puritan'."

Naipaul's works have established his status as one of the English language's most distinguished and perceptive contemporary writers. In his 1976 study of Naipaul, Michael Thorpe offers this overview of the novelist's accomplishments: "While Naipaul is by no means alone in coming from a makeshift colonial society and using the 'metropolitan' language with a native surety, these origins have helped him more than any of his contemporaries from the Commonwealth to develop an inclusive view of many facets of the larger world, a view focused by his intense sense of displacement from society, race or creed. . . . He has gone beyond local conflicts, isolated instances of the colonial experience, to attempt something approaching a world view. . . . His insights and his manner of conveying them carry a persuasive truth."

As a result, continues Thorpe, "Naipaul has spoken from and to more points within that world [of imperial or social oppression] than any English writer—but his is not a comforting or hopeful voice. . . . Asked if he were an optimist [Naipaul] replied: 'I'm not sure. I think I do look for the seeds of regeneration in a situation; I long to find what is good and hopeful and really do hope that by the most brutal sort of analysis one is possibly opening up the situation to some sort of action; an action which is not based on self-deception.'. . . [But] he supplies none of the props even realists let us lean upon in the end: there are no consolations—no religious belief, no humanistic faith in man's future, not even the personal supports of friendship or love. . . . [Thus] Naipaul's is one of the bleakest visions any imaginative observer alive has given us. . . . [He] refuses to leap to positive attitudes he cannot justify. Naipaul would be the last to claim for his work that it represents a final or adequate vision; it is the record of one man's impressions of the world and it does not pretend to be the whole truth about it. . . . Yet Naipaul insists that he is hopeful: as one who has not flinched from harsh reality, he has earned the right to our reciprocal hope that he may yet find a way beyond despair."

BIOGRAPHICAL/CRITICAL SOURCES:

BOOKS

Contemporary Literary Criticism, Gale (Detroit), Volume 4, 1975, Volume 7, 1977, Volume 9, 1978, Volume 13, 1980, Volume 18, 1981, Volume 37, 1986.

Dictionary of Literary Biography, Volume 125:*Twentieth-Century Caribbean and Black African Writers, Second Series,* Gale, 1993.

Dictionary of Literary Biography Yearbook: 1985, Gale, 1986.

Dissanayake, Wimal, *Self and Colonial Desire: Travel Writings of V. S. Naipaul,* Peter Lang (New York City), 1993.

Gorra, Michael Edward, *After Empire: Scott, Naipaul, Rushdie,* University of Chicago Press, 1997.

Jussawalla, Feroza, editor, *Conversations with V. S. Naipaul,* University Press of Mississippi, 1997.

Hamner, Robert D., *V. S. Naipaul,* Twayne, 1973.

Kamra, Shashi, *The Novels of V. S. Naipaul: A Study in Theme and Form,* Prestige Books/Indian Society for Commonwealth Studies, 1990.

Khan, Md. Akhtar Jamal, *V. S. Naipaul: A Critical Study,* Creative Books, 1998.

King, Bruce, *V. S. Naipaul,* St. Martin's (New York City), 1993.

Nixon, Rob, *London Calling: V. S. Naipaul, Postcolonial Mandarin,* Oxford University Press, 1992.

Theroux, Paul, *Sir Vidia's Shadow: A Friendship across Five Continents,* Houghton Mifflin, 1998.

Thorpe, Michael, *V. S. Naipaul,* Longmans, 1976.

Weiss, Timothy, *On the Margins: The Art of Exile in V. S. Naipaul,* University of Massachusetts Press (Amherst), 1992.

PERIODICALS

America, June 15, 1991, pp. 656-57.

Americas (English edition), March-April, 1998, Sandra Chouthi, "House of Worldly Treasures," p. 4.

American Scholar, winter, 1999, Jeffrey Meyers, review of *Beyond Belief,* p. 150.

Atlantic, May, 1970; January, 1976; July, 1977; June, 1979.

Best Sellers, April 15, 1968.

Booklist, January 1, 1999, review of *Beyond Belief,* p. 777.

Books Abroad, winter, 1968; winter, 1969.

Books and Bookmen, October, 1967.

Boston Globe, March 15, 1987; January 22, 1989; December 23, 1990.

Chicago Sunday Tribune, July 12, 1959.

Choice, June, 1973.

Christian Century, September 9, 1998, Jane I. Smith, review of *Beyond Belief,* p. 835.

Christian Science Monitor, July 19, 1962; March 29, 1968; May 28, 1970; February 28, 1991, p. 11.

Commentary, August, 1994, pp. 27-31.

Commonweal, September 9, 1994, pp. 28-29.

Contemporary Literature, winter, 1968.

Economist, July 16, 1977.

Economist (US), September 12, 1998, review of *Beyond Belief,* p. S7.

Forbes, February 23, 1998, Richard C. Morais, "Tribal Tribulations," p. 149.

Foreign Affairs, September-October, 1998, L. Carl Brown, review of *Beyond Belief,* p. 162.

Illustrated London News, May 20, 1967.

Kenyon Review, November, 1967.

Library Journal, May 15, 1998, James F. DeRoche, review of *Beyond Belief,* p. 91.

Listener, May 25, 1967; September 28, 1967; May 23, 1968.

London Magazine, May, 1967.

Los Angeles Times, May 9, 1980; March 15, 1989.

Los Angeles Times Book Review, June 24, 1979; May 22, 1994, pp. 3, 11.

Nation, October 9, 1967; October 5, 1970; December 13, 1975; July 2, 1977; June 30, 1979.

National Review, October 6, 1970; August 29, 1994, pp. 61-62.

New Leader, May 4, 1998, Roger Draper, review of *Beyond Belief,* p. 13.

New Republic, July 9, 1977; June 9, 1979; June 10, 1991, pp. 30-34; June 13, 1994, pp. 40-45; July 13, 1998, Fouad Ajami, review of *Beyond Belief,* p. 27.

New Statesman, May 5, 1967; September 15, 1967; November 7, 1969; October 8, 1971; June 17, 1977.

Newsweek, December 1, 1975; June 6, 1977; May 21, 1979; June 13, 1994, p. 55.

New Yorker, August 4, 1962; August 8, 1970; June 6, 1977; May 21, 1979.

New York Herald Tribune Books, June 24, 1962.

New York Review of Books, October 26, 1967; April 11, 1968; December 30, 1971; May 31, 1979; February 14, 1991, pp. 3-5.

New York Times, December 16, 1967; December 25, 1971; August 17, 1977; May 14, 1979; March 13, 1980; May 17, 1994.

New York Times Book Review, October 15, 1967; April 7, 1968; May 24, 1970; October 17, 1971; November 16, 1975; December 28, 1975; May 1, 1977; June 12, 1977; May 13, 1979; May 22, 1994, p. 1, 42-43.

Observer (London), April 30, 1967; September 10, 1967; October 26, 1969.

Progressive, November, 1998, Edward W. Said, review of *Beyond Belief,* p. 40.

Publishers Weekly, May 25, 1998, review of *Beyond Belief,* p. 82; November 29, 1999, review of *Between Father and Son,* p. 59.

Punch, May 10, 1967.

Saturday Review, July 2, 1960; October 23, 1971; November 15, 1975.

Spectator, September 22, 1967; November 8, 1969; May 14, 1994, p. 36.

Time, May 25, 1970; December 1, 1975; June 20, 1977; May 21, 1979; May 30, 1994, p. 64.

Time International, August 3, 1998, "Journey to Islam," p. 39.

Times Literary Supplement, May 31, 1963; April 27, 1967; September 14, 1967; December 25, 1969; July 30, 1971; November 17, 1972.

Transition, December, 1971.

Tribune Books (Chicago), May 13, 1979; April 20, 1980.

U.S. News & World Report, August 10, 1998, Jonah Blank, "Feuding Literary Titans," p. 39.

Washington Post Book World, April 19, 1970; December 5, 1971; November 28, 1976; June 19, 1977; July 1, 1979; May 15, 1994, pp. 1, 14.

World Press Review, July, 1998, L. K. Sharma, "Faith and Neurosis," p. 41.*

* * *

NANCE, John J. 1946-

PERSONAL: Born July 5, 1946, in Dallas, TX; son of Joseph Turner (an attorney) and Margrette Z. (a poet; maiden name, Grubbs) Nance; married Benita Priest (a school development specialist), July 26, 1968; children: Dawn Michelle, Bridgitte Cathleen, Christopher Sean. *Education:* Southern Methodist University, B.A., 1968, J.D., 1969; U.S. Air Force Undergraduate Pilot Training, distinguished graduate, 1971.

ADDRESSES: Home—4512 87th Ave. W., Tacoma, WA 98466. *Office*—EMEX Corp., P. O. Box 5476, Kent, WA 98064. *Agent*—Wieser & Wieser, 118 East 25th St., New York, NY 10010.

CAREER: Park Cities North Dallas News, writer, columnist, and aviation writer, 1957-64; KAIM-AM/FM, Honolulu, HI, announcer and newsperson, 1964-65; WFAA-AM/FM/TV, Dallas, TX, radio and television newsperson, 1966-70; NEWSCOM News Service, Dallas, news director, 1969-70; admitted to the Bar of the State of Texas, 1970; attorney in private practice, 1970—; Braniff International Airlines, Dallas, pilot, 1975-82; Alaska Airlines, Seattle, WA, pilot, 1985—, professional leave, 1987-93; Simulator Training Incorporated (flight school), Seattle, pilot training consultant and instructor, 1985-92; EMEX Corporation, Tacoma, airline safety analyst and consultant, 1986—; ABC Radio and Television Network, aviation analyst, 1994; *Good Morning America,* ABC, aviation editor, 1995; Nance & Carmichael, PC (law firm), Austin, TX, partner, 1997; writer. Executive Transport Incorporated, president, 1979-85; Preventative Products Incorporated, vice-president of development, 1983-88. Congressional Office of Technology Assessment, consultant, 1987; Foundation for Issues Resolution in Science and Technology, founding board member, 1987-89; National Patient Safety Foundation at American Medical Association, member of board; consultant and analyst on aviation and earthquake safety for major television and radio news networks, including American Broadcasting Companies, National Broadcasting Company, Columbia Broadcasting System, Cable News Network, Public Broadcasting Service, National Public Radio, United Press International, Associated Press, and British Broadcasting Corporation; guest appearances on nationally broadcast television shows, including *Today, This Morning, Macneil-Lehrer Report, CBS Evening News,* and *Nova;* professional speaker on corporate, managerial, aviation, seismic, and other topics. *Military service:* U.S. Air Force, 1970-75; pilot and aircraft commander, 1971-75; entered associate reserve, 1975; present rank, lieutenant colonel. Served in Vietnam War as pilot, 1971-74; project officer, Cockpit Resource Management and Aircrew Flight Safety Program Development and Education, 97th Military Aircraft Squadron, 1988-93; activated and deployed to Operation Desert Storm (Persian Gulf War), 1990-91; Individual Mobilization Augmentee, Randolph AFB, Texas, affiliated with Crew Resource Management (CRM) education, 1993-95.

John J. Nance

MEMBER: American Bar Association, National Speakers Association, Authors Guild of America, Texas Bar Association, Reserve Officers Association, Phi Alpha Delta, Delta Chi.

AWARDS, HONORS: Washington Governor's Outstanding Author Award, 1987, for *Blind Trust;* Pacific Northwest Writers Conference Lifetime Achievement Award, 1996.

WRITINGS:

Splash of Colors: The Self-Destruction of Braniff International (nonfiction), Morrow, 1984.
Blind Trust (nonfiction), edited by Howard Cady, Morrow, 1986.
On Shaky Ground (nonfiction), Morrow, 1988.
Final Approach (novel), Crown, 1990.
What Goes Up (nonfiction), Morrow, 1991.
Scorpion Strike (novel), Crown, 1992.
Phoenix Rising (novel) Crown, 1994.
Pandora's Clock (novel), Doubleday, 1995.
Medusa's Child (novel), Doubleday, 1997.
The Last Hostage (novel), Doubleday, 1998.
Blackout (novel), Putnam, 2000.

Contributor to *Transportation Safety in an Age of Deregulation,* edited by Leon N. Moses and Ian Savage, Oxford University Press, 1989. Contributor to periodicals, including *Los Angeles Times, USA Today, San Francisco Chronicle,* and *Professional Pilot. Braniff Inflight Magazine,* columnist, 1987-89.

ADAPTATIONS: Pandora's Clock was released as a television miniseries by NBC, 1996; *Medusa's Child* was released as a television miniseries by ABC, 1997.

SIDELIGHTS: John J. Nance's background as a journalist, lawyer, and experienced military and commercial pilot has made him a highly respected analyst of the aviation industry and has led him to write several nonfiction and fiction books about airline safety and other societal issues. Born in Dallas, Texas, in 1946, Nance was interested in flying and writing at a young age, becoming the aviation writer for his neighborhood newspaper when he was thirteen. While earning an undergraduate and law degree as an ROTC scholar at Southern Methodist University, Nance worked full-time as a radio broadcast journalist. After receiving a degree in air law, Nance attended the U.S. Air Force Undergraduate Pilot Training at Williams Air Force Base in Arizona, where he was cited as a distinguished graduate. He later served as a pilot and aircraft commander for the U.S. Air Force, flying thirty-four missions in Vietnam. In 1975 Nance left active duty and joined the reserves, serving as an aircraft commander. He was promoted to lieutenant colonel—a rank he still holds—in 1989. Nance worked as a commercial pilot for Braniff International Airlines for seven years, until the corporation went bankrupt in 1982. Byron Acohido in the *Seattle Times* once noted how Nance's career has given him a unique advantage as an aviation analyst: "Reporters gravitate to Nance because he's a rare specimen: an articulate, knowledgeable and well-connected member of the aviation community who owes allegiance to no one save his conscience." Acohido quoted a member of the aviation community, who stated, "Most pilots have a hard time communicating about flying. . . . John has background in law, and he's a wordsmith. He can express our feelings without offending people."

Nance wrote his first book after losing his position as a pilot for Braniff. *Splash of Colors: The Self-Destruction of Braniff International* focuses on the executive decisions to dramatically expand the company after the federal government deregulated the airline industry in 1978, an action that minimized governmental intervention in the airlines, allowing companies to grow rapidly and engage in competitive cost-cutting practices that some people argued would affect safety. Unforseen increases in fuel prices and interest rates on the money Braniff had borrowed for its expansion ultimately led to financial disaster for the company. Mark Potts, in a review of *Splash of Colors* in the *Washington Post,* praised Nance's coverage of the plight of both the workers and the executives of Braniff and called the book "one of the best chronicles of corporate tragedy."

In his next book, *Blind Trust,* Nance explores the importance of the individual aviation employee, whom he cites as a key factor in risk management in modern-day air travel. Analyzing a number of tragic airplane crashes, Nance identifies issues in the airline industry that need to be addressed in order to minimize aviation safety problems caused by human error. Many of the dangers he discusses stem from deregulation; companies hired inexperienced pilots to fly unfamiliar routes and forced pilots to work longer hours. In order to cut costs and offer low passenger fares in further attempts to compete with other airlines, companies also minimized the maintenance of planes and replaced experienced employees with lower-paid newcomers. The industry's new concern with growth, Nance claims, led airline corporations to ignore the effect these changes had on workers and their performance in relation to air safety. Nance concludes in *Blind Trust* that eight-five percent of all airline disasters are due to "stressed-out pilots, overworked air traffic controllers, less-than-vigilant government investigators and cost-conscious maintenance crews." He suggests that government officials and airline executives should put more effort into understanding and remedying these problems. "Deregulation," the author says in the book, "has retarded dramatically and dangerously the spread of a very basic understanding: People will make mistakes; these mistakes can be anticipated through human-factors and human-performance research and investigation; and what the industry can learn from such research can be applied in direct practical ways to prevent those predictable mistakes from causing crashes and killing passengers."

Critics praised Nance for his clear and insightful presentation in *Blind Trust.* Paul Sonnenburg in the *Los Angeles Times Book Review* noted Nance's "discerning aircraft accident analyses—models of deftly sketched detail, compassionate perception of human behavior, and shrewd synthesis of complex relationships and perspectives." Douglas B. Feaver, in his review for the *Washington Post,* called Nance's book "one of the best and most troubling aviation safety books of recent years."

Nance's other writings include a study of the threat of earthquakes to communities in the United States entitled *On Shaky Ground,* and a novel, *Final Approach,* which has been praised as a first-rate exploration of the politics behind an investigation of a fictional airline disaster. Nance became well known in later years for his novels. Such bestsellers as *Medusa's Child* and *Blackout* have helped establish Nance as "arguably the king of the modern-day aviation thriller," as a *Publishers Weekly* reviewer wrote.

In *Pandora's Clock,* the author presents a claustrophobic worst-case scenario: a commercial airplane passenger afflicted with a doomsday virus. *Medusa's Child,* a 1996 release, takes the reader through twelve hours aboard a cargo plane sabotaged with a nuclear device capable of obliterating half the Atlantic seaboard. As the bomb's timer ticks down, the crew struggles to disarm the weapon even as the plane approaches a hurricane. While a *Publishers Weekly* notice marked the author down for "cartoonish characters and comic-book theatrics," *People* reviewer Cynthia Sanz argued that the author "skillfully ratchets up the suspense."

Nance published *The Last Hostage* in 1998, an on-flight hostage drama that provides "a thrilling ride," according to J. D. Reed in *People. Library Journal*'s Maria Perez-Stable agreed, remarking that the novel's "fast-moving plot has more twists than a corkscrew." With *Blackout,* FBI agent Kat Bronsky and news reporter Robert MacCabe team up to investigate why numerous jumbo jets are falling from the sky. In each case a mysterious, blinding flash has preceded the crash, and a corporate jet is in the vicinity of each disaster. The finger is pointed at terrorists bent on disabling the U.S. air industry by orchestrating air tragedies. To *Booklist* critic Gilbert Taylor, Blackout delivered "a glorified chase scene stretched from Hong Kong to Idaho."

While Taylor joined a consensus that Nance's fictional stylings left something to be desired, most critics agree that the thrill factor in *Blackout* compensated for any literary shortcomings. Nance, said a *Publishers Weekly* article on *Blackout,* "continues to craft brilliantly hair-raising in-flight emergency scenes" culminating in "a rousing, well-developed finale that comes together smoothly on final approach."

Nance once told *CA:* "As an author, I'm a communicator with a journalist's responsibility for balance and accuracy, a storyteller's passion to entertain and excite, and an advocate's determination to educate and motivate. I'm very privileged to have gained an audience that seems to enjoy both my nonfiction and fiction, and I'm determined to remain scrupulously faithful to their expectations by structuring the truth (without embellishment) into dynamic, human terms, and by telling exciting tales against the background of strict reality."

BIOGRAPHICAL/CRITICAL SOURCES:

BOOKS

Nance, John J., *Blind Trust,* Morrow, 1986.

PERIODICALS

Booklist, December 15, 1996, p. 693; January 1, 2000, p. 834.
Library Journal, March 15, 1998, p. 95; February 1, 2000, p. 118.
Los Angeles Times Book Review, January 26, 1986, p. 1; October 2, 1988, p. 1.
Morning News Tribune (Tacoma, WA), July 30, 1989, p. E1.
New York Times Book Review, January 19, 1986, p. 10.
People, March 31, 1986, p. 93; March 2, 1998, p. 38.
Publishers Weekly, January 6, 1997, p. 64; January 12, 1998, p. 46; January 3, 2000, p. 60.
Seattle Times, January 16, 1989, p. F1.
Washington Post, September 24, 1984; January 21, 1986.*

* * *

O'GREEN, Jennifer
See ROBERSON, Jennifer

O'GREEN, Jennifer Roberson
See ROBERSON, Jennifer

* * *

OHIYESA
See EASTMAN, Charles A(lexander)

* * *

OSTERWEIS, Rollin G(ustav) 1907-1982

PERSONAL: Born August 15, 1907, in West Haven, CT; died in 1982, in Branford, CT; son of Gustav (a cigar manufacturer and dealer in leaf tobacco) and Rose (Osterweis) Osterweis; married Ruth Mildred Loewenstein, September 27, 1932; children: Sally Jo (Mrs. Charles Kopman), Nancy (Mrs. Myles Alderman), Ruth Mildred (Mrs. Joel Selig), Rollyn Gay (Mrs. Daniel Krichbaum). *Education:* Yale University, B.A., 1930, M.A., 1943, Ph.D., 1946; attended Oxford University, summer, 1931, and Georgetown Foreign Service School, 1931-32. *Politics:* Independent. *Religion:* Reformed Jewish.

CAREER: Lewis Osterweis & Sons, New Haven, CT, salesman, sales manager, and partner in charge of sales, 1932-42; Yale University, New Haven, CT, instructor, 1943-45, 1946-48, assistant professor, 1949-54, associate professor, 1954-68, professor of history, 1968-76, professor emeritus, 1976-82, director of debating and public speaking, 1948-82. Commissioner in charge of publications, Connecticut State Civil War Centennial Commission, 1961-65; president, New Haven Preservation Trust, 1971-82.

MEMBER: American Historical Association, Organization of American Historians, American Forensic Association, Authors Club (London), Connecticut Academy of Arts and Sciences, Elizabethan Club (Yale University), Yale Faculty Club (president, 1970-72), New Haven Colony Historical Society (president, 1962-67).

WRITINGS:

Judah P. Benjamin: Statesman of the Lost Cause, Putnam (New York City), 1933.
Rebecca Gratz: A Study in Charm, Putnam, 1935.
The Sesquicentennial History of the Connecticut Academy of Arts and Sciences, Yale University Press (New Haven, CT), 1949.
Romanticism and Nationalism in the Old South, Yale University Press, 1949.
Three Centuries of New Haven: 1638-1938, Yale University Press, 1953.
(With Jacques Guicharnaud) *Santarem* (historical novel), Librairie Plon, 1959.
Charter No. 2: The Centennial History of the First New Haven National Bank, Printing Office, Yale University Press, 1963.
The Myth of the Lost Cause: 1865-1900, Archon Books (Hamden, CT), 1973.
The New Haven Green and the American Bicentennial, Archon Books, 1976.

SIDELIGHTS: An educator, historian, and author, Rollin G. Osterweis had an interest in the antebellum South that led to his writing several books on the topic, among them *Romanticism and Nationalism in the Old South* and *The Myth of the Lost Cause: 1865-1900.* In addition to his studies of the American South, Osterweis also wrote the biography *Rebecca Gratz: A Study in Charm.* Writing in *Library Journal,* E. G. Detlefsen described Osterweis as "a distinguished Yale historian and orator."

Osterweis argued in his *Romanticism and Nationalism in the Old South* that there were four distinct types of literary romanticism in operation in the pre-Civil War South. These four types were centered in Richmond, Virginia; Charleston, South Carolina; New Orleans, Louisiana; and the fourth in Texas. Each type shared a common belief in a courtly code of chivalry which influenced the style of literature they created. Osterweis especially compares and contrasts the leading Southern literary publications of the time, including the *Southern Literary Messenger, Charleston Quarterly,* and *De Bow's Review.* While H. M. Jones in the *Annals of the American Academy* believed that *Romanticism and Nationalism in the Old South* was "a suggestive, if mildly repetitious, study," the critic for the *U. S. Quarterly Book Review* found that Osterweis's book offered "fresh insight" and concluded that it was "valuable to all those interested in the complexities of American history." Frances Gaither in the *New York Times* judged: "Osterweis has spared himself no pains, and the result makes good reading."

In *The Myth of the Lost Cause* Osterweis deflates the idea that white citizens of the post-Civil War South were gallant in how they handled their defeat. He traces the development of the idea of the Lost Cause, in which aristocratic Southerners accepted their loss like gentlemen, through a careful examination of contemporary periodicals, literature, and political speeches. The critic for *Choice* noted that the book was "disjointed, wandering, and repetitious," while admitting that Osterweis "does use some fascinating popular sources" to back his contentions. Detlefsen in *Library Journal* found *The Myth of the Lost Cause* to be "a well written and solidly researched study."

In addition to his works about the American South, Osterweis also wrote the well-received biography *Rebecca Gratz: A Study in Charm.* Osterweis's book tells the life story of a member of a wealthy Jewish family in Philadelphia who served as the model for Walter Scott's character Rebecca in his novel *Ivanhoe.* Osterweis uses some novelistic techniques, such as invented dialogue, as well as her actual letters, to present Rebecca's story. The reviewer for the *New York Times* wrote that the book "is well documented and has been written with scholarly care." The *Christian Science Monitor* critic found that "Osterweis's greatest contribution to general knowledge is in his interesting portrayal of American Jewry in the days before the great immigrations."

BIOGRAPHICAL/CRITICAL SOURCES:

PERIODICALS

American Historical Review, July, 1949; October, 1953.

Annals of the American Academy, July, 1949.

Books, July 28, 1935, p. 8.

Choice, January, 1974.

Christian Century, March 2, 1949.

Christian Science Monitor, May 28, 1935, p. 16.

Current History, April, 1949.

Library Journal, November 15, 1973.

New Statesman and Nation, September 28, 1935.

New York Herald Tribune Weekly Book Review, September 4, 1949, p. 10.

New York Times, June 2, 1935, p. 15; February 20, 1949, p. 6.

Saturday Review of Literature, June 8, 1935.

Springfield Republican, June 23, 1935, p. E5; May 31, 1953, p. C5.

Times Literary Supplement, July 4, 1935, p. 434.

U.S. Quarterly Book Review, June, 1949; September, 1953.

Yale Review, autumn, 1953.

OBITUARIES:

PERIODICALS

AB Bookman's Weekly, March 29, 1982.*

P-Q

PACHTER, Henry M(aximillian) 1907-1981 (Henri Rabasseire)

PERSONAL: Surname originally Paechter; born February 22, 1907, in Berlin, Germany; came to the United States in 1941, naturalized in 1948; died in 1981; son of Fritz E. (a printer) and Helene (Streisand) Paechter; married Hedwig Roesler (a secretary); children: Renee Vera. *Education:* University of Berlin, Ph.D., 1930.

CAREER: Lived in France, 1933-41, doing research and teaching; *Deutsche Zeitung,* Cologne, Germany, foreign correspondent, 1948-64; New School for Social Research, New York City, 1952-68, became professor of history and chairman of the department; City College of City University of New York, New York City, professor of history, beginning 1968.

MEMBER: American Association of University Professors, Renaissance Society, American Historical Association, Foreign Press Association, United Nations Correspondents Association.

AWARDS, HONORS: Guggenheim fellow, 1951; National Endowment for the Arts awards, 1967, for essay "J.F.K. as an Equestrian Statue."

WRITINGS:

(Under pseudonym Henri Rabasseire) *Espagne Creuset Politique,* Editions Fustier, 1938.

(With Karl O. Paetal and Berta Hellman) *Nazi-Deutsch: German-English Dictionary of New German Terms,* Office of Economic Research, 1943, published as *Nazi-Deutsch: A Glossary of Contemporary German Usage,* Ungar, 1944.

(With others) *German Radio Propaganda,* Cornell University Press (New York City), 1944.

Paracelsus: Magic into Science, Henry Schuman, 1951.

Collision Course: The Cuban Missile Crisis and Coexistence, Praeger (New York City), 1963.

Weltmacht Russland: Aussenpolitische Strategie in drie Jahrhunderten, Stalling, 1968, revised edition published as *Weltmacht Russland: Tradition u. Revolution in d. Sowjetpolitik,* Deutscher-Taschenbuch Verlag, 1970.

(With Robert Boyers) *The Legacy of the German Refugee Intellectuals,* Skidmore College, 1969.

Decline and Greatness of Europe in the Twentieth Century, Praeger, 1971.

The Fall and Rise of Europe: A Political, Social and Cultural History of the Twentieth Century, Praeger, 1975.

Modern Germany: A Social, Cultural, and Political History, Westview Press (Boulder, CO), 1978.

Weimar Etudes, Columbia University Press, 1982.

Socialism in History: Political Essays of Henry Pachter, edited and with an introduction by Stephen Eric Bronner, Columbia University Press, 1984.

Contributor to books, including *The Axis Grand Strategy: Blueprints for the Total War,* Farrar & Rinehart, 1942; *The Third Reich,* Praeger, 1955; and *American Literary Anthology,* Farrar, Straus, 1968. Contributor of articles to *World Politics, Problems of Communism, Social Research, Journal of the History of Medicine, History and Theory, Wort und Wahrheit, Aussenpolitik, Der Monat,* and other publications. Co-editor, *Dissent.*

SIDELIGHTS: Henry M. Pachter was, according to Jim Miller in *Newsweek,* "an activist, a journalist and, in America, a professor of history and political science; in 1954 he helped establish the socialist journal *Dissent.*"

Among Pachter's books are *Collision Course: The Cuban Missile Crisis and Coexistence, The Fall and Rise of Europe: A Political, Social, and Cultural History of the Twentieth Century,* and *Modern Germany: A Social, Cultural, and Political History.*

In *Collision Course* Pachter examines the Cuban missile crisis of 1962, the closest that the United States and the Soviet Union ever came to nuclear war. Pachter details the events leading up to the crisis, including the installation of Russian missiles in Cuba and their discovery by the CIA, and the confrontation which eventually led to a naval blockade of the island nation and the removal of the missiles. Although criticizing Pachter for spinning "the entire story of the crisis around the personalities of [John] Kennedy and [Nikita] Khrushchev," Jean Daniel in *Book Week* found that the thesis is "skillfully developed." Pachter's account of the affair, Donald Wasson noted in the *Library Journal,* is presented "carefully and in quite dramatic fashion." "Pachter," wrote R. F. Delaney in *America,* "gives the reader a sense both of the crisis and of the minute-to-minute policy decisions."

The Fall and Rise of Europe traces the history of Europe during the twentieth century, centering on Pachter's notion that, despite the upheavals and wars of the century, European political unity seems likely to happen in the foreseeable future. Outlining the cultural commonalities shared by all Europeans, Pachter argues that these common values bind Europeans together and will eventually bring them together politically as well. W. J. Greenwald in *Library Journal* believed that Pachter's thesis "recedes from view after the introductory comments." The reviewer for *Choice* called the book "well written" but "skimpy," while noting that Pachter's thesis "is clearly presented."

In *Modern Germany* Pachter presents a broad overview of German history from the time of Bismarck to the 1970s, covering political, social and cultural trends. The reviewer for *Choice* called the volume "an exceptionally well-written history" and an "insightful and lucidly written book." Writing in the *Annals of the American Academy,* J. E. Helmreich praised Pachter for having "skillfully blended erudition with lively writing. The work . . . is stimulating and worthwhile reading."

BIOGRAPHICAL/CRITICAL SOURCES:

PERIODICALS

America, December 21, 1963, R. F. Delaney, review of *Collision Course.*

Annals of the American Academy, November, 1979, J. E. Helmreich, review of *Modern Germany.*

Booklist, May 15, 1951, review of *Paracelsus. Book Week,* June 7, 1964, Jean Daniel, review of *Collision Course,* p. 8.

Choice, December, 1975, review of *The Fall and Rise of Europe;* July-August, 1979, review of *Modern Germany.*

Christian Century, August 8, 1951, W. E. Garrison, review of *Paracelsus.*

Churchman, October 15, 1951, W. P. Sears, review of *Paracelsus. Library Journal,* January 1, 1964, Donald Wasson, review of *Collision Course;* June 15, 1975, W. J. Greenwald, review of *The Fall and Rise of Europe;* February 1, 1979, D. J. Martz, review of *Modern Germany;* July, 1982, G. H. Libbey, review of *Weimar Etudes.*

New Statesman, October 1, 1982, Paul Binding, review of *Weimar Etudes.*

Newsweek, September 6, 1982, Jim Miller, review of *Weimar Etudes.*

New Yorker, May 26, 1951, review of *Paracelsus.*

New York Herald Tribune Book Review, July 8, 1951, J. A. Mazzeo, review of *Paracelsus,* p. 4.

New York Times, April 29, 1951, T. C. Chubb, review of *Paracelsus,* p. 14.*

* * *

PACKER, Herbert L(eslie) 1925-1972

PERSONAL: Born July 24, 1925, in Jersey City, NJ; died December 6, 1972; son of Abraham and Lillian (Lieberman) Packer; married Nancy Huddleston (a university professor), March 15, 1958; children: Ann Elizabeth, George Huddleston. *Education:* Yale University, B.A., 1944, J.D., 1949. *Politics:* Democrat. *Religion:* None.

CAREER: Attorney associated with Washington, DC firm; Stanford University, Stanford, CA, assistant professor, 1956-57, associate professor, 1957-59, professor, 1959-71, Jackson Eli Reynolds Professor of Law, 1971-72, viceprovost, 1967-69. Member of Attorney General's Committee on Poverty and Administration of Federal Criminal Justice, 1961-63; chairman of committee for credential revocation procedures, California State Board of Education, 1962-63; contributor to revision of California penal code, 1964-69. *Military service:* U.S. Navy, 1944-46.

MEMBER: American Law Institute, Elizabethan Club (Yale University), Mory's Association (Yale University), Phi Beta Kappa.

AWARDS, HONORS: Ford Foundation fellow, 1960-61; Rockefeller Foundation fellow, 1963-64; American Council of Learned Societies fellow, 1963-64; Order of the Coif triennial award, 1970, for *The Limits of the Criminal Sanction;* Guggenheim fellowship, 1971.

WRITINGS:

Ex-Communist Witnesses: Four Studies in Fact Finding, Stanford University Press (Stanford, CA), 1962.
The State of Research in Anti-Trust Law, Walter Meyer Institute of Law (New Haven, CT), 1963.
The Limits of the Criminal Sanction, Stanford University Press, 1968.
(With Thomas Ehrlich) *New Directions in Legal Education,* McGraw (New York CIty), 1972, abridged edition, 1973.

Contributor to *American Scholar, Commentary, New Republic,* and *New York Review of Books.*

SIDELIGHTS: Herbert L. Packer wrote two important studies of the American legal system. In *Ex-Communist Witnesses,* Packer examined the usefulness of such approaches as cross-examination, court trials, and Congressional investigation to determine the truth of Communist activities in the United States. In *The Limits of the Criminal Sanction,* Packer studied the question of how society can effectively punish its criminals.

In *Ex-Communist Witnesses,* Packer studies the official testimonies of four prominent former members of the American Communist Party—Whittaker Chambers, Elizabeth Bentley, Louis Budenz, and John Lautner—to determine which investigative method proved the most reliable in extracting the truth from them. According to M. L. Ernst in the *Annals of the American Academy,* Packer's book "creates valid reservation as to present practices in the field of cross-examination." Anthony Lewis, writing for the *New York Times Book Review,* found fault with Packer's proposal to create "a special body something like a British tribunal of inquiry," but J. J. Marke, in his review for the *Library Journal,* concluded that Packer's *Ex-Communist Witnesses* "presents a penetrating study of American legal processes."

A wide-ranging study of the effectiveness of criminal punishment, *The Limits of the Criminal Sanction* "is a probing, clearly written essay," according to Marke, in which Packer concludes that "society depends too much on the criminal sanction and actually is overusing it." R. L. Goldfarb in the *New Republic* called the book "a thorough, scholarly, orderly analysis" which presents "sensible ideas on the limits of the criminal sanction."

BIOGRAPHICAL/CRITICAL SOURCES:

PERIODICALS

Annals of the American Academy, November, 1962, M. L. Ernst, review of *Ex-Communist Witnesses.*
Economist, September 13, 1969, review of *The Limits of the Criminal Sanction.*
Library Journal, September 15, 1962, J. J. Marke, review of *Ex-Communist Witnesses;* March 1, 1969, J. J. Marke, review of *The Limits of the Criminal Sanction.*
Nation, April 21, 1969, C. D. Stone, review of *The Limits of the Criminal Sanction.*
New Republic, January 4, 1969, R. L. Goldfarb, review of *The Limits of the Criminal Sanction.*
New Yorker, June 30, 1962, review of *Ex-Communist Witnesses.*
New York Times Book Review, August 12, 1962, Anthony Lewis, review of *Ex-Communist Witnesses,* p. 3.

OBITUARIES:

PERIODICALS

New York Times, December 8, 1972.
Washington Post, December 15, 1972.*

* * *

PACKER, Joy (Petersen) 1905-1977 (Lady Packer)

PERSONAL: Born February 11, 1905, in Cape Town, South Africa; died, 1977; daughter of Julius (a doctor) and Ellen Magdalen (Marais) Petersen; married Herbert Annesley Packer (an admiral in the Royal Navy), 1925 (deceased); children: Peter. *Education:* Attended University of Cape Town. *Religion:* Anglican. *Avocational interests:* Africa, travel, and the study of wildlife.

CAREER: Writer. Freelance journalist in Cape Town, South Africa, beginning 1924; *Daily Express,* London,

England, news reporter, 1931-32; Hong Kong Radio, Hong Kong, writer of women's features, 1932-35; free-lance correspondent for British publications while living in Balkans, 1936-39; publicity writer for war organizations; broadcaster to South Africa for British Broadcasting Corp., London, 1939-43; affiliated with Ministry of Information, Egypt, 1943, and with Psychological Warfare Branch of Allied Headquarters, Italy, 1944-45.

MEMBER: International PEN, Western Province Sports Club.

WRITINGS:

Pack and Follow: One Person's Adventures in Four Different Worlds, Eyre & Spottiswoode (London), 1945.
Grey Mistress, Eyre & Spottiswoode, 1949.
Apes and Ivory, Eyre & Spottiswoode, 1953.
Home from Sea, Eyre & Spottiswoode, 1963, Dutton (New York City), 1964.
The World Is a Proud Place, Dutton, 1966.
Valley of the Vines, Lippincott (Philadelphia), 1955.
The Moon by Night, Lippincott, 1957.
The High Roof, Lippincott, 1959.
The Glass Barrier, Lippincott, 1961.
The Man in the Mews, Eyre & Spottiswoode, 1964, Dutton, 1965.
The Man out There, Dutton, 1967.
The Blind Spot, Eyre & Spottiswoode, 1967.
Leopard in the Fold, Eyre & Spottiswoode, 1969.
Veronica, Eyre & Spottiswoode, 1970.
Boomerang, Corgi Books, 1972.
Deep as the Sea, Eyre Methuen, 1976.
Dark Curtain, Eyre Methuen, 1977.

Contributor of short stories and articles to magazines. Packer's books have been translated into many languages.

ADAPTATIONS: Valley of the Vines was adapted for a television series in South Africa; *The Moon by Night* was filmed.

SIDELIGHTS: Joy Packer wrote travel books based on her life as the wife of Sir Herbert Packer, an admiral in the British navy. In *Pack and Follow* and *Grey Mistress,* Packer recounted the couple's experiences while living in the Far East, Greece, Yugoslavia, and Turkey. *Deep as the Sea* is based on her husband's letters and chronicles his nearly fifty-year career in the navy. Packer's popular romance novels, including *Valley of the Vines, The Moon by Night,* and *High Roof,* are set in her native South Africa. Speaking of Packer's work as a novelist, La Tourette Stockwell in the *Chicago Sunday Tribune* called the author "a born storyteller who knows how to build up suspense and excitement and to make her characters seem real people whom you remember as friends."

Valley of the Vines is a story of young love set on a South African estate run by matriarch Constance de Valois, known as Grannie Con. In the course of unraveling her plot, Packer makes "the reader familiar with much that is South African," according to Sylvia Stallings in the *New York Herald Tribune Book Review.* While the reviewer for the *Christian Science Monitor* found that the novel "has a haunting charm which gives value and staying power to an otherwise unremarkable story," R. B. Robertson in *Library Journal* believed that the book's "Du Maurier-like plot for the ladies is here given so fresh a setting and lyrical a narration that it should have a very pleasant popularity." *Valley of the Vines* was later adapted for South African television.

In *The Moon by Night,* Packer follows young Alice Lang from her position as a nurse in England to the South African wildlife preserve of Velaba. There she must choose between two men who work amid the ever-present dangers of the preserve. Reviewers especially praised Packer for her realistic portrayal of the people and animals of the South African wilderness. Stockwell noted that "the novel's strength derives from Mrs. Packer's knowledge and love of the bushveld, native people, customs and traditions." Similarly, F. A. Boyle in *Library Journal* found that "Africa is the leading character in this satisfying novel." "Packer," according to Mary Ross in the *New York Herald Tribune Book Review,* "tells a story well; *The Moon by Night* moves swiftly, with the excitement of adventure and suspense." The critic for the *Times Literary Supplement* concluded: "Those who like their travel-books with a romantic thread will enjoy it thoroughly."

Set in the South African city of Cape Town, Packer's novel *High Roof* follows the trials of two married couples during a period of emotional turmoil. The critic for *Kirkus* described the novel as "essentially a romantic drama of attractive people in suspect situations." While the *Times Literary Supplement* reviewer found it to be "written in the style of agonized imminence common to the women's magazine story," Stockwell maintained: "Packer knows how to tell a good story which holds her readers' interest."

BIOGRAPHICAL/CRITICAL SOURCES:

PERIODICALS

Booklist, November 1, 1957, review of *The Moon by Night;* October 15, 1959, review of *High Roof.*

Bookmark, February, 1956, review of *Valley of the Vines;* October, 1957, review of *The Moon by Night;* November, 1959, review of *High Roof.*

Chicago Sunday Tribune, January 22, 1956, La Tourette Stockwell, review of *Valley of the Vines,* p. 3; September 29, 1957, La Tourette Stockwell, review of *The Moon by Night,* p. 4; September 20, 1959, La Tourette Stockwell, review of *High Roof,* p. 9.

Christian Science Monitor, February 16, 1956, review of *Valley of the Vines,* p. 5.

Kirkus, November 15, 1955, review of *Valley of the Vines;* June 1, 1957, review of *The Moon by Night;* July 1, 1959, review of *High Roof.*

Library Journal, December 15, 1955, R. B. Robertson, review of *Valley of the Vines;* August, 1957, F. A. Boyle, review of *The Moon by Night.*

New Yorker, October 5, 1957, review of *The Moon by Night.*

New York Herald Tribune Book Review, January 22, 1956, Sylvia Stallings, review of *Valley of the Vines,* p. 6; September 1, 1957, Mary Ross, review of *The Moon by Night,* p. 4.

New York Times, January 22, 1956, Beverly Grunwald, review of *Valley of the Vines,* p. 28; September 1, 1957, Judith Quehl, review of *The Moon by Night,* p. 16.

San Francisco Chronicle, November 22, 1959, review of *High Roof,* p. 28.

Saturday Review, February 4, 1956, Oliver La Farge, review of *Valley of the Vines;* September 14, 1957, S. P. Mansten, review of *The Moon by Night.*

Springfield Republican, March 11, 1956, review of *Valley of the Vines,* p. C7.

Times Literary Supplement, September 30, 1955, review of *Valley of the Vines,* p. 578; September 27, 1957, review of *The Moon by Night,* p. 573; July 31, 1959, review of *High Roof,* p. 445.*

* * *

PACKER, Lady
See PACKER, Joy (Petersen)

PAINTER, Charlotte 1926-

PERSONAL: Born May 24, 1926, in Baton Rouge, LA; daughter of L. E. and Dillie (Womack) Painter; married Thomas Voorhees, April 28, 1962 (deceased); children: Thomas Gregory. *Education:* Stanford University, M.A., 1965.

ADDRESSES: *Home*—P. O. Box 372-635F, Oakland, CA 94618.

CAREER: Writer. Stanford University, Stanford, CA, lecturer, 1961-65; University of California, Berkeley, lecturer, 1964-71; San Francisco State University, San Francisco, lecturer, 1973-95.

AWARDS, HONORS: Wallace Stegner writing fellowship, Stanford University, 1961-62; Mary Roberts Rinehart fellowship, 1962; Radcliffe Institute for Independent Study fellowship, 1965-67; National Endowment for the Arts fellowship, 1972; D. H. Lawrence fellowship, 1975.

WRITINGS:

The Fortunes of Laurie Breaux, Little, Brown (Boston), 1961.

Who Made the Lamb, McGraw (New York City), 1965.

Confession from the Malaga Madhouse: A Christmas Story, Dial (New York City), 1971.

(Editor with Mary Jane Moffat) *Revelations: Diaries of Women,* Random House (New York City), 1974.

Seeing Things, Random House, 1976.

Gifts of Age: Portraits and Essays of Thirty-two Remarkable Women, Chronicle Books (San Francisco), 1986.

Conjuring Tibet, Mercury Books, 1996.

Contributor to *New Yorker, Redbook, Ladies' Home Journal, Massachusetts Review, Yardbird, Place,* and other periodicals.

SIDELIGHTS: Charlotte Painter's writings are strongly autobiographical. *Who Made the Lamb,* for example, is based on a journal Painter kept while she was pregnant. *Confession from the Malaga Madhouse* recounts her experiences in Spain where, as a widow with a six-year-old son, she was arrested for possession of hashish and confined to a mental hospital. Painter has also co-edited *Revelations: Diaries of Women.*

In *Who Made the Lamb* Painter relates not only her own thoughts and feelings about being pregnant, but also her ideas on the state of the world into which she was bringing a child. Maggie Rennert in *Book Week* found the journal to be both irritating and useful. "The selfish, rejecting, denying personality on display alienates the reader," Rennert believed, "but the integrity and clarity of the account command his respect." Writing in the *New York Times Book Review,* Mark Harris found that Painter's journal of her pregnancy "leads us to our own awakening. . . . If this is first a book about one woman's pregnancy it is finally about nothing less than the way in which the commonplace well-observed informs our total existence."

Arrested for possession of hashish while visiting Spain, Painter spent a week in a Spanish mental asylum, an experience she chronicles in *Confession from the Malaga Madhouse.* Barbara Harte in *Best Sellers* called *Confession* a "feckless, episodic, disjointed narrative about stick figures. . . . Painter's confession does not come off, or comes off as a fraud." Similarly, Felicia Lamport in *Saturday Review* believed that the book "has neither the openness of a confession nor the orderliness of a diary." But according to J. B. Lopez, reviewing the title for *Library Journal,* "Painter is a disturbing and disturbed writer; her unusual book is recommended."

Painter joined with Mary Jane Moffat to edit *Revelations,* a collection of diary excerpts written by over thirty different women. The anthology includes females aged from childhood into old age, and from the tenth century to the present. Joy Macari, reviewing the book for *Library Journal,* described it as "a rich and varied sampling," while Harriett Straus, also reviewing the title for *Library Journal,* called it "a fascinating, coherent collection." "This anthology is a service," wrote June Goodwin in the *Christian Science Monitor.* "It is time the diary be more widely recognized as a vital aspect of literature, especially women's literature."

BIOGRAPHICAL/CRITICAL SOURCES:

PERIODICALS

Best Sellers, December 15, 1971, Barbara Harte, review of *Confession from the Malaga Madhouse.*

Book Week, April 18, 1965, Maggie Rennert, review of *Who Made the Lamb,* p. 13.

Christian Science Monitor, November 7, 1974, June Goodwin, review of *Revelations,* p. 10.

Kirkus, September 1, 1961, review of *The Fortunes of Laurie Breaux.*

Library Journal, October 15, 1961, Irene Gitomer, review of *The Fortunes of Laurie Breaux;* February 1, 1965, M. C. Langner, review of *Who Made the Lamb;* October 15, 1971, J. B. Lopez, review of *Confession from the Malaga Madhouse;* September 15, 1974, Harriett Straus, review of *Revelations;* November 15, 1974, Joy Macari, review of *Revelations.*

New Yorker, November 13, 1971, review of *Confession from the Malaga Madhouse.*

New York Herald Tribune Books, October 29, 1961, Paul Engle, review of *The Fortunes of Laurie Breaux,* p. 6.

New York Times Book Review, November 12, 1961, Martin Levin, review of *The Fortunes of Laurie Breaux,* p. 55; February 7, 1965, Mark Harris, review of *Who Made the Lamb,* p. 10.

Saturday Review, October 28, 1961, Granville Hicks, review of *The Fortunes of Laurie Breaux;* November 6, 1971, review of *Confession from the Malaga Madhouse.**

* * *

PAISH, F(rank) W(alter) 1898-1988

PERSONAL: Surname rhymes with "creche"; born January 15, 1898, in Croydon, England; died May 23, 1988; son of Sir George (an economist and journalist) and Emily Mary (Whitehead) Paish; married Beatrice Marie Eckhard, December 31, 1927; children: Elizabeth Mary (Mrs. Michael Thomson), Anthony George Conrad, Christopher Michael. *Education:* Trinity College, Cambridge, A.B., 1921, M.A., 1930. *Politics:* Liberal.

CAREER: Standard Bank of South Africa Ltd., employee in London, England, 1921-23, Cape Town, South Africa, 1923-32; London School of Economics and Political Science, London, lecturer, 1932-38, reader, 1938-49, professor of economics, 1949-65, professor emeritus, 1965-88; Lloyds Bank, London, economic consultant, 1965-70. Deputy director, British Ministry of Aircraft Production, London, 1941-45; economist, International Monetary Fund, Washington, DC, 1951. *Military service:* British Army, Royal Field Artillery, 1916-19; became lieutenant; received Military Cross.

MEMBER: Royal Economic Society, British Association (section president, 1953), Association of University Teachers of Economics (chairman, 1950-65), Reform Club.

AWARDS, HONORS: Fellow, London School of Economics, 1972.

WRITINGS:

(With G. L. Schwartz) *Insurance Funds and Their Investment,* P. S. King (London), 1934.

The Post-War Financial Problem and Other Essays, Macmillan (London), 1950.

Business Finance, Pitman (London), 1953.

Studies in an Inflationary Economy: The United Kingdom, 1948-1961, Macmillan, 1962.

(Editor) *Benham's Economics,* 7th edition, Pitman, 1964, 9th edition, with A. J. Culyer, 1973.

(With Jossleyn Hennessey) *Policy for Incomes?,* Institute of Economic Affairs (London), 1964.

Long-Term and Short-Term Interest Rates in the United Kingdom, Manchester University Press (Manchester), 1966.

Rise and Fall of Incomes Policy, Institute of Economic Affairs, 1969.

How the Economy Works, and Other Essays, Macmillan, 1970.

Contributor to *Economic Journal, Banker, Irish Banking Review, Scottish Journal of Political Economy, Economica,* and other publications. Editor, London and Cambridge Economic Service, 1947-51.

SIDELIGHTS: A long-time professor at the London School of Economics and Political Science, F. W. Paish is probably best remembered for advocating an unemployment rate of about two or three percent as a means of stabilizing inflation. Called the minimum margin of excess capacity, Paish's notion, unpopular when first introduced in the 1960s, is now accepted by many economists. Among his books are *The Post-War Financial Problem, Studies in an Inflationary Economy,* and *How the Economy Works, and Other Essays.*

The Post-War Financial Problem focuses on England's economic difficulties following the end of World War II. With the Labour Party in power, and socialist programs in effect, the country suffered from a financial slowdown that lasted throughout much of the 1950s. In his book, Paish criticized Labour's continuation of wartime rationing of food and other goods and its raising of tax rates as policies which hindered the country's chances for economic recovery. Writing in the *Journal of Political Economy,* A. I. Bloomfield found that "the essays in this volume are stimulating and lucidly written." The review for the *Times Literary Supplement* believed that "the publication of this collection of papers will establish Mr. Paish's reputation as one of our most distinguished writers on financial topics."

Paish's *Studies in an Inflationary Economy* gathers together a number of his writings about England's economy during the 1950s. His idea of the necessity for a minimum margin of excess capacity—in other words, a small amount of unemployed people—in order to stave off inflation, is first presented in this collection. The reviewer for the *Times Literary Supplement* found the idea to be "at variance with reality." But D. A. Alhadeff in the *American Economic Review* wrote: "This is a stimulating and provocative book in which theoretical insight, statistical interpretation, and historical perspective have been combined to illuminate alternatives for public policy."

How the Economy Works, and Other Essays focuses on the effects of government monetary and fiscal policies on the nation's economy. While the critic for the *Times Literary Supplement* found that the essays in Paish's book should have been made "into a cohesive whole," the *Choice* reviewer believed that the volume "will prove valuable for the monetary and fiscal policy specialists."

BIOGRAPHICAL/CRITICAL SOURCES:

PERIODICALS

American Economics Review, March, 1963, D. A. Alhadeff, review of *Studies in an Inflationary Economy.*

Choice, December, 1971, review of *How the Economy Works.*

Current History, December, 1951, review of *The Post-War Financial Problem.*

Economist, September 5, 1970, review of *How the Economy Works.*

Foreign Affairs, April, 1952, review of *The Post-War Financial Problem.*

Journal of Political Economy, October, 1951, A. I. Bloomfield, review of *The Post-War Financial Problem;* February, 1963, Phillip Cagan, review of *Studies in an Inflationary Economy.*

Times Literary Supplement, March 23, 1951, review of *The Post-War Financial Problem,* p. 183; September 7, 1962, review of *Studies in an Inflationary Economy,* p. 670; August 14, 1970, review of *How the Economy Works,* p. 895.

OBITUARIES:

PERIODICALS

Times (London), May 26, 1988.*

PAKENHAM, Simona Vere 1916-

PERSONAL: Born September 25, 1916, in Taplow, Berkshire, England; daughter of Thomas Compton and Phyllis (Price) Pakenham; married Noel P. D. Iliff, 1938; children: David Anthony. *Education:* Attended Central School of Speech Training and Dramatic Art, 1934, and Old Vic Drama School, 1935-36. *Religion:* Church of England. *Avocational interests:* Music, Biblical studies, gardening.

ADDRESSES: *Agent*—c/o Macmillan, 25 Eccleston Place, London SW1W 9NF, England.

CAREER: Writer. Actress and stage designer in repertory, at theaters in London, Dublin, Edinburgh, and elsewhere in the United Kingdom, 1930-52. Regular broadcaster on British Broadcasting Corp. overseas religious programs.

WRITINGS:

Ralph Vaughan Williams: A Discovery of His Music, St. Martin's (New York City), 1957.
The First Nowell: A Nativity Play, Oxford University Press (London), 1959.
Pigtails and Pernod, St. Martin's, 1961.
Sixty Miles from England: A History of the British Colony in Dieppe, 1814-1914, Macmillan (London), 1967.
In the Absence of the Emperor: London-Paris, 1814-1815, Cresset Press (London), 1968.
Cheltenham: A Biography, Macmillan, 1971.

SIDELIGHTS: Simona Pakenham has written two books on the English colony in Dieppe, France, which has existed since just after the Napoleonic Wars of the early nineteenth century.

In *Pigtails and Pernod,* Pakenham recounts her visits as a young girl to her grandparents' house in Dieppe. As a school girl, Pakenham visited her grandparents about six times each year. In addition to her memories of family events, including their Christmas celebrations, she also details the differing customs, eccentricities, and foibles of the English colonists and their French neighbors. As Aileen Pippett explained in the *Saturday Review,* "the book abounds in good stories . . . , but it is more than a ragbag of anecdotes because everything is seen through the eyes of a shrewd and observant child." Speaking of the book's initial section, Fanny Butcher in the *Chicago Sunday Tribune* claimed: "If there are a more delightful 100 pages about a visit to France I have not encountered them." The critic for the *Times Literary Supplement* found that "Pakenham has just the right approach to her material . . . and the proportions of the book are more delicate, and more exact, than its apparent artlessness might suggest."

Pakenham outlines the history of Dieppe in *Sixty Miles from England.* The town began in 1814, following the last of the Napoleonic Wars, when wealthy English families settled in the French harbor town and created their own community. Dieppe soon developed its own "social life, schools, churches, and celebrities," as the *New Yorker* critic noted. Pakenham's history, the reviewer for the *Times Literary Supplement* believed, "is written with the same eye for absurdity and the same slightly formal elegance as [*Pigtails and Pernod*]."

BIOGRAPHICAL/CRITICAL SOURCES:

PERIODICALS

Booklist, January 15, 1962, review of *Pigtails and Pernod.*
Bookmark, January, 1962, review of *Pigtails and Pernod.*
Chicago Sunday Tribune, November 26, 1961, Fanny Butcher, review of *Pigtails and Pernod,* p. 3.
Book World, February 11, 1968, Alan Pryce-Jones, review of *Sixty Miles from England,* p. 12.
Kirkus, September 1, 1961, review of *Pigtails and Pernod.*
Library Journal, June 1, 1957, C. K. Miller, review of *Ralph Vaughan Williams;* December 1, 1961, Dorothy Nyren, review of *Pigtails and Pernod.*
New Statesman, December 22, 1961, Peter Porter, review of *Pigtails and Pernod.*
New Yorker, February 17, 1962, Naomi Bliven, review of *Pigtails and Pernod;* December 2, 1967, review of *Sixty Miles from England.*
New York Times Book Review, December 3, 1961, Morris Gilbert, review of *Pigtails and Pernod,* p. 34.
Saturday Review, December 23, 1961, Aileen Pippett, review of *Pigtails and Pernod.*
Times Literary Supplement, June 21, 1957, review of *Ralph Vaughan Williams,* p. 376; March 28, 1962, review of *Pigtails and Pernod,* p. 198; July 13, 1967, review of *Sixty Miles from England,* p. 621.*

* * *

PANKEY, Eric 1959-

PERSONAL: Born February 25, 1959, in Kansas City, MO; son of James A. (an accountant) and Frances (an accountant; maiden name, Pierce) Pankey; married Jennifer Atkinson (a writer and editor), July 6, 1985. *Education:* University of Missouri at Columbia, B.S., 1981; University of Iowa, M.F.A., 1983.

ADDRESSES: Office—Department of English, George Mason University, 4400 University Dr., Fairfax, VA 22030-4444.

CAREER: Linn-Mar Community Schools, Marion, IA, teacher, 1983-86; Iowa Arts Council, Des Moines, artist in the schools, 1986; Washington University, St. Louis, MO, director of Master of Fine Arts program, 1987-96; George Mason University, Fairfax, VA, associate professor, 1996-97, professor of English, 1997—.

AWARDS, HONORS: Walt Whitman Award from Academy of American Poets, 1984, for *For the New Year;* recipient of fellowships from Ingram Merrill Foundation, National Endowment for the Arts, and Guggenheim Foundation.

WRITINGS:

For the New Year, Atheneum (New York City), 1984.
Heartwood, Atheneum, 1988.
Apocrypha, Knopf (New York City), 1991.
The Late Romances, Knopf, 1997.
Cenotaph, Knopf, 2000.

Contributor of poems and articles to journals, including *Kenyon Review, Iowa Review, Antioch Review, New Yorker,* and *Ironwood.*

WORK IN PROGRESS: Another volume of poems.

SIDELIGHTS: Eric Pankey is a highly regarded American poet who won the Walt Whitman Award for his first collection, *For the New Year.* A *Publishers Weekly* reviewer places Pankey's work "at a crossroads between lyrical formalism and jazzy modulations akin to the best of Charles Wright." According to *Library Journal* correspondent Tim Gavin, Pankey's poems "reveal his dedication to craft" and are "touching, sincere, and sublime." In her *New Leader* essay on *The Late Romances,* Phoebe Pettingell wrote: "Pankey's art suggests the smokey, sophisticated vocal line of Billie Holiday and Jelly Roll Morton—half rueful, half mocking of audience and self. Nothing is quite as it seems: that is the underlying sensibility." Pettingell concluded that Pankey's "wry lyrics . . . shimmer with ideas the way an opal does with colors in the changing light. Pankey's teasing speculations often move in several directions, leading the reader's attention along a playful path that, not infrequently, ends in a disturbing conclusion."

BIOGRAPHICAL/CRITICAL SOURCES:

PERIODICALS

Library Journal, December, 1984, p. 2285; August, 1988, p. 162; November 1, 1991, p. 103; January, 2000, p. 118.
New Leader, December 16, 1996, p. 30.
Poetry, December, 1992, p. 159.
Publishers Weekly, May 27, 1988, p. 58; December 30, 1996, p. 60; December 6, 1999, p. 72.

* * *

PICANO, Felice 1944-

PERSONAL: Born February 22, 1944, in New York, NY; son of Phillip (a grocer) and Ann (Del Santo) Picano. *Education:* Queens College of the City University of New York, B.A., 1964.

ADDRESSES: Agent—Stephanie Tade, Jane Rotrosen Agency, 226 East 32nd St., New York, NY 10016; and Malaga Baldi, Malaga Baldi Agency, 204 West 84th St., Suite 3C, New York, NY 10024.

CAREER: New York City Department of Welfare, New York City, social worker, 1964-66; *Art Direction,* New York City, assistant editor, 1966-68; Doubleday Bookstore, New York City, assistant manager, 1969-70; free-lance writer, 1970-72; Rizzoli's Bookstore, New York City, assistant manager and buyer, 1972-74; writer, 1974—. Founder and publisher of the Sea Horse Press Ltd., 1977-94; co-founder and co-publisher of the Gay Presses of New York, 1980-94. Instructor of fiction writing classes, YMCA West Side Y Writers Voice Workshop, 1982-83.

MEMBER: Authors Guild, Writers Guild of America, PEN.

AWARDS, HONORS: PEN/Ernest Hemingway Award nomination, 1976, for *Smart as the Devil;* New York State Arts Council Grant, 1981; American Library Association Award, 1982, for *A True Likeness;* Jane Chambers Playwriting Award, 1985, for *One O'Clock Jump;* Chapbook award, Poetry Society of America, 1986; Short Story award, PEN, 1986; *Story* Magazine Award, 1994, for "Love and the She-Lion"; Lambda Literary Award nominations, 1995, for *Dryland's End, 1996, for Like People in History,* 1998, for *A House on the Ocean, a House on the Bay,* and 2000, for *The Book*

Felice Picano

of Lies; Ferro-Grumley Award, 1996, Le Figaro Litteraire Citation, top five foreign language books of the year, 1996, and *Gay Times of England* Award, 1996, for *Like People in History.*

WRITINGS:

Smart as the Devil (novel), Arbor House (New York City), 1975.

Eyes (novel), Arbor House, 1976.

The Mesmerist (novel), Delacorte (New York City), 1977.

The Deformity Lover and Other Poems, Sea Horse Press (New York City), 1978.

The Lure (novel), Delacorte, 1979.

(Editor) *A True Likeness: An Anthology of Lesbian and Gay Writing Today,* Sea Horse Press, 1980.

An Asian Minor: The True Story of Ganymede (novella; also see below), Sea Horse Press, 1981.

Late in the Season (novel), Delacorte, 1981.

Slashed to Ribbons in Defense of Love and Other Stories (also see below), Gay Presses of New York (New York City), 1983.

House of Cards (novel), Delacorte, 1984.

Ambidextrous: The Secret Lives of Children (memoir), Gay Presses of New York, 1985.

Window Elegies (poetry), Close Grip Press, 1986.

Immortal (play with music; based on Picano's novella *An Asian Minor: The True Story of Ganymede*), produced Off-Off Broadway, 1986.

One o'Clock (one-act play), produced Off-Off Broadway, 1986.

Men Who Loved Me: A Memoir in the Form of a Novel, New American Library (New York City), 1989.

To the Seventh Power, Avon Books (New York City), 1990.

(With Charles Silverstein) *The New Joy of Gay Sex,* HarperPerennial (New York City), 1993.

Like People in History (novel), Viking, 1995.

Dryland's End, Masquerade Books, 1995.

A House on the Ocean, A House on the Bay: A Memoir, Faber and Faber (Boston), 1997.

Looking Glass Lives: A Novel, illustrated by F. Ronald Fowler, Alyson Books (Los Angeles, CA), 1998.

The Book of Lies (novel), Little Brown/Abacus (London), 2000.

The New York Years: Stories (contains *An Asian Minor* and *Slashed to Ribbons in Defense of Love),* Alyson Books, 2000.

Onyx (novel), Alyson Books, 2001.

Counting Backwards (short stories and essays), Alyson Books, 2001.

CONTRIBUTOR TO ANTHOLOGIES

Campbell, editor, *New Terrors, Number Two,* Pan Books (England), 1978.

Leland, editor, *Orgasms of Light,* Gay Sunshine, 1979.

Denneny, editor, *Aphrodisiac: Fiction from Christopher Street,* Coward (London), 1980.

Ramsey Campbell, editor, *New Terrors Omnibus,* Pan Books, 1980.

Coffey, editor, *Masters of Modern Horror,* Coward, 1981.

Young, editor, *On the Line,* Crossing Press (Trumansburg, NY), 1982.

F. Grossman, editor, *Getting from Here to There: Writing and Reading Poetry,* Boynton/Cook (Upper Montclair, NJ), 1982.

Ortleb and Denneny, editors, *The Christopher Street Reader,* Coward, 1983.

Stephen Coote, editor, *The Penguin Book of Homosexual Verse,* Penguin (New York City), 1983.

Young, editor, *The Male Muse, Number Two,* Crossing Press, 1983.

Martin Humphries, editor, *Not Love Alone,* Gay Mens Press (London), 1985.

George Stambolian, editor, *Men on Men,* New American Library, 1986.

Michael Klein, editor, *Poets for Life,* Crown, 1989.

Graham Masterson, editor, *Scare Care,* Putnam, 1989.
George Stambolian, editor, *Men on Men,* Volume 3, Dutton, 1990.
George Stambolian, editor, *Men on Men,* Volume 4, Dutton, 1992.
David Bergman, editor, *The Violet Quill Reader,* St. Martin's Press, 1994.
Brian Bouldry, editor, *Wrestling with the Angel,* Riverside Books, 1995.
David Laurents, editor, *The Badboy Book of Erotic Poetry,* Masquerade Publishing, 1995.
Leslea Newman, editor, *Bearing the Unbearable,* Crossing Press, 1995.
Gavin Dillard, editor, *Between the Cracks,* Daedalus Publishing, 1996.
David Laurents, editor, *Wanderlust,* Masquerade Publishing 1996.
William J. Mann, editor, *Grave Passions,* Masquerade Publishing, 1997.
Richard Schneider, Jr., editor, *The Best of The Harvard Gay & Lesbian Review,* Temple University Press, 1997.
Michael Shernoff, editor, *Gay Widowers,* Hayworth Press, 1997.
David Bergman, editor, *Men on Men,* Volume 7, Dutton, 1998.
Lucy Jane Bledsoe, editor, *Gay Travels: A Literary Companion,* Whereabouts Press, 1998.
Lawrence Schimel, editor, *The Mammoth Book of Gay Erotica,* Carrol & Graf, 1998.
Ricahrd Labonte, editor, *Gay Male Erotica, 1999,* Cleis Press, 1999.
Gavin Dillard, *A Day for a Lay: A Century of Gay Poetry,* Barricade Books, 1999.
Jane de Lynn, editor, *New York Sex,* Painted Leaf Press, 1999.
Giovanna Capone, Denise Nico Leto, and Tommi Avicolli-Mercca, editors, *Hey Paesan!,* Three Guineas Press, 2000.

OTHER

Also author of the screenplay *Eyes,* based on the novel of the same title, 1986. Contributor of articles, poems, stories, and reviews to periodicals, including *Los Angeles Times, San Francisco Examiner, The Advocate, Mandate, The Washington Blade, Bay Windows, Genre, Harrington Gay Men's Fiction Quarterly, Lambda Book Report, Harvard Gay & Lesbian Review, Lexicon, Kindred Spirit, Global City Review, Story, Sodomite Invasion Review, OUT, Mouth of the Dragon, Islander, Cumberland Review, Connecticut Poetry Review, Cream City Review,* and *Soho Weekly News,* and to on-line periodicals, including *Vote.com—The Fifth Estate, Barnes & Noble.com,* and *Blithe House Quarterly.com.* Book editor, *New York Native,* 1980-83.

ADAPTATIONS: An Asian Minor, was adapted by Picano and Jerry Campbell for the stage as *Immortal!,* first produced in 1986; *The Lure* has been optioned for a feature film by David Forrest/Sanctuary Films.

SIDELIGHTS: Felice Picano is "a premier voice in gay letters," to quote Malcolm Boyd in the *Advocate.* A novelist, poet, memoirist, and pioneer in gay publishing, Picano was a founding member of New York City's Violet Quill Club, a group of intellectuals and artists who sought to promote gay writing. Picano's own work has been praised for using "the history of gay culture as the subject for popular novels," according to *New York Times Book Review* correspondent Suzanne Berne.

Timing was crucial to Picano's career. He began publishing mainstream novels in the mid-1970s and was earning a wide readership with them when he decided to write gay fiction instead. That decision led him to pen literate works with "well-constructed characters and settings," to quote *Library Journal* contributor Theodore R. Salvadori, while it also brought him friendships with other intellectual gay authors such as Edmund White and Andrew Holleran. Reflecting on his diverse career in an interview released by a recent publisher of his work, Picano said: "I've been accused of committing literary suicide several times over the years, because I keep on doing what I'm not supposed to do in my writing. I was enjoying a very successful mainstream career when I became one of the first openly gay writers. By the mid-eighties, I was writing gay literary novels and, after I had gathered a little bit of a reputation in gay literature, people told me I was making a mistake when I co-authored *The New Joy of Gay Sex.* I always seem to be doing something wrong. But I'm following a trajectory that I more or less understand."

New York Times Book Review contributor David Lipsky called Picano "a word machine" who "approaches the page with a newcomer's joy." In his review of Picano's *The Book of Lies*—a *roman a clef* about the Violet Quill Club—Lipsky noted that the characters are "outsize and the novel is written in a dishy, larger-than-life style. . . . The results are surprisingly entertaining." A *Publishers Weekly* correspondent, assessing the same work, concluded: "Picano is successful in his gossipy recreation of the group of gay literary innovators. In depicting the near future, his amusing assumptions demonstrate a keen tab on trends and the possible new technologies ahead. The surprises at the end keep the reader's head spinning."

Picano has authored several memoirs, one of which is *A House on the Ocean, A House on the Bay.* In this work he recalls the years of the 1960s and 1970s when he lived in Manhattan and partook of the pleasures of Fire Island, New York. "Picano is definitely gifted enough to ensure this book's popularity with lesbian and gay readers everywhere," declared Charles Harmon in *Booklist.* In the *Library Journal,* Richard Violette called Picano "a leading light in the gay literary world," adding that in *A House on the Ocean, a House on the Bay,* "his glints of flashing wit and subtle hints of dark decadence transcend cliches." Robrt L. Pela in the *Advocate* maintained that, considering all of his works—fiction, nonfiction, and poetry—"Picano's destiny . . . has been to lead the way for a generation of gay writers."

Several of Picano's works have been translated into French, Japanese, Spanish, Dutch, Danish, German, Hebrew, Polish, and Portuguese. He described his writing in *CA:* "In my poetry I am keeping a sort of notebook of fragmentary experiences and understandings. In the past, this meant a polarization of subject matter: poems dealing either with perceptions gathered from the world of nature as revealed in Big Sur or Fire Island; or poems dealing with contemporary aspects of urban life and characters— portraits of epileptics, deformity lovers, obscene phone callers, etc. Of late, however, my poetry has become more autobiographical—though not at all confessional—integrating interior and exterior worlds. And forms have changed from lyric and monologic to more experimental structures such as self-interviews, imaginary dialogues, and letters to unknown persons.

"In fiction I write about the possible rather than the actual, and so, I suppose, 'Romances' in Hawthorne's sense of the word, even with 'realistic' settings, characters, and actions. My novels, novellas, and short stories deal with ordinary individuals who are suddenly thrust into extraordinary situations and relationships which test their very existence. Unusual perceptions and abilities, extrasensory powers, and psychological aberrations become tools and weapons in conflicts of mental and emotional control. Previous behavioral patterns are inadequate for such situations and must be changed to enable evolved awareness and survival, or they destroy their possessor. Thus, perspective is of the utmost importance in my fiction, both for structure and meaning. I am dedicated to experimenting with new and old points of view, which seem to have progressed very little since the pioneering work of Henry James and James Joyce."

Picano added that he also works in film and theater, starting with adaptations of previously written works: "These intensely collaborative efforts—apparently so very different than other solitary writing—have proven to be fascinating not only because I've learned the strengths and weaknesses in collaboration, but also because through experienced theater and film director's views of what the public requires, I've learned how completely idiosyncratic I and my perspective has been, is, and will probably continue to be. Few writing experiences can equal the intensity of theater rehearsals leading to opening night, and nothing can equal the simultaneous frustration and elation of having others speak the works you've written."

BIOGRAPHICAL/CRITICAL SOURCES:

BOOKS

Bergman, David, editor, *The Violet Quill Reader,* St. Martin's Press, 1994.

Bouldry, Brian, editor, *Wrestling with the Angel,* Riverside Books, 1995.

Canning, Richard, *Thirty Gay Authors: Interviews,* Columbia University Press, 2000.

Contemporary Authors Autobiography Series, Volume 13, Gale (Detroit), 1991.

Gay & Lesbian Literary Companion, Visible Ink Press, 1995.

Newman, Leslea, editor, *Bearing the Unbearable,* Crossing Press, 1995.

Picano, Felice, *Ambidextrous: The Secret Lives of Children,* Gay Presses of New York, 1985.

Picano, Felice, *Men Who Loved Me,* Dutton, 1989.

Picano, Felice, *A House on the Ocean, a House on the Bay: A Memoir,* Faber and Faber (Boston), 1997.

Schneider, Jr., Richard, editor, *The Best of The Harvard Gay & Lesbian Review,* Temple University Press, 1997.

Shernoff, Michael, editor, *Gay Widowers,* Hayworth Press, 1997.

PERIODICALS

A/B (special issue of *The Modern Language Association Quarterly*), fall, 2000, Kevin Stone Fries and Felice Picano, "Prelude to Process: Sources of Felice Picano's Lifewriting."

Advocate, April 15, 1997, Malcolm Boyd, review of *A House on the Ocean, a House on the Bay,* p. 53; September 15, 1998, Robrt L. Pela, "A Writer's

Journey: Felice Picano Talks about His Latest Novel, a Tale of Love and Travel through Time," p. 64; December 21, 1999, Robrt L. Pela, review of *The Book of Lies,* p. 73.

Art & Understanding, November, 1999, Greg Herren, "Felice Picano: A Retrospective," and Kelly McQuain, "Lies and Lives: Interview with Felice Picano."

Bay Area Reporter, October 7, 1999, Deborah Peifer, "Purple Reign."

Booklist, April 15, 1997, Charles Harmon, review of *A House on the Ocean, a House on the Bay,* p. 1378.

Chiron Review, October, 2000, Robert Peters, "Felice Picano Featured and Interviewed."

Frontiers, October 15, 1999, Doug Sadownick, "Survivor: Felice Picano."

Gay and Lesbian Times of San Diego, November 18, 1999, Salvatore Sapienza, "Tales of a Founding Father."

Harvard Gay & Lesbian Review, fall, 1998.

James White Review, fall, 1999, "Telling the Truth in Fiction—Andrew Holleran and Felice Picano on the Violet Club and After."

Just out in Portland, October 15, 1999, Christopher Cuttone, "Look Back in Lavender," and Flora Sussely, "Talking to Felice Picano."

Library Journal, February 15, 1989; November 1, 1989; June 1, 1997, Richard Violette, review of *A House on the Ocean, a House on the Bay,* p. 100; September 1, 1999, Theodore R. Salvadori, review of *The Book of Lies,* p. 235.

New York Times Book Review, December 2, 1979; July 16, 1995, Suzanne Berne, "Men in Love," p. 21; December 12, 1999, David Lipsky, review of *The Book of Lies,* p. 28.

Publishers Weekly, December 9, 1988; September 22, 1989; June 19, 1995, p. 51; October 25, 1999, review of *The Book of Lies,* p. 49.

Village Voice, December 24, 1979.

OTHER

Alyson Books, http://www.alyson.com/ (May 26, 2000).

* * *

PILLING, Christopher Robert 1936-

PERSONAL: Born April 20, 1936, in Birmingham, Warwickshire, England; married wife, Sylvia, 1960; children: one son, two daughters. *Education:* Attended Institute of French Studies, La Rochelle, France, 1955; University of Leeds, B.A. (with honors), 1957; University of Nottingham, Loughborough College, certificate in education, 1959.

ADDRESSES: Home—25 High Hill, Keswick, Cumbria CA12 5NY, England.

CAREER: Ecole Normale, Moulins, France, assistant in English, 1957-58; teacher of French and physical education at grammar schools on the Wirral, England, 1959-61, in Birmingham, England, 1961-62, and at Quaker school near Pontefract, England, 1962-73; Knottingley High School, England, teacher and head of department of modern languages, 1973-78; University of Newcastle upon Tyne, Newcastle upon Tyne, England, tutor in art and English literature in Department of Adult Education, 1978-80; Keswick School, Keswick, England, head of French department, 1980-88; full-time writer, 1988—. Member of Northern Arts Literature Panel.

MEMBER: Whitwood and District Arts Association (member of committee).

AWARDS, HONORS: New Poets Award, 1970, for *Snakes and Girls;* Arts Council grant, 1971, and translator's grant, 1977; Kate Collingwood Award from Northern Playwrights Society, 1983, for *Torquemada;* Northern Arts grant, 1985; Laureat du Concours Europeen de Creation Litteraire, 1992; Tyrone Guthrie residency, 1993.

WRITINGS:

POETRY

Snakes and Girls, University of Leeds School of English Press, 1970.

Fifteen Poems, University of Leeds School of English Press, 1970.

In All the Spaces on All the Lines, edited by Harry Chambers, Phoenix Pamphlet Press (Manchester, England), 1971.

Wren and Owl, University of Leeds School of English Press, 1971.

Andree's Bloom and the Anemones, Sceptre Press (Rush Den, England), 1973.

Light Leaves, Cellar Press (Hitchin, England), 1975.

War Photographer since the Age of Fourteen, Starwheel Press (Hitchin, England), 1983.

Foreign Bodies, Flambard Press (Newcastle Upon Tyne, England), 1992.

Cross Your Legs and Wish, Red Beck Press (Bradford, England), 1994.

OTHER

These Jaundiced Loves: A Translation of Tristan Corbiere's "Les Amours Jaunes," Peterloo Poets (Cornwall, England), 1995.

Also author of sequence of poems about birds, trees, and insects. Author of plays *Torquemada*(retitled *A Splendid Specimen); Mock Wedding;* and *Maddalena.* Translator of Tristan Corbiere's *Les Amours Jaunes,* Guillevic's *Carnac,* and selected poems of Lucien Becker. Work represented in numerous anthologies, including *Four Poetry and Audience Poets,* edited by Alan Ram, Leeds University Press, 1971; *PA 21: Twenty-one Years of Poetry and Audience,* Aquila, 1976; *Peterloo Anthology 1,* edited by Cambers, Peterloo Poets, 1979; *The Oxford Book of Verse in English Translation,* edited by Charles Tomlinson, Oxford University Press, 1980; *Between Comets: For Norman Nicholson at Seventy,* edited by William Scammell, Taxus Press, 1984; and *The New Lake Poets,* edited by Scammell, Bloodaxe, 1991. Also contributor to *PEN New Poems: 1970-71, New Poetry: Arts Council Anthology,* 1975-78, 1983, *A Mandeville Fifteen,* 1976, *Poets Yearbook Anthology,* 1977, *Lancaster Literature Festival Anthology,* 1983, 1984, 1986, 1990, 1992, and *Lettres d'Europe,* 1992.

SIDELIGHTS: Christopher Pilling's strength as a poet is his ability to plumb "the subjective depths of everyday domestic moments by forming around them multiple concrete and abstract analogies," according to *Contemporary Poets* contributor Anne Cluysenaar. This is particularly apparent in the collections *In All the Spaces on All the Lines* and *Snakes and Girls,* Cluysenaar opines, citing "Partial Ellipse," a poem in *Snakes and Girls,* in which Pilling refers to his wife's wedding ring as "a gold curve . . . on a hand-coloured background." Cluysenaar finds that "Pilling's more discursive poems tend to be less fully achieved. They do, however, suggest the poet's intellectual grasp of his life-loving orientation."

BIOGRAPHICAL/CRITICAL SOURCES:

BOOKS

Contemporary Poets, 6th edition, St. James Press (Detroit), 1996.

PERIODICALS

Poetry and Audience, May 1, 1970.*

POLK, William R(oe) 1929-

PERSONAL: Born March 7, 1929, in Forth Worth, TX; son of George Washington and Adelaide (Roe) Polk; married Joan Cooledge, December 15, 1950 (divorced December, 1960); married Ann Cross, June 9, 1962; children: (first marriage) Milbry Catherine, Alison Elizabeth; (second marriage) George W. IV, Eliza Forbes. *Education:* Attended University of Chile, 1945-46; Harvard University, B.A. (with honors), 1951, Ph.D., 1958; American University of Beirut, graduate study, 1951-52; Oxford University, B.A. (honors), 1955, M.A., 1959.

ADDRESSES: Home—669 Chemin de la Sine, 06140 Vence, France.

CAREER: Harvard University, Cambridge, MA, assistant professor of Middle Eastern studies, 1955-62; U.S. Department of State, Washington, DC, member of Policy Planning Council, 1961-65; University of Chicago, Chicago, IL, professor of Middle Eastern history and director of Center for Middle Eastern Studies, 1965-74; Adlai Stevenson Institute of International Affairs, Chicago, president, 1967-73. Advisory editor, Beacon Press, 1956-60; senior editor and member of board of directors, Arlington Books, Inc., 1959-61. Lecturer in United States and abroad. Member of board of directors of Hyde Park Bank & Trust Co., Microfilm Data System, Moore International, and Rabia Ltd.

MEMBER: Council on Foreign Relations, Middle East Institute (member of board of governors, 1962—), Middle East Studies Association of North America (member of board of directors), Academy on Public Policy (fellow).

AWARDS, HONORS: Four Rockefeller Foundation fellowships, 1951-55; Guggenheim fellowship, 1961-62.

WRITINGS:

What Arabs Think (published with *American Business and the Arab World* by W. Jack Butler), Foreign Policy Association (New York City), 1952.

(With David M. Stamler and Edmund Asfour) *Backdrop to Tragedy: The Struggle for Palestine,* Beacon Press (Boston, MA), 1957.

(Editor with others) *Studies on the Civilization of Islam,* Beacon Press, 1962.

(Editor, and author of introduction) *Developmental Revolution: North Africa, Middle East, South Africa,* Middle East Institute (Washington, DC), 1963.

The Opening of South Lebanon, 1788-1840: A Study of the Impact of the West on the Middle East, Harvard University Press (Cambridge, MA), 1963.

The United States and the Arab World, Harvard University Press, 1965, 5th edition published as *The Arab World Today,* 1991.

(Editor with Richard L. Chambers) *Beginnings of Modernization in the Middle East: The Nineteenth Century,* University of Chicago Press (Chicago, IL), 1968.

Passing Brave, Knopf (New York City), 1972.

(Translator, and author of introduction) *The Golden Ode,* University of Chicago Press, 1974.

The Elusive Peace: The Middle East in the Twentieth Century, St. Martin's (New York City), 1979.

Neighbors and Strangers: The Fundamentals of Foreign Affairs, University of Chicago Press, 1997.

Polk's Folly: An American Family History, Doubleday (New York City), 2000.

Also editor of and contributor to *Perspective of the Arab World,* 1956. Contributor to a report, "Ideology and Foreign Affairs," prepared for U.S. Senate Committee on Foreign Relations. Contributor to *Bulletin of the Atomic Scientists, Foreign Affairs Quarterly, The Atlantic,* and other journals.

WORK IN PROGRESS: Revolution! Miracle at Yorktown and the Good American: The Life, Times and Murder of George Polk.

SIDELIGHTS: William Roe Polk is an internationally recognized expert on Middle Eastern affairs. Polk's professional affiliations have included Harvard University and the University of Chicago, as well as the U.S. Department of State. His book-length assessment of the Middle East, published as *The Arab World Today,* has run through five editions since it was first printed in 1965. More recently, Polk's *Neighbors and Strangers: The Fundamentals of Foreign Affairs* was deemed "a wise, learned, and graceful work" by David C. Hendrickson in *Foreign Affairs.* Hendrickson further called the book "a superb introduction to the origin and logic of the principal areas of transaction among political collectives—defense, trade, espionage, and diplomacy." In *Library Journal,* James Holmes likewise characterized *Neighbors and Strangers* as "a lively and thought-provoking account strongly recommended for academic libraries."

Polk is a member of a distinguished American family of Scotch-Irish origin that includes former president James K. Polk and a veritable host of other military, academic, and business leaders. In *Polk's Folly: An American Family History,* the author profiles his forebears from the earliest immigrants—who landed in Maryland in 1680—to his brother, a journalist who was murdered in 1948. In between, Polk documents his family's success as plantation owners, James K. Polk's commendable presidency—during which the United States won the Mexican War—and Polk family contributions to the Civil War in both the Union and Confederate armies. To quote David Herbert Donald in the *New York Times Book Review,* Polk "demonstrates that the Polks are an underestimated clan, whose members have been involved in nearly every stage of American development and have participated with bravery and determination in every one of the country's wars." Noting that the earliest American generations of the Polk family are not well-documented, and that other generations failed to keep good records of themselves, Donald cited William Roe Polk for his attempts to reconstruct his ancestors' lives based upon histories of what was happening around them. "His method has enabled him to produce a spirited, broad-scale saga of an American family we ought to remember," Donald declared. *Library Journal* correspondent Dale F. Farris likewise praised Polk for his "passionate search for notables in his complex family tree," concluding that *Polk's Folly* is "a fascinating, entertaining saga that illuminates American history."

BIOGRAPHICAL/CRITICAL SOURCES:

PERIODICALS

Foreign Affairs, spring, 1981, p. 960; March-April, 1998, p. 150.

Library Journal, September 1, 1997, p. 201; January, 2000, p. 133.

New Statesman, January 4, 1980, p. 21.

New York Times Book Review, January 16, 2000, p. 18.

Publishers Weekly, September 22, 1997, p. 64; December 6, 1999, p. 65.

* * *

POLLAND, Madeleine A(ngela Cahill) 1918-
(Frances Adrian)

PERSONAL: Born May 31, 1918, in Kinsale, County Cork, Ireland; daughter of Patrick Richard (a civil servant) and Christina (Culkin) Cahill; married Arthur Joseph Polland (an accountant), June 10, 1946 (died, October, 1987); children: Charlotte Frances, Fergus Adrian. *Politics:* Conservative. *Religion:* Roman Catholic. *Avocational interests:* Lawn bowls, travel, museums, art.

ADDRESSES: Home—Edificio Hercules 634, Avenida Gamonal, Arroyo de la Miel, Malaga, Spain.

CAREER: Letchworth Public Library, Letchworth, England, assistant librarian, 1938-42; writer, 1958—. Guest speaker, New York Public Library Children's Book Fair, 1968. *Military service:* Women's Auxiliary Air Force, ground-controlled interception division of radar, 1942-45.

AWARDS, HONORS: New York Herald Tribune Honor Book, 1961, for *Children of the Red King,* and 1962, for *Beorn the Proud.*

WRITINGS:

JUVENILE NOVELS

Children of the Red King, Constable (London), 1960, Holt (New York City), 1961.
The Town across the Water, Constable, 1961, Holt, 1963.
Beorn the Proud, Constable, 1961, Holt, 1962.
Fingal's Quest, Doubleday (New York City), 1961.
The White Twilight, Constable, 1962, Holt, 1965.
Chuiraquimba and the Black Robes, Doubleday, 1962.
The City of the Golden House, Doubleday, 1963.
The Queen's Blessing, Constable, 1963, Holt, 1964.
Flame over Tara, Doubleday, 1964.
Mission to Cathay, Doubleday, 1965.
Queen without Crown, Constable, 1965, Holt, 1966.
Deirdre, Doubleday, 1967.
To Tell My People, Hutchinson, 1968.
Stranger in the Hills, Doubleday, 1968.
Alhambra, Doubleday, 1970.
To Kill a King, Holt, 1971.
A Family Affair, Hutchinson (London), 1971.
Daughter of the Sea, Doubleday, 1972, published in England as *Daughter to Poseidon,* Hutchinson, 1972.
Prince of the Double Axe, Abelard-Schuman (London), 1976.

ADULT NOVELS

Thicker than Water, Holt, 1966.
Minutes of a Murder, Holt, 1967, published in England as *The Little Spot of Bother,* Hutchinson, 1967.
Random Army, Hutchinson, 1969, published as *Shattered Summer,* Doubleday, 1970.
Package to Spain, Walker, 1971.
(Under pseudonym Frances Adrian) *Double Shadow,* Fawcett (New York City), 1978.
All Their Kingdoms, Delacorte (New York City), 1981.
The Heart Speaks Many Ways, Delacorte, 1982.
No Price Too High, Delacorte, 1984.
As It Was in the Beginning, Piatkus (London), 1987.
Rich Man's Flowers, Piatkus, 1990.
The Pomegranate House, Piatkus, 1992.

SIDELIGHTS: Madeleine A. Polland writes novels based on events and people in European, especially Irish, history. "My sense of history," she explained in her article for the *Something about the Author Autobiography Series* (*SAAS*), "has always been an important aspect of my writing: my consciousness of the feet that have walked before mine, and the fact that no matter how early the period, all those concerned were still *people.* Like ourselves."

To make her historical novels as realistic as possible, Polland has often visited the actual places she writes about, and walked the paths the historical people of her stories walked. Except for two stories set in China and Paraguay, she noted in her *SAAS* article, "I had the pleasure of walking through the settings for myself, in Ireland, Scotland, Denmark, England, and Spain, always in the company of some, if not all, of my family."

Of all these places, Ireland is apparently a particular favorite of Polland's according to Pamela Cleaver, a contributor to *Twentieth-Century Romance and Historical Writers.* "Her love for Ireland is very strong and her sympathy for its tribulations shows in books like *As It Was in the Beginning, Thicker than Water,* and *The Little Spot of Bother,*" Cleaver notes. "Her best, most lyrical descriptions, too, are of the Irish countryside." Ireland's struggle for independence from England figures in *As It Was in the Beginning;* its heroine, Kate Mary Pearse, is the cousin of a rebel leader and the lover of the man who is trying to hunt him down for the British government. Also set in Ireland is *Deidre,* a retelling of the legend of a young woman who, in ancient times, is betrothed to High King but falls in love with another man. Polland's preparations for writing this book included visiting the hill where the High King held court and the lakeside location where Deidre and her lover were said to have built their home, a spot where, "even now, the people there will tell the old story of Deidre's tragic love as if it were yesterday," Polland wrote in *SAAS.*

Polland has claimed that on several occasions she has felt odd sensations when visiting an historical site, sensations which gave her a brief vision of earlier times.

Writing in *Horn Book,* she told of visiting Sussex in southern England and suddenly feeling afraid: "I was shivering with a dreadful terror that was certainly not my own, nor could I gain any peace until I left the spot and gone away." Only later did she discover that the early Roman invaders had passed through that part of England and the fear she felt was akin to the fear that the early natives must have felt on confronting the Roman soldiers. In *To Tell My People* Polland writes of that time, and she has her character Lumna feel "the onslaught of terror at the first manifestations of a civilization she had never dreamed of. The same terror that I myself knew in the same spot."

Sometimes Polland draws on her own experience to create her fiction. As a little girl, she remembers the Irish civil war and the turmoil of that period, especially the time when her home town was burned to the ground. In *City of the Golden House,* a story set in ancient Rome, Polland drew on her memories to write of the burning of Rome. She explained in *Horn Book:* "I needed to re-create all the horror and terror of the fire of Rome during the reign of Emperor Nero. . . . I knew quite clearly that although I was writing of the fire of Rome, it was the burning of [my home town of] Kinsale which I recounted: a haunting from my childhood." Her research for this book, she noted in *SAAS,* drove home "the reality of history." She explained, "Even in ancient Rome people had one way or the other, just as we do, to buy their food and make their clothes and put shoes on their feet. And they were families, just as we are, with parents and children and uncles and aunts and grandmothers: some much loved and some not so cared for. I must say it came as a great surprise to me to find that they lived in blocks of apartments. Exactly as we do today."

Polland's insistence that people of times long past are essentially the same as the people of today has allowed her to create realistic characters in all of her historical fiction. The realism of her characters adds to the realism of her settings as well. A reviewer for *Horn Book* finds that in *The White Twilight* Polland "has told an absorbing story with an unusual historical setting and individual, well-realized characters. The beautiful writing and the strong feeling of place make the story rich and rewarding." A reviewer for *Junior Bookshelf* praises the realistic emotions of *Prince of the Double Axe:* "Death is shown as a kindly end to old age and suffering, fear as natural as loyalty and courage. Altogether, a sensitive and well-told story."

Polland's historical research does not impress all commentators; in an essay for *Twentieth-Century Children's Writers,* Graham Hammond contends that this "may seldom provide more than a vivid romanticised background to the drams she unfolds." He also finds her plots at times "implausible" and her pacing in some cases excessively slow, a reservation shared by Cleaver, who sees "more emphasis on emotion than action" in Polland's tales. "Indeed, a book like *The Little Spot of Bother* could easily be condensed into a short story as far as the action is concerned," Cleaver observes. Both essayists, however, find elements to admire in Polland's work. "She portrays her characters in bitter conflict, cruel dilemmas; they suffer pain and permanent injury on the road to self-knowledge," Hammond writes, adding that her books for juvenile readers "may well provide a not inconsiderable bridge" between children's and adult fiction. And Cleaver remarks, "Polland uses conflict of war (especially civil war in both Spain and Ireland), conflict of class, and conflict of cultures in her plotting. Her characters, especially her Irish characters, are realistic, and she is adept at portraying atmosphere such as the claustrophobic closeness of Irish village life. Her descriptions are evocative and beautiful; her love for the places she describes shines through." What is more, Cleaver concludes, "Polland's romances are truly romantic and although the reader is battered by stormy seas of emotion during the books, she reaches the safe harbour of the happy ending eventually."

BIOGRAPHICAL/CRITICAL SOURCES:

BOOKS

Something about the Author Autobiography Series, Volume 8, Gale (Detroit), 1989, pp. 227-242.

Twentieth-Century Children's Writers, 4th edition, St. James Press (Detroit), 1995.

Twentieth-Century Romance and Historical Writers, 3rd edition, St. James Press, 1994.

PERIODICALS

Best Sellers, March 15, 1971; April, 1979; October, 1982.

Books and Bookmen, January, 1973.

British Book News, April, 1987; May, 1987.

Bulletin of the Center for Children's Books, October, 1973.

Christian Science Monitor, November 12, 1970.

Commonweal, May 21, 1971.

Horn Book, June, 1965; June, 1966; August, 1967; April, 1968, pp. 147-150; October, 1968; October, 1970; December, 1970; June, 1971.

Junior Bookshelf, February, 1977.

Library Journal, October 15, 1970.

New York Times Book Review, May 9, 1965; July 18, 1965; July 9, 1967; October 27, 1968; February 6, 1972.
Publishers Weekly, February, 1973.
Punch, April 12, 1967.
Saturday Review, July 17, 1965; July 24, 1965.
Spectator, December 5, 1970.
Times Literary Supplement, May 25, 1967; July 27, 1967; November 30, 1967; October 3, 1968; June 26, 1969; October 30, 1970; April 2, 1971; May 14, 1971; December 8, 1972.

* * *

POLLARD, Sidney 1925-1998

PERSONAL: Born Siegfried Pollak, April 21, 1925, in Vienna, Austria; died November 22, 1998, in England; son of Moses and Leontine (Katz) Pollak; married Eileen Andrews, August 13, 1949 (divorced); married Helen Trippett, November 6, 1982; children: (first marriage) Brian Joseph, David Hugh, Veronica Ruth. *Education:* London School of Economics and Political Science, B.Sc., 1948, Ph.D., 1950. *Avocational interests:* The Cooperative Movement and cooperative education, music, walking, the cinema.

CAREER: University of Sheffield, Sheffield, England, Knoop fellow in economic history, 1950-52, assistant lecturer, 1952-55, lecturer, 1955-60, senior lecturer, 1960-63, professor of economic history, 1963-80; University of Bielefeld, Bielefeld, West Germany, professor of economic history, 1980-90, professor emeritus, 1990-98. Visiting professor of economics at universities in America, Israel, and Australia. *Military service:* Royal Reconnaissance Corps, 1943-47.

MEMBER: Economic History Society, Society for the Study of Labour History (chairman, 1964-66; president 1971-80).

AWARDS, HONORS: Thomas Newcomen Award in business history, 1967, for *The Genesis of Modern Management: A Study of the Industrial Revolution in Great Britain;* honorary senior fellow, University of Sheffield, 1990; honorary D. Litt, University of Sheffield, 1992.

WRITINGS:

Three Centuries of Sheffield Steel, Marsh Brothers (Sheffield), 1954.
A History of Labour in Sheffield, 1850-1939, Liverpool University Press (Liverpool, England), 1959.
The Development of the British Economy, 1914-1950, Edward Arnold (London), 1962, 4th edition published as *The Development of the British Economy, 1914-1990,* E. Arnold, 1992.
The Genesis of Modern Management: A Study of the Industrial Revolution in Great Britain, Harvard University Press (Cambridge, MA), 1965.
(With David W. Crossley) *The Wealth of Britain, 1086-1966,* Batsford (London), 1968, Schocken (New York City), 1969.
(Editor with C. Holmes) *Documents of European Economic History,* St. Martin's, Volume I: *The Process of Industrialization, 1750-1870,* 1968, Volume II: *Industrial Power and National Rivalry, 1870-1914,* 1972, Volume III: *The End of the Old Europe, 1914-1939,* 1973.
The Idea of Progress: History and Society, F. Watts (New York City), 1968.
(Editor and author of introduction) *The Gold Standard and Employment Policies between the Wars,* Methuen (London), 1970.
(Editor with others) *Aspects of Capital Investment in Great Britain, 1750-1850,* Methuen, 1971.
(Editor with John Salt) *Robert Owen: Prophet of the Poor,* Bucknell University Press (Cranbury, NJ), 1971.
European Economic Integration, 1815-1970, Harcourt (San Diego, CA), 1974.
(Editor with Holmes and author of introduction) *Essays in the Economic and Social History of South Yorkshire,* Recreation, Culture, and Health Department, South Yorkshire County Council, 1976.
(With Paul Robertson) *The British Shipbuilding Industry, 1870-1914,* Harvard University Press, 1979.
Peaceful Conquest: The Industrialization of Europe, 1760-1970, Oxford University Press, 1981.
The Integration of the European Economy since 1815, University Association for Contemporary European Studies, 1981.
The Wasting of the British Economy: British Economic Policy, 1945 to the Present, St. Martin's, 1982.
(With Charles H. Feinstein) *Studies in Capital Formation in the United Kingdom, 1750-1920,* Oxford University Press (Clarendon), 1988.
Britain's Prime and Britain's Decline: The British Economy, 1870-1914, E. Arnold, 1988.
Typology of Industrialization Processes in the Nineteenth Century, Gordon & Breach (London), 1990.
(Editor and contributor) *Wealth and Poverty: An Economic History of the twentieth Century,* Harrap (London), 1990.
(Contributor) *Economy and Society: European Industrialisation and Its Social Consequences,* Leicester University Press (Leicester, England), 1991.

(Editor and author of introduction) *The Metal Fabrication and Engineering Industries,* Blackwell (Cambridge, MA), 1994.
(Editor) *Von der Heimarbeit in die Fabrik: Industrialisierung und Arbeiterschaft in Leinen-und Baumwollregionen Westeuropas wahrend des 18. und 19. Jahrhunderts,* Frank Cass & Co. (London), 1995.
Marginal Europe: The Contribution of Marginal Lands since the Middle Ages, Oxford University Press (New York City), 1997.
The International Economy since 1945, Routledge (London), 1997.
Labour History and the Labour Movement in Britain, Ashgate (Brookfield, VT), 1999.
Essays on the Industrial Revolution, Ashgate, 2000.

Also editor of *The Trade Unions Commission: The Sheffield Outrages,* 1971. Contributor to professional journals and the British press. Editor, *Bulletin* of the Society for the Study of Labour History, 1960-71.

SIDELIGHTS: Professor Sidney Pollard's area of expertise was European economic history, and in that course of study he was a seminal figure. According to Albert O. Hirschman in *Economic Development and Cultural Change,* Pollard's work "makes a vital and original contribution to the understanding of development and industrialization of Europe." Professor Pollard not only described the means by which Britain became an industrial power, but he also predicted a period of relative economic decline in the post-World War II years. A London *Times* correspondent wrote of the scholar: "Pollard's was not an effortless ride to academic eminence, but the barriers in his way seemed to spur him on."

Born in Vienna, Austria in 1925, Pollard was sent to England by his Jewish parents in 1938. Both of his parents became Holocaust victims. As a refugee Pollard was put to work on various farms, but he did not like the work and sought to improve his lot through education. After taking some correspondence courses, he qualified for London University, but he did not finish his degree until after World War II. Upon finishing his doctoral degree in 1950, he became a research fellow and then the first professor of economic history at Sheffield University. His formal academic career ended in 1990 when he resigned a professorship at Bielefeld University in Germany, but he continued to write and speak until his death in 1998.

One of Pollard's better-known works is *Marginal Europe: The Contribution of Marginal Lands since the Middle Ages.* Hirschman wrote of the book: "It is immediately evident that we have here a view totally different from the traditional emphasis on the contrast between 'core' and 'periphery,' where core stands for the dynamic center and periphery for the less developed, 'dependant' and impoverished part of a country. Pollard is fully aware that he puts forward theses that are at odds with much conventional wisdom. But it should be said right away that he is not presenting his ideas as totally new, but rather as sequences that did occur and had their importance just as others."

In a *Business History* review of Pollard's *The International Economy since 1945,* B. W. E. Alford cited the professor for his "high standards," adding: "Pollard combines an enormous breadth of scholarship with an ability to condense material . . . whilst still presenting it in an engaging and informative manner." Elsewhere in *Business History,* W. R. Lee declared: "Pollard's espousal of a regional development model for understanding the broader processes of European industrialisation has redirected the focus of a great deal of recent research in this field." Indeed, much of Pollard's body of work has been praised for its originality and—in the case of his writings on postwar England—for its prescience. Although he died in November of 1998, much of his work is still in print, including two posthumously published texts on the industrial revolution.

BIOGRAPHICAL/CRITICAL SOURCES:

PERIODICALS

Business History, April, 1993, M. W. Kirby, review of *The Development of the British Economy,* p. 116; July, 1994, Sabine Spangenberg, review of *Markt, Staat, Planung—Historische Erfahrungen mit Regulierungs- und Deregulierungsversuchen der Wirtschaft,* p. 115; July, 1995, W. R. Lee, review of *Von der Heimarbeit in die Fabrik,* p. 126; April, 1998, B. W. E. Alford, review of *The International Economy since 1945,* p. 153.
Economic Development and Cultural Change, April, 1999, Albert O. Hirschman, review of *Marginal Europe,* p. 688.
Times Literary Supplement, February 19, 1970; April 9, 1971; September 10, 1971; May 26, 1972; June 1, 1973; September 11, 1981.

OBITUARIES:

PERIODICALS

The Independent (London), December 10, 1998, Colin Holmes, p. S6.

Times (London), December 18, 1998."*

* * *

POPKIN, Richard H(enry) 1923-

PERSONAL: Born December 27, 1923, in New York, NY; son of Louis (a public relations specialist) and Zelda (a writer; maiden name, Feinberg) Popkin; married Juliet Greenstone (a teacher), June 9, 1944; children: Jeremy, Margaret, Susan. *Education:* Columbia University, A.B., 1943, A.M., 1945, Ph.D., 1950; graduate study at Yale University, 1945-46. *Religion:* Jewish.

ADDRESSES: *Office*—Department of Philosophy, Washington University, St. Louis, MO 63130.

CAREER: University of Connecticut, Storrs, instructor in philosophy, 1946-47; State University of Iowa, Iowa City, assistant professor, 1947-58, associate professor of philosophy, 1958-60; Harvey Mudd College, Claremont, CA, professor of philosophy, 1960-63; University of California, San Diego, professor of philosophy, 1963-73; Washington University, St. Louis, MO, professor of philosophy, 1973-98, professor emeritus, 1998—; University of California, Los Angeles, adjunct professor of philosophy and history, 1998—. Founding, director, International Archives of the History of Ideas. *Military service:* U.S. Army, 1943.

MEMBER: American Society for Eighteenth-Century Studies (member of executive board, 1973-76), American Philosophical Association (vicepresident of Western Division, 1962), Renaissance Society of America, Phi Beta Kappa.

AWARDS, HONORS: Nicholas Murray Butler Medal from Columbia University, 1977.

WRITINGS:

(With Ayrum Stroll) *Philosophy Made Simple,* Doubleday (Garden City, NJ), 1957, 2nd revised edition, 1993.

The History of Scepticism from Erasmus to Descartes, Van Gorcum & Co., 1960, revised edition, 1964, Harper (New York City), 1968, 4th edition, University of California Press (Berkeley, CA), 1979.

(With Stroll) *Introduction to Philosophy,* Holt (New York City), 1961, revised edition, 1979.

(Editor and translator) Pierre Bayle, *Historical and Critical Dictionary: Selections,* Bobbs-Merrill (New York City), 1965.

(Editor with David Norton) *David Hume's Historical Writings: Selections,* Bobbs-Merrill, 1965.

(Editor and author of introduction) *Readings in the History of Philosophy: The Sixteenth and Seventeenth Centuries,* Free Press (New York City), 1966.

The Second Oswald, Avon (New York City), 1966, revised edition, Andre Deutsch (New York City), 1967.

(Editor with Stroll) *Readings in Philosophy,* Holt, 1972, revised edition, 1979.

(With Stroll) *Philosophy and the Human Spirit: A Brief Introduction,* Holt, 1973.

The High Road to Pyrrhonism, Austin Hill (San Diego, CA), 1980.

Isaac La Peyrere (1596-1676): His Life, Work, and Influence, E. J. Brill (Leiden, the Netherlands), 1987.

(Editor and author of introduction, notes, and bibliography) *Pascal Selections,* Macmillan (New York City), 1989.

The Third Force in Seventeenth-Century Thought, E. J. Brill, 1992.

(With David S. Katz) *Messianic Revolution: Radical Religious Politics to the End of the Second Millennium,* Hill & Wang (New York City), 1999.

(Editor) *The Columbia History of Western Philosophy,* Columbia University Press (New York City), 1999.

CONTRIBUTOR

Frank N. Magill, editor, *Masterpieces of World Philosophy in Summary Form,* Salem Press (Englewood Cliffs, NJ), 1961.

C. M. Turbayne, editor, *Studies on Bishop Berkeley,* Bobbs-Merrill, 1970.

Physics, Logic, and History, Plenum (New York City), 1970.

R. B. Palmer, editor, *Philomathes: Studies and Essays in the Humanities in Memory of Philip Merlan,* Nijhoff (The Netherlands), 1971.

Josiah Thompson, editor, *Kierkegaard: A Collection of Critical Essays,* Doubleday (New York City), 1972.

Craig Walton and John P. Anton, editors, *Philosophy and the Civilizing Arts: Essays Presented to Herbert W. Schneider,* Ohio University Press (Athens), 1974.

Essays in Honor of Ernest C. Mossner, Edinburgh University Press (Edinburgh, Scotland), 1974.

Big Brother and the Holding Company, Ramparts (Palo Alto, CA), 1974.

Woman in the Eighteenth Century, and Other Essays, McMaster University, 1976.

Edward P. Mahoney, editor, *Philosophy and Humanism: Renaissance Essays in Honor of Paul Oskar Kristeller,* E. J. Brill, 1976.

Kenneth R. Merrill and Robert W. Shahan, editors, *David Hume, Many-sided Genius,* University of Oklahoma Press (Norman), 1976.

AUTHOR OF INTRODUCTION

Henry Van Leeuwen, *The Problem of Certainty in English Thought, 1630-1690,* Nijhoff, 1963.

Joseph Glanvill, *Essays on Several Important Subjects in Philosophy and Religion,* Johnson Reprint (New York City), 1970.

Donald Freed and Mark Lane, editors, *Executive Action,* Dell (New York City), 1973.

Isaac La Peyrere, *Men before Adam,* Olms Reprint, 1979.

La Peyrere, *Du Rappel des Juifs* (title means "The Recall of the Jews"), Olms Reprint, 1979.

Stillingfleet, *Three Attacks on Locke,* Olms Reprint, 1980.

OTHER

Also contributor to Paul Dibon, editor, *Pierre Bayle: Le Philosophe de Rotterdam, 1959;* V. C. Chapell, editor, *Hume,* 1966; *Expanding Horizons of Knowledge about Man, Yeshiva University,* 1967; *Naturalism and Historical Understanding: Essays on the Philosophy of John H. Randall, Jr.,* 1967; *The Critical Spirit: Essays in Honor of Herbert Marcuse,* 1967; Imre Lakatos and Alan Musgrave, editors, *Problems in the Philosophy of Science,* 1968; N. S. Carl and R. H. Grimm, editors, *Perception and Personal Identity: Proceedings of the 1967 Oberlin Colloquium in Philosophy,* 1969. Contributor to *Encyclopaedia Britannica, Catholic Encyclopedia, Encyclopedia of Philosophy, Encyclopedia Judaica,* and *Dictionary of the History of Ideas.* Contributor of more than 200 articles and reviews to scholarly journals and popular magazines, including *Ramparts.* Founding editor, *Journal of the History of Philosophy.*

SIDELIGHTS: Richard H. Popkin is an historian of philosophy who is well versed in Western systems of thought stretching back into Classical times. Popkin was based at Washington University in St. Louis, Missouri, for much of his career and has more recently been an adjunct professor at the University of California, Los Angeles. His writings give not only an historic overview of philosophy but also, in some cases, apply it to current events such as messianic cult activity and skepticism. *Library Journal* correspondent Robert Hoffman stated that Popkin's work "ranges over the whole history of Western philosophy, from the pre-Socratics to 20th-century philosophy, both analytic and continental."

Popkin teamed with David S. Katz to write *Messianic Revolution: Radical Religious Politics to the End of the Second Millennium,* appropriately published in 1999. The work explores the history of millenarianism from ancient times to the present, focusing primarily upon Judaic and Christian traditions. The authors see their book as a guide to the basic aims of millennial teaching and the behavior of doomsday cult leaders such as David Koresh, whose followers were fire-bombed by the FBI after a lengthy siege of their compound in 1993. In a *Booklist* review of *Messianic Revolution,* Steven Schroeder commended Popkin and Katz for their "fresh reading of European history and a look at sources often neglected in textbook accounts. . . . Acquaintance with those roots helps in understanding not only messianic movements but also the social and political conversations those movements inform." A *Publishers Weekly* contributor suggested that the book "brings together a potpourri of interesting people who have been fascinated by the interpretation of biblical prophecy." The critic concluded: "Katz and Popkin have produced a book that is clear, concise and comprehensive." *Times Literary Supplement* reviewer David Martin deemed *Messianic Revolution* a "beautifully written and well-timed" study that reveals "the broad relationship of Judaism to its radical Christian revision over the last two millennia."

BIOGRAPHICAL/CRITICAL SOURCES:

PERIODICALS

Booklist, April 15, 1999, p. 1488.

Economist, December 4, 1999, p. 6.

Library Journal, February 1, 1999, p. 92.

Publishers Weekly, March 8, 1999, p. 62.*

* * *

QUEENAN, Joe 1950-

PERSONAL: Born November 3, 1950, in Philadelphia, PA; son of Joseph and Agnes (McNulty) Queenan; married Francesca Jane Spinner (a certified public accountant), January 7, 1977; children: Bridget, Gordon. *Education:* St. Joseph's College, B.A., 1972. *Politics:* Democrat. *Religion:* Roman Catholic.

ADDRESSES: Home—Tarrytown, NY. *Agent*—Joe Vallecy, 320 Riverside Dr., New York, NY 10012.

CAREER: Barron's, New York City, writer, 1987-89; *Forbes,* senior editor, 1989-90; freelance writer, 1990—.

WRITINGS:

Imperial Caddy: The Rise of Dan Quayle in America and the Decline and Fall of Practically Everything Else, Hyperion (New York City), 1992.

If You're Talking to Me, Your Career Must Be in Trouble: Movies, Mayhem, and Malice, Hyperion, 1994.

The Unkindest Cut: How a Hatchet-Man Critic Made His Own $7,000 Movie and Put It All on His Credit Card, Hyperion, 1995.

Red Lobster, White Trash, and the Blue Lagoon: Joe Queenan's America, Hyperion, 1998.

Confessions of a Cineplex Heckler: Celluloid Tirades and Escapades, Hyperion, 1999.

My Goodness: A Cynic's Short-Lived Search for Sainthood, Hyperion, 2000.

Contributor to magazines and newspapers, including *Spy, Gentlemen's Quarterly, TV Guide, Movieline, Chief Executive,* and *Time.*

SIDELIGHTS: Joe Queenan casts a jaundiced eye on popular culture and reports his opinions on everything from film stars to chain restaurants—always using humor to bolster his views. According to Bruce McCall in the *New York Times Book Review,* Queenan has crafted "a lucrative career spent gleefully skewering Hollywood airheads and other hapless patsies for skewering's sake." Like many a humorist before him, Queenan has vented his spleen against easy targets in politics, movies, and music. Unlike others, however, he has taken his vision a step further, making his own low-budget film and setting off to immerse himself in low-brow pleasures. Calling Queenan a "proven comic talent" in the *New York Times Book Review,* Lance Gould noted: "The very fact that a talented cultural critic is devoting time and energy to dissect the creative efforts of known hacks is certainly ripe with humorous possibilities. . . . Queenan's razor-sharp rebukes can be appreciated by anyone who has done time in an elevator, supermarket aisle or dentist's office."

Queenan claims that his upbringing accounts for his cynical mindset. "I grew up in Philadelphia. Everyone from Philly is mean," he told the *Knight-Ridder/Tribune News Service.* Indeed, the author has found a great deal of writing grist in his North Philadelphia Roman Catholic childhood. His favorite pastime as a youngster was attending the movies at the neighborhood theater, and after graduating from St. Joseph's University in Philadelphia he gravitated to film reviewing and political commentary for magazines such as *Spy* and *Rolling Stone.* His disdain for the moviemaking community in Los Angeles won him a readership—and made him a pariah in Hollywood. In the *American Spectator,* Andrew Ferguson wrote: "Movies are a tempting target for the satirist, because most movies are made by dolts and it shows. Queenan was uniquely equipped for sustained labor. Not only is his knowledge of movies encyclopedic, his visual sense highly refined, his nose for cant and sham unerring. And not only is he a gifted stylist whose prose swings effortlessly from scabrous insult to semi-serious praise. Joe Queenan had something more: he was actually willing to stay home and watch movies for uninterrupted weeks at a time."

Queenan's movie criticism is collected in such volumes as *If You're Talking to Me, Your Career Must Be in Trouble: Movies, Mayhem, and Malice* and *Confessions of a Cineplex Heckler: Celluloid Tirades and Escapades.* The books are unsparing in their satire and are particularly unforgiving to some of Hollywood's biggest icons—Barbra Streisand, Woody Allen, and Oliver Stone, to name a few. To quote *Booklist* reviewer Gilbert Taylor, "Queenan's acerbic aspersions upon icons such as [Martin] Scorcese and Streisand have made him persona non grata in Tinseltown, but not to silver screen addicts who love to see overblown egos deflated." In the *New York Times Book Review,* Michael E. Ross deemed Queenan to be a "Jeremiah of the movies, a kind of pop-culture consumer-affairs reporter," and a *Publishers Weekly* correspondent called Queenan "a quirky, often perceptive movie maven" whose "insights are often so on-target that readers may find themselves wishing for more." The critic added: "He is essentially a comic writer who delivers laughs in almost every essay."

In 1995 Queenan set out to prove that he, too, could make a bad movie. Inspired by the independent film *El Mariachi,* purported to have been made for a mere $7,000, Queenan decided to produce his own movie, *Twelve Steps to Death,* for the lesser sum of $6,998. His adventures during production are recounted in *The Unkindest Cut: How a Hatchet-Man Critic Made His Own $7,000 Movie and Put It All on His Credit Card.* Queenan took adult-education courses on film editing and script writing, cast his children and neighbors in the movie, shot it in his backyard, and tried to get the whole project finished in nine days. To quote Julia Phillips in the *New York Times Book Review,* "The bottom line of *Twelve Steps to Death* is a bottomless pit, and [Queenan's] tour de force balloons into a $69,999 farce de frappe." Phillips found *The Unkindest Cut* "an often hilarious, almost always unflinching account of the making of the movie." In *Booklist,* Taylor described the entire adventure as "a pretty atrocious movie with pretty good publicity that just might recoup Queenan's investment. Although *Twelve Steps* may never darken your local international film festival, this hyperbolic spoof of moviemaking shows what you're missing."

Red Lobster, White Trash, and the Blue Lagoon: Joe Queenan's America charts a new goal for the author: complete immersion in pop culture for an entire year. "Queenan sets off to explore the real America," declared Lance Gould in the *New York Times Book Review.* "Only the one Queenan visits is where Billy Joel and Michael Bolton are hailed as musical virtuosos and where a night out at the Olive Garden is considered a fine dining experience." *Insight on the News* contributor Rex Roberts observed: "*Red Lobster* is often funny, although Queenan's shtick consists of one joke. . . . To his credit, Queenan knows that his fusillades against such easy targets won't carry the day, so he invents a plot that has him falling even deeper into the morass of American culture." Roberts concluded: "These days, a little bit of elite-and-effete humor goes a long way. Queenan is funny, but readers are cautioned to take him in small doses." A *Publishers Weekly* reviewer praised the book for its "hilarious venting of spleen," adding: "Cynics in general and fans of Queenan in particular will find many pleasures in this wonderfully comic diatribe."

A moral reckoning awaits Queenan in his work *My Goodness: A Cynic's Short-Lived Search for Sainthood.* Taking stock of his voluminous output of nasty remarks and taking a contrite look around him at all the worthy causes championed by rock musicians and movie stars, Queenan decides to seek redemption by using ethically correct toothpaste and issuing apologies to those who have felt the sting of his pen. As Bruce McCall noted, Queenan "is far from the first writer to identify the pursuit of human virtue as prime satirical fodder, but he's probably the first to do so by working within the system." McCall added: "There's barely a sentence in *My Goodness* without a risible time-out in the wrestling match between the author's guilt and his exertions to become a better person. And apart from the story of his epic struggle, pitting Queenan's congenital iconoclasm against the smug, sappy and hypocritical premises of the moral correctness movement is a book idea whose time has come." A *Publishers Weekly* reviewer cited the work for its "gleefully barbed and insouciant tone that has made [Queenan] famous as an insult-meister." And McCall concluded that *My Goodness* "has to be the year's most sinfully rewarding guilty pleasure."

Joe Queenan told *CA:* "I write because it beats working in a factory. That's it."

BIOGRAPHICAL/CRITICAL SOURCES:

PERIODICALS

American Spectator, June, 1994, Andrew Ferguson, review of *If You're Talking to Me, Your Career Must Be in Trouble: Movies, Mayhem, and Malice,* p. 62.

Booklist, January 1, 1994, Gilbert Taylor, review of *If You're Talking to Me, Your Career Must Be in Trouble: Movies, Mayhem, and Malice,* p. 800; February 1, 1996, Gilbert Taylor, review of *The Unkindest Cut: How a Hatchet-Man Critic Made His Own $7,000 Movie and Put It All on His Credit Card,* p. 910.

Knight-Ridder/Tribune News Service, February 17, 1994, Laurie Busby, "Joe Queenan Has Hollywood in His Satiric Gunsight and No Lack of Ammunition," p. 21.

Insight on the News, August 3, 1998, Rex Roberts, review of *Red Lobster, White Trash, and the Blue Lagoon: Joe Queenan's America,* p. 36.

Nation, November 9, 1992, Douglas McGrath, review of *Imperial Caddy: The Rise of Dan Quayle in America and the Decline and Fall of Practically Everything Else,* p. 547.

National Review, August 31, 1992, Joseph Sobran, review of *Imperial Caddy. The Rise of Dan Quayle in America and the Decline and Fall of Practically Everything Else,* p. 69.

New York Times Book Review, October 11, 1992, Molly Ivins, "A Heartbeat Away," p. 13; January 28, 1996, Julia Phillips, "Movie Madness," p. 34; July 26, 1998, Lance Gould, "Awful! Terrible! Excruciatingly Bad!," p. 10; February 20, 2000, Michael E. Ross, review of *Confessions of a Cineplex Heckler: Celluloid Tirades and Escapades;* March 5, 2000, Bruce McCall, review of *My Goodness: A Cynic's Short-Lived Search for Sainthood.*

Publishers Weekly, June 22, 1998, review of *Red Lobster, White Trash, and the Blue Lagoon: Joe Queenan's America,* p. 77; December 6, 1999, review of *Confessions of a Cineplex Heckler: Celluloid Tirades and Escapades,* p. 60; January 10, 2000, review of *My Goodness: A Cynic's Short-Lived Search for Sainthood,* p. 55.*

R

RABASSEIRE, Henri
See PACHTER, Henry M(aximillian)

* * *

RAKOSI, Carl
See RAWLEY, Callman

* * *

RAMAGE, James A(lfred) 1940-

PERSONAL: Born May 6, 1940, in Paducah, KY; son of Newman (a farmer) and Helen (Culp) Ramage; married Ann Winstead (an accountant), June 6, 1964; children: Andrea Suzanne. *Education:* Murray State University, B.S., 1965, M.A., 1968; University of Kentucky, Ph.D., 1972. *Politics:* Democrat. *Religion:* Baptist.

ADDRESSES: Home—369 Knollwood Dr., Highland Heights, KY 41076. *Office*—Department of History, Northern Kentucky State College, Highland Heights, KY 41076.

CAREER: High school teacher of history in the county schools of St. Louis, MO, 1965-67; Northern Kentucky State College, Highland Heights, assistant professor, 1972-75, associate professor of history, beginning in 1975, assistant to the president, beginning in 1972. City of Highland Heights, chairperson of Citizens Task Force for Planning, 1974-75; Recreation Commission for Highland Heights, chairperson, beginning in 1975. *Military service:* U.S. Air Force, 1958-62.

MEMBER: Southern Historical Association, Kentucky Historical Society, Red River Valley Historical Association, Filson Club, Phi Alpha Theta.

WRITINGS:

John Wesley Hunt: Pioneer Merchant, Manufacturer, and Financier, University Press of Kentucky (Lexington, KY), 1974.
Holman Hamilton: A Biographical Sketch, University Press of Kentucky, 1975.
Rebel Raider: The Life of General John Hunt Morgan, University Press of Kentucky, 1986.
(With Lester V. Horwitz) *The Longest Raid of the Civil War: Little-known and Untold Stories of Morgan's Raid into Kentucky, Indiana, and Ohio,* Farmcourt, 1999.
Gray Ghost: The Life of Colonel John Singleton Mosby, University Press of Kentucky, 1999.

BIOGRAPHICAL/CRITICAL SOURCES:

PERIODICALS

American Historical Review, October, 1987, p. 1037.
Journal of American History, June, 1987, p. 181.
Library Journal, July 16, 1986, p. 77; September 1, 1999, p. 204.
New York Times Book Review, October 24, 1999, p. 36.*

RAWLEY, Callman 1903-
(Carl Rakosi)

PERSONAL: Born Carl Rakosi, November 6, 1903, in Berlin, Germany; name legally changed; came to the United States, 1910; son of Leopold and Flora (Steiner) Rakosi; married Leah Jaffe, May 6, 1939; children: Barbara, George. *Education:* University of Wisconsin, B.A., 1924, M.A., 1926; University of Pennsylvania, Master of Social Work, 1940. *Religion:* Jewish.

ADDRESSES: Home—1464 17th Ave., San Francisco, CA 94122.

CAREER: Family Service, Cleveland, OH, caseworker; involved with Jewish Board of Guardians, New York City, and Massachusetts Society for Prevention of Cruelty to Children, Boston, 1925-26; University of Texas at Austin, instructor, 1928-29; Cook County Bureau of Public Welfare, Chicago, IL, social worker, 1932-33; Federal Transit Bureau, New Orleans, LA, supervisor, 1933-34; Tulane University of Louisiana (now Tulane University), Graduate School of Social Work, New Orleans, field work supervisor, 1934-35; Jewish Family Welfare Society, Brooklyn, NY, caseworker, 1935-40; Jewish Social Service Bureau, St. Louis, MO, case supervisor, 1940-43; assistant director of Jewish Children's Bureau and Bellefaire (residential treatment center for disturbed children), both Cleveland, OH, 1943-45; Jewish Family and Children's Service, Minneapolis, MN, executive director, 1945-68; private practice in psychotherapy and marriage counseling, 1958-68; Yaddo, Saratoga Springs, NY, resident writer, 1968-75. Writer-in-residence, University of Wisconsin, 1969-70; member of faculty, National Poetry Festival, 1973; poet-in-residence, Michigan State University, 1974.

MEMBER: National Association of Social Workers (president of South Minnesota chapter, 1959-61), National Conference of Jewish Communal Service (vice president, 1957-58), Family Service Association of America (chairman of Midwest regional committee, 1961-64; chairman of committee on long-range planning, 1964-66).

AWARDS, HONORS: National Endowment for the Arts award, 1969, fellowship, 1972 and 1979; Distinguished Service award, National Poetry Association, 1988; Penn Award, 1996, for *Poems, 1923-1941.*

WRITINGS:

UNDER NAME CARL RAKOSI

Two Poems, Modern Editions Press (New York City), 1933.

Selected Poems, New Directions (New York City), 1941.

Amulet, New Directions, 1967.

Two Poems, Modern Editions Press, 1971.

Ere-Voice, New Directions, 1971.

Ex-Cranium, Night, Black Sparrow Press (Santa Barbara, CA), 1975.

My Experiences in Parnassus, Black Sparrow Press, 1977.

History, Oasis Books (London), 1981.

Droles de Journal, Toothpaste Press, 1981.

Carl Rakosi: Collected Prose, National Poetry Foundation (Orono, ME), 1983.

Spiritus I, Pig Press (Durham, England), 1983.

Carl Rakosi: Collected Poems, National Poetry Foundation, 1986.

Poems, 1923-1941, Sun and Moon (Los Angeles), 1995.

The Earth Suite, Etruscan Books (England), 1997.

The Old Poet's Tale, Etruscan Books, 1999.

Also author of *The Beasts* and *Early Poems,* both 1994. Contributor to anthologies, including *The American Literary Anthology,* no. 3, edited by Plimpton and Ardery, *Heartland II,* edited by Lucien Stryk, *Modern Things,* edited by Parker Tyler, *An Introduction to Poetry,* edited by Louis Simpson, *The Treasury of American Poetry,* edited by Nancy Sullivan, *A Geography of Poets,* edited by Edward Field, *Inside Outer Space,* edited by Robert Vas Dias, *From the Other Side of the Century,* Sun and Moon, 1994; *Poems for the Mellenium,* University of California Press, 1995, and *The Body Electric,* Norton, 2000. Contributor of poetry to journals, including *Paris Review, Poetry, Massachusetts Review, American Poetry Review, Transition, Exile, Sulfur,* and *Conjunctions.*

SIDELIGHTS: Callman Rawley, known in the literary world as poet Carl Rakosi, is a member of the older Objectivist group of poets, "reflecting the influence" of Ezra Pound and William Carlos Williams, a *Choice* reviewer relates. Objectivist writing is characterized by the presentation of concrete images; direct treatment of the subject without ornamental verbiage; and insistence on a high degree of craftsmanship, such that the poem itself is an object deliberately constructed in a form appropriate to its content. Rakosi once explained to *CA* how he came to be associated with the group: "I received an invitation from Louis Zukofsky to rush him my best poems for a special issue of *Poetry* which he was editing under the sponsorship of Ezra Pound. Here began my association with him and with two of the others in that issue and, later, in *An 'Objectivist' Anthology,* George Oppen and Charles Reznikoff. Zukofsky called us Objectivists. We are still known by that name." Rakosi's early work received some praise, with a *New York Herald Tribune Books* reviewer declaring that in *Selected Poems,* "Rakosi turns out the carefully disciplined and distinguished work of a mature poet."

Rakosi gave up poetry, however, for an extended period. "Between the years 1939 and 1965 I wrote no poetry," Rakosi once told *CA.* Jim Harrison, writing in the *New York Times Book Review,* explains that the poet had stopped writing because he had come to feel "in the wake of the Depression and World War II, his intensely individual lyricism was irrelevant and impossible to continue." Geoffrey O'Brien reports in a *Village Voice* review that the poet remarked of Pound's *Cantos,* "All that pretense and double-dealing are nauseating to me. And irrelevant. People today are not heroes, and modern human nature is not epic. It's just human, and anything else is just playing games." Poetry, he felt, would not accomplish much to alleviate the desperation of the people he wanted to help. He devoted himself to his career in social work and to his family.

A letter from Andrew Crozier, a young British poet, moved Rakosi to begin writing again. The letter, written in 1965, explained how Crozier had admired Rakosi's early poems, and had searched out nearly eighty of them in various journals. When he saw that Rakosi must have stopped writing, he politely inquired why. "I almost wept when I received this," Rakosi once told *CA.* Of his work since then, O'Brien comments, "Rakosi's late phase is not so much a resumption as a rebirth. The 'Ancient image' which he prays will 'restore / my ancient relation / to words / in which I have set / my hope' seems to have answered him generously." In the poems of this second period, Harrison observes, "The positive effect of Rakosi's social concerns are direct and evident. . . . It is a tremendously engaged poetry, humane, attentive to the ordinary until the ordinary ceases to be so, but scarcely ever committing the usual objectivist sin of mere attitude, that of expecting dumb, unequal objects to stand by themselves as poems. These poems are 'made' things and throughout the book we sense the intelligence that directed the craft." Harrison concludes by saying that Rakosi "should be read and saluted by those who care for the life of the poem," and other critics voice similar sentiments. Poems in *Amulet,* comments *Prairie Schooner* contributor Stanley Cooperman, "will, I believe, come as something of an unexpected pleasure to those readers who have been so bullied by academic theorists, and anti-academic academic theorists, that they approach objectivist poetry with the foolish solemnity of society matrons attending a light-show." Cooperman especially enjoys "the ease and comfort and wit of [Rakosi's] work."

W. G. Regier, however, in a *Prairie Schooner* review of *Ere-Voice,* takes exception to Rakosi's tone, calling it "self-satire . . . rising to self-righteousness" and describing the poet as "a self-appointed prophet." He opines, "It is finally this tone that ruins most of Rakosi's work." But in this collection are a few fine poems, such as "In a Warm Bath," which has "substance supporting tone," in Regier's assessment. "Rakosi has as many faults as the California coast," Regier summarizes. "What a wonder that he can be just as attractive. When the passage is made through the wasteland, Rakosi rewards his readers with jewels." Some other negative responses to Rakosi's work focus on his techniques. *Poetry* contributor Laurence Lieberman feels that "the line weave"—a form made of lines alternately aligned to the right, then the left sides of the page—"dominate all other qualities in the poems" in *Amulet.* As a result, he feels, it is more difficult to appreciate the variety of themes and objects Rakosi presents. Other reviewers feel that his sudden shifts between theme, sound patterns, and levels of diction diffuse the lyric energy of the poems. Cooperman, however, responds more favorably. "It is the casual leap into serious thought and back again, that keeps us balancing on the points of our mind, doing a verbal and intellectual jig to a fiddle that sometimes—and unexpectedly—becomes an orchestration. Quickness is needed: the ability to shift tones both on the linguistic and intellectual level. For Rakosi's work is at once irreverent and serious; highly intellectual and simplistic," Cooperman suggests.

This "leaping" between various registers of language is closely related to Rakosi's major theme, "the irreducible tension between a perceiving human and physical reality. . . . His most serious poems try to capture the knowledge of the shifty, duplicitous nature" of the human relationship to the physical world, Michael Heller writes in the *New York Times Book Review* critique of *Collected Poems.* O'Brien also notes this aspect of Rakosi's poetry, saying "his poems thrive on a tensile oscillation between the particularity of raw data and the whimsical unpredictability of the mind's music. . . . Abrupt shifts of tone and perspective become a technique for reminding himself where he is." Heller, in his *Conviction's Net of Branches: Essays on the Objectivist Poets and Poetry,* defines Rakosi as a poet "profoundly in between" his imaginative, emotional life and the objects in his world. Through poetry, he establishes more than a simple link between these two planes of reference; in his variety, he suggests that poetry provides "an infinity of linkages," Heller observes. Therefore, he says, "the substantive quality of [Rakosi's] work lies not in the things it renders but in this arrested quality, the shapely contour of interacting thought and emotion, thought and object." Heller adds, "It is because of this tracing, this linguistic interconnecting, that Rakosi strikes one as, above all, the poet of the lived world, the phenomenal world radiating out from us, the world under the double sign of self and otherness."

"Like Williams's [poetry]," writes *New York Times Book Review* critic R. W. Flint, "his writing has obviously been nourished every step of the way by the rigors and rewards of exacting work well outside the literary orbit." Heller, writing in *Conviction's Net of Branches,* opines that "Rakosi's work is among the most compassionate bodies of poetry, . . . because so much seems to be transformed for the express purposes of communication and seems to have been given over to directness of statement and the recognition that another human is reading it." Adds O'Brien: "I can think of no contemporary poet who radiates such an aura of enjoyment—enjoyment of the mind, of the oddness of language, of the mind's capacity to make something out of nothing."

BIOGRAPHICAL/CRITICAL SOURCES:

BOOKS

Contemporary Authors Autobiography Series, Volume 5, Gale (Detroit), 1987.

Contemporary Literary Criticism, Volume 47, Gale, 1988.

Heller, Michael, *Conviction's Net of Branches: Essays on the Objectivist Poets and Poetry,* Southern Illinois University Press (Carbondale), 1985.

Heller, Michael, editor, *Carl Rakosi: Man and Poet,* National Poetry Foundation, University of Maine (Orono), 1993.

PERIODICALS

American Book Review, May-June, 1982.

Chicago Review, winter, 1979.

Choice, July-August, 1972, review of *Ex Cranium, Night,* p. 73.

Contemporary Literature, spring, 1969.

Iowa Review, winter, 1971.

New York Herald Tribune Books, May 10, 1942, "Objectivism," p. 30.

New York Times Book Review, May 17, 1942, Peter Monro Jack, review of *Selected Poems,* p. 5; January 28, 1968, Jim Harrison, "Gnomic Verse," p. 10; November 16, 1975; March 8, 1987, Michael Heller, "Heaven and the Modern World," p. 22.

Poetry, August, 1968, Laurence Lieberman, review of *Amulet,* pp. 340-342.

Poetry Flash, March, 1987.

Prairie Schooner, fall, 1968, Stanley Cooperman, "The Experience of Having Poemed," pp. 266-272; spring, 1972, W. G. Regier, "The Touring Word," pp. 85-86.

Preview, June, 1975.

Threepenny Review, summer, 1988.

Times Literary Supplement, October 12, 1984, Michael Hulse, "Taking on the Alien," p. 1169.

Village Voice, June 13, 1987, Geoffrey O'Brien, "Enjoy!," pp. 50, 52.

* * *

REDFIELD, James 1950-

PERSONAL: Born March 19, 1950, in Alabama; married Salle Merrill (a massage therapist and writer). *Education:* Studied at Auburn University; M.A. in counseling.

ADDRESSES: *Home*—Florida. *Agent*—c/o Warner Books, Inc., Time & Life Bldg., 9th Floor, 1271 Avenue of the Americas, New York, NY 10020.

CAREER: Children's counselor and therapist; freelance author.

MEMBER: Global Renaissance Alliance.

AWARDS, HONORS: Medal of the Presidency of the Italian Senate, 1997.

WRITINGS:

The Celestine Prophecy (novel), Warner Books (New York City), 1993.

(With Carol Adrienne) *The Celestine Prophecy: An Experiential Guide* (workbook), Warner Books, 1995.

The Tenth Insight: Holding the Vision (novel), Warner Books, 1996.

(With Adrienne) *The Tenth Insight: Holding the Vision; An Experiential Guide* (workbook), Warner Books, 1996.

The Celestine Vision: Living the New Spiritual Awareness, Warner Books, 1997.

(With Dee Lillegard) *The Song of Celestine* (juvenile novel), illustrated by Dean Morrissey, Little, Brown (Boston), 1998.

(Author of introduction) Carol Adrienne, *The Purpose of Your Life: Finding Your Place in the World Using Synchronicity, Intuition, and Uncommon Sense,* Morrow (New York City), 1998.

The Secret of Shambhala: In Search of the Eleventh Insight, Warner Books, 1999.

WORK IN PROGRESS: Further sequels to the *Celestine Prophecy.*

SIDELIGHTS: New Age philosopher and author James Redfield astonished the publishing world with the success of his spiritual vision in novel form, *The Celestine Prophecy.* Redfield first self-published the book, which had been rejected by several conventional firms, and sold copies of it out of the trunk of his car. He attracted sufficient attention in New Age circles, and circulated so many copies, that Warner Books decided to buy *The Celestine Prophecy* for 800,000 dollars in 1993. With a major company behind it, the volume's sales took off. As of June, 1996, according to Marci McDonald in *Maclean's, The Celestine Prophecy* had sold 5.8 million copies in thirty-two countries and had "a stranglehold on the top spot of *The New York Times* best-seller list for . . . 116 weeks." Redfield collaborated with Carol Adrienne on a workbook for the novel, *The Celestine Prophecy: An Experiential Guide,* which saw print in 1995. He also penned a sequel, *The Tenth Insight: Holding the Vision,* and collaborated with Adrienne on a workbook for it, as well.

Redfield was raised a Methodist, but was attracted to Eastern religions such as Taoism and Buddhism from an early age. While attending graduate classes at Auburn University, he also began researching intuition and other related subjects. He told John Leland in *Newsweek:* "For me the '60s weren't about burning down the ROTC building; they were the start of the Human Potential Movement, an explosion in research into consciousness." Leland went on to report that Redfield went to Sedona, Arizona, to "explore energy vortexes," and that he "discovered his past lives among Franciscan monks in the sixteenth century, among Native Americans in the nineteenth."

Though Redfield used some of his arcane knowledge in his career counseling abused children, he became burnt out at this job, and quit it to write and market *The Celestine Prophecy.* The novel follows an unnamed narrator who leaves a post similar to Redfield's own in order to search for an ancient manuscript in Peru. During his search, the narrator has encounters with several spiritually enlightened people, who deliver nine insights to him. He is also pursued while on his quest, by the Peruvian government and by Catholic priests who fear the manuscript will undermine their interpretation of theology.

Literary critics have taken many potshots at the novel, complaining about its bare-bones plot rife with coincidences, its "*Raiders-of-the-Lost-Ark*" flavor, and Redfield's simplistic writing style. The author responded to these criticisms for McDonald however: "I keep explaining it's not a great American novel. It's a parable and you write parables a different way. I wanted it to be as accessible as possible." Other reviewers have condemned *The Celestine Prophecy* along with other New Age literature as being anti-rational, or for offering too easy a spiritual path. But the response from readers has been overwhelming, and many study groups have formed to examine both *The Celestine Prophecy* and *The Tenth Insight.* Leland remarked at the conclusion of his article about Redfield and his writings: "If this is the road to enlightenment . . . deal me in."

The Tenth Insight picks up the still unnamed narrator after the enlightenment he received in *The Celestine Prophecy* has begun to fade—hence the second novel's subtitle, *Holding the Vision.* Set in a valley of the Appalachian Mountains where secret energy experiments are taking place, "the book is, in part," according to McDonald, "a reply to Redfield's critics who argued that, contrary to his Pollyanna-ish prediction of a spiritual renaissance, the world is going to hell in an economic and environmental hand-basket." She went on to assert that in Redfield's view, "the naysayers can only be overcome by keeping the faith."

In *The Song of Celestine* Redfield collaborates with Dee Lillegard to restate the message of *The Celestine Prophecy* in a picture book aimed at younger readers. In this tale, a young Celestine becomes lost in the woods and is soon caught up in a quest for the meaning of life. A reviewer for *Publishers Weekly* found the book "overbearing" and Lillegard's writing to be "lumbering." "There's not enough of a story here to engage the attention of young readers," the reviewer contended, "nor are they likely to grasp the cloaked meaning." While offering high praise to the illustrations of Dean Morrissey, comparing his work to that of the Dutch masters, the *Publishers Weekly* reviewer maintained that "even stellar artwork is not enough to hoist this book out of its pompous mire."

Continuing his unnamed hero's spiritual quest in *The Secret of Shambhala: In Search of the Eleventh Insight,* Redfield serves up another adventure story that involves a trip to the Far East and the search for Shambhala, the legendary utopian city of Tibetan Buddhism more commonly known as Shangri-La. Here the Red Chinese Army assumes the role of villains-in-pursuit who would foil the hero's goal. "All ends happily and hopefully in this transparent takeoff of *Lost Horizon* (1933)," noted Ray Olson of *Booklist,* "that goes James Hilton's escapist perennial one better by claiming to know how all humanity will soon make it to Shambhala/Shangri-La, too." A writer for *Publishers Weekly* described the book as a "slight fable . . . with an appealing spiritual quest . . . soon burdened with Redfield's millennial concerns," going on to add: "Readers will find value in Redfield's simply stated comments abut building energy through nutrition, posture and thought, and refusing to erode one's energy through negative thinking."

Central to the idea of Redfield's New Age philosophy as expressed in his novels are the concepts of "synchronicity," "critical mass," and "a spiritual renaissance." Borrowing a chapter from Swiss psychologist Carl Jung, Redfield maintains that there are meaningful coincidences (synchronicities) in the world that are not random occurrences but a result of our thoughts. Thus by having positive thoughts we can shape a positive reality. Further, Redfield contends that the world is currently undergoing a significant awakening. As more and more individuals become aware of synchronicity and the power of thought a critical mass will eventually be achieved, resulting in a spiritual renaissance that will solve our problems as a species and lead to a new era of social progress. Not relying on faith alone, Redfield uses both observations from the everyday world and the results of scientific research to support his views. In an article in the *Skeptic,* Phil Mole questioned whether or not there is actually any objective evidence to support Redfield's ideas. Examining statistics, probability, the relativity theories of Einstein, particle physics, and cultural anthropology, Mole concluded: "there is absolutely no scientific evidence that Redfield's philosophy is true. There is no mysterious non-locality in the world, and our consciousness has no influence on objective reality." Further, Mole depicted the future that Redfield portrays as one in which our individualities would be lost: "Our personalities and autonomy have been subordinated to the Collective Mind, which will guide us to the truth. What is the truth? Anything the Mind says it is. Redfield's vision is not Utopian—it is an Orwellian nightmare."

Putting some of the beliefs embodied in his writings into practice in his own life, Redfield has been active in campaigning to preserve what remains of America's wilderness areas. In 1999 he became involved with the Global Renaissance Alliance, an organization committed to non-violent change that is attempting to integrate spiritual values into the political process. Although he has been overwhelmed with offers to purchase the film rights to *The Celestine Prophecy,* Redfield has held out for a great deal of control over the project. "This is a spiritual book," he explained to Leland. "I don't want it to become a shoot-'em-up movie."

BIOGRAPHICAL/CRITICAL SOURCES:

PERIODICALS

Atlantic Monthly, July, 1996, pp. 103-106.
Booklist, November 1, 1999, Ray Olson, review of *The Secret of Shambhala,* p. 483.
Entertainment Weekly, May 24, 1996, p. 87.
Maclean's, June 10, 1996, p. 61.
National Review, December 19, 1994, p. 63.
Newsweek, June 24, 1996, p. 70.
New York, August 1, 1994, pp. 50-51.
New Yorker, June 27, 1994, pp. 91-92.
People, December 26, 1994, p. 90.
Publishers Weekly, March 16, 1998, review of *The Purpose of Your Life,* p. 44; June 22, 1998, review of *The Song of Celestine,* p. 90; October 25, 1999, review of *The Secret of Shambhala,* p. 53.
Skeptic, summer, 1999, Phil Mole, "Celestine Profits," p. 76.*

* * *

REED, Ronald F. 1945-

PERSONAL: Born December 1, 1945, in Brooklyn, NY; married Ann Aspden (an English teacher), January 25, 1968; children: Adam, Jeremy, Rebecca. *Education:* St. Francis College, Brooklyn, NY, B.A., 1968; City University of New York, M.A., 1971; University of Western Ontario, Ph.D., 1976.

ADDRESSES: Home—Arlington, TX. *Office*—c/o Texas Wesleyan College, Fort Worth, TX 76105.

CAREER: Texas Wesleyan College, Fort Worth, associate professor of philosophy and education, beginning in 1979, and director of Analytic Teaching Program.

MEMBER: National Book Critics Circle, American Association of University Professors, John Dewey Society, American Philosophical Association, Philosophy of Education Society.

AWARDS, HONORS: Sam Taylor fellow, 1980-82; World Order fellow, 1981-82.

WRITINGS:

Talking with Children, Arden Press (Denver, CO), 1983.
(Editor with Ann Margaret Sharp) *Studies in Philosophy for Children: Harry Stottlemeier's Discovery,* Temple University Press (Philadelphia, PA), 1992.
(Editor with John P. Portelli) *Children, Philosophy, and Democracy,* Detselig Enterprises (Calgary, Alberta), 1995.
(With Johnson) *Friendship and Moral Education: Twin Pillars of Philosophy for Children,* Peter Lang (New York City), 1999.
(Editor with Tony W. Johnson) *Philosophical Documents in Education,* Longman (White Plains, NY), 1996, 2nd edition, 2000.

Contributor of articles and reviews to education and philosophy journals and newspapers. Editor of *Analytic Teaching.*

BIOGRAPHICAL/CRITICAL SOURCES:

PERIODICALS

Choice, November, 1999, p. 594.
Library Journal, February 1, 1992, p. 93.*

* * *

REEVES, James
See REEVES, John Morris

* * *

REEVES, John Morris 1909-1978
(James Reeves)

PERSONAL: Born July 1, 1909, in London, England; died May 1, 1978; son of Albert John and Ethel Mary (Blench) Reeves; married Mary Phillips, 1936 (died 1966); children: Stella, Juliet Mary, Gareth Edward. *Education:* Jesus College, Cambridge, M.A. (honors), 1931.

CAREER: Writer and editor. Teacher in state schools and teacher training college, 1933-52; William Heinemann Ltd. (publishers), London, England, general editor of "Poetry Bookshelf" series, 1951-78; Unicorn Books, London, general editor, 1960-78.

WRITINGS:

POETRY; UNDER NAME JAMES REEVES

The Natural Need, Constable (London), 1935.
The Imprisoned Sea, Editions Poetry (London), 1949.
XIII Poems, privately printed, 1950.
The Password, and Other Poems, Heinemann (London), 1952.
The Talking Skull, Heinemann, 1958.
Collected Poems, 1929-1959, Heinemann, 1960.
The Questioning Tiger, Heinemann, 1964.
Selected Poems, Allison & Busby (London), 1967, revised edition, 1977.
Subsong, Heinemann, 1969.
Poems and Paraphrases, Heinemann, 1972.
Collected Poems, 1929-1974, Heinemann, 1974.
Arcadian Ballads, illustrated by Edward Ardizzone, Whittington Press (Andoversford, Gloucestershire, England), 1977.
The Closed Door, Twinrocker (Brookston, IN), 1977.

CRITICISM; UNDER NAME JAMES REEVES

Man Friday: A Primer of English Composition and Grammar, Heinemann, 1953.
The Critical Sense: Practical Criticism of Prose and Poetry, Heinemann, 1956.
Teaching Poetry: Poetry in Class Five to Fifteen, Heinemann, 1958.
A Short History of English Poetry, 1340-1940, Heinemann, 1961, Dutton (New York City), 1962.
Understanding Poetry, Heinemann, 1965, Barnes & Noble (New York City), 1968.
Commitment to Poetry, Barnes & Noble, 1969.
(With Martin Seymour-Smith) *Inside Poetry,* Barnes & Noble, 1970.
How to Write Poems for Children, Heinemann, 1971.
The Reputation and Writings of Alexander Pope, Barnes & Noble, 1976.
The Writer's Approach to the Ballad, Harrap (London), 1976.

EDITOR; UNDER NAME JAMES REEVES

(With Denys Thompson) J. Bronowski and others, *The Quality of Education: Methods and Purposes in the Secondary Curriculum,* Muller (London), 1947.
The Writer's Way: An Anthology of English Prose, Christophers (London), 1948.

The Poets' World (anthology), Heinemann, 1948, revised edition published as *The Modern Poets' World,* 1957.

(With Norman Culpan) *Dialogue and Drama,* Heinemann, 1950, Plays Inc. (Boston), 1968.

D. H. Lawrence, *Selected Poems,* Heinemann, 1951.

The Speaking Oak: English Poetry and Prose: A Selection, Heinemann, 1951.

John Donne, *Selected Poems,* Heinemann, 1952, 2nd edition, 1957, Macmillan (New York City), 1958.

Gerard Manley Hopkins, *Selected Poems,* Heinemann, 1953, Macmillan, 1957.

John Clare, *Selected Poems,* Heinemann, 1954, Macmillan, 1957.

The Bible in Brief: Selections from the Text of the Authorised Version of 1611, Wingate (London), 1954, published as *The Holy Bible in Brief,* Messner (New York City), 1954.

Robert Browning, *Selected Poems,* Heinemann, 1956, Macmillan, 1957.

Cecil J. Sharp, compiler, *The Idiom of the People: English Traditional Verse,* Macmillan, 1958.

Emily Dickinson, *Selected Poems,* Heinemann, 1959, Barnes & Noble, 1966.

Samuel Taylor Coleridge, *Selected Poems,* Heinemann, 1959.

(With William Vincent Aughterson) *Over the Ranges,* Heinemann (Melbourne), 1959.

The Personal Vision . . . , Poetry Book Supplement (London), 1959.

The Rhyming River, four volumes, Heinemann, 1959.

(And author of introduction and notes) *The Everlasting Circle: English Traditional Verse,* Macmillan, 1960.

(With Desmond Flower) *The Taste of Courage,* Harper (New York City), 1960, published as *The War, 1939-1945,* Cassell (London), 1960.

Stephen Leacock, *The Unicorn Leacock,* Heinemann, 1960.

Great English Essays, Cassell, 1961.

Robert Graves, *Selected Poetry and Prose,* Hutchinson (London), 1961.

Georgian Poetry, Penguin (London), 1962.

The Cassell Book of English Poetry, Harper, 1965.

Jonathan Swift, *Selected Poems,* Heinemann, 1966, Barnes & Noble, 1967.

(With Seymour-Smith) *A New Canon of English Poetry,* Barnes & Noble, 1967.

(With Sean Haldane) *Homage to Trumbull Stickney: Poems,* Heinemann, 1968.

An Anthology of Free Verse, Basil Blackwell (Oxford, England), 1968.

The Reader's Bible, Tandem (London), 1968.

The Sayings of Dr. Johnson, J. Baker (London), 1968.

Poets and Their Critics 3: Arnold to Auden, Hutchinson, 1969.

(With Seymour-Smith) Andrew Marvell, *The Poems of Andrew Marvell,* Barnes & Noble, 1969.

Geoffrey Chaucer, *Chaucer: Lyric and Allegory,* Heinemann, 1970.

A Vein of Mockery: Twentieth-Century Verse Satire, Heinemann, 1973.

Thomas Gray, *The Complete English Poems of Thomas Gray,* Barnes & Noble, 1973, published as *Selected Poems,* Heinemann, 1973.

Five Late Romantic Poets: George Darley, Hartley Coleridge, Thomas Hood, Thomas Lovell Beddoes, Emily Bronte, Heinemann, 1974.

(With Seymour-Smith) Walt Whitman, *Selected Poems of Walt Whitman,* Heinemann, 1976.

(With Robert Gittings) Thomas Hardy, *Selected Poems of Thomas Hardy,* Barnes & Noble, 1981.

CHILDREN'S POETRY; UNDER NAMES JAMES REEVES

The Wandering Moon, illustrated by Evadne Rowan, Heinemann, 1950, 2nd edition, 1957, Dutton (New York City), 1960.

The Blackbird in the Lilac: Verses, illustrated by Ardizzone, Dutton, 1952.

(With others) *A Puffin Quartet of Poets,* edited by Eleanor Graham, illustrated by Diana Bloomfield, Penguin, 1958.

Prefabulous Animiles, illustrated by Ardizzone, Heinemann, 1957, Dutton, 1960.

Ragged Robin: Poems from A to Z, illustrated by Jane Paton, Dutton, 1961.

Hurdy-Gurdy: Selected Poems for Children, illustrated by Ardizzone, Heinemann, 1961.

Complete Poems for Children, illustrated by Ardizzone, Heinemann, 1973.

More Prefabulous Animiles, illustrated by Ardizzone, Heinemann, 1975.

CHILDREN'S FICTION; UNDER NAME JAMES REEVES

Pigeons and Princesses (also see below; stories), illustrated by Ardizzone, Heinemann, 1956.

Mulbridge Manor, illustrated by Geraldine Spence, Heinemann (London), 1958, Penguin, 1963.

Titus in Trouble, illustrated by Ardizzone, Bodley Head (London), 1959, Walck (New York City), 1960.

Sailor Rumbelow and Britannia (also see below), illustrated by Ardizzone, Heinemann, 1962.

Sailor Rumbelow, and Other Stories (includes *Pigeons and Princesses* and *Sailor Rumbelow and Britannia*), illustrated by Ardizzone, Dutton, 1962.

The Story of Jackie Thimble, Dutton, 1964.

The Strange Light, illustrated by Lynton Lamb, Heinemann, 1964, Rand McNally (Chicago), 1966.

The Pillar-Box Thieves, illustrated by Dick Hart, Nelson (London), 1965.

Rhyming Will, illustrated by Ardizzone, Hamish Hamilton (London), 1967, McGraw-Hill (New York City), 1968.

Mr. Horrox and the Gratch, illustrated by Quentin Blake, Abelard-Schuman (London), 1969.

The Path of Gold, illustrated by Krystyna Turska, Hamish Hamilton, 1972.

The Lion That Flew, illustrated by Ardizzone, Chatto & Windus (London), 1974.

The Clever Mouse, illustrated by Barbara Swiderska, Chatto & Windus, 1976.

Eggtime Stories, illustrated by Colin McNaughton, Blackie (London), 1978.

The James Reeves Story Book, illustrated by Ardizzone, Heinemann (London), 1978, published as *The Gnome Factory and Other Stories,* Penguin, 1986.

A Prince in Danger, illustrated by Gareth Floyd, Kaye & Ward (London), 1979.

EDITOR OF CHILDREN'S BOOKS; UNDER NAME JAMES REEVES

Orpheus: A Junior Anthology of English Poetry, two volumes, Heinemann, 1949-50, teacher's book, 1952.

Strawberry Fair, Heinemann, 1954.

Green Broom, Heinemann, 1954.

Yellow Wheels, Heinemann, 1954.

Grey Goose and Gander, Heinemann, 1954.

The Merry-Go-Round: A Collection of Rhymes and Poems for Children, illustrated by John MacKay, Heinemann, 1955.

Heinemann Junior Poetry Books, four volumes, Heinemann, 1955.

A Golden Land: Stories, Poems, Songs, New and Old, Hastings (New York City), 1958.

A First Bible: An Abridgement for Young Readers, illustrated by Geoffrey Fraser, Heinemann, 1962.

The Christmas Book, illustrated by Raymond Briggs, Dutton, 1968.

One's None: Old Rhymes for New Tongues, illustrated by Bernadette Watts, Heinemann, 1968, Watts (New York City), 1969.

The Springtime Book: A Collection of Prose and Poetry, illustrated by McNaughton, Heinemann, 1976.

The Autumn Book: A Collection of Prose and Poetry, illustrated by McNaughton, Heinemann, 1977.

RETELLER; UNDER NAME JAMES REEVES

English Fables and Fairy Tales, Retold, illustrated by Joan Kiddell-Monroe, Oxford University Press (London), 1954, Walck, 1960.

Jonathan Swift, *Gulliver's Travels: The First Three Parts,* Heinemann, 1955.

Jules Verne, *Twenty Thousand Leagues under the Sea,* Chatto & Windus, 1956.

Miguel de Cervantes, *Exploits of Don Quixote, Retold,* Blackie, 1959, Walck, 1960.

Aesop, *Fables from Aesop, Retold,* illustrated by Maurice Wilson, Blackie, 1961, Walck, 1962.

Three Tall Tales, Chosen from Traditional Sources, illustrated by Ardizzone, Abelard-Schuman, 1964.

The Road to a Kingdom: Stories from the Old and New Testaments, illustrated by Richard Kennedy, Heinemann, 1965.

The Secret Shoemakers and Other Stories (adapted from *Kinder und Hausmaerchen* by the Brothers Grimm), illustrated by Ardizzone, Abelard-Schuman, 1966.

The Cold Flame (adapted from tales by the Brothers Grimm), illustrated by Charles Keeping, Hamish Hamilton, 1967, Meredith Press (New York City), 1969.

The Trojan Horse, illustrated by Turska, Hamish Hamilton, 1968, Watts, 1969.

Heroes and Monsters: Legends of Ancient Greece Retold, illustrated by Sarah Nechamkin, Volume 1: *Gods and Voyagers,* Blackie, 1969, Two Continents (New York City), 1978, Volume 2: *Islands and Palaces,* Blackie, 1971, published as *Giants and Warriors,* Blackie, 1977, Two Continents, 1978.

The Angel and the Donkey, illustrated by Ardizzone, Hamish Hamilton, 1969, McGraw-Hill, 1970.

Maildun the Voyager, illustrated by John Lawrence, Hamish Hamilton, 1971, Walck, 1972.

How the Moon Began (based on a folktale by the Brothers Grimm), illustrated by Ardizzone, Abelard-Schuman, 1971.

The Forbidden Forest and Other Stories, illustrated by Raymond Briggs, Heinemann, 1973.

The Voyage of Odysseus: Homer's Odyssey Retold, Blackie, 1973.

Two Greedy Bears (based on a Persian folktale), illustrated by Floyd, Hamish Hamilton, 1974.

Quest and Conquest: Pilgrim's Progress Retold, illustrated by Joanna Troughton, Blackie, 1976.

Snow-White and Rose-Red, illustrated by Jenny Rodwell, Andersen Press (London), 1979.

Fairy Tales from England, illustrated by Rosamund Fowler, Oxford University Press, 2000.

OTHER; UNDER NAME JAMES REEVES

Mulcaster Market: Three Plays for Young People (includes *Mulcaster Market, The Pedlar's Dream,* and *The Stolen Boy*), illustrated by Dudley Cutley, Heinemann, 1951, published as *The Peddler's Dream and Other Plays,* Dutton, 1963.

The King Who Took Sunshine (children's play), Heinemann, 1954.

A Health to John Patch (ballad opera for children), Boosey & Hawkes (London), 1957.

(Translator) Frantisek Hrubin, *Primrose and the Winter Witch,* illustrated by Jiri Trnka, Hamlyn (London), 1964.

(Translator) Alexander Pushkin, *The Golden Cockerel and Other Stories,* illustrated by Jan Lebis, Dent (London), 1969, Watts, 1969.

A. D. One: A Masque for Christmas (play for adults), privately printed, 1974.

(Translator) Marie de France, *Shadow of the Hawk and Other Stories,* illustrated by Anne Dalton, Collins (London), 1975, Seabury Press (New York City), 1977.

SIDELIGHTS: "Since the death of Walter de la Mare in 1956," wrote Charles Causley in the *Times Literary Supplement,* "no British poet or writer of stories has made a more valuable contribution to children's literature in English than the late James Reeves." Reeves wrote poetry and stories for children, edited children's anthologies, and adapted old folktales, fairy tales, and classics. He translated stories from the Czech and the Russian and adapted Old and New Testament stories for young readers. He also wrote poetry for adults and edited books for the "Poetry Bookshelf" series. Writing in the *Dictionary of Literary Biography,* Constance Vidor explained that "Reeves brought a poet's imagination and a scholar's seriousness to his writing for children. . . . Reeve's prose and poetry for children exemplify a wide knowledge of traditional forms and folktale themes, a love of nonsense and whimsy, and an understanding of the musical and rhythmic capacities of the English language."

Reeves's poems for children were popular with readers and critics alike. A reviewer in *New Statesman* described Reeves as "a consistently good performer and . . . his intentionally child-aimed poems are of a piece with his adult ones—both have the same clarity and feeling for clean structure." Reeves inveighed against overly sweet, poorly crafted verse that "mak[es] poetry seem something childish," and according to Margaret Campbell in *St. James Guide to Children's Writers,* "he succeeded in keeping that advice in mind in his own poems." "My interests and upbringing," Reeves once commented, "are reflected in my poems for children." Many of these poems are humorous, and they have "a dancing rhythm and plenty of nonsense," Campbell commented. "They catch a mood quickly and lightly." In Reeves's first children's poetry collection, *The Wandering Moon, Chicago Sunday Tribune* reviewer Jean Baron thought some poems "may seem overly quaint and tea-in-the-nurseryish," but added that these "should not be allowed to detract from the very real delight in this book." A critic for the *Christian Science Monitor* dubbed another collection, *Prefabulous Animiles,* "nonsense verse in the best tradition," while *New York Herald Tribune Book Review* contributor M. S. Libby asserted that this book "will open the door of poetry for many children."

In *How to Write Poems for Children,* Reeves explained how he went about creating verse for a young audience by giving examples of his own work, telling the stories behind the poems, and speculating on the child who might read and appreciate the poems. In a review of the book, the *Times Literary Supplement* critic admitted that "the book's weakness . . . is that Mr. Reeves does not really say much about his own poems, quoted on virtually every page of the book, that cannot be deduced from a careful reading of them." And yet, the reviewer found that "Reeves makes a gentle, autumnal expositor of his own work" and noted that it was the author's "assured sense of what will and what will not appeal to children that is the book's strength."

Both in his original stories and adaptations of traditional folktales, Reeves brought a poet's touch to his fiction. Virginia Haviland in *Book World* described Reeves as "a poet whose gift is reflected in his retellings." She continued, "Mr. Reeves' informal, chatty style and his naming of characters . . . enhance the homely aspects of the old tales, giving them sometimes a here-and-now quality." Writing in *Punch,* Bobbie Ann Mason called Reeves "one of the great children's writers," while Zena Sutherland, writing in *Saturday Review,* praised Reeves's "rugged, spare, eloquent style." Campbell pointed out that in his adaptation of Grimm brothers' tales, *The Forbidden Forest and Other Stories,* Reeves's "short crisp sentences get swiftly to the point; none of the characters bandies words or minces manners." She also lauded his *Exploits of Don Quixote* for sticking close to the original story and preserving its humor. In much the same vein, *Chicago Sunday Tribune* reviewer F. E. Faverty noted that in this work, "the excitement and drama are retained. The mixture of heroism and absurdity in Don Quixote are well shown." The *Saturday Review* critic found *Ex-*

ploits of Don Quixote to be "a highly successful version in which . . . the story's essential wit, humor, and pathos are not sacrificed." In *Maildun the Voyager,* Reeves adapts a traditional Irish tale about a young man who sails off to avenge himself on the pirates who killed his father, becomes lost, and finds himself among fabulous, distant islands. The *Horn Book* critic found that Reeves's version of the tale was "excellent" and "combines tragic and epic elements" in its telling.

Campbell noted that Reeves's original stories for children are marked by "unusual characters and backgrounds." His fertile and playful imagination often produced works that reviewers considered appropriate for both adults and children. Janet Malcolm, reviewing *Rhyming Will* in the *New Yorker,* considered it "an adult entertainment that just might amuse children, too." The book tells the story of Will, a young boy of the eighteenth century who does not speak until he is almost seven, and then only in rhyme. Will runs away to London and becomes famous as a poet—until one day, requested to give a speech in verse at a banquet, he is so nervous that he speaks in prose. Although Will fears he is in disgrace, the man he was supposed to honor with his versifying is greatly relieved at not having to hear any more poetry. He gratefully presents Will with five gold coins. Although Marie Peel of *Books and Bookmen* felt that the story "has a creative central idea but hardly fulfills its potential," the *Book World* critic considered it "a lovely period piece." Reeves's other works of fiction for children demonstrate great variety of subject matter. *The Strange Light* is about characters waiting to be used in books—"an ingenious idea," in the words of Campbell—who become acquainted with a real-life little girl. "From a less light-handed artist than James Reeves," a *Times Literary Supplement* reviewer remarked, "the joke might be painfully artificial, even coy, but his inventive and delicate pen touches off a squib that crackles brightly, if briefly." In *Mulbridge Manor,* written for a somewhat older audience, a group of children assist an old woman and thwart a criminal. "Virtue is rewarded with a happy ending," Campbell related, "but fate plays some funny tricks on the way."

Reeves was also well known for his many anthologies of prose and poetry for children, which included such collections as *The Spring Book, The Autumn Book,* and *The Christmas Book.* Reviewing *The Christmas Book* for the *New York Times Book Review,* Margaret F. O'Connell praised Reeves's "unerring eye for sharp images and the rhythm of words," while the *Christian Science Monitor* critic found it to be "a good introduction to the many celebrated authors whose names decorate its pages like electric candles on an eclectic tree."

Reeves's writing for adults met with more measured praise than did his work for children. A reviewer for the *Times Literary Supplement* found *Commitment to Poetry,* a collection of Reeves's literary criticism, troubling for what it revealed about Reeves's vision: "He is well-read and loves literature, but his thought about it has no edge, no definition. His selections for his own 'Poetry Bookshelf' series show taste: but their introductions, most unadvisedly brought together in his essay collection, are little more than amiable rambles." And, reviewing Reeves's poetry, a *Times Literary Supplement* reviewer expressed some dissatisfaction with *Subsong,* a collection of Reeves' verse: "The volume as a whole reveals a slightly dissatisfying maladjustment between ironic social commentary and more serious preoccupations. . . . He is better on the whole when he can merge his aphoristic skill with a level of deeper insight which suggests shrewdness rather than merely external wit."

Reeves' poetic gifts, however, may not have been so much lacking, as simply unappreciated during the time in which he wrote. That at least was the opinion of the *Times Literary Supplement* critic who reviewed *Poems and Paraphrases.* Noting that "Reeves has had a long career as a poet," the reviewer commented that "as a writer for children . . . he is a prolific and respected figure but his own poetry has never had quite the attention it deserves." Quoting William Butler Yeats, who once called Reeves' poetry "too reasonable, too truthful," the critic commented: "It is a reasonableness and truthfulness that Reeves shares with other recent poets whose work earned respect rather than fashionable enthusiasm but who are beginning to be more warmly assessed."

BIOGRAPHICAL/CRITICAL SOURCES:

BOOKS

Dictionary of Literary Biography, Volume 161: *British Children's Writers since 1960,* Gale (Detroit), 1996.

St. James Guide to Children's Writers, 5th edition, St. James Press (Detroit), 1999.

PERIODICALS

Booklist, May 1, 1959, review of *Blackbird in the Lilac;* December 15, 1960, review of *Prefabulous Animiles;* October 15, 1960, review of *Exploits of Don Quixote.*

Bookmark, October, 1960, review of *Prefabulous Animiles.*

Books & Bookmen, February, 1968, pp. 34-35; November, 1979, p. 59.

Book Week, October 30, 1966, M. S. Libby, review of *The Strange Light,* p. 24.

Book World, November 5, 1967, pp. 23-24; May 4, 1969, J. H. Clarke, review of *The Cold Flame,* p. 26, and W. J. Smith, review of *One's None,* p. 24.

Chicago Sunday Tribune, November 2, 1958, review of *Golden Land,* part 2, p. 32; May 10, 1959, Gerldine Ross, review of *Blackbird in the Lilac,* p. 3; November 6, 1960, Jean Baron, reviews of *Prefabulous Animiles* and *The Wandering Moon,* p. 18, and F. E. Faverty, review of *Exploits of Don Quixote,* p. 22.

Christian Science Monitor, May 14, 1959, review of *Blackbird in the Lilac,* p. 10; November 3, 1960, review of *Prefabulous Animiles,* p. 3B; November 29, 1968; May 1, 1969, review of *One's None,* p. B2, and Susan Kupper, review of *The Trojan Horse,* p. B3; May 7, 1970, review of *The Golden Cockerel,* p. B4.

Commonweal, November 14, 1958, C. H. Bishop, review of *Golden Land.*

Guardian, May 20, 1960, Bernard Bergonzi, review of *The Everlasting Circle,* p. 8.

Guardian Weekly, November 22, 1969, p. 18.

Horn Book, February, 1959, review of *Golden Land;* April, 1959, review of *Blackbird in the Lilac;* December, 1960, reviews of *Prefabulous Animiles* and *The Wandering Moon;* June, 1969, review of *One's None;* August, 1969, review of *The Cold Flame;* August, 1970, review of *The Golden Cockerel;* October, 1972, review of *Maildun the Voyager.*

Kirkus, September 1, 1958, review of *Golden Land;* August 1, 1960, reviews of *Prefabulous Animiles, The Wandering Moon,* and *Exploits of Don Quixote.*

Library Journal, December 15, 1958, Mabel Berry, review of *Golden Land;* May 15, 1959, L. R. Markey, review of *Blackbird in the Lilac;* August, 1960, B. A. Robie, review of *The Everlasting Circle;* September 15, 1960, F. H. Hektoen, reviews of *Prefabulous Animiles* and *The Wandering Moon;* October 15, 1966, M. L. Purucker, review of *The Strange Light;* November 15, 1966, John Montgomery, review of *Understanding Poetry;* April 15, 1969, Priscilla Moxom, review of *The Cold Flame,* and L. D. Molvar, review of *The Trojan Horse;* May 15, 1969, Ginger Brauer, review of *One's None;* October 15, 1970, Lynda McConnell, review of *The Golden Cockerel;* December 15, 1972, Sandra Scheraga, review of *Maildun the Voyager.*

Manchester Guardian, December 5, 1958, Brian Redhead, review of *Golden Land,* p. 9; October 15, 1960, R. M. Hadlow, review of *Exploits of Don Quixote.*

New Statesman, November 15, 1958, Anna Madge, review of *Golden Land;* May 28, 1960, Charles Causley, review of *The Everlasting Circle;* November, 1968; June 4, 1971, John Coleman, review of *Maildun the Voyager,* p. 782.

New Yorker, December 14, 1968.

New York Herald Tribune Book Review, November 2, 1958, M. S. Libby, review of *Golden Land,* p. 26; May 10, 1959, M. S. Libby, review of *Blackbird in the Lilac,* p. 5; September 18, 1960, M. S. Libby, reviews of *Prefabulous Animiles* and *The Wandering Moon,* p. 10.

New York Times, November 2, 1958, Charles and Helen Simmons, review of *Golden Land,* p. 6; May 10, 1959, Paul Engle, review of *Blackbird in the Lilac,* p. 31.

New York Times Book Review, November 13, 1960, Walker Gibson, reviews of *Prefabulous Animiles* and *The Wandering Moon,* p. 56; December 1, 1968; May 18, 1969, Barbara Wersba, review of *The Cold Flame,* p. 26; November 9, 1969, Hugh Nissenson, review of *The Golden Cockerel,* p. 32; January 28, 1973, Feenie Ziner, review of *Maildun the Voyager,* p. 8.

Poetry, May, 1969, M. L. Rosenthal, review of *A New Canon of English Poetry.*

Punch, December 11, 1968.

San Francisco Chronicle, April 26, 1959, Charlotte Jackson, review of *Golden Land,* p. 26; June 21, 1959, review of *Blackbird in the Lilac,* p. 24; November 13, 1960, review of *Exploits of Don Quixote,* p. 18.

Saturday Review, May 9, 1959, review of *Blackbird in the Lilac;* November 12, 1960, review of *Exploits of Don Quixote,* p. 96; November 12, 1966, Zena Sutherland, review of *The Strange Light,* p. 50; April 19, 1969, Zena Sutherland, review of *The Trojan Horse,* pp. 38-39.

Spectator, November 28, 1958, John Coleman, review of *Golden Land,* p. 768; June 10, 1960, Norman MacCaig, review of *The Everlasting Circle,* p. 841.

Times Educational Supplement, December 25, 1987, p. 10.

Times Literary Supplement, November 21, 1958, review of *Golden Land,* p. 17; December 4, 1959, review of *Exploits of Don Quixote,* p. 19; June 24, 1960, review of *The Everlasting Circle,* p. 396; July 9, 1964, review of *The Strange Light,* p. 602; June 17, 1965, review of *Understanding Poetry,* p. 503; November 30, 1967, review of *The Cold Flame,* p. 1142; July 18, 1968, review of *A New Canon of English Poetry,* p. 754; October 3, 1968, review of *One's None,* p. 1112; December 5, 1968, review of *The Trojan Horse,* p. 1374; December 25, 1969, p. 1467; April 16, 1970, review of *The Golden Cockerel,* p. 420; April 23, 1970, p. 450; February 7, 1971, p. 773; August 4, 1972, p. 910; September 28, 1973; November 23, 1973; July 5, 1974; September 29, 1978.

Washington Post Book World, February 9, 1986.

OBITUARIES:

PERIODICALS

Times (London), May 9, 1978.*

* * *

REGIS, Ed
See REGIS, Edward, Jr.

* * *

REGIS, Edward, Jr. 1944-
(Ed Regis)

PERSONAL: Born January 7, 1944, in New York, NY; son of Edward J., Sr. (in business) and Doris (a homemaker; maiden name, Deloye) Regis; married Pamela Thompson (a college teacher), August 25, 1972. *Education:* Hunter College, B.A., 1965; New York University, M.A., 1969, Ph.D., 1972. *Politics:* Independent.

ADDRESSES: *Home*—Sabillasville, MD. *Office*—Western Maryland College, 2 College Hill, Westminster, MD 21157.

CAREER: Salisbury State College, Salisbury, MD, assistant professor of philosophy, 1971-72; Howard University, Washington, DC, assistant professor, 1972-76, associate professor of philosophy, 1976-87; Western Maryland College, Westminster, MD, college scholar, 1988—; writer.

AWARDS, HONORS: Reason Foundation fellow, 1980 and 1982; Earhart Foundation research grant, 1980-81, for work in ethical theory; annual Philosophy Club symposium prize, 1982, for "The Moral Status of Multigenerational Interstellar Exploration."

WRITINGS:

(Editor) *Gewirth's Ethical Rationalism: Critical Essays with a Reply by Alan Gewirth,* University of Chicago Press (Chicago), 1984.

(Editor) *Extraterrestrials: Science and Alien Intelligence,* Cambridge University Press (New York City), 1985.

(Under name Ed Regis) *Who Got Einstein's Office? Eccentricity and Genius at the Institute for Advanced Study,* Addison-Wesley (Reading, MA), 1987.

Great Mambo Chicken and the Transhuman Condition: Science Slightly over the Edge, Addison-Wesley, 1990.

Nano: The Science of Nanotechnology: Remaking the World Molecule by Molecule, Little, Brown (Boston), 1995.

Virus Ground Zero: Stalking the Killer Viruses with the Centers for Disease Control, Pocket Books (New York City), 1996.

The Biology of Doom: America's Greatest Germ Warfare Project, Holt (New York City), 1999.

Contributor to *Interstellar Migration and the Human Experience,* edited by Eric M. Jones and Ben R. Finney, University of California Press, 1985; contributor of articles and reviews to periodicals, including *Air and Space, American Philosophical Quarterly, College English, Discover, Ethics, Journal of Critical Analysis, Journal of Philosophy, Metaphilosophy, New Scholasticism, Omni, Pacific Philosophical Quarterly, Religious Humanism, Review of Metaphysics, Science Digest, Smithsonian, Teaching Philosophy, Thomist,* and *Wired.*

SIDELIGHTS: Philosophy professor and science writer Edward Regis, Jr., explores the workings of some of the greatest theoretical minds of the twentieth century in his book *Who Got Einstein's Office? Eccentricity and Genius at the Institute for Advanced Study.* Funded by East Coast department store magnates Louis Bamberger and Caroline Bamberger Fuld and conceived by education expert Abraham Flexner, the Institute was designed to provide scientists with the ideal environment for purely theoretical pursuits. After reviewing the history of the Institute, Regis concentrates in his nonfiction study on the provocative theories and personalities of the scientists who have given the Institute its reputation as a refuge for eccentric geniuses. From the legendary quirks of American physicist Albert Einstein to the flamboyant brilliance of Hungarian-born mathematician Johnny von Neumann, Regis creates an anecdotal chronicle of the scientists who have made the Institute a theoretical playground for more than fifty years.

Critics responded favorably to *Who Got Einstein's Office.* Jonathan Weiner, writing in *New York Times Book Review,* describes the book as "entertaining" and praises the author's introductions to various scientific theories as being "among the best I have read." Though he feels that Regis might be "manipulating his material" and "reaching for effect," *Washington Post* contributor Robert Kanigel commends the author's competence as a science writer, adding that "readers grounded in science will be propelled through the text." And *Los Angeles Times Book Review* writer Malcolm C. MacPherson judges Regis a "science writer of the first magnitude" who has "a genius for bulldozing through dark thickets of scientific mumbo-jumbo."

In his next book Regis examines some of the more long-range possibilities of science and technology. *The Great Mambo Chicken and the Transhuman Condition: Science Slightly Over the Edge* derives the lead in its title from experiments conducted by Arthur Hamilton Milt in the early 1970s. Milt subjected chickens to increased gravity levels in centrifuges for months at a time. He discovered that the birds developed greater stamina and superior vascular and muscular systems. Some of the other scientists with speculative ideas that Regis portrays in his study include Princeton physicist Gerard K. O'Neill, who envisions cities in space; Freeman Dyson, who projects an artificial biosphere that will completely encompass the solar system; cryonics pioneer Bob Ettinger, who speculates on the possibilities inherent in freezing the human body after death; and Hans Moravec, a robotics expert, who thinks the contents of a human brain,—knowledge, memories, beliefs, feelings—could someday be downloaded onto computer disks. A reviewer from the *Futurist* notes: "With an informal and entertaining style, Regis explores the different scientists' far-out ideas and their commitment to turning science fiction into science fact." Howard Rheingold feels that Regis is "never condescending to his subjects." The *Whole Earth Review* writer adds: "Regis evokes humor, owe, and continued reflection on the sheer chutzpah of Homo sapiens in this informal but well-informed joyride through the territory of high-tech high-hubrists."

In *Nano: The Science of Nanotechnology: Remaking the World Molecule by Molecule,* Regis devotes an entire book to one of the future technologies he touches upon in *The Great Mambo Chicken.* The science of nanotechnology, still in its barest infancy, considers the possibility of engineering atoms and molecules into self-replicating machines, known as "nanobots." Stanford scientist Eric Drexler and other proponents of this technology predict that nanobots could accomplish a nearly endless variety of wondrous tasks: the terraforming of Mars, an end to human disease and aging, and even the transformation of matter (changing dirt into sides of beef or rocket engines). Of course there are also dangers to consider, the possibility of renegade nanobots self-replicating uncontrollably and transforming the entire earth into "grey goo" in a few days. Critics of the movement, such as MIT professor Robert Silbey, feel that Drexler and his supporters are way ahead of themselves. Silbey points out that there exists no means to engineer atoms to perform specifics tasks, either now or in the foreseeable future; the behavior of atoms, as Heisenberg's uncertainty principle states, is unpredictable; and even slight changes in temperature could grossly deform the nanobots that Drexler envisions. Assessing *Nano* for *Technology Review,* Robert J. Crawford notes that Regis does not seriously consider such objections, but dismisses the critics of nanotechnology by accusing them of " 'resisting' some new paradigm, he never clearly defines." Further, Crawford dubs Regis with the pejorative appellation of "techiecultest," and feels that his study represents "a tediously familiar formula: find a flamboyant researcher, broadcast that researcher's claims, explain a little about the technology behind it, and then move on." In contrast, a *Publishers Weekly* critic describes *Nano* as an "engaging report on what may be tomorrow's alchemy."

In *Virus Ground Zero: Stalking the Killer Viruses with the Centers for Disease Control,* Regis relates the history of the CDC and its battles against infectious disease from its birth as a malaria-eradication agency in the 1940s to its contemporary world-wide role as the planet's central disease-fighting organization. Although he praises the CDC for swift responses that have prevented many epidemics, such as the early recognition of the hanta virus on a Navajo reservation in 1993, it is also Regis's contention that the CDC has engaged in "empire-building" by exaggerating the public health threat of many viruses (such as Ebola and Lassa, both of which can be easily combated with traditional methods) in an attempt to increase its own budget and importance. He also points out that the CDC has expanded its purview in recent years to include health problems that do not fall under the category of infectious disease, such as smoking, car crashes, and obesity. A *Publishers Weekly* writer reviewing *Virus Ground Zero* remarks: "This balanced report makes an impressive counterweight to more cautionary books such as Richard Preston's *The Hot Zone* and Laurie Garrett's *The Coming Plague.*" Jacob Sullivan of *Reason* finds Regis's account to be "fast-paced and absorbing . . . lively, engaging, and often amusing." Sullivan also seconds the book's concerns about the CDC's self-aggrandizing use of its power.

In his 1999 study, *The Biology of Doom: America's Greatest Germ Warfare Project,* Regis explores another history, that of the U.S. government's biological warfare program. Begun in the 1930s in response to the threat posed by Nazi Germany, the program was formally terminated by Richard Nixon in 1980. Regis discusses a good deal of information that has only surfaced in recent years, such as accidental sheep kills and the experimental use of psychotropic agents on individuals who did not know they had become human "guinea pigs." He also delineates the different methods explored to deliver biological weapons, including sprays, fleas, and underwater bombs. A writer for *Publishers Weekly* observes: "Regis writes for the layperson, and he is careful to depict the human drama behind the science." Gilbert Taylor of *Booklist* calls *The Biology of Doom* "[a]n objectively handled summary."

Regis is a member of the extropians, described by Gary Chapman of the *New Republic* as "a high-tech human potential cult based in California." In an article in *Wired,* Regis stated: "No ambition, however extravagant, no fantasy, however outlandish, can any longer be dismissed as crazy or impossible. . . . Suddenly, technology has given us powers with which we can manipulate not only external reality . . . but also, and much more portentously, ourselves."

Regis once told *CA:* "I am a private pilot, and I live on a thirty-acre farm five miles from Camp David in rural Maryland."

BIOGRAPHICAL/CRITICAL SOURCES:

PERIODICALS

Booklist, March 1, 1995, p. 1168; October 1, 1999, Gilbert Taylor, review of *The Biology of Doom,* p. 313.

Christian Science Monitor, October 13, 1987.

Futurist, May-June, 1991, review of *Great Mambo Chicken and the Transhuman Condition,* p. 43.

Los Angeles Times Book Review, September 13, 1987.

New Republic, January 9, 1995, Gary Chapman, review of *Wired,* p. 19.

New York Times Book Review, September 27, 1987.

Publishers Weekly, February 6, 1995, review of *Nano,* p. 69; November 20, 1995, Paul Nathan, "On the World Stage," p. 21; October 28, 1996, review of *Virus Ground Zero,* p. 70; October 25, 1999, review of *The Biology of Doom,* p. 61.

Reason, June, 1997, Jacob Sullum, review of *Virus Ground Zero,* p. 62.

Technology Review, May-June, 1996, Robert J. Crawford, review of *Nano,* p. 69.

Washington Post, September 22, 1987.

Whole Earth Review, fall, 1993, Howard Rheingold, review of *Great Mambo Chicken and the Transhuman Condition,* p. 115.*

* * *

RICHARDSON, John 1924- (Richard Johnson)

PERSONAL: Born in 1924, in London, England; father was a general. *Education:* Attended Slade School of Art, London.

ADDRESSES: *Home*—New York, NY. *Office*—c/o Random House, 201 East 50th St., New York, NY 10022.

CAREER: Art critic, editor, and biographer. Oxford University, Oxford, England, Slade Professor of Art, 1994-95. *New Statesman,* London, England, art, ballet, and fiction critic; affiliated with Christie's, New York City; vice president of Knoedler's (an art gallery); managing director of Artemis (a consortium of art dealers); exhibition organizer; art adviser.

AWARDS, HONORS: Received Whitbread Award for *A Life of Picasso: Volume I, 1881-1906.*

WRITINGS:

Manet, Phaidon, 1967, revised edition with notes by Kathleen Adler, Salem House, 1984.

(Editor) *The Collection of Germain Seligman: Paintings, Drawings, and Works of Art,* E. V. Thaw, 1979.

(With the collaboration of Marilyn McCully) *A Life of Picasso: Volume I, 1881-1906,* Random House (New York City), 1991.

(With the collaboration of McCully) *A Life of Picasso: Volume 2, 1907-1917,* Random House, 1996.

The Sorcerer's Apprentice: Picasso, Provence, and Douglas Cooper, Knopf (New York City), 1999.

Contributor to *Late Picasso: Paintings, Sculpture, Drawings, Prints, 1953-1972,* University of Washington Press, 1989; contributor to periodicals, sometimes under the pseudonym Richard Johnson, including *New Statesman, New York Review of Books,* and *House and Garden.*

EXHIBITION CATALOGUES

(Editor with Eric Zafran) *Master Paintings from the Hermitage and the State Russian Museum, Leningrad,* M. Knoedler, 1975.
(Preparer) *Corot and Courbet,* D. Carritt, Ltd., 1979.
Through the Eye of Picasso, 1928-1934: The Dinard Sketchbook and Related Paintings and Sculpture, W. Beadleston, 1985.

Contributor to *Douglas Cooper und die Meister des Kubismus* (title means "Douglas Cooper and the Masters of Cubism"), text and catalogue by Dorothy M. Kosinski, Kunstmuseum Basel, 1987; and *Nicolas de Stael in America,* Phillips Collection, 1990.

WORK IN PROGRESS: The third volume of *A Life of Picasso.*

SIDELIGHTS: John Richardson told Grace Glueck of the *New York Times:* "Writing about Picasso is a minefield. . . . With him, you have to leave everything open-ended, leave room for another interpretation. You can't slam the door on anything." These caveats notwithstanding, Richardson is considered the definitive biographer of the mercurial artist Pablo Picasso, an assessment based on the first two volumes of a planned four-volume work titled *A Life of Picasso.* Himself a respected art historian, Richardson was on intimate terms with Picasso during the artist's later years. Thus, as biographer Richardson brings to his work a close personal study of Picasso as well as a scholar's in-depth interpretation of the art works themselves and their place in twentieth century art history. In *Booklist,* Donna Seaman noted: "Picasso was more like a force of nature than a man, and Richardson is more than a biographer: he is bard, analyst, intimate, and historian."

Picasso allegedly thought of his work as his diary, and, using that belief as a premise, Richardson seeks to link the artist's life with his paintings in *A Life of Picasso: Volume I, 1881-1906,* the first installment of the biography. "Already," he told the *New York Times Book Review,* "people are starting to fictionalize, historicize, politicize, and psychoanalyze [Picasso's] work, and already they are arriving at absurd conclusions because they're not sufficiently familiar with the facts of the artist's life."

Richardson—who has also written a study on the French painter Edouard Manet and criticism for periodicals—became a friend of Picasso while living in the south of France in the 1950s. Because of his relationship with the artist, who died in 1973, the anticipation preceding the publication of *A Life of Picasso* was some of the most heated in the history of biography; both art historians and the general public were anxious to glimpse the intimate look at the revolutionary painter the book promised. The first volume of *A Life of Picasso* examines Picasso's first twenty-five years, beginning with his childhood in Spain and following him to his early years in Paris. Sometimes able to reconstruct day by day accounts of Picasso's life with the help of research provided by the art historian Marilyn McCully, Richardson attempts to reconcile the many versions of the painter's youth into one truthful work.

One of the ways Richardson illuminates truth is by eliminating the myths that surround the artist. Richardson writes that Picasso was not a child prodigy—he has often been compared to the composer Wolfgang Amadeus Mozart—but that his skill was a result of hard practice. He also notes that Picasso's father, an unsuccessful painter of pigeons who encouraged his son's artistic interests, did not surrender his brush to his son upon witnessing Picasso's ability but continued to paint for many years. In addition, Richardson evokes the rough, bohemian lifestyle Picasso adopted when he traveled to Paris in 1900, describing the mistresses and artists with whom Picasso associated at the time, a circle that included the writer Gertrude Stein and fellow painter Henri Matisse. Richardson closes the first volume as Picasso prepares to paint *Les Demoiselles d'Avignon,* the canvas that would revolutionize the world of art by introducing the Cubist movement.

Critics found that *A Life of Picasso* exceeded their expectations. "A remarkable achievement," *New York Times Book Review* contributor John Russell wrote, adding that, "Not only Picasso himself, but all those with whom he came into close contact—friends, lovers, colleagues, nonentities and men and women of genius—are brought to rounded life." In *Maclean's,* Pamela Young commented that Richardson's book "is a remarkably evocative study of a formidable artist's emerging greatness." Comparing *A Life of Picasso* to Richard Ellmann's National Book Award-winning biography *James Joyce, Time* reviewer Robert Hughes wrote: "Richardson is a born storyteller, with a vivid sense of detail and character that enables him to deal with the large cast of players entangled in Picasso's early life."

Aside from these appraisals of Richardson's ability to bring Picasso and the people with whom he associated to life, Hilton Kramer, writing in the *Washington Post Book World,* praised the critical aspect of Richardson's work: "His analysis of the paintings of the Blue period and the Rose period—the high points of Picasso's achievement in the years covered by this first volume—is the best I have read anywhere, and so is his account of the way Picasso responded to certain earlier artists . . . in his own early work." In the *Los Angeles Times Book Review,* Peter Schjeldahl declared: "Richardson's strongest suit is a running analysis of Picasso's stylistic evolution that makes [the painters] El Greco, [Francisco] Goya and [Paul] Gauguin as vividly present in the book as any friend or mistress." Kramer also praised the overall impact of *A Life of Picasso:* "This is a book that shows every sign of changing the course of biographical writing about the major figures of the modern movement. . . . If the sheer brilliance of this first installment can be sustained throughout the remainder of the work, Richardson will have written not only one of the great biographies but a book likely to illuminate a good deal . . . about the life of the spirit in this turbulent century."

The same critical reception attended the publication of *A Life of Picasso, Volume II: 1907-1917.* This volume begins with Picasso's completion of *Les Demoiselles d'Avignon* and explores the decade in which he produced Cubist masterpieces and became interestesd in neoclassicism. Central to the work is Richardson's exposition on the Cubist movement and Picasso's relationship with fellow artist Georges Braque. According to Michael Fitzgerald in *Art in America,* Richardson's distinction "is not so much in portraying the profound seriousness of Picasso's enterprise during this period, a fact no longer in dispute. Rather it is to articulate how his driving ambition and omnivorous curiosity intertwined with his often bawdy, gregarious and conniving behavior without sensationalizing the life or sidelining the art." Fitzgerald added: "Previous studies have devoutly analyzed the intricacies of Cubism, or danced through the love affairs and brushes with the law that spiced those times. None, however, glides so smoothly between them and shows how the arcana of Cubism are inseparable from Picasso's everyday experiences." Deeming the book "as luminous as it is instructive," Richard Howard stated in the *New York Times Book Review:* "This volume can make us understand what the misunderstood label 'Renaissance Man' really means—for it is in analogy to the Renaissance discovery and exploration of new worlds as well as the discovery and exploration of a classical past that Picasso, the inventor of a repertory of forms unparalleled in modern art as well as the exploiter of a tribal and Iberian 'primitive' past, is truly a Renaissance man."

Insight on the News contributor Eric Gibson called *A Life of Picasso, Volume II* a "masterly, insightful and nuanced account." The critic maintained that Richardson "doesn't hesitate to judge his subject harshly when the occasion calls for it. Indeed, aside from its wealth of information, the salient quality of this book is the author's ability to immerse himself in his subject while retaining the requisite detachment. There's a lesson here for many biographers if only they would take it." In the *New York Times,* Michiko Kakutani characterized the book as "magisterial—and masterly" and commended Richardson for making the painter's work the center of the story. Kakutani concluded: "While it's possible to disagree with . . . individual arguments, one thing remains beyond dispute: *A Life of Picasso* is a superior work of portraiture and scholarship. Picasso is lucky indeed to have Mr. Richardson as the writer of what will unquestionably be his definitive biography."

In 1999 Richardson published a more intimate memoir titled *The Sorcerer's Apprentice: Picasso, Provence, and Douglas Cooper.* The book explores Richardson's twelve-year relationship with art historian and collector Douglas Cooper, a period during which the two men restored a chateau in the south of France and frequently spent time with Picasso and other well-known painters. According to Michael Peppiatt in the *New York Times Book Review,* Richardson "recounts the rise and fall of Cooper in his life without much apparent animosity, in a brisk narrative filled with incisive sketches of the many other personalities he came to know." The critic concluded that *The Sorcerer's Apprentice* is an "engaging, witty account of a not so misspent youth." In *Booklist,* Seaman praised the book for helping to remove gay history from the shadows by illuminating "many pertinent aspects of the lives of gay artists and writers previously omitted from historical accounts."

Richardson once told the *New York Times Book Review:* "I wouldn't want to write about any other artist after Picasso. I don't think I could. Picasso was a bit of a cannibal. He had a way of consuming people. I think by the time I've finished this biography, I shall be totally consumed."

BIOGRAPHICAL/CRITICAL SOURCES:

PERIODICALS

Art in America, June, 1997, p. 29.

ARTnews, summer, 1991, p. 23.

Booklist, October 15, 1996, p. 396; November 15, 1999, p. 592.

Economist, February 8, 1997, p. 91.

Insight on the News, December 16, 1996, p. 34.

Los Angeles Times Book Review, February 24, 1991, pp. 1, 9.

Maclean's, April 22, 1991, p. 65.
Nation, May 20, 1991, p. 99.
New Republic, April 22, 1991, p. 38; June 2, 1997, p. 30.
New Yorker, December 16, 1996, p. 92.
New York Review of Books, February 6, 1997, p. 18; December 2, 1999, p. 6.
New York Times, March 19, 1991, pp. C11, C18; May 31, 1991, p. B11; November 8, 1996, p. B14; December 8, 1996, p. H41.
New York Times Book Review, March 3, 1991, pp. 1, 20-21; December 1, 1991, p. 3; November 17, 1996, p. 9; December 12, 1999, p. 8.
Time, February 19, 1991, pp. 65-66; December 2, 1996, p. 85.
Tribune Books (Chicago), February 24, 1991, p. 5.
Washington Post Book World, February 10, 1991, pp. 1, 8.*

* * *

RICHEY, Russell E(arle) 1941-

PERSONAL: Born October 19, 1941, in Asheville, NC; son of McMurry (a professor) and Erika (a teacher; maiden name, Marx) Richey; married Merle Umstead, August 28, 1965; children: William, Elizabeth. *Education:* Wesleyan University, B.A., 1963; Union Theological Seminary, B.D., 1966; Princeton University, M.A., 1968, Ph.D., 1970.

ADDRESSES: Office—Candler School of Theology, Emory University, Atlanta, GA 30322.

CAREER: Drew University, Madison, NJ, 1969-86, began as assistant professor of church history, became professor of church history, assistant to the president, 1978-81; Duke University, Durham, NC, associate dean for academic programs and research professor of church history, 1986-92, associate dean for academic programs and professor of church history, 1992-97, professor of church history, 1997-2000; ordained United Methodist minister, 1971. Florence Ellen Bell Methodist Scholar-in-Residence, Drew University, 1998; Candler School of Theology, dean, 2000—. Member of executive committee, United Methodist Church General Commission on Archives and History, 1992-2000; Member of board of directors, Association for Christian Training and Service, 1996-97; member of probationary process planning team, United Methodist Church board of higher education and ministry.

MEMBER: American Society of Church History (member of council, 1976-78, 1995-97), American Academy of Religion, American Association of University Professors, American Studies Association, Historical Society of the United Methodist Church, Wesleyan Theological Society, Phi Beta Kappa.

AWARDS, HONORS: Lilly Endowment grant, 1991; ecumenical faculty associate grant, General Commission on Christian Unity and Interreligious Concerns, 1992.

WRITINGS:

(Editor with Donald Jones) *American Civil Religion,* Harper (New York City), 1974.
(Editor) *Denominationalism,* Abingdon (Nashville, TN), 1977.
(Editor with Kenneth E. Rowe) *Rethinking Methodist History,* Kingswood (Nashville, TN), 1985.
Early American Methodism, Indiana University Press (Bloomington, IN), 1991.
Ecumenical and Interreligious Perspectives, QR Books (Nashville, TN), 1992.
(Editor with Rowe and Jean Miller Schmidt) *Perspectives on American Methodism: Interpretive Essays,* Kingswood, 1993.
(With R. Bruce Mullin) *Reimagining Denominationalism,* Oxford University Press (New York City), 1994.
The Methodist Conference in America: A History, Abingdon, 1994.
(With Rowe and James Kirby) *The Methodists,* Greenwood Press (Westport, CT), 1996.
(Editor with Dennis M. Campbell and William B. Lawrence) *Connectionalism: Ecclesiology, Mission, and Identity,* Abingdon, 1997.
(Editor with Campbell and Lawrence) *The People(s) Called Methodist: Forms and Reforms of Their Life,* Abingdon, 1998.
(Editor with Campbell and Lawrence) *Doctrines and Discipline,* Abingdon, 1999.
(With Campbell and Lawrence, and co-editor) *Questions for the Twenty-first Century Church,* Abingdon, 1999.

Contributor to *Beyond Establishment: Protestant Identity in a Post-Protestant Age,* Westminster Press (Louisville, KY), 1993; *Methodism in Its Cultural Milieu,* Oxford University Press, 1994; *Theological Education in the Evangelical Tradition,* Baker Books (Grand Rapids, MI), 1997. Also contributor of articles to *Church History, Journal of the American Academy of Religion, Foundations, Eighteenth-Century Studies,* and other periodicals. Member of editorial advisory board, *Quarterly Review, Christian History,* and *Church History.*

WORK IN PROGRESS: Further work on American denominationalism; further volumes with Campbell and Lawrence for the "United Methodism and American Culture" series; *The Methodist Experience in America,* with Rowe and Schmidt.

SIDELIGHTS: Russell E. Richey is an historian of the United Methodist Church in America, as well as a scholar of denominational history in general. Richey's many volumes, whether written or edited, contribute not only to the documentation of Methodism, but also to the ongoing concerns of the denomination as it moves into the twenty-first century. In an *RQ* review of Richey's *The Methodists,* Gregory A. Crawford cited the author as a "well-known Methodist scholar," and declared that the book had a "firm footing within the bounds of scholarship."

Richey told *CA:* "Denominations need to be better understood by those within them. Otherwise bureaucracy, inertias, subservience to authority, apotheosis of the institution immobilize members, stifle the creative religious spirit, inhibit the evolution of new structures to fit new circumstances. With such understanding, members should be freed to make denominations what they once were, means to higher ends. Without such understanding they will remain ends in themselves."

BIOGRAPHICAL/CRITICAL SOURCES:

PERIODICALS

Christian Century, December 7, 1994, Martin E. Marty, review of *Reimagining Denominationalism,* p. 1159.

RQ, summer, 1997, Gregory Crawford, review of *The Methodists,* p. 606.

* * *

RIMLAND, Ingrid 1936-

PERSONAL: Born May 22, 1936, in Halbstadt, Ukraine; daughter of Friedrich and Evelyn (Loetkemann) Brandt; divorced; children: Erwin, Rudy. *Education:* Wichita State University, B.A. (magna cum laude), 1971; University of the Pacific, M.A., 1973, Ed.D., 1979.

ADDRESSES: Home—6301 Herndon Pl., Stockton, CA 95207. *Office*—1931 Kiernan Ave., Modesto, CA 95350.

CAREER: Teacher of German in a private school in Argentina, 1956-58; Stanislaus Union School District, Modesto, CA, psychometrist, 1974—.

AWARDS, HONORS: California Literature Medal Award, Commonwealth Club of San Francisco, for best first novel by a California writer, 1977, and Gold Biennial Award, honorable mention, National League of American Pen Women, both for *The Wanderers;* honorable mention in journalism competition, National League of American Pen Women, for column "Children in Focus"; Soroptimist International Woman of Achievement and Woman of Distinction awards; IADM third prize, association of German-language media, for essay "Spache als Heimat." Recipient of PEN emergency grant and Mary Rinehart Foundation grant.

MEMBER: California Association of School Psychologists and Psychometrists, Phi Kappa Phi, Phi Delta Kappa, Mortar Board, honorary member of MENSA.

WRITINGS:

Psyching out Sex, Westminster Press (Philadelphia), 1975.

The Wanderers: The Saga of Three Women Who Survived (novel), Concordia (St. Louis), 1977, revised edition, Crystal Publications (Stockton, CA), 1988.

The Furies and the Flame: A True Story (autobiography), Arena Press (Novato, CA), 1984.

Demon Doctor, Crystal Publications, 1988.

Lebensraum! A Passion for Land and Peace (historical fiction), Samisdat Publishers (Toronto), 1998.

Lebensraum! The Theft of Land and Peace, Samisdat Publishers, 1998.

Lebensraum! The Dream of Land and Peace, Samisdat Publishers, 1998.

Author of columns "Children in Focus" and "Beautiful People and Books" for *Stockton Record,* Stockton, CA, "Superkids" for *Stockton Magazine,* and "Exclusively Yours" for *Stockton Lifestyle.* Contributor to newspapers, including *Los Angeles Times, Des Moines Register, Fresno Bee,* and *Kansas City Star,* and to anthologies.

SIDELIGHTS: Ingrid Rimland has had a dichotomous career. She was once acclaimed for her writing about her experiences as a World War II refugee and a mother fighting for care for her brain-injured son; she also wrote articles for numerous well-regarded publications and gave lectures to special education professionals. Since 1995, however, she "has been one of the most visible figures in the Holocaust denial movement," according to the *HateWatch* Web site. Her three-part work of historical fiction, *Lebensraum!,* portrays German Christians as the true victims of World War II and Adolf Hitler as a hero. Also, notes *HateWatch,* she is press secretary to Holocaust denier Ernst Zundel and co-Webmaster of the *Zundelsite,* an Internet site that carries extensive antisemitic and pro-Hitler content. She writes daily "Z-grams" consisting of "several pages of text denying the Holocaust or defending Ernst Zundel," *HateWatch* reports. Z-gram samples show her calling the Holocaust "a filthy lie," claiming that Nazi concentration camps were "detention centers . . . NOT killing centers," and alleging that Jews control the American media and use this power to pursue an anti-German agenda. Of Hitler, she says, "For people of my background, the Fuhrer was a tragic figure of mythical historical proportions: A man of great perception of the nature of all evil who threw the finest of his kin against the Antichrist in a futile and desperate war."

Rimland, who is of German Mennonite descent, was born in Ukraine, then part of the Soviet Union, in 1936. During World War II, her family looked on the invading German army as their liberators from the Soviet regime. After Germany's defeat, the family emigrated to Paraguay with a group of Mennonite refugees who set out to pioneer the Paraguayan jungle. She came to Canada with her husband and child in 1960, and came to the United States in 1967. Her novel *The Wanderers,* dealing with Mennonites who flee Ukraine for Paraguay during World War II, draws heavily on her heritage; the Zundelsite describes it as "a fictitious account of her Mennonite grandmother's life." The book was well received and won honors as the best first novel by a California writer in 1977. On the *Zundelsite,* Rimland noted that at the luncheon where she received this award, the guest speaker was *Roots* author Alex Haley: "He was flown in at my request—which tells you where my mindset was in those years. . . . I must admit in those years I did not perceive or appreciate the irony of a black ethnic novel sweeping America before a white ethnic novel." She also commented that "here in America, as far as I know, this was the first book ever of its kind that showed the German soldiers as heroes and not villains." She followed *The Wanderers* with *The Furies and the Flame: A True Story,* an account of her struggle to obtain education and proper care for her son Erwin, born in 1959 and brain-damaged in infancy. When he was thirteen, she placed him in an institution. "The book ends with a chapter that to this day still makes me cry," Rimland wrote on the *Zundelsite.* "It describes my feelings as I had to relinquish Erwin because my emotional reserves simply gave out on me, and I chose to take hold of my own life since I could not live through my child's limitations." Rimland's efforts on behalf of Erwin, who now lives in a private home, contributed to the breakup of her marriage and her estrangement from her other son, Rudy.

Rimland subsequently devoted much of her time to writing *Lebensraum!* She also became "openly anti-Semitic and pro-Hitler, but these are views she hid or suppressed for some time before stating them openly at the 'Zundelsite,' " according to *HateWatch.* This has cost her access to the literary world; the *Lebensraum!* trilogy, *HateWatch* remarks, "was issued only as a subsidy publishing and reviews of it had to be commissioned or written by friends of the 'movement.' " *Lebensraum!* spans two centuries in telling the story of two groups of German Mennonites, one that settled in the Ukraine and another in Kansas. It details the desire of both to create an agrarian utopia, a dream derailed by the two World Wars, the Great Depression, and, in the case of the group in the Ukraine, the Soviet government. A publication called *Instauration* characterizes the sufferings of those in the Ukraine under the Soviet regime as "the fearful Ukrainian Holocaust." The *Instauration* reviewer continues, "Rimland, who gives the official Jewish Holocaust short shrift, categorizes the Ukrainian as authentic and responsible for millions of deaths." The critic praises Rimland's characters as believable and her plot as "uncluttered and right to the point" and further relates that the work contains "brief strands of tribute to Hitler . . . the three volumes portray a Fuhrer with a human face and put the blame on Jewry for much of what has gone wrong in the world."

Rimland apparently believes her work makes her a candidate for martyrdom. "The road I have chosen as an activist for our kin and our cause is not exactly easy," she writes on the *Zundelsite.* "It could well be, one merry day, when, thanks to the 'Zundelsite' and 'Lebensraum!' and other projects yet to come, the enemy will 'take me out'—though, trust me, not without a struggle!"

BIOGRAPHICAL/CRITICAL SOURCES:

PERIODICALS

Instrauration, September, 1998.
Jubilee, July/August, 1998.

OTHER

HateWatch, http://www.hatewatch.org/ (March 1, 1999).*

* * *

ROBERSON, Jennifer 1953-
(Jennifer O'Green, Jennifer Roberson O'Green; Jay Mitchell, a pseudonym)

PERSONAL: Born October 26, 1953, in Kansas City, MO; daughter of Donald and Shera (a literary agent's reader) Roberson; married Mark O'Green (a designer-manager in computer games systems), February 16, 1985. *Education:* Northern Arizona University, B.S., 1982. *Religion:* Christian. *Avocational interests:* Professional dog obedience trainer, exhibitor of Labrador retrievers and Cardigan Welsh Corgis in conformation and obedience.

ADDRESSES: Office—c/o Children of the Firstborn, 610 North Alma School Rd., Suite 18, Box 104, Chandler, AZ. *Agent*—Scott Meredith Literary Agency, 845 Third Ave., New York, NY 10022.

CAREER: Wyoming Eagle, Cheyenne, WY, investigative reporter, 1976; Farnam Companies, Phoenix, AZ, advertising copywriter, 1977; writer, 1982—. Speaker at schools, colleges, professional writers' organizations, and science-fiction conferences.

MEMBER: Science Fiction and Fantasy Writers of America, Novelists, Inc., Cardigan Welsh Corgi Club of America, Southern California Cardigan Welsh Corgi Club, Bluebonnet Cardigan Welsh Corgi Club.

AWARDS, HONORS: Selected best new fantasy author, *Romantic Times* (magazine), 1984, for *Shapechangers;* Junior Alumni Achievement Award, Northern Arizona University, 1985; selected best new historical author, *Romantic Times,* 1987; outstanding young woman of America, 1988; selected as reviewer's choice annual top fantasy novel, *Science Fiction Chronicle,* 1989, for *Sword-Dancer* and *Sword-Singer,* and 1990, for *Sword-Maker;* certificate of appreciation, city of Tempe, 1990, for outstanding volunteer service to the community; Jubilee Year Distinguished Alumnus Award, Northern Arizona University, 1990.

WRITINGS:

"CHRONICLES OF THE CHEYSULI" FANTASY SERIES

Shapechangers, DAW (New York City), 1984.
The Song of Homana, DAW, 1985.
Legacy of the Sword, DAW, 1986.
Track of the White Wolf, DAW, 1987.
A Pride of Princes, DAW, 1988.
Daughter of the Lion, DAW, 1989.
Flight of the Raven, DAW, 1990.
A Tapestry of Lions, DAW, 1992.

"SWORD-DANCER SAGA" FANTASY SERIES

Sword-Dancer, DAW, 1986.
Sword-Singer, DAW, 1988.
Sword-Maker, DAW, 1989.
Sword-Breaker, DAW, 1991.
Sword-Born, DAW, 1998.

OTHER

Smoketree, (romantic suspense), Walker & Co. (New York City), 1985.
(Under pseudonym Jay Mitchell) *Kansas Blood,* Zebra Books (New York City), 1986.
(Under name Jennifer O'Green) *Royal Captive,* Dell (New York City), 1987.
Lady of the Forest, Zebra Books, 1992.
(With Melanie Rawn and Kate Elliot) *The Golden Key,* DAW, 1996.
(Editor) *Return to Avalon: A Celebration of Marion Zimmer Bradley,* DAW, 1996.
Lady of the Glen: A Novel of 17th-Century Scotland and the Massacre of Glencoe, Kensington (New York City), 1996.
Highlander: Scotland the Brave, Warner Books (New York City), 1996.
(Editor) *Highwaymen: Robbers and Rogues,* DAW, 1997.
Lady of Sherwood, Kensington, 1999.

Work represented in several anthologies, including *Sword and Sorceress,* volumes 1-8, edited by Marion Zimmer Bradley, DAW, 1984-91; *Spell Singers,* edited by A. B. Newcomer, DAW, 1988; *Herds of Thunder, Manes of Gold,* edited by Bruce Coville, Doubleday, 1989; *Horse Fantastic,* edited by Martin Greenberg and Rosalind Greenberg, DAW, 1991; and *Christmas Bestiary,* edited by M. Greenberg and R. Greenberg, DAW, 1992. Also columnist (as Jennifer Roberson O'Green) for *Corgi Quarterly* and *AKC Gazette.* Contributor to periodicals, including *Fantasy, Writer,* and *Aboriginal Science Fiction.*

SIDELIGHTS: Jennifer Roberson commented to *CA:* "I was fortunate to grow up in a family of readers; our genealogical chart is filled with bookaholics, including the renowned English author Thomas Hardy. An only child of divorced parents, I discovered very young that siblings and best friends were available at all times between the pages of favorite novels. It was not at all unusual for three generations—grandfather, mother, and daughter—to gather in the living room and while away the hours engrossed in our books of the moment."

This environment also helped foster Roberson's enjoyment of writing. By age fourteen she had already completed her first novel and received her first rejection slip. Even though she was hurt by the rejection, she did not allow it to quell her desire to be published. During the next fourteen years, she wrote three more unpublished novels before settling into the fantasy genre. Her first fantasy series "Chronicles of Cheysuli" was begun while in college; it was during her final semester that she received notice of the sale of her first book, *Shapechangers.*

Shapechangers was followed by seven other novels in the Cheysuli series. The Cheysuli are a race of people in which each member has the power to communicate with a given animal through telepathy and the power to assume that animal's form. The series chronicles the struggles between the oppressed Cheysuli—banished by a jealous ruler after his wife left him for his bodyguard, a Cheysuli—and a race called the Ihlini. The story continues over several generations, with many love affairs and rivalries as well as much use of sorcery and supernatural power. "The action is swift, constant and exciting," comments Debora Hill in the *St. James Guide to Fantasy Writers.*

Roberson is noted for creating strong female characters, both in the Cheysuli series and the Sword-Dancer books. Roberson has said she wanted to feature characters who would help break the traditional, sexist role females had often been assigned by other fantasy authors. The novelist explained: "I wanted to write about a man who, in meeting up with a strong, competent woman in the same line of work, has his consciousness raised during a dangerous journey that taxes them physically as well as emotionally. My personal description was 'Conan the Barbarian meets Gloria Steinem'; the true title was *Sword-Dancer,* and it was published in 1986."

Roberson has since written four more novels featuring what she calls "my Tracy/Hepburn-like duo"—Tiger, a male sword-dancer, or soldier of fortune, and Delilah (Del for short), a female sword-dancer. When they meet, Del is wanted for killing the man who trained her in the art of sword-fighting. She also is searching for her brother, who was taken prisoner by a band of criminals who murdered their parents and raped Del. Over the course of the series, Tiger joins Del in the quest for her brother and on her journey to face her accusers. Along the way, they meet demonic dogs, powerful wizards, false messiahs, and various other strange beings who inhabit their desolate world. "It adds up to a thoroughly enjoyable and well-written series, with pleasing characters and situations," Hill observes.

Roberson expanded her work into other genres by writing a western novel from a woman's viewpoint and a contemporary romantic suspense novel. She added: "But one thing I'd always wanted to try—another 'someday' dream—was a big, sprawling, mainstream historical epic. Russ [Galen, Roberson's agent] won me the chance when I submitted an outline/sample chapter package to him in which I proposed to write a reinterpretation of the Robin Hood legend, but with a twist—I wanted to emphasize Marian's point of view and contribution to the legend." The result was *Lady of the Forest,* which took Roberson a year to research and write; she described it as "in actuality, a 'prequel' to the familiar legend. I wanted very much to write the story of how the legend came to be; the tale of how seven very different people from a rigidly stratified social structure came to join together to fight the inequities of medieval England. To me, the key was *logic*—I interwove historical fact with the fantasy of the classic legend, and developed my own interpretation of how things came to be. I wanted to come to know all of these people; to climb inside their heads and learn what motivated them to do what they did."

In *Lady of Sherwood,* Roberson returns to her characters Marian and Robin Hood to tell the story of what happened after the death of King Richard the Lionhearted, the monarch who had pardoned the Robin Hood gang for their robberies. Suddenly, the sheriff of Nottingham is once again on their trail. The reviewer for *Publishers Weekly* praises Roberson's portrayal of Marian in particular, finding the character to be "thoroughly independent but not burdened with anachronistic feminist ways." Also impressive, the critic continues, is Roberson's "incorporation of historical detail" and her presentation of Marian and Robin's relationship. "Exciting and satisfying," the critic sums up, "Roberson's genre-blending novel may be her best yet."

Roberson once pointed out to *CA:* "One thing I have learned along the way that a writer, to be successful, must *write;* she cannot be satisfied with what she has already done, but must look ahead to what she will do. A writer completely satisfied with her work ceases to grow, and stunts her talent. It is far more important to *write* than it is *to have written.*"

BIOGRAPHICAL/CRITICAL SOURCES:

BOOKS

St. James Guide to Fantasy Writers, St. James Press (Detroit), 1996.

PERIODICALS

Booklist, September 1, 1996, Roland Green, review of *The Golden Key,* p. 69.

Fantasy Review, August, 1984, p. 22; October, 1985, p. 19; September, 1986, p. 30; June, 1987, p.40.

Locus, November, 1989, p. 57; July, 1990, p. 55; June, 1991, p. 50.

Magazine of Fantasy and Science Fiction, April, 1997, Michelle West, review of *Highlander: Scotland the Brave,* p. 132.

Publishers Weekly, February 26, 1996, review of *Lady of the Glen,* p. 87; August 19, 1996, review of *The Golden Key,* p. 57; November 1, 1999, review of *Lady of Sherwood,* p. 78.

Science Fiction Chronicle, March, 1986, p. 36; December, 1986, p. 50; January, 1987, p. 40; October, 1987, p. 27; March, 1989, p. 39; December, 1989, p. 39.

Voice of Youth Advocates, October, 1988, p. 196; August, 1989, p. 167; December, 1990, p. 301.

* * *

ROOS, Audrey (Kelley) 1912-1982
(Kelley Roos, a joint pseudonym)

PERSONAL: Born in 1912 in Elizabeth, NJ; died of cancer, December 11, 1982, on Martha's Vineyard, MA; married William E. Roos (a writer). *Education:* Attended Carnegie Institute of Technology.

CAREER: Writer, 1940-82. Owner of a catering service on Martha's Vineyard, MA.

AWARDS, HONORS: Edgar Allan Poe Award from the Mystery Writers of America, 1961, for television adaptation of John Dickson Carr's novel *The Burning Court.*

WRITINGS:

WITH HUSBAND, WILLIAM ROOS, UNDER JOINT PSEUDONYM KELLEY ROOS

Made up to Kill, Dodd (New York City), 1940, published as *Made up for Murder,* Jarrolds (London), 1941.

If the Shroud Fits, Dodd, 1941, published as *Dangerous Blondes,* Spivak (New York City), 1951.

The Frightened Stiff, Dodd, 1942.

Sailor, Take Warning!, Dodd, 1944.

There Was a Crooked Man, Dodd, 1945.

Ghost of a Chance, A. A. Wyn (New York City), 1947.

Murder in Any Language, A. A. Wyn, 1948.

Triple Threat: Three Jeff and Haila Mysteries (contains *She'd Make a Lovely Corpse, Death of a Trouper,* and *Beauty Marks the Spot*), A. A. Wyn, 1949, reprinted as *Beauty Marks the Spot,* Dell (New York City), 1951.

The Blonde Died Dancing, Dodd, 1956, published as *She Died Dancing,* Eyre & Spottiswoode (London), 1957.

Requiem for a Blonde, Dodd, 1958, published as *Murder Noon and Night,* Eyre & Spottiswoode, 1959.

Scent of Mystery (novelization of screenplay), Dell, 1959.

Necessary Evil, Dodd, 1965.

Grave Danger, Dodd, 1965.

Cry in the Night, Dodd, 1966.

One False Move, Dodd, 1966.

Who Saw Maggie Brown?, Dodd, 1967.

To Save His Life, Dodd, 1968.

Suddenly One Night, Dodd, 1970.

What Did Hattie See?, Dodd, 1970.

Bad Trip, Dodd, 1971.

Murder on Martha's Vineyard, Walker & Co. (New York City), 1981.

OTHER

(With husband William Roos under names Audrey and William Roos) *Speaking of Murder: A Melodrama* (three-act play; first produced on Broadway at the Royale Theater, December 19, 1956), Samuel French (New York City), 1957.

(With husband William Roos) *A Few Days in Madrid,* Scribner, 1965.

(With husband William Roos) *The Mystery Next Door,* Scribner, 1972.

Also author of television play *The Case of the Burning Court,* an adaptation of *The Burning Court* by John Dickson Carr, 1960. Work represented in anthologies, including *Four and Twenty Bloodhounds,* edited by Anthony Boucher, Simon & Schuster, 1950, and *Anthology 1971,* edited by Ellery Queen, 1970. Contributor of numerous short stories to periodicals, including *American Magazine, Mike Shayne Mystery Magazine,* and *Ellery Queen's Mystery Magazine.* A collection of the Rooses' manuscripts is housed at the Mugar Memorial Library at Boston University.

ADAPTATIONS: Some of the Roos' works have been made into motion pictures, including *A Night to Remember,* based on a short story, starring Loretta Young and Brian Aherne, Columbia, 1942; *Dangerous Blondes,* based on the novel *If the Shroud Fits,* with Allyn Joslyn and Evelyn Keyes, Columbia, 1943; *Come Dance with Me!,* based on the novel *The Blonde Died Dancing,* featuring Brigitte Bardot and Henri Vidal, Kingsley International, 1960; and *Scent of Mystery,* based on a short story, starring Denholm Elliott, Peter Lorre, and Elizabeth Taylor in a cameo appearance, Michael Todd, Jr., 1960.

SIDELIGHTS: With the publication of their first novel, *Made up to Kill,* in 1940, the husband-and-wife writing team of William and Audrey Roos began producing numerous mystery and suspense novels praised by critics for their wit, sophistication, and spirit. Written under the joint pseudonym Kelley Roos, the books offer fast-paced plots and well-constructed leading characters, and often feature husband-wife sleuth teams. Appealing more to readers who enjoy romantic mysteries than to those who like hard-boiled detective stories, the novels are usually set in New York City, and they occasionally revolve around the theater. The Roos, noted *Twentieth-Century Crime and Mystery Writers* essayist Fred Dueren, "wrote for those who read for enjoyment, rather than aiming for the analytic or adventuresome reader."

Made up to Kill, the Roos' first novel, introduces series characters Jeff and Haila Troy. While Jeff, a detective-story novelist, alternately hinders and helps the police in his efforts to crack cases, Haila usually solves the mystery one step ahead of him. *New York Times Book Review* critic Isaac Anderson dubbed the couple's initial effort "a mighty good start" and "a story that will keep you guessing until the cows come home." From 1940 to 1949 the Roos wrote Troy novels exclusively, producing eight in nine years, and one was made into a motion picture, *Dangerous Blondes.* Several reviewers thought the Troy books good examples of enjoyable, undemanding mystery fare. For instance, in the *Weekly Book Review,* Will Cuppy called *Sailor, Take Warning!* a "harmless and frequently entertaining pipe-dream" and pronounced the Troys to be "a cut above the standard domestic act so familiar in light mysteries." *Murder in Any Language,* according to the *Saturday Review of Literature* critic, offered an "engrossing plot [and] constant action"; a reviewer for the same publication dubbed *Ghost of a Chance* a "spine-tingler and adequate detective item." In 1966 the Rooses resurrected the characters for *One False Move,* updating the Troys without aging them. Set in a small Texas town rather than in New York, *One False Move* has the recently divorced Troys reconciled at the end.

After the publication of the eighth novel featuring Jeff and Haila was a seven year hiatus before the Roos published another book. *The Blonde Died Dancing,* which is markedly more suspenseful than their earlier mysteries, features a different husband and wife detective couple, Connie and Steve Barton, but still takes place in New York City. *Scent of Mystery,* published three years later, in 1959, involves still another couple in a Spanish setting. Intrigue permeates this and subsequent novels, and a concentration on exotic locales and love interests becomes more important than the mystery in these works. Indeed, the Roos' work, according to Dueren, "is notable as an example of the changes in emphasis in mystery novels" over the period spanned by their career.

Anthony Boucher in the *New York Times Book Review* called the Roos' 1965 offering *Necessary Evil* "one of their best ever." The book shows how one imperfection in a supposedly unsolveable murder plot by a socialite affects a dozen lives on all levels of New York City society. "It's a gay, sprightly book," Boucher continued, "with lively people, clever dialogue and dazzling intermeshing of plots and viewpoints within a tight time-span—a technical tour de force and one of the most sheerly entertaining stories of the season." In a later review for the same publication, Boucher referred to the Roos' mystery *Grave Danger* as "a delight both in its conciseness and in its intricacy, as it explores the complications of a 'perfect' murder in Connecticut."

In *Who Saw Maggie Brown?* one of Broadway's top actresses is kidnapped while relaxing under an assumed name. The woman's boyfriend and a detective come to her rescue in what Boucher, again writing in the *New York Times Book Review,* deemed "a lively, extremely economical, human and attractive thriller." *What Did Hattie See?* focuses on a nearsighted secretary at a New York talent agency who had seen a stolen painting on her boss's mantel. Although Hattie had not recognized the canvas, would-be killers presume otherwise and track her, much to her surprise. Sergeant Cuff in the

Saturday Review called *What Did Hattie See?* "cleverly plotted suspense, pulled off with a light touch," while Allen J. Hubin in the *New York Times Book Review* judged that its events "flow smoothly and absorbingly."

Some of the later Roos books, including their last one, *Murder on Martha's Vineyard,* take the readers inside the killers' minds. The plot has Nancy Brewster returning with her new husband to the Massachusetts island, where three years earlier she had been acquitted of murdering her first husband. Her friends and local townspeople are still wary of her, however, and Nancy hires a private investigator to search for the real murderer and prove her innocence. She subsequently comes face-to-face with the psychopath and learns his motive. Jean M. White in the *Washington Post Book World* stated that the Roos have "a nice feeling for character, from the Irish private eye to a 12-year-old girl trying to acquire a taste for Scotch." She judged *Murder on Martha's Vineyard* "a romantic thriller with a salty New England seashore setting . . . made-to-order for summertime escape reading." Dueren added that the Rooses' entire body of work was tailor-made for escapism; the books "in all cases . . . provided a substantial plot, good characters, and relief from the anxieties of a commonplace world."

BIOGRAPHICAL/CRITICAL SOURCES:

BOOKS

Twentieth-Century Crime and Mystery Writers, 3rd edition, St. James Press (Detroit), 1991.

PERIODICALS

Books, September 28, 1941, Will Cuppy, review of *If the Shroud Fits,* p. 20; October 25, 1942, Will Cuppy, review of *Frightened Stiff,* p. 26.

Book Week, February 6, 1944, Elizabeth Bullock, review of *Sailor, Take Warning!,* p. 10.

Boston Globe, May 23, 1945, review of *There Was a Crooked Man,* p. 13.

Boston Transcript, August 31, 1940, Marian Wiggin, review of *Made up to Kill,* p. 8.

Chicago Sun, November 4, 1949, James Sandoe, review of *Triple Threat.*

Kirkus, March 1, 1947, review of *Ghost of a Chance;* July 15, 1948, review of *Murder in Any Language;* October 1, 1949, review of *Triple Threat.*

New Yorker, January 22, 1944, review of *Sailor, Take Warning!;* September 4, 1948, review of *Murder in Any Language.*

New York Herald Tribune Weekly Book Review, April 27, 1947, Will Cuppy, review of *Ghost of a Chance,* p. 25; November 28, 1948, Will Cuppy, review of *Murder in Any Language,* p. 34; October 16, 1949, review of *Triple Threat,* p. 20.

New York Times, August 25, 1940, Isaac Anderson, review of *Made up to Kill,* p. 22; October 5, 1941, Isaac Anderson, review of *If the Shroud Fits,* p. 22; October 11, 1942, Kay Irvin, review of *Frightened Stiff,* p. 25; January 30, 1944, Isaac Anderson, review of *Sailor, Take Warning!,* p. 8; April 29, 1945, Isaac Anderson, review of *There Was a Crooked Man,* p. 17; April 20, 1947, Isaac Anderson, review of *Ghost of a Chance,* p. 34; September 19, 1948, Isaac Anderson, review of *Murder in Any Language,* p. 31; October 9, 1949, review of *Triple Threat,* p. 27.

New York Times Book Review, April 25, 1965; December 12, 1965, Anthony Boucher, review of *Necessary Evil;* December 17, 1967, Anthony Boucher, review of *Who Saw Maggie Brown?;* October 13, 1968; April 19, 1970, Allen J. Hubin, review of *What Did Hattie See?;* January 17, 1971.

San Francisco Chronicle, October 3, 1948, E. D. Doyle, review of *Murder in Any Language,* p. 14; December 4, 1949, E. D. Doyle, review of *Triple Threat,* p. 32.

Saturday Review, March 28, 1970, Sergeant Cuff, review of *What Did Hattie See?*

Saturday Review of Literature, September 7, 1940, review of *Made up to Kill;* October 18, 1941, review of *If the Shroud Fits;* October 10, 1942, review of *Frightened Stiff;* April 21, 1945, review of *There Was a Crooked Man;* May 17, 1947, review of *Ghost of a Chance;* September 11, 1948, review of *Murder in Any Language.*

Springfield Republican, January 23, 1944, review of *Sailor, Take Warning!,* p. E7.

Stage, April 1, 1971.

Washington Post Book World, August 16, 1981, Jean M. White, review of *Murder on Martha's Vineyard.*

Weekly Book Review, January 23, 1944, Will Cuppy, review of *Sailor, Take Warning!,* p. 22; April 29, 1945, Will Cuppy, review of *There Was a Crooked Man,* p. 16.

OBITUARIES:

PERIODICALS

AB Bookman's Weekly, January 31, 1983.

Chicago Tribune, December 13, 1982.*

ROOS, Kelley
See ROOS, Audrey (Kelley)

* * *

ROOSE-EVANS, James 1927-

PERSONAL: Born November 11, 1927, in England; son of Jack and Catherine Owen (Morgan) Roose-Evans. *Education:* Oxford University, B.A., 1952, M.A., 1957. *Politics:* Liberal. *Religion:* Christian.

ADDRESSES: *Home*—Wales and London, England. *Agent*—David Higham Associates Ltd., 5-8 Lower John St., Golden Square, London W1R 4HA, England.

CAREER: Maddermarket Theatre, Norwich, England, artistic director, 1954-55; Juilliard School of Music, New York City, member of faculty, 1955-56; Royal Academy of Dramatic Art, London, England, staff member and judge, 1957-62; Hampstead Theatre Club, London, founder and artistic director, 1959-71; Middlesex Polytechnic, London, first reader in drama, 1979—. Ordained priest of the Anglican Church, 1982. Pitlochry Festival Theatre, Scotland, artistic director, 1960; Stage Two (theatre workshop and research center), founder and director, beginning 1969. Adjudicator, National Union of Students Drama Festival, 1970, and National Drama Festival of Zambia, 1973. Ohio State University, distinguished visiting fellow, 1991-92. Welsh Arts Council, member of drama committee and dance committee; Southeast Wales Arts Association, member of combined arts panel; Welsh Dance Theatre, council member. The Bleddfa Trust, founder and chairman. Lecturer and conductor of theater workshops in the United States. Director of numerous West End productions, including *Under Milk Wood, Cider with Rosie, Private Lives, The Happy Apple, An Ideal Husband, Spitting Image, 84 Charing Cross Road, The Seven-Year Itch, The Best of Friends,* and *Mate, a Personal Affair;* director of French production of Vaclav Havel's *Temptation;* director of *Oedipus,* produced in Athens at Greek Contemporary Theatre. *Military service:* Royal Army Educational Corps, 1947-49.

MEMBER: Royal Society of Arts (fellow), Garrick Club.

AWARDS, HONORS: Arts Council bursary to Finland, 1968; *The Female Messiah* was chosen by British Broadcasting Corp. as its entry for the 1975 Italia Prize.

WRITINGS:

(Adaptor) *The Little Clay Cart,* Elek Books (London), 1965.

Directing a Play: James Roose-Evans on the Art of Directing and Acting, Theatre Arts Inc. (New York City), 1968.

Experimental Theatre: From Stanislavsky to Today, Universe Books (New York City), 1970, revised edition published as *Experimental Theatre: From Stanislavsky to Peter Brook,* 1984.

(And director) *The Female Messiah* (radio documentary), British Broadcasting Corp. (BBC), 1975.

(And director) *The Third Adam* (radio documentary), BBC, 1976.

London Theatre: From the Globe to the National, Dutton (New York City), 1977.

Acrobats of God (television documentary), BBC, 1977.

Lady Managers (television documentary), BBC, 1980.

(Adaptor) *84 Charing Cross Road* (play; based on the book by Helene Hanff; first produced in England, 1981), Samuel French/Doubleday (New York City), 1983.

Inner Journey, Outer Journey: Finding a Spiritual Centre in Everyday Life, Rider (London), 1987, published as *The Inner Stage: Finding a Center in Prayer and Ritual,* Cowley (Cambridge, MA), 1990.

(Editor and author of introduction) Joyce Grenfell, *Darling Ma: Letters of Joyce Grenfell,* Hodder & Stoughton (London), 1988.

Re: Joyce! (play), first produced on West End, 1988.

(Editor) Grenfell, *The Time of My Life; The Wartime Journals of Joyce Grenfell,* Hodder & Stoughton, 1990.

Passages of the Soul: Ritual Today, Element (Longmead, England), 1994, published as *Passages of the Soul: Rediscovering the Importance of Rituals in Everyday Life,* 1995.

One Foot on the Stage: The Biography of Richard Wilson, Weidenfeld & Nicholson (London), 1997.

FOR CHILDREN

The Adventures of Odd and Elsewhere, Deutsch (London), 1971.

The Secret of the Seven Bright Shiners: An Odd and Elsewhere Story, Deutsch, 1972.

Odd and the Great Bear: An Odd and Elsewhere Story, Deutsch, 1973.

Elsewhere and the Gathering of the Clowns: An Odd and Elsewhere Story, Deutsch, 1974.

The Return of the Great Bear: An Odd and Elsewhere Story, Deutsch, 1975, published as *Odd to the Rescue: An Odd and Elsewhere Story,* 1983.
The Secret of Tippity-Witchit: An Odd and Elsewhere Story, Deutch, 1976.
The Lost Treasure of Wales: An Odd and Elsewhere Story, Deutsch, 1977.

OTHER

Also author of *London Theatre,* 1977, and a dramatic anthology, *Pride of Players,* 1978; author of radio play, *Topsy and Ted,* and of play, *Augustus,* first produced, 1985; author of radio documentary, *A Well-conducted Theatre,* 1979. Author of introduction to Andrew Sinclair's *Adventures in the Skin Trade* (based on the novel by Dylan Thomas), New Directions (New York City), 1968. Contributor to *Actor Training Two,* edited by Richard Brown, Drama Book Specialists, 1976. Author of column, "Something Extra," for *Woman* magazine, 1986—. Contributor of reviews and articles to periodicals, including *Times Educational Supplement* and *Financial Times.*

ADAPTATIONS: A 1987 movie adaptation of *84 Charing Cross Road* was written by Hugh Whitemore and directed by David Jones.

SIDELIGHTS: James Roose-Evans has had a varied career. He has written and directed numerous plays, gaining a reputation as a theatrical innovator; has authored books on spirituality; and has created a popular series of children's books, the "Odd and Elsewhere" stories. Roose-Evans's theatrical experience informs these stories, which focus on a teddy bear named Odd and a toy clown called Elsewhere. "Roose-Evans has spent much of his working life in the theatre, and he is especially good at describing the excitement and anguish of public performance, a constant theme," observed Heather Neill in *Twentieth-Century Children's Writers.* "Circuses and Arthurian myth, liberally modified, have provided inspiration for his stories . . . but the main thread is the traditional one of defeat of Evil by Good."

The books in the series form a continuing story, but they can be read individually. Over the course of their adventures, Odd and Elsewhere progress from toys to living beings, and they learn responsibility and a sense of their goals in life; as Neill put it, "in short, they begin to grow up." The stories teach moral lessons, but not in a heavy-handed fashion, and along the way they offer bits of trivia about nature and other subjects. "Despite a few . . . infelicities—the out-of-place grotesquerie of [the characters] Mr. Goodman and Arbuthnot on their first appearance, the killing off of enemies without regret, and the almost invariable consigning of females to kitchens—these books have a pace and inventiveness, a feeling for language, and an appreciation of lovable eccentricity that will make them delightful companions to generations of children," concluded Neill.

BIOGRAPHICAL/CRITICAL SOURCES:

BOOKS

Twentieth-Century Children's Writers, 4th edition, St. James Press (Detroit), 1995.

PERIODICALS

Camden Journal, February-March, 1968.
Drama, winter, 1968.
Los Angeles Times, March 14, 1986; March 20, 1987.
New York Times, June 3, 1970; February 3, 1987.
Times (London), November 30, 1981; April 1, 1987.
Times Literary Supplement, October 22, 1971; June 15, 1973; July 11, 1975; December 5, 1975; May 25, 1977.*

* * *

ROSECRANCE, Richard (Newton) 1930-

PERSONAL: Born October 24, 1930, in Milwaukee, WI.

ADDRESSES: Office—11383 Bunche Hall, University of California, Los Angeles, CA; fax: 310-206-2582. *E-mail*—rosecran@polisci.ucla.edu.

CAREER: University of California, Los Angeles, teacher, 1957-67, professor of political science, 1988—, director of the Center for International Relations; Cornell University, Ithaca, NY, Walter S. Carpenter Junior professor of international and comparative politics, beginning in 1970; University of California, Berkeley, professor, until 1988. Member of the U.S. Department of State's Policy Planning Council, 1967.

AWARDS, HONORS: Fulbright scholar in Australia, Rockefeller Foundation fellow in England, Guggenheim fellow, Ford fellow.

WRITINGS:

The Dispersion of Nuclear Weapons: Strategy and Politics, Columbia University Press (New York City), 1964.

The Future of the International Strategic System, Chandler Publishing, 1972.

International Relations: Peace or War?, McGraw (New York City), 1973.

Power, Balance of Power, and Status in Nineteenth-Century International Relations, Sage Publications (Beverly Hills, CA), 1974.

Strategic Deterrence Reconsidered, International Institute for Strategic Studies, 1975.

America as an Ordinary Country: U.S. Foreign Policy and the Future, Cornell University Press (Ithaca, NY), 1976.

The Rise of the Trading State: Commerce and Conquest in the Modern World, Basic Books (New York City), 1986.

America's Economic Resurgence: A Bold New Strategy, Harper (New York City), 1990.

(Editor with Arthur A. Stein) *The Domestic Bases of Grand Strategy,* Cornell University Press, 1993.

(Editor with Michael E. Brown) *The Costs of Conflict: Prevention and Cure in the Global Arena,* Rowman & Littlefield (Lanham, MD), 1999.

The Rise of the Virtual State: Wealth and Power in the Coming Century, Basic Books, 1999.

Contributor to *Lessons from the Fall and Rise of Nations: The Future for America,* Woodrow Wilson International Center for Scholars, 1987.

SIDELIGHTS: Political scientist, educator, and author, Richard Rosecrance has published numerous books on international relations and American foreign policy. His 1986 volume, *The Rise of the Trading State: Commerce and Conquest in the Modern World,* puts forth the proposition that in order to compete successfully in the world economy, the United States needs to change its foreign policy from a territorial (military-political) system to that of a trading nation. As historical precedent for his contention, Rosecrance's discussion ranges over hundreds of years, including a comparison between the territorial policies of Louis XIV of France with the earlier trade-based policies of Venice, Genoa, and Amsterdam. He notes that with the Industrial Revolution the link between land and power was broken. Consequently, in the contemporary world a nation's interest can be advanced more successfully by economic development and international trade than by costly and dangerous wars to gain territory. Reviewing *The Rise of the Trading State,* Chalmers Johnson finds a good deal to praise but more to criticize. The *Atlantic* critic states: "Rosecrance's book displays a broad sweep, with an excellent interweaving of historical examples and theoretical conceptualizations . . . a timely and thought-provoking book that is not, in the end, convincing." Johnson's main objection has to do with the fact that he feels Rosecrance knows far more about the territorial state than the trading state. Nor does Rosecrance advance concrete suggestions on how the United States could make the transition to a trading state. Further, according to Johnson, Rosecrance's study contains factual errors, such as his claim that Alexander Hamilton was opposed to the trading state when in truth he was strongly in favor of it. "Rosecrance's real contribution," Johnson concludes, "comes in his depiction of what will happen if we continue on the territorial path. . . . [W]e are likely to end up as the world's leading producers of ICBMs and soybeans while the Japanese make everything in between."

In his 1990 volume, *America's Economic Resurgence: A Bold New Strategy,* Rosecrance states: "The basic contention of this book . . . is that, unlike past powers, the United States can come back from decline." Rosecrance's has numerous suggestions on how this comeback can be accomplished. He thinks that we should reduce the budget deficit by raising taxes and reducing military spending, cut back on entitlement programs such as Social Security and Medicare, establish closer tries between business and government, and provide increased funds for education and research. He also feels the United States should compete more actively for foreign markets and build a trading partnership with Japan. Leonard Silk of the *New Leader* observes: "Rosecrance's perception that a reorientation of America's foreign policy is crucial to its economic revival is an important contribution to national thinking about the problems of the United States in the emerging multipolar world." However, Silk also feels that "no reliable prophecy of future events . . . [can be found in] heavily footnoted, data-laden political science, like Rosecrance's carefully reasoned volume." He sees *America's Economic Resurgence* as a book that hopes America "has not had its day." "Hope," concludes Silk, "when it underrates the depth of problems and dangers, can lead to negligence and inanition."

The Domestic Bases of Grand Strategy, a volume Rosecrance co-edited with Arthur A. Stein, presents a series of chapters by different writers that argue against what is known as the "realist" view of international relations. According to the realist interpretation, power is what all nations seek to gain. *The Domestic Bases of Grand Strategy* contends that the interrelations of nations reflect a complex mix involving culture, history, economics, ideology, and domestic policy. It cites numerous historical examples, such as the end of the Cold War and Anglo-German naval competition before World War I, that cannot be explained solely by the quest for power. In a review for *Foreign Affairs,* Frances Fukuyama notes that "this book is evidence of the fading 'realist' interpretation of international relations," but feels that what is missing from the volume "is a positive theory linking domestic politics to grand strategy."

In *The Rise of the Virtual State: Wealth and Power in the Coming Century,* Rosecrance proposes a new model for the world of the twenty-first century. Whereas throughout history the ownership of land has served as the source of economic power, Rosecrance feels that in the future control over processes and services will supercede it. He envisions a "virtual state" in which land is no longer the main focus of national identity. Since wars have mostly been fought over land, he predicts that the possibility for violent confrontations between nations will be reduced. Citing the multinational corporation as a working model for the virtual state, and listing Japan, Korea, and Switzerland as nations that have already moved in this direction by relocating much of their production abroad, Rosecrance's conclusions are optimistic. He asserts that "the world is making steady progress toward peace and economic security." A *Publishers Weekly* reviewer remarks: "This analysis will likely stand up well as a grand preliminary testament to the changing nature of civilization."

BIOGRAPHICAL/CRITICAL SOURCES:

PERIODICALS

Atlantic, December, 1985, Chalmers Johnson, review of *The Rise of the Trading State,* p. 106.

Foreign Affairs, March-April, 1994, Francis Fukuyama, review of *The Domestic Bases of Grand Strategy,* p. 140.

New Leader, May 14, 1990, Leonard Silk, review of *America's Economic Resurgence,* p. 24.

Publishers Weekly, October 25, 1999, review of *The Rise of the Virtual State,* p. 60.

Times Literary Supplement, November 26, 1976.*

* * *

ROSENBLUM, Robert 1927-

PERSONAL: Born July 24, 1927, in New York, NY; son of Abraham H. (a dentist) and Lily M. (Lipkin) Rosenblum. *Education:* Queens College (now Queens College of the City University of New York), B.A., 1948; Yale University, M.A., 1950; New York University, Ph.D., 1956.

ADDRESSES: Office—Department of Fine Arts, New York University, New York, NY 10003.

CAREER: University of Michigan, Ann Arbor, instructor in fine arts, 1955-56; Princeton University, Princeton, NJ, associate professor of art and archeology, 1956-66; New York University, New York, NY, professor of fine arts, 1966—; Solomon R. Guggenheim Museum, New York, NY, curator, 1996—. Visiting professor, Columbia University, 1960-61, 1963. Lecturer on art at Harvard, Yale, and Columbia Universities, University of California, Riverside, Hamilton College, Metropolitan Museum of Art, Guggenheim Museum, Art Institute of Chicago, Los Angeles County Museum, and Brooklyn Museum/ *Military service:* U.S. Army, 1945-46.

AWARDS, HONORS: Fulbright grant; American Council of Learned Societies fellowship; Proctor and Gamble fellowship at Princeton University; National Book Award nomination, 1976, for *Modern Painting and the Romantic Tradition;* Commandeur de l'Ordre des Arts et des Lettres, 1999; PEN Award nomination, literary writing on the visual arts, 2000, for *On Modern American Art.*

WRITINGS:

Cubism and Twentieth-Century Art, Abrams (New York City), 1960.

Transformations in Late Eighteenth-Century Art, Princeton University Press (Princeton NJ), 1967.

Jean-Auguste-Dominique Ingres, Abrams, 1967.

Frank Stella, Penguin (New York City), 1970.

Modern Painting and the Romantic Tradition: Friedrich to Rothko, Harper (New York City), 1975.

(Author of essay) *The Sculpture of Picasso* (exhibition catalog), Pace Gallery (New York City), 1982.

(With H. W. Janson) *19th Century Art,* Prentice-Hall (Englewood Cliffs, NJ), Abrams, 1984.

The Dog in Art from Rococo to Post-Modernism, Abrams, 1988.

(Author of text) Mike Bidlo, *Masterpieces* (exhibition catalog), Edition Bischofberger (Zurich), 1989.

(Compiler) *L'art au temps de la Revolution francaise* (conference proceedings of the 27th International Congress of the History of Art), Societe alsacienne pour le developpement de l'histoire de l'art (Strasbourg, France), 1989.

The Romantic Child: From Runge to Sendak, Thames & Hudson (New York City), 1989.
Paintings in the Musee d'Orsay, foreword by Francoise Cachin, Stewart, Tabori & Chang (New York City), 1989.
(Conducted interview) *Alan Sonfist, 1969-1989,* Long Island University (Bronxville, NY), 1990.
(Author of essays with Boris I. Asvarishch) Sabine Rewald, editor, *The Romantic Vision of Caspar David Friedrich: Paintings and Drawings from the USSR* (exhibition catalog), Metropolitan Museum of Art (New York City)/Art Institute of Chicago, 1990.
(Author of introduction) Metropolitan Museum of Art, *The Landscape in Twentieth-Century American Art* (exhibition catalog), American Federation of Arts/ Rizzoli (New York City), 1991.
(Author of introduction) Jeff Koons, *Jeff Koons Handbook,* Rizzoli, 1992.
(Author of text) David Bowes, *Julio de 1993* (exhibition catalog), Galeria Ramis Barquet (Garza Garcia, Mexico), 1993.
(Author of text with Carter Ratcliffe) Ratcliffe, *Gilbert & George: The Singing Sculpture,* A. McCall (New York City), 1993.
(Author of additional essay) Sandy Ballatore, *Romantic Modernism, 100 Years* (exhibition catalog), Museum of New Mexico, 1994.
(Author of essay) *Mel Ramos: Pop Art Images,* Benedikt Taschen (Koln), 1994.
Diane Burki: New Painting from Bellasio, Locks Gallery (Philadelphia), 1994.
Dinos and Jake Chapman: Unholy, Gagosian Gallery (New York City), 1997.
Jasper Johns: Loans from the Artist (exhibition catalog), Foundation Beyeler (Riehen), 1997.
(Author of essay) *Messers MacDermott & MacGough: Paintings, Photographs & Time Experiments* (exhibition catalog), Stichting Kunstboek (Bruges, Belgium), 1997.
(Editor with Steven A. Nash) *Picasso and the War Years, 1937-1945,* Thames & Hudson, Fine Arts Museums of San Francisco, 1998.
(Author of essays with Vincent Fremont) *Andy Warhol Knives: Paintings, Polaroids, and Drawings* (exhibition catalog), Salon Verlag (Koln), 1998.
On Modern American Art: Selected Essays, Abrams, 1999.
(With MaryAnne Stevens and Ann Dumas) *1900: Art at the Crossroads,* Abrams, 2000.

Also contributor to numerous books on art, including *Andy Warhol: Portraits of the Seventies,* edited by David Whitney, Random House, 1979; *Art at Work: The Chase Manhattan Collection,* edited by Marshall Lee, Dutton, 1984; and *Andy Warhol: Portraits of the Seventies and Eighties,* Thames & Hudson, 1993. Contributor to *Encyclopedia Britannica* and *Encyclopedia of World Art;* contributor to numerous exhibition catalogues. Contributor to art periodicals.

SIDELIGHTS: In his 1999 collection, *On Modern American Art: Selected Essays,* noted art critic and historian Robert H. Rosenblum states that he is attempting "to translate the visceral experience of art into . . . modes of language and art history." The fifty essays that comprise the book span forty years (1958-1998) of Rosenblum's career and also forty years of contemporary American art. Willem de Kooning, Jasper Johns, Roy Lichtenstein, Jackson Pollack, Andrew Wyeth, and Mark Rothko are only a few of the artists examined in this compilation that Stephen Allan Patrick of *Library Journal* characterizes as "insightful, provocative, and humorous . . . [and] an important work interpreting the American art movement." The volume also includes black and white reproductions of many of the works of art discussed along with a comprehensive bibliography of Rosenblum's other writings. "Equally comfortable with the retrograde, the canonical and the new," a reviewer for *Publishers Weekly* observes, "Rosenblum gravitates in particular to the way in which painters consider the history of their form." In addition to essays on specific artists, often first written as reviews of exhibitions, Rosenblum also tackles broader subjects he considers relevant to recent American art history, such as the significance of memory and retrospection in painting and the question of what is distinctively American about American art. The *Publishers Weekly* reviewer concludes his comments by praising Rosenblum's clarity of expression but also noting that at times his "prose can be less than compelling."

In addition to his role as a critic and observer of contemporary art, which has included authoring the text for numerous exhibition catalogs and book-length collections of many artists' work, Rosenblum has also published a number of books that take a more historical perspective. His *19th Century Art,* co-authored with New York University colleague H. W. Janson, presents a comprehensive survey and interpretation of American and European art movements throughout the nineteenth century. The book includes more than 500 illustrations, many of them in color. A *People Weekly* reviewer comments that it "would be easy to spend weeks just gazing" at these illustrations, and goes on to praise the books thorough index and bibliography, and the "lucid, vivid prose" in which it is written.

In *The Dog in Art,* Rosenblum takes a lighter and less conventional approach to art history, suggesting that the way artists have portrayed dogs may provide as much information on the social and cultural history of the West as an examination of its wars and revolutions. The book ranges from the 1700s through post-modernism and includes studies of a black and white Chin, painted by French impressionists Renoir and Manet, a statue of a defecating dog by Italian sculptor Adriano Cecioni, a shaved and beribboned poodle by eighteenth-century painter Jean-Jacques Bachelier, and Albert Giacometti's 1951 sculpture of a mongrel street dog. Harry Shapiro of *People Weekly* finds *The Dog in Art* "often delightful," but finds Rosenblum's contention that the portrayal of dogs in art can offer significant historical insights to be "overly ambitious."

BIOGRAPHICAL/CRITICAL SOURCES:

PERIODICALS

Entertainment Weekly, November 19, 1993, Rebecca Ascher-Walsh, review of *Andy Warhol Portraits,* p. 86.

Library Journal, June 1, 1998, Eric Bryant, review of *MacDermott and MacGough,* p. 106; May 15, 1999, Perry Jack Brown, review of *Arts of the 19th Century,* Vol. 2: *1850-1905,* p. 92; November 1, 1999, Stephen Allan Patrick, review of *On Modern American Art,* p. 78.

People Weekly, April 9, 1984, review of *19th Century Art,* p. 13; February 6, 1989, Harriet Shapiro, review of *The Dog in Art,* p. 30.

Publishers Weekly, March 8, 1991, review of *The Romantic Vision of Casper David Friedrich,* p. 71; February 1, 1993, review of *The Jeff Koons Handbook,* p. 86; May 24, 1993, review of *Gilbert & George,* p. 76; October 25, 1999, review of *On Modern American Art,* p. 64.

* * *

ROSSMAN, Marlene L. 1948-

PERSONAL: Born in 1948, in Brooklyn, NY; married Elliot Silverman (a lawyer), June 29, 1980. *Education:* Pace University, B.A., 1972, M.B.A., 1982; New York University, M.A., 1974.

ADDRESSES: *Office*—Rossman, Graham Associates, 201 East 17th St., 17th Floor, New York, NY 10003; fax 212-477-2295. *E-mail*—mlrossman@aol.com.

CAREER: Wingate English Academy, New York City, managing director, 1976-80; Rossman, Graham, Associates (marketing, sales, and business planners), New York City, partner, beginning in 1980, and president. New York University, adjunct professor, 1984-86; Pace University, adjunct professor, 1986-94; University of San Diego, visiting professor and executive in residence, 1995.

MEMBER: Financial Women's Association (member of board of directors and chairperson of Professional Development Committee), American Sommeliers Association (founding member), Women for Wine Sense (founding member of New York chapter), Omicron Delta Epsilon.

WRITINGS:

The International Businesswoman: A Guide to Success in the Global Marketplace, Praeger (New York City), 1986.

The International Businesswoman of the 1990s, Praeger, 1990.

Multicultural Marketing: Selling to a Diverse America, AMACOM (New York City), 1994.

Contributor to marketing and business journals, including *Baylor Business Studies* and *Marketing News.* Some writings have been translated into Japanese and Chinese.

SIDELIGHTS: Marlene L. Rossman told *CA:* "I was inspired to write my first book when, in 1984, I was giving a speech about my career as a marketing consultant. I was besieged with questions by women. These women had many of the same questions about the business world and its rigors that I had when I began. In order to help pave the way for other young career women, I decided to write a 'how-to' book."

She added: "My most recent book, *Multicultural Marketing,* comes out of my experience helping large corporate clients (including Dial Corp., Pfizer, Colgate-Palmolive, Nordstrom, and Boise Cascade) market their products to Asian Americans, African Americans, Hispanics, and other diverse segments [of the population]."

BIOGRAPHICAL/CRITICAL SOURCES:

PERIODICALS

Times (London), October 6, 1986.*

RUSE, Michael E. 1940-

PERSONAL: Born June 21, 1940. *Education:* University of Bristol, B.A., 1962, Ph.D., 1970; McMaster University, M.A., 1964.

ADDRESSES: Office—Department of Philosophy, University of Guelph, Guelph, Ontario N1G 2W1 Canada. *E-mail*—mruse@arts.uogelph.ca.

CAREER: University of Guelph, Guelph, Ontario, lecturer, 1965-69, assistant professor, 1969-71, associate professor, 1971-74, professor of philosophy and zoology, 1974—. Associate of Clare Hall, Cambridge, 1972-73; visiting professor at Indiana University, winter, 1976; lecturer in the United States, Canada, and Venezuela.

MEMBER: Royal Society of Canada (fellow), American Association for the Advancement of Science (fellow).

AWARDS, HONORS: Canada Council grants, 1971, 1974, and 1976-77, and fellowship, 1972-73; Guggenheim fellowship; Killam fellowship.

WRITINGS:

The Philosophy of Biology, Hutchinson University Press, 1973.

Sociobiology: Sense or Nonsense?, D. Reidel (Boston), 1979, 2nd edition, 1985.

The Darwinian Revolution: Science Red in Tooth and Claw, University of Chicago Press (Chicago), 1979.

Taking Darwin Seriously: A Naturalistic Approach to Philosophy, Blackwell (New York City), 1986.

Philosophy of Biology Today, State University of New York (Albany), 1988.

(Compiler and author of introduction) *Philosophy of Biology,* Collier (New York City), 1989.

The Darwinian Paradigm: Essays on Its History, Philosophy, and Religious Implications, Routledge (New York City), 1989.

Homosexuality: A Philosophical Inquiry, Blackwell (New York City), 1990.

Evolutionary Naturalism: Selected Essays, Routledge, 1995.

Monad to Man: The Concept of Progress in Evolutionary Biology, Harvard University Press (Cambridge, MA), 1996.

Mystery of Mysteries: Is Evolution a Social Construction?, Harvard University Press, 1999.

EDITOR

Nature Animated: Historical and Philosophical Case Studies in Greek Medicine, Nineteenth-Century and Recent Biology, Psychiatry, and Psychoanalysis: Papers Deriving from the Third International Conference on the History and Philosophy of Science, [Montreal], 1980, D. Reidel, 1983.

But Is It Science?: The Philosophical Question in the Creation/Evolution Controversy, Prometheus Books, 1988.

What the Philosophy of Biology Is: Essays Dedicated to David Hull, Kluwer Academic (Boston), 1989.

Philosophy of Biology, Prometheus Books, 1998.

(With David L. Hull) *The Philosophy of Biology,* Oxford University Press, 1998.

(With June Maienschein) *Biology and the Foundation of Ethics,* Cambridge University Press (New York City), 1999.

OTHER

Contributor to books, including *Laws, Logic, Life,* edited by R. Colodny, University of Pittsburgh Press, 1977; *Matters of Life and Death: Crises in Bio-Medical Ethics,* edited by John E. Thomas, Samuel Stevens, 1978; and *The Sociobiology Debate,* edited by Arthur L. Caplan, Harper, 1979. Editor, "Philosophy and Biology" series, Cambridge University Press. Contributor of about eighty articles and reviews to philosophy journals. Founding editor, *Biology and Philosophy;* member of editorial board of nine journals.

SIDELIGHTS: Michael E. Ruse, a Canadian professor of both philosophy and zoology, has written extensively on the subject of Charles Darwin and his evolutionary theories. Ruse's collection, *The Darwinian Paradigm: Essays on Its History, Philosophy, and Religious Implications,* opens with a discussion of the philosophical ideas that influenced Darwin at the time he was developing his theories and closes with a discussion of the implications those theories hold for theology. The eight essays in between range over a variety of topics, including teleology (the examination of phenomena as displaying purpose or direction) and how different aspects of biology provide contributing evidence for Darwin's ideas. Raymond E. Grizzle's review of *The Darwinian Paradigm* for *BioScience* concentrates its comments on the science-versus-religion aspects of the book. Viewing Ruse as "one of the more well-known and respected philosophers of science," Grizzle feels that many "who fully accept biological evolution as a scientific theory but not as a religion" would be interested in Ruse's opinions on the subject.

However, Grizzle notes: "Ruse . . . sends out conflicting signals with respect to his views in this area, and thus his interpretation of Darwinism. . . . In sum, it is not clear to me where Ruse stands on the overall relationship between science and religion." "My criticisms not withstanding," Grizzle concludes, "I think this book must be read by those interested in the historical development of Darwinism."

In *Monad to Man: The Concept of Progress in Evolutionary Biology* Ruse argues that the belief in moral and social progress, as embodied in the Enlightenment and defined by the writings of philosophers such as Voltaire and Condorcet, has had a profound influence on the science of evolutionary biology from its very origins. Ruse begins his historical survey in the eighteenth century, examining both the research and the attitudes that shaped that research for scientists of the era, including the French naturalist, Lamarck, and Erasmus Darwin, the grandfather of Charles. Moving on to the first half of the nineteenth century, Ruse covers the work of Cuvier, Richard Owen, von Baer, and Agassiz, among others. Writing in *Science,* Francisco J. Ayala remarks: "Ruse skillfully shows how the temper of the times, most particularly optimism about cultural progress, pervaded these early biologists' highly speculative theorizing." Ruse presents a more detailed analysis of Charles Darwin, tracing the gradual acceptance of his theories into the twentieth century and exploring their influence on other scientific disciplines, such as mathematics, genetics, and paleontology. Throughout, he continues to assert that the belief in progress introduced a philosophical bias that tainted the scientific objectivity of both Darwin and those who expanded upon his work. While seemingly impressed with the scholarship of Ruse's study, and in agreement with the central thesis of *Monad to Man,* Ayala takes issue with Ruse's claim that the ideology of progress continues to influence the outcome of biological research today and will continue to do so for the foreseeable future. Ayala feels that contemporary scientists are cognizant of this bias and that they no longer believe that judgments about the "progressiveness" of a species are a relevant topic for scientific inquiry.

Ruse broadens the thesis of *Monad to Man* in his 1999 study, *Mystery of Mysteries: Is Evolution a Social Construction?* Describing the "central question" of the book in *Publishers Weekly,* a reviewer states: "Is science a report on objective reality with special standards of truth finding, as Austrian-born philosopher Karl Popper maintains, or is it a culturally bound enterprise, a sequence of paradigms that subjectively mirror our ever-shifting view of the world?" Beginning his study with the work of Erasmus Darwin (who saw evolution as a work set in motion by a non-interfering God) and ending with contemporary scientists such as Stephen Jay Gould (whose theory of "punctuated equilibrium," according to Ruse, owes a debt to the Marxist views of Gould's father) Ruse presents a detailed examination of ten evolutionary theorists, showing how the individual cultural biases of each influenced both the direction of their researches and the conclusions they reached. However, Ruse goes on to contend that as a science matures the effects of cultural bias decline while the role played by scientific objectivity increases. Mary Carroll of *Booklist* finds *Mystery of Mysteries* to be a "challenging but readable study." Lloyd Davidson, writing in *Library Journal,* dubs it "thoughtful and fascinating . . . a brilliant analysis." John Tyler Bonner of *Natural History* describes Ruse's portraits of individual scientists and their work as "elegant vignettes," but also believes that some of his conclusions are not supported by sufficient evidence. "To attribute to E. O. Wilson," Bonner declares, "affection for religion and 'militarism,' as Ruse does because Wilson grew up in the South, is grasping at straws."

BIOGRAPHICAL/CRITICAL SOURCES:

PERIODICALS

BioScience, September, 1994, Raymond E. Grizzle, review of *The Darwinian Paradigm,* p. 560.

Booklist, April 15, 1999, review of *Mystery of Mysteries,* p. 1495.

Library Journal, April 1, 1999, Lloyd Davidson, review of *Mystery of Mysteries,* p. 125.

National Review, March 8, 1999, Paul R. Gross, "Science Goes Nuts," p. 50.

Natural History, April, 1999, John Tyler Bonner, review of *Mystery of Mysteries,* p. 20.

Publishers Weekly, February 15, 1999, review of *Mystery of Mysteries,* p. 91.

Science, January 24, 1997, Francisco J. Ayala, review of *Monad to Man,* p. 495.*

S

SAFIRE, William 1929-

PERSONAL: Born William Safir, December 17, 1929, in New York, NY; name legally changed to Safire; son of Oliver C. and Ida (Panish) Safir; married Helene Belmar Julius (a jewelry-maker), December 16, 1962; children: Mark Lindsey, Annabel Victoria. *Education:* Attended Syracuse University, 1947-49. *Politics:* Libertarian conservative.

ADDRESSES: *Office—New York Times,* 1627 I St., N.W., Washington, DC 20006. *Agent*—Morton Janklow, 598 Madison Ave., New York, NY 10036.

CAREER: New York Herald-Tribune Syndicate, reporter, 1949-51; WNBC-WNBT, correspondent in Europe and Middle East, 1951; WNBC, New York City, radio-TV producer, 1954-55; Tex McCrary, Inc., vice president, 1955-60; Safire Public Relations, Inc., New York City, president, 1961-68; The White House, Washington, DC, special assistant to the President and speechwriter, 1968-73; *New York Times,* Washington, DC, columnist, 1973—. Member of Pulitzer Prize board, 1995—. Served in *Military service:* U.S. Army, 1952-54.

AWARDS, HONORS: Pulitzer Prize for distinguished commentary, 1978, for articles on Bert Lance.

WRITINGS:

The Relations Explosion, Macmillan (New York City), 1963.

(With M. Loeb) *Plunging into Politics,* McKay (New York City), 1964.

The New Language of Politics, Random House (New York City), 1968, 3rd edition published as *Safire's Political Dictionary: The New Language of Politics,* 1978, revised and enlarged edition published as *Safire's New Political Dictionary: The Definitive Guide to the New Language of Politics,* Random House, 1993.

William Safire

Before the Fall, Doubleday (New York City), 1975, published as *Before the Fall: An Inside View of the Pre-Watergate White House,* Da Capo Press (New York City), 1988.

Full Disclosure (novel), Doubleday, 1977, limited edition with illustrations by George Jones, Franklin Library, 1977.
On Language (collection of weekly columns), Times Books (New York City), 1980.
Safire's Washington, Times Books, 1980.
What's the Good Word?, Times Books, 1982.
(Compiler with brother, Leonard Safir) *Good Advice,* Times Books, 1982.
I Stand Corrected: More on Language (collection of weekly columns), Times Books, 1984.
Take My Word for It: More on Language (collection of weekly columns), Times Books, 1986.
Freedom (novel), Doubleday, 1987.
You Could Look It Up: More on Language, Times Books, 1988.
(Compiler and editor with Leonard Safir) *Words of Wisdom,* Simon and Schuster (New York City), 1989.
Language Maven Strikes Again (collection of weekly columns), Holt (New York City), 1990.
(Compiler and editor with Leonard Safir) *Leadership,* Simon and Schuster, 1990
Coming to Terms (collection of weekly columns), Doubleday, 1991.
The First Dissident: The Book of Job in Today's Politics, Random House, 1992.
(Compiler and author of introduction) *Lend Me Your Ears: Great Speeches in History,* Norton (New York City), 1992.
(Compiler with L. Safir) *Good Advice on Writing: Writers Past and Present on How to Write Well,* Simon & Schuster (New York City), 1992.
Quoth the Maven (collection of weekly columns), Random House, 1993.
In Love with Norma Loquendi (collection of weekly columns), Random House, 1994.
Sleeper Spy (novel), Random House, 1995.
Watching My Language (collection of weekly columns), Random House, 1996.
Spread the Word (collection of weekly columns), Times Books, 1999.
Scandalmonger (novel), Simon & Schuster, 2000.

Also author of *Fumblerules: A Light-hearted Guide to Grammar and Good Usage,* 1990. Author of political column "Essay," in *New York Times,* and "On Language" column in *New York Times Magazine.* Contributor to *Harvard Business Review, Cosmopolitan, Playboy, Esquire, Reader's Digest, Redbook,* and *Collier's.*

SIDELIGHTS: William Safire has worn several hats in his varied career: speechwriter for President Richard Nixon, language commentator for the Sunday *New York Times Magazine,* political commentator for the *New York Times,* novelist, and historian. Safire does not pull his punches, and has made both friends and enemies on all sides of political and linguistic issues. According to J. A. Barnes in the *National Review,* "whether you love [Safire] or you hate him, you cannot afford to skip over him." *Time* contributor Paul Gray appreciates Safire's lack of rigidity: "William Safire has largely made his reputation through epigrammatic feistiness and hit-and-run repartee. . . . His twice-a-week columns continue to display reportorial zeal and refreshing unpredictability." Safire is also quick to alert his readers to governmental figures who run amuck. *Washington Post* contributor Eleanor Randolph notes: "The years in public relations and the White House seem to have given [Safire] an ear for sour notes on both sides—among those in power in the government and those in power in the press." And when speaking of his commentaries on English-language usage, some critics view Safire as an institution. David Thomas in the *Christian Science Monitor* observes that "Safire may be the closest we have to a clearinghouse for hearing, seeing, and testing how we're doing with the language."

Safire began his career as a public relations writer, took a job as speechwriter for Spiro Agnew in the 1968 presidential campaign, and eventually became a senior speechwriter for President Nixon. He left his position, however, before the bugging of Watergate and was finishing his memoir of the Nixon White House when the president resigned. Because of the timing of its completion, *Before the Fall* almost missed publication entirely. The book painted a fairly positive view of the administration and was rejected by William Morrow, who also demanded back their advance. But eventually the book was published by Doubleday.

Newsweek's Walter Clemons calls *Before the Fall* "a puffy, lightweight concoction, served up for the faithful." Clemons complains that "Safire is protective of Nixon, reserving his harshest judgment for the deviousness and drive for power he attributes to Henry Kissinger." But *Atlantic* contributor Richard Todd gives the book credit for being "full of interesting data on the theme that Safire identifies as crucial to the Nixon Administration: its sense of the world as 'us' against 'them.' " And Daniel Schorr, in the *New York Times Book Review,* recounts Safire's description of Nixon's desire for "understanding and perspective," and notes: "If Nixon gets the kind of understanding he wants, this book will surely have helped a lot. In any event [*Before the Fall*] . . . will still be an enormous contribution to understanding the phenomenon called Nixon."

Safire's first novel, *Full Disclosure,* also deals with a president in danger of losing his office. His fictional leader, Sven Ericson, has been blinded from a bump on the head received while closeted in a Pullman berth with a female member of the White House press corps. The plot concerns whether the Twenty-fifth Amendment, regarding disabled presidents, will be used to oust Ericson. *New Republic* contributor Stephen Hess says *Full Disclosure*'s strength comes from the fact that it "is about presidential politics by a man who intimately knows presidential politics." But a *Saturday Review* contributor questions the work's literary value, claiming that the story's political puzzle is "the book's one redeeming feature." The critic adds, however, that by exploring Ericson's uncertain position, "Safire not only cooks up a fiery stewpot of political ambitions, but produces a dramatic warning of the [Twenty-fifth Amendment's] possible abuse."

Safire's columns on language for the *New York Times* are widely read and enjoyed. In several books, he has reprinted column selections and his readers' replies. *On Language* gives examples of correct and incorrect usage, and explores word origins as well. In the *Saturday Review,* John Ciardi explains Safire's position toward communication in *On Language* as "neither an [etymologist] nor an expert on usage. He is a keen reporter at his splendid best in such reports as the one here labeled 'Kissingerese,' a star coverage of the idiom of Henry the Pompous." Ciardi continues: "I am engaged and rewarded by this maculate Safire, and even more so when he is attended by his letterwriters." Other reviewers also enjoy Safire's interaction with his readers. "Although what Safire has discovered about word origins and their current usage made good reading, the inclusion of what his readers have to add makes them even more so," states *Christian Science Monitor* contributor Maria Lenhart. And, according to D. J. Enright in the *Encounter,* "Safire's relations with his Irregulars are highly interesting, and help to generate much of the comedy in this almost continuously entertaining book."

Freedom, a heavily detailed historical novel, is the author's longest work. When Safire submitted the manuscript to his publisher after working on it for seven years, the triple-spaced copy ran 3,300 pages. When Doubleday found the book too large to bind, Safire had to cut at least one section; still, the final product was 1,152 pages. In *Freedom,* Safire again uses his Washington experience to describe the capital between June of 1861 and January 1, 1863. The story opens with Lincoln's issue of the Emancipation Proclamation and focuses on the president's role during the early Civil War years. *New York Review of Books* contributor C. Vann Woodward describes Safire's Lincoln as "a Lincoln racked by debilitating depression (which he called melancholia), agonizing over the daily choice of evils, and seeking relief in one of his that-reminds-me stories. He is by turns Saint Sebastian, Machiavelli, Pericles, and an oversize, countrified Puck."

Safire explained his attitude toward Lincoln to Alvin P. Sanoff for *U.S. News & World Report:* "It's impossible to approach Lincoln honestly with a spirit of reverence and awe. He is a secular and not a religious figure. He wasn't martyred; he was assassinated. Approaching Lincoln as a political figure, which is what he was, you can appreciate him." Still, Safire concluded that "I've come to the conclusion that he was, indeed, the greatest President, with the possible exception of Washington, because he was so complex and so purposeful. When you see him with all the warts, when you see his drawbacks and his failures and his shortcomings, then you see his greatness." The author explained to *Publishers Weekly* contributor Trish Todd that one of the greatest issues facing the U.S. government at that time is the contemporary problem of "how much freedom must be taken away from individuals in order to protect the freedom of the nation." And while Safire feels that Lincoln occasionally went too far in suspending individual liberties, he told Eleanor Randolph for the *Washington Post:* "If [Lincoln] were running today, I'd vote for him. I think he had his priorities straight." Randolph continued, "straight priorities mean having a core of beliefs that are worth all the harassment and trouble that come with leadership."

While *Freedom* has received much popular and critical acclaim, some reviewers dislike the book's focus. Woodward feels Safire has almost neglected the presence of blacks in the Civil War: "One book of the nine into which the novel is divided is indeed entitled 'The Negro,' but it is largely concerned with other matters, with only four or five pages on blacks, and most of that is what whites said or did about them, not what they said and did themselves." Woodward adds, "as a whole [blacks] are granted fewer than twenty-five lines of their own to speak. None of their prominent leaders are introduced, and Frederick Douglass is not mentioned. . . . Nowhere does this huge book face up squarely to the impact of slavery and the complexities of race." Other critics have found the book too lengthy and detailed. But while *Los Angeles Times Book Review* contributor Winston Groom finds the book "often ponderous, tedious and maddening to plow through," he feels that reading *Freedom* is worth the effort: "It's a story that ought to be read by every American, and for that matter everyone else in the world, because it so graphically presents how our grand experiment in democracy has actually worked in a time of extreme stress. . . . [*Freedom*] enlivens and elucidates a period of American history that remains crucial for anyone with the faintest interest in what we, the American people, are all about." And Chicago *Tribune Books* contributor John Calvin Batchelor calls *Freedom* "a mountain to dazzle and assault," states that it is "loving, cogent, bottomlessly researched, [and] passionately argued," and claims the book "is guaranteed to exhaust the reader like no other intellectual endeavor, yet in the end it delivers a miracle."

Safire ventured further into new writing territory with *The First Dissident: The Book of Job in Today's Politics.* Safire had long been fascinated by Job, the Biblical figure whose faith was tested by his many troubles and who sought an explanation from God. Published in a U.S. presidential election year, 1992, the book led Kenneth L. Woodward to report in *Newsweek:* "In this campaign season's most improbable political meditation, Safire has published . . . a sometimes wise and frequently witty demonstration of how Job's confrontation with Ultimate Authority can illuminate the power struggles in Washington and vice versa." Safire's interpretation of Job is a far cry from the most widely held view of him. He is usually held up as a model of long-suffering patience, but Safire views him as a righteous, rebellious, "even blasphemous" figure "who demands that God explain himself or stand guilty of abusing his own authority," explains Woodward. "He is in short, the original political contrarian, a fellow who, in another era, might just find work as a brave, truth-telling columnist."

Christian Science Monitor contributor Marshall Ingwerson notes that extensive study informs the book, and he remarks that "Safire's own concept of God is of a powerful—but not all-powerful—creator who leaves it to man to carve out justice in the world." But while Ingwerson and Woodward both credit the author with serious theological intent, another reviewer, Jonathan Dorfman, finds *The First Dissident* a disappointing, superficial book. Writing in the *Washington Post Book World,* he finds promise in Safire's stated premise, "to discern political lessons in Job and the book's relevance to modern politics," but goes on to say: "You begin the book with high expectations. Five minutes later, you realize that the author reduces the gravity of Job to a trifle with all the moral freight of *Larry King Live."* Dorfman further castigates Safire for trivializing Job's suffering by comparing him to politicians such as Gary Hart and Bert Lance. The reviewer deems Safire's discussion of Job and Lincoln more appropriate, though: "In his meditation on Lincoln and Job, Safire drops his street-smart style; the tone is somber, fit for the gravity of the subject. . . . [The essay is] an elegiac lament that atones for much of his frivolity on the angry howl of Job."

Safire tried another new genre in 1995 with *Sleeper Spy,* a novel of espionage. *New Yorker* reviewer David Remnick characterizes it as "an old-fashioned Washington-Moscow thriller. It features a hundred billion dollars, a sexy network newsie, a K.G.B. mole, lots of secret agents, and a hero who is . . . 'the world's greatest reporter.' " In the story, a Russian spy who has been working in finance in the United States is given a small fortune to invest and increases it many times over. With the breakup of the Soviet Union and the deaths of his spymasters, however, the agent is left on his own, pursued by various factions. Reviewers are mixed in their assessment of Safire's skill in handling this type of thriller. "Interesting as all this is conceptually, it makes for a highly cerebral and talky novel—a mind game," finds Morton Kondracke, contributor to the *New York Times Book Review,* adding, "Toward the end the reader is made to feel that the writer is having most of the fun, some of it at the expense of the reader, who's suddenly told without warning that things presumed to be facts simply aren't." Yet Kondracke allows that *Sleeper Spy* "certainly does engage the mind and, on a few occasions, stir the pulse." *New York Times* reviewer George Stade is critical of Safire's handling of plot and dialogue, saying the author "has the skills of a reporter but not those of a storyteller."

Remnick is more generous, calling *Sleeper Spy* "a great big ice-cream cone of a book: predictable, sweet fun." Jonathan Kirsch also finds much to praise. In the *Los Angeles Times* he dubs *Sleeper Spy* "a smartly done spy story with enough surprises to set it apart from the ordinary run of espionage fiction." The book, he says, "crackles with wit and savvy." Kirsch concludes: "The author enjoys himself most when he gives us the world according to William Safire, a world beset with plots and conspiracies, a world in which brains count and the good guys (and gals) win."

Safire attracted considerable media attention himself in 1996, after he made a comment in his *New York Times* column about the firing of the travel workers in the White House by First Lady Hillary Rodham Clinton. Safire wrote in his column that Mrs. Clinton was a "congenital liar" for claiming that she "hadn't personally insisted on firing the seven-man White House Travel staff," wrote William F. Buckley Jr. in the *National Review.* "In fact, according to her ex-employee and Clinton pal Mr. Watkins, she did want them fired." President Clinton took umbrage at Safire's remarks and responded (through White House spokesman Mike McCurry) that, were he not president, he would punch Mr. Safire in the nose. "What fascinates is that this episode and a few others . . . invite the formal scrutiny of investigating panels, and theoretically, the courts themselves, because perjury is contingently involved," Buckley explained. "To get to the White House one promises one thing, does another. Or else one reaffirms on Monday what one repudiates on Tuesday? Some would go so far as guess that if he were simply 'Mr.' Clinton even then he wouldn't actually go to Mr. Safire's office and poke him in the Republican Party, or Congress, or the voters who vote for the wrong people."

The author reexamined some of the same issues surrounding the Clintons and their relationship with the media in his historical novel *Scandalmonger.* The book details the life and career of journalist James Thomson Callender, who first broke the story of Alexander Hamilton's extramarital affair at Thomas Jefferson's instigation, then a few years later released the story of Jefferson's decades-long affair with his slave Sally Hemings. "In light of the recent White House brouhaha," declared a *Publishers Weekly* reviewer, "it's fascinating to learn that in the days of the founding fathers, politicians were just as licentious and newspapermen even more scurrilous than some players in contemporary media." "Drawing on letters and historical records," Daisy Maryles and Dick Donahue stated in *Publishers Weekly,* "Safire shows how media invasion of private lives—as well as politicians' manipulation of the press—are as old as the Constitution itself." "For any who still believe that sexual scandalmongering is something new in Washington, DC, or that bitter partisanship did not exist in those hollowed days of the Founding Fathers, or that First Amendment issues are something only we in the present day wrestle with," *Booklist* contributor Brad Hooper wrote, "let them read this novel and think again." "This meaty, profoundly engrossing novel," Barbara Conaty revealed in *Library Journal,* "vividly illustrates episodes in the history of American journalism and government."

BIOGRAPHICAL/CRITICAL SOURCES:

BOOKS

Contemporary Literary Criticism, Volume 10, Gale (Detroit), 1979.

PERIODICALS

Atlantic, July, 1975; March, 1979.

Booklist, September 1, 1997, Alice Joyce, review of *Watching My Language,* p. 43; October 15, 1999, Philip Herbst, review of *Spread the Word,* p. 401; December 15, 1999, Brad Hooper, review of *Scandalmonger,* p. 739.

Boston Globe, May 17, 1995, p. 5; July 25, 1995, p. 6.

Chicago Tribune, August 4, 1988; November 10, 1993, section 7, p. 4.

Christian Science Monitor, January 12, 1981; December 31, 1984; January 11, 1993, p. 15.

Commentary, April, 1993, p. 56.

Economist, November 21, 1992, p. 107.

Encounter, April, 1981.

Entertainment Weekly, November 10, 1995, p. 55.

Esquire, April, 1994, p. 84.

Forbes, October 26, 1992, p. 26.

Insight on the News, February 12, 1996, Alan L. Anderson, "The White House and the Liberal, Lawyer, Liar Label," p. 30.

Library Journal, June 1, 1997, Peter A. Dollard, review of *Lend Me Your Ears,* p. 90; July, 1997, Cathy Sabol, review of *Watching My Language,* p. 83; January, 2000, Barbara Conaty, review of *Scandalmonger,* p. 162.

Los Angeles Times, November 14, 1992, p. B4; September 10, 1993, p. E10; September 20, 1995, p. E4.

Los Angeles Times Book Review, August 30, 1987; December 20, 1992, p. 2.

Nation, June 21, 1999, David Sarasohn, "On Safire's Language," p. 10.

National Catholic Reporter, February 5, 1993, p. 25.

National Review, November 28, 1980; March 29, 1993, p. 66; February 12, 1996, William F. Buckley, Jr., "This 'Liar' Business," p. 62.

New Republic, July 9-16, 1977; February 16, 1987.

Newsweek, March 3, 1975; August 31, 1987; November 9, 1992, p. 81; January 31, 1994, p. 41.

New York, December 21, 1992, p. 107.

New Yorker, August 21, 1995, pp. 116, 118.

New York Review of Books, September 24, 1987.

New York Times, November 5, 1992, p. C20; September 4, 1995, p. A15.

New York Times Book Review, February 23, 1975; July 21, 1991, p. 18; November 8, 1992, p. 14; October 31, 1993, p. 9; September 18, 1994, p. 20; September 17, 1995, p. 15.

People, December 4, 1995, p. 36; January 29, 1996, Kim Cunningham, "Hell from the Chief," p. 94.

Playboy, November, 1992, p. 63.

Publishers Weekly, April 30, 1982; March 29, 1987; April 12, 1991, p. 51; August 10, 1992, p. 61; June 7, 1993, p. 58; July 11, 1994, p. 70; July 31, 1995, p. 67; June 30, 1997, review of *Watching My Lan-*

guage, p. 59; December 20, 1999, review of *Scandalmonger,* p. 53; February 14, 2000, Daisy Maryles and Dick Donahue, "A Scandalous Newcomer," p. 85.
Saturday Review, July 9, 1977; November, 1980.
Time, August 31, 1987; February 12, 1990; December 11, 1995, p. 95; January 22, 1996, "Pugilistic Main Event of the Week," p. 11; March 18, 1996, "Verbatim," p. 33.
Tribune Books (Chicago), August 9, 1987; October 17, 1993, p. 8; September 17, 1995, p. 6.
U.S. News & World Report, August 24, 1987.
Vanity Fair, November, 1992, p. 148.
Washingtonian, August, 1991, p. 66.
Washington Post, August 24, 1987; November 23, 1992, p. B2; December 1, 1995, p. F1.
Washington Post Book World, August 27, 1995, p. 5.
Wilson Library Bulletin, March, 1994, p. 95.*

* * *

SAUNDERS, Madelyn
See DAY, Dianne

* * *

SCHAEFFER, Neil 1940-

PERSONAL: Born November 30, 1940, in Brooklyn, NY; son of David (in sales) and Ann (Berkowitz) Schaeffer; married Susan Fromberg (a poet, novelist, and professor), October 11, 1971; children: Benjamin, May. *Education:* Columbia University, B.A., 1962, M.A., 1964, Ph.D., 1971.

ADDRESSES: *Home*—Brooklyn, NY. *Office*—Department of English, 3107 Boylan Hall, Brooklyn College of the City University of New York, Brooklyn, NY 11210. *Email*-102246.3671@compuserve.com.

CAREER: Brooklyn College of the City University of New York, Brooklyn, NY, lecturer, 1966-70, assistant professor, 1971-75, associate professor, 1976-81, professor of English, 1982—, chairman of English department, 1982—.

MEMBER: Modern Language Association of America, American Society for Eighteenth-Century Studies, Columbia University Seminar on Eighteenth-Century European Culture.

WRITINGS:

The Art of Laughter, Columbia University Press (New York City), 1981.
The Marquis de Sade: A Life, Knopf (New York City), 1999.

Contributor of articles and stories to magazines, including *Chicago Review, Mississippi Review,* and *Confrontation.*

WORK IN PROGRESS: The Representation of Time in Literature.

SIDELIGHTS: Neil Schaeffer told *CA:* "As in *The Art of Laughter,* I am interested in critical arguments that enlighten not only particular works, but also the ways by which we arrive at our characteristic responses to them. My present research is in time theory, and specifically for literature, the ways in which time is embodied in language and becomes represented in art."

An interest in Norman Mailer's writings led Schaeffer to the life and works of Donatien-Alphonse-Francois de Sade, better known as the Marquis de Sade. Schaeffer spent more than eleven years researching and writing his biography, *The Marquis de Sade: A Life,* in the process becoming the first to translate many of Sade's letters from French into English. Where other biographers have been morally affronted by Sade's perverse behavior and writings, Schaeffer sought to understand the man's psychology and defended him as a product of his times—late eighteenth-century France. According to Richard Bernstein in the *New York Times,* the finished biography "enables one to see Sade not only as something close to an archetype, a kind of grotesque cardboard figure, but as a man who is both contemptible and, in his way, admirable." Bernstein further remarked: "Central to Mr. Schaeffer's portrait is the idea of a strange, stubborn greatness to Sade, both as a literary adventurer into territory that no other writer had dared explore and as a champion of an extreme libertarian philosophy. . . . [Schaeffer] lays out the facts of Sade's fascinating life and character and leaves it up to the reader to judge."

Almost all those who reviewed *The Marquis de Sade: A Life* noted that it joined a crowded field of books on the notorious Marquis. What distinguishes Schaeffer's treatment is his sympathy for Sade and his attempts to put Sade's behavior—and especially his fictions—in context. "The "90s have been a banner decade for "The Divine Marquis,' " a *Publishers Weekly* reviewer noted. ". . . Schaeffer will suffer for his timing." The reviewer found Schaeffer's book "well researched and accessible," but also an "uneven effort to distill the man from the myth." In the *New York Times Book Review,* Mim Udovitch declared: "Sade's life is, to put it mildly, sufficiently interesting to sustain several retellings and numerous approaches." Udovitch suggested that Schaeffer's book on Sade is "practically poleaxed by devotion." Conversely, Bernstein defended Schaeffer's judgments. "It's certainly possible to ask, as one sits down to read Mr. Schaeffer's treatment of Sade, why another biography of this notorious and already well-researched figure is needed," the critic stated. "But Mr. Schaeffer's book is a welcome addition to the literature. It is both sophisticated and hardheaded about Sade; it has a definitive quality to it." Bernstein concluded: "In all, Sade spent 29 years in prison. There is something powerful and moving in that fact alone, and it is the strength of Mr. Schaeffer's biography that it makes Sade not just a notorious figure but a credibly heroic one as well."

BIOGRAPHICAL/CRITICAL SOURCES:

PERIODICALS

Choice, January, 2000, p. 936.
Library Journal, September 15, 1981, p. 1736.
New York Times, April 28, 1999, p. B8.
New York Times Book Review, June 13, 1999, p. 12.
Publishers Weekly, March 22, 1999, p. 82.
Time, May 17, 1999, p. 90.*

* * *

SCHAMA, Simon (Michael) 1945-

PERSONAL: Surname is pronounced *Sha*-ma; born February 13, 1945, in London, England; came to the United States, 1980; son of Arthur Osias (a textile merchant) and Gertrude Clare (Steinberg) Schama; married Ginny Papaioannou (a professor of anatomy and pathology); children: Chloe, Gabriel. *Education:* Christ's College, Cambridge University, B.A., 1966, M.A., 1969. *Avocational interests:* Claret, the music of Schubert, Red Sox baseball, spring bulbs, Brazilian music, Middle Eastern and Indian cooking.

ADDRESSES: Home—421 Hardscrabble Rd., Briarcliff Manor, NY 10510-1806. *Office*—Department of History, Columbia University, New York, NY 10032-3702.

CAREER: Cambridge University, Cambridge, England, director of studies in history, 1966-76; Oxford University, Oxford, England, 1976-80, tutor in history and lecturer; Harvard University, Cambridge, MA, Erasmus Lecturer in the civilization of the Netherlands, 1978, professor of history, Mellon Professor of Social Sciences and senior associate, Center for European Studies, 1980-93; University of Columbia, New York, NY, professor, 1994—.

MEMBER: American Academy of Arts and Sciences, Christ's College of Cambridge University (fellow), Brasenose College of Oxford University (fellow), Maatschappij voor Nederlandse Letterkunde.

AWARDS, HONORS: Wolfson Literary Prize for History, Wolfson Foundation, 1977, and Leo Gersoy Memorial Prize, American Historical Association, 1978, both for *Patriots and Liberators;* NCR Book Award for Nonfiction, NCR Ltd., and *Yorkshire Post* Book of the Year designation, both 1990, both for *Citizens: A Chronicle of the French Revolution;* Guggenheim fellow, 1983-84.

WRITINGS:

(Editor with Eric Homberger and William Janeway) *The Cambridge Mind,* Little, Brown (Boston), 1970.
Patriots and Liberators: Revolution in the Netherlands, 1780-1813, Knopf, 1977, Vintage (New York City), 1992.
Two Rothschilds and the Land of Israel, Knopf (New York City), 1979.
The Embarrassment of Riches: An Interpretation of Dutch Culture in the Golden Age, Knopf, 1987.
Citizens: A Chronicle of the French Revolution, Knopf, 1989.
Dead Certainties (Unwarranted Speculations) (historical novella), Knopf, 1991, Vintage, 1992.
Landscape and Memory (derived in part from BBC television series written by the author), Knopf, 1995.
(Author of essay) Frederic Brenner, *Jews, America: A Representation* (photographic study), Abrams (New York City), 1996.
Rembrandt's Eyes, Knopf, 1999.

Contributor or articles, essays and criticism to magazines and newspapers, including *Granta, New Republic, New York Times, New Yorker, Times Literary Supplement,* and *The Independent.* Writer and presenter of documentaries for BBC television, including *The Art of the Western World, Rembrandt, Landscape and Memory,* and *The Public Eye and the Private Gaze.* Writer of documentary films.

Work had been translated into ten languages.

SIDELIGHTS: Simon Schama, Mellon professor of history at Harvard University, has combined extensive historical scholarship with his interest in both literature and the fine arts to produce a succession of unique and sometimes controversial volumes of narrative history. Rather than confining himself to specialization within a distinct historical period or place, Schama focuses on the process by which nations have formed cohesive identities, and on the manner in which individuals have become "citizens." Despite finding himself at the center of controversy over his idiosyncratic approach to history, Schama has received widespread professional recognition, and his books have broad popular appeal. "Fizzing with vitality and insight, bubbling over with ideas and perceptions, buzzing with gossip, anecdote and a sense of drama, Schama shuns scholarly neutrality, comes chock-full of personal prejudices, and puts himself on the line with a bravery one can only respectfully salute," observes Colin Jones in the *Times Literary Supplement.* Caryn James, stressing the distinctive quality of Schama's work as a historian, writes in the *New York Times* that he "depends on the most astute recent scholarship while evoking the narrative sweep of his 19th-century predecessors Michelet and Tocqueville, writers who knew that history was a story before it was an academic discipline."

Schama's first book, *Patriots and Liberators: Revolution in the Netherlands, 1780-1813,* a lengthy volume born of ten years of research in Dutch historical archives and requiring Schama's mastery of the Dutch language, recounts the period during which a loosely-knit federation of independent Dutch provinces transformed itself into the United Netherlands under King William I. Most specifically, Schama deals with the French occupation of Holland during that period of French expansion between the Revolution of 1789 and the onset of the Napoleonic Wars. "Anyone aroused by the idea of history or by the spectacle of human complication will by no means be wasting the time it takes to read through this intelligent, analytical narrative," writes Raymond A. Sokolov in the *New York Times Book Review.*

The Embarrassment of Riches: An Interpretation of Dutch Culture in the Golden Age is a vivid portrait of seventeenth-century Holland's social culture and an enlightened look at the moral dilemma of Dutch society—a conspicuous consumption at odds with the restraints imposed by the Calvinist *gereformeerde Kerk.* Called "an event in historical studies" by Jonathan Israel in the *Times Literary Supplement, The Embarrassment of Riches* analyzes one of the most creative and efflorescent periods in European history remarkable for such things as an immense outpouring of Dutch burgher art and the tulip mania of 1636. Schama paints with detailed brush-strokes, using as his medium the many outward manifestations of inner conflicts between material wealth and moral piety unique to this epoch. He uses contemporary art and literature as primary source material, bypassing such exceptional works as those of Rembrandt, Vermeer, de Groot, and Spinoza for works more characteristic of Dutch society at large. John Gross, in a review for the *New York Times,* comments: "[The] use Mr. Schama makes of Dutch art (its feel and its spirit, not just its documentary value) is one of the book's most notable features. He also provides an object lesson in rescuing the study of a culture from the categories imposed on it by historians of a later epoch." Gross concludes, "This is history on the grand scale, and like all generously conceived historical works it leaves us reflecting about the present as well as the past."

Schama's approach to history has been criticized by some reviewers. Harold Beaver, writing in the *New York Times Book Review,* terms Schama's efforts "a quasi-anthropological attempt to describe historical behavior as social process . . . by a compilation of the mental bric-a-brac composing what Emile Durkheim called 'the collective or common conscience' of a culture." Reviewing *The Embarrassment of Riches* for the *Los Angeles Times Book Review,* Johan Pieter Snapper distills Schama's approach: "[He] sees the essence of 17th-century Dutch society as a multi-layered structure of cultural paradoxes that the surprising Dutch transformed into a delicate polarity." Snapper also remarks, "Unfortunately, he tends to turn his insightful perception of the dual (practical and ethical) exercise of Dutch wealth into a paradigm for all other aspects of that society as well. Every image has a counter image, every picture a reflection, every thesis an antithesis. His conclusions, therefore, while persuasively drawn in many instances, tend to lose their impact in overstatement." In *The Embarrassment of Riches,* Schama defends his intent in focusing upon "those social and mental traits that tied Dutch men and women together rather than separated them" and so diverges from the Marxist-inspired approach that reduces historical events to "class struggle." While expressing some reservations about the assumptions upon which Schama grounds his thesis, Israel praises the book for its ability to recreate the energy of the Dutch Golden Age: "It is an immensely compelling book which brings out, often with rare discernment, the flavour and peculiarity of a host of facets and traits of Dutch culture which other historians and art historians have missed, ignored, or had less of a feel for."

More traditional in scope than his other works, *Two Rothschilds and the Land of Israel* is Schama's testament to the contribution made by Edmund de Rothschild and his son, James, towards the creation of a Jewish community in Palestine. The colonization efforts by the Rothschilds, begun in the 1880s and continued into the 1930s, led to the actualization of the modern state of Israel. The book was inspired by an informal seminar on Jewish social and intellectual history that Schama presented while a teacher at Cambridge during the 1960s and 1970s and is based on Schama's research—through the cooperation of James's widow, Dorothy de Rothschild—in the archive of the Palestine Jewish (Israelite) Colonization Association (P.I.C.A). While noting the objectivity and thoroughness of the work, the late historian Barbara Tuchman felt it to be recondite: "[The] text of this solid work is dense, undiscriminating and detailed to the point of indigestible superfluity," she commented in the *New York Times Book Review.* "I am sure that not every transaction of each one of the P.I.C.A. colonies is recorded; it just seems that way." Robert Kirsch views the book from a more personal perspective in the *Los Angeles Times:* "This is not a history of Zionism, nor even . . . complete biographies of the two Rothschilds. . . . But it is a fascinating account of the dedication of father and son."

Schama's epic, *Citizens: A Chronicle of the French Revolution,* was published to coincide with the French bicentennial celebration of the storming of the Bastille on July 14, 1789. The critical acclaim that *Citizens* received upon publication catapulted it onto national bestseller lists, a rare achievement for a volume of history of such length and complexity. One reason for the book's popular appeal is the colorful narrative its author employs. "*Citizens* is an argument told in the form of a story, which as a historian you're not supposed to be doing anymore," writes Paul Galloway in *Tribune Books,* reflecting the reservations of some critics. Robert M. Maniquis expresses concern over what he calls "fast and loose analogizing," noting in the *Los Angeles Times Book Review* that Schama "confuses the issue and for many readers he may even diffuse the importance of past horrors in historical cliches disguised as just another good story." Historian Lawrence Stone, although critical of both the lack of reference notes and the book's vague ideological basis, states in *New Republic:* "The very great virtues of this book do not lie in its profound insights, or in the truth of the underlying premise, or in the depth of the research, but rather in the coruscating brilliance of Schama's style, his dazzling display of erudition and intelligence, his unusual stress on the sheer ferocity and brutality of the events." Richard Cobb, noted with fellow historian Alfred Cobban for his revisionist interpretation of the Revolution, lauds Schama in the London *Times:* "This is the most marvelous book I have read about the French Revolution in the last 50 years."

Citizens is much more than merely a colorful and dramatic tale. Perceiving the "liberal" historical view of the Revolution as the "crucible of modernity" to be at variance with reality, Schama prefaces the book with the contention: "The Revolution begins as a great exercise in patriotic rejuvenation and it ends as the greatest imperial, aggressive war state that Europe has seen for many hundreds of years." *Citizens* refutes much of the mythology surrounding the Revolution and locates its origins in the resistance mounted by the clergy and nobility to Louis XVI's efforts at developing a modern market economy rather than in peasant disaffection with the existing feudal structure. Schama contends that the Revolution interrupted the natural de-feudalization occurring at the same period in England and the American colonies; that in fact the Revolution impeded a trend toward modernization born of the Enlightenment and established human rights only to subsequently repress them. This position places *Citizens* squarely in the center of a debate about the legacy of the revolution that has been going on for over two centuries. While some historians have categorized his position as "conservative," the book is considered a "revisionist" history by many reviewers. Schama disagrees, asking Mervyn Rothstein of the *New York Times,* "What is it that is supposed to be being revised?. . . It has been said that history is an argument without end, and it's always been that way."

"To those who insist that to prosecute is not the historian's job, one may reply that neither is a selective forgetfulness practiced in the interest of scholarly decorum," Schama asserts in *Citizens.* In his close examination of the violence that both ended France's "ancien regime" and became the public policy of Jacobin extremists during the Terror of 1793, he discerns no Revolutionary aim justifying the murder of over forty thousand people. Eugen Weber writes in the *New York Times Book Review* that Schama "reminds us that [Revolutionary] power depended on intimidation: the spectacle of death. Violence was no aberration, no unexpected skid off the highway of revolution: it *was* the Revolution—its motor and, for a while, its end." Historian Stanley Mellon comments in Chicago *Tribune Books,* "Schama's harshest judgements are reserved for the entrenched scholarly tradition that has for a century tried to explain away and apologize for the Reign of Terror—what he characterizes as the 'scholarly normalization of evil.' In contrast, Schama has adopted the view . . . that crime is crime and that the historian, faced with the criminal, must play the moralist and act the judge."

Schama broke from restrictions imposed by writing "history" with the publication of *Dead Certainties (Unwarranted Speculations).* In this historical novella, Schama juxtaposes the deaths of General James Wolfe at the Battle of Quebec in 1759 and the murder of George Parkman that precipitated the arrest, conviction, and execution of a professor of Boston's Harvard Medical College in 1850. "It is a tour de force of storytelling, but is it history?" asks Gordon S. Wood in the *New York Review of Books,* viewing Schama's foray into quasi-fictional narrative as an abrogation of his responsibility as "historian." Schama reconciles his position between "historian" and "novelist," telling Missy Daniel in *Publishers Weekly:* "I wanted the sense that the past comes at one in unpredictable ways, with varying degrees of sharpness; to somehow find a text that would do that." But Wood objects, saying that "Schama cannot have it both ways. He cannot write fiction and still assume that it will have the authenticity and credibility of history." He maintains that readers "are never sure which is which, and therefore come to doubt the truthfulness of the whole."

Dead Certainties is the creative vehicle by which Schama illustrates the historian's function, not merely to accumulate historical fact but in performing the subjective process by which the past is brought back to life in terms of the present. He writes in the book's "Afterword": "[Historians] are left forever chasing shadows, painfully aware of their inability ever to reconstruct a dead world in its completeness, however thorough or revealing their documentation. Of course, they make do with other work: the business of formulating problems, of supplying explanations about cause and effect. But the certainty of such answers always remains contingent on their unavoidable remoteness from their subjects. We are doomed to be forever hailing someone who has just gone around the corner and out of earshot."

Schama's *Landscape and Memory* marked another departure for him. Instead of examining and analyzing a particular historical era, the oversized volume presents a thesis, or rather a group of them, and ranges throughout history to gather supporting evidence. The central theses of *Landscape and Memory* debunk conventional wisdom on at least two counts. First to suffer the assault of Schama's pen is the idea that Man and Nature are distinctly separate entities; rather, the historian-cum-poet argues that the human world and the natural world have always been inextricably intertwined but that our perceptions of nature are thoroughly culturally determined. Second, Schama makes a point that flies in the face of a view considered politically correct by the contemporary environmental movement: namely, the vision of Nature as pristine and Man as its despoiler, particularly over the last hundred years. Schama's own vision proposes that the interactions between humankind and the landscapes of the natural world have existed since time immemorial, and despite the reality of despoliation that relationship has often proved beneficial to both.

Yet Schama's undertaking in *Landscape and Memory* represents more than a list of propositions bolstered by a sum of evidence to support them. In a broader sense the book is a reflection upon and a celebration of the relationship between the human species and nature that is distinctly illuminated by Schama's far-reaching knowledge and artistic sensibility. As with the historian's other books, critical response to the volume is a curious mixture of awe and enthusiasm combined with occasional carping directed at Schama's unconventional approach to the writing of history. Richard Wilson of *History Today* notes: "Others will spot mistakes in the footnotes, quibble about details of interpretation, and object to the vauntedly subjective nature of Professor Schama's approach, but few can doubt that this will turn out to be one of the most memorable and enjoyable of the recent 'big' books." Summing up the achievement of *Landscape and Memory* in an article for the *New Republic,* Anthony Grafton states: "Schama mounts a formidable scholarly expedition into the bright heart of the Construct Called Nature. He carries the reader in space from Egypt to Yosemite, in subject matter from ancient stone cult images to Anselm Kiefer's all-too-modern scorched books, in time from the second millennium BC to the present. He examines an enormous range of individuals, telling their stories easily and vividly." Judging the worth of the book in the same article, Grafton concludes: "Unclassifiable, inimitable, sometimes irritating and often fascinating, *Landscape and Memory* will inform and haunt, chasten and enrage, its readers. It is that rarest of commodities in our cultural marketplace, a work of genuine originality."

Eric Gibson of *National Review* sees *Landscape and Memory* as "a tour de force of insights, connections, and revelations," while John Elson of *Time* remarks: "In sharing the past, Schama does not merely dramatize history, he personalizes it as well. . . . Such intimate touches do not detract from the cosmic scope of *Landscape and Memory;* they are grace notes in what deserves to become a classic." In contrast, commenting on the same personal nature of the book, an *Economist* reviewer declares: "Because *Landscape and Memory* reflects Mr Schama's personality, it is far more than a dry academic tome. Because that personality is dazzling and magpie-like, it is a collection of marvelous parts. Alas, as a whole, it is less than the sum of them."

Schama's 1999 biographical study, *Rembrandt's Eyes,* both portrays the life of the great seventeenth-century Dutch master and provides an exploration of his art. The title is derived from Schama's use throughout the book of the appearance of the eyes in Rembrandt's self-portraits as a means of interpreting the artist's state of mind. Like Schama's other books, *Rembrandt's Eyes* is a storehouse of historical detail rendered in a dense and imagistic style. "Schama's immense, luxurious, and richly contextual portrait of Rembrandt," comments Donna Seaman in *Booklist,* "is not strictly a biography. Instead, like his groundbreaking *Landscape and Memory,* it is a creative synthesis of history, aesthetics, and spirituality." Albert Mobilio of *Fortune* praises the depiction of the book's setting, post-Reformation Amsterdam: "Schama portrays this culture with rich sensory acuity," and goes on to parallel Seaman's assessment by stating: "Equal parts aesthetic meditation, biography, and art criticism, *Rembrandt's Eyes* is cultural history at its best." Discussing the book's interpretation of the art of Rembrandt in *Library Journal,* Robert Cahn observes: "Schama not only comes to grips with the core of the oeuvre but also passionately and insightfully exposes Rembrandt's extraordinary innovations of traditional genre formulae and proffers a subtle and vigorous appreciation of the manipulation of paint so central to the work's expressive essence." Cohn feels that "Schama's is the best synthesis available of the Dutch master's life and will be required by all collections." Steven Henry Madoff of *Time* proclaims, "what a triumph of scholarship and imagination!" while Seaman concludes: "Schama chronicles the ups and downs of Rembrandt's life in vivid detail, and engages so passionately and brilliantly with his paintings and their startling departures from tradition, [that] Rembrandt and his masterpieces seem to be reborn."

BIOGRAPHICAL/CRITICAL SOURCES:

BOOKS

Schama, Simon, *Citizens: A Chronicle of the French Revolution,* Knopf, 1989.

Schama, Simon, *Dead Certainties (Unwarranted Speculations),* Knopf, 1991.

PERIODICALS

Booklist, April 1, 1995, Donna Seaman, review of *Landscape and Memory,* p. 1363; October 15, 1999, Donna Seaman, review of *Rembrandt's Eyes,* p. 406.

Economist, May 6, 1995, review of *Landscape and Memory,* p. 84.

Forbes, September 26, 1994, Katherine A. Powers, review of sound recording of *Citizens,* p. S32.

Fortune, December 6, 1999, Albert Mobilio, "Rembrandt: Method Acting on Canvas," p. 78.

Globe and Mail (Toronto), August 10, 1991, p. C8.

History Today, August, 1996, Richard Wilson, review of *Landscape and Memory,* p. 55.

Insight on the News, May 15, 1995, Witold Rybczynski, review of *Landscape and Memory,* p. 25.

Knight-Ridder/Tribune Business News, November 28, 1999.

Maclean's, April 24, 1995, John Bemrose, review of *Landscape and Memory,* p. 67.

Library Journal, October 15, 1999, Robert Cahn, review of *Rembrandt's Eyes,* p. 68.

Los Angeles Times, January 12, 1979.

Los Angeles Times Book Review, June 14, 1987, p. 12; May 21, 1989, p. 4.

Nation, May 22, 1995, Gregory McNamee, review of *Landscape and Memory,* p. 727.

National Review, July 31, 1995, Eric Gibson, review of *Landscape and Memory,* p. 59.

New Republic, April 17, 1989, pp. 35-38; August 7, 1995, Anthony Grafton, review of *Landscape and Memory,* p. 37.

Newsweek, April 3, 1989, p. 71.

New Statesman & Society, April 21, 1995, Boyd Tonkin, "Big Trees, Small Stories," p. 20, Patrick Curry, review of *Landscape and Memory,* p. 37.

New Yorker, April 17, 1989, pp. 131-135.

New York Review of Books, April 13, 1989, pp. 11-14; June 12, 1991, pp. 12-16.

New York Times, March 15, 1989; April 27, 1989.

New York Times Book Review, May 15, 1977, p. 16; December 17, 1978, pp. 3, 34; June 23, 1987, p. 23; July 5, 1987, pp. 1, 16; March 19, 1989, pp. 1, 31, 33; May 2, 1991, p. 3.

Publishers Weekly, May 17, 1991, pp. 46-47; March 6, 1995, review of *Landscape and Memory,* p. 48.

Time, April 17, 1989, pp. 74, 76; April 24, 1995, John Elton, review of *Landscape and Memory,* p. 73; December 6, 1999, Steven Henry Madoff, review of *Rembrandt's Eyes,* p. 120.

Times (London), September 3, 1987; May 25, 1989; June 1, 1991, p. 21.
Times Literary Supplement, November 20-26, 1987, p. 1267; July 21- 27, 1989, p. 791; June 19, 1991, p. 5.
Tribune Books (Chicago), April 2, 1989, p. 6; July 12, 1989, pp. 1, 4.
Washington Post Book World, June 28, 1987, p. 1; April 2, 1989; May 5, 1991, pp. 8-9.*

* * *

SCHICKEL, Richard (Warren) 1933-

PERSONAL: Born February 10, 1933, in Milwaukee, WI; son of Edward John and Helen (Hendricks) Schickel; married Julia Carroll Whedon, March 11, 1960 (divorced); children: Erika, Jessica. *Education:* University of Wisconsin, B.S., 1956, graduate study, 1956-57.

ADDRESSES: Home—33 Harrison St., New York, NY 10013. *Agent*—Don Congdon Associates, 177 East 70th St., New York, NY 10021.

CAREER: Sports Illustrated, New York City, reporter, 1956-57; *Look,* New York City, senior editor, 1957-60; *Show,* New York City, senior editor, 1960-62, book columnist, 1962-64; book critic for *Sunday,* NBC-TV, 1963-64; Rockefeller Brothers Fund, New York City, consultant, 1963-65; Rockefeller Foundation, New York City, consultant, 1965; *Life,* New York City, film reviewer, 1965-72; *Time,* New York City, film reviewer, 1972—.

MEMBER: National Society of Film Critics, Writers Guild of America, Directors Guild of America, New York Film Critics.

AWARDS, HONORS: New Republic Young Writer Award, 1959; Guggenheim fellowship, 1964-65; British Film Institute Book Award, 1985, and Theatre Library Association Award, 1987, both for *D. W. Griffith: An American Life.*

WRITINGS:

TELEPLAYS AND DOCUMENTARY SCRIPTS

The Film Generation, Public Broadcasting System (PBS-TV), 1969.
The Movie-Crazy Years, PBS-TV, 1971.
(And producer) *Hollywood: You Must Remember This,* PBS-TV, 1972.
(And producer and director) *The Men Who Made the Movies* (eight part series), PBS-TV, 1973.
(And producer) *Life Goes to the Movies,* National Broadcasting Co., 1976.
(And producer) *The Making of Star Wars,* American Broadcasting Co., 1976.
(And producer and director) *Into the Morning: Willa Cather's America,* PBS-TV, 1978.
Funny Business, Columbia Broadcasting System, 1978.
(And producer and director) *The Horror Show,* Columbia Broadcasting System, 1978.
(And producer) *SPFX: The Making of The Empire Strikes Back,* Columbia Broadcasting System, 1980.
(And producer and director) *James Cagney: That Yankee Doodle Dandy,* PBS-TV, 1981.
(And producer) *From Star Wars to Jedi: The Making of a Saga,* Columbia Broadcasting System, 1983.
(And producer and director) *Hollywood on Hollywood,* American Film Institute, 1993.
(With Robert Mundy, and producer and director) *Beyond the Law,* American Film Institute, 1998.

Also writer of syndicated television series *The Coral Jungle,* 1976. 1998. Co-executive producer of television documentary *AFI's 100 Years . . . 100 Movies.*

OTHER

The World of Carnegie Hall, Messner (New York City), 1960.
The Stars, Dial (New York City), 1960.
Movies: The History of an Art and an Institution, Basic Books (New York City), 1964.
The Gentle Knight (juvenile), Abelard (New York City), 1964.
(With Lena Horne) *Lena,* Doubleday (New York City), 1965.
The World of Goya, Time-Life (Alexandria, VA), 1968.
(Editor with John Simon) *Film 67/68,* Simon & Schuster (New York City), 1968.
The Disney Version: The Life, Times, Art, and Commerce of Walt Disney, Simon & Schuster, 1968, revised edition, Touchstone (New York City), 1985, 3rd edition, with new introduction, Ivan R. Dee (Chicago), 1997.
Second Sight: Notes on Some Movies (collection of film criticism), Simon & Schuster, 1972.
His Picture in the Paper, Charterhouse, 1973.
Harold Lloyd: The Shape of Laughter, New York Graphic Society (Boston), 1974.
(With Bob Willoughby) *The Platinum Years,* Random House (New York City), 1974.

The Men Who Made the Movies, Atheneum (New York City), 1975.

The World of Tennis, Random House, 1975.

(With Douglas Fairbanks) *The Fairbanks Album,* New York Graphic Society, 1976.

Another I, Another You: A Love Story for the Once Married, Harper (New York City), 1978.

Singled Out, Viking (New York City), 1981.

Cary Grant: A Celebration, Little-Brown (Boston), 1983.

D. W. Griffith: An American Life, Simon & Shuster, 1984.

Gary Cooper, Little, Brown, 1985.

Intimate Strangers: The Cult of Celebrity, Doubleday, 1985.

James Cagney: A Celebration, Little-Brown, 1985.

(With Michael Walsh) *Carnegie Hall: The First One Hundred Years,* Abrams (New York City), 1987.

Striking Poses, Workman Publishing (New York City), 1987.

Schickel on Film, Morrow (New York City), 1989.

Brando: A Life in out Times, Atheneum (New York City), 1991.

Double Indemnity, BFI Pub. (London), 1992.

Clint Eastwood: A Biography, Knopf (New York City), 1996.

Matinee Idylls: Reflections on the Movies, Ivan R. Dee, 1999.

Contributor to periodicals.

SIDELIGHTS: Richard Schickel is known as both a film critic for *Time* magazine and as a novelist and chronicler of Hollywood history and celebrity. In his 1985 book *Intimate Strangers: The Culture of Celebrity,* Schickel offers an in-depth examination of what it means to be celebrated in a media-conscious society. The result of ten years of thought, *Intimate Strangers* explores the many levels of fame, and how it can be manipulated to serve less-than-noble aims. Alden Whitman, writing in the *Chicago Tribune,* termed the book "entertaining, but not profound." Toronto *Globe and Mail* critic Jay Scott reacted more favorably to the text, calling it a "lively, thoughtful and ultimately chilling social history," whereas Elaine Kendall of the *Los Angeles Times* offered the evaluation that "though Schickel hasn't broken any new trails, he offers numerous alluring side trips to sites not included on the standard tourist route."

Schickel's interest in renowned people and his special preoccupation with film are reflected in numerous "star" biographies, covering such diverse luminaries as Cary Grant and director D. W. Griffith. Michiko Kakutani of the *New York Times* evaluated *Cary Grant: A Celebration* by noting "Mr. Schickel writes about movies with confidence and brio, and he does an admirable job of situating Mr. Grant's work within a cinematic tradition." Similarly, Schickel's *The Disney Version,* a study of animator Walt Disney and his place in popular culture, received high critical praise. "Carefully researched, intelligently organized, [and] expertly written" was the evaluation of Bernard Wolfe in *Harper's.* Katherine Gauss Jackson, writing in *Harper's,* described it as a "discerning biography" which is "a thoroughly satisfying and most informative discussion of all aspects of the Disney legend," while Jonathan Yardley praised the text in the *Washington Post Book World* as "the most provocative study of a man whose influence in American life remains vastly underrated." *D. W. Griffith* was termed "one of the best histories of early movie-making yet published" by Toronto *Globe and Mail* critic Jay Scott. He added: "[Schickel] does not let his respect for the achievements overwhelm his distaste for the flaws: this is a portrait rich in light and shadow, one that follows admirably its internal call for intelligent moderation." Commenting on Schickel's *Clint Eastwood: A Biography* in *Publishers Weekly* a reviewer noted: "No mere celebrity bio, this is a beautifully written, comprehensive and astonishingly insightful study of a man who, seemingly against all odds, has achieved world renown as both a pop culture icon and an accomplished film artist." Reviewing the same book for *Entertainment Weekly,* Gene Lyons found Schickel's treatment overly sympathetic but still found the book entertaining, noting that "Schickel doesn't know how to be dull."

Schickel's 1999 volume, *Matinee Idylls: Reflections on the Movies,* presents twenty essays on cinema. Most of these essays originally appeared in the pages of *Time* and most deal with directors and actors from an earlier era. Gordon Flagg of *Booklist* commented: "Schickel offers fresh insights into such luminaries as Greta Garbo and Bette Davis, but more rewarding are his appraisals of such now less celebrated figures as director King Vidor and Charles Laughton,'a star in a character actor's body.' " "The most provocative essay in the book," according to Flagg, "bemoans the disappearance of the film culture of the '50s through '70s, when a veritable community of cineasts supported foreign movies and serious American films." Dale Thomajian faulted some of Schickel's observations for "betray[ing] a very faint trace of intellectual elitism, a tendency to value satire above poetry and significance above mystery," but added: "Nearly every essay in *Matinee Idylls* is an intelligent and sensitive examination of an important cinema figure or phenomenon." In a similar vein a *Pub-*

lishers Weekly reviewer felt that while Schickel criticizes "the gibberish of post-structural academic criticism" of cinema, he often incorporates its terminology into his observations. Nevertheless the same reviewer concluded: "Evincing a nostalgia for classic Hollywood narrative, his [Schickel's] casual ramblings are not rigorously intellectual, but offer unusually good-natured commentary in the notoriously difficult world of film criticism."

Schickel's first novel, *Another I, Another You,* was also well received. Joseph McLellan of *Time* described it as "a blending of new subject matter with an older kind of style" producing a "Dickens-Thackeray sort of feeling to some of [Schickel's] social observations. . . . Unfortunately," McLellan continued, "there is also a 19th-century flavor in the treatment of secondary characters . . . who are simplified almost to the point of abstraction." McLellan concluded, however, that the book contained "some moments of grown-up tenderness described with uncommon skill and delicacy." Writing in the *New York Times Book Review,* Richard Freedman stated that "rarely has the pathos of the detritus of divorce been more skillfully rendered," and praised the book as "one of those rarities of current storytelling, a genuinely nice—but unsticky—novel."

In addition to his many books, Schickel has also written numerous documentary scripts for television, generally on subjects having to do with the movies. Reviewing Schickel's 1993 *Hollywood on Hollywood* for *Entertainment Weekly,* Lisa Schwarzbaum commented: "Schickel . . . is able to piece together smooth, appealing, all-American, middlebrow TV pieces—his latest being this somewhat airless proof of his thesis that 'the idea of Hollywood is the most original idea Hollywood ever had.' " *Hollywood on Hollywood* presents a series of clips of movies about Hollywood grouped by categories such as "the rise to cinematic stardom," "the fall from stardom," "the life of directors," and "Hollywood movies' contribution to the national effort in World War II." "The best chunk of *Hollywood on Hollywood,"* Schwarzbaum noted, "is the segment about the onscreen image of moviemaking after the war. In the 1950s, as Schickel puts it, the industry that congratulated itself on winning the war lost the peace and underwent a fascinating, bitter, cleansing period of self-hatred." Movies examined in this section include Clifford Odets' 1955 *The Big Knife,* about selling out in Hollywood, and Paddy Cheyefsky's 1958 *The Goddess,* a fictionalized portrait of Marilyn Monroe.

Schickel's 1998 documentary *Beyond the Law,* co-scripted with Robert Mundy, presents a survey of American movies about crime. Steven Gaydos of *Variety* found little of value in the show and stated: "*Law* completely botches the exciting, vibrant story of the evolution of the American crime film." Gaydos criticized the Schickel-Mundy presentation for failing to discuss or in some cases even mention significant influences upon American crime movies, singling out both the German cinematographic advances that made *film noir* possible and Hong Kong action movies as two significant elements that received short shrift. Gaydos concluded: "the analysis of the crime film doesn't include any dissection of the building blocks of filmmaking, other than a few *de rigueur* seconds of the car chase from *The French Connection."*

In his review of *Matinee Idylls* for *Library Journal,* Richard Grefrath stated: "Schickel has become one of America's most influential and widely read film critics. Though he is known as a scholar well grounded in the artistry of cinema as well as the practical considerations of the motion picture industry, Schickel's writing is entertaining and accessible."

Schickel once told *CA* that he hopes "to return to fiction—sooner rather than later, but for the past few years, I have been trying to broaden my range as a film critic. I expect to go on trying to do that in the immediate future, and hope to do more essays about important film artists of the past."

BIOGRAPHICAL/CRITICAL SOURCES:

PERIODICALS

Book World, April 28, 1968.
Booklist, November 1, 1996, Bonnie Smothers, review of *Clint Eastwood,* p. 458; September 1, 1999, Gordon Flagg, review of *Matinee Idylls,* p. 56.
Chicago Tribune, March 17, 1985.
Commentary, September, 1968.
Detroit News, May 10, 1981.
Entertainment Weekly, August 13, 1993, Lisa Schwarzbaum, "Hollywood on Hollywood," p. 60; November 22, 1996, Gene Lyons, review of *Clint Eastwood,* p. 127.
Film Comment, September, 1999, Dale Thomajan, review of *Matinee Idylls,* p. 71.
Film Quarterly, summer, 1968.
Globe and Mail, April 27, 1985.
Harper's, June, 1968.
Library Journal, June 15, 1999, Richard Grefrath, review of *Matinee Idylls,* p. 81.
Los Angeles Times, May 8, 1981; March 11, 1985; July 7, 1985.

New York Times, April 24, 1981; October 14, 1983; April 5, 1984; February 21, 1985; October 5, 1986.
New York Times Book Review, May 5, 1968; July 19, 1981; April 9, 1978; December 4, 1983; April 4, 1984; March 17, 1985; December 6, 1987.
New Republic, July 6, 1968.
New Statesman, February 25, 1977.
Playboy, January, 1965.
Publishers Weekly, September 30, 1996, review of *Clint Eastwood,* p. 68; November 1, 1999, review of *Matinee Idylls,* p. 62.
Time, May 3, 1968; May 1, 1978; May 25, 1981; April 8, 1985; December 2, 1996, "A Biography of Clint Eastwood," p. 89.
Times Literary Supplement, December 16, 1965; July 2, 1976; July 11, 1986.
Tribune Books, March 16, 1986.
Variety, June 22, 1998, Steven Gaydos, review of *AFI's 100 Years,* p. 31.
Wall Street Journal, May 22, 1968; June 5, 1978.
Washington Post, June 12, 1978.
Washington Post Book World, December 6, 1987.*

* * *

SCHWARZ, Ted
See SCHWARZ, Theodore R., Jr.

* * *

SCHWARZ, Theodore R., Jr. 1945-
(Ted Schwarz)

PERSONAL: Born October 12, 1945, in Cleveland, OH; son of Theodore (a salesman) and Ruth (a home economist; maiden name, Stern) Schwarz; married Nancy Clark (a civil servant), December 17, 1966 (divorced, 1978); married Leslie Carroll (a bookkeeper), August 17, 1979. *Education:* Attended Case Western Reserve University, 1964-66, and New York Institute of Photography, 1965.

ADDRESSES: *Office*—Bradley Building, 1220 West sixth St., Suite 800, Cleveland, OH 44113. *Agent*—Bob Tabian, International Creative Management, 40 West 57th St., New York, NY 10019.

CAREER: Freelance writer, 1964—. Radio writer for National Broadcasting Company (NBC), 1966, Storer Broadcasting Co., 1966-74, and Westinghouse Broadcasting Co., 1967; *Akron Beacon Journal,* Akron, OH, reporter, 1967-68, general assignment recorder, 1968-69; freelance commercial photographer, 1969-73. Part-time instructor in writing at Pima College, 1976-87, and Yavapi College, 1982-87. Adjunct professor, Northern Arizona University, 1984-87. Teacher for Writer's Digest School. Worked as heart research technician at Akron City Hospital, as an alternative to military service, 1966-67.

MEMBER: Authors Guild, Authors League of America, Writers Guild of America West, Numismatic Literary Guild, Mystery Writers of America.

WRITINGS:

Coins as Living History, Arco (New York City), 1976.

UNDER NAME TED SCHWARZ

The Successful Promoter, Regnery, 1977.
(With Henry Hawksworth) *The Five of Me,* Regnery, 1977.
(With Christina Peters) *Tell Me Who I Am before I Die,* Rawson Associates, 1978.
(With Ralph Allison) *Mind in Many Pieces: The Making of a Very Special Doctor,* Rawson Associates, 1980.
Beginner's Guide to Coin Collecting, Doubleday (New York City), 1980.
The History of United States Coinage, Barnes, A. S. (San Diego, CA), 1981.
The Hillside Strangler, Doubleday, 1981.
How to Protect Yourself, Your Home, and Your Family, Arco, 1983.
Beginner's Guide to Stamp Collecting, Arco, 1983.
Arnold Friberg: The Passion of a Modern Master, Northland Press (Flagstaff, AZ), 1985.
(With John DeLorean) *DeLorean,* Zondervan (Grand Rapids, MI), 1985.
(With Parichehr Yomtoob) *A Gift of Life,* St. Martin's (New York City), 1985.
(Ghostwriter for Florence Henderson) *A Little Cooking, a Little Talking, and a Whole Lot of Fun with Florence Henderson and Friends from Her Krazy Kountry Kitchen,* Panorama, 1988.
(With Duane Empey) *That Other Church down Your Block,* Zondervan, 1988.
Time Management for Writers, Writer's Digest (Cincinnati, OH,) 1988.
(With Allen Friedman) *Power and Greed: Inside the Teamsters Empire of Corruption,* Watts (New York City), 1989.
The Complete Guide to Writing Biographies, Writer's Digest, 1990.

(With Joyce Lukezic) *False Arrest: The Joyce Lukezic Story,* New Horizon Press (Far Hills, NJ), 1990.

(With Leslie McRay) *Kept Women: Confessions from a Life of Luxury,* Morrow (New York City), 1990.

(With Sherry Clayton Taggett) *Paintbrushes and Pistols: How the Taos Artists Sold the West,* J. Muir Publications (Santa Fe, NM), 1990.

Deadly Whispers (biography), St. Martin's, 1992.

Walking with the Damned: The Shocking Murder of the Man Who Freed 30,000 Prisoners from the Nazis, Paragon House (New York City), 1992.

(With Barbara Gibson) *The Kennedys: The Third Generation,* Thunder's Mouth Press (Emeryville, CA), 1993.

(With Marita Lorenz) *Marita: One Woman's Extraordinary Tale of Love and Espionage from Castro to Kennedy,* Thunder's Mouth Press, 1993.

(With Peter MacDonald) *The Last Warrior: Peter MacDonald and the Navajo Nation,* Orion Books (New York City), 1993.

Healing in the Name of God: Faith or Fraud?, Zondervan, 1993.

(With LaVonne McKee) *Get Ready to Say Goodbye: A Mother's Story of Senseless Violence, Tragedy, and Triumph,* New Horizon Press, 1994.

(With Geraldine Barr) *My Sister Roseanne: The True Story of Roseanne Barr Arnold,* Carol Publishing (Secaucus, NJ), 1994.

(With Gibson) *Rose Kennedy and Her Family: The Best and Worst of Their Lives and Times,* Carol Publishing, 1995.

(With Paul Reed) *Kontum Diary: Captured Writings Bring Peace to a Vietnam Veteran,* Summit Publishing (Arlington, TX), 1996.

Free Speech and False Profits: Ethics in the Media, Pilgrim Press (Cleveland, OH), 1996.

To Love a Child: A Reluctant Father Adopts a "Forgotten" Child, New Horizons Press, 1996.

(With Tom Rybak) *Trust No One: The Glamorous Life and Bizarre Death of Doris Duke,* St. Martin's, 1997.

(With Tonya Flynt-Vega) *Hustled: My Journey from Fear to Faith,* Westminister John Knox Press (Louisville, KY), 1998.

(With Ralph Allison) *Minds in Many Pieces: Revealing the Spiritual Side of Multiple Personality Disorder,* CIE Publishers (Los Osos, CA), 2nd edition, 1999.

Kids and Guns: The History, the Present, the Dangers, and the Remedies, Watts, 1999.

(With Richard E. Goetzke) *Hush! A Demon Sleeps beside Me: A True Story of Violent Secrets, Betrayal, and Courage,* New Horizon Press, 1999.

PHOTOGRAPHY BOOKS; UNDER NAME TED SCHWARZ

The Business Side of Photography, American Photographic Book Publishing Co., 1969.

How to Make Money with Your Camera, H. P. Books (Tucson, AZ), 1974.

How to Start a Professional Photography Business, Regnery, 1977.

(Contributor) *The Encyclopedia of Practical Photography,* Amphoto, 1978.

Amphoto Guide to Modeling, Amphoto, 1979.

How to Be a Freelance Photographer, Contemporary Books (Chicago), 1980.

Consumer Guide to Model Photography, Consumer Guide, 1980.

Careers in Photography, Contemporary Books, 1981.

The Complete Business Guide for the Freelance and Professional Photographer, Focal Press (Woburn, MA), 1983.

The Professional Photographer's Handbook, McGraw (New York City), 1983.

(With Brian Stoppee) *The Photographer's Guide to Using Light,* Amphoto, 1986.

Also co-author of *The Photographer's Business Handbook,* for McGraw-Hill.

OTHER

Also author of *The Peter Lawford Story.* Ghostwriter of a business guide and several books about drug addiction and childhood health, for a number of publishers, including St. Martin's, McGraw, and Bobbs-Merrill. Author of columns, "Tips by Ted," *Rangefinder,* 1970—, and "Civil War Postal History," *Stamp News,* 1976—; also author of syndicated cartoon, "The Badge Guys," Newspaper Enterprise Association, 1971-73. Contributor of approximately two thousand articles to magazines, including *Family Circle, Writer's Market,* and *Studio Photography.* Contributing editor of *Stamp News,* 1976—, and *Physician's Management.*

ADAPTATIONS: False Arrest: The Joyce Lukezic Story was produced as an ABC television miniseries.

WORK IN PROGRESS: A book on California history tentatively titled *The Secret History of California* for Northland Press; mystery books titled *Death Song Singing, Stalker in the Shadows, Dirty Little Secrets,* and *A Perfect Little Murder;* several film projects, including *Salons* with Joe Felice, and *The Godson.*

SIDELIGHTS: Ted Schwarz is a prolific author who has written, co-written, and ghosted books on a wide variety of subjects, including photography, coin collecting, writing, cooking, children and gun safety, ethics in the media, and faith healing. However, he is probably best known for his numerous "celebrity" biographies, often co-written with their subjects or with someone close to their subjects.

In *False Arrest: The Joyce Lukezic Story,* co-written with its subject, Schwarz presents the tale of a woman who fell victim to an Arizona law that allows someone to be convicted of a crime on the basis of charges by someone who has previously confessed to the same crime. The crime in question was the murder of Lukezic's husband's business partner, Patrick Redmond, and Redmond's mother-in-law. The man who confessed to the crime stated that Lukezic had contracted the murders. *False Arrest* not only details the particulars of the murder but Lukezic's two-year ordeal in jail before she was cleared of the charges. It was adapted for an ABC television miniseries.

In his 1992 solo effort, *Walking with the Damned: The Shocking Murder of the Man Who Freed 30,000 Prisoners from the Nazis,* Schwarz tells the tale of Count Folke Bernadotte, a member of a Swedish royal family who, as a Red Cross representative near the end of World War II, managed to negotiate with Heinrich Himmler to gain the release of 30,000 death camp prisoners. Bernadotte later represented the United Nations in Palestine during peace negotiations on the first Arab-Israeli conflict. While working there, he was assassinated by Zionist terrorists in 1948. According to a reviewer from *Publishers Weekly:* "The material which the author has collected on Bernadotte is thin; he has padded it with a rehash of Himmler's rise to power, the development of the death camps and a murky account of internecine struggles among Palestinian Jews."

In another book co-written with its subject, *Marita: One Woman's Extraordinary Tale of Love and Espionage from Castro to Kennedy,* Schwarz relates the bizarre and purportedly true life story of Marita Lorenz, a woman who claims to have had a love affair with Fidel Castro when she was nineteen and subsequently given birth to his baby. According to Marita, the CIA convinced her incorrectly that Castro had been responsible for the infant's death, and she then agreed to try to assassinate the Cuban dictator. Among Marita's many other adventures are gunrunning with Lee Harvey Oswald and an affair with Venezuela dictator Marcos Perez Jimenez. Reviewing the book for *Entertainment Weekly,* Rhonda Johnson feels that "[c]onspiracy buffs and camp enthusiasts alike will appreciate this Cold War memoir," but goes on to note: "Buried in the drama is an important story about covert operations in the U.S., but the complete lack of corroboration tends to undermine the author's credibility, leaving some of her tales . . . just a bit open to question." Chris Chase of *Cosmopolitan* is more skeptical, commenting: "If even half of this is true, the FBI and the CIA are so dumb you can take their money, never do anything they're paying you to do, and still end up sleeping in Queens, instead of with the fishes."

Schwarz co-wrote *Trust No One: The Glamorous Life and Bizarre Death of Doris Duke,* with Tom Rybak, a former employee of infamous heiress Doris Duke. Inheriting a fortune at an early age after the death of her tobacco baron father, Duke embarked on a life of excess that included failed marriages, numerous affairs, drug and alcohol addiction, and jet-setting around the world. The exact cause of her death, at age eighty, though attributed to an overdose of morphine, has long been a subject of speculation. Reviewing *Trust No One* for *Booklist,* Kathleen Hughes states: "This book, while rendering a concise, if extremely dark, portrayal of the lives of the very wealthy, leaves the reader with the feeling of witnessing a bad car accident, horrified and repulsed yet somehow transfixed." Elizabeth Mellett of *Library Journal* observes that "Schwarz has done a competent job, but not everyone would speak with him, and the book becomes repetitive in the final chapters." Mellett also feels that *Trust No One* has nothing new to offer in terms of resolving the puzzle of Duke's death.

Schwarz's 1999 offering, *Hush! A Demon Sleeps beside Me: A True Story of Violent Secrets, Betrayal, and Courage,* was co-written with Richard E. Goetzke. It tells Goetzke's story of his marriage to Lauren Wexler, a woman who turned out to have six alternate personalities, all of them with distinct voices and appearances. Schwarz and Goetzke relate how the latter was violently attacked by Lauren and arrested for spousal abuse when he bruised her wrist trying to defend himself. Goetzke's efforts to help his wife get treatment for her disorder proved to no avail. A reviewer for *Publishers Weekly* remarks: "Ludicrously melodramatic writing and the decision to use demon possession as a metaphor for mental illness are the most glaring of this book's many faults. . . . The events are chilling enough not to have been saddled with the sensationalism the authors appear to have believed necessary to retain a reader's interest."

Schwarz once told *CA* that he began writing during his childhood, compelled by an introvert's need to communicate with a larger number of people than he would "otherwise have the courage to face." After experiencing his first success at age fifteen with the sale of an article to a hobby publication, he concentrated on improving his style and ability, often neglecting his schoolwork in the process. A firm believer that a writer is only as good as his or her next work, he constantly lives with "a very mild case of nervous tension" and feels guilty when away from the typewriter for any length of time.

With perseverance, anyone can become a professional writer, maintains Schwarz: "It is often said that new writers have no chance. This has been said so long that, if it were true, all writing would have stopped after Matthew, Mark, Luke and John died and the Bible was published. There is great opportunity in this field that many writers fear to take advantage of. Other writers worry about talent. Writing is a growth field. I have no idea what talent is or if I have it. A new writer should write, try to understand where mistakes were made, and then write again. If the individual can keep writing, not repeating past mistakes but improving a little each time, at some point that person will be selling. No one succeeds in this field without sitting down and doing the work."

Schwarz additionally wrote to *CA:* "I am getting more involved with fiction, both in developing projects for television and in writing novels. I will probably try to spend between a quarter and a third of my time writing fiction. I not only like the freedom it provides to not have to travel quite so much, I also enjoy the challenge of creating a world which has never existed before, populating it with people no one knew until I created them, then making them all come so alive that the reader wants to spend a couple of hours in that world."

BIOGRAPHICAL/CRITICAL SOURCES:

PERIODICALS

Booklist, March 15, 1994, Sue-Ellen Beauregard, review of *Get Ready to Say Goodbye,* p. 1309; September 15, 1994, Ilene Cooper, review of *My Sister Roseanne,* p. 82; March 15, 1997, Kathleen Hughes, review of *Trust No One,* p. 1223.

Cosmopolitan, November, 1993, Chris Chase, review of *Marita,* p. 30.

Entertainment Weekly, December 3, 1993, Rhonda Johnson, review of *Marita,* p. 66.

Library Journal, March 15, 1997, Elizabeth Mellett, review of *Trust No One,* p. 70.

Publishers Weekly, February 16, 1990, review of *False Arrest,* p. 64; January 13, 1992, review of *Walking with the Damned,* p. 43; October 18, 1993, review of *The Last Warrior,* p. 43; October 25, 1993, review of *The Kennedys,* p. 54; February 7, 1994, review of *Get Ready to Say Goodbye,* p. 77; October 31, 1994, review of *My Sister Roseanne,* p. 51; May 6, 1996, review of *Kontum Diary,* p. 65; February 3, 1997, review of *Trust No One,* p. 86; November 1, 1999, review of *Hush! A Demon Sleeps beside Me,* p. 70.*

* * *

SEAGRAVE, Sterling 1937-

PERSONAL: Born April 15, 1937, in Columbus, OH; son of Gordon (a surgeon, missionary, and writer) and Marion (Morse) Seagrave; married Wendy Law-Yone (a writer), 1967 (divorced, 1972); married Peggy Sawyer (a senior picture editor), July 1, 1983; children: (first marriage) Jocelyn, Sean (twins). *Education:* Attended University of Miami, 1956, University of Mexico, 1957, and National University of Venezuela, 1958. *Avocational interests:* Tae Kwon Do (black belt), sailing, and boatbuilding.

ADDRESSES: Agent—Robert Gottlieb, William Morris Agency, 1350 Avenue of the Americas, New York, NY 10019.

CAREER: Merchant seaman in Latin America during the 1950s; free-lance journalist, covering Cuban revolution with rebel forces of Fidel Castro in Pinar del Rio region of Cuba, 1958; reporter and columnist for various newspapers in the United States, 1959-67; stringer for *Time* (magazine) in Paris, France, 1962; *Washington Post,* Washington, DC, 1962-65, began as reporter, became assistant foreign news editor; freelance journalist in Southeast Asia, 1965-72; worked intermittently as an editor for *Bangkok* (magazine) and as an editorial page editor for *Bangkok Post,* both in Bangkok, Thailand; *St. Petersburg Times,* St. Petersburg, FL, 1973-75, began as feature editor, became foreign news editor; Time-Life Books, Alexandria, VA, editor and writer, 1975-80; writer, 1980—.

MEMBER: Authors Guild.

WRITINGS:

Yellow Rain: A Journey through the Terror of Chemical Warfare, M. Evans (New York City), 1981.

Soldiers of Fortune, Time-Life (Alexandria, VA), 1981.

The Soong Dynasty, Harper (New York City), 1985.

The Marcos Dynasty, Harper, 1988.

Dragon Lady: The Life and Legend of the Last Empress of China, Knopf (New York City), 1992.

Lords of the Rim: The Invisible Empire of the Overseas Chinese, Putnam's (New York City), 1995.

The Yamato Dynasty: The Secret History of Japan's Imperial Family, Bantam (New York City), 1999.

Writer and producer of documentaries on the Vietnam War, including *Holiday from Hell,* American Broadcasting Company (ABC-TV), 1967. Contributor to periodicals, including *Life, Esquire, Atlantic, Saturday Evening Post, Reader's Digest,* and *Far Eastern Economic Review.*

Seagrave's works have been translated into German, French, Spanish, Japanese, Chinese, and Arabic.

SIDELIGHTS: A former *Time* and *Washington Post* reporter who was raised on the China-Burma border, Sterling Seagrave is known for his investigative books about aspects of Far Eastern history. Seagrave's work has been commended for exposing high-level corruption in countries such as China and the Philippines, and it has also enlightened American readers on aspects of Far Eastern culture that factor into business and politics there. As Emily MacFarquhar put it in the *New York Times Book Review,* Seagrave "is at his best when he is debunking conventional certitudes. . . . He does an amateur's demolition job on professional historians and their tainted sources."

Seagrave is the son of the legendary "Burma Surgeon," Gordon Seagrave, a medical missionary who built a major hospital on the remote Chinese border of northern Burma. Sterling Seagrave was born in the United States during his parents' brief visit there in 1936 and was taken at age six weeks to Burma, becoming the sixth generation of Seagraves to live in that country. At the end of 1941, when the Japanese invaded Burma, his mother took him to India and later to the United States. During the ensuing war years, Gordon Seagrave served as chief medical officer for General Joseph W. Stilwell, the U.S. commander of Allied troops in China, Burma, and India. Seagrave and his mother returned to Burma following World War II but returned to the United States in the early 1950s due to civil wars in Burma and China.

The Seagrave family was divided for many years because of the Burmese civil war. During this time Seagrave studied at the University of Miami, the University of Mexico, and the National University of Venezuela. He also worked his way around Latin America as a merchant seaman. In the late 1950s, during a communist revolution led by Fidel Castro in Cuba, Seagrave was arrested by the Zaldivar Batista government's secret police and imprisoned for three days in the dungeons of Havana's infamous el Principe Fortress. Seagrave subsequently chose a career in journalism, and in 1958 he returned to Cuba to spend the last nine months of the revolution following the rebel Fidelistas in the mountains of Pinar del Rio.

Upon returning to the United States, Seagrave wrote stories for a number of publications, including *Time* and the *Washington Post.* In 1965, he returned to Burma where he received word that his father was ill. He was forced to leave the country after his father's death, because Burma had adopted an isolationist policy that discouraged visitors. However, he remained in Asia for seven years, working as a freelance journalist for such periodicals as *Life, Esquire,* and the *Far Eastern Economic Review.* The realities of his personal situation factored into Seagrave's career decisions, and he gave up youthful notions of becoming a novelist. "I was always very poor," he once told *CA* in an interview. "I went to work for newspapers to survive. As it turned out, the newspaper work taught me a lot of discipline, and through it I became interested in investigative journalism. So far, my books have been investigative journalism, constructed and written in the style of novels. Frankly, I find them much more interesting to work on than novels, because the elements are all very real. I enjoy the challenge of presenting difficult factual material in a dramatic form. I think this ends up combining the best of both."

Seagrave resettled in the United States in the mid-1970s and took a position as an editor with the *St. Petersburg Times.* He later joined Time-Life Books as a writer and editor, resigning in 1980 to produce *Soldiers of Fortune* and to write books full time. He first attracted widespread attention the following year with his controversial study *Yellow Rain.* In this 1981 work Seagrave posits that the Soviet Union developed biochemical weapons that they and their allies used to annihilate resisting peoples in isolated areas of Yemen in the mid-1960s, Laos in the late 1970s, and Afghanistan in the early 1980s. Scenario and results were the same in all three instances, Seagrave asserts in the book: Soviet-built or -piloted planes dropped bombs emitting dense smoke in various colors—brown, black, grey green, and yellow—that blistered the skin of those who came in contact with it, caused convulsions, and brought an agonizing death by massive hemorrhaging.

Seagrave estimates that by 1981, between 15,000 and 30,000 people had died from this "yellow rain," which he suspects contained biosynthetic fungal poisons called tricothecene toxins (T-2), a substance occurring naturally in bread molds. Seagrave also maintains that the poisons were tested in marginal areas in preparation for large-scale chemical warfare with the United States and its allies, an allegation that the Soviets fiercely deny. Soil samples tested by French, Norwegian, Belgian, and Canadian scientists revealed the presence of T-2 as Seagrave had predicted, but similar findings in the United States have been the subject of continuing controversy.

"The evidence in the case is the heart of Mr. Seagrave's book, and he has presented it ably," opined Thomas Powers in his *New York Times Book Review* critique of *Yellow Rain.* "A defending lawyer might have a field day with the circumstantial nature of the evidence, but Mr. Seagrave is persuasive in making his case." At least one reviewer was critical of the U.S. government's use of Seagrave's allegations as a means to escalate the cold war. Kathryn Kilgore, writing in the *Village Voice,* bitterly noted: "Seagrave's conjectures have been sanctioned as facts, justifying U.S. production of chemical and bacteriological weapons." Indeed, Seagrave reluctantly admits in *Yellow Rain* that only a buildup of U.S. stores of biotoxins would serve as a deterrent to a Soviet threat. The author subsequently argued, however, that the controversy contributed to the positive outcome of U.S./Soviet nuclear disarmament negotiations, and that the use of chemical weapons by Iraq during the Iran-Iraq War of the 1980s vindicates his warnings.

In his next work, *The Soong Dynasty,* Seagrave turned his investigative eye on Charlie Soong, a wealthy merchant, and his six children, who came to influence Chinese politics and culture for a generation—from the founding of the Chinese republic by Sun Yat-sen in 1911 until its fall to Mao Tse-tung in 1949. "Few families since the Borgias [a corrupt family influential in the papacy and in Italy during the fifteenth and sixteenth centuries] have played such a disturbing role in human destiny," reads the portentous opening of the book, as quoted by Christopher Lehman-Haupt in the *New York Times.* In this family biography, Seagrave first examines patriarch Charlie, a Chinese stowaway educated in the United States by Methodists who made such an enormous fortune selling Bibles and noodles that he financed the insurrections of Sun Yat-sen, the founder of the revolutionary Chinese communist party Kuomintang. Charlie's oldest son, Tse-ven, a financier, was reputedly the richest man in the world at one time. Oldest daughter Ai-ling married H. H. Kung, a fabulously wealthy descendant of the ancient Chinese philosopher Confucious. Middle daughter Ching-ling—the only member of the clan whom Seagrave portrays favorably— married Sun and, after the death of her revolutionary husband, remained loyal to the left and eventually served as vice-chair of Mao's People's Republic of China. Youngest daughter May-ling married Mao's nemesis, Chiang Kai-shek, and became first lady of the Republic of China. Two other banker brothers, Tse-liang and Tse-an, along with Tse-ven, helped Chiang pervert the Kuomintang after Sun's death, turning the party into a vehicle for self-aggrandizement and systematic looting.

Seagrave presents the Soongs as a family of greedy manipulators beholden to the brutal Chinese mafia, the Green Gang, who financed Chiang's Nationalist regime through opium peddling, prostitution, and extortion. But, because "they had a public plumage that was so praiseworthy it dazzled the eye," Seagrave lamented in the book, as quoted by Jonathan Spence in *New York Times Book Review,* the Soongs were able to win U.S. favor. May-ling obtained U.S. congressional support for her husband's corrupt government during World War II by denouncing the communists who threatened her husband's standing. She also beguiled and exploited publishing mogul Henry Luce, owner of *Time* and *Life* magazines, convincing him that the Soongs and Chiang represented a progressive new China.

"To his great credit," John Fraser proclaimed in a *New York Times Book Review* piece on *The Soong Dynasty,* "Sterling Seagrave has tackled a mighty subject with resourcefulness and considerable spirit. This is just as well, for a more ascetic historian might have succumbed to something fatal when confronted with the catalogue of horrors pre-communist China has in its ample storehouse of memories." Although Seagrave relied on many secondary sources, Fraser defended the author's unique purpose, noting that "it is in bringing together the multitudinous threads and weaving them into such a coherent, chronological and dramatic form that has been Seagrave's most significant achievement. . . . It's all here and the cumulative effect is devastating." And, as *New York Times Book Review* contributor Jonathan Spence remarked, Seagrave has "ruffled the plumage most thoroughly, and the eye is no longer dazzled."

After the publication of *The Soong Dynasty,* Seagrave said he received death threats from Taiwan, which prompted him to take his family into hiding for a year. "It's not fear, it's discretion," he told Joseph Berger in the *New York Times Book Review,* explaining that a journalist who wrote a book critical of Chaing's family was shot to death in October, 1984. Seagrave recounted that he had planned for fifteen years to write *The Soong Dynasty,* a motivation stemming from his childhood spent on the China-Burma border. "I would hear lots of things about the Soongs and Chiangs," he commented to Berger, "which didn't jibe with what I saw in *Life* magazine."

Although he and his family could have been in danger, Seagrave continued to produce exposes of corruption in the Far East. In his 1988 book, *The Marcos Dynasty,* which *Times Literary Supplement* contributor Michael Leifer called "a chronicle of the gross abuse of power," Seagrave focuses on the Filipino dictator Ferdinand Marcos and his wife, Imelda. Marcos dominated the Philippines' political scene for two decades and was supported by the U.S. government. The ruler was later accused of robbing his country and terrorizing its citizens. When he was finally forced into exile by a popular revolt in early 1986, it was discovered that Marcos had amassed a fortune of more than one hundred billion dollars.

David C. Unger wrote in his *New York Times Book Review* critique of *The Marcos Dynasty* that the fallen leader emerges from Seagrave's book "as an unscrupulous political schemer with a genius for playing off opposing power centers to his own advantage and profit." Although *Time* reviewer John Elson argued that Seagrave "seems so concerned about building an indictment that he fails to answer the question of what really made Ferdinand and Imelda tick," the critic nonetheless concluded that the author "does persuade us that his subjects, Ferdinand in particular, were paradigmatically venal." *Washington Post Book World* contributor Ross Thomas, deeming the book a "scorching biography," declared: "Seagrave's history of how the Philippines' former president and first lady managed to become so corrupt and so immensely rich and powerful will satisfy the cravings of those addicted to such tales—which may include just about everybody."

Two more Seagrave titles investigate modern Chinese history from varied viewpoints. *Dragon Lady: The Life and Legend of the Last Empress of China* seeks to correct previous biographies of the late empress Tzu Hsi, who ruled with her son and nephew from 1861 until 1908. According to Seagrave, the empress was slandered by British and Chinese writers who, for their own reasons, sought to portray her as a sexually-ravenous, conniving, and murderous ruler. By contrast, to quote a *Publishers Weekly* reviewer, Seagrave "delineates a figurehead empress, a dutiful widow and a frightened matriarch who lost three emperors to conspiracy." *Lords of the Rim: The Invisible Empire of the Overseas Chinese* explores the wealth, numbers, and political influence of some fifty-five million expatriate Chinese, scattered across all of Asia and even the United States and Canada. In Seagrave's view, these powerful men and women retain ties to their homeland and will provide billions of dollars in reinvestment revenue if and when the communist regime crumbles. An *Economist* critic wrote of *Lords of the Rim:* "As an impressionistic picture of the history, wealth, power and, in some cases, skulduggery of the overseas Chinese, [Seagrave] has produced a gripping read." *Nation* correspondent Sara C. Jorgensen likewise contended that the work "is both a valuable tool for understanding recent Chinese history and a means of predicting the future," and a *Publishers Weekly* reviewer concluded that Seagrave "has delivered an engrossing mercantile history."

The 2,500-year-old Japanese imperial dynasty is the focus of Seagrave's attention in *The Yamato Dynasty: The Secret History of Japan's Imperial Family.* Seagrave seeks to penetrate the veils of secrecy that have surrounded the Japanese ruling family for centuries, and in doing so he reveals the idiosyncracies of various emperors and empresses, and also the political intrigues hatched by the rulers and their entourages. An important part of the work, needless to say, concerns Emperor Hirohito and his role in World War II. According to Phyllis Birnbaum in the *Times Literary Supplement,* Seagrave "is good on the backroom machinations which eventually allowed Hirohito to retain his throne and avoid prosecution for war crimes." Birnbaum concluded of the book in full that the reader "is left with the impression of an author struggling to fashion a gripping story from a fairly lacklustre subject. In the main, the mediocrity of these Japanese rulers was such that even Sterling Seagrave's swashbuckling prose cannot rescue them."

Seagrave told *CA:* "Writing books about Asia helps me to sort out the past, to separate the truth from the fiction, the fact from the propaganda, and to see it all a bit more clearly. It keeps me involved with things that have always meant a lot to me."

BIOGRAPHICAL/CRITICAL SOURCES:

BOOKS

Seagrave, Sterling, *The Marcos Dynasty,* Harper (New York City), 1988.

Seagrave, Sterling, *The Soong Dynasty,* Harper, 1985.

PERIODICALS

Booklist, August, 1995, p. 1916.
Commentary, March, 1982, p. 64.
Detroit News, March 17, 1985.
Economist, November 11, 1995, p. S12.
Los Angeles Times Book Review, January 3, 1982, p. 4; May 19, 1985, p. 7.
Maclean's, April 15, 1985, p. 56.
Nation, September 11, 1995, p. 248.
New York Times, March 14, 1985.
New York Times Book Review, October 18, 1981, pp. 11 and 41; March 17, 1985, pp. 1 and 38; December 11, 1988, p. 11; May 3, 1992, p. 12.
People, October 5, 1981, pp. 43-50.
Publishers Weekly, February 24, 1992, p. 35; June 26, 1995, p. 100.
Time, April 29, 1985, p. 82; November 14, 1988, p. 91.
Times Literary Supplement, April 28, 1989, p. 465; December 31, 1999, p. 30.
Village Voice, October 28, 1981, p. 45; March 25, 1986, p. 46.
Washington Post Book World, March 24, 1985, pp. 1, 4; October 16, 1988, p. 5.*

* * *

SEN, Amartya K(umar) 1933-

PERSONAL: Born November 3, 1933, in Santiniketan, India; son of Ashutosh and Amita Sen; married Nabaneeta Dev, 1960 (marriage ended, 1974); married Eva Colorni, 1977 (deceased, 1985); married Emma Rothschild, 1991; children: Antara, Nandana, Indrani, Kabir. *Education:* Presidency College (Calcutta, India), B.A., 1953; Trinity College, Cambridge, B.A., 1955, M.A. and Ph.D., 1959.

ADDRESSES: *Office*—The Master's Lodge, Trinity College, Cambridge CB2 1TQ, England.

CAREER: Jadavpur University, Calcutta, India, professor of economics, 1956- 58; Trinity College, Cambridge, England, fellow, 1957-63; Delhi University, Delhi, India, professor of economics, 1963-71; London School of Economics, London, England, professor of economics, 1971-77; Oxford University, Oxford, England, professor of economics, 1977-80, Drummond Professor of Political Economy, 1980-88; Harvard University, Cambridge, MA, Lamont University Professor and professor of economics and philosophy, 1988-98; Trinity College, Cambridge, England, Master, 1998—. Andrew D. White Professor at Large, Cornell University, 1978-85; fellow of All Souls College, Oxford, England, 1980-88. Chairperson of the United Nations Expert Group on the Role of Advanced Skills and Technology, 1967.

MEMBER: International Economic Association (president, 1986-89, honorary president, 1989—), American Economic Association (president, 1994—), Econometric Society (president, 1984), Royal Economic Society, Indian Economic Association (president, 1989), Development Studies Association (president, 1980-82).

AWARDS, HONORS: Fellow of the British Academy; foreign honorary member of the American Academy of Arts and Sciences; fellow of the Econometric Society; honorary fellow of the Institute of Social Studies (the Hague); Mahalanobis Prize, 1976; honorary doctorate of literature, University of Saskatchewan, 1979; Nobel Prize in economics, 1998.

WRITINGS:

Choice of Techniques: An Aspect of the Theory of Planned Economic Development, Basil Blackwell (Oxford, England), 1960, A. M. Kelley (New York City), 1968.
Collective Choice and Social Welfare, Holden-Day (San Francisco), 1970.
(Editor) *Growth Economics: Selected Readings,* Penguin (Harmondsworth, England), 1970.
Behaviour and the Concept of Preference, London School of Economics and Political Science (London), 1971.
Crisis in Indian Education, Institute of Public Enterprise (Hyderabad, India), 1971.
(With Partha Dasgupta and Stephen Marglin) *Guidelines for Project Evaluation,* United Nations (New York City), 1972.
On Economic Inequality, North-Holland, Oxford University Press, and Norton (New York City), 1973, reprinted, Oxford University Press (New York City), 1997.
Employment, Technology, and Development: A Study Prepared for the International Labour Office within the Framework of the World Employment Programme, Clarendon Press (Oxford, England), 1975.
Levels of Poverty: Policy and Change: A Background Study for World Development Report, 1980, World Bank (Washington, DC), 1980.
Poverty and Famines: An Essay on Entitlement and Deprivation (also see below), Oxford University Press (New York City), 1981.

Choice, Welfare, and Measurement, MIT Press (Cambridge, MA), 1982.

(Editor with Bernard Williams) *Utilitarianism and Beyond,* Cambridge University Press (New York City), 1982.

Resources, Values, and Development, Harvard University Press, 1984, reprinted, Harvard University Press, 1997.

Commodities and Capabilities, North-Holland, 1985.

On Ethics and Economics, Basil Blackwell, 1987.

Food, Economics, and Entitlements, United Nations University (Helsinki), 1987.

Hunger and Entitlements: Research for Action, United Nations University, 1987.

(With others) *The Standard of Living,* Cambridge University Press (New York City), 1987.

(Editor with K. N. Raj and C. H. Hanumantha Rao) *Studies on Indian Agriculture,* Oxford University Press (New Delhi), 1988.

Africa and India: What Do We Have to Learn from Each Other?, WIDER (Helsinki), 1988.

Gender and Cooperative Conflicts, United Nations University, 1988.

(With Jean Dreze) *Hunger and Public Action* (also see below), Oxford University Press (New York City), 1989.

(With Martha Craven Nussbaum) *Internal Criticism and Indian Rationalist Traditions,* United Nations University, 1989.

Jibanayatra o arthaniti, Ananda, 1990.

(Editor with Dreze) *The Political Economy of Hunger* (also see below), 3 vols., Oxford University Press (New York City), 1990-91.

Money and Value: On the Ethics and Economics of Finance/Denaro e valore: etica ed economia della finanza, Edizione dell'elefante (Rome), 1991.

Inequality Reexamined, Harvard University Press, 1992.

(Editor with Nussbaum) *The Quality of Life,* Oxford University Press, 1993.

(Editor with Dreze and Athar Hussain) *The Political Economy of Hunger: Selected Essays,* Oxford University Press, 1995.

(With Dreze) *India: Economic Development and Social Opportunity* (also see below) Oxford University Press (Delhi, India), 1995.

(Editor with Kenneth J. Arrow and Kotaro Suzumura) *Social Choice Re-examined: Proceedings of the IEA Conference Held at Schloss Hernstein, Berndorf,* St. Martin's (New York City), 1996-97.

(Editor with Dreze) *Indian Development: Selected Regional Perspectives,* Oxford University Press (New York City), 1997.

Development as Freedom, Knopf (New York City), 1999.

(With Dreze) *The Amartya Sen and Jean Dreze Omnibus: Comprising Poverty and Famines, Hunger and Public Action, and India: Economic Development and Social Opportunity,* Oxford University Press, 1999.

L'economie est une science morale, Decouverte (Paris), 1999.

Reason before Identity, Oxford University Press, 1999.

Member of editorial board, *Economics and Philosophy, Ethics, Feminist Economics, Gender and Development, Indian Economic and Social History Review, Indian Journal of Quantitative Economics, Journal of Peasant Studies, Pakistan Development Review, Pakistan Journal of Applied Economics, Philosophy and Public Affairs, Social Choice and Welfare, Common Knowledge, Critic & Review, Theory and Decision,* and *Contemporary World.*

SIDELIGHTS: Amartya K. Sen, the 1998 Nobel Prizewinner in economics, is a highly regarded theorist whose works have been credited with reintroducing ethics into economic discourse. Kenneth J. Arrow, himself a well-respected economist, wrote in the *New York Review of Books* that Sen "is a scholar of unusually wide interests in an era in which most economists have become highly specialized." Sen's ground-breaking work has led to the development of more sophisticated techniques for assessing world poverty and the relative wealth of nations. He has studied the causes of famine, the economic impact of literacy and public health initiatives, and the means by which governments can improve the prospects for their poorest citizens. As Jeffrey Sachs put it in *Time,* "In a lifetime of careful scholarship, Sen has repeatedly returned to a basic theme: even impoverished societies can improve the well-being of their least advantaged members. . . . In a world in which 1.5 billion people subsist on less than $1 a day, this Nobel Prize can be not just a celebration of a wonderful scholar but also a clarion call to attend to the urgent needs of the poor." In *Foreign Affairs,* Richard N. Cooper wrote: "Most economists these days eschew moral philosophy—namely, the consideration of social justice—because they consider it too 'soft' for rigorous analytical treatment. But Amartya Sen harks back to the older and richer tradition of evaluating the considerations of economic efficiency—which dominate most modern economic analyses—with respect to their general social consequences. Such judgments require an ethical framework." Cooper concluded: "Sen is a genuine world citizen. Implicit throughout his [work] is the notion that all humanity is connected and that human suffering anywhere holds relevance everywhere."

Sen's work has gained a wide readership due in part to the clarity of his prose style, which makes complex economic theories and arguments accessible to the nonspecialist. In a review of the author's *Resources, Values, and Development* published in the *London Review of Books,* Robert Cassen commented that Sen "has a mind like a searchlight, illuminating his material with an intense lucidity; he has a gift for looking at assumptions his colleagues have long taken for granted, and finding them defective. Economics as it is commonly taught would be somewhat different if the insights propounded here were taken to heart." *Challenge* contributor Kaushik Basu felt that Sen's writings reveal "work of immense elegance, combining formal logic, welfare economics, and moral philosophy. . . . It has influenced the way one thinks of welfare economics and collective decision-making." A correspondent for *Time International* maintained that Sen tries to make his work understandable because he is a champion of wide dissemination of fact. "Whereas previous Nobel laureates were high priests of markets and monetarism, Sen has given economics a human face," the reporter noted. ". . . His concern is not hedge funds, high finance and speculators who shift billions with the click of a computer mouse, but helping the world's poor. And he sees the media as an ally in that noble task. We could do with more such reminders of an almost forgotten mandate."

A *Business Week* reviewer suggested that Sen "is still moved by the extreme want he witnessed as a youth." At the age of ten in 1943, Sen—the grandson of a college professor—personally witnessed a severe famine in Calcutta that at its height claimed 30,000 lives per week. The starvation was not caused by poor harvests, but by stockpiling and misinformation-and, Sen would later conclude, the absence of elected officials who could be called to task by their constituents. Sen earned his advanced degrees from Trinity College, Cambridge, and his subsequent career as a professor and writer has embraced the real-life lessons he was taught at an impressionable age.

One of Sen's most influential books—and the work that most critics feel won him the Nobel Prize—is *Collective Choice and Social Welfare,* first published in 1970. According to Basu, the book "played a significant role in the juxtaposition of welfare economics and moral philosophy." In this and subsequent works, Sen uses the tools of social choice theory to analyze concepts such as fairness, liberty, and justice. He challenges the notion that wealth automatically "buys" happiness, and that a better gauge of well-being might be that of "extended sympathy." Basu claimed that *Collective Choice and Social Welfare* "became a classic," drawing the attention of "not only economists but also professional philosophers." Social choice theory—the area of microeconomics which examines the relation between social judgments and individual preference—is further explored through the essays collected in *Choice, Welfare, and Measurement.* According to A. B. Atkinson in the *New York Review of Books,* Sen argues that individuals incorporate a much larger pool of information in making choices than had been theretofore acknowledged by economists. The author applies this argument to the question of poverty, an area in which, asserted Atkinson, "Sen has opened up an important new line of inquiry and stimulated a large theoretical literature."

Another of Sen's contributions to economic theory can be found in *Poverty and Famines: An Essay on Entitlement and Deprivation.* In that work, the author challenges the accepted notion that famine is primarily caused by a reduction in the food supply caused by drought or disease. Utilizing data gathered from four major twentieth-century famines in Asia and Africa (including the one he witnessed himself), Sen argues that famine results when changes in the economic system deny or reduce the ability of a proportion of the population to acquire an amount of food necessary to keep alive. Michael Lipton remarked in the *Times Literary Supplement:* "Sen has, at last, imposed a sensible structure on our analysis of these tragic events." *On Poverty and Famines* touches on such longstanding economic questions as the definition of relative poverty and the ethics of economic theories. These same questions enliven Sen's *Resources, Values, and Development,* which was praised by Lipton not only for its clarity and wit, but also for the author's effort to bridge the gap between economic theorizing and ethical behavior in public policy matters. In arguing against laissez-faire or trickle-down theories of managing national economies, Lipton noted, "[Sen] is . . . denying that the injunction 'leave it to the market' is a tolerable, or often even a consistent or comprehensible, guide to economic policy." Cassen concluded: "Massively researched, scrupulously referenced, a share of these papers would be a satisfactory lifetime's achievement for many academics; but they are only a fraction of [Sen's] durable and wide-ranging accomplishments. And they are written with a combination of humanity, rigour, elegance and force that puts him in the most rare and distinguished company."

In *On Ethics and Economics,* the author's efforts to reinsert ethical questions into economic discourse take the forefront. John Broome commented in the *London Review of Books:* "Sen has never acknowledged a boundary between economics and ethics. He brings philosophical arguments to bear where they are needed in economics, and combines them skilfully with formal analysis. He has also used the methods of economics to illuminate questions in philosophy." Sen also contributed two essays to *The Standard of Living,* and these pieces serve as the focus of discussion for the remainder of the book, comprising four commentaries by other economists. In this case, Sen argues for an expanded definition of the standard of living that takes into account both a person's abilities and the opportunities presented by the person's life situation. Sen returns to this idea in his *Inequality Reexamined,* in which he discusses poverty and human welfare as more than an expression of monetary income. David Miller wrote in the *Times Literary Supplement:* "Sen's point is that two people may have the same income, but one of them, say because of a handicap, may have many fewer opportunities to achieve valuable goals. We need to look behind external advantages to see how for different categories of people these translate into real capacities." F. W. Musgrave, who reviewed *Inequality Reexamined* for *Choice,* concluded: "Readers could not expect a better, more comprehensive conceptual basis for examining statistical and empirical studies on inequality."

Development as Freedom was the first major title Sen published in the wake of receiving the Nobel Prize. Considered by some critics to be the author's personal manifesto, *Development as Freedom* argues that "development" cannot be measured merely in terms of industrialization or per capita income—it also must take into account the degree of political freedom citizens command, as well as their individual abilities to make informed choices in all aspects of their lives. "If there is an underlying theme in Sen's work—and it takes up a few chapters here—it is skepticism that money is the measure of all things," wrote Fareed Zakaria in the *New York Times Book Review.* Zakaria added: "Sen recognizes that in most countries higher incomes do produce improvements across most measures of the quality of life. But in looking at the exceptions he forces us to examine the connection between income and well-being, between money and happiness." Cooper stated that *Development as Freedom* "provides a framework for thought rather than a formula for reform. It urges readers to ask what the ultimate aims of development should be, arguing that the appropriate aim is enlarging the capabilities of all human beings. In the process, Sen skillfully emphasizes the many dimensions—including freedom of expression—needed to attain that goal. But he is quietly revolutionary in insisting that we keep our eye on the ultimate objectives rather than on the intervening instrumental variables."

Upon awarding Sen his Nobel Prize, the Swedish Academy of Sciences stated that the scholar had "restored an ethical dimension to the discussion of vital economic problems." Indeed, throughout his work the author emphasizes the influence of economic theory in the everyday lives of real people. Critics have applauded not only his arguments but also the manner in which he relates them. Lipton, for one, remarked: "His discussions . . . demonstrate the agreeable equation that wit plus rigour equals clarity." Others emphasize the breadth of the knowledge that Sen brings to economic theory. In the *London Review of Books* Bernard Williams concluded: "Sen's acute analysis and his remarkable powers of making subtle and relevant distinctions combine with his astonishing range of information to make instruments suitable for immediate political application."

BIOGRAPHICAL/CRITICAL SOURCES:

BOOKS

Basu, Kaushik, and others, editors, *Choice, Welfare, and Development: A Festschrift in Honour of Amartya K. Sen,* Oxford University Press (New York City), 1995.

PERIODICALS

Business Week, September 20, 1999, p. 18.
Challenge, March-April, 1999, p. 41.
Choice, March, 1993, p. 1208.
Economist (US), October 17, 1998, p. 87; January 9, 1999, p. 37; September 18, 1999, p. 8.
Foreign Affairs, January-February, 2000, p. 163.
Journal of Development Studies, October, 1995, p. 155; December, 1996, p. 143; June, 1997, p. 719; April, 1998, p. 156.
London Review of Books, May 23, 1985; May 19, 1988, pp. 16-17; November 18, 1993, pp. 7-8.
New Republic, September 30, 1996, p. 38.
New York Review of Books, July 15, 1982, pp. 24-25; October 22, 1987.
New York Times Book Review, November 28, 1999, p. 14.
Time, October 26, 1998, p. 69.
Time International, October 26, 1998, p. 64.
Times Literary Supplement, March 15, 1982, p. 265; July 26, 1985; November 27, 1987, p. 1314; March 12, 1993, p. 23.*

SENELICK, Laurence P(hilip) 1942-

PERSONAL: Born October 12, 1942, in Chicago, IL; son of Theodore (a purchasing agent) and Evelyn (Marder) Senelick. *Education:* Northwestern University, B.A., 1964; Harvard University, A.M., 1968, Ph.D., 1972. *Avocational interests:* Cooking, collecting.

ADDRESSES: Home—117 Mystic St., West Medford, MA 02155. *Office*—Department of Drama, Tufts University, Medford, MA 02155.

CAREER: Emerson College, Boston, MA, assistant professor of English, 1968-72; Tufts University, Medford, MA, assistant professor, 1972-76, associate professor, 1976-83, professor of drama and oratory, beginning 1987, currently Fletcher Professor of Oratory. Professional actor and director, 1963—; director of Proposition Cabaret, 1968-69, and Summer School Theatre Workshop at Harvard University, 1974-75. Member of Russian Research Center at Harvard University. Member of sub-committee on theatre and dance, ACLS-Soviet Ministry of Culture commission on arts and arts research. Honorary curator of Russian Drama and Theatre, Harvard Theatre Collection, 1991—; McGregor Visiting Scholar/Artist, Wabash College, 1992.

MEMBER: International Federation for Theatre Research, American Society for Theatre Research, Actors' Equity Association, Society for Cultural Relations with the USSR, British Music Hall Society, British Theatre Institute.

AWARDS, HONORS: Woodrow Wilson fellow, 1964 and 1965; grant from National Endowment for the Humanities, 1977; Guggenheim fellow, 1979, 1987; Institute for Advanced Studies (West Berlin) fellow, 1984-85; George Freedley Award, Theatre Library Association, for *Gordon Craig's Moscow Hamlet;* Salzburg Seminar fellow, 1988; National Theatre Translation Fund award, 1993; Bernard Hewitt award from American Society for Theatre Research, 1997, for *The Chekhov Theatre: A Century of the Plays in Performance;* St. George medal from Ministry of Culture, Russia, for service to Russian art and scholarship.

WRITINGS:

(Editor and translator) Anton Chekhov, *The Seagull [and] The Cherry Orchard,* AHM Publishing, 1977.

(With David Brownell) *Tchaikovsky's Sleeping Beauty,* Bellerophon Books (Santa Barbara, CA), 1978.

A Cavalcade of Clowns, Bellerophon Books, 1978.

(Editor and translator) *Russian Dramatic Theory from Pushkin to the Symbolists: An Anthology,* University of Texas Press (Austin), 1981.

(With D. F. Cheshire and Ulrich Schneider) *British Music Hall, 1840-1923,* Shoe String (Hamden, CT), 1981.

Gordon Craig's Moscow Hamlet, Greenwood Press (Westport, CT), 1982.

Dead Souls (two-act play; adapted from the novel by Nikolai Gogol), first produced in Medford, MA, at Tufts University, May, 1982.

Serf Actor: A Biography of Mikhail Shchepkin, Greenwood Press, 1984.

Anton Chekhov, Macmillan/Grove (New York City), 1985.

(With P. Haskell) *The Cheese Book,* Simon & Schuster (New York City), 1985.

(Translator) Klaus Mann, *The Pious Dance,* PAJ Press, 1987.

Humpty Dumpty: The Age and Stage of G. L. Fox, University Press of New England (Hanover, NH), 1988.

Cabaret Performance: Volume 1: *Europe, 1890-1940,* PAJ Press, 1988, Volume 2: *Europe, 1920-1940,* Johns Hopkins University Press (Baltimore, MD), 1992.

(Editor) *National Theatre in Northern and Eastern Europe, 1746-1900,* Cambridge University Press (New York City), 1991.

(Editor) *Wandering Stars: Russian Emigre Theatre, 1905-1940,* University of Iowa Press (Iowa City), 1992.

(Editor) *Gender in Performance: The Presentation of Difference in the Performing Arts,* University Press of New England, 1992.

(Editor and author of notes and introduction) Charles Rice, *Tavern Singing in Early Victorian London: The Diaries of Charles Rice for 1840 and 1850,* Society for Theatre Research (London), 1997.

The Chekhov Theatre: A Century of the Plays in Performance, Cambridge University Press, 1997.

Lovesick: Modernist Plays of Same-Sex Love, 1894-1925, Routledge (New York City), 1999.

The Changing Room: Varieties of Theatrical Cross-Dressing, Routledge, 2000.

Also editor and contributor, *Sources and Documents of Western Theatre,* Volume XII, Cambridge University Press. Contributor to *McGraw-Hill Encyclopedia of World Drama, Oxford Companion to the Theatre, Academic American Encyclopedia, International Encyclopedia of Dance, Cambridge Guide to World Theatre, Cambridge Guide to American Theatre, International*

Dictionary of the Theatre, Journal of the History of Sexuality, and *McGill's Critical Survey of Drama.* Contributor to periodicals, including *Russian Review, New Boston Review, Call Boy, After Dark, History of Photography, Cuisine, Theater, Poetics Today, Theatrephile, American Speech, Nineteenth-Century Theatre Research, Theatre Studies,* and *Theatre Quarterly.* Editor of *Dickens Studies,* 1965-69.

WORK IN PROGRESS: A documentary history of Soviet theatre.

SIDELIGHTS: Theatre critic, playwright, and historian Laurence P. Senelick is especially known for his work on European and Russian stage performances, from the plays of Anton Chekhov to the antics of European cabaret. During his wide-ranging career, Senelick has staged plays and published commentary on them. He has collected and translated cabaret routines and has published several works on aspects of gender and homosexuality in the theatre. He once told *CA:* "It is immensely important to inform one's scholarship and research by practical experience in the field. I maintain an active life as an actor, director, playwright, and screenwriter as an adjunct to my investigations of the theatre of the past. The traffic works both ways: the practical experience illuminates the historical study."

Senelick's two-volume collection of cabaret skits, *Cabaret Performance,* translates cabaret texts from all over Europe. Included are dramatic sketches, songs, monologues, show reviews, and occasional commentaries from audience members, gleaned from memoirs and diaries. To quote Karl Toepfer in *TDR,* Senelick "prefaces each part devoted to a country and each section devoted to an author or performer with brief, suave commentary on cultural and biographical details which distinguish cabaret according to national and personal mechanisms of difference." Toepfer concludes that *Cabaret Performance* is "significant in freeing cabaret from the obfuscating aura of mystique, into which it has been cast by a desire for historical affirmation of a modernist performance mode assumed to be more 'daring' yet 'intimate' than recent decades have allowed it to be."

Lovesick: Modernist Plays of Same-Sex Love, 1894-1925 collects a half dozen plays that deal with homosexuality in the context of the times. The anthology contains four full-length and two one-act dramas, reviews of each show, introductions and notes by Selenick, and—in many cases—pictures of performances. According to M. J. Emery in *Choice,* Selenick's commentary enhances the value of the collection. "To read these supplementary materials is to dive headlong into the legal, historical, ethical, and aesthetic contradictions in which homosexuality swirled a century ago," the critic stated. In *Library Journal,* Howard Miller noted that *Lovesick* "provides a valuable introduction to the history of gay theater" and likewise reveals "an important piece of gay and lesbian history." A reviewer for the *Advocate* called the work a "priceless primer" that offers "an entertaining and enlightening look at the lost vernacular and sordid situations of our queer past."

BIOGRAPHICAL/CRITICAL SOURCES:

PERIODICALS

Advocate, May 25, 1999, p. 106.
Choice, January, 2000, p. 926.
Library Journal, July, 1981, p. 1405; December, 1992, p. 142; March 15, 1999, p. 79.
New York Times Book Review, January 10, 1988, p. 21.
TDR, spring, 1982, p. 143; spring, 1983, p. 117; spring, 1994, p. 171; winter, 1995, p. 193.

* * *

SHACHTMAN, Tom 1942-

PERSONAL: Born February 15, 1942, in New York, NY; *Education:* Tufts University, B.S., 1963; Carnegie-Mellon University, M.F.A., 1966.

ADDRESSES: Home—New York, NY. *Agent*—Mel Berger, William Morris Agency, 1350 Avenue of the Americas, New York, NY 10019.

CAREER: Freelance writer, producer, and director for television, 1966—; author, 1979—. Assistant chief of the television division, National Geographic Society, 1969-70; The Writers Room (a non-profit urban writers' colony), president.

MEMBER: Writers Guild of America, East, PEN, Authors Guild.

AWARDS, HONORS: Shubert fellowship, 1965-66; gold award from Atlanta Film Festival, award from New York International Film Festival, and Golden Gate award from San Francisco Film Festival, all 1972, all for *Children of Poverty;* gold award from Virgin Islands Film Festival, and award from New York International Film Festival, both 1973, both for *Children of Trouble;* gold award from Virgin Islands Film Festival, award from New York International Film Festival, and local Emmy awards, all 1975, all for *Children of Violence;* local Emmy award for *Winning Isn't Everything,* 1977, and for other works.

WRITINGS:

The Coming Forth by Day of Osiris Jones (adapted from poem by Conrad Aiken), first produced in New York City at Actors Experimental Theater, 1971.

(Author of dialogue) Werner Herzog, *Nosferatu* (screenplay; adapted from novel *Dracula* by Bram Stoker), Twentieth-Century Fox, 1979.

The Day America Crashed, Putnam (New York City), 1979.

Edith and Woodrow (nonfiction), Putnam, 1980.

Growing up Masai (juvenile), photographs by Donn Renn, Macmillan, 1981.

The Birdman of St. Petersburg: Ralph T. Heath, Jr. (juvenile), Macmillan, 1982.

The Phony War, 1939-1940, Harper (New York City), 1982.

Decade of Shocks: Dallas to Watergate, 1963-1974, Poseidon Press (New York City), 1983.

Parade! (juvenile), photographs by Chuck Saaf, Macmillan, 1985.

(With Robert J. Lamphere) *The FBI-KGB War: A Special Agent's Story,* Random House (New York City), 1986.

America's Birthday: The Fourth of July (juvenile), photographs by Saaf, Macmillan, 1986.

Beachmaster: A Story of Daniel au Fond (juvenile), illustrated by Jamichael Henterly, Holt (New York City), 1988.

(With Harriet Shelare) *Video Power: A Complete Guide to Writing, Planning, and Shooting Videos,* Holt, 1988.

(With Patrick Reynolds) *The Gilded Leaf: Triumph, Tragedy, and Tobacco: Three Generations of the R. J. Reynolds Family and Fortune,* Little, Brown (Boston, MA), 1989.

Wavebender: A Story of Daniel au Fond (juvenile), illustrated by Henterly, Holt, 1989.

The President Builds a House (juvenile), photographs by Margaret Miller, Simon & Schuster (New York City), 1989.

(With Paul G. Stern) *Straight to the Top: Beyond Loyalty, Gamesmanship, Mentors, and Other Corporate Myths,* Warner Books (New York City), 1990.

(With Clive Chajet) *Image by Design: From Corporate Vision to Business Reality,* Addison-Wesley (Reading, MA), 1991.

Driftwhistler: A Story of Daniel au Fond (juvenile), Holt, 1991.

Skyscraper Dreams: The Great Real Estate Dynasties of New York, Little, Brown, 1991.

(With Robert K. Ressler) *Whoever Fights Monsters: A Brilliant FBI Detective's Career-long War against Serial Killers,* St. Martin's (New York City), 1992.

(With Ressler) *Justice Is Served,* St. Martin's, 1994.

The Inarticulate Society: Eloquence and Culture in America, Free Press (New York City), 1995.

(With Ressler) *I Have Lived in the Monster: A Report from the Abyss,* St. Martin's, 1997.

Around the Block: The Business of a Neighborhood, Harcourt (New York City), 1997.

The Most Beautiful Villages of New England, photographs by Len Rubenstein, Thames & Hudson (New York City), 1997.

Absolute Zero and the Conquest of Cold, Houghton (Boston, MA), 1999.

Also author of one-act plays. Contributor of articles to newspapers and magazines.

TELEVISION SCRIPTS

The Twenty-First Century, Columbia Broadcasting System, Inc. (CBS-TV), 1966-69.

The Everglades, American Broadcasting Companies, Inc. (ABC-TV), 1970.

Discovery, ABC-TV, 1970-71.

NBC Reports, National Broadcasting Company, Inc. (NBC-TV), 1971.

Children of Poverty (trilogy; includes *Children of Poverty, Children of Trouble,* and *Children of Violence),* 1972-75.

Broken Treaty at Battle Mountain, Public Broadcasting Service (PBS-TV), 1973.

The Masks We Wear, ABC-TV, 1973.

Rainbow Sundae, ABC-TV, 1973-75.

Sixty Minutes, CBS-TV, 1974.

The Last Frontier, syndicated, 1975.

Decades of Decision, PBS-TV, 1976.

We Are about Caring, Capital Cities stations, 1976.

The Entrepreneurs, syndicated, 1988.

WORK IN PROGRESS: Wizards at War: The Use and Abuse of Science and Technology in World War II, for Avon/Morrow, to be published in 2001.

SIDELIGHTS: Tom Shachtman once told *CA:* "A style and feeling for audience given me by a dozen years' work in documentaries for television has been carried over into my nonfiction books." A respected television writer and producer, Shachtman has also written "two dozen books on a wide range of topics for readers of all ages," to quote David Rouse in *Booklist.* Rouse added: "Mostly biographies and chronological narratives, [Shachtman's] works have proven to be both entertaining and informative." The author is equally at home with arctic seals and New York skyscrapers, with Woodrow Wilson and the troubled heirs of the R. J. Reynolds tobacco fortune, and with former high-ranking officials in the CIA and FBI who want their stories told.

One of Shachtman's early books, *The Day America Crashed,* reconstructs events across America on October 24, 1929, the day of the first large stock market crash. By looking at the day's range of activity in such detail, wrote Christopher Lehmann-Haupt in the *New York Times,* Shachtman "is able to convey the profound and extensive sense of shock that altered the prevailing psychology of the times, which in turn may have contributed as much to the coming of the Depression as actual economic conditions did."

Throughout his career, Shachtman has teamed with various individuals who have used his writing expertise to help craft their stories. Notable among these people are Robert J. Lamphere, a cold war-era CIA agent, Patrick Reynolds, a younger-generation member of the R. J. Reynolds tobacco dynasty, and Robert K. Ressler, the FBI agent who coined the term "serial killer" and helped to track down some of the notorious murderers himself. Lamphere's tale, *The FBI-KGB War: A Special Agent's Story,* was described as "interesting and highly readable" by *New Republic* contributor Ronald Radosh. The critic concluded that the book "is an eye-opener. [Lamphere] has laid bare the antecedents of today's spy cases and showed something of the scope and strength of Soviet espionage." Shachtman completed three books with Ressler, including *I Have Lived in the Monster: A Report from the Abyss.* Citing the work for its "crisp and well paced" writing, Christine A. Moesch noted in *Library Journal:* "Especially harrowing are [Ressler's] interviews with John Wayne Gacy and Jeffrey Dahmer. An absolutely chilling look at the evil that is the mind of a serial killer." *Booklist* correspondent Mike Tribby declared *I Have Lived in the Monster* "well written [and] scary without quite being gruesome," adding that the book "would do any true-crime collection proud." In a *Publishers Weekly* review of the Shachtman-Ressler collaboration *Whoever Fights Monsters: A Brilliant FBI Detective's Career-long War against Serial Killers,* a critic stated: "[Ressler's] quest-catching and understanding criminals-absorbs and unsettles the reader, placing true crime in the real world." The Ressler-Shachtman books have sold several million copies in Japan and throughout the world in translation.

The Gilded Leaf: Triumph, Tragedy, and Tobacco: Three Generations of the R. J. Reynolds Family and Fortune grew out of a collaboration between Shachtman and Patrick Reynolds, a grandson of the founder of the R. J. Reynolds empire. The book details numerous cancer deaths and scandals—including an unsolved shooting—that have marked the Reynolds family since the turn of the century. "Many in the Reynolds clan probably will hope that *The Gilded Leaf* disappears in a puff of cigarette smoke," suggested Andrea Cooper in the *New York Times Book Review.* Cooper went on to call *The Gilded Leaf* "a courageous and worthwhile book. More than an entertainment, it documents the danger of parents who confuse money with love."

A native of New York City, Shachtman has written about Manhattan in many documentaries and in two of his books, *Skyscraper Dreams: The Great Real Estate Dynasties of New York* and *Around the Block: The Business of a Neighborhood. Skyscraper Dreams* gives profiles of the entrepreneurs who shaped Manhattan's skyline and a history of the buildings themselves. "Mr. Shachtman has done an enormous amount of research, and the story of how Manhattan was built is a fascinating one," wrote Jeff Kisseloff in the *New York Times Book Review.* Kisseloff felt that Shachtman tended to portray the real estate barons in an overly positive light. "Mr. Shachtman wants us to like the subjects of his book," the critic concluded. "But more often than not the members of the great real estate dynasties come off as remarkably calculating and self-centered." Larry Light for *Business Week* called the book "a fascinating history, showing how the city has been molded by the edifice complexes of risk-takers. . . . Shachtman ably sketches the rise and fall of these family empires. . . . The feuds of these real estate kingpins are the stuff of grand comedy . . . wonderful fun."

Around the Block sheds light on the business, educational, and residential aspects of life in one square block area of downtown New York, where the businesses range from Cahners Publishing Company to an independent video rental store and a plumbing supply shop. In the *Economist,* a reviewer deemed the work "the sort of business book that is published too rarely. . . . Its subject goes to the heart of modern American business—and in the process tells you more about social conflicts, immigration, education, and, indeed, America itself than countless loftier works." The reviewer went on to call *Around the Block* a "near classic" and "one of the best descriptions of American business in microcosm to come out of the 1990s." A reviewer for the *New Yorker* wrote that the book is "a grand idea, splendidly executed."

Shachtman's *The Inarticulate Society: Eloquence and Culture in America* examines the debasement of America's verbal currency, citing television, popular music, and even political debate as areas in which language has suffered severe devaluation. In the *National Review,* Tracy Lee Simmons maintained: "Mr. Shachtman argues here [that] the primacy of the word in American culture has been replaced by the reign of the visual image, which has diverted even the more judicious among us from attending to words and their meanings." The critic added: "Mr. Shachtman guesses that, in our rush from a word-guided world, we are becoming a culture fueled by emotion rather than thought." *New York Times* columnist Michiko Kakutani faulted the book for its "pretentious assertions, condescending remarks and out-and-out lapses of logic," but she nevertheless observed that Shachtman "raises many valid questions and makes a few astute observations." *Insight on the News* contributor Peter A. Jay found the book a "readable jeremiad," clearly demonstrating that ". . . precise and eloquent language is under attack from all sides." "The book's *piece de resistance* is Mr. Shachtman's sardonic tracing of the decline and fall of TV news, and how it has destroyed eloquence. . . . He coins a sharp phrase when he calls for a 'revolt of the articulate masses,' " wrote Florence King for the *Wall Street Journal.*

Shachtman delves into the realm of science in his book *Absolute Zero and the Conquest of Cold.* The book charts the history of scientific research into cooling, from the Middle Ages to the present, offering brief biographies of some of the important inventors in the field of temperature measurement, refrigeration, and supercooling. According to Simon Singh in the *New York Times Book Review,* the work "analyzes the social impact of the chill factor, explains the science of cold and tells the curious tales behind inventions like the thermometer, the fridge and the thermos flask." The critic continued: "Shachtman, who has written books about a wide variety of subjects, recounts the history of cold with passion and clarity. . . . Shachtman argues that the science of cold, which has so much influenced [the twentieth] century, will continue to revolutionize technology well into the next." To quote a *Publishers Weekly* reviewer, "Shachtman's book comes alive in his highly technical descriptions of the unique and wondrous properties of materials at only a few degrees above absolute zero." And in *Booklist,* Gilbert Taylor sums the title as "an absorbing account to chill out with." Mark Prendergrast for the *Atlanta Journal-Constitution* described *Absolute Zero* as ". . . masterfully told. In many ways an absolute delight, chock-full of quirky characters questing for ever-lower temperatures and discovering fundamental properties of matter along the way. Shachtman has achieved an enormous feat, combining science, biography, and analysis into a compelling narrative full of explosions, obsessed experimentalists and unexpected revelations delivered from a region so cold that no human could survive a single second there."

In addition to his numerous adult books, Shachtman has written books for children, all of them about a sea lion in the Pacific Northwest. In *Beachmaster: A Story of Daniel au Fond, Wavebender: A Story of Daniel au Fond,* and *Driftwhistler: A Story of Daniel au Fond,* Shachtman offers realistic adventures for the adolescent sea lion and his companions. However, the author does allow the sea lion to communicate in speech and thought that is recognizable to young readers. In a *New York Times Book Review* piece on *Beachmaster,* Meg Wolitzer commended Shachtman for making "a clear moral distinction between the violence done to sea creatures by man and the violent struggles among sea creatures that play a large part of life in the ocean." Wolitzer concluded: "Readers will finish the novel with an understanding of the crucial difference between sport and survival. Like the ocean itself, the story is full of life."

BIOGRAPHICAL/CRITICAL SOURCES:

PERIODICALS

Atlanta Journal-Constitution, December 12, 1999, Mark Prendergrast, review of *Absolute Zero.*

Booklist, May 15, 1992, p. 1650; June 1, 1995, p. 1703; May 1, 1997, p. 1466; September 15, 1997, p. 188; November 1, 1999, p. 495.

Business Week, Larry Light, "Skyscraper Dreams," October 7, 1991, p. 18.

Christian Century, May 20, 1981, p. 41; January 25, 1984, p. 84.

Commentary, November, 1986, p. 83.

Dallas Morning News, May 6, 1979.

Economist, December 13, 1997, p. S8.

Foreign Affairs, winter, 1986, p. 400.

Insight on the News, August 14, 1995, p. 25.

Journal of American History, September, 1987, p. 558.

Horn Book, January-February, 1986, p. 72.

Library Journal, June 1, 1986, p. 128; April 1, 1989, p. 97; May 15, 1991, p. 90; July, 1991, p. 111; June 1, 1992, p. 150; May 15, 1997, p. 87; September 15, 1997, p. 84.

Los Angeles Times, May 17, 1979.
National Review, February 12, 1996, p. 55.
New Republic, September 8, 1986, p. 38.
New Yorker, December 1, 1997, review of *Around the Block.*
New York Times, March 26, 1979; July 14, 1995, p. B8; December 1, 1997, p. B6.
New York Times Book Review, March 8, 1981, p. 7; April 26, 1981, p. 56; April 16, 1989, p. 26; August 20, 1989, p. 21; August 25, 1991, p. 15; November 30, 1997, p. 19; December 12, 1999, p. 30.
Publishers Weekly, February 13, 1981, p. 84; March 10, 1989, p. 70; March 9, 1990, p. 55; March 8, 1991, p. 62; May 31, 1991, p. 65; March 30, 1992, p. 93; May 29, 1995, p. 76; May 23, 1986, p. 93; December 6, 1999, p. 67.
School Library Journal, November, 1985, p. 91; December, 1988, p. 112; September, 1989, p. 268; February, 1992, p. 89.
Wall Street Journal, July 31, 1995, Florence King, review of *The Inarticulate Society,* p. A12.
Washington Monthly, September, 1989, p. 58.

* * *

SHAEVITZ, Marjorie Hansen 1943-

PERSONAL: Born May 22, 1943, in Fresno, CA; daughter of Robert Vedsted and Evelyn (Beck) Hansen; married Morton H. Shaevitz (a psychologist and writer), March 11, 1972; children: Geoffrey Hansen, Marejka Hansen. *Education:* Fresno State College (now California State University, Fresno), B.A., 1964; Stanford University, M.A., 1967; participated in student exchange at Keio University, Tokyo, 1967.

ADDRESSES: Home—La Jolla, CA. *Office*—c/o Institute for Family and Work Relationships, 1020 Prospect, Suite 400, La Jolla, CA 92037. *Agent*—Sandy Dijkstra, Dijkstra Agency, 1155 Camino del Mar, Del Mar, CA 92014.

CAREER: East-West Center, Honolulu, HI, orientation officer, 1967-68; University of California, San Diego, La Jolla, instructor in disadvantaged employee development program, 1970, director of counseling and registration services, 1970-73, coordinator of adult vocational counseling program, 1971-76, and Extension Study Skills Institute, 1976-78, director of Programs for Mental Health Professionals, 1973-78; Institute for Family and Work Relationships, La Jolla, co-director, beginning in 1977. Women in Transition, director, 1970-73; California Commission on the Status of Women, gubernatorial appointee, 1984-99; Stanford University, Institute for Research on Women and Gender, chairperson of national advisory panel, 1992—; California Office of Women's Health, gubernatorial appointee on advisory board, 1994—; California Medical Association Board, member of board, 1994—; psychotherapist in private counseling practice; executive coach; public speaker; guest on local and national radio and television programs.

MEMBER: American Psychological Association (associate member), American Personnel and Guidance Association, National Council on Family Relations, California State Personnel and Guidance Association, California Association of Marriage and Family Counselors, California State Psychological Association, La Jolla Farms Community Association (co-president, 1977-78), Charter One Hundred.

WRITINGS:

(With Eleanor Lenz) *So You Want to Go Back to School: Facing the Realities of Re-Entry,* McGraw (New York City), 1977.
(With husband, Morton H. Shaevitz) *Making It Together as a Two-Career Couple,* Houghton (Boston, MA), 1980.
The Superwoman Syndrome, male responses by M. H. Shaevitz, Warner Books (New York City), 1984.
The Confident Woman: Learn the Rules of the Game, Harmony Books (New York City), 1999.

Creator of audio cassettes, including (with M. H. Shaevitz) *The Confident Woman: Asserting Yourself at Work, Love, and Play,* released by Nightingale-Conant Corp. (Chicago, IL), 1989. Contributor to professional journals and local magazines.

WORK IN PROGRESS: Research on couple relationships, family systems, and two-career couples in business.

SIDELIGHTS: Marjorie Hansen Shaevitz told *CA:* "My practice is focused on executive women's leadership skills and to develop health and well-being programs. Also, I work with high school students on choosing and gaining acceptance to college/university, planning for careers, and developing a program for increasing their study skills effectiveness. In association with my husband, I work with couples in dealing more effectively with marital issues, dual-career stresses, and other family systems problems."

BIOGRAPHICAL/CRITICAL SOURCES:

PERIODICALS

DIY Retailing, March, 1985, p. 179.
Isabella, spring, 2000, vol. 2, p. 14.
Library Journal, November 15, 1984, p. 2158.
Ms., March, 1985, p. 88.
People Weekly, February 18, 1985, p. 22.
Publishers Weekly, October 11, 1985, p. 63.
San Diego Magazine, May, 2000, p. 38.
Working Woman, April, 1984, p. 108; November, 1984, p. 124.

OTHER

Women First—The Confident Woman, http://www.womenfirst.com/ (June 19, 2000).

* * *

SHEAHAN, John (B.) 1923-

PERSONAL: Born September 11, 1923, in Toledo, OH; son of Bernard William (an engineer) and Florence (Sheahan) Sheahan; married Denise Eugenie Morlino (a social worker); children: Yvette Marie, Bernard Eugene. *Education:* Stanford University, B.A., 1948; Harvard University, Ph.D., 1954. *Politics:* Democrat.

ADDRESSES: Home—P. O. Box 751, Williamstown, MA 01267. *Office*—c/o Department of Economics, Williams College, Williamstown, MA 01267.

CAREER: U.S. Economic Cooperation Administration, economic analyst in Paris, France, 1951-54; Williams College, Williamstown, MA, faculty member, beginning in 1954, professor of economics, beginning in 1966. Brookings Institution, national research professor, 1959-60; El Colegio de Mexico, visiting professor, 1970-71; Universite de Grenoble, France, Fulbright research professor, 1974-75. Harvard University, economic adviser to Development Advisory Service, Bogota, Colombia, 1963-65; Center for U.S.-Mexican Studies, University of California at San Diego, visiting research fellow, 1991. *Military service:* U.S. Army, 1943-46; received Purple Heart.

MEMBER: Latin American Studies Association.

WRITINGS:

Promotion and Control of Industry in Postwar France, Harvard University Press (Cambridge, MA), 1963.
The Wage-Price Guideposts, Brookings Institution (Washington, DC), 1967.
An Introduction to the French Economy, C. E. Merrill (Columbus, OH), 1969.
Aspects of Planning and Development in Colombia, Office for Public Sector Studies, Institute of Latin American Studies, University of Texas at Austin, 1977.
Alternative International Economic Strategies and Their Relevance for China, World Bank (Washington, DC), 1986.
Patterns of Development in Latin America: Poverty, Repression, and Economic Strategy, Princeton University Press (Princeton, NJ), 1987.
Searching for a Better Society: The Peruvian Economy from 1950, Pennsylvania State University Press (University Park, PA), 1999.

Contributor to professional journals in the United States, Colombia, and France.

SIDELIGHTS: John Sheahan is competent in French and Spanish and is also an economic advisor and consultant for China, South Korea, Sri Lanka, Thailand, and the Federated States of Micronesia.

BIOGRAPHICAL/CRITICAL SOURCES:

PERIODICALS

Annals of the American Academy of Political and Social Science, 1989, p. 156.
Choice, November, 1999, p. 590.
Economic Development and Cultural Change, October, 1989, p. 207.
Foreign Affairs, spring, 1988, p. 878.
Journal of Development Studies, January, 1990, p. 367.
Journal of Economic Literature, March, 1989, p. 100.
Nation's Business, February, 1980, p. 16.

* * *

SHELDRAKE, Rupert 1942-

PERSONAL: Born June 28, 1942, in Newark, England; son of Reginald (a pharmacist) and Doris (Tebbutt) Sheldrake; married Jill Purce (a writer), December 21, 1985; children: Merlin. *Education:* Clare College, Cambridge, B.A., 1963, M.A., 1967, Ph.D., 1968; graduate study at Harvard University, 1963-64; also studied at Royal Society—University of Malaya, 1968. *Politics:* "Green." *Religion:* Anglican.

ADDRESSES: Agent—John Brockman, John Brockman Associates Inc., 2307 Broadway, New York, NY 10024.

CAREER: Clare College, Cambridge University, Cambridge, England, research fellow and director of studies in biochemistry, 1968-73; International Crops Research Institute for the Semi-Arid Tropics, Hyderabad, India, principal plant physiologist, 1974-78, consultant physiologist, 1981-85; writer in India and England, 1978-81; writer and lecturer in Great Britain, Canada, United States, and Western Europe, 1985—.

AWARDS, HONORS: Botany prize from Cambridge University, 1963; Frank Knox Fellow, Harvard University, 1964; Rosenheim research fellowship from the Royal Society, 1973; Book of the Year Award, British Institute for Social Inventions, 1994, for *Seven Experiments That Could Change the World.*

WRITINGS:

(With Satya Pal Yadav and James G. Ryan) *Human Nutritional Needs and Crop Breeding Objectives in the Semi-Arid Tropics: A Further Note,* International Crops Research Institute for the Semi-Arid Tropics (Andhra Pradesh, India), 1974.

A New Science of Life: The Hypothesis of Formative Causation, Blond & Briggs, 1981, new edition, Anthony Blond, 1985, Park Street Press (Rochester, VT), 1995.

The Presence of the Past: Morphic Resonance and the Habits of Nature, Times Books (New York City), 1988.

The Rebirth of Nature: The Greening of Science and God, Bantam (New York City), 1990.

(With Ralph Abraham and Terence McKenna) *Trialogues at the Edge of the West: Chaos, Creativity, and the Resacralization of the World,* Bear & Co (Santa Fe, NM), 1992.

Seven Experiments That Could Change the World: A Do-It-Yourself Guide to Revolutionary Science, Riverhead Books (New York City), 1995.

(With Matthew Fox) *Natural Grace: Dialogues on Creation, Darkness, and the Soul in Spirituality and Science,* Doubleday (Garden City, NY), 1996.

(With Fox) *The Physics of Angels: Exploring the Realm Where Science and Spirit Meet,* Harper (San Francisco), 1996.

(With Abraham and McKenna) *The Evolutionary Mind: Trialogues at the Edge of the Unthinkable,* Dakota Books (Santa Cruz, CA), 1997.

Dogs That Know When Their Owners Are Coming Home: And Other Unexplained Powers of Animals, Crown (New York City), 1999.

SIDELIGHTS: Rupert Sheldrake's theory of formative causation proposes to explain how life forms of the past influence emerging life forms and how these new forms, in turn, influence the patterns of future life. Described by Paul Raeburn in *Psychology Today* as a "masterful storyteller" who "bolsters his contentions with a dazzling collection of observations drawn from all fields of science," Sheldrake introduced his theory in *A New Science of Life: The Hypothesis of Formative Causation* and later elaborated upon it in *The Presence of the Past: Morphic Resonance and the Habits of Nature.* Formative causation asserts that new organisms achieve form through the help of ancestral blueprints, which are contained in "morphogenetic fields" ("morphogenetic" comes from the Greek *morphe,* meaning "form," and *genesis,* meaning "origin" or "coming into being"). Morphogenetic fields contain an inherent memory dependent on "morphic resonance," a transfer of information from previous organisms to subsequent similar organisms through time and space. Sheldrake believes that this form of communication explains why newly synthesized chemical compounds initially take much longer to crystallize than later crystals of the same compound, and why today's rats have been tested to have a much easier time finding their way through mazes than did their ancestors. Put simply, Sheldrake claims it is easier to do something after someone or something has done it before.

Sheldrake and Matthew Fox—an Episcopalian priest and radical theologian—produced a pair of books that provide a dialogue between science and religion. *The Physics of Angels: Exploring the Realm Where Science and Spirit Meet* discusses heavenly beings, drawing on the writings of Thomas Aquinas, Hildegard of Bingen, and others. In *Natural Grace: Dialogues on Creation, Darkness, and the Soul in Spirituality and Science,* Sheldrake and Fox argue that the barriers between science and religion must be broken down, and that mankind must take a more spiritual view of science and a more flexible view of religion. According to Donna Seaman in *Booklist,* the dialogues are "cogent and passionate," and "will inspire fresh perspectives and continued discussion."

Sheldrake returned to his ideas of morphic fields in his 1999 book *Dogs That Know When Their Owners Are Coming Home: And Other Unexplained Powers of Animals.* The book is full of amazing animal anecdotes, including stories about cats who have found their way back to their owners even when separated by hundreds of miles, birds who sensed imminent bomb attacks, and animals who respond to the ringing of the telephone only when specific people are calling. Sheldrake believes animals have many psychic powers that humans have lost, and he theorizes that morphic fields act as a channel for these extrasensory powers. His writings are based on five years of research and interviews with animal handlers. Numerous reviewers declared that the book was good reading, even for readers who did not share Sheldrake's beliefs. *Library Journal* reviewer Peggie Partello noted, "His conclusions may cause you to be surprised, dismayed, or disbelieving, but you will never be bored." Nancy Bent concurred in *Booklist,* "Whether or not the reader believes in the psychic abilities of animals, all will be fascinated by the weight of the evidence and by Sheldrake's clear commentary." And a *Publishers Weekly* writer enthused: "Skeptics may scoff, yet the cumulative weight of evidence Sheldrake assembles is impressive. . . . This pioneering study throws a floodlight on an area largely ignored by institutional science."

Sheldrake once told *CA:* "I believe that we are standing on the threshold of a major scientific revolution—a change from the mechanist notion of the world as an inanimate machine to the holistic paradigm of nature as a living organism. My books are a contribution to this process of change."

BIOGRAPHICAL/CRITICAL SOURCES:

PERIODICALS

America, March 2, 1991, p. 246.
Booklist, September 1, 1995, p. 23; June 1, 1996, Donna Seaman, review of *Natural Grace,* p. 1639; September 15, 1999, Nancy Bent, review of *Dogs That Know When Their Owners Are Coming Home,* p. 196.
Commonweal, June 18, 1982, p. 356.
Esquire, May, 1985, p. 82.
Fate, May, 1983, p. 72; March, 1984, p. 7.
Lancet, April 9, 1994, p. 905.
Library Journal, May 15, 1982, p. 1002; February 1, 1983, p. 190; March 1, 1988, p. 73; December, 1990, p. 156; November 1, 1993, p. 167; August, 1995, p. 112; October 1, 1999, Peggie Partello, review of *Dogs That Know When Their Owners Are Coming Home,* p. 125.
National Review, June 14, 1985, p. 50; June 28, 1985, p. 49.
Nature, September, 1981.
New Realities, July, 1982, p. 38; December, 1983, p. 8.
New Scientist, July 21, 1988.
New Statesman, June 3, 1988, p. 26.
New Statesman & Society, June 10, 1994, p. 39; July 22, 1994, p. 39.
Newsweek, July 7, 1986, p. 64.
Psychology Today, June, 1988; July, 1988, p. 77.
Publishers Weekly, December 18, 1987, p. 49; November 9, 1990, p. 48; June 26, 1995, p. 94; July 29, 1996, review of *The Physics of Angels,* p. 84; August 9, 1999, review of *No Dumb Bunnies Here,* p. 233, review of *Dogs That Know When Their Owners Are Coming Home,* p. 329.
Science Digest, February, 1983, p. 94.
Times (London), April 7, 1988; December 3, 1990, p. 106.
Times Educational Supplement, June 3, 1983; May 12, 1995.
Times Higher Educational Supplement, May 5, 1995.
Times Literary Supplement, March 12, 1982; June 24-30, 1988.
Washington Post Book World, April 3, 1988.*

* * *

SHORT, Philip 1945-

PERSONAL: Born April 17, 1945, in Bristol, England; son of Wilfred (a teacher) and Marion (Edgar) Short; married Christine Victoria Baring-Gould, August 9, 1968; children: Sengan. *Education:* Queen's College, Cambridge, B.A., 1966, M.A., 1968.

ADDRESSES: Office—c/o Lloyds Bank, 20 Badminton Rd., Dowend, Bristol, England. *Agent*—David Higham Associates Ltd., 5/8 Lower John St., Golden Sq., London W1R 4HA, England.

CAREER: Freelance correspondent from Malawi, 1967-70, and Uganda, 1971-73; British Broadcasting Corp., London, correspondent from Moscow, Soviet Union, 1974-76, and Peking, China, beginning in 1977.

WRITINGS:

Banda, Routledge & Kegan Paul (London, England), 1974.
The Dragon, the Bear, and the Future of the West, Hodder & Stoughton (London), 1981, published as *The Dragon and the Bear: Inside China and Russia Today,* 1982, published as *The Dragon and the Bear: China and Russia in the Eighties,* Morrow (New York City), 1982.
Mao, a Life, Holt (New York City), 2000.

BIOGRAPHICAL/CRITICAL SOURCES:

PERIODICALS

American Legion, February, 1983, p. 114.
Foreign Affairs, spring, 1983, p. 986.
New York Times Book Review, February 6, 1983, p. 7; June 12, 1983, p. 24.
Publishers Weekly, November 26, 1982, p. 51; November 15, 1999, p. 49.*

* * *

SIDER, Ronald J(ames) 1939-

PERSONAL: Born September 17, 1939, in Stevensville, Ontario, Canada; immigrated to the United States, 1962; naturalized citizen, 1974; son of James Peter (a minister) and Ida (Cline) Sider; married Arbutus Lichti, August 19, 1961; children: Theodore Ronald, Michael Jay, Sonya Maria. *Education:* Waterloo University, B.A. (with honors), 1962; Yale University, M.A., 1963, B.D., 1967, Ph.D., 1969.

ADDRESSES: Home—312 West Logan St., Philadelphia, PA 19144. *Office*—Department of Theology, Eastern Baptist Theological Seminary, 10 East Lancaster Ave., Wynnewood, PA 19096.

CAREER: Messiah College, Philadelphia, PA, instructor, 1968-70, assistant professor, 1970-74, associate professor of history and religion, 1974-78, dean, 1971-75; Eastern Baptist Theological Seminary, Philadelphia, associate professor, 1978-84, professor of theology and culture, 1984—. National Workshop on Race and Reconciliation, co-chairperson, 1975. Member of board of directors, Mennonite Central Committee, 1978-80, and Bread for the World, 1978-84.

MEMBER: World Evangelical Fellowship (convenor of unit on ethics and society, 1978-87), National Association of Evangelicals, Evangelicals for Social Action (member of board of directors, 1973; chairperson of board of directors, 1973-87; executive director, 1987-92; president, 1993—).

AWARDS, HONORS: Fellow of Institute for Advanced Christian Studies, 1976; award for Distinguished Christian Service in Social Welfare, North American Association of Christians in Social Work, 1990; *Rich Christians in an Age of Hunger* named one of the "top 100 most influential religious works of the twentieth century" by *Christianity Today;* Faithful Servant Award, NAE Social Action Committee, 2000. Honorary D.Div., Westminster College, 1998.

WRITINGS:

Andreas Bodenstein von Karlstadt: The Development of His Thought, 1517-1525, E. J. Brill, 1974.
(Editor and contributor) *The Chicago Declaration,* Creation House (Carol Stream, IL), 1974.
Rich Christians in an Age of Hunger: A Biblical Study, Inter-Varsity Press (Downers Grove, IL), 1977, 20th anniversary revision, 1997.
Evangelism, Salvation, and Social Justice, Grove (New York City), 1977.
(Editor) *Karlstadt's Battle with Luther: Documents in a Liberal-Radical Debate,* Fortress (Philadelphia), 1978.
Christ and Violence, Herald Press (Scottsdale, PA), 1979.
(Editor) *Cry Justice: The Bible on Hunger and Poverty,* Paulist Press (New York City), 1980.
(Editor) *Living More Simply: Biblical Principles and Practical Models,* Inter-Varsity Press, 1980.
(Editor) *Evangelicals and Development: Toward a Theology of Social Change,* Paternoster Press (Exeter, England), 1981, Westminster (Philadelphia), 1982.
(Editor) *Lifestyle in the Eighties: An Evangelical Commitment to Simple Lifestyle,* Westminster, 1982.
(Editor with Darrel Brubaker) *Preaching on Peace,* Fortress (Philadelphia), 1982.
(With Richard K. Taylor) *Nuclear Holocaust and Christian Hope,* Inter-Varsity Press, 1982, published as *Nuclear Holocaust and Christian Hope: A Book for Christian Peacemakers,* Paulist Press, 1983.
(With Oliver O'Donovan) *Peace and War: A Debate about Pacifism,* Grove Books, 1985.
Evangelical Faith and Social Ethics (in Chinese), China Graduate School of Theology (Hong Kong), 1986.
Completely Pro-Life: Building a Consistent Stance, Inter-Varsity Press, 1987.
(With Michael A. King) *Preaching about Life in a Threatening World,* Westminster, 1988.
(With Kathleen Hayes) *JustLife/88: A 1988 Election Study Guide for Justice, Life, and Peace,* Eerdmans (Grand Rapids, MI), 1988.
Testing the Limits of Nonviolence, Hodder & Stoughton, 1988, published as *Non-Violence: The Invincible Weapon?,* Word, 1989.
One-Sided Christianity?: Uniting the Church to Heal a Lost and Broken World, Zondervan (Grand Rap-

ids, MI), 1993, published as *Good News and Good Works: A Theology for the Whole Gospel,* Baker Books (Grand Rapids, MI), 1999.

(Editor with Herbert Scholssberg and Vinay Samuel) *Christianity and Economics in the Post-Cold War Era: The Oxford Declaration and Beyond,* Eerdmans, 1994.

Cup of Water, Bread of Life: Inspiring Stories about Overcoming Lopsided Christianity, Zondervan (Grand Rapids, MI), 1994.

Genuine Christianity, Zondervan, 1996.

(Editor) *For They Shall Be Fed: Scripture Readings and Prayers for a Just World,* Word (Dallas, TX), 1997.

Just Generosity: A New Vision for Overcoming Poverty in America, Baker Books, 1999.

Living like Jesus: Eleven Essentials for Growing a Genuine Faith, Baker Books, 1999.

Contributor to numerous books, including *The Urban Mission,* edited by Craig Ellison, Eerdmans, 1974; *Evangelicalism and Anabaptism,* edited by C. Norman Kraus, Herald Press, 1979; *Sharing Jesus in the Two Thirds World,* edited by Vinay Samuel and Chris Sugden, Partnership in Mission, 1983, Eerdmans, 1985; and *Freedom and Discipleship: Liberation Theology in an Anabaptist Perspective,* edited by Daniel S. Schipani, Orbis Books, 1989. Contributor to *Baker's Dictionary of Christian Ethics.* Contributor to theology journals, including *Christianity Today, Christian Century,* and *New Testament Studies.* Co-editor, *Transformation: An International Dialogue on Evangelical Social Ethics,* 1984-2000; contributing editor, *Christianity Today* and *Sojourners;* publisher, *PRISM* and *Creation Care.*

SIDELIGHTS: Ronald J. Sider has written numerous books on social justice and various aspects of Christianity. In *Cup of Water, Bread of Life: Inspiring Stories about Overcoming Lopsided Christianity,* he opens a discussion of the best way to bear wholistic Christian witness—that is, to meet both the spiritual and the physical needs of people. The book is not a "how-to" manual, but a collection of ten stories about church-based, wholistic ministries in various parts of the world. Half focus on work in inner cities in the United States and the United Kingdom; the other half concern work in undeveloped countries. Sider has considerable practical experience in the field, as he worked extensively in an inner city ministry in Philadelphia for ten years. In the introduction to *Cup of Water,* he "courageously admits that his own efforts . . . flopped after a decade of hard work," notes Amy L. Sherman in *Christian Century.* "He seeks to encourage readers for whom the success stories in this volume are painful reminders of their own frustrating failures in similar efforts. This adds an important element of reality to the book. Indeed, one wishes that Sider had devoted a chapter to his efforts in Philadelphia, chronicling the lessons he learned in the process. . . . this is a valuable resource for Christians eager to imitate Jesus' way of ministry—one that neglected neither spiritual nor material needs."

In *Just Generosity: A New Vision for Overcoming Poverty in America,* Sider offers practical and spiritual balms for the woes of the nation's poor. "With impressive thoroughness, he demonstrates that both Old and New Testaments enjoin believers to help the poor become productive members of society and to use public as well as private resources to do so," informs *Booklist* reviewer Ray Olson. Some of his practical suggestions include increasing the Earned Income Tax Credit, the minimum wage, and the food stamp program. He emphasizes, however, that such changes must be supported by work to meet the spiritual needs of the needy. "Many readers will find his discussion insightful and his proposals for change resonant," assured Leroy Homerding in *Library Journal.* In the opinion of a *Publishers Weekly* contributor, "Sider is more prophet than politician but by basing his policy arguments on something more than political expediency, he makes the somewhat tired idea of Christian politics seem plausible, even exciting, again."

Sider once told *CA:* "I love tennis, jog to stay in shape, and try desperately to kindly decline many speaking invitations in order to stay home with my family. Discipleship begins at home. So does peace and reconciliation. It is a farce to write and speak about peace, love, and justice unless, by God's grace, it is becoming a reality in one's own home and church."

BIOGRAPHICAL/CRITICAL SOURCES:

PERIODICALS

Booklist, October 1, 1999, Ray Olson and Gilbert Taylor, review of *Just Generosity,* p. 313.

Buzz, February, 1979.

Christian Century, July 16, 1980, p. 738; November 10, 1980, p. 1131; January 26, 1983, p. 74; February 15, 1984, p. 174; May 3, 1995, Amy L. Sherman, review of *Cup of Water, Bread of Life,* p. 491.

Christianity Today, June 17, 1983, p. 58; July 10, 1987, pp. 46, 48; October 21, 1988, p. 55; March 19, 1990, p. 62; April 27, 1992; April, 2000.

Eternity, April, 1979.

Human Rights Quarterly, May, 1995, Terry Coonan, review of *Christianity and Economics in the Post-Cold War Era,* pp. 403-405.
Library Journal, August, 1980, p. 1646; September 1, 1999, Leroy Homerding, review of *Just Generosity,* p. 199.
National Catholic Reporter, March 18, 1983, p. 13; October 7, 1983, p. 21; July 20, 1984, p. 10.
Publishers Weekly, August 30, 1999, review of *Just Generosity,* p. 72.
Wittenberg Door, October-November, 1979.

* * *

SILVER, Philip Warnock 1932-

PERSONAL: Born November 12, 1932, in Bryn Mawr, PA; married, 1958; children: two. *Education:* Haverford College, B.A., 1954; Middlebury College, M.A., 1955; Princeton University, M.A., 1960, Ph.D., 1963.

ADDRESSES: Office—c/o Department of Spanish and Portuguese, Columbia University, 612 West 116th St., New York, NY 10027.

CAREER: Rutgers University, New Brunswick, NJ, instructor in Spanish, 1961-63; Oberlin College, Oberlin, OH, assistant professor, 1963-66, associate professor of Spanish and Portuguese, 1967-71; Columbia University, New York City, visiting professor, 1971-72, professor of Spanish and Portuguese, beginning in 1972, chairperson of department, 1973-76.

MEMBER: Modern Language Association of America, American Translators Association.

AWARDS, HONORS: Guggenheim fellow, 1966.

WRITINGS:

(Translator) *Unamuno: A Philosophy of Tragedy,* University of California Press (Berkeley, CA), 1962.
Et in Arcadia Ego: A Study of the Poetry of Luis Cernuda, Tamesis Books, 1965.
Sunlight and Crumbs (poems), Triskelion Press (Oberlin, OH), 1969.
(Translator and author of introduction) Jose Ortega y Gasset, *Phenomenology and Art,* Norton (New York City), 1975.
Ortega as Phenomenologist: The Genesis of "Meditations of Quixote," Columbia University Press (New York City), 1978.
(Editor and author of prologue) Damaso Alonso, *Antologia poetica,* Alianza, 1979.
(Translator) Felix Martinez-Bonati, *Fictive Discourse and the Structures of Literature: A Phenomenological Approach,* Cornell University Press (Ithaca, NY), 1981.

Other books include *Red Doll,* 1987.

BIOGRAPHICAL/CRITICAL SOURCES:

PERIODICALS

Publishers Weekly, October 9, 1987, p. 78.*

* * *

SINCLAIR, Andrew (Annandale) 1935-

PERSONAL: Born January 21, 1935, in Oxford, England; son of Stanley Charles (in the British Colonial Service) and Hilary (a writer; maiden name, Nash-Webber) Sinclair; married Marianne Alexandre, 1960 (divorced); married Miranda Seymour, October 18, 1972 (divorced June 6, 1984); married Sonia Melchett (a writer), July 25, 1984; children: (first marriage) Timon Alexandre; (second marriage) Merlin George. *Education:* Cambridge University, B.A. (double first honors in history), Trinity College, 1958, Ph.D., Cambridge, 1963.

ADDRESSES: Home—Flat 20, Millennium House, 132 Grosvenor Road, London SW1V 3JY, England. *Agent*—Christopher Sinclair, Stevenson, 3 Sount Terrace, London SW7 2TB, England.

CAREER: Churchill College, Cambridge, England, founding fellow and director of historical studies, 1961-63; University of London, London, England, lecturer in American history, 1965-67; Lorrimer Publishing, London, managing director, 1967-91; Timon Films, London, film director and screenwriter, 1969—. Writer and filmmaker. *Military service:* British Army, Coldstream Guards, 1953-55; became lieutenant.

MEMBER: Association of Cinematographers and Television Technicians, Royal Society of Literature (fellow), Society of American Historians (fellow).

AWARDS, HONORS: Commonwealth fellow, Harvard University, 1959-61; American Council of Learned Societies fellow, 1963-64; Somerset Maugham Literary Prize, 1967, for *The Emancipation of the American Woman;* Venice Film Festival award, 1971, and Cannes Film Festival prize, 1972, both for *Under Milk Wood.*

WRITINGS:

NOVELS

The Breaking of Bumbo (also see below), Simon & Schuster (New York City), 1959.

My Friend Judas (also see below), Faber, 1959, Simon & Schuster, 1961.

The Project, Simon & Schuster, 1960.

The Paradise Bum, Atheneum (New York City), 1963, published in England as *The Hallelujah Bum,* Faber, 1963.

The Raker, Atheneum, 1964.

Gog (first volume in trilogy), Macmillan, 1967.

Magog (second volume in trilogy), Harper (New York City), 1972.

The Surrey Cat, M. Joseph, 1976, published as *Cat,* Sphere, 1977.

A Patriot for Hire, M. Joseph, 1978, published as *Sea of the Dead,* Sphere, 1981.

The Facts in the Case of E. A. Poe, Weidenfeld & Nicolson, 1979, Holt (New York City), 1980.

Beau Bumbo, Weidenfeld & Nicolson, 1985.

King Ludd, Hodder & Stoughton, 1988.

The Far Corners of the Earth, Hodder & Stoughton, 1991.

The Strength of the Hills: A Novel Hodder & Stoughton (London), 1992.

King Ludd (third volume of trilogy), Four Walls Eight Windows (New York City), 1993.

NONFICTION

Prohibition: The Era of Excess, introduction by Richard Hofstadter, Atlantic-Little, Brown (Boston), 1962, published as *The Era of Excess: A Social History of the Prohibition Movement,* Harper, 1964.

The Available Man: The Life behind the Masks of Warren Gamaliel Harding, Macmillan, 1965.

The Better Half: The Emancipation of the American Woman, Harper, 1965, published as *The Emancipation of the American Woman,* 1966.

The Last of the Best: The Aristocracy of Europe in the Twentieth Century, Macmillan, 1969.

Che Guevara, Viking, 1970, published in England as *Guevara,* Fontana, 1970.

Dylan Thomas: No Man More Magical, Holt, 1975, published in England as *Dylan Thomas: Poet of His People,* M. Joseph, 1975.

The Savage: A History of Misunderstanding, Weidenfeld & Nicolson, 1977.

Jack: A Biography of Jack London, Harper, 1977.

John Ford: A Biography, Dial (New York City), 1979.

Corsair: The Life of J. Pierpont Morgan, Little, Brown (Boston, MA), 1981.

The Other Victoria: The Princess Royal and the Great Game of Europe, Weidenfeld & Nicolson, 1981.

(With Ladislas Farago) *Royal Web: The Story of Princess Victoria and Frederick of Prussia,* McGraw (New York City), 1982.

Sir Walter Raleigh and the Age of Discovery, Penguin, 1984.

The Red and the Blue: Intelligence, Treason, and the Universities, Weidenfeld & Nicolson, 1985, published as *The Red and the Blue: Cambridge, Treason, and Intelligence,* Little, Brown, 1986.

Spiegel: The Man behind the Pictures, Weidenfeld & Nicolson, 1987, published as *S. P. Eagle: A Biography of Sam Spiegel,* Little, Brown, 1988.

War like a Wasp: The Lost Decade of the Forties, Hamish Hamilton, 1989, Viking, 1990.

The Need to Give: The Patrons and the Arts, Sinclair-Stevenson (London), 1990.

The Sword and the Grail: Of the Grail and the Templars and a True Discovery of America, Crown (New York City), 1992.

Francis Bacon: His Life and Violent Times, Crown, 1993.

In Love and Anger: A View of the '60s, Sinclair-Stevenson, 1993.

Jerusalem: The Endless Crusade, Crown, 1995.

Arts and Cultures: The History of the Fifty Years of the Arts Council, Sinclair-Stevenson, 1995.

The Discovery of the Grail, Century, 1997, Carroll & Graf (New York City), 1998.

Death by Fame: A Life of Elisabeth, Empress of Austria, Constable, 1998, St. Martin's (New York City), 1999.

Dylan the Bard: A Life of Dylan Thomas, Constable, 1999, St. Martins Press (New York City), 2000.

PLAYS

My Friend Judas (adapted from author's novel of same title), produced in London at Arts Theatre, 1959.

(Adapter) Dylan Thomas, *Adventures in the Skin Trade* (first produced at Hampstead Theatre Club, 1965; produced in Washington, DC, at Washington Theatre Club, 1970), Dent, 1967, New Directions, 1968.

The Blue Angel (adapted from screenplay of Josef von Sternberg's film of same title), produced in Liverpool, England, at Liverpool Playhouse, 1983, and Bristol and Brighton, 1992.

SCRIPTS

Before Winter Comes (based on Frederick L. Keefe's short story "The Interpreter"), Columbia, 1969.

(And director) *The Breaking of Bumbo* (based on author's novel of the same title), Associated British Pictures Corp., 1970.

The Voyage of the Beagle (television script), CBS Films, 1970.

(And director) *Under Milk Wood* (based on Dylan Thomas's play of same title; produced by Timon Films, 1971), Simon & Schuster, 1972.

(And director) *Blue Blood,* Timon Films, 1972.

Martin Eden (television script; based on novel by Jack London), RAI, 1981.

Also author of television scripts *The Chocolate Tree,* 1963, and *Old Soldiers,* 1964.

TRANSLATOR

Selections from the Greek Anthology, Weidenfeld & Nicolson, 1967, Macmillan, 1968.

(With Carlos P. Hansen) *Bolivian Diary: Ernesto Che Guevara,* Lorrimer, 1968.

(With former wife, Marianne Alexandre) Jean Renoir, *La Grande Illusion* Lorrimer, 1968.

OTHER

(Author of introduction) Homer, *The Iliad,* translated by W. H. D. Rouse, Heron Books (Portland, OR), 1969.

Inkydoo, the Wild Boy (children's story), Abelard (London), 1976, published as *Carina and the Wild Boy,* Beaver/Hamlyn, 1977.

(Editor) Jack London, *The Call of the Wild, White Fang, and Other Stories,* introduction by James Dickey, Penguin, 1981.

(Editor and author of introduction) Jack London, *The Sea Wolf and Other Stories,* Penguin, 1989.

(Compiler) *The War Decade: An Anthology of the 1940s,* Hamish Hamilton, 1989.

Contributor to *Atlantic, Harper's, Observer, Guardian, Spectator, New Statesman, Granta, Texas Quarterly, Transatlantic Review,* and other periodicals and newspapers.

SIDELIGHTS: British author Andrew Sinclair has produced a voluminous body of work for almost four decades. Ranging from allegorical fiction to biography to historical fiction, Sinclair's writings frequently explore historical figures, periods, and places from a modern perspective.

Among Sinclair's best-known works are the trilogy *Gog, Magog,* and *King Ludd.* A blend of fiction, history, and myth, the novels examine Great Britain's past and present through the eyes of half-brothers Gog and Magog, names that evoke the twin giants of British legend whose statues stood guard over London's Guildhall until they were destroyed by German bombs in 1940. As Richard Freedman explains in the *Saturday Review,* Sinclair's modern versions of these age-old figures "symbolize the best and worst people and events from ancient Albion to Labourite Britain."

In the first novel, which begins just after the end of World War II, a seven-foot-tall man is washed ashore on the coast of Scotland, naked and suffering from amnesia. After a brief convalescence, the man—who remembers only that his name is Gog—sets out for London, hoping to learn more about his identity and, therefore, his past. The rest of the novel chronicles his many adventures as he journeys south. In the picaresque tradition, Gog meets a variety of fictional, historical, and mythological characters along the way. Some display concern and offer him assistance and advice; others (including his own wife and half-brother) regard him as "the perfect victim" and derive much pleasure from making him suffer. By the end of the novel, the one-time innocent has developed a less idealistic, more pragmatic attitude toward life, one that acknowledges the existence of evil and corruption and the need for each person to fight his or her own battles.

In their evaluations of *Gog,* critics have tended to rate it in one of two ways: as an unsuccessful attempt at sophisticated satire or as a highly ambitious and imaginative product of genius. An adherent of the former view is *New Statesman* reviewer Kenith Trodd, who characterizes *Gog* as "a series of funny production numbers: droll, but the laughs are hollow where they need to be edgy; the wrong sort of punch." Frank McGuinness also believes *Gog* lacks the proper "punch." Writing in *London Magazine,* McGuinness declares that the book exhibits "perhaps more satirical pretensions than the author's talent for ribald and extravagant inventiveness can finally support. . . . The truth is that if the novel is not without distinction as a study of a mind hovering between sanity and madness, its satirical aims are lost in a welter of scholarly clowning, crude farce and the sort of glib cynicism that is so often mistaken for cold, hard-headed intellectualism."

A similar opinion is expressed by J. D. Scott in the *New York Times Book Review.* "Mr. Sinclair has too much talent to fail to make an impression," the critic begins. "But the impression is confused by too much frenetic action, and softened by long lapses into flat, sometimes merely clever, sometimes merely banal, prose. *Gog* is a monument of myth and slapstick, violence and parody, drama-of-evil and custard-pie comedy. Like some great Gothic folly seen through the mist, it fails to communicate its meaning."

On the other side of the discussion are those reviewers who regard *Gog* as excitingly original and entertaining. Though he thinks the novel is "much too long," Roger Sale comments in the *Hudson Review* that "the end is rich and satisfying, a book the likes of which I have not seen in a long time." In his study *The Situation of the Novel,* Bernard Bergonzi praises Sinclair's "extraordinary imaginative exuberance" and terms *Gog* "an intensely personal book, whose approach could not be followed by writers who do not share Sinclair's preoccupations, knowledge and temperament." Even more enthusiastic is critic Philip Callow, who asserts in *Books and Bookmen:* "[*Gog*] sears and scalds, it's the vision of a cold, planetary eye, and somehow it all founders in the end, goes mad like a cancer and finally smashes in a blind fury of destruction. I'm still reeling. I think there's genius in it."

Rachel Trickett more or less agrees with this assessment of *Gog,* stating in the *Yale Review* that it is "most extraordinary and ambitious. . . . A mixture of traditional genres, the allegory, the romance, and the picaresque tale, it is at once realistic and a fantasy, didactic and mythical, precise and comprehensive. . . . Confusion and carelessness are its worst faults, but its inclusiveness is also its strength. Self-indulgent and undisciplined, it nevertheless shows a clumsy but powerful genius which can only leave one astonished, occasionally repelled, but consistently grateful for so much imaginative vigor and breadth."

Magog examines many of the same social, political, and moral issues raised in *Gog,* this time from the point of view of Gog's half-brother and spiritual opposite—Magog, the "symbol of power, authority, centralization, the tyranny of material success and fashion," as Trickett describes him. Like *Gog, Magog* begins in 1945, just after the end of the war. Sinclair portrays his title character as a young civil servant whose promising career with the government comes to an abrupt end when an investigation reveals the extent of his dishonest dealings. Despite this apparent setback, Magog moves on to successively more powerful positions as head of a film production company, an urban developer, and, finally, master of a new college at Cambridge. The focus of the book is on these various stages in Magog's career and on what *Dictionary of Literary Biography* writer Judith Vincent refers to as his ultimate realization "that his material success is hollow and that an inevitably changing order must deprive him of power."

Reviewers have greeted *Magog* with somewhat less enthusiasm than *Gog.* "Gobbling great hunks of time, a vast *dramatis personae;* tossing off puns, inside jokes, bits of mythology; insisting that the life of a man and of an empire have much in common, *Magog* trivializes all it touches," declares Patricia Meyer Spacks in the *Hudson Review.* "It's funny sometimes, sometimes even sad, but the lack of sharp authorial perspective makes it seem purposeless."

Commenting in the *New York Times Book Review,* Anthony Thwaite remarks that *Magog* "suffers, as sequels are apt to do, from the disabilities of its predecessor: lumbering in its episodic movement, spotty in its characterization, arbitrary in its action, and megalomaniac in its overview. . . . This book is not an epic, whatever its author's purpose may have been. Nor, despite its blurb, is it a 'wonderfully sardonic morality tale.' Sinclair's juggled universe bears little resemblance to any known world, no matter how hard he tries to reinforce everything with documentary and travelogue. *Magog* is a febrile, self-indulgent, opinionated and finally rather squalidly boring fling at the picaresque."

Unlike their colleagues, reviewers from the *Times Literary Supplement* and *Books and Bookmen* temper their criticism with praise. The *Times Literary Supplement* critic, for example, believes that "too many events" make *Magog* read like "a first-draft synopsis of a twelve-volume novel series, full of bright ideas, sharp comments and ambitions not yet realized." Nevertheless, the critic adds, "Sinclair is always interesting and convincing about [the] details of high life, which he treats with disdain." Oswell Blakeston also has some positive observations, particularly regarding the author's "ear for civil service dialogue." In general, says Blakeston in *Books and Bookmen,* this makes for "a splendid beginning" to the novel. "But then, alas, [Sinclair] plunges into farce," the critic continues. "[And] after one has laughed at a well-aimed poisoned dart of brilliant criticism, it's hard to accept the old custard pie as a devastating weapon."

Kenn Stitt and Lee T. Lemon are among those whose praise for *Magog* is almost without qualification. In a *New Statesman* article, Stitt describes the novel as "a rich and complex book, mirroring the complexities of the world it is set in, its strands intricately and carefully interwoven." Though he finds the theme somewhat trite, Lemon observes in *Prairie Schooner* that the author "does a fine job of showing the reader the peculiar anguish of the successful but hollow man [and] the intricacies of power." Like several other critics, he also finds that Sinclair "has a talent for the memorable turn of phrase." In short, concludes the reviewer, *Magog* "just might be one of the best novels of the past few years"—even better than *Gog*. "The earlier book was a stumbling romp through the history and mythology of the British Isles," says Lemon. "But *Magog* is a different book. Magog . . . is not hindered by his brother [Gog's] ponderous memories. He is a kind of gadfly of meaningless change. . . . By the end of the novel, Magog the manipulator has learned that time brings new and shrewder manipulators, and that one does not have to manipulate for the things which give satisfaction."

In 1988 *King Ludd,* the last novel in the trilogy, appeared. It begins with the story of the Luddites of the early nineteenth century, British workers who, thrown out of work because of the introduction of machines into factories, began an unorganized rebellion against mechanization. King Ludd was the name given to the mythical leader of the Luddite rebellion. In Sinclair's version of British history, Gog discovers that King Ludd was in reality based on one of his ancestors. Gog also believes that he can hear messages from the old Celtic gods, and he sees vestiges of the ancient Gogam script of the Druids in such present-day activities as cryptography. Gog, D. A. N. Jones explains in the *Times Literary Supplement,* "is a mixomythologist." Robert Nye, writing in the London *Times,* states: "What we have here is Gog's version of the history of the Luddites, married to an exhaustive account of the mythology of communications from the time of the Gogam script to the present day." Speaking of the trilogy as a whole, Nye concludes: "Sinclair succeeds in engaging and holding our attention. I think these books are important, and that they'll last."

Writing in the *Contemporary Authors Autobiography Series,* Sinclair noted that he sees *King Ludd* as a story of technology in Britain from the early nineteenth century to the 1980s. The novel covers, Sinclair explained, "the Luddites, who first wrecked the new textile machines, through the story of the printers like Francis Place who defended liberty, on to the sad end of the print unions through new technology. . . . Contemporary events have given *King Ludd* its shape."

In a letter to *CA,* Sinclair commented on the ideas that inspired *Gog* and *Magog* and explained how *King Ludd* completes the trilogy. "*Gog* is based on Eliot's principle that time past and present and future are all the same. It also attempts to bring alive the legendary and mystical history of Britain as seen in the struggle of the people against the power of the government, of London, of King Ludd's town. There is no resolution to the fight of Gog against Magog, of the land against the city, of the ruled against the ruler, but in that fight lies the spirit and the glory of Albion, whatever it may be. *Magog*'s world is the machinations of power, and how its misuse drove Britain down after the end of the Second World War. *King Ludd* deals with England from the time of the Luddites opposing the industrial revolution through the neurosis of the 1930s to the odd conflicts of today, where the descendants of the Tolpuddle martyrs now have their unions and use the workers' power to oppress the rest. When brother fights brother, Magog and King Ludd will always rule."

Sinclair also explores elements of English, international, and biographical history in his nonfiction. *The Sword and the Grail: Of the Grail and the Templars and a True Discovery of America* not only looks at the author's own ancestors (the St. Clairs, Earls of Orkney) but also at their relationship with the Order of the Knights Templar and the reputed expedition of Sir Henry St. Clair to the New World. According to some sources Henry St. Clair, the first St. Clair to be named Earl of Orkney, led a colonial expedition to North America in 1398 to find a place of refuge for the outlawed religious ascetic order—almost one hundred years before Christopher Columbus' famous voyage. Relying on secondary sources and information preserved in the Sinclairs' family church, Sinclair tries to show that Sir Henry's trip did in fact take place. He also suggests that the Templars found their last refuge in the St. Clair Castle in Scotland, and that their rituals were directly linked to later Masonic rituals. Reviewers, however, question the reliability of his sources and the historicity of his conclusions. "The author's major documentary source is widely regarded as fraudulent," explains William F. Young in *Library Journal,* and he adds that the author's work is "compelling but questionable as history." A *Publishers Weekly* reviewer calls the volume "of interest mainly to history buffs and medievalists." "Sinclair wallows in family genealogy and overly dense detail," states a critic in *Kirkus Reviews,* "but his vast knowledge and clever detective work do create a colorful, tantalizing study."

Sinclair turns to social history in *Francis Bacon: His Life and Violent Times* and later works. *Francis Bacon* is a colorful biography of the twentieth-century painter whose work, writes Jeffrey Hogrefe in the *Los Angeles Times Book Review,* "has been equated with the pain and suffering of the 20th Century." Alan Ross, writing in the *Spectator,* characterizes Sinclair's biography as "social [history] rather than . . . art [criticism]." *Jerusalem: The Endless Crusade* recreates the history of the holy city in a way, according to Stephen Howe in *New Statesman,* reminiscent of his fiction—a place steeped in the essence of history. Ilene Cooper, a reviewer for *Booklist,* expresses disappointment with Sinclair's writing style, which in her opinion "never rises much above the level of an earnest Ph.D. thesis"; however, she adds that "it's obvious that Sinclair has not only done his research but also feels the awe that Jerusalem . . . is capable of inspiring." She concludes that "it may take a bit of effort to wade through this slow-moving account, but there is an ultimate payoff: a thoughtful portrait of a city that has fascinated humankind for more than two millennia."

In Love and Anger: A View of the '60s, and *Arts and Cultures: The History of the Fifty Years of the Arts Council* both look at the development of important icons in British social history during the past few decades. Jill Neville, writing in the *Times Literary Supplement,* declares that "*In Love and Anger* is an insider's account which reveals the unconquerable naivety of the period," while *Spectator* contributor Charles Saumarez Smith, reviewing *Arts and Cultures,* asserts that "Sinclair writes from inside the fold, benefitting from access to unpublished information and providing a useful who was who."

The Discovery of the Grail traces the evolution of myths about the Holy Grail, starting with pre-Christian myths and leading all the way to the writings of psychiatrist Carl Jung. While the Grail is commonly defined as the chalice that held Christ's blood, Sinclair widens that definition to include many holy relics, including the philosopher's stone, cornucopias, the Ark of the Covenant, and the dish bearing the severed head of John the Baptist. The texts he analyzes are as diverse as Mary Shelley's *Frankenstein,* Dante's *Divine Comedy,* and the *Aeneid* by Virgil. This wide focus and a presumption of the readers' knowledge on a great many subjects make his book "daunting to the general reader," in the estimation of a *Publishers Weekly* writer, who also finds Sinclair's writing inelegant. Yet the reviewer concludes that "no one . . . can doubt Sinclair's religious fervor and the sincerity of his deeply personal quest." More critical is Henry L. Carrigan, Jr., who states in *Library Journal* that "the book is unsure whether it wants to be pop psychology, literary history, or a New Age religious tract." Carrigan finds *The Discovery of the Grail* to be full of "simplistic pronouncements" that are "closer to the ethereal musings of Deepak Chopra than a serious study of the Grail."

In the biography *Death by Fame: A Life of Elisabeth, Empress of Austria,* Sinclair draws parallels between his subject, who lived from 1837 to 1898, and Princess Diana of Wales. Like Diana, Elisabeth was beautiful, had an eating disorder, was trapped in a poor marriage, and sought to alleviate her unhappiness by constant travel and charity work. Elisabeth met her doom at the hands of an assassin whose only goal was to kill a member of royalty—any member. Some reviewers find the comparison of the two women to be strained, and *New York Times Book Review* contributor Margaret Van Dagens declares that *Death by Fame* disintegrates into "rambling thoughts about many celebrities, from Elton John to Carole Lombard." A *Kirkus Reviews* contributor is more charitable, describing *Death by Fame* as "a well-written, thoroughly researched story of a popular and beautiful empress, who, while self-indulgent, sought a life of privacy and peace."

BIOGRAPHICAL/CRITICAL SOURCES:

BOOKS

Bergonzi, Bernard, *The Situation of the Novel,* University of Pittsburgh Press (Pittsburgh), 1970.

Contemporary Literary Criticism, Gale (Detroit, MI), Volume 2, 1974, Volume 14, 1980.

Dictionary of Literary Biography, Volume 14: *British Novelists since 1960,* Gale, 1982.

Morris, Robert K., editor, *Old Lines, New Forces: Essays on the Contemporary British Novel, 1960-1970,* Fairleigh Dickinson University Press, 1976.

Sinclair, Andrew, essay in *Contemporary Authors Autobiography Series,* Gale, Volume 5, 1987.

PERIODICALS

America, August 3, 1996, Alan J. Avery-Peck, review of *Jerusalem,* p. 28.

Art in America, December, 1994, Faye Hirsch, review of *Francis Bacon,* p. 31.

Best Sellers, October 1, 1967.

Booklist, September 15, 1995, Ilene Cooper, review of *Jerusalem,* p. 139.

Books and Bookmen, May, 1967; June, 1967; June, 1972.

Book World, September 24, 1967.

Drama, summer, 1967.

Hudson Review, winter, 1967; autumn, 1972.

Kirkus Reviews, September 1, 1992, p. 1118; July 15, 1995, pp. 1012-13; September 15, 1998, review of *The Discovery of the Grail.*

Library Journal, May 15, 1990, p. 78; September 15, 1992, p. 76; May 1, 1993, p. 118; September 15, 1995, p. 82; November 15, 1998, Henry L. Carrigan, review of *The Discovery of the Grail,* p. 68.

Listener, April 4, 1968.

London Magazine, June, 1967.

Los Angeles Times, April 7, 1981.

Los Angeles Times Book Review, April 10, 1994, p. 4.

New Statesman, June 9, 1967; May 5, 1972; February 5, 1988, p. 33; August 18, 1995, pp. 30-31; February 9, 1996, pp. 36-37.

New Statesman and Society, August 18, 1995, pp. 30-31; February 9, 1996, pp. 36-37.

New York Times, April 21, 1981.

New York Times Book Review, January 22, 1967; September 10, 1967; October 8, 1967; July 2, 1972; October 12, 1980; March 8, 1987; May 8, 1988, p. 11; March 17, 1988, p. 33; September 5, 1999, Margaret Van Dagens, review of *Death by Fame,* p. 17.

Observer (London), June 1, 1967; January 1, 1970; August 13, 1995, p. 13.

Prairie Schooner, spring, 1974.

Publishers Weekly, May 11, 1990, p. 241; August 17, 1992, p. 481; March 29, 1993, review of *King Ludd,* p. 48; August 7, 1995, review of *Jerusalem,* p. 451; October 19, 1998, review of *Discovery of the Grail,* p. 67.

Punch, January 20, 1970.

Saturday Review, September 16, 1967.

Spectator, April 25, 1969; September 18, 1993, pp. 37-38; August 9, 1995, pp. 28-29; February 10, 1996, pp. 33-34.

Time, September 1, 1967.

Times (London), January 21, 1982; June 20, 1985; June 29, 1985; October 21, 1989.

Times Literary Supplement, June 8, 1967; July 13, 1967; May 5, 1970; June 26, 1981; July 12, 1985; July 25, 1986; December 18, 1987; September 16, 1988; November 10, 1989; September 24, 1993, p. 17; June 3, 1994, p. 36; September 8, 1995, p. 24.

Tribune Books (Chicago), April 1, 1979; October 5, 1981.

Variety, January 15, 1969.

Washington Post, April 30, 1981.

Washington Post Book World, February 15, 1987; July 8, 1990.

Yale Review, spring, 1968.*

SOBEL, Dava 1947-

PERSONAL: Born June 15, 1947, in New York, NY; daughter of Samuel H. (a physician) and Betty (a chemist; maiden name, Gruber) Sobel; married Arthur C. Klein (an author); divorced, December 14, 1995; children: Zoe Rachel, Issac. *Education:* State University of New York at Binghamton, Bx.H.S. of Science, 1969. *Politics:* Democrat. *Religion:* Jewish. *Avocational interests:* Ballroom dancing, amateur astronomy.

ADDRESSES: Agent—Michael Carlisle, William Morris Agency, 1325 Avenue of the Americas, New York, NY 10019-6011.

CAREER: Author. *New York Times,* New York City, science reporter, 1979-82; astronomy columnist for *East Hampton Independent,* East Hampton, NY, 1994—, and for The Discovery Channel On-Line, 1996—.

MEMBER: Planetary Society, National Association of Watch and Clock Collectors, American Association of University Women.

AWARDS, HONORS: American Psychological Foundation National Media Award, 1980; Lowell Thomas Award from Society of American Travel Writers, 1992; gold medal, Council for the Advancement and Support of Education (CASE), 1994, for an article on longitude published in *Harvard Magazine.*

WRITINGS:

(With Frank D. Drake) *Is Anyone Out There?: The Scientific Search for Extraterrestrial Intelligence,* Delacorte (New York City), 1992.

Longitude: The True Story of a Lone Genius Who Solved the Greatest Scientific Problem of His Time, Walker & Co. (New York City), 1995, new edition with William J. H. Andrewes published as *The Illustrated Longitude,* 1998.

Galileo's Daughter: A Historical Memoir of Science, Faith, and Love, Walker & Co., 1999.

WITH FORMER HUSBAND, ARTHUR C. KLEIN

Backache Relief: The Ultimate Second Opinion from Back-Pain Sufferers Nationwide Who Share Their Successful Healing Experiences, Times Books (New York City), 1985.

Arthritis: What Works, St. Martin's Press (New York City), 1989.

Arthritis: What Exercises Work, St. Martin's Press, 1993, published with foreword by John Bland as

Arthritis: What Works; Breakthrough Relief for the Rest of Your Life, Even after Drugs and Surgery Have Failed, St. Martin's Press, 1995.
Backache: What Exercises Work, St. Martin's Press, 1994.

OTHER

Contributor of articles to periodicals, including *Astronomy, Audubon, Discover, Harvard Magazine, Ladies Home Journal, Life, New York Times Magazine, New Yorker, New Woman, Omni, Redbook, Vogue,* and *Working Woman.*

ADAPTATIONS: Longitude was adapted for television.

WORK IN PROGRESS: A book about the solar system; a book of astronomical essays.

SIDELIGHTS: Former *New York Times* science reporter Dava Sobel has earned great critical recognition for the books *Longitude: The True Story of a Lone Genius Who Solved the Greatest Scientific Problem of His Time* and *Galileo's Daughter: A Historical Memoir of Science, Faith, and Love.* Both are highly unusual books that became international bestsellers. *Longitude* is the true story of the quest to devise a reliable navigational instrument for sailors; *Galileo's Daughter* creates a unique portrait of the famous astronomer Galileo Galilei, using letters from his cloistered daughter as its foundation. *Entertainment Weekly* writer Gillian Flynn praised Sobel as someone who is able to "write lyrically about decidedly unlyrical topics."

Described as an "elegant history" by *New York Times* critic Christopher Lehmann-Haupt, *Longitude* is the story of an eighteenth-century clockmaker's persistence in developing a sea-worthy clock by which sailors might determine longitude, the distance east or west on the earth. Throughout history, without a tool or method of determining their positions, many sailors sailed off-course, which, at best, delayed their deliveries of goods. Tragically, however, thousands of sailors perished at sea, due to their inability to calculate the location of land.

In 1714, Sobel relates, England's parliament addressed the dire problem by promising a reward of 20,000 pounds (the equivalent of millions of dollars by modern standards) to anyone who could solve the problem of determining longitude. Scientists knew that every hour's time difference between a ship and its destination (or port of origin) equaled a change in longitude of fifteen degrees east or west; the solution, therefore, was to create an instrument that would withstand the erratic changes in climate and humidity aboard a ship so that sailors could determine their position by the time.

John Harrison, a self-educated clockmaker, accepted the challenge, devoting some forty-six years of his life to the building of weather- and motion-proof clocks. His effort produced the chronometer and earned admiration and a monetary prize from King George III. His work, however, was not without obstacles, and Sobel shares many of those obstacles, along with often amusing stories of solutions offered by others to the longitude problem, in her book, which, according to John Ellsworth, writing in the *New York Times Book Review,* "captures John Harrison's extraordinary character: brilliant, persevering and heroic in the face of adversity. He is a man you won't forget."

Longitude elicited further praise from critics, including Lehmann-Haupt, who lauded Sobel's "remarkable ability to tell a story with clarity and perfect pacing." Touched by Sobel's account of being reduced to tears upon visiting the maritime museum that houses Harrison's clocks, Lehmann-Haupt wrote: "Such is the eloquence of this gem of a book that it makes you understand exactly how she felt." Bruno Maddox expressed similar sentiments in his *Washington Post Book World* review: "*Longitude* is a simple tale, brilliantly told," Maddox wrote. "Perhaps one of the most impressive things about the book—given its subject matter—is the sheer simplicity of the whole thing. . . . She offers us no attack on the modern assumption that time is solid and objective; she wholly refrains from rubbing readers' noses in the artificiality of meaning, etc.; she offers us nothing, in short, but measured, nearly perfect prose and a magnificent story, an extraordinary book." *Longitude* spent forty weeks on the *New York Times* bestseller list and sold more than a million copies.

While researching *Longitude,* Sobel came across a letter written to the seventeenth-century astronomer Galileo—who supported Nicholas Copernicus's revolutionary theory that the earth moved around the sun instead of vice versa—from his daughter. She was surprised to know that he had a child at all; further investigation revealed that he had three illegitimate offspring. His two daughters, deemed unmarriageable due to their illegitimacy, had been placed in a convent during their teenage years. The elder of the pair, who took the name Sister Maria Celeste, was a truly remarkable woman who served as herbalist and accountant to the convent. Hundreds of letters to her father showed her great intelligence and devotion to her father, who returned her affection.

It is well known that Galileo's theories put him in opposition with the Roman Catholic church; the Court of the Inquisition forced him to recant, but he cleverly succeeded in setting down his works for posterity by recasting them as a fictional dialogue. He is frequently portrayed as a defiant figure, "a scientific Martin Luther," in the words of *Library Journal* contributor Wilda Williams, but that image is incorrect. He was a true believer who experienced a real crisis within himself over the conflict between his work and the authority of the Church. Williams quoted Sobel as saying, "Galileo remained a good Catholic to his dying day. His scientific discoveries actually strengthened his faith."

Sobel has stated that as a Jew raised in the Bronx, she had a difficult time understanding the religious world of her story—particularly Maria Celeste's life as a member of the Poor Clares, a Franciscan order dedicated to poverty and seclusion. A rich correspondence with the mother abbess of a contemporary Poor Clares convent was so enlightening to her that she told Williams, "I could now understand why even today a young woman would enter a convent and live in poverty." Many reviewers credit *Galileo's Daughter* with providing a fascinating look into this kind of life, as well as providing a wonderful portrait of Galileo, his family, and his world. It is a "creative and compelling work" that reveals Sobel's "technical insight and originality," according to Hilary Burton in *Library Journal.* The author "has a remarkable ability to explain technical subjects without being simplistic or pedantic. There is a tremendous amount of fascinating detail in this work, and yet it reads as smoothly and compellingly as fiction."

"Retelling the story of Galileo's famous battle with the Inquisition over geocentricism, [Sobel] brings it to life by concentrating on the everyday—his professional feuds, his own sincere religious beliefs and—most important—his intense relationship with his eldest daughter," noted Malcolm Jones in *Newsweek,* who deemed the book as portraying "an epic battle over our place in the cosmos." On the strength of *Galileo's Daughter* and *Longitude,* Flynn lauded Sobel as someone of great talent and insight, "a writer who has reached through the brambled, layered detritus of hundreds of years, retrieved a forgotten clock maker and a lost daughter, and gently restored these strangers to all their joyful, proud, petulant, toothachy genuineness."

Sobel is also the co-author, with her former husband Arthur C. Klein, of several books on back pain and arthritis, including 1989's *Arthritis: What Works.* Based on the authors' interviews with more than 1,000 arthritis sufferers, *Arthritis: What Works* discusses various methods of treatment that patients report have alleviated their pain, from traditional therapy offered by physicians and drugs, to less conventional treatments used by holistic healers. In addition, the authors share recipes and diet plans considered to be helpful in attacking arthritis through nutrition. A companion of sorts to *Arthritis: What Works* is *Arthritis: What Exercises Work,* in which Sobel and Klein describe and illustrate exercises that were reported by the arthritis sufferers they interviewed to relieve symptoms of arthritis. The authors issued a similar book, *Backache: What Exercises Work,* after speaking with some five hundred sufferers of back injury about activities that eased their pain and hastened their return to normal activity.

BIOGRAPHICAL/CRITICAL SOURCES:

PERIODICALS

American Scientist, March, 2000, "Renaissance Nun, Over Newton's Shoulder, Chesapeake Dent," p. 173.

Analog: Science Fiction and Fact, September, 1993, p. 165.

Astronomy, June, 1993, p. 92; December, 1995, p. 103; March, 2000, review of *Galileo's Daughter,* p. 103.

The Beaver: Exploring Canada's History, August-September, 1999.

Booklist, September 1, 1995, p. 23; August, 1999, Gilbert Taylor, review of *Galileo's Daughter,* p. 1983; March 15, 2000, Whitney Scott, review of *Galileo's Daughter,* p. 1397.

Discover, December, 1999, Josie Glausiusz, review of *Galileo's Daughter,* p. 116.

Economist, October 19, 1996, p. S13; November 13, 1999, "Heroes of Modern Science: Loyal Child," p. 9.

Entertainment Weekly, December 11, 1998, p. 71; November 19, 1999, Gillian Flynn, review of *Galileo's Daughter,* p. 91.

Geographical, May, 2000, review of *The Illustrated Longitude,* p. 93.

Hindu, May 16, 2000, review of *Longitude.*

Library Journal, February 15, 1985, p. 175; August, 1989, p. 156; October 1, 1992, p. 113; November 15, 1993, p. 94; September 15, 1995, p. 90; August, 1996, p. 136; February 1, 1999, Michael Rogers, review of *The Illustrated Longitude,* p. 126; October 1, 1999, Wilda Williams, "A Father of Science, A Daughter of God," p. 128, Hilary Burton, review of *Galileo's Daughter,* p. 131.

Los Angeles Times Book Review, November 22, 1992, p. 6.
New Statesman, August 9, 1996, Boyd Tonkin, review of *Longitude,* p. 45.
Newsweek, October 11, 1999, Malcolm Jones, "When the Earth Moved: Dava Sobel Pairs Galileo's Story with His Daughter's to Give Us 17th-Century Italian Life in the Round," p. 83.
New York Times, November 2, 1995, p. C 21.
New York Times Book Review, October 11, 1992, p. 18; November 26, 1995, p. 15; October 17, 1999, p. 6.
New York Times Magazine, December 19, 1982, p. 110.
Public Opinion Quarterly, spring, 1989, p. 149.
Publishers Weekly, August 18, 1989, p. 60; September 7, 1992, p. 89; June 27, 1994, p. 74; September 18, 1995, p. 119; February 5, 1996, p. 24; July 19, 1999, review of *Galileo's Daughter,* p. 170; October 4, 1999, John F. Baker, "Dava Sobel: Matters of and Faith," p. 48; November 1, 1999, Daisy Maryles, "A Scientific Find," p. 24; November 29, 1999, Daisy Maryles, "A Father's Pride," p. 30.
School Library Journal, February, 1996, p. 135.
Science, November 6, 1992, p. 1012; October 8, 1999, p. 248.
Scientific American, January, 1993, p. 155.
Skeptical Inquirer, May, 2000, James C. Sullivan, "Galileo's Daughter Speaks," p. 51.
Sky & Telescope, December, 1992, p. 650; July, 1996, p. 60.
Sunday Times, December 26, 1999, "Lucky Timing from the First Lady of Longitude," p. 11.
Time, November 15, 1999, R. Z. Sheppard, "Footsteps No Longer: As Women's History Takes Root in the Canon, More Stories about the Past Take on a Female Voice," p. 108.
Washington Monthly, January-February, 1996, p. 53.
Washington Post Book World, November 26, 1995, p. 2.*

* * *

SPENCE, Jonathan D(ermot) 1936-

PERSONAL: Born August 11, 1936, in England; son of Dermot Gordon Chesson (a poet) and Muriel (Crailsham) Spence; married Helen Alexander, September 15, 1962; children: Colin Chesson, Ian Alexander. *Education:* Cambridge University, B.A., 1959; Yale University, Ph.D., 1965.

ADDRESSES: *Office*—Department of History, Yale University, New Haven, CT 06520. *E-mail*—jonathan.spence@yale.edu.

CAREER: Yale University, New Haven, CT, assistant professor, 1965-71, professor of Chinese history, beginning 1971, became George Burton Adams Professor of History and chair of department. Wiles Lecturer, Queens University, Belfast, 1985; Gauss Lecturer, Princeton University, 1987; visiting professor, Peking University, 1987. *Military service:* British Army, 1954-56; became first lieutenant.

MEMBER: Council on East Asian Studies (chair).

AWARDS, HONORS: Christopher Book Award, 1975, for *Emperor of China: Self-Portrait of K'ang-Hsi; Los Angeles Times* Book Award, 1982, and Harold D. Vursell Memorial Award, American Academy-Institute of Arts and Letters, 1983, both for *The Gate of Heavenly Peace: The Chinese and Their Revolution, 1895-1980;* Gelber Prize, 1990, and Best Book of the Year, American Association for Chinese Studies, 1996, both for *Chinese Roundabout: Essays in History and Culture;* notable book, *New York Times,* 1998, for *The Chan's Great Continent: China in Western Minds.*

WRITINGS:

Ts'ao Yin and the K'ang-Hsi Emperor, Bondservant and Master, Yale University Press (New Haven, CT), 1966.
To Change China: Western Advisers to China, 1620-1960, Little, Brown (Boston), 1969, published as *The China Helpers: Western Advisers to China, 1620-1960,* Bodley Head (London), 1969.
Emperor of China: Self-Portrait of K'ang-Hsi, Knopf (New York City), 1974.
The Death of Woman Wang (novel), Viking (New York City), 1978.
(With John E. Wills, Jr.) *From Ming to Ch'ing: Conquest, Region, and Continuity in Seventeenth-Century China,* Yale University Press, 1979.
(With Paul Cohen and Steven Levine) *The Historical Precedents for Our New Regulations with China,* East Asia Program (Washington, DC), 1980.
The Gate of Heavenly Peace: The Chinese and Their Revolution, 1895-1980, Viking, 1981.
The Memory Palace of Matteo Ricci, Viking, 1984.
The Question of Hu (biography), Knopf, 1988.
(Editor with Pei-kai Cheng and Michael Lestz) *The Search for Modern China: A Documentary Collection,* Norton (New York City), 1990.
Chinese Roundabout: Essays in History and Culture, Norton, 1992.
God's Chinese Son: The Taiping Heavenly Kingdom of Hong Xiuquan, Norton, 1996.

(With Annping Chin) *The Chinese Century: The Photographic History of the Last Hundred Years,* Random House, 1996.

The Chan's Great Continent: China in Western Minds, Norton, 1998.

The Taiping Vision of a Christian China, 1836-1864, Markahm Press Fund, Baylor University Press (Waco, TX), 1998.

Mao Zedong, Viking, 1999.

Also contributor to books, including *A Century in Crisis: Modernity and Tradition in the Art of Twentieth-Century China,* Guggenheim Museum (New York City), 1998.

SIDELIGHTS: Jonathan D. Spence writes books of Chinese history that employ various styles of organization and approach. "No one writes history—Chinese or any other kind—exactly as Spence does," Harrison E. Salisbury claims in Chicago's *Tribune Books.* In his *Emperor of China: Self-Portrait of K'ang-Hsi,* Spence splices together contemporary accounts of a seventeenth-century Chinese ruler to fashion a kind of autobiography. In *The Death of Woman Wang,* he fuses the official history of a seventeenth-century Chinese province, the memoirs of a local magistrate, and a collection of contemporary short stories into an historical novel. *The Gate of Heavenly Peace: The Chinese and Their Revolution, 1895-1980* presents recent Chinese history as seen and lived by China's writers and artists. And *The Memory Palace of Matteo Ricci* is a biography of a sixteenth-century Jesuit missionary to China organized around the mental images used in a Medieval memory system. Because he "brings imagination and literary flair to his material," these books have won Spence "a high reputation," John Gross reports in the *New York Times.*

One of Spence's most successful books is *The Gate of Heavenly Peace,* winner of two major awards in the field of historical writing. Tracing the turbulent history of modern China, *The Gate of Heavenly Peace* does not tell of the political leaders of the time nor of the common people. It focuses instead on China's intelligentsia and records how they both inspired and served the forces of political change and were often the first victims of those changes. As Kenneth J. Atchity explains in the *Los Angeles Times Book Review,* "Spence shows us history through the perceptions of individuals who—in a more or less minor key, relative to Sun Yatsen and Mao—were affected by these movements and whose souls helped shape these dreams." In particular, the book follows the careers of three people: the Confucian scholar Kang Youwei, the writer Lu Xun, and the novelist Ding Ling.

"No one has quite done Chinese history like this before," Jay Mathews writes in the *Washington Post Book World.* Mathews believes that Spence "brings alive the men and women who made the revolution, uncovering their bedtime fantasies, personality conflicts, sexual weaknesses and irrational rages." Similarly, Richard Harris of the London *Times* calls *The Gate of Heavenly Peace* "a book that brings China to life better than almost any other written about China since [the revolution]."

Spence's book also provides a valuable insight into the nature of the Chinese revolution. As Stuart Schram writes in the *Times Literary Supplement,* "Spence illuminates in a way no one else has done before, important aspects of the revolution, and in the process brings us closer to a full understanding of its meaning." "Spence has woven a magical symphony," Salisbury writes, "that tells us as no conventional history could of the agony of a nation in awesome labor, giving birth, as it were, to its own future."

In *The Memory Palace of Matteo Ricci,* Spence recreates the China of the sixteenth century and the work of the Jesuit missionaries of the time. In doing so, he also sketches a panoramic overview of the relationship between Europe and the East. The book's title comes from Ricci's memory system, which he used to remember vast amounts of information. His memory feats astounded his Chinese friends. At one gathering, Ricci was given a list of 500 Chinese characters to memorize. He read them back correctly and then, to the astonishment of the Chinese, recited them correctly in backward order as well. The system he used was based on a mental "memory palace"—a series of vividly imagined rooms. In each room was stored visual representations of the items to be remembered. As the user of the system imagines a walk through these rooms, the visual images trigger the proper memories in the proper order.

The Memory Palace of Matteo Ricci is organized around eight pictures—four used in Ricci's memory system and four religious wood-cuts he chose to illustrate one of his books. Spence uses these pictures as starting-points to discuss such topics as sixteenth-century warfare, commerce, and religious thought. "Spence cuts across the fabric of history from many different angles and directions," H. J. Kirchhoff writes in the Toronto *Globe and Mail,* "allowing Ricci's choices of illustration and explication to direct our gaze toward the Chinese of the sixteenth century, and toward the Jesuits who so determinedly and imaginatively proselytized them." As Marvin R. O'Connell observes in the *Washington Post Book World,* "Spence has employed Ricci's preoccupation with mnemonics to fashion an ingenious structure in which to bring together a history of China and Europe during Ricci's lifetime. . . . [It is] a genuine tour de force."

Spence employed a more conventional structure in *The Search for Modern China.* The author begins this study in 1600, during the era when the Ming dynasty was crumbling. Progressing chronologically through the centuries, he demonstrates that since that time, China has continually struggled to hold together a vast nation which seems always to be on the verge of falling apart. Fear of such fragmentation is one of the major sources of China's traditional closed-door policy. Spence examines the many ways in which China has attempted to protect itself from outsiders and their influence, and analyzes the ways that these attitudes come into play in modern China.

"To understand the burdens and opportunities embedded in China's past there is no better place to start than Jonathan D. Spence's excellent new book," asserts Vera Schwarcz in the *New York Times Book Review.* Nicholas R. Clifford concurs in *Commonweal* that Spence's book offers unusually clear insights into "*China's* history, rather than a China seen through Western eyes, or a China that simply responds to the actions of others." Writing in *Publishers Weekly,* Chris Goodrich names *The Search for Modern China* "a significant contribution to the history of our time." Originally conceived as a textbook, Spence's book proved to have wide appeal; it was on the *New York Times* bestseller list for three weeks.

Spence followed *The Search for Modern China* with *Chinese Roundabout: Essays in History and Culture.* "A new book by Jonathan Spence is always a cause for celebration," enthuses Kate Lowe in *History Today,* "and this volume, containing a collection of twenty-five of what he considers some of his best articles and review essays, will allow new generations to catch up easily on missed treats. The range [of the book] is breathtaking, from Confucianism to sea slugs, and from Tianamen under the Ming and Qing, to an appreciation of Arthur Waley." Lowe points out that although his books are popular, Spence has sacrificed none of his academic integrity. J. D. Brown makes a similar point in a Chicago *Tribune Books* review, describing Spence as "a clear and lively writer who is also inventive and witty, [and] at the same time a painstaking scholar." Allowing that Spence's style is occasionally "a bit dry," Brown goes on to add: "It is also various and possesses an element of unpredictability, which can produce results that are, at once, surprising, entertaining and inspired. As these essays show, Spence at his best employs an adventurous imagination to blow away the layers of dust that have obscured China's past and made the present so bewildering."

In his next offering, *God's Chinese Son: The Taiping Heavenly Kingdom of Hong Xiuquan,* Spence chose to focus on one bizarre, violent episode in nineteenth-century China—the Taiping Rebellion, instigated by Hong Xiuquan. The son of a farming couple, Hong aspired to become a mandarin, and so traveled as a young man to Canton to take the Confucian examinations. After failing several times, he fell ill and experienced a baffling, vision-filled delirium. Beginning to read a Bible given to him by a missionary, Hong came to believe that he was the Second Son of God. He became an itinerant preacher and attracted legions of followers. Eventually, he called for the destruction of the government, and nearly achieved it; however, his own cult was eventually wiped out by religious excesses and self-destructive paranoia.

A *Publishers Weekly* reviewer calls it a "strange, compelling tale" and credits Spence with being "a first-rate storyteller [who] recounts this extraordinary event with verve, offering sharp insights into the political dangers of religious fanaticism." Marie Arana-Ward also commends the author on his achievement. She writes in the *Washington Post Book World,* "Weaving what is already well known about the Taiping Rebellion with information from newly discovered documents inscribed by Hong, Spence gives us a magnificent tapestry of those apocalyptic days. It is a story that reaches beyond China into our world and time: a story of faith, hope, passion, and a fatal grandiosity."

Spence presented a sweeping overview of the ways in which China has been viewed by outsiders in *The Chan's Great Continent: China in Western Minds.* Observations from the first Jesuit missionaries, Marco Polo, Voltaire, Mark Twain, Richard Nixon, and a host of others are offered as a means of analyzing the ways in which Western minds have perceived China. Some of the writers actually went there, others did not, but in either case, Spence notes, China always seems to have stood for a mysterious "otherness," a country that was everything the West was not. Images of perfect order mingle with tales of outlandish decadence. Spence "brilliantly demonstrates [that] these competing hypotheses, already in play centuries ago, continue to find expression in the reflections of contemporary scholars and statesmen," comments Stephen Greenblatt in *New York Times Book Review.* "The overriding theme is that most Western thought on China has been colored by the religious, political, economic or personal agendas of those doing the observing," notes a *Publishers Weekly* reviewer. "Spence's book will appeal not only to those interested in history and literature, but to anyone looking for a perspective on contemporary discourse about China." Steven I. Levine, writing in *Library Journal,* contends that "only Spence, the Yale historian and master storyteller . . . could have woven such a brilliant tapestry from the threads of these Western travelogs, novels, stories, and plays. . . . This graceful book reminds us of the need to reflect upon our understanding of so protean a history and culture as China's."

Spence examined the life of one of modern China's most influential players in the biography *Mao Zedong.* Mixing historical fact with cultural analysis, the author creates "a work that is fluid and informative," in the opinion of a *Publishers Weekly* reviewer. By focusing on the cultural rather than political commentary, Spence is able to consider how Mao, a simple farm boy, rose to rule the most populous country in the world. The book is brief, a fact which "enables—or requires—Spence to accelerate the pace of Mao's life, thus adding drama to the sea of change in Mao's character from naive idealist to cunning political infighter and center of a personality cult."

Spence's unique presentations of history, Michael Feingold maintains in the *Voice Literary Supplement,* "may be on the thin edge of ethical procedure. For the lay reader, however, they're infinitely more entertaining than the ponderous sobriety, overlaid with econometric tables and French theorizing, that history as a field has become. . . . If Spence's tactics are maddening, they're also revelatory, making us think about the life behind history as a drier recitation of facts never could." David Lattimore of the *New York Times Book Review* cites *Emperor of China, The Death of Woman Wang,* and *The Gate of Heavenly Peace* as works in which Spence "employs a similar method of delicate interweaving and transition. These are works of carefully thought out, accurately annotated history, which, with their well-observed detail and extensive quotations, propel us among the very sights and sounds and emotions of the time. They exemplify a high historical art, worthy tributes to Clio, muse of history." Salisbury describes Spence as "a poet-historian of China, whose images bring to us the true fragrance of the East, the limitless breadth of China, the deep wells of its culture, the harshness of its cruelties, the continuity of the Chinese ethos."

BIOGRAPHICAL/CRITICAL SOURCES:

PERIODICALS

America, September 29, 1990, p. 190.
American Spectator, December, 1990, p. 52.
Booklist, September 15, 1998, Brad Hooper, review of *The Chan's Great Continent,* p. 172.
Boston Globe, November 16, 1988, p. 85; May 6, 1990, p. B51; July 2, 1992, p. 67.
Charlotte Observer, January 11, 1999.
Chicago Tribune, May 13, 1990, section 14, p. 1; July 12, 1992, section 14, p. 3.
Commonweal, August 10, 1990, pp. 462-63.
Economist, June 2, 1990, pp. 95-96; October 2, 1999, "Gazing at China," p. 91.
Far Eastern Economic Review, March 13, 1997, p. 47.
Foreign Affairs, March, 1999, Lucian W. Pye, review of *The Chan's Great Continent,* p. 156.
Globe and Mail (Toronto), June 29, 1985.
Historian, spring, 1995, pp. 626-27.
History and Theory: Studies in the Philosophy of History, May, 1992, pp. 143-52.
History Today, February, 1993, p. 57; December, 1993, pp. 55, 57.
Library Journal, May 15, 1992, p. 103; December, 1998, Steven I. Levine, review of *The Chan's Great Continent,* p. 128.
Los Angeles Times, November 20, 1988, p. B1.
Los Angeles Times Book Review, December 27, 1981; November 25, 1984; May 27, 1990, p. 1.
Nation, September 2, 1978.
New Leader, July 9, 1990, p. 17; January 4, 1999, p. 29.
New Republic, January 4, 1999, Ian Buruma, "Two Cheers for Orientalism," p. 29.
New Statesman & Society, September 29, 1989, p. 38; June 8, 1990, p. 34.
Newsweek, May 22, 1978; November 9, 1981.
New Yorker, April 3, 1989, pp. 109-115.
New York Review of Books, May 18, 1978; May 31, 1990, p. 16; November 5, 1992, pp. 51-53; February 29, 1996, pp. 39- 42; December 3, 1998, p. 21.
New York Times, October 12, 1981; November 21, 1984; May 10, 1990, p. C19.
New York Times Book Review, July 16, 1969; June 11, 1978; October 18, 1981; December 2, 1984; December 18, 1988, p. 7; May 13, 1990, pp. 1, 32; November 15, 1998, Stephen Greenblatt, "Orienteering," p. 19; December 2, 1990, p. 81; February 4, 1996, p. 6; November 15, 1998.
Philadelphia Inquirer, October 18, 1998.
Publishers Weekly, March 16, 1990, p. 56; May 4, 1990, pp. 48-49; April 20, 1992, p. 42; November 27, 1995, p. 62; August 3, 1998, review of *The*

Chan's Great Continent, p. 62; September 20, 1999, review of *Mao Zedong,* p. 61.
Time International, April 5, 1999, Hannah Beech, "Through Western Eyes," p. 56.
Times (London), February 18, 1982.
Times Literary Supplement, August 19, 1983; September 27, 1985; February 12, 1993, p. 26.
Tribune Books (Chicago), October 11, 1981; July 12, 1992, pp. 3, 9.
U.S. News and World Report, May 28, 1990, p. 62.
Voice Literary Supplement, December, 1984.
Washington Post Book World, November 22, 1981; December 23, 1984; April 22, 1990, p. 1; January 21, 1996, pp. 1, 14.
Yale Review, autumn, 1969.*

* * *

SPINRAD, Norman (Richard) 1940-

PERSONAL: Born September 15, 1940, in New York, NY; son of Morris and Ray (Greenhut) Spinrad. *Education:* City College of the City University of New York, B.S., 1961. *Politics:* "Independent Conservative Radical."

ADDRESSES: Agent—Jane Rotrosen, 318 East 51st St., New York, NY 10022.

CAREER: Writer, 1963—. Worked as a sandalmaker, welfare investigator, and radio talk show host; literary agent, Scott Meredith Literary Agency, New York, NY, 1965-66.

MEMBER: Writers Guild of America, Science Fiction Writers of America (vice president, 1972-74; president, 1980-81; western regional director).

AWARDS, HONORS: Hugo Award nominations, World Science Fiction Society, 1968, for the teleplay "The Doomsday Machine," 1970, for *Bug Jack Barron,* and 1975, for "Riding the Torch"; Nebula Award nominations, Science Fiction Writers of America, 1969, for "The Big Flash" and *Bug Jack Barron,* 1972, for *The Iron Dream,* and 1984, for *The Void Captain's Tale;* Association of American Publishers, National Book Award nomination, 1973, for *The Iron Dream,* and American Book Award nomination, 1980, for *The Star Spangled Future;* Prix Apollo, 1974, for *The Iron Dream;* Jupiter Award for best science fiction novella, 1975, for "Riding the Torch."

WRITINGS:

The Solarians, Paperback Library (New York City), 1966.
Agent of Chaos, Belmont Books (New York City), 1967, introduction by Barry Malzberg, F. Watts (New York City), 1988.
The Men in the Jungle, Doubleday (New York City), 1967.
"The Doomsday Machine" (teleplay; episode of *Star Trek* series), National Broadcasting Co. (NBC-TV)/Paramount, 1967.
Bug Jack Barron, Walker Co. (New York City), 1969.
Fragments of America, Now Library Press, 1970.
The Last Hurrah of the Golden Horde (short stories), Doubleday, 1970.
(Editor, author of introduction, and contributor) *The New Tomorrows,* Belmont Books, 1971.
The Iron Dream, Avon (New York City), 1972, hardcover edition published with a new introduction by Theodore Sturgeon, Gregg Press (Boston), 1977.
(Editor, author of introduction, and contributor) *Modern Science Fiction,* Anchor Press, 1974, hardcover edition, Gregg Press, 1976.
"Tag Team" (teleplay; episode of *Land of the Lost*), NBC-TV, 1974.
No Direction Home: An Anthology of Science-Fiction Stories (includes "The Big Flash"), Pocket Books (New York City), 1975, hardcover edition, Millington Books (London), 1976.
Passing through the Flame: The Last Hollywood Novel, Berkley (New York City), 1975.
Riding the Torch (bound with *Destiny Times Three,* by Fritz Leiber), Dell (New York City), 1978, published separately, Bluejay (New York City), 1984.
The Star Spangled Future (short stories), Ace, 1979.
A World Between, Pocket Books, 1979.
Songs from the Stars, Simon Schuster (New York City), 1980.
The Void Captain's Tale, Timescape Books (New York City), 1983.
Staying Alive: A Writer's Guide, Donning (Norfolk, VA), 1983.
The Mind Game, Bantam (New York City), 1985.
Child of Fortune, Bantam, 1986.
Little Heroes, Bantam, 1987.
Science Fiction in the Real World, Southern Illinois University Press (Carbondale), 1990.
Russian Spring, Bantam, 1991.
Pictures at Eleven, Bantam, 1994.
Journals of the Plague Years, Bantam, 1995.
Greenhouse Summer, Tor (New York City), 1999.
He Walked among Us (Heyne Verlag, Germany), forthcoming.

Also author of *Other Americas* (novellas), 1988, and the novel *The Children of Hamlin,* 1991. Author of weekly column on politics for Los Angeles *Free Press,* 1970-71; author of monthly column on writing and publishing for *Locus,* 1979-85. Author of review column for *Asimov's Science Fiction Magazine.* Contributor to numerous science fiction anthologies and books about science fiction, including *SF: The Other Side of Realism,* edited by Thomas D. Clareson, Bowling Green University Popular Press, 1971; *Threads of Time: Three Original Novellas of Science Fiction,* edited by Robert Silverberg, Thomas Nelson, 1974; *Experiment Perilous: Three Essays on Science Fiction,* edited by Andrew Porter, Algol Press, 1976; and *The Craft of Science Fiction,* edited by Reginald Bretnor, Harper, 1976. Contributor of political and social essays to *Knight* magazine, of film criticism to Los Angeles *Free Press, Cinema,* and *Staff,* and of fiction to *Playboy, New Worlds, Analog Science Fiction/Science Fact,* and other periodicals.

ADAPTATIONS: The film rights to *Bug Jack Barron* were purchased by Universal.

SIDELIGHTS: As a member of the science fiction new wave of the 1960s and more recently as president of the Science Fiction Writers of America, Norman Spinrad has campaigned for a new acceptance of the genre and its writers. He suggested in a *CA* interview that the emergence of science fiction in pulp magazines and its subsequent categorization as popular culture has proven a barrier to its consideration as serious literature. Critics and innovators have emerged to broaden the scope of the genre, but as Spinrad explained to Robert Dahlin in a *Publishers Weekly* interview, categorization persists because it serves the interests of publishers. "These categories are a publisher's trip," he said. "What I'd like to do, but can't in this country, is just have my books published as books."

Added to the struggle for acceptance, Spinrad notes in *SF: The Other Side of Realism,* the science fiction writer faces creative challenges. The science fiction novelist "must not only create characters, theme, forces of destiny and plot but (unlike the mainstream novelist) must create from scratch a universe entire in which character, plot and destiny interact with each other and with the postulated environment." This, in turn, presents technical obstacles, he points out. "While one is in the process of creating in detail the sf context, the characters and plot hang in limbo; while one is advancing plot and characterization, one's grip on one's created universe tends to loosen." Yet, as the author indicates in *Modern Science Fiction,* science fiction is "the only fiction that deals with modern reality in the only way that it can be comprehended—as the interface between a rapidly evolving and fissioning environment and the resultant continuously mutating human consciousness."

"Science fiction, for me, is relating the total external environment to the inner psyche, something I find missing in many contemporary books," he told Dahlin. "The media, technology, politics—all these are part of us, and what I care about is the way people are changed by external means." Spinrad's first three novels, *The Solarians, Agent of Chaos,* and *The Men in the Jungle,* as well as his short fiction of this period, show a progression away from traditional science fiction forms and concerns toward the external/internal approach and an awareness of contemporary issues. According to *Dictionary of Literary Biography* contributor Ina Rae Hark, a recurring theme in much of this early fiction is one in which "a home world that seems a source of security and power must by willingly or unwillingly sacrificed in order to liberate human potential, thus enabling men to rise from its ashes and conquer the stars."

With his fourth novel, *Bug Jack Barron,* Spinrad separated himself from pulp science fiction forever. The host of a popular weekly phone-in television show set in the near future, Jack Barron has made his reputation by placing viewers, who call in their complaints on videophones, face to face with their alleged offender for a nationally televised debate of the issue. One phoned-in tip puts the television muckraker on the trail of a millionaire scheming to control cryogenic operations and research into immortality. In order to expose the hideous side of the millionaire's obsession, Barron must first free himself from the seduction of the immortality offered him as a bribe. In this book, Spinrad scrutinizes the powerful, notes a *Times Literary Supplement* contributor, especially those outside politics; he "writes about two of the most potentially dangerous elites: the super-television inquisitors and the men with the scientific power to control and extend human life for ever."

Locating the book along the science fiction spectrum, Hark writes that "besides its lack of traditional pulp accessories, *Bug Jack Barron* leans toward the New Wave by including elements traditionally foreign to the science-fiction genre: an experimental, stream-of-consciousness style . . . abundant obscenity, and explicitly detailed sexual encounters." In the larger framework of contemporary fiction, "*Bug Jack Barron* remains a novel of considerable strengths and considerable flaws," comments Hark. "Most of its faults stem from the 'wicked mad businessman' plot, most of the strengths from the sociological observations for whose expression the plot provides a framework." And, concludes the *Times Literary Supplement* contributor: "Mr. Spinrad writes with verve and has a lively ear for current idiom. His 'political science fiction' has a deadly plausibility."

Spinrad's *The Iron Dream,* an alternate history, presents itself as the second edition of the book, *Lord of the Swastika,* complete with an informative introduction and a scholarly afterword. This fictitious science fiction classic from the 1950s was written by the illustrator and Hugo Award winning science fiction writer Adolf Hitler, who immigrated to the United States from Germany in 1919. "Spinrad's craft is sure and imaginative," observes Albert I. Berger in the *Science Fiction and Fantasy Book Review.* "He makes astonishingly good and thoroughly logical and consistent use of an old science fiction device, the parallel time-track, to examine the individual and mass psychology of fascism."

"*Lord of the Swastika* is a very badly written sword-and-sorcery opus, full of nauseating battles and grotesque and obsessive phallic and scatological imagery," writes Hark. "The book mythopoeticizes Hitler's actual rise to power, with the military victory he would have desired substituting for the actual course of World War II." She adds that *The Iron Dream* "is, despite being a rather unpleasant reading experience, far and away Spinrad's best novel because its format emphasizes his virtues as an ironist and social moralist and minimizes—even uses to advantage—his weaknesses as a stylist and plot constructor."

"At the very least, *The Iron Dream* must be admired as a remarkable tour de force, a dazzling display of ingenuity and originality," H. Bruce Franklin maintains in *Washington Post Book World.* "But it is much more than that, for it forces us to confront elements of fascism within our own culture, low and high." As Berger notes, "The forward . . . nicely ties Spinrad's examination of Nazism to contemporary popular culture." Franklin agrees, writing that "we recognize the similarities between [the protagonist's] brutal omnipotent maleness and the diseased fantasies of both fascism and the latest sword-and-sorcery epics." Furthermore, adds Berger, "the afterword similarly skewers the easy academic acceptance of fundamentally barbaric principles if they can be made to fit preconceived notions or anti-communist cant." This reviewer reaches the conclusion that "as a thoughtful, incisive satire on the roots of fascism and an example of the thoroughgoing fashion in which Spinrad maintains the internal logic of his parallel time-track to serve his ends, *The Iron Dream* belongs in any serious science fiction collection."

Two of Spinrad's novels from the 1980s, *The Void Captain's Tale* and *Child of Fortune*—both set in a far future universe filled with exotic and distant worlds made closer by an erotic form of space travel—received considerable attention. "Spinrad's ingenious space-drive," explains Theodore Sturgeon in the *Los Angeles Times Book Review,* "has the ship's machine create a field . . . which at peak and at captain's command melds with the pilot's psyche, causing the ship to cease to exist in one spatial locus and reappear in another." The captain of the first book tell the story of his forbidden relationship with his ship's Void Pilot, the woman whose special training facilitates the hyperspace jumps—jumps during which she experiences transcendent orgasm, unity with the cosmos.

Drawn by her desire to remain in this higher state, the Void Pilot proposes to her captain that he commit her to the hyperspace jump forever. To do so, however, he must sacrifice himself, his crew, and passengers. As Sturgeon points out, the captain comes to a "slow realization, and ultimate conviction, that there may be a value in the release of a single human being into a higher consciousness far greater than the worth of any number of . . . people." The reviewer, himself a well-known science fiction writer, believes that "what makes this book important . . . is its demand that our most deeply conditioned ethics be examined as freely—as meticulously and courageously—as anything else."

In *The Void Captain's Tale,* writes Howard Waldrop in *Washington Post Book World,* "Spinrad has written a . . . book, dark and somber in tone, subject matter and method." And, comments Waldrop, "he has come up with an idea, a style and a narrative that perfectly fits his talent." The book generated some controversy because of its eroticism and some criticism of Spinrad's future language. Yet, as Gerald Jonas concludes in the *New York Times Book Review,* "Norman Spinrad, like his characters, takes great risks; the rewards for readers willing to meet him halfway are commensurate."

Child of Fortune is the story of a flower child of the future who sets out on a journey of self-discovery that takes her to many of the exotic worlds of Spinrad's future universe; one is a garden of pleasures from which no one has ever returned. "How the heroine regains her freedom—and discovers her true calling—by wielding the peculiarly human weapon of speech—is the core of the story," observes Jonas in another *New York Times Book Review* article. Though he faults Spinrad's future language, Toronto *Globe and Mail* contributor H. J. Kirchhoff finds this novel "complex, colorful, zesty and bawdy. The characters are drawn in such depth that it is hard not to empathize with them, and the settings are flamboyant, even sensational." Finally, maintains Gary K. Wolfe in *Fantasy Review:* "Despite echoes of Cordwainer Smith—as well as Henry Miller, Baudelaire, and perhaps even Octave Mirbeau—*Child of Fortune* is a highly original work and one of considerable merit. . . . I hope the book achieves the audience it deserves."

In the 1990s Spinrad continued to publish novels at an undiminished rate. His 1991 *Russian Spring,* set in the twenty-first century, relates the story of two generations of a family over a thirty-year period. The books opens on a world in which the United States has remained a military power but has incurred a heavy national debt while becoming increasingly isolationist and hostile in its foreign policy. Would-be astronaut Jerry Reed must travel to Common Europe, the only place where space exploration is being planned, in an attempt to fulfill his ambitions. In Paris he meets and falls in love with Soviet career bureaucrat Sonya Gagarin. Once the couple are married, Spinrad's narrative leaps twenty years into the future. While Jerry's plans for a career in space have been foiled by a pervasive anti-Americanism, Sonya's career has steadily progressed. The couple now have two children, daughter Franja, who has inherited her father's space wanderlust, and son Bob, who is enamored by a vision of America as it once existed in the twentieth century. After Franja enrolls in a Russian space academy and Bob takes off to discover the current state of the United States, the story takes another ten-year jump into the future. Commenting on the resolution of the novel, a *Publishers Weekly* reviewer observes: "A series of odd, occasionally tragic events brings the family (and the world) together. Despite some tech-talk this is not science fiction: the first two-thirds of this hefty book is chillingly logical, if sometimes very funny, and while the happy ending may seem forced, Spinrad gives us a wild, exhilarating ride into the next century."

In *The Children of Hamlin,* also published in 1991, Spinrad presents a loosely autobiographical novel set in the '60s counterculture of New York City. The action revolves around Tom Hollander, ex-junkie and a reader for a literary agency. Tom's best friends, a couple named Ted and Doris, are obsessed with therapy and consciousness expansion. He is torn between two lovers, the free-spirited drug-dealer Robin, and Arlene, a woman who is as obsessed with therapy as his friends. A *Publishers Weekly* reviewer notes: "If this . . . novel . . . had been published . . . during the era that it reflects, it would have achieved cult status by now." On a more negative note, the reviewer adds: "The stumbling block here is the determined use of slang; overindulgence in such words as 'bummers' and 'groovies' quickly becomes tiresome."

Spinrad's 1995 *Pictures at Eleven* presents a thriller revolving around ecoterrorism. Radical environmental activists seize a television station in Los Angeles and negotiate with their hostages about program changes, including a show for terrorists. Spinrad puts a Hollywood agent in charge of the team of outside negotiators who are trying to gain the hostages' freedom. D. A. Ball of *Entertainment Weekly* finds the idea for the book to be "brilliant . . . unbelievably interesting," but also feels that Spinrad's execution fails to realize the promise in that idea. "Spinrad writes with an outsider's notion of police procedure, the news media, and hostage behavior," Ball states, also noting that much of the writing is "cliched." In direct contrast, Dennis Winters of *Booklist* decries Spinrad's plot as "tired and hackneyed," but concludes: "Along the way, Spinrad gets beyond the cliched faces of his characters and even beyond the conventionally unconventional faces behind them. The characters turn into real people, able to carry the action where it's going. Spinrad has shown his mastery of this genre as well as his preferred haunts along its edges yet again."

Spinrad's books have been translated into a number of languages, including French, Italian, and German.

BIOGRAPHICAL/CRITICAL SOURCES:

BOOKS

Bretnor, Reginald, editor, *The Craft of Science Fiction,* Harper, 1976.

Clareson, Thomas D., editor, *SF: The Other Side of Realism,* Bowling Green University, 1971.

Dictionary of Literary Biography, Volume VIII: *Twentieth-Century Science- Fiction Writers,* Gale, 1981.

Platt, Charles, *Dream Makers: The Uncommon People Who Write Science Fiction,* Berkley Publishing, 1980.

Spinrad, Norman, editor, *The New Tomorrows,* Belmont Books, 1971.

Spinrad, Norman, editor, *Modern Science Fiction,* Anchor Books (New York City), 1974.

PERIODICALS

Analog Science Fiction/Science Fact, April, 1983.

Best Sellers, March, 1983.

Booklist, November 1, 1994, Dennis Winters, review of *Pictures at 11,* p. 482.

Entertainment Weekly, December 2, 1994, D. A. Ball, review of *Pictures at Eleven,* p. 66.

Extrapolation, winter, 1995, Wendy E. Erisman, "Inverting the Ideal World: Carnival and the Carnivalesque in Contemporary Utopian Science Fiction," pp. 333-344; spring, 1995, Jennifer Lynn Browning, "Science Fiction in the Real World," pp. 70-74.

Fantasy Review, July, 1985; August, 1985.

Globe and Mail (Toronto), August 24, 1985.

Los Angeles Times Book Review, April 3, 1983; October 27, 1985.

New York Times Book Review, May 22, 1983; September 8, 1985.

Publishers Weekly, January 2, 1981; August 16, 1991, review of *Russian Spring,* p. 46; September 13, 1991, p. 62; October 18, 1999, review of *Greenhouse Summer,* p. 75.

Science Fiction and Fantasy Book Review, October, 1982.

Science Fiction Chronicle, December, 1985.

Science Fiction Studies, spring, 1973.

Times Literary Supplement, March 26, 1970.

Washington Post Book World, July 27, 1980; July 25, 1982; February 27, 1983.

OTHER

Norman Spinrad's Home Page, http://ourworld.compuserve/homepages/normanspinrad/ (December 2, 1999).*

*   *   *

SPIVAK, Gayatri Chakravorty 1942-

PERSONAL: Born in 1942, in India. *Education:* University of Calcutta, B.A., 1959; Cornell University, M.A., 1962, Ph.D., 1967.

ADDRESSES: Office—Department of English, Columbia University, 2960 Broadway, New York, NY 10027-6902; fax 212-854-6465. *E-mail*—gcs4@columbia.edu.

CAREER: Writer and educator. Has taught English and comparative literature at several universities, including University of Iowa and University of Texas; served as Longstreet Professor of English, Emory University; and Andrew K. Mellon Professor of English, University of Pittsburgh; Columbia University, New York City, Avalon Foundation Professor in the Humanities, 1991—. Has been a fellow at several institutes and universities, including the National Humanities Institute, the Center for the Humanities at Wesleyan, the Center for the Study of Social Sciences, Calcutta, and the Davis Center for Historical Studies, Princeton University.

AWARDS, HONORS: Guggenheim fellowship; Kent fellowship; Translation Prize, Sahitya Akademi (National Academy of Literature in India), 1997.

WRITINGS:

NONFICTION

Myself Must I Remake: The Life and Poetry of W. B. Yeats (juvenile), Crowell (New York City), 1974.

In Other Worlds: Essays in Cultural Politics, Methuen (London), 1987, Routledge (New York City), 1988.

(Editor, with Ranajit Guha) *Selected Subaltern Studies,* Oxford University Press (New York City), 1988.

The Post-Colonial Critic: Interviews, Strategies, Dialogues, edited by Sarah Harasym, Routledge, 1990.

Outside in the Teaching Machine, Routledge, 1993.

The Spivak Reader, edited by Donna Landry and George McLean, Routledge (London), 1995.

A Critique of Post-Colonial Reason: Toward a History of the Vanishing Present, Harvard University Press (Cambridge, MA), 1999.

TRANSLATOR

Derrida, Jacques, *Of Grammatology,* Johns Hopkins University Press (Baltimore), 1976.

Hassan, Jamelie, *Inscription,* Dunlop Art Gallery (Regina, Canada), 1990.

Devi, Mahasweta, *Imaginary Maps,* Routledge, 1995.

Devi, Mahasweta, *Breast Stories,* Seagull Books (Calcutta), 1997.

OTHER

Contributor to anthologies, including *Displacement: Derrida and After,* Indiana University Press (Bloomington), 1983; *Philosophical Approaches to Literature: New Essays on Nineteenth and Twentieth-Century Texts,* Bucknell University Press (Lewisburg), 1984; *For Alma Mater: Theory and Practice in Feminist Scholarship,* edited by Paula Treichler, Cheris Kramarae, and Beth Stafford, University of Illinois Press (Urbana), 1985; *Post-Structuralism and the Question of History,* edited by Derek Attridge, Robert Young, and Geoff Bennington, Cambridge University Press, 1987; *Marxism and the Interpretation of Culture,* edited by

Cary Nelson and Lawrence Grossberg, Macmillan (London), 1988; *The New Historicism,* edited by H. Aram Vesser and Stanley Fish, Routledge, 1989; *Feminists Theorize the Political,* edited by Judith Butler and Joan Scott, Routledge, 1992; and *Colonial Discourse/ Postcolonial Theory,* Manchester University Press, 1994.

Contributor to journals, including *Boundary 2, Critical Inquiry, Diacritics, Differences, Harper's, Journal of South Asian Literature, Modern Language Notes, New Literary History, Oxford Literary Review,* and *Socialist Review.* Has served on editorial boards of many journals, including *New Formations, Diaspora, Parallax,* and *Interventions.*

SIDELIGHTS: Indian literary theorist and educator Gayatri Chakravorty Spivak is concerned with the work of postcolonial and third-world writers. A self-proclaimed feminist Marxist deconstructivist, she is one of the most outspoken proponents of a revision of postcolonial literary theory. In her books, which include 1987's *In Other Worlds: Essays in Cultural Politics* and *The Post-Colonial Critic: Interviews, Strategies, Dialogues,* published in 1990, Spivak addresses the importance of acknowledging a writer's "positionality"—the unique multiple cultural, economic, racial, and political influences or perspectives that influence one's writing. Spivak is also known for her work in translating Jacques Derrida's *Of Grammatology* and the stories of Indian writer Mahasweta Devi.

The assumption held by many critics that, for every way of thinking, there is a single, unique voice is an integral aspect of Spivak's work. In her influential essay "Can the Subaltern Speak?," published in *Marxism and the Interpretation of Culture,* Spivak explores the ways in which the "subaltern"—members of the non-ruling class—express the oppression they encounter. In attempting to speak for the subaltern, members of the intellectual elite can only present an interpretation of the subalternal voice filtered through an intellectual/elitist viewpoint. The subaltern are relegated to the position of subjects rather than participants in a two-way dialogue. Spivak encourages academics to understand how their positions of intellectual and economic privilege limit their integrity in serving as a spokesperson for the subaltern. In other discussions, the critic posits women in the role of subaltern, questioning the male-constructed voice of women within a patriarchal society.

The Post-Colonial Critic contains twelve interviews with Spivak; she expresses her views on a variety of subjects and includes a cogent analysis of the works of both Derrida and Karl Marx. A collection of essays, *In Other Worlds* is organized into three areas: a criticism of major literary works, a discussion of literary theory, and a critique of the diverse theoretical representations of the subaltern in literature. Calling Spivak's critique of Marxist analysis "acute, unusual, and scholarly," Roger Fowler notes in *Modern Language Review* that *In Other Worlds* "is a challenging and highly intelligent volume." Several of Spivak's most well-known essays were collected as *The Spivak Reader* and published in 1995.

Writing at length and in great detail on Spivak's 1999 volume *A Critique of Post-Colonial Reason: Toward a History of the Vanishing Present,* Terry Eagleton of the *London Review of Books* praises the author on some counts and offers extensive criticism of the book on others. Eagleton begins his essay by noting that there must be "a secret handbook for post-colonial critics" that sets down two basic rules about their writing: first, reject the worth of your own discipline; second, be as obscure "as you can decently get away with." Spivak, according to Eagleton, obeys both rules. She states "that a good deal of US post-colonial theory is 'bogus.' " She makes numerous statements "inaccessible" to the general reader, such as "the in-choate in-fans ab-original para-subject cannot be theorized as a functionally *completely* frozen in a world where teleology is schematized into geo-geography." Eagleton finds Spivak's prose to be "overstuffed" and "excessively elliptical," and states of the book as whole: "The endless digressions and self-interruptions of this study, as it meanders from Kant to Krishna, Schiller to Sati, belong, among other places, to a politically directionless Left." This lack of direction, by which Eagleton means the tendency of post-colonial critics to condemn Western policy in the Third World without offering specific political alternatives, is another count on which he faults *A Critique of Post-Colonial Reason.* He also feels that despite Spivak's "withering criticism of the post-colonial Western liberals," and her "keen nose for Western cant, patronage and hypocrisy, she is notably reluctant to break ranks." On the positive side, Eagleton comments: "Spivak has a quite formidable span of reference, which leaves most other cultural theorists looking dismally parochial. Few of them could remotely match the range and versatility of this book, which stretches from Hegelian philosophy and the historical archives of colonial India to Post-Modern culture and international trade." He notes that "[i]n the course of this book, Spivak writes with great theoretical brilliance on Charlotte Bronte and Mary Shelley, Jean Rhys and Mahasweta Devi" He also praises her recognition of the fact that essays of cultural criticism do not represent a threat to the transnational corporations that define much of Western policy toward the Third World. "The relations between North and South," as Eagleton puts it, "are not primarily about discourse, language, or identity but about armaments, commodities, exploitation, migrant labour, debt and drugs; and this study boldly addresses the economic realities which too many post-colonial critics culturalise away."

BIOGRAPHICAL/CRITICAL SOURCES:

BOOKS

Feminist Writers, St. James Press (Detroit, MI), 1996.

PERIODICALS

Arena, Volume 97, 1991.
Choice, March, 1995, p. 1059.
London Review of Books, May 13, 1999, pp. 3, 5-6.
Modern Language Review, October, 1989, p. 897; January, 1993, p. 160.
Publishers Weekly, April 26, 1999, p. 72.
Oxford Literary Review, Volume 12, numbers 1-2, 1991.

OTHER

Comparative Literature: The Intellectual Foundations, http://web.columbia.edu/ (July 8, 1999).
Gayatri Chakravorty Spivak: An Introduction, http://www.stg.brown.edu (July 8, 1999).*

* * *

STANCYKOWNA
See SZYMBORSKA, Wislawa

* * *

STEEL, Ronald (Lewis) 1931-

PERSONAL: Born March 25, 1931, in Morris, IL. *Education:* Northwestern University, B.A., 1953; Sorbonne, University of Paris, graduate study, 1953; Harvard University, M.A., 1955.

ADDRESSES: Office—University of Southern California School of International Relations, Von KleinSmid Center, Room 304, Los Angeles, CA 90089-0043.

CAREER: Writer. University of Southern California, Los Angeles, CA, professor of international relations, 1986—. Vice consul in U.S. Foreign Service, 1957-58; Scholastic Magazines, New York, NY, editor, 1959-62. Visiting fellow, Jonathan Edwards College, Yale University, 1970-73; visiting professor, University of California, Irvine, University of California, Los Angeles, Yale University, Wellesley College, Dartmouth, Rutgers University, and the University of Texas at Austin. Senior associate of Carnegie Endowment for International Peace, Washington, DC. *Military service:* U.S. Army, 1954-56.

AWARDS, HONORS: American Political Science Association Congressional fellow, 1962-63; Sidney Hillman Foundation Award for best nonfiction book, 1967, for *Pax Americana;* Guggenheim fellow, 1973; National Book Critics Circle Award for nonfiction, Bancroft Prize from Columbia University Board of Trustees, *Los Angeles Times* Book Award, *Washington Monthly* Book Award, American Book Award and Pulitzer Prize nominations, and named a notable book by the American Library Association, all 1981, all for *Walter Lippmann and the American Century;* American Book Award, 1982, for paperback edition of *Walter Lippmann and the American Century.*

WRITINGS:

The End of the Alliance: America and the Future of Europe, Viking (New York City), 1964.
(With George H. T. Kimble) *Tropical Africa Today,* McGraw (New York City), 1966.
Pax Americana, Viking, 1967, published with introduction by D. W. Brogan, Hamish Hamilton (London), 1968, revised edition, Viking, 1970.
Imperialists and Other Heroes: A Chronicle of the American Empire, Random House (New York City), 1971.
Walter Lippmann and the American Century, Little, Brown (Boston), 1980, with a new introduction by the author, Transaction (New Brunswick, NJ), 1998.
(Contributor) Nitza Rosovsky, *The Jewish Experience at Harvard and Radcliffe: An Introduction to an Exhibition Presented by the Harvard Semitic Museum on the Occasion of Harvard's 350th Anniversary, September, 1986,* Harvard University Press (Cambridge, MA), 1986.
Temptations of a Superpower, Harvard University Press, 1995.
In Love with Night: The American Romance with Robert Kennedy, Simon & Schuster (New York City), 2000.

Regular contributor to *New York Review of Books*. Contributing editor, *New Republic.*

EDITOR

Federal Aid to Education, Wilson (New York City), 1961.
U.S. Foreign Trade Policy, Wilson, 1962.
Italy, Wilson, 1963.
New Light on Juvenile Delinquency, Wilson, 1967.
North Africa, Wilson, 1967.

SIDELIGHTS: Ronald Steel is a scholar and commentator upon America's role in foreign affairs with special emphasis on the post-cold war era. To quote Alan Tonelson in the *New York Times Book Review,* Steel's work "deserves a wide readership among both foreign policy experts and laymen. . . . His biggest contribution to our public life has been his dogged effort to bring American foreign policy making down from the clouds." In the *Nation,* Warren Cohen called Steel "one of the finest writers on foreign affairs of the past thirty years," an analyst "with little if any faith in the foreign policy elite."

Perhaps not surprisingly, Steel began to question American policies of intervention as early as the 1960s. In 1967 he published *Pax Americana,* a critical study of the motives and consequences of American foreign policy in the two decades following World War II. *New York Times* columnist Michiko Kakutani deemed the book "a classic," noting that, in Steel's view, "America's fear of Communism and its moralistic desire to spread its own values to the world at large had had serious repercussions, including an infatuation with global power and influence." Henry Steele Commager, writing in the *New York Times Book Review,* called *Pax Americana* "the most ardent and, to my mind, the most persuasive critique of American foreign policy over the last twenty years that has yet appeared." In her review, Kakutani concluded that *Pax Americana* and Steel's subsequent works offer "a provocative prescription for a new foreign policy based on humility and a recognition of limits, a prescription that is bound to be hotly debated."

Steel is perhaps equally well known for his biographies, including *Walter Lippmann and the American Century,* to which he devoted ten years of labor. The book met with a great deal of critical enthusiasm upon its publication in the fall of 1980. Joseph Epstein, writing in the *Times Literary Supplement,* noted: "The critical reception accorded . . . . *Walter Lippmann and the American Century* has been overwhelming in its conclusion that Steel has written a brilliant book." This acclaim was soon made official: The following year the volume won a number of prestigious awards and also received Pulitzer Prize and American Book Award nominations.

Walter Lippmann and the American Century recounts the career of one of America's most influential twentieth-century journalists. From his undergraduate days at Harvard to his death in 1974, Lippmann was either reporting the news or making headlines himself. As a political columnist from 1931 to 1967, he wrote the syndicated "Today and Tomorrow," which at its peak appeared in over 200 newspapers. Lippmann was also one of the founders of the *New Republic,* editor of the *New York World,* author of a number of influential books, and advisor to presidents through the decades. Paul Gray commented in *Time* magazine: "Getting such a long and varied life between the covers of a single volume seems challenging enough; harder still to record the vast panorama of history that Lippmann observed and, in some instances helped shape. Author Ronald Steel performs these two tasks brilliantly."

Even before Steel began the task of putting Walter Lippmann's life into print, all the ingredients for a successful biography seemed to be present. Foremost was Lippmann's full cooperation. Steel conducted a series of personal interviews with Lippmann and had access to Lippmann's private papers, a huge collection including diaries and some 100,000 letters now at Yale University. Yet another reason for Steel's success was his "own immersion in the currents of twentieth-century thought," according to Janet Mandelstam of the *Detroit News.*

Some reviewers felt that Steel's views on foreign policy account for the shortcomings of *Walter Lippmann and the American Century.* In *Commentary,* for instance, Kenneth Lynn declared: "Inasmuch as Ronald Steel's previous work . . . has been in the realm of political analysis, one would expect that he would be at his best in demonstrating how remarkably well Lippmann's political commentaries have stood the test of time. Steel, however, is an ideologue whose approach to the issues of twentieth-century American politics is as predetermined as Lippmann's was exploratory."

Epstein characterized Steel's biography as "a whole-earth catalogue of revisionist presuppositions, assumptions and notions," adding: "*Walter Lippmann and the American Century* is a political biography in the full sense of the term. Not only is it about a political figure but it is also written out of a quite specific political point of view. . . . Much of his biography is scarcely more than a checklist of Walter Lippmann's opinions. . . . When Lippmann's opinions and Steel's are not congruent, Lippmann's are found wanting."

J. A. Thompson, in his *Journal of American Studies* review of *Walter Lippmann and the American Century,* refuted Epstein's criticism, claiming that his comments "give a distorted and inadequate idea of the book." Thompson explained: "Generally speaking, there is no doubt that Steel writes most approvingly when Lippmann's opinions come closest to those of an American liberal or radical in the 1960s, but such editorializing is not obtrusive." Other reviewers also praised Steel's objectivity. In the *New Republic,* Alfred Kazin stated: "Steel's book is a strong performance. Steel, although considerably left of Lippmann, does justice to the man's resilient intelligence." And David Halberstam, writing in the *Los Angeles Times Book Review,* said that Steel "has clearly worked diligently to master the era; he has also worked to restrain his own politics."

Some critics pointed out that *Walter Lippmann and the American Century* is more than just a retelling of a famous person's life. Anthony Lewis of the *New York Review of Books* observed that the biography "is a fascinating book: on journalism, on America in the world, on a mysterious human being. . . . Steel explores the possible psychological origins of Lippmann's contradictory qualities, and does so with skill." *New York Times* contributor John Leonard commented: "I think Mr. Steel has written a different book from the one he thought he was writing. *Walter Lippmann* is less about the failure of 20th-century American liberalism than it is about the failure of 20th-century American journalism as journalism hunkered down with government. The book I read is extremely good."

Steel's *Temptations of a Superpower* grew from a lecture he delivered at the Library of Congress. The work is "an eloquent meditation on the role of the United States in the world," to quote *Foreign Affairs* correspondent David C. Hendrickson. Steel suggests that America's globalist vision, and hence its military spending, has not only become archaic since the end of the cold war, it has also had a negative impact on domestic reforms and business innovations. In *Washington Monthly,* Doyle McManus wrote, "Put bluntly, Steel's message in this nicely crafted series of essays is: Forget most of what you learned during the past half-century. The United States may be the world's only superpower, but it is far less "super' than before, and the honor may be more trouble than it's worth. The notion that the United States "must lead' in virtually every circumstance is a terrible mistake." McManus added: ". . . This is, in short, a Walter Lippmann view of the post-Cold War world: a brief for a new realism and against reflexive idealism."

Steel does not prescribe complete isolationism for the United States. As he sees it, America must intervene in foreign situations on moral grounds when genocide is taking place, and on political grounds when American interests or the safety of American borders are threatened. As Tonelson put it, "Rather than drain our resources and energies pursuing stability (even where it has never existed), Mr. Steel suggests we would be better off exploring policy options that enable us to live satisfactorily with considerable instability."

Temptations of a Superpower was well received by most critics. Kakutani praised the work for its "persuasive and carefully considered arguments." Noting that Steel's suggestions "do not satisfy my American exceptionalist desire to do good in the world," Cohen nonetheless admitted that they "would keep the United States from doing much harm. And if, as he hopes, the time, energy and resources thus saved are used to cure some of the ills of American society, we will all benefit." Tonelson concluded that *Temptations of a Superpower* affords "a rare example of clarity, wisdom and intellectual integrity. It would stand out even in a time when the nation's chattering classes were able to distinguish argument from invective."

Less a biography than an extended commentary, Steel's *In Love with Night: The American Romance with Robert Kennedy* takes a realistic look at the Massachusetts senator, who was killed while campaigning for president in 1968. Steel portrays Kennedy as a ruthless and moody individual, willing to make deals to further his career and in thrall to his family's myth-especially in the wake of brother John F. Kennedy's assassination. Steel questions Kennedy's zeal for liberal politics, civil rights, and unilateral withdrawal from Vietnam, ultimately contending that Kennedy's core views did not differ much from those of Richard M. Nixon. According to Sean Wilentz in the *New York Times Book Review,* Steel seeks "to debunk what he calls a liberal myth, the assumption that Robert Kennedy embodied the motivating values of American liberalism and would have pursued them with passionate conviction if he had been elected president." Wilentz added: "At bottom, Steel charges, the crusader against war and injustice remained a cynical, self-interested politician." In *Time,* John F. Stacks described *In Love with Night* as "a hard-eyed rumination on the difference between the real (and of course flawed) Robert Kennedy and the popular memory of his greatness."

While most critics agreed with Steel that Robert Kennedy's assassination "has prevented people from taking a hard, candid look at the man," to quote a *Publishers Weekly* reviewer, they differed on whether or not the Bobby Kennedy myth has enriched America in the decades since his death. Stacks felt that Steel successfully "makes Robert seem less than we remember," but Kakutani stated that the author's observations "are not exactly earthshaking, especially in light of all the revisionist portraits of the Kennedys in recent years." Wilentz concluded: "What might have happened had Kennedy lived is, of course, unknowable. We are left, instead with speculations—and with the arguments that Kennedy provoked. Had Steel tried to understand R. F. K. the political man instead of merely deconstructing the myth, he might have spent more time thinking about those arguments, and about how Kennedy tried to open up fresh possibilities in American political life." The *Publishers Weekly* reviewer, conversely, declared that *In Love with Night* "is absorbing because of the intensity of Kennedy himself-and for the intensity of feelings that many Americans still have for what they thought he represented."

BIOGRAPHICAL/CRITICAL SOURCES:

PERIODICALS

Boston Globe, November 3, 1980.
Commentary, October, 1980.
Commonweal, June 26, 1964; October 27, 1967; November 7, 1980.
Detroit News, September 28, 1980.
Foreign Affairs, fall, 1980; May-June, 1995, p. 174.
Journal of American Studies, December, 1981.
Los Angeles Times Book Review, August 31, 1980.
Nation, November 8, 1980; May 8, 1995, p. 640.
New Republic, August 16, 1980.
New York, September 15, 1980.
Newsweek, July 24, 1967; September 8, 1980.
New York Review of Books, October 9, 1980.
New York Times, August 22, 1980; May 23, 1995; December 17, 1999.
New York Times Book Review, March 29, 1964; July 16, 1967; September 12, 1971; August 24, 1980; April 9, 1995, p. 8; January 9, 2000, p. 13.
Publishers Weekly, December 13, 1999, p. 75.
Saturday Review, July 3, 1971; September, 1980.
Time, September 8, 1980; December 6, 1999, p. 105.
Times (London), February 19, 1981.
Times Literary Supplement, August 3, 1967; February 20, 1981.
Washington Monthly, May, 1995, p. 50.
Washington Post Book World, August 24, 1980.
Washington Star, August 31, 1980.*

* * *

STEWART, James B. 1957(?)-

PERSONAL: Born c. 1957, in Quincy, IL. *Education:* Attended DePauw University; Harvard Law School, LLB.

ADDRESSES: Agent—c/o Simon & Schuster, 1230 Avenue of the Americas, New York, NY 10020.

CAREER: Cravath, Swaine, & Moore (law firm), New York City, attorney; *Wall Street Journal,* senior writer and front page editor, 1983-92; writer.

AWARDS, HONORS: George Polk Award, Long Island University (journalism department), 1987, Gerald Loeb Award, University of California, Los Angeles (John E. Anderson Graduate School of Management), and Pulitzer Prize, Columbia University (graduate school of journalism), all 1988, all with Daniel Hertzberg, all for *Wall Street Journal* coverage of the October, 1987, stock market crash and Wall Street insider trading.

WRITINGS:

The Partners: Inside America's Most Powerful Law Firms, Simon & Schuster (New York City), 1983.
The Prosecutors: Inside the Offices of the Government's Most Powerful Lawyers, Simon & Schuster, 1987.
Den of Thieves, Simon & Schuster, 1991.
The Housing Status of Black Americans, Transaction (New Brunswick, NJ), 1992.
Blacks in Rural America, Transaction, 1995.
Blood Sport: The President and His Adversaries, Simon & Schuster, 1996, published with a new afterword by the author, Touchstone (New York City), 1997.
(Editor, with others) *W. E. B. DuBois on Race and Culture: Philosophy, Politics, and Poetics,* Routledge (New York City), 1996.
(Editor) *African Americans and Post-Industrial Labor Markets,* Transaction, 1997.
Follow the Story: How to Write Successful Nonfiction, Simon & Schuster, 1998.
Blind Eye: How the Medical Establishment Let a Doctor Get Away with Murder, Simon & Schuster, 1999.

Contributor to periodicals, including the *New Yorker.* Served as executive editor of *American Lawyer.*

SIDELIGHTS: James B. Stewart, a former attorney and editor for the *Wall Street Journal,* is the author of three critically acclaimed books on law and financial investment. The first two volumes, *The Partners: Inside America's Most Powerful Law Firms,* published in 1983, and *The Prosecutors: Inside the Offices of the Government's Most Powerful Lawyers,* published in 1987, offer insights into some of the most powerful operators in the American legal system. Stewart's third book, 1991's *Den of Thieves,* probes insider trading as well as other illegal activities which have scandalized the investment world in the 1980s.

The Partners profiles eight of the largest and most powerful law firms in the United States, with the focus on each firm being a major legal battle it has been involved with. The book opens with the story of clandestine negotiations between two large firms—under the direction of their American banking clients—for the release of fifty-two American hostages held in Iran by Islamic extremists. Stewart also tells of the ten-year defense of the IBM Corporation against a barrage of private and governmental anti-trust suits; the restructuring of Chrysler Corporation's enormous debt; and the settling of American millionaire Nelson Rockefeller's large estate following his sudden death. As Stewart relates in *The Partners,* the attorneys in these firms stopped at nothing in their quest to win, a devotion which prompted them to work seven days a week, employ questionable tactics, and bill exorbitant amounts. One lawyer, who worked an entire day and billed the client for twenty-four hours, was soon topped by a colleague who also worked an entire day, but then took a transcontinental flight which enabled him to bill twenty-seven hours in a one-day period.

The Partners was well received by critics, with many reviewers praising the volume's insights and strong narrative qualities. In the *New Republic,* James J. Cramer admired Stewart's research and presentation of detail while offering minor criticism regarding the emphasis on attorneys over the clients who employ them. In summation, Cramer proclaimed the book a useful text: "Considering how little the public, including many noncorporate lawyers, knows about the crucial roles these corporate lawyers can play, Stewart's efforts can only be saluted." Calling *The Partners*'s collection of legal dramas "first rate," *Newsweek* contributor Aric Press praised Stewart's ability to tell a story, but expressed a desire for more analysis and editorial commentary from the author. John Jay Osborn, Jr., writing in the *Washington Post Book World,* stated that "Stewart has written a fascinating, fast moving narrative study of a vital American institution." In the *New York Times Book Review,* Neal Johnston commented that the author "has done an effective job of illuminating the realities of those institutions which continue to shape America."

Stewart's follow-up, *The Prosecutors,* examines several complicated cases brought by federal prosecutors during the 1980s, including the McDonnell Douglas Corporation's bribes to Pakistani officials and charges of impropriety leveled against Reagan administration Attorney General Edwin Meese. Employing a format similar to *The Partners,* Stewart presents each case as a separate story, relating the key players and events. As Walter Walker wrote in the *Washington Post Book World:* "Stewart has written a highly entertaining account of several of the more notorious prosecutions conducted in this country over the past ten years." *New York Times Book Review* contributor Seymour Wishman found the historical content of *The Prosecutors* important, yet also highly readable: "Each of the stories unfolds with the suspense of a terrific detective novel, but the book is even better than that because the stories are true."

For his next book, *Den of Thieves,* Stewart shifts focus from the legal community to America's financial system, taking account of the greed and dirty-dealing that marred the stock market landscape during the 1980s. The volume examines numerous scandals which erupted during the decade, with special attention paid to insider trading scams (the practice of using secret information regarding impending business transactions as an advantage in buying and selling). At the height of the decade's avarice, players such as Ivan Boesky and Michael Milken were reaping tremendous profits at the expense of nearly all stock market investors, a majority of whom were unsuspecting middle- and lower-income Americans.

Boesky, who specialized in insider trading, was able to "predict" which mergers, buyouts, and takeovers would actually occur and thus invest and profit from the most lucrative outcome. Working out of the investment firm Drexel Burnham Lambert, Milken came to be Boesky's closest ally in the world of merger-making, earning the moniker of junk bond king (junk bonds are securities that advertise high yield but are better described as high risk; they are often sold as quick financing for takeover maneuvers). In Milken's case, junk bonds rarely rewarded their buyers with anything; they suffered the downside of "high risk" while Milken and Boesky profited from their sale by way of a skilled cycle of duplicity. Artificially reducing the value of certain securities, Milken bought up the holdings of his clients (who had no way of knowing the actual values) and then sold them to Boesky for a small profit. Boesky then sold the securities back to Drexel Burnham Lambert at a higher price and profit. The firm would then resell the same securities to their clients for even higher prices. As Stewart recounts in *Den of Thieves,* Boesky and Milken's reign ended with a string of indictments that rocked the very foundations of the investment world and resulted in lengthy prison terms for both men—and a large clean-up bill that fell on the shoulders of the American taxpayers.

Reviewers praised *Den of Thieves* as an historically significant record of Wall Street plundering; the account, some noted, shed new light on the complicity of the financial news media and government regulators in these financial misdealings. A reviewer for the *New Yorker* termed the book a "fascinating account," while *New Republic* contributor Cramer stated that Stewart's work "stand[s] as the definitive history of the financial depredations of the decade. *Den of Thieves* provides details of manipulations that will jolt even the most knowing observers of the period." Investment banker and financial columnist Michael M. Thomas observed in the *New York Times Book Review* that *Den of Thieves* "is an absolutely splendid book and a tremendously important book, as good a book on Wall Street as I have ever read." Appraising its informational content, Thomas wrote that "the genius of this book is that it lets the larger questions emerge entirely from the narrative."

Den of Thieves embroiled Stewart in several controversies. In October, 1991, Alan Dershowitz, Michael Milken's defense lawyer, launched a public campaign accusing Stewart of anti-Semitism, bias, and factual inaccuracy. Following Dershowitz's publication of a full-page advertisement in the *New York Times,* Stewart and his defenders waged a war of words, exchanging volleys with Milken's sympathizers through articles and letters to the editor in the *New York Times* and the *Wall Street Journal.* In the *Nation,* Cramer defended Stewart's identification of the religious backgrounds of various players as presentation of fact and specifically termed Dershowitz's charges as "thoroughly shabby allegations." In September, 1992, Michael F. Armstrong, a prominent New York lawyer, sued Stewart for libel, claiming to have been wrongly accused in the book of preparing a false affidavit for a client. Despite these troubles *Den of Thieves* earned the respect of numerous critics and financial insiders, and went on to become a bestseller.

The tangled story of Bill and Hillary Clinton's involvement in the Whitewater land investment scandal is the subject of *Blood Sport: The President and His Adversaries. Blood Sport* illustrates both that the matter was blown out of proportion and that the Clintons indeed demonstrated some serious character flaws, both in their illegal land deals and in their handling of the investigation into their activities. "Only a staff apologist for the Clintons could come away from Stewart's portrayal without feeling a little ashamed of having their ilk in the White House," claimed Jeff A. Taylor in *Reason.* "The new information Stewart adds to the Whitewater canon will not jump out at most readers. Instead what Stewart has described as the Clintons' 'pattern of deceit' will." *New Republic* writer Sean Wilentz called Stewart a "painstaking journalist" whose book "winds up confirming that the significance of the Whitewater matter has been exaggerated out of proportion to its actual importance." Several reviewers concurred that the character portrait of the Clintons—particularly Hillary—is the greatest strength of *Blood Sport.* Thomas Powers concluded in *New York Times Book Review:* "This is narrative writing of a high order. [The book] is rich with beautifully drawn characters and dramatic incidents."

Stewart reported on the horrific story of Dr. Michael Swango in his 1999 book *Blind Eye: How the Medical Establishment Let a Doctor Get Away with Murder.* According to the author, Swango is a serial killer responsible for the deaths of at least fifty people. Yet he has only been convicted of lesser charges, partly because of the medical establishment's eagerness to cover up his wrongdoing. During his internship he may have injected a mixture of poisons into five patients, some of whom died; yet nurses who reported his suspicious behavior were discounted by the hospital administration. He was known to have a fascination with car crashes and kept a scrapbook of grisly accident-scene photos. Working as a paramedic, he laced his co-workers' food with ant poison, a crime for which he eventually served two years in prison. Even after this incident, which was publicized on prime-time television, he succeeded in landing further medical positions in other states. In 1994, when the FBI began to close in on him for more poisonings, he fled to Africa, where he again used a falsified resume and a suave demeanor to gain more appointments. When finally apprehended, he was only convicted of falsifying a job application and sentenced to forty-two months in jail. Stewart charges that again and again, hospital administrators chose to simply run the killer out of town rather than bring censure down on their profession by thoroughly investigating his misdeeds.

Blind Eye is "a harrowing and exhaustively researched account of neglect by the medical profession," in the opinion of a reviewer for *Publishers Weekly. Business Week*'s writer praised Stewart as "an excellent writer and reporter" who uses "court documents and hundreds of interviews to meticulously document Swango's trail." That commentator does fault Stewart for failing to adequately cover the larger issues raised in the book, saying, "Although he provides a few examples of other docs rum amok, the extent of the problem of dangerous physicians isn't comprehensively considered or analyzed. Still, this is a brave and passionate book. Whether Swango is ever tried for murder, his poisoning conviction—not to mention the disturbing events that dogged his career—should have kept him from attending any more patient bedsides. Physicians may feel embattled on many fronts, but circling the wagons on matters of patient safety is intolerable."

BIOGRAPHICAL/CRITICAL SOURCES:

PERIODICALS

Atlantic Monthly, October, 1996, Martin Walker, review of *Blood Sport,* p. 114.
Arkansas Business, March 25, 1996, pp. 6, 34.
Booklist, September 1, 1999, William Beatty, review of *Blind Eye,* p. 6.
Book Week, September 1, 1999.
Business Week, October 28, 1991, p. 16; December 9, 1991, p. 12; April 1, 1996, p. 15; September 6, 1999, "White Coats, Black Hat," p. 17.
Commentary, March, 1992, p. 54.
Economist, September 18, 1999, "Curative Killer," p. 13.
Entertainment Weekly, April 5, 1996, Mark Harris, review of *Blood Sport,* p. 73.
Financial World, November 12, 1991, p. 104.
Fortune, October 21, 1991, p. 195.
Gentlemen's Quarterly, August, 1992, p. 66.
Industrial and Labor Relations Review, July, 1998, Jessica Gordon Nembhard, review of *African Americans and Post-Industrial Labor Markets,* p. 714.
Journal of Economic Issues, September, 1998, Robert Cherry, review of *African Americans and Post-Industrial Labor Markets,* p. 887.
Journal of Regional Science, February, 1998, p. 183.
Maclean's, March 25, 1996, "New Chapters on Whitewater," p. 33.
Management Today, April, 1992, p. 106.
Nation, December 16, 1991, p. 783-785; April 22, 1996, Doug Ireland, review of *Blood Sport,* p. 25.
National Review, May 6, 1996, Michael Isikoff, review of *Blood Sport,* p. 47.
New Republic, March 21, 1983, pp. 38-39; December 16, 1991, pp. 50-53; May 20, 1996, Sean Wilentz, review of *Blood Sport,* p. 35.
Newsweek, February 14, 1983, p. 77; October 14, 1991, p. 48; March 18, 1996, Michael Isikoff & Mark Hosenball, "Picking up the Scent: A New Book Chases Hillary's Whitewater Money Trail," p. 29.
New Yorker, November 18, 1991, p. 135.
New York Review of Books, April 18, 1996, p. 59.
New York Times, February 3, 1983; September 27, 1987, section 7, p. 20; April 1, 1988, section B, p. 4.
New York Times Book Review, March 6, 1983, pp. 13, 20; September 27, 1987, p. 20; October 13, 1991, pp. 1, 36-37; March 24, 1996, Thomas Powers, "Muddy Water"; August 29, 1999, p. 9.
People Weekly, December 16, 1991, p. 45; April 15, 1996, Jane Sims Podesta, "Bill and Hillary's Big Flaw? An 'Obsession with Being Perfect,' " p. 32.
Publishers Weekly, August 9, 1999, review of *Blind Eye,* p. 332; October 4, 1999, review of audio version of *Blind Eye,* p. 37.
Reason, June, 1996, Jeff A. Taylor, review of *Blood Sport,* p. 59.
Time, March 18, 1996, "Contributors," p. 4, James B. Stewart, "On the Road to Scandal," p. 48; September 13, 1999, R. Z. Sheppard, "Bad Medicine: The Diagnosis Is Murder in a Real-Life Doctor Drama," p. 76.
USA Today, December 8, 1987, section B, p. 7; September 13, 1988, section B, p. 2.
Wall Street Journal, May 1, 1987, p. 26; February 29, 1988, p. 26; April 1, 1988, p. 2; May 11, 1988, p. 26; September 13, 1988, p. 42.
Washington Post Book World, February 20, 1983, pp. 5, 15; September 20, 1987, pp. 5, 9.
Washington Monthly, January/February, 1992, p. 48.*

* * *

STONE, Ruth 1915-

PERSONAL: Born June 8, 1915, in Roanoke, VA; daughter of Roger McDowell (a musician) and Ruth (Ferguson) Perkins; married second husband, Walter B. Stone (deceased); children: Marcia (Mrs. Donald Croll, Jr.), Phoebe, Blue-Jay Abigail. *Education:* Attended University of Illinois; Harvard University, B.A. *Avocational interests:* Drum music, the women's liberation movement.

ADDRESSES: Home—R.F.D. 3, Brandon, VT 05733. *Office*—Paris Press, Inc., P.O. Box 487, Ashfield, MA 01330.

CAREER: Radcliffe College, Cambridge, MA, seminar teacher, 1963-65; Wellesley College, Wellesley, MA, member of faculty of department of English, 1965; Brandeis University, Waltham, MA, member of faculty of department of English, 1965-66; University of Wisconsin—Madison, member of faculty of department of English, 1967-69; University of Illinois at Urbana-Champaign, member of faculty of department of English, 1971-73; Indiana University at Bloomington, visiting professor, 1973-74; Center College, Danville, KY, Creative Writing Chair, winter, 1975; Brandeis University, Hurst Visiting Professor, 1976; University of Virginia, Charlottesville, visiting professor, 1977-78; University of California, Davis, Regent's Lecturer, spring, 1978, visiting lecturer, fall, 1978, 1981; Old Dominion University, visiting professor, 1989-90; State University of New York, Binghamton, professor of English and creative writing, 1990—. Poet.

AWARDS, HONORS: Bess Hoskin Prize, *Poetry* magazine, 1954; Radcliffe Institute fellowship, Harvard University, 1963-65; Robert Frost fellow at Breadloaf Writers' Conference, summer, 1963; Shelley Memorial Award, Poetry Society of America, 1964; Kenyon Review fellowship, 1965; grant from Academy of Arts and Letters, 1970; Guggenheim fellowships, 1971-72, 1975-76; PEN Award, 1974; Delmore Schwartz Award, 1983-84; Whiting Award, 1986; Paterson Prize, 1988, National Book Critics Circle Award, 2000, for *Ordinary Words.*

WRITINGS:

POETRY

In an Iridescent Time (poems), Harcourt (New York City), 1959.
Topography and Other Poems, Harcourt, 1971.
Unknown Messages, Nemesis Press, 1973.
Cheap: New Poems and Ballads, Harcourt, 1975.
American Milk, From Here Press (Fanwood, NJ), 1986.
Second-Hand Coat: Poems New and Selected, David R. Godine (Boston), 1987.
Simplicity, Paris Press (Northampton, MA), 1995.
Ordinary Words, Paris Press (Ashfield, MA), 1999.

Also contributor to numerous anthologies, including *Erotic Poetry,* edited by William Cole, Random House (New York City), 1964, *No More Masks,* edited by Florence Howe, Anchor Books (New York City), 1973, *The Poetry Anthology, 1912-1972,* Houghton (Boston), 1978.

OTHER

(Editor) *Garland Encyclopedia of World Music: Africa* (nonfiction), Garland, 1997.

Contributor of poetry to periodicals, including *Accent, Iowa Review, Kenyon Review, Partisan, Poetry,* and other periodicals; contributor of short stories to *Commentary* and *New Yorker.*

WORK IN PROGRESS: A book of short stories; a book on bus travel, tentatively titled *Desperate Buses.*

SIDELIGHTS: Ruth Stone is an important, if relatively unknown, American poet. Commenting on the "odd neglect" of this "major talent," Sandra Gilbert mused in *Women's Review of Books* that "sheer bad luck" is in part to blame for Stone's obscurity. Stone's first book of verse, *In an Iridescent Time,* was published in 1958. The poems in it "reveal a witty, sophisticated artist with exceptional verbal energy and, complementing her sophistication, a vein of visionary naivete," according to Gilbert. Shortly after the book came out, Stone was left a widow with three young children. She embarked on a difficult life journey, alternately living on a primitive farm in Vermont and moving around the country from one university to another in short-term teaching positions. It was during theses "years of trouble, of impoverished wandering and widowhood" that her poetry took on the "depth and daring" that characterize her work.

Reviewing *Ordinary Words,* a *Publishers Weekly* writer called it "well worth discovering, consistent and forthright in its explorations of the quotidian and the dream-life it can produce. . . . the ordinary, for Stone, turns out to be more than enough." Gilbert noted the "special boldness" of the poet's work and conjectured that it is "at least in part a product of the pain and loss she's had to confront, the perilous life she's lived at the edge of comforts most other people of letters take for granted in our society. . . . I would like Ruth Stone's achievements . . . to be more widely celebrated. But in any case I'm happy to celebrate my own certainty that her extraordinary words are among those that will flow through the valley of our saying from here to there, from now to then, into the farthest reaches of the twenty-first century and beyond."

Stone has recorded five long-playing tapes and two long-playing records of poetry and commentary.

BIOGRAPHICAL/CRITICAL SOURCES:

BOOKS

Leslie Fiedler, *Waiting for the End,* Stein & Day (New York City), 1964.

Barker, Wendy, and Sandra M. Gilbert, editors, *The House Is Made of Poetry: The Art of Ruth Stone,* Southern Illinois University Press (Carbondale), 1996.

PERIODICALS

Booklist, November 15, 1997, review of *Garland Encyclopedia of World Music: Africa,* p. 578.

Feminist Studies, fall, 1999, Alicia Ostriker, "Ruth Stone," p. 662.

Library Journal, September 1, 1997, review of *Garland Encyclopedia of World Music: Africa,* p. 184.

Publishers Weekly, July 26, 1999, review of *Ordinary Words,* p. 86; January 31, 2000, Judy Quinn, "Nominations for 1999 NBCC Awards," p. 17; March 20, 2000, John F. Baker, "Critics Circle Awards Surprise Winners," p. 16.

Reference & User Services Quarterly, summer, 1998, Anthony J. Adam, review of *Garland Encyclopedia of World Music: Africa,* p. 357.

Women's Review of Books, October, 1999, Sandra Gilbert, "Extraordinary Words," pp. 6-7.*

* * *

STUDD, Stephen (Allen) 1946-

PERSONAL: Born December 7, 1946, in London, England; son of Robert William (a driver) and Sarah Amelia (a homemaker; maiden name, Gardiner) Studd. *Education:* Attended Trinity College of Music, 1963-71; Fitzwilliam College, Cambridge, M.A. (with honors), 1969; Royal Academy of Music, L.R.A.M., 1971. *Avocational interests:* Music, opera, sports history, archaeology, travel.

ADDRESSES: Home—Diana Rd., Walthamstow, London E17, England. *Office*—c/o *Waltham Forest Guardian,* Fulbourne Rd., Walthamstow, London, England.

CAREER: Building, London, England, journalist, 1970-72; *Education,* London, journalist, 1972-75; freelance journalist, 1975-76; Peat, Marwick, Mitchell (accountants), London, editor of house journal, 1976-77; *Waltham Forest Guardian,* London, journalist, beginning in 1977, deputy editor, beginning in 1984.

WRITINGS:

Puddle Dock (history), Peat, Marwick, Mitchell (London, England), 1977.

Herbert Chapman, Football Emperor, P. Owen, 1981.

Fleeting Years (poems), Merlin Books, 1982.

Saint-Saens: A Critical Biography, Cygnus Arts, 1999.

Also author of short stories.

WORK IN PROGRESS: A novel about the future.

SIDELIGHTS: Stephen Studd told *CA:* "I set out to be a professional concert pianist, but I decided, for reasons of job security, to study history at Cambridge and take up a career in journalism. I pursued music as an amateur, studied piano part-time at Trinity College of Music, London, and became a Licentiate of the Royal Academy in 1971.

"My interest in football led me to research the life of Herbert Chapman, the manager who shaped the legendary Arsenal team of the 1930s and who revolutionized the game. I have also written short stories and poetry, but my work as an editor restricts literary activities. My favorite poets are Shakespeare, Keats, and Edward Thomas; favorite authors include Dickens and Dostoyevsky.

"My projected novel depicts a twenty-first century Europe whose society is one of extreme affluence, but it is completely amoral and decimated by disease. I have brooded on this subject for many years; considering the nature of work and class division and the political and social developments that occurred during this time has only served to confirm the image I have built up. It is a vision of the future that is also very much a comment on the contemporary world."

BIOGRAPHICAL/CRITICAL SOURCES:

PERIODICALS

Times Literary Supplement, November 19, 1999.*

* * *

SYRUC, J.
See MILOSZ, Czeslaw

SZYMBORSKA, Wislawa 1923-
(Stancykowna, a pseudonym)

PERSONAL: Born July 2, 1923, in Prowent-Bnin, near Poznan, Poland; married (husband deceased). *Education:* Attended Jagellonian University, 1945-48.

ADDRESSES: Home—Ul. Krolewska 82/89, 30-079, Cracow, Poland.

CAREER: Poet and critic. Poetry editor and columnist, *Zycie literackie* (literary weekly magazine), 1953-81.

MEMBER: Polish Writers' Association (member of general board, 1978-83).

AWARDS, HONORS: Cracow literary prize, 1954; Gold Cross of Merit, 1955; Ministry of Culture prize, 1963; Knight's Cross, Order of Polonia Resituta, 1974; Goethe Prize, 1991; Herder Prize, 1995; Polish PEN Club prize, 1996; Nobel Prize for Literature, 1996.

WRITINGS:

POETRY

Dlatego zyjemy (title means "That's Why We Are Alive"), [Warsaw], 1952.

Pytania zadawane sobie (title means "Questions Put to Myself"), [Warsaw], 1954.

Wolanie do Yeti (title means "Calling out to Yeti"), [Warsaw], 1957.

Sol (title means "Salt"), Panstwowy Instytut Wydawniczy (Warsaw), 1962.

Wiersze wybrane (collection), Panstwowy Instytut Wydawniczy, 1964.

Sto pociech (title means "A Hundred Joys"), Panstwowy Instytut Wydawniczy, 1967.

Poezje wybrane (title means "Selected Poems"), Ludowa Spoldzielnia Wydawnicza (Warsaw), 1967.

Poezje (title means "Poems"), Przedmowa Jerzego Kwiatkowskiego (Warsaw), 1970.

Wybor poezje (collection), Czytelnik, 1970.

Wszelki wypadek (title means "There but for the Grace"), Czytelnik, 1972.

Wybor wierszy (collection), Panstwowy Instytut Wydawniczy, 1973.

Tarsjusz I inne wiersze (title means "Tarsius and Other Poems"), Krajowa Agencja Wydawnicza (Warsaw), 1976.

Wielka liczba (title means "A Great Number"), Czytelnik, 1976.

Sounds, Feelings, Thoughts: Seventy Poems, translated by Magnus J. Krynski and Robert A. Maguire, Princeton University Press (Princeton, NJ), 1981.

Poezje wybrane (II), (title means "Selected Poems II"), Ludowa Spoldzielnia Wydawnicza (Warsaw), 1983.

Ludzie na moscie, Czytelnik, 1986, translation by Adam Czerniawski published as *People on a Bridge: Poems,* Forest (Boston, MA), 1990.

Poezje = Poems (bilingual edition), translated by Krynski and Maguire, Wydawnictwo Literackie (Cracow), 1989.

Wieczor autorski: wiersze (title means "Authors' Evening: Poems"), Anagram (Warsaw), 1992.

Koniec I poczatek (title means "The End and the Beginning"), Wydawnictwo Literackie, 1993.

View with a Grain of Sand: Selected Poems, translated by Stanislaw Baranczak and Clare Cavanagh, Harcourt (New York City), 1995.

Widok z ziarnkiem piasku: 102 Wiersze, Wydawn, 1996.

Nothing Twice: Selected Poems, selected and translated by Stanislaw Baraanczak and Clare Cavanagh, Literackie, 1997.

Hundert Gedichte, Hundert Freuden, Literackie, 1997.

O asmierci bez przesady = de la mort sans exagerer, Literackie, 1997.

Nulla e in regalo, Literackie, 1998.

Poems, New and Collected, 1957-1997, translated from the Polish by Stanislaw Baraanczak and Clare Cavanagh, Harcourt Brace (New York City), 1998.

Work represented in anthologies, including *Polish Writing Today,* Penguin (New York City), 1967; *The New Polish Poetry,* University of Pittsburgh Press (Pittsburgh), 1978; and *Anthologie de la poesie polonaise: 1400-1980,* revised edition, Age d'homme, 1981. Also contributor, under pseudonym Stancykowna, to *Arka* (underground publication) and *Kultura* (exile magazine; published in Paris).

OTHER

Lektury nadobowiazkowe (collection of book reviews; title means "Non-Compulsory Reading"), Wydawnictwo Literackie, 1973.

Zycie na poczekaniu: Lekcja literatury z Jerzym Kwiatowskim I Marianem Stala, Literackie, 1996.

Also translator of French poetry.

SIDELIGHTS: Wislawa Szymborska was thrust into the international spotlight in 1996 after receiving the Nobel Prize for Literature. The reclusive and private Szymborska was cited by the Swedish Academy for "poetry that with ironic precision allows the historical and biological context to come to light in fragments of human reality." Her poetry, described by *Los Angeles Times* critic Dean E. Murphy, is "seductively simple verse . . . [which has] captured the wit and wisdom of everyday life for the past half century."

Though not widely known outside her native Poland, Szymborska received critical acclaim for the first collection of her work to appear in English translation, *Sounds, Feelings, Thoughts: Seventy Poems.* "Of the poetic voices to come out of Poland after 1945 Wislawa Szymborska's is probably the most elusive as well as the most distinctive," writes Jaroslaw Anders in the *New York Review of Books.* Anders comments: "*Sounds, Feelings, Thoughts* contains poems from [Szymborska's] five books written since 1957, comprising more or less half of what the poet herself considers her canon. Its publication is of interest not only because of Szymborska's importance as a poet, but also because her work demonstrates that the diversity of poetic modes in Poland is much greater than is usually perceived."

Alice-Catherine Carls, in a review of *Sounds, Feelings, Thoughts* in *Library Journal,* calls the work "one of those rare books which put one in a state of 'grace.' " Robert Hudzik, also in *Library Journal,* claims: "This volume reveals a poet of startling originality and deep sympathy."

The 1995 collection *Views with a Grain of Sand: Selected Poems* was also praised by many critics who laud Szymborska's directness and distinctive voice. Stephen Dobyns in the *Washington Post Book World* praises both the humor of Szymborska's work as well as the translation by Stanislaw Baranczak and Clare Cavanagh. Edward Hirsch in a *New York Review of Books* review concurs, arguing that the volume reveals "the full force of [Szymborska's] fierce and unexpected wit." Louis McKee, in a *Library Journal* review also praises the "wonderfully wicked" wit of Szymborska. Dobyns concludes: "The poems are surprising, funny and deeply moving. Szymborska is a world-class poet, and this book will go far to make her known in the United States."

Publication of *Poems New and Collected, 1957-1997* inspired further critical acclaim. "It may seem superfluous to praise a Nobel Laureate in literature, but Szymborska is a splendid writer richly deserving of her recent renown," affirmed Graham Christian in *Library Journal.* Noting the poet's "unflinching examination of torture and other wrongs inflicted by repressive regimes," Christian went on to say that Szymborska's verse contains "the exhilarating power of a kind of serious laughter." Despite the poems' frequently grim subject matter, "Syzmborska's tough naturalism does allow rays of light to penetrate its bleak landscapes, leaving lasting, sustaining impressions," declared a reviewer for *Publishers Weekly.*

Many commentators remark on the deceptively simple quality of Syzmborska's work. In simple language, she speaks of ordinary things, only to reveal extraordinary truths. In a *Publishers Weekly* article about Szymborska, Joanna Trzeciak praises "the wit and clarity of Szymborska's turns of phrase. Under her pen, simple language becomes striking. Ever the gentle subversive, she stubbornly refuses to see anything in the world as ordinary. The result is a poetry of elegance and irony, full of surprising turns." And Denise Wiloch, a contributor to *Contemporary Women Poets,* points out that "the seemingly casual musings she captures in her poems are deceptive and full of irony. Her work reverberates long after it is read."

"She knows philosophy, literature, and history, but mostly she knows common human experience," concludes *Booklist* writer Ray Olson. "Her work is ultimately wisdom literature, written in a first person that expresses a universal humanity that American poets—lockstep individualists all—haven't dared essay since early in this century. She is like Brecht without hatred, Sandburg without socialist posturing, Dickinson without hermetism, Whitman without illusory optimism: a great poet."

Szymborska's works have been translated into Arabic, Hebrew, Japanese, Chinese, and other languages.

BIOGRAPHICAL/CRITICAL SOURCES:

BOOKS

Balbus, Stanislaw, *Swiat ze wszystkich stron swiata: O Wislawie Szymborski,* Literackie, 1996.

Baranczak, Stanislaw, *Breathing under Water and Other East European Essays,* Harvard University Press (Cambridge, MA), 1990.

Contemporary Women Poets, St. James Press (Detroit, MI), 1998.

Levine, Madeline, *Contemporary Polish Poetry: 1925-1975,* Twayne (Boston, MA), 1981.

PERIODICALS

Booklist, April 15, 1998, Ray Olson, review of *Poems New and Collected 1957-1997;* March 15, 1999,

Ray Olson, review of *Poems New and Collected 1957-1997,* p. 1276.

Humanities Review, spring, 1982, p. 141.

Library Journal, September 1, 1981, p. 1636; July, 1995, p. 85; April 1, 1998, Graham Christian, review of *Poems New and Collected 1957-1997,* p. 92.

Los Angeles Times, October 4, 1996; October 13, 1996.

Maclean's, October 14, 1996, p. 11.

New Republic, January 1, 1996, p. 36; December 30, 1996, p. 27.

New Yorker, December 14, 1992, p. 94; March 1, 1993, p. 86.

New York Review of Books, October 21, 1982, p. 47; November 14, 1996, p. 17; October 21, 1993, p. 42; April 18, 1996, p. 35; October 8, 1998, p. 37.

New York Times, October 4, 1996.

New York Times Book Review, October 27, 1996, p. 51.

New York Times Magazine, December 1, 1996, p. 46.

Observer (London), August 18, 1991, p. 51.

People, May 5, 1997, review of *View with a Grain of Sand,* p. 41.

Publishers Weekly, April 7, 1997, Joanna Trzeciak, "Wislawa Szymborska: The Enchantment of Everyday Objects," p. 68; March 30, 1998, review of *Poems New and Collected 1957-1997,* p. 77.

Time, October 14, 1996, p. 33.

Times Literary Supplement, September 17, 1999, Clair Wills, "How Real Is Reality?" p. 25.

U.S. News and World Report, October 14, 1996, p. 32.

Wall Street Journal, October 4, 1996.

Washington Post Book World, July 30, 1995, p. 8.

World Literature Today, spring, 1982, p. 368; winter, 1997.*

T-V

TAYLOR, Duncan (Burnett) 1912-

PERSONAL: Born October 7, 1912, in Edinburgh, Scotland; son of William Macrae (a physician) and Hermina (Henderson) Taylor; married Barbara Kuczynski (a freelance writer), January 21, 1937; children: Neil Macrae. *Education:* Attended Clifton College, Bristol, 1926-31; King's College, Cambridge, B.A., 1934, M.A., 1938; University of London, Diploma of Institute of Education, 1935.

ADDRESSES: *Home*—103 Corringham Rd., London NW11, England.

CAREER: Teacher in London, England, 1935-41; British Broadcasting Corp., London producer for school radio, 1947-72. British Library, guide and lecturer, beginning in 1975. *Military service:* Royal Air Force, 1941-46; became flight lieutenant.

WRITINGS:

(Translator) *Wolf Dog,* Thomas Nelson (London), 1938.

(Translator with wife, Barbara Kuczynski) *Gypsies,* Methuen (London), 1938.

The Elizabethan Age, Roy (New York City), 1955, enlarged edition, Dobson (London), 1968.

Jim Bartholomew of the R.A.F., Chatto & Windus (London), 1956.

Ancient Greece, illustrated by Katerina Wilczynski, Methuen, 1957, Roy, 1958.

Bob in Local Government, Chatto & Windus, 1958.

Chaucer's England (for juveniles), Dobson, 1959, Roy, 1960, enlarged edition, Dobson, 1968.

Ancient Rome (for juveniles), Methuen, 1960, Roy, 1961, enlarged edition, Methuen, 1963.

A Soldier on Hadrian's Wall, Oxford University Press (Oxford, England), 1962.

(With Louise Cochrane) *The World of Nations,* Whitman Publishing, 1963.

Fieldings' England, Dobson, 1966, Roy, 1967.

A Story of Pompeii and Vesuvius from BBC Radiovision, paintings by Justin Todd, British Broadcasting Corp. (London), 1969.

A Short History of the Post-War World: 1945-1970, Dobson, 1977.

SIDELIGHTS: Among Duncan Taylor's publications are the works *Ancient Greece, Ancient Rome,* and *Chaucer's England. Ancient Greece* is a book which, according to H. F. Graff's *New York Times* review, "makes Greek history and mythology viable again." The book was described by *Commonweal* contributor C. H. Bishop with such terms as "concise" and "lively." In another work, explained F. C. Stickles in a *Library Journal* review of *Ancient Rome,* Taylor uses "short chronological vignettes" that are "told with simplicity and humor" to give juveniles a "concise" overview of the city spanning its beginnings to 410 A.D. M. S. Libby complimented Taylor in the *New York Herald Tribune Book Review* for offering "young people from eleven to fifteen a thorough start toward understanding [a great civilization]." In the *New York Times Book Review,* W. H. Armstrong maintained that Taylor once again provides great detail "to bring history alive for the more mature young reader."

Chaucer's England, Taylor's 1959 work, presents a "survey of life in Chaucerian England," including the subjects of London, the home, religion, work, and crime, outlined T. C. Hines in *Library Journal.* A *Booklist* reviewer reported that Taylor offers "a well-rounded picture of fourteenth-century England," one that, even though "directed to British young people," is helpful for American young adult students as well in the junior high or early high school years. *Chaucer's England* has a "pleasant style and occasional wry humor [which] might give it a wider audience," determined T. C. Hines in his *Library Journal* review. A critic for the *Times Literary Supplement* complained that *Chaucer's England* was confusing, citing "utterly unmedieval [drawings]" that were "obviously taken from nineteenth-century sources" and Taylor's combination of content. However, a critic writing in *Kirkus Reviews* complimented Taylor's technique of "[linking history] with literature and . . . view[ing] it through a poet's eyes." A *Horn Book* critic argued that Taylor writes on the book's subjects "in a brisk and illuminating manner." Armstrong declared in a *New York Times Book Review* report that "Taylor has done young readers a service by writing this book."

BIOGRAPHICAL/CRITICAL SOURCES:

PERIODICALS

Booklist, September 15, 1960.
Books & Bookmen, December, 1968.
Commonweal, November 14, 1958.
Horn Book, August, 1960.
Kirkus Reviews, April 1, 1960; February 1, 1961.
Library Journal, May 15, 1960; April 15, 1961.
New York Herald Tribune Book Review, November 6, 1960; July 30, 1961.
New York Times, November 2, 1958.
New York Times Book Review, May 29, 1960; May 28, 1961.
Times Literary Supplement, December 4, 1959; May 25, 1967.*

* * *

TAYLOR, John Russell 1935-

PERSONAL: Born June 19, 1935, in Dover, Kent, England; son of Arthur Russell and Kathleen (Picker) Taylor. *Education:* Jesus College, Cambridge, B.A., 1956.

ADDRESSES: Home—11 Hollytree Close, Inner Park Rd., London SW19, England. *Office*—c/o *Times,* 1 Pennington St., London E1, England. *Agent*—A. D. Peters, 10 Buckingham St., London WC2, England.

CAREER: Times Educational Supplement, London, England, sub-editor, 1959-60; *Times Literary Supplement,* London, editorial assistant, 1961-63; *Times,* London, entertainment correspondent, 1959-63, film critic, 1963-73, art critic, beginning in 1978. University of London, Courtauld Institute of Art, researcher on art nouveau book illustration, 1956-58; Tufts University, lecturer in film, 1970-71; University of Southern California, professor of cinema, 1972-78.

MEMBER: Film and Television Press Guild (London), Critics Circle (London), Society of Cinematologists (New York City).

WRITINGS:

Joseph L. Mankiewicz: An Index to His Work, British Film Institute, 1960.
The Angry Theatre: New British Drama, Hill & Wang (New York City), 1962, revised edition, 1969, published as *Anger and After: A Guide to the New British Drama,* Methuen, 1962, 2nd revised edition, 1969.
Anatomy of a Television Play; An Inquiry into the Production of Two ABC Armchair Theatre Plays: "The Rose Affair" by Alun Owen, and "Afternoon of a Nymph" by Robert Muller, Weidenfeld & Nicolson, 1962.
Cinema Eye, Cinema Ear: Some Key Film-Makers of the Sixties, Hill & Wang, 1964.
(Contributor) *Shakespeare: A Celebration,* Penguin (New York City), 1964.
(Editor and author of introduction) *John Arden: Three Plays,* Penguin, 1965.
(Editor and author of introduction) *New English Dramatists 8,* Penguin, 1966.
The Penguin Dictionary of the Theatre, Penguin, 1966, 2nd revised edition published as *A Dictionary of the Theatre,* 1976.
The Art Nouveau Book in Britain, Methuen (London, England), 1966, MIT Press (Cambridge, MA), 1967, reprinted with new preface, P. Harris (Edinburgh, Scotland), 1979.
The Rise and Fall of the Well-Made Play, Hill & Wang, 1967.
Preston Sturges, Secker & Warburg (London), 1967.
(Editor) *John Osborne: "Look Back in Anger"; A Casebook,* Macmillan (London), 1968, Aurora Publishers (Nashville, TN), 1970.
(With Brian Brooke) *The Art Dealers,* Scribner (New York City), 1969.
Harold Pinter, edited by Ian Scott-Kilvert, Longman (London), 1969.
(With Arthur Jackson) *The Hollywood Musical,* McGraw (New York City), 1971.

The Second Wave: British Drama for the Seventies, Hill & Wang, 1971, revised edition, Eyre Methuen (London), 1978.

(Editor) Graham Greene, *The Pleasure-Dome: The Collected Film Criticism, 1935-40,* Secker & Warburg, 1972, Oxford University Press (New York City), 1980.

(Editor) Greene, *Graham Greene on Film,* Simon & Schuster (New York City), 1973.

David Storey, edited by Scott-Kilvert, Longman, 1974.

Peter Shaffer, edited by Scott-Kilvert, Longman, 1974.

(Author of introduction) John Kobal, editor, *Fifty Super Stars,* Hamlyn (New York City), 1974.

Directors and Directions: Cinema for the Seventies, Hill & Wang, 1975.

Hitch: The Life and Times of Alfred Hitchcock, Pantheon (New York City), 1978, published as *Hitch: The Life and Work of Alfred Hitchcock,* Faber (London), 1978.

(With Hugh Hunt and Kenneth Richards) *The Revels History of Drama in English,* Volume 7: *1880 to the Present Day,* edited by Clifford Leech and T. W. Craik, Methuen, 1978.

Impressionism, Hennerwood Publications, 1981.

Strangers in Paradise: The Hollywood Emigres, 1933-1950, Holt (New York City), 1983.

Ingrid Bergman, photographs from the Kobal collection, St. Martin's (New York City), 1983.

Alec Guinness: A Celebration, Little, Brown (Boston, MA), 1984.

Vivien Leigh, Elm Tree (London), 1984.

(With Kobal) *Portraits of the British Cinema: Sixty Glorious Years, 1925-1985,* photographs from the Kobal collection, Aurum Press, 1985, Salem House (Salem, NH), 1986.

Orson Welles: A Celebration, Little, Brown, 1986.

Edward Wolfe, Trefoil Books, 1986.

(Author of introduction) Roberto Gonzalez Fernandez, *Journeys: Artworks,* GMP (London), 1988.

Bernard Meninsky, Redcliffe (Bristol, England), 1990.

Art for Sale, Barrie & Jenkins, 1990.

Impressionist Dreams: The Artists and the World They Painted, Little, Brown, 1990.

Claude Monet: Impressions of France, from Le Havre to Giverny, Collins & Brown (London), 1995.

Bill Jacklin, Phaidon (Oxford, England), 1997.

The Sun Is God: The Life and Work of Cyril Mann (1911-80), Lund Humphries (London), 1999.

Contributor to periodicals. Editor, *Films and Filming,* 1983-90.

SIDELIGHTS: John Russell Taylor, best known for his film and art reviews for the London *Times,* has been called an "impartial critic" by a *Times Literary Supplement* reviewer; and in 1967, a *Drama* contributor referred to him as "possibly the best cinema reviewer writing in [England], immensely well informed, objective, sane and mostly uninfluenced by current intellectual foibles." Taylor continues to examine the topics of his reviews—the theatre, the film world, and the art world—in his books; and major Hollywood personalities, such as Alfred Hitchcock, are among the many subjects discussed.

Eliot Fremont-Smith maintains in *Village Voice* that Hitchcock's "sense of fun, lust for the macabre, psychological daring, technical innovation, exacting orderliness, authority with actors, rubber face, and long brilliant career" make him "the most immediately fascinating of directors." The "comprehensive" *Hitch: The Life and Times of Alfred Hitchcock,* continues Fremont-Smith, "serves him and us superbly." Focusing mainly on Hitchcock's career, "Taylor has written a very useful book about a professional at work," observes *New York Times Book Review* contributor Nora Sayre. However, comparing Taylor's work with Francois Truffaut's book-length interview with Hitchcock, Christopher Lehmann-Haupt of the *New York Times* finds that "almost all of the vast detail concerning the films that appears in Taylor's book is also present in Truffaut's. . . . in short, Taylor's biography is necessary only to demonstrate that such a book is not really necessary." Fremont-Smith claims, however: "Taylor deals with everything—the Catholic upbringing, the early silent films, the frustrations with Korda and Selznick, the transplant to Hollywood, the private life, . . . the uncertain periods in his career, the constant experimentation, and the triumphs. . . . The writing is clear, the subject nifty, the book admiring but not fawning. And you come out happy."

Strangers in Paradise: The Hollywood Emigres 1933-1950 deals with the refugees from Nazi Germany and other parts of Europe who flocked to Hollywood during the 1930s and 1940s, explains a *Publishers Weekly* contributor. "From oceans of research the author distills a fresh essence, a detailed study on the flight to Hollywood, from their culturally fettering homelands, of Europe's film makers, and what happened to those who flew," comments Basil Boothroyd in the London *Times.* In addition to the filmmakers, Taylor also discusses refugee artists, writers, and intellectuals, prompting S. S. Prawer to claim in the *Times Literary Supplement:* "One cannot help feeling that Taylor has cast his net too wide; that he would have done better to confine himself to emigres connected with the film-world." Jonathan Yardley, though, writes in the *Washington Post* that

"Taylor tells this story gracefully and engagingly, and he has many perceptive observations to make." And the *Publishers Weekly* contributor concludes that *Strangers in Paradise* is an "enjoyable, well-researched story," adding that "by turns funny and sad, this is a book that is consistently interesting."

BIOGRAPHICAL/CRITICAL SOURCES:

PERIODICALS

Booklist, September 1, 1994, p. 15.
California, May, 1983, p. 124.
Drama, winter, 1967.
Economist, March 5, 1983, p. 100.
Film Quarterly, summer, 1984, p. 32.
Library Journal, April 1, 1983, p. 740; October 15, 1990, p. 87.
Los Angeles Times Book Review, May 15, 1983; March 11, 1984; February 24, 1985.
Newsweek, December 16, 1985.
New York Times, November 28, 1978.
New York Times Book Review, November 19, 1978; July 10, 1983, p. 19; December 8, 1985, p. 17.
People Weekly, February 6, 1984, p. 12; May 21, 1984, p. 16.
Publishers Weekly, February 4, 1983, p. 361.
Time, June 20, 1983, p. 76.
Times (London), March 3, 1978.
Times Literary Supplement, December 14, 1967; March 11, 1983; December 7, 1984; November 28, 1986; November 5, 1999.
Variety, February 23, 1983, p. 112; June 6, 1984, p. 92; April 22, 1987, p. 92.
Village Voice, October 9, 1978.
Washington Post, January 5, 1978; April 13, 1983.
Washington Post Book World, July 8, 1984.*

* * *

THAROOR, Shashi 1956-

PERSONAL: Born in 1956, in London, England; son of Chandran Tharoor (a newspaper executive) and Lily Tharoor (a homemaker and free-lance writer; maiden name, Menon); married Tilottama Mukherji (a scholar), August 3, 1977; children: Ishaan, Kanishk (twin sons). *Education:* Delhi University, B.A. (history, with honors), 1975; Tufts University, M.A., 1976, M.A.L.D., 1977, Ph.D. 1978. *Politics:* Independent. *Religion:* Hindu. *Avocational interests:* Cricket, theater, Indian political affairs.

ADDRESSES: Home—401 East 34th St., Apt N-7C, New York, NY 10016. *Office*—United Nations, Office of the Secretary-General, New York, NY 10017. *Agent*—Ann Rittenberg, 14 Montgomery Place, Brooklyn, NY 11215.

CAREER: United Nations High Commissioner for Refugees, Geneva, Switzerland, assistant to the director of external affairs, 1978-79, public information officer, 1980-81, head of Singapore office, 1981-84, senior external affairs officer, 1985-87, executive assistant to the deputy high commissioner, 1987-89; United Nations headquarters, New York, NY, special assistant to the undersecretary general for peacekeeping operations, 1989-96, executive assistant to the Secretary-General, 1997—.

MEMBER: International Institute of Strategic Studies, India International Centre, PEN American Centre, New York Institute of the Humanities (elected fellow, 1995-96).

AWARDS, HONORS: Rajika Kripalani Young Journalist Award, Rajika Kripalani Memorial Foundation, 1976; best book of the year, Federation of Indian Publishers and *Hindustan Times,* 1990, for *The Great Indian Novel;* Commonwealth Writers Prize (Eurasian region), Commonwealth Foundation, 1990, for *The Great Indian Novel.*

WRITINGS:

Reasons of State: Political Development and India's Foreign Policy under Indira Gandhi, 1966-1977, Vikas (New Delhi), 1982.
The Great Indian Novel (novel), Arcade (New York), 1989.
The Five-Dollar Smile: Fourteen Early Stories and a Farce in Two Acts, Viking (New Delhi), 1990, published as *The Five-Dollar Smile and Other Stories,* Arcade, 1993.
Show Business (novel), Viking (New Delhi), 1991, Arcade, 1992.
India: From Midnight to the Millennium, Little, Brown (Boston), 1997.

Columnist, *Indian Express.* Contributor of hundreds of articles, reviews, and commentaries to publications, including *New York Times, Washington Post,* and *Indian Review of Books.*

ADAPTATIONS: Show Business was adapted to film by B. J. Kahn and released as *Bollywood,* 1994.

SIDELIGHTS: Shashi Tharoor recasts the traditional Indian epic poem *Mahabharata* in *The Great Indian Novel,* his first published work of fiction. Tharoor uses the ancient story as a framework upon which to satirize India's political history through the use of allusions. Major characters appear as thinly-veiled reincarnations of Jawaharlal Nehru, Indira Gandhi, and Mohandas K. Gandhi. The author also weaves into the narrative occasionally mocking references to certain British novels that have dealt with India; for instance, there is a chapter titled "The Bungle Book," after Rudyard Kipling's *Jungle Book,* and *The Jewel in the Crown* by Paul Scott is transformed into "The Duel with the Crown." An E. M. Forster character from *A Passage to India,* Ronald Heaslop, reappears frequently throughout *The Great Indian Novel.* And contemporary Indian writers such as Salman Rushdie come under Tharoor's wit, with Rushdie's novel *Midnight's Children* recalled as *Midnight's Parents.*

The narrator of *The Great Indian Novel,* Ved Vyas, is an elder statesman of the Indian nationalist movement who both describes and participates in the events of the novel, which retells the political history of twentieth-century India. Ved is "the progenitor of every grasping politician since liberty and he's the half-brother of the virgin-coddling, toilet-scrubbing, Untouchable-petting and all-star obtuse Gangaji (read M. K. Gandhi)," explained John Calvin Batchelor in the *Washington Post Book World.* "Gangaji," Ved remarks in the book, "was the kind of person it is more convenient to forget. The principles he stood for and the way he asserted them were always easier to admire than to follow. While he was alive, he was impossible to ignore; once he had gone, he was impossible to imitate."

Tharoor's plot details fictional events that closely resemble actual occurrences during India's struggle toward independence. India's political background is also the subject of Tharoor's first book, *Reasons of State: Political Development and India's Foreign Policy under Indira Gandhi, 1966-1977.* Edward Hower, writing in the Chicago *Tribune Books,* found *The Great Indian Novel* "ambitious and often eloquent," adding "we need no special knowledge of India to find Tharoor's book fascinating." *New York Times Book Review* contributor Michael Gorra complimented the author on his wit, remarking, "I loved the complicated joke Mr. Tharoor builds out of Kipling's 'Gunga Din' and the sense of comic resignation with which he describes bureaucracy as 'simultaneously the most crippling of Indian diseases and the highest of Indian art-forms.' "

In his second novel, *Show Business,* Tharoor writes about a fictional actor who catapults to fame in India's thriving film industry. "Year in, year out, [in India] hundreds of gaudy, fantastical, escapist, preposterous action-musical-romance-epics are churned out," explained reviewer William Boyd in the *New York Times Book Review.* Cast as a leading man in these matinee-style movies, Ashok Banjara becomes a box-office sensation, growing rich and marrying his co-star. He is also a prolific womanizer, seducing his next co-star while his wife is pregnant with triplets. Described by Sybil Steinberg in *Publishers Weekly* as "a personable, egotistical cad," Ashok next trades on his fame to enter politics, which eventually brings about his downfall and public disgrace. Critic Jonathan Yardley, reviewing *Show Business* in the *Washington Post Book World,* considered it "a splendid novel." Yardley stated, "Eschewing the temptations of magical realism to which other Indian writers have succumbed, he has written a witty, ironic novel in which Indian film—and India itself—is seen from any number of revealing angles." Boyd praised *Show Business* for its stylistic flair, perceiving the novel as "a mix of first-person narration, synopses of Ashok's dreadful Hindi films and resentful and accusatory monologues by the supporting cast. The effect is to fragment and rearrange the chronology . . . of Ashok Banjara in a way that replicates the razzle-dazzle of the Hindi film world, but that also permits Mr. Tharoor to comment, with telling irony and insight, on the curious parallels between India's unique film culture and the . . . serenity and chaos . . . of India itself."

Tharoor offered "an engaging reflection on the fiftieth anniversary of India's independence" with *India: From Midnight to the Millennium,* according to *Foreign Affairs* reviewer Donald Zagoria. Outstanding photographs and sparkling commentary combine in a volume that "blends academic analysis and personal observation on a whole range of topics and problems that India confronts—caste, religion, and economics." *Booklist* writer Donna Seaman found *India: From Midnight to the Millennium* "an ideal introduction to India's diversity and mesh of past and present," and a "captivating survey." Donald Johnson, a contributor to *Library Journal,* wrote that Tharoor's *India,* "like his earlier work . . . is an insightful and provocative analysis of the accomplishments and failures of the past fifty years. . . . Superbly written, this work will be useful to anyone interested in modern India." John F. Burns for the *New York Times Book Review* noted that Tharoor "show[s] an encyclopedic command of what has gone wrong with Indian democracy over the past half-century." Burns further related his opinion that "Tharoor is a fluid and powerful writer, one of the best in a generation of Indian writers."

Tharoor's prose style is singled out for praise by *Contemporary Novelists* essayist Ralph J. Crane. Discussing *The Great Indian Novel,* Crane noted the historical and political aspects of the book, but went on to say: "Perhaps of even greater importance than the history and politics in this novel is Tharoor's interest in language. Through his many linguistic and literary games—such as the novel's self-reflexivity and the frequent spot-the allusion games—Tharoor exposes the power of language as a tool of the colonial process while at the same time pointing the reader back to the literature." Crane concluded: "While Tharoor's work has so far received scant critical attention, *The Great Indian Novel* alone suggests that he deserves to be considered among the major Indian writers of recent decades."

Tharoor once told *CA:* "Ever since my birth—to Indian parents in London—was marked by the casting of two mutually-irreconcilable horoscopes, I have led a 'double life,' only one part of which has been devoted to writing. But it has been an important, even vital part. I wrote fiction from a very young age, my first story emerging when I was six. I was an asthmatic child, often bedridden with severe attacks, who rapidly exhausted the diversions available to me. Like every first child, I found few books on the family's shelves that appealed to me, and those I read inconveniently fast. Purchases were expensive and libraries limited; many let you borrow only one book at a time, and I had an awkward tendency to finish that in the car on the way home. Perhaps the ultimate clincher was that there was no television in the Bombay of my boyhood. So I wrote.

"I often had to sit up in bed to do so, but my imagination overcame my wheezing. My first stories were imitative school mysteries in the Enid Blyton tradition, but without the Enid Blyton flair. By the time I was nine I was attempting to churn out heroic tales of wartime derring-do. Here I was more than derivative; I abandoned any patriotic pretensions and wrote about an RAF fighter pilot called Reginald Bellows. When the first installment of 'Operation Bellows' appeared, in a Calcutta teen magazine, I was a month short of my eleventh birthday. I had found my metier.

"As I became a teenager, I started trying to depict the world I knew in India. Improbable fantasies about distant lands and times seemed suddenly less interesting than writing about people like myself. The audience was ready made—Indians who read Indian mass-circulation magazines. I was writing to be published and to be read, not to pursue an obscure literary aesthetic. This in turn helped define the nature, and limitations, of my early work. My stories (subsequently collected in *The Five-Dollar Smile*) largely reflect an adolescent sensibility; with one or two exceptions the stories' concerns, assumptions, and language all emerge from the consciousness of an urban Indian male in his late teens.

"India is, of course, a vast and complex country; in Walt Whitman's phrase, it contains multitudes. If the world depicted in my short stories is a very narrow slice of it, the scope of my first novel may have taken my writing to the other extreme. In *The Great Indian Novel* I attempted to reinvent the political history of twentieth-century India through a recasting of characters, events and themes from the two-thousand-year-old Indian epic *Mahabharata.* I hoped in the process to cast a satirical light on the myths and legends of India's traditional culture as well as of its contemporary history. My second novel, *Show Business,* is, like its predecessor, also concerned with the kinds of stories a society tells about itself—in this case, the stories of India's popular cinema. In retelling, reinterpreting, and remaking national myths both ancient and modern, the two novels attempt an irreverent treatment of some fairly serious questions—the nature of India as society and nation, as well as the issues of destiny and predestination, reality and illusion, public morality and human values, even karma and dharma. But the irreverence was essential, both because of its capacity to provoke and because I unashamedly want people to *enjoy* my books.

"The other feature of my writing that I hope readers will appreciate is the liberties I take with conventional narrative technique. The interpolation of verse (mock epic doggerel in *The Great Indian Novel,* parodied film lyrics in *Show Business*) is a stylistic device that I hope proves as pleasurable to readers as it did to me, and it also serves a literary purpose within the context of the novel.

"I have always seen myself as a human being with a number of concerns about—and responses to—the world, some of which I express in my work for the United Nations (I'm leading the team at United Nations headquarters handling the peacekeeping operation in Yugoslavia) and some of which emerge in my writing. This is why, in my fiction so far, my concern has been more with the mores than the men, and less with the individual than the issues.

"My life as a writer has been somewhat crippled by the demands of my work on Yugoslavia for the United Nations (as the *New York Times* pithily put it in their brief profile, 'The More War, The Less Writing'). I used to write on evenings and weekends; since late 1991 I haven't had enough of either to permit progress on a third novel."

BIOGRAPHICAL/CRITICAL SOURCES:

BOOKS

Contemporary Literary Criticism, Volume 70, Gale (Detroit), 1991.

Contemporary Novelists, St. James (Detroit), 1996.

Tharoor, Shashi, *The Great Indian Novel,* Viking, 1989.

PERIODICALS

Booklist, June 15, 1992; August, 1997, p. 1872.

Discovery, February, 1992.

Far Eastern Economic Review, November 16, 1989.

Foreign Affairs, March 22, 1983; July 1, 1998, p. 139.

India Currents, October, 1992.

India West, February 12, 1993.

Library Journal, May 15, 1992; July, 1993; June 15, 1997, p. 86; July, 1997, p. 102.

Los Angeles Times, July 25, 1991, section E, p. 10.

New York Times, February 13, 1990.

New York Times Book Review, March 24, 1991, p. 16; September 27, 1992, pp. 1, 22; October 12, 1997.

Publishers Weekly, February 15, 1991, p. 76; March 16, 1992, p. 62; May 31, 1993, p. 41; June 23, 1997, p. 78; July, 1997.

Statesman, July 8, 1990.

Times Literary Supplement, September 8-14, 1989, p. 969.

Tribune Books (Chicago), June 16, 1991, p. 5.

Village Voice, May 21, 1991, p. 72.

Washington Post Book World, March 24, 1991, pp. 1-2; August 30, 1992, p. 3.

World and I, July, 1991, pp. 343-49, 351-61.*

* * *

TOPPING, Seymour 1921-

PERSONAL: Born December 11, 1921, in New York, NY; son of Joseph and Anna (Seidman) Topolsky; married Audrey Elaine Ronning (a photo-journalist), November 19, 1949; children: Susan, Karen, Lesley, Rebecca, Joanna. *Education:* University of Missouri, B.J., 1943; also attended College of Chinese Studies, Peking, China.

ADDRESSES: Home—5 Heathcote Rd., Scarsdale, NY 10583. *Office*—Pulitzer Prize Board, Journalism 709, Columbia University, New York, NY 10027. *E-mail*—st122@columbia.edu.

CAREER: International News Service, 1946-48, correspondent in North China covering civil war there, 1946-47, later chief of bureau based in Nanking; Associated Press (AP), correspondent in Nanking, 1948-49, head of Indo-china war staff in Saigon, 1950-51, London correspondent, 1952, diplomatic correspondent for London and the Continent, 1952-56, chief of Berlin Bureau, 1956-59; *New York Times,* New York, City, member of metropolitan staff, 1959, chief correspondent, Moscow, 1960-63, and Southeast Asia, 1963-66, foreign editor, 1966-69, assistant managing editor, 1969-76, deputy managing editor, 1976-77, managing editor, 1977-87, director of editorial development regional newspapers, 1987-93; Columbia University Graduate School of Journalism, New York City, professor of journalism, 1993—, Sanpaolo Professor of International Journalism, 1994—. Administrator, Pulitzer Prizes, 1993—. *Military service:* U.S. Army, infantry, 1943-46; served in Philippines; became captain.

MEMBER: American Society of Newspaper Editors (president, 1992-93), Council on Foreign Relations, Asia Society, National Committee for United States-China Relations, Century Association.

AWARDS, HONORS: Distinguished service award from University of Missouri School of Journalism, 1968; honorary Litt.D., Rider College, 1983.

WRITINGS:

Journey between Two Chinas, Harper (New York City), 1972.

The Peking Letter: A Novel of the Chinese Civil War, Public Affairs (New York City), 1999.

Also author of foreword to *The Splendor of Tibet,* by wife, Audrey Topping, SINO Publishing (New York City), 1981. Member of board of directors of *New York Quarterly.*

SIDELIGHTS: Seymour Topping drew on his considerable experience of the Far East when writing his novel *The Peking Letter: A Novel of the Chinese Civil War.* Topping worked as a journalist covering China and Indochina for many years. His story is set in the late 1940s, when Beijing was still the walled, mysterious city of Peking and when the forces of Mao Tse-tung and Chiang Kai-shek battled for supremacy. The protagonist of *The Peking Letter* is Eric Jensen, who was raised in China by his missionary parents. Somewhat self-indulgent and more interested in art and culture than in politics, Jensen nevertheless finds himself blackmailed into working as a CIA agent. The Chinese woman he loves, medical student Lilian Yang, is a leftist sympathizer who wants him to deliver a letter negotiating the peaceful surrender of Peking. His involvement deepens until he is pursued by the CIA, the Nationalist secret police, and the Communist military police. "The depth of detail, Topping's knowledge of China, and the unseen twists in plot make for an entertaining read," enthused Carolyn Kubisz in *Booklist. New York Times Book Review* writer Lisa See approved of the realistic way Topping showed how many Americans in China at that time professed the superiority of traditional American values, even as they enjoyed the such luxuries such as live-in prostitutes and the easy acquisition of valuable antiques. "Although Topping is writing about events a half-century ago, many of the issues are very much in the headlines today. The arguments over democracy and Communism may, in fact, be even more germane now as China grapples with its free-market economy, the United States holds its annual debate over China's most-favored-nation status and the two countries continue to struggle with their mutual feelings of distrust," See explains. "Topping has shown in the way only a veteran reporter can that the infatuation—or, conversely, the xenophobic distrust—Americans have always felt for China is just another instance where the more things change, the more they remain the same."

Topping, a former editor at the *New York Times,* has given many lectures to newspapers professionals about ways to cope with the changing media world. In order to compete with television, he declares, newspapers must dedicate themselves to what they can provide best: in-depth coverage and hard news. He also points to the challenge of overcoming a growing apathy toward news in general. "It is time for newspapers, rather than suffering discouragement in the face of this bypass tendency, to recognize that they are being presented with a historic opportunity to enhance their role in American life," Topping was quoted as saying in an *Editor & Publisher* article by Debra Gersh. "Television may be the prime source for breaking spot news, but no medium is better equipped than newspapers for analysis and serious discussion of the rectification of our society."

BIOGRAPHICAL/CRITICAL SOURCES:

PERIODICALS

Booklist, September 15, 1999.

Center Magazine, May-June, 1985, pp. 15, 29; July-August, 1985, p. 36.

Editor & Publisher, January 14, 1989, p. 26; January 12, 1991, Ann Marie Kerwin, "Newspapers' Glass Half Full or Half Empty?," p. 18; March 2, 1991, M. L. Stein, "Mainstream Papers' 'Worst Nightmare,' " p. 14; April 17, 1993, Debra Gersh, "Advice to Editors," p. 25.

New York Times Book Review, January 4, 1981, p. 6; September 5, 1999, Lisa See, "Gang of One," p. 18.

New York Times Magazine, January 17, 1982, p. 94.

Publishers Weekly, August 9, 1999, review of *The Peking Letter,* p. 341.

* * *

TOWNES, Charles H(ard) 1915-

PERSONAL: Born July 28, 1915, in Greenville, SC; son of Henry Keith and Ellen Sumter (Hard) Townes; married Frances H. Brown, May 4, 1941; children: Linda Lewis Townes, Ellen Screven Townes, Carla Keith Townes, Holly Robinson Townes. *Education:* Furman University, B.A. (modern languages) and B.S. (physics), both with highest honors, 1935; Duke University, M.A., 1937; California Institute of Technology, Ph.D., 1939.

ADDRESSES: Office—c/o Department of Physics, University of California, Berkeley, CA 94720.

CAREER: Bell Telephone Laboratories, member of technical staff, 1939-47; Columbia University, New York City, associate professor, 1948-50, professor of physics, 1950-61, department head, 1952-55, executive director of Columbia Radiation Laboratory, 1950-52; Massachusetts Institute of Technology, Cambridge, professor of physics, 1961-67, provost of the university, 1961-66; University of California, Berkeley, university professor of physics, 1967-86, professor emeritus, 1986-96, professor in graduate school, 1996—. Institute of Defense Analyses, vice president and director of research, 1959-61; Woods Hole Oceanographic Institution, member of corporation; Max-Planck Institute for Physics and Astrophysics, foreign member. University of Paris, Fulbright lecturer, 1955-56; University of Tokyo, Fulbright lecturer, 1956; Enrico Fermi International School of Physics, director, 1963; Cambridge University, Scott Lecturer, 1963; University of Toronto, Centennial Lecturer, 1967; served in various positions for other institutions, including Lincoln Lecturer, 1972-73, Halley Lecturer, 1976, Krishman Lecturer, 1992, Nishina Lecturer, 1992, and Henry Norris Russell Lecturer, 1999; member of board of trustees of California Institute of Technology, Carnegie Institution of Washington, Graduate Theological Union, and California Academy of Sciences. General Motors Corp., member of board of directors, 1973-86. President's Scientific Advisory Committee, member, 1966-69, vice chairperson, 1967-69; National Aeronautics and Space Administration, chairperson of scientific and technical advisory committee for manned space flight, 1964-69; National Academy of Sciences, council member, 1968-72, 1978-81; chairperson of space science board, 1970-73; President's Committee on Science and Technology, member, 1976. Holder of patents related to masers and lasers.

MEMBER: Institute of Electrical and Electronic Engineers (life member), American Physical Society (Richtmeyer Lecturer, 1959; president, 1967), Optical Society of America (honorary member), American Philosophical Society, American Astronomical Society, American Academy of Arts and Sciences, Royal Society (foreign member), Indian National Science Academy, Russian Academy of Sciences (foreign member), Pontifical Academy of Sciences, National Academy of Engineering, National Academy of Achievement, California Academy of Sciences.

AWARDS, HONORS: Guggenheim fellow, 1955-56; Stuart Ballantine Medal, Franklin Institute, 1959, 1962; National Academy of Sciences, Comstock Award, 1959, and John J. Carty Medal; Thomas Young Medal and prize, Institute of Physics and Physical Society of England, 1963; Nobel Prize, physics, 1964, for work on masers and lasers; Medal of Honor, Institute of Electrical and Electronic Engineers, 1967; Optical Society of America, C. E. K. Mees Medal, 1968, Frederic Ives Medal, 1996; Distinguished Public Service Medal, National Aeronautics and Space Administration, 1969; Wilhelm Exner Award of Austria, 1970; inducted into National Inventors Hall of Fame, 1976; Plyler Prize, American Physical Society, 1977; Niels Bohr International Gold Medal, 1979; National Science Medal, 1983; inducted into Engineering and Science Hall of Fame, 1983; Commonwealth Award, 1993; ADION Medal, Nice Observatory, 1995; Rabindranath Tagore Commemorative Plaque, East Asian Society, 1999; Frank Annunzio Award, Columbus Foundation, 1999; Rumford Premium, American Academy of Arts and Sciences; more than twenty-five honorary degrees from colleges and universities; officier, French Legion of Honor; inducted into South Carolina Hall of Fame.

WRITINGS:

(With Paul Kisliuk) *Molecular Microwave Spectra Tables,* U.S. Government Printing Office (Washington, DC), 1952.

(With A. L. Schawlow) *Microwave Spectroscopy,* McGraw (New York City), 1955.

(Editor and contributor) *International Quantum Electronics Conference,* Columbia University Press (New York City), 1960.

Making Waves, American Institute of Physics (Woodbury, NY), 1995.

How the Laser Happened: Adventures of a Scientist, Oxford University Press (New York City), 1999.

Also co-editor and contributor, *Quantum Electronics and Coherent Light,* 1964. Contributor to scientific journals. Member of editorial board, *Review of Scientific Instruments,* 1950-52, *Physical Review,* 1951-53, *Journal of Molecular Spectroscopy,* 1957-60, and *Proceedings of the National Academy of Sciences,* 1978-84. The papers of Charles H. Townes are stored at the Library of Congress, Washington, DC.

BIOGRAPHICAL/CRITICAL SOURCES:

BOOKS

Backer, Donald C., editor, *The Galactic Center: Proceedings of the Symposium Honoring C. H. Townes,* American Institute of Physics, 1987.

PERIODICALS

California, September, 1982, p. 82.

Choice, November, 1999, p. 563.

Physics Today, September, 1983, p. 89; October, 1988, p. 26.

* * *

TREFIL, James S. 1938-

PERSONAL: Born September 10, 1938, in Chicago, IL; son of Stanley (a personnel manager) and Sylvia (a social worker; maiden name, Mestek) Trefil; married Elinor Pletka, September 2, 1960 (divorced, January, 1972); married Jeanne Waples, October 20, 1973 (divorced June, 1997); married Kim Gareiss, June 21, 1999; children: James Karel, Stefan James, Dominique Katherine, Flora Jeanne, Tomas. *Education:* University of Illinois, B.A., 1960; Oxford University, B.A., 1962, M.A., 1962; Stanford University, M.S., 1964, Ph.D., 1966.

ADDRESSES: *Home*—4210 Ann Fitz Hugh Dr., Annandale, VA 22003. *Office*—Department of Physics, George Mason University, Fairfax, VA 22030.

CAREER: Stanford Linear Accelerator Center, Stanford, CA, fellow, 1966; European Center for Nuclear Research, Geneva, Switzerland, fellow, 1966-67; Massachusetts Institute of Technology, Cambridge, fellow at Laboratory for Nuclear Science, 1967-68; University of Illinois, Urbana, assistant professor of physics, 1968-70; University of Virginia, Charlottesville, fellow, Center for Advanced Studies, and associate professor, 1970-75, professor of physics, 1975-88; George Mason University, Fairfax, VA, Clarence J. Robinson Professor of Physics, 1988—. Science advisor to National Public Radio; consultant to *Smithsonian* magazine; contributing editor for *Science* and *USA Weekend.*

MEMBER: American Physical Society (fellow), World Economic Forum (fellow), American Association for the Advancement of Science (fellow).

AWARDS, HONORS: Marshall Scholar, 1960-62; Air Force Office of Scientific Research postdoctoral fellow, 1966-67; President and Visitor's Research Prize, University of Virginia, 1979; American Association for the Advancement of Science/Westinghouse Science Journalism Award, 1983; Andrew Gement Award for science and humanities, 2000.

WRITINGS:

Introduction to the Physics of Fluids and Solids, Pergamon (Elmsford, NY), 1975.

Physics as a Liberal Art, Pergamon, 1978.

From Atoms to Quarks: An Introduction to the Strange World of Particle Physics, Scribner (New York City), 1980.

(With Robert T. Rood) *Are We Alone?: The Possibility of Extraterrestrial Civilizations,* Scribner, 1981.

Living in Space, Scribner, 1981.

The Unexpected Vista: A Physicist's View of Nature, Scribner, 1983.

The Moment of Creation: Big Bang Physics from before the First Millisecond to the Present Universe, Scribner, 1983.

A Scientist at the Seashore, Scribner, 1984.

Space, Time, Infinity: The Smithsonian Views the Universe, Pantheon/Smithsonian Books (New York City), 1985.

Meditations at Ten Thousand Feet: A Scientist in the Mountains, Scribner, 1986.

Meditations at Sunset: A Scientist Looks at the Sky, Scribner, 1987.

(Contributor and co-author of appendix) E. D. Hirsch Jr., *Cultural Literacy: What Every American Needs to Know,* Houghton (New York City), 1987.

The Dark Side of the Universe: A Scientist Explores the Mysteries of the Cosmos, Scribner, 1988.

(With E. D. Hirsch) *Dictionary of Cultural Literacy,* Houghton, 1988, revised edition, 1993.

Reading the Mind of God: In Search of the Principle of Universality, Scribner, 1989.

(With Robert M. Hazen) *Science Matters: Achieving Scientific Literacy,* Doubleday (New York City), 1991.

1001 Things Everyone Should Know about Science, Doubleday, 1992.

The Facts of Life: Science and the Abortion Controversy, Oxford University Press (New York City), 1992.

Sharks Have No Bones: 1001 Things You Should Know about Science, Simon & Schuster (New York City), 1993.

A Scientist in the City, Doubleday, 1994.

(With R. Hazen) *The Physical Sciences: An Integrated Approach,* Wiley (New York City), 1995, 2nd edition published as *The Sciences: An Integrated Approach,* Wiley, 1998.

The Edge of the Unknown: 101 Things You Don't Know about Science and No One Else Does Either, Houghton, 1996.

Are We Unique?: A Scientist Explores the Unparalleled Intelligence of the Human Mind, Wiley, 1997.

Other Worlds: The Solar System and Beyond, National Geographic Society (Washington, DC), 1999.

SIDELIGHTS: In one respect, James S. Trefil "surpasses almost all other scientists writing about science for the public," notes Alan P. Lightman in the *New York Times Book Review.* He elaborates: "As in his previous books and articles, we feel a real person talking to us about the physical world. . . . Such immediacy must be treasured in science communication." Through his books and articles, Trefil has clarified such subjects as atomic theory and the big bang for popular audiences; in his "Natural Philosopher" series, Trefil explores everyday questions about man's surroundings and applies physical theory in obtaining their answers. In *A Scientist at the Seashore,* the first book in the series, Trefil begins at a beach and investigates the influence of physics on tides, waves, sailing, skipping stones, and other topics. Similarly, *Meditations at Ten Thousand Feet: A Scientist in the Mountains* includes examinations of geology, such as the formation of mountains and glaciers, plate tectonics, and the age of the earth. A theoretical approach to topics such as the color of light, clouds, and thunderstorms characterizes *Meditations at Sunset: A Scientist Looks at the Sky,* while *A Scientist in the City* explores the urban setting. All of these books have been praised for explanations that are comprehensible without being condescending or oversimplified.

One reason for the success of Trefil's trilogy is that his essays "are lucidly written in a style that is personal and discursive rather than technical," comments Gerald Feinberg in the *New York Times Book Review.* "Whether he is writing about the oceans, the cosmos or the Earth itself," observes Lee Dembart of the *Los Angeles Times,* "he exudes awe and wonder that things are as they are. He is the best kind of teacher," continues the critic. "His knowledge of the subject is expert, but he conveys it with the enthusiasm of a beginner." Jonathan Weiner similarly remarks upon the author's approach: "Trefil . . . seems to be an ideal physics teacher: clear, affable and as pleased by the beauty of natural laws as most people are by sunsets," the critic writes in the *New York Times Book Review.* "He holds your attention without begging for it, and he almost always knows when a point has been made or when an analogy is needed. I enjoyed reading even stories I already knew well . . . because of the superb clarity of the explanations," adds Weiner.

Analyzing the proficiency of Trefil's explanations, Ellen W. Chu states in the *New York Times Book Review* that they "omit nothing crucial and, most important, engage our active participation. Without patronizing," continues Chu, "he makes the 'scientific method' a real step-by-step process of discovery he invites us to share with him, not a rigid intellectual exercise performed only by fully registered scientists." Part of this process includes connecting the various elements of his analyses so that they form a coherent whole. "This is science writing at its best," comments Dembart, "a broad sweep over many disciplines that helps make the outlines of the jigsaw puzzle of the universe clearer." Chu similarly observes that "no matter how far afield [Trefil] takes us, he ties everything back to something familiar; his direct, unpretentious style makes the book painless and enjoyable reading.""Taken as a whole," writes Feinberg, "I found *Meditations at 10,000 Feet* an impressive achievement in science writing for the general public." The critic concludes that Trefil's readers "will learn a good deal about science. They will also have a chance to see something that is much less common in science writing than clear exposition—how a scientist can use his training to understand his everyday experience."

In *The Edge of the Unknown: 101 Things You Don't Know about Science and No One Else Does Either,* Trefil gathered information from a wide range of scientific disciplines and presented it in an entertaining, brief format. Each topic addresses a new discovery, an age-old question, or a scientific development that has had, or will have, far-reaching societal implications. Many of the three-page essays are about health matters; seven of the ten problems Trefil designates as the most important facing mankind today are related to the human body. A *Publishers Weekly* reviewer finds *The Edge of the Unknown* "a competent and sometimes fascinating tour of the frontiers of scientific inquiry" and notes that "Trefil has a gift for constructing useful analogies" Readers will have "respect and awe" for those who have made the great scientific advances.

Are We Unique? A Scientist Explores the Unparalleled Intelligence of the Human Mind examines the characteristics that differentiate humans from other living creatures and from computers. Another *Publishers Weekly* reviewer finds that Trefil "demonstrates his skill in translating academic notions into language accessible to the educated general reader," yet he cautions that the author's "fine science writing . . . is undercut at times by Trefil's tone." This "self-importance" is offset by the author's "insight and clarity," concedes the reviewer.

Trefil once told *CA:* "I regard my writing as an outgrowth of my work as a teacher. Both involve explaining concepts clearly. I write about physical science, which is the area of my research, and about energy, a subject which I teach. I am particularly interested in wood heating, as I have used it myself for a number of years.

"I feel that science has come to play such a large role in our lives that it is absolutely crucial that the general public know what is happening. Unfortunately, very few scientists involve themselves in this sort of work. The situation may be changing, but not fast enough."

BIOGRAPHICAL/CRITICAL SOURCES:

PERIODICALS

America, January 14, 1984, p. 5.
Astronomy, March, 1989, p. 98.

Booklist, January 1, 1994, p. 795; December 15, 1995, p. 717; September 15, 1996, Gilbert Taylor, review of *The Edge of the Unknown,* p. 194; December 1, 1996, review of *The Edge of the Unknown,* p. 664.

Chatelaine, April, 1989, p. 12.

Chemical & Engineering News, January 2, 1989, p. 34; December 2, 1991, p. 47.

Discover, January, 1992, p. 69.

Education Digest, January, 1997, p. 75.

Library Journal, January, 1985, p. 93; March 1, 1986, p. 51; March 15, 1986, p. 74; June 1, 1987, p. 111; June 15, 1987, p. 78; March 1, 1989, pp. 40, 45; June 15, 1989, p. 75; January, 1991, p. 142; December, 1991, p. 190; November 15, 1993, p. 96; October 1, 1995, p. 133; October 1, 1996, p. 122; February 3, 1997, p. 86; March 15, 1997, Laurie Bartolini, review of *Are We Unique?,* p. 86.z

Los Angeles Times, April 16, 1986.

Los Angeles Times Book Review, July 5, 1987.

New York Times Book Review, April 24, 1983; September 25, 1983; February 24, 1985, p. 9; November 17, 1985; May 11, 1986, p. 27; July 12, 1987, p. 7; April 26, 1987, p. 36; October 16, 1988, p. 14; January 16, 1994, p. 27; November 10, 1996, p. 57; May 25, 1997, p. 17.

Oceans, July-August, 1985, p. 59.

Physics Today, April, 1988, p. 88.

Publishers Weekly, March 7, 1986, p. 89; May 19, 1989, p. 76; December 14, 1990, p. 58; December 6, 1993, p. 66; August 5, 1996, review of *Edge of the Unknown,* p. 422; February 3, 1997, review of *Are We Unique?,* p. 86; September 20, 1999, review of *Other Worlds,* p. 59.

Science, January 18, 1991, p. 266; March 15, 1991, p. 1308.

Science '83, July-August, 1983, p. 97; December, 1983, p. 116.

Science Digest, June, 1986, p. 73.

Sky & Telescope, April, 1989, p. 382.

School Library Journal, September, 1994, p. 258.

Science News, February 6, 1982, p. 92.

Smithsonian, May, 1983, p. 33.

Times Literary Supplement, February 20, 1981.

Washingtonian, August, 1985, p. 62; September, 1997, p. 37.

Washington Monthly, March, 1991, p. 60.

Washington Post, July 14, 1987.

Washington Post Book World, July 24, 1983; March 17, 1985; April 20, 1986.

Wilson Library Bulletin, December, 1993, p. 76.

TROW, George W. S. 1943-

PERSONAL: Surname rhymes with "throw"; born September 28, 1943, in Greenwich, CT; son of George Swift (in the newspaper business) and Anne (a homemaker; maiden name, Carter) Trow. *Education:* Harvard College, A.B., 1965. *Religion:* Episcopalian.

ADDRESSES: *Office*—c/o Pantheon Books, 201 East 50th St., New York, NY 10022.

CAREER: *New Yorker,* New York City, staff writer, 1966-94.

AWARDS, HONORS: Jean Stein Award for fiction from the American Academy and Institute of Arts and Letters, 1986, for essays "Within the Context of No Context" and "The Harvard Black Rock Forest" and for novel *The City in the Mist.*

WRITINGS:

Prairie Avenue (three-act play), first produced Off-Broadway at the South Street Theater, April, 1979.

The Tennis Game (three-act play; first produced Off-Broadway at the Theater of the Open Eye, February, 1978), Dramatists Play Service (New York City), 1979.

Elizabeth Dead (one-act play), first produced in New York City at the Cubiculo Theater, November, 1980.

Bullies (collection of stories), Little, Brown (Boston), 1980.

Within the Context of No Context (nonfiction essays; contains "Within the Context of No Context" and "Within That Context, One Style"), Little, Brown, 1981, revised edition (contains "Within the Context of No Context" and "Collapsing Dominant"), Atlantic Monthly Press (New York City), 1997.

The City in the Mist (novel), Little, Brown, 1984.

My Pilgrim's Progress: Media Studies, 1950-1998 (nonfiction), 1999.

Contributor to periodicals, including *New Yorker* and *Harper's Magazine.*

SIDELIGHTS: A longtime contributor to the *New Yorker,* George W. S. Trow is known both as an innovator in the school of fiction and a witty critic of the media and popular culture. Trow's plays, short stories, and novel exhibit what Roger Dionne, writing for the *Los Angeles Times,* called "a truly new way of perceiving the world." These writings, likened by critics to the works of controversial American writer Gertrude Stein for their anti-establishment themes and abstract style, take a satiric look at a vapid and pretentious society. Trow has also taken aim at the vapidness of society in his nonfiction works *Within the Context of No Context* and *My Pilgrim's Progress: Media Studies, 1950-1998.* "I was brought up in the shadow of the Victorian world," Trow once told *CA.* "In all my work, I am thinking about how we got from that world to the one we live in."

Early in his career, two of Trow's plays enjoyed Off-Broadway runs and brought the young author critical attention. *The Tennis Game,* staged in 1978, used tennis as a metaphor for society, evolving from a genteel nineteenth-century sport to a contemporary display of frenzied competition. *New York Times* critic Mel Gussow hailed the play as a "clever" work of "literate as well as literary quality." Similarly, the 1980 production *Elizabeth Dead*—consisting solely of a seventy-five minute soliloquy spoken by a dying Queen Elizabeth—won praise as an imaginative effort. Jennifer Dunning noted in the *New York Times* that the play contained "some touching, deft conceits." Dunning and Gussow suggested, however, that each stage work was obscured by an overly self-conscious posture.

In 1980, the same year in which *Elizabeth Dead* was staged, sixteen of the author's short fiction pieces for the *New Yorker* were published in a volume titled *Bullies.* According to Trow on the book's jacket copy, "The stories in *Bullies* take place in a landscape rather like history with the tide out." The writings are populated by a wide array of personalities, including an Upper East Side divorcee who likes to throw dinner parties, members of the Rock Critic Establishment, aging stars, and faded royalty: in short, both the *bullies* who set the fashion and the bullied who feel compelled to follow it. Eve Babitz, writing for the *New York Times Book Review,* lauded *Bullies* as "a victory for things exactly as they are" and proof "that style, taste, those little refinements used in everyday life to separate the elegant and delightful from the rest of us, are nothing more than 'specifics.' "

In an article for the *Village Voice,* however, Eve Ottenberg accused Trow of creating "an in-joke," thereby falling victim to the same pretentious vice that he purports to expose. Ottenberg argued that many readers would miss the significance of Trow's recurring Alani Beach setting. "The spirit of the gossip column haunts these stories," she wrote, and those "who are expected to know what [the Hotel Reine American] is without being told, will probably not be amused." But in a review for *Harper's Magazine,* Jeffrey Burke viewed the "crumbling resort" of Alani Beach as a source of illumination in the stories rather than obscurity or condescension: Trow created an appropriate backdrop for his dark satire by shifting to a "surreal" context colored with "malevolence," assessed Burke.

In 1984 Trow published his first novel, a short volume titled *The City in the Mist.* It chronicles a century in the lives of the Coonlons and the Aspairs, two wealthy New York families. The central figure is sixty-year-old bachelor Edward Coonlon Jones, grandson of the Coonlon patriarch. Schooled from an early age in the art of materialism, the unemployed Edward's main occupation involves looking after his legacy, especially his mother's precious Adam-Sheraton chairs. Although several critics faulted the book for its self-contained chapters, confusing myriad of characters, and general lack of direction, Richard Eder, writing for the *Los Angeles Times Book Review,* judged *The City in the Mist* "a witty and powerful vision of our contemporary disarray." He went on to say that "it devises a golden and magical legend for New York's rackety energy and confusion; and seeks in that legend the means to restore to us our sense of who we might really be."

Some critics contend that Trow's black humor, deadpan style, and often harsh evaluation of society at large can only appeal to a limited audience. But Joseph McLellan of the *Washington Post Book World* ventured that "in the rarefied, eccentric field he cultivates, his writing is consistently good and sometimes brilliant." Commenting on the author's ability to unearth the "mold, rot, [and] terror" that exist beneath elitist pretensions, Dionne asserted, "The measure of Trow's achievement is that such chilling themes as his become in his stories so damnably amusing."

Trow offered more observations on the state of contemporary American society in his 1981 essay collection *Within the Context of No Context.* The volume consists of two nonfiction pieces that originally appeared in the *New Yorker.* Several critics considered the title essay more relevant and insightful than its companion. "Within the Context of No Context" presents a generation without a past, a generation raised on television, whose members lack a sense of history beyond their personal recollections. Eva Hoffman explained in the *New York Times Book Review* that Trow has diagnosed an "elusive middle-class malaise" as a chronic case of "reality anemia." The second essay, "Within That Context, One Style," profiles Turkish-born Atlantic Records president Ahmet Ertegun as an individual embedded within Trow's "context of no context." While pointing out that the author "sometimes risks glibness" in his essays, Hoffman appraised *Within the Context of No Context* as a "penetrating" and "convincing" work of criticism that is "diametrically opposed to the myth . . . of America the raw, America the energetic." Barry Gewen, reviewing the book for the *New Leader,* thought Trow, an "intelligent and subtle" writer, nevertheless had not found quite the right tone for his material: "Irony by itself, no matter how well expressed, is ultimately unsatisfying."

There was a receptive audience, however, for the 1997 edition of *Within the Context of No Context,* which contains the title essay and a new one called "Collapsing Dominant" but not the Ertegun piece. "What is impressive and eerie about reading the [title] essay now is not only how well the quality of George Trow's writing holds up but also his virtually prophetic indictment of American culture—its ignorance of history, its lack of content," declared John Irving in the *New York Times Book Review.* Irving continued, "What makes *In the Context of No Context* even more scathing now than it seemed in 1980 is that everything has worsened; the culture has become even more puerile." He concluded that "this elegant little book is essential reading for anyone interested in the demise, the terminal silliness, of our culture."

My Pilgrim's Progress: Media Studies, 1950-1998 is in many ways a follow-up to *Within the Context of No Context.* In this volume Trow jumps from subject to subject—including his hero, Dwight D. Eisenhower; Elvis Presley and the Beatles; the film *All About Eve;* mindless television shows and talentless celebrities—but his overall point is that American culture has declined precipitously in the latter half of the twentieth century. "The main idea, largely developed in Mr. Trow's examination of *Mainstream American Cultural Artifacts,* is that the protective solidity of the American culture that existed at mid-century has vanished, even if we do not realize just how complete the disappearance was," explained *New York Times* critic Richard Bernstein, who deemed the book "original, provocative and possibly prophetic" and its author "an old-fashioned curmudgeon who writes with hip, new-fashioned flair." Trow laments the media's undermining of the masculine authority—what he calls "civilized masculine dominance energy"—he believes the country sorely needs. For him, this energy was personified by such figures as Eisenhower, Franklin D. Roosevelt, and some non-Americans, including British prime minister Winston Churchill. Richard Brookhiser, a contributor to the conservative journal *National Review,* noted that Trow's book "is not a neoconservative critique"—Trow is sympathetic to some liberal ideas—but asserted that "what all conservatives can appreciate is Trow's compass-needle yearning for adults who know what they are doing." *New York Times Book Review* commentator Gerald Marzorati, though, warned that "not all civilized masculine dominance energy is for the best" and complained that Trow often fails to explain his ideas thoroughly: "One of Trow's favorite formulations . . . is "You'll have to trust me on that one." Among the things you have to trust him on are just about everything having to do with his thesis."

James Wolcott, writing in the *New Republic,* found the book too long on nostalgia; "Sugarcoating the past," he contended, "is unworthy of someone with Trow's brilliance." He remarked that "*In the Context of No Context* and *My Pilgrim's Progress* are both rooted in an Edenic myth of America," the concept that the nation was a paradise, now lost. But, he averred, "Some might argue that paradise lost began with the introduction of slavery to our shores and the extermination of Indian nations, but to Trow and his admirers, creatures of their time as much as anyone else, America's wrong turn happened before their eyes, with the primitive advent of television." Trow, he said, exaggerates the importance of TV and other media: "If the century is a failure, an epic disaster, it is difficult to see how popular entertainment or the tabloid mentality deserves the primary blame. The wholesale slaughter of the First World War, the Holocaust, the Stalinist terror: none of these horrors were the product of show business run amok. . . . In our own time, Matt Drudge and Jerry Springer, novelty-store items of plastic vomit though they may be to many, are minor pests compared to Pinochet or Pol Pot."

BIOGRAPHICAL/CRITICAL SOURCES:

PERIODICALS

Atlantic Monthly, June, 1984.
Detroit News, October 4, 1981.
Harper's Magazine, May, 1980.
Los Angeles Times, June 3, 1980.
Los Angeles Times Book Review, February 12, 1984.
National Review, April 5, 1999, p. 50.
New Leader, November 2, 1981, pp. 14-15.
New Republic, February 8, 1999.
New York Times, February 15, 1978; April 26, 1980; November 27, 1980; February 10, 1999.
New York Times Book Review, April 20, 1980; October 11, 1981; February 5, 1984, p. 12; April 6, 1997; February 14, 1999.
Saturday Review, September, 1981.
Village Voice, July 9-15, 1980; December 23-29, 1981.

Washington Post, June 12, 1980.
Washington Post Book World, March 25, 1984.*

* * *

UNWIN, Stanley 1884-1968

PERSONAL: Born December 19, 1884; died October 13, 1968; son of Edward and Elizabeth (Spicer) Unwin; married Alice Mary Storr, 1914; children: David Storr, Ruth Severn Unwin Brodrick, Rayner Stephens. *Education:* Educated at schools in England and Germany.

CAREER: Bought the George Allen & Co. Ltd. publishing business and founded the London publishing firm of George Allen & Unwin Ltd. in 1914; served as chairman until his death. British Council, member of executive; Equitable Life Assurance Society, director; Sir Halley Stewart Trust, chairman.

MEMBER: International Publishers' Congress (president, 1936-38, 1946-54), Publishers' Association of Great Britain and Ireland (president, 1933-35), Royal Society of Literature (fellow), Royal Geographical Society, Royal Zoological Society, Royal Economic Society, Royal Institute of International Affairs, American Academy of Arts and Sciences (honorary), Reform Club.

AWARDS, HONORS: Honorary LL.D. from Aberdeen University, 1945; Accolade from King George VI, 1946; palmes en gold de l'ordre de la Couronne; officer d'Academie Francais; Order of White Lion of Czechoslovakia; officer in the Order of Orange Nassau (Netherlands); Knight Commander of the Order of the Falcon (Iceland); Knight Commander of Order of St. Michael and St. George, 1966.

WRITINGS:

The Truth about Publishing, Allen & Unwin (London), 1926, revised and partially rewritten by son, Philip Unwin, for 8th edition, 1976.

(With Severn Storr) *Two Young Men See the World,* Allen & Unwin, 1934.

Best Sellers: Are They Born or Made?, Allen & Unwin, 1939.

Publishing in Peace and War, Allen & Unwin, 1944.

How Governments Treat Books, Allen & Unwin, 1950.

The Truth about a Publisher: An Autobiographical Record, Macmillan (New York City), 1960.

SIDELIGHTS: In 1914 Stanley Unwin purchased George Allen & Co., Ltd. and created the still-existing publishing firm of George Allen & Unwin Ltd. Before founding the business, Unwin traveled with Severn Storr throughout the world to explore the bookselling market. During their journey, both Unwin and his friend and future brother-in-law wrote letters and kept journals. Although not intended for publication at the time, a writer for the *New York Times* reported that those early writings were later "fused . . . into one continuous narrative from which careful editing . . . eliminated everything [without] inherent consequence" and published as *Two Young Men See the World* in 1934.

"Of their adventures among booksellers [Unwin and Storr] tell us nothing, which is regrettable," commented a *New Statesman* reviewer, "for to know who and what was in demand in Africa, Australia, Japan and the Pacific Islands in the year 1912 would probably have been both entertaining and instructive." "But," continued the reviewer, "that is the only complaint that may be made against a book that is packed with vivid description, set down without any thought of publication, and consequently lacking the naive self-consciousness that mars so much of our literature of travel." The two young men wrote about "obvious things, which are the permanent things, . . . and they know that the little adventure, which is the typical adventure, will meet with a sympathetic reception."

In 1926 Unwin published his most successful book, *The Truth about Publishing,* which has gone into eight editions and been reprinted numerous times. Oliver Harrison explained in the *Nation* that the book presents "in concrete form every detail of [the publishing] business." Critics have praised the book highly for its detail, accuracy, and honest presentation of book publishing business information. The critic for the *Times Literary Supplement* claimed that Unwin "has a genius for detail, and never before, to the best of our knowledge, have all [the book publishing] processes, the reasons for them, and the best methods of carrying them out been set forth with anything like the same fullness and accuracy." The critic for the *Saturday Review of Literature* found that Unwin "has done a real service to publishers, authors, and the general public. Probably no other man in the English speaking world has so many of the qualifications necessary for the writing of this valuable book. . . . He has written a thoroughly delightful and interesting book."

In 1960 Unwin published another book documenting his life experiences, *The Truth about a Publisher: An Autobiographical Record.* While Unwin's main purpose in writing his book is to recounting the story of his publishing company, "around it he has pleasantly woven his own life story, personal and professional," as P. J. Henniker-Heaton wrote in the *Christian Science Monitor.* "The self-portraiture is candid, almost naively so, and not so much immodest as non-modest," Isabel Quigly wrote in the *Guardian.* Writing in the *New York Times Book Review,* V. S. Pritchett noted that *The Truth about a Publisher* "as the charm of good-humored honesty, presenting its author without affectation or vanity as a busy, alert, conservative businessman in a trade as peculiar as horse racing." S. B. Lunt in the *New York Herald Tribune Book Review* concluded that Unwin "has most surely lived the writing of this book as he has lived life itself—with zest, wisdom, and integrity—all seasoned with flashes of wit." According to Daniel Metcher in *Saturday Review,* the book is "a remarkable introduction to a remarkable man."

BIOGRAPHICAL/CRITICAL SOURCES:

PERIODICALS

Booklist, June, 1927, review of *The Truth about Publishing;* September 1, 1960, review of *The Truth about a Publisher.*

Boston Transcript, November 28, 1934, review of *Two Young Men See the World.*

Christian Science Monitor, July 14, 1960, P. J. Henniker-Heaton, review of *The Truth about a Publisher,* p. 7.

Guardian, April 22, 1960, Isabel Quigly, review of *The Truth about a Publisher.*

Kirkus, April 1, 1960, review of *The Truth about a Publisher.*

Library Journal, August, 1960, H. F. Berolzheimer, review of *The Truth about a Publisher.*

Nation, March 23, 1927, Oliver Harrison, review of *The Truth about Publishing.*

New Statesman, November 13, 1926, review of *The Truth about Publishing;* July 21, 1934, review of *Two Young Men See the World;* April 2, 1960, Maurice Richardson, review of *The Truth about a Publisher.*

New York Herald Tribune Book Review, April 10, 1927, C. N. Hitchcock, review of *The Truth about Publishing,* p. 21; June 12, 1960, S. B. Lunt, review of *The Truth about a Publisher.*

New York Times, March 13, 1927, review of *The Truth about Publishing;* January 20, 1935, review of *Two Young Men See the World,* p. 16.

New York Times Book Review, September 11, 1960, V. S. Pritchett, review of *The Truth about a Publisher,* p. 30.

San Francisco Chronicle, August 28, 1960, review of *The Truth about a Publisher,* p. 25.

Saturday Review, June 16, 1934, review of *Two Young Men See the World;* July 30, 1960, Daniel Melcher, review of *The Truth about a Publisher.*

Saturday Review of Literature, May 21, 1927, review of *The Truth about Publishing.*

Spectator, October 30, 1926, review of *The Truth about Publishing;* April 15, 1960, Iain Hamilton, review of *The Truth about a Publisher.*

Springfield Republican, April 8, 1927, review of *The Truth about Publishing,* p. 10.

Times Literary Supplement, October 21, 1926, review of *The Truth about Publishing;* May 17, 1934, review of *Two Young Men See the World,* p. 353; April 1, 1960, review of *The Truth about a Publisher.**

* * *

USSHER, (Percival) Arland 1899-1980
(Percy Arland Ussher)

PERSONAL: Born September 9, 1899, in London, England; died December 24, 1980, in Dublin, Ireland; son of Beverley and Emily (Jebb) Ussher; married Emily Whitehead, May, 1925 (died, 1974); married Margaret Keith, September 2, 1975; children: (first marriage) Henrietta Owen (Mrs. Gerald Arland Staples). *Education:* Attended Trinity College, Dublin, 1917-19, and St. John's College, Cambridge, 1920. *Politics:* Liberal. *Religion:* Protestant.

CAREER: Freelance writer.

MEMBER: Irish Academy of Letters, Philosophical Society and Metaphysical Society (both Dublin).

AWARDS, HONORS: Gregory Medal, Academy of Letters.

WRITINGS:

(Under name Percy Arland Ussher; translator in verse from the Gaelic) Brian Merriman, *The Midnight Court and the Adventures of a Luckless Fellow,* preface by W. B. Yeats, Boni & Liveright, 1926, published as *Two Poems Translated from the Gaelic,* AMS (New York City), 1982.

Cainnt an Tsean Shaoghail (title means "Old World Speech"), Government Publications Office, 1942.

Postscript on Existentialism, and Other Essays, Sandymount Press, 1946.

The Twilight of the Ideas, and Other Essays, Sandymount Press, 1948.

Cursai an Tsean-Shaoghail (title means "Life on a Farm in the Old World"), Government Publications Office, 1948.

The Face and Mind of Ireland, Devin-Adair (Greenwich, CT), 1950, reprinted, 1979.

The Magic People, Devin-Adair, 1952.

Three Great Irishmen: Shaw, Yeats, Joyce, Gollancz (London), 1952, Devin-Adair, 1953.

Alphabet of Aphorisms, Dolmen Press, 1953.

Journey through Dread: Kierkegaard, Heidegger, and Sartre, Darwen Finlayson, 1955, Devin-Adair, 1956.

(With Carl von Metzradt) *Enter These Enchanted Woods: Grimm's Fairy Tales,* Dolmen Press, 1955.

The Thoughts of Wi Wong, Dolmen Press, 1955.

The Mines of Siberiay: A New Ballad of Rooshian Rodie and Pawnbroker Liz, Dolmen Press, 1956.

The Twenty-two Keys of the Tarot, Dolmen Press, 1957, new edition, 1976.

Spanish Mercy, Gollancz, 1960.

Sages and Schoolmen, Dufour (Chester Springs, PA), 1967.

Eros and Psyche: Essays, Runa Press (Dublin), 1977.

From a Dark Lantern: A Journal, edited by Roger Nyle Parisious Ussher, Cuala Press (Dalkey, Ireland), 1978.

The Journal of Arland Ussher, edited by Adrian Kenny, Raven Arts (Dublin), 1980.

The Juggler: Selections from a Journal, Dolmen Press, 1980.

Contributor to *New English Weekly, Adelphi, Dublin Magazine,* and other periodicals.

SIDELIGHTS: Arland Ussher, an Irish author, philosopher, and critic, was known for his acerbic wit, his observations on Irish culture, his studies of different national characters, his philosophical viewpoints, and his beautiful English translations of Gaelic poetry. Although well respected by critics, Ussher's refusal to condescend to popular tastes in his work limited his readership. However, his later writings gained greater public attention and this "hard-won recognition that Arland Ussher enjoyed in later life came from his gifts as a prose stylist, his all-round appreciation of complex issues through 'the constantly shifting viewpoint,' and his philosophic stance above the tides and tumults of the age," commented David Buxton in the London *Times.*

Ussher's work includes *The Face and Mind of Ireland,* a publication that "sketches the history of Ireland in his lifetime as seen from the shifting viewpoints of a man who has tried to clear his mind of youthful prejudices and impatience and to show events and men and women in the proper perspective [as well as attempting] the more ambitious task of explaining the inward make-up of the Irish Roman Catholic, his attitude to his religion, and its relation to his morals, manners, and actions, and to Irish social life," reported J. T. Gwynn in the *Manchester Guardian.* "These matters," noted J. C. Lehane in the *Chicago Sunday Tribune,* "are discussed with such objectivity and detachment that *The Face and Mind of Ireland* merits the respectful attention of all parties." James Stern in the *New York Times* found the book to be "wholly admirable for its freshness, objectivity and wisdom."

Another of Ussher's books, *Three Great Irishmen: Shaw, Yeats, Joyce,* reflects on "the Irish background of these three geniuses," stated a *Christian Century* critic. The critic praised Ussher: "He does not unduly exploit their common ethnic quality, though he relates them clearly enough to their racial and cultural origin." In a *New York Times* review, Horace Reynolds found that "Ussher writes with learning, wit, clarity and imagination. If at times he is capriciously personal, if occasionally he is seduced into ornament by his virtuosity in analogy, the caprice is often engaging, the ornament exciting and amusing."

Ussher also wrote *The Magic People,* which H. L. Roth described in *Library Journal* as "an appraisal of the Jews [which is concerned] not so much with present day Jews as it is with the whole background of Jewish civilization, relationships with non-Jews throughout history, Jesus and the Jews and an analysis of anti-Semitism." Readers of *The Magic People* who were unfamiliar with Jewish history, according to Roth, might "have difficulty understanding many of the allusions and divining the points made. However, it is well worth reading with Bible in hand." Reviewing the book for the *New York Times,* N. K. Burger stated that "much of what Mr. Ussher has to say will produce argument. His thought is personal and eclectic, but it is also lively and stimulating." A critic for the *Times Literary Supplement* declared *The Magic People* to be a "very entertaining and often uncommonly shrewd work."

BIOGRAPHICAL/CRITICAL SOURCES:

PERIODICALS

Catholic World, October, 1953, Katherine Bregy, review of *Three Great Irishmen: Shaw, Yeats, Joyce.*

Chicago Sunday Tribune, August 13, 1950, J. C. Lehane, review of *The Face and Mind of Ireland,* p.

5; August 16, 1953, J. M. Flynn, review of *Three Great Irishmen: Shaw, Yeats, Joyce,* p. 4.

Christian Century, August 26, 1953, review of *Three Great Irishmen: Shaw, Yeats, Joyce.*

Christian Science Monitor, September 23, 1950, Horace Reynolds, review of *The Face and Mind of Ireland,* p. 7.

Commonweal, October 6, 1950, Vivian Mercier, review of *The Face and Mind of Ireland;* August 7, 1953, Walter Kerr, review of *Three Great Irishmen: Shaw, Yeats, Joyce.*

Kirkus, June 1, 1951, review of *The Magic People.*

Library Journal, September 1, 1951, H. L. Roth, review of *The Magic People;* July, 1953, Herbert Cahoon, review of *Three Great Irishmen: Shaw, Yeats, Joyce.*

Manchester Guardian, August 16, 1949, J. T. Gwynn, review of *The Face and Mind of Ireland,* p. 4; August 26, 1952, Gerard Fay, review of *Three Great Irishmen: Shaw, Yeats, Joyce.*

Nation, November 10, 1951, review of *The Magic People.*

New Statesman, November 5, 1949, W. R. Rodgers, review of *The Face and Mind of Ireland;* December 23, 1950, C. E. M. Joad, review of *The Magic People;* September 27, 1952, W. R. Rodgers, review of *Three Great Irishmen: Shaw, Yeats, Joyce.*

New York Times, July 30, 1950, James Stern, review of *The Face and Mind of Ireland,* p. 5; September 9, 1951, N. K. Burger, review of *The Magic People,* p. 10; July 26, 1953, Horace Reynolds, review of *Three Great Irishmen: Shaw, Yeats, Joyce,* p. 3.

San Francisco Chronicle, October 1, 1950, review of *The Face and Mind of Ireland,* p. 18; July 26, 1953, review of *Three Great Irishmen: Shaw, Yeats, Joyce.*

Saturday Review of Literature, December 16, 1950, Padraic Colum, review of *The Face and Mind of Ireland;* September 5, 1953, Padraic Colum, review of *Three Great Irishmen: Shaw, Yeats, Joyce.*

Spectator, September 2, 1949, Austin Clarke, review of *The Face and Mind of Ireland;* August 15, 1952, Patrick Kavanagh, review of *Three Great Irishmen: Shaw, Yeats, Joyce.*

Time, September 17, 1951, review of *The Magic People.*

Times Literary Supplement, September 2, 1949, review of *The Face and Mind of Ireland,* p. 571; December 22, 1950, review of *The Magic People,* p. 818; August 29, 1952, review of *Three Great Irishmen: Shaw, Yeats, Joyce,* p. 560.

OBITUARIES:

PERIODICALS

Times (London), December 31, 1980.*

* * *

USSHER, Percy Arland
See USSHER, (Percival) Arland

* * *

VIOLA, Herman J(oseph) 1938-

PERSONAL: Born February 24, 1938, in Chicago, IL; son of Joseph (a carpenter) and Mary (Incollingo) Viola; married Susan Patricia Bennett (a librarian), June 13, 1964; children: Joseph, Paul, Peter. *Education:* Marquette University, B.A., 1960, M.A., 1964; Indiana University, Ph.D., 1970.

ADDRESSES: *Home*—7307 Pinewood St., Falls Church, VA 22046-2725. *Office*—Museum of Natural History, Smithsonian Institution, Washington, DC 20560.

CAREER: National Archives, Washington, DC, archivist, 1966-68; *Prologue: Journal of the National Archives,* Washington, DC, founding editor, 1968-72; Smithsonian Institution, Washington, DC, director of National Anthropological Archives, 1972-86, director of quincentenary programs at Museum of Natural History, 1986-ca. 1998, curator emeritus, ca. 1998—. *Military service:* U.S. Navy, 1962-64.

MEMBER: Society of American Archivists (program chair, 1972), Organization of American Historians, American History Association, Western History Association.

WRITINGS:

Thomas L. McKenney: Architect of America's Early Indian Policy, 1816-1830, Swallow Press (Athens, OH), 1974.

The Indian Legacy of Charles Bird King, Smithsonian Institution Press (Washington, DC), 1976.

Diplomats in Buckskins: A History of Indian Delegations in Washington City, Smithsonian Institution Press, 1981.

The National Archives of the United States, Abrams (New York City), 1984.

Exploring the West: A Smithsonian Book, Smithsonian Institution Press, 1987.

After Columbus: The Smithsonian Chronicle of the North American Indians, Smithsonian Books (Washington, DC), 1990.

Ben Nighthorse Campbell: An American Warrior, Orion Books (New York City), 1993.

Why We Remember: United States History through Reconstruction, teacher's edition, Addison-Wesley (Menlo Park, CA), 1997.

Warrior Artists: Historica Cheyenne and Kiowa Indian Ledger Art: Drawn by Making Medicine and Zotum, National Geographic Society (Washington, DC), 1998.

Little Bighorn Remembered: The Untold Indian Story of Custer's Last Stand, Random House (New York City), 1999.

EDITOR

(With Robert Kvasnicka) *The Commissioners of Indian Affairs,* University of Nebraska Press (Lincoln), 1979.

(With Carolyn Margolis) *Magnificent Voyagers: The U.S. Exploring Expedition, 1938-1942,* Smithsonian Institution Press, 1985.

(With Margolis) *Seeds of Change: A Quincentennial Commemoration,* Smithsonian Institution Press, 1991.

(And author of introduction) *The Memoirs of Charles Henry Veil: A Soldier's Recollections of the Civil War and the Arizona Territory,* Orion Books, 1993.

FOR CHILDREN

(With wife, Susan P. Viola) *Giuseppe Garibaldi,* Chelsea House (New York City), 1988.

Sitting Bull, illustrations by Charles Shaw, Raintree Publishers (Milwaukee, WI), 1990.

After Columbus: The Horse's Return to America, illustrations by Deborah Howland, Soundprints (Norwalk, CT), 1992.

Osceola, illustrations by Yoshi Miyake, Raintree Steck-Vaughn (Austin, TX), 1993.

It Is a Good Day to Die: Indian Eyewitnesses Tell the Story of the Battle of Little Bighorn (juvenile), Random House, 1998.

Why We Remember: United States History, Addison-Wesley, 1998.

SIDELIGHTS: Herman J. Viola has parlayed a childhood fascination with Native Americans into a lifetime career as a curator of Indian documents and an author of histories of the American West. For much of his professional life Viola was associated with the National Archives-and later the Smithsonian Institution-where he worked with the visual, oral, and written artifacts of American Indians. His writings spun out of the documents he cared for, and many of his books abound with Indian eyewitness accounts of major episodes in their tribal histories.

Little Bighorn Remembered: The Untold Story of Custer's Last Stand is one of those books. Viola persuaded the descendants of the Cheyenne, Sioux, Crow, and Arikara warriors who took part in the battle to talk about their ancestors' recollections. The book contains these oral histories as well as archaeological evidence, drawings, maps, and photographs of the battle in which Custer and his troops were soundly defeated. *Wild West* reviewer Louis Hart noted that the Indian accounts in *Little Bighorn Remembered* are "fascinating" and that the work is "certainly another welcome addition to the field . . . a book that makes the battle come alive." In the *Library Journal,* Charles V. Cowling stated that Viola "creates an interesting overview by collecting accounts of the battle by descendants of Indians who fought on both sides." Viola also published a children's version of the same book, titled *It Is a Good Day to Die: Indian Eyewitnesses Tell the Story of the Battle of Little Bighorn. Horn Book* correspondent Barbara Bader praised Viola's efforts for younger readers, concluding: "No other juvenile treatment of the battle is nearly as full, authentic, and immediate."

In an interview with *Insight on the News,* Viola said: "All of the Indian communities have a history that we should have worked hard to help preserve. That's what I was involved with here at the Smithsonian. I would like to see history programs conducted on all the reservations before the memory is lost. I don't think it's too late, even at this moment, to collect things that are still out there."

BIOGRAPHICAL/CRITICAL SOURCES:

PERIODICALS

American Spectator, April-May, 1994, p. 74.

Booklist, September 1, 1998, p. 118.

Horn Book Magazine, September-October, 1998, p. 625.

Insight on the News, January 3, 2000, p. 37.

Library Journal, August, 1998, p. 86; September 1, 1999, p. 213.

Los Angeles Times Book Review, September 30, 1984.

Publishers Weekly, August 16, 1999, p. 74.

School Library Journal, March, 1997, p. 210.
Washington Post Book World, August 23, 1981; December 5-11, 1999, p. 4.
Wild West, February, 2000, p. 62.*

W

WARDLAW, Lee 1955-

PERSONAL: Born November 20, 1955, in Salina, KS; daughter of Joseph Patterson (a radio station owner) and Margaret (a homemaker and community volunteer; maiden name, Laux) Wardlaw; married Craig Zeisloft Jaffurs (wine maker), August 27, 1983; children: one son, Patterson Wardlaw Jaffurs. *Education:* California Polytechnic State University, B.A. (with honors), 1977. *Religion:* Atheist. *Avocational interests:* Reading "especially mystery or suspense/thrillers," bodysurfing and swimming, wine tasting, cats, Hawaii; "I also enjoy studying philosophy and chewing bubble gum!"

ADDRESSES: *Home*—P.O. Box 1452, Summerland, CA 93067. *Agent*—Virginia Knowlton, Curtis Brown Ltd., 10 Astor Pl., New York, NY 10003.

CAREER: Los Ninos Head Start Pre-School, Santa Barbara, CA, director's assistant, 1977-78; Goleta Head Start Pre-School, Goleta, CA, director/head teacher, 1978-79; Cornelia Moore Memorial Dental Foundation, Santa Barbara, director/teacher, 1979-82; Outlaw Communications, Santa Barbara, owner, 1982-85; children's book author, 1985—. Lecturer, workshop leader at various conferences, schools and associations within California and out of state, 1986—; Santa Barbara Community College, Santa Barbara, writing instructor, 1988—; Mountain View Elementary and Ellwood Elementary, Santa Barbara and Goleta, teacher of creative writing courses for children, 1990-91. KIST radio, Santa Barbara, public ascertainment coordinator, 1974-81; reading tutor, 1975-79; Girl Scout Leader, 1977-78; Montecito Library, storyteller, 1978-79; Peabody Elementary School, library volunteer, 1985-93; Santa Barbara County Schools library committee, children's book reviewer, 1986-90.

MEMBER: Society of Children's Book Writers and Illustrators (Santa Barbara/Ventura Chapter, advisory board, 1996—), California Reading Association, Children's Literature Council of Southern California, Ventura County Reading Association, Cornelia Moore Dental Foundation Board of Directors (education advisor, 1982-1992), Santa Barbara Writers for Children, Cal Poly Alumni Association, Santa Barbara High School Alumni Association, Southern California Children's Booksellers Association, Author's Guild, California Readers, Cat Writer's Association.

AWARDS, HONORS: Creative Service Award, Cornelia Moore Dental Foundation, 1982; selected as Grand Marshal, DownTown Organization/Santa Barbara Chamber of Commerce Christmas Parade, 1989; Best Local Author, Santa Barbara News-Press/KCQR radio community poll, 1990; Recommended for Reluctant Young Adult Readers Award, American Library Association (ALA), and Children's Choice Award, International Reading Association/Children's Book Council, both 1991, both for *Corey's Fire;* Recommended for Reluctant Young Adult Readers Award, ALA, 1992, for *Cowabunga! The Complete Book of Surfing;* Distinguished Alumni Award, Santa Barbara High School Alumni Association, 1993; Texas Lone Star Recommended Reading List, and Florida Sunshine State Young Reader's Award, both 1996, for *Seventh-Grade Weirdo;* Junior Library Guild selection, 1997, Notable Children's Trade Book in the Field of Social Studies, Children's Book Council/National Council of Social Studies, 1998, and nomination for Treasure State (Montana) Children's Choice Award, 2000, all for *Punia and the King of Sharks;* South Carolina Children's Book Award finalist, Garden State (New Jersey) Children's Book Award finalist, Florida Sunshine State Young Reader Award, The Great Stone Face (New Hampshire) Children's Book Award, and Oklahoma Sequoyah Children's Book Award, all 1999, and nomination for Maryland Black-Eyed Susan Award, 2000, all for *101 Ways to Bug Your Parents.*

WRITINGS:

NONFICTION

Giggles & Grins: A Dental Health and Nutrition Curriculum Guide for Pre-School Teachers, C. M. Dental Foundation, 1985.
Cowabunga! The Complete Book of Surfing, Avon Sports, 1991.
Bubblemania: A Kid's Book of Bubble Gum, Aladdin/Simon & Schuster, 1997.
We All Scream for Ice Cream!, HarperCollins, 2000.

FOR CHILDREN

Me + Math = Headache, illustrated by Joanne Hoy, Red Hen Press, 1986, revised edition illustrated by Deborah Stouffer, 1989.
The Eye and I, illustrated by Stouffer, Red Hen Press, 1988.
Operation Rhinoceros, illustrated by Stouffer, Red Hen Press, 1992.
Seventh-Grade Weirdo, Scholastic, 1992, republished as *My Life as a Weirdo,* Troll, 2000.
The Tales of Grandpa Cat, illustrated by Ronald Searle, Dial, 1994.
(Reteller) *Punia and the King of Sharks: A Hawaiian Folktale,* illustrated by Felipe Davalos, Dial, 1995.
101 Ways to Bug Your Parents, Dial, 1996.
The Ghoul Brothers, illustrated by Brian Floca, Troll, 1996.
Dinosaur Pizza, illustrated by Julie Durrell, Troll, 1998.
Bow-Wow Birthday, illustrated by Arden Johnson-Petrov, Boyds Mill Press, 1998.
Hector's Hiccups, illustrated by Joan Holub, Random House, 1999.
First Steps, illustrated by Julie Paschkis, HarperCollins, 1999.
Saturday Night Jamboree, illustrated by Barry Root, Dial, 2000.

FOR YOUNG ADULTS

Alley Cat, Simon & Schuster, 1987.
Corey's Fire, Avon/Flare, 1990.
Don't Look Back, Avon/Flare, 1993.

Alley Cat has been translated into French, German, Italian, and Hungarian. Also contributor of the short story "Shadow Girl" to the anthology *See You in September,* Avon, 1995, and reteller of the "Legend of the Menehune Ditch," published in *Cricket* magazine, September, 1999.

ADAPTATIONS: Corey's Fire was recorded for the blind, 1991.

WORK IN PROGRESS: The Chair Where Bear Sits (picture book) for Winslow Press, due in 2001; *Peek-a-Book* (picture book), for Dial, due in 2002.

SIDELIGHTS: Lee Wardlaw is the author of over twenty titles for young readers of all ages. They include coming-of-age novels for young adults, humorous tales for middle graders, and picture books for toddlers. She has also written three popular nonfiction titles extolling the joys of surfing, in *Cowabunga!,* of bubble gum, in *Bubblemania,* and America's favorite dessert in *We All Scream for Ice Cream!* Wardlaw is noted for her humorous viewpoint on growing up and for characters that display inner resiliency and determination in both serious and silly situations.

A long-time resident of Santa Barbara, California, Wardlaw has been an author for much of her life. "I've been writing since age seven, and it was something I always wanted to do," Wardlaw told Russ Spencer of the *Santa Barbara News Press.* She worked as a tutor, a radio commercial copywriter, fashion model, tooth fairy, and a school teacher before committing herself to a career as a writer. As she told Spencer, "I thought if I did it full time it would get boring. . . . I thought that if you did something you really loved, it would get old after a while. But after teaching, I realized writing is really what I should be doing, and I'm still at it."

One of Wardlaw's most celebrated books, *Corey's Fire,* is based on a true story. She once told *CA* about the pivotal event that changed her life and inspired *Corey's Fire:* "On a hot summer evening in 1977, a young man was flying a kite in the foothills of Santa Barbara, California. A gust of wind tangled the kite in some power lines, showering sparks into the dry weeds below. Although firefighters rushed to the scene, the blaze soon flared out of control. The fire burned for more [than] twenty-four hours, destroying 200 homes. My family's home was one of those that burned to the ground. We lost everything—including my cat. Days later, while sifting through the wreckage and ash, I found only two recognizable items: a blackened baby spoon and our front door knob! I kept both as souvenirs of what I call the 'before time.' "

To deal with her feelings about the fire, Wardlaw wrote the story about Corey, the fourteen-year-old protagonist, who is a dependent, immature girl, full of self-pity. *Corey's Fire* tells of her change after the fire. "It is not the disaster that changes Corey," Wardlaw once explained to *CA*. "She chooses to change. That's her first step to becoming an independent young woman. And the newfound 'fire' inside her becomes the guiding force behind convincing her parents to rebuild and get on with their lives.

"I started making notes and doing research for *Corey's Fire* in 1978. I interviewed family and friends, re-read newspaper articles, and listened to tape recordings of more than twelve hours of live radio broadcasts from news reporters at the scene. Reliving the fire was painful—so painful that I was unable to begin writing the book until March of 1982, five years after the disaster. Eight years after that, the book was finally published. I dedicated it to my mother and my two brothers, who also endured the fire."

Romance is at the center of the novel, although next door neighbor Topher (short for Christopher) is anything but romantic at the beginning. Topher is good-looking, but Corey can't stand him because he is sarcastic and chases her cat with his motorcycle. It is Topher, however, who understands Corey's rage when her house is destroyed in a brush fire, and he helps her look for her cat, losing his tough-guy facade in the process. Corey also learns about friendship from her neighbor, Ericka. Ericka sticks by Corey, even when Corey is mean to her because her home was left standing when Corey's was burned. Appreciated by the Santa Barbara community, *Corey's Fire* was praised by critics as well. A reviewer for *Publishers Weekly* described it as a "refreshing twist on the standard love story." The reviewer continued, "The author's unflinching realism in describing the fire and its aftermath adds sizzle to an already appealing romance." Diana Watkins of *Voice of Youth Advocates* wrote, "Middle school students will easily identify with Corey, Christopher West, and Ericka." The International Reading Association/Children's Book Council awarded the book a Children's Choice Award.

Wardlaw has written two other novels for young adults, *Alley Cat* and *Don't Look Back,* neither of which was as well received as *Corey's Fire.* In *Alley Cat,* the author used her experiences in radio to tell the story of an awkward teen, Allison Blake, who finds opportunity and respect for her abilities as a weekend disk jockey on a local radio station. In *Don't Look Back,* Drew faces her inner demons during a summer in Hawaii with her estranged father. A romantic liaison with a sensitive surfer helps her come to terms with her father. A contributor for *Publishers Weekly* commented that "Wardlaw once again combines coming-of-age struggles with a predictable but pleasing romance."

Wardlaw's experience of feeling like a misfit in junior high formed the basis for *Seventh-Grade Weirdo* (later republished as *My Life as a Weirdo*). It tells the story of Christopher Robin, who has a mother who loves Winnie-the-Pooh (hence Rob's name), a father who is a former professional surfer, and a five-year-old sister, Winnie, the family genius, who impersonates storybook characters and invents a game that promises to make her a millionaire. Rob worries that with a family like his, everyone will think he is a weirdo too. To add to his troubles, on the first day of seventh grade, Rob makes an enemy of the school bully, "The Shark," and must, in the end, confront him.

According to Susie Wilde in the *Independent Weekly,* "Wardlaw's masterful dialogue maintains a perfect balance of funny, fresh, realistic kid-talk. . . . Rob makes a comfortingly comic role model for kids shifting gears into middle school." Carrol McCarthy, writing for *School Library Journal,* said, "This entertaining, sometimes touching story of self-realization is successful despite the exaggerated qualities of the characters." Esther Sinofsky of *Voice of Youth Advocates* wrote that Wardlaw's "light touch keeps a smile on your lips as you read."

Wardlaw has made a minor specialty of middle-grader and beginning reader books that blend humor and realistic situations. In *Me + Math = Headache,* she tells of young Jeffrey who hates math; in *The Eye and I,* Jeffrey is paralyzed with fear when he has to be video-taped giving a speech in front of his fifth-grade class. Jeffrey makes a further appearance in *Operation Rhinoceros,* in which he fears he is losing his friends because the new teacher is none other than his mother. In *The Ghoul Brothers,* two friends dress up as a two-headed monster and get a big surprise from a little sister. Hiccups and their cure form the plot line of *Hector's Hiccups* in which an Hispanic boy is helped by his sister and brother to get rid of his bothersome condition.

Wardlaw introduces twelve-year-old Steve Wyatt, alias Sneeze, an inveterate inventor, in *101 Ways to Bug Your Parents.* His parents deny him the opportunity of attending the annual Invention Conference in San Francisco by enrolling him in a summer writing program, but Sneeze finds a fine way to feel better and make some money at the same time. Out of revenge for his ruined summer, he creates a how-to manual in his writing class, titled *101 Ways to Bug Your Parents.* It is an instant hit with the other kids in the class, and they are desperate to buy copies. "Three-dimensional characters . . . populate this fast, fun read," commented Lisa Van Drasek in *School Library Journal,* who added, "Readers will hope for further adventures with Sneeze and his friends." *Booklist*'s Frances Bradburn remarked, "Wardlaw has written a funny story with more substance than is evident initially . . . The death of a parent, job insecurity, gifted children, teacher respect, true friendship, and even intellectual freedom all find play here."

Wardlaw told *CA* the story behind *101 Ways to Bug Your Parents:* "Kids are often surprised to learn that I didn't start writing *101 Ways* when I was a kid. Oh, I definitely had my favorites: I alternated between using #35—'Give them the silent treatment'—and #101: 'Beg them to death.' (Pleasepleaseplease, PUH-LEEEEEZE, Mom?!)

"But the idea for *101 Ways to Bug Your Parents* actually came from an amusing article I read in our local Santa Barbara newspaper.

"The article was called '101 Reasons for Staying Single,' and told the story of a teacher who gave her 4th grade students a unique journal writing assignment: *Write about ten things you've done that really bugged your parents.*

"Immediately the kids started scribbling furiously, and at the end of only 15 minutes, they had hundreds of ideas! The class then compiled 101 of their favorites, and wrote them on the blackboard. A teacher's aide thought the list was funny, and sent it into the newspaper, which published it the following week . . . where I read it and instantly thought: *What a great idea!*

"Of course, no matter how great an idea is, it's not enough to make a great book. I had a title—*101 Ways to Bug Your Parents*—but no story. So the first thing I did was arrange to meet the teacher and the kids who'd written the list.

"I found out from them that the teacher, Nancy Revlin, had been scared to death that she was going to get into trouble. Seems that the newspaper received dozens of letters from parents and one ex-principal, saying things like: 'What a terrible assignment! Is this what our schools are coming to today? This teacher should be fired! Parents have enough trouble raising children without giving them assignments like this!' and blah, blah, blah.

"Poor Mrs. Revlin. This was her first year teaching, and she was really afraid that she'd get fired. But her principal laughed it off. He understood that she'd given the assignment in fun, and that the list wasn't hurting anybody—except maybe a few parents who were getting bugged a little more than usual.

"But the complaints Mrs. Revlin received started me thinking and playing my favorite game: *what if?* What if the teacher *had* gotten into trouble? What if one of her students had turned the writing assignment into an entire book called *101 Ways to Bug Your Parents?* What if he started selling it on school property, causing public outcry against him and the teacher? What if the main theme of this story wasn't just a few kids being obnoxious toward their parents, but one of intellectual freedom? What would happen then?

"The rest, as they say, is history.

"I got the idea for the main character, Sneeze, from another newspaper article, this one about a ten-year-old boy who won a college scholarship for inventing the world's first glow-in-the-dark toilet seat to keep his parents from falling in the you-know-what when they got up in the middle of the night.

"But Sneeze's inventiveness is also based on me. No, I haven't invented a glow-in-the-dark toilet seat, or a Keep Kool Baseball Kap, or bubble gum that never loses it's flavor.

"But I *am* an inventor of stories . . . and the passion and pleasure Sneeze has for his crazy creations is exactly how I feel about writing. Sneeze sums it up this way at the end of the book: 'Inventing is who I am, and who I want to be. Always. Sure, making money, being famous and all that stuff is nice. But it's just icing on the cake. Doing something right because you enjoy it, because you believe in it, because it's *right*—that's what counts.

"That's what it feels like to be an author. Yes, I'm a mother, and a teacher, and a wife . . . but I'm also a writer. I've been a writer since I was seven years old. I enjoy writing more than any other job I've ever had . . . and getting to live and work as a writer is a dream come true."

In addition to fiction, Wardlaw has written two nonfiction books, *Cowabunga! The Complete Book of Surfing* and *Bubblemania. Cowabunga!* was inspired by Wardlaw's husband, a surfer for twenty-five years, who suggested that young people would enjoy a book about the sport. Wardlaw found that the only books about surfing available for young people in libraries were "hopelessly out of date," as she told *Los Angeles Times* interviewer Jane Hulse. "Surfboards had one fin, and swimsuits came above the bellybutton." Wardlaw began her research by going through her husband's collection of surfing magazines, interviewing surfers and surfboard makers, and reading about surfing in libraries. After putting together some sample chapters, she contracted with Avon to write the book.

Cowabunga! The Complete Book of Surfing is an overview of the sport rather than a how-to book. "It's difficult to surf by reading a book," Wardlaw told Hulse. "I'm not a great surfer. . . . I didn't feel I should teach kids to do it." Wardlaw begins her book with the history of the sport in Polynesia and Hawaii, then describes the culture surrounding it in California in the 1960s, explains the construction of surfboards, lists hot surfing spots, shops, camps, and schools, and even provides a glossary of surfing words. George Delalis, writing for *School Library Journal,* called Wardlaw's book a "comprehensive introduction to the sport," and concluded that the work is "a useful resource for both veterans and beginners." Writing in *Voice of Youth Advocates,* Drue Wagner-Mees commented, "*Cowabunga!* has just about everything you ever wanted to know about surfing . . . The text reads easily, flows, and catches the spirit of the sport."

More playful in spirit, but equally well researched, is Wardlaw's *Bubblemania,* a "zany history of the discovery and development of the bubble-gum industry," according to Jennifer Oyama of *School Library Journal.* Wardlaw traces the history of chewing gum from the tree bark of Mayan Indians to major companies such as Adams, Curtis, and Wrigley. She also details the manufacture and distribution of chewing gum, explains the connection between ball players and bubble gum, and gives handy tips about blowing the perfect bubble. "Young readers will marvel at the detail in this fun book," remarked Susan DeRonne in *Booklist.*

Wardlaw has also found success in writing picture books, such as *The Tales of Grandpa Cat, Punia and the King of Sharks, Bow-Wow Birthday,* and *First Steps.* In *The Tales of Grandpa Cat,* she teamed up with the well-known illustrator Ronald Searle to create a tall tale with a new twist for middle graders. Expecting to be bored out of their wits at a visit to Grandma and Grandpa Cat's retirement home, the grandcats instead are held spellbound by the old cat's tales of former friends and exploits. *Booklist*'s Janice Del Negro said that the book was for "kids ready to venture beyond vocabulary-controlled materials, as well as for those who can't get enough about cats." A reviewer for *Publishers Weekly* wrote, "Antic illustrations by *New Yorker* cover artist Searle accentuate the hilarity of Wardlaw's . . . brisk cat-tale." In the opinion of a critic for *Kirkus Reviews,* "The stories are . . . playful attention-getters and come to a fine, loopy conclusion."

Describing *Punia and the King of Sharks,* a reviewer for *Publishers Weekly* commented, "Jaunty prose and artwork join forces in this adaptation of a Hawaiian folktale." Punia, a clever boy, outwits the sharks and gets away with some delicious lobsters. "Wardlaw's simple, direct retelling of a little-known Hawaiian folktale combines a popular topic (sharks), an action-filled plot, and the triumph of the weak over the strong," according to *Booklist*'s Julie Corsaro.

On a very different subject, *Bow-Wow Birthday* tells of a party for a favorite pet, a dog who sleeps through its own party. Helen Rosenberg, writing in *Booklist,* commented, "The hilarious story includes a host of children's favorite dog puns . . . and Johnson-Petrov's bold illustrations work wonderfully with the humorous text to make the book a fun-filled romp through an unusual birthday party." Personal experiences also figure in Wardlaw's picture books. The birth of her own son inspired Wardlaw to write the briskly rhythmic text of *First Steps,* a 1999 picture book for the very young.

Wardlaw lives in Santa Barbara with her husband Craig, her son, and her two cats, Riesling and Beaujolais. She writes at home, teaches courses on writing for young adults, and visits children in schools throughout California and in other states. She once told *CA* that the best things about being an author are "working at home, seeing my books in bookstores, creating people I'd like to meet in real life, and getting fan mail." The worst things are "getting bad reviews, not having anybody to talk to during the day (except my cats, who don't say much), [and] waiting two to three years from the time my book is bought by a publisher to when it is actually published." Wardlaw continues to write because "it's fun. . . . First and foremost, I write to entertain myself. But I also write to show my readers a world they can delight in, a world of wonder and awe, a world where so much is possible. Around any bend, at any moment, might come Mystery! Adventure! Romance!"

BIOGRAPHICAL/CRITICAL SOURCES:

PERIODICALS

Booklist, August, 1992; October 1, 1994, Jance Del Negro, review of *The Tales of Grandpa Cat,* p. 440; October 1, 1996, Frances Bradburn, review of *101 Ways to Bug Your Parents,* p. 128; December 1, 1996, Julia Corsaro, review of *Punia and the King of Sharks,* p. 667; October 1, 1997, Susan DeRonne, review of *Bubblemania,* p. 326; March 1, 1998, Helen Rosenberg, review of *Bow-Wow Birthday,* p. 1142.

Bookpage, September, 1992, p. 23.

Camarillo Daily News, March 13, 1992, pp. A1-A2.

Independent Weekly, August 19, 1992, Susie Wilde, review of *Seventh-Grade Weirdo,* p. 21.

Kirkus Reviews, September 15, 1994, review of *The Tales of Grandpa Cat,* p. 1285; October 1, 1996, p. 1475.

Los Angeles Times, August 2, 1991, Jane Hulse, "Hanging 10."

Publishers Weekly, December 22, 1989, review of *Corey's Fire,* p. 57; June 29, 1992, pp. 63-64; November 15, 1993, review of *Don't Look Back,* p. 80; September 12, 1994, review of *The Tales of Grandpa Cat,* p. 89; December 9, 1996, review of *Punia and the King of Sharks,* p. 68.

Santa Barbara News Press, July 21, 1987, Marilyn McMahon, "Fiery Inspiration," pp. D1-D2; March 15, 1991, Russ Spencer, "Catching a New Wave," pp. 25-26.

School Library Journal, February, 1992, George Delalis, review of *Cowabunga! The Complete Book of Surfing,* p. 117; September, 1992, Carrol McCarthy, review of *Seventh-Grade Weirdo,* p. 261; February, 1995, p. 83; October, 1996, Lisa Van Drasek, review of *101 Ways to Bug Your Parents,* p. 128; January, 1998, Jennifer Oyama, review of *Bubblemania,* p. 135; May, 1998, p. 128.

Voice Literary Supplement, July-August, 1991, p. 15.

Voice of Youth Advocates, August-September, 1987, p. 126; April, 1991, Diana Watkins, review of *Corey's Fire,* p. 38; December, 1991, Drue Wagner-Mees, review of *Cowabunga!,* p. 343; April, 1993, Esther Sinofsky, review of *Seventh-Grade Weirdo.*

Wilson Library Bulletin, February, 1995, pp. 94-95.

OTHER

Lee Wardlaw Children's Author Home Page, http://www.leewardlaw.com/ (June 23, 2000).*

WEST, Cornel (Ronald) 1953-

PERSONAL: Born June 2, 1953, in Tulsa, OK; son of Clifton L. Jr. (a civilian Air Force administrator), and Irene (a school teacher; maiden name, Bias) West; divorced twice; married; third wife's name, Elleni (a social worker); children: (first marriage) Clifton Louis. *Education:* Harvard University, A.B. (magna cum laude), 1973; Princeton University, M.A., 1975, Ph.D., 1980. *Politics:* Democratic Socialists of America. *Religion:* Baptist.

ADDRESSES: *Office*—Barker Center, 2nd Floor, Department of Afro-American Studies, Harvard University, Cambridge, MA 02138; fax 617-496-2871.

CAREER: Union Theological Seminary, New York City, assistant professor of philosophy of religion, 1977-83 and 1988; affiliated with Yale University Divinity School, New Haven, CT, 1984-87, and University of Paris, Paris, France, spring, 1987; Princeton University, Princeton, NJ, professor of religion and director of African American Studies, beginning in 1989; Harvard University, Cambridge, MA, professor of religion and Afro-American studies.

AWARDS, HONORS: Du Bois fellow at Harvard University.

WRITINGS:

Prophesy Deliverance!: An Afro-American Revolutionary Christianity, Westminster (Philadelphia), 1982.

Prophetic Fragments, Eerdmans (Grand Rapids, MI), 1988.

The American Evasion of Philosophy: A Genealogy of Pragmatism, University of Wisconsin Press (Madison, WI), 1989.

(With bell hooks) *Breaking Bread: Insurgent Black Intellectual Life,* South End Press (Boston), 1991.

The Ethical Dimensions of Marxist Thought, Monthly Review Press, 1991.

Race Matters, Beacon (Boston), 1993.

Beyond Eurocentrism and Multiculturalism, Volume 1, *Prophetic Thoughts in Postmodern Times,* Volume 2, *Prophetic Reflections, Notes on Race and Power in America,* Common Cause Press, 1993.

Keeping Faith: Philosophy and Race in America, Routledge (New York City), 1994.

(With Michael Lerner) *Jews and Blacks: Let the Healing Begin,* G. P. Putnam's Sons (New York City), 1995.

(With Lerner) *Jews & Blacks: A Dialogue on Race, Religion, and Culture in America,* Plume (New York City), 1996.

(With Henry Louis Gates Jr.) *The Future of the Race,* Knopf (New York City), 1996.

(With Mumia Abu-Jamal) *Death Blossoms: Reflections from a Prisoner of Conscience,* Plough, 1996.

Restoring Hope: Conversations on the Future of Black America, edited by Kelvin Shawn Sealey, Beacon, 1997.

(With Roberto Mangabeira Unger) *The Future of American Progressivism: An Initiative for Political and Economic Reform,* Beacon, 1998.

(With Sylvia Ann Hewlett) *The War against Parents: What We Can Do for America's Beleaguered Moms and Dads,* Houghton (Boston), 1998.

The Cornel West Reader, Basic Civitas Books (New York City), 1999.

EDITOR

(With Caridad Guidote and Margaret Coakley) *Theology in the Americas: Detroit II Conference Papers,* Orbis Books (Maryknoll, NY), 1982.

(With John Rajchman) *Post-Analytic Philosophy,* Columbia University Press (New York City), 1985.

(With Colin MacCabe) James Snead, *White Screens, Black Images: Hollywood from the Dark Side,* Routledge (New York City), 1994.

(With Jack Salzman and David Lionel Smith), *Encyclopedia of African-*

American Culture and History, Macmillan (New York City), 1996.

(With Salzman) *Struggles in the Promised Land: Toward a History of Black-Jewish Relations in the United States,* Oxford University Press, (New York City), 1997.

(With Quinton Hosford Dixie) *The Courage to Hope: From Black Suffering to Human Redemption,* Beacon, 1999.

OTHER

Co-editor of *Out There: Marginalization and Contemporary Cultures,* 1991; contributor to periodicals, including *Monthly Review, Critical Quarterly, Nation, Tikkun, New York Times Book Review,* and *New York Times.* Contributor to *The Affirmative Action Debate,* edited by George E. Curry, Addison, Wesley, 1996.

SIDELIGHTS: As a philosopher, director of African American studies, social critic, educator, Christian, and Marxist, Cornel West is considered by many to be among the foremost modern intellectuals. West has issued numerous books and articles that address such subjects as multiculturalism, Eurocentrism, racism, and socialism. "If West hasn't written *the* book," claimed Robert S. Boynton in the *New York Times,* "he has made his influence felt as a speaker in classrooms, churches and protest rallies all across the country; he's a significant intellectual presence, scholarly enough to be cited in footnotes yet so charismatic that colleagues have compared him to Martin Luther King Jr. . . . He brings a religious zeal to intellectual issues. He makes the life of the mind exciting."

Central to West's message is his belief that Christianity, combined with the doctrine of Marxism, is a powerful weapon against white racism and oppression. One of West's earliest books, *Prophecy Deliverance!: An Afro-American Revolutionary Christianity,* expounds on his theory that this combination of philosophies has the ability to affect major social change. *Prophecy Deliverance!* was praised by a *Choice* critic who wrote, "West has written a brilliant and provocative manifesto, which marks an entirely new stage of development in the movement of black liberation theology."

Additional essays on West's thoughts about Marxism and Christianity, as well as sex, suicide, and violence in modern-day America can be found in West's *Prophetic Fragments.* In an *Essence* review of *Prophetic Fragments,* Paula Giddings contended, "With his exceptionally wide-ranging knowledge and crisp prose, West should certainly command every thinking person's attention."

As a graduate student at Princeton, West was fascinated by the work of Princeton philosopher Richard Rorty, who has written extensively about American pragmatism. Inspired by Rorty, West developed his own version of pragmatism, which he calls "prophetic pragmatism." Commenting on West's *The American Evasion of Philosophy: A Genealogy of Pragmatism,* philosopher K. Anthony Appiah asserted in *Nation:* "If there is much that is appealing in Rorty's antifoundationalism, his liberal revulsion against human cruelty and his arguments for pluralism, there is something worrisome, too, in his deliberate ethnocentrism and the conservatism that flows from his political pessimism. Cornel West's engaging and engaged *The American Evasion of Philosophy* needs to be read as a subtle polemic against the dangers of the highly influential new pragmatism as it celebrates and expands Rorty's insights." Appiah added that West's work is "rooted in a sense of the continuing relevance of Christianity and socialism," and that it "displays an inexhaustible appetite for ideas and a compelling moral vision." Appiah deemed *The*

American Evasion of Philosophy "the most ambitious and original project that [West] has undertaken."

Most of West's writings seek to inspire individuals to use the power of their minds to better themselves and their communities. *Breaking Bread: Insurgent Black Intellectual Life* is no exception, but it also covers much more. Written with educator bell hooks, *Breaking Bread* includes the authors' thoughts on sexism, racism, and individualism, but also offers their critiques of aspects of black modern culture, including fashion and arts. *Black Enterprise* writer Tonya Bolden recommended *Breaking Bread* to "those who value the life of the mind," and observed that "the book lacks malice and carries a message of hope attesting to the authors' love for their people and commitment to their salvation." A *Publishers Weekly* reviewer similarly found that *Breaking Bread* "is of enormous importance and offers rewarding reading."

Another of West's books aimed at promoting social change is *Race Matters,* a collection of essays in which West discusses how various groups (including liberals and conservatives, blacks and whites) are to blame for poor race relations in the United States. Paul Delaney, writing for the *New York Times Book Review,* suggested, "Mr. West's solutions [to race relations] are basic, indeed old-fashioned, resting on a kind of coming together of the minds to resolve to change things. His specific recommendations include coalition building, redistribution of wealth, 'large-scale public intervention to insure access to basic social goods,' and courageous leaders." A *Publishers Weekly* reviewer portrayed West as "more healing visionary than historian," and opined: "These essays . . . solidify his position as one of the nation's leading public intellectuals."

Reviewing West's next volume of essays, *Keeping Faith: Philosophy and Race in America,* for the *Christian Century,* Donald E. Messer observed: "In contrast to his best-selling *Race Matters,* the book lacks a clear focus. Rather, it illustrates the incredible scope of the author's interests and intellect." Some of the subjects West tackles in *Keeping Faith* include architecture, social theory, art criticism, and legal studies. Messer noted that West's "concern for the marginalized" members of society and the "maldistribution of resources, wealth and power" in American pervades his analysis. At the same time, the *Christian Century* contributor continued, "West doesn't hesitate to criticize his own African-American community." To overcome racism in American, West calls for African-Americans to form "alliances and coalitions with progressive Latino, Asian, Native American and white peoples."

In an extensive 1995 article in the *New Republic,* subsequently described in *Tikkun* as "a racist attack on a prominent Afro-American intellectual," literary editor Leon Wieseltier examined six of West's books, including *Race Matters* and *Keeping the Faith.* Wieseltier's negative assessment of West went so far as to condemn his work as "completely worthless." Quoting extensively from the volumes he was examining to support his contentions, Wieseltier further characterized West's writing as "noisy, tedious, slippery . . . sectarian, humorless, pedantic and self-endeared," and West himself as "a homiletical figure, a socialist divine, who has come to lift the spirits of the progressives." An editorial in the *Nation* by Jon Wiener described Wieseltier's article as being "highly and inexplicably critical" of West. Wiener went on to note that West, in addition to his writings, has proven a significant political force who "has been working tirelessly to revive the progressive alliance of blacks and Jews that animated the civil rights movement and, before that, the liberal and left causes of the 1930s and 1940s." It was Wiener's contention that Wieseltier's negative assessment of West had little to do with the quality of West's writings and everything to do with the positions West expresses and the active political role he plays. Wiener concluded: "Cornel West views the gross inequities in our society as despicable; he argues that individual greed is destroying whatever community we have left; he calls for a renewal of the struggle for social justice and democratic community. And he argues that Jews and blacks ought to join together to fight. That's what Wieseltier—and the *New Republic*—don't like about him."

In an article appearing a few months later the *New Republic* again castigated West, this time for betraying his own views by making an appearance at the National African-American Leadership Summit, an event sponsored by Reverend Benjamin Chavis, an avowed black separatist. West defended his appearance by stating: "I'm not a black nationalist or separatist, but the common focus here is on black suffering and pain."

Despite the controversy generated by Wieseltier's extreme castigation of West, the long-range impact of the article appears to have been negligible in terms of West's reputation, his continue activism, and his productivity as an author. Two books written in collaboration with *Tikkun* editor Michael Lerner, both calling for greater co-operation between the Jewish and Black communities, soon followed. In 1996 West joined with fellow Harvard academician Henry Louis Gates Jr. to publish *The Future of the Race,* an examination of and response to W. E. B. Du Bois's famous work of 1903, "The Talented Tenth," which promulgated the idea of educated blacks devoting themselves to uplifting the lives of less fortunate Afro-Americans. The West-Gates collaboration also included portraits of contemporary Afro-Americans, educated and successful, and how they have fulfilled the promise of a "Talented Tenth." Bonnie Smothers of *Booklist* felt that *The Future of the Race* presents "an argument that compels one to think about sacrifice for the good of humanity, whatever its rewards." However, Eric J. Sundquist of *Commentary* found the book's presentation of Du Bois's views to be incomplete and consequently inaccurate, and concludes: "Even if there is plenty to choose here between West's doomsaying and Gate's pragmatism, neither tells us much about the future of the race."

The War against Parents: What We Can Do for America's Beleaguered Moms and Dads, marked something of a change of pace for West in that its central concern was not a racial one. Written in collaboration with Sylvia Ann Hewlett the book contended that both American government policy and American popular media are forces that work against people trying to raise children. West and Hewlett singled out both corporate greed unrestricted by government controls and an entertainment industry that plays to the youth market with no concern for its effects as significant factors that have made raising children in American so difficult. Their suggested solutions included the founding of a national organization of concerned parents, similar to the American Association of Retired Persons, and the establishment of a "Parents' Bill of Rights." A *Publishers Weekly* reviewer described the book as "strongly polemical" but at the same time found that "it offers a strong, well-reasoned position on an issue of national importance, and calls for action in a sober but compelling way." E. J. Dionne of *Nation's Cities Weekly* commented that "Hewlett and West have not worked out all the answers . . . they do not pretend to have solved all the problems. But their collaboration is a hopeful sign, and their effort to link values and economics is a needed tonic."

In 1999 *The Cornel West Reader* appeared, a book that a *Publishers Weekly* reviewer described as a "mammoth collection of social commentary, interviews, essays and memoir [that] details his [West's] evolution as a social analyst and public figure." The collection contains both selections from West's earlier books and previously uncollected work. The reviewer felt that although "the range of his [West's] philosophical sermons can occasionally be overwhelming, his eclectic interests and original observations are quite rewarding," and concluded: "This collection amply attests that West's reputation as a brilliant, humane voice in American intellectual discourse is richly deserved."

BIOGRAPHICAL/CRITICAL SOURCES:

PERIODICALS

Black Enterprise, June, 1992, p. 23.
Booklist, February 15, 1996, Bonnie Smothers, review of *The Future of the Race,* p. 96.
Choice, April, 1983, p. 1156.
Christian Century, September 21, 1994, Donald E. Messer, review of *Keeping Faith,* p. 864.
Commentary, July, 1996, Eric J. Sundquist, review of *The Future of the Race,* p. 60.
Essence, January, 1989, p. 30.
Library Journal, January 15, 1983, p. 138; March 1, 1988, p. 70.
Nation, April 9, 1990, pp. 496-98; March 27, 1995, Jon Wiener, "Jews. Blacks, TNR," p. 404.
Nation's Cities Weekly, June 15, 1998, E. J. Dionne, review of *The War against Parents,* p. 8.
New Republic, March 6, 1995, Leon Wieseltier, "All and Nothing at All: The Unreal World of Cornel West," p. 31; July 10, 1995, "The Decline of One (Repeat, One) African American Intellectual," p. 9.
Newsweek, June 7, 1993, p. 71.
New York Times, September 15, 1991.
New York Times Book Review, May 16, 1993, p. 11.
Publishers Weekly, November 22, 1991; February 15, 1993, p. 218; March 30, 1998, review of *The War against Parents,* p. 60; October 25, 1999, review of *The Cornel West Reader,* p. 57.
Tikkun, March-April, 1995, "The Attack on Cornel West," p. 7.*

* * *

WHEELIS, Allen B. 1915-

PERSONAL: Born October 23, 1915, in Marion, LA; son of Allen and Olive Minnie (Thompson) Wheelis; married Joyce Margaret Mitchell, November 20, 1937 (divorced, 1954); married Ilse Kaulbach (a psychiatrist and psychoanalyst), April 19, 1954; children: (first marriage) Mark Lewis, Victoria Lorelei (Mrs. Mark Jenkins); (second marriage) Joan. *Education:* University of Texas, A.B., 1937; Columbia University, M.D., 1943; New York Psychoanalytic Institute, graduate, 1952.

ADDRESSES: Home and Office—3731 Jackson St., San Francisco, CA 94118.

CAREER: Psychiatrist and writer. Austen Riggs Center, Stockbridge, MA, staff member, 1947-54; private practice of psychiatry and psychoanalysis, San Francisco, CA, 1954—. *Military service:* U.S. Navy, 1943-46, surgeon; became lieutenant senior grade.

MEMBER: American Psychiatric Association, American Psychoanalytic Association, American Medical Association, San Francisco Psychoanalytic Society.

WRITINGS:

The Quest for Identity, Norton (New York City), 1958.
The Seeker, Random House (New York City), 1960.
The Illusionless Man, Norton, 1966.
The Desert (novel), Basic Books (New York City), 1969.
The End of the Modern Age, Basic Books, 1971.
The Moralist, Basic Books, 1973.
How People Change, Harper (New York City), 1973.
On Not Knowing How to Live, Harper, 1975.
The Scheme of Things, Harcourt (New York City), 1980.
The Doctor of Desire, Norton, 1987.
The Path Not Taken: Reflections on Power and Fear, Norton, 1990.
The Life and Death of My Mother, Norton, 1992.
The Way Things Are: A Novel, Baskerville Publishers (Dallas, TX), 1994.
The Listener: A Psychoanalyst Examines His Life, Norton, 1999.

Writer of scientific articles and short stories.

SIDELIGHTS: Allen Wheelis is a psychiatrist and writer. In *The Way Things Are* (1994), he uses his knowledge of the human mind to write a novel about a seventy-year-old intellectual's heated affair with a twenty-eight-year-old woman, and her ties to a doomsday prophet who was her former lover and professor. Kathleen Chrysler, a reviewer for *Booklist,* finds that *The Way Things Are* is "is a realistic, though unsympathetic, portrayal of humankind's denial of its own fragility and the paralysis born of that revelation." A *Publishers Weekly* reviewer observes that "Wheelis skillfully uses his characters' dreams and interior monologues to lay bare their unspoken thoughts and feelings."

Wheelis's background is exposed in *The Listener: A Psychoanalyst Examines His Life* (1999). Wheelis relates his life as a psychoanalyst practicing in San Francisco. David Mehegan in the *Boston Globe* relates what he feels Wheelis reveals: "A view of a sample of meaningful relationships and events, from great to small, with which he forges his withering, bleak outlook on existence." However, he expresses his appreciation of the work by calling it a "strange, beautiful, awkward puzzle of a book." Wheelis's rural Texas home was dominated by his father, who controlled his family even as his health deteriorated from tuberculosis. His father passed away in 1925. As Wheelis enters his adult life, his mother, once "a resourceful and sturdy wife and mother . . . slipped into a kind of infantilism" Mehegan relates. *Library Journal* contributor Lucille M. Boone remarks: "A listener by trade, Wheelis is also a powerful yet disturbing storyteller with a gift for evoking compassion and sympathy in his listener—the reader." Mehegan also finds a strong "compassion" underneath the "pity and sadness": "There is something beautiful and touching about the heart of Allen Wheelis."

BIOGRAPHICAL/CRITICAL SOURCES:

PERIODICALS

Booklist, April 1, 1994, Kathleen Chrysler, review of *The Way Things Are,* p. 1425; April 15, 1994, Kathleen Chrysler, review of *The Way Things Are,* p. 1516.
Boston Globe, September 5, 1999, David Mehegan, review of *The Listener,* pp. L1-L2.
Library Journal, March 15, 1987, p. 92; December, 1992, Joan L. Weber, review of *The Life and Death of My Mother,* p. 224; April 1, 1994, Ellen R. Cohen, review of *The Way Things Are,* p. 135; September 15, 1999, Lucille M. Boone, review of *The Listener,* p. 101.
New York Times Book Review, May 10, 1987, Bettina L. Knapp, "The Doctor of Desire," p. 20; May 24, 1992, Louis Begley, review of *The Life and Death of My Mother,* p. 21.
Publishers Weekly, July 4, 1980, p. 79; March 6, 1987, p. 102; April 20, 1990, p. 63; December 13, 1991, review of *The Life and Death of My Mother,* p. 42; March 7, 1994, review of *The Way Things Are,* p. 55; August 9, 1999, review of *The Listener,* p. 331.

* * *

WHITFIELD, Stephen J(ack) 1942-

PERSONAL: Born December 3, 1942, in Houston, TX; son of Bert (a salesman) and Joan (Schwarz) Whitfield. *Education:* Tulane University, B.A., 1964; Yale University, M.A., 1966; Brandeis University, Ph.D., 1972. *Politics:* Democrat. *Religion:* Judaism.

ADDRESSES: Office—Department of American Studies, Brandeis University, Waltham, MA 02454. *E-mail*—swhitfield@brandeis.edu

CAREER: Southern University, New Orleans, LA, instructor in history, 1966-68; high school teacher of history in the public schools of Jacksonville, FL, 1968-69; Brandeis University, Waltham, MA, began as assistant professor of American studies, 1972, became professor and chairperson of American studies, and Max Richter Chair in American Civilization.

WRITINGS:

Scott Nearing: Apostle of American Radicalism, Columbia University Press (New York City), 1974.

Into the Dark: Hannah Arendt and Totalitarianism, Temple University Press (Philadelphia), 1980.

(Editor) *Meditations of a Maverick Rabbi: Selected Writings of Albert S. Axelrad: Published on the Occasion of His Twentieth Anniversary in the Rabbinate,* introduction by Nahum N. Glatzer, Rossel Books (Chappaqua, NY), 1984.

A Critical American: The Politics of Dwight Macdonald, Archon Books (Hamden, CN), 1984.

Voices of Jacob, Hands of Esau: Jews in American Life and Thought, Archon Books, 1984.

American Space, Jewish Time: Essays in Modern Culture and Politics, Archon Books, 1988, North Castle Books (Armonk, NY), 1996.

A Death in the Delta: The Story of Emmett Till, Free Press (New York City), 1988, Johns Hopkins University Press (Baltimore, MD), 1991.

The Culture of the Cold War, Johns Hopkins University Press (Baltimore, MD), 1991, 2nd edition, 1996.

(Author of introduction) Horace M. Kallen, *Culture and Democracy in the United States,* Transaction Publishers (New Brunswick, NJ), 1998.

In Search of American Jewish Culture, Brandeis University Press (Hanover, NH), 1999.

Also book reviewer for *New Leader,* 1971-75.

SIDELIGHTS: The writings of professor Stephen J. Whitfield have explored such subjects as totalitarianism, Jewish culture in America, the Cold War, and radical politics in America. His 1984 study, *A Critical American: The Politics of Dwight Macdonald,* dwells upon the writings and ideas of the radical political journalist/cultural critic rather than the biographical details of his life. Known for his acerbic style and independent views, Macdonald worked for a number of publications during his career, including *Fortune* and the *Partisan Review.* In the late 1940s he published his own journal, *Politics.* Having embraced and later challenged the views of Trotsky in the 1930s, and the Socialist Workers Party in the early 1940s, Macdonald eventually emerged as an anti-Communist without relinquishing his own critical stance toward the politics and culture of the United States. Macdonald's views made a significant contribution to the leftist dialogue in American for several decades. Reviewing *A Critical American* for the *Nation,* Casey Blake offers his own extensive assessment of Macdonald's work and thought. According to Blake, to understand Macdonald one must grasp the "connection between his political and cultural criticism," and also be aware of MacDonald's own "important distinction between 'progressive' and 'radical' politics." Blake contends that Whitfield's account "really only scratches the surface of his [Macdonald's] career, omitting any discussion of his cultural criticism."

In 1955 a black teenager from Chicago, while visiting his relatives in the Mississippi Delta, whistled at, and possibly propositioned, a white woman. Later the woman's husband, along with a relative, kidnapped the teenager, beat him and shot him, and disposed of his body in the Tallahatchie River. Acquitted of the crime by an all-white jury, the two men later sold their story to *Look,* where they essentially confessed to the crime. These events are recounted in book form for the first time in Whitfield's 1988 *A Death in the Delta: The Story of Emmett Till.* In addition to detailing the events described, Whitfield goes on to show how this crime, coming on the heels of the *Brown v. Board of Education* decision that put a legal end to segregation, both shocked the nation and prompted many young people to become more involved in combating racism. Jennifer Howard of *Washington Monthly* remarks, "for more than thirty years, Till has been relegated to the status of a footnote. Whitfield's book places Till's murder as a crucial, if hidden, event in the history of civil rights." Howard also comments that *A Death in the Delta* "indicates that, in killing Till, two white Southerners only put another nail in the coffin of the very thing they were trying to keep alive."

Whitfield's *In Search of American Jewish Culture* examines how American culture has been effected by its Jewish population and also explores the unique Jewish culture that has evolved within the American context. He feels that American Jewish identity, no longer defined in a religious sense, has both manifested and characterized itself most distinctively in the arts. Some chapters deal with the performing arts, such as popular and symphonic music or the theater. Others examine books such as *The Diary of Anne Frank* or films such as *Schindler's List.* George Cohen, writing in *Booklist,* assesses Whitfield's study as a "lucid and absorbing work." However, Idelle Rudman of *Library Journal* faults Whitfield for failing to address "the daily life of American Jews or what Jewishness inherently means." A *Publishers Weekly* reviewer finds much to criticize in *In Search of American Jewish Culture,* describing it as a "scholarly and entertaining yet confusing book." "While cultural studies at its best offers analysis of the interplay between historical and cultural trends," the reviewer states, "this book abandons historical analysis and degenerates into stereotyped ethnic triumphalism." In the later chapters of the book, Whitfield centers his attention on changes in Jewish identity and their sociological impact. While granting that here Whitfield is "more on target," the *Publishers Weekly* reviewer maintains that "resting on the book's shaky conceptual foundation, these reflections come to late."

BIOGRAPHICAL/CRITICAL SOURCES:

PERIODICALS

American Historical Review, December, 1985, review of *A Critical American: The Politics of Dwight Macdonald,* p. 1296.

American Scholar, summer, 1990, review of *A Death in the Delta,* p. 455.

Booklist, August, 1999, George Cohen, review of *In Search of American Jewish Culture,* p. 2000.

Journal of American History, September, 1985, review of *A Critical American: The Politics of Dwight Macdonald,* p. 450; March, 1990, Leonard Dinnerstein, *American Space, Jewish Time,* p. 1234.

Library Journal, August, 1999, Idelle Rudman, review of *In Search of American Jewish Culture,* p. 101.

Nation, February 21, 1981, Elisabeth Young-Bruehl, review of *Into the Dark,* p. 214; January 12, 1985, Casey Blake, review of *A Critical American: The Politics of Dwight Macdonald,* p. 21.

New Leader, December 29, 1980, Sol Gittleman, review of *Into the Dark,* p. 12; February 11, 1985, review of *A Critical American: The Politics of Dwight Macdonald,* p. 13.

New York Times Book Review, February 10, 1985, review of *A Critical American: The Politics of Dwight Macdonald,* p. 3.

Publishers Weekly, August 9, 1999, review of *In Search of American Jewish Culture,* p. 337.

Washington Monthly, June, 1989, Jennifer Howard, review of *A Death in the Delta,* p. 57.

WILKES, Paul 1938-

PERSONAL: Born September 12, 1938, in Cleveland, OH; son of Paul Thomas (a carpenter) and Margaret (Salansky) Wilkes; married Tracy Gochberg; children: Paul Noah, Daniel Thomas. *Education:* Marquette University, B.A., 1960; Columbia University, M.A., 1967.

ADDRESSES: Home and Office—Star Route, Gilbertville, MA 01031. *Agent*—Alison Bond, 171 West 79th St., New York, NY 10024.

CAREER: Freelance writer. *Boulder Daily Camera,* Boulder, CO, staff member, 1964-66; *Baltimore Sun,* Baltimore, MD, writer, 1967-68; Harper & Row, New York City, editor, 1969; Harper's Magazine Press, New York City, editor, 1970. Lecturer in feature writing, Brooklyn College, 1973-75; visiting writer, University of Pittsburgh, 1979-89; lecturer in documentary filmmaking, Boston University, 1981; visiting writer, College of the Holy Cross, 1986; visiting writer, Clark University, 1989—. Co-founder of Christian Help in Park Slope (CHIPS), 1973-75. *Military service:* U.S. Navy, communications officer, 1961-64; became lieutenant junior grade.

MEMBER: Slovak Studies Association (president, 1985-87).

AWARDS, HONORS: Julius Ochs Adler fellow, 1966; best nonfiction awards from Society of Midland Authors and Friends of American Writers, both 1974, both for *Fitzgo: The Wild Dog of Central Park;* By-Line Award, Marquette University, 1977, for distinguished service in journalism; alumni award, Columbia University Graduate School of Journalism, 1978, for distinguished service in journalism; Alfred I. DuPont-Columbia Survey and Award in Broadcast Journalism, 1978, for *Six American Families;* Matica Slovenska fellow, 1979; Christopher Award, 1991.

WRITINGS:

Fitzgo: The Wild Dog of Central Park (nonfiction), Lippincott (Philadelphia), 1973.

These Priests Stay (biography), Simon & Schuster (New York City), 1973.

You Don't Have to be Rich to Own a Brownstone, Quadrangle (New York City), 1973.

Trying out the Dream: A Year in the Life of an American Family (nonfiction), Lippincott, 1975.

Six American Families (based on his television documentary series of the same title; also see below),

Office of Communication, United Church of Christ (New York City), 1977.

Merton: By Those Who Knew Him Best (biography), Harper (San Francisco), 1984.

In Mysterious Ways: The Death and Life of a Parish Priest (biography), Random House (New York City), 1990.

Companions along the Way (essays), Thomas More Press (Chicago), 1990.

My Book of Bedtime Prayers (illustrated by Sandra S. Shields), Augsburg (Minneapolis), 1992.

The Education of an Archbishop: Travels with Rembert Weakland (biography), Orbis (Maryknoll, NY), 1992.

Temptations, Random House, 1993.

And They Shall Be My People: An American Rabbi and His Congregation, Atlantic Monthly (New York City), 1994.

The Good Enough Catholic: A Guide for the Perplexed, Ballantine (New York City), 1996.

The Seven Secrets of Successful Catholics, Paulist Press (New York City), 1998.

Beyond the Walls: Monastic Wisdom for Everyday Life, Doubleday (New York City), 1999.

TELEPLAYS

Six American Families (documentary), Public Broadcasting Service (PBS), 1977.

Men of Iron (drama), PBS, 1978.

(Co-author) *The Molders of Troy* (drama), PBS, 1980.

Merton (documentary), PBS, 1984.

OTHER

Contributor to numerous periodicals, including *New York, New Yorker, New York Times Magazine, Atlantic, America,* and *Commonweal.*

SIDELIGHTS: In *The Good Enough Catholic,* Paul Wilkes offers palatable answers to some difficult questions faced by many American Catholics. The Roman Catholic Church faces a deep crisis in the United States, where many members have abandoned it or pick and choose from its beliefs as it suits them. Many see the church as too rigid and, if they find official teachings on sexuality, birth control, and other matters too confining, they see nothing wrong in ignoring them. Wilkes encourages this course; in the words of *Commonweal* contributor R. Scott Appleby, he "sets himself up as a kind of friendly one-man magisterium, espousing his own personal solutions to complex, controverted questions, ignoring inconvenient historical or doctrinal claims against his assertions" and advising that one "need not attempt to become a spiritual paragon or saint." Wilkes examines the catechetical teachings in four areas: "Inner Life," "Daily Life," "Life with Others," and "The Church and You." Taking a look at the contemporary issues in each realm, Wilkes gives historical and modern illustrations of how to deal with them. John J. O'Keefe, a reviewer for *America,* finds *The Good Enough Catholic* to be "a very good book," adding: "Wilkes writes beautifully about the joys and rewards of a life or prayer. He offers concrete and useful suggestions about how Catholic families might live the Christian life more deeply in the context of their own homes." O'Keefe notes, however, that "Wilke's basic strategy for dealing with the tension in the American church and conflict with the magisterium, however, is 'love and do what you will.' For many Catholics in America, this strategy no longer satisfies."

Wilkes looked at another aspect of Catholicism in *Beyond the Walls: Monastic Wisdom for Everyday Life.* Describing his year of monthly visits to a Trappist monastery, with the focus changing each month to a different aspect of monastic life, the author attempts to share the wisdom he gained on such topics as prayer, faith, discernment, and community. "Each chapter ends with his exit from the cloister, as he tries to incorporate insights gained into his cluttered world as father, husband, teacher, and lay minister," writes a *Publishers Weekly* contributor. "Wilkes has created a loving book that will help laypeople find—or learn to create—peace in their busy lives."

BIOGRAPHICAL/CRITICAL SOURCES:

PERIODICALS

America, June 2, 1984, p. 422; November 17, 1990, p. 364; March 20, 1993, p. 20; June 4, 1994, p. 27; June 3, 1995, p. 26; February 8, 1997, John J. O'Keefe, review of *The Good Enough Catholic,* p. 35.

Best Sellers, August 1, 1973; March 1, 1974.

Booklist, January 15, 1993, p. 880; September 1, 1994, p. 7.

Christian Century, February 6, 1991, p. 133.

Christian Science Monitor, June 13, 1973; April 2, 1975.

Commentary, December, 1994, p. 63.

Commonweal, November 9, 1990, p. 655; March 26, 1993, p. 27; June 18, 1993, p. 24; March 14, 1997, R. Scott Applebny, review of *The Good Enough Catholic,* p. 17.

Humanist, September-October, 1985, p. 34.

Library Journal, September 1, 1990, p. 225; January, 1993, p. 168; September 15, 1994, p. 74; November 15, 1996, p. 67.
Los Angeles Times Book Review, March 17, 1985, p. 10.
National Catholic Reporter, May 25, 1984, p. 16; November 9, 1990, p. 29; May 7, 1999, William C. Graham, "Bookshelf," p. 36.
National Review, December 5, 1994, p. 80.
New Republic, April 26, 1975.
Newsweek, March 24, 1975.
New Yorker, February 18, 1985, p. 121; December 17, 1990, p. 122.
New York Times Book Review, December 23, 1984, p. 1; October 30, 1994, p. 28; December 1, 1996, p. 22.
Publishers Weekly, October 19, 1984, p. 34; July 13, 1990, p. 45; December 28, 1992, p. 58; August 29, 1994, p. 56; August 30, 1999, review of *Beyond the Walls,* p. 74.
Tribune Books (Chicago), January 27, 1984, p. 24.
Wilson Library Bulletin, April, 1985, p. 62.*

* * *

WILLIAMS, Emmett 1925-

PERSONAL: Born April 4, 1925, in Greenville, SC; son of Julian Eugene and Leokadia (Kowalewska) Williams; married Laura Powell MacCarteney, September 14, 1949; married Ann Noel Stevenson, May 9, 1970; children: (first marriage) Laura Katherine, Penelope, Eugene Ward; (second marriage) Garry Julian. *Education:* Kenyon College, B.A., 1949; also attended University of Paris.

ADDRESSES: Office—Carpenter Visual Arts Center, Harvard University, Cambridge, MA 02138.

CAREER: Something Else Press, New York City, editor-in-chief, 1966-70; California Institute of the Arts, Valencia, School of Critical Studies, professor of art, 1970-72; Nova Scotia College of Art and Design, Halifax, visiting professor of art, 1972-74; International Symposium of the Arts, Warsaw, co-founder and director, 1987-88; The Artists' Museum, Lodz, Poland, president, 1990—.

Artist-in-residence at the following: Fairleigh Dickinson University, Madison, NJ, 1968; University of Kentucky, Lexington, 1969; Mount Holyoke College, South Hadley, MA, artist-in-residence, 1975-77; (and research fellow) Harvard University, Cambridge, MA, Carpenter Center for the Visual Arts, 1977-80; (and guest professor) Hochschule der Kunste, Berlin, and Hochschule fur bildender Kunste, Hamburg, 1981-1985; Machida-shi Museum of Graphic Arts, Tokyo, 1987; Malindi Artists' Proof, Malindi, Kenya, 1990, 1992.

Lived in Europe from 1949-66, worked on staff of European *Stars & Stripes* in Darmstadt; assistant to ethnologist Paul Radin in Lugano; collaborated in Darmstadt circle of concrete poetry and dynamic theatre, 1957-59; founding member, Domaine Poetique, Paris; founding member of the international Fluxus group since 1962, was European coordinator in the early sixties. *Military service:* U.S. Army, 1943-46.

AWARDS, HONORS: National Endowment for the Arts fellowship, 1977.

WRITINGS:

POETRY

Konkretionen, Material (Darmstadt, Germany), 1958.
Thirteen Variations on Six Words of Gertrude Stein (1958), Galerie der Speigel (Cologne), 1965.
Rotapoems, Edition Hansjoerg Mayer (Stuttgart), 1966.
The Last French-Fried Potato and Other Poems, Something Else Press (New York City), 1967.
Sweethearts (poem cycle), Edition Hansjoerg Mayer, 1967, Something Else Press, 1968.
The Book of Thorn and Eth, Edition Hansjoerg Mayer, 1968.
The Boy and the Bird (poem cycle), illustrated by Tom Wasmuth, Wittenborn (New York City), 1968, new edition illustrated by Williams, Edition Hansjoerg Mayer, 1979.
A Valentine for Noel: Four Variations on a Scheme, Something Else Press (Barton, VT), 1973.
Selected Shorter Poems, 1950-1970, Edition Hansjoerg Mayer, 1974, New Directions (New York City), 1975.
The Voyage, Edition Hansjoerg Mayer, 1975.
Faustzeichnungen, illustrated by Williams, Rainer (Berlin), 1983.
A Little Night Book, illustrated by Keith Goddard, Works (New York City), 1983.
Deutsche Gedichte und Lichtskulpturen, illustrated by Williams, Rainer, 1988.
Aleph, Alpha, and Alfalfa, Haus am Lutzowplatz (Berlin), 1993.

PLAYS

Ja, Es war noch da (produced in Darmstadt, Germany, 1960), published in Nota 4 (Munich), 1960; produced in New York City as *Yes It was Still There,* 1965.

A Cellar Song for Five Voices, produced in New York City, 1961.

Four-Directional Song of Doubt for Five Voices, produced in Wiesbaden, Germany, 1962.

The Ultimate Poem, produced in Arras France, 1964.

EDITOR

Poesie et cetera americaine (poetry anthology), Biennale (Paris), 1963.

(Translator and editor) Daniel Spoerri, *An Anecdoted Topography of Chance,* Something Else Press (New York City), 1966.

(With Claes Oldenburg) Oldenburg, *Store Days,* Something Else Press, 1967.

An Anthology of Concrete Poetry, Something Else Press, 1967.

(Contributing editor) *Open Poetry: Four Anthologies of Expanded Poems,* Simon & Schuster (New York City), 1973.

TRANSLATOR

Daniel Spoerri, *An Anecdoted Topography of Chance. . . ,* Something Else Press, 1966.

(And author of introduction) Spoerri, *The Mythological Travels of a Modern Sir John Mandeville,* Something Else Press, 1970.

Spoerri, *Mythology and Meatballs: A Greek Island Diary-Cookbook,* Aris (Berkeley, CA), 1982.

OTHER

Six Variations upon a Spoerri Landscape: A Suite of Lithographs (includes text), Nova Scotia College of Art and Design (Halifx), 1973.

Zodiac (lithographs), Gallery Birthday Star (Tokyo), 1974.

(With Keith Godard) *Holdup* (photo-drama), Works, 1980.

Schemes and Variations (autobiographical essays and illustrations), Edition Hansjoerg Mayer (Stutggart and London), 1981.

Chicken Feet, Duck Limbs, and Dada Handshakes, Western Front (Vancouver), 1984.

Schutzengel/l'ange gardien/guardian angel/angelo custode, Edition Hundertmark (Cologne), 1985.

My Life in Flux—and Vice Versa, Thames & Hudson (New York City), 1992.

(Gatheror with Ay-O and editor with Ann Noel) *Mr. Fluxus: A Collective Portrait of George Maciunas, 1931-1978: Based upon Personal Reminiscences,* Thames & Hudson (New York City), 1998.

Williams' manuscript collections are held at Sohm Archive, Staatsgalerie, Stuttgart, and Sackner Archive, Miami Beach, FL. Authors works have been translated into French.

SIDELIGHTS: Emmett Williams studied poetry with John Crowe Ransom, was an assistant to ethnologist Paul Radin, and has been remarkably involved in both concrete poetry and Fluxus. In addition to being "an initiator of Fluxus, an international post-Dada, mixed means movement," stated Richard Kostelanetz in a *Contemporary Poets* essay, Williams has "pioneered the art of 'concrete poetry,' in which the poet eschews conventional syntax (and related devices) to organize language in other ways." Explaining Fluxus, concrete poetry, and Williams' relation between the two, Alain Arias-Misson wrote in the *American Book Review:* "Fluxus on the one hand, Concrete & Visual Poetry on the other, have been two divergent tracks on the same psychic landscape, and divergent means that at some point they intersect, and the person in whom they intersect is [Williams]."

Williams generally "favor[s] such severe constraints as repetition, permutation, and linguistic minimalism," indicated Kostelanetz. Although much of Williams' poetry is unpublished, "his masterpiece, the book-length *Sweethearts,*" judged Kostelanetz, was first published in the late 1960s. *Sweethearts,* described Kostelanetz, "consists of one word (the title) whose 11 letters are visually distributed over 150 or so sequentially expressive pages, the work as a whole relating the evolution of a man-woman relationship. Like Williams's other work, *Sweethearts* is extremely witty: and like much else in experimental writing, it must be seen (and read) for its magic to be believed."

Williams is both a writer and editor of works containing concrete poetry, which a *Times Literary Supplement* reviewer defined as "a deviation from poetry, graphic design, and typography alike [which focuses on] a hitherto little-cultivated area where those three arts mix." His 1967 *An Anthology of Concrete Poetry* "has outsold its competitors;" this is one reason "Williams' name is better known than his poetry" according to Kostelanetz in *Contemporary Poets.* Jerome Cushman recommended Williams' anthology in *Library Journal,* acknowledging its "variety of poems" by "poets [who] want the reader to become involved in the poem. . . .

Interest in the text is not as important as the poem's structure [which uses] visual, semantic, and phonetic elements of language." "To Emmett Williams 'concrete poetry, then, is what poets in this anthology make,' and with that circular reasoning," reported *Commonweal* contributor Richard Kostelanetz, "no one dare risk an extended debate."

Williams addresses Fluxus in two of his more recent works, *My Life in Flux—and Vice Versa* and *Mr. Fluxus: A Collective Portrait of George Maciunas, 1931-1978: Based upon Personal Reminiscences. My Life in Flux,* "with a kind of concreteness of language in which words and names jump and run and dance and play on the page," suggested Arias-Misson, "is the clearest, most demystifying and ultimately most mystical (because indecipherable) account of Fluxus yet published. Perhaps because Emmett Williams has had the ingenuity and poetic instinct to present it as in and of his life." The work "is not an autobiography . . . [for it is] only about [Williams'] life in Fluxus. . . . But," added Arias-Misson, "where the subject is touched tangentially by great swerves of digression, one picks up quite a bit of [Williams] along the way." Arias-Misson further mentioned that "this big, warm-hearted fiesta of a book . . . is perhaps above all the memory of the friendships and ingenious inventions and antics of a group of very gifted friends." George Maciunas, the "ideologue, taskmaster, manager, and ingenious inventor of . . . most of the repertoire of Fluxus objects," described Arias-Misson, is discussed in *My Life in Flux;* he is also the focus of *Mr. Fluxus: A Collective Portrait of George Maciunas, 1931-1978: Based upon Personal Reminiscences,* which a *Publishers Weekly* critic denounced as a "bloated and badly blurred" portrait that presents "vague recollections" which Williams edited with Ann Noel such that the contents "[lack] any sense of proportion."

BIOGRAPHICAL/CRITICAL SOURCES:

BOOKS

Contemporary Poets, Sixth Edition, St. James (Detroit), 1996.

Solt, M. E., *Concrete Poetry: A World View,* University of Indiana (Bloomington), 1968.

PERIODICALS

Afterimage (Rochester, NY), Volume 12, number 6, 1985.

American Book Collector, April, 1968.

American Book Review, April-May, 1994.

American Poetry Review (Philadelphia), April-May, 1992.

Commonweal, March 20, 1970.

Library Journal, December 1, 1967.

National Observer, January 25, 1971.

New York Times, December 20, 1967.

New York Times Book Review, February 25, 1968.

Publishers Weekly, April 6, 1998.

Quarterly Journal of Speech, February, 1970.

Time, April 12, 1968.

Times Literary Supplement, February 29, 1968; October 2, 1970; February 10, 1979.*

* * *

WILLIAMS, Joan 1928-

PERSONAL: Born September 26, 1928, in Memphis, TN; died January 5, 1994; daughter of Priestly H. and Maude (Moore) Williams; married Ezra Drinker Bowen, 1954 (divorced, 1970); married John Fargason, 1970; children: (first marriage) Ezra Drinker, Matthew Williams. *Education:* Bard College, B.A., 1950; Fairfield University, M.A., 1985. *Avocational interests:* Sailing and skiing.

ADDRESSES: Home—6 Old Farm Rd., Charlottesville, VA 22903. *Agent*—Harold Ober Associates, 425 Madison, New York, NY 10017.

CAREER: Worked at Double Day Bookshop in New Orleans; *Look Magazine,* answered letters to the editor; full-time writer.

MEMBER: PEN, Authors Guild.

AWARDS, HONORS: Grant in literature, National Institute of Arts and Letters, 1962; John P. Marquand First Novel Award, 1962, for *The Morning and the Evening;* Guggenheim fellow, 1986.

WRITINGS:

The Morning and the Evening, Atheneum (New York City), 1961.

Old Powder Man, Harcourt (New York City), 1966.

The Wintering, Harcourt, 1971.

County Woman, Little, Brown (Boston, MA), 1982.

Pariah and Other Stories, Little, Brown, 1983.

Pay the Piper, Dutton (New York City), 1988.

Co-author with William Faulkner of the teleplay *The Graduation Dress,* produced on General Electric Theater for Columbia Broadcasting System, October 30, 1960. Also author of short stories published in various publications, including *Atlantic Monthly, Saturday Evening Post, Esquire, Virginia Quarterly Review,* and *Mademoiselle.*

SIDELIGHTS: Joan Williams' literary career began in 1949 when, following the publication of her first story titled "Rain Later," she met and initiated a correspondence with William Faulkner. Williams soon became a protegee of Faulkner and the two developed a close friendship, which included a brief love affair. They collaborated to write the script for the teleplay *The Graduation Dress.* Faulkner provided the title for Williams' second story, "The Morning and the Evening," and also recommended it to his agent Harold Ober. Ober sold the story to the *Atlantic,* it appeared there in January, 1953, and Williams' career was formerly launched.

In addition to frequent comparisons to Faulkner, Williams, who died in 1994, was highly regarded by many critics for both her individual voice and her interpretations of the Southern genre. Essayist Alphonse Vinh of *Contemporary Southern Writers* once remarked: "Williams is a writer of genuine talent and possessor of a distinctive voice. She has the ability to conjure the sights, smells, and sounds of the world in which she grew up—that is Memphis and the hard scrabbled area around Arkabutla where her mother's people came from." Tracing her own literary influences, Williams once stated that her inspiration came more from Eudora Welty and Katherine Anne Porter than from Faulkner.

William's second story became the first chapter of her first novel, also titled *The Morning and the Evening.* It is the tale of a retarded mute named Jake Darby and how the residents of the small Mississippi town where he lives deal with him. Although many of them are well-meaning, they fail to integrate Jake into their community and make him self-sufficient. According to Vinh: "In Williams' first novel, she establishes the recurring themes of her later works: loneliness and isolation of individuals pitted against the narrowness and unforgiving social conventions of Southern life." Williams' work took a semi-autobiographical turn with her second novel, *Old Powder Man.* Detailing the difficult relationship between dynamite salesman Frank Wynn and his daughter, Laurel, the work parallels Williams' own relationship with her father. The novel covers thirty years in Wynn's life, including his career obsession, two failed marriages, and his deathbed realizations about how his personal relationships have failed. In the final chapters of the book the point of view shifts from Wynn to Laurel, who gains some understanding of her father and manages a partial reconciliation with him. Vinh felt that "a sense of profound regret and loss permeates the ending of" the book. Gail M. Morrison of the *Dictionary of Literary Biography* characterized *Old Powder Man* as "equally effective in its portrayal of its protagonist's loneliness, but considerably more mature" than *The Morning and the Evening.* Noted novelist Robert Penn Warren praised *Old Powder Man* and considered it to be the Southern version of Arthur Miller's *Death of a Salesman.*

Williams' 1971 novel *The Wintering,* a barely disguised rendition of her love affair and relationship with Faulkner, coupled with her own struggles to become a writer, fared less well with critics. The novel was suggested by Faulkner, including the name of his fictional character, Jeffrey Almoner, that appears therein. "[W]hile some details are recognizable representations of reality," Morrison stated, "others are obviously added to disguise the truth so that the novel is a work torn between two genres, neither fact nor fiction. Instead, it hovers uneasily somewhere in between." Other critics faulted the novel's shifting point of view, its style, and the character of Almoner as never appearing more than two-dimensional. Vinh saw *The Wintering* as a departure for Williams, noting: "Normally a writer of straightforward fiction, Williams is at her most experimental in this novel with her frequent use of letters . . . juxtaposition of time and space, and her use of interior monologue to describe the inner states of her characters."

Despite Williams' early success and established reputation, her fourth novel *County Woman* also received mixed reviews. Set in Mississippi in 1962, the book is, in the words of *Chicago Tribune* reviewer Polly Morrice, about a "middle-aged woman searching for true direction" during the turmoil of "the Old South giving way to the New." Allie McCall's conventional way of life is dramatically transformed when she decides to run for constable of Itna Homa, a small farming community near Oxford. Her decision alters her traditional lifestyle, which includes caring for both her elderly father and her husband. The Southern political climate of the 1960s becomes the backdrop and parallel to Allie's change. As one of the characters says when she hears the radio announcement about James Meredith's admission to the University of Mississippi, "Then it's the end. The end of living the way us Southern white people have." A reviewer for the *New Yorker* remarked, "Allie's new restlessness is not only mirrored in but magnified by the events in the news." However, Morrice concluded: "Whole lot of shakin' up goes on in the few months' span of *County Woman,* too much for us to read it as a plausible chronicle of social evolution." *Los Angeles Times* reviewer Elizabeth Wheeler called it a "put-down-housewife-wakes-and-smells-the-coffee" plot, typical of a "new genre of fiction" emerging in the 1980s. While she found all but Williams' writing "a bit unsatisfactory" and Allie McCall's transformation overly dramatic, she praised Williams' prose, especially the "lively and authentic-sounding Southern voices."

Other critics commended Williams for her authentic setting and knowledge of subject. *Detroit News* reviewer Anne Tyler believed the novel's "drawbacks don't amount to a hill of beans (as one of the Itna Homas might put it)." She goes on to praise Williams' "faultless ear and eye" for rural community settings and characters and believes *County Woman* to be a "wide, deep window upon a fascinating little world." *Washington Post Book World* critic Jonathan Yardley agreed, calling it "an intelligent and well-written novel, one with a secure grasp on time, place and character. . . . Williams remembers precisely what the rural South was like two decades ago, not merely the details but the attitudes, and she gets it down exactly right."

A *Washington Post Book World* critic called Williams' *Pariah and Other Stories* a collection which "charts the territory of the rural and small-town South—the land where porches sag on tenant houses, where screen doors slap on summer days, where matrons while away hot afternoons over bridge games." The *New York Times Book Review*'s Edith Milton claimed: "At [the stories'] deepest level, they have an apocalyptic resonance; the affection and warmth at their center is surrounded by a sense of universal and ever intensifying darkness." Tyler in the *Detroit News* found "endurance" to be "the thread running through this book. Most of the stories (whether the early ones or the later, generally more polished ones) explore the ways in which people manage to trudge along in spite of everything—poverty, loneliness, change, injustice, old age, or simple exhaustion." She called the story "Jesse" "perhaps the best piece in the book" and believed it to be "not so much a story as a poem, and an absolutely beautiful one." Vinh believed: "In some important way, Williams' gifts as a writer . . . [are] best suited to the short story form and it is to be regretted that she has not decided to pursue more seriously this genre so close to poetry."

Reviewing Williams' 1988 novel *Pay the Piper* for *Publishers Weekly,* Sybil Steinberg observed: "Williams is an accomplished novelist who seems here to have muted a potentially engrossing story." The plot of the book centers around Laurel Perry, a writer of novels that are critically acclaimed but fail to sell. Laurel, who grew up on the wrong side of the tracks in the small town of Delton, Mississippi, married above her origins and now lives in Connecticut with a husband who is well-bred but unfaithful. During her annual visit to her hometown, Laurel meets Hal MacDonald, local scion of a socially prominent family. MacDonald is in prison for shooting and murdering his stepson. Laurel not only decides to rehabilitate MacDonald, but falls in love with him. She leaves her first husband and marries MacDonald once he is released from prison. The marriage is a disaster: MacDonald turns out to be not only a murderer, but a psychopath and an alcoholic. Vinh saw Laurel's actions as "a vain attempt to recover her Southerness," and also remarked: "Despite its gripping psychological intensity, the novel fails to engage the reader wholly." Steinberg concluded: "Laurel's passivity and lifelong subservience to men make her a rather colorless character. . . . It is only when she realizes she has thrown away her life, discovers herself alone in middle age and makes muddled attempts to find companionship and happiness that she becomes an appealing figure. At this point the novel acquires depth and poignancy."

Summing up Williams' career, Morrison once stated: "Neglected today, Williams' novels are limited in range; but the best of them are noteworthy in their recreation of Southern settings and in their depiction of characters alienated from themselves and others in their loneliness. They deserve attention more serious than has been accorded them thus far."

BIOGRAPHICAL/CRITICAL SOURCES:

BOOKS

Contemporary Southern Writers, Gale (Detroit , MI), 1999.

Dictionary of Literary Biography, Volume 6: *American Novelists since World War II, Second Series,* Gale, 1980, pp. 367-70.

Lloyd, James B., editor, *Lives of Mississippi Authors, 1817-1967,* University Press of Mississippi (Jackson), 1981.

Williams, Joan, *County Woman,* Little, Brown, 1982.

PERIODICALS

America, December 31, 1988, "Joan Williams: Struggling Fiction Writer," p. 544.

Best Sellers, June 15, 1971, p. 138.

Booklist, May 15, 1961; September 1, 1971, p. 39; February 15, 1982, p. 746; August 1983, p. 1450; May 15, 1988, p. 1573.
Chicago Tribune, May 9, 1982, p. 2.
Christian Science Monitor, May 18, 1961.
Detroit News, February 7, 1982; September 4, 1983.
Hudson Review, spring 1972, p. 166.
Kirkus Review, February 1, 1971, p. 138; December 1, 1981, p. 1489; June 1, 1983, p. 638; March 15, 1988, p. 407.
Library Journal, March 15, 1971, p. 978; March 1, 1982, p. 564; June 15, 1983, p. 1276.
Los Angeles Times Book Review, September 15, 1985, p. 8.
National Review, February 5, 1982, p. 116.
New York Times Book Review, May 21, 1961; September 18, 1983, p. 14.
New Yorker, March 15, 1982, p. 143; October 10, 1983, p. 167.
People Weekly, October 31, 1983, review of *Pariah and Other Stories,* p. 14.
Publishers Weekly, January 25, 1971, p. 260; December 18, 1981, p. 58; June 10, 1983, p. 56; March 25, 1988, Sybil Steinberg, review of *Pay the Piper,* p. 52.
San Francisco Chronicle, May 30, 1961.
Saturday Review, May 13, 1961.
Time, May 19, 1961.
Village Voice Literary Supplement, February 1982, p. 4.
Virginia Quarterly Review, summer 1971, p. R96.
Washington Post Book World, February 7, 1982, p. 3; August 7, 1983, p. 8; October 13, 1985, p. 16; May 29, 1988, p. 3.

* * *

WILLIAMSON, Marianne 1952-

PERSONAL: Born in 1952 in Houston, TX; daughter of Alan Vishnevetsky (an attorney); children: India Emmaline. *Education:* Attended Pomona College. *Religion:* Jewish.

ADDRESSES: *Home*—West Hollywood, CA. *Office*—Los Angeles Center for Living, Los Angeles, CA. *Agent*—Al Loman, Authors and Artists Group, 19 West 44th St., New York, NY 10036.

CAREER: Lecturer and writer. Founded Los Angeles Center for Living and Manhattan Center for Living.

WRITINGS:

A Return to Love: Reflections on the Principles of "A Course in Miracles", HarperCollins (New York City), 1992.
A Woman's Worth, Random House (New York City), 1993.
Illuminata: Thoughts, Prayers, Rites of Passage, Random House, 1994, published as *Illuminata: A Return to Prayer,* Riverhead Books (New York City), 1995.
(With daughter, Emma Williamson) *Emma and Mommy Talk to God,* HarperCollins (New York City), 1996.
The Healing of America, Simon & Schuster (New York City), 1997.
Illuminated Prayers, Simon & Schuster, 1997.
Healing the Soul of America: Reclaiming Our Voices as Spiritual Citizens, Simon & Schuster, 1997.
Enchanted Love: The Mystical Power of Intimate Relationships, Simon & Schuster, 1999.

Williamson has released numerous audiocassettes, including *Romantic Delusions, Love, Passion, and Soul, Positive Relationships—Music, Meditation, and Prayer,* and *Letting Go and Becoming: Talks on Spirituality and Modern Life.*

SIDELIGHTS: Marianne Williamson is a popular spirituality speaker who has been regarded in *Newsweek* as a "pop guru" and in the *New York Times* as the "Prophet of Love." She became involved in spirituality in 1977 while living a life that she described to *Newsweek* as a "mess." By that time she had already been in and out of various relationships, survived drug use, and failed as a jazz singer. While at a friend's house that year, Williamson discovered *A Course in Miracles,* psychologist Helen Schucman's work on finding happiness and inner peace in contemporary times. Schucman's multivolume publication, which *Newsweek* described as "a gassy modern-day gospel," proved inspirational to Williamson. She soon became immersed in Schucman's ideology, which she summarized to the *New York Times* as "a self-study program of spiritual psychotherapy," and by the early 1980s Williamson was sharing her expertise before gatherings of the Philosophical Research Society.

Throughout the 1980s, Williamson grew increasingly successful in sharing her spirituality with others. She synthesized the tenets of various religions in her lectures and, like Schucman, counseled her audience to find contentment by replacing feelings of fear and hate with those of happiness and love. Williamson's message has won her particular acceptance among celebrities, including recording industry entrepreneur David Geffen. But this affiliation with show business, while adding to Williamson's fame, has provided fuel for her detractors. One such critic, quoted in Leslie Bennetts's *Vanity Fair* article, spoke on Williamson's possible ulterior motives in proclaiming her message: "She's playing a win-win game for herself. . . . She's preaching the gospel of giving and love and goodness, and what she's getting out of it is fame."

Celebrities, meanwhile, are quick to note that Williamson has brought comfort to many people. One supporter, Geffen, was quoted in *Newsmakers 91* as saying that Williamson "does a lot of good work," and he added: "She's also able to articulate things that are valuable for people to hear. People are alienated from their families, from religion, and she's found a way to bring them together."

Williamson's work has, on occasion, even inspired involvement from other celebrities. In Los Angeles, for instance, Williamson's activities as principal fundraiser for Project Angel Food, wherein gourmet food is delivered to the area's dying victims of acquired immunodeficiency syndrome (AIDS), spurred involvement from a number of show-business figures, including Shirley MacLaine, Bette Midler, and Geffen. And when Williamson's Manhattan Center for Living neared dissolution following board strife, singer-actress Cher interceded with a donation that kept the center functional. In 1991 Williamson won further attention with *A Return to Love: A Reflection on the Principles of "A Course in Miracles."* In this book Williamson reiterates Schucman's earlier message and provides autobiographical accounts relating the effectiveness of adopting a more positive, peaceful outlook. By the spring of 1992, Williamson's book had become a best-seller across the United States.

In 1997, she turned her attention from personal fulfillment to a broader world view with her book *The Healing of America.* In this volume, Williamson "produced what might be the first manifesto of New Age politics," in the opinion of *New Republic* commentator Margaret Talbot, offering "a diagnosis of what ails the nation and a prescription for making it better, or rather, for making it feel better." Talbot commends Williamson's good intentions, but warns that it is her "citizenly duty to remark upon the nonsense" found in *The Healing of America.* The author "orders and classifies the world into absurdly stereotyped feminine and masculine qualities," and she frequently shows a disregard for logic and rationality. Talbot summarizes: "In this pious book, you will find a delegitimation of judgement and a delegitimation of conflict; a promiscuous intermingling of the personal and spiritual realms with the public and political realms; a dalliance with conspiracy theories; and a distrust of rationality and the intellect that would make democratic deliberation meaningless. Williamson is caring and inclusive and pained and tender-hearted and intensely concerned about children and the poor; but her prescriptions for politics give compassion a bad name."

The Healing of America is taken more seriously by Lynda Gorov, a writer for *Mother Jones.* Allowing that Williamson sometimes seems to offer "religion without rules, salvation without sacrifice," Gorov nonetheless finds that *The Healing of America* is "a daring departure for Williamson, even if she says it is merely an extension of her belief that love and prayer will save individuals and maybe even the world. The hefty manuscript almost—but not quite—dares to state that navel gazing alone is not enough; that it's time to move from self-absorbed me-ism to a more civic-minded we-ism. This message runs the real risk of turning off an audience that appears to be looking for easy answers to earthly salvation. Williamson says that doesn't matter."

Williamson returned to the personal realm with the 1999 book *Enchanted Love: The Mystical Power of Intimate Relationships.* Prefacing each chapter with an excerpt of conversation between herself and her lover, the author then goes on to explore different aspects of love, including forgiveness, romance, monogamy, and marriage. *Booklist* reviewer Ilene Cooper notes that "there are some interesting insights and nuggets of information here," but she complains that "they get lost in a text that is overwritten and at times repetitious." Cooper concludes that "the most affecting parts of the book are the sweet, simple prayers that punctuate each chapter."

BIOGRAPHICAL/CRITICAL SOURCES:

BOOKS

Newsmakers 91, Gale (Detroit, MI), 1991, pp. 463-64.

PERIODICALS

Booklist, February 15, 1992, p. 1069; April 1, 1993, p. 1386; May 15, 1995, p. 1664; June 1, 1996, p. 1732; September 1, 1997, Ilene Cooper, review of *The Healing of America,* p. 5; August, 1998, Nancy Spillman, review of *Positive Relationships,* p.

2029; September 1, 1999, Ilene Cooper, review of *Enchanted Love,* p. 7.
Commentary, August, 1992, p. 59.
Commonweal, September 9, 1994, p. 20.
Entertainment Weekly, March 15, 1992, p. 150; June 25, 1993, p. 99.
Forbes, May 9, 1994, p. S104.
Library Journal, January, 1992, p. 136; March 15, 1992, p. 150; April 15, 1993, p. 114; June 1, 1993, p. 212; September 1, 1993, p. 244; May 15, 1998, Linda Bredengerd, review of *Love, Passion, and Soul,* p. 135; May 15, 1999, Nancy Paul, review of *Letting Go and Becoming,* p. 148.
Mademoiselle, March, 1992, p. 162.
Mother Jones, November, 1997, Lynda Gorov, "Faith: Marianne Williamson Is Full of It," p. 52, Paul Rogat Loeb, "When Sorry Is Good Enough," p. 56.
New Republic, December 8, 1997, Margaret Talbot, review of *The Healing of America,* p. 31.
Newsweek, March 23, 1992, p. 65; June 7, 1993, p. 56.
New York Times, February 19, 1992, p. C1.
People, October 13, 1997, Francine Prose, review of *The Healing of America,* p. 35.
Psychology Today, July, 1992, p. 28.
Publishers Weekly, December 20, 1991, p. 72; April 6, 1992, p. 27; April 12, 1993, p. 52; October 3, 1994, p. 36; April 8, 1996, p. 62; December 2, 1996, p. 31; August 18, 1997, review of *The Healing of America,* p. 80; August 30, 1999, review of *Enchanted Love,* p. 61.
Redbook, May 1993, p. 48.
School Library Journal, June, 1996, p. 112.
Skeptical Inquirer, fall, 1992, p. 17.
Time, July 29, 1991, p. 60; January 23, 1995, p. 10.
Utne Reader, November, 1997, p. 21.
Vanity Fair, June, 1991, p. 130.
Women in Business, May-June, 1994, p. 5.*

* * *

WILLIS, Connie 1945-

PERSONAL: Born December 31, 1945, in Denver, CO; stepdaughter of William and LaMarlys Crook (a homemaker) Trimmer; married Courtney W. Willis (a physics teacher), August 23, 1967; children: Cordelia. *Education:* Colorado State College (now University of Northern Colorado), B.A., 1967.

ADDRESSES: Home—1716 13th Ave., Greeley, CO 80631. *Agent*—Ralph Vicinanza, 111 Eighth Ave., Suite 1501, New York, NY 10011.

CAREER: Branford Public Schools, Branford, CT, teacher of fifth and seventh grades, 1967-69; freelance writer, 1969—.

MEMBER: Science Fiction Writers of America.

AWARDS, HONORS: Grant from National Endowment for the Humanities, 1980; Colorado Artist-in-Residence; Hugo Awards, World Science Fiction Convention, 1982, for novelette "Fire Watch," 1988, for novella "The Last of the Winnebagos," 1992, for novel *Doomsday Book;* John W. Campbell Memorial Award, World Science Fiction Convention, 1988, for novel *Lincoln's Dreams;* Nebula Awards, Science Fiction Writers of America, both 1982, for "Fire Watch" and short story "A Letter from the Clearys," 1988, for "The Last of the Winnebagos," 1989, for novelette "At the Rialto," both 1992, for novel *Doomsday Book* and short story "Even the Queen."

WRITINGS:

SCIENCE FICTION NOVELS

(With Cynthia Felice) *Water Witch,* Ace Books (New York City), 1980.
Lincoln's Dreams, Bantam (New York City), 1988.
(With Felice) *Light Raid,* Ace Books, 1989.
Doomsday Book, Bantam, 1992.
Uncharted Territory, Spectra, 1994.
Remake, M. V. Ziesing (Shingletown, CA), 1994.
Bellwether, Bantam, 1996.
(With Felice) *Promised Land,* Ace Books, 1997.
To Say Nothing of the Dog, or, How We Found the Bishop's Bird Stump at Last, Bantam, 1997.

OTHER

Fire Watch (science fiction stories), Bluejay (New York City), 1984.
(With Poul Anderson, Ed Bryant, Stephen R. Donaldson, Larry Niven, Fred Saberhagen, and Roger Zelazny) *Berserker Base,* Tor Books (New York City), 1985.
Impossible Things (science fiction stories), Bantam, 1993.
Miracle, and Other Christmas Stories, Bantam, 1999.
(Editor and author of commentary) *Nebula Awards 33: The Year's Best SF and Fantasy Chosen by the Science-Fiction and Fantasy Writers of America,* Harcourt (New York City), 1999.

Also author and reader of the sound recording, *Even the Queen and Other Short Stories,* 1997. Contributor of stories to science fiction magazines including *Omni* and *Isaac Asimov's Science Fiction Magazine.*

WORK IN PROGRESS: Working Cape Race, a novel.

SIDELIGHTS: The recipient of numerous Hugo and Nebula Awards, author Connie Willis has written novels and stories that have not only been acclaimed by critics and readers but by her fellow science-fiction writers as well. Willis's first solo novel, *Lincoln's Dreams,* focuses on Annie, a young woman plagued by dreams about the Civil War, and Jeff, a researcher who helps identify the source of those dreams. The nightmares are so detailed that they could only be the dreams of someone else—most likely Robert E. Lee, dead for over a century. In a *New York Times Book Review* article, Gerald Jonas says the book "literally gave me dreams—strange narrative fantasies that left me with a not unpleasant sense of being on the verge of some important revelation. As the book itself did." Willis conceals nothing, and the mystery of *Lincoln's Dreams* is solved. David Brin indicates in the *Los Angeles Times Book Review* that "whether writing drama or witty humor or, in this case, a poignant examination of duty, Willis conveys through her characters a sense of transcendent pity that few modern authors ever attempt."

Willis followed *Lincoln's Dreams* with *Doomsday Book,* a time-travel novel set in England in both the mid-twenty-first century and the fourteenth-century. Against the wishes of her tutor, Kivrin, an Oxford history student, decides to travel back to the year 1320. An error in the time-travel procedure sends her back to 1348 instead, a time when the Black Death was raging through England. Kivrin becomes deeply involved with the people of the era and in fighting the epidemic. Meanwhile, a plague also breaks out in the world from which Kivrin had traveled, revealing that although science has progressed in its ability to combat contagious disease the human reaction to it has not. While noting some errors in Willis's historical research, David V. Barrett of *New Statesman* nevertheless calls *Doomsday Book* "one of the harshest yet most beautiful novels I have read for years." A *Publishers Weekly* reviewer finds the novel to be "an intelligent and satisfying blend of classic science fiction and historical reconstruction," and concludes: "This book finds villains and heroes in all ages, and love, too, which Kivrin hears in the revealing and quietly touching deathbed confession of a village priest."

Willis's third novel, *Uncharted Territory,* offers a far-future farce. On the backwater world of Bhoote two gently feuding planetary surveyors and a visiting "socioexozoologist" who is studying alien mating customs are taken on a tour of the planet (on horseback!) by a larcenous native guide who makes up violations of native customs, and the fines that accompany them, as they proceed. The slapstick narrative eventually leads to a revelation about the geology of Bhoote. A critic for *Publishers Weekly* describes *Uncharted Territory* as "a pleasant diversion," while noting "there's little for the reader to take away." However, Carl Hays of *Booklist* observes: "Willis proves unsurpassed in sf in her ability to unload, within a short but thoroughly satisfying narrative space, a full literary bag of tricks ranging from wry dialogue to extraterrestrial intrigue."

Willis shifts tone again with the 1994 *Remake.* In a near-future Hollywood traditional movie-making has been replaced by computer graphics. Tom, the narrator of the story, is in charge of mining old films to create new ones, often starring dead actors. It is also his job to make sure the remakes adhere to the politically correct attitudes of the times. Tom falls in love with Alis, a young woman who has come to Hollywood to become a star in the kind of movies that are no longer made. Before Tom knows it, Alis begins turning up as a dancer in the old movies he watches to create new ones. To pursue his love, Tom must unravel this mystery. While commenting that "Willis's writing, as usual, is transparently clean and deft," a *Publishers Weekly* writer concludes with tempered praise: "One flaw is a scene of requited love that neither the form nor tone of this bittersweet romance can support. But if the characters are mostly stock and the sentimentality easy, this is still popular fiction at a high level, entertaining, thoughtful and often touching."

According to a *Publishers Weekly* reviewer: "In Willis's fifth solo novel, her practiced screwball style yields a clever story which, while imperfect, is a sheer pleasure to read." *Bellwether* takes place in the near future at a corporation known as Hi-Tek. Sociologist/statistician Sandy Foster is joined by a mail girl and an expert in chaos theory in her research into the source of fads. According to a critic from *Publishers Weekly:* "Where the story's headed becomes transparent too early. . . . But none of that counts much against this bright romantic comedy, where the real pleasure is the thick layers of detail . . . and the wryly disdainful commentary on human stupidity."

In *To Say Nothing of the Dog,* Willis returns to England and the theme of time travel. The plot revolves around time-traveler Ned Henry, a rich dowager who wants to rebuild Coventry Cathedral by scavenging the past, and a supposed vacation back to 1888 where Ned discovers that he must correct an incongruity in time with the help of love-interest and fellow time-traveler Verity Kindle. "What a stitch!" proclaims Sally Estes of *Booklist,* "Take an excursion though time, add chaos theory, romance, plenty of humor, a dollop of mystery, and a spoof of the Victorian novel and you end up with what seems like a comedy of errors but is actually a grand scheme 'involving the entire course of history and all of time and space.' " "While thematically not the major novel that Willis's much-acclaimed *Domesday Book* was,"opines a *Publishers Weekly* writer, "her newest shares its universe as well as its near flawlessness of plot, character and prose."

In addition to her solo novels, Willis has collaborated on three novels with Cynthia Felice, and has also published several collections of stories. Reviewing Willis's third collaboration with Felice, the 1997 *Promised Land,* a *Publishers Weekly* reviewer remarks: "Since they first teamed up, in *Water Witch,* Willis and Felice have been a solidly successful pair known for smoothly mixing SF adventure with humor and light romance." The reviewer finds *Promised Land,* a young woman's coming-of-age story set on a desolate colony planet, to be no exception: "Lively characters, a well-defined setting and sure-handed storytelling add up to a novel that's bound to capture readers' imaginations." Commenting in *Booklist* on Willis's collection, *Impossible Things,* Hays states: "Ranging in style from biting satire to speculative history, Willis' second collection of short fiction displays a versatility of form and conception few in the genre can match." Willis's third collection, the 1999 *Miracle, and Other Christmas Stories,* provides strange twists on some traditional Christmas icons, including Frank Capra's *It's a Wonderful Life* and Dickens's *A Christmas Carol.* A writer for *Publishers Weekly* states: "The witty, literate Willis offers a wonderfully enjoyable ode to Christmas with this collection of eight fantastic seasonal titles."

Willis once told *CA:* "I have been writing for . . . years, beginning with confessions and settling in science fiction, where I am happy to be able to write whatever I want: screwball comedies, stories about the distant past and the distant future, fairy tales, serious science stories, horror and fantasy and romance, almost anything. I love the short form best and never intend to abandon it, even though I am working on novels. I have been an Anglophile forever and write a great many of my stories about England."

BIOGRAPHICAL/CRITICAL SOURCES:

PERIODICALS

Booklist, December 15, 1993, Carl Hays, review of *Impossible Things,* p. 741; May 1, 1994, Carl Hays, review of *Uncharted Territory,* p. 1586; July, 1997, Laurie Hartshorn, review of *Even the Queen and Other Short Stories,* p. 1829; January 1, 1999, Sally Estes, review of *To Say Nothing of the Dog,* p. 786; April 15, 1999, Roland Green, review of *Nebula Awards 33,* p. 1518.

Globe and Mail (Toronto), August 16, 1986.

Library Journal, February 15, 1997, Susan Hamburger, review of *The Promised Land,* p. 165; December, 1998, review of *To Say Nothing of the Dog,* p. 188; April 1, 1999, Laurel Bliss, review of *Nebula Awards 33,* p. 132.

Los Angeles Times Book Review, February 7, 1988.

New Statesman,, November 27, 1992, David V. Barrett, review of *Doomsday Book,* p. 38.

New York Times Book Review, June 7, 1987.

Publishers Weekly, May 4, 1992, review of *Doomsday Book,* p. 54; November 29, 1993, p. 59; January 18, 1985; April 14, 1989; November 29, 1993, review of *Impossible Things,* p. 59; June 6, 1994, review of *Uncharted Territory,* p. 62; December 19, 1994, review of *Remake,* p. 51; January 29, 1996, review of *Bellwether,* p. 96; January 27, 1997, review of *The Promised Land,* p. 82; October 27, 1997, review of *To Say Nothing of the Dog,* p. 56; March 8, 1999, review of *Nebula Awards 33,* p. 51; October 25, 1999, review of *Miracle, and Other Christmas Stories,* p. 55.

Washington Post Book World, July 31, 1988; May 28, 1989.*

* * *

WONG, Jade Snow 1922-

PERSONAL: Born January 21, 1922, in San Francisco, CA; daughter of Hong (a manufacturer) and Hing Kwai (Tong) Wong; married Woodrow Ong (a travel agent), August 29, 1950; children: Mark Stuart, Tyi Elizabeth, Ellora Louise, Lance Orion. *Education:* San Francisco Junior College, A.A., 1940; Mills College, B.A., 1942. *Politics:* Democrat. *Religion:* Methodist.

ADDRESSES: *Office*—2123-2125 Polk St., San Francisco, CA 94109. *Agent*—Curtis Brown Ltd., 575 Madison Ave., New York, NY 10022.

CAREER: Worked as secretary in San Francisco, CA, 1943-45; proprietor of ceramics gallery, 1946—; co-owner of travel agency, 1957—; writer. Director of Chinese Culture Center, 1978-81.

MEMBER: International Air Traffic Association, Norcal Pacific Area Travel Association, Museum Society (director, 1976-81). Member of California Council for the Humanities, 1975-81; member of advisory councils for China Institute of New York and Friends of the San Francisco Libraries.

AWARDS, HONORS: Award for pottery from California State Fair, 1947; Silver Medal for craftsmanship from *Mademoiselle;* award for enamel from California State Fair, 1949; Silver Medal for nonfiction from Commonwealth Club of San Francisco, 1976, for *Fifth Chinese Daughter;* honorary doctorate of humane letters from Mills College, 1976.

WRITINGS:

Fifth Chinese Daughter (autobiography), Harper, 1950, reprinted with a new introduction by the author, illustrated by Kathryn Uhl, University of Washington Press, 1989.

The Immigrant Experience (nonfiction), Dial, 1971.

No Chinese Stranger (nonfiction), illustrated by Deng Ming-Dao, Harper, 1975.

Also author of column in *San Francisco Examiner.* Contributor to periodicals, including *Holiday* and *Horn Book.*

SIDELIGHTS: Jade Snow Wong once commented: "My writing is nonfiction based on personal experiences. So few Chinese American have published that I think it is my responsibility to try to create understanding between Chinese and Americans. In my work with ceramics and travel, I follow the same philosophy. Because I am innovative and unconventional, I am often far ahead of my time. Thirty-two years after publication, *Fifth Chinese Daughter* is still in print and used by schools everywhere. I am fluent in English, Cantonese, and have studied Mandarin since beginning my travels in the People's Republic of China. Though I don't think being a woman has been any problem, I give priority to women's responsibility for a good home life; hence, I put my husband and four children before my writing or ceramics. I also believe in serving my community and this work has taken more time than writing a book."

With the release in 1950 of her autobiography, *Fifth Chinese Daughter,* Jade Snow Wong became one of the first Chinese-American women ever to be published. When her book first appeared, Wong was praised for the candor with which she described her struggle to balance both Chinese and American influences. Wong's resolution of the conflict between the traditions of her ancestors and those of her adopted country forms the core of *Fifth Chinese Daughter.* Critics also praised the book for its preservation of a part of Chinese-American history in the first half of the twentieth century and as an engaging coming-of-age story. A second volume of autobiography, *No Chinese Stranger,* appeared twenty-five years later, offering an account of Wong's marriage, the birth of four children, the establishment of a travel agency with her husband, and a description of their 1972 trip to the People's Republic of China, among other travel narratives. Like *Fifth Chinese Daughter, No Chinese Stranger* also contains detailed instructions on the preparation of several Chinese dishes, making it a valuable resource of information on Chinese cooking. Although both fictional and nonfictional accounts of the Chinese-American experience are more common at the end of the twentieth century than when Wong first became an author, the historical merit of, in particular, her first book, with its rare depiction of pre-World War II Chinatown in San Francisco, is considered invaluable, as is her account of the prejudice she faced, both as a Chinese American and as a woman, when she sought first education and then employment in mid-twentieth-century America.

Fifth Chinese Daughter is an "account of how a young woman of notable intelligence, good humor, and talent handled the job of dovetailing American ways with a Chinese upbringing," began a reviewer for the *New Yorker* in 1950. Wong wrote and published her first book when she was still in her twenties, and it generated much commentary. Wong responded to some of this criticism in an essay published in *Horn Book,* where she wrote, in part:

"I do not think of myself as a writer, and I am not an authority in the field of intercultural relations. I was born in San Francisco of parents who had come from China and I speak only as one individual who was raised in the old-world Chinese standards and who found outside the confines of Chinatown a new American world waiting for her. The new world was full of light and promised independence, but the path between the two worlds was untrod and, as I later found, a rough one."

Wong continued: "As I made clear in the author's note for *Fifth Chinese Daughter,* I am not saying that mine is a typical story, not even typical of the experiences of other members of my family. But I am speaking the truth as I know it, and the conservatives who have been angered at my book cannot denounce it on the grounds that it is untrue, only on grounds that the truth should not have been told—least of all, by me."

Fifth Chinese Daughter has been continuously in print for half a century. Over the years it has gathered comparisons to Henry Adams's *The Education of Henry Adams,* as the model for an autobiographical narrative told in the third person, and to Maxine Hong Kingston's *The Woman Warrior,* published a generation after Wong's book, as an example of an utterly different portrait, in both form and content, of growing up Chinese in America. Much has been made in the years since its first publication of Wong's choice to rely on the third-person singular voice to tell her own life story, a choice the author explained in an introduction by reference to the shocking immodesty of telling a story in the first person in Chinese tradition. For Kathleen Loh Swee Yin and Kristoffer F. Paulson, writing in *MELUS* in 1982, Wong's choice to write an autobiography in the third person "effectively renders the divided consciousness of dual-heritage," and thus is at the heart of the genius of her book. "Wong's achievement . . . is a foundation stone for ethnic literature, for feminist literature and for American literature," Yin and Paulson concluded. With the publication of a new edition of *Fifth Chinese Daughter* nearly fifty years after the appearance of the first, critics responded equally to the historical value of Wong's intimate and detailed description of life in San Francisco's Chinatown in the 1920s and 1930s and to her struggle to gain American-style independence and self-respect while retaining her Chinese heritage.

In *No Chinese Stranger,* Wong's second volume of autobiography, the author briefly retraces in third person the story of her upbringing and education, then, with the death of her father, turns to the first person to recount the story of forming her own family, setting up a business as a ceramicist, and then another with her travel agent husband, raising their four children, and traveling to Hong Kong, Thailand, and the People's Republic of China. Throughout, "the lively, forthright prose makes for delightful reading," contended Elizabeth A. Teo in *Library Journal.* The attractions of *No Chinese Stranger* for *Publishers Weekly* reviewer Barbara A. Bannon included the author's commentary on the San Francisco Bay Area, cooking, ceramics, and travel.

BIOGRAPHICAL/CRITICAL SOURCES:

BOOKS

Contemporary Literary Criticism, Volume 17, Gale (Detroit), 1981.

Culley, Margo, editor, *American Women's Autobiography: Fea(s)ts of Memory,* University of Wisconsin Press, 1992, pp. 252-67.

Kim, Elaine H., *Asian American Literature: An Introduction to the Writings and Their Social Context,* Temple University Press, 1982, pp. 58-90.

Who's Who among Asian Americans, Gale, 1994.

PERIODICALS

Amerasia Journal, vol. 15, no. 2, 1989, pp. 224-26.

Booklist, September 1, 1975, p. 18.

Christian Science Monitor, March 31, 1981, p. 23.

Commonweal, November 24, 1950, p. 182.

Horn Book, December, 1951, Jade Snow Wong, Growing up between the Old World and the New, pp. 440-445.

Interracial Books for Children Bulletin, Vol. 7, nos. 2-3, 1976, pp. 13-14.

Kliatt, September, 1989, p. 33.

Library Journal, June 15, 1975, Elizabeth A. Teo, review of *No Chinese Stranger,* pp. 1211-1212.

MELUS, fall, 1979, pp. 51-71; spring, 1982, Kathleen Loh Swee Yin and Kristoffer F. Paulson, "The Divided Voice of Chinese-American Narration: Jade Snow Wong's *Fifth Chinese Daughter,"* pp. 53-59.

New Yorker, October 7, 1950, review of *Fifth Chinese Daughter,* p. 118.

New York Herald Tribune Book Review, September 24, 1950.

New York Times Book Review, October 29, 1950, p. 27.

Publishers Weekly, April 21, 1975, Barbara A. Bannon, review of *No Chinese Stranger,* p. 45.*

* * *

WRIGHT, J. B.
See BARKAN, Joanne

Y-Z

YOLEN, Jane (Hyatt) 1939- (Jane H. Yolen)

PERSONAL: Married name Jane Yolen Stemple; born February 11, 1939, in New York, NY; daughter of Will Hyatt (an author and publicist) and Isabelle (a social worker, puzzle-maker, and homemaker; maiden name, Berlin) Yolen; married David W. Stemple (a retired professor of computer science and ornithologist), September 2, 1962; children: Heidi Elisabet, Adam Douglas, Jason Frederic. *Education:* Smith College, B.A., 1960; University of Massachusetts, M.Ed., 1976; also completed course work for doctorate in children's literature at the University of Massachusetts. *Politics:* Liberal Democrat. *Religion:* Jewish/Quaker. *Avocational interests:* "Folk music and dancing, reading, camping, politics, all things Scottish."

ADDRESSES: Home—Phoenix Farm, 31 School Street, Box 27, Hatfield, MA 01038, and Wayside, 96 Hepburn Gardens, St. Andrews, Fife, Scotland KY16 9LN. *Agent*—Marilyn Marlow, Curtis Brown Ltd., 10 Astor Place, New York, NY 10003.

CAREER: Saturday Review, New York City, production assistant, 1960-61; Gold Medal Books (publishers), New York City, assistant editor, 1961-62; Rutledge Books (publishers), New York City, associate editor, 1962-63; Alfred A. Knopf, Inc. (publishers), New York City, assistant juvenile editor, 1963-65; full-time professional writer, 1965—. Editor of imprint, Jane Yolen Books, for Harcourt Brace Jovanovich, 1988-98. Teacher of writing and lecturer, 1966—; has taught children's literature at Smith College. Chairman of board of library trustees, Hatfield, MA, 1976-83; member of Arts Council, Hatfield.

MEMBER: International Kitefliers Association, Society of Children's Book Writers (member of board of directors, 1974—), Science Fiction Writers of America (president, 1986-88), Children's Literature Association (member of board of directors, 1977-79), Science Fiction Poetry Association, National Association for the Preservation and Perpetuation of Storytelling, Western New England Storyteller's Guild (founder), Bay State Writers Guild, Western Massachusetts Illustrators Guild (founder), Smith College Alumnae Association.

AWARDS, HONORS: Boys' Club of America Junior Book Award, 1968, for *The Minstrel and the Mountain;* Lewis Carroll Shelf Award, 1968, for *The Emperor and the Kite,* and 1973, for *The Girl Who Loved the Wind;* Best Books of the Year selection, *New York Times,* 1968, for *The Emperor Flies a Kite; World on a String: The Story of Kites* was named an American Library Association (ALA) Notable Book, 1968; Children's Book Showcase of the Children's Book Council citations, 1973, for *The Girl Who Loved the Wind,* and 1976, for *The Little Spotted Fish;* Golden Kite Award, Society of Children's Book Writers, 1974, ALA Notable Book, 1975, and National Book Award nomination, 1975, all for *The Girl Who Cried Flowers and Other Tales;* Golden Kite Honor Book, 1975, for *The Transfigured Hart,* and 1976, for *The Moon Ribbon and Other* Tales; Christopher Medal, 1978, for *The Seeing Stick.*

Children's Choice from the International Reading Association and the Children's Book Council, 1980, for *Mice on Ice,* and 1983, for *Dragon's Blood;* Parents' Choice Awards, Parents' Choice Foundation, 1982, for *Dragon's Blood,* 1984, for *The Stone Silenus,* and 1989, for *Piggins* and *The Three Bears Rhyme Book; School Library Journal* Best Books for Young Adults citations, 1982, for *The Gift of Sarah Barker,* and 1985, for *Heart's Blood;* Garden State Children's Book Award, New Jersey Library Association, 1983, for *Commander*

Toad in Space; CRABbery Award from Acton Public Library (MD), 1983, for *Dragon's Blood; Heart's Blood* was selected one of ALA's Best Books for Young Adults, 1984; Mythopoeic Society's Fantasy Award, 1984, for *Cards of Grief; The Lullaby Songbook* and *The Sleeping Beauty* were each selected one of Child Study Association of America's Children's Books of the Year, 1987; World Fantasy Award, 1988, for *Favorite Folktales from around the World;* Parents' Choice Silver Seal Award, Jewish Book Council Award, Association of Jewish Libraries Award, all 1988, Judy Lopez Honor Book, Nebula Award finalist, both 1989, and Maude Haude Lovlace Award, 1996, all for *The Devil's Arithmetic;* Golden Sower Award from the Nebraska Library Association, 1989, and Charlotte Award from New York State Reading Association, both for *Piggins.* Yolen has received several awards for her body of work, including the Chandler Book Talk Reward of Merit, 1970; LL.D. from College of Our Lady of the Elms, Chicopee, MA, 1981; Daedelus Award, 1986, for her fantasy and short fiction; Kerlan Award for "singular achievements in the creation of children's literature," 1988; Smith College Medal, 1990; Skylark Award, New England Science Fiction Association, 1990; the Regina Medal for her body of writing in children's literature, 1992; the Keen State Children's Book Award, 1998; Literary Light Award, Boston Library, 1998; and the Anna V. Zarrow Award, 1999. Thirteen of Yolen's books have been selected by the Junior Literary Guild. In addition, *The Emperor and the Kite* was named a Caldecott Medal Honor Book, 1968, for its illustrations by Ed Young, and *Owl Moon* received the Caldecott Medal, 1988, for its illustrations by John Schoenherr.

WRITINGS:

FOR CHILDREN; PICTURE BOOKS AND FICTION

The Witch Who Wasn't, illustrated by Arnold Roth, Macmillan, 1964.

Gwinellen, the Princess Who Could Not Sleep, illustrated by Ed Renfro, Macmillan, 1965.

The Emperor and the Kite, illustrated by Ed Young, World Publishing (Cleveland, OH), 1967, Philomel, 1988.

The Minstrel and the Mountain: A Tale of Peace, illustrated by Anne Rockwell, World Publishing, 1967.

Isabel's Noel, illustrated by Roth, Funk and Wagnalls (New York), 1967.

Greyling: A Picture Story from the Islands of Shetland, illustrated by William Stobbs, World Publishing, 1968, illustrated by David Ray, Philomel, 1991.

The Longest Name on the Block, illustrated by Peter Madden, Funk and Wagnalls, 1968.

The Wizard of Washington Square, illustrated by Ray Cruz, World Publishing, 1969.

The Inway Investigators; or, The Mystery at McCracken's Place, illustrated by Allan Eitzen, Seabury (New York), 1969.

Hobo Toad and the Motorcycle Gang, illustrated by Emily McCully, World Publishing, 1970.

The Seventh Mandarin, illustrated by Young, Seabury, 1970.

The Bird of Time, illustrated by Mercer Mayer, Crowell (New York), 1971.

The Girl Who Loved the Wind, illustrated by Young, Crowell, 1972.

The Girl Who Cried Flowers and Other Tales, illustrated by David Palladini, Crowell, 1974.

The Boy Who Had Wings, illustrated by Helga Aichinger, Crowell, 1974.

The Adventures of Eeka Mouse, illustrated by Myra McKee, Xerox Education Publications (Middletown, CT), 1974.

The Rainbow Rider, illustrated by Michael Foreman, Crowell, 1974.

The Little Spotted Fish, illustrated by Friso Henstra, Seabury, 1975.

The Transfigured Hart, illustrated by Donna Diamond, Crowell, 1975, Magic Carpet Books/Harcourt, 1997.

Milkweed Days, photographs by Gabriel Amadeus Cooney, Crowell, 1976.

The Moon Ribbon and Other Tales, illustrated by Palladini, Crowell, 1976.

The Seeing Stick, illustrated by Remy Charlip and Demetra Maraslis, Crowell, 1977.

The Sultan's Perfect Tree, illustrated by Barbara Garrison, *Parents'* Magazine Press (New York), 1977.

The Hundredth Dove and Other Tales, illustrated by Palladini, Crowell, 1977.

Hannah Dreaming, photographs by Alan R. Epstein, Museum of Fine Art (Springfield, MA), 1977.

The Lady and the Merman, illustrated by Barry Moser, Pennyroyal, 1977.

Spider Jane, illustrated by Stefan Bernath, Coward, 1978.

The Simple Prince, illustrated by Jack Kent, *Parents'* Magazine Press, 1978.

No Bath Tonight, illustrated by Nancy Winslow Parker, Crowell, 1978.

The Mermaid's Three Wisdoms, illustrated by Laura Rader, Collins (New York), 1978.

Dream Weaver and Other Tales, illustrated by Michael Hague, Collins, 1979, reissued as *Dream Weaver,* 1989.

Spider Jane on the Move, illustrated by Bernath, Coward, 1980.

Mice on Ice, illustrated by Lawrence DiFiori, Dutton, 1980.

Shirlick Holmes and the Case of the Wandering Wardrobe, illustrated by Anthony Rao, Coward, 1981.

The Acorn Quest, illustrated by Susanna Natti, Harper, 1981.

Brothers of the Wind, illustrated by Barbara Berger, Philomel, 1981.

Sleeping Ugly, illustrated by Diane Stanley, Coward, 1981.

The Boy Who Spoke Chimp, illustrated by David Wiesner, Knopf, 1981.

Uncle Lemon's Spring, illustrated by Glen Rounds, Dutton, 1981.

Owl Moon, illustrated by John Schoenherr, Philomel (New York), 1987.

(Reteller) *The Sleeping Beauty,* illustrated by Ruth Sanderson, Knopf, 1986.

Dove Isabeau, illustrated by Dennis Nolan, Harcourt, 1989.

Baby Bear's Bedtime Book, illustrated by Dyer, Harcourt, 1990.

Sky Dogs, illustrated by Barry Moser, Harcourt, 1990.

(Reteller) *Tam Lin: An Old Ballad,* illustrated by Mikolaycak, Harcourt, 1990.

Elfabet: An ABC of Elves, illustrated by Lauren Mills, Little, Brown, 1990.

Letting Swift River Go, illustrated by Barbara Cooney, Little, Brown, 1990.

The Dragon's Boy, Harper, 1990.

Wizard's Hall, Harcourt, 1991.

Hark! A Christmas Sampler, illustrated by Tomie dePaola, music by Adam Stemple, Putnam, 1991.

(Reteller) *Wings,* Harcourt, 1991.

All Those Secrets of the World (autobiographical fiction), illustrated by Leslie Baker, Little, Brown, 1991.

Encounter, illustrated by David Shannon, Harcourt, 1992.

Mouse's Birthday, illustrated by Degen, Putnam, 1993.

Hands, illustrated by Chi Chung, Sundance Publishing, 1993, also published as *Hands: Big Book,* 1993.

Beneath the Ghost Moon, illustrated by Laurel Molk, Little, Brown, 1994.

Honkers, illustrated by Leslie Baker, Little, Brown, 1993.

Travelers Rose, Putnam, 1993.

Grandad Bill's Song, illustrated by Melissa Bay Mathis, Philomel, 1994.

And Twelve Chinese Acrobats (autobiographical fiction), illustrated by Jean Gralley, Philomel, 1994.

Good Griselle, illustrated by David Christiana, Harcourt, 1994.

The Girl in the Golden Bower, illustrated by Dyer, Little, Brown, 1994.

Old Dame Counterpane, illustrated by Ruth Tietjen Councell, Putnam, 1994.

(Reteller) *Little Mouse and Elephant: A Tale from Turkey,* illustrated by John Segal, Simon & Schuster, 1994.

(Reteller) *The Musicians of Bremen: A Tale from Germany,* illustrated by Segal, Simon & Schuster, 1994.

The Ballad of the Pirate Queen, illustrated by Shannon, Harcourt, 1995.

Before the Storm, illustrated by Georgia Pugh, Boyds Mills Press, 1995.

(Reteller) *A Sip of Aesop,* illustrated by Karen Barbour, Blue Sky Press, 1995.

Merlin and the Dragons, illustrated by Ming Li, Dutton, 1995.

The Wild Hunt, illustrated by Francisco Mora, Harcourt, 1995.

(With daughter Heidi E. Y. Stemple) *Meet the Monsters,* illustrated by Patricia Ludlow, Walker, 1996.

Nocturne, illustrated by Anne Hunter, Harcourt, 1997.

Child of Faerie, Child of Earth, illustrated by Dyer, Little, Brown, 1997.

Miz Berlin Walks, illustrated by Floyd Cooper, Philomel, 1997.

(Reteller) *Once upon a Bedtime Story: Classic Tales,* illustrated by Councell, 1997.

The Sea Man, illustrated by Christopher Denise, Putnam, 1997.

Twelve Impossible Things Before Breakfast (short stories), Harcourt, 1997.

House, House, illustrated with photographs by the Howes Brothers and Jason Stemple, Marshall Cavendish (New York), 1998.

King Long Shanks, illustrated by Victoria Chess, Harcourt, 1998.

(Reteller) *Pegasus, the Flying Horse,* illustrated by Ming, Dutton, 1998.

Raising Yoder's Barn, illustrated by Bernie Fuchs, Little, Brown, 1998.

(Reteller) *Prince of Egypt,* Dutton, 1998.

(With Heidi E. Y. Stemple) *Mary Celeste: An Unsolved Mystery from History,* illustrated by Roger Roth, Simon & Schuster, 1999.

Moonball, illustrated by Greg Couch, Simon & Schuster, 1999.

Dinosaurs Say Goodnight, illustrated by Mark Teague, Blue Sky Press, 2000.

Off We Go! illustrated by Laurel Molk, Little, Brown, 2000.

The Book of Fairy Holidays, illustrated by Christiana, Blue Sky Press (New York), in press.
Harvest Home, illustrated by Greg Shed, Harcourt, in press.
(Compiler with Linda Mannheim) *Stretching the Truth,* illustrated by Kevin Hawkes, Blue Sky Press, in press.

"GIANTS" SERIES; PICTURE BOOKS, ILLUSTRATED BY TOMIE DePAOLA, PUBLISHED BY SEABURY

The Giants' Farm, 1977.
The Giants Go Camping, 1979.

"COMMANDER TOAD" SERIES; FICTION, ILLUSTRATED BY BRUCE DEGEN

Commander Toad in Space, Coward, 1980.
Commander Toad and the Planet of the Grapes, Coward, 1982.
Commander Toad and the Big Black Hole, Coward, 1983.
Commander Toad and the Dis-Asteroid, Coward, 1985.
Commander Toad and the Intergalactic Spy, Coward, 1986.
Commander Toad and the Space Pirates, Putnam, 1987.
Commander Toad and the Voyage Home, Putnam, 1998.

"ROBOT AND REBECCA" SERIES; FICTION

The Robot and Rebecca: The Mystery of the Code-Carrying Kids, illustrated by Jurg Obrist, Knopf, 1980, student book club edition illustrated by Catherine Deeter, Random House, 1980.
The Robot and Rebecca and the Missing Owser, illustrated by Lady McCrady, Knopf, 1981.

"PIGGINS" SERIES; PICTURE BOOKS, ILLUSTRATED BY JANE DYER, PUBLISHED BY HARCOURT

Piggins, 1987.
Picnic with Piggins, 1988.
Piggins and the Royal Wedding, 1988.

"MOLE" SERIES; FICTION, ILLUSTRATED BY KATHRYN BROWN, PUBLISHED BY HARCOURT

Eeny, Meeny, Miney Mole, 1992.
Eeny Up Above, in press.

"YOUNG MERLIN" SERIES; FICTION, PUBLISHED BY HARCOURT

Passager, 1996.
Hobby, 1996.
Merlin, 1997.

"TARTAN MAGIC" SERIES; FICTION, PUBLISHED BY HARCOURT

The Wizard's Map, 1998.
The Pictish Child, 1999.

FOR CHILDREN; NONFICTION

Pirates in Petticoats, illustrated by Leonard Vosburgh, McKay, 1963.
World on a String: The Story of Kites, World Publishing, 1968.
Friend: The Story of George Fox and the Quakers, Seabury, 1972.
(Editor with Barbara Green) *The Fireside Song Book of Birds and Beasts,* illustrated by Peter Parnall, Simon & Schuster, 1972.
The Wizard Islands, illustrated by Robert Quackenbush, Crowell, 1973.
Ring Out! A Book of Bells, illustrated by Richard Cuffari, Seabury, 1974.
Simple Gifts: The Story of the Shakers, illustrated by Betty Fraser, Viking, 1976.
(Compiler) *Rounds about Rounds,* music by Barbara Green, illustrated by Gail Gibbons, Watts (New York), 1977.
The Lap-Time Song and Play Book, musical arrangements by son Adam Stemple, illustrated by Margot Tomes, Harcourt, 1989.
A Letter from Phoenix Farm (autobiography), illustrated with photographs by son Jason Stemple, Richard C. Owen (Katonah, NY), 1992.
Jane Yolen's Songs of Summer, musical arrangements by Adam Stemple, illustrated by Cyd Moore, Boyds Mills Press, 1993.
Welcome to the Green House, illustrated by Laura Regan, Putnam, 1993.
Jane Yolen's Old MacDonald Songbook, illustrated by Rosekrans Hoffman, Boyds Mills Press, 1994.
Sing Noel, musical arrangements by Stemple, illustrated by Nancy Carpenter, Boyds Mills Press, 1996.
Milk and Honey: A Year of Jewish Holidays, illustrations by Louise August, musical arrangements by Stemple, Putnam, 1996.
Welcome to the Sea of Sand, illustrated by Laura Regan, Putnam, 1996.

Welcome to the Ice House, illustrated by Regan, Putnam, 1998.

Tea with an Old Dragon: A Story of Sophia Smith, Founder of Smith College, illustrated by Monica Vachula, Boyds Mills Press, 1998.

FOR CHILDREN; POETRY

See This Little Line?, illustrated by Kathleen Elgin, McKay (New York), 1963.

It All Depends, illustrated by Don Bolognese, Funk and Wagnalls, 1970.

An Invitation to the Butterfly Ball: A Counting Rhyme, illustrated by Jane Breskin Zalben, *Parents'* Magazine Press, 1976.

All in the Woodland Early: An ABC Book, illustrated by Zalben, Collins, 1979, Caroline House (Honesdale, PA), 1991.

How Beastly!: A Menagerie of Nonsense Poems, illustrated by James Marshall, Philomel, 1980.

Dragon Night and Other Lullabies, illustrated by Demi, Methuen (New York), 1980.

(Editor) *The Lullaby Songbook,* musical arrangements by Adam Stemple, illustrated by Charles Mikolaycak, Harcourt, 1986.

Ring of Earth: A Child's Book of Seasons, illustrated by John Wallner, Harcourt, 1986.

The Three Bears Rhyme Book, illustrated by Dyer, Harcourt, 1987.

Best Witches: Poems for Halloween, illustrated by Elise Primavera, Putnam, 1989.

Bird Watch, illustrated by Ted Lewin, Philomel, 1990.

Dinosaur Dances, illustrated by Degen, Putnam, 1990.

An Invitation to the Butterfly Ball: A Counting Rhyme, illustrated by Jane Breskin Zalben, Caroline House, 1991.

(Compiler) *Street Rhymes around the World,* illustrated by seventeen artists, Wordsong (Honesdale, PA), 1992.

Jane Yolen's Mother Goose Songbook, musical arrangements by Stemple, illustrated by Rosecrans Hoffman, Boyds Mill Press, 1992.

(Compiler) *Weather Report,* illustrated by Annie Gusman, Boyds Mills Press, 1993.

Mouse's Birthday, illustrated by Degen, Putnam, 1993.

Raining Cats and Dogs, illustrated by Janet Street, Harcourt, 1993.

What Rhymes with Moon?, illustrated by Councell, Philomel, 1993.

(Editor) *Sleep Rhymes Around the World,* illustrated by seventeen artists, Boyds Mills Press, 1993.

(Compiler and contributor) *Alphabestiary: Animal Poems from A to Z,* illustrated by Allan Eitzen, Boyds Mills Press, 1994.

Sacred Places, illustrated by David Shannon, Harcourt, 1994.

Animal Fare: Zoological Nonsense Poems, illustrated by Street, Harcourt, 1994.

The Three Bears Holiday Rhyme Book, illustrated by Dyer, Harcourt, 1995.

Water Music: Poems for Children, illustrated with photographs by Jason Stemple, Boyds Mills Press, 1995.

(Compiler) *Mother Earth, Father Sky: Poems of Our Planet,* illustrated by Jennifer Hewitson, Boyds Mills Press, 1996.

O Jerusalem, illustrated by John Thompson, Scholastic, 1996.

Sea Watch: A Book of Poetry, illustrated by Lewin, Putnam, 1996.

(Compiler and contributor) *Sky Scrape/City Scape: Poems of City Life,* illustrated by Ken Condon, Boyds Mills Press, 1996.

(Compiler) *Once upon Ice and Other Frozen Poems,* illustrated with photographs by Stemple, Boyds Mills Press, 1997.

Snow, Snow: Winter Poems for Children, illustrated with photographs by Stemple, Wordsong (Honesdale, PA), 1998.

The Originals: Animals That Time Forgot, illustrated by Lewin, Philomel, 1998.

FOR YOUNG ADULTS; FICTION

(With Anne Huston) *Trust a City Kid,* illustrated by J. C. Kocsis, Lothrop, 1966.

(Editor) *Zoo 2000: Twelve Stories of Science Fiction and Fantasy Beasts,* Seabury, 1973.

The Magic Three of Solatia, illustrated by Julia Noonan, Crowell, 1974.

(Editor and contributor) *Shape Shifters: Fantasy and Science Fiction Tales about Humans Who Can Change Their Shape,* Seabury, 1978.

The Gift of Sarah Barker, Viking, 1981.

Neptune Rising: Songs and Tales of the Undersea Folk (story collection), illustrated by Wiesner, Philomel, 1982.

The Stone Silenus, Philomel, 1984.

Children of the Wolf, Viking, 1984.

(Editor and contributor with Martin H. Greenberg and Charles G. Waugh) *Dragons and Dreams,* Harper, 1986.

(Editor and contributor with Greenberg and Waugh) *Spaceships and Spells,* Harper, 1987.

The Devil's Arithmetic, Viking, 1988.

(Editor and contributor with Martin H. Greenberg) *Werewolves: A Collection of Original Stories,* Harper, 1988.

The Faery Flag: Stories and Poems of Fantasy and the Supernatural, Orchard Books (New York), 1989.
(Editor and contributor with Greenberg) *Things That Go Bump in the Night,* Harper, 1989.
(Editor and contributor) *2041 AD: Twelve Stories about the Future by Top Science Fiction Writers* (anthology), Delacorte, 1990, reprinted as *2041,* Delacorte, 1991.
(Editor and contributor with Greenberg) *Vampires,* HarperCollins, 1991.
Here There Be Dragons (original stories and poetry), illustrated by David Wilgus, Harcourt, 1993.
Here There Be Unicorns (stories and poetry), illustrated by Wilgus, Harcourt, 1994.
Here There Be Witches (stories and poetry), illustrated by Wilgus, Harcourt, 1995.
(Editor and contributor) *Camelot: A Collection of Original Arthurian Tales,* illustrated by Winslow Pels, Putnam, 1995.
(Editor with Greenberg and contributor) *The Haunted House: A Collection of Original Stories,* illustrated by Doron Ben-Ami, HarperCollins, 1995.
Here There Be Angels (stories and poetry), illustrated by Wilgus, Harcourt, 1996.
Here There Be Ghosts (stories and poetry), illustrated by Wilgus, Harcourt, 1998.
(With Bruce Coville) *Armageddon Summer,* Harcourt, 1998.

"PIT DRAGON" SERIES; FICTION

Dragon's Blood: A Fantasy, Delacorte, 1982.
Heart's Blood, Delacorte, 1984.
A Sending of Dragons, illustrated by Tom McKeveny, Delacorte, 1987.

FOR ADULTS; FICTION

Tales of Wonder (short stories), Schocken (New York City), 1983.
Cards of Grief (science fiction), Ace Books, 1984.
Merlin's Booke (short stories), illustrated by Thomas Canty, Ace Books, 1982.
Dragonfield and Other Stories (story collection), Ace Books, 1985.
(Editor) *Favorite Folktales from around the World,* Pantheon, 1986.
Sword and the Stone, Pulphouse (Eugene, OR), 1991.
Briar Rose, Tor Books, 1992.
Storyteller, New England Science Fiction Association Press (Cambridge, MA), 1992, boxed edition illustrated by Merle Insinga.
(Editor and contributor with Greenberg) *Xanadu,* Tor Books, 1993.
(Editor and contributor with Greenberg) *Xanadu Two,* Tor Books, 1994.
(Editor and contributor with Greenberg) *Xanadu Three,* Tor Books, 1995.
The Books of Great Alta, St. Martin's Press (New York City), 1997.
(Editor) *Gray Heroes: Elder Tales from around the World,* Viking Penguin, 1998.
Not One Damsel in Distress, Harcourt, 2000.
(With daughter Heidi E. L. Stemple) *Mirror, Mirror,* Viking, 2000.
(Editor and contributor) *Sherwood: A Collection of Original Robin Hood Stories,* illustrated by Dennis Nolan, Philomel, 2000.
(With Robert J. Harris) *Queen's Own Fool,* Philomel, 2000.

"WHITE JENNA" SERIES; FICTION

Sister Light, Sister Dark, Tor Books, 1988.
White Jenna, Tor Books, 1989.
The One-armed Queen, with music by son Adam Stemple, Tor Books, 1998.

FOR ADULTS; NONFICTION

Writing Books for Children, The Writer (Boston), 1973, revised edition, 1983.
Touch Magic: Fantasy, Faerie and Folklore in the Literature of Childhood, Philomel, 1981, revised edition, August House, 2000.
Guide to Writing for Children, Writer, 1989.
(With Nancy Willard) *Among Angels* (poetry), illustrated by S. Saelig Gallagher, Harcourt, 1995.

OTHER

Also author of the play *Robin Hood,* a musical with music by Barbara Greene first produced in Boston, MA, 1967, and of the chapbook *The Whitethorn Wood.* Ghostwriter of a number of books for Rutledge Press that were distributed by other publishing houses, including *One, Two, Buckle My Shoe,* a counting rhyme book published by Doubleday, and a series of activity books. Editor of *A Plague of Sorcerers* by Mary Frances Zambreno, *Appleblossom* by Shulamith L. Oppenheim, *Jeremy Thatcher, Dragon Hatcher* by Bruce Coville, *The Jewel of Life* by Anna Kirwan-Vogel, *The Patchwork Lady* by Mary K. Whittington, *The Red Ball* by Joanna Yardley, all Harcourt, 1991. Contributor to many books, including *Dragons of Light,* edited by Orson Scott Card, Ace Books, 1981; *Elsewhere,* edited by Terri Windling and Mark Alan Arnold, Ace Books, Volume 1, 1981, Volume 2, 1982; *Hecate's Cauldron,* edited by Susan Schwartz, DAW Books, 1982; *Heroic Visions,* edited by Jessica Amanda Salmonson, Ace Books, 1983; *Faery!,* edited by Windling, Ace Books, 1985; *Liavek,* edited by Will Shetterly and Emma Bull, Ace Books, 1985; *Moonsinger's Friends,* edited by Schwartz, Bluejay, 1985; *Imaginary Lands,* edited by Robin McKinley, Greenwillow, 1985; *Don't Bet on the Prince: Contemporary Feminist Fairy Tales in North America and England,* by Jack Zipes, Methuen, 1986; *Liavek: Players of Luck,* edited by Shetterly and Bull, Ace Books, 1986; *Liavek: Wizard's Row,* edited by Shetterly and Bull, Ace Books, 1987; *Visions,* by Donald R. Gallo, Delacorte, 1987; *Liavek: Spells of Binding,* edited by Shetterly and Bull, Ace Books, 1988; *Invitation to Camelot,* by Parke Godwin, Ace Books, 1988; and *The Unicorn Treasury,* by Bruce Coville, Doubleday, 1988, and dozens more. Author of introduction for *Cut from the Same Cloth: American Women of Myth, Legend, and Tall Tale,* collected and told by Robert D. San Souci, Philomel, 1993; *Best-Loved Stories Told at the National Storytelling Festival,* National Storytelling Association, 1996; and *Fearless Girls, Wise Women, and Beloved Sisters: Heroines in Folktales from around the World* by Kathleen Ragan, Norton, 1998. Yolen has also written songs and lyrics for folksingers, some of which have been recorded. Her papers are housed at the Kerlan Collection, University of Minnesota.

Author of column "Children's Bookfare" for *Daily Hampshire Gazette* during the 1970s. Contributor of articles, reviews, poems, and short stories to periodicals, including *Chicago Jewish Forum, Horn Book, Isaac Asimov's Science Fiction Magazine, Language Arts, Los Angeles Times, Magazine of Fantasy and Science Fiction, New Advocate, New York Times, Parabola, Parents' Choice, Washington Post Book World, Wilson Library Bulletin,* and *Writer.* Member of editorial board, *Advocate* (now *New Advocate*) and *National Storytelling Journal,* until 1989. Some of Yolen's books have been published in Australia, Austria, Brazil, Denmark, England, France, Germany, Japan, South Africa, Spain, and Sweden. Also writes as Jane H. Yoden.

ADAPTATIONS: The Seventh Mandarin was produced as a motion picture by Xerox Films, 1973; *The Emperor and the Kite* was produced as a filmstrip with cassette by Listening Library, 1976; *The Bird of Time* was adapted into a play and was first produced in Northampton, MA, 1982; *The Girl Who Cried Flowers and Other Tales* was released on audio cassette by Weston Woods, 1983; *Dragon's Blood* was produced as an animated television movie by Columbia Broadcasting System (CBS), 1985, and shown on *CBS Storybreak; Commander Toad in Space* was released on audio cassette by Listening Library, 1986; *Touch Magic . . . Pass It On,* a selection of Yolen's short stories, was released on audio cassette by Weston Woods, 1987; *Owl Moon* was produced as a filmstrip with cassette by Weston Woods, 1988, and as both a read-along cassette, 1990, and a video; *Owl Moon* was also adapted as part of the video *Owl Moon and Other Stories* produced by Children's Circle; *Piggins and Picnic with Piggins* was released on audio cassette by Caedmon, 1988; *Best of Science Fiction and Fantasy* was released on audio cassette by NewStar Media, 1991; *Merlin and the Dragons* was released on audio cassette by Lightyear Entertainment, 1991, was produced as a video by Coronet, 1991, and was released as *What's a Good Story? Merlin and the Dragon* with commentary by Yolen; *Greyling* was released on audio cassette by Spoken Arts, 1993; *Hands* was released on audio cassette by Sundance Publishing, 1993; Beneath the Ghost Moon was produced as a video by Spoken Arts, 1996; *Wizard's Hall* was released on audio cassette by "Words Take Wines," narrated by Yolen, 1997. Recorded Books has also issued audio cassettes of three of Yolen's books: *Briar Rose, The Devil's Arithmetic,* and *Good Griselle.* Yolen is the subject of the audio cassette *The Children's Writer at Work—Jane Yolen,* produced by Real Life Productions; in addition, she is the subject of the videos *Good Conversation: A Talk with Jane Yolen,* produced by Weston Woods, and *The Children's Writer at Work,* produced by Reel Life, 1997.

WORK IN PROGRESS: Many Mansions, a novel; *The Sword of the Rightful King,* a novel; *Books and the Seven Leagues,* a novel; *Wild Wings,* a book of poetry; several screenplays.

SIDELIGHTS: Dubbed "the American Hans Christian Andersen" by editor/publisher Ann K. Beneduce and "a modern equivalent of Aesop" by Noel Perrin in the *New York Times Book Review,* Jane Yolen is considered a gifted, versatile author who has developed a stellar reputation as a fantasist while contributing successfully to many other genres. An exceptionally prolific writer, she is the creator of approximately three hundred books for children and young adults and approximately twenty-five for adults. Yolen has written fiction for young adults and adults as well as poetry, criticism, and books on the art of writing and the genre of fantasy for an adult audience. She has also edited and compiled a number of works for both younger and older readers and has also contributed to several collections and anthologies. As a writer of juvenile literature, Yolen addresses her books to an audience ranging from preschool through high school and has written works ranging from picture books and easy readers to young adult novels. She is the creator of realistic fiction, mysteries, verse, animal tales, concept books, historical fiction, humorous stories, and lyrical prose poems, as well as informational books on such subjects as kites, bells, the Shakers, the Quakers, and the environment. Several of Yolen's books have been published in series, and she is particularly well known for the "Pit Dragon" series of young adult fantasy novels in which she created a mythological world based around cockfighting dragons on an arid planet. A folksinger and storyteller, Yolen has created several works that reflect her love of music and oral folklore, including compilations of international songs, rhymes, and stories. Several of the author's books are autobiographical or incorporate elements from her life or the lives of her family, and her three children all contribute to her works—daughter Heidi as a writer and sons Adam and Jason as a musical arranger and photographer, respectively. Yolen has also worked with a number of outstanding illustrators such as Mercer Mayer, Michael Foreman, Barbara Cooney, Michael Hague, Glen Rounds, Nancy Winslow Parker, Barry Moser, Charles Mikolaycak, Demi, Tomie dePaola, Jane Dyer, David Wiesner, Bruce Degen, Victoria Chess, James Marshall, and Ted Lewin. In addition, two of Yolen's books have received prizes from the Caldecott Medal committee: *Owl Moon* won the Caldecott Medal for its illustrations by John Schoenherr while *The Emperor and the Kite* was named a Caldecott honor book for its illustrations by Ed Young.

Yolen is perhaps best known as a writer of original folk and fairy tales and fables with a strong moral core. She has received special recognition for her literary fairy tales, works in the tradition of Oscar Wilde and Laurence Houseman that combine familiar fantasy motifs with contemporary elements and philosophical themes. As a fantasist, Yolen is noted for creating elegant, eloquent tales with deep psychological insights that evoke a timeless sense of wonder while having relevance to contemporary life. She includes figures such as dragons, unicorns, witches, and mermaids as characters, and her stories often revolve around shape-shifters, animals who have the ability to transform into humans or humans into animals. As a writer, Yolen invests her works with images, symbols, and allusions as well as with wordplay—especially puns—and metaphors. She is considered an exceptional prose stylist whose fluid, musical writing is both polished and easy to read aloud. As a writer of nonfiction, the author is credited for capturing the spirit of her subjects as well as for the enthusiasm with which she invests her books. Although her fiction is occasionally criticized for unlikely plots and sketchy characterizations and her fairy tales are sometimes considered too mannered, Yolen is generally praised as a writer of consistent quality whose books are evocative, moving, and enjoyable. Peter D. Sieruta of *Children's Books and Their Creators* stated: "With a confident writing style and inexhaustible imagination, Jane Yolen has proven herself one of the most prolific and diverse creators in the field of children's literature." In her entry in *Twentieth-Century Children's Writers,* Marcia G. Fuchs commented: "Faerie, fiction, fact, or horrible fantasy, Yolen's lyrical and magical tales are indeed tales to read and to listen to, to share, to remember, and to pass on." Jane Langton, herself a noted writer of fantasy, stated in the *New York Times Book Review* that Yolen's fables "are told with sober strength and native wit. They are simple and perfect, without a word too much." Writing in *Teaching and Learning Literature,* Lee Bennett Hopkins toasted the author: "May the pen of Yolen never run dry. The world of children's literature has been, and will continue to be, richer for her vast talents."

Writing in the *Fourth Book of Junior Authors and Illustrators (FBJAI),* Yolen said, "I come from a long line of storytellers. My great-grandfather was the Reb, the storyteller in a small village in Finno-Russia, my father an author, my mother a mostly unpublished writer." Born in New York City, Yolen is the daughter of Will Hyatt Yolen, a writer, newspaperman, and publicist who was an international kite-flying champion, and Isabelle Berlin Yolen, a social worker whose crossword puzzles appeared in children's magazines. Yolen once remarked for *CA:* "My father's family were merchants and storytellers (some called them well-off liars!). My mother's family were intellectuals. I seem to have gotten a bit of both, though not enough of either." Yolen's father publicized the sport of kite flying so successfully that, according to his daughter in *CA,* he "forced a renaissance in kiting that is still going on"; in 1968, Yolen published *World on a String: The Story of Kites,* a well-received informational book about the subject. The author's mother quit her job as a social worker in order to raise Jane and her younger brother, Steven; in her free time, Isabelle Yolen wrote short stories and created crossword puzzles and double acrostics. Jane spent most of her childhood in New York City. She also spent summers in Virginia, the birthplace of her mother, and lived for a year and a half in California, where her father did publicity for Warner Brothers.

Yolen told *CA,* "I was a writer from the time I learned to write." An early reader as well as a tomboy, Yolen played games in Central Park while being encouraged in her reading and writing by her teachers. "I was," she recalled "the gold star star. And I was also pretty impossibly full of myself. In first or second grade, I wrote the school musical, lyrics and music, in which everyone was some kind of vegetable. I played the lead carrot. Our finale was a salad. Another gold star." Yolen wrote in *FBJAI,* "[I]f I had to point to my primary source of inspiration, it would be to the folk culture. My earliest readings were the folk tales and fairy stories I took home from the library by the dozens. Even when I was old enough to make the trip across Central Park by myself, I was still not too old for those folk fantasies." Yolen once told *CA* that she read "all the Andrew Lang fairy books as a child and any kind of fairy stories I could get my hands on. I vividly remember *Treasure Island* and the Louisa May Alcott books. All of the Alcott books, *Jo's Boys,* and even the Alcott books that nobody else had heard of, became part of my adolescent reading. I read *The Wind in the Willows* and the Mowgli stories. We didn't have 'young adult' fiction, so I skipped right into adult books which tended to be very morose Russian novels—my Dostoevsky phase—then I got hooked on Joseph Conrad. Adventure novels or lugubrious emotional books are what I preferred. Then I went back into my fairy tale and fantasy stage. Tolkien and C. S. Lewis, metaphysical and folkloric fantasy." In a transcript of a speech in *Judaica Librarianship,* Yolen commented that she was raised "on tales of King Arthur and Robin Hood. I was a fanatical reader of fantasy and magic, history and adventure." She also began to develop her musical abilities, singing with a friend and earning enough money by passing the hat to buy sodas and ice cream. In sixth grade, Yolen was accepted by Hunter, a girls' school for what were called "intelligently gifted" students. The author said: "With my gold stars and my writing ability, I expected to be a superior gift to Hunter. To my surprise—and horror—I was barely in the middle of my class and managed to stay there by studying extremely hard."

While at Hunter, Yolen wrote in *CA,* "[m]usic became a mainstay in my life." Her father, who sang and played the guitar, introduced Yolen to folk songs. She wrote in *FBJAI:* "I went him some better in learning every old English, Scottish, Irish, and Appalachian love song and ballad I ever heard." Yolen starred as Hansel in the school production of Engelbert Humperdinck's opera *Hansel and Gretel,* played the piano, and wrote songs; in addition, she became the lead dancer in her class at Balanchine's American School of Ballet. She also developed her interest in writing. In eighth grade, Yolen wrote her first two books, a nonfiction book on pirates, and a novel about a trip across the West by covered wagon. She described this work, which is seventeen pages long and includes a plague of locusts, death by snake bite, and the birth of a baby on the trail, as "a masterpiece of economy." Her experience writing the novel helped Yolen to develop an appreciation for the short form. She wrote in *CA* that short stories and poetry "have remained my first loves." During her twelfth and thirteenth summers, Yolen attended Indianbrook (now Farm and Wilderness), a Quaker camp in Vermont. Here, she said, "I learned about pacifism, swimming, storytelling, mucking out horse stalls, planting a garden, and kissing, not necessarily in that order."

After returning from her second summer at Indianbrook, Yolen moved with her family to Westport, Connecticut. As a student at Staples High School, she became captain of the girls' basketball team; news editor of the school paper; head of the Jewish Youth Group; vice president of the Spanish, Latin, and jazz clubs; a member of the school's top singing group; and a contributor to the school literary magazine. She also won a Scholastic Writing Award for one of her poems, a contest called "I Speak for Democracy," and her school's English prize. Before graduation, her class named Yolen "The Perfect Senior." A high school friend, Stella Colandrea, introduced Yolen to the Catholic Mass. "It was because of Stella's influence that I became enamored of different religions. My own Judaism and camp-discovered Quakerism were the most morally appealing, but the panoply of Catholic rites seem to have taken hold of my imagination and wind in and out of many of the elaborate religious rituals I write about in my fantasy tales. And, since I am an Arthurian buff and a lover of things medieval, knowing a bit about the church helps," Yolen wrote in *CA.* However, Yolen's greatest influence in high school was her cousin-in-law Honey Knopp, a pacifist and peace activist who held hootenannies at her home and gave Yolen a copy of *Journal* by George Fox, the founder of the Quaker faith. Fox later became the subject of Yolen's biography *Friend: The Story of George Fox and the Quakers.* The home that Honey Knopp shared with her husband, Burt, according to Yolen, "became my haven. Oh, I still went to basketball games and dances and parties, wisecracking with my friends and being outrageous. But Honey called out another side of me." Honey's influence is present in many of Yolen's most well-known books, such as *The Gift of Sarah Barker* and *The Transfigured Hart.*

After graduating from high school, Yolen attended Smith College, a prestigious institution for women in western Massachusetts. Going to Smith, Yolen wrote in *CA,* "was a choice that would, all unknowingly, change my life. It made me aware of friendships possible—and impossible—with women. It created in me a longing for a particular countryside, that of New England. It charged me with a sense of leftsidedness, of an alien or changeling awareness. And it taught me, really, about poetry and literature and the written word." At Smith, Yolen majored in English and Russian literature and minored in religion. She ran several campus organizations, authored and performed in the class musicals, and wrote her final exam in American intellectual history in verse, receiving an A+ as her grade. She also wrote poetry: between her junior and senior year, one of Yolen's poems was published in *Poetry Digest,* and her verse was also published in other small literary magazines.

Although poetry was in her soul, Yolen decided to become a journalist. During the summer between her freshman and sophomore years, Yolen worked as a cub reporter for the *Bridgeport Sunday Herald.* "It was there," Yolen recalled in *CA,* "I wrote my first signed pieces for a newspaper. My very first byline read 'by Joan Yolen.' I did not take it as a sign." Other vacations were spent as a junior counselor in New Jersey and working for *Newsweek* magazine as an intern; she also contributed to the *New Haven Register* and published an article on kites in *Popular Mechanics.* Yolen dismissed the idea of being a journalist when she found herself making up facts and writing stories off the top of her head; she also found that she was emotional when it came to interviewing the poor. "It became clear," she told *CA,* "that I was a fiction writer." However, Yolen did continue her musical pursuits, writing in *FBJAI* that she "made an unhappy college career bearable by singing with a guitar-playing boyfriend at fraternity parties and mixers. We made a little money, a lot of friends, and imprinted hundreds of folk tunes on our hungry minds." After graduating from Smith, Yolen moved to New York City and worked briefly for *This Week* magazine and *Saturday Review* before launching her career as a freelance writer. She helped her father write his book *The Young Sportsman's Guide to Kite Flying* and did a number of small freelance jobs. Yolen took an apartment in Greenwich Village with two roommates. At a wild party there in the summer of 1960, she met her future husband, David Stemple, who was a friend of one of her roommates; the couple were married in 1962. Yolen has noted that one of her most popular books, *The Girl Who Loved the Wind,* is about her meeting with David, a computer expert and photographer who is Yolen's chief advisor on her books. "In it," she stated in *CA,* "a Persian girl is kept in a walled-in palace by an overprotective father until the day the wind leaps over the garden wall and sweeps her away into the wide, everchanging world."

Approached by an editor from the publishers Alfred A. Knopf, Yolen fibbed and said that she had a book-length manuscript ready for review. She recalled in *CA:* "Caught in the web of this deceit, I, who always prided myself on my honesty, realized there was nothing to do but sit down at my typewriter and get something done quickly. Children's books! I thought. They'd be quickest and easiest." Yolen soon learned that writing books for children was not as quick and easy as she first thought. She collaborated with a high school friend, illustrator Susan Purdy, on several manuscripts, none of which were accepted by the editor at Knopf. Then, Yolen and Purdy sent their manuscripts to other publishers, but with no success. In 1961, Yolen became an assistant editor at Gold Medal Books, a paperback house known for its western novels and spy thrillers. She wrote in *CA:* "I was famous for about a moment in publishing as the one who coined 'she was all things to two men' for some Gothic novel." Her father introduced Yolen to Eleanor Rawson, the vicepresident of David McKay Publishing Company. In turn, Rawson introduced the fledgling author to Rose Dobbs, the editor in charge of children's books. Yolen's first book, the nonfiction title *Pirates in Petticoats,* was accepted by Dobbs and published by McKay in 1963; Dobbs also bought Yolen's second work, *See This Little Line?,* a picture book in rhyme that was published the same year.

After leaving Gold Medal Books, where she got to know such authors as Kurt Vonnegut and Harlan Ellison, Yolen became an associate editor at Rutledge Press, a small packaging house that created books and then sold them to larger publishing companies for distribution. Yolen became a ghostwriter for Rutledge, authoring several books—often concept and activity books—that were published under different names. While at Rutledge, Yolen met Frances Keene, an editor who became head of the children's book department at Macmillan. Writing in *CA,* Yolen called Keene, who was to publish five of her books, "a great teacher as well as a fine editor. She taught me to trust my storytelling ability and to work against being too quick. . . . She also pushed me into delving deeply into folklore while at the same time recognizing my comedic talents." Yolen described her association with Keene as the "beginning of an editorial relationship that I *really* count as the start of my writing career." In 1963, Yolen became an assistant editor in the children's department at Knopf, where she met authors and illustrators such as Roald Dahl and Roger Duvoisin and learned about juvenile literature. She formed a writers' group with such aspiring authors and editors as Jean van Leeuwen, Alice Bach, and James Cross Giblin; one of the members of the group, Anne Huston, collaborated with Yolen on *Trust a City Kid,* a realistic story published in 1966.

In 1965, the Stemples decided to spend a year traveling. For nine months, they trekked across Europe and then sailed for Israel and Greece. Yolen wrote in *CA* that bits and pieces "of our wanderings have already found their way into my stories." She added that "places and people we met were stored away in my memory, and months, even years, later were transformed into the magical landscape of my tales." While they were traveling, Yolen discovered that she was pregnant; Heidi Stemple arrived in 1966, shortly after her parents returned to America. David Stemple took a job at the University of Massachusetts Computer Center in Amherst, so he and Jane relocated to western Massachusetts. Adam Stemple was born in 1968 and Jason Stemple in 1970. During the late 1960s, Yolen met editor Ann K. Beneduce, whom the author described in *CA* as "another seminal influence in my writing life." Yolen and Beneduce, who, according to the author, "produced book after book in the handsomest way possible," worked on approximately thirty books together.

The Emperor and the Kite, a picture book that was among the first of Yolen's works to be edited by Beneduce, is the first of the author's titles to receive major awards. The story outlines how Djeow Seow, the youngest and smallest daughter of an ancient Chinese emperor, saves her father after he is kidnapped by sending him a kite to which is attached a rope made of grass, vines, and strands of her hair. Writing in *Dictionary of Literary Biography (DLB),* William E. Krueger noted that the story "is simply told in the folk tradition, with traditional motifs which provide an aura both of antiquity and of familiarity to the tale." The critic also observed the theme—"that those whom society considers deficient are capable and perhaps more proficient than others—recurs in subsequent tales." A critic in *Publishers Weekly* said that *The Emperor and the Kite* "is easily one of the most distinguished [books with Oriental backgrounds]—and distinguished proof that extravagance, intelligence, premeditated extravagance, always justifies itself." A reviewer in *Children's Book News* commented: "Here is a writer who delights in words and can use them in a controlled way to beautiful effect." In 1968, *The Emperor and the Kite* received the Lewis Carroll Shelf Award and was named a Caldecott Honor Book. Yolen received a second Lewis Carroll Shelf Award for *The Girl Who Loved the Wind,* a picture book, again illustrated by Ed Young, that was published in 1972. In this work, a widowed merchant tries to protect his beautiful daughter from unhappiness but ends up making her a virtual prisoner. The wind visits her and sings to her about life, how it is always full of change and challenges. Finally, the princess escapes with the wind into the world. Writing in *School Library Journal,* Marilyn R. Singer stated that Yolen "produced a treasure. The story has the grace and wisdom of a folk tale, the polish that usually comes from centuries of telling." Eleanor Von Schweinitz of *Children's Book Review* added that the author "has an especial gift for the invention of traditional-type tales and this is complemented by her rare ability to use language creatively. Here she has used the simple rhythms of the storyteller to conjure up the distinctive flavour of an Eastern tale." Writing in *CA,* Yolen said that she wrote *The Girl Who Loved the Wind* "for myself, out of my own history. But recently I received a letter from a nurse who told me that she had read the story to a dying child, and the story had eased the little girl through her final pain. The story did that—not me. But if I can continue to write with as much honesty and love as I can muster, I will truly have touched magic—and passed it on."

When she was sixteen, her aunt's sister by marriage, Honey Knopp, gave Yolen a copy of the journal of George Fox, the founder of the Quakers. "Since then," Yolen told *CA,* "I've been interested in the Quakers." Yolen became a member of the Religious Society of Friends (Quakers) in 1971. The next year, she published another of her most well-received titles, *Friend: The Story of George Fox and the Quakers.* A biography of the seventeenth-century Englishman who founded the movement that came to be known as Quakerism as part of his own quest for religious freedom, the book is noted for portraying Fox—with his long hair and pronouncements in favor of women's rights and against war and slavery—as a kindred spirit to the young radicals of today. William E. Krueger of *DLB* called *Friend* "a quite readable biography, interesting and, in places, quite touching, without fictionalization." Writing in *Library Journal,* Janet G. Polacheck noted: "Even where the subject is not in great demand, this beautifully written, valuable biography is an essential purchase." *The Girl Who Cried Flowers and Other Tales,* a book published in 1974, won the Golden Kite Award that year; it was also nominated for the National Book Award the next year. It is a collection of five stories that, according to a reviewer in *Publishers Weekly,* "could be called modern folk- or fairy tales, since they boast all the usual ingredients—supernatural beings, inexplicable happenings, the struggle between good and evil forces." The critic concluded that Yolen's "artistry with words . . . makes a striking book." A critic in *Kirkus Reviews* called *The Girl Who Cried Flowers* a "showpiece, for those who can forego the tough wisdom of traditional fairy tales for a masterful imitation of the manner." Reflective of a clear moral tone, *The Girl Who Cried Flowers* is also considered notable for suggesting the close relationship of humanity and nature. William E. Krueger of *DLB* called the book "haunting in its mythic implications" and stated that "the tone and poetic elements are Yolen's unique contributions."

All in the Woodland Early, a concept book that teaches the alphabet through the author's verses and musical score, appeared in 1978. The book outlines a little boy's hunting expedition in the woods; each letter represents the animal, bird, or insect—both familiar and unfamiliar—for which he is searching. At the end of the last verse, readers discover that the boy is gathering the animals to play with him and a little girl. Yolen also provides music to go with her words. Writing in the *Washington Post Book World,* Jerome Beatty Jr. said: "Count on versatile Jane Yolen to invent something special and intriguing." He summed up his review by saying: "So clever! It adds another dimension to a lesson in the ABCs, does it not?" A reviewer in *Publishers Weekly* called *All in the Woodland Early* "an outstanding alphabet book," while William E. Krueger of *DLB* called it a "beautifully composed book, reminiscent of cumulative nursery rhymes. . . . This work exhibits Yolen's delightful handling of image, verse, and music."

In 1980, Yolen published the first of her popular "Commander Toad" series, *Commander Toad in Space.* Beginning readers that poke fun at the popular "Star Wars" films—for example, Commander Toad's ship is called the *Star Warts*—and the "Star Trek" television show, the series is usually considered a humorous and entertaining way of introducing children to literature. In *Commander Toad in Space,* the brave captain and his frog crew discover a watery planet and an evil monster, Deep Wader, who is defeated by being engaged in a sing-along. Judith Goldberger of *Booklist* stated: "Any beginning-to-read book with brave space explorers, a ship named the *Star Warts,* and a monster who calls himself Deep Wader would be popular almost by definition. The bonus here is that the adventure of Commander Toad and his colleagues is a clever spoof and really funny reading." A reviewer in *School Library Journal* called the book a "hoppy combination of good story and clever media exploitation" before concluding: "This one holds water."

In 1976, Yolen published *Simple Gifts: The Story of the Shakers,* an informational book about the history of Shakerism, a millennium religion that grew out of Quakerism but has different beliefs. In 1981, she published *The Gift of Sarah Barker,* an historical novel for young adults that is set in a Shaker community. The story features two teenagers, Abel and Sarah, who have grown up in the Society of Believers, a celibate religious community, and now find that they are sexually attracted to each other. As the young people struggle with their feelings, Yolen depicts the contradiction between the religious ecstasy of the Shakers—whose dances and celebrations gave the group their nickname—and the repressive quality of their lifestyle. Sarah and Abel decide to leave the community, but not before Sister Agatha, Sarah's abusive mother, commits suicide. Writing in *Children's Book Review Service,* Barbara Baker called *The Gift of Sarah Barker* "an absorbing tale" and a "jewel of a historical novel," while Stephanie Zvirin of *Booklist* stated: "Into the fabric of a teenage romance [Yolen] weaves complicated and disturbing—at times violent—undercurrents that add a dimension both powerful and provocative." Before writing *Sarah Barker,* Yolen interviewed some of the few remaining Shakers for background information. She also used her daughter, Heidi, who was becoming interested in boys, as the prototype for Sarah. Yolen told *CA,* "I kept wondering how, in a Shaker community, you could keep the boys away from a girl like Heidi or keep Heidi away from the boys. I imagined a Romeo and Juliet story within the Shaker setting."

In 1982, Yolen published *Dragon's Blood: A Fantasy,* the first volume in her "Pit Dragon" series. High fantasy for young adults that incorporates elements of science fiction and is often compared favorably to the "Pern" books by Anne McCaffrey, the "Pit Dragon" series is acknowledged for Yolen's imaginative creation of a completely realized world. *Dragon's Blood* features Jakkin, a fifteen-year-old slave boy whose master is the best dragon breeder on the planet Austar IV, a former penal colony where inhabitants train and fight dragons domesticated by the early colonists. Jakkin steals a female dragon hatchling to train in secret for the gaming pits, a cockfighting ritual that contributes largely to the planet's economy. Hoping to win his freedom by raising a superior fighting dragon, Jakkin establishes an amazing mental link with his "snatchling," which he names Heart's Blood. The story ends with the dragon's first win; Jakkin—now free—learns that his master knew about his theft and that Akki, a bond girl training in medicine whom Jakkin loves, is his master's illegitimate daughter. Writing in *Horn Book,* Ann A. Flowers called *Dragon's Blood* an "original and engrossing fantasy," while Patricia Manning of *School Library Journal* said that the novel provides a "fascinating glimpse of a brand new world." Pauline Thomas of the *School Librarian* called the book "[s]plendid entertainment," adding, "the author explains little, letting the reader work out the details of geography, natural history, social structure, and sexual mores. The result is remarkably convincing. Austar IV is a world as real as [Ursula K. Le Guin's] Earthsea. "

In the second volume of the series, *Heart's Blood,* Jakkin is the new Dragon Master and Heart's Blood has given birth to five hatchlings. Jakkin becomes involved in Austar politics when he is asked to infiltrate rebel forces and rescue Akki. Becoming the pawns in a deadly game, Jakkin and Akki flee with Heart's Blood into the freezing cold of night, called Dark After. Cornered by the authorities after inadvertently blowing up a major city, the trio fight for their lives. In the battle, Heart's Blood is killed. In order to survive the freezing temperatures, Jakkin and Akki enter her carcass; when they emerge, they have been given the gift of dragon's sight—telepathy—and the ability to withstand the cold. Charlotte W. Draper of *Horn Book* stated: "Rich in symbolism, eloquent in the evocation of a culture which carries within it the seeds of its own destruction, the book stretches the reader's conception of human capability." In *A Sending of Dragons,* the third volume in the series, Jakkin and Akki avoid capture by running into the wilderness with Heart's Blood's five babies. When they enter a hidden tunnel, the group encounter an underground tribe of primitives who have discovered the way to extract metals on Austar IV. Jakkin and Akki also learn that these people, who, like them, are bonded to dragons, have developed a bloody, terrifying ritual of dragon sacrifice. At the end of the novel, Akki, Jakkin, and Heart's Blood's fledglings escape with two of the primitive community's dragons. Confronted by their pursuers from above ground, they decide to return to the city and use their new knowledge to bring about an end to the feudalism and enslavement on Austar IV. A reviewer in *Publishers Weekly* stated: "Yolen's tightly plotted, adventurous trilogy constitutes superb storytelling. She incorporates elements of freedom and rebellion, power and control, love and friendship in a masterfully crafted context of a society sick with perversion." Writing in *School Library Journal,* Michael Cart said that, like the two volumes preceding it, the particular strengths of *A Sending of Dragons* are in "the almost encyclopedic detail which Yolen has lavished upon her fully realized alternative world of Austar IV, in her sympathetic portrayal of the dragons as both victims and telepathic partners, and in the symbolic subtext which enriches her narrative and reinforces her universal theme of the inter-dependency and unique value of all life forms."

One of Yolen's most highly acclaimed books is *The Devil's Arithmetic,* a young adult novel published in 1988. A time travel fantasy that is rooted in one of the darkest episodes of history, the novel features Hannah Stern, a twelve-year-old Jewish girl who is transported from contemporary New York to rural Poland in 1942 when she opens the door for Elijah during her family's Seder celebration. Captured by the Nazis, Hannah—now called Chaya—is taken to a death camp, where she meets Rivka, a spirited young girl who teaches her to fight against the dehumanization of the camp and tells her that some must live to bear witness. When Rivka is chosen to be taken to the gas chamber, Chaya, in an act of self-sacrifice, goes in her place; as the doors of the gas chamber close, Chaya—now Hannah again—is returned to the door of her grandparents's apartment, waiting for Elijah. Hannah realizes that her Aunt Eva is her friend Rivka and that she also knew her grandfather in the camp. A critic in *Kirkus Reviews* wrote of *The Devil's Arithmetic:* "Yolen is the author of a hundred books, many of which have been praised for their originality, humor, or poetic vision, but this thoughtful, compelling novel is unique among them." Writing in *Bulletin of the Center for Children's Books,* Roger Sutton noted that Yolen's depiction of the horrors in the camp "is more graphic than any we've seen in holocaust fiction for children before." Confirming that Yolen has brought the "time travel convention to a new and ambitious level," Cynthia Samuels of the *New York Times Book Review* concluded that "sooner or later, all our children must know what happened in the days of the Holocaust. *The Devil's Arithmetic* offers an affecting way to begin." Yolen, who has said that she wrote *The Devil's Arithmetic* for her own children, stated in her acceptance speech for the Sydney Taylor Book Award: "There are books one writes because they are a delight. There are books one writes because one is asked to. There are books one writes because . . . they are there. And there are books one writes simply because *the book has to be written. The Devil's Arithmetic* is this last kind of book. I did not just write it. The book itself was a mitzvah." In addition to the Taylor Award, which was given to the novel in 1989, Yolen received the Parents' Choice Silver Seal Award, the Jewish Book Council Award, and the Association of Jewish Libraries Award for *The Devil's Arithmetic,* which was also a finalist for the Nebula Award.

With *Encounter,* a picture book published to coincide with the five-hundredth anniversary of the discovery of America, Yolen created what is perhaps her most controversial work. Written as the remembrance of an elderly Taino Indian man, the story, which describes the first encounter of Native Americans with Columbus, depicts the man's experience as a small boy. The narrator awakens from a terrifying dream about three predatory birds riding the waves to see three anchored ships. Frightened yet fascinated by the strangers who come ashore, the boy tells his chief not to welcome the men, but he is ignored. The boy and several other Indians are taken aboard the ships as slaves. After he escapes by jumping overboard, the boy tries to warn other tribes, but to no avail; the Taino are wiped out. Calling *Encounter* an "unusual picture book," Carolyn Phelan of *Booklist* noted that "while the portrayal of Columbus as evil may strike traditionalists as heresy, he did hunger for gold, abduct native people, and ultimately (though unintentionally), destroy the Taino. This book effectively presents their point of view." Writing in the *New Advocate,* James C. Junhke called *Encounter* "among the most powerful and disturbing publications of the Columbus Quincentennial." Noting the "pioneering brilliance" of the book, the critic called Yolen's greatest achievement "the reversal of perspective. This book forces us to confront what a disaster it was for the Taino people to be discovered and destroyed by Europeans. Readers young and old will fervently wish never to be encountered by such 'strangers from the sky.' " Writing in response to Junhke's review in the same publication, Yolen said, "If my book becomes a first step towards the exploration of the meeting between Columbus and the indigenous peoples—and its tragic aftermath—then it has done its work, whatever its flaws, perceived or real." The author concluded, "We cannot change history. But we—and most especially our children—can learn from it so that the next encounters, be they at home, abroad, or in space, may be gentler and mutually respectful. It is a large hope but it is, perhaps, all that we have."

Throughout her career, Yolen has woven bits and pieces of her personal history—and that of her family and friends—into her works. She was quoted in *DLB* as saying that she uses "these scraps the way a bird makes a nest and a mouse makes a house—snippet by snippet, leaf and bough and cotton batting and all." Several of the author's books are directly autobiographical. For example, *All Those Secrets of the World,* a picture book published in 1991, is set during the two years that her father was away at war. Yolen recalls how, as a four-year-old, she watched her father depart by ship. The next day, Janie and her five-year-old cousin Michael see some tiny specks on the horizon while they are playing on the beach; the specks are ships. Michael teaches Janie a secret of the world, that as he moves farther away, he gets smaller. Two years later, when her father returns, Janie whispers Michael's secret after he tells her that she seems bigger: that when he was so far away, everything seemed smaller, but now that he is here, she is big. A reviewer in *Publishers Weekly* wrote: "Yolen here relates a bittersweet memory from an important period in her childhood. . . . This timely nostalgic story is told with simple grace, and Janie's thoughts and experiences are believably childlike." Phyllis G. Sidorsky of *School Library Journal* called *All Those Secrets of the World* an "affecting piece without an extraneous word and one that is particularly timely today."

In 1995, Yolen published *And Twelve Chinese Acrobats,* a tale for middle graders based on family stories about her father's older brother. Set in a Russian village in 1910, the book features Lou the Rascal, a charming troublemaker who keeps getting into scrapes. When Lou is sent to a military school in Kiev, the family—especially narrator Wolf, Lou's youngest brother (and Yolen's father)—is sad. Lou is expelled from military school. Months later, he surprises everyone by bringing home a troupe of twelve Chinese acrobats he met while working in a Moscow circus. The acrobats fascinate the locals with their descriptions of an exotic world far removed from the little village. When the acrobats leave the *shtel* in the spring, Lou's father, recognizing his son's managerial ability, sends him to America to find a place for the family. Writing in *Bulletin of the Center for Children's Books,* Betsy Hearne said: "The relationship between the two brothers, Lou and Wolf, lends an immediate dynamic to the historical setting." The critic concluded that the compressed narrative, brief chapters, spacious format, large print, and "vivaciously detailed pen-and-ink illustrations dancing across almost every page [by Jean Gralley] make this a prime choice for young readers venturing into historical fiction for the first time, or, for that matter, considering a probe into their own family stories." A critic in *Kirkus Reviews* called *And Twelve Chinese Acrobats* a book "radiating family warmth, in words, art, and remembrance."

In an article for *Horn Book,* Yolen stated: "As a writer I am the empress of thieves, taking characters like gargoyles off Parisian churches, the *ki-lin* (or unicorn) from China, swords in stones from the Celts, landscapes from the Taino people. I have pulled threads from magic tapestries to weave my own new cloth." The author concluded, "Children's literature is about growth. Just as we do not put heavy weights on our children's heads to stunt their growth, we should not put weights on our writers' heads. To do so is to stunt story forever. Stories go beyond race, beyond religion—even when they are about race and religion. The book speaks to individuals in an individual voice. But then it is taken into the reader's life and recreated, re-invigorated, revisioned. That is what literature is about." Writing in *CA,* Yolen mused that her life, "like anyone else's is a patchwork of past and present. . . . I can also see a pattern that might tell me my future—as long as I remain consistent. I consider myself a poet and a storyteller. Being 'America's Hans Christian Andersen' means trying to walk in much-too-large seven-league boots. I just want to go on writing and discovering my stories for the rest of my life because I know that in my tales I make public what is private, transforming my own joy and sadness into tales for the people. The folk."

BIOGRAPHICAL/CRITICAL SOURCES:

BOOKS

Authors and Artists for Young Adults, Volume 4, Gale (Detroit), 1990, pp. 229-241.

Children's Literature Review, Volume 4, Gale, 1982, pp. 255-269; Volume 44, 1997, pp. 167-211.

de Montreville, Doris, and Elizabeth D. Crawford, editors, *Fourth Book of Junior Authors and Illustrators,* Wilson, 1978, pp. 365-367.

Dictionary of Literary Biography, Volume 52: *American Writers for Children since 1960: Fiction,* Gale, 1986, pp. 398-405.

Drew, Bernard A., *The One Hundred Most Popular Young Adult Authors,* Libraries Unlimited, 1996.

Roginski, Jim, *Behind the Covers: Interviews with Authors and Illustrators of Books for Children and Young Adults,* Libraries Unlimited, 1985.

St. James Guide to Fantasy Writers, St. James Press (Detroit), 1996.

St. James Guide to Young Adult Writers, St. James Press, 1999.

Silvey, Anita, editor, *Children's Books and Their Creators,* Houghton Mifflin, 1995, pp. 700-701.

Twentieth-Century Children's Writers, St. James Press, 1989, pp. 1075-1078.

Yolen, Jane, *Guide to Writing for Children,* The Writer, 1989.

Yolen, *Touch Magic: Fantasy, Faerie, and Folktale in the Literature of Childhood,* Philomel, 1981.

Yolen, *Writing Books for Children,* The Writer, 1973, revised edition, 1983.

PERIODICALS

Booklist, November 15, 1980, Judith Goldberger, review of *Commander Toad in Space,* p. 464; May 15, 1981, Stephanie Zvirin, review of *The Gift of Sarah Barker,* p. 1250; March 1, 1992, Carolyn Phelan, review of *Encounter,* p. 1281.

Bulletin of the Center for Children's Books, October, 1988, Roger Sutton, review of *The Devil's Arithmetic,* pp. 23-24; June, 1995, Betsy Hearne, review of *And Twelve Chinese Acrobats,* p. 365.

Children's Book News, January-February, 1970, review of *The Emperor and the Kite,* pp. 23-24.

Children's Book Review, December, 1973, Eleanor Von Schweinitz, review of *The Girl Who Loved the Wind,* pp. 172-173.

Children's Book Review Service, June, 1981, Barbara Baker, review of *The Gift of Sarah Barker,* p. 100.

Horn Book, August, 1982, Ann A. Flowers, review of *Dragon's Blood,* pp. 418-419; April, 1984, Charlotte W. Draper, review of *Heart's Blood,* p. 206; November-December, 1994, Yolen, "An Empress of Thieves," pp. 702-705.

Judaica Librarianship, spring, 1989-winter, 1990, transcript of Yolen's acceptance speech for the Sydney Taylor Book Award, pp. 52-53.

Kirkus Reviews, July 15, 1974, review of *The Girl Who Cried Flowers and Other Tales,* p. 741; August 15, 1988, review of *The Devil's Arithmetic,* p. 1248; April 15, 1995, review of *And Twelve Chinese Acrobats,* p. 564.

Library Journal, June 15, 1972, Janet G. Polacheck, review of *Friend: The Story of George Fox and the Quakers,* p. 2245.

New Advocate, spring, 1993, James C. Juhnke and Jane Yolen, "An Exchange on *Encounter,*" pp. 94-96.

New York Times Book Review, November 20, 1977, Jane Langton, review of *The Hundredth Dove and Other Tales,* p. 30; November 13, 1988, Cynthia Samuels, "Hannah Learns to Remember," p. 62; November 8, 1992, Noel Perrin, "Bulldozer Blues," p. 54; May 17, 1998.

Publishers Weekly, August 14, 1967, review of *The Emperor and the Kite,* p. 50; July 22, 1974, review of *The Girl Who Cried Flowers and Other Tales,* p. 70; January 11, 1980, review of *All in the Woodland Early,* p. 88; October 9, 1987, review of *A Sending of Dragons,* p. 90; March 22, 1991, review of *All Those Secrets of the World,* p. 80; June 15, 1998, p. 60.

School Librarian, December, 1983, Pauline Thomas, review of *Dragon's Blood,* p. 384.

School Library Journal, March, 1973, Marilyn r. Singer, review of *The Girl Who Loved the Wind,* p. 102; December, 1980, review of *Commander Toad in Space,* p. 66; September, 1982, Patricia Manning, review of *Dragon's Blood,* p. 146; January, 1988, Michael Cart, review of *A Sending of Dragons,* pp. 87-88; July, 1991, Phyllis G. Sidorsky, review of *All Those Secrets of the World,* p. 66; March, 1998, p. 207.

Teaching and Learning Literature (TALL), November-December, 1996, Lee Bennett Hopkins, "O Yolen: A Look at the Poetry of Jane Yolen," pp. 66-68.
Washington Post Book World, April 13, 1980, Jerome Beatty Jr., "Herds of Hungry Hogs Hurrying Home," p. 10.*

* * *

YOLEN, Jane H.
See YOLEN, Jane (Hyatt)

* * *

ZIMROTH, Evan 1943-

PERSONAL: Born February 24, 1943, in Philadelphia, PA; daughter of Lester (an international lawyer and banker) and Janet (in child development) Nurick; married Peter Zimroth (marriage ended); married Henry Wollman (an architect), October 29, 1977; children: (second marriage) Lilly Sophia, Else Kathryn. *Education:* Barnard College, B.A., 1965; Columbia University, Ph.D., 1972. *Religion:* Jewish.

ADDRESSES: Home—600 West 115th St., New York, NY 10025. *Office*—Department of English, Queens College of the City University of New York, Flushing, NY 11367.

CAREER: Washington Ballet, Washington, DC, professional dancer, 1957-61; Queens College of the City University of New York, Flushing, NY, 1969—, currently professor of English. Visiting professor at University of Paris—Vincennes, 1975.

MEMBER: Poets and Writers.

AWARDS, HONORS: National Jewish Book Award, 1996.

WRITINGS:

Giselle Considers Her Future (poems), Ohio State University Press, 1978.
Dead, Dinner, or Naked (poems), TriQuarterly Books (Evanston, IL), 1993.
Gangsters (novel), Crown (New York City), 1996.
Collusion: Memoir of a Young Girl and Her Ballet Master, Harper (New York City), 1999.

Co-founder of *Poesie Vincennes,* 1975; member of editorial staff of *Little Magazine.*

SIDELIGHTS: Evan Zimroth has published two accounts of troubled relationships: the novel *Gangsters,* about an adulterous affair between a Jewish woman and a Christian man, and the memoir *Collusion,* in which she recounts her ballet training as a young girl under a famous Russian dancer.

Gangsters tells of the illicit relationship between Nicole Wolfe, a married woman who teaches literature at a New York college, and Tom, an architect estranged from his wife. The couple's erotic episodes are spiced with theological discussions about the religious practices of their respective faiths. Writing in the *New York Times Book Review,* Bill Kent believed *Gangsters* to be "awkward and embarrassing." The critic for *Publishers Weekly* was more positive; calling *Gangsters* a "lurid, erotic, at times overwrought debut novel," the critic concluded that "the ending is worth the wait, a genuine shocker."

In *Collusion* Zimroth recounts her ballet training under a demanding ballet master and the sado-masochistic relationship that formed between the two. "In beautiful, seductive prose, Zimroth makes readers privy to the delicate balance of pain and pleasure that ruled her life," according to Stephanie Zvirin in *Booklist.* Joan Stahl in *Library Journal* found that Zimroth is "still ambivalent about her early and haunting experiences," while the critic for *Publishers Weekly* described *Collusion* as "an interesting backstage look at the seamier side of an art form." Writing in the *American Book Review,* Lorna Harbus concluded that Zimroth's "writing is sincere, direct, and imaginative, and the result is a coming-of-age story enhanced by the details of a dancer's life—sweat, blood, tears, and sexual innuendo."

BIOGRAPHICAL/CRITICAL SOURCES:

PERIODICALS

American Book Review, January-February, 2000, Lorna Harbus, review of *Collusion,* p. 20.
Booklist, January 1, 1999, Stephanie Zvirin, review of *Collusion,* p. 821.
Library Journal, September 15, 1996, p. 99; March 1, 1999, Joan Stahl, review of *Collusion,* p. 88.
New York Times Book Review, October 13, 1996, Bill Kent, review of *Gangsters,* p. 21; January 10, 1999, Mary Grace Butler, review of *Collusion.*
Poetry, October, 1981, p. 40.
Publishers Weekly, February 15, 1993, review of *Dead, Dinner, or Naked,* p. 234; August 12, 1996, review

of *Gangsters,* p. 66; December 14, 1998, review of *Collusion,* p. 65.*